Fodor's 2003

Italy

Fodor's Travel Publications • New York, Toronto, London, Sydney, Auckland

www.fodors.com

CONTENTS

MAPS

Circled letters in text correspond to letters on the photographs. For more information on the sights pictured, turn
to the indicated page number ④> on each photograph.

DESTINATION ITALY

No less an observer of life than Goethe once exhaled into the now-famous diaries he kept of his 18th-century journey through Italy, "I can honestly say I've never been as happy in my life as now." The great German poet was neither the first nor the last visitor to fall blissfully under the spell of this justifiably fabled land, with its stunning landscapes, stupendous contributions to Western civilization, and unabashed enthusiasm for life's pleasures. Be prepared to be swept away. It may be while witnessing the conspiracy of dreamlike light and seductive sea from the Belvedere of Infinity at the Villa Cimbrone in Ravello or, for that matter, while encountering any of the many other uniquely Italian scenes—but sooner or later on your own Italian journey, you're bound to succumb to Italy's charms.

VENICE

Arriving in Venice for the first time, the humorist Robert Benchley shot off a telegram to his editor at the *New Yorker*, "Streets full of water. Please advise." Water captures the imagination here, rendering the city dreamlike. Above all, watery

Ⓐ 44

Venice is a city of fantasy, and its lavish palaces and churches —such as the domed Chiesa di Santa Maria della Salute, gracing the entrance to the Ⓐ**Grand Canal**—rise out of the lagoon like mirages. The prosaic becomes extraordinary here. The fishermen and lace makers who live on the nearby, low-lying island of Ⓑ**Burano** paint their simple houses in playfully bright hues. The city's symbol, perched among Moors and angels on the enameled facade of the Ⓒ**Torre dell'Orologio** in Piazza San Marco, is not just a lion but a supernatural leonine creature that sprouts wings.

Ⓑ 55

Ⓒ 44

VENETIAN ARC

When the sad moment comes to leave Venice, console yourself by seeking out the masterworks of the art-rich cities that spread in an arc to the north and the west. In Padua's Ⓐ**Cappella degli Scrovegni,** the great 14th-century master Giotto introduced a graphic dose of reality to his fresco cycle, including the first blue skies to appear in Western painting. But it was Palladio, the greatest architect of the Renaissance, who endowed the region with its most-visited treasures. In Vicenza his Ⓑ**Villa La Rotonda** and Ⓒ**Palazzo della Ragione,** known simply as the Basilica, bear the telltale and much-imitated hallmarks of Palladian style—serenity, symmetry, order, and harmony.

Ⓑ 90

Ⓒ 87

THE DOLOMITES: TRENTINO-ALTO ADIGE

Ⓐ 133

"The most beautiful work of architecture ever seen" is how the great 20th-century architect Le Corbusier described the Dolomites, northeast Italy's domain of rocky mountain spires. In unspoiled villages, such as Ⓐ**Santa Maddalena,** nestled beneath the raw, craggy peaks and tucked into verdant Alpine valleys, the architecture is of the quaint, centuries-old South Tyrolean variety, at once Italian and Austrian. Whatever the culture, the common asset is snow, on literally hundreds of miles of ski runs at such world-famous resorts as Ⓑ**Madonna di Campiglio.**

Ⓑ 121

Poets, royals, Roman emperors, and mere mortals have long swooned over the Italian lakes, where deep blue waters and verdant hillsides clad with voluptuous gardens offer respite for the world-weary at Europe's toniest resorts, including the Ⓐ**Villa d'Este** on Lake Como. Other sophisticated pleasures are less than an hour away in Milan. The fashions you see on the runway here can be had (for a price, of course) in the city's chic shops, including those

MILAN, LOMBARDY & THE LAKES

beneath the belle epoque glass vaults of one of the world's first shopping centers, the Ⓑ**Galleria Vittorio Emanuele.** Easy living is relatively new to these parts: explore the region's turbulent past in the cities of the Po plain. At places like the Ⓒ**Castello Visconteo** in Pavia you'll soon discover that rule often demanded a firm hand—and a well-fortified palace.

Ⓐ 185

Ⓑ 154

Ⓒ 167

PIEDMONT
VALLE D'AOSTA

"Foot of the mountains" is what Piedmont means, and rare is the patch of earth in this bountiful northern region that doesn't afford at least a glimpse of the Alps. To the south, on the plains of the Po River, well-tended vineyards that surround fortified hill towns produce sparkling Spumanti and hearty Barolos, a formidable match for the region's white truffles. In the center of it all is Turin, where the Savoy legacy is palpable in the Rococo Palazzo Reale, and the legendary Holy Shroud draws pilgrims and scientific controversy. To the north, the highest Alps soar skyward and hem in the Valle d'Aosta. Castles right out of storybooks, like the one at Ⓑ**Fénis,** guard the passes, and renowned resorts, among them Ⓐ**Breuil-Cervinia,** afford the chance to ski on the slopes of the mightiest Alp of them all, the Matterhorn. In the shadow of the pistes are Aosta, a Roman outpost of 1st-century BC fame, and the Parco Nazionale del Gran Paradiso, where ibex, chamois, and a flurry of May blossoms flourish.

Ⓐ⟩**216**

Ⓑ⟩**217**

Not nearly as worldly as its counterpart across the French border, the "other" Riviera more than compensates by being a little balmier, a lot less discovered, a little sweeter, and, well, more enticingly Italian. The charm of this region, officially

ITALIAN RIVIERA

known as Liguria and forming an arc around the helter-skelter port city of Genoa, can be as subtle as the soft ocher-color facade of a palazzo in the faded, genteel resort of Ⓐ**Rapallo.** For more drama you need only travel to the easternmost edge of the region, where the Riviera attains a picturesque crescendo. Here, Ⓑ**Riomaggiore** and its four sibling villages cling to seaside cliffs and give a name to one of Europe's most breathtaking coastlines—and most popular walking terrain—the Cinque Terre, or Five Lands.

Ⓐ 241

FLORENCE

Ⓐ▷ 281

Ⓑ▷ 292

Florence, the "Athens of Italy" and the key to the Renaissance, hugs the banks of the Arno River. Folded among the emerald cypress-studded hills of north-central Tuscany, the city is anchored by the Ⓓ**Duomo,** with its Brunelleschi dome, an engineering tour de force. Elegant and somewhat aloof, as if set apart by its past greatness, Florence shares with Rome the honor of first place among Italian cities for the magnitude of its artistic works. Among them is the Renaissance masterpiece started by Masaccio and Masolino and finished by Filippino Lippi, the Ⓑ**Santa Maria del Carmine** fresco cycle in the Cappella Brancacci. Through its innovative style, their creation changed the course of art forever. In the Galleria dell'Accademia, you will find one of the most-visited and powerful works of art in the world, Michelangelo's *David*. You can wander among the great works here or visit the reproduction in the Ⓒ**Piazzale Michelangelo** and enjoy it among the throngs of Florentines sipping aperitifs at one of the outdoor

Ⓒ▷ 294

cafés. Down every *via* (street) and *vicolo* (alley) and in every piazza you'll make new discoveries of Romanesque, Gothic, or Renaissance architecture. Sheltered within the churches, cloisters, and towers are the masterful paintings and sculptures of the Quattrocento and Cinquecento periods. These marvels retain their potency even in the Florence of the Ⓐ**Ponte Vecchio,** with its goldsmiths and jewelry shops and its fine view downriver to the Ponte Santa Trinita, which Florentines call the most beautiful bridge in the world. Pause a moment and judge for yourself.

Without a doubt, Mother Nature outdid herself in Tuscany, the region on the Ligurian and Tyrrhenian seas that radiates from Florence. Punctuated by thickly wooded hills, snow-capped peaks, sun-drenched vineyards, olive groves, and

TUSCANY

Ⓐ〉352

dramatic hill towns, Tuscany's milk-and-honey vistas have changed little since Renaissance artists first beheld them. Not surprisingly, you'll find some of Italy's greatest art treasures here, including the

12th-century Leaning Tower of Pisa and Piero della Francesca's fresco cycle in Arezzo. Travelers are also entranced by medieval Siena, "the Pompeii of the Middle Ages," as it was called by the philosopher Taine. With its Ⓐ**Piazza del Campo** delimited by the austere Palazzo Pubblico, Siena symbolizes the grace and power of a proud city, and its age-old rivalry with

Ⓑ〉343

Ⓒ〉354

Florence still fires its citizenry's tongues and souls. During the ©**Palio,** the square explodes in a frenzy of pageantry and passion and a dizzying horse race amid colorful flags.

Sunny vineyards and olive groves embrace and characterize Tuscany's bucolic landscape. In ®**San Gimignano,** the quintessential Tuscan town, linger over a glass of Vernaccia di San Gimignano, then stand on the steps of the Collegiata at sunset as the swallows, twittering softly in the air, swoop in and out of the famous medieval towers. Or travel farther afield to the Gothic ©**Abbazia di San Galgano** and look up to the sky through the missing rooftop, a haunting suggestion of time past.

©>**362**

15

EMILIA-ROMAGNA

(A) 382

Emilia-Romagna owes its beginnings to the Romans, who in 187 BC built the Via Aemilia; today the road spans the region, from Piacenza to the beaches of Rimini. Mosaics in nearby Ravenna are glittery treasures left from Byzantine rule. In (A)**Bologna,** the region's principal city and intellectual center, arcades lining the streets double as municipal umbrellas on rainy days. You can contemplate the harmony of Piazzas Maggiore and Nettuno and the grandeur of Giambologna's (B)**Fontana del Nettuno** while tucking into ricotta-stuffed ravioli or nut- and cream-rich tortellini. This region of gastronomic fame invented the balsamic vinegar of Modena, prosciutto, and buttery, complex Parmigiano Reggiano from the (C)**Parma** area, sprinkled all around Italy, and the world.

(B) 383

(C) 376

UMBRIA,
THE MARCHES,
AND ABRUZZO

Ⓐ 416

Ⓑ 420

The bluish haze that tints the landscape lends a mystical, ethereal element to Umbria, which bears the legends of saints and the rich artistic inheritance of Giotto. The spirit of St. Francis permeates Assisi and its Ⓐ**Piazza del Comune,** aflutter with birds. The Festival of Two Worlds draws artists to Spoleto, and Orvieto's Gothic Duomo is simply stunning. To the east the turreted castles of the Marches hulk among the Apennines, and the Renaissance Ⓑ**Palazzo Ducale** guards majestic Urbino. Rugged Abruzzo to the south holds remnants of the Roman empire as well as the gifts of nature in its national park. Drive among Umbria's hill towns, stopping for dishes perfumed with black truffles and sun-kissed olive oil.

Rome—antique, Renaissance, Baroque, always papal—is a veritable Grand Canyon of culture, built of stratified layers of ancient, medieval, and modern. It's the mixture of old and new that gives Rome its vibrancy, with Vespas and

ROME

Ⓐ 451

compact cars buzzing past the famous sights and subtle details that tell the stories of the city. Walk through Old Rome, taking in the Baroque splendor. Continue along the Via Portico d'Ottavia of the Jewish Ghetto, past the Ⓑ **Bocca della Verità,** set into the vestibule of a 12th-century church, and cross the Tiber River to the cobblestone alleys of Trastevere. Stop for a Campari break at a café in the timeless 17th-century Piazza Navona, take pleasure in an hour stolen alongside Bernini's splashing

Ⓑ 472

Ⓒ 451

Ⓓ**Fontana dei Quattro Fiumi,** or wander through the colorful Ⓔ**Campo dei Fiori market** to savor the aromas of fresh produce blessed by the balm of the Roman sun. Few places are as visited as the Vatican and its collection of buildings—an estimated 14,000 rooms, chapels, and galleries. Decorated in uniforms designed by Michelangelo using the colors of the Medici popes, the Ⓐ**Swiss Guards,** entrusted with protecting the pope, stand guard as you make your way to the impressive Piazza San Pietro. Enter Ⓒ**St. Peter's Basilica** and let the sheer size of the world's most famous Catholic church engulf you. Climb the narrow, winding staircase to the top of the dome for a view of the terra-cotta hues of the city below—a glorious reward.

Ⓔ▷457

19

CAMPANIA

Mount Vesuvius may grumble, the earth around Naples may shoot steaming gases, the dark waters of Lago d'Averno may lend credence to the ancients' belief that this was the entrance to the underworld, the port cities of Pompeii and Herculaneum may be frozen in time forever by a catastrophic volcanic eruption. But blessed by gentle light and washed by warm seas, Campania defies these omens. A vast treasury of Baroque architecture, classical antiquities, and Renaissance masterpieces, it is above all appreciated for its beauty and easygoing ways: It's no coincidence that Pompeii's **ⒷVilla dei Misteri** frescoes—perhaps our most astonishing paintings from the ancient world—depict a young woman's initiation into the cult of Dionysus, the god of wine. The very names here—Capri, Positano, Amalfi, and even Naples, the operatic city at center stage—evoke sybaritic pleasures and hedonism, fragrant lemon groves and turquoise seas. Campania delivers on these promises in spades. "The sun, the moon, the stars and Amalfi," it is said, and who could think of anything else, given the atmospheric village's romantic

Ⓐ 536

perch on Europe's most beautiful coast, and with such a **ⒶDuomo**—a mind-bending blend of Moorish, Romanesque, and Baroque elements—in its midst?

Ⓑ 554

"Viva San Gennaro!" rings the cry when the blood of Naples's patron saint liquifies, a miracle that repeats itself with encouraging regularity three times a year—the first Saturday in May, September 19, and December 16. A good thing, too, because failure to do so portends disaster for the city. Despite its proximity to such fateful proceedings, as well as to the spewings of Mt. Vesuvius, the hilltop town of ©**Ravello** seems immune to any calamity more serious than the intrusion of a cloud on its otherwise seamless vista.

Ⓐ 602

APULIA & MOLISE

En route to Brindisi and Greece-bound ferries, many travelers speed heedlessly through the 250 miles (402½ km) of coast that comprises Italy's heel. (Passing through is something of a tradition here; the crusaders did it on their way to and from the Holy Land.) Linger awhile, though, and you'll discover that the sun-baked landscape yields more than olives and grapes. Greeks, Romans, Holy Roman Emperors, and numerous other conquerors have stayed long enough to leave their mark on little-known places like the Baroque Ⓐ**Duomo** in Ⓒ**Gallipoli,** a coastal city whose whitewashed, Casbah-like fishing port evokes northern Africa. Even more exotic are the eye-catching Ⓓ*trulli,* conical roofed dwellings built

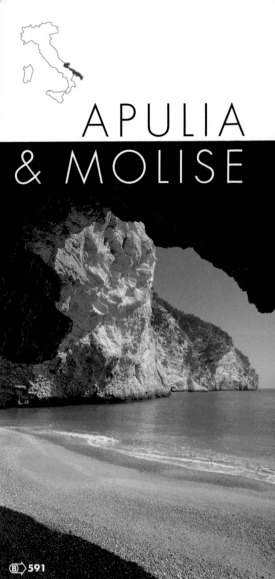

Ⓑ 591

efficiently in the shape of igloos, without mortar, from blocks of local limestone. Lore has it that this construction allowed the trulli to be disassembled in a hurry when the royal tax collector came around. However they came into being, more than 1,000 of these eccentric structures add a quirky charm to the inland town of Alberobello. One of the greatest appeals of the region is what isn't here—large-scale development along the seductive coastline, at its most alluring along the Ⓑ**Gargano Promontory,** studded with coves.

Ⓓ 596

Ⓒ 602

BASILICATA & CALABRIA

The southernmost regions of the peninsula, the toe of the boot, are known informally as the *Mezzogiorno*—literally "midday," for the blazing sun that casts the white villages, shimmering seas, and barren landscapes in a harsh light that will render your impressions all the more vivid. The pleasure of traveling through this untrodden terrain is stumbling upon largely undiscovered places far off the beaten path—the simple *sassi*, dwellings partially hewn from caves, in the Basilicata village of Ⓐ**Matera,** perhaps, or the ©**Chiesa di Santa Maria della Isola,** atop its rocky promontory in Tropea, on the Calabrian coast. In fact some of the major treasures of the Mezzogiorno are only now being unearthed. Dredged

Ⓐ⟩**614**

Ⓑ⟩**622**

from the sea in 1972, the 5th-century BC Ⓑ**Bronzi di Riace,** some of the finest examples of Greek art, command pride of place in the dazzling collection of antiquities in the Museo Nazionale della Magna Grecia in Reggio di Calabria.

©⟩**620**

SICILY

Ⓐ 661

Ⓑ 662

The architecture of magical Sicily reflects the island's centuries of changing dominion under the Greeks, Arabs, Normans, and Spaniards. Baroque church-hopping could be a sport in the cacophonous streets of Palermo, seafaring Siracusa, and the ceramics center of Ⓐ**Caltagirone.** The breezes are sultry and everyday life is without pretense, as witnessed in the workaday stalls of Palermo's Vucciria market and in Ⓑ**Catania,** its fish market piled high with the island's ubiquitous sardines. A phalanx of Greek temples stands sentinel in Agrigento's Valley of the Temples, blanketed in almond, oleander, and juniper blossoms. Dating from the 5th century BC, the Ⓒ**Tempio di Giunone** retains many of its original sandstone columns even after the wrath of Carthage.

Ⓒ 652

Savagely beautiful landscapes of dense and mountainous bush, rock-strewn beaches, and weathered coves with wind-sculpted granite formations intensify Sardinia's aura of isolation. This Mediterranean island west of mainland Italy is far enough from imperial and

SARDINIA

papal Rome to have its own enigmatic character, which has been shaped by an amalgam of peoples and architectural styles: Phoenician, Spanish, Moorish, Turkish, Genoan, and Pisan. If here in midsummer, you've been cast in the role of an Italian movie star, so grab your yacht and wraparounds and tack to the

Ⓐ 698

Costa Smeralda, where the international jet set slips into resorts such as Ⓐ**Cala di Volpe** in Porto Cervo. For theatrics of a historical nature, venture inland to Su Nuraxi, the ruins of a prehistoric fortified village. In early May the Ⓑ**Festa di Sant'Efisio,** a four-day procession celebrating the island's patron saint, culminates as worshipers in regional dress parade down Cagliari's main street.

Ⓑ 688

GREAT ITINERARIES

Ⓐ ▷ 181

Italian Gardens

7 to 9 days

Using the living materials and elements of nature to achieve studied aesthetic effects, Italians are masters at creating gardens, and have been from the Renaissance and Baroque ages until well into the 19th century. Usually framing country villas or grand city palaces, the most spectacular gardens are laid out with an artist's eye for perspective and color; many are studded with statuary and fanciful fountains. A tour of some of Italy's most beautiful gardens begins in Milan, gateway to the Lake District—ideally in spring, when azaleas and rhododendrons are in glorious bloom. Note that some gardens are not open in winter or in inclement weather; always call ahead.

STRESA

3 days. Spend the better part of one day on an excursion from the stately Lake Maggiore resort town of Stresa, exploring the Borromean Islands, from the decorative Baroque palace and terraced gardens on Isola Bella to the Renaissance-style villa on Isola Madre, surrounded by a lush park where peacocks strut amid banks of azaleas, rhododendrons, and camellias. To plant the elaborately tiered gardens of Isola Bella and Isola Madre, a 16th-century count had laborers haul soil to the islands in boats. The next day hop on a ferry to Verbania and get off

at the embarcadero of the Villa Taranto. Adorned with terraces, cascades, and fountains, its vast garden was laid out in the 20th century and remains one of Europe's finest. Some 20,000 plant species—many rare and exotic—grow here.
☞ *Chapter 4, Lake Maggiore and Lake Orta.*

BELLAGIO

2 or 3 days. Settle into this beauty spot on Ⓐ Lake Como surrounded by romantic vistas. At Villa Melzi, which some regard as the most serendipitous site in the entire Lake District, a fabulous staircase blooms with azaleas in spring and is topped by a neoclassic palace. Just across the lake in Tremezzo, one stop away on the ferry, is Villa Carlotta, a wedding present to Charlotte of Russia in 1843. The luxuriant gardens and park are known for their spectacular rhododendrons and azaleas. From Tremezzo, take the ferry to Sala Comacina, where, during visiting hours, there is regular ferry service to Villa Balbaniello, one of the most romantic sites of all. Check opening times with the Bellagio or Tremezzo tourist offices. Afterward, if you have time, take the leisurely ferry trip around the Maggiore or Como lakes to get glimpses of many more villa gardens from the boat.
☞ *Chapter 4, Lake Como.*

FLORENCE

2 or 3 days. Make Florence your base for a series of visits to the gardens of the Medici villas on the city's outskirts. These gardens feel somewhat austere, their beauty lying in the artful arrangements of evergreens. Roam through the Giardini Boboli, behind Palazzo Pitti, laid out for Eleanor of Toledo, wife of Medici Grand Duke Cosimo I, noting how the plan was ingeniously adapted to a very irregular site. Then, together with some city sightseeing to help you focus on the Medici influence in Florence, con-

tinue your villa touring in half-day excursions. Villa Gamberaia, a legacy of the wealthy Capponi family, is an elegant Italian garden set in olive groves in the hills of Settignano. North of Florence, toward Sesto Fiorentino, the vast Medici gardens of Villa di Castello are festooned with more than 500 lemon trees. At the Medici Villa La Petraia, sculptures by Renaissance masters adorn the 16th-century Italian garden and a park is landscaped in 19th-century style.
☞ *Chapter 7, Side Trips from Florence.*

VALLE D'AOSTA

Turin

Asti

60 km
(37 mi)

30 km
(18 mi)

Alba

San Remo

By Public Transportation
Trains make frequent runs between Milan and Stresa (about 60 minutes), Como (30 minutes), and Lecco (30 minutes). The good lake ferry service makes it easy to explore villages on the Maggiore and Como lakes (ferry trips are no more than 30 minutes). Travel by bus from Como to Bellagio and between Lecco and Bellagio (both trips about 75 minutes, depending on traffic). By train it takes about 3½ hours to travel between Milan and Florence. To reach Villa Gamberaia from Florence, take Bus 10, marked Settignano. To reach Villa La Petraia take Bus 28; Villa di Castello is within walking distance.

A Food Lover's Tour
10 to 14 days

Sampling Italy's best food and wines in the very places they are produced will enrich your understanding of the country and its people. On this itinerary through a country where good eating and drinking is the rule, you'll take in the birthplace of some wonderful wines, a gracious city renowned for exquisite chocolates and its grand fin-de-siècle cafés, truffle country, and, last but not least, Emilia-Romagna's Parma, which is as rich in history and art as in its culinary delights. In northern Italy, near the

Ⓑ▷376

Dolomites, you'll see how irresistible cooking mixes Italian and Austrian accents.

TURIN

1 or 2 days. Dine on as many as 30 antipasti followed by a creamy risotto, and top off your meal with a delectable dessert. Then head for one of the city's historic cafés to savor the wonderful pastries along with your espresso. And don't forget to pick up some of the city's celebrated hazelnut chocolates, called *gianduiotti*. Southeast of Turin in the Monferrato and Langhe districts, rolling hills are blanketed with the vineyards that produce Barolo, "king of the wines and wine of kings," in addition to Barbaresco and others.
☞ *Chapter 5, Turin and Fortified Cities of the Po Plain.*

ASTI, ALBA, AND PARMA

2 days. Spend a day exploring the wineries in the area. Asti has lent its name to Spumante, a sparkling white that brings bubbles of gaiety to every kind of celebration in Italy. Some like it sweet,

especially as a dessert wine, but many choose the brut version, much like champagne and made by the same method. Spend another day in Alba, stopping at the Castello di Barolo to sample the wine and visit the wine museum. While in the area, let the aroma of white truffles tickle your senses, and treat your taste buds to a range of culinary specialties that exalt this regal tuber. Alba is the capital of the Langhe wine country; its October wine and truffle fair features a rousing medieval-style tournament. En route to Verona, make a detour to Ⓑ Parma for a quintessential Italian meal.
☞ *Chapter 5, Fortified Cities of the Po Plain* and *Chapter 9, On the Road to Parma and Modena.*

VERONA

1 or 2 days. This could be your base for an excursion north to Trento, where some of Italy's best Spumanti are produced. Verona's ancient Roman Arena, medieval buildings, and characteristic restaurants deserve some attention, too.
☞ *Chapter 2, Padua, Verona, Vicenza* and *Chapter 3, Western Trentino.*

San Remo

LIGURIAN SEA

Pisa

Livorno

Lucca

Florence

BOLZANO

1 or 2 days. If you spend the night here, you'll have time to enjoy the area's distinctive Austrian-Italian cuisine and to follow the Strada del Vino (Wine Road) that starts at Caldaro, 9 miles (15 km) south of Bolzano.
☞ *Chapter 3, Alto Adige and Cortina* and *Heart of the Dolomites.*

TREVISO

2 days. Medieval buildings, canals, mill wheels, and an abundance of inns where you can savor local dishes and wines make this a good base for exploring the area. Spend a day on an excursion to Udine, or follow the Strada del Vino Rosso (Red Wine Road) through cabernet and merlot country along the Piave River from Conegliano, where sparkling, fruity Prosecco is made. A bowl of *pasta e fagioli,* the hearty bean-and-pasta soup, a specialty of the Veneto region, will sustain you.
☞ *Chapter 2, Villa Barbaro, Treviso, and the Hillside Towns* and *Udine and Trieste.*

UDINE

1 day. Another optional overnight stop, this attractive city was ruled by Venice and shows it, with stone Venetian lions rampant on graceful buildings and columns in pretty piazzas. The Collio wine district nearby is known for its amazing and utterly distinctive local cheeses.
☞ *Chapter 2, Udine and Trieste.*

CHIANTI

2 or 3 days. Spend at least two days roaming through

the Chianti district between Florence and Siena, where you can delve into the subtle differences in vintages and perhaps swerve out of the district's official confines into the realm of Brunello di Montalcino. Here, it seems that even the tiniest village harbors a precious artwork or two by Tuscan masters. Many wineries offer guided tours of their cellars, often part of historic estates belonging to families that can trace their origins back to the Middle Ages or the Renaissance.
☞ *Chapter 8, Chianti and Southern Tuscany.*

By Public Transportation
Local trains and buses make the 45-minute run from Turin to Asti and Alba. Parma is on the Milan line; switch at Piacenza (30 minutes). Return to Turin to get a train on the main east–west line to Verona (3 hours from Turin). In Verona you'll find frequent service on another main line to Trento (1 hour) and Bolzano (a 2-hour trip). Return to Verona for a train to Padua, 60 minutes away. Treviso can be reached by train (60 minutes) or bus (70 minutes) from Padua. Udine is on a main line that passes through Padua; journey time is 2½ hours. There is fast service on the same line to Florence (2¾ hours from Venice), where you can get a local train or bus to make the 90-minute trip to Siena. Local buses serve the Chianti district.

Classical Highlights
8 to 12 days

Well colonized by the ancient Greeks, then epicenter of the Roman Empire, Italy has a wealth of classical sites, many of them in an excellent state of preservation. Rome was, of course, the capital of the Roman Empire, and a number of ancient sites remain here today, seemingly plunked down in the middle of the modern metropolis. Campania, too, is full of important classical landmarks, from both the Roman

©444

and the Greek eras, and Pompeii is not the only vestige of the eruption of nearby Mt. Vesuvius. If you have more time and a more intense interest in ancient history, you'll want to travel all the way to Sicily, the large island just off the toe of Italy's boot. Settled by the Greeks, it was a center of trade and culture in the Hellenic world, and it still is richly endowed with remarkable sites.

ROME

2 or 3 days. Spend at least a day exploring Ancient Rome—the Capitoline Hill, the Roman Forum, the Circus Maximus, the ©Colosseum, the Pantheon—and on subsequent days, venture out to the Via Appia and the Catacombs, or study classical sculptures in the Vatican Museums and antiquities in the Museo Nazionale Romano in Palazzo Altemps. It is quite an experience to turn a corner and see a famous building, such as the Colosseum, across the street, with traffic whizzing blithely past its crumbling arches.
☞ *Chapter 11, Exploring Rome.*

NAPLES AND CAMPANIA

2 or 3 days. After arriving in Naples from Rome, spend the afternoon at the Museo Archeologico Nazionale. Herculaneum and Pompeii can be visited in one day from Naples, but it would be a very full day, and it is best to break it into two separate excursions. The relics being unearthed from the lava at Herculaneum are even better preserved than the once-buried ruins at Pompeii. On another day, enjoy an excursion down the Amalfi Coast or take the A3 to Paestum, with its still-intact Greek temples. Take an optional day to tour the area just west of Naples—the Roman

amphitheater at Pozzuoli, spooky Lake Avernus, the Roman resort town at Baia, with its excavated baths, and the Sibyl's Cave at Cumae, perhaps the oldest Greek colony in Italy. ☞ *Chapter 12, Naples; The Phlegrean Fields; Herculaneum, Vesuvius, Pompeii; and The Amalfi Coast.*

TAORMINA

1 day. Get a fine view of Mt. Etna and see the town's Greek theater, its backdrop the shimmering Mediterranean; the theater is still used for a summer arts festival. ☞ *Chapter 15, Eastern Sicily.*

By Public Transportation Train service between Rome and Naples is fast and frequent, taking less than two hours on express trains. The Circumvesuviana train line can take you conveniently from Naples to Pompeii (a 35-minute trip) and Herculaneum (about 20 minutes' travel time). There is a train station right in Paestum (1½ hours from Naples). A ferry operates from Naples to Palermo, Sicily (it's a 4- to 9-hour trip), and a main train line makes the five-hour run between Palermo and Siracusa, which is also reached from Messina (a 3-hour trip) and Catania (1½ hours). Taormina is a one-hour train ride from Messina. Other sites on Sicily—such as Agrigento (2 hours from Palermo)—are better reached by bus than by the unreliable local train service.

PALERMO, SICILY

1 day. Visit the Museo Archeologico Regionale and nearby Segesta, with its fine Doric Greek temple. ☞ *Chapter 15, Palermo and Western Coast to Agrigento.*

AGRIGENTO

1 or 2 days. Explore the Valley of the Temples, an extensive Greek site, and if you have time, make your way up the coast to see the spectacular Greek temple complex at ⒹSelinunte. ☞ *Chapter 15, Western Coast to Agrigento.*

SIRACUSA

1 or 2 days. Visit the Parco Archeologico in town, the splendid Museo Archeologico, and, if there's time, take an excursion to see the mosaics at the Imperial Roman Villa at Casale, just south of Piazza Armerina. ☞ *Chapter 15, Siracusa and Eastern Sicily.*

FODOR'S
CHOICE

QUINTESSENTIAL ITALY

Even with so many special places in Italy, Fodor's writers and editors have their favorites. Here are a few that stand out.

Bellagio, Lake Como. Once called "Italy's prettiest town," Como still seems to be more of an operetta set than a resort. Surrounded by sumptuous villas and gardens, the town has long played host to honeymooners, kings, and other celebrated visitors. ☞ p. 182

Ⓒ **Lecce, Apulia.** Extravagant Baroque churches, a flowering of golden stone, are the showpieces of this city in Italy's deep south, stomping ground of the ancient Greeks, the crusaders, and a 17th-century landed aristocracy. All left their marks. ☞ p. 600

Ⓗ **Piazza del Campo, Siena.** This shell-shaped piazza dominated by the austere Palazzo Pubblico symbolizes the grace and power of the proud medieval city whose prominence in the banking and wool trades spurred a bitter rivalry with Florence. ☞ p. 352

SPECIAL MEMORIES

Festa di San Efisio, Cagliari. Tradition isn't just a cliché in Sardinia's lexicon, and none of the island's other time-honored festivals has the passion of Cagliari's annual May binge, when a processional round-trip from Cagliari to Pula and back takes four days. ☞ p. 688

Passeggiata, **Taormina.** For perfect people-watching in a dazzling seaside setting, head for Corso Umberto at dusk. All turn out for the promenade, pausing for gelato or a *caffè* and casting a vigilant eye toward magnificent Mt. Etna. ☞ p. 667

Ⓘ **Sunset gondola ride, Grand Canal, Venice.** For a truly magic moment, travel this surrealistic waterway, lined with fairy-tale palazzi veiled in silvery mists. ☞ p. 78

Ⓐ **Twilight, Positano.** The utter tranquillity of Positano at sunset is a balm to the soul. Whitewashed houses tumble down to the azure sea, shimmering under a blood-orange sky. Reserve an alfresco table at a café and let it all soak in. ☞ p. 569

WHERE ART COMES FIRST

Basilica di San Francesco, Assisi. The Giotto fresco cycle illustrating the life of St. Francis is counted among the masterpieces of the Renaissance, and the soaring double basilica, still recovering from damage sustained in a 1997 earthquake, makes them a majestic home. ☞ p. 416

Ⓙ **Chiesa dei Frari, Venice.** In this great Venetian Gothic church, you'll find two of Titian's most spectacular altarpieces; their blazing colors and luminosity cast 20th-century electricity into shadow. ☞ p. 53

Galleria degli Uffizi, Florence. A repository of unparalleled Italian masterpieces—including Botticelli's *Birth of Venus* and Leonardo da Vinci's *Adoration of the Magi*—stands steps from the Arno in the offices Vasari designed for the Medici Grand Duke Cosimo I. ☞ p. 278

Ⓓ **La Rotonda, Vicenza.** Italy's most famous Palladian villa inspired Thomas Jefferson's Monticello. If you run into the delightfully friendly owner, Count Ludovico di Valmarana, he'll direct you to the peerless Tiepolo frescoes at his family's Villa of the Dwarfs down the road. ☞ p. 90

Museo e Galleria Borghese, Rome. Cardinal Scipione Borghese's lovely 17th-century villa is an artistic treasure, and its collection of lush Baroque statuary and paintings makes it one of Italy's crown jewels. ☞ p. 469

Land of Temples, Agrigento, Sicily. More than 20 centuries of silence and solitude greet you at this archaeological site, where evocative temples built before the year AD 1 still rise out of the crests of a valley that undulates down to the blue sea. ☞ p. 647

FLAVORS

Ⓕ **Gualtiero Marchesi, Erbusco, Lago d'Iseo.** Spectacular flights of fancy are handled with classic Lombardian finesse by Italy's first proponent of *la cucina nuova*. Creativity has no limits here; accents range from the whimsy of origami to caviar garnishes. *$$$$* ☞ p. 179

Ⓑ **Da Cesari, Bologna.** Emilia-Romagna is hailed as Italy's greatest culinary region, and dining here will make you understand why. From balsamic vinegar to white truffles to Parmigiana Reggiana, the area's riches are put to masterful use in an array of traditional dishes. A wine made by the owner's family completes the experience. *$$–$$$* ☞ p. 386

Cibreo, Florence. A favorite of critics and locals for its takes on Italian standards, this classic eatery gives diners a unique choice: the front room, with high style and prices to match, or the trattoria, with a pared-down menu and table setting but the same marvelous food. *$$–$$$$* ☞ p. 300

Ⓔ **Tazza d'Oro, Rome.** Those who claim that the national coffee habit is the key to the Italian disposition find conclusive proof here in Italy's best cup of coffee. Do as the Romans do: order a glass of water as a chaser. *$* ☞ p. 484

COMFORTS

Certosa di Maggiano, Siena. A 14th-century monastery with a chapel and bucolic garden are now an exquisite country hotel. Rooms are a study in understated luxury and comfort, with fine woods, leathers, and traditional prints. *$$$$* ☞ p. 353

Ⓖ **Accademia, Venice.** Just beyond the hotel's iron gate, a secret garden awaits, complete with a diminutive Palladian-style villa, a canal parterre, and verdant trees. It's enchanting and cheery, although, alas, no secret. *$$–$$$* ☞ p. 67

La Fenice, Positano. Kissed by sunlight, embraced by bougainvillea, this tiny hotel is an oasis by the sea. Whitewashed rooms and cottages give way to a turquoise pool; away from the center of town, tranquility is assured. *$$* ☞ p. 572

31

1 VENICE

It's easy to forgive Venice for its eternal preoccupation with its own beauty. All the picture books in the world won't prepare you for the city's exotic landmarks, among them the Basilica di San Marco and the Palazzo Ducale, rising like mirages from the lagoon. With sumptuous palaces and romantic waterways, Venice is straight out of an 18th-century Canaletto masterpiece.

Updated by
Carla Lionello

I T IS CALLED LA SERENISSIMA, or "the most serene," a reference to
the monstrous power, majesty, and wisdom of this city that was for
centuries the unrivaled mistress of trade between Europe and the Orient and the staunch bulwark of Christendom against the tides of Turkish expansion. "The most serene" also refers to the way in which
those visiting have looked upon Venice, a miraculous city imper-
turbably floating on its calm blue lagoon.

Entirely built on water by men who dared defy the sea, Venice is unlike any other town. No matter how many times you have seen it in
movies or TV commercials, the real thing is more surreal and dreamlike than you ever imagined. Its landmarks, the Basilica di San Marco
and the Palazzo Ducale, seem hardly Italian: delightfully idiosyncratic,
they are exotic mélanges of Byzantine, Gothic, and Renaissance styles.
Sunlight shimmers and silvery mist softens every perspective here, and
you understand how the city became renowned in the Renaissance for
its artists' rendering of color. It is full of secrets, inexpressibly romantic, and—at times—given over entirely to pleasure.

Founded in the 5th century on the marshes by the Veneti escaping from
the barbarians, Venice rose from the waters to dominate the Adriatic
and hold the gorgeous East in fee. Early in its history the city called in
Byzantine artists to decorate its churches with brilliant mosaics, still
glittering today. In the 13th through 15th centuries, the influence of
Gothic architecture produced the characteristic type of palace in the
Florid Gothic style, with the finely wrought facades for which the town
is famous. The Renaissance arrived in Venice relatively late, at a time
when the city had reached its peak in power and prosperity. In its early
phase the style is referred to as Lombardesque, after the Lombardo family, who elaborated a specific kind of colored marble decoration made
of intertwined discs, roundels, and crosses. The city's greatest Renaissance artists—the Bellini brothers, Carpaccio, and Giorgione—were
all active between the late 15th and early 16th centuries. Along with
the stars of the next generation—Veronese, Titian, and Tintoretto—
they played a decisive role in the development of Western art, and their
work still covers walls and ceilings all over the city.

Venice's height of political and economic importance came in the 15th
and 16th centuries, when it extended its domain inland to include all
of what is now known as the Veneto region and part of Lombardy.
For 400 years the great maritime city-republic had been growing in
power, but after the 16th century the tide changed. The Ottoman Empire blocked Venice's Mediterranean trade routes, and newly emerging sea powers such as Britain and the Netherlands broke Venice's
monopoly by opening oceanic trading routes. Like its steadily dwin-
dling fortunes, Venice's art and culture began a prolonged decline, leaving only the splendid monuments to recall a fabled past, with the
18th-century paintings of Canaletto and frescoes of Giambattista
Tiepolo striking a glorious swan song.

You must walk everywhere in Venice (Venezia, in Italian) and where
you cannot walk, you go by water. Occasionally, from fall to spring,
you have to walk *in* water, when extraordinarily high tides known as
acqua alta invade the lower parts of the city, flooding Piazza San
Marco for a few hours. The problem of protecting Venice and its lagoon from dangerously high tides has generated extravagant plans and
so many committee reports that the city may sink as much under the
weight of paper as under water. Progress is being made, however. For
centuries Venice's canals were regularly dredged to keep them clean

and navigable. After nearly 30 years' neglect, the dredging of canals was finally resumed in 1993. It is hoped that waterless and malodorous canals (caused by *acqua bassa*—exceptionally low tides) will soon be a thing of the past.

In spite of these problems, Venetians have mastered the art of living well in their singular city. You'll see them going about their daily affairs in *vaporetti* (water buses), aboard the *traghetti* (traditional gondola ferries) that ply between the banks of the Grand Canal, in the *campi* (squares), and along the *calli* (narrow Venetian streets). They are nothing if not skilled—and remarkably tolerant—in dealing with the veritable armies of tourists from all over the world that at peak times inundate the city.

Pleasures and Pastimes

Carnevale

" . . . All the world repaire to Venice to see the folly and madnesse of the Carnevall . . .'tis impossible to recount the universal madnesses of this place during this time of licence," commented traveler John Evelyn in 1646. Indeed, Carnevale (Carnival) was once an excuse for all manner of carnal indulgence. In its 18th-century heyday, festivities began on December 26 and lasted two months; the festival has since traded some of its more outlandish flavor for vast commercialization and lasts only for the 10 days preceding Ash Wednesday.

Dining

The general standard of Venetian restaurants has suffered from the effects of mass tourism, but it is still possible to eat well in Venice at moderate prices. A great Venetian tradition revolves around *bacari,* the local name for the little watering holes—called *osterie* elsewhere in Italy— where locals have gone for centuries to have a glass of wine, *cicheti* (little savory snacks), and a chat. Venetian fish specialties include *sarde in saor* (layers of fried sardines, onions, pine nuts, and raisins), *baccalà mantecato* (dried cod with milk and olive oil), *moeche* (soft-shell crabs), and *seppie in umido* (cuttlefish braised in tomato sauce). For general information and price categories, *see* Dining *in* Smart Travel Tips A to Z.

Lodging

Most of Venice's hotels are in renovated palaces, but space is at a premium—and comes for a price—with all Venice lodging. The most exclusive hotels are indeed palatial, although even they may have some small, dowdy, Cinderella-type rooms. In lower categories, rooms may be cramped, and not all hotels have lounging areas. Because of preservation laws, some hotels are not allowed to have elevators. Air-conditioning can be essential if you suffer in summer heat; some hotels charge a supplement for it. Although the city has no cars, it does have boats plying the canals and pedestrians chattering in the streets, even late at night, so ask for a quiet room if noise bothers you. During the summer months, don't leave your room lights on at night *and* your window wide open: mosquitoes can descend en masse. For general information and price categories, *see* Lodging *in* Smart Travel Tips A to Z.

EXPLORING VENICE

Piazza San Marco is unquestionably the heart of Venice. The city is made up of six *sestieri*, or neighborhoods: San Marco, west of Piazza San Marco; Castello, east of San Marco; Cannaregio, to the northwest; Santa Croce and San Polo, roughly between the station and the Grand Canal; and Dorsoduro, diagonally across the Grand Canal from San

Marco. Canals, called *rii* (singular *rio*), are spanned by frequent bridges, but the Grand Canal can be crossed on foot only at three points—Ponte degli Scalzi (near the train station), Ponte di Rialto, and Ponte dell'Accademia—which decidedly complicates matters. It's supremely maddening to find yourself on the wrong bank of the Grand Canal with no bridge in sight, but taking the nearest traghetto is a wonderful way to save your legs and heal your mood.

A street is called a *calle,* but a street that runs alongside a canal is called either a *riva* or a *fondamenta.* The closed-in streets of Venice make it hard to see any reference point, such as the spire of the Campanile, above the rooftops, and the winding backstreets can confuse your sense of direction. Streets and canals may look deceptively familiar, only to make sudden dead ends. Taking a trip on one of the town's public water buses along the Grand Canal is a wonderful way to get to know the city's unique landscape, but the city should really be explored on foot; sestieri are best savored by strolling from a Renaissance church to a chatty *bacaro* (wine shop), stopping on the way to admire the boats parked in a small canal, or sitting at a café for a cappuccino and a piece of pastry while watching Venice's still-sweet dolce vita unfold before your eyes. However, a map of vaporetto routes, available at the ACTV office (☏ 041/5287886), is always helpful.

A group of 13 Venetian churches (known as Chorus churches) selected for their artistic merit charge admission of 3,000 lire/€1.55 during fixed hours that do not interfere with church services; they are Santa Maria del Giglio, Santo Stefano, Santa Maria Formosa, Santa Maria dei Miracoli, Santa Maria Gloriosa dei Frari, San Polo, San Giacomo dall'Orio, San Stae, Sant'Alvise, La Madonna dell'Orto, San Pietro di Castello, Il Redentore, and San Sebastiano. At these times there should always be someone there to provide information and a free leaflet (available in English). Postcards and booklets about these important sights are on sale. If you plan to visit more than a few, consider the cumulative ticket for 15,000 lire/€7.75 (10,000 lire/€5.15 for students under 30), valid at all churches. Audio guides for each church cost 3,000 lire/€1.55; for 6,000 lire/€3.10 you can rent audio guides to all of the churches. The artwork has been clearly labeled and free lighting systems have been installed (ask the staff to point out switches for you) in all of the Chorus churches, but you will need 200-lire/€0.10 to 500-lire/€0.25 coins to turn on the lights in other churches.

A combined museum ticket (18,000 lire/€9.30) is good for the Palazzo Ducale, Museo Correr, Museo Archeologico, Palazzo Mocenigo, Biblioteca Marciana, Museo del Merletto on Burano, and Museo Vetrario on Murano. This ticket can be bought only at the Museo Correr and Palazzo Ducale, and it is valid for one visit to each museum over the course of three months. A different combined ticket (18,000 lire/€9.30, also valid for three months) includes admission to the Galleria Franchetti, the Gallerie dell'Accademia, and the Museo Orientale. Note that Venetian museums, with the exception of the Peggy Guggenheim Collection, have no cafés inside and that you are not permitted to bring food or drink with you. The reception staff might allow you to run out to the nearest bar and return without having to pay a second admission, but this is left to their discretion—there are no set rules.

Numbers in the text correspond to numbers in the margin and on the Venice map.

Great Itineraries

IF YOU HAVE 2 DAYS

Spend your first day visiting the sights in and around that most famous of squares, Piazza San Marco, including the Basilica di San Marco. Explore the adjoining neighborhoods San Zaccaria, the Mercerie (shopping district), and Sant'Angelo–Santo Stefano central quarters if you want to catch a glimpse of Venetian life. Make an early start the following day to explore the Rialto fish and produce market, and then spend the rest of the morning cruising down the Grand Canal, stopping to visit the Gallerie dell'Accademia and the Ca' Rezzonico. End your day with a visit to San Pietro di Castello, a neighborhood particularly characteristic of Venice.

IF YOU HAVE 4 DAYS

Follow the itinerary above for the first two days. On the third day, visit the Campo dei Santi Giovanni e Paolo, northwest of Castello, and the Campo dell'Arsenale, only a short walk from your next stop, the Museo Storico Navale in Castello. Return to Piazza San Marco and take the 52 or 82 vaporetto line from San Zaccaria for a look at the impressive churches of San Giorgio Maggiore (on the island of San Giorgio Maggiore) and Redentore (on the Giudecca), both particularly beautiful at sunset. On your final day visit the islands of the lagoon: be sure not to miss Murano and its glass museums, along with the islands of Burano and Torcello.

IF YOU HAVE 6 DAYS

Start at Piazza San Marco, ending your day on the Ponte dei Sospiri next door. The next day cruise the Grand Canal, stopping first at the Ponte di Rialto to explore the market, then at the church of Santa Maria della Salute, which is a short walk from the Peggy Guggenheim Collection. Next, visit the Gallerie dell'Accademia and the nearby Ca' Rezzonico, or stroll along the romantic Zattere promenade to catch the sunset. On the third day, visit Santa Maria dei Miracoli, Campo dei Santi Giovanni e Paolo, Campo dell'Arsenale, and finally the Museo Storico Navale. If you have time, try to visit San Pietro di Castello before returning to Piazza San Marco via the Scuola di San Giorgio degli Schiavoni. On the fourth day, take the 52 or 82 vaporetto line from San Zaccaria to explore San Giorgio Maggiore and the Giudecca. Head directly across from the Giudecca to the Zattere, where you can treat yourself to an ice cream with a view. Spend the afternoon exploring the streets around Piazza San Marco and the squares of San Luca, Sant' Angelo, and Santo Stefano to catch a glimpse of busy Venetian life and the best window-shopping in town. On the fifth day, head for the Scuola dei Carmini—famous for Tiepolo's frescoes—and the Chiesa di San Sebastiano, with an impressive cycle of paintings by Veronese. A must is the Frari, home of some of Titian's best works. Next, visit the Scuola Grande di San Rocco, with dramatic pieces by Tintoretto. On your final day explore the islands of the lagoon. If you can, squeeze in a visit to the cemetery island, Cimitero di San Michele.

Piazza San Marco, the Heart of Venice

The most evocative square in the world, Piazza San Marco is the heart of Venice, a vast open square enclosed by an orderly procession of arcades marching toward the fairy-tale cupolas and marble lacework of the Basilica di San Marco. Perpetually animated during the day when it's filled with people and crowds of fluttering pigeons, it can be magical at night, especially in the winter, when melancholy mists swirl around the lampposts and bell tower.

A Good Walk

Start your day in the **Piazza San Marco** ① with a morning visit to the **Basilica di San Marco** ②, home of the Pala d'Oro and the Museo di San Marco. Next, get a bird's-eye view of the piazza and city from the **Campanile** ③. Move on to the smaller Piazzetta San Marco for a visit to the glorious **Palazzo Ducale** ④ and a look at the Ponte dei Sospiri at the east wing of the palace. Return to Piazza San Marco, where directly opposite the facade of the basilica you will find the **Museo Correr** ⑤ in the Ala Napoleonica.

TIMING

You'll need a full day to visit each sight thoroughly. If you have limited time, you will need to discipline yourself. A half day should be enough to see the essential sights: do not miss the Pala d'Oro in the basilica, the Palazzo Ducale, and, of course, the piazza itself. If you come in summer, you will have to adapt to the crowds, like the Venetians. Try visiting at odd hours to avoid tour groups.

Sights to See

★ ❷ **Basilica di San Marco.** An opulent synthesis of Byzantine and Romanesque styles, Venice's gem is laid out in the form of a Greek cross topped off with five plump domes. The basilica did not actually become the cathedral of Venice until as late as 1807, but its role as the church of the doge gave it immense power and wealth. It was begun in 1063 to house the remains of St. Mark the Evangelist, which had been filched from Alexandria two centuries earlier by two agents of the doge. The story goes that they stole the saint's remains and hid them in a barrel under layers of pickled pork to get them past the Muslim guards. The escapade is illustrated in a mosaic in the semicircular lunette over the front door on the far left. This 13th-century mosaic is the earliest one on this heavily decorated facade; look at it closely to see a picture of the church as it appeared at that time.

Over the years, this church stood as a symbol of Venetian wealth and power, and it was endowed with all the riches the Republic's admirals and merchants could carry off from the Orient, earning it the nickname Chiesa d'Oro (Golden Church). The four bronze horses that prance and snort over the central doorway (copies only, but the originals are on view indoors in the Museo di San Marco) were classical sculptures that victorious Venetians took away from Constantinople in 1204, along with lots of other loot on display here. Just inside the central front doors in the church porch is a medallion of red porphyry set in the floor to mark the spot of another of Venice's political coups: the reconciliation between Barbarossa, the Holy Roman Emperor, and Pope Alexander III (circa 1105–81), brought about by Doge Sebastiano Ziani in 1177.

The Basilica is famous for its 43,055 square ft of stunning mosaics. They continue across the ceilings, as the roof is made up of brick vaulting rather than wood. Many of the original windows were filled in to make room for even more mosaics, resulting in an interior so dark that candlelight is necessary even in daytime. The soft light shimmering against the tiny gold tiles, each mounted at a slight angle to enhance this effect, is nothing short of magical. The earliest mosaics are from the 11th and 12th centuries; later ones were done as late as the 16th century, such as the *Last Judgment* on the arch between the porch and the nave, said to be based on drawings by Tintoretto (1518–94). The dim light, the galleries high above the naves—they served as the *matroneum* (women's gallery)—the massive altar screen (or iconostasis), the single massive Byzantine chandelier, and even the Greek cross floor plan give San Marco an exotic feeling quite unlike that of most other Western churches. The pomp and mystery of the Orient are wedded to Christian belief, with awe-inspiring results.

Just off the porch to the right, step into the **Cappella Zen** (Zen Chapel), named after a local cardinal rather than a form of Buddhism, to see some earlier (13th-century) mosaics telling the story of the life of St. Mark. Next to it, the **Battistero** (Baptistery) contains a bronze font cover by Sansovino (1486–1570) and the tomb of Doge Andrea Dandolo (1307–54), a friend of Petrarch (1304–74) and a writer in his own right. Several of the earlier doges were buried here, and later ones were interred in the Chiesa dei Santi Giovanni e Paolo. Two more chapels in the left transept are worth a special look: the **Cappella della Madonna di Nicopeia** (Chapel of the Madonna of Nicopeia), which holds a precious icon (part of the loot from Constantinople) that many consider Venice's most powerful protector. Nearby is the **Cappella della Madonna dei Mascoli,** where the Virgin Mary was worshiped by a confraternity (*mascoli*), with fine 15th-century mosaics depicting her life, possibly based on drawings by Jacopo Bellini (1400–70).

The **Santuario** (Sanctuary) in the Basilica of San Marco is well worth the modest admission fee. The main altar, with its green marble canopy lifted high on carved alabaster columns, covers the tomb of St. Mark. Behind this is the real attraction: the extraordinarily sumptuous **Pala d'Oro** (Golden Altarpiece), a dazzling gilded silver screen encrusted with 1,927 precious gems and 255 enameled panels. It was originally made in Constantinople in the 11th century and then continually embellished over the next three centuries by Byzantine and Venetian master craftsmen. The bronze door leading from the sanctuary back into the sacristy is another work by Sansovino; check out the top left corner, where the artist included a self-portrait and, above that, a picture of his friend and fellow artist Titian (circa 1485–1576). The **Tesoro** (Treasury), entered from the right transept, contains many exquisite treasures borne away from Constantinople and other conquests.

From the atrium, climb the steep stairway to the **Galleria** and the **Museo di San Marco** for a look at the interior of the church from the organ gallery and a sweeping view of Piazza San Marco and the Piazzetta dei Leoncini from the outdoor gallery. The highlight of the museum is the close-up look afforded of the four gilded bronze horses that once stood outside on the gallery. The originals were probably cast in imperial Rome and later transported to the New Rome, Constantinople. Napoléon took them to Paris after he conquered Venice in 1797, but they were returned after the fall of the French Empire. Be warned: guards at the door turn away any visitors wearing shorts, short skirts, tank tops, and other attire considered inappropriate. If you want to take a free guided tour in English in summer (with less certainty in winter, since the guides are volunteers), wait on the left in the porch for a group to form. ⊠ *Piazza San Marco,* ☎ *041/5225697. Basilica:* ▨ *Free.* ☉ *May–Oct., Mon.–Sat. 9:45–5:30, Sun. 1–5:30; Nov.–Apr., Mon.–Sat. 9:45–4:30, Sun. 1–4:30. Sanctuary and Pala d'Oro:* ▨ *3,000 lire/€1.55.* ☉ *Same as basilica, last entry 30 mins before closing. Treasury:* ☎ *041/5225697.* ▨ *4,000 lire/€2.70.* ☉ *Same as basilica, last entry 30 mins before closing. Gallery and museum:* ☎ *041/5225205.* ▨ *3,000 lire/€1.55.* ☉ *Same as basilica, last entry 30 mins before closing. Tours:* ▨ *Free.* ☉ *June–Aug., Mon.–Sat. several tours daily.*

★ ❸ **Campanile.** Venice's famous brick bell tower (325 ft tall, plus the angel) stood here for 1,000 years before it collapsed one morning in 1912, practically without warning. It was swiftly rebuilt according to the old plan. Jacopo Sansovino's pretty marble loggia below, dating from the early 16th century, was crushed and promptly restored. In

Venice

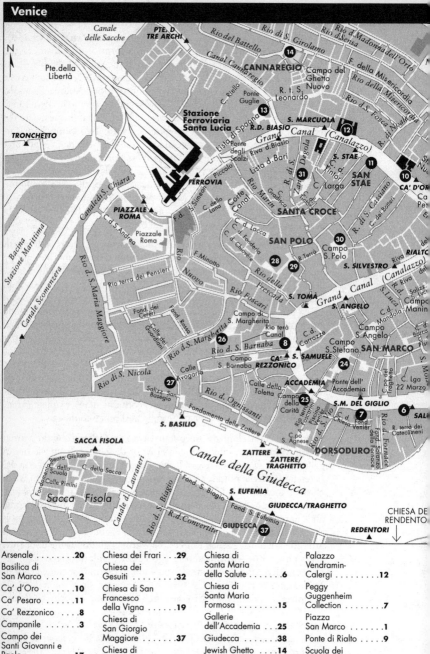

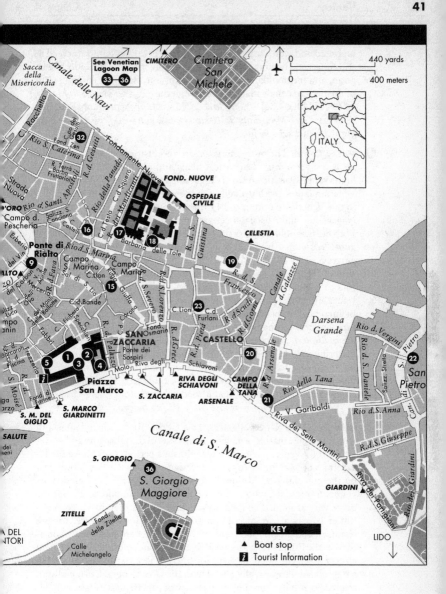

See Venetian Lagoon Map
③③ ③⑥

CIMITERO

Cimitero San Michele

0 — 440 yards
0 — 400 meters

ITALY

Sacca della Misericordia

Canale delle Navi

C. Racchetta

Fond. Zen

③②

Rio S. Caterina

R. d. Gatti

Strada Nuova

R. Terra Barba Fruttariol

Fondamente Nuove

FOND. NUOVE

C. d' Oro

Campo d. Pescheria

Rio d. Santi

Salizz. S. Canciano

C. d. Testa

C. d. Panada

C. d. Squero

C. dei Gesuiti

OSPEDALE CIVILE

CELESTIA

'ORO

Elberia

C. d. Vin

Ponte di Rialto

⑨

S. Giustina

Barbaria delle Tole

Calle Larga G. Gallina

①⑥

①⑦

①⑧

R. d. S.

④⑨

ALTO

Campo S. Marina

C. Lion

R. d. S. Marina

Campo RS. Maria

②⑩

R. d. S. Francesco

R. d. S.

R. d. S. Lorenzo

①⑤

C. d. Bande

C. Lion

②③

C. d. Furlani

CASTELLO

R. d. Scudi

R. d. S.

R. d. Greci

R. d. Pieta

Darsena Grande

Rio d. Vergini

S. Pietro

②②

San Pietro

Canale d. Galeazze

Rio d. S. Daniele

Salizz. Straila

SANO ZACCARIA

Ponte dei Sospiri

Riva degli Schiavoni

RIVA DEGLI SCHIAVONI

②⓪

②①

CAMPO DELLA TANA

R. d. Arsenale

V. Garibaldi

Rio della Tana

Rio d. S. Anna

⑤ ① ③ ② ④

Piazza San Marco

ℹ

S. ZACCARIA

ARSENALE

S. MARCO GIARDINETTI

S. M. DEL GIGLIO

Fond. d. Farine

Riva dei Sette Martiri

R. d. S. Giuseppe

Rio dei Giardini

SALUTE

Canale di S. Marco

LIDO

S. GIORGIO

③⑥

S. Giorgio Maggiore

GIARDINI

Riva dei Partigiani

ZITELLE

Fond. delle Zitelle

Calle Michelangelo

DEL NTORI

KEY

▲ Boat stop

ℹ Tourist Information

the 15th century, clerics found guilty of immoral behavior were suspended in wooden cages from the tower, sometimes forced to subsist on bread and water for as long as a year, other times left to starve. The stunning view from the tower on a clear day includes the Lido, the lagoon, and the mainland as far as the Alps but, strangely enough, none of the myriad canals that snake through the city. ⊠ *Piazza San Marco,* ☎ *041/5224064.* ⌷ *10,000 lire/€5.15.* ⊙ *June–Sept., daily 9:30 AM–9:30 PM; Oct.–May, daily 9:30–sunset; last entry 30 mins before closing. Closed 2 wks in Jan.*

❺ **Museo Correr.** The museum of the art and history of Venice, the Correr is a diverse mix of historical items and old master paintings. Exhibits range from the absurdly high-soled shoes worn by 16th-century Venetian ladies (who walked with the aid of a servant on either side) to fine Venetian painting and 11 rooms illustrating the period from the Napoleonic and Austrian occupation through the unification of Italy. Map buffs should not miss the huge, exceptionally detailed *Grande Pianta Prospettica* by Jacopo de' Barberi (about 1440–1515), which portrays every inch of 16th-century Venice. You can see the older version of the Rialto Bridge, a topless campanile on Piazza San Marco (the roof had been destroyed in a fire), and the many churches, convents, and hostels that stood in the area that is now the Giardini della Biennale before being demolished by Napoléon. The **Quadreria** (Picture Gallery) on the second floor features stunning Gothic works by the *madoneri,* a group of Greek-Venetian painters who specialized in glittering gold Madonnas. ⊠ *Piazza San Marco, Ala Napoleonica,* ☎ *041/5225625.* ⌷ *18,000 lire/€9.30 combined ticket includes entrance to Palazzo Ducale, Museo Archeologico, Biblioteca Marciana, Palazzo Mocenigo, Museo Vetrario, and Museo del Merletto.* ⊙ *Apr.–Oct., daily 9–7; Nov.–Mar., daily 9–5; last entry 1½ hrs before closing.*

★ ❹ **Palazzo Ducale** (Doge's Palace). This Gothic-Renaissance fantasia of pink-and-white marble, a majestic expression of the prosperity and power attained by Venice during its most glorious period, rises above the Piazzetta San Marco. Its top-heavy design (the dense upper floors rest on the graceful ground-floor colonnade) has always confounded architectural purists, who contend that buildings should be set out the other way around. The Palazzo was much more than just a palace—rather it was a sort of combination White House, Senate, torture chamber, and prison rolled into one. Venice's government, set up sometime in the 7th century as a participatory democracy, provided for an elected ruler, the doge, to serve for life, but in practice he was simply a figurehead. Power really rested with the Great Council, originally an elected body but, from the 13th century on, an aristocratic stronghold, with members inheriting their seats from their noble ancestors. Laws were passed by the Senate, a group of 200 elected from the Great Council (which could have as many as 1,700 members). Executive powers belonged to the College, a committee of 25 leaders. In the 14th century, the Council of Ten was formed to deal with emergency situations; it was often more powerful than the Senate, but its members could serve only for limited terms.

A fortress for the doge existed on this spot in the early 9th century; the building you see today was a product of the 12th century, although, like the basilica next door, it was continually added to and transformed over the course of time. You enter the palace at the ornate Gothic **Porta della Carta** (Gate of the Paper), where official decrees were traditionally posted; it opens onto an immense courtyard. Ahead is the **Scala dei Giganti** (Stairway of the Giants), guarded by huge statues of Mars and Neptune by Sansovino. Ordinary mortals do not get to climb these stairs, however; after paying your fee, walk along the arcade to reach the central interior staircase. Its upper flight, called the **Scala d'Oro** (Golden Staircase) and also designed by Sansovino, has lavish gilt decoration. Although it may seem odd that the government's main council rooms and reception halls would be so far upstairs, imagine how effectively foreign emissaries must have been intimidated by this arduous climb.

Visitors must also have been overwhelmed by the sumptuous decoration of these chambers, their walls and ceilings covered with works by Venice's greatest artists. Among the grand rooms you can visit are the **Anticollegio,** a waiting room outside the Collegio's chamber with two fine paintings, Tintoretto's *Bacchus and Ariadne Crowned by Venus* and the *Rape of Europa* by Veronese (1528–88); the **Sala del Collegio** (College Chamber), its ceiling magnificently painted by Veronese; and the **Sala del Senato** (Senate Chamber), with Tintoretto's *Triumph of Venice* on the ceiling. The huge *Paradise* on the end wall of the **Sala del Maggiore Consiglio** (Great Council Hall) is by Tintoretto; it is a dark, dynamic masterpiece. This is the world's largest oil painting (23 by 75 ft), a vast work commissioned for a vast hall. The massive carved and gilded ceiling is breathtaking, even dizzying, as you wheel around searching for the best vantage point from which to admire Veronese's majestic *Apotheosis of Venice* filling one of the center panels. Look at the frieze of portraits of the first 76 doges around the upper part of the walls. One portrait is missing: a black painted curtain near the left-hand corner of the wall opposite Tintoretto's painting marks the spot where the portrait of doge Marin Falier should be. A Latin inscription bluntly explains that Falier was executed for treason in 1355. The Republic never forgave him.

A guided tour of the palace's secret rooms takes you to the doge's private apartments, up into the attic and Piombi prison, and through hidden passageways to the torture chambers, where prisoners were interrogated. The 18th-century writer and libertine Casanova, a native of Venice, was imprisoned here in 1755, having somehow offended someone in power (the official accusation was of being a Freemason); he made a daring escape 15 months later and fled to France, where he continued his career of intrigue and scandal. From the east wing of the Doge's Palace, the enclosed marble **Ponte dei Sospiri** (Bridge of Sighs) arches over a narrow canal to the cramped, gloomy cell blocks of the so-called Nuova Prigione (New Prison). During the Romantic era of the 19th century, the bridge's tragic and melancholy history made it one of the prize sights for tourists. The bridge's name comes from the sighs of those being led to execution. Take a look out its windows to see the last earthly view many of these prisoners had. ✉ *Palazzo Ducale, Piazzetta San Marco,* ☎ *041/5224951.* ✉ *18,000 lire/€9.30 combined ticket includes entrance to Museo Correr, Museo Archeologico, Biblioteca Marciana, Palazzo Mocenigo, Museo Vetrario, and Museo del Merletto.* ☉ *Apr.–Oct., daily 9–7; Nov.–Mar., daily 9–5; last entry 1½ hrs before closing. "Secret Itineraries" tour:* ✉ *24,000 lire/€12.40.* ☉ *English-language tours usually daily at 10:30, reservations mandatory.*

★ ❶ **Piazza San Marco** (St. Mark's Square). If you stand at the far end of the piazza (facing the basilica), you'll notice that rather than being a strict rectangle, it opens wider at the basilica end, distorting the perspective and creating the illusion that the square is even larger than it is. On your left, the long, arcaded building is the **Procuratie Vecchie,** built in the early 16th century as offices and residences for the powerful Procurators of San Marco. Across the piazza, on your right-hand side, is the **Procuratie Nuove,** built half a century later in a more grandiose classical style. The Procuratie Nuove has impeccable architectural lineage: it was originally planned by perhaps Venice's greatest Renaissance architect, Sansovino, to carry on the look of his **Libreria Sansoviniana** (Sansovinian Library), where the **Biblioteca Nazionale Marciana** (Marciana National Library) is now housed, though Sansovino died before the building had begun. The actual designer was Vincenzo Scamozzi (circa 1552–1616), a pupil of Andrea Palladio (1508–80) and a devout neoclassicist who also completed the Libreria; later sections were completed by Baldassare Longhena (1598–1682), Venice's other great architect, who belonged firmly to the Baroque tradition. The old section of the Libreria Sansoviniana, the **Biblioteca Marciana,** contains precious manuscripts and antique hand-printed books. ⊠ *Piazza San Marco, entrance through Museo Correr,* ☎ *041/5208788.* ▨ *18,000 lire/€9.30 combined ticket includes entrance to Museo Correr, Museo Archeologico, Palazzo Ducale, Palazzo Mocenigo, Museo Vetrario, and Museo del Merletto.* ☉ *Daily 9–7.*

When Napoléon (1769–1821) entered Venice with his troops in 1797, he called Piazza San Marco "the world's most beautiful drawing room"—and promptly gave orders to redecorate it. His architects demolished a 16th-century church, with a facade designed by Sansovino, that stood at the end of the square farthest from the basilica, and put up the **Ala Napoleonica** (Napoleonic Wing), or Fabbrica Nuova (New Building), to unite the two 16th-century buildings on either side.

NEED A BREAK?	On the Procuratie Vecchie side of Piazza San Marco is the historic **Caffè Quadri** (☎ 041/5289299), shunned by Venetians during the 19th century when the occupying Austrians made it their gathering place. It's closed on Monday in November–March except during Carnival and Christmas holidays. **Caffè Florian** (☎ 041/5285338), on the Procuratie Nuove side, was regularly frequented by Casanova, Wagner, and Proust. It's closed on Wednesday in November–March.

Piazzetta San Marco. This square leads from Piazza San Marco down to the waters of the Bacino di San Marco (St. Mark's Basin). Now crowded with excursion boats, the landing was once the grand entrance to the Republic. Two tall columns rise here on the waterfront: one is topped by the winged lion, a traditional emblem of St. Mark that became by extension the symbol of Venice itself; the other bears aloft a statue of St. Theodore (the first patron saint of Venice) and his dragon.

Torre dell'Orologio. Erected in 1496, the Clock Tower has an enameled timepiece and animated figures of Moors that strike the hour (HORAS NON NUMERO NISI SERENAS states the inscription—"Only happy hours"). During Ascension Week (40 days after Easter) and on Epiphany (January 6), an angel and three wise men go in and out of the doors and bow to the Virgin Mary. It is closed for restoration until at least 2002. ⊠ *Northern side of Piazza San Marco.*

Along the Grand Canal

Venetians call it the Canalazzo, but to the rest of the world it's the Grand Canal, the city's main thoroughfare. A ribbon of water 3 km (2 mi) long and 40 to 76 yards wide, it wends from San Marco to the Stazione Ferroviaria Santa Lucia like an inverted letter S. It used to be, and to some extent still is, the 5th Avenue of Venice. It was here, from the 14th to 18th centuries, that the city's richest families lived, building for themselves a series of magnificent Venetian Gothic and Renaissance palaces—nearly 200 in number—remarkable even by the city's standards. Here the most opulent and fantastic creations of a people obsessed with opulence and fantasy appear before you in a seemingly endless panorama of unique architectural richness. It makes sense to attempt little more at first than to sample, to breathe in, the unparalleled magnificence of the Grand Canal, letting it wash over you—only metaphorically, of course; it may not be deep (average depth is 9 ft) but it's very dirty. To begin your exploration, catch Vaporetto 1 at the San Marco landing stage. (Return for a romantic gondola ride an hour or so before sunset, but for sightseeing on the canal, you get a better, more extensive, and less expensive view from a vaporetto.) Try to get one of the coveted seats in the prow, where you have an unencumbered view. Once off the vaporetto, keep in mind that the two-man traghetti allow you at many points along the Canalazzo to ferry across from one bank to the other for only 700 lire/€0.35.

A Good Boat Trip

As you leave Piazza San Marco on the vaporetto, **Chiesa di Santa Maria della Salute** ⑥, the huge, white, domed 17th-century Baroque church designed by Longhena, is on the left. Not far from this stop is the small **Peggy Guggenheim Collection** ⑦, filled with engaging 20th-century works, a nice departure from the cinquecento. Across the canal you can see the imposing terraced front of the Gritti Palace hotel, which occupies the former Palazzo Pisani. A few minutes farther on (after passing the Gallerie dell'Accademia), on the left bank at the Ca' Rezzonico stop is Longhena's Baroque **Ca' Rezzonico** ⑧. Be sure to visit the Museo del Settecento Veneziano, housed here in gilded salons. The canal narrows and boat traffic increases as you approach the **Ponte di Rialto** ⑨, arched high over the canal. The landing on the right, just beyond the Rialto, marks the lovely Venetian Gothic palace of **Ca' d'Oro** ⑩. Across the canal from the Ca' d'Oro, you'll see the classical facade, with loggias on two stories, of the Ca' Corner della Regina. Just beyond the Corner della Regina you can't miss the imposing bulk of the grand Baroque **Ca' Pesaro** ⑪, designed by Longhena. Not far beyond, on the left, another white church is adorned with Baroque statues; this is the Chiesa di San Stae, and the landing here is a gateway to an untrammeled San Stae neighborhood, with its narrow canals and airy squares. Back on the right bank, the Renaissance **Palazzo Vendramin-Calergi** ⑫ is the home of Venice's glamorous Casino. Continuing along the Grand Canal, winding toward the railway station, you will see on your right the 16th-century Ponte delle Guglie, famed for its spires, and adjacent to it the elegant facade of **Palazzo Labia** ⑬. Upon disembarking you'll be within striking distance of Venice's **Jewish Ghetto** ⑭ in the Cannaregio district.

TIMING

The sights on and along the Grand Canal can be comfortably visited in one day. Jumping on and off the vaporetto is easy, although you may be tempted just to take the ride and view the sights from the canal.

Sights to See

⑩ **Ca' d'Oro.** This lovely Venetian Gothic palace is adorned with marble traceries and ornaments once embellished with pure gold. Today it houses the **Galleria Franchetti**, a fine collection of tapestries, sculptures, and paintings. ⊠ *Calle della Ca' d'Oro, 3933 Cannaregio,* ☎ *041/5238790.* 🎟 *6,000 lire/€3.10, 18,000 lire/€9.30 combined ticket includes entrance to Museo Orientale and Gallerie dell'Accademia.* ⊙ *Tues.–Sun. 8:15–7:15, Mon. 8:15–2; last entry 30 mins before closing.*

⑪ **Ca' Pesaro.** Designed by Longhena in grand Baroque style, the palace is now home to two rather dull art collections, the **Museo Orientale** (Oriental Art Museum) and the **Galleria d'Arte Moderna** (Modern Art

Gallery), containing mostly 19th-century and some 20th-century works. ✉ *San Stae, Santa Croce,* ☎ *041/5241173.* ✆ *4,000 lire/€2.05, 18,000 lire/€9.30 combined ticket includes entrance to Galleria Franchetti and Gallerie dell'Accademia.* ☉ *Museo Orientale Tues.–Sun. 8:15–2; last entry 30 mins before closing. Galleria d'Arte Moderna closed for restoration until at least 2002.*

★ ❽ **Ca' Rezzonico.** In this huge Baroque mansion you'll find Venice's most magnificent ballroom—site of the city's greatest costume balls, the last of which was held in the 1960s to honor Elizabeth Taylor and Richard Burton. Architect Baldassare Longhena began work on it in the 1660s, and it was completed by Giorgio Massari in the 1740s. This was the last home of English poet Robert Browning (1812–89), who died here. The **Museo del Settecento Veneziano** (Museum of 18th-Century Venice), housed in gilded salons, reopened in 2001 after extensive renovations. ✉ *Fondamenta Pedrocco, 3136 Dorsoduro,* ☎ *041/2410100.* ✆ *12,000 lire/€6.20.*

❻ **Chiesa di Santa Maria della Salute.** The view of "La Salute"—as Venetians affectionately call it—from the Riva degli Schiavoni at sunset or from the Accademia Bridge by moonlight is simply unforgettable. The architect Baldassare Longhena was only 32 years old when he participated in the design competition to build a great shrine dedicated to the Virgin Mary, in gratitude for liberation from the terrible plague of 1630 and 1631 that killed 47,000 victims in Venice alone. His original idea of a classically inspired white octagonal temple covered by a colossal cupola, with a Palladian-style facade and bizarre Baroque decorations, won over the avant-garde judges of the competition. The luminous interior features six chapels with one altar each and a beautiful polychrome marble floor. Look for Titian's *Pentecost* across the aisle to the left. Since it was brought from Crete by Francesco Morosini in 1672, the Byzantine icon above the main altar has been venerated as the Madonna della Salute (of Health). The **Sacrestia Maggiore** contains a wealth of art, including five works by Titian—the best of which is the *Five Saints* altarpiece—a large *Nozze di Canaan* by Tintoretto, and a precious 15th-century *paliotto* (tapestry) with an image of the Pentecost in the style of Mantegna (1431–1506) and Giovanni Bellini (circa 1435–1516) made from wool, silk, and silver thread. A traditional thanksgiving pilgrimage during November's Festa della Madonna della Salute is one of the most evocative Venetian festivals. ✉ *Punta della Dogana, Dorsoduro,* ☎ *041/5225558.* ✆ *Church free, sacristy 2,000 lire/€1.05.* ☉ *June–Sept., daily 9:30–5:30; Oct.–May, daily 9:30–11:30 and 3–5:30.*

⓮ **Jewish Ghetto.** The neighborhood that gave the world the word "ghetto" is today a quiet warren of streets off the main arteries, away from the tourist flow, and still home to Jewish institutions, a kosher restaurant, a rabbinical school, and five synagogues. The first Jews probably came to Venice in the 11th century, although they were not granted resident status. The Rialto commercial district, as vividly recounted in Shakespeare's *The Merchant of Venice,* was dependent upon Jewish merchants and moneylenders to finance ship cargos and to help cover the government's ever-increasing war expenses. The circumstances of an extremely expensive battle against nearby Chioggia prompted the doge to allow Jews to live and work in the city.

Opposition of priests and a few prominent families never ceased, and in 1516 the Senate was compelled to confine Jews to the periphery of town. The island of Cannaregio, named then for the foundry ("geto" in Venetian) there that produced cannon for the Republic, was selected. Gates at the entrance to the neighborhood were locked at night, and two boats patrolled the surrounding canals. The first residents were Central European Jews who spoke with a German accent, and thus "geto" came to be pronounced as "ghetto." They were allowed only to lend money at low interest, operate pawnshops controlled by the government, trade in textiles, and practice medicine. (Jewish doctors were highly respected and could leave the ghetto at any hour when on duty.) Jews felt relatively safe in Venice, and in the 16th centuries the community grew considerably, with refugees arriving from the Near East, southern and central Italy, Spain, and Portugal. The ghetto was allowed to expand twice, but with the densest population in the city, still there wasn't room for everyone: notice the slanting nine-story apartment blocks on Campo del Ghetto Nuovo. Although the gates were pulled down during Napoleonic rule, the Jews realized full freedom only in the late 19th century with the founding of the Italian state. On the eve of World War II there were about 1,500 Jews left in the ghetto: 289 were deported by the Nazis. Eight returned.

Centuries of Jewish culture fill the tiny but well-arranged **Museo Ebraico,** which contains splendid silver Hanukkah lamps and torahs, Passover plates, and beautifully decorated wedding contracts in Hebrew. Guided synagogue tours in Italian and English leave hourly from the museum. €*Campo del Ghetto Nuovo, 2902/b Cannaregio,* ☎ *041/715359.* ⊠ *5,000 lire/€2.60, 12,000 lire/€6.20 with guided tour.* ☿ *Weekdays 9–5, Sun. 9–5:40; tours Sun.–Thurs., hourly 9:30–3:30.*

⑬ Palazzo Labia. Once the palatial stomping grounds of Venice's showiest 18th-century family, the palace is today the Venetian headquarters of RAI, the Italian radio and television giant. It's hard to imagine a broadcasting company in any other country establishing itself amid such opulence, but in Italy it somehow makes sense. The **Tiepolo Room,** a gorgeous ballroom in the palazzo, exhibits the final flowering of Venetian painting: illusionistic frescoes of Antony and Cleopatra by Giambattista Tiepolo (1696–1770), teeming with dwarfs, Barbary pirates, and toy dogs. The artist's true sense of pleasure is evident. ⊠ *Campo San Geremia, Cannaregio,* ☎ *041/781277 or 041/781203.* ⊠ *Free.* ☿ *Wed.–Fri. 3–4 (by appointment only).*

⑫ Palazzo Vendramin-Calergi. In 1883, composer Richard Wagner (born 1813) died in this Renaissance palazzo, which was designed by Mauro Coducci (1440–1504) in white stone with red marble medallions and an imposing carved frieze. Today it houses Venice's Casino, and if you want to see the historic rooms inside you must do so as a player.

⑦ Peggy Guggenheim Collection. Visit and delight in this small but choice gallery of 20th-century painting and sculpture, in the heiress Guggenheim's lavish former apartments in the Palazzo Venier dei Leoni. Through wealth and social connections, Guggenheim (1898–1979) became a serious patron of art, and her holdings here include several works by Picasso, Kandinsky, Pollock, Motherwell, and Ernst (who was at one time her husband). ⊠ *Entrance on Calle San Cristoforo, 701 Dorsoduro,* ☎ *041/5206288.* ⊠ *12,000 lire/€6.20.* ☿ *Wed.–Mon. 10–6.*

★ **⑨ Ponte di Rialto** (Rialto Bridge). A competition to design a permanent stone bridge across the Grand Canal (replacing earlier wooden versions) attracted the best architects of the late 1500s, including Michelangelo, Palladio, and Sansovino. But the job went to the appropriately named Antonio da Ponte. His plan focused on structure rather than elaborate decoration, and kept costs down at a time when the Republic's coffers were low due to continual wars against the Turks and the opening of oceanic trade routes. The side paths offer one of the city's most famous views: the Grand Canal full of gondolas and boats.

San Marco to Castello

For those who have been to Rome and visited the once working-class quarter of Trastevere, perhaps it will make sense to learn that the east side of Castello has been called "the Trastevere of Venice," for it has no palaces, only a dense concentration of humble houses around which neighborhood life turns. Adventurous tourists who get out of San Pietro di Castello and the Arsenale face an almost total absence of bars and shops, with the exception of Via Garibaldi, with its tiny morning produce market, low-key shop windows, and watering holes. Churches that could make a Renaissance pope jealous await as you leave Piazza San Marco behind you. The Chiesa dei Santi Giovanni e Paolo, Santa Maria dei Miracoli, San Francesco della Vigna, and San Pietro di Castello all deserve a visit, as does the Scuola di San Giorgio degli Schiavoni for its remarkable paintings by Carpaccio.

A Good Walk

Head out of Piazza San Marco under the clock tower onto the Mercerie, a mesh of upscale shopping streets that lead more or less directly to Campo San Zulian. Take Calle Guerra and Calle delle Bande to reach the white-marble **Chiesa di Santa Maria Formosa** ⑮. Follow Calle Borgoloco into Campo San Marina, where you turn right, cross the little canal, and take Calle Castelli to the **Chiesa di Santa Maria dei Miracoli** ⑯. Bear right to Calle Larga Giacinto Gallina, which leads to **Campo dei Santi Giovanni e Paolo** ⑰, site of the massive Dominican Chiesa dei Santi Giovanni e Paolo, or San Zanipolo. A powerful equestrian monument to Bartolomeo Colleoni by Florentine sculptor Andrea del Verrocchio (1435–88) stands in the square.

Leave the square by way of Salizzada dei Santi Giovanni e Paolo, where you find the church of Santa Maria dei Derelitti, better known as the **Ospedaletto** ⑱, with its over-the-top Baroque facade by Longhena. Continue along Barbaria de le Tole, Calle del Cafetier, and Calle Zen. Down Ponte Santa Giustina make a left on Salizzada Santa Giustina to reach **Chiesa di San Francesco della Vigna** ⑲, with its stern, classical facade. Find your way to Campo dell'Arsenale, preferably via Campo della Celestia and Campiello Do Pozzi, to see the main entrance to the **Arsenale** ⑳, the immense shipyard of the Republic. The **Museo Storico Navale** ㉑ on nearby Campo San Biagio has four floors of scale boat models. If you still have time and energy, go east to the island of San Pietro and the **Chiesa di San Pietro di Castello** ㉒, which, with its small harbor and a long wooden bridge straddling the canal that separates it from the rest of town, is one of Venice's most picturesque corners. On your way back from the eastern district, about midway between the Arsenale and Piazza San Marco, finish up your tour at the **Scuola di San Giorgio degli Schiavoni** ㉓.

TIMING

An exploration of this neighborhood and as far east as the island of San Pietro should take five to six hours. Try to avoid walking around this mostly open neighborhood during the hottest hours of the day in summer. Allow some time to browse through the Mercerie district.

Sights to See

⑳ **Arsenale.** The immense Arsenal dockyard was founded, tradition holds, by Doge Falier in 1104, and it was built up considerably throughout the 16th century. For a republic founded on sea power, having a huge, state-of-the-art shipyard was of paramount importance, and this one was legendary for its size and efficiency. Galleys 200 ft long were built here, capable of carrying 300 tons of ginger, pepper, silk, and silver. Until the middle of the 16th century, when slaves began to be used in the galleys, crews were made up of men who volunteered in exchange for an opportunity to amass pounds and pounds of precious merchandise from ports all around the eastern Mediterranean, to be resold if they survived the perils of the trip. With 16,000 "Arsenalotti" on the payroll, a perfectly armed warship could be built in just 12 hours; 100 ships were built in 60 days in 1597 for the battle against the Turks at Cyprus. After that war, the old Venetian word *arzanà* (from the Arabic *darsina'a*, meaning workshop) was adopted by another 14 languages. Dante visited the shipyards several times, and the half-naked bodies of the workers, armed with pitches and boiling tar, inspired his vision of the seventh level of Hell in his *Inferno*. ✉ *Campo dell'Arsenale, Castello.*

★ ⓱ **Campo dei Santi Giovanni e Paolo.** This large square has the massive Dominican **Chiesa dei Santi Giovanni e Paolo**—or San Zanipolo as it's known in Venetian dialect—on one side and the powerful equestrian **Monumento di Bartolomeo Colleoni** by Florentine sculptor Andrea del Verrocchio on the other. Colleoni had served Venice well as a *condottiere,* or mercenary commander (the Venetians preferred to pay others to fight for them on land). When he died in 1475, he left his fortune to the city on the condition that a statue be erected in his honor "in the piazza before St. Mark's." The republic's shrewd administrators coveted Colleoni's ducats but had no intention of honoring anyone, no matter how valorous, with a statue in Piazza San Marco. So they commissioned the statue and put it up before the Scuola di San Marco, which is off to the side, enabling them to collect the loot. San Zanipolo contains tombs of several doges, as well as a wealth of art. Don't miss the Cappella del Rosario (Rosary Chapel), off the left transept; with its Veronese ceiling paintings, it's a sumptuous study in decoration, built in the 16th century to commemorate the 1571 victory of Lepanto, in western Greece, in which Venice and a combined European fleet destroyed the Turkish navy. ✉ *Campo dei Santi Giovanni e Paolo,* ☎ 041/5235913. ⏱ *Mon.–Sat. 7:30–12:30 and 3:30–6, Sun. 3:30–6.*

⓳ **Chiesa di San Francesco della Vigna** (Church of St. Francis of the Vineyard). The original 13th-century church, surrounded by a vineyard kept by the Franciscans, was enlarged and rebuilt by Sansovino in 1534. Don't come all the way without a pocket full of 500-lire coins—you'll need them to turn on the lights, which bring to life the surprising artwork inside. All labeled paintings are worth at least a look, especially the triptych with the Sts. Girolamo, Bernardino da Siena, and Ludovico by Antonio Vivarini (circa 1415–76 or '84), on the wall to the left of the main door, and Giovanni Bellini's *Madonna with Saints and Patron,* down the steps to the left, inside the Cappella Santa. The highlight is the glittering gold *Madonna Adoring the Child* by Antonio da Negroponte, an inspiring work that invites contemplation. Painted in the second half of the 15th century, this masterpiece marks the transition from the Gothic style, which it preserves in a certain formal rigidity, to that of the Renaissance, which is seen in the elaborately detailed decoration and naturalistic subjects. Two pretty cloisters open out from the left nave, their pavement constructed entirely of tombstones of patricians, admirals, and cardinals, testimony to the fact that San Francesco della Vigna was once favored by noble Venetian circles. ✉ *Campo San Francesco della Vigna, Castello,* ☎ 041/5206102. ⏱ *Mon.–Sat. 8–noon and 3–7, Sun. 3–7.*

⓴ **Chiesa di San Pietro di Castello.** This church is famous for its imposing campanile, the first in Venice to be built from the marblelike Istrian stone rather than from brick. It stands out against the peaceful Renaissance cloister, for years a sort of squatters colony, and the rather picturesque, workaday slips along the Canale di San Pietro. The Veneti had settled here long before Venice ever existed as a city in its own right, but now the "island" is a particularly tranquil, almost forgotten place, with nothing to suggest that for more than 1,000 years this church served as Venice's cathedral—until the Basilica di San Marco superseded it in 1807. The interior features some minor 17th-century art and the archaic Cattedra di San Pietro. ⊠ *Campo San Pietro Apostolo, Castello,* ☎ *041/5238950.* ⊒ *3,000 lire/€1.55, 13-church ticket 15,000 lire/€7.75.* ☉ *Mon.–Sat. 10–5, Sun. 1–5.*

⑯ Chiesa di Santa Maria dei Miracoli. Perfectly proportioned and sheathed in marble, this church is an early Renaissance gem, decorated inside with exquisite marble reliefs. Notice how the architect, Pietro Lombardo (circa 1435–1515), made the church look bigger with various optical illusions: varying the color of the exterior marble to create the effect of distance; using extra pilasters to make the building's canal side look longer; slightly offsetting the arcade windows to make the arches look deeper. The church was built in the 1480s to house an image of the Virgin Mary that is said to perform miracles—look for this icon on the high altar. The church reopened in 1998 after a three-year restoration to slow down the effects of saltwater erosion. ⊠ *Calle delle Erbe, Castello,* ☎ *041/5235293.* ⊒ *3,000 lire/€1.55, 13-church ticket 15,000 lire/€7.75.* ☉ *Mon.–Sat. 10–5, Sun. 1–5.*

⑮ Chiesa di Santa Maria Formosa. This graceful white marble church was inspired by a vision of *una Madonna formosa* (a buxom Madonna) that St. Magno experienced in the 7th century. The Madonna told him to follow a small white cloud and build a church wherever it settled. The present building, built by Coducci in 1492, was grafted onto the foundations of an earlier 11th-century church that replaced Magno's original. The church's interior is a unique architectural blend, merging a welter of Renaissance decoration with Coducci's ersatz collection of Byzantine cupolas, barrel vaults, and narrow-columned screens. Of interest are two fine paintings, Bartolomeo Vivarini's *Madonna of the Misericordia* and Palma Vecchio's *Santa Barbara.* Outside, there is a lively square with a few sidewalk cafés and a small vegetable market on weekday mornings. ⊠ *Campo Santa Maria Formosa, Castello,* ☎ *041/5234645.* ⊒ *3,000 lire/€1.55, 13-church ticket 15,000 lire/€7.75.* ☉ *Mon.–Sat. 10–5, Sun. 1–5.*

🖐 ㉑ Museo Storico Navale (Museum of Naval History). Four floors of scale boat models and an annex containing actual boats—from gondolas to the famous doges' ceremonial boat, *Bucintoro*—are guaranteed to fascinate children and boat lovers. ⊠ *Campo San Biagio, Arsenale, Castello,* ☎ *041/5200276.* ⊒ *3,000 lire/€1.55.* ☉ *Weekdays 8:45–1:30, Sat. 8:45–1.*

⑱ Ospedaletto. This "little hospital" (as the name translates) dates from the 16th century and was one of Venice's four foundling hospitals set up in church's annexes, in this case that of Santa Maria dei Derelitti (St. Mary of the Destitute). Each hospital had an orchestra and choir of orphans, who performed regularly for the faithful. Note the large gallery above the Derelitti's altar, built to accommodate the young musicians. The orphanage is now a home for the elderly. The beautiful 18th-century **Sala della Musica** (Music Room), where rehearsals took place and patrons and honored guests were received, is the only one of its kind to survive. It has been magnificently restored and can be visited (enter through the church). On the Music Room's far wall is a lovely fresco by Jacopo Guarana (1720–1808), depicting Apollo, god of music, surrounded by the orphan musicians conducted by their master, Pasquale Anfossi. Note that at press time the Ospedaletto was closed indefinitely for restoration; call ahead for the current status. ✉ *Barbaria de le Tole, Castello.* 🖅 *3,000 lire/€1.55.* ☉ *Church and Music Room Apr.–Sept., Thurs.–Sat. 4–7; Oct.–Mar., Thurs.–Sat. 3–6. Closed for restoration; call 041/2702464 or 041/520063.*

㉓ **Scuola di San Giorgio degli Schiavoni.** This is one of numerous *scuole* built during the time of the Republic. These weren't schools, as the present-day Italian word would imply, but instead an important network of institutions that were established by different social groups—enclaves of foreigners, tradesmen, followers of a particular saint, and parishioners. The Scuola di San Giorgio dei Greci was founded in 1451 by the local Dalmatian community, which still owns it. Many scuole were decorated lavishly by the most fashionable artists of the day. Here, one master did it all, creating an unpretentious, harmonious ambience and one of the most beautiful rooms in all of Italy. Although not well known outside Venice, where he spent all his life, Vittore Carpaccio (circa 1465–1525) painted devotional *teleri* (large narrative canvases of legendary and religious scenes) against a background of Venetian architecture, combining observation, fantasy, and a warm sense of color. For this scuola, Carpaccio concentrated on scenes from the lives of three saints especially venerated in Dalmatia: St. George, St. Tryphone, and St. Jerome. Study the exuberance of *St. George Slaying the Dragon* or the vivid colors and details in *The Funeral of St. Jerome* and *St. Augustine in His Study.* ✉ *325/a Castello, near Ponte dei Greci,* ☎ *041/5228828.* 🖅 *5,000 lire/€2.60.* ☉ *Nov.–Mar., Tues.–Sat. 10–12:30 and 3–6, Sun. 10–12:30; Apr.–Oct., Tues.–Sat. 9:30–12:30 and 3:30–6:30, Sun. 9:30–12:30.*

Dorsoduro, San Polo, and Santa Croce

If churches, further ramblings along dreamy canals, and masterpieces by great Venetian artists such as Titian and Tintoretto capture your interest, head out of Piazza San Marco to explore the sestieri on the other side of the Grand Canal.

A Good Walk

Leave Piazza San Marco via Bocca di Piazza. Next take Calle Larga XXII Marzo to **Campo Santo Stefano** ㉔, dominated by the 14th-century church of Santo Stefano. Join the stream of pedestrians crossing the Grand Canal on the Ponte dell'Accademia to the Dorsoduro (literally "hard back" for its strong clay foundation) district. The bridge leads you directly to the **Gallerie dell'Accademia** ㉕, displaying an unparalleled collection of Venetian painting. Continue toward Campo Santa Margherita, passing Mondonovo, one of Venice's best mask shops. Stop at the **Scuola dei Carmini** ㉖ to see Giambattista Tiepolo's ceiling paintings. Tiepolo was strongly influenced by Paolo Veronese, some of whose finest works can be seen if you take a short and rewarding canalside detour along Fondamenta del Soccorso, making a sharp left turn along Fondamenta di San Sebastiano, and crossing the second bridge on the right, which leads to the **Chiesa di San Sebastiano** ㉗.

Retracing your steps, continue from Campo Santa Margherita (via Calle San Pantalon to Calle dei Preti to Calle della Scuola) to the **Scuola Grande di San Rocco** ㉘, filled with dark, dramatic canvases by the mannerist Tintoretto. At the end of Salizzada San Rocco, turn left to find the entrance to the Franciscan **Chiesa dei Frari** ㉙. The streets between Campo Santa Margherita and the Frari have attractive cafés, pubs, ice cream shops, and pastry shops catering to the students of nearby University Ca' Foscari. From the Frari, head south to Campo San Tomà to reach

Campo San Polo ㉚, via Rio terà dei Nomboli, Calle dei Saoneri, and Salizzada San Polo, all lined with crafts shops. From here follow the main drag along Calle della Madonetta, Calle dell'Olio, Ruga del Ravano, and Ruga Vecchia San Giovanni to the Rialto shopping district, where you can cross the Grand Canal for the shortcut back to San Marco. Alternatively, you can go north from Campo San Polo by way of Calle Bernardo, Calle dello Scaleter, Rio terà Parrucchetta, and Calle del Tintor to **Campo San Giacomo dall'Orio** ㉛, where the 13th-century church of San Giacomo stands in an enchanting square. Here you're not far from the San Stae vaporetto landing, so you can take the boat back along the Grand Canal to the heart of the city.

TIMING

The value of a detailed map and a sense of patience when navigating the streets of this walk can't be overemphasized. Not including time spent in the Gallerie dell'Accademia and time to get lost, the route will take three to four hours to cover. There are fewer people out and about in the early afternoon, which makes it easier to get around, but keep in mind that many of the shops and some churches are also closed at that time. Also remember: only three bridges span the Grand Canal—the Ponte degli Scalzi, Ponte di Rialto, and the Ponte dell'Accademia—so be sure to be near one of them when you're ready to call it a day. If you're not, you may have to backtrack.

Sights to See

㉛ **Campo San Giacomo dall'Orio.** The several streets that lead to this square all approach it laterally, giving no sense of this pleasantly odd-shaped campo. Trees, benches, a public fountain—so rare on Venetian campi—make this a perfect place to rest, relax, or even have a picnic. Founded according to legend in the 9th century on an island still populated by wolves, the church as it presently stands here was built in 1225 and modified in the Renaissance, but it still retains a distinctly archaic atmosphere. Perhaps it's the low, monumental, and unmatched Byzantine columns that make this place seem like an old pagan temple set beneath a beautiful 15th-century ship's-keel roof. In the sanctuary, the large, mystical Lombardesque crosses in marble and gilded wood restore a religious sense to the space, surrounded and protected by a bevy of small medieval Madonnas. The two sacristies contain works by Palma il Giovane (circa 1544–1628) and Veronese. ⊠ *Campo San Giacomo dall'Orio.* 🎟 *3,000 lire/€1.55, 13-church ticket 15,000 lire/€7.75.* ☉ *Mon.–Sat. 10–5, Sun. 1–5.*

㉚ **Campo San Polo.** Only Piazza San Marco is larger than this square, where not even the pigeons manage to look cozy and the echo of the children's voices bouncing off the surrounding palaces makes the space seem even more cavernous. But not so long ago this campo was a throbbing center of activity, animated by shows, bull races, fairs, military parades, and packed markets. The **Chiesa di San Polo**, founded in the 9th century, underwent a major reconstruction in the late Gothic period and a neoclassical makeover in the early 1800s. Extensive restoration in the 1930s brought back the wonderful wooden ship's-keel roof, as well as the earlier Byzantine window on the facade. The artwork inside is not particularly engaging, as the 19th-century alterations were so costly that the friars had to sell the best paintings in order to pay the bills. The *Stations of the Cross* in the Oratory to the left of the entrance is the remaining gem: painted by Giambattista Tiepolo's son Giandomenico (1727–1804), the 14 scenes are remarkably expressive and theatrical. ⊠ *Campo San Polo.* 🎟 *3,000 lire/€1.55, 13-church ticket 15,000 lire/€7.75.* ☉ *Mon.–Sat. 10–5, Sun. 1–5.*

㉔ **Campo Santo Stefano.** One of the busiest campi in all of Venice, this now-fashionable square was once used for bullfights, during which bulls (or oxen) were tied to a stake and baited by dogs. For centuries the square was grassy, all except for a stone avenue known as the *liston*. This became such a popular place to stroll that it led to a Venetian expression *andare al liston,* which means "go for a walk." Check out the 14th-century **Chiesa di Santo Stefano** and its bell tower—the tipsiest in all Venice—and stop in to see the ship's-keel roof, a type found in several of Venice's older churches and the work of master shipbuilders. The most valuable art, including three paintings by Tintoretto and a cross by Paolo Veneziano, is kept in the **Sacristy.** *Church:* ✉ *Campo Santo Stefano,* ☎ *041/5225061.* 🎟 *Sacristy: 3,000 lire/€1.55, 13-church ticket 15,000 lire/€7.75.* ⊘ *Mon.–Sat. 10–5, Sun. 1–5.*

NEED A BREAK? **Caffè Paolin** (✉ 3464 Campo Santo Stefano, ☎ 041/5220710), closed Saturday, makes some of the best gelato in Venice and is a pleasant spot from which to watch the passing parade.

★ ㉙ **Chiesa dei Frari** (Church of the Friars). This immense Gothic church of russet-color brick was built in the 14th century for the Franciscans. I Frari, as it is known locally, is deliberately austere, befitting the simplicity of the Franciscan rule, in which spirituality and poverty were key tenets. Paradoxically, the Frari also contains a number of the most sumptuous and brilliant pictures in any Venetian church. Chief among them are the magnificent **Titian altarpieces,** arguably the most dazzling works that the prolific artist produced. For its mellow luminosity, first check out Giovanni Bellini's *Madonna and Four Saints* in the sacristy, painted in 1488 for precisely this spot. The contrast with the heroic energy of Titian's large *Assumption* over the main altar—painted little more than 30 years later—is startling and clearly illustrates the immense and rapid development of Venetian Renaissance painting. This work caused a sensation when unveiled in 1519 and was immediately acclaimed for its winning combination of Venetian color—especially the glowing reds—and classical Roman figure style.

The *Pesaro Madonna* over the first altar on the left near the main altar is also by Titian; his wife, who died shortly afterward in childbirth, posed for the figure of Mary. The Madonna was radical for its time because the main figure was not placed squarely in the center of the painting, creating an unusual dynamism. On the same side of the church, look at the spooky, pyramid-shape monument to the sculptor Antonio Canova (1757–1822), which contains his heart. Across the nave is a neoclassical 19th-century monument to Titian, executed by two of Canova's pupils. ✉ *Campo dei Frari, San Polo,* ☎ *041/5222637.* 🎟 *3,000 lire/€1.55, 13-church ticket 15,000 lire/€7.75.* ⊘ *Mon.–Sat. 9–6, Sun. 1–6.*

㉗ **Chiesa di San Sebastiano.** Veronese established his reputation with the frescoes he painted at this church when still in his twenties, after leaving his native Verona. He continued to embellish the interior for more than a decade with amazing perspective and trompe-l'oeil scenes. In 1588 he was buried here. ✉ *Campo San Sebastiano, Dorsoduro,* ☎ *041/5282487.* 🎟 *3,000 lire/€1.55, 13-church ticket 15,000 lire/€7.75.* ⊘ *Mon.–Sat. 10–5.*

★ ㉕ **Gallerie dell'Accademia** (Accademia Galleries). Housed in this magnificent museum is unquestionably the most extraordinary collection of Venetian art. Highlights include Giovanni Bellini's altarpiece from the church of San Giobbe (notice how he carried the church's architectural details right into the frame of the painting) and his moving

Madonna with St. Catherine and the Magdalen; a fine *St. George* by Andrea Mantegna (1431–1506), Bellini's brother-in-law from Padua; and Veronese's monumental *Feast in the House of Levi.* Here is the Venetian High Renaissance in all its richness, even glamour. The third painting was commissioned as a Last Supper, but the Inquisition took issue with Veronese's inclusion of jesters and German soldiers in it. Veronese avoided the charge of profanity by changing the title, and the picture was then supposed to depict the bawdy but still biblical feast of Levi. A room preserved from the Scuola della Carità—which previously occupied the museum's site—holds on one wall its original masterpiece, Titian's *Presentation of the Virgin.*

Don't miss the room containing various views of 15th- and 16th-century Venice by Vittore Carpaccio and Giovanni Bellini's brother, Gentile—study them to see how little the city has changed since then. Room V holds one of the gallery's most famous paintings, the *Tempest* by Giorgione (1477–1510), a work that has consistently baffled art historians while charming them with its magical painterly qualities and exquisite landscape. The work is nothing if not ambiguous (what exactly is going on between this impassive young soldier and naked woman suckling a child?) and provokes a sense of menace with its gathering summer storm in the background. For the first time in art, the atmosphere of a painting became as important as the figures. More works by Giovanni Bellini, Cima da Conegliano, Carpaccio, Titian, Tintoretto, and Veronese are housed in the **Quadreria** on the top floor, which can be visited every Tuesday afternoon by reservation (☎ 041/5222247, no extra charge) or daily by appointment as part of a **guided tour** (☎ 041/713498); it is essential to agree on the guide's fee before starting the tour). The audio guide (7,000 lire/€3.60 for one, 10,000 lire/€5.15 for two) is well done, but quite selective, and should be considered only if you have very limited time, as it doesn't add anything to the excellent annotation (in English) in each room. ✉ *Campo della Carità, Accademia, Dorsoduro,* ☎ *041/5222247.* 🎫 *12,000 lire/€6.20.* ☉ *Tues.–Sun. 8:15–7:15, Mon. 8:15–2; longer hrs in summer.*

㉖ Scuola dei Carmini. This scuola is home to Giambattista Tiepolo's ceiling paintings, commissioned to honor the Carmelite order by depicting prominent Carmelites in conversation with saints and angels. Of the three great Venetian painters whose names start with *T* (Titian, Tintoretto, and Tiepolo), Tiepolo came last chronologically (he painted in the 18th century, the others in the 16th century) and achieved the greatest international fame in his own time. An underlying melancholy in his ethereal, brightly colored paintings betrays a man of sober piety. Tiepolo's vivid technique transformed some unpromising religious themes into flamboyant displays of color and movement. Mirrors on the benches make it easier to see the ceilings. ✉ *Campo dei Carmini, Dorsoduro,* ☎ *041/5289420.* 🎫 *8,000 lire/€4.15.* ☉ *Nov.–Mar., daily 9–4; Apr.–Oct., Mon.–Sat. 9–6, Sun. 9–4.*

㉘ Scuola Grande di San Rocco. This workshop is famed for its many dark, dramatic canvases by Tintoretto. Born some 30 years after Titian, Jacopo Robusti—called Tintoretto because his father was a dyer—was more mystical and devout than the sophisticated older painter. Though his colors are equally brilliant, he carried Titian's love of motion and odd composition to almost surreal levels, in the same mannerist vein as El Greco (who was at one time a pupil of Titian). In 1564, Tintoretto edged out the other painters competing for the commission to decorate this building by submitting not a sketch but a finished work, which he moreover offered free of charge. The series of more than 50 paintings he ultimately created took a total of 23 years to complete.

These works on Old and New Testament themes were restored in the 1970s, and Tintoretto's inventive use of light has once more been revealed. The Sala del Tesoro holds a collection of precious artworks dedicated to San Rocco. ⊠ *Campo San Rocco, Frari,* ☎ *041/5234864.* 🔲 *10,000 lire/€5.15.* ⊙ *Nov. 3–Mar., daily 10–4; Apr.–Nov. 2, daily 9–5:30; last entrance ½ hr before closing.*

Islands of the Lagoon

The perfect vacation from your Venetian vacation is an escape to the magical islands of the city's lagoon—Murano, Burano, and Torcello—which can provide welcome relief after the brooding, enclosed charms of Venice itself. Far from the madding crowd, Torcello is the actual birthplace of Venice. Today it is visited for its haunting melancholy, its great Byzantine-era church, and that famous outpost of elegance, the Locanda Cipriani. The island is also perfect for picnics, but bring food from Venice. Burano is a toy town of little houses all painted in a riot of color—blue, yellow, pink, ocher, and dark red; here visitors love to shop for the best in Venetian lace. Murano is known the world over for its glass—but guided tours usually involve high-pressure attempts to make you buy, with little time left for anything else. It's worth the extra effort to make your own way around the islands, using the good vaporetto connections. There are several options for getting to these islands: Lines 12 and 14 to Murano, Burano, and Torcello from the landing stage at Fondamente Nuove, almost due north of San Marco; and Line 41, which you can pick up in town, runs to Fondamente Nuove, San Michele, and Murano, where you change to Line 14 to continue to Torcello.

A Good Boat Trip

Take Line 41 from Piazza San Marco to the Fondamente Nuove stop. Here, in the Campo dei Gesuiti, is the **Chiesa dei Gesuiti** ㉜. It's only a five-minute ride from here to **San Michele** ㉝, the cemetery island and the church of San Michele in Isola. Another five minutes on Line 52 takes you to **Murano** ㉞, either the Navagero or the Museo stops. From the Navagero stop, it's a five-minute walk to the Museo Vetrario: follow Fondamenta Navagero, cross Ponte San Donato, and turn left onto Fondamenta Giustinian. The museum has a fascinating display of glass objects dating from the oldest Roman period (AD 1st–3rd centuries) to the 19th century. Make your way to the Faro stop and take Line 12 to **Burano** ㉟, about 30 minutes farther, where you can see traditional lace making at the Scuola di Merletti di Burano. Line 12 continues from the Burano landing stage to the sleepy green island of **Torcello** ㊱, only five minutes away. A brick-paved lane leads up from the landing stage and follows the curve of the canal toward the center of the island. You pass the Locanda Cipriani, one of Hemingway's haunts. Just beyond is the grassy square that holds the island's only surviving monuments. Next to it is the cathedral of Santa Maria Assunta, built in the 11th century.

TIMING

Boats leave every hour and the trip takes about 50 minutes each way. Stopping on every island and visiting the various sights will take a full day. If, however, you limit yourself to Torcello, Burano, and Murano, a full morning or a full afternoon will suffice.

Sights to See

★ ㉟ **Burano.** Dotting this quiet fishing village are well-maintained houses painted in cheerful colors. Lace is to Burano what glass is to Murano, but be prepared to pay a lot for the real thing—$1,000 to $2,000 for a 10-inch doily. Stalls line the roughly 100 yards from the landing stage to Piazza Galuppi, the main square. The vendors, many of them fish-

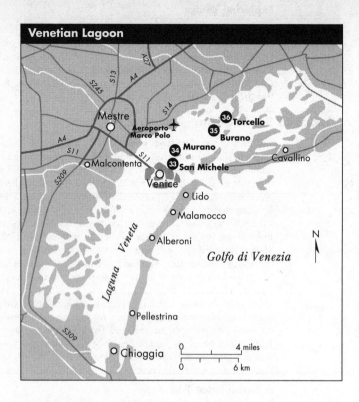

Venetian Lagoon

ermen's wives, are generally good-natured and blessedly unfamiliar with the techniques of the hard sell.

The **Museo del Merletto** (Lace Museum) is the best place to learn about the lace-making traditions of Burano and the skills needed to make the more expensive lace. ⊠ *Piazza Galuppi,* ☎ *041/730034.* ◱ *8,000 lire/€4.15, 18,000 lire/€9.30 combined ticket includes entry to Museo Correr, Palazzo Ducale, Museo Archeologico, Biblioteca Marciana, Palazzo Mocenigo, and Museo Vetrario.* ☉ *Apr.–Oct., Wed.–Mon. 9– 5; Nov.–Mar., Wed.–Mon. 10–4.*

㉜ Chiesa dei Gesuiti. This 18th-century church dominating the Campo dei Gesuiti is extravagantly Baroque in style; the classical arches and straight lines of the Renaissance have been abandoned in favor of flowing, twisting forms. The marble of the gray-and-white interior is used like brocade, carved into swags and drapes. Titian's *Martyrdom of St. Lawrence,* over the first altar on the left, is a dramatic example of the artist's feeling for light and movement. ⊠ *Campo dei Gesuiti,* ☎ *041/5231610.* ☉ *Daily 10–noon and 5–7.*

★ **㉞ Murano.** Like Venice, Murano is made up of a number of smaller islands linked by bridges. It is known for its glassworks, which you can visit to see how glass is made. Many of these line the **Fondamenta dei Vetrai,** the canalside walkway leading away from the Colonna landing stage. The houses are simpler than many of their Venetian counterparts; traditionally they were workmen's cottages. Just before the junction with Murano's Grand Canal—250 yards up from the landing stage—is the **Chiesa di San Pietro Martire.** This 16th-century reconstruction of an earlier Gothic church has several works by Venetian masters, notably a *Madonna and Child* by Giovanni Bellini and *St. Jerome* by Veronese.

The Venetian glass at the **Museo Vetrario** (Glass Museum) ranges from priceless antique to only slightly less-expensive modern. The museum details authentic Venetian styles and patterns and the history of Murano's glassworks, moved here from Venice in the 13th century because they were a fire hazard. ⊠ *Murano*, ☎ *041/739586.* ⊠ *8,000 lire/€4.15, 18,000 lire/€9.30 combined ticket includes entry to Museo Correr, Palazzo Ducale, Museo Archeologico, Biblioteca Marciana, Palazzo Mocenigo, and Museo del Merletto.* ⊙ *Apr.–Oct., Thurs.–Tues. 10–5; Nov.–Mar., Thurs.–Tues. 10–4.*

③③ **San Michele.** Venice's cypress-lined cemetery island is home to the pretty Renaissance church of **San Michele in Isola,** designed by Coducci in 1478, and Venice's cemetery. It is sobering to walk among the gravestones with the sound of water lapping on all sides. American poet Ezra Pound (1885–1972), Russian impresario and art critic Sergey Diaghilev (1872–1929), and composer Igor Stravinsky (1882–1971) are all buried here. For most Venetians, however, the stay here is short-lived, as the cemetery has a policy of transferring those interred more than 10 years to another, less grandiose cemetery, so as to make room for new arrivals. ☎ *041/2730111.* ⊙ *Nov.–Mar., daily 7:30–4; Apr.–Oct., daily 7:30–6.*

★ **③⑥** **Torcello.** This is where the first Venetians landed in their flight from the barbarians 1,500 years ago. Even after many settlers left to found the city of Venice on the island of Rivo Alto (Rialto), Torcello continued to grow and prosper until its main source of income, wool manufacturing, was priced out of the marketplace. It's hard to believe now, looking at this almost deserted island, that in the 16th century it had 20,000 inhabitants and 10 churches.

Santa Maria Assunta, the cathedral for Torcello, dates from the 11th century. The ornate Byzantine mosaics are testimony to the importance and wealth of an island that could attract the best artists and craftsmen of its day. The vast mosaic on the inside of the facade depicts the *Last Judgment* as artists of the 11th and 12th centuries imagined it: figures writhe in vividly depicted contortions of pain. Facing it, as if in mitigation, is the calm mosaic figure of the Madonna, alone in a field of gold above the staunch array of Apostles. The bell tower can be climbed by appointment. ⊠ *Torcello*, ☎ *041/730084.* ⊠ *5,000 lire/€2.60.* ⊙ *June–Sept., daily 10:30–6; Oct.–May, daily 10–4.*

NEED A BREAK?	**Locanda Cipriani** (⊠ Torcello, ☎ 041/730150), closed Tuesday and early January–early February, is an inn famous for its good food and the patronage of Ernest Hemingway, who often came to Torcello for the solitude. These days, Locanda Cipriani—not to be confused with the Cipriani hotel on the Giudecca—is about the busiest spot on the island, as well-heeled customers arrive on high-speed powerboats.

San Giorgio Maggiore and the Giudecca

Beckoning all travelers across St. Mark's Basin like some sort of Venetian Bali Hai is the island of San Giorgio Maggiore, separated by a canal from the Giudecca. A tall brick campanile on that distant bank perfectly complements the Campanile of San Marco. Behind it looms the stately dome of one of Venice's greatest churches, San Giorgio Maggiore. The island of Giudecca, a crescent cupped around the southern shore of Venice, is one of the most mysterious neighborhoods in all of Venice, with an obscure history and a somber feel.

A Good Boat Trip

Take Line 82 from San Zaccaria across St. Mark's Basin to the island of San Giorgio. Here you should visit Palladio's **Chiesa di San Giorgio Maggiore** ㊲. Return to the pier and proceed by vaporetto (still Line 82) to the island of **Giudecca** ㊳. Explore the neighborhood and visit the Chiesa del Redentore, also by Palladio. Continue on the vaporetto to the next stop, Zattere, opposite the Giudecca. The promenade here is enchanting; you can eat in one of the many pizzerias that line the promenade, taking in the lively atmosphere.

TIMING

A half day should give you plenty of time to enjoy the sights. Allow at least an hour to visit each of the churches, and another hour or two to visit the Giudecca neighborhood and the Zattere promenade.

Sights to See

㊲ **Chiesa di San Giorgio Maggiore.** A church has been on this island since the late 8th century, with a Benedictine monastery added in the 10th century (closed to the public). The present church, San Giorgio Maggiore, was begun in 1566 by Palladio, the greatest architect of his time. Two of Palladio's hallmarks are mathematical harmony and architectural elements borrowed from classical antiquity, both of which are demonstrated in this superbly proportioned neoclassical church of red brick and white marble. Its interior is refreshingly airy and simply decorated. Two important late Tintoretto paintings hang on either side of the chancel: the *Last Supper* and the *Gathering of Manna*. Over the first altar on the right side of the nave is an *Adoration of the Shepherds* by Jacopo Bassano (1517–92), a painter from Bassano del Grappa on the mainland who possessed considerable originality and was especially adept at portraying nature and country life. The campanile is so high that it was struck by a lightning bolt in 1993. The elevator ride to the top is well worth the 3,000 lire/€1.55 offering, as the views are some of the finest in town. ⊠ *Isola di San Giorgio,* ☎ 041/5227827. ☉ *June–Sept., daily 9–12:30 and 2:30–6; Oct.–May, daily 10–12:30 and 3–5; bell-tower 3,000 lire/€1.55.*

㊳ **Giudecca.** The island's name is something of a mystery. According to some, it derives from the possible settlement of Jews here in the 14th century; others believe it was so called because in the 9th century nobles condemned to exile (*giudicato*) were sent here. It became a pleasure garden for wealthy Venetians during the long and luxurious decline of the Republic. In one regard it is still the province of the wealthy: the exclusive Cipriani hotel lies secluded on its eastern tip.

DINING

Venetian cuisine is based on fish and seafood—*granseola* (crab), *moeche* (small, soft-shelled crabs), and *seppie* or *seppioline* (cuttlefish). Fish, usually priced by the *etto* (100 grams, or about ¼ pound), can be quite expensive. Antipasti may take the form of a seafood salad, prosciutto *di San Daniele* (of the Friuli region), or pickled vegetables. As a first course, Venetians favor risotto, the creamy rice dish, prepared here with vegetables or shellfish. Pasta, too, is paired with seafood sauces—Venice is *not* the place to order spaghetti with tomato sauce. *Pasticcio di pesce* is pasta baked with fish, usually *baccalà* (salt cod). A classic first course here and elsewhere in the Veneto is *pasta e fagioli* (thick bean soup with pasta). *Bigoli* is strictly a local pasta shaped like short, fat spaghetti, usually served with *nero di seppia* (squid-ink sauce). Polenta, a creamy cornmeal dish, is another pillar of regional cooking. It's often served with *fegato alla veneziana* (liver with onions).

Though it originated on the mainland, tiramisu is Venice's favorite dessert, a heavenly concoction of mascarpone (a rich, soft double-cream cheese), espresso, chocolate, and *savoiardi* (ladyfingers). Local wines are the dry white Tocai and Pinot from the Friuli region and bubbly white Prosecco, a naturally fermented sparkling wine that is a shade less dry. Some of the best Prosecco comes from Valdobbiadene, rivaled only by the slightly more expensive Cartizze. Popular red wines include merlot, cabernet, Raboso, and Refosco. You can sample all of these in Venice's bacari (local watering holes), where wine is served by the glass (known as an *ombra* in Venetian dialect) and accompanied by *cicheti* (assorted tidbits), often substantial enough for a light meal.

It's always a good idea to reserve your table or have your hotel *portiere* (concierge) do it for you. Dining hours are short, starting at 12:30 or 1 for lunch and ending at 2:30 or 3, when restaurants close for the afternoon, opening up again to start serving at about 7:30 and closing again at 11 or midnight. Most close one day a week and are also likely to close without notice for vacation or renovation. Few have signs on the outside, so when the metal blinds are shut tight you can't tell a closed restaurant from a closed TV-repair shop.

Cannaregio

$$$ ✕ **Fiaschetteria Toscana.** This warm restaurant in a former Tuscan wine and oil storehouse merits a jaunt from terra firma to Cannaregio for its cheerful and courteous service, fine cucina, and rose-hued walls. Gastronomic highlights include a delicate *tagliolini* (noodles), perhaps prepared *alla buranella* (with shrimp); the zabaglione; and the wine list. In warm weather, the best tables are in the arbor on the square. ✉ *Campo San Giovanni Crisostomo 5719, Cannaregio,* ☎ *041/5285281. AE, DC, MC, V. Closed Tues. and 4 wks in July–Aug. No lunch Mon.*

$$ ✕ **Vini da Gigio.** A quaint, friendly, family-run trattoria on the quay
★ side of a canal just off the Strada Nuova, da Gigio is very popular with Venetians and other visiting Italians who appreciate the affable service; well-prepared homemade pasta, fish, and meat dishes; and imaginative and varied cellar and good-quality draft wine. It's good, too, for a cheap, simple lunch at tables in the bar. ✉ *Fondamenta de la Chiesa 3628/a, Cannaregio,* ☎ *041/5285140. AE, DC, MC, V. Closed Mon., 3 wks in Jan.–Feb., 1 wk in June, and 3 wks in Aug.–Sept.*

Castello

$$$ ✕ **Al Covo.** This small and charming osteria changes its menu accord-
★ ing to the day's bounty—mostly local seafood caught just hours before and specialties from other European waters. Cesare Benelli and his American wife, Diane, insist on the freshest ingredients and claim not to use butter or animal fats. Try the *zuppa di pesce* (fish broth) followed by the fish of the day either grilled, baked, or steamed. Diane will guide you through some of her homemade desserts and the extensive wine selection. At lunch, only a prix-fixe menu (at 57,000 lire/€29.45, with several options) is served; dinner is à la carte. ✉ *Campiello della Pescaria 3968, Castello,* ☎ *041/5223812. No credit cards. Closed Wed. and Thurs., 2 wks in Aug., and 4 wks in Dec.–Jan.*

$$ **Alle Testiere.** A strong local following can make it tough to get one of
★ the five tables at this tiny trattoria near Campo Santa Maria Formosa. Some flea-market touches, such as the two wrought-iron headboards that give the place its name, make Alle Testiere seem older than its mid-1990s provenance. Chef Bruno Gavagnin's dishes stand out for lightness and balance. Try the *gnocchetti con moscardini* (little gnocchi with

Venice Dining and Lodging

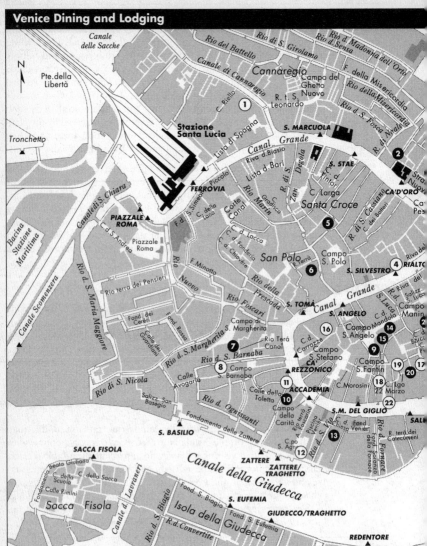

Dining ●

Al Covo **42**
Al Mascaron **26**
Alle Testiere **27**
Antico Martini **9**
Cantinone
Storico **13**
Da Arturo **14**
Da Ignazio **6**
Da Ivo **21**
Da Remigio **40**
Fiaschetteria
Toscana **23**
Grand Canal **33**
Harry's Bar **32**
La Caravella **20**

Le Bistrot **31**
L'Incontro **7**
Osteria Da Fiore . . .**5**
San Trovaso **10**
Vini da Gigio **2**
Vino Vino **15**

Lodging ○

Accademia **11**
Ala **18**
Bernardi
Semenzato **3**
Bucintoro **43**
Cipriani **35**
Concordia **30**
Danieli **36**
Gritti Palace **22**
Hesperia **1**
Hotel Pausania . . .**8**
Istituto
San Giuseppe . . .**28**
La Calcina **12**
La Residenza **37**

Londra Palace **38**
Luna Baglioni **34**
Metropole **41**
Quattro Fontane . . .**44**
Riva **29**
San Moisè **17**
San Samuele **16**
Santa Marina **24**
Saturnia
Internazionale . . .**19**
Scandinavia **25**
Sturion **4**
Wildner **39**

CIMITERO ▲

Cimitero
San
Michele

Sacca
della
Misericordia

Canale delle Navi

0 ____ 440 yards
0 ____ 400 meters

C. Racchetta

Rio S. Caterina

C.

R. Terra
Barba
Fruttarol

R. d. Gesuiti

Fondamenta Nuove

Rio della Panada

C. d. Squero

C. del Mendicanti

FOND. NUOVE ▲

FOND. NUOVE

③

Rio d'Santi Apostoli

vo

Salizz. S.
Canciano

C. Castellani

C. d. Tesio

Rio d. S. Marina

OSPEDALE
CIVILE

campo d.
scheria

R. d. S.
Gustina

❷❸

Campo
S. Bartolomio

❷❹

Campo
S. Marina

Rugo Giuffa

Barbaria delle Tole

CELESTIA ▲

Calbo'il vide

Calle
Sol di
borgoloco

❷❺ ❷❻
❷❼

R. d. S. Lorenzo

R. d. S. Severo

R. d. S.
Francesco

R. d. S.

Canale d. Galeazze

Darsena
Grande

Rio d. Vergini

San
Pietro

R. d. Rava

❷❽

C. d. Bande

❷❾

San
Zaccaria

C. Lion

C. d.
Furlani

C. d.
Pestrin

R. d. Scudi

R. d. Gorna

❸①

Fond.
Osmarin

❸⓪

R. d. Palazzo

R. d. Fabbri

Specchieri

❸❻ ❸❾ ❸❽

Molo

Riva degli

❸❶

Schiavoni

❸⑦

Castello

❸❷

Rio d. S. Daniele

Saliz. S.zatta di S.

Rio d. S. Anna

Can.

R. d. S. Giuseppe

❹❹

❸❹ ❸❷

Piazza
San Marco

S. ZACCARIA ▲

RIVA DEGLI
SCHIAVONI

❹❷

R. d'Arsenale

Rio della Tana

V. Garibaldi

S. MARCO
GIARDINETTI

ARSENALE

❹❸

Riva dei Sette Martiri

S. M. DEL
GIGLIO

UTE

Canale di S. Marco

S. GIORGIO ▲

Isola di
S. Giorgio
Maggiore

ℹ

ZITELLE ▲

Fond.
delle Zitelle

❸❺

Calle
Michelangelo

Riva dei Partigiani

Rio Ant. Giardini

KEY

▲ Boat Stop

ℹ Tourist Information

tender baby octopus), or the baked *rombo* (turbot) with radicchio di Treviso. A short but well-assembled wine list allows for some interesting combinations. Save room for a slice of pear tart. ⊠ *Calle del Mondo Novo 5081, Castello,* ☎ *041/5227220. Reservations essential. MC, V. Closed Sun., 3 wks in Aug., and 3 wks Dec.–Jan.*

$$ ✕ **Da Remigio.** This very popular, family-run local trattoria near San Giorgio dei Greci turns out reliable and tasty fish and meat dishes. It's the ideal place to enjoy an informal meal in the company of hungry, chatty Venetians. ⊠ *Salizzada dei Greci 3416, Castello,* ☎ *041/ 5230089. Reservations essential. AE, DC, MC, V. Closed Tues., 2 wks in July–Aug., and 4 wks in Dec.–Jan. No dinner Mon.*

$ ✕ **Al Mascaron.** The convivial, crowded Al Mascaron, with its paper tablecloths and very informal atmosphere, is a regular stop for Venetians who drop in to gossip, drink, play cards, and eat cicheti at the bar. You can bet on delicious seafood, pastas, risottos, and seafood salads. So popular has Al Mascaron become that the owners, Gigi and Momi, have opened an offshoot called Mascareta a few doors down the calle (at No. 5183), where you can enjoy a glass of wine and cold snacks. ⊠ *Calle Lunga Santa Maria Formosa 5225, Castello,* ☎ *041/ 5225995. No credit cards. Closed Sun. and mid-Dec.–mid-Jan.*

Dorsoduro

$$ ✕ **Cantinone Storico.** On a quiet, romantic canal near the Accademia, this comfortable trattoria with tables alfresco serves well-prepared specialties such as risotto *terra mare* (with seafood, vegetables, and porcini mushrooms) and *tagliolini alla granseola* (narrow fettuccine-shape pasta with crab sauce). Heavily advertised, the Cantinone draws mostly tourists, yet it's hard to beat the good location, and the prices are reasonable. The house wines are good. ⊠ *Fondamenta di Ca' Bragadin 660/1, Dorsoduro,* ☎ *041/5239577. AE, MC, V. Closed Sun. and 2 wks in Nov.*

$ ✕ **L'Incontro.** This trattoria has a faithful clientele of Venetians and vis-
★ itors, attracted by flavorful food, friendly service, and reasonable prices. Menu choices include freshly made Sardinian pastas, juicy steaks, wild duck, boar, and (with advance notice) roast suckling pig. You'll find it between San Barnaba and Campo Santa Margherita. ⊠ *Rio terà Canal 3062/a, Dorsoduro,* ☎ *041/5222404. AE, D, MC, V. Closed Mon., Jan., and 2 wks in Aug. No lunch Tues.*

$ ✕ **San Trovaso.** A wide choice of Venetian dishes served in robust portions, economical prix-fixe menus, pizzas, and house wine by the glass or pitcher keep this two-floor, no-nonsense tavern abuzz with young Venetians and low-budget visitors in the know. It's always packed, and table turnover is fast. Not far from the Gallerie dell'Accademia, this is a good place to slip into while sightseeing in Dorsoduro. ⊠ *Fondamenta Priuli 1016, Dorsoduro,* ☎ *041/5203703. AE, MC, V. Closed Mon. and 1 wk in Dec. or Jan.*

San Marco

$$$$ ✕ **Antico Martini.** This place was born as a café in 1720, and some 70 years later its fortunes soared with the opening of the Teatro La Fenice on the same campo. It became a restaurant in all respects only in the early 20th century, and its original quarters are impeccably maintained by the current owner, Emilio Baldi. Intimate tables, candlelight, antique oil canvases, and a patrician air are paired with traditional yet inventive dishes. Salmon rolls filled with caviar and sour cream might be followed by tagliatelle with prawn and arugula and angelfish with black peppercorns. Finish your meal with a slice of apple and raspberry tart, or consider booking a soufflè. There's no need to rush out, as the Antico Martini has a piano bar open until 3 AM. ⊠ *Campo San Fantin, 1983 San Marco,* ☎ *041/5224121. Reservations essential. Jacket required. AE, DC, MC, V. Closed Tues. No lunch Wed.*

$$$$ ✕ **Grand Canal.** The Grand Canal restaurant at the Hotel Monaco and Grand Canal is a favorite with Venetians, who enjoy eating in summer on the lovely canal-side terrace looking across the mouth of the Grand Canal to San Giorgio Maggiore and in the cozy dining room in winter. All the pasta is made fresh daily on the premises, and the smoked and marinated salmon are also prepared on-site. The chef's traditional Venetian dishes are top-flight; you'll marvel over savory meat and fish dishes such as *scampi alla Buséra* (shrimp in a cognac sauce). ⊠ *Hotel Monaco and Grand Canal, Calle Vallaresso 1325, San Marco,* ☎ *041/5200211. Jacket required for dinner. AE, DC, MC, V.*

$$$$ ✕ **Harry's Bar.** The humble door of this very less-than-humble watering hole leads to the legendary Venetian hangout of such notables as Hemingway, Maugham, and Onassis, not to mention Barbara Hutton, Peggy Guggenheim, and Orson Welles. Such company doesn't come cheap, but Harry's is still known for the best and driest martinis in town, the most heavenly Bellinis (fresh peach juice and Prosecco), and its kitchen's fine, if overpriced, Venetian cuisine. The decor is boring beige-on-beige, but the "pictures" on the walls upstairs—windows that look out on spectacular Chiesa di Santa Maria della Salute—easily compete with the finest Canaletto *vedute* (scenic paintings). ⊠ *Calle Vallaresso 1323, San Marco,* ☎ *041/5285777. Reservations essential. AE, DC, MC, V.*

$$$$ ✕ **La Caravella.** Confronted with chateaubriand, bouillabaisse, and fegato alla veneziana, you might think you had wandered into a temple of French haute cuisine. Continue reading the very extensive menu to discover some of the best Venetian specialties in town, such as *tagliarini* (delicate narrow fettuccine-shape pasta) alla granseola and fillets of local sea bass and sole. The front room of this old favorite—long admired for its fine wine list and cordial, gracious service—is like the dining saloon of an old Venetian sailing ship. The pretty garden courtyard is open from May to September. ⊠ *Calle Larga XXII Marzo 2397, Saturnia Internazionale hotel, San Marco,* ☎ *041/5208901. Reservations essential. AE, DC, MC, V.*

$$$ ✕ **Da Arturo.** On the Calle degli Assassini—a name common to several Venetian streets and a reminder of the centuries gone by when violence and betrayal were everyday occurrences—this tiny restaurant can offer a most peaceful and enjoyable evening. It has the distinction (in Venice) of *not* serving seafood. Instead, you'll choose from among fresh vegetable and salad dishes; tasty, tender, and generous meat courses, including the delicately pungent *braciola alla veneziana* (pork chop schnitzel with vinegar); and an authentic, creamy homemade tiramisu to finish. ⊠ *Calle degli Assassini 3656, San Marco,* ☎ *041/ 5286974. Reservations essential. No credit cards. Closed Sun., 10 days after Carnival, and 4 wks in Aug.*

$$$ ✕ **Da Ivo.** An enclave of Tuscan cuisine two minutes from Piazza San Marco, Da Ivo is more than a cozy, relaxing trattoria hanging off the Rio dei Fuseri. It appeals to both residents and visitors—the latter often come by gondola, making a romantic use of the private landing. Paintings and copper pots hang on white walls; there is candlelight at dinnertime. The wine list focuses on reds from the Piedmont, Veneto, and Tuscany. Start with a vegetable soup, or the less Tuscan tagliolini *alla bottarga* (with roe); to follow, consider that the reputation of the restaurant has been built on its famous grill *con carbone d'olivo* (with charcoal made from olive wood) of *fiorentine* (T-bone steak, cooked rare), game, or fish. A warm zabaglione with ricotta is a worthy

dessert. ⊠ *Calle dei Fuseri 1809, San Marco,* ☎ *041/5285004. AE, DC, MC, V. Closed Sun. and Jan.*

$ ✕ **Le Bistrot.** Live music, poetry readings, and art exhibits attract the younger crowd to this café-brasserie. Centrally located, it's open until 1 AM and features 16th-century Venetian cuisine, such as *l'ambroyno* (spiced chicken with nuts and raisins) and *capirotta* (meat soup). ⊠ *Calle dei Fabbri 4685, San Marco,* ☎ *041/5236651. MC, V.*

$ ✕ **Vino Vino.** The annex of the extremely expensive Antico Martini restaurant is a highly informal wine bar where you can sample Italian vintages and munch on a limited selection of (microwaved) dishes from the kitchens of its upscale big sister next door. ⊠ *Calle delle Veste 2007/a, near Campo San Fantin, San Marco,* ☎ *041/5237027. Reservations not accepted. AE, DC, MC, V. Closed Tues.*

San Polo

$$$ ✕ **Osteria Da Fiore.** Tucked away in a little calle off the top of Campo
★   San Polo, Da Fiore is always packed. It's imperative to reserve for a superlative seafood lunch or dinner, which might include delicate hors d'oeuvres of moeche, scallops, and tiny octopus, followed by a succulent risotto or tagliolini *con scampi e zucchine* (with shrimp and zucchini), and a perfectly cooked main course of *rombo* (turbot) or *branzino* (sea bass). ⊠ *Calle del Scaleter 2202/a, San Polo,* ☎ *041/ 721308. Reservations essential. AE, DC, MC, V. Closed Sun. and Mon., Aug., and Dec. 24–Jan. 16.*

$$ ✕ **Da Ignazio.** In a smallish, pleasant, and unadorned space near Campo San Polo, Ignazio is reliable for good food at reasonable prices (except for the expensive fish dishes). The cuisine is classic Venetian, from seafood risotto to fegato alla veneziana, but there are standard Italian items as well. ⊠ *Calle dei Saoneri 2749, San Polo,* ☎ *041/ 5234852. AE, DC, MC, V. Closed Sat., 2 wks over Christmas, and 2 wks in July.*

LODGING

Everyone loves Venice, and hotels here can cater to all tastes and price ranges. Rates are a little higher than in Rome and Milan, but you can save off-season (November–March, excluding Christmas and Carnevale). Most rates include breakfast. It is *essential* to know how to get to your hotel when you arrive, as transport can range from arriving in a water taxi or gondola to wandering alleys and side streets—luggage in hand—with relapses of déjà vu. The busiest times for hotels are spring and autumn; December 20–January 2; and the two-week Carnival period leading up to Ash Wednesday. Book well in advance. If you don't have reservations, you can almost always get a room in any category by going to the **AVA** (Venetian Hoteliers Association, ☎ 041/5228004 administration), which will make same-day, free reservations for those who come in person to their booths at Piazzale Roma (☎ 041/5231397, open daily 9 AM–10 PM); Santa Lucia train station (☎ 041/715288 and 041/ 715016, open daily 8 AM–9 PM); and Marco Polo Airport (☎ 041/ 5415133, open daily 9 AM–10 PM). A deposit, which will be deducted from your hotel bill, is required to hold the room (20,000 lire/€10.35– 90,000 lire/€46.50 per person; MC and V accepted). Alternatively, **Venezia Sì** offers free reservations over the phone: in Italy, call toll-free ☎ 800/843006, Mon.–Sat. 9 AM–7 PM; from abroad, call ☎ 0039/ 0415222264 or FAX 0039/0415221242. Many hotels accept reservations on-line; the site www.veniceinfo.it offers free (with pictures) about most hotels.

HOW TO
USE THIS GUIDE

Great trips begin with great planning, and this guide makes planning easy. It's packed with everything you need—insider advice on hotels and restaurants, cool tools, practical tips, essential maps, and much more.

COOL TOOLS

Fodor's Choice Top picks are marked throughout with a star.

Great Itineraries These tours, planned by Fodor's experts, give you the skinny on what you can see and do in the time you have.

Smart Travel Tips A to Z This special section is packed with important contacts and advice on everything from how to get around to what to pack.

Good Walks You won't miss a thing if you follow the numbered bullets on our maps.

Need a Break? Looking for a quick bite to eat or a spot to rest? These sure bets are along the way.

Off the Beaten Path Some lesser-known sights are worth a detour. We've marked those you should make time for.

POST-IT® FLAGS
Dog-ear no more!

"Post-it" is a registered trademark of 3M.

ICONS AND SYMBOLS

Watch for these symbols throughout:

★   Our special recommendations

✕   Restaurant

🏨   Lodging establishment

✕🏨   Lodging establishment whose restaurant warrants a special trip

☾   Good for kids

☞   Sends you to another section of the guide for more information

✉   Address

☎   Telephone number

FAX   Fax number

WEB   Web site

🎟   Admission price

🕑   Opening hours

$-$$$$ Lodging and dining price categories, keyed to strategically sited price charts. Check the index for locations.

①❶   Numbers in white and black circles on the maps, in the margins, and within tours correspond to one another.

ON THE WEB

Continue your planning with these useful tools found at **www.fodors.com**, the Web's best source for travel information.

"Rich with resources." —*New York Times*

"Navigation is a cinch." —*Forbes* "Best of the Web" list

"Put together by people bursting with know-how."
                         —*Sunday Times* (London)

Create a Miniguide Pinpoint hotels, restaurants, and attractions that have what you want at the price you want to pay.

Rants and Raves Find out what readers say about Fodor's picks—or write your own reviews of hotels and restaurants you've just visited.

Travel Talk Post your questions and get answers from fellow travelers, or share your own experiences.

On-Line Booking Find the best prices on airline tickets, rental cars, cruises, or vacations, and book them on the spot.

About our Books Learn about other Fodor's guides to your destination and many others.

Expert Advice and Trip Ideas From what to tip to how to take great photos, from the national parks to Nepal, Fodors.com has suggestions that'll make your trip a breeze. Log on and get informed and inspired.

Smart Resources Check the weather in your destination or convert your currency. Learn the local language or link to the latest event listings. Or consult hundreds of detailed maps—all in one place.

Cannaregio

$$ ⊞ **Hesperia.** A quiet, friendly hotel with some rooms overlooking the wide (and clean!) Canale di Cannaregio, the Hesperia is within convenient walking distance from the train station and right across from the Jewish Ghetto. Its restaurant, Il Melograno, has tables outside in summer. ✉ *459 Cannaregio, 30121,* ☎ *041/715251,* FAX *041/715112,* WEB *www.veniceinfo.it. 16 rooms, 2 with private bath on the corridor. Restaurant. AE, DC, MC, V.*

$ ⊞ **Bernardi Semenzato.** This is a particularly inviting little hotel just
★ off Strada Nuova and near the Rialto. All rooms in the main hotel are well maintained, making the Bernardi a better value than ever. Prices are even lower in the nearby annex, with six standard-size rooms and one large one with a lovely canal view. ✉ *Calle dell'Oca, 4366 Cannaregio, 30121,* ☎ *041/5211052,* FAX *041/5222424,* WEB *www.veniceinfo.it. 24 rooms, 14 with bath. AE, MC, V.*

Castello

$$$$ ⊞ **Danieli.** You'll feel like a doge in Venice's largest luxury hotel, a collage of newer buildings around a 15th-century palazzo built for the doge Dandolo—all oozing with sumptuous Venetian decor and atmosphere. Some suites are positively palatial, but some of the less attractive rooms are still overpriced. The four-story-high lobby is supreme, its chic salons and bar offering relaxation and celebrity sightings. The rooftop terrace restaurant is justly famous for top-notch cuisine and its heavenly view of San Giorgio Maggiore and St. Mark's Basin. From May through October, guests have access to the pool and tennis courts of the hotels Des Bains and Excelsior on the Lido. ✉ *Riva degli Schiavoni 4196, Castello, 30122,* ☎ *041/5226480,* FAX *041/5200208,* WEB *www.luxurycollection.com. 219 rooms, 11 suites. Restaurant, bar, air-conditioning. AE, DC, MC, V.*

$$$$ ⊞ **Metropole.** Only a few minutes' stroll from Piazza San Marco, the Metropole offers spacious rooms and sitting areas furnished with style and panache from the owner's impressive collection of antiques. Many rooms have a view of the lagoon, but the others overlooking a canal and peaceful gardens are also inviting. You can step from your water taxi or gondola directly into the hotel lobby. ✉ *Riva degli Schiavoni 4149, Castello, 30122,* ☎ *041/5205044,* FAX *041/5223679,* WEB *www.hotelmetropole.com. 67 rooms, 7 suites. Restaurant, bar, air-conditioning. AE, DC, MC, V.*

$$$–$$$$ ⊞ **Londra Palace.** Fine views of the lagoon and the church of San Giorgio offer a soothing balance to the concoction of plush carpets and costly tapestries in a thousand and one patterns that fill the over-the-top interiors of the Londra Palace, one of the long-established grand hotels of Venice. Handsome Biedermeier tables, couches, and writing desks stand out against the numerous marble columns used support such heavy luxury. Rooms overlooking the Riva cost 10% more than the smaller, top-floor rooms with mansard ceilings. The hotel's ground-floor restaurant offers pricey but solid Venetian cuisine. Extras include a complimentary Mercedes for a one-day excursion to the mainland. ✉ *Riva degli Schiavoni 4171, Castello, 30122,* ☎ *041/5200533,* FAX *041/5225032,* WEB *www.hotelondra.it. 36 rooms, 17 suites. Restaurant, piano bar, air-conditioning. AE, DC, MC, V.*

$$$ ⊞ **Santa Marina.** In the small neighborhood campo that is home to this hotel, five minutes from the Rialto Bridge, you will probably see more Venetians than tourists passing by. Immaculate rooms are outfitted in pastel colors and lacquered Venetian-style furniture. The staff is helpful and kind, and breakfast is served on the veranda in summer.

   ⊠ *Campo Santa Marina, 6068 Castello, 30122,* ☎ *041/5239202,* FAX *041/5200907,* WEB *www.hotelsantamarina.com. 20 rooms. Breakfast room. AE, DC, MC, V.*

\$\$\$ ⚎ **Scandinavia.** Central but off the main tourist arteries, the Scandinavia is housed in a building dating from the 11th century. Despite the name, the rooms are done in Venetian style with brocade tapestry and Murano chandeliers. Ask for a room with a view onto the cheerful campo below. The top suite has a beautiful, private covered veranda with a view of the nearby church. ⊠ *Campo Santa Maria Formosa 5240, Castello, 30122,* ☎ *041/5223507,* FAX *041/5235232,* WEB *www.scandinaviahotel. com. 33 rooms, 1 suite. Breakfast room. AE, MC, V.*

\$\$ ⚎ **Bucintoro.** Whistler once stayed here, and today the Bucintoro is still favored by artists drawn by the lagoon views from each room. Off the tourist track, this friendly, family-run hotel on the waterfront by the Arsenal has clean, simple rooms and prices that are unbeatable for such a spectacular location. (Note that this multifloor hotel has no elevator.) ⊠ *Riva San Biagio, 2135 Castello, 30122,* ☎ *041/5223240,* FAX *041/5235224. 28 rooms, 25 with bath. Breakfast room. No credit cards. Closed mid-Dec.–early Feb.*

\$\$ ⚎ **La Residenza.** The word *residenza* in Italian connotes aristocratic elegance, and this hotel does not disappoint, with the atmosphere more of a noble's private house rather than a hotel. The hall occupies the whole *portego* (entry hall) of the patrician apartment of Palazzo dei Badoari-Partecipazi già Gritti and looks almost disproportionately opulent for this quiet hotel at the low end of its price category. Well-preserved 18th-century stuccowork adorns the ceilings and walls, along with precious oil paintings. Oriental carpets partially hide the beautiful Venetian floor. Breakfast is served on the many coffee tables surrounded by couches and armchairs in the hall. Rooms are done in faux-antique style; the choice ones overlook the pretty campo below. ⊠ *Campo San Giovanni in Bragora 3608, Castello, 30122,* ☎ *041/ 5285315,* FAX *041/5238859,* WEB *www.veniceinfo.it. 14 rooms. AE, DC, MC, V.*

\$\$ ⚎ **Wildner.** Right between the superdeluxe Danieli and Londra hotels, this pleasant, family-run, unpretentious pensione enjoys the same views. The rooms are spread over four floors (no elevator), half with a view of San Giorgio. The quieter ones look out onto Campo San Zaccaria. ⊠ *Riva degli Schiavoni 4161, Castello, 30122,* ☎ *041/5227463,* FAX *041/5265615,* WEB *www.veneziahotels.com. 16 rooms. Breakfast room. AE, DC, MC, V.*

 \$ ⚎ **Istituto San Giuseppe.** This is one of several religious institutions in Venice run by nuns—and it's in an excellent location north of Piazza San Marco. Rooms are spartan, but spotless and very quiet, as they overlook the inner cloister. Book well ahead, as the unbeatable prices draw crowds of guests, mostly Italians in the know. Curfew is at 11 PM (10:30 in the winter), and no breakfast is served. ⊠ *5402 Castello, 30122,* ☎ *041/5225352,* FAX *041/5224891. 16 rooms. No credit cards.*

 \$ ⚎ **Riva.** This small hotel, close to San Marco, is at the junction of three canals much used by all manner of Venetian watercraft. Although they are endlessly fascinating to watch, here you take the good with the bad, as the passing gondolier at sunset is replaced by the buzz of a water taxi at dawn. Rooms differ in size, and climbing up to the top floor (no elevator) wins you a better view. The decor is typical of Venetian hotels—the usual mix of Murano chandeliers, 18th-century-style furniture, exposed ceiling beams, and beds lacquered in pastel shades. ⊠ *Ponte dell'Angelo 5310, Castello, 30122,* ☎ *041/5227034,* FAX *041/ 5285551. 12 rooms, 10 with bath. No credit cards. Closed mid-Nov.– Carnevale, except 2 wks at Christmas.*

Dorsoduro

$$-$$$ 🏨 **Accademia.** Probably the most enchanting hotel in Venice, the Ac-
★ cademia is also one of the most popular, so early reservations are a must.
Just beyond an iron gate, a secret garden awaits, complete with mini
Palladian-style villa, canal parterre, and verdant trees—all rarities in
Venice. Lounges, the bar, and a wood-paneled breakfast room are
cheery, and breakfast outside on the garden terrace is a special treat.
⊠ *Fondamenta Bollani 1058, Dorsoduro, 30123,* ☎ *041/5210188,*
FAX *041/5239152,* WEB *www.pensioneaccademia.it. 27 rooms. Bar,
breakfast room, air-conditioning. AE, DC, MC, V.*

$$-$$$ 🏨 **Hotel Pausania.** This 14th-century palazzo delivers all of the mod-
ern comforts with taste, from the moment you ascend the grand staircase rising above a fountain. Light-shaded rooms are spacious, with
comfortable furniture and carpets with rugs thrown over them. Some
rooms face the small canal (which can become a bit noisy early in the
morning) in front of the hotel, whereas others look out over the large
garden courtyard. The hotel has a convenient car service (75,000
lire/€38.70) to and from the airport. ⊠ *2824 Dorsoduro, 30123,* ☎
041/5222083, FAX *041/5222989,* WEB *www.veniceinfo.it. 26 rooms.
Bar, breakfast room, air-conditioning. AE, DC, MC, V.*

$$ 🏨 **La Calcina.** The Calcina sits in an enviable position along the sunny
★ Zattere with views across the wide Giudecca Canal. You can sunbathe
on the *altana* (wooden-roof terrace) or enjoy an afternoon tea in one
of the reading corners of the shadowy, intimate hall with flickering can-
dlelight and barely perceptible classical music. A stone staircase leads
to the rooms upstairs (no elevator), with shiny wooden floors, origi-
nal Art Deco furniture and lamps, and firm beds; some suffer from a
lack of storage space. A courteous and helpful staff makes this one of
Venice's most comfortable and serene places to lay your head. The annex
nearby offers lower-priced rooms without a view. ⊠ *780 Dorsoduro,
30123,* ☎ *041/5206466,* FAX *041/5227045,* WEB *www.veniceinfo.it. 42
rooms. Breakfast room. AE, DC, MC, V.*

Giudecca

$$$$ 🏨 **Cipriani.** It's impossible to feel stressed in this sybaritic oasis of stun-
ning rooms and suites, some with garden patios. The hotel launch whisks
you to Giudecca from San Marco and back at any hour; those just din-
ing at the exceptional Ristorante Harry Cipriani can use it as well. The
restored and subtly integrated 17th-century-style Palazzo Vendramin
is more charming than the main hotel and the Palazzetto, a modern
annex of five rooms and four junior suites facing the Canale della
Giudecca. Prices are high even by Venetian standards, but this is the
only place in town with such extensive facilities and services, from an
Olympic-size pool and tennis courts to cooking courses and fitness pro-
grams. ⊠ *Giudecca 10, 30133,* ☎ *041/5207744,* FAX *041/5207745,* WEB
*cipriani.orient-express.com. 54 rooms, 50 suites. Restaurant, bar, air-
conditioning, pool, tennis court. AE, DC, MC, V. Main hotel closed
Dec.–Apr., Palazzo Vendramin and Palazzetto closed Jan.*

Lido

$$$ 🏨 **Quattro Fontane.** This fine hotel in a well-maintained mansion run
★ by a Danish couple offers the serenity of the Lido, although you will
be a 15-minute walk and a 20-minute boat ride from Piazza San
Marco. Well-decorated rooms, with period furniture and tasteful
tapestries, overlook the surrounding garden. Common areas contain
an odd collection of mason's aprons, pipes, ex-votos, masks from

Jakarta, Roman seals, and seashells. A huge fireplace adds warmth and
character in the colder months. After a full day you can relax in the
library, which holds books in many languages. ⊠ *Via delle Quattro
Fontane 16, Lido, 30126,* ☎ *041/5260227,* FAX *041/5260726,* WEB
www.veniceinfo.it. 59 rooms. Library. AE, DC, MC, V.

San Marco

$$$$ 🏨 **Concordia.** Half of the rooms in this central, attractive, and well-run
hotel overlook the Basilica of San Marco, as does the spacious breakfast room–bar, where light meals and snacks are also available all day.
The romantic *mansarda* (rooftop room) has a panoramic view over the
Piazza San Marco. The management offers discounted prices at off-peak
times, so check when booking. ⊠ *Calle Larga San Marco 367, San Marco,
30124,* ☎ *041/5206866,* FAX *041/5206775,* WEB *www.hotelconcordia.
com. 54 rooms, 3 suites. Bar, breakfast room, air-conditioning. AE, DC,
MC, V.*

$$$$ 🏨 **Gritti Palace.** Queen Elizabeth, Greta Garbo, and Winston Churchill
 ★   made this their Venetian address. The feeling of being in an aristocratic
private home pervades this legendary hotel, replete with fresh flowers,
fine antiques, sumptuous appointments, and old-fashioned service.
The dining terrace on the Grand Canal is best in the evening when the
boat traffic dies down. Guests have access to a pool and tennis courts.
⊠ *Campo Santa Maria del Giglio 2467, San Marco, 30124,* ☎ *041/
794611,* FAX *041/5200942,* WEB *www.luxurycollection.com. 87 rooms,
6 suites. Restaurant, bar, café, air-conditioning. AE, DC, MC, V.*

$$$$ 🏨 **Luna Baglioni.** Two minutes from San Marco, this handsome hotel
has elegant rooms, several with a view of the Grand Canal. Breakfast
is served in a salon fit for a king, with frescoes by the school of Tiepolo,
18th-century furniture, and Venetian floors. Most suites feature fireplaces, hot tubs, and terraces. Restaurant Canova offers modern Venetian cuisine. ⊠ *1243 San Marco, 30124,* ☎ *041/5289840,* FAX *041/
5287160,* WEB *www.baglionihotels.com. 111 rooms, 7 suites. Restaurant. AE, DC, MC, V.*

$$$–$$$$ 🏨 **Saturnia Internazionale.** There's lots of patinated charm in this his-
toric palace near Piazza San Marco, but it's peaceful and tranquil. Beamed
ceilings, damask-hung walls, and authentic Venetian decor impart real
character to the solid comfort of its rooms and salons. Many rooms
have glamorous, large bathrooms. La Caravella is a restaurant of spe-
cial note. ⊠ *Calle Larga XXII Marzo 2398, San Marco, 30124,* ☎
041/5208377, FAX *041/5207131,* WEB *www.hotelsaturnia.it. 95 rooms.
Restaurant, bar, air-conditioning. AE, MC, V.*

$$ 🏨 **Ala.** The Ala is in the "aristocratic" part of town, between Piazza
San Marco and Campo Santo Stefano, a few steps from the Santa Maria
del Giglio vaporetto and traghetto stop. The owner's collection of
armor is displayed in the hall and sitting rooms, where English-language newspapers are at your disposal. Some rooms are large, with coffered ceilings and old-style furnishings; others are smaller with
more modern decor. Most come with a view of either the campo below or
the side canal. ⊠ *2494 San Marco, 30124,* ☎ *041/5208333,* FAX *041/
5206390,* WEB *www.hotelala.it. 85 rooms. Breakfast room. AE, DC,
MC, V.*

$$ 🏨 **San Moisè.** The closest you can get to staying in an 18th-century
Venetian house, the San Moisè deserves special mention for its warm
decor, which in this part of town usually comes at a much higher
price. Rooms share the same motifs as the cozy portego: Oriental rugs,
glass chandeliers, rich tapestries, handsome furniture, and in some cases
a pleasantly irregular structure. Some rooms have a view of the *rio* (small

canal), and others face a small inner courtyard, home to a lush wisteria tree. There is no elevator, but you won't have to climb any higher than to the second floor. ⊠ *Piscina San Moisè, 2058 San Marco, 30124,* ☎ *041/5203755,* FAX *041/5210670,* WEB *www.sanmoise.it. 16 rooms. Bar, air-conditioning. AE, DC, MC, V.*

$ 🖭 **San Samuele.** Near the Grand Canal and Palazzo Grassi, this friendly hotel has clean, sunny rooms in surprisingly good shape for the price. Five of the bathrooms, with white and gray-blue tiles, are new, and the walls are painted in crisp, pleasant shades of pale pink or blue. Curtains and bedspreads are made out of antique-looking fabrics, and although the furniture is of the boxy modern kind, the owners are gradually adding more interesting-looking pieces. ⊠ *Salizzada San Samuele 3358, San Marco, 30124,* ☎ FAX *041/5228045,* WEB *www. veniceinfo.it. 10 rooms, 7 with bath. No credit cards.*

San Polo

$$ 🖭 **Sturion.** You might recognize the facade of this hotel in a painting by Carpaccio that hangs at the Gallerie dell'Accademia. Once frequented by merchants who traded at the nearby Rialto market, the small, family-run hotel has two rooms overlooking the Grand Canal and a small but pretty breakfast room. Some rooms are reserved for nonsmokers. There's no elevator. ⊠ *Calle del Sturion 679, San Polo, 30125,* ☎ *041/ 5236243,* FAX *041/5228378,* WEB *www.locandasturion.com. 11 rooms. Breakfast room, no-smoking rooms. AE, DC, MC, V.*

NIGHTLIFE AND THE ARTS

The Arts

For a detailed listing of what's going on, pick up the monthly *Venezia News* from a newsstand. It has plenty of information in English about concerts, opera, ballet, theater, exhibitions, movies, sports, sightseeing, and a useful "Servizi" section with late-night pharmacies, operating hours for the busiest vaporetto and bus lines, and a listing of the main trains and flights from Venice. The tourist office puts out "Leo," a seasonal brochure in Italian and English with a list of events and updated museum hours. A similar publication is the *Guest in Venice* booklet, free at your hotel. On the Internet you can get a preview of what's going on in Venice—try www.ombra.net and www.venicepages. com (the latter in Italian). The **Biennale,** a cultural institution, organizes events throughout the year, including the film festival, which begins at the end of August. The big Biennale international art exhibition, usually held from mid-June to early November, has been held since 1993 on odd-numbered years at the **Giardini della Biennale** (Castello Gardens).

Festivals

Carnevale takes place the 10 (or more) days leading up to Ash Wednesday. Crowds of revelers make the city almost impossible to visit, so unless you are intent on joining in, stay away. For information about Carnival, check with the Venice tourist office (☎ 041/5298711). On the third Sunday of July, the **Festa del Redentore** (Feast of the Redeemer) is celebrated with the building of a pontoon bridge over the channel to the Giudecca, commemorating the doge's annual visit to this church to offer thanks for the end of a 16th-century plague. At midnight on Saturday fireworks explode over the lagoon as many Venetians take to the water in boats to enjoy the show. The following day there is procession to the church.

Music

Although there are occasional jazz and Italian pop concerts in clubs around town, the vast majority of music played in Venice is classical. Vivaldi (Venice's most famous composer) tends to be on the playbill; the churches of the Pietà, San Stae, Santo Stefano, and San Bartolomeo are frequent venues. For information on these often impromptu events, ask at the APT office, consult the *Venezia News* or other arts and tourism publications, and look for posters on walls and in restaurants and shops. Tickets for some events are handled by the following: **Kele e Teo Agency** (⊠ Ponte dei Bareteri 4930, San Marco, ☎ 041/5208722, FAX 041/5208913), **Nalesso** (⊠ Calle dello Spezier off Campo Santo Stefano 2765, San Marco, ☎ 041/5203329).

Opera and Ballet

Teatro La Fenice (⊠ Campo San Fantin) is one of Italy's oldest opera houses, a pilgrimage shrine for opera lovers everywhere and the scene of many memorable operatic premieres, including, in 1853, the dismal first-night flop of Verdi's *La Traviata*. The great opera house was badly damaged by fire in January 1996, and the meticulous restoration work—helped in large part by donations from opera-lovers around the world—is expected to last for several years. Until the Fenice reopens, opera, symphony, and ballet performances are held year-round at the **Palafenice** (⊠ near the Tronchetto parking area, ☎ 041/786511, 041/5204010 last-minute booking, WEB www.teatrolafenice.it); call for ticket information or go to the Cassa di Risparmio bank (⊠ Campo San Luca, ☎ 041/5210161).

Nightlife

Piazza San Marco is a meeting place in fair weather, when the cafés stay open late, though young Venetians tend to gravitate toward Campo Santa Margherita and Fondamenta della Misericordia, off the Strada Nuova.

Bars

Devil's Forest Pub (⊠ Calle dei Stagneri 5185, off Campo San Bartolomeo, ☎ 041/5200623) is a favored hangout of many young Venetians. **Fiddler's Elbow** (⊠ Strada Nuova 3847, Cannaregio, ☎ 041/5239930) offers all the typical trappings of an Irish pub: gab, grub, and frothy Guinness. The **Martini Scala Club** (⊠ Campo San Fantin 1983, San Marco, ☎ 041/5224121) is an elegant piano bar in the Antico Martini restaurant. Tunes start at 10 and go until the wee hours; it's closed on Tuesday. A nightspot with food, drinks, and music, **Paradiso Perduto** (⊠ Fondamenta della Misericordia 2540, Cannaregio, ☎ 041/720581) serves up inexpensive fish dishes and usually has live music on Sunday and Monday; it's closed on Tuesday and Wednesday.

Casinos

The city-run gambling casino at the splendid **Palazzo Vendramin-Calergi** reopened in 2000 after restoration. It's a classic scene of well-dressed high-rollers (and those who just look the part) playing French roulette, Caribbean poker, chemin de fer, 30–40, and slots. (By request, it's possible to eat at the restaurant without paying casino admission.) ⊠ *San Marcuola vaporetto stop*, ☎ 041/5297111. ⊿ *15,000 lire/€7.75.* ⊘ *Daily 11 AM–2:30 AM.*

A casino in **Ca' Noghera on Mestre,** near the airport, has slots, blackjack, craps, poker, and roulette. ⊠ *Via Triestina 222, Tessera,* ☎ 041/5297111. ⊿ *5,000 lire/€2.60.* ⊘ *Daily 11 AM–3:30 AM.*

There's a minimum admission age of 18 at both casinos.

Nightclubs

For dancing, try the tiny **Disco Club Piccolo Mondo** (✉ 1056/A Dorsoduro, ☎ 041/5200371), near the Accademia Gallery. The larger **Casanova** (✉ Lista di Spagna 158/a, Cannaregio, ☎ 041/2750199) is a relatively new restaurant-cabaret-disco with big projection screens, metallic walls, and red-leather couches. Outside Venice on the nearby Lido is **Piazza Caffè** (✉ Lungomare Marconi 22, Lido, ☎ 041/5260466), one of the more trendy, hip spots, with disco and live performances. It's open daily May–September and on the weekends October–April.

OUTDOOR ACTIVITIES AND SPORTS

Participant Sports

Golf

The 18-hole **Golf Club Lido di Venezia** (✉ Via del Forte, Alberoni, Lido, ☎ 041/731333), closed Monday, is on Lido island. The course isn't exceptional, but it fulfills the basic needs of golf addicts.

Horseback Riding

Circolo Ippico Veneziano (✉ Ca' Bianca, the Lido, ☎ 041/5265162), closed Sunday afternoon and Monday, rents horses for riding trails on the premises and can refer you to terra firma clubs around the Veneto.

Running

The best running route (6–7 km [4–4½ mi] long) heads east from Piazza San Marco, and skirts the lagoon along the Riva degli Schiavoni and the Riva dei Sette Martiri to the pine wood of Sant'Elena. You can run back to the center cutting across the picturesque neighborhood of Castello and the island of San Pietro di Castello. Note that from late spring to early fall, from 9 AM to 7 PM, there are likely to be many passersby to dodge in the San Marco–Riva degli Schiavoni tract. It's wise to consult with your concierge for further guidance.

Swimming

Venice's best public pool is the **Piscina Comunale** (✉ Island of Sacca Fisola, far end of Giudecca, ☎ 041/5285430), open daily mid-September–June; call ahead for hours. Take Line 82 to Sacca Fisola. (Note that there are no lockers available.) There's a public pool in **Cannaregio at Sant'Alvise** (☎ 041/713567), housed in a well-preserved building that once served as the community laundry. (No lockers are available.) Admission for each of the pools is 8,000 lire/€4.15.

Tennis

The **Hotel des Bains** (✉ Lungomare Marconi 17, Lido, ☎ 041/5265921) rents courts to nonguests from March through November. **Hotel Excelsior** (✉ Lungomare Marconi 41, Lido, ☎ 041/5260201) has courts available from March through November as well. There are several tennis clubs on the Lido, but they are rarely open to nonmembers. One is the **Lido Tennis Club** (✉ Via Sandro Gallo 163, ☎ 041/5260954).

SHOPPING

You're sure to find plenty of pleasant shops and boutiques as you explore Venice. It's always a good idea to mark the location of a shop that interests you on your map; otherwise you may not be able to find it again in the maze of tiny streets. Regular store hours are usually 9–12:30 and 3:30 or 4–7:30 PM; some stores are closed on Saturday afternoon or Monday morning. Food shops are open 8–1 and 5–7:30, and are closed all day Sunday and on Wednesday afternoon. However, many tourist-oriented shops are open all day, every day. Some shops close for both a summer and a winter vacation.

Markets

The morning open-air fruit and vegetable market at **Rialto** offers animated local color and commerce. On Tuesday through Saturday mornings, the **fish market** (adjacent to the Rialto produce market) teaches an impressive lesson in ichthyology, with species you've probably never seen before. In the Castello district is **Via Garibaldi,** the scene of a lively food market on weekday mornings. Another small market is near the train station.

Shopping Districts

The **San Marco** area is full of shops and couture boutiques such as Armani, Missoni, Valentino, Fendi, and Versace. **Le Mercerie,** along with the Frezzeria and Calle dei Fabbri, leading from Piazza San Marco, are some of Venice's busiest shopping streets. Other good shopping areas surround Calle del Teatro and Campi San Salvador, Manin, San Fantin, and San Bartolomeo. Less-expensive shops are between the Rialto Bridge and San Polo.

Specialty Stores

Glassware

Glass, most of it made in Murano, is Venice's number one product, and you'll be confronted by mind-boggling displays of traditional and contemporary glassware, often kitsch. Take your time and be selective. You will probably find that prices in Venice's shops and the showrooms of Murano's factories are pretty much the same. However, because of competition, shops in Venice with wares from various glassworks may charge slightly less. **Domus** (⊠ Fondamenta dei Vetrai, Murano, ☎ 041/739215) has a selection of smaller objects and jewelry from the best glassworks. **Galleria San Nicolò** (⊠ Calle del Traghetto 2793, Dorsoduro, by the Ca' Rezzonico vaporetto stop, ☎ 041/5221535) is owned by the American glass expert Louise Berndt. It shows the best of contemporary glass, including superb work by Yoichi Ohira, a Japanese designer and longtime Venice resident. For chic, contemporary glassware, Carlo Moretti is a good choice; his designs are on display at **L'Isola** (⊠ Campo San Moisè 1468, San Marco, ☎ 041/5231973).

Marina Barovier's gallery (⊠ Calle delle Botteghe 3172, San Marco, just off Campo Santo Stefano, ☎ 041/5236748) has an excellent selection of collectors' contemporary glass. Go to Michel Paciello's **Paropàmiso** (⊠ Frezzeria 1701, near Piazza San Marco, ☎ 041/5227120) for stunning Venetian glass beads and traditional jewelry from all over the world. **Pauly** (⊠ Piazza San Marco 73–77, ☎ 041/5209899) is central, with a wide array of glassware. In a category all his own is **Gianfranco Penzo** (⊠ Campo del Ghetto Nuovo 2895, ☎ no phone), who decorates Jewish ritual vessels in glass and makes commemorative plates; he takes special orders. **Tre Erre** (⊠ Piazza San Marco 79/b, ☎ 041/5201715) is a reliable and respected firm. **Venini** (⊠ Piazzetta dei Leoncini 314, ☎ 041/5224045) has been an institution since the 1930s, attracting some of the foremost names in glass design. **Vetri d'Arte** (⊠ Piazza San Marco 140, ☎ 041/5200205) offers moderately priced glass jewelry.

VENETIAN MASKS UNVEILED

VENETIAN MASK-MAKING has experienced a rebirth. In the time of the Republic, the mask trade was vibrant—Venetians used masks all year long to go about town incognito—but it was suppressed by Napoléon, a by-product of his effort to end Carnival and other Venetian holidays. When Carnival was revived in the late 1970s, mask-making returned as well. Though many of the current workshops stick to centuries-old techniques, none have been in business for more than 30 years.

A landmark date in the history of Venetian masks is 1436, when the *mascareri* (mask makers) founded their own guild. By then the techniques that are replicated today were well established: a mask is first modeled in clay, then a chalk cast is made from it and lined with layers of papier-mâché, glue, gauze, and wax. (You can buy a molded mask at this stage of production and paint it yourself.)

But masks were popular well before the mascareri's guild was established. Local laws regulating their use appeared as early as 1268, often intended to prevent people from carrying weapons when masked or in a vain attempt to prohibit the then-common practice of masked men disguised as women entering convents to seduce nuns. Even on religious holidays—when masks were theoretically prohibited—they were commonly used by Venetians going to the theater or attempting to avoid identification at the city's numerous brothels and gaming tables.

In the 18th century masks started being used by actors playing the traditional roles of the commedia dell'arte. Arlecchino, Pantalone, Pulcinella, and company would wear leather masks designed to amplify or change their voices. Inexpensive papier-mâché versions of these traditional, all-black masks can be found everywhere. Arlecchino has the round face and surprised expression, Pantalone is the one with the curved nose and long moustache, and Pulcinella has the protruding nose.

The least expensive mask is the white Bauta, smooth and plain with a short, pointed nose. It's also reproduced in ceramic and brass. Invented in the 18th century as a disguise, a properly made Bauta will also alter the tone of the wearer's voice. It was particularly popular for women going to the theater, and whether worn by a man or woman, it was always accompanied by a black three-cornered hat and an ample black cloak. The pretty Gnaga, which resembles a cat's face, was used by gay men to "meow" compliments and proposals to good-looking boys. The basic Moretta is just a black oval with eyeholes. The most interesting-looking of the traditional masks is perhaps the Medico della Peste (the Plague's Doctor), with an enormous nose shaped like a bird's beak and surmounted by a pair of glasses. During the terrible plague of 1630 and 1631, doctors took some protective measures against infection: as well as wearing masks, they examined patients with a rod to avoid touching contagious bodies and wore waxed coats that didn't "absorb" the disease. Inside the nose of the mask they put medical herbs and fragrances thought to filter and clean the infected air, while the glasses protected the eyes.

Following the boom of mask shops, numerous costume rental stores opened in the 1990s. Here you'll find an assortment of masks and simplified versions of 18th-century costumes (for men both civil and military) that are warm enough to be worn outdoors and at the same time suitable for dances and parties. They can be rented for one or more days (with reduced rates for longer periods), and most models are also for sale. If you plan to rent a costume during Carnival, it's a good idea to make a reservation several months in advance.

—Carla Lionello

Lace and Embroidered Fabrics

Much of the lace and embroidered linen sold in Venice and on Burano is really made in China or Taiwan. However, at **Il Merletto** (⊠ Sotoportego del Cavalletto, under the Procuratie Vecchie, Piazza San Marco 95–96, ☎ 041/5208406), you can ask for the authentic, handmade lace kept in the drawers behind the counter. This is the only place in Venice connected with the students of the Scuola del Merletto in Burano, who, officially, do not sell to the public. A top address for linen is **Jesurum** (⊠ Piazza San Marco 60–61, ☎ 041/5229864). Go to **Lorenzo Rubelli** (⊠ Campo San Gallo 1089, just off Piazza San Marco, ☎ 041/5236110) for the same brocades, damasks, and cut velvets used by the world's most prestigious decorators. At **Norelene** (⊠ Calle della Chiesa 727, ☎ 041/5237605) you'll find wonderful hand-printed fabrics.

Masks

Laboratorio Artigiano Maschere (⊠ Barbaria delle Tole, near Campo dei Santi Giovanni e Paolo, ☎ 041/5223110) is home to Giorgio Clanetti, credited with starting the revival in mask making. **Mondonovo** (⊠ Rio terà Canal, ☎ 041/5287344) is a cut above most other mask stores.

VENICE A TO Z

To research prices, get advice from other travelers, and book travel arrangements, visit www.fodors.com.

AIRPORTS AND TRANSFERS

Aeroporto Marco Polo is served by domestic and international flights, including connections from London, Amsterdam, Brussels, Frankfurt, Munich, Paris, Vienna, and Zurich.

Taking a boat may be the best way to get to Venice from the airport. The most direct way is by the Alilaguna launch, with regularly scheduled service until midnight; it takes about an hour to get to the landing (just off Piazza San Marco), stopping at the Lido on the way, and the fare is 17,000 lire/€8.80 per person, including bags. A water taxi—a sleek, modern motorboat known as a *motoscafo*—from the airport costs about 140,000 lire/€72.30 for two people (more for larger groups), but it is always essential to agree on a fare before boarding.

Blue ATVO buses make the 25-minute nonstop trip from the airport to Piazzale Roma; from here you can get a vaporetto to the landing nearest your hotel. The ATVO fare is 5,000 lire/€2.60, and tickets are available on the bus when the airport ticket booth is closed. The local ACTV bus (Line 5) runs from the airport to Piazzale Roma every 30 minutes (every hour after 8:10 PM), but you need a ticket (1,500 lire/€0.75) before boarding, which can only be purchased at the airport tobacconist-newsstand, open daily 6:30 AM–9 PM. Luggage can be a hassle on the bus, which is usually crowded with local commuters. A yellow taxi from the airport to Piazzale Roma costs about 55,000 lire/€28.40.

➤ AIRPORT INFORMATION: **Aeroporto Marco Polo** (⊠ Tessera, about 10 km [6 mi] north of the city on the mainland, ☎ 041/2609260, WEB www.veniceairport.it).

➤ TAXIS AND SHUTTLES: **Alilaguna** (☎ 041/5235775). **ATVO** (☎ 041/929500). **Motoscafo** (☎ 041/5415084). **Yellow Taxi** (☎ 041/5237774).

BOAT AND FERRY TRAVEL
BY GONDOLA

If you simply can't leave Venice without a gondola ride, the best time is in the late afternoon or early evening, when the Grand Canal isn't so heavily trafficked. Try to avoid low tide, when the foul odors of the canals are at their worst. It's best to start from a station on the Grand Canal because the lagoon is usually choppy. Make it clear that you want to see the smaller canals, and come to terms on the cost and duration of the ride before you start. Gondoliers are supposed to charge a fixed minimum of about 120,000 lire/€62 for up to six passengers for 50 minutes. From 8 PM to 8 AM the rate increases to approximately 150,000 lire/€77. Bargaining may get you a better price.

BY MOTOSCAFO

These stylish powerboat water taxis are extremely expensive, and the fare system is as complex as Venice's layout. Plan on spending at least 80,000 lire/€41 for a short trip in town. Always agree on the fare before starting out, and beware of other additions such as handling luggage and late or early hours.

BY TRAGHETTO

Few tourists know about the two-man gondolas that ferry people across the Grand Canal at various fixed points. They are the cheapest and shortest gondola ride in Venice and can save a lot of walking. The fare is 700 lire/€0.35, which you hand to the gondolier when you get on. Look for TRAGHETTO signs.

BY VAPORETTO

ACTV water buses, open daily 7:30 AM–8 PM, run the length of the Grand Canal and circle the city. There are several lines, some of which connect Venice with the major and minor islands in the lagoon. Landing stages are clearly marked with name and line number, but check before boarding, particularly with Lines 52 and 82, to make sure the boat is going in your direction.

Line 1 is the Grand Canal local, calling at every stop, and continuing via San Marco to the Lido. (The trip takes about 45 minutes from the station to San Marco.) Line 41 and Line 42 follow long loop routes in opposite directions: take Line 41 from San Zaccaria to Murano, but Line 42 from Murano to San Zaccaria; Line 42 from San Zaccaria to the Redentore, but Line 41 from the Redentore back to San Zaccaria. Line 51 runs from the railway station to San Zaccaria via Piazzale Roma and Zattere and continues to the Lido. Line 52 goes along the same route but in the opposite direction, so from the Lido it makes stops at the Giardini, San Zaccaria, Zattere, Piazzale Roma, the train station, Fondamente Nuove (where boats leave for the islands of the northern lagoon), San Pietro, and back to the Lido. Line 82 runs in a loop from San Zaccaria to Giudecca, Zattere, Piazzale Roma, the train station, Rialto (with fewer stops along the Grand Canal than Line 1), and back to San Zaccaria, and out to the Lido in the summer. Line N runs from roughly midnight to 5 AM, stopping at the Lido, San Marco, Rialto, the train station, Piazzale Roma, Giudecca, Zattere, and San Zaccaria, then returning back the opposite direction.

FARES AND SCHEDULES

The one-way fare for the ACTV water bus is 6,000 lire/€3.10 on all lines (return 10,000 lire/€5.15). A 24-hour tourist ticket costs 18,000 lire/€9.30, a three-day ticket 35,000 lire/€18.10, and a seven-day ticket 60,000 lire/€31.00; these are especially worthwhile if you are planning to visit the islands. Groups of three to five people traveling together are eligible for reduced fares (ask for the *biglietto famiglia*).

With the *traghetto* ticket you can go from one stop to the next for only 3,000 lire/€1.55 (return 5,000 lire/€2.60); note that this also includes the San Zaccaria–San Giorgio and Lido–Sant'Elena routes. You can also buy a *blocchetto* (book of 10 tickets) for 50,000 lire/€25.80, but don't throw away used tickets, as the blocchetto must always be shown whole to the controller. Free timetables are available at the main ticket office at Piazzale Roma.

Timetables are also posted at every landing stage, and there is a ticket booth at each stop. After 9 PM, tickets are available on the boats, but you must immediately inform the controller that you need a ticket. For this reason, it may be useful to buy your tickets in advance. Be sure to validate tickets in the time-stamp machines before getting on board, or you could be subject to a fine.

➤ BOAT AND FERRY INFORMATION: **ACTV** (☎ 041/5287886, WEB www.actv.it). **Motoscafo** (☎ 041/5222303 airport transfers).

BUS TRAVEL TO AND FROM VENICE
Buses connect the bus terminal to Mestre, the Brenta Riviera, Padua, Treviso, Cortina d'Ampezzo, and other destinations in the region.

FARES AND SCHEDULES
ACTV buses to Mestre (1,500 lire/€0.75) are very frequent, and there's night service; ACTV buses to Padua stop along the Brenta Riviera (two departures per hour, 3,000 lire/€1.55–6,000 lire/€3.10). ATVO buses to Cortina (19,000 lire/€9.80) operate weekends only September– May with one departure early in the morning from Venice, and one departure around 3 PM from Cortina; from June to August, these departures are daily. La Marca buses have two departures hourly to Treviso, 4,000 lire/€2.70.

➤ BUS INFORMATION: **ACTV** (☎ 041/287886). **ATVO** (☎ 041/5205530). **La Marca** (☎ 0422/57731). **Bus Terminal** (✉ Piazzale Roma, across the Grand Canal from the train station).

CAR RENTAL
➤ LOCAL AGENCIES: **Avis** (✉ Piazzale Roma, ☎ 041/5225825; ✉ Aeroporto Marco Polo, ☎ 041/5415030, WEB www.avisautonoleggio.it). **Hertz** (✉ Piazzale Roma, ☎ 041/5284091; ✉ Aeroporto Marco Polo, ☎ 041/5416075, WEB www.hertz.com). **Sixt Rent-a-Car** (✉ Aeroporto Marco Polo, ☎ 041/5415570, WEB www.sixt.it).

CAR TRAVEL
Venice is on the east–west A4 autostrada, which connects with Padua, Verona, Brescia, Milan, and Turin. If you bring a car to Venice, you will have to pay for a garage or parking space. Warning: do not be waylaid by illegal touts, often wearing fake uniforms, who may try to flag you down and offer to arrange parking and hotels; their activities have become a scandal in a city generally free of con men and criminals. Ignore them and continue on until you reach the automatic ticket machines. Do not leave valuables in the car. There is a luggage-check office, open daily 8 AM–8 PM, next to the Pullman Bar on the ground floor of the municipal garage at Piazzale Roma. You can take your car to the Lido; the car ferry (Line 17) makes the half-hour trip about every 50 minutes from a landing at Tronchetto, but in summer there can be long lines. It costs 17,000–35,000 lire/€8.75–18.10, depending on the size of the car. Line 82 runs from Tronchetto to Piazzale Roma and Piazza San Marco and also goes on to the Lido in summer. (When there is thick fog or extreme tides, a bus runs to Piazzale Roma instead.) Avoid private boats—they are a rip-off.

PARKING

Parking at Autorimessa Comunale costs 36,000 lire/€18.60 for 24 hours. The private Garage San Marco costs 35,000 lire/€18.10 for 12 hours and 48,000 lire/€24.80 per 24 hours. To reach the privately run Tronchetto parking area, follow the signs to turn right before Piazzale Roma. Parking costs 30,000 lire/€15.50 for 24 hours. The AVA has arranged a discount of 20% per day for hotel guests who use the Garage San Marco or the Tronchetto facility. Ask for a voucher upon checking into your hotel and present it at the parking area when you pay. Only Garage San Marco accepts reservations.

➤ CONTACTS: **Autorimessa Comunale** (✉ Piazzale Roma, end of S11 road, ☎ 041/2727301). **Garage San Marco** (✉ Piazzale Roma 467/f, end of S11 road, ☎ 041/5232213). **Tronchetto** (☎ 041/5207555).

DISABILITIES AND ACCESSIBILITY

In Venice, bridges, narrow streets, historic buildings that cannot be renovated, high-tide, and uneven access to vaporetto landings complicate matters for people with mobility problems. Contact Informahandicap for details about routes with facilities for people with disabilities; the Venice tourist information office can identify for you hotels with facilities for people with disabilities. Palazzo Ducale, the Campanile di San Marco, Gallerie dell'Accademia, Ca' Rezzonico, Palazzo Grassi, Galleria Franchetti inside the Ca' d'Oro, and the Scuola di San Rocco have either lifts or ramps for wheelchairs. Most churches, including the Basilica di San Marco, have one or two low steps to overcome.

➤ CONTACTS: **Informahandicap** (✉ Viale Garibaldi 155, 30100, Mestre, ☎ 041/5341700).

EMBASSIES AND CONSULATES

There is no U.S. or Canadian consular service.

➤ UNITED KINGDOM: **U.K. Consulate** (✉ Campo della Carità 1051, Dorsoduro, ☎ 041/5227207).

EMERGENCIES

The U.K. Consulate can recommend doctors and dentists. Your hotel or any pharmacy should also be able to offer advice. The nearest pharmacy is never far, and they take turns staying open at night, on Saturday afternoon, and on Sunday; the weekly list of after-hours pharmacies is posted on the front of every pharmacy.

➤ EMERGENCY SERVICES: **General Emergencies** (☎ 113). **Ambulance** (☎ 118). **Carabinieri** (☎ 112).

➤ HOSPITALS: **Venice Hospital First Aid** (☎ 041/5230000).

ENGLISH-LANGUAGE MEDIA

BOOKS

Cafoscarina is the bookstore of nearby Università di Venezia Ca' Foscari, with the town's largest selection of books in English. Emiliana Editrice, Fantoni, and Studium have a small selection of books about Venice and Italian food.

NEWSPAPERS AND MAGAZINES

The newspaper stall to the right of the San Marco post office has English-language newspapers.

➤ CONTACTS: **Cafoscarina** (✉ Campiello Squellini 3259, Dorsoduro, ☎ 041/5229602). **Emiliana Editrice** (✉ Calle Goldoni, between Piazza San Marco and Campo San Luca, ☎ 041/5220793). **Fantoni** (✉ on Salizzada San Luca, ☎ 041/5220700). **Studium** (✉ Calle de la Canonica, off Piazzetta dei Leoncini, ☎ 041/5222382).

MAIL AND SHIPPING

Venice's main post office is housed in the Fondaco dei Tedecchi, near the Rialto bridge.

TOURS

BOAT TOURS

The Cooperativa San Marco organizes tours of the islands of Murano, Burano, and Torcello. April through November, the 3½-hour tours depart daily at 9:30 and 2:30 (December–March daily at 2) from the landing stage in front of the Giardini Reali, just off Piazza San Marco; they cost about 30,000 lire/€15.50. Tours tend to be annoyingly commercial and emphasize glass-factory showrooms, pressuring you to buy, sometimes at higher prices than normal.

American Express offers group gondola rides with serenades from May through October nightly at 7:30 and 8:30 and from November through March daily at 3:30 (about 50,000 lire/€25.80).

➤ FEES AND SCHEDULES: **American Express** (⊠ Salizzada San Moisè 1471, San Marco, ☎ 041/5200844, FAX 041/5229937). **Cooperativa San Marco** (⊠ just off San Marco, ☎ 041/5235775 or 041/2406736).

PRIVATE GUIDES

Cooperativa Guide Turistiche Autorizzate has a list of nearly a hundred licensed guides. Venicescapes is an Italo-American cultural association that offers a choice of five "theme" itineraries. Tours are all private and can accommodate a maximum of six people. Reservations are necessary (book at least a couple of months ahead). Custom-designed itineraries are available on request.

➤ CONTACTS: **Cooperativa Guide Turistiche Autorizzate** (⊠ San Marco 750, near San Zulian, ☎ 041/5209038, FAX 041/5210762). **Venicescapes** (⊠ Campo San Provolo 4954, Castello, 30122, ☎ FAX 041/5206361, WEB www.venicescapes.org).

TOURS OF THE SURROUNDING REGION

American Express offers several worthwhile excursions. A day trip to Padua goes by boat along the Brenta River, with stops at three Palladian villas, and a return to Venice by bus. The tours run three days a week from March to October and cost 120,000 lire/€62.00 per person (170,000 lire/€87.80 with lunch); bookings need to be made the day before.

The Palladio Villa Tour (by minibus, maximum eight people), besides a visit to the Palladian villas, includes a walking tour of Vicenza (Wednesday only; 190,000 lire/€98.10 per person; optional lunch 20,000 lire/€10.30 per person).

The interesting Hills of the Veneto tour (by minibus, maximum eight people) focuses on the little-known, picturesque hill towns of Marostica, Bassano del Grappa, and Asolo; with stops at Villa Barbaro at Maser and at a vineyard along the Strada del Prosecco for a Prosecco wine tasting (Tuesday, Thursday, and weekends; 175,000 lire/€90.40 per person, optional lunch 25,000 lire/€12.90 per person).

For a break from the heat, consider the Dolomite Tour (by minibus, maximum eight people) through the stupendous scenery in the Dolomite mountains; stops include Titian's birthplace Pieve di Cadore, the Santa Caterina and Misurina lakes, the famous Cime di Lavaredo peaks, and Cortina d'Ampezzo (Monday and Friday, 180,000 lire/€92.95 per person includes packet lunch). For these last three tours it is essential to make reservations a couple of weeks in advance.

➤ FEES AND SCHEDULES: **American Express** (⊠ Salizzada San Moisè 1471, San Marco, ☎ 041/5200844, FAX 041/5229937).

Two-hour walking tours of the San Marco area can be booked through American Express. Its daily "Jewels of the Venetian Republic" tour (about 45,000 lire/€23.25) ends with a glassblowing demonstration. From April 25 to November 15, American Express also offers an afternoon walking tour that ends with a gondola ride (about 50,000 lire/€25.80). From June through August, free guided tours (some in English) of the Basilica di San Marco are offered from Monday to Saturday by the Procuratoria; information is available in the atrium of the church.

➤ FEES AND SCHEDULES: **American Express** (✉ Salizzada San Moisè 1471, San Marco, ☎ 041/5200844, FAX 041/5229937). **Procuratoria** (☎ 041/5225205).

TRAIN TRAVEL
Venice has rail connections with every major city in Italy and Europe. Some trains do not terminate at Stazione Ferroviaria Santa Lucia. Instead, they stop only at the Stazione Ferroviaria Venezia-Mestre, which is then 10 minutes by train to Venice. All trains traveling to and from Santa Lucia stop at Mestre; to get from Venezia-Mestre to Santa Lucia, take the first available train, remembering there is a *supplemento* (extra charge) for traveling on Intercity and Eurocity and Eurostar trains and that if you do not purchase your ticket at the station booth and validate it in the machine on the platform before boarding, you are liable for a hefty fine.

➤ TRAIN INFORMATION: **Stazione Ferroviaria Santa Lucia** (✉ on the Grand Canal in the northwest corner of the city, ☎ 8488/88088, WEB www.fs-on-line.com). **Stazione Ferroviaria Venezia-Mestre** (✉ Mestre, 12 km [7 mi] north of Venice, ☎ 1478/88088, WEB www.fs-on-line.com).

TRANSPORTATION AROUND VENICE
First-time visitors find that getting around Venice presents some unusual problems: the layout is complex; the waterborne transportation can be bewildering; the house-numbering system is baffling; many street names in the *sestieri* (six districts) of San Marco, Cannaregio, Castello, Dorsoduro, Santa Croce, and San Polo are duplicated; and often you must walk, whether you want to or not. It's essential to have a good map showing all street names and vaporetto routes; buy one at a newsstand. Signs are posted on many corners pointing you in the right direction for the nearest major landmark—San Marco, Rialto, Accademia, etc.—but don't count on finding such signs once you're deep into residential neighborhoods.

TRAVEL AGENCIES
➤ LOCAL AGENT REFERRALS: **Albatravel** (✉ Calle dei Fabbri 4538, San Marco, ☎ 041/5210123, FAX 041/5200781). **American Express** (✉ Salizzada San Moisè 1471, San Marco, ☎ 041/5200844, FAX 041/5229937). **Gran Canal** (✉ Ponte del Ovo, near the Rialto Bridge, 4759 San Marco, ☎ 041/2712111, FAX 041/5223380).

VISITOR INFORMATION
For those ages 14–28, the "Rolling Venice" youth card (5,000 lire/€2.60) includes handy guidebooks to the city and offers discounts for ACTV vaporetto passes and a few museums, as well as some hotels, restaurants, and shops. It is available from the Assessorato alla Gioventù, open weekdays 9:30–1, Tuesday and Thursday 9:30–1 and 3–5; from the Arte e Storia travel agency, open weekdays 9–12:45 and 3–6:15; and from the Associazione Italiana Alberghi per la Gioventù, open Monday–Saturday 8:30–1:30. You must show your passport to qualify.

➤ TOURIST INFORMATION: **Arte e Storia travel agency** (✉ Campo della Lana, ☎ 041/5240232). **Assessorato alla Gioventù** (✉ Corte Contarini 1529, behind Piazza San Marco post office, ☎ 041/2747651). **Associazione Italiana Alberghi per la Gioventù** (✉ Calle Castelforte, near San Rocco, ☎ 041/5204414). **Venice Tourist Offices** (✉ Santa Lucia train station, ☎ 041/5298727; ✉ San Marco 71/f, near the Museo Correr; Venice Pavillon next to the ex Giardinetti Reali; Venice Pavillon inside Garage Comunale; Gran Viale S. Maria Elisabetta 6/a, Lido. Telephone information line, weekdays 8:30–5, ☎ 041/5298711; WEB www.venezia.provincia/apt.it).

2 VENETIAN ARC

PADUA, VERONA, VICENZA,
UDINE, TRIESTE

In the Veneto and Friuli-Venezia Giulia regions you'll see much that looks Venetian, but there's more here than Gothic buildings and winged lions. You'll find Asolo, the City of a Hundred Horizons; Padua, ennobled by Giotto's frescoes; the romantic Verona of *Romeo and Juliet*; and the villas of Andrea Palladio, where 16th-century aristocrats led the privileged life. To the east are Udine, with what has been called "the most beautiful Venetian square on terra firma," and the border town of Trieste, famous for its Austrian-like coffeehouses and winding streets.

Updated by
Carla Lionello

AS ROME PRESIDES OVER LAZIO, the arc around Venice stretching from Verona east to Trieste falls under the historical and spiritual influence of its namesake city. No lagoons, perhaps, but the region's architecture, paintings, and way of life all reflect the splendor of La Serenissima. Much of the pleasure of exploring this area comes from discovering the individual variations on the overall Venetian theme that confer special charm on each of the towns you'll visit. Some, such as Verona, Treviso, and Udine, have a solid medieval look; Asolo has an idyllic setting; Bassano combines a bit of both. If you are a confirmed or fledgling oenophile, you'll enjoy tasting local wines within view of the vineyards that produce some of the best-known Italian vintages—among them, Soave, Valpolicella, Bardolino, and Prosecco. But most of all, you'll find artistic jewels everywhere, from the great Venetian masters in Verona to Veronese's lighthearted frescoes in Villa Barbaro at Maser.

Udine, home to the first important frescoes by Giambattista Tiepolo, is one of Italy's least-known towns: small and pleasantly bourgeois, it makes for quiet walks, great meals, and is a good base from which to explore the rest of the Friuli region. In Trieste, after a climb to the hill of San Giusto with its cathedral and castle, the aroma of freshly roasted coffee that fills the city center is hard to resist: a cappuccino (here called caffelatte) and a piece of Austro-Hungarian pastry are de rigueur.

Pleasures and Pastimes

Concerts and Opera
The love of Italian culture need not stop at Venice. Verona, Trieste, and Vicenza offer some of the most spectacular opportunities for enjoying open-air operas and concerts.

Dining
In the main cities of the Veneto region, restaurants are in the middle to upper ranges of each price category, but in smaller towns and in the countryside you can find some real bargains. At the eastern end of the Arc, in less-trafficked Friuli–Venezia Giulia, prices are generally lower. Seafood is the specialty along the coast, of course, while inland the cuisine varies from the delicate risotto of the Veneto to the more decisively flavored cooking of the Trieste area, heavily influenced by Austria and Slovenia. San Daniele del Friuli, near Udine, is famous for its delicious prosciutto of the same name. Polenta, made of cornmeal, is a staple throughout the area; it is served with thick, rich sauces or grilled as an accompaniment to meat or fish dishes. In the Veneto, a bowl of thick *pasta e fagioli* (pasta and bean soup), here typically prepared with the addition of wide pieces of fresh pasta, is all you might want to eat on a cold winter's night.

The best local wines are Soave, Tocai, Prosecco, Riesling, and pinot—all white; and reds Bardolino, Valpolicella, merlot, cabernet, and pinot nero. The Collio designation indicates wines from vineyards in the eastern part of Friuli, up against the Slovenian border. One of the most famous wines produced here is the Picolit, similar to sauterne and made in very limited quantities. The Veneto and Friuli regions are renowned for their grappas. Justifiably popular are those made by the families Nardini, in Bassano, and Nonino, at Udine. Trieste is the home of the famous Stock liqueur.

For general information and price categories, *see* Dining *in* Smart Travel Tips A to Z.

Lodging

The area around Venice has been playing host to visitors for centuries, and as a result there is a range of comfortable accommodations at every price. As with dining, common sense should tell you that the slightly out-of-the-way small hotel will cost you less than its counterpart in a stylish Adriatic resort. Hotels in nearby Vicenza, Bassano del Grappa, along the Brenta, and in Venice are better in terms of variety and quality than in Padua itself, which caters primarily to business travelers. Many hotels in Trieste offer substantial discounts on weekends. Expect to pay more as you approach Venice, since many of the mainland towns absorb the overflow during the times when Venice becomes most crowded, such as Carnevale (Carnival, held two weeks preceding Lent), and from mid-spring to early autumn. For general information and price categories, *see* Lodging *in* Smart Travel Tips A to Z.

Shopping

Many of the goods associated with Venice are actually produced in the surrounding areas of the Venetian Arc—which means that with a bit of diligence or luck you can pick up a bargain from the source. Mountain towns and villages such as Bassano del Grappa and Asolo have the strongest handicraft tradition, but you can find a wide range of goods—from ceramics to musical instruments—also on the side streets of less-known places like Arquà Petrarca, Marostica, and Bagnano di Asolo. Itinerant antiques markets are customarily held throughout the region, usually on Sunday. Finally, food shops, wine shops, and open-air produce markets are some of Italy's best.

Villas and Palazzi

The countless villas and palaces sprinkled throughout the Venetian hinterland and the Palladian villas along the Brenta River should not be missed. These gracious country homes give insight into the way wealthy Venetians used to—and still do—spend leisure time. Many of the villas are privately owned but are open to the public at certain times or by special request. Local tourist offices can be helpful in providing information on visiting these jewels.

Exploring the Venetian Arc

The Venetian Arc encompasses the coastal crescent and the inland plain that stretches from the mouths of the Po and Adige rivers southwest of Venice to Trieste and the Slovenian to Venice's east. It bridges two Italian regions—the Veneto and Friuli–Venezia Giulia—and is mainly flat green farmland spotted with low hills that swell and rise steeply inland in a succession of plateaus and high meadows to the snow-tipped Alps.

Numbers in the text correspond to numbers in the margin and on the Venetian Arc and Verona maps.

Great Itineraries

Hard as it may seem to leave the unique beauty of Venice behind, the Venetian Arc is the perfect last course to round off your stay. The towns are all beautiful, mixing grandiose architecture and medieval aristocracy flawlessly. One of these towns, Verona, also unknowingly produced the most tragic of all *storie d'amore* (love stories)—*Romeo and Juliet*. The sorrow that this tale inspires can be drowned in the delights of some of the best-known Italian wines.

Many towns can be seen on one- or two-day excursions from Venice itself. A three-day itinerary will exclude Trieste and restrict you to the other principal sights. A five-day exploration will give you plenty to remember and savor, but you will have to discipline yourself to keep up a swift pace. A seven-day trip will give you the time to fully experience the architecture, history, and culture of this beautiful region.

IF YOU HAVE 3 DAYS

Begin your drive at **Villa Pisani** ①, the most splendid of all Veneto villas. Move on to **Padua** ②, taking in the Cappella degli Scrovegni. Continue toward ⊡ **Verona** ④–⑱, the city of *Romeo and Juliet*. The following day, see some of Palladio's works in **Vicenza** ③ and head for **Marostica** ⑲, ⊡ **Bassano del Grappa** ⑳, and **Asolo** ㉑. Save the last day for **Treviso** ㉓ and **Conegliano** ㉔, and stop for a tour of **Udine** ㉕. Return to Venice along the A4.

IF YOU HAVE 5 DAYS

Follow the three-day itinerary until Asolo, but at a slower pace. Stop in ⊡ **Verona** ④–⑱ for the first two nights; then, after visiting **Bassano del Grappa** ⑳ on the third day, instead of moving on directly to Treviso, travel toward **Villa Barbaro** ㉒ in Maser and then on to **Treviso** ㉓ and ⊡ **Conegliano** ㉔, where you can overnight. On the fourth day, head for **Udine** ㉕ and **Cividale** ㉖; then go down to ⊡ **Trieste** ㉘. Spend the evening and most of the following day in this border city; then move on to **Castello di Miramare** ㉗ before taking the A4 back to Venice.

IF YOU HAVE 7 DAYS

Follow the itinerary described above; in **Bassano del Grappa** ⑳ take the time to visit the famous Nardini distillery on the edge of town. ⊡ **Treviso** ㉓, where you can spend the third and fourth nights, makes a good base for exploring the Marca Trevigiana, famous for its three Strade del Vino (wine roads): the Strada del Prosecco, which cuts across the hills between **Conegliano** ㉔ and Valdobbiadene; the Strada dei Vini del Piave, which winds along the Piave River between Conegliano, Campodipietra, Zenson, and Roncade; and the Strada dei Vini del Montello e dei Colli Asolani, which runs to the south of the Piave River between the Montello and **Asolo** ㉑. On the fifth day, visit Conegliano, **Udine** ㉕, and **Cividale** ㉖; then head for ⊡ **Trieste** ㉘. Spend two nights and a full day there; then move on to **Castello di Miramare** ㉗ before taking the A4 back to Venice.

When to Tour the Venetian Arc

There is no particular good or bad time to see the sights around the Venetian Arc. Most of the year the area is relatively free from very heavy traffic and congestion. If, however, you want to get the most out of your stay, come during the late spring and early summer months (May, June, July) or in early September. Winter is a good time to avoid travel to the region; foggy conditions and wet, bone-chilling cold are not unusual from November through March. Opera and theater buffs should come in spring and summer, when outdoor performances are held.

ON THE ROAD TO PADUA AND VICENZA

Foremost among the treasures of the Veneto region are the beautiful villas of Andrea Palladio (1508–80) built to render *la vita* all the more *dolce* for 16th-century aristocrats. Other important sights include Giotto's 14th-century frescoes in Padua's Cappella degli Scrovegni and many of Donatello's greatest sculptures.

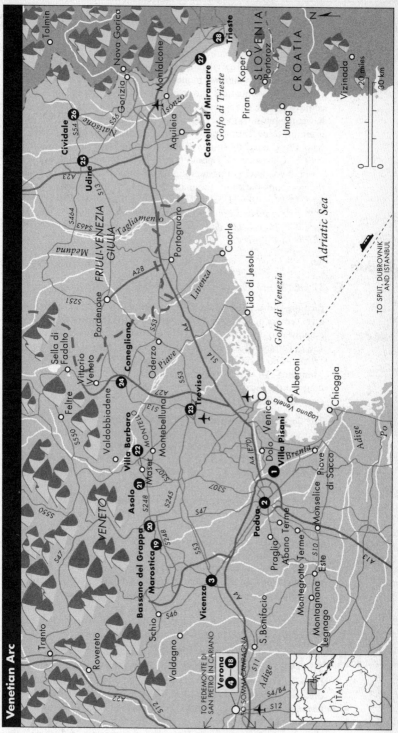

Venetian Arc

TO PEDEMONTE DI
SAN PIETRO IN CARIANO

TO SPLIT, DUBROVNIK
AND ISTANBUL

Adriatic Sea

SLOVENIA

CROATIA

FRIULI-VENEZIA
GIULIA

VENETO

ITALY

20 miles
30 km

Tolmin
Nova Gorica
Gorizia
Cividale
Udine
Montfalcone
Trieste
Castello di Miramare
Golfo di Trieste
Koper
Portoroz
Piran
Umag
Vizinada
Aquileia
Isonzo
Natisone
Tagliamento
Meduna
Sella di
Fadalto
Vittorio
Veneto
Feltre
Conegliano
Valdobbiadene
Villa Barbaro
Asolo
Maser
Montebelluna
Treviso
Bassano del Grappa
Marostica
Vicenza
Verona
SOMMACAMPAGNA
S.Bonifacio
Valdagno
Schio
Trento
Rovereto
Pordenone
Oderzo
Piave
Portogruaro
Livenza
Caorle
Lido di Jesolo
Golfo di Venezia
Laguna Veneta
Alberoni
Chioggia
Venice
Dolo
Villa Pisani
Brenta
Padua
Praglia
Abano Terme
Montegrotto Terme
Monselice
Este
Montagnana
Legnago
Adige
Po
Piave
di Sacco
Adige
S.10

1
2
3
4 – 18
19
20
21
22
23
24
25
26
27
28

N

Villa Pisani

○ ❶ *10 km (6 mi) southeast of Padua.*

This extraordinary house in Stra, also called Villa Nazionale, is the most spectacular of all the villas in the region. Through the 16th to 18th centuries, in sultry summer months wealthy Venetians would spend their *villeggiatura*—vacation and escape from harried city life—on their country estates. Many stately residences were constructed on the Brenta River, the main waterway used by Venetians to go inland. Villa Pisani is an imposing 18th-century edifice that once belonged to Napoléon, who appreciated its similarities to Versailles. See the grandiose frescoes by Giambattista Tiepolo (1696–1770) on the ceiling of the ballroom. If you have youngsters surfeited with old masters in tow, explore the gorgeous **park** and the **maze** (open April to September only). ⊠ *Stra,* ☎ *049/502074.* ▦ *Villa, maze, and grounds 10,000 lire/€5.15; maze and grounds 5,000 lire/€2.60.* ۞ *Apr., Tues.–Sun. 9–5; May, Tues.–Sun. 9–6; June–Sept., daily 9–7; Oct.–Mar., Tues.–Sun. 9–4; last entry 1 hr before closing.*

Padua

❷ *37 km (23 mi) west of Venice, 92 km (57 mi) east of Verona.*

Bustling Padua (Padova, in Italian) has long been one of the major cultural centers in northern Italy. It's home to the peninsula's second-oldest university, founded in 1222, which attracted the likes of Dante (1265–1321), Petrarch (1304–74), and Galileo Galilei (1564–1642). Three great artists—Giotto (1266/67–1337), Donatello (circa 1386–1466), and Mantegna (1431–1506)—left great works here. If you will be visiting many of the local sights, plan on getting the Padua Biglietto Unico, a cumulative ticket (15,000 lire/7.75€).

★ The **Cappella degli Scrovegni** (Scrovegni Chapel) was erected in 1303 by a wealthy Paduan, Enrico Scrovegni, in atonement for his father's sins. Giotto was immediately commissioned to decorate its interior, a task that occupied the great artist and his helpers until 1305–6. They created a magnificent fresco cycle illustrating the lives of Mary and Christ; in typical medieval comic-strip fashion, the 38 panels are arranged in tightly knit tiers to be read from left to right. On the wall to the right of today's entrance is a powerful *Last Judgment*. The realism in these frescoes—which include the first blue skies in Western painting—at the time was considered revolutionary. As only a limited number of people are admitted inside, it's advisable to make a reservation (2000 lire/€1.05) a few days ahead either in person at the ticket office or, weekdays only, by phone. Entrances are scheduled every 20 minutes, and punctuality is mandatory. In any season it's a good idea to bring along a heavy sweater, as the frescoes are preserved at a rather cold temperature. Visits last 40 minutes. ⊠ *Piazza degli Eremitani 8,* ☎ *049/8204550.* ▦ *10,000 lire/€5.15 (includes admission to Museo Civico).* ۞ *Daily 9–7 (last visit starts at 6:40).*

The 13th-century **Chiesa degli Eremitani** contains some fragments of frescoes (most were destroyed by the Allied bombing of 1944) by Andrea Mantegna, the brilliant locally born artist, some of whose masterpieces are in nearby Mantua. The **Museo Civico di Padova** (Civic Museum of Padua), housed in what used to be the monastery of the church, has its quota of works by Venetian masters, as well as a fine collection of ancient relics. ⊠ *Piazza Eremitani 8,* ☎ *049/8204550.* ▦ *Museo Civico: 10,000 lire/€5.15 (includes admission to Cappella degli Scrovegni).* ۞ *Daily 9–7.*

The 16th-century **Palazzo del Bo'** houses the Università di Padova, founded in 1222. The building, which now features an 18th-century facade, is named after the Osteria del Bo' (*bo* means ox), an inn that once stood on the site. This is worth a visit to see the exquisite and perfectly proportioned anatomy theater and a hall with a lectern used by Galileo. Reservations are mandatory; tickets must be bought in advance at the tourist information office located a few steps away in the Galleria Pedrocchi (☎ 049/87767927). Tours are normally given in Italian only. English-speaking guides are available at an extra cost of about 100,000 lire/€51.65. ☒ *Via VIII Febbraio,* ☎ *049/8209711.* ☎ *5,000 lire/€2.60.* ⊙ *Guided tours only. Nov.–Feb., Mon. and Fri. at 3 and 4; Wed. at 9, 10, 3, and 4; Thurs. and Sat. at 9 and 10. Mar.– Oct., Mon. and Fri. at 3, 4, and 5; Wed. at 9, 10, 11, 3, 4, and 5; Thurs. and Sat. at 9, 10, and 11.*

Palazzo della Ragione, also called Il Salone, was built in the Middle Ages as the seat of Padua's parliament. Today its street-level arcades shelter shops and cafés. In the frescoed **Salone** (Salon) on the upper level is an enormous wooden horse, a 15th-century replica of the bronze steed in Donatello's statue of Gattamelata. ☒ *Piazza della Ragione,* ☎ *049/8205006.* ☎ *7,000 lire/€3.60.* ⊙ *Tues.–Sun. 9–7.*

The huge **Basilica di Sant'Antonio** is a cluster of Byzantine domes and slender, minaret-like towers that gives the church an Asian-inspired style reminiscent of San Marco in Venice. The interior is sumptuous, too, with marble reliefs by Tullio Lombardo (circa 1455–1532), the greatest in a talented family of marble carvers who decorated many churches in the area, among them Santa Maria dei Miracoli in Venice. The artistic highlights here, however, all bear Donatello's name: the 15th-century Florentine master did the remarkable series of bronze reliefs illustrating the life of St. Anthony—whose feast day, Festa di Sant'Antonio on June 13, draws pilgrims from all over Europe—as well as the bronze statues of the Madonna and saints on the high altar. ☒ *Piazza del Santo,* ☎ *049/8242811.* ⊙ *Daily 6:30 AM–7 PM.*

To mark the 800th anniversary of the birth of St. Anthony in 1195, the **Mostra Antoniana,** a museum with some 300 exhibits and a multilingual documentary film relating to the image of the saint and of the Basilica di Sant'Antonio, was opened in 1995 on the first floor of the church cloister building. Standing in front of the church is Donatello's powerful statue of the *condottiere* (mercenary general) Erasmo da Narni, called Gattamelata, which was cast in bronze—a monumental technical achievement—in 1453 and was to have an enormous influence on the development of Italian Renaissance sculpture. ☒ *Piazza del Santo,* ☎ *049/8242811.* ☎ *5,000 lire/€2.60.* ⊙ *Easter–Oct., daily 9–12:30 and 2:30–6; Nov.–Easter, Sat.–Mon., Wed., and Thurs. 9–12:30 and 2–5:30.*

The **Orto Botanico** (Botanic Garden) was founded in 1545 by order of the Venetian Republic to supply the university with medicinal plants. The garden is in front of Sant'Antonio. ☒ *Via Orto Botanico 15,* ☎ *049/8272119.* ☎ *5,000 lire/€2.60.* ⊙ *Apr.–Oct., daily 9–1 and 3–6; Nov.–Mar., Mon.–Sat. 9–1.*

Piazza dei Signori exhibits some fine examples of 15th- and 16th-century buildings. On the west side, the **Palazzo del Capitanio** has an impressive **Torre dell'Orologio,** which has a fine astronomical clock dating from 1344. The **Cathedral** is just a few steps away.

Laid out in 1775, **Prato della Valle** is an unusual and attractive piazza with a central wooded oval park, encircled by a canal, called Isola Memmia. A market is featured here weekends. The abbey of **Santa Giustina,** at the southwest end of the Prato della Valle, has finely inlaid choir stalls and a colossal altarpiece, the *Martyrdom of St. Justine*, by Veronese (1528–88). ⊠ *Prato della Valle*, ☎ *049/8220411*. ☉ *Daily 9–noon and 3–8*.

OFF THE
BEATEN PATH

ABANO TERME AND MONTEGROTTO TERME – These two spas, about 12 km (7 mi) south of Padua, are set in the dreamy landscape of the Euganean Hills. Colorful gardens and fresh summer breezes make them havens if you are looking for a respite from city life.

PRAGLIA – You can tour the evocative 15th-century halls and cloisters of this Benedictine monastery hidden in the hills. Wine and honey produced by the monks are for sale. Head 12 km (7 mi) southwest of Padua, following signs for Abano Terme on the south side of the city. The monastery closes to the public when the monks withdraw in meditation, as well as on holy days, so it's advisable to call ahead before making a visit. ☎ *049/9900010*. ☑ *Free; donations appreciated*. ☉ *Tours Apr.–Oct., Tues.–Sun. every ½ hr 3:30–5:30; Nov.–Mar., Tues.–Sun. every ½ hr 2:30–4:30*.

MONTAGNANA – The surrounding walls of this medieval city 50 km (30 mi) southwest of Padua are remarkably well preserved, and there are 24 towers, a moat, and four city gates. Its former rivals, Este and Monselice, are only 20 km (12 mi) east on the same road.

Dining and Lodging

$$$ ✕ **Angelo Rasi.** Perfect for a light dinner on a breezy summer evening, this wine bar with tables along the river offers delicious fish salads and also serves a few pasta dishes and simple meat courses. ⊠ *Riviera Paleocapa 7*, ☎ *049/8719797*. *V. Closed Mon. No lunch*.

$$$ ✕ **Antico Brolo.** Housed in a 16th-century building not far from central Piazza dei Signori, charming Antico Brolo is one of the best restaurants in town. Seasonal specialties are prepared with flair and might include starters like tiny flans with wild mushrooms and herbs or fresh pasta dressed with zucchini flowers. The wine list isn't likely to disappoint you. ⊠ *Corso Milano 22*, ☎ *049/664555. AE, DC, MC, V. Closed Mon. and 1 wk in Aug. No lunch Tues.*

$$ ✕ **Cavalca.** A family-run establishment with a long tradition, Cavalca is just off Piazza dei Signori in the heart of Padua. Classic decor and simple but courteous service are hallmarks here. The specialties are *pasta e fagioli* (pasta and bean soup), *capretto arrosto* (roast kid), and the platter of *arrosti misti* (assorted roast meats). ⊠ *Via Manin 8*, ☎ *049/8760061. Reservations essential. AE, DC, MC, V. Closed Wed., 2 wks in mid-Jan., 3 last wks in July. No dinner Tues.*

$$$ 🏨 **Donatello.** Directly opposite the Basilica di Sant'Antonio, Donatello has rooms with a view of the square and church, but it can be noisy. Rooms are contemporary, with TVs. ⊠ *Via del Santo 102, 35100*, ☎ *049/8750634*, ⅜ *049/8750829*, ⅦⅢ *www.hoteldonatello.net. 49 rooms. Restaurant. AE, DC, MC, V. Closed mid-Dec.–mid-Jan.*.

$$$ 🏨 **Villa Ducale.** Set in its own statuesque gardens, one of the country residences built along the Brenta River by Venetian noblemen has been turned into a stylish hotel with stuccoed walls and ceilings, Murano glass chandeliers and mirrors, and Venetian-style marble flooring. This is not in Padua but in Dolo, halfway between Venice and Padua, and is connected to both by regular local train service. ⊠ *Riviera Martiri della Libertà 75, Dolo, 30031, 10 km (6 mi) east of Padua*, ☎ *041/5608020*, ⅜ *041/5608004*, ⅦⅢ *www.villaducale.it. 11 rooms. Restaurant. AE, DC, MC, V.*

$$$ 🏨 **Villa Pisani.** Housed in a wing of the historical residence of the same
★   name, Villa Pisani is a refined hotel in nearby Vescovana with original 16th-century frescoes, period furniture, and the exclusive atmosphere of a doge's farm. Built in the 16th century by Padua's bishop Francesco

Pisani, a member of the ducal Pisani family of Venice, the villa is surrounded by a magnificent park set out in the neo-Gothic English style. ⊠ *Via Roma 19, Vescovana, 35040, 30 km (19 mi) south of Padua,* ☎ FAX *0425/920016,* WEB *www.villapisani.com. 8 rooms, 1 suite. Bar, pool, meeting room. AE, DC, MC, V.*

Nightlife and the Arts

CAFFÈ

The ever-popular **Caffè Pedrocchi** (⊠ Piazzetta Pedrocchi, ☎ 049/8781231), in a 19th-century neoclassical coffeehouse that looks like a cross between a museum and a stage set, serves up an excellent cappuccino. The upstairs rooms, with their frescoed ceilings brightly restored in 1998, often house art shows (☎ 049/8205007). The *caffè* downstairs is open daily until 11. Admission to upstairs shows, open Tuesday–Sunday 9:30–12:30 and 3:30–6, is 5,000 lire/€2.60.

NIGHTCLUBS AND BARS

An over-25 crowd fills the small **Le Petit Palais** (⊠ Via Vecellio 1, ☎ 049/600134), with a dance floor and commercial house music downstairs and a lounge upstairs. It's closed Monday and mid-July to mid-August. **Victoria** (⊠ Via Savonarola 149, ☎ 049/8721530) is a *birreria* (a bar that serves primarily beer) with live jazz concerts on Thursday; it's closed on Monday. **Limbo** (⊠ Via San Fermo 44, ☎ 049/656882), closed on Monday and Tuesday, is a restaurant-pizzeria open late with live music and a disco downstairs.

Outdoor Activities and Sports

GOLF

The 18-hole course at **Golf Club Padova** (⊠ Via Noiera 57, Valsanzibio di Galzignano Terme, ☎ 049/9130078) is 23 km (15 mi) south of Padua.

TENNIS

Green Tennis (⊠ Via Pilade Bronzetti 33, ☎ 049/8719774) has public courts. Book in advance.

Shopping

Padua's Saturday market in **Prato della Valle** has a wide range of goods, from garments and shoes to fabric, kitchenware, and handmade baskets. An antiques market is held there the third Sunday of every month.

Vicenza

❸ *60 km (37 mi) east of Verona, 32 km (19 mi) west of Padua.*

Vicenza bears the distinctive signature of the 16th-century architect Andrea Palladio and was designated by UNESCO in 1994 as a preeminent site of world cultural heritage. The architect, whose name is the root of the style referred to as "Palladian," gracefully incorporated elements of classical architecture—columns, porticoes, and domes—into a style that reflected the Renaissance celebration of order and harmony. His elegant villas and palaces were influential in propagating classical architecture in Europe, especially Britain, and later in America—most notably at Thomas Jefferson's Monticello.

In the mid-16th century, Palladio was given the opportunity to rebuild much of Vicenza, which had suffered great damage during the bloody wars waged against Venice by the League of Cambrai, an alliance consisting of the papacy, France, the Holy Roman Empire, and several neighboring city-states. Palladio imposed upon the city a number of his grand Roman-style buildings—rather an overstatement, considering the town's status. With the basilica, begun in 1549 in the very heart of Vicenza, he ensured his reputation, then embarked on a series of lordly buildings, all of which proclaim the same rigorous classicism.

The Gothic **Duomo** contains a gleaming altarpiece by Lorenzo Veneziano, a 14th-century Venetian painter. The cathedral itself was partly destroyed in World War II, but nearly all the damaged areas have been restored. Although the Duomo is open daily, tourists are asked not to visit on Saturday afternoon and Sunday. ⊠ *Piazza Duomo,* ☎ *0444/320996.* ⊙ *Daily 10:30–noon and 2:30–5:30.*

The **Corso Palladio** is lined with imposing palaces and churches that run the gamut from Venetian Gothic to Baroque. Many of the palaces were designed by Palladio. The church of **Santa Corona** holds an exceptionally fine *Baptism of Christ* (1500) by Giovanni Bellini (1430–1516) over the altar on the left, just in front of the transept. ⊠ *Contrà S. Corona.* ⊙ *Mon. 4–6, Tues.–Fri. 9–noon and 3–6.*

The exquisite and unmistakably Palladian **Palazzo Chiericati** houses the Vicenza municipal art gallery and holds a representative collection of Venetian paintings. ⊠ *Piazza Matteotti,* ☎ *0444/321348.* ☎ *13,000 lire/€6.70 (includes admission to Teatro Olimpico).* ⊙ *July–mid-Aug., Tues.–Sun. 10–7; mid-Aug.–June, Tues.–Sun. 9–5.*

★ The **Teatro Olimpico** is Palladio's last, and perhaps most exciting, work. Based closely on the model of an ancient Roman theater, it represents an important development in theater and stage design and is noteworthy for its acoustics and the cunningly devised false perspective of a classical street in the permanent backdrop. The anterooms are all frescoed with images of important figures in Venetian history. ⊠ *Piazza Matteotti,* ☎ *0444/323781.* ☎ *13,000 lire/€6.70 (includes admission to Palazzo Chiericati).* ⊙ *July–mid-Aug., Tues.–Sun. 10–7; mid-Aug.–June, Tues.–Sun. 9–5.*

At the heart of Vicenza is **Piazza dei Signori,** also the site of **Palazzo della Ragione,** or Palladio's "basilica"—a confusing way to refer to it, since it is not a church but a courthouse and public meeting hall. An early Palladian masterpiece, it was actually a medieval building that the architect modernized, and the skill with which he wedded the graceful two-story exterior loggias to the existing Gothic structure is remarkable. Also note the **Loggia del Capitaniato,** opposite, which Palladio designed but never completed. ⊠ *Piazza dei Signori,* ☎ *0444/323681.* ☎ *10,000 lire/€5.15, loggias only 2,000 lire/€1.05.* ⊙ *Tues.–Sun. 9–5 (hrs can vary depending on exhibition).*

OFF THE BEATEN PATH

VILLA LA ROTONDA – This is the most famous Palladian villa of all. In truth, it can hardly be called a villa, since Palladio was inspired by ancient Roman temples. Take the time to admire it from all sides, and you'll see that it was the inspiration not just for Monticello but for nearly every state capitol in the United States. The interior is typical of Palladio's grand style, with a distinctive use of negative space. You can walk 3 km (2 mi) along the Riviera Berica from Vicenza, or take Bus 8 from Viale Roma and ask the driver to let you off at the villa. Note that the interior is open only on Wednesday, from mid-March through mid-October. ⊠ *Via della Rotonda 29,* ☎ *0444/321793.* ☎ *10,000 lire/€5.15, grounds only 5,000 lire/€2.60.* ⊙ *Grounds mid-Mar.–mid-Oct., Tues.–Sun. 10–noon and 2:30–5; villa mid-Mar.–mid-Oct., Wed. 10–noon and 3–6.*

VILLA VALMARANA AI NANI – This 18th-century country house, a short walk from Palladio's Villa La Rotonda, is decorated with a series of marvelous frescoes by Giambattista Tiepolo: these are fantastic visions of a mythological world, including one of his most stunning works, the *Sacrifice of Iphigenia.* The neighboring Foresteria, or guest house, holds more frescoes, showing 18th-century Veneto life at its most charming, by Tiepolo's son, Giandomenico (1727–1804). ⊠ *Via dei Nani 2/8,* ☎

*0444/321803. ⚏ 10,000 lire/€5.15. ⊙ Mid-Mar.–mid-Nov., Wed.,
Thurs., and weekends 10–noon; mid-Mar.–Apr. and Oct.–mid-Nov., also
Tues.–Sun. 2:30–5:30; May–Sept., also Tues.–Sun. 3–6.*

Dining and Lodging

$$ ✕ **Al Paradiso.** This pizzeria-trattoria just off the Piazza dei Signori is
one of a pair next door to each other and owned by two brothers; the
other is **Vecchia Guardia** (⊠ Via Vecchia Guardia 15, ☎ 0444/321231),
which is closed on Thursday. The setting is particularly attractive in
summer, when you can sit outside. The pizzas and other dishes are tasty
and very reasonably priced. ⊠ *Via Pescherie Vecchie 5, ☎ 0444/
322320. AE, DC, MC, V. Closed Mon. and 1 wk in Nov.*

$$ ✕ **Antico Ristorante agli Schioppi.** Gli Schioppi is an attractive, family-
run restaurant established in 1897. The low-key decor in the Veneto
country style matches the simple, traditional cuisine. The *baccalà* is a
must, as are the *bigoli al sugo* (homemade, thick spaghetti dressed with
a light meat sauce). Desserts include ever-so-light fruit mousse and *panna
cotta* (a sort of eggless cream custard). ⊠ *Contra' del Castello 26-28,
☎ 0444/543701. AE, DC, MC, V. Closed Sun., mid-July–mid-Aug.,
and Dec. 24–Jan. 6. No dinner Sat.*

$$ ✕ **Da Remo.** About a kilometer (½ mi) outside town, Da Remo is worth
the taxi ride—it's one of Vicenza's best restaurants. In an attractive
country-house setting, with light, airy dining rooms and a garden ter-
race, you can enjoy a relaxing meal of Venetian specialties, among
them *faraona* (guinea hen) with radicchio, and risotto with seasonal veg-
etables. ⊠ *Via Ca'Impenta 14, ☎ 0444/911007. AE, DC, MC, V.
Closed Mon., 3 wks in Aug., and Dec. 23–Jan. 6. No dinner Sun.*

$$-$$$ 🏨 **Campo Marzio.** This elegant, luxurious hotel sits right in the cen-
ter of the city. The rooms are furnished in different styles; choose from
Chinese, modern, and floral themes, all with bathrooms that have
nice ceramic sinks. A special perk is the availability of bicycles free of
charge. The price increases at trade-fair times, but you'll always get a
good buffet breakfast. ⊠ *Via Roma 27, 36100, ☎ 0444/545700,* FAX
0444/320495, WEB *www.hotelcampomarzio.com. 35 rooms. Restaurant,
bar, bicycles, free parking. AE, DC, MC, V.*

$$ 🏨 **Due Mori.** In the heart of Vicenza just off Piazza dei Signori, this
small hotel is a favorite with regular visitors and a very good value.
It's light and airy, yet at the same time cozy. The rooms are individually furnished with nice antiques and wood detail in the bathrooms.
⊠ *Contrá Do Rode 26, 36100, ☎ 0444/321886,* FAX *0444/326127.
26 rooms. AE, MC, V.*

Nightlife and the Arts

MUSIC AND THEATER

Teatro Olimpico has a concert season in May and June, as well as a classical drama season in September. Even if your Italian is dismal, it's
thrilling to see a performance in Palladio's magnificent theater.

Outdoor Activities and Sports

BIKING

Bikes can be rented from the luggage lost-and-found at the **train station** (☎ 0444/392528) for a very reasonable 1,500 lire/€0.75 per hour
or 15,000 lire/€7.75 per day (from 8 AM to 8 PM).

VERONA

On the banks of the fast-flowing Adige River, enchanting Verona lays
claim to classical and medieval monuments, a picturesque town center where bright geraniums bloom in window boxes, and a romantic
reputation, thanks to its being the setting of Shakespeare's *Romeo and*

Juliet. It is one of Italy's most alluring cities, despite extensive industrialization and urban development in its newer sections. Inevitably, with its lively Venetian air, proximity to Lake Garda, and renowned summer opera season, it attracts hordes of tourists, especially vacationing Germans and Austrians, who arrive via the Brenner Pass to the north. Since 1967, Verona has housed Vinitaly, one of the world's most important wine expos. When it was first held, Vinitaly counted hardly 60 stalls—the 2001 edition hosted 3,300 stands from 21 countries.

Verona grew to power and prosperity within the Roman Empire as a result of its key commercial and military position in northern Italy. After the fall of the Empire, the city continued to flourish under the guidance of Barbarian kings such as Theodoric, Alboin, Pepin, and Berenger I, reaching its cultural and artistic peak in the 13th and 14th centuries under the della Scala dynasty. (You'll see the *scala*, or ladder, emblem all over town.) In 1404, however, Verona traded its independence for security and placed itself under the control of Venice. (The other recurring architectural motif is the lion of St. Mark, symbol of Venetian rule.) Verona remained under Venetian protection until 1797, when Napoléon invaded. In 1814 the entire Veneto region was won by the Austrians, and it was finally united with the rest of Italy in 1866.

Exploring Verona

Note that the Duomo and churches in Verona enforce a strict dress code: no tanks, sleeveless shirts, shorts, or short skirts. You might want to consider buying the 8,000-lire/€4.15 combined ticket that includes admission to most churches in town, including the Duomo, San Zeno, and Sant'Anastasia. For updated information about these churches call Associazione Chiese Vive (☎ 045/592813). Alternatively, the 22,000 lire/€11.35 Verona Card ticket gives admittance to most sights in town, including churches.

A Good Walk

Start at the **Arena di Verona** ④ in Piazza Brà, the vast and airy square at the center of the city. Built by the Romans in the 1st century AD, the arena is one of the largest and best-preserved Roman amphitheaters anywhere. Take Via Mazzini, the main shopping street in town, to **Piazza delle Erbe** ⑤, a busy square with an open-air market. The **Casa di Giulietta** ⑥, with the most famous balcony in Italy, is a block down Via del Cappello. Return and take a few moments to stroll around **Piazza dei Signori** ⑦, and admire the **Palazzo della Ragione** ⑧, **Loggia del Consiglio** ⑨, and **Palazzo degli Scaligeri** ⑩. It's a short walk through Piazza Indipendenza to Ponte Nuova and across the river toward the church of **Santa Maria in Organo** ⑪ and the **Giardino Giusti** ⑫. Follow Via Santa Maria in Organo up to the Teatro Romano and **Museo Archeologico** ⑬. The Romanesque **Duomo** ⑭ is just over Ponte Pietra. From here either walk down Via Duomo and Corso Sant'Anastasia to **Sant'Anastasia** ⑮, and Via Forti and the **Galleria d'Arte Moderna** ⑯, or turn toward the riverbank and stroll (or alternately take Bus 76) down to the 14th-century **Castelvecchio** ⑰, looking like a fairy-tale castle guarding the bridge reaching over the Adige. The stunning Romanesque **San Zeno Maggiore** ⑱ church is another few minutes' walk downriver.

TIMING

It takes about 40 minutes to walk the route and three hours to see all the sights.

Sights to See

★ ❹ **Arena di Verona.** Only four arches remain of the outer rings of the arena, but the main structure is so complete that it takes little imagination to

Verona

Arena di Verona ...**4**
Casa di Giulietta ...**6**
Castelvecchio ...**17**
Duomo ...**14**
Galleria d'Arte
Moderna ...**16**
Giardino Giusti ...**12**

Loggia del
Consiglio ...**9**
Museo
Archeologico ...**13**
Palazzo degli
Scaligeri ...**10**
Palazzo della
Ragione ...**8**

Piazza dei
Signori ...**7**
Piazza delle
Erbe ...**5**
San Zeno
Maggiore ...**18**
Santa Maria in
Organo ...**11**
Sant'Anastasia ...**15**

picture it as the site of the cruel deaths of countless gladiators, wild beasts, and Christians. Today it hosts Verona's summer opera, famous for spectacular productions and audiences of as many as 16,000. The best operas to see here are the big, splashy ones that demand huge choruses, Cinerama sets, lots of color and movement, and, if possible, camels, horses, and/or elephants. The music can be excellent, and the acoustics are fine, too. If you go, be sure to take or rent a cushion—four hours on 2,000-year-old marble can be an ordeal. ⊠ *Arena di Verona, Piazza Brà 5,* ☎ *045/8003204.* ☒ *6,000 lire/€3.10 or Verona Card, 2,000 lire/€1.05 1st Sun. of month.* ☯ *Tues.–Sun. 9–6:30 (on performance days 9–3); closed 10 days Sept.*

❻ Casa di Giulietta (Juliet's House). The balcony in the small courtyard will help to bring Shakespeare's play to life, even if it was built in the 20th century. Historians now believe that the couple had no real-life counterparts, but this hasn't discouraged anyone from imagining that they did. After all, historians are not as renowned for their storytelling as Shakespeare is. ⊠ *Via Cappello 23,* ☎ *045/8034303.* ☒ *6,000 lire/€3.10 or Verona Card.* ☯ *Tues.–Sun. 9–6:30.*

OFF THE
BEATEN PATH   **TOMBA DI GIULIETTA** – Romantic souls may want to see the pretty spot claimed to be Juliet's Tomb. Authentic or not, it is still popular with lovesick Italian teenagers, who leave notes for the tragic lover. ⊠ *Via del Pontiere 35,* ☎ *045/8000361.* ☒ *5,000 lire/€2.60 or Verona Card, free 1st Sun. of month.* ☯ *Tues.–Sun. 9–6:30.*

GIARDINI DI VILLA ARVEDI – The 17th-century Villa Arvedi is surrounded by historic gardens that have preserved their original layout, with well-kept alleys, a spectacular fountain, and a frescoed church. Parts of the villa are open to the public, and the garden tour includes a visit to the Salone dei Titani (Salon of the Titans), with frescoes by L. Dorigny (1654–1742) depicting mythological scenes, and to the Salone dei Cesari, named after the portraits of Roman emperors derived from the more famous Titian originals at the Palazzo Te in Mantua. ⊠ *Statale per Grezzana, 8 km (5 mi) northeast of town,* ☎ *045/907045,* WEB *www.villarvedi.it.* ☒ *10,000 lire/€5.15.* ☯ *By appointment, minimum 10 people (for 100,000 lire/€51.65, smaller groups are also taken).*

⑰ Castelvecchio (Old Castle). This crenellated, russet brick building with massive walls, towers, turrets, and a vast courtyard was built for Cangrande II della Scala in 1354. It presides over a street lined with attractive old buildings and palaces of the nobility. Inside, the **Museo di Castelvecchio** gives you a good look at the castle's vaulted halls and the treasures of Venetian painting and sculpture that they contain. ⊠ *Corso Castelvecchio,* ☎ *045/594734.* ☒ *6,000 lire/€3.10 or Verona Card, free 1st Sun. of month.* ☯ *Tues.–Sun. 9–6:30; hrs and admission may change during special exhibitions.*

⑭ Duomo. The ornate Romanesque Duomo has not only architectural characteristics typical of the Venetian style but also some Byzantine attributes. A strict dress code is enforced (no tanks, sleeveless shirts, shorts, or short skirts). ⊠ *Via Duomo.* ☒ *3,000 lire/€1.55, 8,000 lire/€4.15 for combined churches ticket, or Verona Card.* ☯ *Mon.–Sat. 11–1, Sun. 1:30–5, longer hrs in summer.*

⑯ Galleria d'Arte Moderna (Gallery of Modern Art). The handsome Palazzo Forti, where Napoléon once stayed, frequently hosts contemporary painting exhibitions of well-known artists; past shows have included the works of Marcel Duchamp (1887–1968) and Andy Warhol (1928–87). At press time it was closed for restoration; call for the current status. ⊠ *Via Forti 1,* ☎ *045/8001903.*

⑫ **Giardino Giusti.** The formal Giusti Gardens, laid out on several levels around a 16th-century villa, are a symbol of things long past. There's a fine view of the city from the terrace, where the German poet and dramatist Johann Wolfgang von Goethe (1749–1832) recorded his impressions of them. ⊠ *Via Giardino Giusti 2,* ☎ *045/8034029.* ⊠ 🎫 *8,000 lire/€4.15.* ◎ *Daily 9–sunset.*

⑨ **Loggia del Consiglio.** The graceful structure was built in the 12th century to house city council meetings and still serves as the seat of the provincial government. ⊠ *Piazza dei Signori.* ◎ *Closed to the public.*

⑬ **Museo Archeologico.** The museum is housed in an old monastery above the Teatro Romano, which was built in the same era as the Arena di Verona. The Roman Theater is sometimes used for dramatic productions. From here there are good views over the entire city. ⊠ *Rigaste del Redentore,* ☎ *045/8000360.* 🎫 *5,000 lire/€2.60 or Verona Card, free 1st Sun. of month.* ◎ *Tues.–Sun. 9–6:30.*

⑩ **Palazzo degli Scaligeri.** This was the medieval stronghold from which the della Scalas ruled Verona with an iron fist. ⊠ *Piazza dei Signori.* ◎ *Closed to the public.*

⑧ **Palazzo della Ragione.** The 12th-century palace has a somber courtyard, Gothic staircase, and medieval tower overlooking the piazza. ⊠ *Piazza dei Signori.* ◎ *Closed to the public.*

⑦ **Piazza dei Signori.** Verona's great piazza has been at the center of things for more than a thousand years, but the impressive facades and arched entrances surrounding it date from the early Renaissance.

⑤ **Piazza delle Erbe** (Vegetable Market Square). This square is the site of the ancient Roman forum and today hosts a colorful morning market, with huge rectangular umbrellas raised to shade the neat ranks of produce.

★ ⑱ **San Zeno Maggiore.** Possibly the finest example of a Romanesque church in Italy, with a 13th-century rose window and 12th-century portal, San Zeno is set between two medieval bell towers. The light-gray and white-brick color scheme—typical of Italy's Romanesque churches—is especially impressive here. Inside, look for Mantegna's *Madonna* over the main altar; a peaceful cloister is off the nave to the left. ⊠ *Piazza San Zeno,* ☎ *045/8006120.* 🎫 *3,000 lire/€1.55, 8,000 lire/€4.15 for combined churches ticket, or Verona Card.* ◎ *Tues.–Sat. 10–1 and 1:30–4, Sun. 1–5, longer hrs in summer.*

⑪ **Santa Maria in Organo.** The choir and sacristy of this medieval church are decorated with inlaid-wood masterpieces by the 15th-century monk Fra Giovanni. A series of panels depicts varied scenes—local buildings, an idealized Renaissance town, wildlife, and fruit—that radiate a love of life and reveal the artist's eye for detail. ⊠ *Via Interrato dell'Acqua Morta,* ☎ *045/591440.* ◎ *Apr.–Oct., daily 7:30–noon and 3–6; Nov.–Mar., daily 7:30–noon.*

⑮ **Sant'Anastasia.** Not far from the Duomo, Sant'Anastasia is Verona's largest church. In stark contrast to the simple, vaguely Romanesque facade, the impressive Gothic doorway is surrounded by elaborate carvings illustrating scenes from the New Testament, and down the steps you'll meet the famous *Gobbi,* two sculptures of crouching humpbacks supporting the holy-water stoups. The highlight, on display inside the sacristy and sadly damaged, is a detached fresco painted in blue and gray pastel shades by Pisanello (1377–1455), called *St. George and the Princess.* ⊠ *Vicolo Sotto Riva 4,* ☎ *045/8004325.* 🎫 *3,000 lire/€1.55,*

combined ticket 8,000 lire/€4.15, or Verona Card. ☉ *Tues.–Sat. 10–
1 and 1:30–4, Sun. 1–5, longer hrs in summer.*

Dining and Lodging

$$$$ ✕ **Le Arche.** True to its name, this elegant restaurant is in a medieval
building a step away from the della Scala tombs. The Art Nouveau dining room features candlelight and flowers. Only seafood is served, absolutely fresh and superlatively prepared. Try the *raviolone al branzino
e spinaci in salsa di foie gras e tartufo* (large ravioli stuffed with sea
bass and spinach with foie gras and truffle sauce) and the unusual *salsiccia di pesce* (fish sausage made with sea scorpion, sea bass, and
salmon). ✉ *Via Arche Scaligere 6,* ☎ *045/8007415. AE, DC, MC, V.
Closed Sun. and 3 wks in Jan.–Feb. No lunch Mon.*

$$$–$$$$ ✕ **Dodici Apostoli.** Vaulted ceilings, frescoed walls, and a medieval am-
bience make this an exceptional place to enjoy classic local and regional
dishes. Near Piazza delle Erbe, it stands on the foundations of a Roman
temple. Specialties include *zuppa scaligera* (soup of meat stock with
vegetables and bread) and *vitello Lessinia* (veal with mushrooms,
cheese, and truffles). ✉ *Vicolo Corticella San Marco 3,* ☎ *045/596999.
AE, DC, MC, V. Closed Mon., Jan. 1–7, and mid-June–July 7. No din-
ner Sun.*

$$$–$$$$ ✕ **Osteria All'Oste Scuro.** Two local gourmets turned what was once
a family trattoria into a first-class fish restaurant. Specials might in-
clude *spaghettini ai gamberetti e cannellini* (thin spaghetti with shrimp
and Tuscan beans), and more traditional dishes like grilled crab and
prawns or baked fish with potatoes are always on the menu. ✉ *Vi-
colo San Silvestro 10,* ☎ *045/592650. V. Closed Sun., 2 wks in Aug.,
and Dec. 25–Jan. 8. No lunch Mon.*

$$ ✕ **Al Calmiere.** This congenial trattoria on the lovely piazza in front
of San Zeno Maggiore is the ideal place to enjoy tagliatelle *con fega-
tini di pollo* (with chicken-liver sauce), various types of pasta in *brodo*
(broth), meats, and local wines—there are some 20 different Valpoli-
cellas alone available—at reasonable prices. The interior, with an enormous open fireplace used for cooking, is especially cozy in winter. ✉
Piazza San Zeno 10, ☎ *045/8030765. AE, DC, MC, V. Closed Thurs.,
1st wk in Jan., and 2–3 wks in July. No dinner Wed.*

$$ ✕ **La Greppia.** The classic decor with vaulted ceilings sets the tone in
this bustling restaurant off Via Mazzini between the Arena and Piazza
delle Erbe. The kitchen produces fine versions of local and regional dishes,
especially *tortelli di zucca* (pasta filled with squash) and *bolliti* (assorted
boiled meats served with a choice of sauces). Service is courteous and
efficient. ✉ *Vicolo Samaritana 3,* ☎ *045/8004577. AE, DC, MC, V.
Closed Mon., 2nd wk of Jan., and last 2 wks in June.*

$$ ✕ **La Stueta.** Perhaps the best bargain in town (prices are at the lower
end of this category), La Stueta is a friendly trattoria not far from the
Giardino Giusti across the river. Try the gnocchi *con la pastisada* (with
a horse-meat sauce), *baccalà* (salt cod), or *maiale all'amarone* (pork
shin in a red wine sauce, served with polenta). ✉ *Via del Redentore
4/b,* ☎ *045/8032462. AE, DC, MC, V. Closed Mon. and 3 wks in July.
No lunch Tues.*

$ ✕ **Pizzeria Vesuvio.** Between Castelvecchio and San Zeno Maggiore,
this authentic Neapolitan pizzeria has tables on the riverbank in summer and a lovely, breezy view of the Adige. ✉ *Via Rigaste 41,* ☎ *045/
595634. AE, DC, MC, V. Closed Mon.*

$$$$ ▥ **Gabbia d'Oro.** Set in a historic building off Piazza delle Erbe in the
★ ancient heart of Verona, this hotel is a tasteful fantasia of romantic ornamentation, lavish trimmings, exquisite fabrics, and gorgeous period
pieces. Rooms—each one different and more attractive than the last—

have frescoes, beamed ceilings, pretty wallpaper, antique prints and furnishings, and canopy beds, some festooned with rosy-cheeked cherubs. You can relax outdoors in the medieval courtyard, in the comfortable orangerie, or on the roof terrace. The breakfast spread is to die for. ⊠ *Corso Porta Borsari 4/a, 37121,* ☎ *045/8003060,* 𝖥𝖠𝖷 *045/590293,* 𝖶𝖤𝖡 *www.hotelgabbiadoro.it. 19 rooms, 8 suites. Breakfast room. AE, DC, MC, V.*

$$$$ 🏨 **Villa del Quar.** This tranquil 16th-century villa is surrounded by gar-
★ dens and vineyards in the Valpolicella country, 10 minutes by car from the city. Architect Leopoldo Montresor and his wife, Evelina, who live here with their children, converted part of the villa into a stylish and sophisticated hotel. No expense has been spared: all rooms have marble bathrooms (some with whirlpool baths) and European antiques. ⊠ *Via Quar 12, Pedemonte di San Pietro in Cariano, 37020, 5 km (3 mi) northwest of Verona,* ☎ *045/6800681,* 𝖥𝖠𝖷 *045/6800604,* 𝖶𝖤𝖡 *www.integra.fr/relaischateaux/delquar. 18 rooms, 4 suites. Restaurant, pool, gym. AE, DC, MC, V.*

$$$ 🏨 **Colomba d'Oro.** This attractive four-star hotel right by the Arena occupies a building dating from the 14th century. It's retained a clubby atmosphere and European charm while providing up-to-date comforts. ⊠ *Via Cattaneo 10, 37121,* ☎ *045/595300,* 𝖥𝖠𝖷 *045/594974,* 𝖶𝖤𝖡 *www.colombahotel.com. 41 rooms, 10 suites. Parking (fee). AE, DC, MC, V.*

$$ 🏨 **Torcolo.** The warm welcome extended by the owners, Signoras
★ Diana and Silvia, the pleasant rooms unfussily decorated, and the central location on a peaceful street close to Piazza Brà and the Arena make the Torcolo outstanding value in its class. Breakfast is served outside on the terrace in front of the hotel in summer. ⊠ *Vicolo Listone 3, 37121,* ☎ *045/8007512,* 𝖥𝖠𝖷 *045/8004058. 19 rooms. AE, MC, V.*

Nightlife and the Arts

Nightclubs

On weekend nights, **Alter Ego** (⊠ Via Torricelle 9, ☎ 045/915130) packs a twentysomething crowd that might call itself alternative. **Berfi's** (⊠ Via Lussemburgo 1, ☎ 045/508024, is a popular and expensive spot with a restaurant and piano bar. From mid-September to mid-May it's open on weekends only.

Opera

Of all the venues for enjoying opera in the region, pride of place must go to the **Arena di Verona.** Its summer opera season runs from July through August, and the 16,000 in the audience sit on the original stone terraces dating from the time when gladiators fought to the death. The opera stage is huge and best suited to grand operas such as *Aïda,* but the experience is memorable no matter what is being performed. Sometimes, while sipping a drink in a café at **Piazza Brà,** you can hear the performance. *Ente Lirico Arena di Verona:* ⊠ *Piazza Brà 28, Verona, 37121; box office: Via Dietro Anfiteatro 6/b,* ☎ *045/8005151,* 𝖶𝖤𝖡 *www.arena.it.* ⊘ *Weekdays 9–noon and 3:15–5:45, Sat. 9–noon.*

Outdoor Activities and Sports

Biking

Bikes are available for rent from **Noleggio Bici** (no phone), on Via Roma at the corner with Piazza Brà, between April and September.

Golf

The 18-hole course at **Golf Club Verona** (⊠ Ca' del Sale 15, Sommacampagna, ☎ 045/510060) is 16 km (10 mi) west of Verona and 2 km (1 mi) from the Sommacampagna exit on the A4 autostrada. It's closed on Tuesday.

Shopping

Antiques and Housewares

The area around the Gothic church of Sant'Anastasia is full of antiques shops, most of them catering to serious collectors. You can picnic on the Piazza dei Signori in the cool breeze after a strenuous day of antiques hunting. The perfect place to splurge on a modern gift or imaginative decorative piece is **Alternative** (⊠ vicolo San Marco in Foro 2, ☎ 045/8010910), with trendy glass artworks and design objects.

Markets

Verona's two markets, located on **Piazza delle Erbe** and on **Piazza Cittadella,** both open Monday–Saturday 8–1 and 3:30–sundown, have a selection of food, wine, clothing, antiques, and even pets.

Wine

Vinitaly (☎ 045/8298111, WEB www.veronafiere.it), the famous international trade fair for wine producers, takes place at the Fiera di Verona on Viale del Lavoro 8 each year in early April. The public is welcome, although booths are only open to dealers.

VILLA BARBARO, TREVISO, AND THE HILLSIDE TOWNS

In this area directly north of Venice, market towns cling to the steep foothills of the Alps and the Dolomites alongside streams raging down from the mountains. Villa Barbaro, Palladio's most beautiful creation, is here, as are the arcaded streets of Treviso and the graceful Venetian Gothic structures of smaller hill towns.

Marostica

⑲ *7 km (4½ mi) west of Bassano del Grappa, 26 km (16 mi) northeast of Vicenza.*

The first and most evident feature of Marostica is its Castello Superiore, perched on a hillside overlooking the surrounding countryside. But the most famous sight in town is Piazza Castello, the main square, paved in checkerboard fashion.

Outdoor Activities and Sports

A game of **human-scale chess** is acted out in Piazza Castello by players in medieval costume on the second weekend in September in even-numbered years (tickets go on sale in April); for information and bookings, contact Marostica's tourist office (☞ Visitor Information *in* Venetian Arc A to Z, *below*).

Bassano del Grappa

⑳ *7 km (4½ mi) east of Marostica, 37 km (23 mi) north of Venice.*

Beautifully positioned directly above the swift-flowing waters of the Brenta River and at the foot of the Mt. Grappa massif (5,880 ft), Bassano has old streets lined with low-slung buildings adorned with wooden balconies and pretty flowerpots. Bright ceramic wares produced here and in nearby Nove are displayed in shops along byways that curve uphill toward a centuries-old square and, even higher, to a belvedere with a good view of Mt. Grappa and the beginning of the Val Sugana.

Bassano's most famous landmark is the **covered bridge** that has spanned the Brenta since the 13th century. Rebuilt countless times (floods are frequent), the present bridge is a postwar reconstruction using Andrea Palladio's 16th-century design. The great architect astutely chose to use wood as his medium, knowing that it could be replaced quickly and cheaply.

Bassano is home to the famous **Nardini** distillery, where the grappa liqueur has been distilled for more than a century. Stop in for a sniff or a snifter at any of the local cafés.

Dining and Lodging

$$-$$$ ✕ **Da Renzo alla Trinità.** This popular family-run restaurant has a view of the hills and olive groves of Bassano and a pleasant terrace used year-round. Seafood antipasti and grilled fish fresh from the Adriatic are specialties. You can also enjoy regional dishes made with fresh seasonal ingredients. ⊠ *Via Santissima Trinità 9,* ☎ *0424/503055. AE, D, MC, V. Closed Tues. and 2 wks in Aug. No lunch Wed.*

$$ ✕ **Ristorante Birreria Ottone.** This old-world restaurant in town center is a favorite with the locals, who tout the excellent cuisine, the draft wine and beer, and the friendly Wipflinger family, headed by Otto, whose Austrian forebear founded this beer hall about 100 years ago. Equally good for a simple lunch or a more elaborate dinner, Ottone offers specialties that include a delicious goulash cooked with cumin. ⊠ *Via Matteotti 47/50,* ☎ *0424/522206. AE, D, MC, V. Closed Tues. and 3 wks in Aug. No dinner Mon.*

$$$-$$$$ 🏠 **Villa Palma.** This gracefully refurbished 18th-century country villa, only a short drive from Asolo (10 km/6 mi) and Bassano (5 km/3 mi), combines modern comforts and conveniences with rural calm and old-fashioned style and charm—wooden beams, vaulted brick ceilings, and tasteful furnishings. Creature comforts include whirlpool baths or sauna showers and fax and computer facilities. In summer, meals are served on the terrace overlooking the splendid garden. ⊠ *Via Chemin Palma 30, Mussolente, 36065,* ☎ *0424/577407,* FAX *0424/87687,* WEB *www.larosina.it. 20 rooms, 1 suite. Restaurant. AE, DC, MC, V.*

$$$ 🏠 **Belvedere.** This historic hotel has richly decorated public rooms with
★   period furnishings and Oriental rugs. A fireplace and piano music in the lounge and an excellent restaurant with a garden make for a very pleasant stay. The rooms are decorated in traditional Venetian or chic contemporary style. ⊠ *Piazzale G. Giardino 14, 36061,* ☎ *0424/ 529845,* FAX *0424/529849,* WEB *www.bonotto.it. 81 rooms, 6 suites. Restaurant. AE, DC, MC, V.*

$$ 🏠 **Al Castello.** In a restored town house at the foot of the medieval Torre Civica (Civic Tower), the Cattapan family's Castello is a reasonably priced, attractive choice. Rooms are furnished simply but well equipped. ⊠ *Piazza Terraglio 19, 36061,* ☎ FAX *0424/228665. 11 rooms. Café. AE, MC, V.*

Shopping

Bassano del Grappa and nearby Nove are famous for ceramics. A large number of shops in town also feature wrought-iron and copper utensils, many of them made on the premises. At **L'arte della Ceramica** (⊠ Via Angarano 21, ☎ 0424/503901)) you'll find some of the best handmade ceramics from Bassano: plates, bowls, jugs, and apothecary jars are decorated in traditional flowery and fruity patterns. If you're looking for something distinctive, pay a visit to **Al Galletto Nero** (⊠ Via Macello 12, ☎ 0424/502509), where $1 cuchi (terra-cotta whistles) sit side by side with $1,000 collector's items.

Asolo

★ **㉑** *11 km (7 mi) east of Bassano del Grappa, 33 km (20½ mi) northwest of Treviso.*

The romantic, charming hillside hamlet of Asolo was the consolation prize of an exiled queen. At the end of the 15th century, Venetian-born Caterina Cornaro was sent here by Venice's doge to keep her from interfering with Venetian administration of her former kingdom of Cyprus, which she had inherited from her husband. To soothe the pain of exile, she established a lively and brilliant court in Asolo. Over the centuries, Venetian aristocrats continued to build gracious villas on the hillside, and in the 19th century Asolo once again became the idyllic haunt of musicians, poets, and painters. From the outside, you can explore villas once inhabited by Robert Browning and the actress Eleonora Duse. Be warned that Asolo's old-world atmosphere vaporizes on holiday weekends when the crowds pour in. In the town center is **Piazza Maggiore,** with Renaissance palaces and fin-de-siècle cafés. Uphill from the piazza, past Caterina's ruined castle and some Gothic-style houses, is the empty **Rocca** (⊙ Saturday–Sunday 9–12:30 and 3–dusk), a medieval fortress from which you get a view of Asolo's hundred horizons.

Dining

$$$ ✕ **Hosteria Ca'Derton.** Right on the main square, Ca'Derton has a pleasant, old-fashioned ambience, with early photos of Asolo and bouquets of dried flowers. The friendly proprietor takes pride in the homemade pasta and desserts and offers a good selection of both local and international dishes. ⊠ *Piazza D'Annunzio 11,* ☎ *0423/529648. AE, DC, MC, V. Closed Mon., last wk in July, and 1st wk in Aug. No dinner Sun.*

Shopping

Asolo center hosts an antiques market on the weekend of the first Sunday of every month except July and August.

Villa Barbaro

㉒ *7 km (4½ mi) northeast of Asolo, 33 km (20½ mi) northwest of Treviso.*

Villa Barbaro is one of Palladio's most gracious creations. The fully furnished villa just outside the town of Maser is still inhabited by its owners, who make you slip heavy felt scuffs over your shoes to protect the highly polished floors. The elaborate stuccowork and opulent frescoes by Paolo Veronese bring the 16th century to life. After La Rotonda, this is Palladio's greatest villa and is definitely worth going out of your way to see. (Before making the trip, note the restricted hours.) ⊠ *Via Cornuda 2,* ☎ *0423/923004.* ⊡ *9,500 lire/€4.90.* ⊙ *Mar.–Oct., Tues. and weekends 3–6; Nov.–Feb., weekends 2:30–5.*

Dining and Lodging

$$ ✕ **Agnoletti.** In the town of Giavera del Montello, about 25 km (16
★ mi) east of Maser, Agnoletti is an 18th-century inn of a bygone era with a lovely summer garden. The kitchen can produce an all-mushroom menu; but if you order something else, at least try the mushroom zuppa or *crostata di funghi* (mushroom tart). ⊠ *Via della Vittoria 190, Giavera del Montello,* ☎ *0422/776009. No credit cards. Closed Tues. and 2–3 wks in Jan.*

$$ ✕ **Da Bastian.** A good place to stop for lunch in Maser before visiting the Villa Barbaro, this contemporary restaurant has a pleasant garden for outdoor dining. Highlights of the menu include varied antipasti, grilled mushrooms, homemade vegetarian ravioli, and, for second courses, baccalà, snails, and broiled meat with delicious sauces. ⊠ *Via*

Cornuda (follow signs), ☎ 0423/565400. No credit cards. Closed Thurs. and Aug. No dinner Wed.

$$$$ 🏨 **Villa Cipriani.** This historic villa is set in a romantic garden on the hillside and surrounded by other gracious country homes. Tastefully furnished with 19th-century antiques, it offers atmosphere, creature comforts, and attentive service. The superb restaurant has a terrace overlooking the garden. ⊠ Via Canova 298, 31011, ☎ 0423/952166, FAX 0423/952095, WEB www.sheraton.com/villacipriani. 31 rooms. Restaurant. AE, DC, MC, V.

Treviso

㉓ 35 km (22 mi) southeast of Maser, 30 km (19 mi) north of Venice.

The arcaded streets, frescoed houses, and channeled streams that run through the center of Treviso date mostly from the 15th century. The most important church in Treviso is **San Nicolò,** an impressive Gothic structure with an ornate vaulted ceiling. San Nicolò has frescoes of the saints by 14th-century artist Tommaso da Modena on the columns. But the highlight is the remarkable series of 40 portraits of Dominican friars by the same artist in the seminary next door. They are astoundingly realistic, considering that some were painted as early as 1352, and include one of the earliest-known portraits of a subject wearing glasses. ⊠ Capitolo dei Domenicani, Seminario Vescovile, Via San Nicolò, ☎ 0422/56725. ☉ Mon.–Sat. 9–noon and 3–6:30, Sun. 3–6:30.

Inside Treviso's **Duomo,** on the altar of one of the chapels to the right, is an Annunciation by Titian (circa 1488–1576). ⊠ Piazza del Duomo. ☉ Daily 10:30–12:30.

Piazza dei Signori is the heart of medieval Treviso and still the town's social center, with outdoor cafés and some impressive public buildings. One of these, the Palazzo dei Trecento, has a small alley behind it. Follow the alley for about 200 yards to the pescheria (fish market), on an island in one of the small rivers that flow through town. Shops in Treviso feature wrought-iron and copper utensils.

Dining and Lodging

$$$-$$$$ ✕ **Da Alfredo.** This restaurant belongs to the El Toulà group, a small
★ chain of high-class restaurants in Italy and abroad. This is your chance to enjoy the Art Noveau decor and fine cuisine that's made the chain famous. The menu focuses on dishes from the Veneto and on Italian classics prepared with flair. Among regional dishes are calf's liver with apples and three risottos, ai funghi (with mushrooms), agli asparagi (with asparagus), and alle cicale di mare (with a shrimplike crustacean). Italian classics include ravioli filled with ricotta cheese and fresh mint, and grilled meats and fish. For ambience and service, it's one of the region's best. ⊠ Via Collalto 26, ☎ 0422/540275. AE, DC, MC, V. Closed Mon. and Aug. No dinner Sun.

$$-$$$ ✕ **Beccherie.** In a town known for good eating, this rustic inn is a fa-
★ vorite. It's in the heart of old Treviso, behind the main square, and there are tables outside for fair-weather dining under the portico. Specialties vary with the season. In winter, look for crespelle al radicchi (crepes with radicchio) and faraona in salsa peverada (guinea with a peppery sauce). Spring heralds risotto with spring vegetables, stinco di vitello (veal shin), and pasticcio di melanzane (eggplant casserole). ⊠ Piazza Ancilotto 10, ☎ 0422/56601. AE, DC, MC, V. Closed Mon. and 2 wks in July. No dinner Sun.

$$$ 🏨 **Al Fogher.** On the outskirts of town, Al Fogher is handy if you're traveling by car. This outpost of the Best Western chain has a bright contemporary look, with lots of modern art and room decor about

equally divided between classic and modern. ⊠ *Viale della Repubblica 10, 31100,* ☎ *0422/432950,* 𝔽𝔸𝕏 *0422/430391,* 𝕎𝔼𝔹 *www.sevenon-line.it/fogher. 54 rooms, 1 suite. AE, DC, MC, V.*

$$$ 🔟 **Continental.** You'll find this hotel within the old city walls, between the train station and the sights. It is a traditional four-star hotel offering reliable comfort. Rich fabrics and Oriental rugs lend an air of opulence. ⊠ *Via Roma 16, 31100,* ☎ *0422/411216,* 𝔽𝔸𝕏 *0422/55054,* 𝕎𝔼𝔹 *www.sevenonline.it/continental. 80 rooms. Parking (fee). AE, DC, MC, V.*

Conegliano

㉔ *23 km (14 mi) north of Treviso, 60 km (37 mi) north of Venice.*

Conegliano is in the heart of wine-producing country. The town itself is attractive, with Venetian-style villas and frescoed houses, but the real draw is the wine, particularly the effervescent Prosecco di Conegliano.

Dining and Lodging

$$ ✕🔟 **Canon d'Oro.** The town's oldest inn, the Canon d'Oro is in a 15th-century building in a central location near the train station. Guest rooms are decorated in the 18th-century style; bathrooms are on the small side. The restaurant's tranquil decor lets you concentrate on the good food, mainly regional specialties such as risotto, smoked pork chop, *baccalà alla vicentina* (dried cod prepared in a creamy stew with anchovies and Parmesan), and *fegato alla veneziana* (liver with onions). ⊠ *Via XX Settembre 129, 31015,* ☎ *0438/34246, 0438/415166 restaurant,* 𝔽𝔸𝕏 *0438/34249,* 𝕎𝔼𝔹 *www.sevenonline.it/canondoro. 35 rooms. Restaurant. AE, MC, V. Restaurant closed Fri. and 3 wks in late July–early Aug.*

En Route Leading southeast from Conegliano, the well-marked **Strada dei Vini del Piave** wends its way through cabernet and merlot country along the Piave River. There are dozens of places to stop, sample, and buy the red—and sometimes rosé—wines. The road ends at Oderzo.

FRIULI-VENEZIA GIULIA

Italy's northeastern corner is an ethnically mixed cocktail of Italian, Slavic, and central European cultures. Its peripheral location often puts this potentially fascinating area beyond the range of most visitors. The old Austrian port of Trieste—a symbol of Italian nationalist aspirations for so long—and the medieval city of Udine are perfect bases for local excursions.

Udine

㉕ *71 km (44 mi) east of Conegliano, 127 km (79 mi) northeast of Venice.*

Udine, in Italy's Friuli–Venezia Giulia region, commands a view of the surrounding plain and the Alpine foothills; according to legend, it stands on a mound erected by Attila the Hun so he could watch the burning of the important Roman center of Aquileia to the south. Udine flourished in the Middle Ages, thanks to its location, favorable to trade, and the rights it gained from the local patriarch to hold regular markets. There is a distinctly Venetian feel to the city, noticeable in the architecture of Piazza della Libertà, under the stern gaze of the lion of St. Mark, symbol of Venetian power.

The **Galleria d'Arte Antica** is a wide-ranging collection of local and Italian art including canvases by the prolific Neapolitan Luca Giordano (1632–1705), the Venetians Vittore Carpaccio (circa 1460–1525) and Tiepolo, and a painting of St. Francis receiving the stigmata attributed to Caravaggio (circa 1571–1610). ⊠ *Piazzale del Castello,* ☎ *0432/ 502872.* ⊡ *4,000 lire/€2.05, free Sun.* ⊙ *Tues.–Sat. 9:30–12:30 and 3–6, Sun. 9:30–12:30.*

Dining and Lodging

$$$ ✕ **Antica Maddalena.** Just a few steps from Udine's pretty Piazza del-
★ l'Unità you'll find this elegant eating place, defined by its owner as a deluxe trattoria. Lots of warm wood tones, fresh flowers, and stained glass complement a menu of regional and Italian specialties, among them *zuppa di funghi porcini* (porcini mushroom soup) and gnocchi *con zucca e ricotta* (with squash and ricotta cheese). Second courses focus on fish. ⊠ *Via Pellicerie 4,* ☎ *0432/25111. DC, MC, V. Closed Mon. and 1 wk in Aug. No lunch Sun.*

$$ ✕ **Trattoria al Lepre.** A characteristic *focolare* (hearth) in one of the dining rooms is a symbol of traditional local cooking, and that's what you'll enjoy in this simple establishment. The specialties include tagliatelle *con funghi* (with mushrooms) and *stinco di maiale* (roast pork shin with polenta). ⊠ *Via Poscolle 27,* ☎ *0432/295798. AE, DC, MC, V. Closed Tues. and 2 wks in Aug.*

$ ✕ **Al Vecchio Stallo.** Hidden away in a narrow alley, this popular osteria offers a great selection of wine by the glass and a few well-prepared traditional soups and meat dishes, including *zuppa d'orzo* (barley soup) and *cinghiale in umido* (stewed wild boar). Seasonal vegetables, *frittate* (thick omelets), and fish on Friday round out the menu. ⊠ *Via Viola 7,* ☎ *0432/21296. No credit cards. Closed Sun. and 2 wks in late Dec.–early Jan.*

$$$ ▣ **Astoria Hotel Italia.** Centrally located, the Italia offers soundproof rooms furnished in traditional style. Public rooms have Venetian glass chandeliers and comfortable armchairs. ⊠ *Piazza XX Settembre 24, 33100,* ☎ *0432/505091,* FAX *0432/509070,* WEB *www.hotelastoria.udine.it. 73 rooms, 2 suites. Restaurant, minibars. AE, DC, MC, V.*

Cividale

㉖ *17 km (11 mi) east of Udine, 144 km (89 mi) northeast of Venice.*

Cividale dates from the time of Julius Caesar. It is popularly supposed (particularly by locals) that it was built by Caesar when he was commander of Roman legions in the area. The city straddles the Natisone River and contains many examples of Venetian Gothic buildings, particularly the **Palazzo Comunale.** The Renaissance **Duomo** has a striking silver-gilt altar. ⊠ *Piazza Duomo,* ☎ *0432/731144.* ⊙ *Mon.–Sat. 9–noon and 3:30–6, Sun. 3–6.*

The **Museo Archeologico** is the best place to trace the history of the area and the importance of Cividale and Udine in the formative period following the collapse of the Roman Empire. A large collection of Lombard artifacts includes weapons, jewelry, and domestic wares from this warrior race, which swept into what is now Italy in the 6th century. ⊠ *Piazza Duomo 7,* ☎ *0432/700700.* ⊡ *4,000 lire/€2.05.* ⊙ *Oct.–May, Mon. 9–7, Tues.–Fri. 8:30–7:30, weekends 8:30–8; June–Sept., Mon. 9–2, Tues.–Fri. 8:30–7, Sat. 8:30 AM–11 PM, Sun. 8:30–8.*

En Route From Cividale, head south to Monfalcone, and then take the scenic S14 road eastward along the coast, under the shadow of the huge geological formation called the Carso, a barren expanse of limestone that forms a giant ledge, most of which is across the border in Slovenia. Italian territory goes only a few kilometers inland in this strip, and Italy's small Slovenian minority ekes out an agricultural existence in the region, which has changed hands countless times since the final days of imperial Rome.

Castello di Miramare

★ ㉗ *78 km (48 mi) south of Cividale, 7 km (4½ mi) north of Trieste.*

This seafront castle in Miramare is a 19th-century extravaganza in white stone, built for the Archduke Maximilian of Habsburg (brother of Emperor Franz Josef). Maximilian spent a brief, happy time here until Napoléon III of France took Trieste from the Habsburgs and sent the archduke packing. He was given the title of Emperor of Mexico in 1864 as a compensation but met his death before a Mexican firing squad in 1867. You can visit the lush grounds and admire the memorable views over the Adriatic. ✉ *Miramare,* ☎ *040/224143.* ✇ *Castle 8,000 lire/€4.15, plus 4,000 lire/€2.05 for guided visit (reservation mandatory, call 040/2247013); grounds free.* ☉ *Castle and grounds daily 9–6, longer hrs in summer.*

Trieste

㉘ *64 km (40 mi) southeast of Udine, 163 km (101 mi) east of Venice.*

Surrounded by rugged countryside and beautiful coastline, Trieste is built on a hillside above what was once the chief port of the Austro-Hungarian Empire. Typical of Trieste are its belle-epoque cafés. Like Vienna's coffeehouses, these are social and cultural centers and much-beloved refuges from the prevailing northeast wind, the chilling *bora*.

The sidewalk cafés on the vast seaside **Piazza dell'Unità d'Italia** are popular meeting places in the summer months. The square is similar to Piazzetta San Marco in Venice; both are focal points of architectural interest and command fine views of the sea. Behind the **Palazzo Comunale** (Town Hall; ✉ at the end of Piazza dell'Unità d'Italia), going away from the sea, steps lead uphill, following the city's pattern of upward expansion from its roots as a coastal fishing port in Roman times.

The **Civico Museo Revoltella e Galleria d'Arte Moderna** (Revoltella Museum and Gallery of Modern Art) was founded in 1872 when the Venetian Baron Revoltella left the city his palazzo, library, and art collection. The gallery has one of the most important collections of 19th- and 20th-century art in Italy, with Italian artists particularly well represented. ✉ *Via Diaz 27,* ☎ *040/311361.* ✇ *10,000 lire/€5.15.* ☉ *Oct.–Apr., Wed.–Mon. 10–7; May–Sept., Wed.–Mon. 10–8.*

The solid Romanesque construction of the church of **San Silvestro** (✉ Via San Silvestro), open Monday–Saturday 10–1, dates from the 11th century. The Baroque extravagance of **Santa Maria Maggiore,** just beyond San Silvestro, backs onto a network of alleys closed to traffic.

The 14th-century **Cattedrale di San Giusto** incorporates two much older churches, one dating from as far back as the 5th century. The exterior adds even more to the jumble of styles involved by using fragments of Roman tombs and temples: you can see these most clearly on the pillars of the main doorway. The highlights of the interior are the 13th-century mosaics and frescoes. ✉ *Piazza Cattedrale.* ☉ *Apr.–Sept., Mon.–Sat. 8–noon and 3:30–7:30, Sun. 8–1 and 3:30–8; Oct.–Mar., Mon.–Sat. 8–noon and 2:30–6:30, Sun. 8–1 and 3:30–8.*

From the hilltop **Castello di San Giusto** you can take in some of the best views of the area. In the 15th century, this castle was built by the Venetians, who always had an eye for the best vantage point in the cities they conquered or controlled. The Habsburgs, subsequent rulers of Trieste, enlarged it to its present size. Some of the best exhibits in the **Museo Civico del Castello di San Giusto** are the displays of weaponry and armor. ✉ *Piazza Cattedrale,* ☎ *040/309362 castle, 040/308686 museum,*

CAFFÈ CULTURE

SINCE TRIESTE IS ONE of the most famous coffee towns in the world, perhaps it's no coincidence that its mayor is Riccardo Illy, patriarch of the famous *über*-roaster, Illycaffè, which can be credited with supplying caffeine fixes to most Italians and much of the free world. The elegant civility of Trieste plays out beautifully in a caffè culture that rivals that of Vienna. Know that in Trieste your cappuccino will come in an espresso cup, with only half as much frothy milk and a dollop of whipped cream. Many caffè are part of a *torrefazione* (roasting shop), so you can sample the beans before you buy. Few caffè in Trieste, in Italy, or in the world, can rival **Antico Caffè San Marco** (✉ Via Cesare Battisti 18, ☎ 040/363538) for its glimmering Art Deco style and old-world atmosphere. On Friday and Saturday there is live music. **Cremecaffè** (✉ Piazza Goldoni 10, ☎ 040/636555) may not be the place to sit down and read the paper, but it's nonetheless one of the most frequented caffè in town, with 20 different blends to choose from. One of the city's finest roasting shops, **Caffè La Colombiana** (✉ Via Carducci 12, ☎ 040/370855), has been in the same location since the 1940s. There is no better locale in town than at **Caffè Piazza Grande** (✉ Piazza dell'Unità d'Italia 5, ☎ 040/369878), with a great view of the great piazza. **Il Gran Bar Malabar** (✉ Piazza San Giovanni 6, ☎ 040/636226) is yet another wonderful stop for a coffee or an aperitif, with an excellent wine list and tastings every Friday after 6:30 PM.

WEB *www.retecivica.trieste.it.* ✉ *Museum and castle 3,000 lire/€1.55.* ☉ *Museum Tues.–Sun. 9–1. Castle June–Sept., daily 9–7; Oct.–May, daily 9–5.*

The **Piazza della Borsa** contains Trieste's original stock exchange, the **Borsa Vecchia,** a neoclassical building now serving as the chamber of commerce. A **statue of Leopold I** is at one end of the square.

OFF THE BEATEN PATH

GROTTA GIGANTE – More than 300 ft high, 900 ft long, and 200 ft wide, this gigantic cave is dripping with spectacular stalactites and stalagmites. Allow 45 minutes for the tour (which is required). It is not far from Trieste, about 10 km (6 mi) north of the city (take Bus 42 from Piazza Oberdan). ☎ *040/327312.* ✉ *13,000 lire/€6.70.* ☉ *Nov.–Feb., Tues.–Sun. tours leave at 10, 11, noon, 2, and 3; Mar. and Oct., Tues.–Sun. 10–4, tours leave on the hr; Apr.–Sept., Tues.–Sun. 10–6, tours leave every 30 mins, last tour at 5:30.*

Dining and Lodging

$$–$$$ **✗ Suban.** Though in the hills on the edge of town, this historic trattoria is worth the taxi ride. The rustic decor is rich in dark wood, stone, and wrought iron, and you'll find typical regional fare with imaginative variations. Among the specialties are *jota carsolina* (typical local minestrone made of cabbage, potatoes, and beans) and duck breast in Tokay sauce. ✉ *Via Emilio Comici 2,* ☎ *040/54368. AE, DC, MC, V. Closed Tues., 3 wks in Aug., and 1 wk in Jan. No lunch Mon.*

$$$–$$$$ **✗▣ Duchi d'Aosta.** On the spacious Piazza dell'Unità d'Italia, this hotel is beautifully furnished in lavish Venetian-Renaissance style. Its restaurant, Harry's Grill (closed Monday), is one of the city's most elegant.

⊠ *Piazza dell'Unità d'Italia 2, 34121,* ☎ *040/7600011,* ℻ *040/ 366092,* WEB *www.magesta.com. 50 rooms, 2 suites Restaurant, bar. AE, DC, MC, V.*

$$–$$$ 🖬 **Colombia.** Unpretentious but adequate, this small hotel caters mainly to a business clientele. There is no restaurant, but there's a typical beer-cellar restaurant close by. ⊠ *Via della Geppa 18, 34121,* ☎ *040/369333,* ℻ *040/369644,* WEB *www.hotelcolombia.it. 40 rooms. AE, DC, MC, V.*

Nightlife and the Arts

The **opera** season in Trieste runs from October through May, with a brief operetta festival in July and August. Contact the tourist information office (⊠ Riva III Novembre 9, ☎ 040/3478312) or the opera house (⊠ Piazza Verdi, ☎ 040/6722111) for further details on events.

Outdoor Activities and Sports

GOLF

The nine-hole course at **Golf Club Trieste** (⊠ Padriciano 80, ☎ 040/ 226159) is 6 km (4 mi) from the town center. It's closed on Tuesday.

HORSEBACK RIDING

Ippodromo di Montebello (⊠ Piazzale de Gasperi 4, ☎ 040/393176) is a stable with rides available throughout the year.

SCUBA DIVING

For scuba diving in the Riserva Naturale Marina di Miramare, contact **Riserva Naturale** (☎ 040/224147), which also provides scuba diving equipment.

SWIMMING

The **Piscina Bianchi** (⊠ Riva Gulli 3, ☎ 040/301456), is a centrally located, 25-meter long pool. It's open Monday–Friday 7 AM–9 AM and noon–3; weekends 7 AM–noon when there aren't competitions. Daily tickets cost 6,000 lire/€3.10; no lockers are available.

Shopping

Trieste's busy shopping street, **Corso Italia,** is reached from Piazza della Borsa. There are antiques markets on the streets of the city's old center on the third Sunday of each month. Trieste has some 60 antiques dealers, jewelers, and secondhand shops, and a large antiques fair is held in the city at the end of October.

VENETIAN ARC A TO Z

To research prices, get advice from other travelers, and book travel arrangements, visit www.fodors.com.

AIRPORTS

The main airport serving the Venetian Arc is Aeroporto Marco Polo, 10 km (6 mi) north of Venice, which handles international and domestic flights to the region. A few European airlines schedule flights to Aeroporto di Villafranca, which is also served by a number of charter flights. A regular bus service connects Villafranca with Verona's Porta Nuova railway station.

Treviso's Aeroporto San Giuseppe, 5 km (3 mi) southeast of Treviso, 32 km (19 mi) north of Venice, is also served by charter flights (check www.ryanair.com for flights to and from London). Flights to Treviso usually include transportation from the airport to Venice or other destinations; otherwise there is ATVO local bus service to Treviso every 20 minutes during the day, or a taxi will come to the airport to pick you up from Treviso, only 6 km (4 mi) away. There are domestic flights to Aeroporto Ronchi dei Legionari, 35 km (22 mi) northwest of Trieste, linked with Via Flavio Gioia near Trieste's train station by regular SAITA bus service, or for 15,000 lire/€7.75 you can take the more convenient *servizio navetta* (shuttle).

➤ AIRPORT INFORMATION: **Aeroporto Marco Polo** (☎ 041/2609260). **Aeroporto di Villafranca** (✉ 11 km [7 mi] southwest of Verona, ☎ 045/8095666, WEB www.areoportoverona.it). **Aeroporto Ronchi dei Legionari** (☎ 0481/773224, WEB www.areoporto.fvg.it). **Aeroporto San Giuseppe** (☎ 0422/315111 or 0422/315131).

➤ TAXIS AND SHUTTLES: **SAITA** (☎ 040/425001). **Servizio Navetta** (☎ 0335/5606987 or 0348/4235865 shutttle). **Taxi** (☎ 0422/431515).

BUS TRAVEL

There are interurban and interregional connections throughout the Veneto and Friuli. Local tourist offices may be able to provide details of timetables and routes; otherwise contact the local bus station or, in some cases, the individual bus companies operating from the station, listed below.

➤ BUS INFORMATION: **ACTV buses** (✉ Piazzale Roma, Venice, ☎ 041/5287886 buses to Brenta Riviera). **APT buses** (✉ Porta Nuova, Verona, ☎ 045/8057911). **ATVO buses** (✉ Piazzale Roma, Venice, ☎ 041/5205530 buses to Cortina weekends only). **FVG buses** (✉ Piazza Libertà, Trieste, ☎ 040/425020; ✉ Stazione FS, Piazzale della Stazione, near Campo Marzio, Vicenza, ☎ 0444/223115 or 166/845010, WEB www.ftv.vi.it). **La Marca buses** (✉ Via Lungosile Mattei, Treviso, ☎ 0422/577311). **SITA buses** (✉ Piazzale Boschetti, Padua, ☎ 049/8206844 Mon.–Sat., 049/8206834 Sun.)

CAR RENTAL

➤ LOCAL AGENCIES: **Avis** (✉ Piazzale della Stazione 1, Padua, ☎ 049/664198; ✉ Stazione Marittima, Molo Bersaglieri, Trieste, ☎ 040/300820; ✉ Aeroporto Ronchi dei Legionari, Trieste, ☎ 0481/777085; ✉ Viale Leopardi 5/a, Udine, ☎ 0432/501149; ✉ Stazione FS, Verona, ☎ 045/8006636; ✉ Viale Milano 88, Vicenza, ☎ 0444/321622). **Hertz** (✉ Piazzale della Stazione 5/4, Padua, ☎ 049/657877; ✉ Molo dei Bersaglieri 3, Trieste, ☎ 040/3220098; ✉ Aeroporto Ronchi dei Legionari, Trieste, ☎ 0481/777025; ✉ Via Crispi 17, Udine, ☎ 0432/511211; ✉ Stazione FS, Verona, ☎ 045/8000832; ✉ Stazione FS, Vicenza, ☎ 0444/321313).

CAR TRAVEL

The main access roads to the Venetian Arc from southern Italy are both linked to the A1 (Autostrada del Sole), which connects Bologna, Florence, and Rome. They are the A13, which culminates in Padua, and the A22, which passes through Verona in a north–south direction. The road linking the region from east to west is the A4, the primary route from Milan to as far as Trieste, skirting Verona, Padua, and Venice along the way. The distance from Verona, in the west, to Trieste is 263 km (163 mi). Branches link the A4 with Treviso (A27), Pordenone (A28), and Udine (A23).

EMERGENCY SERVICES
ACI Emergency Service offers 24-hour roadside assistance.
➤ CONTACTS: **ACI dispatchers** (☎ 116).

EMERGENCIES

For first aid, dial the general emergency number (113) and ask for *pronto soccorso*. Be prepared to give your address. (If you can find a concierge or some other Italian-speaker to call on your behalf, do so, as not all 113 operators speak English.) All pharmacies post signs on the door with addresses of pharmacies that stay open at night, on Saturday afternoon, and on Sunday.

➤ CONTACTS: **Police, Ambulance, Fire** (☎ 113).

TOURS

Many of the best tours begin and end in Venice, because so much of the region is accessible from there. The Burchiello excursion boat makes an all-day villa tour along the Brenta River Canal; contact American Express for information. For those who prefer to go it alone, the most practical way is to hire a car for the day. Local tourist offices will be able to put you in contact with the Tourist Guides Association or provide you with a list of authorized guides, for whom there is an official tariff rate.

Trieste offers special weekend package deals ("T for You") that include discounts in hotels and restaurants, free or reduced-price entrance to a selection of the city's main tourist attractions, and some guided tours (to reserve tours call the Association of Trieste Authorized Guides). All of the Trieste hotels listed in this chapter are part of "T for You." Contact the Trieste tourist office (☞ Visitor Information, *below*) for further information.

➤ CONTACTS: **American Express** (✉ Salizzada San Moisè 1471, San Marco, Venice, ☎ 041/5200844, FAX 041/5229937). **Association of Trieste Authorized Guides** (☎ 040/365248 or 040/366280).

TRAIN TRAVEL

The most important train routes arriving from the south will stop almost every hour in either Verona, Padua, or Venice. From northern Italy and the rest of Europe, trains usually enter via Milan or through Porta Nuova station in Verona. To the west of Venice, on the main line running across the north of Italy, are Padua (30 mins from Venice), Vicenza (1 hr), and Verona (1½ hrs); to the east is Trieste (2 hrs). Local trains link Venice to Bassano del Grappa (1 hr), Padua to Bassano del Grappa (1 hr), Vicenza to Treviso (1 hr), and Udine to Trieste (1 hr). Treviso and Udine both lie on the main line from Venice to Tarvisio, on which Eurocity trains continue to Vienna and Prague. Call Ferrovie dello Stato (FS), for information, or check out their Web site.

➤ TRAIN INFORMATION: **Ferrovie dello Stato** (☎ 848/888088, WEB www.fs-on-line.com).

TRAVEL AGENCIES

➤ LOCAL AGENT REFERRALS: **American Express** (✉ Fabretto Viaggi/American Express, Via Risorgimento 20, Padua, ☎ 049/666133; ✉ Paterniti Viaggi/American Express, Corso Cavour 7, Trieste, ☎ 040/366161; ✉ Fabretto Viaggi/American Express, Corso Porta Nuova 11/f, Verona, ☎ 045/8009040).

VISITOR INFORMATION

➤ TOURIST INFORMATION: **Marostica** (✉ Piazza Castello 1, 36063, ☎ 0424/72127, WEB www.telemar.it/marostica.htm). **Padua** (✉ Stazione Ferroviaria, 35100, ☎ 049/8752077, WEB www.padovanet.it/apt). **Treviso** (✉ Piazzetta Monte di Pietà 8, 31100, ☎ 0422/547632, WEB www.sevenonline.it/tvapt). **Trieste** (✉ Riva III Novembre 9, 34100, ☎ 040/3478312; also inside the Eurostar lounge at the train station [no phone], WEB www.triestetourism.it). **Udine** (✉ Piazza Primo Maggio 7, 33100, ☎ 0432/295972, WEB www.regione.fvg.it). **Verona** (✉ Piazza Bra, 37100, ☎ 045/8068680; ✉ Stazione FS, ☎ 045/8000861, WEB www.verona-apt.net). **Vicenza** (✉ Piazza Matteotti 12, 36100, ☎ 0444/320854, WEB www.ascom.vi.it/aptvicenza).

3 THE DOLOMITES: TRENTINO-ALTO ADIGE

TRENTO, BOLZANO, MERANO, CORTINA D'AMPEZZO

Little wonder Leonardo da Vinci depicted the Dolomites behind his Mona Lisa. Nature's skyscrapers, they are hemmed in by stupefying cliffs, emerald-green meadows, and crystal-clear lakes. Dramatic rose-color peaks take on a purple hue at summer's sunset; in winter, the lures are the ski-and-be-seen resorts of Cortina d'Ampezzo and Madonna di Campiglio. In the valleys bustle the history-rich cities of Trento, Rovereto, Merano, and Bolzano.

Updated by
Robin
Goldstein

U NLIKE OTHER FAMOUS ALPINE RANGES, this vast, mountainous domain in northeast Italy has remained relatively undeveloped. The virginal landscape is the ultimate playground for the family or traveler on a quest for an original adventure. Ski fanatics travel across the world to dare some of the steep slopes that test Olympic champions. Mountaineers risk the climb up sheer rock faces. For calmer souls, the seduction of a landscape painted from a palette of extreme colors prevails. The lowland valleys are laced with rivers spanned by awkward bridges and are dotted with secluded villages, picture-book castles, and unexpected historic sites.

The Dolomites, sprawling over the Trentino-Alto Adige region and into parts of Lombardy by the Swiss border and the Veneto along the Austrian border, became known to Americans as a winter sports center after Cortina d'Ampezzo catapulted to fame by hosting the Winter Olympics of 1956. Today, scores of funiculars, chairlifts, and ski lifts provide access to 1,200 km (750 mi) of ski runs, as well as ski jumps and bobsled runs.

Then there are the "untouchable" zones—inaccessible by means of chairlift or ski lift. These are the famous plateaus topping some of the highest mountains, from which you can see Italy on one side and Austria or Switzerland on the other. To enjoy such a rare spectacle, you must spend arduous hours climbing beyond where the lifts end; you may well reach the top only to find cows casually grazing on the grass beneath the implausibly formed peaks (it may make you dizzy just thinking of how they got there). It's perhaps not surprising that Reinhold Messer, the first man to climb Everest without oxygen, lives in the Dolomites.

Yet those that come to the region seeking perilous adventure also often find beauty and tranquillity. Called "the most beautiful work of architecture ever seen" by Le Corbusier, this expansive land of rocks and valleys is marked by a profusion of brilliant colors, architectural styles, and languages. A meander through the valleys becomes a botanical escapade, with rare plant species abounding; high above you on the cliffs are ancient castles and remote fortresses protected by their size and position. There, on the higher levels, are some rarely seen animals: bears, deer, mountain goats, and birds of prey.

Straddling the Brenner Pass—the main access point between Italy and central Europe—the Dolomites play host to a mixture of cultures and languages. Too often overlooked by travelers through the Brenner Pass are the picturesque and prosperous alpine towns of Trento, Bolzano, and Merano. All three are marked by a departure in architectural style, with surrounding mountains dominating an architectural landscape of onion-bulb roofs and jutting spires uncharacteristic of the rest of Italy. The people of Alto Adige are predominantly German-speaking, and their crafts and food have an Austrian accent (until World War I, the area was Austria's South Tirol); in Bolzano and Merano you will get plenty of opportunities to practice your German. (The region of Trentino, on the other hand, is largely Italian-speaking.) Pastry shops; dark, lively beer halls; frigid winter temperatures; a hearty meat-and-dumpling cuisine; and an earlier daily schedule round out the Austro-German influence.

Reflecting the diversity of this part of Italy, the area since 1848 has enjoyed special status as the Autonomous Region of Trentino-Alto Adige, made up of the independent provinces of Trento and Bolzano. And there is still another language to be heard in the area: Ladin, an offshoot of Latin still spoken by a small Ladin community primarily in the Val Gardena. The language can credit centuries of isolation in mountain strongholds for its survival. Signs throughout much of the Dolomites are bilingual. Place-names are given in Italian with German equivalents, where useful, in parentheses below.

Pleasures and Pastimes

Cross-Country Skiing

The Dolomites are an ideal place to learn or improve your *sci di fondo* (cross-country skiing). The major Alpine resorts, and even many out-of-the-way villages, have prepared trails (usually loops marked off by kilometers) appropriate for differing degrees of ability. Two of the best are at Ortisei and Dobbiaco. You can have a lot of fun blazing new trails across virgin snowfields; you can usually get permission by asking at the nearest farmhouse or inquiring at local tourist offices.

Dining

Encompassing the Germanic Alto Adige province and the Italian Trentino province, the Dolomite region combines Italian cuisine with local Tirolean specialties, which are much like the dishes of Austria and central Europe. Local *alimentari* (food shops) stock a bounty of regional cheeses, pickles, salami, and smoked meats—perfect for picnics—and local bakeries turn out a wide selection of crusty dark rolls and caraway-studded rye breads. The best of the local cheeses are the mild *asiago* and *fontal* and the more pungent *puzzone di Moena* (literally, "stinkpot"). Local dishes vary from one isolated mountain valley to the next. Don't miss *speck,* the local smoked ham. Other specialties include *canederli,* or *knoedel,* a type of dumpling with many variations, served either in broth or with a sauce; würstel and hot sauerkraut; ravioli made from rye flour, stuffed with spinach, and fried; and apple or pear strudel. And—as befits a wine-producing region—the local vintages (and fruit brandies) are delicious. In the fall in the South Tirol, when autumn colors beautify the mountains and valleys, it's a tradition to make a tour of the cozy country wine taverns to drink the new wine and eat hot roasted chestnuts.

For general information and price categories, *see* Dining *in* Smart Travel Tips A to Z.

Downhill Skiing

The craggy peaks of the Dolomites have some of the best, and most beautiful, downhill skiing environments and facilities in Europe. The ski season generally runs from late November to April, by which time some people prefer to ski in shirtsleeves. The beginning of the season often suffers from light snowfall, though, and the best skiing often isn't seen until late February; some centers are equipped for summer skiing. The most comprehensive centers are Cortina d'Ampezzo, in the heart of the Dolomites to the east of Bolzano, and Madonna di Campiglio, west of Trento. These resorts are unabashedly upscale, but you get the extras you expect from world-class centers: miles of interconnecting runs linked by cable cars and lifts, plus skating rinks, heated indoor pools, and lively après-ski. Less-expensive adventures can be had at Alta Badia, south from Brunico; Val Gardena; and Ortisei, a popular resort.

Folk Festivals

Essentially rural in character, the Dolomite region offers a rich selection of folk festivals, harvest fairs, and religious celebrations. Chief among these is Trento's weeklong festival of San Vigilio held the last week of June, when marching bands and costumed choirs perform in the streets and squares of the heart of the city. The other major towns have sim-

The Dolomites: Trentino-Alto Adige

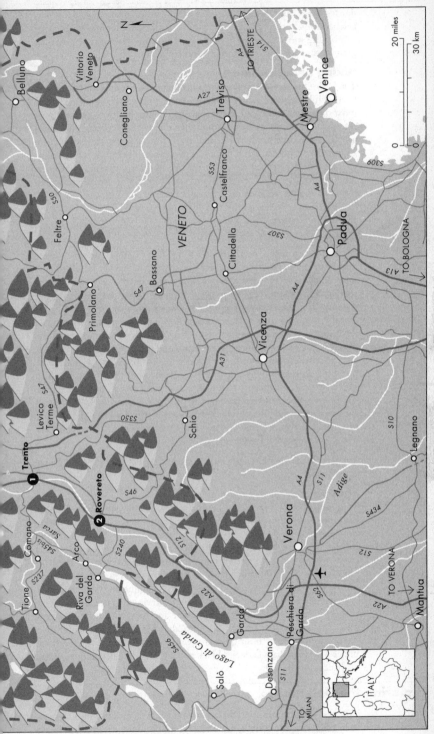

ilar festivals, but equally enjoyable are the more informal and low-key celebrations in the villages of the many valleys, sometimes amounting to nothing more than excuses for hardworking mountain farmers to get together for some local wine and song.

Hiking and Climbing

The Dolomites have a well-maintained network of trails for hiking and rock climbing, with *rifugi* (huts) in both hiking terrain and near the most difficult ascents. At these spartan accommodations you can just refuel with a meal or stay overnight in a dormitory-style room. Routes are designated by grades of difficulty (T, tourist path; H, hiking path; EE for expert hikers; EEA, for equipped expert hikers). It is important to follow safety procedures, have the necessary equipment, and obtain the latest information on trails and conditions. For information, call the **Club Alpino Italiano** (✉ Piazza delle Erbe 46, Bolzano, ☎ 0471/978172; ✉ Corso della Libertà 188, Merano, ☎ 0473/448944; ✉ Via Manci 57, Trento; WEB www.cai.it).

Lodging

Accommodations in the Dolomites range from restored castles to spic-and-span chalet guest houses, from stately 19th-century hotels to chic modern ski resorts. Even a small village may have scores of places to stay, many of them very inexpensive. Hotel information offices at train stations and tourist offices can help you sidestep the language problem if you arrive without reservations: the Bolzano train station has a 24-hour hotel service, and tourist offices will give you a list of all the hotels in the area, arranged by location and price. We've tried to mention hotels in towns that make good bases for travel, as well as some notable hotels found outside of towns. Remember that many hotels in ski resorts cater primarily to longer stays at full or half board: it's wise to book ski vacations as packages in advance. A word of warning: although spring and fall are wonderful times to travel in the region, many mountain hotels are closed for a month or two after Easter and for about six weeks before Christmas.

For general information and price categories, *see* Lodging *in* Smart Travel Tips A to Z.

Shopping

Shopping is an event in the Dolomites, where larger towns such as Bolzano, Bressanone, and Brunico have shops clustered in arcaded streets designed to keep shoppers dry on rainy or snowy days. The ethnic mixture, with its strong Tirolean influence, makes for local products and crafts that are quite different from those elsewhere in Italy. Tirolean clothing—loden goods, lederhosen, dirndls, and linen suits with horn buttons—is a good buy, costing less than in neighboring Austria. Local crafts, such as embroidered goods, wood carvings, figures for nativity scenes, pottery, and handcrafted copper and iron objects, make good gifts. And of course, Trento, Bolzano, and Merano in particular also have no shortage of boutiques stocking items that meet the requisite under-35 Italian dress code: jet-black and icy-gray designer clothes, shoes, and accessories.

Exploring the Dolomites

The best—and only—way to get around in this mountainous region is by following the course of the valleys that find their way to the heart of the massifs of the Dolomites. Two of the most important valleys are those formed by the Isarco and Adige rivers. The Isarco River begins at the Brenner Pass and runs due south to Bolzano, where it joins the Adige River. The Adige itself originates near the Swiss border and also runs south through Bolzano. Italy's main road and rail connections to north-central Europe follow the same rivers northward en route to the Brenner Pass. Note that it is very difficult, if not impossible, to reach the ski areas—or any town outside of Trento, Bolzano, and Merano—without a car.

Numbers in the text correspond to numbers in the margin and on the Dolomites: Trentino-Alto Adige and Bolzano maps.

Great Itineraries

The area of the Dolomites is a vast expanse of valleys, mountain roads, and hillside towns. Although roads can be windy and sometimes snowy in winter, they are generally of excellent quality and well maintained. Instead of rushing to get all the sights into your travels, try to be discerning and stick to the areas you would most like to see. A further note of caution involves the closure of some roads during the winter season, which can begin as early as November and continue until May, in particular the high mountain passes such as Passo di Gavia and Passo dello Stelvio in the east.

IF YOU HAVE 3 DAYS

Start in **Trento** ① and head south to **Rovereto** ② and **Riva del Garda** on the tip of Lake Garda, then on to the quaint towns of **Pinzolo** ③ and **Madonna di Campiglio** ④ for a bird's-eye view of the Dolomites, ending your day via Dimaro in ⛏ **Bolzano** ⑦–⑫. The next day head for the lovely town of **Bressanone** ⑰ and onward via **Brunico** ⑱ to the historic resort of ⛏ **Cortina d'Ampezzo** ⑳. The last day take the Grande Strada delle Dolomiti, passing **Lago di Carezza** ㉕, and return to Trento.

IF YOU HAVE 5 DAYS

Follow the three-day itinerary above as far as Dimaro, but instead of going directly to Bolzano, swing east and head for the dizzyingly high Passo di Gavia and down then to the small town of ⛏ **Bormio** ⑤. The next day proceed to the breathtaking **Passo dello Stelvio** ⑥ and on down to **Naturno** ⑬ before stopping in one of the pearls of the Alto Adige region, **Merano** ⑭. Continue on to ⛏ **Bolzano** ⑦–⑫, the principal city in this region. The next day head for **Cornedo** ⑮, **Chiusa** ⑯, and **Bressanone** ⑰. Move on to Brunico and ⛏ **Cortina d'Ampezzo** ⑳. The next day head to **Canazei** ㉑ via the beautiful Passo di Sella and on to **Ortisei** ㉒, in the heart of the Val Gardena. Return to Trento via **Fiè** ㉓ and **Caldaro** ㉔.

IF YOU HAVE 8 DAYS

Follow the five-day itinerary as far as ⛏ **Bressanone** ⑰. The following day stroll through **Brunico** ⑱ and **Dobbiaco** ⑲ before moving on to ⛏ **Cortina d'Ampezzo** ⑳ for the night. From here follow the Grande Strada delle Dolomiti through the Passo di Falzarego and slightly north through the Passo di Sella and into the Val Gardena and ⛏ **Ortisei** ㉒. On the last day, drive to **Fiè** ㉓ and south on the A22. Just south of Cornedo, turn left onto the S241 to get to **Lago di Carezza** ㉕. Continue along the road until you reach Vigo di Fassa, veering south onto the S48, passing through the small towns of Predazzo, Cavalese, and Ora, until you rejoin the A22 and continue south back to Trento.

When to Tour the Dolomites

If you are coming here for the skiing, your best time to visit is between mid-December to April, when most resorts open. Powder hounds, beware: snowfall in early winter is unreliable; scrutinize snow reports if it's before mid- to late February. The Dolomites do not receive as much consistent snow as the Alps and some years accumulate little snow for the whole season. With the exception of the main bargain period known to Italians as *settimane bianche* (white weeks)—popular ski-package weeks in January or February—the slopes are relatively crowd-free. Booking well in advance of your ski holiday is highly recommended, as lack of snow in the early part of the season can sometimes cause overcrowding later on. During the rest of the year, accommodations are easier to find, but booking is still recommended. Summer is the best time for hiking. Note that nearly all hotels and guest houses outside the main urban centers close from early November to mid- or late December.

WESTERN TRENTINO

The areas east and west of Trento are collectively known as Trentino, a region shaped roughly like a butterfly. The west side includes the peaks of the Brenta Massif, the Stelvio Pass, and the Val Venosta. Some of the passes in this region close during the winter months, so if you are traveling during this period you will not be able to follow the entire itinerary outlined above.

Trento

❶ *51 km (32 mi) south of Bolzano, 24 km (15 mi) north of Rovereto.*

Capital of the autonomous Trentino province, Trento has somehow escaped the ravages of commercialization and retains its architectural charm, artistic attractions, and historic importance. Trento's stunning Piazza del Duomo is splendidly preserved, and its enormous medieval castle dominates the city landscape in virtually original form. It was here, from 1545 to 1563, that the structure of the Catholic Church was redefined at the famous Council of Trent. This was the starting point of the Counter-Reformation, which brought half of Europe back to Catholicism. Trento itself was ruled by prince-bishops until 1803 when they were overthrown by Napoléon's armies. You'll see the word *consiglio* (council) everywhere in Trento—in hotel, restaurant, and street names, and even on wine labels. The modern city, though, has much more to offer than history—it is a prosperous and fashionable university town of growing interest to tourists and businesspeople alike.

Free guided tours of Trento are given on Saturday by the local **tourist office** (✉ Via Manci 2, ☎ 0461/983880). Tours leave at 10 AM for a trip to the Castello del Buonconsiglio and at 3 PM for a tour of the city center. All tours begin in front of the tourist office. In Piazza del Duomo is a Baroque **Fontana del Nettuno.** The massive, low, Romanesque **Duomo,** also known as the Cathedral of San Virgilio, forms the southern edge of the square. Locals refer to the piazza as the city's *salotto,* or sitting room, as in fine weather it is always filled with students and residents drinking coffee, enjoying an aperitif, or reading the newspaper. When skies are clear, pause to savor the view of the mountaintops, ranged majestically around the city in every direction, before entering the cathedral.

Step inside to see the unusual arcaded stone stairways on either side of the austere nave. Ahead of you is the *baldacchino* (altar canopy), a clear copy of Bernini's masterpiece in St. Peter's in Rome. In the small Chapel of the Crucifix to the right is a mournful 15th-century crucifixion, with the Virgin Mary and John the Apostle. This crucifix, built by German artist Sixtus Frei, was a focal point of the Council of Trent: each decree agreed on during the two decades of deliberations was solemnly read out in front of it. Outside, walk around to the back of the cathedral to see an exquisite display of 14th-century stonemasons' art, from the small porch to the intriguing knotted columns on the graceful apse. Within the Duomo grounds is an **archaeological area,** displaying ancient ruins of a 6th-century Christian basilica and a gate dating from the 9th century. ✉ *Piazza del Duomo.* 🎟 *Archaeological area 2,000 lire/€1.05.* 🕓 *Weekdays 10–noon and 2–6, Sat. 10–noon.*

★ The crenellated **Palazzo Pretorio,** which seems to be a wing of the Trento cathedral, was built in the 13th century as the prudently fortified residence of the prince-bishops. Endowed with considerable power and autonomy, these clerics enjoyed a unique position in the medieval hierarchy. A remarkable sight, the Palazzo now guards over the center of Trento in virtually original form—it has lost none of its medieval splendor. The crenellations are not merely decorative: the square pattern represented ancient allegiance to the Guelphs, while the more triangular crenellations seen elsewhere in town represented Ghibelline loyalty. The Palazzo Pretorio now houses the **Museo Diocesano Tridentino,** where you can see paintings showing the seating plan of the prelates during the Council of Trent; early 16th-century tapestries by Pieter van Aelst, the Belgian artist who carried out Raphael's 15th-century designs for the Vatican tapestries; carved wood altars and statues; and an 11th-century sacramentary, or book of services. These and other precious objects all come from the cathedral's treasury. ✉ *Piazza del Duomo 18,* ☎ *0461/234419.* 🎟 *5,000 lire/€2.60 includes Duomo archaeological area.* 🕓 *Mon.–Sat. 9:30–12:30 and 2:30–6.*

Off the northwest side of the Piazza del Duomo, about 650 ft down Via Cavour, is the Renaissance church of **Santa Maria Maggiore,** where many sessions of the Council of Trent were held. The only light in the church comes from a beautifully simple rose window over the main door, so you'll have to strain to see the magnificent ceiling, an intricate combination of stucco and frescoes. ✉ *Via Cavour.* 🕓 *Daily 8:30–noon and 2:30–8.*

Locals refer to **Via Belenzani** as Trento's outdoor gallery because of the frescoed facades of the hallmark Renaissance palazzi. It's an easy 50-yard walk up the lane behind the church of Santa Maria Maggiore. The climb up **Via Manci** is pleasant, past 200 yards of souvenir shops and glassware outlets.

Castello del Buonconsiglio (Castle of Good Counsel), at the end of Via Manci, was once the stronghold of the prince-bishops; its position and size made it easier to defend than the Palazzo Pretorio. As you stand facing it, you can see the evolution of architectural styles, starting with the medieval fortifications of the Castelvecchio section on the far left, down to the more decorative Renaissance **Magno Palazzo,** built three centuries later in 1530. The Castello now houses the **Museo Provinciale d'Arte** (Provincial Art Museum), where permanent and visiting exhibits of art and archaeology are displayed in frescoed medieval halls or under Renaissance coffered ceilings. The 13th-century **Torre dell'Aquila** (Eagle's Tower) holds the highlight of the museum, a medieval fresco cycle of the months of the year called the *Ciclo dei Mesi.* It is full of charming and informatively detailed scenes of 15th-century life in both court and countryside. ✉ *Via Bernardo Clesio 5,* ☎ *0461/233770.* 🎟 *5,000 lire/€2.60.* 🕓 *Tues.–Sun. 9–noon and 2–5. Admission and hrs vary when exhibitions are held.*

The emphasis of the **Museo Storico in Trento** (Trento Historical Museum), housed in the former joiner's shop inside the castle walls, is on modern Trentino history, with displays, dioramas, and the occasional exhibition on the region from the unification of Italy in 1861 up to and including World War II. ✉ *Via Bernardo Clesio 3,* ☎ *0461/230482.* 🎟 *5,000 lire/€2.60.* 🕓 *Tues.–Sun. 9–noon and 2–5.*

The **Torre Verde,** or Green Tower (✉ Piazza Raffaello Sanzio), is part of Trento's 13th-century fortifications, standing alongside other fragments of the city walls. The **Torre Vanga** (⊠ Via Torre Vanga) dates from the 13th century and guards the medieval bridge across the Adige, Ponte San Lorenzo.

The progressive, modern works in the collection of the **Museo d'Arte Moderna e Contemporanea di Trento** are installed in a Renaissance villa, Palazzo delle Albere, next to the Adige river. Permanent works date from the 19th and 20th centuries; rotating exhibitions feature the work of modern and contemporary artists. ⊠ *Palazzo delle Albere, Via Ruggero da Sanseverino 45,* ☎ *0461/234860,* WEB *www.mart.tn.it.* ✉ *8,000 lire/€4.15.* ⏱ *Tues.–Sun. 10–6.*

OFF THE
BEATEN PATH

BELVEDERE DI SARDAGNA – Take the cable car from the station at the Ponte San Lorenzo bridge to this scenic spot, a vantage point 1,200 ft above Trento.

LEVICO TERME – About 20 km (13 mi) southeast of Trento and just east of the summer resorts of Lago di Caldonazzo is the undiscovered Levico Terme, a medieval *terme* (thermal bath) town nestled in the Val Sugana; the valley was inhabited by the Celts and then conquered by the Romans, and today the Latin-derived Ladin is still spoken by remote peoples in a valley enclave. Today, settle into a hotel here for summer sports and relaxation. For cosseting, spa treatment, and modern comforts, the gracious **Imperial Grand Hotel Terme** (*$$$$*; ⊠ Via Silva Domini 1, 38056 Levico Terme, ☎ 0461/706104, FAX 0261/706350) is in a lordly, restored Austrian noble estate, with a beautiful indoor pool, garden, and a fine Tuscan restaurant.

Dining and Lodging

$$$–$$$$ ✕ **Le Due Spade.** Near the Duomo, small, upscale, and romantic, with
★   wood paneling and chairs and an antique stove, this typical Tirolean tavern, which in theory dates back to 1585, has an atmosphere of warmth and comfort, able service, and superb, locally inspired food. You can sample traditional *gnocchetti di ricotta* (ricotta cheese dumplings) and polenta *ai funghi* (with mushroom sauce), and such savory *secondi* (second courses) as *tagliata di Angus alla griglia* (grilled slivers of beef) served with an aromatic herb sauce. Don't miss the outstanding wine list. Given its deserved popularity with locals and limited seating, reservations are a must. ⊠ *Via Don Arcangelo Rizzi 11,* ☎ *0461/234343. Reservations essential. AE, DC, MC, V. Closed Sun. No lunch Mon.*

$$$ ✕ **Chiesa.** Near the castle, a building that dates from about 1400 conceals a bright interior that is purely modern, if not trendy. The restaurant attracts romantic couples and power lunchers alike. Apple prints and excellent risotto *alle mele* (with apples) celebrate the local produce. There is even a set meal featuring apples in every course. Otherwise, the food is traditional: *maccheroncini con salsiccia e verze* (short, narrow pasta tubes with sausage and cabbage) and *tonco de Pontesel* (a stew of mixed meat served with polenta and made according to a 15th-century recipe). ⊠ *Via San Marco 64,* ☎ *0461/238766. AE, DC, MC, V. Closed Sun.*

$ ✕ **Trattoria Pizzeria Laste.** Owner Guido Rizzi invented pizza Calabrese, a white pizza with garlic, mozzarella, and hot red-pepper flakes. He's also a national pizza-making champion, and the proof is in the pudding: each of his 35 pies—including the *sedano* (mozzarella, celery root, *grana* cheese, oregano)—is delectable. Save room for dessert: pizza *dolce*, with bananas, strawberries, kiwi, and caramel. The pizzeria is housed in a pleasant villa in the hills above city center. ⊠ *Via alle Laste 39, Cognola,* ☎ *0461/231570. MC, V. Closed Tues.*

$$ ✕🏠 **Castel Pergine.** On a hilltop 12 km (7 mi) outside of town toward Levico looms this castle, which in the 13th century was transformed into a fort and in the 16th century was occupied by the prince-bishop Bernardo Clesio. Today, the Swiss Schneider-Neffs manage it. Amid the labyrinth of brooding stone and brick chambers, prisons, and chapels you'll find sparse, rustic rooms with carved-wood trim, lace curtains, and heavy wooden beds, some canopied. The grounds often have brightly colored modern-art installations—an interesting juxtaposition. The candlelit restaurant, which serves ages-old seasonal recipes from Trento in lighter guises, is a favorite of locals and visitors alike. ✉ *38057 Pergine Val Sugana, about 10 km (6 mi) east of Trento,* ☎ *0461/531158,* FAX *0461/531329. 21 rooms, 14 with bath. Restaurant, horseback riding, library. AE, MC, V. Closed Nov. 5–Apr. 5. No lunch Mon.*

$$$ 🏠 **Grand Hotel Trento.** Its contemporary rounded facade amid ancient palaces makes this hotel on Piazza Dante an anomaly. Inside, it is lush with modern appointments, from the marble and woodwork in the lobby and lounges to the Clesio restaurant's rich drapery. Rooms are ample and have thick carpets in blues and creams with clubby, wood-trim furniture. ✉ *Via Alfieri 1/3, 38100,* ☎ *0461/271000,* FAX *0461/271001,* WEB *www.venere.it/trento/grandhoteltrento/. 121 rooms, 15 suites. Restaurant, bar, minibars, sauna, meeting room, parking (fee). AE, DC, MC, V. Closed Dec. 24–Jan. 6.*

$$–$$$ 🏠 **Accademia.** This friendly, character-filled hotel occupies an ancient
★ house in the historic center of Trento, close to Piazza del Duomo. Framed by a beautiful arched entryway, the public rooms retain the ancient vaulting, but the bedrooms are modern and comfortably equipped. There's a courtyard garden. ✉ *Vicolo Colico 4/6, 38100,* ☎ *0461/233600,* FAX *0461/230174. 40 rooms, 2 suites. Restaurant, air-conditioning, minibars. AE, DC, MC, V. Closed Dec. 24–Jan. 6.*

$$ 🏠 **Aquila d'Oro.** This small hotel offers comfort, efficiency, and a prime location in the historic town center. Most rooms have nondescript contemporary furniture in somber colors. The owner is more than willing to pitch in names of places for lunch and dinner. ✉ *Via Belenzani 76, 38100,* ☎ FAX *0461/986282. 20 rooms. Bar, breakfast room. AE, DC, MC, V. Closed Dec. 24–Jan. 6.*

$$ 🏠 **Buonconsiglio.** Near the train station, this elegant hotel offers well-kept, sizable rooms and efficient service, perfect for the business traveler. The public spaces are decorated with modern art. ✉ *Via Romagnosi 16–18, 38100,* ☎ *0461/272888,* FAX *0461/272889. 46 rooms, 2 suites. Restaurant, bar. AE, DC, MC, V. Closed Aug. 10–25.*

Nightlife and the Arts

FESTIVALS

From late June to late September, a regional **Superfestival** highlights historic castles as venues for performances and evocations of fact and legend. The festival features music, costumes, banquets, and train excursions to the castles. The **Festivale di Musica Sacra** (Sacred Music Festival)—a monthlong series of concerts held in the churches of Trento and the Trentino—takes place in May and June; for information, call ☎ 0462/983880.

A summer bonus is the weeklong **Festive Vigiliane,** a spectacular pageant in the Piazza del Duomo, culminating on June 26, when townspeople don medieval clothing in honor of their patron saint. For more than 60 years, the May wine festival **Mostra dei Vini** has attracted every Bacchus, from farmers of surrounding hillside towns to sommeliers from all over Italy. The weeklong festival includes tastings, sommelier tours, and prizes; for information, call ☎ 0461/983880. Wine buffs visiting in summer need not be disappointed, however. In July and August, wine buffs can take part in the **Vinum Bonum** program offering music and wine tastings for 15,000 lire/€7.75 at different cellars in Trentino each Tuesday, Thursday, and Friday from 4:30 to 7. Call ☎ 0461/822820 for information.

I Suoni delle Dolomiti, held in June and July, offer the idyllic experience of chamber music played in grassy meadows, echoing through the mountain air. A series of concerts is held at a number of refuges high in the hills of Trentino. Best of all, the concerts and accompanying hikes are free. For more information, contact the Trento APT (☎ 0461/497326).

Shopping

FOODSTUFFS

The **Enoteca di Corso** (✉ Corso 3 Novembre 54) is an extraordinary shop laden with local products, including cheese, salami, and wine.

MARKETS

The small morning **Mercato di Piazza Lodron** is held in Piazza Allessandro Vittoria, where you can pick up meats, cheeses, produce, local truffles, and porcini mushrooms. On **Piazza Arogno** a flea market is held on the third Sunday of every month; there is also a crafts market every Friday and Saturday; but the big shopping day is Thursday, when the weekly market spreads out around this piazza and winds down next to the cathedral.

WOODEN CRAFTS AND CERAMICS

Il Pozzo (✉ Piazza Pasi 14/l) sells excellent handcrafted wooden objects. **Il Laboratorio** (✉ Via Roma 12) specializes in terra-cotta pieces molded by local artists.

Rovereto

❷ *24 km (15 mi) south of Trento, 75 km (47 mi) south of Bolzano.*

A 15th-century castle looks down on the medieval town of Rovereto, in the main north–south valley of the Adige. Some of the fiercest fighting of World War I took place in the wooded hills around Rovereto, with Italian and Austrian troops bogged down in prolonged and costly conflict. Every evening at nightfall you're reminded of the thousands who fell by the ringing of the Campana dei Caduti (Bell of the Fallen). Today, it's a noble, peaceful city filled with children and bright geraniums. Crumbling pastel-color medieval villas inhabit long-shadowed piazzas and winding streets.

The work of native son Fortunato Depero (1892–1960), a prominent Futurist painter, is featured at various spots throughout town. At press time, Casa Museo Depero, a gallery dedicated only to Depero, was closed indefinitely for renovation, but you'll find a good selection of his work at the **Archivio del '900,** a museum dedicated primarily to the Futurist movement. You'll also find works there by Severni and Mazzoni, as well as rotating exhibits. ✉ *Corso Rosmini 58,* ☎ *0464/438887,* WEB *www.mart.tn.it.* 🎟 *7,000 lire/€3.60.* ☉ *Tues.–Thurs. and weekends 10–6, Fri. 10–6 and 8–10.*

Dining

$$$–$$$$ ✕ **Ristorante Al Borgo.** Renowned throughout Italy for its creative cuisine, Al Borgo has a modernist take on each classic it prepares, even the simple black *tagliolini ai frutti di mare*. Trentino specialties on the menu might include *strangola preti* (literally "priest-chokers," a heavy pasta dish). In fall, you might find *polentina* with a fondue of Trentino cheeses and truffle. The restaurant's interior is elegant and calm, with attractive art adorning the walls. ✉ *Via Garibaldi 13,* ☎ *0464/436300.*

Reservations essential. AE, DC, MC, V. Closed Mon., Jan. 15–26, and July 2–27. No dinner Sun., no lunch Sun. in Aug.

\$\$–\$\$\$ ✕ **Ristorante Novecento.** Co-owner Marco Zani can't for the life of him persuade his grandmother, Wanda, to stop cooking. But after a superb dinner in this airy, candlelit restaurant, part of Hotel Rovereto, you'll be happy she still reigns in the kitchen. Luscious dishes, paired with local wines, include *tortelli con fonduta di formaggi* (pasta squares with spinach and ricotta bathed in a butter sauce) and *quaglia con finferli e polenta* (quail with wild mushrooms and polenta). Top it off with warm apple strudel. ✉ *Corso Rosmini 82/d,* ☎ *0464/435222,* WEB *www.rovhotels.com/Rovereto/Dining/dining.html. AE, DC, MC, V. Closed Sun., 2 wks in Aug., 2 wks in Jan.*

Nightlife and the Arts

The **Rovereto Festival** (☎ 0464/452159) in early September offers modern dance and art exhibitions. Late September welcomes the **Festival Internazionale W. A. Mozart** (☎ 0464/452159), with classical performances at the exquisite **Teatro Zadonai** (✉ Corso Bettini 82, ☎ 0464/452159).

En Route   Traveling south from Rovereto, head west on S240, passing the lovely lakeside town of Riva del Garda, and then north on S45 bis to Comano, a small but locally renowned spa. The road continues to Tione, a small farming community. From here, head north on S239 to reach Pinzolo.

Pinzolo

❸ *75 km (47 mi) northwest of Rovereto, 59 km (37) mi northwest of Trento.*

In this quaint mountain village you can see a remarkable 16th-century fresco on the side of a small church. Follow the signs for the church of **San Vigilio,** which you'll come to after a short walk through the pines. On an exterior wall, a vivid fresco painted in 1539 by the artist Simone Baschenis describes the Dance of Death, with 40 ghoulish figures offering a stern rebuke to potential sinners. Unfortunately, the church is usually closed to the public.

Madonna di Campiglio

★ ❹ *14 km (9 mi) north of Pinzolo, 88 km (55 mi) southwest of Bolzano.*

The chichi winter resort of Madonna di Campiglio has surpassed Cortina d'Ampezzo as the most fashionable place to see and be seen on and off the slopes in the Dolomites. Madonna's popularity is well deserved: more than 130 km (80 mi) of ski runs are groomed and 39 lifts operated. The resort itself is at a 5,000-ft altitude, and some of the ski runs, summer hiking paths, and mountain-biking routes venture onto the surrounding peaks, including Pietra Grande, more than 9,700 ft up. An excursion to the Punta Spinale (Spinale Peak) on the year-round cable car affords magnificent views of the Brenta Dolomites.

Lodging

\$\$\$\$ 🏨 **Golf Hotel.** You'll have to make your way up to Campo Carlo ★ Magno, the famous pass just north of town, to reach this grand hotel, the former summer residence of Habsburg emperor Franz Josef. A modern wing has been added to the more-than-a-century-old structure, but old-world charm persists: Rooms 114 and 214 still exhibit the lavish imperial style. The rest of the resort is replete with verandas, Persian rugs, and bay windows. In summer, the golf course attracts a tony crowd. Note that Golf Hotel offers only half- or full-board packages. ✉ *Via*

Cima Tosa 3, 38084, ☎ 0465/441003, FAX 0465/440294, WEB www. golfhotelcampiglio.it. 111 rooms, 4 suites. Restaurant, bar, minibars, 9-hole golf course. AE, DC, MC, V. Closed mid-Apr.–June and mid-Sept.–mid-Dec. FAP, MAP.

$$$–$$$$ 🏨 **Savoia Palace.** This is one of the more traditional hotels at the resort, full of mountain-style furnishings with lots of carved wood and an intimate atmosphere. Two fireplaces blaze away in the bar, where guests recall the day's exploits on the ski slopes. The elegant restaurant serves a mixture of local specialties and rich dishes drawing on Italian and Austrian influences. Guests stay on full- or half-board terms only. ⊠ *Via Dolomiti di Brenta, 38084, ☎ 0465/441004, FAX 0465/440549. 55 rooms. Restaurant, bar, minibars. AE, DC, MC, V. Closed mid-Apr.–June and mid-Sept.–Nov. FAP, MAP.*

$$–$$$ 🏨 **Grifone.** A comfortable Alpine lodge that catches the sun, the Grifone has distinctive wood paneling on the outside, flower-decorated balconies, and rooms with views of the forested slopes. The restaurant serves home cooking as well as international dishes. The hotel is south of the lake, a bit out of town, but the Spinale cable car is very nearby. Half- or full-board packages are required. ⊠ *Via Vallesinella 7, 38084, ☎ 0465/ 442002 or 0339/2798333, FAX 0465/440540, WEB www.hotelgrifone.it. 40 rooms. Restaurant, bar, in-room safes. AE, DC, MC, V. Closed Apr. 20–June and mid-Sept.–Nov. FAP, MAP.*

Outdoor Activities and Sports

GOLF

On **Campo Carlo Magno** (☎ 0465/441003) is a nine-hole course, set in the mountains near Madonna di Campiglio, open from July through mid-September.

HIKING

The local **tourist office** (☞ Visitor Information *in* The Dolomites: Trentino-Alto Adige A to Z, *below*) supplies maps of the dozen or so treks for walking to waterfalls, lakes, and stupefying views.

SKIING

Madonna di Campiglio offers some of the best skiing in the Dolomites, with kilometers of interconnecting runs linked by cable cars and lifts, a quite respectable vertical drop, and plenty of off-piste opportunities. Advanced skiers will delight in the extremely difficult terrain found on certain mountain faces accessible from town. Of course, there are also many intermediate and beginner runs. Madonna's newfound cachet as the ski resort of choice among young Italians is evident in its increasingly well-organized lodging, skiing, and trekking facilities. Ski passes (40,000 lire/€20.65–45,000 lire/€23.25) can be purchased at the *funivia* (cable car) in town. For more information, call ☎ 0465/ 447744 or visit the web site WEB www.campiglio.net/mcsciait.html.

En Route Just a couple of miles north of Madonna di Campiglio is one of the highest points in the Dolomites, the **Campo Carlo Magno** pass. This is where Charlemagne is said to have stopped in AD 800 on his way to Rome to be crowned emperor. Stop here to glance over the whole of northern Italy. Resume your descent with caution (in the space of a mile or so, you will descend more than 2,000 ft via hairpin turns and switchbacks). The strange, rocky pinnacles of the Dolomites, which jut straight up like chimneys and look at times more like Utah's Monument Valley than any European ranges, loom over scattered mountain lakes. Turn left at Dimaro and continue 37 km (23 mi) east to Ponte di Legno through another high pass, **Passo del Tonale** (5,600 ft). Here turn right on S300 and, passing the so-called Black Lake on your left, head for Bormio, the famous Lombard skiing center, through the **Passo di Gavia,** which also must be approached carefully.

Bormio

❺ *20 km (12 mi) south of Passo dello Stelvio, 100 km (60 mi) southwest of Merano.*

At the foot of the Stelvio Pass, in the Valtellina, Bormio is one of the most famous ski resorts on the western side of the Dolomites, with 38 km (24 mi) of long pistes and a 5,000-ft-plus vertical drop. It differs greatly from Madonna di Campiglio in that it is both a town and a summer resort. With an altitude of close to 4,000 ft Bormio has clean, fresh air that in summer draws Italians escaping the humidity of the cities. There are plenty of shops, restaurants, and hotels throughout the town. Bormio has also been known for the therapeutic qualities of its waters since the Roman era. You'll find spas throughout the town.

Bormio is the place to enter the Alps' biggest national park, the **Parco Nazionale dello Stelvio,** spread over 1,350 square km (520 square mi) and four provinces. Opened in 1935 with the express intent to preserve flora and protect fauna, today it thrives, with more than 1,200 types of plants—not to mention 600 different mushrooms—and more than 160 species of animals, including the chamois, ibex, and roe deer. ✉ *Visitor center, Via Monte Braulio 56,* ☎ *0342/901582,* WEB *www.stelviopark.it.* 🎫 *Free.*

Lodging

$$–$$$ 🏨 **Posta.** Ostelli della Posta hotels, staging inns of days gone by, are a time-honored tradition in northern Italy. The reception and atmosphere of this town-center hotel, with its warm wood detail in the low-vaulted areas, will temper the cold. The rooms are cozy and comfortable, with heavy drapery and bed linens. Perks include a small health center with a pool, sauna, gym, and Turkish bath—and a shuttle bus to the slopes. ✉ *Via Roma 66, 23032,* ☎ *0342/904753,* FAX *0342/904484,* WEB *www.valtline.it/hotelposta. 50 rooms. Restaurant, pub, indoor pool, sauna, Turkish bath, health club. AE, DC, MC, V. Closed May–June 20 and Sept.–Nov.*

$$ 🏨 **Nazionale.** Bordering the Stelvio National Park, this central hotel caters to the winter and summer crowd. Rooms are small but well equipped, with TVs and safes. The exterior is, for the most part, wood, with balconies on nearly all floors except the top. The hotel operates a shuttle bus to and from the cable cars. ✉ *Via al Forte 14, 23032,* ☎ *0342/903361,* FAX *0342/905294,* WEB *www.italiahotel.com/hotel-nazionale. 48 rooms. 2 restaurants, bar, minibars, sauna, shops, recreation room. AE, DC, MC, V. Closed Oct.–Dec.*

Outdoor Activities and Sports

SKIING

Skiing is the main winter activity at Bormio. The main mountain above the town is **Vallecetta,** and the secondary ski area is called San Colombano. The base funivia (☎ 0342/901451) is in the center of Bormio and connects you to a network of lifts above. You can buy a ski pass (48,000 lire/€24.80–52,000 lire/€26.85) and pick up a lift map at the base. From there, the funivia takes you to the Bormio 2000 station, from where you can either ski down easy trails, or (better) get another funivia up to the Cima Bianca station. Bormio is a typical Italian ski resort in that, first, you can ski from the top of the mountain all the way down to the valley, and second, trails are not as well marked or easily discernible as their American counterparts. Terrain is mostly intermediate. As elsewhere in the Dolomites, the most reliable time to ski at Bormio is late February or after, as early season snowfall is variable.

Passo dello Stelvio

★ ⑥ *20 km (12 mi) north of Bormio, 80 km (48 mi) west of Merano.*

At just over 9,000 ft, the Passo dello Stelvio (Stelvio Pass) is the second-highest pass in Europe. The view from the top is worth the effort because the pass connects the Val Venosta with the Valtellina in neighboring Lombardy. Just to the left as you enter the pass is Switzerland. Stelvio is a year-round skiing center, with summer skiing on many of its runs.

En Route   Between the Stelvio Pass and Spondigna are 30 km (19 mi) of picturesque, winding road, with 48 hairpin turns. This section of road can be a bit hair-raising if you don't like mountain driving. In Spondigna keep to the right for the road to Naturno.

BOLZANO

32 km (19 mi) south of Merano, 50 km (31 mi) north of Trento.

Bolzano (Bozen), the capital of the autonomous province of Alto Adige, is nestled among craggy peaks in a Dolomite valley just 77 km (48 mi) from the Brenner Pass to Austria. It is protected by the mountains to the north and the east and is on the main north–south artery between northern Europe and Italy—both by car (the A22 *autostrada*) and by rail (on the well-traveled route to Innsbruck and Munich). Tirolean culture dominates Bolzano's language, food, architecture, and people. It may be hard to remember that you're in Italy and not Austria when walking along the city's colorful, cobblestone streets and visiting its lantern-lit cafés, where you may enjoy sauerkraut and a *Weissbier* among a lively crowd of blond-haired, blue-eyed German-speakers. However, fine Italian espresso, fashionable boutiques, and reasonable prices will help remind you where you are. With castles and steeples topping the landscape instead of high-rises, this quiet city at the confluence of the Isarco (Eisack) and Talvera rivers has retained a provincial appeal. Proximity to fabulous skiing and mountain climbing and pleasant coffee shops and bars make this city a worthwhile, if little-known, tourist stop. And its streets are immaculate: with the highest per capita earnings of any city in Italy and a standard of living that is second to none, Bolzano was voted the best place to live in Italy in a 1996 poll conducted by *L'Espresso* magazine.

Exploring Bolzano

A Good Walk

Begin in **Piazza Walther** ⑦, Bolzano's geographical and cultural center. From the plaza, head to the striking **Duomo** ⑧. Exit the church to your left, heading away from Piazza Walther, and continue to the **Chiesa dei Domenicani** ⑨ (Dominican Church) and connected Cappella di San Giovanni, in Piazza dei Domenicani, where you can see Bolzano's best collection of paintings and frescoes. Exit the church, cross Piazza Domenicani (to the northwest), and head up the charming medieval Via Goethe to the colorful **Piazza delle Erbe** ⑩. At the corner of Via dei Portici is the 1745 bronze Fontana del Nettuno (Fountain of Neptune). Next, head to Via dei Portici, Bolzano's most important shopping street. To your left, at the intersection with Vicolo della Pesa, you will pass Piazza del Grano, the old grain market, and the beautiful Casa della Pesa, on the north side of the plaza, which was the seat of public weighings until 1780. If you want, you can continue through Piazza del Grano and exit to your left onto Via Argentieri, another *vicolo* (ancient street), or continue down Via Portici. Lastly, walk over

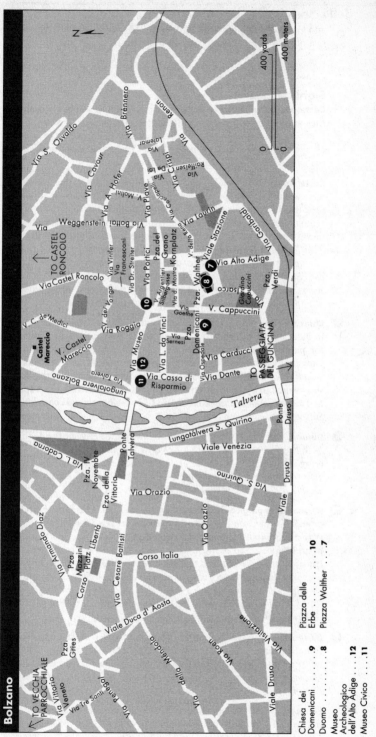

Bolzano

N

400 yards
400 meters

0
0

TO VECCHIA
PARROCCHIALE

Via Vittorio
Veneto

Pza.
Gries

Via Armando Diaz

Via Cesare Battisti

Corso

Via Mazzini
Platz

Via della
Libertà

Pza.
della
Vittoria

Corso Italia

Via Duca d' Aosta

Via Roen

Via Mendola

Viale Druso

Via delle

Via Visitazione

Via Tre Santi la Strada

Via Orazio

Viale Venezia

Via S. Quirino

Viale Druso

Viale Druso

Via Orazio

Pza. IV
Novembre

Via L. Cadorna

Ponte
Talvera

Lungotálvera S. Quirino

Talvera

Ponte
Druso

TO
PASSEGGIATA
DEL GUNCINA

Via Talvera

Lungotalvera Bolzano

Castel
Mareccio

V. C. de' Medici

V. Castel
Mareccio

Via Roggia

Via Museo

Via L. da Vinci

Via Cassa di
Risparmio

Via Sernesi

Pza.
Domenicani

Via Ospedale

Via Dante

Via Carducci

Via della

TO CASTEL
RONCOLO

Via Castel Roncolo

Via Weggenstein

Via

Via S. Osvaldo

Via Brénnero

Via Cavour

Via A. Hofer

Via V. Molini

Via Piave

Via Bottai

Via Vintler

Via
Francescani

Via Dr. Streiter

V. de Vanga

Via Portici

Pza. del
Grano

V. Argentieri
Silbergasse

Via d. Mostra Komplatz

Pza.
Goethe

Via
Goethe

Via Laurin

Raiffeisenstrasse

Via Vanga

Via Dr.

Via Renon

Pza. Walther

Viale Stazione

Via Alto Adige

Giardino
Cappuccini

V. Cappuccini

Via Verdi

Pza.
Verdi

Via Gorbaldi

Via
Laiemar

Via Cristal

Via

Renon

⑩

⑫

⑪

⑧

⑦

⑨

Chiesa dei
Domenicani **9**

Duomo **8**

Museo
Archeologico
dell'Alto Adige **12**

Museo Civico **11**

Piazza delle
Erbe **10**

Piazza Walther **7**

to Via Museo, which will eventually take you to the **Museo Civico** ⑪ and **Museo Archeologico** ⑫, with its 5,300-year-old iceman. Spend the rest of your day enjoying these two museums.

TIMING
Allow at least half a day for this walk.

Sights to See

Castel Mareccio (Schloss Maretsch). The castle dates from the 13th century and is nestled under mountains and surrounded by vineyards. It is now a well-equipped conference center with a restaurant and bar, all open to the public. ⊠ *Lungotalvera Promenade (head north along the river)*, ☎ *0471/976615. Closed Tues.*

Castel Roncolo (Schloss Runkelstein). Restored in 2000, this red-roofed, meticulously kept castle sits among green hills and farmhouses just north of town. It was built in 1237, destroyed half a century later, and then rebuilt soon thereafter. A beautifully preserved cycle of chivalrous medieval frescoes can be viewed inside. A tavern in the courtyard (☎ 0471/324073) serves local food and wines. ⊠ *Via San Antonio, in the San Genesio neighborhood (from Piazza delle Erbe, head north along Via Francescani and continue through Piazza Madonna, connecting to Via Castel Roncolo)*, ☎ *0471/329808*, WEB *www.comune.bolzano.it/roncolo/ie.* 🖾 *10,000 lire/€5.15, guided tour 5,000 lire/€2.60.* ☉ *Tues.–Sun. 10–6.*

❾ **Chiesa dei Domenicani** (Dominican Church). This 13th-century church in Piazza dei Domenicani is renowned as Bolzano's main repository for paintings, especially frescoes. In the adjoining **Cappella di San Giovanni** you can see frescoes of the Giotto school, one of which is a *Triumph of Death* (circa 1340). Despite its macabre title, this fresco shows the birth of a pre-Renaissance sense of depth and individuality. ⊠ *Piazza Domenicani*, ☎ *0471/973133.* ☉ *Church and chapel Mon.–Sat. 9:30–6.*

❽ **Duomo.** The city's Gothic cathedral was built between the 12th and 14th centuries; its lacy spire looks down on the mosaic-like tiles covering its pitched roof. Inside are 14th- and 15th-century frescoes and an intricately carved stone pulpit dating from 1514. ⊠ *Piazza Walther,* ☎ *0471/978676.* ☉ *Weekdays 9:45–noon and 2–5, Sat. 9:45–noon.*

★ ⑫ **Museo Archeologico dell'Alto Adige** (South Tirol Museum of Archeology). This museum has gained international fame for Ötzi, its 5,300-year-old Similaun iceman, discovered in 1991 as the world's oldest naturally preserved body. In 1998, Italy acquired the body from Austria after it was determined that the body lay 200 yards inside Italy. The iceman is displayed in a freezer, complete with his longbow, ax, and even clothing. ⊠ *Museumstrasse 14*, ☎ *0471/982098*, WEB *www.iceman.it.* 🖾 *13,000 lire/€6.70, guided tours 3000 lire/€1.55.* ☉ *Fri.–Wed. 10–6, Thurs. 10–8.*

⑪ **Museo Civico** (Civic Museum). You'll find a rich collection of traditional costumes, wood carvings, and archaeological exhibits here. The mixture of styles reflects the region's cultural cross-fertilization. ⊠ *Via Cassa di Risparmio 14*, ☎ *0471/974625.* 🖾 *7,000 lire/€3.60.* ☉ *May–Oct., Tues.–Sat. 9–12:30 and 2:30–5:30, Sun. 9–1.*

Passeggiata del Guncina is an 8-km (5-mi) botanical promenade, dating from 1892, that culminates in a panoramic view of Bolzano. ⊠ *Quartiere di Gries, follow Via Dante south.*

❿ **Piazza delle Erbe.** A bronze statue of Neptune, which dates back to 1745, presides over a bountiful fruit and vegetable market in this square. The stalls spill over with colorful displays of local produce; bakeries and grocery stores showcase hot breads, pastries, cheeses, and delicatessen meats—a complete range of picnic supplies. Try the speck and the Tirolean-style apple strudel.

❼ Piazza Walther. This pedestrian-only square is Bolzano's heart; it serves as an open-air living room where locals and tourists alike can be found at all hours sipping a drink (perhaps a glass of chilled Riesling) at café tables. This lively square is named after the 12th-century German wandering minstrel Walther von der Vogelweide, whose songs lampooned the papacy and praised the Holy Roman Emperor. In the middle of the plaza is Heinrich Natter's white marble, neo-romanesque **Monument to Walther,** built in 1889.

Vecchia Parrocchiale (Old Parish Church). Said to have been built in 1141, this church in Gries is worth a visit, if only for the elaborately carved 15th-century wooden altar of Michael Pacher, considered a masterpiece of the Gothic style. The 11th-century wooden Romanesque crucifix was probably brought here from France. ⊠ *V. Martin Knoller, in Gries, across the river and down V. della Libertà.* ⊘ *Apr.–Oct., weekdays 10:30–noon and 2:30–4.*

OFF THE BEATEN PATH — **RENON (RITTEN) PLATEAU** – The Earth Pyramids of Renon Plateau make up a bizarre geological formation where erosion has left a forest of tall, thin, needlelike spires of rock, each topped with a boulder. The Soprabolzano funicular leaves from Via Renon, about 300 yards left of the Bolzano train station. At the top, an electric train takes you to the site, which is at Collalbo, just above Bolzano.

Dining and Lodging

$$$ ✕ Abramo. Although outside Bolzano's attractive old center, this restaurant is the best in town. Chef Abramo Pantezi offers an Italian variation of nouvelle cuisine in an attractive setting. At tables set with crystal and silver, you'll choose from seafood dishes such as *salmone allo champagne*. There's a vegetarian antipasto selection. The extensive wine cellar features top-quality California vintages, among others. You can dine alfresco in summer. ⊠ *Piazza Gries 16,* ☎ *0471/280141. AE, DC, MC, V. Closed Sun., Jan. 1–7, and Aug. 1–20.*

$$–$$$ ✕ Zür Kaiserkron. Old-world Tirolean opulence and attentive service set the stage for some of the best food in town. Appetizers might include potato blini with salmon caviar and marinated artichokes with butter (not to be missed if available). Main dishes, such as veal with black truffle and spinach *canederli* (dumplings) make use of ingredients from the local valleys. This restaurant is patronized by dignified local businesspeople and their spouses. ⊠ *Piazzetta Mostra,* ☎ *0471/970770. AE, DC, MC, V. Closed Sun. No dinner Sat.*

$$ ✕ Alexander. Typical Tirolean dishes are served up in a convivial atmosphere at this city-center restaurant. The venison ham and the lamb cutlets *al timo con salsa all'aglio* (with thyme and garlic sauce) are particularly delicious, but make sure to leave room for the rich chocolate cake. ⊠ *Via Aosta 37,* ☎ *0471/918608. AE, DC, MC, V. Closed Sat. No dinner Sun.*

$$ ✕ Gostner Flora's Bistrot. In a medieval tower on Bolzano's market square, this tiny tavern has been around for centuries, and it has been lovingly restored. There is no menu; you choose from a limited number of typical homey Tirolean specialties, different every day. They may include canederli or *schlutzkrapfen* (ravioli). The desserts are homemade, too. The young owner takes pride in a selection of good wine. ⊠ *Piazza delle Erbe 17,* ☎ *0471/974086. No credit cards. Closed Sun. No dinner Sat.*

$ ✕ **Batzenhausl.** A medieval building in the center of town houses this crowded stübe (Tirolean-style drinking hall). It's a popular hangout for the local intellectual set, who hold long, animated conversations over glasses of local wine and tasty local South Tirolean specialties, such as *herrngröstl* (beef on a bed of boiled potatoes) and apple pancakes with ice cream. Try the fried Camembert. ⊠ *Via Andreas Hofer 30,* ☎ *0471/976183. No credit cards. Closed Tues. and 3 wks in June–July. No lunch.*

$ ✕ **Hopfen & Co. Wirtshaus und Brauerie (Bozner Bier).** Authentic and
★ tasty Tirolean specialties like fried white würstel, sauerkraut, and grilled ribs are only a sidelight to the excellent home-brewed Austrian-style pilsner and wheat beer on tap at this lively pub-restaurant, which will transport you from Italy to the north. A stylish young crowd discusses the day's angst at dimly lit dark-wood tables. Live music is played some nights. ⊠ *Piazza delle Erbe 17,* ☎ *0471/300788. AE, MC, V.*

$$$$ ▦ **Hotel Greif.** Even in a hospitable region, the Greif is a rare gem. This
★ small, picturesque, and supremely central hotel has been a Bolzano landmark for centuries, but a beautiful and artistic renovation has now set a standard for modern amenities in Alto Adige. In-room ISDN Internet connections, workstations, and private whirlpool baths are just a few of the perks. Not only are all public and private spaces light, airy, and immaculate, but every room also has a uniquely designed installation by one of a host of South Tirolean artists. ⊠ *Piazza Walther 1, 39100,* ☎ *0471/318000,* 𝔽𝔸𝕏 *0471/318148,* 𝕎𝔼𝔹 *www.greif.it. 33 rooms. Bar, in-room data ports, in-room safes, minibars. AE, DC, MC, V.*

$$$$ ▦ **Park Hotel Laurin.** This hotel, an exercise in Art Nouveau opulence, is set in a large park in the middle of town. Its history is speckled with visits from Europe's grand nobility, including the archduke Franz Ferdinand (whose murder in Sarajevo sparked World War I), King Leopold of Belgium, and Field Marshall Montgomery. Today, it is considered the finest hotel in all of Alto Adige. Some rooms carry through the Belle Epoque decor; others are more modern; all have original paintings by such artists as Oskar Kokoschka, Max Klinger, and Ernst Nepo. A room upgrade has added modern connections. The popular Belle Epoque restaurant prides itself on its use of fresh seasonal ingredients. ⊠ *Via Laurin 4, 39100,* ☎ *0471/311000,* 𝔽𝔸𝕏 *0471/311148,* 𝕎𝔼𝔹 *www.laurin.it. 96 rooms. Restaurant, bar, no-smoking room, in-room safes, minibars, pool, convention center. AE, DC, MC, V.*

$$$–$$$$ ▦ **Schloss Korb.** It's worth the 5-km (3-mi) drive west from Bolzano
★ to reach this hotel. It's set in a romantic 13th-century castle with crenellations and a massive central tower, perched in a park amid vine-covered hills. Much of the ancient decor is preserved, and the public rooms are filled with Tirolean antiques, elaborate wood carvings, old paintings, and attractive plants. The rooms are comfortably furnished—some tower rooms have Romanesque arched windows. ⊠ *Missiano, Strada Castel d'Appiano 5, 39050,* ☎ *0471/636000,* 𝔽𝔸𝕏 *0471/ 636033. 57 rooms, 5 suites. Indoor pool, sauna, 2 tennis courts. No credit cards. Closed Nov.–Easter.*

$$$ ▦ **Luna-Mondschein.** This central yet secluded hotel was built in 1798. Set in a lovely garden, it washes a tranquil, friendly calm over its guests. The rooms are comfortable, with wood paneling throughout. Some rooms overlooking the garden have balconies, but even the rooms overlooking the garage have good views of the mountains. The two restaurants include a typical Tirolean weinstube that serves inexpensive local specialties in a cozy, convivial setting. ⊠ *Via Piave 15, 39100,* ☎ *0471/975642,* 𝔽𝔸𝕏 *0471/975577,* 𝕎𝔼𝔹 *www.hotel-luna.it. 85 rooms. Restaurant, weinstube. AE, DC, MC, V.*

Nightlife and the Arts

Fairs

Spring is heralded each May with large flower markets and events, including concerts and folklore and art exhibits. On August 24 is the **Bartolomeo Horse Fair,** on Renon Mountain just northeast of the town. Hundreds of farmers converge for a day of serious trading and frivolous merriment.

Music

There is a lively music scene in town. Information is available at the tourist office. For opera information and schedules, call **Friends of Opera** (☎ 0471/913223)). Orchestra concerts are often held at **Haus der Kultur** (⌂ Via Sciliar 1, ☎ 0471/977520). The **Park Hotel Laurin Bar** (⌂ Via Laurin 4, ☎ 0471/311000) is a good place to hear jazz.

Theater

Theater is popular in Bolzano—contact the tourist office for a weekly schedule. A frequently used venue is the imposing **Nuovo Teatro Comunale** (⌂ Piazza Verdi, ☎ 0471/304112). **Cortile Theater im Hof** (⌂ Piazza delle Erbe 37, ☎ 0471/980756) specializes in children's theater. Note that performances may be in German.

Outdoor Activities and Sports

Biking

If you're in decent shape, a great way to see some of the surrounding castles, lakes, and forested valleys of the Dolomites is by bike. **Alp Bike** (☎ 0471/272024) offers guided excursions leaving from Piazzale dello Stadio Druso for 15,000 lire/€7.75 per person. Different trips are offered virtually every day, at all levels, but you must reserve a week or more ahead for the more ambitious trips.

Hiking

Club Alpino Italiano (⌂ Piazza delle Erbe 46, ☎ 0471/978172, WEB www. cai.it) is a helpful organization that provides information for hiking and rock climbing. It is important to follow safety procedures and to have all the latest information on trails and conditions.

Tennis

Courts can be found in Bolzano at **Circolo Tennis Bolzano** (⌂ Via Maso della Pieve, ☎ 0471/250598).

Shopping

Local Crafts

The long, narrow arcades of **Via dei Portici** house shops that specialize in Tirolean crafts and clothing—lederhosen, loden goods, linen suits, and dirndls. The best store for locally made handcrafted goods is **Artigiani Atesini** (⌂ Via Portici 39).

Markets

From the end of November to Christmas Eve there is a traditional **Christkindlmarkt** in the main square of Bolzano, with stalls selling all kinds of Christmas decorations and local handcrafted goods. An outdoor fruit and vegetable market takes over the central **Piazza delle Erbe** on Monday through Saturday from 8 to 1. A big weekly flea market takes place Saturday morning in **Piazza della Vittoria.**

ALTO ADIGE AND CORTINA

Alto Adige (Südtirol), the northern half of the region and for centuries part of the Austro-Hungarian Empire, was ceded to Italy at the end of

World War I. As a result, everything here has more than a tinge of the Teutonic, which is nowhere more apparent than in the fact that the majority of the inhabitants speak German. Ethnic differences have led to inevitable tensions (including, alas, acts of terrorism), though a large measure of autonomy has, for the most part, kept the lid on nationalist ambitions.

Naturno

⑬ *61 km (38 mi) east of Passo dello Stelvio, 44 km (27 mi) northwest of Bolzano.*

Colorful houses with painted murals on their walls line the streets of Naturno, a major horticultural center. Art lovers will appreciate the church of **San Procolo,** which is frescoed inside and out and has wall paintings that are the oldest in the German-speaking world, dating from the 8th century. ☉ *Sun. 8–8.*

Above the town, a short distance away, is the 13th-century **Castello Juval,** since 1983 the home of the South Tirolese climber and polar adventurer Reinhold Messner—the first man to conquer Everest solo and the first to scale all 14 of the world's highest peaks without oxygen. Since 1995, part of the castle has been a museum, showing Messner's collection of Tibetan art, mountaineering illustrations, and masks from around the world. ✉ *Viale Europa 2,* ☎ *0473/221852.* 💶 *12,000 lire/€6.20.* ☉ *Mid-Apr.–June and Sept.–mid-Nov., daily 9–5.*

Dining

$$ ✕ **Juval Inn.** Just below Castello Juval, Reinhold Messner's Juval Inn is an old-style hostelry in a restored farmhouse, serving traditional local dishes and wines provisioned from his own farm. ✉ *Schlosswirt-Juval,* ☎ *0473/668238. No credit cards. Closed Wed., July, and Nov.–Easter.*

Merano

★ **⑭** *24 km (15 mi) north of Bolzano, 100 km (62 mi) northeast of Bormio.*

The second-largest town in the Alto Adige, Merano was once the capital of the Austrian region of Tirol; when the town and surrounding area were ceded to Italy as part of the 1919 Treaty of Versailles, Innsbruck became the capital. Merano, however, continued to be known as a spa town, attracting European nobility for its therapeutic waters and its peculiar grape cure, which consists simply of eating the grapes grown on the surrounding hillsides. Sheltered by mountains, Merano has an unusually mild climate, with summer temperatures rarely exceeding 80°F and winters that usually stay above freezing, despite the skiing that is within easy reach. Chairlifts and cable cars connect Merano with the high Alpine slopes of Avelengo and San Vigilio. Along the narrow streets of Merano's Old Town, houses have little towers and huge wooden doors, and the pointed arches of the Gothic cathedral sit next to neoclassical and Art Nouveau–style buildings. Whether you come to be healed by grapes and thermal springs or simply to take in the town's fresh Alpine air, pretty cobblestone streets, and fashionable boutiques, Merano will serve as a good respite from either skiing or capital-hopping.

In the heart of the Old Town, on **Piazza del Duomo,** is the 14th-century Gothic **cathedral,** with a crenellated facade and an ornate campanile. The Capella di Santa Barbara, just behind the cathedral, is an octagonal church containing a 15th-century Pietà. ✉ *Piazza del Duomo.* ☉ *Easter–Sept., daily 8–noon and 2:30–8; Oct.–Easter, daily 8–noon and 2:30–7.*

The **Terme di Merano** (thermal baths) are a huge complex of spa facilities; although some hotels have their own, these separate *terme* are unique. Technicians are trained to treat you with mud packs, massages, and inhalation and sauna routines, or just with the thermal waters, which are said to be especially good for coronary and circulatory problems. Other cures include the famous grape cure at harvesttime in the fall, when a two-week diet of fresh grapes has, since Roman times, been reputed to tone up digestive, liver, and urinary tract functions. ⊠ *Via Piave 9,* ☎ *0473/237724.* ⊠ *15,000 lire/€7.75 for baths; other treatments extra.* ⊗ *Mon.–Sat. 8–noon and 3–7.*

Overlooking the town atop Mt. Tappeinerweg is a castle that was the home of poet Ezra Pound from 1958 to 1964. Still in the Pound family, the castle now houses the **Brunnenburg Agrarian Museum,** devoted to Tirolean country life. Among its exhibits are a blacksmith's shop and, not surprisingly, a room with Pound memorabilia. To get there, take Bus 3, which departs every hour on the hour, from Merano to Dorf Tirol. ⊠ *Ezra Pound Weg 6,* ☎ *0473/923533.* ⊠ *4,000 lire/€2.05.* ⊗ *Apr.–Oct., Wed.–Mon. 9:30–5.*

Dining and Lodging

$$$–$$$$ ✕ **Andrea.** This relaxed but splendid showcase for fine cuisine and service is just off Via dei Portici and right by a cable-car station. Surrounded by wood paneling and lots of green plants, you can dine on creative local and international dishes, such as risotto *alle erbe* (with herbs) and *filetto di vitello con salsa di alloro* (veal fillet with bay-leaf sauce). A set menu (about 100,000 lire/€52) offers a complete five-course dinner, including superb wine. ⊠ *Via Galilei 44,* ☎ *0473/237400. Reservations essential. Jacket and tie. AE, DC, MC, V. Closed Mon. and Feb. No dinner Sun. in Nov.–Mar.*

$$$–$$$$ ✕ **Schloss Maur.** Stained-glass lamps and wood paneling create a warm
★ Art Nouveau ambience in this restaurant in the Hotel Palace. Schloss Maur is the height of elegance—with huge marble columns, high ceilings, and crystal chandeliers—and the prices reflect it. Italian and international dishes include the signature spaghetti with a sauce of zucchini, sage, and green pepper as well as roast saddle of lamb with lobster. ⊠ *Hotel Palace, Via Cavour 2,* ☎ *0473/271000. Reservations essential. AE, DC, MC, V. Closed Wed., 10 days in Mar., June 20–July 20, and Nov. No lunch.*

$$–$$$ ✕ **Flora.** There's room for only about 20 diners in this intimate candlelit restaurant under the historic arcades of Merano's ancient center. Chef Louis Oberstolz serves a creative seven-course set menu using only natural ingredients. Among the specialties are *quaglia ripiena con fegato d'oca grasso* (boned quail stuffed with foie gras) and *schlutzkrapfen* (fresh ravioli with various fillings). ⊠ *Via dei Portici 75,* ☎ *0473/231484. Reservations essential. AE, DC, MC, V. Closed Sun. and mid-Jan.–mid-Feb. No lunch Mon.*

$–$$ ✕ **Terlaner Weinstube Putz.** This local favorite is a rustic stübe in Merano's Old Town. The seasonal menu focuses on Tirolean specialties. Try *zuppa al vino bianco* (stew with white wine) and the various risottos, including the ones with asparagus in the spring and with Barolo in chillier months. ⊠ *Via dei Portici 231,* ☎ *0473/235571. No credit cards. Closed Wed. in Feb.–Mar., and July.*

$$$$ ⊞ **Castel Labers.** On a hilltop amid forested slopes about 3 km (2 mi) northeast of Merano's center, this castle hotel with red-tile gables, towers, and turrets is unmistakably Tirolean in style. Ceiling beams, painted fresco decorations, and crossed halberds on the walls complete the look. The hospitable Stapf-Neubert family owns the hotel and takes an active part in its management. ⊠ *Via Labers 25, 39012,* ☎

0473/234484, FAX *0473/234146. 32 rooms. Restaurant, pool, tennis court. No credit cards. Closed Dec.–Mar.*

$$$$ ⊞ **Hotel Palace.** Merano's grandest hotel is an opulent old-world in-
★ stitution set in an extensive garden. The public rooms are attractive and comfortable, with Art Nouveau touches, Tiffany glass, marble pillars, and high ceilings; the guest rooms are spacious. The impressive spa features various baths, massages, mud treatments, and other cures. A lovely fountain gurgles with thermal Merano water. Rooftop suites have balconies with stunning views of Merano's steeples and the surrounding mountains. The excellent Schloss Maur restaurant serves a wide variety of local and international dishes. ⊠ *Via Cavour 2, 39012,* ☎ *0473/271000,* FAX *0473/271100,* WEB *www.palace.it. 136 rooms. 2 restaurants, bar, indoor-outdoor pool, spa. AE, DC, MC, V.*

$$ ⊞ **Hotel Minerva.** If you don't feel like dishing out for the prices charged by Merano's better-known resort hotels but still want a bit of luxury, then this classic hotel might be your best bet. All rooms are done in the Germanic, heavy-wood style of the area and are very warm in winter; most have balconies that afford lovely views over the town. ⊠ *Via Cavon 95, 39012,* ☎ *0473/236712,* FAX *0473/230460. 46 rooms. Restaurant, bar, pool. AE, DC, MC, V.*

Nightlife and the Arts

There are plenty of nighttime options in and around Merano. Younger visitors might enjoy a night at the **Manhattan Disco** (⊠ Corso della Libertà, ☎ 0471/449655), which has the latest in dance music. More mellow cafés line **Passerpromenade,** along the river. If you can do without ultramodern sound and you have a car, you might want to check out **Dancing Club Exclusif** (☎ 0471/561711), 10 km (6 mi) east in the tiny village of Lana, which caters to an older, more sedate crowd. The **Grape Festival** on the second Sunday of October has parades and wine tastings in Piazza del Duomo.

Outdoor Activities and Sports

Farmers test their horses in the highly charged **horse race** on Easter Monday. **Tennis Club Merano** (⊠ Via Piave 46, ☎ 0473/230313) maintains nine clay courts (four indoor) and two hard courts that are open to the public. Lessons are given at the tennis university.

Shopping

Merano's main shopping street, the narrow, arcaded **Via dei Portici** (Laubengasse), runs west from the cathedral. It features most of the best regional products—wood carvings, Tirolean-style clothing, embroidery, cheeses, salami, and fruit schnapps—along with more standard clothing-boutique shopping. From the end of November until Christmas Eve, Merano holds a traditional **Christkindlmarkt** (Christmas market) in the main square.

Cornedo

🕕 *6 km (4 mi) east of Bolzano.*

At the mouth of the Ega Valley (Eggental), Cornedo is a place to savor the view of the Catinaccio Mountains. Craggy peaks seem to be props for a lighting display, as pink and purple reflections dance over huge rocks. Their creation is the subject of a local German legend that tells of King Laurin, who lived in a vast palace on the Catinaccio, at a time when the mountain was covered with roses. King Laurin became infatuated with the daughter of a neighboring king, Similde, and kidnapped her, but Similde, searching for his daughter, recognized her place of imprisonment by the red roses that grew there. Laurin freed the girl and was made Similde's prisoner. When Laurin finally escaped he decreed that the betraying roses should be turned to rocks, so that they could be seen neither by day nor by night. Today, the spectacular pinkish-red display is at its best at dawn and at sunset.

Chiusa

 24 km (15 mi) north of Cornedo, 30 km (19 mi) northeast of Bolzano.

Beautiful narrow streets lined with houses built in the 15th and 16th centuries best characterize Chiusa (Klausen), the main town in the Val Isarco. Geraniums and begonias fill window boxes beneath the carved wooden shutters. From here you can catch a bus east to Val di Funes, where **Santa Maddalena** is spectacularly hemmed in by the Geisler Peaks and offers good walking terrain and hotels.

Above the town of Chiusa is the Benedictine monastery of **Saviona** (Saeben), built as a castle in the 10th century but occupying a site that was fortified in Roman times. The monastery buildings date from the late Middle Ages and are a mixture of Romanesque and Gothic architecture, surrounded by walls and turrets. Guided visits are organized by the Tourist Association in Chiusa; contact the local **tourist office** (⊠ Piazza Tinne 6, ☎ 0472/847424).

Bressanone

14 km (9 mi) north of Chiusa, 40 km (25 mi) northeast of Bolzano.

Bressanone (Brixen) is an important artistic center of the Alto Adige and was the seat of prince-bishops for centuries. Like their counterparts in Trento, these medieval administrators had the delicate task of serving two opposing masters—the pope (the ultimate spiritual supervisor) and the Holy Roman Emperor (the civil and military leader). Since the papacy and the Holy Roman Empire were virtually at war throughout the Middle Ages, Bressanone's prince-bishops became experts at tact and diplomacy in order to survive. As you arrive from Brunico, you enter the town on Via Mercato Vecchio, a broad road leading to the imposing **Duomo.** It was built in the 13th century but acquired a Baroque facade 500 years later, and its 14th-century cloister is decorated with medieval frescoes. ⊠ *Piazza Duomo.* ☉ *Easter–Sept., daily 8–8; Oct.–Easter, daily 8–7.*

The Bishop's Palace, which now houses the **Museo Diocesano** (Diocesan Museum), is a treasure trove of local medieval art, particularly Gothic wood carving. The wooden statues and liturgical objects were all collected from the cathedral treasury. During the Christmas season, the curators highlight displays of the museum's large collection of antique nativity scenes; look for the shepherds wearing Tirolean hats. ⊠ *Palazzo Vescovile,* ☎ *0472/830505,* ⓦⒺⒷ *www.dioezesanmuseum.bz.it.* 🎟 *8,000 lire/€4.15, nativity scenes exhibition only 3,000 lire/€1.55.* ☉ *Mar. 15–Oct., Mon.–Sun. 10–5; nativity scenes Dec. 15–Feb. 10, Mon.–Sat. 2–5.*

Dining and Lodging

$$ ✕ **Fink.** This restaurant under the arcades in the pedestrians-only town
★ center has a friendly staff and offers an affordable daily set menu. It has a rustic ambience upstairs with lots of wood paneling and serves international as well as hearty Tirolean specialties. Try the *carré di maiale gratinato* (pork roasted with cheese and served with cabbage and potatoes) or the *castrato alla paesana* (a kind of lamb stew). ⊠ *Via Portici Minori 4,* ☎ *0472/834883. AE, MC, V. Closed Wed., July 1–14, and Feb. 1–14. No dinner Tues. in Oct.–June.*

$$$–$$$$ 🏨 **Elephant.** This cozy inn, one of the area's best hotels, is in a historic
★ 16th-century building. The hotel takes its name from an incident in

1550, when King John III of Portugal stopped here for a few days while leading an elephant over the Alps as a present for Austria's Emperor Ferdinand. Each room is different, many with antiques and paintings. Housed on the park property is the separate Villa Marzari, with 14 rooms. The hotel restaurant is known as one of the region's best. ⊠ *Via Rio Bianco 4, 39042,* ☎ *0472/832750,* FAX *0472/836579,* WEB *www.acs.it/elephant. 45 rooms. Restaurant, pool, tennis court. DC, MC, V. Closed Nov. 15–Dec. 25 and Jan. 10–Mar. 17.*

$$ ⊡ **Croce d'Oro** (Goldenes Kreuz). A five-centuries-old tradition of hospitality is still practiced by the Reiserer family at this centrally placed hotel. Shops line the ground floor of the pink building, with styles inside ranging from the more modern, tasteful reception area to the tavern-style bar. The rooms are spacious with sturdy wood appointments. ⊠ *Bastioni Minori 8, 30042,* ☎ *0472/836155,* FAX *0472/ 834255. 72 rooms. Restaurant, bar. No credit cards.*

Shopping
From the end of November until Christmas Eve there is a traditional **Christkindlmarkt** (Christmas market) in the main square of Bressanone, with stalls selling all kinds of Christmas decorations and local handcrafted goods.

Brunico (Bruneck)

★ ⑱ *33 km (20 mi) east of Bressanone, 65 km (40 mi) northwest of Cortina d'Ampezzo.*

With its medieval quarter nestling below the 13th-century bishop's castle, Brunico (Bruneck) is in the heart of the Val Pusteria. This picturesque little town, noted for its quiet and relaxing qualities, is divided by the Rienza River, with the old quarter on one side and the modern quarter on the other.

The **Museo degli Usi e Costumi della Provincia di Bolzano** (Bolzano Province Customs and Costumes Museum, or Ethnographic Museum) re-creates a typical local village and is built around an authentic 300-year-old mansion. The wood-carving displays are the most interesting. It's in the district of Teodone, just outside the town. ⊠ *Via Duca Teodone 24,* ☎ *0474/550781.* ☞ *6,000 lire/€3.10.* ◷ *Mid-Apr.–Oct., Tues.–Sat. 9:30–5:30, Sun. 2–6.*

Lodging
$$ ⊡ **Andreas Hofer.** There's a Tirolean feel to this bright, comfortable hotel set in a large garden outside the center of town. Rooms are modern, with chalet-style balconies overlooking the Val Pusteria. ⊠ *Via Campo Tures 1, 39031,* ☎ *0474/551469,* FAX *0474/551283,* WEB *www.andreashofer.it. 54 rooms. Restaurant, weinstube, sauna. MC, V. Closed Dec. 10–24 and May 1–20.*

$$ ⊡ **Post.** This traditional, homey, yellow-and-blue hotel is distinguished by its friendly rates and restaurant, café, and pastry shop. It has its own parking, which is important because of the pedestrians-only rules in effect throughout much of the central area. ⊠ *Via Bastioni 9, 39031,* ☎ *0474/555127,* FAX *0474/551603,* WEB *www.hotelpost-bruneck.com. 54 rooms, 45 with bath. Restaurant, café, weinstube, free parking. MC, V. Closed Nov.*

Outdoor Activities and Sports
On January 22, locals turn up for the **dogsled race,** and there seems nary a soul without a flask of hot mulled wine to back a favorite. A comparatively inexpensive **ski area** is at Badia Valley, reached by heading south on S244 from Brunico.

Dobbiaco (Toblach)

⑲ *25 km (16 mi) east of Brunico, 34 km (21 mi) north of Cortina d'Ampezzo.*

In Dobbiaco (Toblach), just 12 km (7 mi) to the east along the Drau Valley, Austria's influence intensifies. Italian is spoken grudgingly here, Austrian money is accepted at most shops and restaurants, and the locals appear more blond and blue-eyed than the average Italian. The atmosphere is almost more Austrian than Austria—it is not surprising that Gustav Mahler (1860–1911), the great Austrian composer, came here often for inspiration.

Lodging

$$$–$$$$ 🏨 **Cristallo.** Wood beams and paneling lend an Old Tirolean patina to this small hotel set in a garden just outside town. The architecture and furnishings reflect the local preference for combining traditional chalet design with functional, comfortable modern furniture. You can relax in the cozy and informal stübe. ✉ *Viale S. Giovanni 37, 39034,* ☎ *0474/972138,* 🖷 *0474/972755,* 🌐 *www.hotelcristallo.com/. 30 rooms. Restaurant, bar, indoor pool. AE, MC, V. Closed mid-Apr.–mid-May and mid-Oct.–mid-Dec.*

$$–$$$ 🏨 **Alpino Monte Rota/Alpengasthof Ratsberg.** To reach this hotel, ★ you can take the 10-minute cable-car ride to Monte Rota or drive up by car. It is in traditional style, with the timeless look of local chalets. Front rooms have stunning mountain views from balconies, and those in the back look out over the dense mountain forest. You needn't take the cable car back down for sustenance: the Alpino has a good restaurant, a bar, and a Tirolean-style stübe. ✉ *Monte Rota 10, 39034,* ☎ *0474/972916,* 🖷 *0474/972213,* 🌐 *www.alpenhotel-ratsberg.com. 30 rooms. Restaurant, bar, pool, sauna. No credit cards. Closed Easter–May and Oct. 20–mid-Dec.*

Outdoor Activities and Sports

SKIING

Prepared trails for cross-country skiing (usually loops marked off by kilometers) accommodate differing degrees of ability. One of the best of this kind can be found at **Dobbiaco.** Inquire at the local tourist office. Downhill skiing can be found at **Monte Rota** slopes, accessible from Dobbiaco. These offer considerably lower rates than in many of the more exclusive resorts.

Cortina d'Ampezzo

★ **⑳** *30 km (19 mi) south of Dobbiaco, 140 km (87 mi) east of Bolzano.*

Cortina d'Ampezzo, for many, is what an Italian ski resort is all about. It has been the mountain resort of choice for much of the northern Italian elite for more than a hundred years and was host to the 1956 Winter Olympics. While Cortina is still drawing plenty of visitors, some of its glamour has faded. In recent years, this destination has been eclipsed by Madonna di Campiglio in terms of popularity, especially among younger Italians and soccer stars.

"The Pearl of the Dolomites" is set in a lush meadow 4,000 ft above sea level. Dense forests adjoin the town, and mountains completely encircle the valley. The town sprawls across the slopes along a fast-moving stream; a public park extends along one bank. Luxury hotels and the villas of the rich are conspicuously scattered over the slopes above the town—identifiable by their attempts to hide behind stands of firs and spruces. Cortina's long and picturesque ski runs will delight intermediates, although advanced carvers might lust for steeper terrain (which can only be found off-piste). The bustling center of Cortina d'Ampezzo has little nostalgia for old-time atmosphere, despite its Alpine appearance. The tone is set by fancy shops and stylish cafés, as opulent as their well-dressed patrons, whose corduroy knickerbockers may well have been tailored by Armani. Cortina is the place to go for a whiff of the heady aroma of wealth and sophistication and retains a more Italian feel than most of its Alto Adige neighbors; if you want authentic Tirolean gemütlichkeit, pass through Cortina and stop at one of the more low-key resorts.

On Via Cantore, a winding road heading up out of town to the northeast (becoming SS 48), you can stop and see the **Olympic Bobsled Course,** a leftover from the 1956 Winter Games. The course is open for bobsledding at certain unpredictable times. To get to the **Olympic Ice Stadium,** head north on Via Dello Stadio at the north end of town.

Dining and Lodging

$$$–$$$$ ✕ **De la Poste.** There are two restaurants in the exclusive De la Poste hotel on Cortina's main square—both have a casually chic clientele and a lively atmosphere. There's a refined, high-ceiling main dining room with three big chandeliers where you can dine on soufflés and nouvelle cuisine dishes (every Friday fresh fish is served). There's also a more informal grill room with wood paneling and the family pewter collection. ⊠ *Piazza Roma 14,* ☎ *0436/4271,* WEB *www.hotels.cortina.it/delaposte. Reservations essential. Jacket and tie in dining room. AE, DC, MC, V.*

$$–$$$ ✕ **Tavernetta.** Near the Olympic ice-skating rink, this popular restaurant has an authentic Tirolean ambience, with wood-paneled dining rooms and a local clientele. Here you can try Cortina specialties such as *zuppa di porcini* (porcini mushroom soup), ravioli *di cervo* (stuffed with venison), and game. ⊠ *Via dello Stadio 27/a,* ☎ *0436/867494. AE, DC, MC, V. Closed Wed., mid-June–mid-July, and Nov. No lunch Thurs. in May and Sept.*

$$$$ 🏠 **De la Poste.** Skiers who want to see and be seen return year after year to this lively hotel; one of Cortina's social centers, the hotel's main terrace bar is always crowded. The hotel has been under the same family management since 1826, and the furnishings feature antiques in characteristic Dolomite style. Almost all rooms have wooden balconies. In winter, the hotel offers pricier half-board plans only. ⊠ *Piazza Roma 62, 32043,* ☎ *0436/4271,* FAX *0436/868435,* WEB *www.hotels.cortina.it/ delaposte. 83 rooms. Restaurant, bar. AE, DC, MC, V. Closed mid-Apr.–mid-June and mid-Oct.–mid-Dec.*

$$$$ 🏠 **Miramonti Majestic.** This imposing and luxe hotel, over a century old, has a magnificent mountain-valley position about 1 km (½ mi) south of town. A touch of old-world formality comes through in the imperial Austrian design, and the interior reflects the period style throughout. There's always a roaring fire in the splendid bar, and the hotel's recreation rooms are framed by windows overlooking mountain vistas. The history of Cortina is intricately tied into the Miramonti, and you'll feel a part of it all here. ⊠ *Località Peziè 103, 32043,* ☎ *0436/ 4201,* FAX *0436/867019,* WEB *cortina.dolomiti.org/hmiramonti. 105 rooms. Restaurant, pool, sauna, golf course, tennis court, gym. AE, DC, MC, V. Closed Easter–June and Sept. 15–Dec. 20.*

$$$–$$$$ 🏠 **Corona.** This cozy Alpine lodge is run by Luciano Rimoldi, a noted ski instructor who has coached such luminaries as downhiller Alberto Tomba. Modern art adorns small but comfortable pine-paneled rooms. The bar is a pleasant place to sit, and the hotel—across the river from town—is a five-minute walk to the town center and a 10-minute bus ride to the lifts (a ski bus stops at the hotel). Note that half-board is required. ⊠ *Via Val di Sotto 12, 32040,* ☎ *0436/3251,* FAX *0436/867339,*

WEB *www.sunrise.it/cortina/link/hcorona.html. 44 rooms. Restaurant, bar. AE, DC, MC, V. Closed Apr.–June and Sept. 10–Dec. 5. MAP.*

Nightlife and the Arts

At the **Europa** hotel (⊠ Corso Italia 207, ☎ 0436/3221) you can expect to mingle with the couture set at the VIP disco; nonguests are welcome, but don't expect to spend less than 50,000 lire/€26.

Outdoor Activities and Sports

SKIING

Cortina d'Ampezzo has downhill slopes to challenge all levels of skiers. The most impressive views (and steepest slopes) in town are on **Monte Cristallo**, based at **Misurina**. The **Faloria** gondola runs from the center of town. From its top, you can get up to most of the other central mountains. Farther out of town, don't miss the **Cinque Torri** and **Passo Falzarego** runs either. All runs are covered by the **Dolomiti Superski** pass (☎ 0471/795397, WEB www.dolomitisuperski.com), good for the entire region.

En Route   As you enter the Crepa Tunnel along the S48 from Cortina d'Ampezzo, the ascent for the Passo di Falzarego begins. The **Passo Pordoi** will lead to the so-called Heart of the Dolomites. The roads around this region of the Sella mountains are deemed to be among the most spectacular in Europe, and many consider their rugged beauty to be unparalleled. A fork in the road farther ahead will lead left to Canazei and right into Val Gardena.

HEART OF THE DOLOMITES

The area between Cortina d'Ampezzo east to Bolzano is dominated by two major valleys, the Val di Fassa and the famous Val Gardena. Both share the spectacular panorama of the Sella mountain range, known because of its circular shape as the Heart of the Dolomites. Val di Fassa is made up primarily of the Grande Strada delle Dolomiti (Great Dolomites Road), which runs from the mountain resort of Cortina d'Ampezzo as far as Bolzano. The route, opened in 1909, now comprises 110 km (68 mi) of easy grades and smooth driving between the two cities.

With some of the best views of the Dolomites, Val Gardena is famous as a ski resort, freckled with well-equipped, picturesque towns overlooked by the oblong Sasso Lungo (Long Rock), which is more than 10,000 ft above sea level. It is also home of the Ladins, descendants of soldiers sent by the Roman emperor Tiberius to conquer the Celtic population of the area in the 1st century AD. Forgotten in the narrow cul-de-sacs of isolated mountain valleys, the Ladins have developed their own folk traditions and speak an ancient dialect that is derived from Latin and is similar to Romansch, spoken in some high valleys in Switzerland.

Canazei

㉑   *60 km (37 mi) west of Cortina d'Ampezzo, 52 km (32 mi) east of Bolzano.*

Of the towns in the Val di Fassa, Canazei is the most popular ski resort as well as a summer haven. The slopes around this small town are threaded with mountain trails and ski slopes, surrounded by large pockets of conifers.

OFF THE
BEATEN PATH

COL RODELLA – An excursion from Campitello di Fassa to the vantage point at Col Rodella is a must. The cable car rises some 3,000 ft up the mountain to this most panoramic of vistas. From the balcony at the top you can see full circle around the region, including the Sasso Lungo and the rest of the Sella range.

Lodging

$$–$$$ 🏠 **Alla Rosa.** Centrally located, the hotel has a modest restaurant with a choice of either local or international cuisine, and a cozy bar. The three-story building has balconies on half the rooms and large reception areas. The bedrooms are well laid out with a pleasant rustic and modern mix, but the real attraction is the view over the imposing Dolomites. Half-board is required. ✉ *Via Dolomite 142, 39046,* ☎ *0462/601107,* FAX *0462/601481. 37 rooms. Restaurant, bar, recreation room. MC, V. Closed Oct. MAP.*

En Route   **Passo di Sella** is one of the most famous mountain passes in the Dolomites. It can be approached from the S48 and continues into Val Gardena through the most panoramic mountain scenery in Europe. The road descends to Ortisei, passing the small ski resort of Santa Cristina.

Ortisei (St. Ulrich)

㉒   *28 km (17 mi) north of Canazei, 35 km (22 mi) northeast of Bolzano.*

Ortisei (St. Ulrich), the jewel in the crown of Val Gardena's ski resorts, is a hub of activity in summer as well as winter. There are hundreds of miles of hiking trails and several hundred miles of accessible ski slopes, including the Siusi slopes to the south. Hotels are everywhere and facilities are excellent, with swimming pools, ice rinks, health spas, tennis courts, and bowling. Most impressive of all is the location, a valley surrounded by formidable views in all directions. The Val Gardena comes alive with a parade of horse-drawn sleighs on January 1. For further information on activities in Val Gardena, contact the main tourist office in Ortisei (☞ Visitor Information *in* The Dolomites: Trentino-Alto Adige A to Z, *below*).

For centuries, Ortisei has also been famous for the expertise of its woodcarvers, and there are still numerous workshops here. Apart from making religious sculptures—particularly the wayside Calvaries you come upon everywhere in the Dolomites—Ortisei's carvers were long famous for producing wooden dolls, horses, and other toys. As itinerant peddlers, they traveled every spring on foot with their loaded packs as far as Paris, London, and St. Petersburg to sell their wares. Fine historic and contemporary examples of all kinds of locally carved wooden sculptures and artifacts can be seen at the **Museo della Val Gardena** at Cesa di Ladins. ✉ *Via Rezia 83, Ortisei,* ☎ *0471/797554,* WEB *www.val-gardena.com/italiano/art/museum-ladin.htm.* 🎫 *5,000 lire/€2.60.* ☉ *July–Aug., Mon., Tues., and Thurs.–Sat. 10–noon and 2:30–6; Wed. 10–noon, 2:30–6, and 8:30–10; June and Sept., Tues.–Fri. 2:30–6:30; Feb. 6–Mar. 16, Tues.–Fri. 2:30–5:30.*

Lodging

$$$–$$$$ 🏠 **Adler.** Since 1810, this hotel, one of the best in the valley, has been under the same family management. Set in a large park, the original building has been enlarged several times in the intervening years, yielding spacious guest rooms, but it retains a lot of the old turreted-castle appeal. The Tirolean character is carried through in special parties held once a week for guests. Note that half-board is required here. ✉ *Via Rezia 7, 39046,* ☎ *0471/775000,* FAX *0471/775555,* WEB *www.hotel-adler.com. 101 rooms, most with bath. Restaurant, bar, pool, hair salon, sauna, tennis court, health club. AE, DC, MC, V. Closed mid-Apr.–mid-May and mid-Oct.–mid-Dec. MAP.*

$$$–$$$$ 🏨 **Posta-Cavallino Bianco.** In the town center—and only a five-minute walk from the main ski facilities—this hotel looks like a gigantic dollhouse, with delicate wooden balconies and an eye-catching wooden gable. Inside, the decor is made up of deep colors and ornate carpets and drapery. Wood is incorporated throughout the interior, most notable in the cozy hotel bar with a large handcrafted fireplace. The rooms are good sized. Note that half-board is required. ✉ *Via Rezia 22, 39046,* ☎ *0471/783333,* 📠 *0471/797517,* 🌐 *www.hotel-posta.com. 94 rooms. Restaurant, bar, coffee shop, dance club. MC, V. Closed mid-Apr.–mid-May and mid-Oct.–mid-Dec. MAP.*

Outdoor Activities and Sports

With almost 600 km (370 mi) of accessible downhill slopes, Ortisei is one of the most popular ski resorts in the Dolomites. Prices are good and facilities are among the most modern. A huge and immensely popular circle route, the long, intermediate, and beautiful **Sella Ronda** run will take you through several towns and bend around the entire valley. Begin in nearby **Selva Gardena;** allow a whole day for this popular jaunt. Going with a guide is highly advised; consult the tourist office in **Selva** (☎ 0471/795122) or **Ortisei** (☎ 0471/796328) for more information.

There are more than 90 km (56 mi) of cross-country skiing tracks. The **Val Gardena Ski** cooperative (☎ 0471/792092, 🌐 www.val-gardena.com) has snow reports and information on seasonal events.

Fiè allo Sciliar (Völs am Schlern)

㉓ *26 km (16 mi) southwest of Ortisei, 18 km (11 mi) east of Bolzano.*

Fiè (Völs) is set in a valley with the Renon mountains on one side and the Siusi on the other. The town is surrounded by acres of green coniferous forests. In the town is the parish church of **Santa Maria Assunta,** built in the 16th century in the late Gothic style. The church is being perpetually restored and is closed to the public.

Lodging

$$$–$$$$ 🏨 **Turm.** The *turm* (tower) that houses this welcoming hotel on the edge
★ of Sciliar National Park dates from the 13th century and has been used as a courthouse, dungeon, and tavern. Now owned and run by the Pramstrahler family, it's furnished with their charming collection of paintings and antiques. The picturesque, onion-domed hostelry also has an excellent restaurant. ✉ *Piazza della Chiesa 9, 39040,* ☎ *0471/725014,* 📠 *0471/725474. 25 rooms. Restaurant, indoor and outdoor pool, sauna. MC, V. Closed early Nov.–Dec. 19.*

Outdoor Activities and Sports

The **Oswald von Wolkenstein Cavalcade,** named after the medieval South Tirolese knight and troubadour, is held every year over the first or second weekend of June. After a colorful procession, teams of local horseback riders compete in fast-paced events.

Caldaro

㉔ *22 km (14 mi) south of Fiè, 15 km (9 mi) south of Bolzano.*

Caldaro is a vineyard village with clear views of castles high up on the surrounding mountains, a backdrop that reflects the centuries of division that forged the unique character of the area. Caldaro architecture is famous for the way it blends Italian Renaissance elements of balance and harmony with the soaring windows and peaked arches of the local Gothic tradition. The church of **Santa Caterina,** on the main square, is a good example. ☉ *Daily dawn–dusk.*

Close to Caldaro's main square is the **Museo Provinciale del Vino** (South Tirolean Museum of Wine), illustrating the history of wine production in this region. To further your wine tour, take a ramble along the **Strada del Vino** (Wine Road), which starts in Caldaro. ⊠ *Vicolo dell'Oro 1,* ☎ *0471/963168,* WEB *www.provinz.bz.it/volkskunde-museen/Wm_it_0.htm.* 🎫 *4,000 lire/€2.05.* ☉ *Easter–Oct., Tues.–Sat. 9:30–noon and 2–6, Sun. 10–noon.*

Lago di Carezza

㉕ *35 km (22 mi) east of Caldaro, 29 km (18 mi) east of Bolzano.*

A lake of icy-cold glacial waters, Lake Carezza is some 5,000 ft above sea level. The azure blue of the waters can at times change to magical greens and purples, reflections of the surrounding forest and rosy peaks of the Dolomites.

THE DOLOMITES: TRENTINO-ALTO ADIGE A TO Z

To research prices, get advice from other travelers, and book travel arrangements, visit www.fodors.com.

AIRPORTS

The nearest airport, but the least well connected, is the Aeroporto Bolzano Dolomiti, with flights to Rome, Vienna, Düsseldorf, and Frankfurt. A bit farther, Verona's Aeroporto Villafranca and Munich's Franz Josef Strauss (FJS) Airport in Germany are both well connected by road and rail with the Dolomite area. Milan's Malpensa Airport, the largest in Italy, is about a 3½-hour drive from Bolzano.

➤ AIRPORT INFORMATION: **Aeroporto Bolzano Dolomiti** (☎ 0471/ 254070). **Aeroporto Villafranca** (⊠ 11 km [7 mi] southwest of Verona, ☎ 045/8095666).

BUS TRAVEL

Only a handful of buses link Bolzano with Milan and Venice; the service between these cities and Trento is more frequent (for instance, there is an hourly bus service between Riva del Garda and Trento), but if you want to get to Merano or Cortina d'Ampezzo you will have to change in either Trento or Bolzano. For information, call the number listed below.

Local buses connect the train stations at Trento, Bolzano, and Merano with the mountain resorts. The service is fairly frequent between most main towns during the day. Though some parts of the region remain out of the reach of public transportation, it is possible to visit even the remotest villages without a car if you are equipped with the local bus timetables, available from regional and local tourist offices, and lots of time. Still, most towns are designed for people with cars, and getting between your hotel, ski lifts, and après-ski locales without a vehicle can be very tricky.

➤ BUS INFORMATION: **SASA** (Società Autobus Servizi d'Area, ☎ 0471/ 974292).

CAR RENTAL

➤ LOCAL AGENCIES: **Avis** (⊠ Piazza Verdi 18, Bolzano, ☎ 0471/ 971467, WEB www.avis.com). **Hertz** (⊠ Via Garibaldi 22, Bolzano, ☎ 0471/981411, WEB www.hertz.com).

CAR TRAVEL

The most important route in the region, A22, is the main north–south autostrada linking Italy with northern Europe by way of the Brenner

Pass. It connects Bressanone, Bolzano, Trento, and Rovereto, and at Verona joins the A4, running east–west across northern Italy from Trieste to Turin.

A car is highly recommended for the region. Autostrada A22 connects Bressanone, Bolzano, Trento, and Rovereto. Roads in the broad mountain valleys are usually wide two-lane routes, but the roads up into the highest passes can be narrow, winding, and, especially in winter, subject to sudden closure. (Some are closed to traffic entirely during the winter months.) Call Autostrada Weather Information Service in Bolzano for information on weather-related closures.

EMERGENCY SERVICES
ACI Emergency Service offers 24-hour roadside assistance.
➤ CONTACTS: **ACI dispatchers** (☎ 116). **Autostrada Weather Information Service** (☎ 0471/413810).

EMERGENCIES
For first aid, ask for "Pronto Soccorso," and be prepared to give your address. Pharmacies take turns staying open late and on Sunday; for the latest information, consult the current list posted on the front door of each pharmacy or ask at the local tourist office.
➤ CONTACTS: **Carabinieri** (☎ 112). **Police, Ambulance** (☎ 113).

LANGUAGE
Alto Adige is the only region in Italy with two official languages: Italian and German. In Bolzano, Merano, and environs, street signs, menus, city names, and street chatter are completely bilingual, and depending on your features you may be spoken to in a local dialect of German rather than Italian upon entering a shop or café. Meanwhile, all of Trentino and the ski resorts of Madonna di Campiglio and Cortina d'Ampezzo are strictly Italian-speaking, but the regional accent—most noticeable in the "r," which is guttural rather than rolled—is still quite distinctive.

MAIL AND SHIPPING
Post offices are open on weekdays 8–6:30 and Saturday 8–12:30.
➤ POST OFFICES: **Bolzano** (✉ Piazza Parrocchia, 15). **Cortina d'Ampezzo** (✉ Largo Poste 18/a). **Rovereto** (✉ Via Vittorio Veneto 1). **Trento** (✉ Piazza a. Vittoria 20).

OUTDOORS AND SPORTS
HIKING AND CLIMBING
Local tourist offices can provide information on less-demanding trails.
➤ HIKING AND CLIMBING: **Società degli Alpinisti Tridentini** (✉ Via Manci 57, 38100 Trento, ☎ 0461/981871). **Club Alpino Italiano** (✉ Piazza delle Erbe 46, Bolzano, ☎ 0471/978172; ✉ Corso della Libertà 188, Merano, ☎ 0473/448944; WEB www.cai.it). **Associazione Rifugi del Trentino** (✉ Piazza Centa 13/7, 38100 Trento, ☎ FAX 0461/826066).

TOURS
If you are without a car or if you don't care to drive over mountain roads, guided tours from Bolzano or Trento can show you the Dolomites the easy way. However, the sudden and frequent snowfalls mean that tours are offered in summer only.

BUS TOURS
In Bolzano, city sightseeing and local excursions are organized by the SAD bus company, near the train station. In Trento, city sightseeing can be arranged through the city tourist office.
➤ FEES AND SCHEDULES: **SAD** (✉ Via Conciapelli 60, ☎ 167/846047).

SINGLE-DAY TOURS

In July and August, the SAD bus company's full-day mountain tours include a "Great Dolomites Tour" from Bolzano to Cortina and a tour of the Val Venosta that climbs over the Stelvio Pass into Switzerland. A tour of the Val Gardena and the Siusi Alps is available from April to October.

From June through September, the Calderari e Moggioli travel agency offers a full-day guided bus tour of the Brenta Dolomites and the "Great Dolomites Tour," a full-day drive over the Pordoi and Falzarego passes to Cortina d'Ampezzo and Lake Misurina. The Trentino tourist office also organizes guided tours and excursions by train to castles in the region.

➤ FEES AND SCHEDULES: **Calderari e Moggioli** (✉ Via Manci 46, ☎ 0461/980275).

TRAIN TRAVEL

The express train line that links the towns of Bolzano, Trento, and Rovereto connects with other main lines at Verona, just south of the region. Eurocity trains on the Dortmund–Venice and Munich–Innsbruck–Rome routes also stop at these stations. An express train line follows the course of the Adige Valley from Munich and Innsbruck to the Brenner Pass southward past Bolzano, Trento, and Rovereto. Branch lines from Trento and Bolzano go to some of the smaller valleys, but most of the mountain attractions described above are beyond the reach of trains. Contact Ferrovie dello Stato, the national train operator, for more information.

➤ TRAIN INFORMATION: **Ferrovie dello Stato** (☎ 848/888088, WEB www.fs-on-line.com).

VISITOR INFORMATION

➤ TOURIST INFORMATION: **Alto Adige province** (✉ Piazza Parrocchia 11–12, Bolzano, ☎ 0471/993808, FAX 0471/993899, WEB www.provincia.bz.it/turismo). **Bolzano** (✉ Piazza Walther 8, ☎ 0471/307000-1-2, WEB www.bolzano-bozen.it). **Bormio** (✉ Via Roma 131/b, ☎ 0342/903300, WEB www.valtellinaonline.com). **Bressanone** (✉ Viale Stazione 9, ☎ 0472/836401). **Chiusa** (✉ Piazza Tinne 6, ☎ 0472/847424). **Cortina d'Ampezzo** (✉ Piazzetta San Francesco 8, ☎ 0436/3231). **Dobbiaco** (✉ Via Dolomiti 3, ☎ 0474/972132). **Madonna di Campiglio** (✉ Via Pradalago 4, ☎ 0465/442000). **Merano** (✉ Corso della Libertà 45, ☎ 0473/235223). **Naturno** (✉ Via Municipio 1, ☎ 0473/666077). **Ortisei** (✉ Via Rezia 1, ☎ 0471/796328). **Rovereto** (✉ Via Dante 63, ☎ 0464/430363, WEB www.apt.rovereto.tn.it). **Santa Cristina** (✉ Via Chemun 9, ☎ 0471/793046). **Selva Gardena** (✉ Via Mëisules 213, ☎ 0471/795122). **Trentino Tourist Board** (✉ Via Alfieri 4, Trento, ☎ 0461/983880, FAX 0461/984508, WEB www.provincia.tn.it/APT). **Trento** (✉ Via Alri 4, ☎ 0461/983880).

4 MILAN, LOMBARDY, AND THE LAKES

Old and new are often unexpectedly fused in Italy, and in Lombardy, they marry magnificently. Lakes Como, Maggiore, and Garda—of opulent 19th-century villas, exotic gardens, and Alpine vistas—remain the perfect escapes from Milan, Italy's business hub and crucible of chic. Pavia, Cremona, and Mantua, once proud medieval fortress towns dictating the fortunes of northern Italy, are today bustling centers of industry and commerce, still playing a key role in Italy's richest region.

Updated by
Heather
O'Brian

ONE IS TEMPTED TO DESCRIBE LOMBARDY as a place with something for everyone—Milan, capital of all that is new in Italy; the great Renaissance cities of the Po plain, Pavia, Cremona, and Mantua, where even the height of summer can be comparatively peaceful; and the lakes, where glacial waters framed by the Alps have been praised as the closest thing to paradise by writers as varied as Virgil, Tennyson, and Hemingway.

"Nothing in the world," wrote Stendhal in 1817, "can be compared to the fascination of those burning summer days passed on the Milanese lakes, in the middle of those chestnut groves so green that they immerse their branches in the waves . . ." Millions of travelers have since agreed that, for sheer beauty, the lakes of northern Italy—Como, Maggiore, Garda, and Orta—have few equals. Where else can you find magnificent 18th- and 19th-century villas on the shores of lakes bordered by toy villages and nestled under the foothills of mountains of true Alpine grandeur? From Pliny to d'Annunzio, visitors have found this region—to quote Stendhal—"elegant, picturesque, and voluptuous."

The truth, of course, is more complicated. The lakes, home to dozens of resorts that were once Italy's—and Europe's—most fashionable, have preserved an astonishingly unspoiled beauty, often enhanced by sumptuous summer palaces and exotic formal gardens. Still, one cannot imagine Catullus returning to his "jewel" Sirmione, on Lago di Garda (Lake Garda), without being a little daunted by its development as a lively resort town. Milan can be disappointingly modern—rather too much like the place you have come here to escape—but it is also the perfect blend of old and new, with historic buildings and art collections rivaling those in Florence and Rome.

More than 3,000 years ago—the date and the details are lost in the mysteries of Etruscan inscriptions—explorers from the highly civilized realm of Etruria in central Italy wandered northward beyond the River Po. The Etruscans extended their dominance into this region for hundreds of years but left little of their culture. They were succeeded by the Cenomanic Gauls, who, in turn, were conquered by the legions of Rome in the latter days of the Republic. The region became known as Cisalpine Gaul, and under the rule of Augustus it became a Roman province. Its warlike, independent people became citizens of Rome. Virgil, Catullus, and both Plinys were born in the region during this relatively tranquil era.

The decline of the Roman Empire was followed by the invasions of the Huns and the Goths. Attila and Theodoric, in turn, gave way to the Lombards, who ceded their iron crown to Charlemagne as the emblem of his vast but unstable empire. Even before the fragile bonds that held this empire together had begun to snap, the cities of Lombardy were erecting walls in defense against the Hungarians and against each other. These communes did, however, form the Lombard League, which, in the 12th century, finally defeated Frederick Barbarossa.

Once the invaders had been defeated, new and even bloodier strife began. In each city the Guelphs (bourgeois supporters of the popes) and the Ghibellines (noble adherents to the so-called emperors) clashed with each other. The communes declined, and each fell under the yoke of powerful local rulers. The Republic of Venice dominated Brescia and Bergamo. Mantua was ruled by the Gonzaga, and the Visconti and Sforza families took over Como, Cremona, Milan, and Pavia.

The Battle of Pavia in 1525, when the generals of Charles V (1500–58) defeated the French (and gave Francis I the chance to coin the famous phrase "All is lost save honor"), brought on 200 years of Spanish occupation. The Spaniards were, on the whole, less cruel than the local tyrants and were hardly resisted by the Lombards. The War of the Spanish Succession, in the early years of the 18th century, threw out the Spaniards and brought in the Austrians instead, whose dominion was "neither liked nor loathed" during the nearly 100 years of its existence.

Napoléon and his generals routed the Austrians. The Treaty of Campoformio resulted in the proclamation of the Cisalpine Republic, which quickly became the Republic of Italy and, just as rapidly, the Kingdom of Italy, which lasted only until Napoléon's defeat brought back the Austrians. But Milan, as the capital of Napoléon's republic and of the Kingdom of Italy, had a taste of glory, and the city's inherently independent citizens, along with those of the other Lombard cities, were not slow to resent and combat the loss of "national" pride.

From 1820 on, the Lombards joined the Piedmontese and the house of Savoy in a long struggle against the Habsburgs and, in 1859, finally defeated Austria and brought about the re-creation of the Kingdom of Italy two years later.

Milan and other cities of Lombardy have not lost their independence and their hatred of domination. Nowhere in Italy was the partisan insurrection against Mussolini—to whom they first gave power—and the German regime better organized or more successful. And it was in the city's Piazza Loreto, the same spot where a group of partisans had been shot a few weeks before, that the dead bodies of Mussolini and his lover, Claretta Petacci, were put on display. Milan was liberated from the Germans by its own partisan organization before the entrance of Allied troops; escaping Allied prisoners could find sanctuary there when fighting was still going on to the south. In recent years, the independent Milanesi spirit has been demonstrated in the political movement known as the Lega Nord (Northern League). In 1994, the Lega even enjoyed a brief and colorful stint in a fragile coalition government with center-right party Forza Italia. However, while the Lega's accusations that revenue from the prosperous north are squandered on ill-fated projects in the poorer south continue to strike a note in some northern quarters, other aspects of the party—including calls for secession—were less widely accepted. For the moment, the Lega has rejected this aim but has once again been relegated to being a minor political force.

Pleasures and Pastimes

Car Racing

Lombardy Formula I fans are passionate, living and dying with the fortunes of beloved team Ferrari. A Formula 1 race is held in Monza, 15 km (9 mi) from Milan, the second Sunday in September. The track was built in 1922 in the Parco di Monza, where there are also a hippodrome, a golf course, and other facilities.

Dining

Unlike most other Italian regions, Lombardy traditionally exhibits a northern European preference for butter rather than oil as its cooking medium, which imparts a rich and distinctive flavor to the cuisine. *Alla milanese*–style cooking means the food is usually dipped in egg and bread crumbs mixed with grated Parmesan, then sautéed in butter. One of the most popular specialties here, osso buco, is almost always paired with risotto—its alla milanese preparation enriching it with chicken broth and saffron, imparting a rich flavor and yellow hue. At the same time, Lombardy's capital is becoming increasingly cosmopolitan; Chinese restaurants abound, and it's also possible to dine on Japanese, Mexican, and Middle Eastern dishes and delicacies among other diverse offerings. The lakes are a good source of fish, particularly trout and pike. Gorgonzola, a strong, creamy, veined cheese, and panettone, a sweet yeast bread with raisins, citron, and anise, both hail from the Milan area and can be enjoyed throughout Lombardy. Although most of the wines in Lombardy can be paired well with the cuisine, search wine lists for red Grumello and Sangue di Giuda (Blood of Judas) and the delicious light sparkling whites from the Franciacorta area.

For general information and price categories, *see* Dining *in* Smart Travel Tips A to Z.

Golf

Golf is a recent addition to Italy's sporting roster, and the success of Italy's most famous professional golfer, Constantino Rocca, has added to the sport's popularity among Italians. Facilities have improved dramatically over the last decade, resulting in a proliferation of courses groomed into northern Italy's landscape. Several courses are convenient to Milan and to Lake Como.

Lodging

Lombardy is one of Italy's most prosperous regions, and hotels cater to a clientele of high standards, willing to pay for extra comfort. Many Lombardy hotels are converted from handsome old villas with well-landscaped grounds. Try to visit one or two, even if they are out of your price range as accommodations. Most of the famous lake resorts are expensive, although more basic—and reasonably priced—accommodations can be found in the smaller towns and villages. Milan may seem to have fewer tourists than other large Italian cities, but there is always competition for rooms, generated by the nearly year-round trade fairs and other business-related bookings. It is best—and almost essential in spring and summer—to make reservations.

For general information and price categories, *see* Lodging *in* Smart Travel Tips A to Z.

Soccer

Like the rest of Italy, Lombardy is soccer mad. Fans from all over Italy exhibit fierce support for Milan's soccer teams, AC Milan and Inter Milan, two of the most successful in Europe. Matches are usually played on Sunday, with both teams using the San Siro soccer stadium in Milan for home matches. On match day, as many as 85,000 fans pile into the San Siro to watch, cheer, and boo the performances of each team. For the rest of the week, Sunday's performance is debated and scrutinized in bars, cafés, and restaurants (not to mention the home, workplace, barbershop . . .).

Water Sports

Schools for sailing, scuba diving, waterskiing, and windsurfing are in Riva del Garda, on Lake Garda. Torbole, 5 km (3 mi) east of Riva del Garda on S240, is a prime spot for windsurfing. At Lake Como, there are well-equipped sailing and windsurfing schools as well as waterskiing.

Exploring Milan, Lombardy, and the Lakes

This area of northern Italy is dominated by the region of Lombardy and especially by Milan, which lies at its heart. Many of the region's most important cities—Pavia, Cremona, and Mantua—are to the south and southeast of Milan. These cities all have in common flat geographical surroundings bordered by the Po River, hence they are categorized here as cities of the plain. "The lakes" actually denotes a vast region spread over the middle third of the northern border region. The roads that connect major cities are excellent and are supported by several major highways (autostrade) as well as by secondary routes.

From the north to the east of Milan lie all of the region's lakes. Some border Switzerland; others are at the foot of the Dolomites, Italy's foremost mountain range. The best way to see the lake country is to rent a car in fall or spring and thread a path, at as leisurely a pace as possible, along the small mountain roads that link the lakes' least-spoiled northern tips. This is splendid mountain-driving country, with some of the most beautiful and challenging roads in the world. Without a car, however, it is still possible to see many of the region's sights, thanks to extensive bus routes and the many *vaporetti* (water taxis) that thread the lakes. The throngs that descend upon the lakes in July and August, weekends particularly, make reservations absolutely necessary—especially at Lake Como, the quintessential Italian lake resort.

Numbers in the text correspond to numbers in the margin and on the Milan and Lombardy and the Lakes maps.

Great Itineraries

Traveling by car is usually the best way to get around and to fully appreciate the beauty of the landscape. Allow plenty of time to travel the winding lake roads at leisure, as photo opportunities abound. A week is enough to see the area thoroughly, and although five days will not exclude any sights, you have to keep on the move. Three days will give you a taste of the major sights in the area, but time will be precious and morning starts will have to be early.

IF YOU HAVE 3 DAYS

Begin in **Milan** ①–⑯, taking in the city's major sights, before heading south on the A7 autostrada to the cities of **Pavia** ⑰ and **Cremona** ⑱, home to Stradivari, violin maker extraordinaire. End your day in **Mantua** ⑳. The next day head north on the A22 as far as **Riva del Garda** ㉔ and make your way back through **Gargnano** ㉕, **Gardone Riviera** ㉖, and down into the jewel of Lake Garda's crown, **Sirmione** ㉗. Overnight in ⌧ **Bergamo** ㉙. The next day go as far as **Madonna del Ghisallo** ㉚ and **Bellagio** ㉛ on Lake Como. Finally, move on to Lake Maggiore via **Cernobbio** ㉞, taking time out to cruise the lake on one of the steamers.

IF YOU HAVE 5 DAYS

Travel south along the A7 to **Pavia** ⑰ and **Cremona** ⑱, and then move on to the star-shape fortress city of **Sabbioneta** ⑲, ending your day in ⌧ **Mantua** ⑳, where you can enjoy Mantegna's masterpieces. The next day head north to Lake Garda through the lakefront towns of **Punta di San Vigilio** ㉒, **Malcesine** ㉓, and, at the top of the lake, the pretty town of **Riva del Garda** ㉔. Head down the western side of the lake through **Gargnano** ㉕ and **Gardone Riviera** ㉖, where you should visit Gabriele d'Annunzio's former home, Il Vittoriale, before reaching ⌧ **Sirmione** ㉗. The next day pass through the wealthy city of **Brescia** ㉘ and on to **Bergamo** ㉙. From here head via **Madonna del Ghisallo** ㉚ to ⌧ **Bellagio** ㉛ on Lake Como, said to be the prettiest town in Europe—you'll bed down here for the night. Take time in the afternoon to explore the lake towns of **Varenna** ㉜ and **Tremezzo** ㉝, where you'll find the magnificent Villa Carlotta. If you can manage an early start the following morning, head for **Cernobbio** ㉞ and then west to **Orta San Giulio** ㊱ on Lake Orta. It's only a short hop to Lake Maggiore. You can explore the area from here by steamer, traveling north to ⌧ **Stresa** ㊲ on the western side of the lake. From here it's a short excursion to the town of **Verbania** ㊳, across the bay of the same name. That

Lombardy and the Lakes

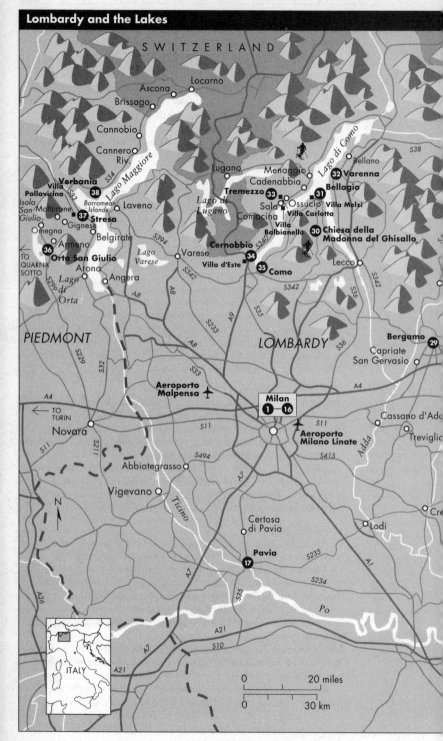

SWITZERLAND

Locarno
Ascona
Brissago
Cannobio
Cannero Riv.
Lugano
Menaggio
Cadenabbia
Bellano
Lago di Como
S38
Verbania
Villa Pallavicino
Borromean Islands
Laveno
Lago di Lugano
Tremezzo **33**
Sala
Ossucio
Comacina
Villa Balbianello
Varenna **32**
Bellagio **31**
Villa Carlotta
Villa Melzi
Chiesa della Madonna del Ghisallo **30**
Stresa **37**
Gignese
Belgirate
Isola San Giulio
Mottarone
Omegna
Armeno
Orta San Giulio **36**
TO QUARNA SOTTO
Arona
Angera
Lago di Orta
Lago Varese
Varese
Cernobbio
Villa d'Este
Como **35**
34
Lecco
S36
S342
S35
PIEDMONT
S229
S32
A8
A8
A9
S233
LOMBARDY
S36
Bergamo **29**
Capriate San Gervasio
A4
Aeroporto Malpensa
S33
S11
Milan **1** **16**
TO TURIN
Novara
S11
S211
S494
Abbiategrasso
Vigevano
Ticino
Certosa di Pavia
Pavia **17**
S235
A7
Aeroporto Milano Linate
S11
Adda
Cassano d'Ad
Treviglio
Cre
Lodi
A1
S234
Po
A7
A26
A21
S10
A7
N
ITALY
0   20 miles
0   30 km
A21
A34
S394
S340
S342

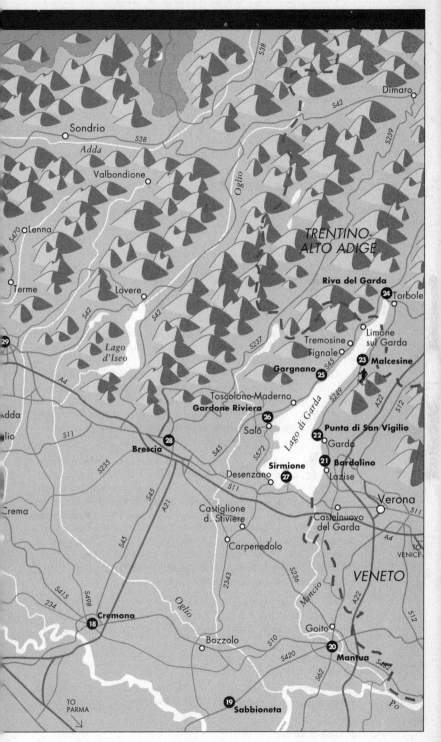

Dimaro

Sondrio

Adda

S38

S42

S239

Valbondione

Oglio

S470 Lenna

**TRENTINO-
ALTO ADIGE**

Terme

Lovere

S42

S42

Riva del Garda

24 Torbole

Limone
sul Garda

29

*Lago
d'Iseo*

S237

Tremosine

Tignale

23 **Malcesine**

Gargnano

25

S45

Toscolano-Maderno

A4

adda

Gardone Riviera

Lago di Garda

S249

26

Salò

Punta di San Vigilio

lio

S11

A22

S12

22

Garda

Brescia

28

S45

S572

21 **Bardolino**

Desenzano

Sirmione

27

Lazise

S235

Verona

S11

Crema

A21

Castelnuovo
del Garda

**Castiglione
d. Stiviere**

A4

TO
VENICE

Carpenedolo

VENETO

2343

S236

S45

Mincio

A22

S12

S415

234

S498

Oglio

Cremona

18

S10

Goito

Bozzolo

20

S420

Mantua

S62

Po

TO
PARMA

19 **Sabbioneta**

afternoon or the following day (alternatively staying in Stresa) head for ⛏ **Milan** ①–⑯ to see the main sights. You could also visit Milan first before setting off on your tour of the rest of the region.

IF YOU HAVE 7 DAYS

If you have the luxury of seven days to tour the area, follow the five-day plan above, but linger in some of the lake towns, especially **Riva del Garda** ㉔ and ⛏ **Sirmione** ㉗ on Lake Garda, ⛏ **Bellagio** ㉛ on Lake Como, and Lake Maggiore's **Verbania** ㊳, where you can explore the magnificent botanical gardens of Villa Taranto. Take an extra day to visit ⛏ **Milan** ①–⑯, which may appear to be just an industrialized city at first glance but reveals artistic and architectural treasures once you scratch its surface.

When to Tour Milan, Lombardy, and the Lakes

In summer months, particularly July and August, lake roads can become congested, especially on evenings and weekends. Fewer people visit in fall, winter, and spring, so many of the lakeside towns are deserted and some restaurants and hotels close. Note that many of the ferry and steamer services stop running in October and recommence in May. Early summer, late summer, and early fall are the best times to see the area, though October can be a tad chilly for swimming.

MILAN

Milan's history as a capital city goes back at least 2,500 years. Its fortunes ever since—both as a great commercial trading center and as the object of regular conquest and occupation—are readily explained by its strategic position at the center of the Lombard plain. Directly south of the central passes across the Alps, Milan is bordered by three highly navigable rivers—the Po, the Ticino, and the Adda—for centuries the main arteries of an ingenious network of canals crisscrossing all Lombardy (and ultimately reaching most of northern Italy).

Virtually every invader in European history—Gaul, Roman, Goth, Longobard, and Frank—as well as a long series of rulers from France, Spain, and Austria, has taken a turn at ruling the city and the region. Milan's glorious heyday of self-rule proved comparatively brief, from 1277 until 1500, during which it was ruled by its two great family dynasties, the Visconti and subsequently the Sforza. These families were known, justly or not, for a peculiarly aristocratic mixture of refinement, classical learning, and cruelty, and much of the surviving grandeur of Gothic and Renaissance art and architecture is their doing. Be on the lookout in your wanderings for the Visconti family emblem—a viper, its jaws straining wide, devouring a child.

If you are wondering why so little seems to have survived from Milan's antiquity, the answer is simple—war. Three times in the city's history, partial or total destruction has followed conflict, in AD 539, 1157, and 1944.

Exploring Milan

The subway system, known as the Metropolitana, is a good way to get around, but staying aboveground in the trolley cars or buses gives a better view.

A Good Walk

Start at the **Duomo** ① and visit its roof, museum, and the **Battistero Paleocristiano** ②. Then move on to **Galleria Vittorio Emanuele** ③, just beyond the northern tip of the cathedral's facade. Continue across the transepts of the Galleria and head north to **Teatro alla Scala** ④, where

Milan

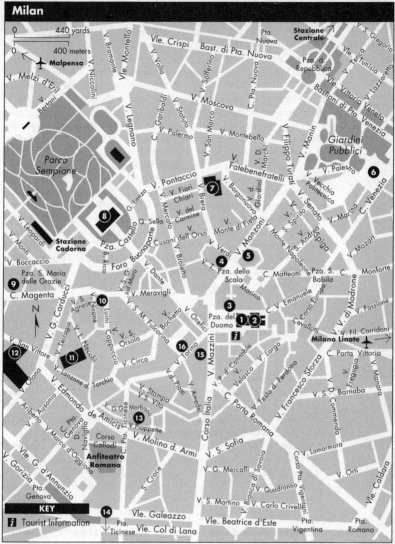

Verdi attained his fame. Head northeast on Via Manzoni, stopping in the **Museo Poldi–Pezzoli** ⑤ to see some fine Renaissance paintings. Via Manzoni leads to the Giardini Pubblici (great for kids), with the **Museo Civico di Storia Naturale** ⑥ on the eastern side of the park. Backtrack to Via Manzoni; take Via Fatebenefratelli west to Via Pontaccio and then to Via Brera to the **Pinacoteca di Brera** ⑦. Next, a brisk walk west along Via Pontaccio will bring you to the imposing **Castello Sforzesco** ⑧. A few blocks southwest of the Castello on Corso Magenta is **Santa Maria delle Grazie** ⑨, home to the renowned *Last Supper*. Go east on Corso Magenta, across Via Carducci, to visit the city's **Museo Civico Archeologico** ⑩. Next to the museum, Via Sant'Agnese leads to the **Basilica di Sant'Ambrogio** ⑪. Across from the church's main doors, turn left on Via San Vittore to see the **Museo Nazionale della Scienza e Tecnica** ⑫. From the museum, take a right and walk down Via Edmondo de Amicis; then take a left on Corso Porta Ticinese to reach the church of **San Lorenzo Maggiore** ⑬. South of Corso Porta Ticinese is the bustling **Navigli district** ⑭. From San Lorenzo Maggiore, take Corso Porta Ticinese north to Via Torino, where, after a few blocks, you'll find **San Satiro** ⑮, yet another of Bramante's Renaissance masterpieces. Turn left on Via Spadari and then turn left on Via Cantu, which takes you to Piazza Pio XI—here you can end your tour at the beautiful **Pinacoteca Ambrosiana** ⑯ museum and attached library.

TIMING

To visit all of the sights in Milan will take a couple of days, but the most important ones can be seen in one day. Note that some churches and museums are closed Monday, including Santa Maria delle Grazie (home of *The Last Supper*).

Sights to See

⑪ **Basilica di Sant'Ambrogio** (Basilica of St. Ambrose). Noted for its medieval architecture, the church was consecrated by St. Ambrose in AD 387, and is the model for all Lombard Romanesque churches. The **Museo della Basilica di Sant'Ambrogio** contains ancient pieces such as a remarkable 9th-century altar in precious metals and enamels. The museum trove also includes paintings, sculptures, and a couple of Flemish tapestries. ✉ *Piazza Sant'Ambrogio 15,* ☎ *02/86450895.* ☑ *Museum 3,000 lire/€1.55.* ☉ *Basilica Mon.–Sat. 7–noon and 2:30–7; museum Sept.–July, Mon. and Wed.–Fri. 10–noon and 3–5, weekends 3–5. Metro: Sant'Ambrogio.*

② **Battistero Paleocristiano.** This subterranean ruin of the baptistery dating from the 4th century is beneath the Duomo's piazza. Although opinion remains divided, it is widely believed that this may have been where Ambrose, Milan's first bishop and patron saint, baptized Augustine. ✉ *Enter through Duomo, Piazza Duomo,* ☎ *02/86463456.* ☑ *3,000 lire/€1.55.* ☉ *Daily 9:30–5:15. Metro: Duomo.*

⑧ **Castello Sforzesco.** For the serious student of Renaissance military engineering, the imposing Castello must be something of a travesty, so often has it been remodeled or rebuilt since it was begun in 1450 by the *condottiere* (hired mercenary) who founded the city's second dynastic family, Francesco Sforza, fourth duke of Milan. Though today the word "mercenary" has a strongly pejorative ring, during the Renaissance all Italy's great soldier-heroes were professionals hired by the cities and principalities that they served. Of them—and there were thousands—Francesco Sforza (1401–66) is considered one of the greatest and most honest. It is said he could remember not only the names of all his men but of their horses as well. And it is with his era, and the building of the Castello, that we know we have entered the enlightened age of the Renaissance. It took barely half a century before it and the city were under foreign rule.

Today, the Castello houses municipal museums devoted variously to Egyptian and other antiquities, musical instruments, paintings, and sculpture. Highlights are the **Salle delle Asse,** a frescoed room still sometimes attributed to Leonardo da Vinci (1690–1730), and Michelangelo's unfinished *Rondanini Pietà,* believed to be his last work—an astounding achievement for a man nearly 90 and a moving coda of his life. ⊠ *Piazza Castello,* ☎ *02/86461404.* ⬚ *Free.* ⊗ *Tues.–Sun. 9–5:30. Metro: Cairoli.*

★ ❶ **Duomo.** This intricate Gothic structure—Italy's largest—has been fascinating and exasperating visitors and conquerors alike since it was begun by Galeazzo Visconti III (1351–1402), first duke of Milan, in 1386. Consecrated in 1577, it was not wholly completed until 1897. Whether you concur with travel writer H. V. Morton, writing in 1964, that the cathedral is "one of the mightiest Gothic buildings ever created," or regard it as a spiny pastiche of centuries, there is no denying that for sheer size and complexity it is unequaled; its very size and appearance suggest Gotham rather than Milan. Its capacity—though it is hard to imagine the church filled—is reckoned to be 40,000. Usually it is empty, a perfect sanctuary from the frenetic pace of life outside and the perfect place for solitary contemplation. The poet Shelley swore by it—claiming it was the only place to read Dante.

The building is adorned with 135 marble spires and 2,245 marble statues. The oldest part is the **apse.** Its three colossal bays of curving and counter-curved tracery, especially the bay adorning the exterior of the stained-glass windows, should not be missed. Step inside and walk down the right aisle to the southern transept, to the **tomb of Gian Giacomo Medici.** The tomb owes something to Michelangelo but was executed by Leone Leoni (1509–90) and is generally considered to be his masterpiece; it dates from the 1560s. Directly ahead is the Duomo's most famous sculpture, the rather gruesome but anatomically instructive figure of **San Bartolomeo** (St. Bartholomew), whose glorious martyrdom consisted of being flayed alive. It is usually said the saint stands "holding" his skin, but this is not quite accurate. It would appear more that he is luxuriating in it, much as a 1950s matron might have shown off a new fur stole.

As you enter the apse to admire those splendid windows, glance at the **sacristy doors** to the right and left of the altar. The lunette on the right dates from 1393 and was decorated by Hans von Fernach. That on the left also dates from the 14th century and is ascribed jointly to Giacomo da Campione and Giovanni dei Grassi. Don't miss the view from the Duomo's **roof;** walk out the left (north) transept to the stairs and elevator. Sadly, on all but the rarest days air pollution drastically reduces the view. As you stand among the forest of marble pinnacles, remember that virtually every inch of this gargantuan edifice, including the roof itself, is decorated with precious white marble. ⊠ *Piazza del Duomo,* ☎ *02/86463456.* ⬚ *Stairs to roof 6,000 lire/€3.10, elevator 9,000 lire/€4.65.* ⊗ *Mid-Feb.–mid-Nov., daily 9–5:45; mid-Nov.–mid-Feb., daily 9–4:15. Metro: Duomo.*

Exhibits at the **Museo del Duomo** shed more light on the cathedral's history and include some of the treasures removed for safety from the exterior. ⊠ *Piazza del Duomo 14,* ☎ *02/860358.* ⬚ *10,000 lire/€5.15.* ⊗ *Tues.–Sun. 9:30–12:30 and 3–6. Metro: Duomo.*

NEED A
BREAK?

Peck, one of Italy's, if not the world's, most irresistible food emporiums, provides an alternative to conventional restaurant dining and also lends its name to one of Milan's best restaurants. In the Duomo area, it is something better than a shop—it's several shops. **Peck Rosticceria** (✉ Via Cantù 3, ☎ 02/8693017), closed Monday, offers grilled delicacies to go and slices of pizza. Best for a quick lunch is **Bottega del Vino** (✉ Via Victor Hugo 4, ☎ 02/861040), which pours almost 200 wines by the glass. Downstairs you will find the highly rated **Il Restaurant** (✉ Via Victor Hugo 4, ☎ 02/876774), closed on Sunday. For do-it-yourself, try the **Delicatessen** (✉ Via Spadari 9, ☎ 02/860842).

★ ❸ **Galleria Vittorio Emanuele.** Anyone who has grown up on the periphery of a contemporary American city should recognize this spectacularly extravagant, late-19th-century glass-topped, barrel-vaulted tunnel for what it is—one of the planet's earliest and most select shopping malls. It may be rivaled perhaps only by GUM, off Red Square in Moscow, for sheer Belle Epoque splendor. Its architect, Giuseppe Mengoni, accidently lost his footing while on the roof and tumbled to his death on the floor of his own creation, just days before its opening.

Like its suburban American cousins, the Galleria fulfills a variety of social functions vastly more important than its ostensible commercial purpose. This is the city's heart, midway between the cathedral and La Scala, and it is sometimes called *Il Salotto* (the Living Room). It teems with life, inviting people-watching from the tables that spill from the Galleria's bars and restaurants, where you can enjoy a ridiculously overpriced coffee.

Like the cathedral, the Galleria is cruciform in shape. The space at the crossing, however, forms an octagon. If this is where you're standing, don't be afraid to look up and gawk. Even in poor weather, the great glass dome makes for a splendid sight. And the mosaics, usually unnoticed, are a vastly underrated source of pleasure, even if they are not to be taken too seriously. They represent Europe, Asia, Africa, and America; those at the entrance arch are devoted to science, industry, art, and agriculture. Books, records, clothing, food, wine, pens, jewelry, and myriad other goods are all for sale in the Galleria, and one of Milan's most traditional restaurants, Savini, is here. ✉ *Piazza del Duomo, beyond northern tip of cathedral's facade.* ☉ *Most shops 9:30–1 and 3:30–7, others later or all day. Metro: Duomo.*

❿ **Museo Civico Archeologico** (Municipal Archaeological Museum). Housed in a former monastery, this museum has some enlightening relics from Milan's Roman past—from everyday utensils and jewelry to several fine examples of mosaic pavement. ✉ *Corso Magenta 15,* ☎ *02/ 86450011.* 🎟 *Free.* ☉ *Tues.–Sun. 9–5:30. Metro: Cadorna.*

🐾 ❻ **Museo Civico di Storia Naturale** (Municipal Natural History Museum). Exhibits here appeal to animal and nature lovers. Just behind the museum are the **Giardini Pubblici** (Public Gardens), a refuge for active young children. ✉ *Corso Venezia 55,* ☎ *02/88463289.* 🎟 *Free.* ☉ *Tues.– Fri. 9–6, weekends 9:30–6:30. Metro: Palestro.*

🐾 ⑫ **Museo Nazionale della Scienza e Tecnica** (National Museum of Science and Technology). Models based on technical projects by Leonardo da Vinci and collections of locomotives, planes, and cars are the highlights here, as well as a recent addition, a submarine. Other attractions in this spacious museum are a picture gallery, which includes some of Leonardo's own paintings, and an interactive scientific laboratory. The museum also houses temporary exhibits. ✉ *Via San Vittore 21,*

near Sant'Ambrogio, ☎ *02/485551,* WEB *www.museoscienza.org.* ✉
10,000 lire/€5.15. ☉ *Tues.–Sun. 9–5. Metro: Sant'Ambrogio.*

⑤ Museo Poldi–Pezzoli. The highlight of this extraordinary museum is undoubtedly the *Portrait of a Lady* by Antonio Pollaiuolo (circa 1431–
98), one of the city's most-prized treasures and the museum's symbol.
The collection also includes masterpieces by Andrea Mantegna (1431–
1506), Giovanni Bellini (1430–1516), and Fra Filippo Lippi (circa
1406–69), whose uncomplicated, heartrending style won him the favor
and patronage of Piero de' Medici, son of Cosimo and father of
Lorenzo Il Magnifico (1449–92). ✉ *Via Manzoni 12,* ☎ *02/794889.*
✉ *10,000 lire/€5.15.* ☉ *Tues.–Sun. 10–6. Metro: Duomo.*

⑭ Navigli district. In medieval times a network of navigable canals, called
navigli, crisscrossed Milan. Almost all have been covered over, but in
this romantic, bohemian neighborhood two long canals—Naviglio
Grande and Naviglio Pavese—and part of a third—Darsena—survive.
They're lined with quaint shops, art galleries, cafés, restaurants, and
clubs. ✉ *South of Corso Porta Ticinese.*

⑯ Pinacoteca Ambrosiana. This museum, founded in the 17th century by
Cardinal Federico Borromeo, is one of the city's treasures. Here you
can contemplate works of art like Caravaggio's simple—yet revolutionary—*Basket of Fruit* and Raphael's awesome preparatory drawing for *The School of Athens* in the Vatican, as well as paintings by
Leonardo, Botticelli, Luini, Titian, and Brueghel, among others. The
adjacent library, the Biblioteca Ambrosiana, also sometimes hosts exhibits and is considered to be the oldest Italian public library. ✉ *Piazza Pio XI 2,* ☎ *02/80692225,* WEB *www.ambrosiana.it.* ✉ *12,000
lire/€6.2.* ☉ *Museum Tues.–Sun. 10–5:30, library weekdays 9:30–5.*

★ ⑦ Pinacoteca di Brera (Brera Gallery). The picture collection in this art
gallery is star-studded, even by Italian standards. Start with the best,
while you're still fresh, and leave the charming minor masterpieces for
afterward. In Room 22, note that Raphael (1483–1520) painted *Be-
trothal of the Virgin* when he was 22. The other painting, *Madonna
with Saints and Angels* by Piero della Francesca (1420?-92) is just as
lovely, much enhanced by a skillful cleaning and restoration.

The somber, beautiful, and moving *Dead Christ* by Mantegna, in Room
6, is by far the smallest painting in the room, but it dominates, with its
sparse palette of gray and terra-cotta and especially with its original perspective. Mantegna's shocking, almost surgical precision—in the rendering
of Christ's wounds, the face propped up on a pillow, the day's growth
of beard—tells of an all-too-human agony. It is one of Renaissance
painting's most quietly wondrous achievements, finding an unsuspected
middle ground between the excesses of conventional gore and beauty in
representing the Passion's saddest moment. On your way out, pause a
moment to view the fine paintings by Carlo Carrà (1881–1966)—especially *La Musa Metafisica,* or *Metaphysical Muse*—suggesting Italy's con-
fident and stylish response to the likes of Picasso and Max Ernst and the
schools of Cubism and Surrealism. ✉ *Via Brera 28,* ☎ *02/722631.* ✉
8,000 lire/€4.15, 12,000 lire/€6.20 when housing exhibitions. ☉ *Tues.–
Sun. 8:30–7. Metro: Cairoli, Lanza, or Monte Napoleone.*

OFF THE
BEATEN PATH
LATIN QUARTER – Take time to wander around the lively quarter surrounding the Pinacoteca di Brera. The narrow streets, lined with boutiques, crafts shops, cafés, restaurants, and music clubs, make up what's
often referred to as Milan's Greenwich Village. A longtime haunt of
artists and musicians, it has a number of clubs and cafés offering live
music late into the night.

⑬ San Lorenzo Maggiore. Sixteen ancient Roman columns line the front of this sanctuary, and 4th-century mosaics still survive in the Cappella di Sant'Aquilino (Chapel of St. Aquilino). ⊠ *Corso di Porta Ticinese.* ⊙ *Daily 7:30–6:45, mosaics 9:30–6:30.*

⑮ San Satiro. This church is an architectural gem created by Bramante (1444–1514), demonstrating his perfect command of proportion and perspective, keynotes of Renaissance architecture. Bramante tricks the eye with a famous optical illusion that makes a small interior seem extraordinarily spacious and airy. ⊠ *Via Torino.* ⊙ *Weekdays 7:30–11:30 and 3:30–6:30, weekends 9–noon and 3:30–7.*

★ ❾ **Santa Maria delle Grazie.** *The Last Supper,* housed in the church and former Dominican monastery of Santa Maria delle Grazie, has had an almost unbelievable history of bad luck and neglect—its near destruction in an American bombing raid in August 1943 was only the latest chapter in a series of misadventures, including, if one 19th-century source is to be believed, being whitewashed over by monks. Well-meant but disastrous attempts at restoration have done little to rectify the problem of the work's placement: it was executed on a wall unusually vulnerable to climatic dampness. Yet the artist chose to work slowly and patiently in oil pigments—which demand dry plaster—instead of proceeding hastily on wet plaster according to the conventional fresco technique. Novelist and critic Aldous Huxley (1894–1963) called it "the saddest work of art in the world." After years of restorers' patiently shifting from one square centimeter to another, Leonardo's famous masterpiece is free of the shroud of scaffolding—and centuries of retouching, grime, and dust. Astonishing clarity and luminosity have been regained.

Despite Leonardo's carefully preserved preparatory sketches in which the apostles are clearly labeled by name, there still remains some small debate about a few identities in the final arrangement. But there can be no mistaking Judas, small and dark, his hand calmly reaching forward toward the bread, isolated from the terrible confusion that has taken the hearts of the others. One critic, Professor Frederick Hartt, offers an elegantly terse explanation for why the composition works: it combines "dramatic confusion" with "mathematical order." Certainly, the amazingly skillful and unobtrusive repetition of threes, when first you see it—in the windows, in the grouping of the figures, and in their placement—adds a mystical aspect to what at first seems simply the perfect observation of spontaneous human gesture.

The painting was executed in what was the order's refectory, now called the **Cenacolo Vinciano.** Take at least a moment to visit Santa Maria delle Grazie itself. It's a handsome church, with a fine dome by Bramante, which was added along with a cloister about the time that Leonardo was commissioned to paint *The Last Supper.* If you're wondering how two such giants came to be employed decorating and remodeling the refectory and church of a comparatively modest religious order, and not, say, the Duomo, the answer lies in the ambitious but largely unrealized plan to turn Santa Maria delle Grazie into a magnificent Sforza family mausoleum. Though Ludovico il Moro Sforza (1452–1508), seventh duke of Milan, was but one generation away from the founding of the Sforza dynasty, he was its last ruler. Two years after Leonardo finished his painting, Ludovico was defeated and imprisoned in a French dungeon for the remaining eight years of his life. Reservations are strongly recommended; you can make them by phoning between 9 AM and 6 PM Monday through Friday. A new group of people is allowed in to view *The Last Supper* every 15 minutes. ⊠ *Piazza Santa Maria delle Grazie 2, off Corso Magenta,* ☎ 02/89421146. ⌑ 12,000 *lire/€6.20 plus 2,000 lire/€1.05 reservation fee.* ⊙ *Tues.–Sun. 8–7. Metro: Cadorna.*

NEED A
BREAK?

Sometimes a bit overcrowded at night, the **Bar Magenta** (⊠ Via Carducci 13 at Corso Magenta, ☎ 02/8053808) can be a good stop en route during the day. Beyond lunch, beer, or coffee, the real attraction is its casual but civilized, quintessentially Milanese ambience.

❹ Teatro alla Scala. You need know nothing of opera to sense that, like Carnegie Hall, La Scala is something rather more than an auditorium. Here Verdi established his reputation and Maria Callas sang her way into opera lore. It looms as a symbol—both for the performer who dreams one day of singing here and for the buff who knows every note of *Rigoletto* by heart. Audiences here can be notoriously fickle and have been known to jeer performers who do not do appropriate justice to their beloved *opera lirica*, as it is known in Italian. The opera house was completely renovated after its destruction by Allied bombs in 1943 and reopened at a performance led by the great Arturo Toscanini in 1946.

If you are lucky enough to be here during the opera season, which runs for approximately six months beginning each December 7, St. Ambrose Day, do whatever is necessary to attend—even if it requires perching among the rafters in one of the dreaded gallery seats. Hearing a Verdi or Puccini opera sung in Italian by Italians in Italy is a magical experience. Plans for a renovation of the theater's stage—intended to bring it into line with the more modern stages at l'Opéra Bastille in Paris and New York's Met—were expected to proceed shortly after the special events marking the 100th anniversary of Verdi's death in 2001, with performances relocated for two or three years to the Teatro Arcimboldi on the outskirts of Milan. However, delays are possible, so be sure to call for information.

During a quick stroll through the theater's small **Museo Teatrale alla Scala,** you get a peek at the gilded grandeur of the boxes and admire the excellent collection of original, hand-painted Art Nouveau posters. Also on display are original scores by Giuseppe Verdi and a small gallery devoted to Toscanini. The museum is expected to be closed while the theater's stage is being renovated, so call ahead before visiting. ⊠ *Piazza della Scala,* ☎ *02/8053418.* 🎫 *6,000 lire/€3.10.* ⊙ *May.–Oct., daily 9–noon and 2–5; Nov.–Apr., Mon.–Sat. 9–noon and 2–5; no theater viewing during rehearsals. Metro: Duomo.*

OFF THE
BEATEN PATH

LEONARDO'S HORSE – At Milan's racetrack, near San Siro, Leonardo's Horse found a home in the autumn of 1999. A gift to the Italian people, the bronze sculpture is based on drawings prepared by Leonardo da Vinci in the 15th century. The idea for the project was first developed by Charles Dent of Allenstown, Pennsylvania, in 1977. The horse was sculpted by Nina Akamu.

MINITALIA PARK – Between Milan and Bergamo, this theme park has a 1:500-scale relief model of Italy, with about 200 replicas of the country's most important monuments. ⊠ *A4 autostrada toward Bergamo, Capriate San Gervasio, 35 km (22 mi) east of Milan,* ☎ *02/909 1341.* 🎫 *22,000 lire/€11.35.* ⊙ *Mar.–Oct., daily 9:30–dusk.*

PARCO DELLA PREISTORIA – Kids of all ages marvel at the 70-ft-long brontosaurus, the fierce Tyrannosaurus, and the 20 other full-size replicas of prehistoric animals lining a path 4 km (2½ mi) long. There are two cafés and a picnic area. ⊠ *25 km (16 mi) east of Milan on S11 near Cassano d'Adda,* ☎ *0363/78184.* 🎫 *Adults 14,000 lire/€7.25, children 12,000 lire/ €6.20.* ⊙ *Mid-Feb.–Nov., daily 9–7; ticket office closes at 6.*

Dining and Lodging

$$$$ ✕ **Da Aimo e Nadia.** It's a little bit out of the way, but it's worth it.
The freshest ingredients are one of the keys behind Aimo and Nadia's
consistently high ranking among Italian restaurants. In the year 2000,
its sommelier was named as the best in Italy, so you'll be able to find
just the perfect wine to go with your meal. The restaurant is warm and
welcoming and serves specialties like *risotto al tartufo* (risotto with truffles) and *tagliolini con totani peperoni dolci e delizie dell'orto* (tagliolini pasta with calamari, sweet peppers, and garden delights). The
fixed-price menu is a good way to go. It starts with a glass of spumante
and an appetizer and ends up with dessert, with a first and two second courses along the way. ⊠ *Via Montecuccoli, 6,* ☎ *02/416886. Reservations essential. Jacket and tie. AE, DC, MC, V. Metro: Primaticcio.
Closed Sun. and Aug. No lunch Sat.*

$$$$ ✕ **Giannino.** This century-old institution is a beautiful place to have
a meal, with the kitchen on view and a winter garden among its aesthetic attractions. You would be hard pressed to find a better version
of the Milanese classic *cotoletta alla milanese* (breaded veal cutlet) anywhere in the city. Giannino also serves a particularly fine risotto, and
you'll find other regional specialties on the vast menu, as well as some
excellent Florentine dishes, among them a succulent version of the *bistecca alla fiorentina* (grilled Chianina beef). ⊠ *Via Amatore Sciesa 8,*
☎ *02/55195582. Reservations essential. AE, DC, MC, V. Closed Sun.
No lunch Mon.*

$$$$ ✕ **L'Antica Osteria del Ponte.** Rich, imaginative seasonal cuisine at the
★   whim of chef Ezio Santin is reason enough to make your way 20 km
(12 mi) southwest of Milan to one of Italy's finest (and most expensive) restaurants. It is set in a traditional country inn with attractive
ceiling beams; a blazing fire makes the interior especially cozy in chilly
weather. The menu changes frequently depending on seasonal specialities.
In the autumn, prized wild porcini mushrooms are among the favored
ingredients. ⊠ *Cassinetta di Lugagnano, 3 km (2 mi) north of Abbiategrasso,* ☎ *02/9420034. Reservations essential. Jacket and tie. AE,
DC, MC, V. Closed Sun., Mon., Dec. 25–Jan. 15, and Aug.*

$$$$ ✕ **Nobu.** A high-end addition to the Japanese dining scene, Milan's
Nobu comes from the creators of the highly acclaimed restaurants of
the same name in New York and London. Here, traditional Japanese
cuisine is combined with South American and Californian influences.
The decor is minimalist Armani, and the sushi is simply delicious. On
the ground floor there's a bar and lounge area where you can have cocktails and light snacks. Call ahead: getting a reservation at Nobu can
be a challenge. ⊠ *Via Pisoni, 1, corner of Via Manzoni 31,* ☎ *02/
72318645. Reservations essential. AE, DC, MC, V. Metro: Montenapoleone. Closed Sun.*

$$$–$$$$ ✕ **Savini.** The Savini, in the Galleria Vittorio Emanuele, is a Milanese
institution, with red carpets and cut-glass chandeliers characteristic of
its late-19th-century roots. The Milanese specialty *risotto al salto* (rice
cooked as a pancake, grilled in the pan) is excellent here, as are the
cotoletta di vitello (veal cutlets) and osso buco. ⊠ *Galleria Vittorio
Emanuele,* ☎ *02/72003433. AE, DC, MC, V. Metro: Duomo. Closed
Sun., Jan. 1–6, and 3 wks in Aug.*

$$$ ✕ **Joia.** At this haute-cuisine restaurant near Piazza della Repubblica,
delicious vegetarian dishes are artistically prepared by chef Pietro Lee-
mann, who creates a new menu every three months. Dishes might include ravioli with basil, potatoes, pine nuts, and crisp green beans, or
purple tagliolini with spring vegetables. A fish menu is also available,
and there is a no-smoking dining room. ⊠ *Via Panfilo Castaldi 18,* ☎

02/29522124. *AE, DC, MC, V. Metro: Repubblica. Closed weekends, Aug., and Dec. 24–Jan. 8.*

\$\$–\$\$\$ ✕ **Antica Trattoria della Pesa.** Fin-de-siècle decor, dark-wood paneling, and old-fashioned lamps re-create the atmosphere of this restaurant at its opening more than 100 years ago. This is authentic Old Milan, as the menu confirms, offering risotto, minestrone, and osso buco. ⊠ *Viale Pasubio, 10,* ☎ *02/6555741. AE, DC, MC, V. Metro: Porta Garibaldi. Closed Sun., Aug., and Dec. 24–Jan. 6.*

\$\$–\$\$\$ ✕ **Boeucc.** Milan's oldest restaurant, opened in 1696, is on the same sug-
★ gestive square as novelist Alessandro Manzoni's house, not far from La Scala. Subtly lit, with cream-color fluted columns, chandeliers, thick carpets, and a garden for warm-weather dining, it has come a long way from the time when it was simply a basement "hole" (*boeucc,* pronounced "birch," is old Milanese for *buco,* or hole). You'll savor typical Milanese and Italian dishes like penne *al branzino e zucchini* (with sea bass and zucchini sauce) and *gelato di castagne con zabaglione caldo* (chestnut ice cream with hot zabaglione). ⊠ *Piazza Belgioso 2,* ☎ *02/76020224. Reservations essential. AE. Metro: Montenapoleone, Duomo. Closed Sat., Aug., Dec. 24–Jan. 2, and Easter holiday. No lunch Sun.*

\$\$ ✕ **La Capanna.** Signora cooks and her husband pours wine and sees that everything goes smoothly in this popular trattoria near the Piola Metro stop (and the university). The food is predominantly Tuscan—Tuscan salami, pappardelle, fish, and steak—but some Milanese specialties are also on the menu. Year-round it is possible to dine on the restaurant's veranda. ⊠ *Via Donatello 9,* ☎ *02/29400884. AE, DC, MC, V. Metro: Piola. Closed Sat. and Aug.*

\$\$ ✕ **La Libera.** Although this establishment in the heart of Brera bills itself as a *birreria con cucina* (beer cellar with kitchen), its young clientele comes here for the excellent food and convivial atmosphere. A soft current of jazz soothes the ripple of conversation amid restful dark green decor. Sample the creative cooking, which varies from season to season but might include such dishes as *insalata esotica* (avocado, chicken, rice, and papaya salad) and *rognone di vitello con broccoletti e ginepro* (veal kidneys with broccoli and juniper berries). ⊠ *Via Palermo 21,* ☎ *02/8053603. AE, DC, MC, V. Metro: Moscova. No lunch.*

\$\$ ✕ **Nabucco.** This smart, tasteful restaurant in the Brera offers such delights as risotto *alla milanese,* an excellent range of salads, and home-made pastries and desserts. ⊠ *Via Fiori Chiari 10,* ☎ *02/860663. AE, DC, MC, V. Metro: Lanza.*

\$–\$\$ ✕ **Al Rifiugio Pugliese.** Just outside the center of town (close to the Wagner metro station), this restaurant is a fun, lively place to sample Apulian specialties like homemade *orecchiette* (a small, ear-shape pasta) with a variety of sauces. ⊠ *Via Costanza 2, corner of Via Boni 16,* ☎ *02/48000917. AE, DC, MC, V. Closed Aug. and late Dec.–early Jan.*

\$–\$\$ ✕ **Taverna Moriggi.** Near the stock exchange, this dusky, wood-paneled wine bar is the perfect spot to enjoy a glass of wine with cheese and cold cuts. At lunch, pasta dishes and select entrées are available, while pasta is the only hot dish served in the evening. You can drop in any time for a bite, but if you're coming for a meal, a reservation is a good idea. ⊠ *Via Moriggi 8,* ☎ *02/86450880. Reservations essential. MC, V. Metro: Cordusio, Missori. Closed Sun. and Aug. No lunch Sat.*

\$–\$\$ ✕ **Trattoria dei Magnani Al Cantinone.** In between La Scala and the Duomo, Cantinone's bar is a relaxing place to sip a glass of wine. The decor is classic Milanese, the service is fast, and the food is homey and reliable. Try the *cotoletta al Cantinone* (veal cutlets with mushrooms, olives, and a cream-and-tomato sauce) accompanied by one of the some 300 wines the proprietor stocks. ⊠ *Via Agnello 19, entrance on Via Ragazzi del 99,* ☎ *02/86461338. AE, DC, MC, V. Metro: Duomo. Closed Sun., Aug., and Dec. 23–Jan. 3. No lunch Sat.*

$–$$ ✕ Trattoria Milanese. Between the Duomo and the Basilica of Sant'Ambrogio, this small, popular trattoria has been run by the same family in the same location since 1933. It's crowded with businesspeople for lunch and with regulars, and the occasional Milanese celebrity, at dinner. Food is authentic regional; good choices include risotto and *cotoletta alla milanese* (Milan-style breaded veal cutlet). ⊠ *Via Santa Marta 11,* ☎ *02/86451991. AE, DC, MC, V. Metro: Duomo, Cordusio, Missori. Closed Tues., Aug., and Dec. 24–Jan. 6.*

$ ✕ Al Tempio d'Oro. It may be noisy, it may have the ambience of an Italian pub, but the food is very good, filling, and—for Milan—surprisingly cheap. It is also near the train station, which makes it a great place to eat before embarking on a journey or, indeed, before beginning your visit to Milan. The food is hardly haute cuisine, but here you'll find an excellent selection of Mediterranean dishes, ranging from a plain pasta to a more exotic Maghrebin couscous. The paella is delicious. ⊠ *Via delle Leghe 23,* ☎ *02/26145709. DC, MC, V. Metro: Pasteur. Closed Sun. and 2 wks in Aug.*

$ ✕ La Bruschetta. This tiny, bustling first-class pizzeria near the Duomo features specialties from Tuscany and other parts of Italy. The wood oven is in full view, so you can see your pizza cooking in front of you, although there are plenty of nonpizza dishes available, too, such as spaghetti *alle cozze e vongole* (with a clam and mussel sauce) and grilled and skewered meats. ⊠ *Piazza Beccaria 12,* ☎ *02/8692494. AE, V. Metro: Duomo. Closed Mon., 3 wks in Aug., and late Dec.–early Jan.*

$ ✕ Pizza Ok. Pizza is almost the only item on the menu at this popular spot near Corso Buenos Aires, but it's very good and the dining experience will be easy on your pocketbook. Possibilities for toppings seem endless. ⊠ *Via Lambro 15,* ☎ *02/29401272. No credit cards. Metro: Porta Venezia. Closed Mon., Aug., and Dec. 24–Jan. 7.*

$$$$ ▥ Carlton-Baglioni. This hotel is the ideal choice for visitors who intend to spend time shopping—or window-shopping—in the nearby high-fashion streets Via della Spiga, Via Sant'Andrea, and Via Monte Napoleone. The hotel is very light and airy, with double-thick windows, a garage with direct access to the hotel, and lots of little touches—gratis chocolates and liqueurs—to make up for the rather functional rooms. Some have terraces large enough for a table, chair, and potted shrubs. ⊠ *Via Senato 5, 20121,* ☎ *02/77077,* FAX *02/783300,* WEB *www.baglionhotel. com. 63 rooms. Restaurant, bar, parking (fee). AE, DC, MC, V.*

$$$$ ▥ Duomo. Your comfort is the important thing at this spacious, modern hotel: celebrities have been turned away when it was thought they would attract noisy fans and paparazzi. This is the obvious choice if a central location is also your priority: you're only 20 yards from the cathedral itself, yet within a quiet pedestrian-only zone. Air-conditioned rooms and duplex suites are swankily done in golds, creams, and browns. If in a room on the second, fourth, or fifth floor, you'll be eye to eye with the Gothic gargoyles and pinnacles of the Duomo. ⊠ *Via San Raffaele 1, 20121,* ☎ *02/8833,* FAX *02/86460454 or 02/86462027,* WEB *www.grandhotelduomo.com. 153 rooms. Restaurant, bar, air-conditioning, parking (fee). AE, DC, MC, V.*

$$$$ ▥ Four Seasons. The renaissance of a 15th-century monastery on an exclusive shopping street in the center of Milan has produced a precious gem—for which you'll pay dearly. The hotel blends European sophistication with American comfort. Individually decorated rooms have opulent marble bathrooms; most rooms face the quiet courtyard. Downstairs is the hotel's well-regarded Il Teatro restaurant. ⊠ *Via Gesù 8, 20121,* ☎ *02/77088,* FAX *02/7708500,* WEB *www.fourseasons.com. 118 rooms. 2 restaurants, bar, health club, business services, meeting room. AE, DC, MC, V.*

$$$$ ⊞ **Grand Hotel et de Milan.** This elegant, central hotel opened its doors in 1863 and has housed famous guests over the years, including the composer Giuseppe Verdi and Maria Callas, and other visiting stars of the nearby La Scala opera house. Rooms are decorated with beautiful antiques and the hotel is also convenient to Milan's exclusive shopping district and the Duomo. The staff is helpful and professional. ⊠ *Via Manzoni, 29, 20100,* ☎ *02/723141,* FAX *02/86460868,* WEB *www. grandhoteletdemilan.it. 95 rooms. 2 restaurants, bar. AE, DC, MC, V.*

$$$$ ⊞ **Palace.** The rather unprepossessing 1950s Milanese exterior is no
★ indication of what lies within, a truly superior hotel with personalized service. Beyond the sumptuous Renaissance and postmodern lobby, rooms reveal precious Empire-style antiques. Exquisite bathrooms are done in Portugal pink and Issoire green marble. Its aim is to be Milan's premier business hotel, with Internet and modem connections in every room, and more. Mediterranean cuisine is served in the Casanova Grill. ⊠ *Piazza della Repubblica 20, 20124,* ☎ *02/6336,* FAX *02/ 654485. 244 rooms. Restaurant, bar, in-room data ports, in-room safes, minibars, laundry service, business services, meeting room, parking (fee). AE, DC, MC, V.*

$$$$ ⊞ **Principe di Savoia.** Of the three deluxe ITT-Sheraton Luxury Col-
★ lection hotels in Milan, this is the most posh. Opened in 1923, it has set and borne the standards for European hotels. Behind the Liberty-style facade, the prevailing decor is 19th-century Lombard, with lavish mirrors, drapes, and carpets. The understated, gracious bedrooms are designed to reflect the eclectic architectural styles of the fin de siècle. If you want to spoil yourself in full Roman-emperor fashion, book the Presidential Suite, complete with private marbled pool. The hotel isn't cheap, but if you stay here you're in good company: this is the favorite Milanese destination of such notables as Queen Elizabeth, the Sultan of Brunei, George Bush, Demi Moore, and Woody Allen. You can dine alfresco in the refined Galleria restaurant. In the year 2000, the hotel was greatly expanded it by taking over the former Duca di Milan hotel next door. The new rooms are also elegant, but decorated in an English style, with floral wallpaper throughout. ⊠ *Piazza della Repubblica 17, 20124,* ☎ *02/62301,* FAX *02/6595838,* WEB *www. luxurycollection.com/property.taf. 399 rooms. Restaurant, bar, health club, dry cleaning, laundry service, business services, convention center, meeting room. AE, DC, MC, V.*

$$$–$$$$ ⊞ **Hotel Spadari al Duomo.** This charming, intimate hotel near the Duomo and the Pinacoteca Ambrosiana also houses its own private art collection. Junior suites on the seventh floor have views of the cathedral. Friendly and helpful management is a plus. Simple dishes are served in the bar. ⊠ *Via Spadari 11, 20123,* ☎ *02/72002371,* FAX *02/861184.,* WEB *www.spadarihotel.com 39 rooms. Bar. AE, DC, MC, V. CP.*

$$$–$$$$ ⊞ **Pierre.** No expense was spared to furnish each room of this luxury hotel in a different style, with lavish color-coordinated fabrics and a variety of modern and antique furniture. Everything is electronic: you can open the curtains, turn off the lights, get personal messages on your TV screen—all at the touch of a button. It's on the inner beltway, near the medieval church of Sant'Ambrogio. ⊠ *Via de Amicis 32, 20123,* ☎ *02/72000581,* FAX *02/8052157. 51 rooms. Restaurant, bar, in-room safes, minibars, parking (fee). AE, DC, MC, V.*

$$ ⊞ **Ariston.** This hotel near the Duomo was built according to bio-architectural principles, using natural materials, and it treats air with ionizers to improve its quality. A warm, informal atmosphere pervades. The buffet breakfast includes organic foods, and bicycles are made available for guests to use in the summer. ⊠ *Largo Carrobbio 2, 20123,* ☎ *02/72000556,* FAX *02/72000914. 46 rooms. Bar, breakfast room, bicycles. AE, DC, MC, V. Closed Aug.*

$$ ⊞ **Canada.** This friendly, small hotel is close to Piazza del Duomo on the edge of a district full of shops and restaurants. It offers good value, with rooms that are furnished in a nondescript fashion but have the usual modern trappings. ⊠ *Via Santa Sofia 16, 20122,* ☎ *02/58304844,* FAX *02/58300282,* WEB *www.canadahotel.it. 35 rooms. Bar. AE, DC, MC, V.*

$$ ⊞ **Gritti.** The Gritti is a bright hotel with a cheerful atmosphere, adequate rooms, and good views (from the inside upper floors) of tiled roofs and the gold Madonnina statue on top of the Duomo, only a few hundred yards away. ⊠ *Piazza Santa Maria Beltrade 4, north end of Via Torino, 20123,* ☎ *02/801056,* FAX *02/89010999,* WEB *www.hotelgritti. com. 48 rooms. Bar, breakfast room, meeting room. AE, DC, MC, V.*

$$ ⊞ **Hotel Vittoria.** This family-owned hotel is on a quiet residential street only minutes from the Galleria Vittorio Emanuele and the Duomo. The guest rooms are tiny but in pristine condition. The courteous, friendly staff is extremely eager to do whatever it can to ensure your comfort and satisfaction. In summer, breakfast is served in the small garden at the back. ⊠ *Via Pietro Calvi 32, 20129,* ☎ *02/5456520,* FAX *02/ 55190246. 20 rooms. Breakfast room, in-room safes, minibars, no-smoking room. AE, DC, MC, V.*

$$ ⊞ **London.** Close to the Duomo, the London has clean, spacious rooms
★ and a staff unfailing in its politeness and efficiency, attending to guests' every need. ⊠ *Via Rovello 3, 20121,* ☎ *02/72020166,* FAX *02/8057037. 29 rooms. Bar. MC, V. Closed Aug. and Dec. 23–Jan. 3.*

$ ⊞ **Antica Locanda Leonardo.** This small hotel is convenient to Santa Maria delle Grazie (home of *The Last Supper*) and the city center. There is a peaceful inner courtyard, and staff is happy to help in getting tickets to the opera, soccer games, and other Milan events. Many of the charming rooms look out onto the courtyard. ⊠ *Corso Magenta 78, 20123,* ☎ *02/463317,* FAX *02/48019012,* WEB *www.leoloc.com. 20 rooms. Restaurant, bar. AE, DC, MC, V. Closed Dec. 27–Jan. 1, and 3 wks in Aug.*

$ ⊞ **San Francisco.** Near Metro stations on two lines (Loreto or Piola stop) and not far from the central station, this modern hotel has a functional, flag-bedecked lobby; simply furnished rooms; and a small garden. ⊠ *Viale Lombardia 55, 20131,* ☎ *02/2361009,* FAX *02/26680377,* WEB *www.hotel-sanfrancisco.it. 31 rooms. AE, DC, MC, V.*

Nightlife and the Arts

The Arts

MUSIC

The Teatro alla Scala is a venue for classical concerts, ballet, and recitals interspersed through the opera season. The **Conservatorio** (⊠ Via del Conservatorio 12, ☎ 02/7621101) is the best place in the city for classical concerts and is a popular venue for the well-heeled all year long. The recently completed **Auditorium di Milano** (⊠ Corso San Gottardo, corner with Via Torricelli, ☎ 02/83389201) houses the **Orchestra Verdi** during its concert season.

OPERA

The season at Milan's famous **Teatro alla Scala** runs from December 7 (St. Ambrose Day) through May or later. Seats are frequently sold out well in advance, but if you are prepared to pay the desk clerk at your hotel, you will probably be able to get hold of a pair of tickets. For information on schedules, ticket availability, and how to buy tickets, there is an **Infotel Scala Service** (with English-speaking staff) at the ticket office (⊠ Teatro alla Scala, Ufficio Biglietteria, Via Filodrammatici 2, ☎ 02/72003744), open daily 9–6 (9–8 when there are performances).

Otherwise, ticket availability may be checked and purchases made by credit card on the opera house's Web site, WEB www.teatroallascala.org, or through the 24-hour automated phone reservation system (☎ 02/860775). Both services charge a 20% advance booking fee. Consult the listings in the informative monthly *Milano Mese,* free at APT (tourist board) offices, or in the weekly *Vivi Milano* (sold with the Wednesday edition of *Corriere della Sera*).

THEATER

Milan's **Piccolo Teatro** (☎ 02/723331) is now made up of three separate venues, each of which is noted for its excellent productions. Intimate **Teatro Paolo Grassi** (✉ Via Rovello 2) is the historical headquarters of the theater, named after its founder. The spacious new **Teatro Giorgio Strehler** (✉ Largo Greppi 1) takes its name from a famous Italian theater director and holds dance and musical performances as well as plays. The horseshoe-shape **Teatro Studio** (✉ Via Rivoli, 6) is a popular venue for experimental theater and music concerts.

Nightlife

BARS

El Brellin (✉ Vicolo Lavandai at Alzaia Naviglio Grande, ☎ 02/58101351) is one of the many bars in the Navigli district. (It also serves brunch, fast becoming a Milanese tradition, on Sunday; it is closed Sunday evening.) In the Brera quarter, check out the **Orient Express** (✉ Via Fiori Chiari 8, ☎ 02/8056227), where it is also possible to get a bite to eat and listen to live music. **Nordest Caffe** (✉ Via P. Borsieri 35, ☎ 02/69001910, closed Sat. evening) is an elegant bar featuring jazz concerts Wednesday and Thursday evenings and classical music on Friday.

NIGHTCLUBS

For an evening of jazz in the heart of the Navigli district, head to **Le Scimmie** (✉ Via Ascanio Sforza 49, ☎ 02/89402874). **Capolinea** (✉ Via Ludovico Il Moro 119, ☎ 02/89122024) is open every night of the week and features an eclectic range of jazz, from Dixieland to the ultramodern New Beat style. **Hollywood** (✉ Corso Como 15/c, ☎ 02/6598996) continues to be one of the most popular places for the fashion set.

La Banque (✉ Via Bassano Porrone, 6, ☎ 02/86996565), near Piazza La Scala, is an exclusive and expensive bar, disco, and restaurant popular for anything from an *aperitivo* to a night on the town. **Magazzini Generali** (✉ Via Pietrasanta 14, ☎ 02/55211313), in what was an old warehouse, is a fun, futuristic place to go for dancing and concerts. It's closed on Sunday. Dancing can be enjoyed to the fullest on the spacious dance floor at **Propaganda** (✉ Via Castelbarco 11, ☎ 02/58310682), near the Bocconi University. Music varies depending on the night but includes Latin American and revival nights.

The hip **Café l'Atlantique** (✉ Viale Umbria 42, ☎ 02/55193906) is a popular place for dancing the night away and enjoying a generous buffet brunch on a lazy Sunday afternoon.

Outdoor Activities and Sports

Participant Sports

GOLF

The **Parco di Monza** (✉ 15 km/9 mi from Milan) has a 27-hole golf course, where it is possible to play 9, 18, or all 27 holes. Contact the Golf Club Milano (☎ 039/303081). You must have a golf-club membership at home in order to play here.

HEALTH CLUB

The best-equipped of Milan's many sports centers is the **Centro Saini** (⌖ Via Corelli 136, ☎ 02/7561280), in the vast Parco Forlanini. Much like a municipal gym, it offers tennis courts, squash, and volleyball facilities, weight rooms, and a track. It's outside the city center; take Bus 38.

Spectator Sports

SOCCER

AC Milan and Inter Milan share the use of the **San Siro Stadium** (⌖ Via Piccolomini). With more than 60,000 of the 85,000 seats allocated to season ticket holders, and another couple of thousand tickets made available to visiting fans (which means they are on sale outside of Milan), tickets can be difficult to come by, especially for the high-profile games. However, the stadium does have tickets on sale for a couple of hours before each game, usually played on Sunday. Otherwise, you can purchase AC Milan tickets at **Cariplo** bank branches, including one in Via Verdi 8. **Inter** tickets can be purchased at the Piazza Meda, 4, branch of Banca Popolare di Milano or at other branches of the bank or at Ticketweb.it, in Via Cappuccini 11 (☎ 02/76009131). If you can't get in to see a game, **stadium tours** (☎ 02/4042432) are also conducted, including a visit to the Milan-Inter museum. Tours meet Monday–Saturday on the hour from 10 AM to 5 PM at Gate 4; they cost 18,000 lire/€9.30.

Shopping

Milan's fortissimo occurs twice a year, at the end of February and October (for women) and June and January (for men), when the world's fashion elite descend on the city for the famous ready-to-wear designer shows that invariably set next season's international styles.

Department Stores

La Rinascente (⌖ Piazza del Duomo, ☎ 02/88521) is one of the bigger department stores in Milan. **Coin** (⌖ Piazza Cinque Giornate, ☎ 02/55192083) offers stylish shopping opportunities.

Markets

Food and a vast array of items, new and old, are displayed in open-air stalls all over Milan. In many markets, bargaining is no longer the custom. You can try to haggle, but if you fear getting ripped off, go to the stalls where prices are clearly marked. On Saturday and Tuesday morning, there is the huge **Mercato Papiniano** (⌖ Viale Papiniano, and the Fiera di Senigallia, on Via Calatafimi) with old and new bargains. If you collect coins, stamps, or telephone cards (now collected in Italy like baseball cards in the United States), go on Sunday morning to the market at **Via Armorari** (⌖ Near Piazza Cordusio). The best antiques markets are held on the last Sunday of each month along the **Navigli** and the third Saturday of each month on **Via Fiori Chiari** (⌖ Near Via Brera).

Shopping Districts

At the northern end of Piazza della Scala, **Via Manzoni** leads into the heart of Milan's most luxurious shopping district, perhaps the most luxurious shopping district in Italy. Right here, in a few small streets laid out like a game of hopscotch—Via Monte Napoleone, Via Sant'-Andrea, Via della Spiga—are the shops of the great Italian designers, such as Armani, Versace, and Gianfranco Ferré. Don't come here looking for affordable fashion—that has been relegated to the other side of the Duomo. Shops are usually open 9–1 (except Monday morning) and 4–7:30; many are closed in August. A good locator map of the best boutiques in the area can be found mounted on a pole at the corner of Via della Spiga and Via Borgospesso.

CLOTHES MAKE THE CITY

WHEN DESIGNER MARIUCCIA Mandelli decided in 1954 to stamp her collection with the name "Krizia," she anticipated fashion-mad Milan with an uncanny foresight. The name adopted by the former teacher is derived from a character in one of Plato's dialogues who spends all of his money on clothes and jewelry for fatuous and vain women; while this may be a designer's dream consumer, the name remains an ironic reminder of the fashion world's constant clash of art and commerce. Nowhere do the two come together so tumultuously as in Milan's Golden Triangle, the approximately 1-km (½-mi) area spanning Via della Spiga, Via Monte Napoleone, and Via Sant'Andrea, which is home to most of Italy's high-fashion houses and the source of several billion dollars of revenue each year. It's here that top designers like Miuccia Prada, Gianfranco Ferré, and Giorgio Armani have their chic boutiques and here that the fashion world's attention is focused four weeks a year on the men's and women's summer and winter collection shows. The city has outgrown its long-standing rivalry with Florence, home to Gucci and Salvatore Ferragamo, for the title of Italy's fashion capital. Milan's designers, Mandelli among them, are known for a subversive attitude toward the conventions of fashion. Legends abound: Missoni's famous 1967 show, in which the black silk dresses of braless models became transparent on the catwalk; Moschino's 1980s-era anti-fashion Minnie Mouse dresses and fried-egg buttons; the late Gianni Versace's rock-and-roll aesthetic that put chains and leather on the catwalk. Italian style is still Italian style, however; one notable exception to this revolutionary fervor is Giorgio Armani, the former medical student whose fluid, elegant designs have made him not only one of the world's leading stylists but also a top Hollywood designer, for films including *American Gigolo* (1980), *True Romance* (1993),

Rising Sun (1993), and *Prêt-à-Porter* (1994), the Robert Altman fashion-world spoof.

Unfortunately, it's all but impossible for the general public to get in to see fashion history being made at the collections, held at the start of January (Men's Spring-Summer), at the end of February (Women's Spring-Summer), at the beginning of October (Women's Fall-Winter), and the end of June (Men's Fall-Winter). Houses hold their own lavish, celebrity-studded presentations, and admission is by jealously guarded invitation only. The national trade organization, the **Camera Nazionale della Moda Italiana,** suggests giving it a go anyway. If you contact design houses in Milan directly before the shows, you may be able to wheedle your way in among the glitterati. **Dolce & Gabbana** dresses the Mediterranean woman (⊠ Via Santa Cecilia, 7, 20122, ☎ 02/774271). **Gianfranco Ferré** traditionally shows in his spacious headquarters (⊠ Via Pontaccio, 21, 20121, ☎ 02/72134201). **Gianni Versace** shows appeal to the rock-and-roll crowd (⊠ Via della Spiga, 25, 20121, ☎ 02/723181). **Giorgio Armani** fashion shows are always celebrity events (⊠ Via Borgonuovo 11, 20121, ☎ 02/723181), and **Gucci** fashion shows are watched closely for new trends (⊠ Via Monte Napoleone 5, 20121, ☎ 02/723141). To see one of Milan's longtimers, you can go to a show of **Krizia** (⊠ Palazzo Melzi d'Eril, Viale Manin 19, 20121, ☎ 02/6596415). **Missoni** shows are known for their bright colors (⊠ Via T. Salvini 1, 20122, ☎ 02/76001479) and **Moschino** for a young, trendy look (⊠ Via Ceradini 11/a, 20129, ☎ 02/7610200). **Prada** (⊠ Via A. Maffei 2, 20135, ☎ 02/546701) has made an international name with simple lines and solid colors. Since his 1999 death, Nicola Trussardi's children have been capably carrying on with tradition at **Trussardi** (⊠ Piazza Duse 4, 20122, ☎ 02/760641).

Brera is a Milanese neighborhood with many unique shops. Walk along Via Brera, Via Solferino, Corso Garibaldi, and Via Paolo Sarpi. **Corso Buenos Aires** is a wide avenue with a variety of shops, several offering moderately priced items. **Corso Vittorio Emanuele** has clothing, leather goods, and shoe shops, some with goods at reasonable prices. **Via Monte Napoleone** has several top-notch jewelers and a profusion of antiques stores and designer fashion boutiques.

Specialty Stores

CLOTHING

For the constant redefinition of cut, design, and style, **Giorgio Armani** (⊠ Via Sant'Andrea 9, ☎ 02/76003234) is the fashion temple. The flashy Armani megastore **Armani Manzoni 31** encompasses a number of shops and restaurants, including **Emporio Armani**(⊠ Via Manzoni, 31, ☎ 02/72318600). **Cerruti 1881** (⊠ Via della Spiga 20, ☎ 02/76009777) has elegant styles with an edge for men and women. Head to **Prada** (⊠ Via della Spiga 1, ☎ 02/76002019) for Miuccia's bewitching minimalist designs (a celebrity favorite), smart leather goods, and the famous series of fin-de-siècle murals. **Gucci** (⊠ Via Monte Napoleone 5 and 27, ☎ 02/795467, 02/771271) has designer Tom Ford's take on fashion and leather goods. **Gianfranco Ferré** (⊠ Via Sant'Andrea 15, ☎ 02/794864) concentrates on swank, ready-to-wear apparel. Daring design is the fashion at **Gianni Versace** (⊠ Via Monte Napoleone 11, ☎ 02/76008528). **Moschino** (⊠ Via Sant'Andrea 12, ☎ 02/76000832) endlessly challenges convention. **Roberto Cavalli** (⊠ Via della Spiga 42, ☎ 02/76020900) is the place for zebra stripes and sexy prints. **Fendi** (⊠ Via Sant'Andrea 16, ☎ 02/76110328) is known for smart purses, fur, and leather. Designer duo **Dolce & Gabbana** (⊠ Via della Spiga, 2, ☎ 02/76001155) create sexy, feminine clothes. If you want the look without designer prices, **Salvagente** (⊠ Via F. Bronzetti 16, ☎ 02/76110328) has brand names at about a third of retail.

HOUSEWARES

L'Utile e il Dilettevole (⊠ Via della Spiga) sells enchanting Italian country-style items for the home. **Alessi** (⊠ Corso Matteotti 9) sells mainly kitchenware by famous Italian and international designers. **High-Tech** (⊠ Piazza XXV Aprile, 12) has everything you can think of for the house, from kitchen utensils to televisions.

SHOES AND LEATHER ACCESSORIES

For top-quality, classic women's shoes, choose **Ferragamo** (⊠ Via Monte Napoleone 3, ☎ 02/76000054). Ferragamo men's shoes can be found down the street (⊠ Via Monte Napoleone 20/5, ☎ 02/76006660). For a mix of style and tradition, try **Fratelli Rossetti** (⊠ Via Monte Napoleone 1, ☎ 02/76021650). Shoe addicts will want a gorgeous pair from **Lario 1898** (⊠ Via Monte Napoleone 21, ☎ 02/76002641) to add to their collection. Comfortable but stylish shoes are found at **Casadei** (⊠ Via Sant'Andrea 17, ☎ 02/76318293). Python shoes are a trademark of **Sergio Rossi,** now owned by Gucci (⊠ Via Monte Napoleone 9, ☎ 02/76006140).

PAVIA, CREMONA, AND MANTUA

Cities of the Po Plain

Great Lombard cities of the Po River plain south of Milan are worth discovering. Pavia is celebrated for its Certosa, a Carthusian monastery. In Cremona, history's great violin makers lived and worked. A diminutive utopian Renaissance city, Sabbioneta was the fruit of one man's obsession. Mantua was the home of the fantastically wealthy Gonzaga dynasty for almost 300 years.

Pavia

⑰ *57 km (35 mi) west of Cremona, 38 km (24 mi) south of Milan.*

Pavia was once Milan's chief regional rival. The city dates from at least the Roman era and was the capital of the Lombard kings for two centuries (572–774). Pavia came to be known as "the city of a hundred towers" (of which only a handful have survived). Its prestigious university was founded in 1361 on the site of a 10th-century law school but has roots dating from antiquity.

The 14th-century **Castello Visconteo** now houses the local **Museo Civico** (Municipal Museum), with an interesting archaeological collection and a picture gallery featuring works by Correggio. ⊠ *Viale 11 Febbraio, near Piazza Castello,* ☎ *0382/33853.* 🎫 *8,000 lire/€4.15.* ☉ *Mar.–June and Sept.–Nov., Tues.–Fri. 9–1:30, weekends 10–7; Dec.– Feb. and July–Aug., Tues.–Sat. 9–1:30.*

In the Romanesque church of **San Pietro in Ciel d'Oro,** you can visit the tomb of Christianity's most celebrated convert, St. Augustine, housed in a Gothic marble ark on the high altar. ⊠ *Via Matteotti.* ☉ *Mon.–Sat. 9–noon and 3–5, Sun. mass.*

The draw in Pavia is the **Certosa** (the Carthusian monastery), 8 km (5 mi) north of the city center. Its elaborate facade shows the same relish for ornamentation as the Duomo in Milan. The Certosa's extravagant grandeur was due, in part, to the plan to have it house the tombs of the family of the first duke of Milan, Galeazzo Visconti III (who died during a plague, at age 49, in 1402). And extravagant it was—almost unimaginably so in an age before modern transport. The very best marble was used, taken undoubtedly by barge from the quarries of Carrara, roughly 240 km (150 mi) away. Though the floor plan may be Gothic—a cruciform divided into a series of squares—the gorgeous fabric that rises above it is triumphantly Renaissance. On the facade, in the lower frieze, are medallions of Roman emperors and Eastern monarchs; above them are low reliefs of the life of Christ and scenes from the career of Galeazzo Visconti III.

The first duke was the only Visconti to be interred here, and then only some 75 years after his death, in a tomb designed by Gian Cristoforo Romano. Look for it in the right transept. In the left transept is a more appealing tomb—that of a rather stern middle-aged man and a beautiful young woman. The man is Ludovico il Moro Sforza (1452–1508), seventh duke of Milan, who commissioned Leonardo to paint *The Last Supper.* The woman is his wife, Beatrice d'Este (1475–97), one of the most celebrated women of her day, the embodiment of brains, culture, birth, and beauty. Married when he was 40 and she was 16, they had enjoyed six years together when she died suddenly, while giving birth to a stillborn child. Ludovico commissioned the sculptor Cristoforo Solari to design a joint tomb for the high altar of Santa Maria delle Grazie in Milan. Originally much larger, the tomb for some years occupied the honored place in Santa Maria delle Grazie as planned. Then, for reasons that are still mysterious, the Dominican monks, who seemed to care no more for their former patron than they did for their faded Leonardo fresco, sold the tomb to their Carthusian brothers to the south. Sadly, part of the tomb and its remains were lost. ⊠ *Certosa, 8 km (5 mi) north of Pavia,* ☎ *0382/925613,* WEB *www. comune.pv.it/certosadipavia/index.html.* 🎫 *Free, donation requested.* ☉ *Oct.–Mar., Tues.–Sat. 9–11:30 and 2:30–4:30, Sun. 9–11:30 and 2:30–5; Apr., Tues.–Sun. 9–11:30 and 2:30–5:30; May–Sept., Tues.– Sun. 9:30–11:30 and 2:30–6.*

Dining

$$$$ ✕ **Locanda Vecchia Pavia al Mulino.** At this sophisticated, art nouveau–
★   style restaurant just 150 yards from the Certosa, you'll find creative
versions of traditional regional cuisine, including *rane* (frogs), the local
specialty, in risotto or cooked on a spit. *Casoncelli* (stuffed pasta), *petto
d'anatra* (duck breast), and veal cutlet alla milanese are done with style,
as are more imaginative seafood dishes. For dessert, consider the hot
chocolate pudding with white chocolate sauce. ✉ *Via al Monumento,*
☎ *0382/925894. Reservations essential. AE, DC, MC, V. Closed
Mon., 2 wks in Aug., and 3 wks in Jan. No lunch Wed.*

Nightlife and the Arts

During the first half of September, Pavia's **Settembre Pavese** festival
presents street processions, displays, and concerts.

Cremona

⑱ *86 km (53 mi) east of Pavia, 93 km (60 mi) southeast of Milan.*

The premier place in Italy to buy a violin is Cremona—as true today
as when Andrea Amati (1510–80) opened up shop here in the 16th
century. Though cognoscenti continue to revere the Amati name, it was
an apprentice of Amati's nephew for whom the fates had reserved wide
and lasting fame. In a career that spanned an incredible 68 years, Antonio Stradivari (1644–1737) made more than 1,200 instruments—including violas, cellos, harps, guitars, and mandolins, in addition to his
fabled violins. Labeled simply with a small printed slip reading ANTO-
NIUS ATRADIVARIUS CREMONENSIS. FACIEBAT ANNO . . .—(the date inserted
in a neat italic hand)—they remain the best, most coveted, and most
expensive stringed instruments in the world.

Cremona's Romanesque **Duomo** was consecrated in 1190 and is home
to the beautiful *Story of the Virgin Mary and the Passion of Christ,*
the central fresco of an extraordinary cycle commissioned in 1514 and
featuring the work of primarily local artists, including Boccacio Boc-
cancino, Giovan Francesco Bembo, and Altobello Melone. ✉ *Piazza
del Comune.* ☉ *Tues.–Sat. 8:30–6, Sun. 10–6.*

If you would like to see original Stradivarius instruments, go to the
second floor of the **Palazzo del Comune** (City Hall), where five masterpieces by Cremonese *liutai* (violin makers), dating from the 16th to
the 18th century, are on view. ✉ *Piazza del Comune,* ☎ *0372/4071.*
🎟 *6,000 lire/€3.10.* ☉ *Tues.–Fri. 8:30–1 and 2:30–4:30, Sat. 9–11:30.*

The **Piazza del Comune,** with its Duomo, campanile, baptistery, and
city hall, is particularly distinctive and harmonious. The combination
of old brick, rose- and cream-color marble, terra-cotta, and old copper roofs brings Romanesque, Gothic, and Renaissance together with
unusual success.

Dominating Cremona's square is the **Torrazzo** (Big Tower), one of
Cremona's symbols and perhaps the tallest campanile in Italy, visible
for a considerable distance across the Po plain. It's open to visitors,
but in winter hours can fluctuate depending on the weather. ✉ *Piazza
del Comune.* 🎟 *8,000 lire/€4.15.* ☉ *Mon.–Sat. 10:30–12:30 and 3–
6, Sun. 10:30–12:30 and 3–7.*

At No. 1 **Piazza Roma,** legendary violin maker Antonio Stradivari lived,
worked, and died. It's a lovely square of gardens, trees, and lawns. According to local lore, Stradivari liked to keep each new instrument in
his bedroom for a month before varnishing it. This way, he claimed,
by virtue of a mysterious transmigration, he gave a soul to each of his

creations. In the center of the park is **Stradivari's grave,** marked by a simple tombstone.

The small **Museo Stradivariano** (Stradivarius Museum) has an informative display of Stradivari's plans and models as well as violins made by Cremona's more modern masters. ⊠ *Via Palestro 17,* ☎ *0372/461886.* 🖼 *6,000 lire/€3.10.* 🕙 *Tues.–Sat. 8:30–6, Sun. 10–6.*

Strolling about town, you may notice that violin making continues to flourish here. There are, in fact, more than 50 liutai, many of them graduates of the Scuola Internazionale di Liuteria (International School of Violin Making), who continue to work by traditional methods in shops scattered throughout Cremona. You are usually welcome to these ateliers, especially if contemplating the acquisition of your own Cremonese violin. (The tourist office has addresses of noted violin makers.)

Dining

$$–$$$ ✕ **La Sosta.** This traditional Cremonese restaurant goes back to the 16th century for some of its culinary inspiration, following a time-tested recipe for a favored first course, gnocchi *Vecchia Cremona.* To finish off the evening, try the *semifreddo al torroncino* and a dessert wine. ⊠ *Via Sicardo, 9,* ☎ *0372/456656. AE, DC, MC, V. Closed Mon. and 3 wks in Aug. No dinner Sun.*

$$ ✕ **Centrale.** Close to the cathedral, this old-style trattoria is a favorite
★ among locals for traditional Cremonese fare, such as succulent *cotecchino con mostarda* (pork sausage and candied fruit with mustard seed) and *tortelli di zucca* (a small stuffed pasta with pumpkin filling), at moderate prices. ⊠ *Vicolo Pertusio 4,* ☎ *0372/28701. AE, DC, MC, V. Closed Thurs. and July.*

Shopping

Cremona is famous throughout Europe as the home of nougat, known here as *torrone.* If the thought of sweet, tooth-crunching nougat is too much to resist, go to **Sperlari** (⊠ Via Solferino 26), home of *the* best nougat in the world. The store also sells all kinds of mostarda.

Sabbioneta

19 *53 km (33 mi) southeast of Cremona, 142 km (88 mi) southeast of Milan.*

Vespasiano Gonzaga (1531–91), Sabbioneta's lord, founder, and chief architect, was not a particularly sympathetic figure. The glory of his attainments in public service is said to have been exceeded only by the ignominy of his treatment of three wives and his only son. Upon retiring from military life at 47, he resolved to turn an old castle and a few squalid cottages into the perfect city—a tiny, urbane metropolis where the most gifted artists and greatest writers would live in perfect harmony with a perfect patron. After some five years of planning and another five of work, the village was transformed into an elegant, star-shape, walled fortress, dubbed Little Athens, with a rational grid of streets, two palaces, two squares, two churches, an exquisite theater (said to be the first in Europe with a roof) by Vincenzo Scamozzi (1552–1616), and a noble gallery of antiquities (a forerunner of today's art galleries). Gonzaga died four years later, survived by the last of his wives.

The **Ufficio Turistico del Comune di Sabioneta** (☎ 0375/221044) leads tours to the Palazzo Ducale, the theater, and the Palazzo del Giardino. Tours begin whenever enough people have assembled. The tourist promotion office (APT; ☞ Visitor Information *in* Milan, Lombardy, and the Lakes A to Z, *below*) leads tours to religious sites, including the city's synagogue.

In the majestic **Palazzo Ducale** (Ducal Palace) are four fine equestrian figures of Vespasiano and his Gonzaga forebears. The little **theater** (an adaptation of Palladio's, at Vicenza, by the man who helped him build it) has been restored, and its frescoes, once whitewashed, have been uncovered. The **Palazzo del Giardino** has a dusty but impressive gallery of antique sculptures. The **synagogue** is now a shuttered and derelict building, the sole surviving trace of Sabbioneta's prosperous 16th-century Jewish community. You'll have to ask someone to point it out. ⊠ *Town center.*

Dining and Lodging

$ ×🏠 **Al Duca.** In Sabbioneta's historical center, this restaurant and small inn serves local specialties like risotto *alla mantovana* (with sausage), *stracotto di asino con polenta* (donkey roast with polenta), and tortelli di zucca. The reasonably priced rooms are comfortable. ⊠ *Via della Stamperia 18, 46018,* ☎ 📠 *0375/220021. 10 rooms. MC, V. Closed Jan. Restaurant closed Mon.*

Mantua

⑳ *37 km (23 mi) east of Sabbioneta, 160 km (102 mi) southeast of Milan.*

Mantua (Mantova, to Italians) is known as the seat of the Gonzagas, who, like the Viscontis and Sforzas of Milan (with whom they intermarried), lived with the regal pomp and circumstance befitting Italy's richest dynasties. Their reign, first as marquesses and later as dukes, was a long one—stretching from the first half of the 14th century into the beginning of the 18th.

Even if you've had enough of old palaces, you may still wish to come to Mantua. First, Virgil was born near here. Second, Mantegna (painter of the poignant *Dead Christ* in Milan's Pinacoteca di Brera) served the Gonzaga as court painter for 50 years, and his best-known and only large surviving fresco cycle can be seen here. In addition, there are two fine churches by Leon Battista Alberti (1404–72). Much like Mantegna's work here, both proved highly influential and were widely emulated later in the Renaissance.

Home to the Gonzagas for centuries, the 500-room **Palazzo Ducale** gives one the sense that it took centuries to build. From a distance, the group of buildings dominates the skyline, and the effect is fascinating. The **Appartamento dei Nani** (Dwarfs' Apartments) were literally that, dwarf-collecting being one of the more bizarre occupations of Renaissance princes. According to historians, the dwarfs were not mistreated but were considered to be something between members of the family and celebrity comics. The apartments were built both for the dwarfs' enjoyment and for that of the court.

The **Appartamento del Paradiso** is praised for its view but is somewhat more interesting for its decorator and first resident, Isabella d'Este (1474–1539). Not only was she married at 16, like her younger sister Beatrice (of the tomb in the Certosa at Pavia), she was apparently also Ludovico il Moro Sforza's first choice for a wife—until he learned she was already affianced to a Gonzaga rival. Isabella was one of the great patrons of the Renaissance. She survived her sister by more than 40 years, and the archives of her correspondence, totaling more than 2,000 letters, are considered some of the most valuable records of the era.

The high point of all 500 rooms, if not of the city, is the **Camera degli Sposi**—literally, "Chamber of the Wedded Couple," because Duke Ludovico and his wife are the focus of attention; it was actually an audience chamber. It was painted by Mantegna over a nine-year period, when he was at the height of his power, and finished when he was 44. Here, Mantegna made a startling advance in painting by organizing the picture plane in a way that systematically mimics the experience of human vision. Even now, more than five centuries later, you can almost sense the excitement of a mature artist, fully aware of the great importance of his painting, expressing his vision with a masterly, joyous confidence. The interiors of Mantua's Palazzo Ducale may be seen today only on a rigorous guided tour normally conducted in Italian by the museum. However, if you wish to be accompanied by an English-speaking guide, call the Mantua Tourist Guide Association or the tourist office (☞ Visitor Information *in* Milan, Lombardy, and the Lakes A to Z, *below*). ⊠ *Piazza Sordello,* ☎ *0376/382150.* ☞ *12,000 lire/€6.20.* ☉ *Tues.–Sun. 8:45–7:15.*

The most serious Mantegna aficionados will want to visit the **Casa di Andrea Mantegna,** designed by the artist himself and built around an intriguing circular courtyard, usually open to view (the interior can only be seen by appointment or during occasional art exhibitions). ⊠ *Via Acerbi 47,* ☎ *0376/360506.* ☞ *Free.* ☉ *Tues.–Sun. 10–12:30 and 3–6 when exhibitions are scheduled.*

Mantegna's tomb is in the first chapel on the left in the church of **Sant'-Andrea** (1471, some sections earlier or later), a masterwork by the architect Alberti. The church is considered Mantua's most important Renaissance creation. ⊠ *Piazza delle Erbe, south of Piazza Sordello.* ☉ *Daily 8–12:30 and 3–6.*

NEED A
BREAK?

Bar Caravatti (⊠ Portico Broletto 16 on Piazza delle Erbe, ☎ 0376/321653) is Mantua's oldest café and continues to be well known for its *aperitivi.* **Bar Sociale** (⊠ Piazza Cavallotta 16 ☎ 0376/322122) is a favored meeting place for Mantovani.

Palazzo Te is one of the greatest of all Renaissance palaces, built by Isabella d'Este's son, Federigo II Gonzaga (1500–40), for his mistress between 1525 and 1535. It is the singular mannerist creation of artist-architect Giulio Romano, decorated with mythological trompe-l'oeil paintings not to every visitor's taste. Nevertheless, as the magnificently frescoed **Sala dei Giganti** (Room of Giants) proves, the palace does not skimp on pictorial drama. ⊠ *Viale Tè, south of town walls,* ☎ *0376/323266,* WEB *www.centropalazzote.it.* ☞ *12,000 lire/€6.20.* ☉ *Mon. 1:30–6, Tues.–Sun. 9–6.*

Dining and Lodging

$$$$ ★ ✕ **Al Bersagliere.** One of Lombardy's best restaurants is this rustic four-room inn in the tiny riverside hamlet of Goito, some 16 km (10 mi) north of Mantua on Route 236 (the main Mantua–Brescia road). It has been run by a single family for more than 150 years. The fish in particular is excellent, as is a Mantuan classic, frog soup. ⊠ *Via Goitese 258, Goito,* ☎ *0376/60007. Reservations essential. AE, DC, MC, V. Closed 3 wks in Aug., Mon., Tues. in Jan.–Feb.; Mar.–Dec. no lunch Mon., Tues.*

$$$$ ★ ✕ **Ambasciata.** Heralded by food critics the world over as one of Italy's finest restaurants, Ambasciata takes elegance and service to extremes rarely, if ever, achieved outside Europe. Yet it is the food and wine that ultimately take center stage. After stints at Le Cirque in New York and the Bellagio in Las Vegas, world-renowned head chef Romano Tamani has returned home to tiny Quistello, about 20 km (12 mi) southeast of Mantua, where he offers to those willing to make the trek (and pay the bill) an ever-changing array of superlative creations

like *timballo di lasagne verdi con petto di piccione sauté alla crème de Cassis* (a mesmerizing meld of green *lasagne*, breast of pigeon, and red currant). Every aspect of the meal—visual and gustatory—is like a finely orchestrated show. You'll feel lucky just to play a bit part. ⊠ *Via Martiri di Belfiore 33, Quistello,* ☎ *0376/619169,* FAX *0376/618255. Reservations essential. AE, DC, MC, V. Closed Mon., Jan. 1–20, and Aug. 5–25. No dinner Sun.*

$$$ ✕ **L'Aquila Nigra.** Down a small side street opposite the Palazzo Ducale, this popular restaurant is set in a former medieval convent, where frescoes grace the walls. Diners choose from such local dishes as *medaglione di anguilla all'aceto balsamico* (medallion of eel with balsamic vinegar), *saltarelli e frittata di zucchine* (lightly fried freshwater shrimp and zucchini), and *petto di faraona in pane grattinata con rosmarino* (breaded guinea fowl with rosemary). Reservations are recommended. ⊠ *Vicolo Bonacolsi 4,* ☎ *0376/327180. AE, DC, MC, V. Closed Sun. and Mon. in Jan.–Mar., June–Aug., and Nov.–Dec.; 1 wk in Jan.; and 3 wks in Aug.*

$$–$$$ ✕ **Trattoria dei Martini–Il Cigno.** In a romantic 16th-century palazzo featuring period frescoes, this restaurant scores well for atmosphere. The menu features local specialties such as tortelli di zucca, *insalata di cappone* (capon salad), *luccio in salsa di verdura all'aceto* (pike with vegetable and vinegar sauce), and variations on the Lombard favorite risotto. ⊠ *Piazza Carlo d'Arco 1,* ☎ *0376/327101. Reservations essential. AE, DC, MC, V. Closed Mon., Tues., 1 wk in Jan., and Aug.*

$ ✕ **Trattoria Due Cavallini.** This friendly family-owned restaurant a bit outside the center of town is the spot for Mantuan specialties like tortelli di zucca. Prices are affordable and portions are abundant. ⊠ *Via Salnitro 5,* ☎ *0376/322084. AE. Closed Tues. and mid-July–mid-Aug.*

$$$ ▥ **San Lorenzo.** Rooms in this city-center hotel known for comfort and individual attention are large, with authentic early 19th-century decor. You're within easy walking distance of many restaurants, which is an advantage, since the hotel's restaurant is not yet open to the public at large, and are only used for private parties. Some people may find the rooms in the front a little noisy at night, when locals indulge in *passeggiata* (early evening promenade). Be sure to visit the rooftop terrace. ⊠ *Piazza Concordia 14, 46100,* ☎ *0376/220500,* FAX *0376/327194,* WEB *www.hotelsanlorenzo.it. 23 rooms, 9 suites. Minibars, meeting rooms, parking (fee). AE, DC, MC, V.*

Nightlife and the Arts

Each year on the Feast of the Assumption (August 15), a contest is held in Mantua to determine who is the best *madonnaro* (street artist). Some of the painters can re-create masterpieces in a matter of minutes.

Outdoor Activities and Sports

The Mantua tourist office provides information on biking in the area and boat rides on the Mincio River.

LAKE GARDA, BRESCIA, BERGAMO

One of the curious things about Lake Garda is its perennial attraction for writers. Even essayist Michel de Montaigne (1533–92), whose 15 months of travel journals contain not a single other reference to nature, paused to admire the view down the lake from Torbole, which he called "boundless."

Lake Garda is 50 km (31 mi) long, ranges roughly 1 km–16 km (½ mi–10 mi) wide, and is as much as 1,135 ft deep. The terrain is flat at the lake's southern base and mountainous at its northern tip. As a consequence, the standard descriptions of it vary from stormy inland sea to crystalline Nordic fjord. It is the biggest lake in the region and by most accounts the cleanest. If you are traveling by car, you should be particularly careful when driving in and out of the hairpin turns on the lake road, where there have been several fatal accidents.

Bardolino

㉑ *64 km (40 mi) north of Mantua, 147 km (91 mi) northeast of Milan.*

Bardolino, which makes unremarkable but famous red wine, is one of the biggest summer resorts on the lake. It stands on the eastern shore at the wider end of the lake. Here there are two handsome Romanesque churches: **San Severo,** from the 11th century, and **San Zeno,** from the 9th. Both are in the center of the small town. Bardolino is very lively at night, especially compared to other towns on the lake.

Nightlife and the Arts

Bardolino is host to several festivals, but the best one is the **Cura'del Grappolo** (Grape Cure Festival), a great excuse to indulge in some of the local vino, since the idea is that the more you drink the better the cure will be. Bring aspirin, just in case.

Punta di San Vigilio

㉒ *6 km (4 mi) north of Bardolino, 70 km (44 mi) north of Mantua.*

Punta di San Vigilio, which just about everyone agrees is the prettiest spot on Garda's eastern shore, is full of cypresses from the gardens of the 15th-century **Villa Guarienti di Brenzone.**

Malcesine

㉓ *28 km (17 mi) north of Punta di San Vigilio, 179 km (111 mi) northeast of Milan.*

One of the loveliest areas along the upper eastern shore of Lake Garda, Malcesine is principally known as a summer resort with sailing and windsurfing schools. The 13 campsites and tourist villages do tend to make the town a little crowded in summer. There are, however, some nice walks from the town toward the mountains behind.

Dominating the town is the 13th- to 14th-century **Castello Scaligero,** built by the Della Scalas.

OFF THE BEATEN PATH **MONTE BALDO –** You're in the Veneto now, and if you are fond of cable cars, take the 15-minute *funivia* (funicular) ride to the top of Monte Baldo (5,791 ft) for a great view of the whole lake in summer, or possibly a short ski run in winter. Call ☎ 0457/400206 for information.

Outdoor Activities and Sports
SKIING
Malcesine is a well-equipped resort with six lifts and more than 11 km (7 mi) of runs of varying degrees of difficulty.

Riva del Garda

㉔ *21 km (13 mi) north of Malcesine, 170 km (106 mi) northeast of Milan.*

One of the biggest towns on the northern tip of the lake, Riva del Garda is large and prosperous, and if you're here in summer, you may want to stay here if the towns farther south seem too crowded. Many of the town's public buildings date from the 15th century, when it was a strategic outpost of the Venetian Republic. The heart of town, the lakeside

Piazza 3 Novembre, is surrounded by medieval *palazzi*. Standing in the piazza and looking out onto the lake, you can understand Riva del Garda's importance as a windsurfing center. Mountain air currents ensure good breezes on even the sultriest midsummer days. The **Torre Apponale,** predating the Venetian period by three centuries, looms above the medieval residences of Riva del Garda's main square; its crenellations recall its defensive purpose. The fortress of **La Rocca,** formerly a residence of the Scaligeri princes of Verona, is now a small museum, which frankly is only worth going into if you have time on your hands. Inside you'll find work of varying quality by local artists. ☎ 0464/573869. 🎫 4,000 *lire/€2.10.* ⊘ *Tues.–Sun. 9:30–5:30.*

OFF THE BEATEN PATH

CASCATA DEL VARONE – This waterfall, some 295 ft high, is 4 km (2½ mi) north of town on the road to Tenno. You can walk up to an observation platform and look up at the water plummeting down the cavity it has carved over time; bring a waterproof jacket.

CASTEL TOBLINO – A lovely stop for a lakeside drink or a romantic dinner is this castle, right on a lake in Sarche, about 20 km (12 mi) north of Riva toward Trento. The compound is fabled to have been a prehistoric, then Roman, village and was later associated with the Church of Trento. Bernardo Clesio had it rebuilt in the 16th century in the Renaissance style. It is now a sanctuary of fine food, serving such dishes as *garganelli alla salsa di carciofi* (grooved tubular-shape pasta with artichoke sauce) and *faraone ripieno alla castagna con salsa al timo* (guinea fowl stuffed with chestnuts in thyme sauce). Lake fish are also among the restaurant's specialties. The 55,000 lire/€28.40 prix-fixe menu is a good way to go. ✉ *Via Caffaro 1, Sarche,* ☎ *0461/864036. MC, V. Closed Tues., mid-Nov.–Feb. No dinner some Mon.*

Lodging

$$$$ 🏨 **Hotel du Lac et du Parc.** Perhaps the French name is intended to evoke the lake's 19th-century grandeur, when it was a favorite destination of European aristocracy. Whatever the reason, it works: Riva's most splendid hotel has elegance, personalized service, and luxury rarely found on Lake Garda. The airy, comfortable public spaces include a large dining room, a delightful bar, and a beautifully manicured private garden that leads to the public beach. The rooms are well appointed and comfortable; be sure to ask for one with air-conditioning. ✉ *Viale Rovereto 44, 38066,* ☎ *0464/551500,* 🏠 *0464/555200. 170 rooms, 5 suites. 2 restaurants, bar, dining room, indoor pool, hair salon, sauna, Turkish baths, 2 tennis courts, gym, beach. AE, DC, MC, V.*

$$$ 🏨 **Hotel Sole.** Occupying a restored 15th-century palazzo, this lovely, understated hotel offers comfortable, well-appointed rooms at affordable rates, which these days is a rare combination for the ever-popular Lake Garda. The terraced rooms in front have breathtaking views of the lake, mountains, and the medieval rooftops of the town. In summer, sun worshipers who despair at the often-crowded beaches can sun themselves in the secluded privacy of the roof terrace. The hotel allows guests to use its city and mountain bikes for free. ✉ *Piazza 3 Novembre 35, 38066,* ☎ *0464/552686,* 🏠 *0464/552811,* 🌐 *www.hotelsole. net. 49 rooms, 3 suites. Restaurant, bar, in-room safes, refrigerators, room service, sauna, bicycles, solarium, parking (fee). AE, DC, MC, V.*

$$$ 🏨 **Luise.** This cozy, reasonably priced hotel has great amenities, including a big garden and a large swimming pool. Luise's restaurant, La Limonaia, is recommended for its Trentino specialties. ✉ *Viale Rovereto 9, 38066,* ☎ *0464/552796,* 🏠 *0464/554250,* 🌐 *www.hotelluise.com. 70 rooms. Restaurant, pool, tennis court. AE, DC, MC, V.*

Outdoor Activities and Sports

WINDSURFING

Contact **Circolo Surf Torbole** (⌧ Colonia Pavese, ☎ 0464/505385) for news on windsurfing in the area.

En Route After passing the town of Limone—where it is said the first lemon trees in Europe were planted—take the fork to the right about 5 km (3 mi) north of Gargnano and head to Tignale. The view from the Madonna di Monte Castello church, some 2,000 ft above the lake, is spectacular. Adventurous travelers will want to follow this pretty inland mountain road to Tremosine; the road winds its way up the mountain through hairpin turns and blind corners that can test even the most experienced drivers.

Gargnano

㉕ *27 km (17 mi) south of Riva del Garda, 141 km (88 mi) northeast of Milan.*

This small port town was an important Franciscan center in the 13th century. One of the two houses owned and lived in by Mussolini is now a language school; the other, **Villa Feltrinelli,** has not yet been opened to the public. An Austrian flotilla bombarded the town in 1866, and some of the houses still bear signs of cannon fire. The town comes alive in the summer months when mostly German tourists, many of whom have villas here, invade the small pebble beach.

Dining and Lodging

$$$$ ✕ **La Tortuga.** This highly acclaimed restaurant may have the appear-
★ ance of a rustic trattoria, but the decor belies the sophisticated, nouvelle-style twists on local dishes. The six-course meals are divine. Specialties include *agnello con rosmarino e timo* (lamb with rosemary and thyme), *persico con rosmarino* (perch with rosemary), and *carpaccio d'anatra all'aceto balsamico* (goose carpaccio with balsamic vinegar). Tempting desserts include hot chocolate soufflé smothered in white-and-dark chocolate sauce. There's an extensive wine cellar; try the local white Lugana. ⌧ *Via XXIV Maggio,* ☎ *0365/71251. AE, DC, MC, V. Closed Tues. and Jan.–mid-Mar. No dinner Mon. in Oct.–May.*

$ 🏨 **Hotel Bartabel.** This cozy hotel on the main street offers comfortable, basic accommodations at a reasonable price. The restaurant has an elegant terrace overlooking the lake. ⌧ *Via Roma 39, 25084,* ☎ *0365/71330,* 🖷 *0365/790009. 10 rooms. Restaurant. AE, DC, MC, V. Closed mid.–late Nov., restaurant closed Mon.*

Outdoor Activities and Sports

BICYCLING AND HIKING

The **Upper Brescian Garda Park** stretches over nine municipalities on the western side of the lake, from Salò to Limone (the northernmost town in the park), covering 38,000 hectares (147 square mi). The **Limone Hotel Owners Association** (⌧ Via Quattro Novembre 2/C, ☎ 0365/954720) can provide trail and bicycle-rental information. From June to September, the **Gruppo Alpini Limone** leads free treks every Sunday.

En Route Going from Gargnano to Gardone, you pass the small town of **Toscolano-Maderno,** which has a delightful lakefront piazza and one of the oldest paper-recycling factories in Italy. The town itself hails from Etruscan times, but there are also remnants of Roman influence.

Gardone Riviera

26 *12 km (7 mi) south of Gargnano, 90 km (56 mi) north Mantua.*

Gardone Riviera, a once-fashionable 19th-century resort (now delightfully faded) is the former home of the flamboyant Gabriele d'Annunzio (1863–1938), one of Italy's greatest modern poets. D'Annunzio's estate, **Il Vittoriale,** perched on the hills above the town, is an elaborate memorial to himself, clogged with the trappings of conquests in art, love, and war (of which the largest is a ship's prow in the garden, which is open 8 AM–8:30 PM in summer, 9–5 in winter), and complete with an imposing mausoleum. ⊠ *Gardone Riviera,* ☎ *0365/296511,* WEB *www.vittoriale.it.* 🎟 *20,000 lire/€10.35 (includes tour of house), 10,000 lire/€5.15 for museum and Vittoriale grounds alone.* ☉ *House Oct.–Mar., Tues.–Sun. 9–1 and 2–5; Apr.–Sept., Tues.–Sun. 10–6.*

When you're in Gardone, it's worth a visit to the **Giardino Botanico Hruska,** where more than 2,000 Alpine, subtropical, and Mediterranean species thrive. ⊠ *Via Roma,* ☎ *0365/20347.* 🎟 *10,000 lire/€5.15.* ☉ *Mar. 15–Oct. 15, daily 9–6.*

OFF THE BEATEN PATH | **SALÒ MARKET** – Four kilometers (2½ miles) south of Gardone Riviera is the pretty lakeside town of Salò, which history buffs may recognize as the capital of the ill-fated Social Republic set up in 1943 by the Germans after they liberated Mussolini from the Gran Sasso. Every Saturday morning, in the Piazza dei Martiri della Libertà, an enormous market is held, with great bargains on everything from household items to clothing to foodstuffs. In August or September, a lone vendor often sells locally unearthed *tartufi neri* (black truffles) at affordable prices.

Dining and Lodging

$$$$ ✕🏨 **Villa Fiordaliso.** The pink-and-white lakeside Villa Fiordaliso—
★ once home to Claretta Petacci, given to her by her lover Benito Mussolini—is a high-quality restaurant, but it also has seven tastefully furnished rooms, some overlooking the lake. The Claretta Suite is where Mussolini and Petacci were said to have carried on their affair. The art nouveau–style restaurant (no lunch Tuesday) features seasonal ingredients like zucchini flowers and porcini mushrooms, paramount in salads and soups. ⊠ *Via Zanardelli 150, 25083,* ☎ *0365/20158,* FAX *0365/290011,* WEB *www.villafiordalisa.it. 7 rooms. Restaurant. AE, DC, MC, V. Closed Mon. and Jan.–Feb..*

$$$$ 🏨 **Villa del Sogno.** A small, winding road takes you from the village
★ to this imposing villa, which surveys the valley and the lake below it. The large hotel terrace and the quiet surrounding grounds add to the feeling of getting away from it all, and you'll probably think twice about a busy sightseeing itinerary once you've settled into position in the sun, cool drink in hand. ⊠ *Corso Zanardelli 107, 25083,* ☎ *0365/290181,* FAX *0365/290230. 28 rooms, 5 suites. Restaurant, pool, tennis court, gym. AE, DC, MC, V. Closed Oct. 31–Mar.*

$$$–$$$$ 🏨 **Grand Hotel Fasano.** A former 19th-century hunting lodge on the lakefront, the Fasano has matured into a seasonal hotel of a high standard. The location, between Gardone and Maderno, is choice. To one side you face the deep blue waters of Lake Garda; otherwise, you're surrounded by a lush, green, 12,000 square m private park where the original Austrian owners no doubt spent their days chasing game. The staff is friendly, as are most of the guests, who seem to be keen on making the most use of the water sports at their disposal. As well as the activities on the water, there are two golf courses in the vicinity. It's worth paying a bit extra to get one of the larger rooms with a lake view and balcony. ⊠ *Corso Zanardelli 190, 25083,* ☎ *0365/290220,*

FAX 0365/290221, WEB *www.grand-hotel-fasano.it. 68 rooms. Restaurant, bar, pool, beach, tennis court, waterskiing. No credit cards. Closed Oct.–early May.*

$$ ⌂ **Villa Maria Elisabetta.** Many of the rooms in this charming hotel, run by a group of hospitable nuns, have views of Lago di Garda. You can sit in the hotel's garden or take one of the ground's trails down to the lakeside for a dip in the lake or a bask in the sun. ⊠ *Viale Zanardelli 180, 25083,* ☎ FAX *0365/20206. 45 rooms. Restaurant, bar, chapel, parking. No credit cards. Closed Oct. 15–Nov. CP, FAP, MAP.*

Nightlife and the Arts

BAR

Gardone's tranquillity is its greatest attraction. Visitors and locals alike relish a passeggiata along the lakefront, stopping perhaps to enjoy an ice cream or aperitif at a bar. **Winnie's Bar,** in the Grand Hotel Fasano, is particularly elegant. It's named after Winston Churchill, who reputedly enjoyed more than just a couple of brandies in the Belle Epoque surroundings.

CONCERTS

Il Vittoriale (☎ 0365/296506) holds a series of concerts and other performing arts in its outdoor theater during July and August.

Sirmione

★ ㉗ *32 km (19 mi) south of Gardone Riviera, 127 km (79 mi) east of Brescia.*

The ruins at this enchanting town on an isthmus at the southwestern shore of Lake Garda, complete with narrow, cobbled streets that wind their way through medieval arches, are a reminder that Garda has been a holiday resort for the well-to-do since the height of the Roman era. Most of the historic town, which stretches the length of the spit, is inaccessible to cars, so you must park the car at the bottom of the historic center and walk the rest of the way. The locals will almost certainly tell you that the so-called **Grotte di Catullo** (Grottoes of Catullus) were once the site of the villa of Catullus, one of the greatest pleasure-seeking poets of all time. Present archaeological wisdom, however, does not concur, and there is some consensus that this was the site of two villas of slightly different periods, dating from about the 1st century AD. But never mind—the view through the cypresses and olive trees is lovely, and even if Catullus didn't have a villa here, he is closely associated with the area and undoubtedly did have a villa somewhere nearby. The ruins are at the top of the isthmus and are badly signposted: walk through the historic center and past the various villas to the top of the spit; the grottoes are on the right. ⊠ *Grotte di Catullo,* ☎ *030/916157.* 🎫 *8,000 lire/€4.15.* ⊙ *Mar.–mid-Oct., Tues.–Sun. 8:30–7; mid-Oct.–Feb., Tues.–Sun. 8:30–4:30.*

The **Castello Scaligera** was built, along with almost all the other castles on the lake, by the Della Scala family. As hereditary rulers of Verona for more than a century before control of the city was seized by the Visconti in 1402, they counted Garda among their possessions. You may wish to go inside, since there is a nice view of the lake from the tower. Or you may want to go for a swim at the nearby beach before continuing on. Entry to the old part of town is gained through the castle's gates, over what was originally a drawbridge. ⊠ *Piazza Castello, Sirmione,* ☎ *030/916468.* 🎫 *8,000 lire/€4.15.* ⊙ *Apr.–Sept. Tues–Sun. 8:30–7; Oct., Tues.–Sun., 8:30–5:30; Nov.–Feb., Tues.–Sun, 8:30–4:30; Mar. Tues.–Sun., 8:30–5:30. Hours are subject to variations.*

OFF THE	**GARDALAND AMUSEMENT PARK –** This park has more than 40 different

OFF THE
BEATEN PATH

GARDALAND AMUSEMENT PARK – This park has more than 40 different rides and water slides, making it one of Italy's biggest amusement parks and a favorite with kids. It is 16 km (10 mi) east of Sirmione. ⊠ *Castelnuovo del Garda,* ☎ *045/6449777.* 📧 *38,000 lire/€19.65.* ☉ *July– Aug., daily 9 AM–midnight; Apr.–June and Sept., daily 9:30–6:30; Oct., weekends 9:30–6:30.*

Dining and Lodging

$$$$ ✕ **La Rucola.** Next to Sirmione's castle, this elegant, intimate restaurant has a creative menu, with seafood and meat dishes accompanied by a good choice of wines. Two fixed-price menus are available. ⊠ *Via Strentelle 3,* ☎ *030/916326. Jacket and tie. AE, DC, MC, V. Closed Jan.–mid-Feb. No lunch Thurs. or Fri.*

$$$ ✕ **Vecchia Lugana.** At the base of the peninsula and outside the town,
★   this restaurant is often touted as among Italy's best. Fish from the lake, grilled trout, and fillet of perch with artichokes are especially good. There's also an elegant garden. ⊠ *Piazzale Vecchia Lugana 1, Lugana di Sirmione,* ☎ *030/919012. AE, DC, MC, V. Closed Tues. and Jan. No dinner Mon.*

$$ ✕ **Ristorante Al Pescatore.** Lake fish is the specialty of this simple, rustic-looking, but very popular restaurant in Sirmione's historical center. Try grilled trout with a bottle of local white wine and finish your meal with a walk in the nearby public park. ⊠ *Via Piana 20,* ☎ *030/ 916216. AE, DC, MC, V. Closed Wed. and Jan.*

$$$$ ☷ **Villa Cortine Palace.** This former private villa in a secluded park risks
★   being just plain ostentatious, but it's saved by the sheer luxury of its setting and the extraordinary professionalism of its staff. The hotel dominates a low hill, and the grounds—a colorful mixture of lawns, trees, statues, and fountains—go down to the lake. The villa itself dates from the early part of the 19th century, although a wing was added in 1952: the trade-off is between the more charming old-world decor in the older rooms and the better lake views from the newer ones. ⊠ *Via Grotte 6, 25019,* ☎ *030/9905890,* 📠 *030/916390,* 🌐 *www.hotelvillacortine. com. 54 rooms, 6 suites. Restaurant, bar, pool, tennis court, beach. AE, DC, MC, V. Closed late Oct.–mid-Apr..*

$$$–$$$$ ☷ **Continental.** On the lakefront, the Continental, with a pool and a lakeside terrace, has the feel of a much more expensive establishment. Most rooms have balconies; ask specifically for a lake view. ⊠ *Via Punta Staffalo 7, 25019,* ☎ *030/9905711,* 📠 *030/916278. 51 rooms. Restaurant, air-conditioning, beach, pool. AE, DC, MC, V. Closed Nov.–Feb. CP, FAP, MAP.*

$$$–$$$$ ☷ **Hotel Sirmione.** Just inside the city walls, near the Castello, this hotel
★   and spa sits amid lakeside gardens and terraces. Rooms are furnished with comfortable Scandinavian slat beds, matching floral draperies and wall coverings, and built-in white furniture. Many guests have been returning for years, largely due to the homespun feel and the attentiveness of its staff. Full and half pension are offered. ⊠ *Piazza Castello 19, 25019,* ☎ *030/916331,* 📠 *030/916558,* 🌐 *www.termedisirmione.com. 101 rooms. Restaurant, 2 bars, pool, spa. AE, DC, MC, V. FAP, MAP.*

Brescia

㉘   *40 km (25 mi) west of Sirmione, 50 km (31 mi) east of Milan.*

The ruins of the **Capitolino,** a temple built by the Emperor Vespasian in AD 73, testify to Brescia's Roman origin. The adjoining Museo Romano is closed indefinitely for restoration, but its outstanding exhibits—including the famed 1st-century bronze *Winged Victory*—can be viewed in the **Monasterio di Santa Giulia** down the street. ⊠ *Via*

dei Musei 81/b, ☎ *030/2977834.* 🖾 *10,000 lire/€5.15.* ☉ *June–Sept.,
Tues.–Sun. 10–8; Oct.–May, Tues.–Sun. 9:30–5:30.*

In addition to the Brescia School, the **Pinacoteca Civica Tosio-Martinengo**
houses paintings by Raphael, Tintoretto (1518–94), Tiepolo (1727–
1804), and Jean Clouet (1485–1540). ✉ *Piazza Moretto, 4,* ☎ *030/
3774999.* 🖾 *5,000 lire/€2.60.* ☉ *June–Sept., Tues.–Sun. 10–5; Oct.–
May, Tues.–Sun. 9:30–1 and 2:30–5.*

Palladio (1508–80) and Sansovino (1486–1570) contributed to the splendid **Palazzo della Loggia,** the Lombard-Venetian palace of marble
overlooking the Piazza della Loggia. The **Torre dell'Orologio** (Clock
Tower; ✉ Piazza della Loggia) dates from the 16th century and is modeled on the campanile in Venice's Piazza San Marco. In the church of
Madonna del Carmine is a flight of stairs that climbs to the ramparts
of the Venetian Castello, high enough to give a panoramic view over
the town and across the plain to the distant Alps. ✉ *Piazza del Duomo.
Closed Mon. and Wed.*

Dining and Lodging

$$$$ ✕ **Gualtiero Marchesi.** Never afraid to try something new, owner-chef
★ Gualtiero Marchesi is celebrated as the founder of *la cucina nuova* (nouvelle cuisine). Since 1993, the kitchen in this deluxe hotel villa has been
revered for its spectacular flights of fantasy executed with classic Lombardian finesse. Tiny lake fish are served in paper, folded origami fashion; soups are garnished with caviar; and ravioli are served *aperto*
(unsealed at the edges) or *fazzoletto* (folded handkerchief-style). The
desserts—and prices—are stellar. ✉ *Via Vittorio Emanuele 11, Erbusco,
inside the Albereta Hotel,* ☎ *030/7760562. Reservations essential. Jacket
and tie. AE, DC, MC, V. Closed Jan. 10–Feb. 20.*

$$$$ ✕ **La Sosta.** Just south of Brescia's cathedral, La Sosta occupies a
17th-century building. The cuisine and service suggest a more expensive establishment. On offer are international dishes and Brescian specialties, including *casoncelli* (large meat-filled ravioli). *Capretto alla
bresciana* (roast kid with polenta) is an outstanding, and substantial,
main course. ✉ *Via San Martino della Battaglia 20,* ☎ *030/295603,*
FAX *030/292589. AE, DC, MC, V. Closed Mon., 1st wk in Jan., and 3
wks in Aug. No dinner Sun.*

$$$$ ▥ **Palazzo Arzaga.** No expense was spared converting this 15th-cen-
tury monastery into the luxury hotel, which opened in 1999. To add
to the historic atmosphere, rooms are decorated with antiques; some
have original frescos. There's also plenty to do. Twenty kilometers (12
miles) from Brescia in a nature reserve near Lake Garda, Arzaga arranges picnics in the surrounding hills, as well as wine-tasting, gas-
tronomical, and sightseeing tours. If you want to stay on site, there is
a PGA-approved Golf Academy with two courses, one designed by Gary
Player, the other by Jack Nicklaus. If golf's not your thing, you might
try the hotel's Saturnia Spa. ✉ *Carzago di Calvagese della Riviera, 25080,*
☎ *030/680600,* FAX *030/6806270., WEB www.palazzoarzaga.com. 81
rooms, 3 suites. 3 restaurants, 2 bars, minibars, 2 pools, sauna, spa,
2 18-hole golf courses, 2 tennis courses, health club, hiking, horseback
riding, jogging, baby-sitting, meeting room, car rental, parking (free).
AE, DC, MC, V.*

$$$$ ▥ **Vittoria.** Centrally located among 16th-century buildings, Vittoria
has more than its share of atmosphere. Erected in 1933, the hotel is in
the Venetian style, with a hint of Byzantium and the Spice Routes in
its pointed arches and windows. Many of the rooms are adorned with
antiques, and the service is on a high level. ✉ *Via delle X Giornate
20, 25121,* ☎ *030/280061,* FAX *030/280065, WEB www.hotelvittoria.com.
66 rooms. Restaurant, bar, meeting room. AE, DC, MC, V.*

Nightlife and the Arts

Brescia's **Teatro Grande** (☎ 030/2979311) has a series of classical-music concerts from April through June, a piano festival in May, and an opera season October through December.

En Route Less touristy than some of Italy's other northern lakes, **Lago d'Iseo** has nonetheless provided an inspirational setting for poets over the years. It's the site of the largest European island situated on a lake, **Monte Isola**, which can be reached by boat with **Navigazione Lago d'Iseo** (☎ 035/971483). The approximately 5-km (3-mi) walk around the island is a pleasant way to spend a few hours in the spring, summer, or fall. If you choose to stay the night, the friendly management of **Bella Vista** ($) will gladly point out hikes and other excursions. ⊠ *Via Siviano, 88,* ☎ *030/9886106.*

On the mainland, a nice and reasonably priced place to stay is the charming hotel in the hills overlooking Iseo, **Relais I Due Roccoli** ($$$). The hotel has just 13 rooms, but its high-quality restaurant attracts outside guests. May is a particularly beautiful time to stay, when the 6,000 rosebushes on the hotel's grounds come into bloom. ⊠ *Via Silvio Bonamelli, road for Polavena,* ☎ *030/9822977.*

Bergamo

㉙ *49 km (30 mi) west of Brescia, 58 km (36 mi) southeast of Bellagio.*

Bergamo is two cities—**Bergamo Bassa** (Lower Bergamo) and **Bergamo Alta** (Upper Bergamo)—connected by a funicular. High on the hillside, surrounded by the ruins of ancient Venetian walls surmounted by a fortress, Bergamo Alta is one of northern Italy's most charming medieval centers. Above it are the Bergamese Alps.

The massive **Torre Civica** offers a great view of the two cities. ⊠ *Piazza Vecchia,* ☎ *035/224700.* ☉ *Mar.–Apr., Wed.–Sat. 10:30–12:30 and 2–6, Sun. 10:30–6; May–mid-Sept., daily 10–8; mid-Sept.–Oct., weekdays 9:30–12:30 and 2–7, weekends 10–7.*

Bergamo's **Duomo** and **Battistero** are the most substantial buildings in Piazza Duomo. But the most impressive is the **Cappella Colleoni,** with resplendent marble decoration. ⊠ *Piazza Duomo,* ☎ *035/217317.* ☉ *Cappella Colleoni weekdays 8–noon and 3–6:30.*

NEED A
BREAK?
Wine Bar Donizetti (⊠ Via Gombito 17/a, ☎ 035/242661) has a cantina stocked with some 600 different bottles of wine, which can be accompanied by salami, local cheese, or a heartier lunch.

★ In the **Accademia Carrara** you will find one of Italy's most important art collections. Many of the Venetian masters are represented—Mantegna, Carpaccio (circa 1460–1525/26), Tiepolo, Francesco Guardi (1712–93), Canaletto (1697–1768)—and there are also magnificent paintings by Bellini and Botticelli (1445–1510). ⊠ *Bergamo Bassa, Piazza Carrara,* ☎ *035/247149,* ⦿ *www.accademiacarrara.it.* ⊡ *5,000 lire/€2.60, free Sun.* ☉ *Apr.–Sept., Tues.–Sun. 10–1 and 3–6:45; Oct.–Mar., Tues.–Sun. 9:30–1 and 2:30–5:45.*

Dining and Lodging

$$–$$$ ✕ **Agnello d'Oro.** A 17th-century tavern on a main street in Upper Bergamo, with wooden booths and walls hung with copper utensils and ceramic plates, Agnello d'Oro is a good place to imbibe the atmosphere as well as the good local wine. Specialties are typical Bergamasque risotto and varieties of polenta served with game and mushrooms. The same establishment also has 20 modestly priced rooms. ⊠ *Via Gombito 22,*

☎ 035/249883. AE, DC, MC, V. Closed Mon. and mid-Jan.–mid-Feb. No dinner Sun.

$$–$$$ ✕ **Dell'Angelo–Taverna del Colleoni.** Angelo Cornaro is the name be-
★ hind the Taverna del Colleoni, on the Piazza Vecchia, right behind the Duomo. He serves a wide and imaginative range of fish and meat dishes, both regional and international, all expertly prepared. ⊠ *Piazza Vecchia 7,* ☎ *035/232596. AE, DC, MC, V. Closed Mon., 1 wk in Jan., and 2 wks in Aug.*

$$ ✕ **Da Ornella.** On the main street in the upper town, this popular trattoria has vaulted ceilings, wooden beams, and antique ceramics on the walls, giving it an old-world ambience. Ornella herself is in the kitchen, turning out casoncelli in butter and sage and platters of assorted roast meats. Three prix-fixe menus are available during the week, two on the weekend. ⊠ *Via Gombito 15,* ☎ *035/232736. Reservations essential. AE, DC, MC, V. Closed Thurs.*

$$ ✕ **La Trattoria del Teatro.** Traditional regional food tops the bill at this good-value restaurant in the upper town. The polenta is a silky delight, and game is recommended in season. Fettuccine *con funghi* (with mushrooms) is a deceptively simple but rich and memorable specialty. ⊠ *Piazza Mascheroni 3,* ☎ *035/238862. No credit cards. Closed Mon. and July 15–30.*

$$$$ ⊞ **Excelsior San Marco.** The most comfortable hotel in the lower part of Bergamo, the Excelsior San Marco is only a short walk from the walls of the upper town. The rooms are surprisingly quiet, considering the central location. The breakfast room has a rooftop terrace. ⊠ *Piazza della Repubblica 6, 24122,* ☎ *035/366111,* FAX *035/223201. 155 rooms. Restaurant, bar, breakfast room, in-room safes, minibars. AE, DC, MC, V.*

$$$–$$$$ ⊞ **Cappello d'Oro.** This hotel, renovated during 1999 and 2000, comes with modern trappings and a century-long tradition of service. Near Porta Nuova in lower Bergamo, the location is convenient. ⊠ *Viale Papa Giovanni XXIII 12, 24121,* ☎ *035/232503,* FAX *035/242946,* WEB *www.hotelcappellodoro.it. 100 rooms. Restaurant, bar, meeting room. AE, DC, MC, V.*

Nightlife and the Arts

The annual **Festival Internazionale del Pianoforte** (International Piano Festival) is held in Bergamo's Teatro Donizetti (⊠ Piazza Cavour 14, ☎ 035/4160611, WEB teatro.gaetano.donizetti.com) in summer. Call the theater for information about drama, opera, and ballet events throughout the year.

LAKE COMO

For those whose idea of heaven is palatial villas, rose-laden belvederes, operetta-set towns, hanging wisteria and bougainvillea, lanterns casting a glow over lakeshore restaurants, and majestic Alpine vistas, heaven is Lake Como. Virgil called it simply "our greatest" lake. In his *Charterhouse of Parma*, Stendhal described it as an "enchanting spot, unequaled on earth in its loveliness." Though summer crowds do their best to vanquish the lake's dreamy mystery and slightly faded old-money gentility, they fail. Como remains a consummate pairing of natural and man-made beauty. Como's villa gardens, like so many in Italy, are a union of two landscape traditions: that of Renaissance Italy, which values order, and of Victorian England, which strives to create the illusion of natural wildness. Such gardens are often framed by vast areas of picturesque farmland—notably olive groves, fruit trees, and vineyards.

Lake Como is some 47 km (30 mi) long north to south and is Europe's deepest lake (almost 1,350 ft). Rarely out of sight to visitors, it looks like a burnished mirror—until it's ruffled by a breeze. In the *centro di lago* (center region of the lake), travelers have long headed for Bellagio, known as the *"punta di Bellagio"* because it's at the hub of the lake's three branches. It's an enchanting location, one that inspired Gabriel Faure to call Bellagio "a diamond contrasting brilliantly with the sapphires of the three lakes in which it is set." After just a few days on Lake Como, you'll understand why Verdi chose to compose *La Traviata* in Cadenabbia, across the lake from Bellagio. Today, for Milanese weekend-trippers, countless honeymooners, and visitors from around the world, going to Lake Como is not so much getting away from it all as recovering the *douceur de vie,* the sweetness of life so rarely encountered today.

If not driving, you arrive at the lake by pulling into the railway station at Como, a leading textile center famous for its silks. Most hasten to the vaporetti waiting to take them to the centro di lago, the most beautiful part of the lake. Art lovers, however, should note that 15 or so blocks south of the station is one of the greatest Italian Romanesque churches, Sant'Abbondio, with a gigantic, awe-inspiring nave. Although you can take a bus up either shoreline, most people take a ferry to Bellagio, the key town of the centro di lago; be sure to take an express ferry, as the local vaporetti can turn a half-hour ride into a three-hour ordeal. From Bellagio, vaporetti and car ferries traverse the lake, making it easy for travelers to get to the other main towns, Cernobbio, Cadenabbia, and Varenna.

Madonna del Ghisallo

18 km (11 mi) north of Cernobbio, 48 km (30 mi) northwest of Bergamo.

㉚ The **Chiesa della Madonna del Ghisallo** (Church of the Patroness of Bicyclists) is not far from the shores of Lake Como and offers a fine view. You will often see cyclists parked outside taking a breather after their uphill struggle, but many come simply in homage to this unique Madonna. From Bergamo, you pass it on the road to Bellagio. ⊠ *Magreglio.* ☉ *Mar.–Nov., daily 8–7.*

Bellagio

★ **㉛** *58 km (36 mi) northwest of Bergamo, 28 km (17 mi) north of Cernobbio.*

Sometimes called the prettiest town in Europe, Bellagio always seems to be flag bedecked, with geraniums ablaze in every window and bougainvillea veiling the staircases, or *montées,* that thread through the town. At dusk, Bellagio's nightspots—including the wharf, where an orchestra serenades dancers under the stars—beckon you to come and make merry.

★ **Villa Serbelloni,** a property of the Rockefeller Foundation, has celebrated gardens on the site of Pliny the Elder's villa overlooking Bellagio. There are only two guided visits per day, restricted to 30 people each, and in May these tend to be commandeered by group bookings. ⊠ *Near Palazza della Chiesa,* ☎ *031/950204.* ☞ *10,000 lire/€5.15.* ☉ *Guided visits Apr.–Oct., Tues.–Sun. at 11 and 4; tours gather 15 mins before start.*

The famous gardens of the **Villa Melzi** were once a favorite picnic spot for Franz Lizst, who advised author Louis de Ronchaud in 1837: "When you write the story of two happy lovers, place them on the shores of Lake Como. I do not know of any land so conspicuously blessed by heaven." The gardens are open to the public, and though you can't get into the 19th-century villa, don't miss the lavish Empire-style family chapel. The Melzi were Napoléon's greatest allies in Italy (the family has passed down the name of Josephine to the present). Directly across the lake is the Villa Carlotta, once the residence of Count Sommariva, Napoléon's worst Italian enemy. ⊠ *3 km (2 mi) outside Bellagio,* 🖃 *8,000 lire/€4.15.* ☉ *Mar.–Nov., daily 9–6.*

OFF THE
BEATEN PATH

VILLA BALBIANELLO – This may be the most magical house in all of Italy. It sits on its own little promontory, Il Dosso d'Avedo—separating the bays of Venus and Diana—around the bend from the tiny fishing village of Ossuccio. Relentlessly picturesque, the villa is composed of loggias, terraces, and *palazzini* (tiny palaces), all spilling down verdant slopes to the lakeshore, where you'll find an old Franciscan church, a magnificent stone staircase, and statue of San Carlo Borromeo blessing the waters. Designed in 1596 by Pellegrino Pelligrini, it was enlarged by Count Lambertenghi (who insisted on calling all his guests "Count" but refused the title himself). In 1974 it was sold to Count Monzino, who willed it to the Fondo Ambiente Italiano, which has opened it to the public. The villa is most frequently reached by launch, arriving from Sala Comacina. Check with the Como tourist office (☞ Visitor Information *in* Milan, Lombardy, and the Lakes A to Z, *below*) for the hours of launch tours. Every Saturday and Sunday, the villa is also reachable on foot from the nearby town of Lenno. If you plan in advance, it is also possible to take a guided tour. You pay 60,000 lire/€31 for the guide—regardless of how many are in your party—and an additional 6,000 lire/€3.10 to enter the villa. To reserve an English-speaking guide, send a fax (FAX 0344/55575) with your request. ⊠ *Il Dosso d'Avedo,* ☎ *0344/56110.* 🖃 *Gardens 8,000 lire/€4.15, gardens and villa 15,000 lire/€7.75.* ☉ *Tues. and Thurs.–Sun. 10–12:30 and 3:30–6:30.*

Dining and Lodging

$$ ✕ **La Pergola.** In Pescallo, about 1 km (½ mi) from Bellagio on the other side of the peninsula, La Pergola is a popular lakeside restaurant. Try to reserve a table on the lakeside terrace and order the daily special of freshly caught lake fish. You can also stay in one of the inn's 11 rooms, all of which have baths. ⊠ *Pescallo,* ☎ *031/950263. AE, MC, V. Closed Tues. and 2–3 wks in Jan.*

$$ ✕ **Silvio.** At the edge of town, this family-owned trattoria with a terrace on the lakeshore is for those who love fresh fish. Served cooked or marinated, with risotto or as a ravioli stuffing, the fish is caught by Silvio's family. This is local cooking at its best. There are also 17 modestly priced rooms. ⊠ *Lòppia di Bellagio, Via Carcano 10,* ☎ *031/950322. MC, V. Closed Jan.–Feb.*

$$$$ ★ 🏨 **Grand Hotel Villa Serbelloni.** Designed to cradle dukes and duchesses in high luxury, this hotel is now a refined haven for the discreetly wealthy, set within a pretty park just down the road from the punta di Bellagio. Inside, the atmosphere of 19th-century luxury has not so much faded as mellowed: the rooms are immaculate and plush. The public rooms are a mix of gilt and marble, with thick, colorful carpets. Service is unobtrusive, and the staff is particularly good about arranging transportation around the lake. The best rooms—where Churchill and Kennedy stayed—face the lake and the Tremezzina, a group of towns on the opposite shore. ⊠ *Via Roma 1, 22021,* ☎ *031/950216,* FAX *031/951529,* WEB *www.villaserbelloni.it. 83 rooms. 2 restaurants, 2 pools, hair salon, sauna, Turkish bath, tennis court, health club. AE, DC, MC, V. Closed mid-Nov.–early Apr.*

$$$–$$$$ 🏨 **Belvedere.** In Italian, the name means "beautiful view," and from the gardens of this enchanting hotel you can see just how apt a name it is. The hotel has been in the Martinelli-Manoni family since 1880, and the unbroken tradition of service makes it one of the best places to stay in town. The house is simple, though not plain; the rooms are understated but comfortable. Antique chairs and eye-catching rugs complement the modern fittings. The bathrooms are expertly designed for maximum comfort. Once vineyards surrounded the house; these have been transformed into the hotel's outstanding feature, the terraced gardens. The restaurant is very good. ✉ *Via Valassina 31, 22021,* ☎ *031/950410,* FAX *031/950102,* WEB *www.belvederebellaggio.com. 70 rooms. Restaurant, bar, pool, meeting rooms. AE, DC, MC, V.*

$$$–$$$$ 🏨 **Du Lac.** In the center of Bellagio, by the landing dock, Du Lac is a comfortable medium-size hotel owned by an Anglo-Italian family that sets a relaxed and congenial tone. Most rooms have views of the lake and mountains, and there is a rooftop terrace garden for drinks or just unwinding. ✉ *Piazza Mazzini 32, 22021,* ☎ *031/950320,* FAX *031/951624. 48 rooms. Restaurant, bar, minibars, air-conditioning. MC, V. Closed early Nov.–late Mar.*

$$$–$$$$ 🏨 **Hotel Florence.** If there is a bargain to be had amid all of Bellagio's opulence, this lakeside villa is it. Originally constructed at the beginning of the 18th century, the mainstay of the house as it appears today dates from the 1880s, including the impressive lobby with its vaulted ceiling and imposing Florentine fireplace. Most of the rooms, furnished with interesting antiques, are large and comfortable and have splendid views of the lake. The restaurant and bar draw locals and visitors alike with live music on weekends. ✉ *Piazza Mazzini 45, 22021,* ☎ *031/950342,* FAX *031/951722. 36 rooms. Restaurant, bar. AE, DC, MC, V. FAP, MAP.*

$$ 🏨 **Excelsior-Splendide.** Chances are you'll be lulled to sleep at night here by the lilting sounds of an orchestra directly under your window—this hotel is opposite Bellagio's enchanting quay, where live music beckons one and all on summer nights. It's in the town center, handy to restaurants and just a five-minute walk from the stunning gardens of Villa Melzi. ✉ *Lungo Lario Mazzoni, 22021,* ☎ *031/950225,* FAX *031/951224. 47 rooms. Restaurant, pool. AE, DC, MC, V. Closed Nov.–mid-Mar.*

Varenna

③②   *10 km (6 mi) north of Bellagio, 78 km (48 mi) north of Milan.*

You can reach Varenna by ferry from Bellagio. The principal sight here is the spellbinding garden of the **Villa Monastero,** which, as its name suggests, was originally a monastery. Now it's an international science and convention center. ✉ *Varenna,* ☎ *0341/295459.* 🎫 *3,000 lire/€1.55.* ☉ *Mar.–May and Sept.–Oct., daily 10–6 (may close for lunch, call ahead); June–Aug., daily 9–7.*

Tremezzo

③③   *34 km (21 mi) north of Cernobbio, 78 km (48 mi) north of Milan.*

If you are lucky enough to visit this small lakeside town in late spring or very early summer, you will find the magnificent **Villa Carlotta** a riot of color, with more than 14 acres of azaleas and dozens of varieties of rhododendrons in full bloom. The villa itself was built between 1690 and 1743 for the luxury-loving Marquis Giorgio Clerici. The range of the garden's collection is remarkable, particularly considering the difficulties of transporting delicate plants before the age of aircraft. Palms, banana trees, cacti, eucalyptus, a sequoia, orchids, and camellias are counted among the more than 500 species.

According to local lore, one reason for the Villa Carlotta's magnificence was a competition between the marquis's son-in-law, who inherited the estate, and the son-in-law's arch-rival, who built *his* summer palace directly across the lake. Whenever either added to his villa and garden, it was tantamount to taunting the other in public. Eventually the son-in-law's insatiable taste for self-aggrandizement prevailed. The villa's last (and final) owners were Prussian royalty (including the "Carlotta" of the villa's name); the property was confiscated during World War I.

The villa's interior is worth a visit, particularly if you have a taste for the romantic sculptures of Antonio Canova (1757–1822). The best known is his *Cupid and Psyche,* which depicts the lovers locked in an odd but graceful embrace, with the young god above and behind, his wings extended, while Psyche awaits a kiss that will never come. Check with the Bellagio tourist office (☞ Visitor Information *in* Milan, Lombardy, and the Lakes A to Z, *below*) for the hours of the launch to Tremezzo. It's also possible to arrive by car or bus. ☎ *0344/40405,* WEB *www.uni.com//villacarlotta/.* ☒ *Villa and gardens 12,000 lire/€6.20.* ☉ *Apr.–Sept., daily 9–6; mid- to late Mar. and Oct., daily 9–11:30 and 2–4:30.*

Lodging

$$$$ 🏨 **Grand Hotel Tremezzo.** One hundred windows face the lake in this charming turn-of-the-20th-century hotel, in the middle of a private park stretching over 12½ acres, has a wide range of creature comforts, from a heated swimming pool and private landing on the lake to a hillside for jogging. All rooms have a view of the lake or the park. The 18-hole Menaggio & Cadenabbia golf course is about five minutes away by car. ☒ *Via Regina 8, 22019,* ☎ *0344/42491,* FAX *0344/40201. 100 rooms, 2 suites. 3 restaurants, 3 bars, 2 pools, hair salon, sauna, tennis court, gym, jogging, Ping-Pong, billiards, meeting room, solarium, helipad. AE, DC, MC, V. Closed mid-Nov.–Feb.*

$ 🏨 **Rusall.** Located on the hillside above Tremezzo in the midst of a large garden, this small and reasonably priced hotel offers a good place to get away from it all. Lie out on the terrace and enjoy the view. Rooms are simple and comfortable. ☒ *Via S. Martino, 2, Frazione Rogaro, 22019,* ☎ *0344/40408,* FAX *0344/40447,* WEB *www.rusallhotel.com. 19. Restaurant, bar, tennis court. AE, DC, MC, V.*

Cernobbio

➌➍ *34 km (21 mi) south of Tremezzo, 53 km (3 mi) north of Milan.*

Cernobbio is the first town you come to as you head north from Como. Although many of the villas of the southwest branch—the lake's most overbuilt district—remain private and closed to the public, they can be enjoyed from a boat. If you're planning to say "budget be damned" in only one place, the **Villa d'Este** could be it. If you can't stay at this legendary lakeside resort hotel, call ahead and ask to see the grounds or have a meal in the hotel's restaurant.

Built over the course of roughly 45 years (completed in 1615) for Cardinal Tolomeo Gallio, who began life humbly as a fisherman, the Villa d'Este has had a colorful and somewhat checkered history, swinging wildly between extremes of grandeur and dereliction. Its tenants have included the Jesuits, two generals, a ballerina, the disgraced and estranged wife of a future king of England (Caroline of Brunswick and George IV, respectively), a family of ordinary Italian nobles, and, finally, a czarina of Russia. Its life as a private summer residence ended in 1873, when it was turned into the fashionable hotel it has remained ever since.

Though the gardens are not as grand as they are reputed to have been during the villa's best days as a private residence, and though they have suffered some modification to permit the addition of tennis courts and swimming pools, they still have a stately dignity. The alley of cypresses is a fine example of a proudly repeated Italian garden theme. The fanciful pavilions, temples, miniature forts, and mock ruins make for an afternoon's walk of quietly whimsical surprises.

Dining and Lodging

$$$ ✕ **Il Gatto Nero.** This restaurant is set in the hills above Cernobbio and has a splendid view of the lake. Specialties include risotto *ai funghi porcini* (with porcini mushrooms), *papardelle al ragù di selvaggini* (bow-tie pasta with wild game sauce), wild game, and lake fish. ⊠ *Via Monte Santo, 69, Rovenna,* ☎ *031/512042. AE, DC, MC, V. No lunch Mon. or Tues.*

$$$$ 🏠 **Villa d'Este.** From Napoléon to the Duchess of Windsor, this grand
★   establishment has long welcomed Europe's rich and famous. One of the most luxurious hotels in Italy, the 17th-century Villa d'Este provides just about every conceivable comfort, even a nightclub. The sparkling chandeliers in the vast lobby cast their light on the broad, marble staircases that lead to the guest rooms. The rooms are furnished in the Empire style preferred by wealthy Italians: walnut paneling, sofas in striped silk, and many gorgeous antiques. A broad veranda sweeps out to the lakefront, where a large swimming pool juts out above the water. Across the lake, blue, snowcapped mountains blend into the deep green of the slopes leading down to the shore. La Veranda is the hotel's formal restaurant, while the Grill is more relaxed and Kisho offers Japanese cuisine. ⊠ *Via Regina 40, 22012,* ☎ *031/3481,* 🆔 *031/348844,* 🆆🅴🅱 *www. villadeste.it. 166 rooms. 3 restaurants, bar, indoor pool, sauna, 8 tennis courts, squash, nightclub. AE, DC, MC, V. Closed mid-Nov.–Feb..*

Como

③⑤   *5 km (3 mi) south of Cernobbio, 61 km (38 mi) north of Milan.*

Como, on the south shore of the lake, is only part elegant resort, with cobbled pedestrian streets winding their way past parks and bustling cafés and away from the lakefront. The other part is an industrial town, renowned for its silk production. If you're traveling by car, leave it outside town center, as traffic can be mayhem and streets are often closed.

The splendid 15th-century Renaissance-Gothic **Duomo** was begun in 1396, the facade was added in 1455, and the transepts completed in the mid-18th century. The dome was designed in 1744 by Filippo Juvara (1678–1736), chief architect of many of the sumptuous palaces of the royal house of Savoy. The facade features statues of two of Como's most famous sons, Pliny the Elder and Pliny the Younger, whose chronicles are some of the most important documents of antiquity. Inside, the works of art include Luini's *Holy Conversation,* a fresco cycle by Morazzone, and the *Marriage of the Virgin Mary* by Ferrari. ⊠ *Piazza del Duomo.* ☉ *Daily 7–noon and 3–7.*

At the heart of Como's medieval quarter, the city's first cathedral, **San Fedele,** is worth a peek, if only because it is one of the oldest churches in the region. ⊠ *Piazza San Fedele.* ☉ *Daily 7–noon and 3–7.*

If you brave Como's industrial quarter, you will find the beautiful church of **Sant'Abbondio,** a gem of Romanesque architecture begun by Benedictine monks in 1013 and consecrated by Pope Urban II (circa 1035–99) in 1095. Inside, the five aisles of the church converge on a presbytery with a semicircular apse decorated with a cycle of 14th-century frescoes—all of which have been restored to their original magnificence—by Lombard artists heavily influenced by the Sienese school. In the nave, the cubical capitals supporting the pillars are the earliest example of this style in Italy. ✉ *Via Sant'Abbondio.* ◷ *Daily 7–6.*

OFF THE
BEATEN PATH **CASTIGLIONE OLONA** – Just 18 km (11 mi) west of Como are a Gothic *collegiata* (collegiate church) and baptistery with superlative frescoes by Giotto's pupil Masolino da Panicale. ☎ *0331/858903.* ◷ *Apr.–Sept., Tues.–Sat. 9:30–12 and 3–6:30; Oct.–Mar., Tues.–Sat. 10–12 and 2:30–5:30. Open by appointment Sun.* 🖃 *5,000 lire/eur 2.60.*

Dining and Lodging

\$\$\$\$ ✕ **La Locanda dell'Isola.** Isola Comacina, Lake Como's only island, five minutes by boat from Sala Comacina, is rustic and restful but at times crowded. The same could be said for the Locanda. Forget any notions of choosing from a menu, because here the deal is a set price for a set meal, with drinks included. The good news is that the food is delicious, the service is friendly, and the setting is magnificent. You'll have to pace yourself through a mixed antipasto, salmon, trout, chicken, salad, cheese, coffee, and dessert. ✉ *Isola Comacina, Sala Comacina,* ☎ *0344/55083. No credit cards. Closed Nov.–Feb. and Tues. in mid-Sept.–mid-May.*

\$\$\$\$ 🏨 **Barchetta Excelsior.** Despite its rather unprepossessing exterior, this central, modern hotel is comfortable, with many rooms looking directly across Piazza Cavour to Lake Como. The rooms are airy and spacious, with those on the upper floors commanding the best views. Ask for a lake view because not all rooms have one, although the noise of the piazza can be a distraction. The Barchetta is run by the same group that owns Villa d'Este. ✉ *Piazza Cavour 1, 22100,* ☎ *031/3221,* 𝖥𝖠𝖷 *031/302622,* 𝖶𝖤𝖡 *www.villadeste.it. 84 rooms. 2 restaurants, bar, breakfast room, minibars, no-smoking room. AE, DC, MC, V.*

\$\$\$–\$\$\$\$ 🏨 **Terminus.** Commanding a panoramic view over Lake Como, this
★ early 20th-century, Liberty-style building is perhaps the city's finest hotel. The public spaces have an understated elegance, with plenty of marble and high ceilings. The guest rooms are done in floral patterns and are tastefully furnished with large, walnut wardrobes and silk-covered sofas. Room 500, in a small tower, is the best in the hotel: the split-level room is divided by a spiral staircase, and the three-sided view from the bedroom is magnificent. In summer, the garden terrace is perfect for relaxing over a drink. ✉ *Lungo Lario Trieste 14, 22100,* ☎ *031/ 329111,* 𝖥𝖠𝖷 *031/302550,* 𝖶𝖤𝖡 *www.albergoterminus.com. 38 rooms. Restaurant, bar, breakfast room, in-room data ports, in-room safes, minibars, no-smoking room, massage, sauna, meeting room. AE, DC, MC, V.*

\$\$\$–\$\$\$\$ 🏨 **Villa Flori.** Italian patriot Garibaldi spent his wedding night here, in a suite that now bears his name. The hotel enjoys a panoramic view and has a highly acclaimed restaurant, Raimondi. ✉ *Via Cernobbio 12, 22100,* ☎ *0315/73105,* 𝖥𝖠𝖷 *031/33820,* 𝖶𝖤𝖡 *www.hotelvillaflori.com. 45 rooms. Restaurant, meeting room. AE, DC, MC, V.*

\$\$–\$\$\$ 🏨 **Tre Re.** This clean, spacious, welcoming hotel is just a few steps west of the cathedral and convenient to the lake. Although the exterior gives away the age of this 16th-century former convent, the rooms are airy, comfortable, and modern. The moderately priced restaurant shares an ample terrace with the hotel. ✉ *Via Boldoni 20, 22100,* ☎ *031/ 265374,* 𝖥𝖠𝖷 *031/241349,* 𝖶𝖤𝖡 *www.hoteltrere.com. 40 rooms. Restaurant, bar, free parking. MC, V. Closed Dec. 15–Jan. 10.*

Outdoor Activities and Sports

SKIING

In the province of Como, fine skiing facilities abound at Valsassina, Val Lesina, Valvarrone, Valcavargna, and Val d'Intelvi. For information, call the Provincial Tourist Board in Como (☞ Visitor Information *in* Milan, Lombardy, and the Lakes A to Z, *below*).

WATERSKIING

Various facilities for waterskiing and all water sports can be found on the lake; contact the Provincial Tourist Board in Como (☞ Visitor Information *in* Milan, Lombardy, and the Lakes A to Z, *below*).

Shopping

MARKET

Every Saturday (except the first Saturday of every month), Piazza San Fedele holds a **local crafts market** from 9 to 7.

SILK

Como is renowned for its high-quality silk; it's responsible for around three-fourths of Europe's production. **Mantero** (⊠ Via Volta) sells a wide range of locally made silks. **Binda** (⊠ Viale Geno) is a silk wholesale store, with great prices on a variety of items, including shirts, ties, and scarves. Bargains can also be found at Binda's **retail store** (⊠ Via Cadorna).

LAKE MAGGIORE AND LAKE ORTA

Magnificently scenic, Lake Maggiore has its less mountainous eastern shore in Lombardy, its higher western shore in Piedmont, and its northern tip in Switzerland. Never more than 5 km (3 mi) wide, the lake is almost 50 km (30 mi) long. The better-known resorts are on the Piedmontese shore, particularly Stresa, a well-established tourist town that provided a setting for Hemingway's *A Farewell to Arms*. A mountainous strip of land separates Lake Maggiore from Lago di Orta (Lake Orta), its smaller neighbor to the west, in Piedmont. Orta attracts fewer visitors than the three larger lakes, and a tour around it can be a pleasant alternative in the summer. Stresa is the main town on Lake Maggiore, and Orta San Giulio is the largest center on Lake Orta; all points of interest on the two lakes are reached from these towns.

Orta San Giulio

㊱ *15 km (9 mi) west of Stresa, 76 km (47 mi) northwest of Milan.*

Orta San Giulio is at the end of a small peninsula jutting out into Lake Orta about a third of the way up its eastern shore. Intricate wrought-iron balustrades and balconies adorn the 18th-century buildings of the charming town. The shady main square looks out across the lake to the small island of San Giulio. There are few more relaxing experiences than sipping a drink at one of the piazza cafés and looking out at the languid waters stirred by a mountain breeze, with sailboats making their way to nowhere in particular.

OFF THE
BEATEN PATH

SACRO MONTE – Rising up behind Orta and looking down on the lake, Sacred Mountain is an enjoyable and interesting hike. Pass the Church of the Assumption, and just ahead you see a gateway marked Sacro Monte. This leads to the path up the hill, a comfortable climb that takes about 40 minutes round-trip. As you approach the top, you pass no fewer than 20 17th-century chapels, all devoted to St. Francis of Assisi. They are decorated with frescoes and striking, life-size terra-cotta statue groups (a total of almost 400 figures) illustrating incidents from the saint's life. You can climb the campanile of the last chapel for a view over the lake and the town, about 350 ft below.

The island of **San Giulio,** just offshore, is accessible by hired boat. The lake is no more than 2 km (1 mi) wide, and most boats charge about

10,000 lire/€5.15 for up to four people to make the round-trip. The island takes its name from the 4th-century St. Julius, who—like St. Patrick in Ireland—is said to have banished snakes from the island. Julius is also said to have founded the Basilica in AD 390, although the present building shows more signs of its renovations in the 10th and 15th centuries. Inside, there is a black-marble pulpit (12th century) with elaborate carvings, and downstairs you'll find the crypt containing relics of the saint. In the sacristy of the church is a large bone said to be from one of the beasts destroyed by the saint, but on closer examination it seems to be a whalebone.

Much of the area is taken up by private villas; it only takes a few minutes to walk around the parts of the island open to the public. The view back across the lake to Orta, with Sacro Monte behind it, is memorable, particularly in the late afternoon, when the light picks up the glint of the wrought-iron traceries. Signs laud the virtues of silence and contemplation, and the island's quiet is broken only by the pealing of the basilica's bells.

Dining and Lodging

$$$-$$$$ ✕ 🏨 **Hotel San Rocco.** Half of the rooms in this converted 17th-century convent in a lakeside garden on the edge of town have views of the water, garden, and surrounding mountains. Many have balconies and are furnished in modern style. The restaurant ($$$) features international cuisine and has beautiful views of the lake. Among the specialties is *pesce persico* (perch). ⊠ *Via Gippini da Verona 11, 28016,* ☎ *0322/911977,* 🆃🆇 *0322/911964,* 🆆🅴🅱 *www.hotelsanrocco.it. 80 rooms. Restaurant, bar, hair salon, pool. AE, DC, MC, V.*

En Route Follow the shore drive from Orta San Giulio north to Omegna, at the head of Lake Orta. A mile or so west of Omegna, in the village of Quarna Sotto, there's a musical-instrument factory that's worth a stop. The shore drive continues around the rest of the lake, and at the southern end you can pick up S229, which will take you back to the A4 autostrada.

If you're going to Stresa from Lake Orta, take the twisting mountain road past Mottarone, the tallest peak between the lakes, to Gignese, where you'll be about 2,300 ft above sea level and can take in a last dramatic view of Maggiore. Follow the road up to Lake Orta, through the town of Armeno, shaded first by forests of evergreens, then oaks. In the late summer and early fall, you're likely to see whole families out in these woods, crouched down in their hunt for wild mushrooms, or—if they're lucky—truffles.

Stresa

③⑦ *16 km (10 mi) east of Orta San Giulio, 80 km (50 mi) northwest of Milan.*

Stresa, which has capitalized on its central lakeside position and its good connections to the Isole Borromee (Borromean Islands) in Lake Maggiore, has to some extent become a victim of its own success. The luxurious elegance that distinguished it in its heyday has faded; the grand hotels are still grand, but their surrounding parks and gardens are now encroached by traffic. Even the undeniable loveliness of the lakeshore drive has been threatened by the roar of diesel trucks and BMW traffic. One way to escape is to head for the Isole Borromee.

As you wander around the grounds of **Villa Pallavicino,** with their palms and semitropical shrubs, don't be surprised if you're followed by a peacock or even an ostrich: they're part of the zoological garden and are allowed to roam almost at will. From the top of the hill on which the villa stands, you can see the gentle hills of the Lombardy shore of Lake Maggiore and, nearer and to the left, the jewel-like Borromean Islands. In addition to a bar and restaurant, the grounds also have picnic spots. ⊠ *Via Sempione Sund 8,* ☎ *0323/31533.* 🎟 *12,000 lire/€6.20.* ☉ *Early Mar.–Oct., daily 9–6.*

Boats to the **Borromean Islands** leave every 15–30 minutes from the dock at Stresa's Piazza Marconi. Although you can hire a boatman to take you, it's cheaper and just as convenient to use the regular service. Make sure you buy a ticket allowing you to visit all the islands—Bella, Dei Pescatori, and Madre. The islands take their name from the Borromeo family, which has owned them since the 12th century. **Isola Bella** (Beautiful Island) is the most famous of the three, and the first that you'll visit. Its name is actually a shortened form of Isabella, wife of the 16th-century Count Carlo III Borromeo (1538–84), who built the palace and terraced gardens for her. Few wedding presents have been more romantic. Wander up the 10 terraces of the gardens, where peacocks roam among the scented shrubs, statues, and fountains. The view of the lake is splendid from the top terrace. Before Count Carlo began his project, the island was rocky and almost devoid of vegetation; the soil for the garden had to be transported from the mainland. Visit the palazzo to see the rooms where famous guests—including Napoléon and Mussolini—stayed in 18th-century splendor. ☎ *0323/30556.* 🎟 *Garden and palazzo 15,000 lire/€7.75.* ☉ *Mar. 27–Sept., daily 9–noon and 1:30–5:30; Oct. 1–24, daily 1:30–5.*

Stop for a while at the tiny **Isola dei Pescatori** (Island of the Fishermen), less than 100 yards wide and only about ½ km (¼ mi) long. Of the three islands, this one has remained closest to the way it was before the Borromeos began building. The island's little lanes, strung with fishing nets and dotted with shrines to the Madonna, are the definition of picturesque; little wonder that in high season the village is crowded with postcard stands.

Isola Madre (Mother Island) is the largest of the three and, like Isola Bella, has a large botanical garden. Even dedicated nongardeners should take time to see the profusion of exotic trees and shrubs running down to the shore in every direction. Two special times to visit are April (for the camellias) and May (when azaleas and rhododendrons are in bloom). Also on the island is a 16th-century palazzo, where an antique puppet theater is on display, complete with string puppets, prompt books, and elaborate scenery designed by Alessandro Sanquirico, who was a scenographer at La Scala in Milan. ☎ *0323/31261.* 🎟 *12,000 lire/€6.20.* ☉ *Apr.–Oct., daily 8:30–noon and 2–5:30.*

For more information about the islands and how to get there, contact the tourist office in Stresa (☞ Visitor Information *in* Milan, Lombardy, and the Lakes, *below*) or ask at the landing stages (look for Navigazione Lago Maggiore signs).

Every August and September, Stresa hosts the **Settimane Musicali di Stresa,** which attracts some world-famous musicians. Contact the Stresa tourist office (☞ Visitor Information *in* Milan, Lombardy, and the Lakes A to Z, *below*) for information.

Lodging

$$$$ 🏨 **Grand Hotel des Iles Borromees.** A palatial old-world hotel, this princely establishment has catered to a demanding European clientele since 1863. And though it still has the spacious salons and lavish decor of the turn of the 20th century, it has been discreetly modernized. Rooms have luxurious bathrooms. ⊠ *Lungolago Umberto I 67, 28838,* ☎ *0323/*

30431, FAX *0323/32405,* WEB *www.borromees.it. 172 rooms. Restaurant, bar, indoor pool, spa, tennis court, convention center, helipad. AE, DC, MC, V.*

$$ 🏨 **Primavera.** In a plain 1950s building in the heart of Stresa, Primavera has balconies embellished with flower boxes. It has the advantage of a location in a quiet pedestrian zone only three minutes from the lake and embarcadero. Rooms are compact and simply furnished. ✉ *Via Cavour 39, 28838 Stresa,* ☎ *0323/31286,* FAX *0323/33458. 32 rooms. AE, DC, MC, V. Closed Jan.–Feb. and mid-Nov.–mid-Dec.*

Verbania

38   *16 km (10 mi) north of Stresa, 95 km (59 mi) northwest of Milan.*

Verbania lies across the Gulf of Pallanza from Stresa. It's known for the **Villa Taranto,** which has magnificent botanical gardens containing some 20,000 species. Created by the enthusiastic Scotsman captain Neil McEachern, these gardens rank among Europe's finest. ✉ *Verbania,* ☎ *0323/556667.* 🎫 *12,000 lire/€6.20.* ☉ *Apr.–Oct., daily 8:30–7:30; last tickets sold at 6:30.*

Dining and Lodging

$$$$ ✕ **Ristorante del Sole.** This lakeside inn has been run by the same fam-
★   ily for more than 150 years. The present chefs, the infectiously cheerful Carlo Brovelli and son Davide, do the family proud. The lake figures into the menu in the form of trout and perch carpaccio. The seasonal menu is heavy on artichoke dishes in spring and eggplant in summer. There are also 15 apartments if you'd like to stay the night. ✉ *Piazza Venezia 5, Ranco, near Angera,* ☎ *0331/976507,* FAX *0331/976620. Reservations essential. AE, DC, MC, V. Closed Tues. and Jan.–mid-Feb. No dinner Mon. in mid-Feb.–mid-Mar.*

$$ ✕ **Del Cesare.** Off Piazza Cadorna and close to the embarcadero, this hotel restaurant serves tasty risotto *con filetti di persico* (with perch fillets) and typical Piedmontese meat dishes, such as beef braised in Barolo wine. ✉ *Via Mazzini 14,* ☎ *0323/31386. AE, DC, MC, V. Closed Tues. and mid-Dec.–late Feb.*

$$ 🏨 **Il Chiostro.** Part of this charming hotel, not far from the lake, was carved out of a 15th-century convent, as the name Il Chiostro ("the cloister") suggests. Some rooms have original frescos, and the chapel in the older part of the hotel is still used. The hotel's other section, originally a textile factory, dates to the start of the 19th century. Some rooms face out onto a lovely garden. A full meal plan is available. ✉ *Via Fratelli Cervi 14, 28921,* ☎ *0323/404077,* FAX *0323/401231. 100 rooms. Restaurant, bar, chapel, meeting room. AE, DC, MC, V. CP, FAP.*

OFF THE   **SANTA CATERINA DEL SASSO BALLARO** – Near the town of Laveno, this
BEATEN PATH   beautiful lakeside hermitage was constructed in the 12th century by a local merchant to express his gratitude for being saved from the wrath of a storm. About 20 km (12 mi) farther north on the eastern side of the lake, you will find comfortable and charming Liberty-style lodgings at the family-run **Camin Hotel Luino** ($$$). ✉ *Via Dante 35, 21016 Luino,* ☎ *0332/530118,* FAX *0332/537226. AE, DC, MC, V.*

MILAN, LOMBARDY, AND THE LAKES A TO Z

To research prices, get advice from other travelers, and book travel arrangements, visit www.fodors.com.

AIRPORTS AND TRANSFERS

Aeroporto Malpensa, about 50 km (31 mi) northwest of Milan, services intercontinental flights. Aeroporto Milano Linate, less than 10 km (6 mi) east of Milan, handles international and domestic flights. Malpensa Shuttle Buses run twice daily between the two airports. The fare is 18,000 lire/€9.30, and the trip takes about 75 minutes.

The Malpensa Express Train connects Malpensa airport with the Cadorna train station near downtown Milan. The ride takes about 40 minutes and costs 15,000 lire/€7.75 one-way or 20,000 lire/€10.35 for a round-trip ride on the same day. Trains run to Cadorna from Malpensa every half hour 7:45 AM–9:45 PM; trains run from Cadorna to Malpensa every half hour 6:50 AM–8:20 PM. Malpensa Express Buses run on the same route outside of these hours. In addition, Malpensa Shuttle Buses go to and from the central train station, Milano Centrale. The fare is 8,000 lire/eur 4.15. STAM buses run between Linate and the central train station every half hour. Phone is 02/717106. The fare from Linate is 3,500 lire/€1.80 on the special airport bus or 1,500 lire/€0.75 on municipal Bus 73 (to Piazza San Babila); from Malpensa the cost is 13,000 lire/€6.70. Call for schedule information.

To get from Malpensa to Milan by car, take Route S336 east to the A8 autostrada southeast. The drive takes about 40 minutes, depending on traffic and destination. From Linate, take what was once the Old Brescia Road west into the central downtown area; the trip takes less than 20 minutes.

A taxi stand is directly outside the arrivals building doors at Malpensa. Approximate taxi fare is 130,000 lire/€67.15. From Linate, the approximate fare is 30,000 lire/€15.50.

➤ AIRPORT INFORMATION: **Aeroporto Malpensa** (☎ 02/74851). **Aeroporto Milano Linate** (☎ 02/74851).

➤ TAXIS AND SHUTTLES: **Malpensa Express Train** (☎ 02/27763). **Malpensa Shuttle Buses** (☎ 02/58583158). **STAN** (☎ 02/717106).

BOAT AND FERRY TRAVEL

There is frequent daily ferry and hydrofoil service between towns on the lakes and a range of round-trip excursions with dining service (optional) aboard.

FARES AND SCHEDULES

➤ BOAT AND FERRY INFORMATION: **Navigazione Laghi** (✉ Via Ariosto 21, Milan, ☎ 02/4676101). **Navigazione Lago di Como** (✉ Via Per Cernobbio 18, Tavernola, near Como, ☎ 031/579211). **Navigazione Lago di Garda** (✉ Piazza Matteotti 2, Desenzano, ☎ 030/9149511). **Navigazione Lago Maggiore** (✉ Viale Baracca 1, Arona, ☎ 0322/46651).

BUS TRAVEL

Italian bus service is best avoided on intercity routes, since it is neither faster, cheaper, nor more convenient than the railways; trains are generally better than buses for getting around the cities of the plain. Most bus companies use Milan's Piazza Castello as a terminus, as the city has no central bus terminal. For bus information, call Autostradale; you can also try Zani Viaggi.

There is regular bus service between the small towns on the lakes, and it tends to be a cheaper way of getting around than ferry or hydrofoil service. The bus service around Lake Garda serves mostly towns on the western shore. Call SIA for information.

➤ Bus Information: **Autostradale** (☎ 166/845010). **SIA** (☎ 030/3774237). **Zani Viaggi** (☎ 02/867131).

CAR RENTAL
➤ Local Agencies: **Avis** (✉ Piazza Diaz, Milan, ☎ 02/89010645; ✉ Aeroporto Milano Linate, Milan, ☎ 02/717214; ✉ Aeroporto Malpensa, Milan, ☎ 02/58581137). **Europcar** (✉ Via Galbani 12, Milan, ☎ 02/66710491; ✉ Aeroporto Milano Linate, Milan, ☎ 02/76110277; ✉ Aeroporto Malpensa, Milan, ☎ 02/58581142). **Hertz** (✉ Aeroporto Milano Linate, Milan, ☎ 02/70200256; ✉ Aeroporto Malpensa, Milan, ☎ 02/58581081).

CAR TRAVEL
Two major autostrada routes cross at Milan: the A1, which leads south to Bologna, Florence, and Rome, and the A4, which runs west–east from Turin to Venice. A7 angles southwest down to Genoa from Milan. Milan is ringed by a bypass road (the *tangenziale*). The A8 travels northwest to Lago Maggiore and beyond to Domodossola. The A9 leads north past Como to Chiasso and the Saint Gotthard Pass into Switzerland.

The A4 autostrada is the main east–west highway for this region. The A22 is a major north–south highway running just east of Lake Garda. Although these major highways will allow you to make good time between the cities of the plain, you'll have to follow secondary roads—often of great beauty—around the lakes. S572 follows the southern and western shores of Lake Garda, S45b edges the northernmost section of the western shore, and S249 runs along the eastern shore. Around Lake Como, follow S340 along the western shore, S36 on the eastern shore, and S583 on the lower arms. S33 and S34 trace the western shore of Lake Maggiore.

EMERGENCY SERVICES
ACI, the Italian auto club, offers 24-hour roadside assistance (free to members, for a fee to nonmembers).
➤ Contacts: **ACI dispatchers** (☎ 116).

EMBASSIES AND CONSULATES
➤ Australia: **Australian Consulate** (✉ Via Borgogna 2, Milan, ☎ 02/777041).
➤ Canada: **Canadian Consulate** (✉ Via Vittorio Pisani 19, Milan, ☎ 02/67581).
➤ New Zealand: **New Zealand Consulate** (✉ Via Guido d'Arezzo, Milan, ☎ 02/48012544).
➤ United Kingdom: **U.K. Consulate** (✉ Via San Paolo 7, Milan, ☎ 02/723001).
➤ United States: **U.S. Consulate** (✉ Via Principe Amedeo 2, Milan, ☎ 02/290351).

EMERGENCIES
English-speaking officers with the carabinieri (the national police) are available 24 hours a day to deal with every kind of emergency. You can dial the ambulance number wherever you are, and it will connect you to the nearest local emergency service. For first aid, ask for *pronto soccorso*, and be prepared to give your address.

There are a number of pharmacies open 24 hours a day, including one on the upper level of Stazione Centrale in Milan. Others take turns staying open late and on weekends; to find the nearest one, check the roster outside any pharmacy or the list published in the *Corriere della Sera*.

➤ CONTACTS: **Ambulance** (☎ 118). **Carabinieri** (☎ 112). **Police** (☎ 62261).
➤ 24-HOUR PHARMACIES: **Stazione Centrale** (☎ 02/6690735).

ENGLISH-LANGUAGE MEDIA

BOOKS

American Bookshop (✉ Largo Cairoli at Via Camperio, Milan, ☎ 02/878920). **English Bookshop** (✉ Via Ariosto at Mascheroni, Milan, ☎ 02/4694468). **Feltrinelli Bookstore** (✉ Piazza del Duomo, Milan, ☎ 02/86996897). **FNAC** (✉ Via Torino, corner of Via della Palla, Milan, ☎ 02/720821). **Hoepli** (✉ Via Hoepli 5, Milan, ☎ 02/864871).

MAIL AND SHIPPING

➤ OVERNIGHT SERVICES: **DHL** (✉ Via Agnello, 15, Milan, ☎ 800/345345). **Federal Express Europe** (✉ 10, Via Albricci, Milan, ☎ 800/123800). **United Parcel Service** (✉ 15/2 Via Fantoli, Milan, ☎ 800/877877).
➤ POST OFFICES: **Milan** (✉ Via Cordusio 4, Milan, ☎ 02/8690460).

SAFETY

While the problem is less serious than in Rome, Milan has its share of petty theft. In parts of the city with heavy tourist traffic and on the metro you should keep a close eye on your purse or wallet. Also note that in August, when many of the locals leave town on holiday, tourists become more conspicuous targets for crime.

TAXIS

Taxi fares in Milan seem expensive compared with those in American cities, but drivers are honest (to an extreme, compared with those in some cities). A short downtown hop averages 16,000 lire/€8.25. Taxis wait at stands or can be called at the number below.
➤ TAXI COMPANIES: **Code Blue** (☎ 02/4040). **Radio Taxi** (☎ 02/8383).

TOURS

For tours in Milan, contact the tourist office (☞ Visitor Information *below*). Lake tours can often be arranged by private launches at lakeside hotels.

TRAIN TRAVEL

Although Milan has a bewildering number of railway stations, only one is of concern, Milano Centrale, unless you travel on local routes at peculiar hours—in which case service can begin or terminate in suburban stations (most notably Milano Lambrate for Bergamo, and Stazione Nord for Como). Premium international (EC) service and premium (IC) domestic service connect Milano Centrale with major European cities. Metro Line 3 links Milano Centrale with Piazza Duomo. For general information on trains and hours, check the state railroad Internet site. From Milan, there is frequent direct service to Cremona, Bergamo, Pavia, Brescia, Mantua, Desenzano del Garda–Sirmione, and Como. Call Ferrovie dello Stato (FS), for information, or check out their Web site.
➤ TRAIN INFORMATION: **Ferrovie dello Stato** (☎ 848/888088, WEB www.fs-on-line.com). **Milano Centrale** (✉ about 5 km [3 mi] northwest of the Duomo and Galleria, ☎ 848/888088 for toll-free information; 02/72524370 for APT office).

TRANSPORTATION AROUND MILAN

Milan has an excellent system of public transport (for information call ATM), consisting of trolley cars, buses, and a subway system, the Metropolitana, which runs on three lines. Tickets for each must be purchased before you board and must be canceled by machines at underground station entrances and mounted on poles inside trolleys and buses. Tickets cost 1,500 lire/€0.75 and can be purchased from news vendors, tobacconists, and machines at larger stops. Buy several at once—they remain valid until canceled. One ticket is valid for 75 minutes on all surface lines, or for one subway trip. A 24-hour ticket valid on all public transport lines costs 5,000 lire/€2.58, and one ticket valid for 48 hours costs 9,000 lire/€4.65; they are sold at Duomo Metro and Stazione Centrale Metro stations.

Serious pollution is responsible for a rigorous effort to control excessive traffic in and out of Milan. Cars lacking a special resident's permit will be stopped and ticketed. Parking in the city center is possible 7 AM–8 PM for a fee. If age or infirmity entitles you to special dispensation, ask your rental agency or hotel concierge about car permits for special cases. For car service with a driver, call Autonoleggio Pini.

➤ CONTACTS: **ATM** (☎ 800/016857). **Autonoleggio Pini** (☎ 02/29400555, FAX 02/2047843).

TRAVEL AGENCIES

➤ LOCAL AGENT REFERRALS: **Compagnia Italiana Turismo** (CIT; ✉ Galleria Vittorio Emanuele, Milan, ☎ 02/863701). **American Express Travel Agency** (✉ Via Brera 3, Milan, ☎ 02/72003693).

VISITOR INFORMATION

➤ TOURIST INFORMATION: **Bellagio** (✉ Piazza della Chiesa 14, ☎ 031/950204). **Bergamo** (✉ Vicolo Aquila Nera at Piazza Vecchia, Upper Bergamo, ☎ 035/232730; ✉ Viale Vittorio Emanuele 20, Bergamo Bassa, ☎ 035/210204). **Brescia** (✉ Corso Zanardelli 34, ☎ 030/43418). **Como** (✉ Via Borgovico 148, Como, ☎ 031/230329 or 031/230111). **Cremona** (✉ Piazza del Comune 8, ☎ 0372/23233). **Malcesine** (✉ Via Capitanato del Porto 6, ☎ 045/7400555). **Mantua** (✉ Piazza A. Mantegna 6, ☎ 0376/328253). **Milan** (✉ Via Marconi 1, ☎ 02/72524300; ✉ Stazione Centrale, ☎ 02/72524370). **Pavia** (✉ Via Fabio Filzi 2, ☎ 0382/22156). **Riva del Garda** (✉ Giardini di Porta Orientale 8, ☎ 0464/554444). **Sabbioneta** (✉ Via Vespasiano Gonzaga 27, ☎ 0375/52039). **Sirmione** (✉ Viale Marconi 8, ☎ 030/916245 or 030/916114). **Stresa** (✉ Via Canonica 8, ☎ 0323/30150).

5 PIEDMONT/ VALLE D'AOSTA

TURIN, THE COLLINE, THE ALPS, THE PO PLAIN

Italy's windows on France and Switzerland are delightful surprises even in a land of natural beauty. Snowcapped Monte Bianco and Monte Cervino climb to the highest heights in Europe, and below them, Alpine valleys cradle storybook castles. From here come Alba's truffles, Barolo's wine, and the FIATs, Borsalino hats, and Asti Spumante of Turin, the city sparkling at the center of it all.

F
ROM ALPINE VALLEYS hemming the highest mountains in Europe to the mist-shrouded lowlands skirting the Po River, from pulsating industrial centers turning out the best of Italian design to tiny stone villages isolated above the clouds, and from hearty peasant cooking in farmhouse kitchens to French-accented delicacies accompanied by some of Italy's finest wines, Piedmont and the spectacular Valle d'Aosta present you with a store of historical, cultural, and natural riches.

Updated by
Heather
O'Brian

The Valle d'Aosta's Italian Alps afford excellent skiing and climbing at renowned resort towns such as Courmayeur and Breuil-Cervinia. In the Piedmontese lowlands, Turin, the regional capital, is a historical center that today also serves as the heart of Italy's booming auto industry. Don't be put off by Turin's industrial reputation—it's also home to elegant piazzas, high fashion, fine chocolate, and worthwhile museums. And now, the city is busy highlighting its attractions as it prepares to host the Winter Olympics of 2006. Near Turin are Alba, home of fragrant Italian white truffles, seasonal delicacies that sell for more than $1,000 per pound; Asti, Barolo, and Barbaresco, the famous wine centers; and the modern business hubs Ivrea, Novara, and Alessandria.

Tucked away at the foot of the Pennine, Graian, Cottian, and Maritime Alps (Piemonte, in Italian, means "foot of the mountains"), Piedmont and the autonomous region of Valle d'Aosta just north of it seem more akin to neighboring France and Switzerland. Well-dressed women in the refined cafés of Turin are addressed more often as *madama* than *signora,* and French is often used in the more remote mountain hamlets.

Piedmont was originally inhabited by Celtic tribes who were absorbed by the conquering Romans. As allies of Rome, the Celts held off Hannibal when he came down through the Alpine passes with his elephants but were eventually defeated, and their capital—Taurasia, the present Turin—was destroyed. The Romans rebuilt the city, giving its streets the grid pattern that survives today. Roman ruins can be found throughout both regions and are particularly conspicuous in the town of Aosta. With the fall of the Roman empire, Piedmont suffered the fate of the rest of Italy and was successively occupied and ravaged by barbarians from the east and the north. In the 11th century, a feudal French family named Savoy ruled Turin briefly; toward the end of the 13th century they returned to the area, where they would remain, almost continuously, for 500 years. In 1798 the French Republican armies invaded Italy, but when Napoléon's empire fell, the house of Savoy returned to power.

Beginning in 1848, Piedmont was one of the principal centers of the Risorgimento, the movement for Italian unity. In 1861 the Chamber of Deputies of Turin declared Italy a united kingdom. Rome became the capital in 1870, marking the end of Piedmont's importance in the political sphere. Nevertheless, the architectural splendors of Turin, together with some unheralded but excellent museums, continue to draw travelers.

Piedmont became one of the first industrialized regions in Italy, and the automotive giant FIAT—the Fabbrica Italiana Automobili Torino—was established here in 1899. Today the region is the center of Italy's automobile, metalworking, chemical, and candy industries, having attracted thousands of workers from Italy's impoverished south. The FIAT dynasty, led by the Agnelli family—Italy's equivalent of the Kennedys—has been perhaps the most important player in the region's rise to power and affluence.

The Valle d'Aosta, to the north, is famous for its impressive fortified castles and splendid Alpine beauty. It was settled in the 3rd millennium

BC by people from the Mediterranean and later by a Celtic tribe known as the Salassi, who eventually fell to the Romans. The Saracens were here in the 10th century; by the 12th century, the Savoy family had established itself, and the region's feudal nobles moved into the countryside, building the massive castles that still stand. Valle d'Aosta enjoyed relative autonomy as part of the Savoy kingdom and was briefly ruled by the French four separate times. The region is still officially bilingual, so you will hear both Italian and French.

Pleasures and Pastimes

Dining

These two regions offer rustic specialties from farmhouse hearths, fine cuisine with a French accent—and everything in between. The area's best-known dish is probably polenta, a creamy cornmeal concoction often served with *carbonada* (veal stew), local sausages, melted cheese, or wild mushrooms. The favorite form of pasta is *agnolotti* (filled with meat, spinach, or ricotta cheese), often served in melted butter and shaved truffles. Another regional specialty is *fonduta,* a local version of fondue, made with melted fontina (a cheese from the Valle d'Aosta), eggs, and sometimes grated truffles. Fontina and ham also often deck out the ubiquitous, French-style *crepes alla valdostana,* served piping hot and casserole style. Alba is the home of *tartufi bianchi* (white truffles), much rarer and more expensive than black ones and considered the tastiest by connoisseurs. They sell for at least $1,000 a pound wholesale. Another local dish is *bagna cauda* (literally, "hot bath"), a heated sauce made from butter, oil, anchovies, cream, and shredded garlic; it is served with *cardi* (edible thistles) or other raw vegetables for dipping.

Although as a rule desserts here are less sweet than in some other Italian regions, treats like *panna cotta* (a cooked milk custard) and *torta di nocciole* (hazelnut torte) still delight. Turin is renowned for its delicate pastries and fine chocolates, especially for the hazelnut *gianduiotti.* Valle d'Aosta is famous for a variety of schnappslike brandies made from fruits or herbs. Piedmont is one of Italy's most important wine-producing regions. Most of the wines are full-bodied reds, such as Barolo, Nebbiolo, Freisa, Barbera, and the lighter Barbaresco. Asti Spumante, a sparkling wine, comes from the region, as does vermouth, which was developed in Piedmont by A. B. Carpano in 1786. Many prefer dry (brut) Spumante to the sweet Asti varietal.

For general information and price categories, *see* Dining *in* Smart Travel Tips A to Z.

Lodging

There is a high standard of old-world opulence in Turin's better hotels, and it is translated into the Alpine idiom in the top resort hotels in the mountains. Less-expensive hotels in cities and towns are generally geared to business travelers. You can usually count on a measure of charm at resorts and the Italian brand of gemütlichkeit even in more modest resort hotels. Summer and winter occupancy rates and prices are usually quite high at resorts, with summer vacationers and skiers, respectively, monopolizing available accommodations. Hotels in mountain resorts may offer attractive half-board or off-season rates that can sometimes reduce the cost by a full price category. Many mountain resort hotels cater primarily to half- or full-board guests only, for stays of at least a week. It's a good idea to take a package deal on a ski vacation; it may give you a break on the price of lift tickets.

For general information and price categories, *see* Lodging *in* Smart Travel Tips A to Z.

Skiing

This is the major sport in both Piedmont and the Valle d'Aosta. Resorts with excellent facilities abound near the highest mountains in Europe—Monte Bianco (Mont Blanc), Monte Rosa, Monte Cervino (the Matterhorn), and the Gran Paradiso. Lift tickets, running around 50,000 lire/€25.80 for a day's pass, are significantly less expensive than at major U.S. resorts (though often for fewer trails).

Exploring Piedmont/Valle d'Aosta

The vast Po plain, which stretches eastward in a wide belt across the top of the Italian peninsula, begins in Piedmont, where the Po River has its source in the Coolidge Glacier on 11,000-ft-high Monviso. But Piedmont is primarily a mountainous region. The Maritime Alps lie to the south of Turin, and the rolling hills of the Monferrato and Langhe districts fold the landscape southeast of Turin. High Alpine crests of the Valle d'Aosta rise to the north and west of the plain. As you wind your way northeast into the Valle d'Aosta, you are in the Italian Loire, where solid, imposing castles sit in the shadow of Europe's most impressive peaks, Mont Blanc and the Matterhorn. Nature has endowed Piedmont and the Valle d'Aosta with some of the most striking scenery in Italy.

Like any rugged, mountainous region, the Alps of Piemonte and the Valle d'Aosta can be tricky to navigate. Roads that look like superhighways on the map can be narrow and twisting, with steep slopes and cliff-side drops. Generally, roads are well maintained, but the sheer distance covered by all of those curves tends to take longer than you might have anticipated, and so it's best to figure in extra time for getting around. This is especially true in winter, when weather conditions can cause slow traffic and road closings. Be sure to check with local tourist offices and police before venturing off the beaten path, and find out whether you may need tire chains for snowy and icy roads. Train routes, on the other hand, are more or less reliable in the region.

Numbers in the text correspond to numbers in the margin and on the Piedmont/Valle d'Aosta and Turin maps.

Great Itineraries

With the exception of the mountain resorts, which may be packed at the height of the season, much of Piedmont and Valle d'Aosta is off the beaten track. These regions of Italy offer the pleasures of discovery: uncrowded, unhurried samplings of scenery, art, food, and some of Italy's finest wines. The amount of time you choose to spend here depends on your interests. If you want to admire the highest mountains in the Alps from the pistes or the deck of a chalet, sneak up on the chamois in the Parco Nazionale del Gran Paradiso, and still have time to devote to Turin and the wine country, a total of seven days should be ideal. Five days would give you a chance to visit Turin's attractions, make an excursion into the mountains, and discover some of the smaller cities. In three days you can see Turin and then head to Aosta for a look at some impressive Roman ruins and a quick trip into the mountains. If you budget your time carefully, you can spend half a day in Asti.

IF YOU HAVE 3 DAYS

If you have limited time, you should concentrate first on ⓘ **Turin** ①–⑮, including the **Duomo di San Giovanni** ①, where the famous shroud is housed; the 17th-century **Palazzo Reale** ②, former residence of the Savoy royal family; and the churches of **San Carlo** ⑤ and **Santa Cristina** ⑥, which flank the impressive **Piazza San Carlo** ⑦, considered by some to be Italy's finest square. Take time to enjoy one or more of the city's authentic old-world cafés and walk by the striking **Mole An-**

Piedmont/Valle d'Aosta

SWITZERLAND

Monte Cervino (Matterhorn)

Monte Bianco (Mont Blanc)

Breuil-Cervinia **26**

Great St. Bernard Pass

Monte Rosa

29 Courmayeur

S406 Valtournanche

S27

Gressoney-la-Trinité

S526

Dora

Aosta

Little St. Bernard Pass

28

Nus Châtillon

St. Vincent

S526

Baltéa

VALLE D'AOSTA

27

25

Castello Fénis

Verrès

VALLE D'AOSTA

S505

30 Cogne

Bard **24**

Parco Nazionale del Gran Paradiso

Pont St. Martin

FRANCE

Ceresole Reale

S26

S460

Ivrea

Forno Alpi Gràie

Orco

A5

Dora

Cuorgnè

Balme

Baltéa

S26

Céres

Chivasso

S25

S460

Susa

A4

23 Bardonecchia

Sacra di San Michele **20** **19**

Abbazia di Sant'Antonio di Ranverso

S23

Avigliana

18 **17**

Rivoli

Turin

1 — **15**

Sestriere **22** TO CLAVIERE

Stupinigi

16

S589

S10

A21

N

S23

Pinerolo

Carignano

S20

ITALY

0   10 miles
0   15 km

Saluzzo **21**

A6

TO BRA

S29

TO ALBA

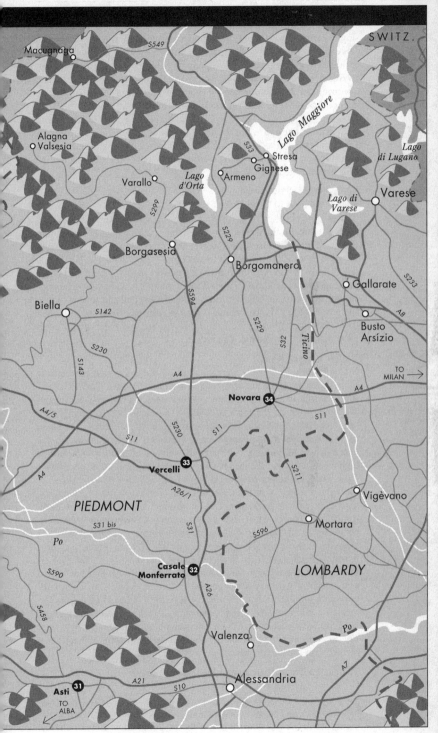

tonelliana ⑩, an odd structure that was once the world's tallest building and now houses a new, extensive cinema museum. On the second day, head northeast along the A5 motorway to ⛰ **Aosta** ㉘ to see its large and well-preserved Roman ruins and enjoy some regional French-influenced cooking. If you have a couple of hours to spare on your way to Aosta, see **Castello Fénis** ㉗, well worth the detour. On the third day, continue on to ⛰ **Courmayeur** ㉙ for magnificent views of Monte Bianco and, if time allows, **Breuil-Cervinia** ㉖ for a look at the Matterhorn. Alternatively, you can catch a glimpse of one or the other and then double back through Aosta to **Cogne** ㉚, where you can make a foray into the Parco Nazionale Gran Paradiso. Another alternative is to return to Turin and head southeast into the vineyard-blanketed hills around medieval ⛰ **Asti** ㉛.

IF YOU HAVE 5 DAYS
Spend two days in ⛰ **Turin** ①–⑮, and then head for the Roman city of ⛰ **Aosta** ㉘, perhaps stopping on the way to see the fairy-tale **Castello Fénis** ㉗. On the third day, you can drink in the views of the Monte Bianco from ⛰ **Courmayeur** ㉙, see the Matterhorn from ⛰ **Breuil-Cervinia** ㉖, or follow the trails from **Cogne** ㉚ into the Parco Nazionale del Gran Paradiso. On the fourth day double back to Turin and make an excursion to **Saluzzo** ㉑, an old town steeped in 15th-century atmosphere. Alpine fans might choose instead to spend the fourth day in the mountains, at Gran Paradiso. On the fifth day continue southeast to ⛰ **Asti** ㉛, exploring the rolling hills where great wines and good food make this a gourmet's paradise.

IF YOU HAVE 7 DAYS
Make ⛰ **Turin** ①–⑮ your base for three days, from which you can explore the city and the outlying towns, including **Saluzzo** ㉑, with its picturesque hilltop center and castles. Another second-day excursion from Turin takes you to the castle at **Rivoli** ⑰, a sanctuary of contemporary art, and then over a pilgrim's route to two medieval abbeys, **Abbazia di Sant'Antonio di Ranverso** ⑱ and Umberto Eco's inspiration, the **Sacra di San Michele** ⑳. Alternatively, travel westward to Piedmont's high mountains and see the resorts of **Sestriere** ㉒ and **Bardonecchia** ㉓, close to the French border. On the third day head for the mountains of the Valle d'Aosta; visit the **Castello Fénis** ㉗ on the way to ⛰ **Aosta** ㉘, a good base for excursions into the mountains that will keep you moving on the fourth and fifth days between **Courmayeur** ㉙, **Breuil-Cervinia** ㉖, and **Cogne** ㉚. Devote the better part of a day to the stunning Gran Paradiso national park, near Cogne. Head south on the sixth day, doubling back past Turin and continuing southeast to ⛰ **Asti** ㉛. Follow the provincial roads through the vineyards of the hilly Monferrato and Langhe districts of south-central Piedmont, delving into their culinary and enological delights. On the seventh day head east across the fertile Po plain toward the rice-growing capital of **Vercelli** ㉝, making sure you see the Duomo, the final resting place of several Savoy rulers. The easternmost city of Piedmont is **Novara** ㉞, of little interest but a rest stop on the way to Milan, only 50 km (30 mi) away.

When to Tour Piedmont/Valle d'Aosta

Unless you are dead set on skiing, the region can be visited in either summer or winter (and for that matter, there's summer skiing at Monte Cervino). In winter, road conditions can be treacherous, especially higher up in the mountains, requiring the use of snow tires or chains. The ski resorts of the Valle d'Aosta are popular with Italians and non-Italians alike, so book your accommodations in advance. Snow conditions for skiing vary drastically year to year—there is nothing approaching the consistency of, say, the Colorado and Utah Rockies—

so keep apprised of weather conditions. If you are visiting in summer, try to avoid coming in August, the holiday month for the vast majority of Italians, many of whom will come here for an Alpine vacation of walking, hiking, and relaxing.

TURIN

Turin—Torino, in Italian—is roughly in the center of Piedmont/Valle d'Aosta and is 128 km (80 mi) west of Milan; it is on the Po River, on the edge of the Po plain, which stretches eastward all the way to the Adriatic. Turin's flatness and wide, angular, tree-lined boulevards are a far cry from Italian *metropoli* to the south; the region's decidedly northern European bent is quite evident in its nerve center. Apart from its role as northwest Italy's major industrial, cultural, and administrative hub, Turin is a center of education, science, and the arts. It also has a reputation as Italy's capital of black magic and the supernatural. This distinction is enhanced by the presence of Turin's most famous, controversial, and unsettling relic, the Sacra Sindone (Holy Shroud), still believed by many Catholics to be the cloth in which Christ's body was wrapped when he was taken down from the cross.

Downtown Turin

Many of Turin's major sights are clustered around Piazza Castello, and others are on or just off the porticoed Via Roma, one of the city's main thoroughfares, which leads 1 km (½ mi) from Piazza Castello south to Piazza Carlo Felice, a landscaped park with a fountain in front of the train station. First opened in 1615, Via Roma was largely rebuilt in the 1930s, during the time of Premier Benito Mussolini.

A Good Walk

Start on Piazza San Giovanni at the **Duomo di San Giovanni** ①, the hushed and shadowy repository of a controversial relic. Step into the **Palazzo Reale** ②, adjacent to the Duomo, to see the sumptuous interiors and, in a separate wing also on Piazza Castello, the Armeria Reale. The massive building occupying an entire block at the center of Piazza Castello is **Palazzo Madama** ③, parts of which were reopened to the public in the spring of 2001. In the northwest corner of the same square, take time to observe Guarini's lively architectural vision in the church of **San Lorenzo** ④. Go southwest on Via Roma, a street rebuilt with arcades in the 1930s. Continuing a few blocks, you come to the twin churches of **San Carlo** ⑤ and **Santa Cristina** ⑥ on the **Piazza San Carlo** ⑦. Just off the northeast end of Piazza San Carlo is the imposing **Palazzo dell'Accademia delle Scienze** ⑧, where you may devote an hour or two to the collections in the Museo Egizio and Galleria Sabauda. To the east, across the street, is the graceful **Palazzo Carignano** ⑨, not only historic but also an example of Piedmontese Baroque. The east facade of the palace faces Piazza Carlo Alberto, where you turn onto Via Po, heading east to Via Montebello, where you turn left to reach the **Mole Antonelliana** ⑩, Turin's oddest and most conspicuous building and the site of a cinema museum.

TIMING
This walk takes the better part of a day if you allow plenty of time for the museums. Since it includes the most important of Turin's sights, it can constitute a satisfactory, albeit speedy, visit.

Sights to See

❶ **Duomo di San Giovanni.** The most impressive piece in Turin's 15th-century cathedral is the shadowy, black marble–walled **Cappella della Sacra Sindone** (Chapel of the Holy Shroud), where the famous relic was housed before a fire in 1997. The chapel was designed by the priest and architect Guarino Guarini (1604–83), a genius of the Baroque style who was official engineer and mathematician to the court of Duke Carlo Emanuele II of Savoy. The fire was a major setback to ongoing restorations; the chapel is expected to remain closed for many years as a result of the damage.

The Sacra Sindone (Holy Shroud) is a 4-yard-long sheet of linen, unremarkable except for the fact that it is thought by millions to be the burial shroud of Christ, bearing the light imprint of His crucified body. The shroud first made an appearance around the middle of the 15th century, when it was presented to Ludovico of Savoy in Chambéry. In 1578 it was brought to Turin by another member of the Savoy royal family, Duke Emanuele Filiberto. It is only in the last few years that the Catholic Church has allowed rigorous scientific study of the shroud. Not surprisingly, results have bolstered both sides of the argument. On the one hand, three separate university teams—in Switzerland, Britain, and the United States—have concluded, as a result of carbon 14 dating, that the cloth is a forgery dating from between 1260 and 1390. On the other hand, they are unable to explain how medieval forgers could have created the shroud's image, which is like a photographic negative, and how they could have had the knowledge or means to incorporate traces of Roman coins covering the eyelids and endemic Middle Eastern pollen woven into the cloth. Either way, the shroud continues to be revered as a holy relic. The shroud is rarely displayed and was last hung from August to October 2000 for the Jubilee, the religious ceremony to mark the beginning of the third millennium. For those who miss the official hangings, a photocopy of the Sindone is on permanent display near the altar of the Duomo. ⊠ *Piazza San Giovanni,* ☎ *011/4361540.* ⊙ *Mon.–Sat. 6:30–noon and 3–7, Sun. 8–noon and 3–7.*

★ ⑩ **Mole Antonelliana.** You won't miss the unusual square dome and thin, elaborate spire tower of this Turin landmark above the city's rooftops. This odd structure, built between 1863 and 1897, was originally intended to be a synagogue, but costs escalated and eventually it was bought by the city of Turin. In its time it was the tallest building in the world. You can take the crystal elevator to the reach the terrace at the top of the dome for an excellent view of the city, the plain, and the Alps beyond. Also worth a visit is the Mole's **Museum of Cinema,** which extends over 34,000 square ft and houses many items of film memorabilia as well as a film library with some 7,000 titles. ⊠ *Via Montebello 20,* ☎ *011/8154230.* 🎫 *Museum 10,000 lire/€5.15; elevator 7,000 lire/€3.60; combination ticket 13,000 lire/€6.70.* ⊙ *Museum Tues.–Fri. and Sun. 9–8, Sat. 9 AM–11 PM, (ticket counter closes 75 mins before closing); elevator Tues.–Fri. and Sun. 10–8, Sat. 10 AM–11 PM.*

⑨ **Palazzo Carignano.** A Baroque triumph of Guarino Guarini, this red-brick palace was built from 1679 to 1685 and is one of Turin's and Italy's most historic buildings. The kings of Savoy Carlo Alberto (1798–1849) and Vittorio Emanuele II (1820–78) were born within its walls. Italy's first parliament met here from 1860 to 1865. The palace is now occupied by the **Museo del Risorgimento,** a museum honoring the 19th-century movement for Italian unity. ⊠ *Via Accademia delle Scienze 5,* ☎ *011/5621147.* 🎫 *8,000 lire/€4.15.* ⊙ *Tues.–Sun. 9–7.*

⑧ **Palazzo dell'Accademia delle Scienze** (Palace of the Academy of Sciences). Guarini's large Baroque tour de force, prefiguring the 18th century's preoccupation with logic and science, houses two of Turin's most famous museums, the Museo Egizio and the Galleria Sabauda. The **Museo Egizio** (Egyptian Museum) is one of the finest outside Cairo. Its superb collection includes statues of pharaohs and mummies, and

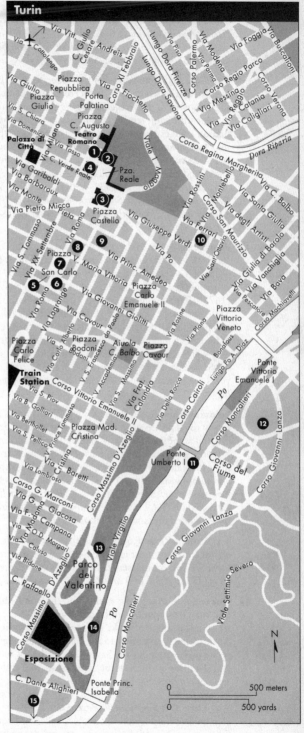

Turin

entire frescoes taken from royal tombs. Look for the 13th-century BC statue of Ramses II, which still glistens in its original colors. ⊠ *Via Accademia delle Scienze 6,* ☎ *011/5617776,* WEB *www.museoegizio.it.* 🎟 *12,000 lire/€6.20; 15,000 lire/€7.75 combined ticket includes Galleria Sabauda.* ☉ *Tues.–Sun. 9–7:30.*

The **Galleria Sabauda** houses the collections of the house of Savoy. It is particularly rich in 16th- and 17th-century Dutch and Flemish paintings: note the *St. Francis with Stigmata* by Jan Van Eyck (1395–1441), in which the saint receives the marks of Christ's wounds while a companion cringes beside him. Other Dutch masterpieces include paintings by Anthony Van Dyck (1599–1641) and Rembrandt (1606–69). A *Tobias and the Angel* by Piero del Pollaiuolo (circa 1443–96) is showcased, and other featured Italian artists include Fra Angelico (circa 1400–55), Andrea Mantegna (1431–1506), and Paolo Veronese (1528–88). ⊠ *Via Accademia delle Scienze 6,* ☎ *011/547440.* 🎟 *8,000 lire/€4.15; 15,000 lire/€7.75 combined ticket includes Museo Egizio.* ☉ *Tues.–Fri. and Sun. 8:30–7:30, Sat. 8:30 AM–11 PM.*

❸ **Palazzo Madama.** In the center of Piazza Castello, this castle was named for the French queen Maria Cristina, who made it her home in the 17th century. The castle incorporates the remains of a Roman gate, as well as medieval and Renaissance additions. The architect Filippo Juvarra (1678–1736) designed the castle's elaborate Baroque facade in the early 18th century: he was intent on dispelling the idea that Italy's importance as a producer of contemporary art and architecture was in decline. Parts of the castle's interior—including the atrium, the large central room known as Il Voltone, a large Baroque staircase, and the Salone del Senato, where the Senate once met—were opened in spring 2001 after being closed 13 years for restoration. ⊠ *Piazza Castello.* 🎟 *Free; exhibitions 12,000 lire/€6.20* ☉ *Tues.–Fri. 10–7, Sat. 10 AM–11 PM, Sun. 10–7.*

❷ **Palazzo Reale** (Royal Palace). This 17th-century palace is the former Savoy royal residence. It is an imposing work of brick, stone, and marble that stands on the site of one of Turin's ancient Roman city gates. In contrast to its austere exterior, the palace's interior is swathed in luxurious, mostly rococo trappings, including tapestries, gilt ceilings, and sumptuous 17th- to 19th-century furniture. Behind the palace, take time to relax in the royal gardens. ⊠ *Piazza Castello,* ☎ *011/4361455.* 🎟 *8,000 lire/€4.15.* ☉ *Tues.–Sun. 8:30–6:30; groups leave every 40 mins (guided visits sometimes available).*

The **Armeria Reale** (Royal Armory), in a wing of the Royal Palace, holds one of Europe's most extensive collections of arms and armor. It is a must-see for connoisseurs. ⊠ *Entrance at Piazza Castello 191,* ☎ *011/543889.* 🎟 *8,000 lire/€4.15.* ☉ *Tues.–Sun. 8:30–7:30.*

❼ **Piazza San Carlo.** While standing in the stately, formal expanse, you, too, may proclaim this to be the grandest square in Italy. In the center stands a **statue of Duke Emanuele Filiberto of Savoy,** victor at the battle of San Quintino in 1557. The melee heralded the peaceful resurgence of Turin under the Savoy, after years of bloody dynastic fighting. The fine bronze statue, erected in the 19th century, is one of Turin's symbols.

NEED A BREAK? | The historic **Café San Carlo** (⊠ Piazza San Carlo) is usually lively with locals, gathered at the marble-top tables under the huge crystal chandelier. On the opposite side of the square, **Stratta,** one of Turin's most famous chocolate shops, open since 1836, sells confections of all kinds—not just the chocolates in the lavish window displays but also fancy cookies, rum-laced fudges, chocolate truffles, and magnificent cakes.

❺ San Carlo. The ornate Baroque facade of this 17th-century church was enhanced in the latter part of the 19th century to harmonize with the facade of Santa Cristina. ⊠ *Piazza San Carlo, entrance on southern end of square.*

❹ San Lorenzo. The cupola and vividly painted interior of this church are standouts. Guarino Guarini was in his mid-sixties when he began work on the church in 1668, but the sprightly collection of domes, columns, and florid Baroque features seems more the work of a younger architect cutting his teeth with a daring display of mathematical invention. ⊠ *Piazza Castello.*

NEED A
BREAK? **Baratti e Milano** (⊠ just east of Piazza Castello, ☎ 011/5613060), in the glass-roofed Galleria Subalpina near Via Po, is another one of Turin's charming old-world cafés. It's famous for its chocolates, so you can indulge your sweet tooth here or buy some gianduiotti or candied chestnuts to take home to friends.

❻ Santa Cristina. Built in the mid-17th century, this church received a Baroque-style face-lift by Juvarra in 1715. ⊠ *Piazza San Carlo.* ☉ *Daily 7–noon and 3–7.*

Along the Po

The Po River is narrow and unprepossessing here in Turin, only a hint of the broad and mighty watercourse that it becomes as it flows eastward toward the Adriatic. It is flanked, however, by formidable edifices, a park, and a lovely pedestrian path.

A Good Tour

Start at the east end of Piazza Vittorio Veneto, at the end of Via Po. Cross the river on Ponte Vittorio Emanuele I, the bridge leading to the church of **Gran Madre di Dio** ⑪, a replica of Rome's Pantheon. To reach the church of **Santa Maria del Monte** ⑫, follow Corso Moncalieri south and then wend your way upward to the top of the hill. Then return to Corso Moncalieri and cross the next bridge downstream, Ponte Umberto I, to the Parco del Valentino, opened in 1856. One of the city's many pretty pedestrian paths, Viale Virgilio runs parallel to the river and leads to the **Castello del Valentino** ⑬, reminiscent of castles on the Loire. Go south on Viale Virgilio to the **Borgo Medioevale** ⑭, a replica of a medieval hamlet and castle. From the park, catch a bus or taxi or just keep on walking south on Corso Massimo d'Azeglio to the **Museo dell'Automobile** ⑮, a low, modern building that sweeps you into a world of nostalgia for the sleek, glamorous cars of yesteryear.

TIMING

Three hours should be enough to allow you to cover the ground with ease, but if you are an automobile buff, allow well over an hour for the Museo dell'Automobile.

Sights to See

 Borgo Medioevale (Medieval Village). A forerunner to today's theme parks, this village, a faithful reproduction of medieval Piedmontese buildings, was created for the Turin Exposition of 1884. Visiting here is like stepping back into the Middle Ages, with craftsmen's shops, houses, churches, and stores clustered along narrow streets and lanes. The centerpiece is the **Rocca Medievale**, a medieval castle in the heart of the village. ⊠ *Riverside, southern edge of the Parco del Valentino,* ☎ 011/4431701. ☜ *Rocca Medievale 5,000 lire/€2.60.* ☉ *Village daily 9–7, Rocca Medievale Tues.–Sun. 9–7 (groups of a maximum of 25 enter the castle every ½ hr).*

⑬ **Castello del Valentino.** The design of this 17th-century castle, built more for appearance than for defense, is based on models of 16th-century French châteaux. Now home to Turin's Polytechnical University's Faculty of Architecture, it stands on the left bank of the Po, in the pretty **Parco del Valentino,** laid out in 1856, which includes botanical gardens. The interior, which now houses a school, is elaborate, with frescoed walls and rich decoration. The real attraction of the castle is its riverside setting amid the greenery of the park. ⊠ *Parco del Valentino,* ☎ *011/ 6707446 botanical gardens.* ▦ *Botanical gardens 5,000 lire/€2.60.* ☉ *Botanical gardens Apr. 11–Sept., weekends 9–1 and 3–7.*

⑪ **Gran Madre di Dio** (Great Mother of God). This 19th-century church was built in a neoclassical style based on the Pantheon in Rome. ⊠ *East bank of the Po, west of Piazza Castello.* ☉ *Mon.–Sat. 7:30–noon and 3:30–7, Sun. 7:30–1 and 3:30–7.*

⑮ **Museo dell'Automobile** (Car Museum). No visit to car-manufacturing Turin would be complete without a pilgrimage to see perfectly conserved Bugattis, Ferraris, and Isotta Fraschinis. Here you'll get an idea of the importance of FIAT—and automobiles in general—to Turin's economy. There's a collection of antique cars from as early as 1893, and displays show how the city has changed over the years as a result of its premier industry. ⊠ *Corso Unita d'Italia 40,* ☎ *011/677666.* ▦ *10,000 lire/€5.15.* ☉ *Tues.–Sun. 10–6:30.*

⑫ **Santa Maria del Monte.** The church and convent standing on top of 150-ft Monte dei Cappuccini date from 1583. Don't be surprised if you find yourself in the middle of a wedding party: local couples often come here to have their pictures taken. ⊠ *Monte dei Cappuccini, above Corso Moncalieri.* ☉ *Daily 9–noon and 2:30–6.*

Dining and Lodging

$$$$ ✕ **Balbo.** Considered by many to be Turin's best restaurant, Balbo is
★ set in an 18th-century palace in Turin's historic center. Some of the more creative takes on traditional regional fare include *tagliatelline al rosso d'uovo con intingolo di verdure, pinoli e uvetta* (fresh pasta with egg yolk, vegetables, pine nuts, and raisins) and *insalata di astice e riso selvaggio* (crawfish and wild-rice salad). In spite of Turin's inland location, Balbo has a nice array of seafood. Both meat and seafood prix-fixe menus are available. ⊠ *Via Andrea Doria 11,* ☎ *011/8395775. Reservations essential. AE, DC, MC, V. Closed Mon. and Aug.*

$$$$ ✕ **La Prima Smarrita.** Intimate and elegant, this restaurant sits on the
★ fringe of the Lingotto neighborhood, a short taxi ride from the city center. Host Moreno Grossi's light, innovative versions of Mediterranean dishes are influenced by the Piedmontese setting, his Tuscan roots, and culinary creativity. Try *tortelli di borragine* (fresh pasta filled with borage and served with fresh tomato sauce) or sea bass with artichokes, potatoes, and olives. And for dessert try the *gianduia* (hazelnut chocolate) mousse. The wine cellar is one of the best in town. ⊠ *Corso Unione Sovietica 244,* ☎ *011/3179657. Reservations essential. Jacket and tie. AE, DC, MC, V. No lunch Mon.*

$$$–$$$$ ✕ **Del Cambio.** The setting and atmosphere of this town-center restaurant in a palace dating from 1757 are incomparable. It is one of Europe's
★ most beautiful and historic restaurants, with decorative moldings, mirrors, and hanging lamps that look just as they did when Italian national hero Cavour dined here more than a century ago. The cuisine draws heavily on Piedmontese tradition and is paired with a wide array of fine Piedmontese wines. Agnolotti in an *arrosto* (roast veal) sauce is a recommended first course. ⊠ *Piazza Carignano 2,* ☎ *011/546690. Jacket and tie. AE, DC, MC, V. Closed Sun., Jan. 1–6, and 3 wks in Aug.*

$$$–$$$$ ✗ **Vintage 1997.** Since opening up for business in 1997, this sophisticated, centrally located restaurant has become a favorite. You might try such specialties as *chateaubriant al tonno* (tuna chateaubriand) and *tortelli di melanzane e mozzarella di bufalo* (pasta with eggplant and mozzarella). Both meat and seafood fixed-price menus are available. ⊠ *Piazza Solferino 16/h,* ☎ *011/535948. AE, DC, MC, V. Closed Sun. and 3 wks in Aug. No lunch Sat.*

$$$ ✗ **Savoia.** This elegantly understated restaurant is divided into three small rooms, decorated with a few choice pictures and antique furniture. The kitchen turns out creative takes on Piedmontese specialties. Try the agnolotti to start, perhaps finishing the evening with *semifreddo a torroncino* (gelato mixed with whipped cream and nougat). The prix-fixe menu is a good way to sample the Savoia's specialties. ⊠ *Via Corta d'Appello, 13,* ☎ *011/4362288, AE, DC, MC, V. Closed Sun. No lunch Sat.*

$$–$$$ ✗ **L'Agrifoglio.** This intimate local favorite has just 10 tables. Specialties change with the seasons, but you might find such delicacies as risotto *alla Barbaresco* (with Barbaresco wine) and agnolotti *del plin al sugo d'arrosto* (with roast veal sauce) on the menu. L'Agrifoglio stays open late for the after-theater and after-cinema crowd. ⊠ *Via Accademia Albertina 38,* ☎ *011/837064. AE, DC, MC, V. Closed Sun.–Mon. No lunch.*

$$–$$$ ✗ **Tre Galline.** Set in a portion of the ancient Roman wall only a few blocks northwest of Piazza Castello, this trattoria has a long history of good Piedmontese cooking. The menu changes regularly, but whatever's available will be flavorfully prepared. The *insalata di gallina* (chicken salad) has the tang of mustard, and the *stinco di vitello* (veal shin) is redolent of thyme. ⊠ *Via Bellezia 37,* ☎ *011/4366553. AE, DC, MC, V. Closed Sun. and briefly in Aug. No lunch Mon.*

$–$$ ✗ **Da Mauro.** Tuscan and Piedmontese dishes are served at this lively, popular family-run trattoria. Specialties include cannelloni *alla Mirella* (baked with mozzarella, prosciutto, and tomato), *involtini di Gorgonzola* (veal roulades with Gorgonzola and a sauce of peppers and olives), and famous grilled Florentine beef. ⊠ *Via Maria Vittoria 21,* ☎ *011/8170604. No credit cards. Closed Mon. and July.*

$–$$ ✗ **Pizzeria Bochicchio Rodolfo.** About 300 types of pizza are served from the wood-burning oven or this excellent pizzeria near the Piazza Gran Madre. Some second courses and antipasti are also available. ⊠ *Via Monferrato 7/C,* ☎ *011/8190688. No credit cards. Closed Thurs.*

$ ✗ **Porto di Savona.** Look for this centuries-old tavern under the arcades of vast Piazza Vittorio Veneto, where it once served as a terminal for the Turin–Savona stagecoach line. The small street-level and upstairs dining rooms have a decidedly old-fashioned air; the marble stairs are well worn, and the walls are decked with photos of Old Turin. Customers sit at long wooden tables to eat home-style Piedmontese cooking, including gnocchi with Gorgonzola and *bollito misto* (mixed boiled meats, appropriately served only in winter). The Barbera house wine is good. ⊠ *Piazza Vittorio Veneto 2,* ☎ *011/8173500. MC, V. Closed Mon., 1st 2 wks in Jan., and last 2 wks in Aug. No lunch Tues.*

$$$$ 🏨 **Jolly Hotel Principi di Piemonte.** Dating back to the 1930s, the central Principi is one of the best hotels in town and often caters to a famous clientele. The rooms, elegantly furnished in antique style, are spacious and light, with high ceilings. ⊠ *Via Gobetti 15, 10123,* ☎ *011/5629693,* ℻ *011/5620270,* 🌐 *www.jollyhotels.it. 104 rooms. Restaurant, bar, minibars. AE, DC, MC, V.*

$$$$ 🏨 **Turin Palace.** You're right across from the train station at this grand, century-old building in the center of town. Quiet, spacious, and well-furnished rooms have high ceilings and feature either leather-and-wood classic modern style or imperial Louis XV furnishings. ⊠ *Via Sacchi 8, 10128,* ☎ *011/5625511,* ℻ *011/5612187,* 🌐 *www.thi.it. 122 rooms. Restaurant, bar, minibars. AE, DC, MC, V.*

$$$ ★ ⊞ **Victoria.** Uncommon style and comfort are the hallmarks of this boutique hotel, personally decorated and supervised by the caring management to create the atmosphere of a refined town house. The newer wing has a grand marble staircase and rooms individually decorated according to a theme, from romantic to clubby. The same attention to detail is given to the older rooms and to the attractive sitting room and breakfast room overlooking a small park. ⊠ *Via Nino Costa 4, 10123,* ☎ *011/5611909,* FAX *011/5611806,* WEB *www.hotelvictoria-torino.com. 94 rooms, 4 suites. Bar, breakfast room. AE, DC, MC, V.*

$$–$$$ ⊞ **Astoria.** Convenient to the city center and the Porta Nuova train station, the Astoria dates back to the 19th century. Rooms are affordable and modern, and there's a little interior garden. ⊠ *Via XX Settembre 4, 10121,* ☎ *011/5620653,* FAX *011/5625866,* WEB *www.astoriahotel.it. 57 rooms. Bar, breakfast room. AE, DC, MC, V.*

$$–$$$ ⊞ **Liberty.** *Liberty* is a term used by Italians to refer to the Art Nouveau style, and this small, conveniently located hotel maintains that style in old-world furnishings and atmosphere, enhanced by the Anfossi family's attentive courtesy. The hotel is a favorite of academics, artists, and others who appreciate its solid, old-fashioned comfort. You must reserve ahead for the restaurant. ⊠ *Via Pietro Micca 15, 10121,* ☎ *011/5628801,* FAX *011/5628163,* WEB *www.turismhotel.com. 35 rooms. Restaurant, bar. AE, DC, MC, V.*

Nightlife and the Arts

The Arts

MUSIC

Classical music concerts are held in the famous **Conservatorio Giuseppe Verdi** (⊠ Via Mazzini 11, ☎ 011/8121268; ⊠ Piazza Bodoni, ☎ 011/888470) throughout the year but primarily in the winter months. The **Settembre Musica Festival** (☎ 011/4424703), held for three weeks in September, highlights classical music; call for specifics. Sacred music and some modern religious pieces are performed in the **Duomo** (⊠ Via Montebello 20, ☎ 011/8154230) on Sunday evening; these are usually advertized in the vestibule or in the local edition of Turin's nationally distributed newspaper *La Stampa*. The Thursday edition comes with a supplement on music and other entertainment possibilities.

OPERA

The **Teatro Regio** (⊠ Piazza Castello 215 I-10124, Turin, ☎ 011/88151, FAX 011/8815214, WEB www.teatroregio.torino.it), one of Italy's leading opera houses, begins its season in December. You can buy tickets for most performances (premieres sell well in advance) at the box office or on the Web site, where discounts are offered on the day of the show. It is also possible to book tickets via post or fax. Payment for confirmed reservations must be made within 20 days of confirmation by credit card, international postal order, or eurocheque.

Nightlife

A plush after-hours venue for Turin's smart set, **Hennessy** (⊠ Via Mongreno 23, Pino Torinese, ☎ 011/8998522) is in a large hotel in the upscale Superga residential district; it's open Friday and Saturday nights until late. A popular meeting place, the wine bar **Caffè Elena** (⊠ Piazza Vittorio Veneto 5, ☎ 011/8123341) is open until two in the morning every night but Wednesday. At the **Zoobar** (⊠ Corso Casale 127, ☎ 011/8194347) it is possible to listen to live music, get a drink, or dance to music played by DJs. It's open Thursday to Saturday. Hot Latin music, often live, is dished up with gusto at **Sabor Latino** (⊠ Via Stradella 10, ☎ 011/852327) every night except Monday. **Pick Up** (⊠ Via Barge 8, ☎ 011/4472204) is a bar and dance club catering to a mixed crowd of young Turinese, university students, and visitors, from Thursday to Sunday. **Alcatraz** (✉ Murazzi del Pol 37/41, ☎ 011/812570) is open for dancing seven days a week in summer months and from Thursday to Sunday in the fall and spring and offers world music, along with other types of music.

Outdoor Activities and Sports

Boating
Turin makes good use of the Po's recreational potential for boating. The **Lega Navale di Torino** (Turin Boating League; ✉ Corso Unione Sovietica 316, ☎ 011/6197643), open daily 3:30–7 PM, organizes courses and special races throughout the summer.

Golf
There are several 18-hole golf courses in the Turin area, including one of Italy's best, **Associazione Sportiva I Roveri** (☎ 011/9235719), in La Mandria, 18 km (11 mi) northwest of the city. It's necessary to have a membership card from your home golf club to play. **Golf Club I Girasoli** (☎ 011/9795088), about 25 km (16 mi) south of the city, is open to the public at large. It's also the site of a small country inn.

Soccer
Turin's two professional soccer clubs, Juventus and Torino, play their games in the **Stadio delle Alpi** (✉ 6 km [4 mi] northwest of city). Juventus is one of Italy's best teams and historically the most popular. There is fierce rivalry between its supporters and those of visiting clubs, especially Inter Milan and AC Milan. Home matches are usually played on Sunday afternoon during the season, which runs from late August to mid-May. It's possible to purchase tickets for Juventus games in any *tabaccheria* (tobacco shop) with a sign bearing a capital "T."

Shopping

Markets
Go to the famous **Balon Flea Market** (✉ Piazza Repubblica) on Saturday morning for excellent bargains on secondhand books and clothing and browsing among stalls selling local specialties such as gianduiotti. The second Sunday of every month, a special antiques market, appropriately called the **Gran Balon,** sets up shop in Piazza Repubblica.

Specialty Stores
Most people know that Turin produces more than 75% of Italy's cars, but they are often unaware that it is also a clothing manufacturing city. Top-quality boutiques stocking local, national, and international lines are clustered along **Via Roma** and **Via Garibaldi.** Piazza San Carlo, Via Po, and Via Maria Vittoria are lined with **antiques shops,** some—but not all—specializing in 18th-century furniture and domestic items.

THE COLLINE AND SAVOY PALACES

As you head west from Turin toward France, into the Colline ("little hills"), castles and medieval fortifications begin to pepper the former dominion of the house of Savoy, and the Alps come into better and better view. In the region lie the storybook medieval towns of Avigliana, Rivoli, and Saluzzo; 12th-century abbeys; and, farther west and into the mountains, the venerable, if not flashy, ski resorts of Bardonecchia and Sestriere.

Stupinigi

⑯ *8 km (5 mi) southwest of Turin.*

The **Palazzina di Caccia,** in the town of Stupinigi, is an elaborate building built by Juvarra in 1729 as a hunting lodge for the house of Savoy. It is more like a royal villa, with its many wings, landscaped gardens, and surrounding forests. This regal aspect was not lost on Napoléon, who lived here before claiming the crown of Italy. The castle interior is sumptuously decorated and today houses the matter-of-factly named **Museo d'Arte e Ammobiliamento** (Museum of Art and Furniture). Take Bus 41 from Stazione Porta Nuova. ✉ *Stupinigi,* ☎ *011/3581220.* 🎟 *10,000 lire/€5.15.* ☉ *Apr.–Oct., Tues.–Sun. 10–5:20; Nov.–Mar., 10–4:20.*

Rivoli

⑰ *16 km (10 mi) north of Stupinigi, 13 km (8 mi) west of Turin.*

The Savoy court was based in Rivoli in the Middle Ages. The 14th- to 15th-century **Casa del Conte Verde,** right in the center of town, is a good example of medieval architecture of the transitional period, when its defensive function was giving way to the decorative. To get to Rivoli, take Tram 1 from downtown Turin, then Bus 36. The 18th-century Savoy castle, built in the Baroque style under the direction of Juvarra, now houses the **Museo d'Arte Contemporaneo** (Modern Art Museum), which contains many examples of 20th-century Italian art. The Futurist movement is particularly well represented. ✉ *Piazzale Masalda di Savoia,* ☎ *011/9565222.* 🎟 *12,000 lire/€6.20.* ☉ *Tues.–Fri. 10–5, weekends 10–7; 1st and 3rd Sat. of month 10–10.*

Abbazia di Sant'Antonio di Ranverso

⑱ *10 km (6 mi) west of Rivoli, 23 km (14 mi) west of Turin.*

The abbey was originally an abbey hospital, founded in the 12th century by the Hospitalers of St. Anthony to care for victims of St. Anthony's Fire, a crippling disease contracted by eating contaminated grains. Pilgrims came here over the centuries for cures or, sometimes, to offer thanks for a miraculous recovery. The 15th-century frescoes, with their lifelike depictions of pilgrims and saints, retain their original colors. ✉ *Buttigliera Alta, Rosta exit off autostrada and Buttigliera Alta exit off S25,* ☎ *011/9367450.* 🎟 *5,000 lire/€2.60.* ☉ *Sept.–May, Tues.–Sun. 9–noon and 2–4:30; June–Aug., Tues.–Sun. 9–noon and 2–5:30.*

Avigliana

⑲ *6 km (4 mi) west of the Abbazia di Sant'Antonio di Ranverso, 29 km (18 mi) west of Turin.*

Perhaps because of its attractive setting, Avigliana was a favorite of the Savoys up until the mid-15th century. Medieval houses still line the narrow, twisting streets. **Casa della Porta Ferrata,** on the street of the same name, is a well-preserved example of Piedmontese Gothic domestic architecture: notice how the fascination with narrow, pointed arches is carried through even to private houses.

Outdoor Activities and Sports

GOLF

Avigliana has a well-laid-out 18-hole golf course, **Le Fronde** (☎ 011/9328053, closed Tues., and Dec.–Feb.), which can be used with a golf-club membership from your hometown.

Sacra di San Michele

★ ⑳   *14 km (8½ mi) west of Avigliana, 43 km (27 mi) west of Turin.*

Unless you plan a 14-km (9-mi) hike from Avigliana, a car is essential for an excursion to the Abbey of St. Michael, perhaps best known as the inspiration for the dramatic setting of Umberto Eco's *The Name of the Rose.* San Michele was built on Monte Pirchiriano in the 11th century to stand out: it is the most prominent location for miles around, hanging over a 3,280-ft bluff. When monks came to enlarge the abbey, they had to build part of the structure on supports more than 90 ft high—an engineering feat that was famous in medieval Europe and is still impressive today. By the 12th century, this important abbey controlled 176 churches in Italy, France, and Spain; one of the abbeys under its influence was Mont-Saint-Michel in France. Because of the abbey's strategic position, it came under numerous attacks over the next five centuries, and it was eventually abandoned in 1622. It was restored in the late 19th and early 20th centuries.

From **Porta dello Zodiaco,** a splendid Romanesque doorway decorated with the signs of the zodiac, you climb 150 steps, past 12th-century sculptures, to reach the church. On the left side of the interior are 16th-century frescoes representing New Testament themes; on the right are stories depicting the founding of the church. Go down to the crypt to see the 9th- to 12th-century chapels. WEB *www.sacradisanmichele.com* 🖃 *5,000 lire/€2.60.* ☉ *Mar. 16–Oct. 15, Tues.–Sat. 9:30–12:30 and 3–6, Sun. 9:30–noon and 2:40–6; Oct. 16–Mar. 15, Tues.–Sat. 9:30–12:30 and 3–5, Sun. 9:30–noon and 2:40–5.*

Saluzzo

㉑   *58 km (36 mi) southwest of Turin.*

Saluzzo is a well-preserved medieval gem. The older and more interesting part of the town hugs a hilltop in the Po Valley and is crowned by a castle. This town of timeworn russet brick was once a flourishing medieval center and was seat of a ducal court during the Renaissance. The narrow, winding streets and frescoed houses, the Gothic cathedral and church of **San Giovanni,** and the 15th-century **Casa Cavassa,** a richly decorated palace that now houses a museum, take you back in time to the age of chivalry.

Knights and damsels of old, heroes and heroines of an allegorical poem written by Marquis Tommaso III of Saluzzo, humanist lord of the castle, parade in full costume in the 15th-century frescoes in the **Sala del Barone** (Baron's Hall) of the **Castello di Manta** (Castle of Manta), 4 km (2½ mi) south of Saluzzo. The castle's exterior is austere, but inside are the frescoes and other decorations. The castle sometimes hosts exhibits, at which time higher admission is charged. ⊠ *Via al Castello 14, Manta,* ☎ *0175/87822.* 🖃 *8,000 lire/€4.15.* ☉ *Mar.–mid-Dec., Tues.–Sun. 10–1 and 2–6.*

Sestriere

㉒   *32 km (20 mi) east of Briançon, 93 km (58 mi) west of Turin.*

In the early 1930s, before skiing became a sport for commoners, the patriarch of the FIAT automobile dynasty had this resort built, with two distinctive tower hotels and ski facilities that have been developed into some of the best in the Alps. The resort lacks the charm of other, older Alpine centers; overdevelopment added some eyesores, and the mountains don't have the striking beauty of those in the Valle d'Aosta.

But skiers have an excellent choice of trails, some of them crossing the border into France.

Lodging

$$$$ 🏨 **Principi di Piemonte.** Large and elegant, this luxurious hotel is on the slopes above the town, near the lifts and the town's golf course. Its secluded location heightens the sense of exclusivity, a quality appreciated by a very stylish clientele. The restaurant and a cozy bar invite après-ski relaxation. ⊠ *Via Sauze, 10058,* ☎ *0122/7941,* 🗚 *0122/755411,* WEB *www.framon-hotels.com. 95 rooms, 5 suites. Restaurant, bar, pool, hot tub, sauna, Turkish baths. AE, MC, V. Closed early Apr.–June and Sept.–Nov..*

$$ 🏨 **Miramonti.** Nearly every room has a terrace at this pleasant, central, modern chalet. The ample, comfortable rooms are done in traditional mountain style, featuring lots of wood paneling and coordinated floral-print fabrics. ⊠ *Via Cesana 3, 10058,* ☎ *0122/755333,* 🗚 *0122/755375. 30 rooms. Restaurant, bar, minibars. AE, DC, MC, V.*

Outdoor Activities and Sports

GOLF

Sestriere's 18-hole **golf course** (☎ 0122/76243) is open from mid-June to mid-September.

SKIING

At 6,670 ft, this resort was built in the late 1920s under the auspices of Turin's Agnelli clan. Although it's near the French border, it is just 93 km (58 mi) west of Turin. The slopes get good snow some years from November through May, others from February through May. For snow conditions, call ☎ 0122/799411. A quaint village with slate-roof houses, **Claviere** (⊠ 17 km [11 mi] west of Sestriere) is one of Italy's oldest ski resorts. Its slopes overlap with those of the French resort of Montgenèvre.

Bardonecchia

㉓ *36 km (22 mi) northwest of Sestriere, 89 km (55 mi) west of Turin.*

This sunny town is one of Italy's oldest winter ski resorts, attracting hardy sports enthusiasts from Turin ever since the 1920s. It is near the entrance to the Fréjus train and automobile tunnels.

Lodging

$$ 🏨 **Asplenia.** Skiers love this small, modern version of a mountain
★   chalet, near the town center and the ski lifts. The ample rooms are comfortably furnished, with a small entryway and a balcony affording beautiful views. ⊠ *Viale della Vittoria 31, 10052,* ☎ *0122/999870,* 🗚 *0122/901968. 17 rooms, 4 suites. Restaurant. No credit cards. Closed May–June and Oct.–Nov.*

$$ 🏨 **Bucaneve.** Just a short walk from the ski lift, this small, family-owned hotel is popular with the ski crowd. A cozy reading room and restaurant add to the allure of these affordable lodgings. ⊠ *Viale della Vecchia 2, 10052,* ☎ *0122/999332,* 🗚 *0122/999980. 17 rooms, 4 suites. Restaurant, bar. AE, MC, V. Closed Oct.–Nov. FAP, MAP.*

$$ 🏨 **Des Geneys-Splendid.** One of the best hotels in the area is in a pine-filled private park near the town center. Its 1930s style is evident in the arched windows on the ground floor, the stucco walls, and the long wrought-iron balconies. The public rooms are spacious and comfortable, and there's a playroom for children. ⊠ *Via Einaudi 21, 10052,* ☎ *0122/99001,* 🗚 *0122/999295. 57 rooms. Restaurant, bar, gym. AE, DC, MC, V. Closed mid-Apr.–mid-June and mid-Sept.–mid-Dec.*

VALLE D'AOSTA, THE MATTERHORN, AND MONT BLANC

The unspoiled beauty of the highest peaks in the Alps competes with the magnificent scenery of Italy's oldest national park in the Valle d'Aosta, a semiautonomous, French-speaking region tucked away at the border with France and Switzerland. Luckily, you don't have to choose—the region is small, so you can fit ski, après-ski, and wild ibex into one memorable trip. The main Aosta Valley, largely on an east–west axis, is hemmed in by high mountains where glaciers have gouged out 14 tributary valleys, six to the north and eight to the south. A car is very helpful here, but take care: distances are relatively short as the crow flies, but steep slopes and winding roads add to your distance and travel time.

En Route   Coming up from Turin, beyond Ivrea, the road takes you through countryside that becomes hillier and hillier, passing through steep ravines guarded by brooding, romantic castles. Pont St. Martin, about 18 km (11 mi) north of Ivrea, is the beginning of French-speaking territory.

Bard

㉔ *65 km (40 mi) north of Turin.*

A few minutes beyond the French-speaking village of Pont St. Martin, you pass through the narrow Gorge de Bard and reach the **Forte di Bard** (closed to the public), a 19th-century reconstruction of a fort that stood for eight centuries, serving the Savoys for six of them. In 1800 Napoléon entered Italy through this valley and used the cover of darkness to get his artillery units past the castle unnoticed. Ten years later he remembered this inconvenience and had the fortress destroyed.

St. Vincent

㉕ *28 km (17 mi) north of Bard, 93 km (58 mi) north of Turin.*

The town of St. Vincent has been a popular spa resort since the late 18th century. Its main game these days is the **Casinò de la Vallée,** one of Europe's largest gambling casinos. Remember to pack your black tie—and plenty of lire.

Dining and Lodging

$$$$ ✕ **Batezar.** This tiny restaurant of only eight tables ranks among the
★   best in all of Italy. The ambience is rustic yet elegant, with arches and beamed ceilings enhanced by local antiques, fine crystal, and silver place settings. The menu, which changes on a weekly basis, is Valdostana and Piemontese, with creative variations. Mushrooms, fish, fresh game, and truffles often play a prominent role. For a starter, try the *pazzarella* (a small pizza with porcini mushrooms, mozzarella, and truffles) or fettuccine with herbs, artichokes, and fillet of rabbit. If you have trouble choosing, put yourself in the chef's hands and order a set menu. Reservations are advised. ⊠ *Via Marconi 1, steps from casino,* ☎ *0166/ 513164. Jacket and tie. AE, DC, MC, V. Closed Wed., 3 wks in June, and Nov. 15–30. No lunch weekdays.*

$$$$ 🏨 **Billia.** A luxury Belle Epoque hotel with faux-Gothic touches, the Billia is in a park in the middle of town and connected directly to the casino by a passageway. Half the rooms are done in modern and half in period decor, replete with all creature comforts. The hotel has extensive facilities, including a conference center and a health club. ⊠ *Viale Piemonte 72, 11027,* ☎ *0166/5231,* 🆑 *0166/523799. 239 rooms, 6 suites. Restaurant, bar, pool, sauna, tennis court, health club, convention center. AE, DC, MC, V.*

$$ **☐ Elena.** The central location is the selling point of this hotel near the casino. The spacious rooms, some with balconies and/or king-size beds, are decorated with color-coordinated fabrics in a comfortable modern style. ⊠ *Via Biavaz 2 (Piazza Zerbion), 11027,* ☎ *0166/512140,* FAX *0166/537459. 48 rooms. Restaurant, bar, air-conditioning, minibars. AE, DC, MC, V.*

Nightlife

A top nighttime entertainment attraction is the **Casinò de la Vallée,** one of only four casinos in Italy, and one of the largest in Europe. You must present identification and be at least 18 years old to enter. (⊠ Via Italo Mus, ☎ 0165/5221; ☉ Sun.–Thurs. 2 PM–2:30 AM, Fri. 2 PM–3 AM, Sat. 2 PM–3:30 AM).

Breuil-Cervinia

㉖ *30 km (18 mi) north of St. Vincent, 116 km (72 mi) north of Turin.*

Breuil-Cervinia is a village at the base of the **Matterhorn** (Monte Cervino in Italian; Mont Cervin in French). Like the village, the famous peak straddles the border between Italy and Switzerland, and all sightseeing and skiing facilities are operated jointly. Splendid views of the peak can be seen from **Plateau Rosa** and the **Cresta del Furggen,** both of which can be reached by cable car from the center of Breuil-Cervinia. While many locals complain that the tourist facilities and the condominiums in the village have changed the face of their beloved Breuil, most would agree that the cable car has given them access to climbing and off-trail skiing in ridges that were once inaccessible.

Dining and Lodging

$$$ ✕☐ **Les Neiges d'Antan.** In a pine wood at Perrères, just outside
★   Cervinia, this small, rustic family-run inn is quiet and cozy, with lots of wood, three big fireplaces, and a nice view of the Matterhorn. The idyllic atmosphere is also preserved by the fact that there are no TVs in the rooms. An excellent restaurant ($$) serves French dishes and local specialties, such as fonduta, *zuppa Valpellinentze* (a peasant soup of bread, cabbage, and Fontina cheese), and an opulent antipasto (local salami, country pâté, and tomino cheese). ⊠ *Località Perrères, 3½ km (2 mi) outside Cervinia, 11021,* ☎ *0166/948775,* FAX *0166/948852. 28 rooms. Restaurant, bar. AE, MC, V. Closed May –June 25 and Sept. 10–early Dec.*

$$–$$$ ✕☐ **Cime Bianche.** This calm, quiet mountain-lodge restaurant is one of the few dining spots in town to offer regional Valdostana cuisine, serving fonduta, polenta, and wild-game dishes in a rustic setting. A range of pasta dishes is also offered. The wood beams and tables are typical of a ski resort, only meals are much less chaotic than your average après-ski affairs. The commanding view covers the Matterhorn and Grandes Murailles. Reservations are strongly recommended. There are also 15 guest rooms, all with private bathrooms, TVs, and balconies. ⊠ *Località La Vieille,44, toward the ski area, near the base lift,* ☎ *0166/949046. MC, V. Closed Mon. and May–June.*

$$$$ ☐ **Hermitage.** A marble relief of St. Theodolus at the entrance re-
★   minds you that this was the site of the saint's hermitage. But asceticism has given way to sybaritic comfort and elegance in what is now one of the most exclusive hotels in this Alpine region. It has the look and atmosphere of a relaxed but posh family chalet, with a fire always glowing in the enormous hearth and a romantic, candlelit dining room. The decor includes rustic antiques, petit-point upholstery, and the Neyroz family's collection of paintings of the Matterhorn. The bright bedrooms have balconies; suites have antique fireplaces

and 18th-century furnishings. Guests pay half price at the Cervinia Golf Club. Or they might choose to get a massage or take advantage of the numerous services offered at the beauty center. ⊠ *Via Piolet, 11021,* ☎ *0166/948998,* FAX *0166/949032,* WEB *www.hotelher-mitage.com. 35 rooms, 5 suites. Restaurant, bar, indoor pool, hair salon, sauna, golf privileges, health club, meeting room. AE, DC, MC, V. Closed May–June and Sept.–Nov.*

$$$–$$$$ 🏨 **Bucaneve.** This small, central hotel, catering to longer stays, is decorated in typical mountain style, with lots of wood paneling throughout, cheery floral upholstery in spacious lounges, and terraces dripping with geraniums. Après-ski, there's a restaurant (half board is required) and a cozy bar with a big fireplace and pianist in the evening. ⊠ *Piazza Jumeaux 10, 11021,* ☎ *0166/949119,* FAX *0166/948308,* WEB *www.hotel-bucaneve.it. 20 rooms, 6 suites. Restaurant, bar, piano bar, hot tub, sauna, gym, solarium. AE, MC, V. Closed May–late June and Sept.–Nov. (depending on weather). MAP.*

$$–$$$$ 🏨 **Chalet Valdotain.** About 2 km (1 mi) outside of town on the road from Châtillon, this Alpine chalet has wooden balconies and snug rooms with terrific views of the Matterhorn. It is known for good food and a friendly atmosphere. ⊠ *Località Lago Bleu 2, 11021,* ☎ *0166/ 949428,* FAX *0166/948874. 35 rooms. Restaurant, bar, pool, sauna, Turkish baths, gym. AE, DC, MC, V. Closed May–mid-June and mid-Sept.–early Dec.*

Outdoor Activities and Sports

CLIMBING

Serious climbers can make the ascent of the **Matterhorn** from Breuil-Cervinia after registering with the local mountaineering officials at the tourist office (⊠ Via Carrel 29, ☎ 0166/949136). This climb is for skilled and experienced climbers only.

SKIING

Because its slopes border the Cervino glacier, this resort at the foot of the Matterhorn offers year-round skiing. Contact the **Breuil-Cervinia tourist office** (☎ 0166/949136) for information.

Castello Fénis

★ ㉗ *11 km (7 mi) west of St. Vincent, 104 km (65 mi) north of Turin.*

The best-preserved fortress in the Valle d'Aosta, the many-turreted Castello Fénis was built in the mid-14th century by Aimone di Chal-lant, a member of a prolific family related to the Savoys. This castle is the sort imagined by schoolchildren, with pointed turrets, portcullises, and spiral staircases. The 15th-century courtyard has a stairway leading to a loggia (open walkway) with wooden balconies. Inside you can see the medieval kitchen, with much of the original cooking equipment, and a collection of weapons in the armory. If you have time to visit only one castle in the Valle d'Aosta, this should be it, even though parts may be closed for restoration. ☎ *0165/764263.* 🎟 *6,000 lire/€3.10.* ☺ *Mar.–June, daily 9–6:30; July–Aug., daily 9–7:30; Sept., daily 9–6:30; Oct.–Feb., Wed.–Mon. 10–5. (Maximum number of 25 people allowed to enter every 1/2 hr.)*

En Route The highway continues climbing through the Valle d'Aosta to the town of Aosta itself. The road at this point is heading almost due west, with rivulets from the wilderness reserve Parco Nazionale del Gran Paradiso streaming down from the left to join the Dora Baltea River, one of the major tributaries of the Po and an increasingly popular spot for rafting. Be careful driving here in late spring, when melting snow can turn some of these streams into torrents.

Aosta

㉘ *12 km (7 mi) west of Castello Fénis, 113 km (70 mi) north of Turin.*

Aosta stands at the junction of two important trade routes from France to Italy—the valleys of the Rhône and the Isère. Its significance as a trading post was recognized by the Romans, who built a garrison here in the 1st century BC. The present-day layout of streets in this small city, tucked away in the Alps more than 644 km (400 mi) from Rome, is the clearest example of Roman street planning in Italy. Well-preserved Roman walls form a perfect rectangle around the center of Aosta, and the regular pattern of streets reflects its role as a military stronghold. St. Anselm, born in Aosta, later became archbishop of Canterbury in England. At the eastern entrance to town, in the Piazza Arco d'Augusto and commanding a fine view over Aosta and the mountains, is the **Arco di Augusto** (Arch of Augustus), built in 25 BC to mark Rome's victory over the Celtic Salassi tribe. The sloping roof, quite clearly, is not original—an early effort at preservation of the site, it was added in 1716 in an attempt to keep rain from seeping between the stones.

The **Collegiata di Sant'Orso** (Collegiate Church of St. Orso) is the sort of church that has layers of history in its architecture. Originally there was a 6th-century chapel on this site, founded by the Archdeacon Orso, a local saint. Most of this structure was destroyed or hidden when an 11th-century church was erected over it. This church, in turn, was encrusted with Gothic, and later Baroque, features, resulting in a jigsaw puzzle of styles, but, surprisingly, not a chaotic jumble. The 11th-century features are almost untouched in the crypt, and if you go up the stairs on the left from the main church you can see the 11th-century frescoes (ask the sacristan for entrance). These restored frescoes depict the life of Christ and the Apostles: although only the tops are visible, you can see the expressions on the faces of the disciples. Take the outside doorway to the right of the main entrance to see the church's crowning glory, its 12th-century **cloister.** Next to the church, it's enclosed by some 40 stone columns with masterfully carved capitals depicting scenes from the Old and New Testaments and the life of St. Orso. The turrets and spires of Aosta peek out above. ⊠ *Via Sant'Orso,* ☎ *0165/40614.* ⊙ *Apr.–Sept., daily 9–5; Oct.–Mar., daily 10–5.*

The huge **Roman Porta Pretoria,** regally guarding over the city, is a remarkable relic from the Roman era. The area between the inner and outer gates was used as a small parade ground for the changing of the guard. ⊠ *West end of Via Sant'Anselmo.*

The 72-ft-high ruin of the facade of the **Teatro Romano** (Roman Theater) guards the ruins of the 1st-century BC amphitheater, which once held 20,000 spectators. Only a bit of the outside wall and seven of the amphitheater's original 60 arches remain, and these are built into the facade of the adjacent convent of the sisters of San Giuseppe. The convent usually allows visitors in to see these arches (ask at the entrance). ⊠ *Via Anfiteatro 4.*

Aosta's **Duomo** dates from the 10th century, but all that remains from that period are the campaniles. The decoration inside is primarily Gothic, but the main attraction of the cathedral predates that era by 1,000 years: a carved ivory diptych showing the Roman Emperor Honorius and dating from AD 406 is among the many ornate objects housed in the treasury. ⊠ *Via Monsignor de Sales,* ☎ *0165/40251.* ⊙ *Treasury Apr.–Sept., Tues.–Sun. 9–11:30 and 3–5:30; Oct.–Mar., Sun. 3–5:30.*

Dining and Lodging

$$–$$$ ✕ **Taverna Nando.** A wine cellar with wooden floors and vaulted ceilings, this family-run tavern is in the center of Aosta, and it has a terrace for outdoor dining. Try regional specialties such as fonduta, carbonada, and *cervo* (venison) with mushrooms. Reservations are recommended. ⊠ *Via de Tillier 41,* ☎ *0165/44455. AE, DC, MC, V. Closed Mon. and June 20–July 10.*

$$–$$$ ✕ **Vecchio Ristoro.** The chef-proprietor of this central converted mill furnished with antiques and a large ceramic stove takes pride in creative versions of regional favorites. Among them may be *petto di faraona in crosta* (breast of guinea hen in a crisp potato crust) and *pizzoccheri* (buckwheat pasta), a specialty of his native Lombardy. ⊠ *Via Tourneuve 4,* ☎ *0165/33238. AE, DC, MC, V. Closed Sun., June, and 1 wk in Nov. No lunch Mon.*

$$ ✕ **La Brasserie du Commerce.** Small, lively, and informal, this place is in the heart of Aosta, near central Piazza E. Chanoux. On a sunny summer day try to get a table on the terrace. Typical valley dishes, such as fonduta, are on the menu, together with a wide range of vegetable dishes and salads. ⊠ *Via de Tillier 10,* ☎ *0165/35613. Reservations not accepted. AE, DC, MC, V. Closed Sun.*

$–$$ ✕ **Piemonte.** A small restaurant in the center of town, the Piemonte
★ has a welcoming atmosphere and rustic decor. Hearty dishes might include *crespelle alla valdostana* (crepes with cheese and ham) and *camoscio* (chamois) with polenta. ⊠ *Via Porta Pretoria 13,* ☎ *0165/ 40111. MC, V. Closed Sun. and Feb.*

$$$–$$$$ ▦ **Holiday Inn Aosta.** This modern, comfortable, highly regarded hotel has the advantages of a central location and rooms with the chain's predictable amenities. There's local color, however, in the attractive Provençal fabrics and the views of the mountains. There are rooms equipped for people with disabilities. ⊠ *Corso Battaglione Aosta 30, 11100,* ☎ *0165/236356,* FAX *0165/236837. 45 rooms, 5 suites. Restaurant, bar, business services. AE, DC, MC, V.*

$$ ▦ **Casa Ospitaliera del Gran San Bernardo.** Run by a monks from the Order of St. Bernard, this charming pension outside Aosta is a good base for cross-country skiing or hiking; perhaps you'll head out to see the order's Saint Bernards. The bargain price includes a full meal plan. ⊠ *Via Flassin 1, Saint-Oyen (Aosta), 11010,* ☎ *0165/78247. 30 rooms. No credit cards. Closed May. FAP.*

$$ ▦ **Milleluci.** A small, cozy, family-run hotel, Milleluci is set in its own
★ garden on a hillside overlooking Aosta, next to Castello Jocteau and with good views of the city and mountains. A huge brick hearth and rustic wooden beams highlight the lounge. Ask for a room in the new wing (opened in 1998); all have their own balconies or terraces. Bedrooms are bright, with prints *de Provence* and attractive wood fittings. The hotel provides breakfast only. There are rooms equipped for people with disabilities and lots of amenities, including a pool and sauna. ⊠ *Località Roppoz 15, 11100,* ☎ *0165/235278,* FAX *0165/235284,* WEB *www.hotelmilleluci.com. 31 rooms, 2 suites. Bar, pool, sauna, tennis court, solarium. AE, MC, V.*

Nightlife and the Arts

Each summer, a series of **concerts** is held in different venues around the city. Organ recitals in July and August attract performers of world renown. Call the tourist board (⊠ Piazza E. Chanoux 8, ☎ 0165/ 236627) for information.

Outdoor Activities and Sports

HORSEBACK RIDING

The area around Aosta is a center for horseback riding. **Centro Turismo Equestre Val di Rhemes** (☎ 0165/907667), 20 km (12½ mi) outside of

Aosta, offers three-hour and all-day guided horseback outings in the Parco Nazionale del Gran Paradiso. If you're too tired to continue your travels after a horseback outing, the center also rents apartments on a daily and weekly basis.

RAFTING

Although world-class rafting competitions have been held on the Dora Baltea, guides can lead you on trips suitable for neophytes. **Rafting Aventure Vallé d'Aosta** (✉ Frazione Vegne, Villeneuve, ☎ 0165/95082), about 10 km (6¼ mi) outside of Aosta, conducts tours June–August.

Shopping

Aosta and the surrounding countryside are famous for wood carvings and wrought iron. There is a permanent **crafts exhibition** in the arcades of Piazza E. Chanoux, in the heart of Aosta; it's a good place to pick up a bargain. Each year, on the last two days of January, all of Aosta turns out for the **Sant'Orso Fair,** where all sorts of crafts are on sale, including handmade lace from nearby Cogne, carved wood and stonework, and brightly colored woolens.

Courmayeur/Monte Bianco

★ ㉙ *35 km (21 mi) northwest of Aosta, 150 km (93 mi) northwest of Turin.*

The main attraction of Courmayeur is a knock-'em-dead view of Europe's tallest peak, Monte Bianco, or Mont Blanc. Jet-set celebrities flock here, following a tradition that dates from the late 17th century, when Courmayeur's natural springs first began to draw visitors. The spectacle of the Alps gradually surpassed the springs as the biggest draw (the Alpine letters of the English poet Shelley were almost advertisements for the region), but the biggest change in the history of Courmayeur came in 1965, when the Mont Blanc tunnel opened. The tunnel was closed after a devastating fire in 1999, and its reopening has been delayed several times. At press time, it was scheduled to reopen at the end of 2001. Contact the Courmayeur tourist board (✉ Piazzale Monte Bianco 13, ☎ 0165/842060) for updates. (For alternate driving routes, *see* Car Travel *in* Piedmont/Valle d'Aosta A to Z, *below*).

Luckily, planners have managed to keep some restrictions on wholesale development within the town, and its angled rooftops and immaculate cobblestone streets maintain a cozy (if prepackaged) feeling. There is no train directly into Courmayeur, so if you don't have a car, you'll have to bus it from nearby Pré-Saint-Didier, accessible by train from Aosta.

At La Palud you can catch the cable car up to the top of **Monte Bianco.** In the summertime, if you get the inclination, once up top you can switch cable cars and descend into Chamonix, in France. In winter, you can ski parts of the route off-piste. The Funivie La Palud whisks you up first to the Pavillon du Mont Fréty—a starting point for many beautiful hikes—and then to the Rifugio di Torino, before arriving at to the viewing platform at **Punta (Pointe) Helbronner** (more than 11,000 ft), which is also the border post with France. Mont Blanc's attraction is not so much its shape (much less distinctive than that of the Matterhorn) as its expanse and the vistas from the top. The next stage—only in the summer months—on the **Télépherique de L'Aiguille du Midi,** as you pass into French territory, is particularly impressive: you dangle over a huge glacial snowfield (more than 2,000 ft below) and make your way slowly to the viewing station above Chamonix. It is one of the most dramatic rides in Europe. From this point you're looking down into France, and if you change cable cars at the Aigu-

ille du Midi station you can make your way down to Chamonix itself. The return trip covers the same route. Schedules are unpredictable, changing depending on weather conditions and demand;
you can get information by sending an e-mail to cable car operators
or calling the Courmayeur tourist office (☎ 0165/842060). ⊠ *Funivie La Palud,* ☎ *0165/89925 Italian side (La Palud); 00/33450536210
French side (Aiguille du Midi),* WEB *www.montebianco.com.* 🖼 *19,000
lire/€9.80 round-trip to Pavillon du Mont Fréty, 47,000 lire/€24.25
round-trip to Helbronner, 90,000 lire/€46.50 round-trip to Aiguille
du Midi, 140,000 lire/€72.30 round-trip to Chamonix.* ☉ *Call for
hrs, which vary throughout year. Closed mid-Oct.–mid-Dec., depending on demand.*

Dining and Lodging

$$$$ ✕ **Maison de Filippo.** Here you'll find country-style home cooking in
a picturesque mountain house furnished with antiques. Reserve in advance, for it's one of the most popular restaurants in the Valle d'Aosta.
There is a set menu only, featuring a daily selection of specialties including a wide choice of antipasti and pasta dishes, such as agnolotti
in various sauces and spaghetti *affumicata* (with salami and bacon).
⊠ *Entreves,* ☎ *0165/869797. Reservations essential. MC, V. Closed
Tues., mid-May–mid-June, and Oct.–mid-Nov.*

$$$ ✕ **Cadran Solaire.** This warm and inviting restaurant is in the town
★ center, in what was the oldest tavern in Courmayeur. It's been reno-
vated by the Garin family, owners of the Maison de Filippo, in such a
way as to highlight the 17th-century stone vault, the old wooden floor,
and the huge fireplace. The menu offers seasonal specialties and in-
novative interpretations of regional dishes, such as gnocchi *gratinati*
(with ricotta) and *filetto di trota alle nocciole* (fillet of trout with
hazelnuts). The stylish bar-lounge is also a relaxing place for a before-
dinner drink. ⊠ *Via Roma 122,* ☎ *0165/844609. Reservations essential.
AE, MC, V. Closed Tues., May, and Oct.*

$ ✕ **Snack Bar du Tunnel.** This cozy restaurant near the center of town
★ had to convert one room into two neck-ducking minifloors in order
to accommodate more of the hungry throngs who show up each night
begging for tables. Those in the know come from miles around for the
pizza, which is among the best in northern Italy. Valdostana special-
ties, such as carbonada with polenta, are also served. ⊠ *Via Circon-
vallazione 80,* ☎ *0165/841705. Reservations essential. AE, DC, MC,
V. Closed Wed.; June 10–July 15; Nov.*

$$$$ ✕🏠 **Royal.** A grand Courmayeur landmark in the town center, the Royal
rises high above the modest surrounding townscape. Decorated with
terraces, flowers, and wood paneling, it is the most elegant, upscale
spot in town, with modern rooms and an evening piano bar. The hotel
caters to longer stays with half- or full-board service. The main restau-
rant, Grill Royal e Golf, is a sight in itself, locally renowned for its culi-
nary creations like frogs' legs in a basil fish broth. Reservations (and
jacket and tie) are required at the Grill, which is open for dinner only
and is closed Monday. ⊠ *Via Roma 87, 11013,* ☎ *0165/831611,* FAX
0165/842093, WEB *www.hotelroyalgolf.com. 70 rooms, 16 suites. 2
restaurants, bar, piano bar, minibars, pool, sauna, health club. AE, DC,
MC, V. Closed wk after Easter–mid-June and mid-Sept.–Nov. FAP, MAP.*

$$$–$$$$ 🏠 **Palace Bron.** Set in a lovely stand of pines above the town, this posh,
★ comfortable hotel is an ideal spot to relax. Guest rooms are bright and
pretty, furnished with antiques and local designs. The sitting room has
picture windows with magnificent views of Mont Blanc, and for chilly
nights the high-quality restaurant offers a cozy fireplace. In winter, there's
a free shuttle between the hotel, the town center, and ski lifts. ⊠ *Via
Plan Gorret 41, 11013,* ☎ *0165/846742,* FAX *0165/844015. 27 rooms.*

Restaurant, bar, piano bar, minibars, meeting room. AE, DC, MC, V. Closed May–June and Oct.–Nov.

$$$–$$$$ ⌂ **Pavillon.** This is an elegant modern version of rustic chalet architecture, complete with warm golden-toned wood paneling, stylish furnishings, a clubby bar, and some stunning contemporary stained glass in the public areas and in the well-equipped health center. ⌂ *Strada Regionale 62, 11013,* ☎ *0165/846120,* ℻ *0165/846122. 40 rooms, 10 suites. Restaurant, bar, indoor pool, hot tub, massage, sauna, steam room, health club, solarium, meeting room. AE, DC, MC, V. Closed end Apr.–June 15, Oct.–Nov. FAP.*

$$$ ⌂ **Auberge de la Maison.** All the rooms at this hotel, built in 1996, have views of Monte Bianco. A massage here can be the perfect ending to a day of hiking or skiing. ⌂ *Via Passerin d'Entreves, 11013,* ☎ *0165/869811,* ℻ *0165/869759. 30 rooms, 3 suites. Hot tub, massage, sauna, gym. AC, DC, MC, V. Closed May.*

$$ ⌂ **Croux.** This bright, comfortable hotel, completely renovated in the autumn of 1999, is near the town center on the road leading to Mont Blanc. Friendly management makes it feel like a more intimate place than you'd expect for its size. Half the rooms have balconies, the other half great views of Mont Blanc. ⌂ *Via Circonvallazione 94, 11013,* ☎ *0165/846735,* ℻ *0165/845180,* 🌐 *www.hotelcroux.it. 33 rooms. Bar, breakfast room. AE, DC, MC, V. Closed Apr.–June 20 and Sept. 15–Dec. 15.*

Outdoor Activities and Sports

SKIING

The famous Courmayeur, for the well-heeled, is well equipped and easy to reach, just outside the Italian end of the Mont Blanc tunnel (which was closed at press time but due to open by late 2001). With only 24 trails, Courmayeur pales in comparison to its French neighbor, Chamonix, in both number and quality of trails. Nevertheless, especially with good natural snow cover, trails and Alpine vistas are spectacular. A huge gondola leads from the center of Courmayeur to Plan Checrouit, where gondolas and lifts lead to the actual ski slopes. The skiing around Mont Blanc is particularly good, and the off-piste options are among the best in Europe. The off-piste routes from Cresta d'Arp (the local peak) to Dolonne, and from the La Palud area into France, should be done with a guide.

SPORTS CENTER

The **Courmayer Sports Center** has something for everyone. There are courts for squash, tennis, basketball, and volleyball, as well as a rock-climbing wall, a skating rink, a five-a-side soccer field, and an indoor golf course. ⌂ *Località Plan de Lizzes,* ☎ *0165/844096.* ☼ *Daily 10 AM–11 PM.*

Cogne and the Parco Nazionale del Gran Paradiso

➌⓪ *52 km (32 mi) southeast of Courmayeur, 134 km (83 mi) northwest of Turin.*

Cogne is the gateway to the Parco Nazionale del Gran Paradiso. This huge park, once the domain of King Vittorio Emanuele II (1820–78) and bequeathed to the nation after World War I, is one of Europe's most rugged and unspoiled wilderness areas, with wildlife and many plant species protected by law. Try to visit in May, when spring flowers are in bloom and most of the meadows are clear of snow. This is one of the few places in Europe where you can see the ibex (a mountain goat with horns up to 3 ft long) or the chamois (a small antelope).

Outdoor Activities and Sports

HIKING

There's wonderful hiking to be done here, both on daylong excursions and longer journeys with overnight stops in the park's mountain refuges. The Cogne tourist office (⊠ Piazza E. Chanoux 36, ☎ 0165/ 74040) has a wealth of information and trail maps to help.

FORTIFIED CITIES OF THE PO PLAIN

Southeast of Turin, in the hilly wooded area around Asti known as the Monferrato and farther south in a similar area around Alba known as the Langhe, the rolling landscape is a patchwork of vineyards and dark woods dotted with hill towns and castles. This is wine country, producing some of Italy's most famous reds and sparkling whites. And hidden away in the woods are the secret places where hunters and their dogs unearth the precious, aromatic truffles worth their weight in gold at Alba's truffle fair. To the north of these hills, across the Po, are the cities of the plain. Beyond them lies Lago Maggiore, and eastward, across the Ticino River, is Milan.

Asti

③ *60 km (37 mi) southeast of Turin.*

Asti is best known outside of Italy for its wines—excellent reds as well as the famous sparkling white Spumante—but its strategic position on trade routes between Turin, Milan, and Genoa has given it a broad economic base. In the 12th century, Asti began to develop as a republic, at a time when other Italian cities were also flexing their economic and military muscles. It flourished in the following century, when the inhabitants began erecting lofty towers for its defense, giving rise to the medieval nickname "city of 100 towers." In the center of Asti, some of these remain, among them the 13th-century **Torre Cometini** and the well-preserved **Torre Troyana,** a tall, slender tower attached to the **Palazzo Troya.**

Corso Vittorio Alfieri is Asti's main thoroughfare, running west–east across the city. This road, known in medieval times as Contrada Maestra, was built by the Romans. The 18th-century church of **Santa Caterina** (⊠ west end of Corso Vittorio Alfieri) has incorporated one of Asti's medieval towers, the **Torre Romana** (itself built on an ancient Roman base), as its bell tower.

The **Duomo** is an object lesson in the evolution of the Gothic architectural style. Built in the early 14th century, the cathedral is decorated so as to emphasize geometry and verticality: pointed arches and narrow vaults are counterbalanced by the earlier, Romanesque attention to balance and symmetry. The porch, on the south side of the cathedral facing the square, was built in 1470 and represents Gothic at its most florid and excessive. ⊠ *Piazza Catedrale.* ☉ *Daily 8–noon and 3:30–7.*

The Gothic church of **San Secondo** (⊠ south of Corso Vittorio Alfieri) is dedicated to Asti's patron saint, reputedly decapitated on the spot where the church now stands. Secondo is also the patron of the city's favorite folklore and sporting event, the annual **Palio,** the colorful medieval-style horse race (similar to Siena's), held each year on the third Sunday of September in the vast Campo del Palio to the south of the church.

OFF THE
BEATEN PATH

ALBA – Thirty kilometers (18 miles) southwest of Asti, this small town has a compact core studded with medieval towers and Gothic buildings, and a gracious old-world atmosphere. In addition to being a wine center of the region, Alba is known as the "City of the White Truffle" for the dirty little tubers that command a higher price per ounce than diamonds. For picking out your truffle and having a few wisps shaved on top of your course, you shell out an extra $16—which is well worth it. Visit in October for the Fiera del Tartufo (National Truffle Fair), Cento Torri Joust (a medieval jousting festival), and the Palio degli Asini (donkey races), held the first Sunday of the month.

If Alba catches your fancy, you might want to spend the night in the reasonably priced Belle Epoque–style bed-and-breakfast **Reinè** (⊠ Località Altavilla 9, ☎ FAX 0173/4401122), on a hill overlooking the historic center in the midst of Dolcetto and Nebbiolo grape vines. There are five rooms and two apartments.

BAROLO – Some of Italy's finest wines are made within a radius of about 16 km (10 mi) of Alba. The zone is dotted with castles, and every town has a shop where you can sample the local vino. The **Castello di Barolo** houses a wineshop and a museum of wine making. ☉ Fri.–Wed. 10–12:30 and 3–6:30. Closed Jan. and part of Feb.

Dining and Lodging

$$$$ ✕ **Gener Neuv.** The family-run Gener Neuv is one of Italy's top restau-
★ rants. It offers a sumptuous menu of regional specialties served in a warm atmosphere of rustic elegance, highlighted by excellent service, fine linen, silver, and crystal. The setting in a park on the bank of the Tanaro River is splendid, although it brought severe flood damage in 1994; the restaurant had to be rebuilt. Your choices may include ag-nolotti *ai tre stufati* (with a filling of ground rabbit, veal, and pork), and you can finish with *composta di prugne e uva* (prune and grape compote). The prix-fixe menu is good value but does not include beverages. ⊠ Lungo Tanaro 4, ☎ 0141/557270, FAX 0141/436723. AE, DC, MC, V. Closed Sun.–Mon. in Jan.–July, Mon. in Sept.–Dec., and Aug. No dinner Sun.

$$ ✕ **L'Angolo del Beato.** Regional specialties like bagna cauda and tagli-olini *al ragu di anatra* (with a duck sauce) are the main attraction here. This central Asti restaurant, housed in a building that dates back to the 12th century, also has a good wine list. ⊠ Via Guttuari 12, ☎ 0141/531668. AE, DC, MC, V. Closed Sun., last wk of Dec., first wk of Jan., and 3 wks in Aug.

$$–$$$ 🏨 **Reale.** This centrally located hotel, which opened its doors in 1793, has spacious and comfortable rooms. Despite its long heritage, it offers modern conveniences like satellite TV. The neighboring restaurant, also called Reale but under different ownership, has classic Piedmontese dishes like agnolotti. ⊠ Piazza Alfieri 6, 14100, ☎ 0141/530240, FAX 0141/3435, WEB www.hotel-reale.com. 27 rooms. AE, DC, MC, V.

$$ 🏨 **Rainero.** An older hotel in the town center, near the station, Rainero has been under the same family management for three generations. It's fitted with cheerful modern furnishings but has no restaurant. Ask for one of the "green rooms," done in a green and white theme. ⊠ Via Cavour 85, 14100, ☎ 0141/353866, FAX 0141/594985, WEB www.hotel-rainero.com. 55 rooms. DC, MC, V. Closed Jan. 1–15.

Nightlife and the Arts

September is a month of fairs and celebrations in this famous wine city, and the **Asti Competition** in the middle of the month brings musicians who perform in churches and concert halls. For 10 days in September, Asti is host to the **Douja d'Or National Wine Festival**—an opportunity to see Asti and celebrate the product that made it famous.

Shopping

The **Enoteca** on Piazza Alfieri, a square adjacent to Campo del Palio, is a wine center and shop, open Monday–Saturday 9–4:30, where you can try a range of Asti vintages, buy a bottle, and even have a light snack. Be aware, though, that prices for Spumante in Asti are not necessarily lower than those elsewhere.

The **McArthur Glen designer outlet** (✉ Serravalle, 30 km [19 mi] south of Alessandria, ☎ 0143/609000, WEB www.mcarthurglen.com) is a bit of a detour from Asti but may be worth it for fans of designer labels. Discounts are on the order of 50% at more than 60 shops, including Armani, Burberry, Ralph Lauren, Versace, Levi's, and Marina Yachting. Directions can be found on the Web site.

En Route From Alba, double back to Asti to pick up the A21 autostrada. The road east from Asti to Alessandria is straight, skirting the southern edge of the Po plain, but for the first half of the drive you see to the south green hillsides covered with vineyards. If you find yourself driving along this road during a thunderstorm (quite common on late-summer afternoons), don't be surprised by the sound of explosions. Wine growers will often let off cannons loaded with blanks to persuade heavy clouds to rain rather than build up and develop destructive hailstones.

Casale Monferrato

㉜ *42 km (26 mi) northeast of Asti, 75 km (46½ mi) southwest of Milan.*

Casale Monferrato, strategically situated on the southern bank of the Po, was held by the Gonzagas, rulers of Mantua, before falling into the hands of the Savoys. The 16th-century **Torre Civica,** marking the heart of Casale Monferrato in Piazza Mazzini, commands extensive views up and down the Po. It's open the second Saturday and Sunday of every month for free guided visits. In the second half of March, the **Festa di San Giuseppe** brings artisans, musicians, and vendors of traditional sweets to the central Piazza del Castello.

Casale's most enlightening sight is the **Museo Israelitico** (Jewish Museum) in the women's section of its synagogue. Inside is a collection of documents and sacred art of a community that was vital to the prosperity of this mercantile city. The synagogue dates from the late 16th century, and neighboring buildings on the same street formed the Jewish ghetto of that period. ✉ *Vicolo Olper 44, south of Torre Civica,* ☎ *0142/71807.* ☉ *Mar.–Dec., Sun. 10–noon and 3:30–5:30; at other times by appointment. Closed Sat.*

Vercelli

㉝ *23 km (14 mi) north of Casale Monferrato, 80 km (50 mi) northeast of Turin.*

Vercelli is the rice capital of Italy and of Europe. Northern Italy's mainstay, risotto, owes its existence to the crop that was introduced to this fertile area in the late Middle Ages. **Piazza Cavour** is the heart of the medieval city and former market square. It was to this small square that merchants across northern Italy came in the 15th century to buy bags of rice, then a novelty grain from the East. Rising above the low rooftops around the piazza is the **Torre dell'Angelo** (Tower of the Angel), whose forbidding military appearance reflects its origins as a watchtower.

The **Duomo,** a mainly late-16th-century construction on the site of what was a 5th-century church, contains tombs of several Savoy rulers in an octagonal chapel along the south (right) wall. The cathedral's **Biblioteca** (chapter library; for entrance, see cathedral office) contains the *Gospel of St. Eusebius,* a 4th-century manuscript, and the *Codex Vercellensis,* an 11th-century collection of Anglo-Saxon poetry. ✉ *Piazza*

Sant'Eusebio, ☎ 0161/255205. ⊙ *Daily 8–12:30 and 3–6:30, except during mass on Sun.*

The **Basilica di Sant'Andrea,** a Cistercian abbey church built in the early 13th century with funds from another Abbey of St. Andrew (in England), witnessed the growing influence of northern Europe on Italy. Sant'Andrea is one of Italy's earliest examples of Gothic architecture, which spread from the north but ran out of steam before getting much beyond the Po plain. The church interior is a soaring flight of Gothic imagination, with slender columns rising up to the ribbed vaults of the high ceiling. The gardens on the north side of the basilica hold the remains of the abbey itself and some of its secondary buildings. It is only here that the Gothic style is interrupted. The buildings surround a cloister in which you can see pointed Gothic arches resting on severe and more solid 12th-century Romanesque bases. ⊠ *Piazza G. Bicheri,* ☎ *0161/255513.* ⊙ *Daily 8–noon and 3–6:30.*

The **Città Vecchia** is a collection of narrow streets and alleys that includes the Basilica di Sant'Andrea. Many of the houses are five centuries old, and you can see partly hidden gardens and courtyards beyond the wrought-iron gates.

OFF THE
BEATEN PATH

BORSA MERCI – On Tuesday and Friday mornings you can take an unusual guided tour of the commodities market (⊠ Via Zumaglini 4, ☎ 0161/5981), where rice has been traded for centuries. Vercelli's is the largest rice market in Europe. Contact the Vercelli tourist office (⊠ Viale Garibaldi 90, 13100, ☎ 0161/58002) for more information.

Novara

❸ *23 km (14 mi) northeast of Vercelli, 95 km (59 mi) northeast of Turin.*

Novara is the easternmost city in Piedmont, only about 10 km (6 mi) west of the Ticino River, which forms the border with Lombardy. Milan is only 32 km (20 mi) beyond the border, and over the centuries the opposing attractions of this neighboring giant and of the regional capital, Turin, have given Novara a bit of an identity crisis. In the Middle Ages, Novara's pivotal position made it a battlefield. A major engagement took place as recently as 1849, when the Austrian forces from the east defeated the Piedmontese armies.

Much of the present city dates from the late 19th and early 20th centuries, although there are interesting buildings from earlier periods scattered about. Novara's most famous landmark is the tall, slender cupola of **San Gaudenzio.** The church itself, built between 1577 and 1690, is wholly Baroque in design, with twisted columns and sumptuous statues. The main attraction, though, is its **cupola,** built from 1840 to 1888 and soaring to a height of just under 400 ft. This spire is visible everywhere in the city and in the surrounding countryside and has become as much a symbol of Novara as the Mole Antonelliana is of Turin— not a complete coincidence, since Antonelli designed this cupola and spire as well. ☎ *0321/629894.* ⊙ *Daily 8–noon and 3–7.*

The **Duomo** is medieval in its origins but reconstructed in neoclassical style. The **Battistero** (Baptistery), just outside the entrance to the cathedral, shows its august age much more clearly. This rotunda-shape building dates from the 5th century, although it was substantially enlarged in the 10th and 11th centuries. Recent restoration work has uncovered pre-Romanesque frescoes more than 1,000 years old on the interior walls. Their flat, two-dimensional style reflects the influence of Byzantine icons, and their vivid colors make the apocalyptic scenes depicted all the more frightening. Also neighboring the cathedral is the **Broletto**, a cluster of well-preserved late-medieval buildings. ✉ *Piazza Martiri della Libertà,* ☎ *0321/35634.* ⊙ *Daily 8–noon.*

Lodging

$$$ 🏨 **Italia.** This modern hotel in the center of the city offers comfortable rooms and efficient service. The facilities cater mainly to businesspeople and include a restaurant, one of Novara's best. Some rooms have good views of the town. ✉ *Via Solaroli 8, 28100,* ☎ *0321/ 399316,* 🖷 *0321/399310. 59 rooms, 4 suites. Restaurant, bar, minibars, meeting rooms. AE, DC, MC, V.*

PIEDMONT/VALLE D'AOSTA A TO Z

To research prices, get advice from other travelers, and book travel arrangements, visit www.fodors.com.

AIRPORTS

The region's only international airport, Aeroporto Torino Caselle, is 18 km (11 mi) north of Turin. It's notoriously foggy in winter, and many flights are diverted to Genoa, on the coast, with bus connections provided to Turin. From Aeroporto Caselle, local buses to Turin arrive at the bus station on Corso Inghilterra in the city center.

➤ AIRPORT INFORMATION: **Aeroporto Torino Caselle** (☎ 011/5676361).

BUS TRAVEL

Turin's main bus station is on the corner of Corso Inghilterra and Corso Vittorio Emanuele. The Turin-based SADEM line services the autostrada network to Milan and other destinations in Italy. Turin-based SAPAV services the same area—both specialize in bus transportation in Piedmont and the Valle d'Aosta. SAVDA specializes in mountain service, providing frequent links between Aosta, Turin, and Courmayeur as well as Milan. SITA buses, part of the nationwide system, also connect Turin with the rest of Italy. There is also a major bus station at Aosta, across the street from the train station. General bus information is available for 1,524-lire/€0.80 per minute (plus tax) at the number below.

➤ BUS INFORMATION: **SADEM** (✉ Via della Repubblica 14, 10095 Grugliasco, Turin, ☎ 011/3000611). **SAPAV** (✉ Corso Torino 396, 10064 Pinerolo, Turin, ☎ 0121/322032). **SAVDA** (✉ Strada Ponte Suaz 6, 11100 Aosta, ☎ 0165/361244).

CAR RENTAL

➤ LOCAL AGENCIES: **Avis** (✉ Porto Nuova, Turin, ☎ 011/6699800; ✉ Corso Turati 37, Turin, ☎ 011/500852; ✉ Aeroporto Torino Caselle, Turin, ☎ 011/4701528). **Hertz** (✉ Via Magellano 12, Turin, ☎ 011/ 502080; ✉ Aeroporto Torino Caselle, Turin, ☎ 011/5678166; ✉ Via Ascoli 39, Turin, ☎ 011/4378175).

CAR TRAVEL

Italy's autostrada network links the region with the rest of Italy and neighboring France. Aosta, Turin, and Alessandria all have autostrada connections, with the A4 heading east to Milan and the A6 heading south to the Ligurian coast and Genoa. Turin is the hub of all the transportation systems in Piedmont, with autostrada connections to the north, south, and east. If you drive in from France or Switzerland, you pass through either the Mont Blanc or Grand St. Bernard tunnel: these are two of the most dramatic entrances to Italy in terms of scenery.

For travel between the French and Italian borders, only a few passes are usable year-round in Piedmont/Valle d'Aosta: the Colle del Gran

San Bernardo/Col du Grand St. Bernard (Martigny to Aosta on Swiss Highway E27 to Italian Highway S27, with 6-km [4-mi] tunnel) and the Traforo del Fréjus, which follows the Italian S335 west through a 13-km (8-mi) tunnel. The 12-km (7-mi) Mont Blanc tunnel from Chamonix to Courmayeur has been closed due to a fire in March 1999 but as of press time was scheduled to reopen at the end of 2001. There are plenty of other passes, but they are not reliable from at least November through April.

EMERGENCY SERVICES

If you have a breakdown on the road, you can walk to one of the roadside stations marked SOS and push the button. You'll be connected to the Automobile Club of Italy (ACI), which will come and assist you, for free if you have a membership card for the automobile club in your home country. (Otherwise, you must pay a fee.) ACI can also be reached at the phone numbers below.
➤ CONTACTS: **ACI** (☎ 116 or 803000).

ROAD CONDITIONS

Well-paved secondary roads (*superstrade*) run through the region, following the course of mountain valleys in many places. Sudden winter storms can close off some of the mountain stretches; contact local tourist offices for up-to-date road information before you set out. Bear in mind that this is very rough country, so no matter what time of year and what route you choose, you are always advised to check with the tourist office or, in a pinch, with the police, to make sure roads are passable and safe.

EMBASSIES AND CONSULATES

➤ UNITED KINGDOM: **U.K. Consulate** (✉ Via Saluzzo 60, Turin, ☎ 011/6509202), open Monday and Thursday 9–noon.

EMERGENCIES

Pharmacies throughout the region take turns staying open late and on Sunday. Dial 192 for the latest information (in Italian) on which are open. The Farmacia Boniscontro in Turin takes a lunch break between 12:30 and 3 but is open all night.
➤ CONTACTS: **Emergencies** (☎ 113). **Police** (☎ 112). **Farmacia Boniscontro** (✉ Corso Vittorio Emanuele II, 66, Turin, ☎ 011/538271).

MAIL AND SHIPPING

➤ POST OFFICES: **Turin** (✉ Via Alfieri 10, ☎ 011/5060040).

OVERNIGHT SERVICES

➤ MAJOR SERVICES: **DHL** (✉ Via Bertolla all'Abbadia Stura, 176, Turin, ☎ 800/345345).

PASSPORTS AND VISAS

You should have your passport with you when day-tripping into France, even though it's unlikely you'll be asked to show it.

TOURS

Turin's group and personally guided tours are organized by the city's tourist office. Here you can also get information about the Touristibus, a two-hour guided bus trip that leaves from Piazza Castello, at the corner of Via Po, every day but Tuesday at 2:30. Touristibus goes through the historic center of Turin, including Via Roma and Porta Nuova, and then out to view such locations as the Palazzina di Caccia in Stupinigi and the Parco Valentino.

PRIVATE GUIDES

Alpine guides are not only recommended, they're essential if you're planning to traverse some of the dramatic ranges outside St. Vincent, Courmayeur, or Breuil-Cervinia. Before embarking on an excursion (however short) into the mountains in these areas, contact the representative of the CAI (Club Alpinisti Italiani) for information about hikes and the risks. Guides from the Alpine Guides Association will accompany you on treks and also lead skiing, canyoning, and ice climbing excursions.

➤ CONTACTS: **Alpine Guides Association** (⊠ Piazza Abbe Henri 2, Courmayeur, ☎ 0165/842064). **CAI** (⊠ Piazza E. Chanoux 8, Aosta, ☎ 0165/40194).

TRAIN TRAVEL

Turin is on the main Paris–Rome TGV express line and is also connected with Milan, only 90 minutes away on the fast train. The fastest (Eurostar) trains cover the 667-km (400-mi) trip to Rome in about six hours, but most take about nine.

Services to the larger cities east of Turin are part of the extensive and reliable train network serving the Lombard Plain. West of the region's capital, however, the train services soon peter out in the steep mountain valleys. Continuing connections by bus serve these valleys, and information about train-bus mountain services can be obtained from train stations and tourist information offices, of contact FS, the Italian national train service.

➤ TRAIN INFORMATION: **FS** (☎ 848/888088, WEB www.trenitalia.com).

VISITOR INFORMATION

➤ TOURIST INFORMATION: **Alba** (⊠ Piazza Medford 3, 12051, ☎ 0173/35833). **Aosta** (⊠ Piazza E. Chanoux 8, 11100, ☎ 0165/236627). **Asti** (⊠ Piazza Alfieri 29, 14100, ☎ 0141/530357). **Bardonecchia** (⊠ Viale Vittoria 44, 10052, ☎ 0122/99032). **Breuil-Cervinia** (⊠ Via Carrel 29, 11021, ☎ 0166/949136). **Cogne** (⊠ Piazza E. Chanoux 36, 11012, ☎ 0165/74040). **Courmayeur** (⊠ Piazzale Monte Bianco 13, 11013, ☎ 0165/842060). **Novara** (⊠ Baluardo Quintino Sella 40, 28100, ☎ 0321/394059). **Saluzzo** (⊠ Via Griselda 6, 12037, ☎ 0175/240352). **Turin** (⊠ Piazza Castello 161, 10122, ☎ 011/535181; ⊠ Stazione Porta Nuova, 10121, ☎ 011/531327). **Vercelli** (⊠ Viale Garibaldi 90, 13100, ☎ 0161/58002).

6 ITALIAN RIVIERA

GENOA, CINQUE TERRE,
PORTOFINO, SAN REMO

It was the Italians who perfected *il dolce far niente*—the sweet art of idleness—and all signs show they did it in Liguria. Flanking Genoa, an art-filled city of long-decaying splendor, the twin Rivieras bask in the sun, dotted with seaside summer resorts and quaint pastel villages. Rapallo, Portovenere, and the Cinque Terre glisten like pearls on a string, but Portofino still wins the beauty contest, as it has since the days of Bogie and Bacall.

Updated by
Robin S.
Goldstein

IKE THE FAMILY JEWELS THAT BEDECK its habitual visitors, the Italian Riviera is glamorous, but in the old-fashioned way. The resort towns and pastel coastal villages that stake intermittent claims on the rocky shores of the Ligurian Sea are the long-lost cousins of newer and more overbuilt seaside paradises. Here the grandest palazzi share space with frescoed, angular, late-19th-century apartment buildings, and high-rise glitz seems as foreign as the Maine lobster that some of the region's tiniest restaurants incongruously fly in for dinner. The rustic and elegant, the provincial and chic, the cosmopolitan and the small-town are blended together here in a sun-drenched pastiche that makes up this, the "other" Riviera.

The serpentine arc of Liguria's coastline, sweeping serenely from Ventimiglia to La Spezia, is the defining mark of the region's identity. Although the province technically extends inland to the tops of the Ligurian Alps, Liguria is Italy's seaside region, and its greatest charms are those of the sea (the "Mare Ligure," never the "Mediterraneo"). For centuries, the region has inspired poets and artists. This is where a captivated Shelley praised the "soft blue Spezian bay" and the daredevil Lord Byron swam from Portovenere to Lerici. Today, travelers escaping the conceits of civilization still head to the Italian Riviera for a cure. Mellowed by the balmy breezes blowing off the sea, they bask in the sun and explore the tiny coastal towns whose greatest treasures—peace, quiet, and dramatic natural beauty—remain for the most part undiscovered.

Liguria's narrow strip of mountain-protected coastline varies considerably between the two Rivieras. The western Riviera di Ponente (Riviera of the Setting Sun), which reaches from the French border to Genoa, has protected bays and wide sandy beaches and is generally more developed and commercialized than its counterpart to the east, the Riviera di Levante (Riviera of the Rising Sun). Beginning at the French border, the Ponente is home to the fanciful seaside resorts of Bordighera and San Remo, similar to their glittery French cousins to the west in their unabashed dedication to the pursuit of pleasure. Much of the eastward sweep of the Ponente coastline has been developed for the packs of sun worshipers who descend upon it in the summer. The minuscule bays and inlets spanning the Levante coastline from Genoa to Portovenere become steeper, sculpted by nature into rocky cliffs.

If this coast is a necklace hung with jewels, the most dazzling pendant is the Portofino promontory. This must be the most photographed village in the world, and one look is enough to tell you why. Smooth-faced, brightly painted houses frame the port in a burst of color that becomes sheer enchantment at sunset, when the houses are reflected in the dancing waters of the harbor. And the people you encounter are attractions in themselves—it was, after all, Bogart and Bacall and Taylor and Burton who put the place on the map.

Farther east is a second peninsula; here the road weaves inland, leaving you to hike or take a train or boat to explore the Cinque Terre, a collective community of five fishing villages perched on bluffs above the sea. Here are some of Liguria's least-crowded beaches, its sweetest white wine, its most picturesque village squares, and certainly its best views. From the hiking trails that link the Cinque Terre, the tiny villages seem like colorful blooms of flowers clinging to hulking black cliffs that plunge into the sea. Though this is still the Italian Riviera at its unbuttoned best, Vernazza's growing trinket-shop trade and Monterosso's ever-booked hotels are signs that even Cinque Terre has been "discovered" in recent years—especially by Americans.

Set in the heart of the region is Genoa, Italy's largest commercial port, where magnificent Renaissance palaces wearing the dusty patina of time attest to the wealth of the city's seafaring past, intermixed with layers of loud urbanity. Every schoolchild knows Genoa as the birthplace of Christopher Columbus, and many would become wide-eyed upon learning it's also the home of Europe's largest aquarium. Despite the curiously seamy city's considerable charm, most visitors to Liguria are more interested in the less historic waters found up or down the coast—not surprising, given the relaxed, easy lifestyle found along their shores.

Pleasures and Pastimes

Boating

With so much coastline—350 km (217 mi)—and so many pretty little harbors, it's no wonder that the Riviera attracts pleasure craft of all shapes and sizes, from rowboats to mega-yachts. San Remo, Rapallo, Santa Margherita Ligure, Chiavari, Finale Ligure, and Sestri Levante have large, well-equipped marinas, and nearly every town has a harbor and at least one marine shop. Kayaking is also popular along Ligurian shores on calmer days. Every October, Genoa hosts a mammoth international boat show.

Dining

Liguria's cooking might surprise you. It employs all sorts of seafood—especially anchovies, sea bass, squid, and octopus—but it makes even wider use of vegetables and the aromatic herbs that grow wild on the hillsides, together with liberal amounts of olive oil and garlic. Basil-and garlic-rich pesto is Liguria's classic pasta sauce. You will also find *pansoti* (round pockets of pasta filled with a cheese mixture) and *trofie* (doughy, short pasta twists sometimes made with chestnut flour) with *salsa di noci,* an intense sauce of garlic, walnuts, and cream that, as with pesto, is ideally pounded with a mortar and pestle. Spaghetti *allo scoglio* is mixed with a tomato-based seafood sauce containing an assortment of local *frutti di mare.* Seafood is the best bet for second courses—the classic preparation is a whole grilled or baked whitefish (*branzino,* sea bass, and *orata,* dorado, are good choices) with olives, potatoes, Ligurian spices, and a drizzle of olive oil. A popular meat is *cima alla Genovese,* breast of veal stuffed with a mixture of eggs and vegetables and rolled, served as a cold cut. You should also try the succulent *agnello* (lamb), *coniglio* (rabbit), and fresh wild mushrooms foraged from the hills.

When not snacking on pizza sold by the slice or by weight, the Genovese and other Ligurians eat *torta pasqualina* (vegetable pie) or *focaccia,* the salty and oily pizzalike bread with various toppings. Focaccia *alla Genovese* is usually served plain, and focaccia *di Recco,* or focaccia *al formaggio,* is topped with melted cheese. Local vineyards produce mostly light and refreshing whites such as Pigato, Vermentino, and Cinque Terre. Rossese di Dolceacqua, from near the French border, is the best red wine the region has to offer, but for a more robust accompaniment to meats, opt for the fuller-bodied reds of the neighboring Piedmont region. *Vini frizzanti* (sparkling wines), both red and white, are ubiquitous in the region, though their quality varies. Sweets are less rich than those in other parts of Italy; *panna cotta* (creamy egg custard, often flavored with caramel, served cold), *semifreddo* (a soft ice cream), and sorbet are favorites for dessert, and *canestralli* (light almond cookies with powdered sugar) and various *frittelle* (crispy fried sweet dough cookies) are perfect with a *caffè* (espresso). For general information and price categories, *see* Dining *in* Smart Travel Tips.

Hiking and Walking

Liguria's hilly terrain makes walking strenuous but rewarding, with stunning views of the sea and castles and little villages dotting the coast. Portofino invites walking, whether you opt for the popular and relatively easy walk from Portofino to the Abbazia di San Fruttuoso or the more challenging hike from Ruta to the top of Monte Portofino. One of the best treks is between the Cinque Terre fishing towns, all the while thumbing your nose at the tourists on the sightseeing boats. Everywhere in Liguria roads, mule paths, or footpaths lead into the hills, where you can discover the region at its unspoiled best.

Lodging

Most good hotels in Genoa are set in pretty modern buildings, not the grand old restored villas you might hope for. When choosing a hotel in Genoa, you should know that in its center it is one of Italy's noisiest cities; make sure your windows are double-glazed (*doppi vetri*). Lodging in Genoa and Liguria, as in much of the north, is somewhat expensive, especially in summer. If visiting in the fall, winter, or spring, be sure to ask for a *sconto bassa stagione* (low-season discount rate). The best bargains and the warmest welcomes, however, can be found in the less-visited inland areas; there aren't a great number of hotels in this part of Liguria, but many of them are family-run and special because of it. Reserve ahead year-round for Genoa, and during peak Easter and summer seasons for resorts. Beware also of unexpected conferences and conventions for which lodging fills up far in advance. Note that many hotels and resorts in the area close for a number of weeks each year, usually late fall and early winter, and some in summer; it's best to call ahead. For general information and price categories, *see* Lodging *in* Smart Travel Tips.

Exploring the Italian Riviera

Liguria's cities, towns, and resorts are nestled into the elongated coastal strip and connected by a highway stretching 260 km (161 mi) from La Spezia and Sarzana to Ventimiglia on the French border. At the center, Genoa separates the eastern (Levante) from the western (Ponente) Riviera, forming two distinct geographic areas to explore (three, including Genoa itself). The hilly and mountainous hinterland, very different in scenery and character from the Riviera, can easily be explored from towns along the coast. From the sea, a series of narrow valleys extend inland, giving access to the sparsely settled interior.

Getting around the Riviera is an expedient affair, though the pace here is leisurely. Public transportation in the region is excellent: trains connect all sights along the coast and buses snake inland. It takes two hours for a fast train to cover the entire coast (though local trains make innumerable stops and take upward of five hours). With the freedom of a car, you could drive from one end of the Riviera to the other on the autostrada in less than three hours. The A10 and A12 on either side of Genoa, engineering wonders with literally hundreds of long tunnels and towering viaducts, skirt the coast, avoiding local traffic on the beautiful Via Aurelia, which was laid out by the ancient Romans. The Via Aurelia, now known as national highway S1, connects practically all the towns along the coast.

Numbers in the text correspond to numbers in the margin and on the Italian Riviera and Genoa maps.

Great Itineraries

If urban artistic and historic treasures are your passion but you also want some seaside relief, stay in Genoa and make it your base for exploring the rest of the region on day trips. For a more relaxed approach, sea views, and recreation, settle into a resort and take a day trip into Genoa. Be forewarned: driving in Genoa is harrowing and should be avoided whenever possible—if you want to see the city on a day trip, go by train; if you're staying in the city, park in a garage or by valet and traverse the city by foot and taxi throughout your stay.

IF YOU HAVE 3 DAYS

Tour time is limited, and you should rent a car and concentrate on select towns. On your first day begin on the eastern Riviera di Levante. Stop at the delightful fishing villages of Vernazza in the **Cinque Terre** ④ and **Camogli** ⑩, detouring for a look at romantic **Portofino** ⑨. For a more cosmopolitan resort atmosphere, opt instead for **Rapallo** ⑦ or 🏨 **Santa Margherita Ligure** ⑧, with a short jaunt from Santa Margherita to Portofino. On the second day see 🏨 **Genoa** ⑪–㉜, exploring the historic center and old harbor. The western Riviera should be the focus of the third day; head for glitzy **San Remo** ㊸ or the more sedate **Bordighera** ㊹, but allow about a half day along the way to visit the medieval centers of **Albenga** ㊴ and **Cervo** ㊵. Naturally, you can follow this itinerary in the opposite direction if you enter in the region from the west.

IF YOU HAVE 5 DAYS

In five days you can go from one end of the Riviera to the other, or start in Genoa and head east or west from there. If you make Genoa your base you can alternate excursions along the coast and into the interior with city sightseeing. On your first day explore 🏨 **Genoa** ⑪– ㉜. If the day is a clear one, take the **Zecca-Righi funicular** ⑭ to the top for an aerial view of the city. On the second day head west, making a detour to Spotorno, and proceed to Noli, one of the best-preserved medieval towns on the entire Riviera. Then see the medieval delights of Cervo before going on to sophisticated 🏨 **San Remo** ㊸ and palm-studded 🏨 **Bordighera** ㊹ for the night. Bask in the sun on the third day or venture inland to the well-preserved medieval villages of Dolcedo and Valloria instead. On the fourth and fifth days explore the eastern Riviera, starting with stately **Nervi** ㉝, near Genoa. Among the many allurements on the Portofino promontory, explore the fishing village of **Camogli** ⑩ and chichi **Portofino** ⑨; don't miss the hamlets of San Rocco, San Niccolò, and Punta Chiappa, accessible on foot from Camogli. You can overnight in a stylish resort such as 🏨 **Santa Margherita Ligure** ⑧ or 🏨 **Rapallo** ⑦. On the fifth day, an excursion by train or boat to the five rock-perched coastal villages of the 🏨 **Cinque Terre** ④ is highly recommended, with Vernazza the first priority.

IF YOU HAVE 7 DAYS

If you begin your visit of the region in 🏨 **Genoa** ⑪–㉜, spend two days there. You will have time for an excursion to **Nervi** ㉝. On the third day head west from Genoa, either working your way gradually to Ventimiglia or going directly to Ventimiglia and then heading back to Genoa. See the extraordinary cactus collection in the **Giardino Botanici Hanbury** ㊻ near **Ventimiglia** ㊾; then turn inland to medieval Dolceacqua, only 10 km (6 mi) away. Stop for tea in genteel 🏨 **Bordighera** ㊹ before continuing on to the much busier and more commercial resort of 🏨 **San Remo** ㊸; San Remo or Bordighera is a good choice for an overnight stay. On the fourth day, discover Noli and Spotorno (bus transport to Noli is via Spotorno). With the exception of **Albisola Marina** ㉟ and **Pegli** ㉞, you can skip the industrialized coast between **Savona** ㊱ and Genoa.

On the fifth day, see the offhand charm of **Camogli** ⑩. Take the turnoff for **Rapallo** ⑦ and **Santa Margherita Ligure** ⑧ and, if the traffic isn't heavy, head for 🏨 **Portofino** ⑨. At the height of the season an excursion boat to Portofino from Camogli, Santa Margherita Ligure, or Rapallo may

Italian Riviera

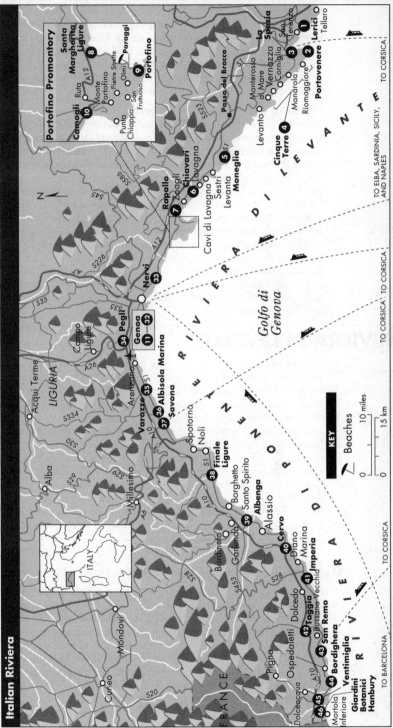

Portofino Promontory

- 8 Santa Margherita Ligure
- 9 Portofino
- 10 Camogli

Santa Margherita Ligure
Ruta
Monte Portofino
Pietre Strette
San Olmi **Paraggi**
Fruttuoso
Portofino
Punta Chiappa
A12

Portofino Promontory

LIGURIA

Acqui Terme

Campo Ligure

Alba

Millesimo

Mondovì

Cuneo

Pigna

Dolceacqua

Ospedaletti

Mortola Inferiore

FRANCE

RIVIERA DI PONENTE

Rapallo
7 Zoagli
6 Lavagna
Chiavari

Cavi di Lavagna

Sestri
Levante
Moneglia
5 Cinque Terre

Nervi 33

Genoa
34 Pegli
11 32

Arenzano
35 Varazze
36 Albisola Marina
Savona
37

Spotorno
Noli

Finale Ligure 38

Borghetto
Santo Spirito
Albenga
39 Cervo
Alassio

40 Diano Marina
Imperia
41

Taggia
42 San Remo
43 Bordighera
Ventimiglia
44 Giardini Botanici Hanbury
45 46

Bardineto
Garlenda

Dolcedo
Bussana Vecchia

La Spezia
1 Lerici
3 2 Portovenere
San Terenzo
Tellaro

Monterosso al Mare
Vernazza
Corniglia
Manarola
Riomaggiore
4 Cinque Terre

Passo del Bracco

Levanto

RIVIERA DI LEVANTE

Golfo di Genova

ITALY

KEY

Beaches

0 — 10 miles
0 — 15 km

N

TO ELBA, SARDINIA, SICILY, AND NAPLES

TO CORSICA

TO CORSICA: TO CORSICA

TO CORSICA

TO BARCELONA

avoid the traffic jams on the narrow access road and parking problems once you arrive. On the fifth or sixth night, stay in the ⛰ **Cinque Terre** ④ and experience its magical nocturnal calm. Hike the paths in Cinque Terre on your sixth or seventh day; then head east to **La Spezia** ③ and look for signs to **Portovenere** ②. Doubling back to La Spezia, take the coast road to charming **Lerici** ①. The La Spezia turnoff on the A12 and S1 highways is only about 15 km (9 mi) from the Tuscany border.

When to Tour the Italian Riviera

Perhaps more than anywhere else in Italy, season is crucial on the Italian Riviera. Though shops, cafés, clubs, and restaurants stay open late in resorts during high season (at Easter and in the summer), during the rest of the year they close early, if they're open at all. Liguria is one of the most seasonal places in the world, and everything from the yacht-dotted playground of Portofino to the rows of seaside restaurants and bars that line the Riviera's quieter shores shuts down from October to February (with the occasional exception of the week around Christmas), leaving little more than starkly barren coasts, boarded-up cafés, and crashing waves. April, May, and September are the best times to visit, with flowers in bloom, pleasant weather, and moderate levels of activity. October and November often bring torrential rains, floods, and landslides to the region, making such excursions as the Cinque Terre walk temporarily impossible. Avoid driving through Ventimiglia on Friday, the busy market day.

RIVIERA DI LEVANTE

Of the two Ligurian Rivieras, the Riviera di Levante, east of Genoa, is overall the wilder and more rugged, yet here you will also find towns like Portofino and Rapallo, world famous for their classic, elegant style. Around every turn of this area's twisting roads, the hills plummet sharply to the sea, forming deep, hidden bays and inlets. Beaches on this coast are rocky, backed by spectacular sheer cliffs. The Portofino promontory has one sandy beach, on the east side, at Paraggi. From Chiavari to Cavi di Lavagna, the coast becomes a bit gentler, with a few sandy areas. Sailing conditions along the rugged coast from Sestri Levante down to Portovenere are good. Waterskiing, tennis, and golf are also popular. You may want to choose a base and take short day trips or explore the area by boat from the larger towns. You can anchor your boat in the relatively calm waters of small *ciazze* (coves) found all along the coast.

Lerici

① *11 km (7 mi) east of La Spezia, 65 km (40 mi) west of Lucca.*

Lerici, near Liguria's border with Tuscany, is set on a magnificent coastline of gray cliffs and pine forests. The town once belonged to Tuscan Pisa, and the 13th-century Pisan **Castello Doria** standing above the splendid bay has attracted lovers of nature for centuries. Shelley was one of Lerici's best-known visitors and spent some of the happiest months of his life in the lovely white village of **San Terenzo**, 2 km (1 mi) away. The **Villa Magni,** where he lived, has a museum devoted to him. After Shelley drowned at sea here in 1822, the bay was renamed Golfo dei Poeti, in his and Byron's honor.

Dining and Lodging

$$$–$$$$ ✕⛰ **Miranda.** Perched amid the clustered old houses in the seaside hamlet of Tellaro, 4 km (2½ mi) southeast of Lerici, this small family-run inn has become a pricey gourmets' destination because of chef Angelo Cabani's imaginative way with Ligurian cooking. His unusual seafood menu changes daily but might include *insalata di gamberoni e aragosta*

con finocchio (shrimp and lobster salad with fennel) and risotto *mantecato con asparagi e gamberi* (with butter, asparagus, and shrimp). Reservations are a must. If you stay in one of the seven comfortable rooms with bath, you can take half board for 200,000 lire/€103 per person. ⊠ *Via Fiascherino 92, Tellaro,* ☎ *0187/964012. 5 rooms, 2 suites. Restaurant, bar. Reservations essential. AE, DC, MC, V. Restaurant closed Mon. Hotel and restaurant closed Jan. 12–Feb. 18. MAP.*

$$$ 🏨 **Florida.** This seafront, family-run establishment is not the most beautiful from the outside, but it has bright rooms with all the extras you would expect in a higher category, including soundproofing and a balcony with a sea view. For an even better view, loll in one of the deck chairs on the roof terrace. The Florida overlooks a small beach area and is close to tennis courts and a golf course; a solarium is also on the premises. ⊠ *Lungomare Biaggini 35, 19032,* ☎ *0187/967332,* FAX *0187/967344,* WEB *www.hotelflorida.it. 37 rooms. Breakfast room, bar, minibars, beach. AE, DC, MC, V. Closed Jan. 6–mid-Mar.*

Portovenere

★ ❷   *12 km (7 mi) south of La Spezia, 114 km (70 mi) southeast of Genoa.*

Portovenere's small, colorful houses, some dating from the 12th century, were once all connected to the 12th- to 16th-century citadel, so that in times of attack the villagers could reach the safety of the battlements. The town commands a strategic position at the end of a peninsula that extends southeast from the Cinque Terre and forms the western border of the Gulf of La Spezia. Lord Byron (1788–1824) is said to have written *Childe Harold's Pilgrimage* here. Near the entrance to the huge, strange **Grotto Arpaia,** at the base of the sea-swept cliff, is a plaque recounting the poet's strength and courage as he swam across the gulf to the village of San Terenzo, near Lerici, to visit his friend Shelley (1792–1822); the feat is commemorated as well by the name of the stretch of water, "Golfo dei Poeti," or Poets' Gulf. On a formidable solid mass of rock above the Grotto Arpaia is **San Pietro,** a 13th-century Gothic church built on the site of an ancient pagan shrine. With its black-and-white-stripe exterior, it is a landmark recognizable from far out at sea. ☉ *Daily 7–6.*

Dining and Lodging

$$$ ✕ **Da Iseo.** Try to get one of the tables outside at this waterfront restaurant with bistro accents and paintings of Portovenere. Seafood is the only choice, but it's fresh and plentiful. Pasta courses are inventive; try spaghetti *alla Giuseppe* (with shellfish and fresh tomato) or *alla Iseo* (with a seafood curry sauce). ⊠ *Waterfront,* ☎ *0187/790610. AE, DC, MC, V. Closed Wed. and Jan. 2–Feb. 15.*

$ ✕ **Antica Osteria del Carrugio.** Near the castle built to defend the coast from Pisan incursions is this 100-year-old tavern with maritime decor. The menu features seafood, which varies from day to day. Specialties include *mescina* (soup of beans, chickpeas, and wheat) and *polpo in insalata* (octopus salad). ⊠ *Via Cappellini 66,* ☎ *0187/790617. Reservations not accepted. No credit cards. Closed Thurs. and Nov.–Dec.*

$$$–$$$$ 🏨 **Royal Sporting.** Appearances are deceptive at this modern hotel on
★   the beach about a 10-minute walk from the village. From the outside, the stone construction seems austere and unwelcoming, but the courtyards and interior—with fresh flowers, potted plants, and cool, airy rooms—are colorful and vibrant. The sports facilities are among the best in the area. ⊠ *Via dell'Olivo 345, 19025,* ☎ *0187/790326,* FAX *0187/777707,* WEB *www.royalsporting.com. 60 rooms. Restaurant, bar, minibars, saltwater pool, tennis court, beach. AE, DC, MC, V. Closed Jan. 21–Feb. 19, Mar. 1–16, and Oct. 29–Dec. 28.*

La Spezia

❸ *103 km (64 mi) southeast of Genoa.*

La Spezia is a large, industrialized naval port on routes to the Cinque Terre and to Portovenere. It lacks the quiet charm of the smaller towns. However, its decaying palm-lined Morin promenade, fertile citrus parks, and lively, balcony-lined streets make parts of La Spezia surprisingly beautiful. The remains of the massive 13th-century **Castel San Giorgio** (⊠ Via XX Settembre) are noteworthy.

Outdoor Activities and Sports

WATERSKIING

La Spezia Motorboat Club (⊠ Via della Marina 224, ☎ 0187/50401) will get you up and skiing.

Cinque Terre

★ **❹** *Monterosso al Mare 93 km (58 mi) southeast of Genoa, Riomaggiore 14 km (9 mi) west of La Spezia.*

The aura of isolation that has surrounded five coastal villages known as the Cinque Terre, together with their dramatic coastal scenery, has made them one of the eastern Riviera's most stunning attractions. However, that aura has been rapidly disappearing (especially in summer) as the Cinque Terre have turned into a common, if not requisite, stop on Italy's tourist trail, in spite of their relative inaccessibility. Clinging haphazardly to steep cliffs, these five enchanting villages are linked by ocean-side footpaths, by train, and by narrow, unpaved, and rather tortuous roads, a fairly recent development. The local train on the Genoa–La Spezia line stops at each town between Levanto and Riomaggiore. The easiest to reach by car is Riomaggiore, easternmost of the villages and closest to La Spezia and the A12 autostrada.

All five of the tiny Cinque Terre enclaves are linked by well-established and -groomed hiking footpaths—for much of their history, these were the only way to get from town to town on land. Although today the train and, to a certain extent, the road have replaced the footpaths, they still provide breathtaking ocean views as well as access to the rugged, secluded beaches and grottoes that will never have a train station. The most famous and easiest of the Cinque Terre trails is the **Via dell'Amore** (Lover's Lane), which links Riomaggiore with Manarola (2 km [1 mi], 30 minutes) by a flat path cut into the cliff side. The same trail continues to Corniglia (3 km [2 mi], 1 hour), then becomes more difficult between Corniglia and Vernazza (3 km [2 mi], 1½ hours) and even more difficult from Vernazza to Monterosso (2 km [1 mi], 1½ hours). Still, because of the relative elevations, walking east to west is easier than walking west to east. Additionally, trails lead from Monterosso up the mountainside and back down to Vernazza, and into the mountains from Corniglia, Manarola, and Riomaggiore, with historic churches and great views along the way. Trail maps are available at the Monterosso tourist office. Be sure to wear sturdy shoes (hiking boots are best) and a hat, and bring a water bottle, as there is little shade. But also check weather reports before hiking; especially in fall and winter, frequent thunderstorms flying in off the coast can send townspeople running for cover and make the shelterless trails slippery and dangerous. Also be aware that, depending on the year, rainfall in October and November can cause landslides and close the hiking paths for periods of the fall and winter.

Try to see the Cinque Terre in early fall or spring, when the weather is good but the waves of tourists aren't so great and the towns can be seen in a somewhat more natural state. Consult the excellent Web site www.cinqueterre.it for a schedule of events and updated information.

Riomaggiore

116 km (72 mi) east of Genoa.

In Riomaggiore, where you'll find the same sorts of flowery little squares that bedeck the town's four siblings, interspersed with modern stucco houses and a sense that the population is less isolated here. This may be because Riomaggiore is comparatively convenient to La Spezia; get here by car, following signs from La Spezia's port.

Manarola

1½ km (1 mi) west of Riomaggiore.

In photogenic Manarola, multicolor houses spill down a dark hillside to town squares that hang over the port like balconies overlooking the tiny turquoise harbor. This is the center of Cinque Terre wine making, and you can taste the fruits of local labor in a number of *cantine*, as well as the **Cooperativa Agricoltura di Riomaggiore, Manarola, Corniglia, Vernazza e Monterosso** (☎ 0187/920435), just outside town.

Corniglia

3 km (2 mi) west of Manarola.

Tiny, isolated Corniglia is unquestionably the most difficult of the Cinque Terre to visit: it has no port and no (usable) access road for automobiles, so you will have to arrive by local train or on foot, along the difficult trail from Vernazza or the easy one from Manarola. The town is strung back from a hilltop overlooking the sea to the mountainside behind it; within it you'll find pretty pastel squares and the 14th-century **San Pietro church.** The rose window of marble imported from Carrara is particularly impressive considering the work it must have taken merely to get it to Corniglia.

$ ✕🏠 **Cecio.** On the winding road between Corniglia and Vernazza, this little, family-run restaurant rents spotless, if small, rooms upstairs, many of which have spectacular views of Corniglia clinging to the cliffs above the bay. That same memorable vista can be taken in while dining on local seafood dishes alfresco at the good and inexpensive restaurant downstairs. ⊠ *200 yards along the road to Vernazza, 19010 Corniglia,* ☎ *0187/812043,* 🖷 *1087/812138. 12 rooms. Restaurant. MC, V. Closed Nov.–Feb.*

Vernazza

3 km (2 mi) west of Corniglia.

Lovely Vernazza has the largest and best-equipped port of the Cinque Terre towns. Its pink, slate-roofed houses and picturesque squares contrast with the remains of a medieval fort and castle. The castle's tower was struck by lightning in 1896; it's been rebuilt and today offers some of the best views in Cinque Terre. Summertime in Vernazza brings smart-set Italians to the town's cafés and restaurants. Stay in town and delve right in, escape on one of the many footpaths leading up through the hillsides' terraced vineyards, or head to one of the other towns on a relaxing boat ride from the port.

DINING

$$$ ✕ **Gambero Rosso.** On Vernazza's main square, looking out at the church, this fine trattoria serves such delectable dishes as shrimp salad, vegetable torte, and squid-ink risotto. The creamy pesto, served atop spaghetti, is some of the best in the area. For dessert don't miss the Cinque Terre's own *schiacchetrà*, a dessert wine served with semisweet *biscotti* (hard cookies). Don't drink it out of the glass—dip the biscotti

in the wine instead. ⊠ *Piazza Marconi 7,* ☎ *0187/812265. AE, DC, MC, V. Closed Mon. in Oct.–Mar., and 1st 3 wks in Nov.*

Monterosso al Mare
3½ km (2 mi) west of Vernazza, 12 km (7 mi) east of Levanto.

Monterosso is the largest, most developed, and least pretty of the five fishing towns, with the Cinque Terre's biggest beach, its only sizable hotels, and most of its restaurants. The narrow alleys and colorful houses of the historic center are clustered on a hilltop above the port and its seaside promenade. Stone stairways link the two areas of town, affording lovely views of the mountains that tumble down onto a wide, sandy beach below, which is mobbed in summer. In Monterosso's historic center, the 12th-century **church** (⊠ Piazza Garibaldi) is striped black and white in the Ligurian Gothic fashion. On Thursday morning the town comes alive with its weekly **market,** where you can pick up local anchovies and lemons, among other delicacies. The **Pro Loco** tourist office (⊠ Via Fegina 38, below train station, ☎ 0187/817506) can help with trail maps and boat schedules.

DINING AND LODGING

$$$ ✕ **Il Gigante.** A good introduction to Ligurian seafood is the *zuppa di pesce* served at this traditional trattoria. This soup is usually offered as a first course but is filling enough to be an entrée. Daily specials might include risotto *ai frutti di mare* and spaghetti with an octopus sauce. Reservations are essential on weekends and in the summer. ⊠ *Monterosso al Mare,* ☎ *0187/817401. AE, DC, MC, V. Closed Mon.*

$$$ ✕ **Il Pirata.** Bright and rustic, this trattoria near the port should be the
★ first stop for lunchtime visitors, especially those who make it in time to grab a seat at the long tables on the front porch outside. Specialties are those of the region, with a few surprising gourmet touches, like the French wines lining the shelves and Maine lobster. Reservations are essential on weekends and in the summer. ⊠ *Via Molinelli 6/8,* ☎ *0187/817536. MC, V. Closed Wed. and mid-Jan.–mid.-Feb.*

$$$$ ▦ **Porto Roca.** In a panoramic position above the sea, Porta Roca is set slightly apart, blessedly removed from the crowds. It has the look of a well-kept villa; its interiors have authentic antique pieces and there are ample terraces (excellent for breakfast with a view). Many rooms are bright and airy, with sea breezes, but avoid the cheaper back rooms, which are dark, dank, and offer no view. Porto Roca is on a network of not-too-demanding hill walks and has a faithful American clientele. ⊠ *Via Corone 1, 19016,* ☎ *0187/817502,* ℻ *0187/817692,* ⅏ *www.portoroca.it. 43 rooms. Restaurant, bar. AE, MC, V. Closed Nov. 4–Mar. 18.*

En Route   From the Cinque Terre, small highways connect back out through the edge of La Spezia to state highway S1, which heads inland to the spectacular Passo del Bracco and then turns back out to toward the sea at Sestri Levante. After Sestri, S1 (which also becomes Via Aurelia) hugs the coast, affording dazzling seaside scenery all the way to Genoa, the Riviera Ponente, and the French border.

Moneglia

❺ *12 km (7 mi) southeast of Sestri Levante, 58 km (36 mi) northwest of La Spezia.*

The town of Moneglia, sheltered by the wooded hills of a nature preserve, faces a little bay guarded by ruined castles. An out-of-the-way alternative to fussier resorts, it's a quiet base for walks and excursions by boat, car, or train to Portofino and the Cinque Terre towns. A classical guitar festival is held here in September.

Lodging

$$ ⊞ **Villa Edera.** Ingeniously merging an older building on a verdant hill-side with a smart contemporary stone-and-glass wing, this hotel is owned by a family that gives guests personal and caring attention. Terraces, a garden, luminous bedrooms, and lounges with stylish wicker arm-chairs are among the comforts. Mamma Ida's cooking is special, too. ⊠ *Via Venino 12, 16030,* ☎ *0185/49291,* FAX *0185/49470,* WEB *www.villaedera.com. 27 rooms. Restaurant, parking (fee). AE, D, MC, V. Closed Nov. 6–Mar. 17.*

Chiavari

❻ *22 km (13 mi) east of Portofino, 38 km (23 mi) southeast of Genoa.*

Chiavari is a fishing town, rather than village, and it has considerable character, with narrow, twisting streets and a good harbor. Chiavari's citizens were intrepid explorers, and many emigrated to South America in the 19th century. The town boomed, thanks to the wealth of the returning voyagers, but Chiavari still retains many medieval traces in its buildings.

In the town center, the **Museo Archeologico** (Archaeological Museum) displays objects from an 8th-century BC necropolis, or ancient cemetery, excavated nearby. ⊠ *Palazzo Costaguta, Via Costaguta 4, Piazza Matteotti,* ☎ *0185/320829.* 🎟 *Free.* ☉ *Tues.–Thurs. 9–1, Fri.–Sun. 2–7. Closed 1st and 3rd Sun. of month.*

Outdoor Activities and Sports

HORSEBACK RIDING

Riding is a rewarding way to explore the wooded hills framing Chiavari. **Rivarola Carasco** (⊠ Via Veneto 212, ☎ 0185/382204) provides mounts.

Shopping

The traditional, light—they weigh only 3 pounds—*campanine* chairs made of olive wood or walnut are still produced by a few Chiavari craftsmen. Macramé lace can also be found here.

Rapallo

❼ *12 km (7 mi) east of Camogli, 28 km (17 mi) east of Genoa.*

Rapallo was once one of Europe's most fashionable resorts, but it passed its heyday before World War II and has suffered from the building boom brought on by tourism. Ezra Pound and D. H. Lawrence lived here, and many other writers, poets, and artists have been drawn to it. Today, the town's harbor is filled with yachts. A single-span bridge on the eastern side of the bay is named after Hannibal, who is said to have passed through the area after crossing the Alps.

Two ancient buildings are highlights in the town center. The cathedral of **Santi Gervasio e Protasio** (☎ 0185/52375), at the western end of Via Mazzini, was founded in the 6th century. It's open daily 6:30–noon and 3–6:30. The **Lazzaretto di Banna,** located across the road from Santi Gervasio e Protasio, was originally a leper house and still retains parts of its original medieval frescoes on its exterior walls.

The **Museo del Pizzo a Tombolo,** in a 19th-century mansion, has a collection of antique lace for which Rapallo was renowned. ⊠ *Villa Tigullio,* ☎ *0185/63305.* 🎟 *Free.* ☉ *Oct.–Aug., Tues.–Wed. and Fri.–Sat. 3–6, Thurs. 10–11:30.*

Dining and Lodging

$$$ ✕ **Roccabruna.** In a splendid villa outside Rapallo, seafood specialties adorn an abundant menu that changes constantly. Take the Casello–Savagna highway from Rapallo; Savagna is only about 2 km (1 mi)

away. Reservations are recommended. ⊠ *Via Sotto la Croce 6, Savagna,* ☎ *0185/261400. MC, V. Closed Mon. and late Nov.–early Dec. No lunch, except Sun. Oct.–June.*

$$$–$$$$ 🏨 **Grand Hotel Bristol.** This large Victorian showcase is in an elevated position overlooking road and sea outside Rapallo and is set in lush gardens with a huge seawater pool. Spacious rooms, many with balcony and sea view, are decorated in soft colors in a smart, contemporary style and have extralarge beds. You can choose between a Rapallo view and a Portofino view. In summer, dinner is served on the roof terrace. ⊠ *Via Aurelia Orientale 369, 16035,* ☎ *0185/273313,* ䷚ *0185/ 55800,* WEB *www.tigullio.net/bristol/. 85 rooms, 6 suites. 2 restaurants, bar, minibars, saltwater pool, hot tub, sauna, game room, horseback riding, meeting room. AE, MC, V. Closed Dec.–Feb.*

$–$$ 🏨 **Giulio Cesare.** Only a block from the sea, this old town house was transformed into a hotel that offers rooms with modern furnishings and sea views. Many rooms have balconies, but noise may be a problem, since the hotel is on a main street. ⊠ *Corso Colombo 52, 16035,* ☎ *0185/50685,* ䷚ *0185/60896. 33 rooms. Restaurant, bar, in-room safes. AE, MC, V. Closed Nov.–Dec. 20.*

Outdoor Activities and Sports
GOLF

The **Rapallo Golf Club** (☎ 0185/261777) has a lush 18-hole course about 2 km (1 mi) northwest of town center.

Shopping

The attractive coastal village of **Zoagli** (⊠ on S1, 4 km [2½ mi] east of Rapallo) has been famous for silk, velvet, and damask since the Middle Ages.

Santa Margherita Ligure

❽ *3 km (2 mi) south of Rapallo, 31 km (19 mi) southeast of Genoa.*

A beautiful old-world resort favored by well-to-do Italians, Santa Margherita Ligure has everything a Riviera playground should have— plenty of palm trees and attractive hotels, cafés, and a marina packed with yachts. Some of the older buildings here are still decorated on the outside with the trompe-l'oeil frescoes typical of this part of the Riviera. This is a pleasant and convenient base for excursions by land and by sea and, for many visitors, represents the perfect balance in the Italian Riviera—less Americanized, younger, and bigger than Cinque Terre; less glitzy than San Remo; more relaxing than Genoa and environs; and perfectly situated for a day trip to Portofino.

Dining and Lodging

$$$–$$$$ ✕ **La Stalla.** Set in an old hilltop palazzo in the hills of the Riviera, this
★   restaurant is worth the harrowing 3-km (2-mi) drive from Santa Margherita's port. The windows command breathtaking views of Santa Margherita and the surrounding mountains and sea, and the restaurant's horse-theme interior is over the top in the most charming Levante style, leaving no wall space undecorated. The traditional Ligurian menu, highlighting local catches like scampi and baked sea bass, complements the view nicely. Don't miss the delectable fried zucchini and stuffed vegetable torte appetizers. ⊠ *Via G. Pino 27, Nozarego,* ☎ *0185/ 289447. AE, DC, MC, V. Closed Mon. and Nov.*

$$$ ✕ **La Paranza.** As befits a spot just off Santa Margherita's port, the specialty here is fresh seafood in every shape and form, from the piles of tiny *bianchetti* (whitebait) in oil and lemon in the antipasto *di mare* (of the sea) to a simple, perfectly grilled whole sole. In between you'll find mussels, clams, octopus, salmon, and whatever else is fresh that

day. Locals say this is the town's best restaurant, but if you're looking for a stylish evening out, look elsewhere—La Paranza is about food, not fashion. ⊠ *Via Jacopo Ruffini 46,* ☎ *0185/283686. Reservations essential. AE, DC, MC, V. Closed Mon. and Nov. 10–25.*

$$$ ✕ **Trattoria Cesarina.** This typical *trattoria* offers classic local fare— and that means seafood. The white interior is refreshingly free of bric-a-brac, allowing you to focus on your meal. Don't expect a menu; instead, allow the friendly staff to tell you what to eat. Among other treats, you will likely encounter a delectable antipasto of local *frutti di mare,* a seafood-theme pasta dish, and the catch of the day delicately grilled or baked in that laissez-faire Ligurian style. ⊠ *Via Mameli 2/C,* ☎ *0185/ 286059. MC, V. Closed Tues. and Dec.–Jan.*

$$$$ 🏨 **Grand Hotel Miramare.** Take the shore road south from town to reach
★ this palatial old-world hotel overlooking the bay. It has a lush garden, swimming pool, and private swimming area on the sea. The bright and airy rooms are furnished with antique furniture and marble bathrooms. ⊠ *Lungomare Milite Ignoto 30, 16038,* ☎ *0185/287013,* FAX *0185/284651,* WEB *www.grandhotelmiramare.it: 82 rooms, 9 suites. 2 restaurants, 2 bars, in-room safes, minibars, pool, beach, waterskiing, meeting room. AE, DC, MC, V.*

$$$$ 🏨 **Imperiale Palace.** Via Pagana climbs north out of Santa Margherita Ligure on its way toward Rapallo; just outside town it passes this old-world luxury hotel, set in an extensive park. Reception rooms with tall windows, plush chairs, and potted plants create a warm welcome. The rooms are furnished with antiques; many overlook the shore drive to the sea. Note that though only 3 km (2 mi) from Portofino, the hotel is not a short walk from any town center. ⊠ *Via Pagana 19, 16038,* ☎ *0185/288991,* FAX *0185/284223,* WEB *www.hotelimperiale.com. 83 rooms, 14 suites. Restaurant, 2 bars, in-room safes, minibars, pool, beach, baby-sitting, parking. AE, DC, MC, V. Closed Nov.–Mar.*

$$$–$$$$ 🏨 **Continental.** This stately seaside mansion with a columned portico was built in the early 1900s and is set in a lush garden shaded by tall palms and pine trees. The decor is a blend of traditional furnishings, mostly in 19th-century style, with some more functional pieces. There is also a modern wing. The hotel's own cabanas and swimming area are at the bottom of the garden. ⊠ *Via Pagana 8, 16038,* ☎ *0185/ 286512,* FAX *0185/284463,* WEB *www.hotel-continental.it. 76 rooms. Restaurant, bar, in-room safes, parking. AE, DC, MC, V. Closed Nov.– Dec. 23.*

Portofino

★ ❾ *5 km (3 mi) south of Santa Margherita Ligure, 36 km (22 mi) east of Genoa.*

One of the most picturesque villages along the coast, with a decidedly romantic and affluent aura, Portofino is also precious, in the true sense of the word. Unless you are traveling on a deluxe level and can keep up with the Agnellis and Berlusconis, you should probably choose to stay in Rapallo or Santa Margherita Ligure rather than at one of Portofino's few and very expensive hotels. Restaurants and cafés are good but also pricey (don't expect to have a beer here for much under 15,000 lire/€7.75). Some of Europe's wealthiest lay anchor in Portofino in the summer, but they stay out of sight by day, appearing in the evening after buses and boats have carried off the day-trippers.

Portofino has long been a popular destination for foreigners. Once an ancient Roman colony and taken by the Republic of Genoa in 1229, it has also been ruled by the French, English, Spanish, and Austrians, as well as marauding bands of 16th-century pirates. Elite British tourists first flocked to the lush harbor in the mid-1800s. At first glance, you may wonder what all the fuss is about. There's not actually much to *do* in Portofino, other than stroll around the wee harbor, see the castle, walk to Punta del Capo, look at the pricey boutiques, and sip a coffee while people-watching. However, weaving through picture-perfect cliff-side gardens and gazing at yachts framed by the turquoise Ligurian Sea and the cliffs of Santa Margherita can make for quite a relaxing afternoon. There are also several tame, photo-friendly hikes into the hills from Portofino to nearby villages. Note the meticulous upkeep of streets and public flora in what is surely Italy's cleanest town. Trying to reach Portofino by bus or car on the single narrow road can be a nightmare in the summer and on holiday weekends. No trains go directly to Portofino; if traveling by rail, you must stop at Santa Margherita and take the public bus from there (5,000 lire/€2.60). An alternative is to take a boat from Santa Margherita.

From the harbor, follow the signs for the climb to the **Castello di San Giorgio,** the most worthwhile sight in Portofino, with its medieval relics, impeccable gardens, and sweeping views. The castle was founded in the Middle Ages but restored in the 16th through 18th centuries; in true Portofino form, it was owned by Genoa's English consul from 1870 until its opening to the public in 1961. ⚏ *3,000 lire/€1.55.* ☉ *Apr.–Sept., Wed.–Mon. 10–6; Oct.–Mar., Wed.–Mon. 10–5.*

Sitting on a ridge above the harbor is the small church of **San Giorgio,** rebuilt four times during World War II, which is supposed to contain the relics of its namesake, brought back from the Holy Land by the Crusaders. Portofino enthusiastically celebrates St. George's Day every April 23. ☎ *0185/269337.* ☉ *Daily 7–6.*

Pristine views can be had from the deteriorating lighthouse, or *Faro,* at **Punta Portofino,** a 15-minute walk along a marked path from the village. Along the seaside path you can see numerous impressive, sprawling private residences behind high iron gates.

The only sand beach near Portofino is at **Paraggi,** a cove on the road between Santa Margherita and Portofino (the bus will stop there on request).

OFF THE BEATEN PATH

ABBAZIA DI SAN FRUTTUOSO – On the sea at the foot of Monte Portofino, the medieval Abbey of San Fruttuoso—built by the Benedictines of Monte Cassino—protects a minuscule fishing village that can be reached only on foot or by water (a 20-minute boat ride from Portofino and also reachable from Camogli, Santa Margherita Ligure, and Rapallo). The restored abbey is now the property of a national conservation fund (FAI). The church holds the tombs of some illustrious members of the Doria family. The historic abbey and its grounds are a delightful place to spend a few hours, perhaps lunching at one of the modest beach trattorias nearby (open only in summer). But boatloads of visitors can make it very crowded very fast; you might appreciate it most off-season. ☎ *0185/772703.* ⚏ *6,000 lire/€3.10.* ☉ *Mar.–Apr. and Oct., Tues.–Sun. 10–4; Dec.–Feb., weekends 10–4; May–Sept., daily 10–6. Call ahead to check hrs.*

Dining and Lodging

$$$$ ✕ **Il Pitosforo.** A chic, tan clientele, many with luxury yachts in the harbor, gives this waterfront restaurant a glamorous atmosphere augmented by outlandish prices. Spaghetti *ai frutti di mare* (with seafood) is recommended; adventurous diners might want to try *lo stocco accomodou* (dried cod in a savory sauce of tomatoes, raisins, and pine nuts). ✉ *Molo Umberto I 9,* ☎ *0185/269020 or 0335/5615833. Reser-*

vations essential. AE, DC, MC, V. Closed Mon.–Tues. and Jan.–mid-Feb. No lunch June–Sept.

$$$
★

✕ **Ristorante Puny.** A table at this tiny restaurant is difficult to get in summer, as the manager caters mostly to friends and regulars. If you are lucky enough to get in, however, the food will not disappoint you, nor will the cozy but elegant yellow interior. The unforgettable *pappardelle al portofino* (large, flat noodles) delicately blends two of Liguria's tastes: tomato and pesto. Ligurian seafood specialties include baked fish with laurel, potatoes, and olives as well as the inventive *moscardini al forno,* baked octopus with lemon and rosemary in tomato sauce. ✉ *P. Martiri dell'Olivetta 4–5 (on the harbor),* ☎ *0185/269037. Reservations essential. No credit cards. Closed Thurs. and Jan.–Feb.*

$$$$
★

☷ **Splendido.** People resort to superlatives when trying to describe this luxury hotel, built in the 1920s on a hill overlooking the sea. The abiding theme is color, from the coordinated fabrics and room furnishings to the fresh flowers in the reception rooms and on the large terrace. It's like a Jazz Age film set—you almost expect to see a Bugatti or Daimler roll up the winding drive from Portofino below. Even grander than the hotel are its prices, making this a place for very special occasions indeed. Rates are off the charts. ✉ *Salita Baratta 16, 16034,* ☎ *0185/267801,* ℻ *0185/267806,* WEB *splendido.orient-express.com. 47 rooms, 22 suites. Restaurant, 2 bars, pool, tennis court, parking. AE, DC, MC, V. Closed Nov. 13–Mar.*

$$$–$$$$

☷ **Eden.** If you must stay in Portofino, this is your only affordable option. Small, unexciting, but comfortable rooms have all the basic amenities, with clean bathrooms, working showers, pinkish walls, and views onto the street but not the bay. Anywhere else, this hotel would be overpriced. But in Portofino it's a good deal. ✉ *Via Vico Dritto 18, near the harbor, 16034,* ☎ *0185/269091,* ℻ *0185/269047. 12 rooms. Restaurant (closed mid-Sept.). AE, MC, V. Closed Dec. 1–25.*

Outdoor Activities and Sports

HIKING

If you have the stamina, you can hike to the Abbazia di San Fruttuoso from Portofino. It's a steep climb at first, and the walk takes about 2½ hours one-way. If you are extremely ambitious and want to make a whole day of it, you can then hike another 2½ hours all the way to Camogli. Much more modest hikes from Portofino include a one-hour uphill walk to Cappella delle Gave, a bit inland in the hills, from where you can continue downhill to Santa Margherita Ligure (another 1½ hours). Finally, there is a 2½-hour hike from Portofino that heads farther inland to Ruta, through Olmi and Pietre Strette.

Camogli

★ ⑩ *20 km (12 mi) east of Genoa, 23 km (14 mi) west of Chiavari.*

Camogli, at the edge of the large promontory and nature reserve known as the Portofino peninsula, has always been a town of sailors. By the 19th century it was leasing its ships throughout the continent. Today, multicolor houses, remarkably deceptive trompe-l'oeil frescoes, and a massive 17th-century seawall mark this picturesque harbor community, perhaps as beautiful as Portofino but without the glamour. When exploring on foot, don't miss the boat-filled second harbor, which is reached by ducking under a narrow archway at the end of the first one.

The **Castello Dragone,** built onto the sheer rock face near the harbor, is home to the **Acquario** (Aquarium), which has display tanks of local marine life actually built into the ramparts. ☷ *4,000 lire/€2.05.* ☉ *May–Sept., daily 10–noon and 3–7; Oct.–Apr., Fri.–Sun. 10–noon and 2:30–6, Tues.–Thurs. 10–noon.*

SAN ROCCO, SAN NICCOLÒ, AND PUNTA CHIAPPA – You can reach these hamlets along the western coast of the peninsula on foot or by boat from Camogli. They are more natural and less fashionable than those facing south on the eastern coast. In the small Romanesque church at San Niccolò, sailors who survived dangerous voyages came to offer thanks.

RUTA – The footpaths that leave from Ruta, 4 km (2½ mi) east of Camogli, up to and around Monte Portofino and Camogli thread through rugged terrain, home to a wide variety of plant species. Weary hikers will be sustained by stunning views of the Riviera di Levante from the various vantage points along the way.

Dining and Lodging

$$$ ✕ **Vento Ariel.** This tiny, friendly restaurant right on the port has informal but impressive decor. It serves seafood only and regularly runs out of items because it relies on the day's catch. Try the spaghetti *alle vongole* (with clams) or the grilled mixed fish. ✉ *Calata Porto,* ☎ *0185/771080. AE, DC, MC, V. Closed Wed. and Jan. 2–15.*

$$$–$$$$ 🏨 **Cenobio dei Dogi.** It is easy to see why this villa once served as the
★ summer home of Genoa's doges. Perched majestically a step above Camogli on its eastern edge, overlooking harbor, peninsula, and sea, but only a few steps from the center of town, Cenobio dei Dogi is indisputably the best address in town. Ask for one of the rooms with expansive balconies, which offer the most commanding vistas of Camogli's cozy port. You can relax in the well-kept park affording outstanding views of the Portofino peninsula or enjoy numerous sporting activities. ✉ *Via Cuneo 34, 16032,* ☎ *0185/7241,* 🖷 *0185/772796,* 🌐 *www.cenobio.it. 108 rooms. Restaurant, bar, pool, tennis court, beach, parking. AE, DC, MC, V.*

Nightlife and the Arts

During the festival of San Fortunato, held on the second Sunday of May each year, is the **Sagra del Pesce,** a crowded, festive, and free-to-the-public feast of freshly caught fish, cooked outside at the port in a frying pan 12 ft wide.

GENOA

Ligurian beach bums, beware: Genoa (Genova, in Italian) is a busy, sprawling, and cosmopolitan city, apt to break the spell of the coastal towns in a hurry. This isn't necessarily bad news, though; with more than a millennium of history under its belt, magnificent palaces and art, and an elaborate network of ancient hilltop fortresses, Genoa may be just the dose of curious culture you were looking for. The city's faded splendor can still be seen through dark shadows and centuries of grime in the narrow alleyways of the city's brooding historic center—the largest in Europe.

Genoa's winding streets haven't always been so haunted and obscure. This is the birthplace of Columbus, but the city's proud history of trade and navigation predates him by several hundred years. Known as *La Superba* (The Proud), Genoa was from the 13th century a great maritime center rivaling Venice and Pisa in power and splendor. Loud and modern container ships now unload at docks that centuries before served galleons and vessels bound for the spice routes. By the 3rd century BC, when the Romans conquered Liguria, Genoa was already an important trading station. The Middle Ages and the Renaissance saw its rise into a jumping-off place for the Crusaders, a commercial center of tremendous wealth and prestige, and a strategic bone of international contention. A network of fortresses defending the city connected by a wall second only in length to the Great Wall of China was constructed in the hills above, and Genoa's bankers, merchants, and princes adorned the city with palaces, churches, and impressive art collections.

Genoa's downfall began more than 500 years ago as it became eclipsed by other Mediterranean ports and northern Italian powerhouses. By the 17th century, Genoa was no longer a great sea power—but more modern enemies were yet to arrive. The city has more recently fought with—and often lost to—every evil associated with industrialization and urbanity. Crammed into a thin crescent of land between sea and mountains, Genoa has expanded up rather than out, taking on the form of a multilayer wedding cake, with streets, highways, churches, and entire residential neighborhoods built on others' rooftops. Public elevators and funiculars are as common as buses and trains in this vertical metropolis. Traffic-, pollution-, and crime-ridden (by Italian standards), Genoa has lost precious tourist revenue due to its urban-planning follies, while the export trade has suffered excessive Italian shipping taxes.

And yet, Europe's biggest boat show, the annual Salone Nautico Internazionale, takes place here. Fine restaurants are abundant, and classical dance and music are richly represented; the Teatro Carlo Felice is the local opera venue, and the internationally renowned annual Niccolò Paganini Violin Contest takes place here. Due to its location and its shipping industry, Genoa is also the most diverse city in Italy; it's where one of the only places on the mostly homogeneous boot you'll find well-established North African, Asian, and South American communities. Just steps away from the port, the darkly shadowed Via del Prè, with its street bazaars and spooky branching alleyways, offers a momentary excursion to a third-world country.

In recent years Genoa has struggled, mostly unsuccessfully, to change its seamy image. A port-side promenade, spider-shape elevator ride with a harbor view, and Europe's largest aquarium were installed for the expensive, much-criticized Columbus Quincentennial celebrations of 1992. Another harbor face-lift is under way in preparation for Genoa's designation as one of the "Cultural Capitals of Europe" for the year 2004. It will take more than a flattering label to rescue this once proud, still fascinating city. But should it be rescued? Perhaps the time to visit is now—before tourists discover Genoa, before the old port is completely overbuilt, and before the city's gritty charm is gone.

Exploring Genoa

The ancient center of Genoa, threaded with little streets flanked by 11th-century portals, is roughly the area between the port and Piazza de Ferrari; this pedestrian-only zone goes by many names: *centro storico* (historic center), Caruggi District, and the Vicoli. Stazione Principe marks the west end of the center, and Stazione Brignole more or less marks the east end. In the middle are the Old Port and Piazza de Ferrari, which you can use as a starting point for city walks. Note that at press time, the whole of Piazza de Ferrari was under construction. Thus you must circumnavigate the piazza rather than crossing it.

A Good Walk: Medieval and Renaissance Genoa

The best way to start your exploration of Genoa is to see it from above. From Piazza Acquaverde, behind Stazione Principe, start your walk along Via Balbi, which runs southeast from Stazione Principe toward the medieval town. On Via Balbi you pass Palazzo Balbi Durazzo, also known as **Palazzo Reale** ⑪, and **Palazzo dell'Università** ⑫. Continue straight past Piazza della Nunziata, stopping at **Santissima Annunziata** ⑬, to

Close-Up

THE ART OF THE PESTO PESTLE

ALTHOUGH YOU MAY HAVE KNOWN Genoa primarily for its salami or its brash explorer, the city's most direct impact on your life away from Italy may be through its cultivation of one of the world's best, and trendiest, pasta sauces. The sublime blend of basil, extra-virgin olive oil, garlic, pine nuts, and grated *fiore sardo* and *parmigiano reggiano* cheeses that forms *pesto alla Genovese* is one of Italy's crowning culinary achievements, a concoction that Italian food guru Marcella Hazan has called "the most seductive of all sauces for pasta." Unlike in the United States, where various versions of pesto bedeck everything from pizza to grilled-chicken sandwiches, Ligurian pesto is served only over spaghetti, gnocchi, lasagne, or—most authentically—Genoese *trofie* or *trenette* (doughy, potato-based pasta twists), and the pasta is most typically mixed with boiled potatoes and green beans. Pesto is also occasionally used to flavor minestrone. The small-leafed basil grown in the region's sunny seaside hills is considered by many to be the best in the world, and your visit to Liguria will afford you the chance to savor pesto in its original form. Pesto sauce was invented primarily as a showcase for that singular flavor, and the best pesto brings out the fresh basil's alluring aroma and taste rather than masking it with the complementary ingredients. The simplicity and rawness of pesto is one of its virtues, as cooking (or even heating) basil immediately ruins its delicate flavor. In fact, pesto aficionados refuse even to subject the basil leaves to an electric blender; Genoese (and other) foodies insist that true pesto can only be made with mortar and pestle. While satisfactory versions can surely be prepared less laboriously, the pesto purists' culinary conservatism is supported by etymology: the word *pesto* is derived from the Italian verb *pestare* (to pound or grind).

Largo di Zecca, from where you can take the **Zecca-Righi Funicular** ⑭ up to a marvelous lookout point on the edge of Genoa's network of fortresses. From Righi you can also walk along the ancient city walls in either direction. After descending, go southeast on Via Cairoli to reach the famed Via Garibaldi, a majestic street where you can pause to see the collections in the museums of **Palazzo Rosso** ⑮ and **Palazzo Bianco** ⑯. Stop in at **Palazzo Tursi** ⑰, Genoa's town hall, and ask the guard at the door if it happens to be open to visitors that day; if it is, you can see one of Paganini's violins. At the end of Via Garibaldi go left and left again to Piazza del Portello, where you can take the **Castelletto** ⑱ elevator for another view of the city, this one offering a closer look at the new port. Returning to Piazza Fontane Marose at the end of Via Garibaldi, turn southwest, taking Via Luccoli into the medieval Caruggi District. Beyond Piazza Soziglia, detour to the left, taking Via Campetto to Piazza San Matteo, flanked by the well-preserved houses of the Dorias and the church of **San Matteo** ⑲. Follow Salita Arcivescovado and turn right on Via Reggio to the cathedral of **San Lorenzo** ⑳, medieval Genoa's religious heart. North of the cathedral is Vico degli Indoratori, onto which you turn northwest. Follow it to Via degli Orefici, on which you turn left to reach the **Loggia dei Mercanti** ㉑. Head north on Via San Luca, Genoa's best shopping street (hopping on weekend afternoons), to the **Galleria Nazionale** ㉒. At the northern end of Via San Luca is the spooky church of **San Siro** ㉓. From there, if it is daytime, if you're adventurous you can continue onto Via del Campo back toward Principe until the street becomes Via del Prè, where you'll find Genoa's seamy, multicultural underbelly, in some senses the true center of the ancient port. Prepare yourself for a tour through the human vices; women should not walk alone on Via del Prè.

TIMING

Allow a full day for this walk. Note that the Galleria Nazionale is open until 7 every day except Monday, when it closes at 1 PM.

Sights to See

Caruggi District. The winding, picturesque alleys—known as *caruggi*—that make up the popular side of medieval Genoa are the city's heart and soul. Wealthy Genovese built their homes in this quarter in the 16th century, and prosperous guilds, such as the goldsmiths for whom Vico dei Indoratori and Via Orefici were named, set up shop here. In this warren of narrow, cobbled streets, extending north from Piazza Caricamento, you'll find the city's oldest churches punctuating blocks of 500-year-old apartment buildings, and tiny shops selling antique furniture, coffee, rifles, cheese, wine, gilt picture frames, camping gear, even live fish. The apartment buildings along the tiny streets lean in so precariously that penthouse balconies in some cases nearly touch those across the street, blocking what little sunlight would have shone down onto the cobblestones. When exploring these shady passageways, bear in mind that this quarter is the city's most disreputable. Don't come here at night or on holidays, when shops are closed and the alleys deserted, unless you're willing to part with your valuables.

⑱ Castelletto. One of Genoa's handy municipal elevators whisks you skyward from Piazza Portello, at the end of Via Garibaldi, for a good view of the old city. ⊠ *Piazza Portello.* 🎫 *600 lire/€0.30 one-way.* ☉ *Continuous service 6:40 AM–midnight.*

OFF THE
BEATEN PATH

MUSEO D'ARTE ORIENTALE CHIOSSONE – In the Villetta di Negro park on the hillside above Piazza Portello, the Chiossone Oriental Art Museum has one of Europe's most extensive and noteworthy collections of Japanese, Chinese, and Thai objects. You can get a fine view of the city from the museum's terrace. ⊠ *Piazzale Mazzini (Piazza Corvetto),* 🕿 *010/ 542285.* 🎫 *6,000 lire/€3.10, free Sun.; guided tour 7,000 lire/€3.60.* ☉ *Tues. and Thurs.–Sun. 9–1.*

㉒ Galleria Nazionale (National Gallery). This collection, housed in the richly adorned **Palazzo Spinola** north of Piazza Soziglia, contains masterpieces by Luca Giordano and Guido Reni. The *Ecce Homo,* by Antonello da Messina, is a hauntingly beautiful painting and is also of historical interest because it was the Sicilian da Messina who first brought Flemish oil paints and techniques to Italy from his sojourns in the Low Countries. ⊠ *Piazza Pellicceria 1,* 🕿 *010/2705300.* 🎫 *8,000 lire/€4.15.* ☉ *Tues.–Sat. 9–8, Sun. 1–8.*

Granarolo funicular. Actually a cog railway, this tram takes you up the steeply rising terrain to another part of the city's fortified walls. It takes 15 minutes to hoist you from Stazione Principe, on Piazza Acquaverde, to **Porta Granarolo,** 1,000 ft above, where the sweeping view gives you a sense of Genoa's size. ⊠ *Piazza del Principe.* 🎫 *1,600 lire/€0.80; bus tickets valid.* ☉ *Departs on the ¼ hr, 6 AM–11:45 PM.*

㉑ Loggia dei Mercanti. This merchants' row dating from the 16th century is lined with shops selling local foods and gifts as well as raincoats, rubber boots, and fishing line. ⊠ *Piazza Banchi.*

⑯ Palazzo Bianco. Originally white, as its name suggests, this palace—a mainstay of the regal Via Garibaldi—has become considerably dark-

250

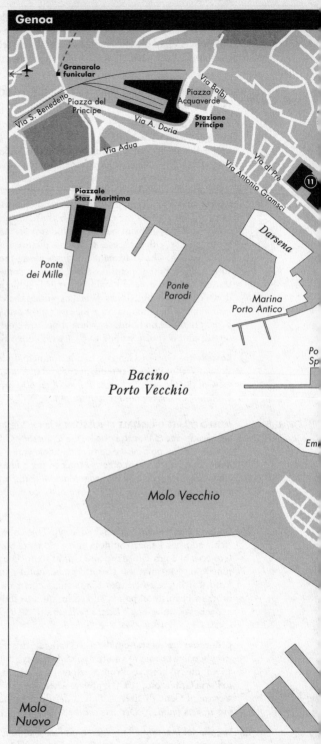

Genoa

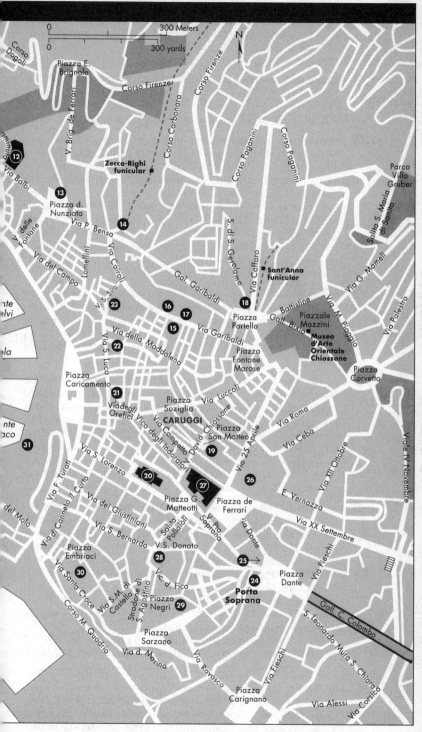

0 300 Meters

0 300 yards

N

Corso Dogali

Piazza E. Brignole

Corso Firenze

Corso Firenze

Corso Carbonara

Corso Paganini

Corso Paganini

Parco Villa Gruber

V. Brig. de Ferrari

12

Via Balbi

13

Piazza d. Nunziata

Via P. Bensa

14

Zecca-Righi funicular

Salita S. Maria di Sanità

V. delle Fontane

Via del Campo

Via Cairoli

Lomellini

Gal. Garibaldi

S. di S. Gerolamo

Via Caffaro

Sant'Anna funicular

18

Battistine

Gall. Bixio

Piazza Portello

Piazzale Mazzini

Museo d'Arte Orientale Chiossone

Via M. Piaggio

Via G. Mameli

Via Palestro

Parco Villa Gruber

V. S. Siro

23

16

17

15

Via Garibaldi

Piazza Fontane Marose

Piazza Corvetto

Via della Maddalena

Via S. Luca

22

Piazza Caricamento

21

Via degli Orefici

Vico degli Indoratori

Piazza Soziglia

Via Luccoli

Via David Chiossone

CARUGGI

Piazza San Matteo

Via Roma

Via Ceba

31

Via Campetto

19

Via 25 Aprile

Via XII Ottobre

Viale IV Novembre

Via S. Lorenzo

20

27

26

E. Vernazza

del Molo

Via F. Turati

Via di Canneto il Curto

Via dei Giustiniani

Piazza G. Matteotti

Piazza de Ferrari

Via Dante

Via XX Settembre

Via S. Bernardo

Salita Pollaiuoli

V. Pta Soprana

Via Fieschi

Piazza Embriaci

30

V.S. Donato

28

25

Piazza Dante

Via Santa Croce

Vico d. Fico

24

Porta Soprana

Gall. C. Colombo

Corso M. Quadrio

Via S.M. di Castello

Stradone di S. Agostino

Piazza Negri

29

S. Leonardo Mura S. Chiara

Piazza Sarzano

Via d. Marina

Via Ravasco

Via Fieschi

Via Alessi

Via Corsica

Piazza Carignano

ened from age and grime. It has a fine art collection, with the Spanish and Flemish schools well represented. ⊠ *Via Garibaldi 11,* ☎ *010/ 5572013.* 🎟 *6,000 lire/€3.10, 10,000 lire/€5.15 combined ticket with Palazzo Rosso.* ☉ *Tues. and Thurs.–Fri. 9–1, Wed. and Sat. 9– 7, Sun. 10–6.*

⑫ **Palazzo dell'Università.** Built in the 1630s as a Jesuit college, this institution has been Genoa's university since 1803. The exterior is unassuming, but climb the stairway flanked by lions to visit the handsome courtyard, with its portico of double Doric columns. ⊠ *Via Balbi 5.*

★ ⑪ **Palazzo Reale.** In a city where conspicuous consumption was a hobby of high society, this sumptuous 17th-century palace—also known as Palazzo Balbi Durazzo—contains lavish, frivolous rococo rooms displaying paintings, sculptures, tapestries, and Oriental ceramics. The former royal digs were inhabited by Italy's rulers, then bought by the royal house of Savoy in the early 19th century. The gallery of mirrors and the ballroom on the upper floor are particularly decadent. You'll also find works by Sir Anthony Van Dyck, who lived in Genoa for six years, beginning in 1621, and painted many fine portraits of the Genovese nobility. ⊠ *Via Balbi 10,* ☎ *010/2710272.* 🎟 *8,000 lire/€4.15.* ☉ *Sun.–Tues. 8:15–1:45, Wed.–Sat. 8:15–7:15.*

⑮ **Palazzo Rosso.** The 17th-century Baroque palace was named for the red stone used in its construction. It now contains, apart from a number of lavishly frescoed suites, works by Titian, Veronese, Reni, and Van Dyck. ⊠ *Via Garibaldi 18,* ☎ *010/2476351.* 🎟 *6,000 lire/€3.10, 10,000 lire/€5.15 combined ticket with Palazzo Bianco.* ☉ *Tues. and Thurs.–Fri. 9–1, Wed. and Sat. 9–7, Sun. 10–6.*

⑰ **Palazzo Tursi.** In the 16th century, wealthy Nicolò Grimaldi had this palace built of pink stone quarried in the region. It's been reincarnated as Genoa's Palazzo Municipale (Municipal Building), and so most of the goings-on inside are the stuff of local politics and quickie weddings. When the rooms aren't in use by Genovese officialdom, however, you are welcome to view the richly decorated rooms and the famous Guarnerius violin that belonged to Niccolò Paganini (1782–1840), which is played once a year on Columbus Day (October 12). ⊠ *Via Garibaldi 9,* ☎ *010/557111.* 🎟 *Free.* ☉ *Weekdays 8–noon (call in advance).*

⑳ **San Lorenzo.** This cathedral, at the heart of medieval Genoa, is embellished inside and out with the contrasting black slate and white marble so common in Liguria. It was consecrated in 1118 to St. Lawrence, who passed through the city on his way to Rome in the 3rd century; the last campanile dates from the early 16th century. For hundreds of years the building was used for state and religious purposes such as civic elections. Note the 13th-century Gothic portal, fascinating twisted barbershop columns, and the 15th- to 17th-century frescoes inside. The **Museo del Tesoro di San Lorenzo** (San Lorenzo Treasury Museum) has some stunning pieces from medieval goldsmiths and silversmiths, for which medieval Genoa was renowned. ⊠ *Piazza San Lorenzo,* ☎ *010/2471831 museum.* 🎟 *Cathedral free, museum 10,000 lire/€5.15.* ☉ *Guided visits only, every ½ hr Mon.–Sat. 9–11:30 and 3–5:30.*

⑲ **San Matteo.** This typically Genovese black-and-white-striped church dates from the 12th century; its crypt contains the tomb of Andrea Doria (1466–1560), the Genovese admiral and statesman who maintained the independence of his native city. ⊠ *Piazza San Matteo,* ☎ *010/ 2474361.* ☉ *Mon.–Sat. 8–noon and 4–7, Sun. 9:30–10:30 and 4–5.*

㉓ **San Siro.** Genoa's oldest church served as the city's cathedral from the 4th to the 9th century. Rebuilt in the 16th and 17th centuries, it now feels like a haunted house—imposing frescoes line the dank hallways, and chandeliers with crooked candles iterate through the darkness. ⊠ *Via San Luca,* ☎ *010/22461468.* ⊙ *Daily 7:30–noon and 4–7.*

⓭ Santissima Annunziata. The 16th- to 17th-century church has exuberantly frescoed vaults and is an excellent example of Genovese Baroque architecture. ⊠ *Piazza della Nunziata,* ☎ *010/297662.* ⊙ *Daily 9–noon and 3–7.*

★ Via Garibaldi. Thirteen palaces were built along what was once known as the Via Aurea (Golden Street) in just 10 years. Genoa's leading patrician families built their residences here from 1554 onward to escape the cramped conditions of the medieval section. It is one of the most impressive streets in Italy, and the palace-museums house some of the finest art collections in the country. Most of the palaces without museums on Via Garibaldi can be visited only by special application, but many have courtyards open to the public. ⊠ *West from Piazza Fontane Marose.*

⓮ Zecca-Righi funicular. This is a seven-stop commuter funicular, beginning at Piazza della Nunziata and ending up at a high lookout on the fortified gates in the 17th-century city walls. Ringed around the circumference of the city are a number of huge fortresses, and this gate was part of the city's system of defenses. From Righi you can undertake scenic all-day hikes from one fortress to the next. ☞ *1,800 lire/€0.95; bus tickets valid.* ⊙ *Departs every ¼ hr 6 AM–11:45 PM.*

A Good Walk: The Southern Districts and the Aquarium

Start just downhill from **Porta Soprana** ㉔ and pay homage to the purported **childhood home of Christopher Columbus** ㉕ on the square. Then head under the Porta Soprana (ancient city gate) and follow Via Dante into Piazza de Ferrari (or around it to the right, as the case may be; at press time the entire Piazza was blocked off for construction) to **Teatro Carlo Felice** ㉖. From Piazza de Ferrari, Genoa's unofficial center, you can make a detour and head down and back up Via XX Settembre, Genoa's wide main thoroughfare, with leading-name boutiques, cafés, and bookstores. Back in Piazza de Ferrari, on the west side of the piazza stands the **Palazzo Ducale** ㉗. Follow the palazzo around to its back side, which bears a neoclassic facade on Piazza Matteotti. Leading uphill from Piazza Matteotti, Salita Pollaiuoli takes you to **San Donato** ㉘. On the west side of the church is Stradone Sant'Agostino, which leads to Piazza Negri and **Sant'Agostino** ㉙. At the top of Stradone Sant'Agostino, from the west end of elongated Piazza Sarzano, take Via Santa Croce and turn right and then left onto Via Santa Maria di Castello, climbing up to the church of **Santa Maria di Castello** ㉚ atop the hill. From Piazza Embriaci turn west and follow the little streets downhill to Via Canneto il Curto, turning downhill on Via San Lorenzo to reach Piazza Caricamento and the Old Port, where you can take a ride in the panoramic **Il Bigo** ㉛ elevator, visit the **Acquario di Genova** ㉜, or take a boat tour of the port.

TIMING

This walk will take from 2½ to 4 hours, with stops at churches and the museum at Sant'Agostino; add an hour or two if you are stopping at the Acquario di Genova.

Sights to See

♻ ㉜ Acquario di Genova. Europe's biggest aquarium, second in the world only to Osaka's in Japan, is the third-most-visited museum in Italy and a must for children. Fifty tanks of marine species, including sea turtles, dolphins, seals, eels, penguins, and sharks, share space with educational displays and re-creations of marine ecosystems, including a tank for live corals from the Red Sea. If coming in by car just for the aquarium, take the Genova Ovest exit from the autostrada. ⊠ *Ponte Spinola,* ☎ *010/2481205; 010/2465535 reservations,* WEB *www.acquario.ge.it.* ⬚ *20,000 lire/€10.30.* ☉ *Sept.–June, Mon.–Wed. and Fri. 9:30–7:30, Thurs. 9:30 AM–11 PM, weekends 9:30–8:30; July–Aug., daily 9:30 AM–11 PM. Closed Mon. Nov.–Feb. Ticket office closes 1½–2 hrs before aquarium.*

㉕ **Childhood home of Christopher Columbus.** The ivy-covered ruins of this fabled medieval house stand, strangely all alone, in the gardens adjacent to the Porta Soprana. ⊠ *Piazza Dante.*

Harbor. A boat tour gives you a good perspective on the layout of the harbor, which dates back to Roman times. The Genoa inlet, the largest along the Italian Riviera, was also used by the Phoenicians and Greeks as a harbor and a vantage point from which they could penetrate inland to form settlements and to trade. The port is guarded by the Diga Foranea, a striking wall 5 km (3 mi) long built into the ocean. Boat tours are available for 10,000 lire/€5.15. The **Lanterna,** a lighthouse more than 360 ft high, was built in 1544 at the height of Andrea Doria's career; it is one of Italy's oldest lighthouses and a traditional emblem of Genoa. WEB *www.portoantico.it*

㉛ **Il Bigo.** This bizarre white structure, erected as a symbol of the 1992 Columbus Quincentennial events, looks like either a radioactive spider or an overgrown potato spore, depending on your point of view. Fortunately, its scenic **Ascensore Panoramico Bigo** (Bigo Panoramic Elevator) takes in the harbor, city, and sea. There is also ice skating November–March. ⊠ *Ponte Spinola, next to Acquario,* ☎ *010/2485710; 010/2461319 ice-skating.* ⬚ *4,000 lire/€2.05, 3,000 lire/€1.55 combined ticket with Acquario.* ☉ *Tues.–Fri. 11:30–1 and 2:30–4, weekends 11:30–1 and 2:30–5.*

㉗ **Palazzo Ducale.** This palace was built in the 16th century over a medieval hall, and its facade was rebuilt in the late 18th century and later restored. It now houses temporary exhibitions and a restaurant-bar serving fusion cuisine. Reservations are necessary to visit the dungeons and tower. ⊠ *Piazza Matteotti 9 and Piazza de Ferrari,* ☎ *010/5774000,* WEB *www.palazzoducale.genova.it.* ⬚ *12,000 lire/€6.20.* ☉ *Tues.–Sun. 9–9; guided tours every hr Fri.–Sun. 3–6.*

Piazza San Matteo. The excellently preserved medieval square was, for 500 years, the seat of the Doria family, which ruled Genoa and much of Liguria from the 16th to the 18th century. The square is bounded by 13th- to 15th-century houses decorated with portals and loggias. ⊠ *South of Piazza Soziglia.*

㉔ **Porta Soprana.** The striking, twin-towered, 12th-century edifice also known as Porta di Sant'Andrea stands at the old gateway to the Roman road that led through Genoa. Just uphill from Columbus's boyhood home, Porta Soprana supposedly employed the explorer's father as a gatekeeper. ⊠ *Piazza Dante.*

㉘ **San Donato.** The 12th-century Romanesque church with its original portal and octagonal campanile is slightly north of Sant'Agostino. ⊠ *Piazza San Donato,* ☎ *010/2468869.* ☉ *Mon.–Sat. 8–noon and 3–7, Sun. 9–12:30 and 3–7.*

㉙ **Sant'Agostino.** This 13th-century Gothic church was damaged during World War II, but it still has a fine campanile and two well-preserved cloisters, which now house an excellent sculpture museum. ⊠ *Piazza Sarzano 35/r,* ☎ *010/2511263.* ⬚ *6,000 lire/€3.10, free Sun.* ☉ *Tues.– Sat. 9–7, Sun. 9–12:30.*

30 Santa Maria di Castello. One of Genoa's most significant religious buildings, an early Christian church, was rebuilt in the 12th century and finally completed in 1513. You can visit the adjacent cloisters and see the fine artwork contained in the museum. ⊠ *Salita di Santa Maria di Castello 15,* ☎ *010/2549511.* ☉ *Daily 9–noon and 3:30–6; call ahead.*

26 Teatro Carlo Felice. The World War II–ravaged opera house in Genoa's modern center, Piazza de Ferrari, was rebuilt and reopened in 1991 to host the fine Genoese opera company; its massive tower has been the subject of much criticism. It stands next to the **Accademia delle Belle Arti** (Academy of Fine Arts), which contains a collection of Ligurian paintings from the 13th to the 19th century. *Theater:* ⊠ *Passo al Teatro 4,* ☎ *010/53811. Academy:* ⊠ *Largo Pertini 4,* ☎ *010/581957,* WEB *www.carlofelice.it.* ☎ *Free.* ☉ *Mon.–Sat. 9–1.*

OFF THE BEATEN PATH

CIMITERO MONUMENTALE DI STAGLIENO – One of the most famous of Genovese landmarks is this bizarrely beautiful cemetery; its fanciful marble and bronze sculptures sprawl haphazardly across a hillside on the outskirts of town. A **Pantheon** holds indoor tombs and some remarkable works like an 1878 *Eve* by Villa. Don't miss Rovelli's 1896 **Tomba Raggio**, which shoots Gothic spires out of the hillside forest. The cemetery began operation in 1851 and has been lauded by such visitors as Mark Twain and Evelyn Waugh. It covers a good deal of ground; allow at least half a day to explore. It's difficult to locate; the 12, 13, and 14 buses, or a taxi, will take you there. ⊠ *Piazzale Resasco,* ☎ *010/870184.* ☎ *Free.* ☉ *Daily 7:30–5. Mass Sun. at 10 AM.*

GENOVA-CASELLA RAILROAD – In continuous operation since 1929, the historic Genova-Casella rail line heads from Piazza Manin in Genoa (follow Via Montaldo from the center of town, or take Bus 33 or 34 to Piazza Manin) through the beautiful countryside that towers above the city, finally arriving in the rural hill town of Casella. On the way, the tiny train traverses a series of precarious switchbacks that afford sweeping views of the forested Ligurian hills. In Casella Paese (the last stop), you can hike, eat lunch, or just check out the view and ride back. There are two restaurants and two pizzerias near the Casella station; try local cuisine at Trattoria Teresin, in Località Avosso (☎ 010/9677708). From the Canova stop, two stops from the end of the line, there are two possible hikes through the hills, one a two-hour trek to a small sanctuary, **Santuario della Vittoria**, and the other a more grueling four-hour hike to the hill town of Creto (which requires a return trip of four hours as well, or an additional 2½–hour hike to the *pino* railway station). Another worthwhile stop along the rail line is Sant'Olcese Tullo, where you can take a half-hour walk, one-way, along a river and through the **Sentiero Botanico di Ciaé**, a botanical garden and forest refuge with labeled specimens of Ligurian flora and a tiny medieval castle. For Canova and Sant'Olcese, inform your conductor that you want him to stop. The Casella railroad is a good way to get a sense of the rugged landscape around Genoa, and you're often likely to have it all to yourself. ☎ *010/837321,* WEB *www.ferroviagenovacasella.it.* ☎ *6,200 lire/€3.20 round-trip, 8,600 lire/€4.45 Sun.* ☉ *Train runs about every hr Mon.–Sat. 7:30–6:30, Sun. 9–6.*

Dining and Lodging

$$$$ ✕ **Antica Osteria del Bai.** The historic Quarto dei Mille district is the setting for this romantic, upscale seaside restaurant perched on a cliff. One large, dark-wood-paneled room offers plate-glass views straight out over the Ligurian sea. A seafaring theme pervades the wall decorations and menu, which might include black gnocchi with lobster sauce, and ravioli *ai frutti di mare* (with mixed seafood). The restaurant's old-world elegance is reflected in its dress and its prices. ⊠ *Via Quarto 16,* ☎ *010/387478. Jacket and tie. AE, DC, MC, V. Closed Mon., Jan. 10–20, and Aug. 1–20.*

$$$–$$$$ ✕ **Gran Gotto.** Innovative classic regional dishes are served in this posh, spacious restaurant festooned with contemporary paintings. The service is quick and helpful. Try *pesce in salsa di zucca e parri* (fish in squash and leek sauce) and the sumptuous *flan di cioccolato* (dark chocolate flan with white chocolate sauce), one of the many excellent homemade desserts. Gran Gotto is in Piazza della Vittoria, near Stazione Brignole, in the modern part of town. ⊠ *Viale Brigata Bisagno 69/r,* ☎ *010/564344. Reservations essential. Jacket and tie. AE, DC, MC, V. Closed Sun. and Aug. 12–31. No lunch Sat.*

$$$–$$$$ ✕ **Zeffirino.** The five Belloni brothers share chef duties at this well-known restaurant full of odd combinations, including decor that ranges from rustic wood to modern metallic. Try the *passutelli* (ravioli stuffed with ricotta cheese and fruit) or any of the homemade pasta dishes. The enterprising Bellonis have expanded westward—there is now a Zeffirino in Las Vegas. Jackets, but not ties, are required here for men. ⊠ *Via XX Settembre 20,* ☎ *010/591990. Reservations essential. AE, DC, MC, V.*

$$–$$$ ✕ **Enoteca Sola.** Meals are made specifically to complement wines at Pino Sola's airy, casually elegant *enoteca* (wine bar) in the heart of the new town. The short menu emphasizes seafood and varies daily but might include stuffed artichokes or baked stockfish. The real draw, though, is the wine list, which includes some of the best *tre bicchieri* wines in Italy (winners of the coveted three-glass award). Ask the waiters for advice on wine pairings. ⊠ *Via C. Barabino 120/r,* ☎ *010/594513. AE, DC, MC, V. Closed Sun. and Aug. 1–22.*

$$ ✕ **Bakari.** Hip styling and ambient lighting hint at the creative, even daring, takes on Ligurian classics offered at this casual centro storico restaurant. Sure bets are the stuffed spinach-and-cheese gnocchi, any of several carpaccios, and the delicate beef dishes. Reserve ahead, requesting a table on the ground floor for a better atmosphere. ⊠ *Vico del Fieno 16/r, northwest of P. San Matteo,* ☎ *010/291936. AE, MC, V. Closed Sun. No dinner Wed. or Fri.*

$–$$ ✕ **Da Genio.** At the top of a pedestrian stairway near Piazza Dante in the Caruggi District, this is a classic trattoria serving classic Genovese dishes, including an assortment of fried vegetable appetizers, *trenette al pesto* (pasta with pesto sauce), and minestrone with a dollop of pesto. *Secondi* (main courses) with fish are well prepared. Reservations are recommended. ⊠ *Salita San Leonardo 61/r,* ☎ *010/588463. AE, MC, V. Closed Sun. and Aug.*

$$$$ ▦ **Bristol Palace.** This grand hotel was built in the 19th century and maintains the old-fashioned traditions of courtesy and discretion. The rooms are large, with high ceilings; paintings decorate the large reception rooms. There's no restaurant, but you're in the heart of the shopping district. ⊠ *Via XX Settembre 35, 16121,* ☎ *010/592541,* 🅵🅰🆇 *010/561756,* 🆆🅴🅱 *www.hotelbristolpalace.com. 133 rooms. Bar, café, snack bar, meeting room. AE, DC, MC, V.*

$$$–$$$$ ▦ **City.** The location of this hotel can't be beat—it's just off Via Roma, the grand shopping street, and one block from Piazza de Ferrari, which divides New Genoa from Old Genoa in the heart of the city. A bland apartment-building exterior gives way to a polished lobby and light, modern rooms that are a bit small but very comfortable. Some windows offer only mediocre views; try for a street-side room on a high floor. ⊠ *Via San Sebastiano 6, 16123,* ☎ *010/5545,* 🅵🅰🆇 *010/586301,* 🆆🅴🅱 *www.bestwestern.it/city ge. 65 rooms. Bar, café, in-room safes, parking (fee). AE, DC, MC, V.*

$$ 🏨 **Agnello d'Oro.** In Genoa's centro storico, about 100 yards from
★   Stazione Principe and next to the Palazzo Reale, this hotel has simple
and modern rooms, and several have a balcony with a view. The
friendly owner does double duty as a travel agent and is happy to help
you with plane reservations and travel plans. ✉ *Vico delle Monachette
6, 16126,* ☎ *010/2462084,* ℻ *010/2462327. 25 rooms. Restaurant,
bar, parking. AE, DC, MC, V.*

$$ 🏨 **Cairoli.** This family-run, central hotel is on a historic street near
Stazione Principe and the aquarium. It is neatly furnished and has a
roof terrace. Happily, the rooms have been soundproofed so you'll get
a good night's sleep—not always the easiest thing to do in this noisy
city. ✉ *Via Cairoli 14/4, 16124,* ☎ *010/2461454,* ℻ *010/2467512.
14 rooms. Bar, breakfast room. AE, DC, MC, V.*

Nightlife and the Arts

Opera
The opera season (October–May) at **Teatro Carlo Felice** (✉ Passo al
Teatro 4, ☎ 010/53811) attracts many lavish productions and occasionally sees the debut of a new work. Genoa's opera company, Fondazione Teatro Carlo Felice, is well respected.

Live Music and Dancing
Especially in the summer months, the place for nightlife is on the waterfront to the *levante* (southeast) side of the city. From the center, take
Corso Italia in the direction of Quarto, Quinto, and Nervi to reach
the outdoor nighttime hub. Extraordinarily popular with locals, **Sen-
hor do Bonfim** (✉ Passeggiata Anita Garibaldi, Nervi, ☎ 010/3726312),
along the water on Nervi's beautiful seaside promenade, offers live music
late into the night on weekends, and mellower-than-disco dancing
every night. Several beachfront *bagni* (literally, baths) and their accompanying restaurants and bars in the area serve as nighttime summer hangouts. Bigger and better-known discotheques such as the
famous **Makò** (✉ Corso Italia 28/r, ☎ 010/367652), perched on a cliff
about halfway to Nervi, attract most of the nighttime attention from
Genoese twenty- and thirtysomethings.

Shopping

Liguria is famous for its fine laces, silver and gold filigree work, and
ceramics. Look also for bargains in velvet, macramé, olive wood, and
marble. Genoa is the best spot to find all these specialties. In the heart
of the medieval quarter, **Via Soziglia** is lined with shops selling handicrafts and tempting foods. **Via XX Settembre** is famous for its wide
range of exclusive shops. You'll find high-end shops lining **Via Luccoli**.
The best shopping area for trendy (read: black) but inexpensive Italian clothing is near San Siro, on **Via San Luca,** which runs through the
centro storico parallel to the port.

Clothing and Leather Goods
At the fancy **Pescetto** (✉ Via Scurreria 8, ☎ 010/2473433), you'll find
designer clothes, perfumes, and gift ideas. **Stefanel** (✉ Via XX Settembre
36–39, ☎ 010/714755) is the venue of choice for modern Italian
women's clothing. Bologna-based **Bruno Magli** (✉ Via XX Settembre
135, ☎ 010/561890) makes an impeccable line of leather shoes and
boots for men and women, beautiful handbags, and leather jackets.

Jewelry
The well-established **Codevilla** (✉ Via Orefici 53, ☎ 010/2472567) is
one of the best jewelers on a street swarming with goldsmiths.

Wines

Vinoteca Sola (⊠ Piazza Colombo 13–15/r, near Stazione Brignole, ☏ 010/561329, WEB www.vinotecasola.it), open daily 9:30–12:30 and 3:30–7, stocks a selection of Italian and Ligurian wines. You can even buy futures for advance purchase and have wine shipped overseas.

Side Trip from Genoa

Nervi

㉝ *11 km (7 mi) east of Genoa, 23 km (14 mi) northwest of Chiavari.*

The true identity of this stately late-19th-century-style resort, famous for its seaside promenade, the Passeggiata Anita Garibaldi (1½ km [1 mi] long), its palm-lined roads, and 300 acres of parks rich in orange trees and exotics, is given away only by the sign on the sleepy train station in the center of town: it's technically part of the city of Genoa. Nervi's secret is an easy one to keep, though: its attractions are peace and quiet, its lush gardens, and the dramatic black cliffs that drop into the sea, as different from Genoa's hustle and bustle as Nervi's clear blue water is from Genoa's crowded port. Despite the contrast, it's easy to visit this remarkable part of the city for a stroll along the water or a day at the beach. Nervi—and the road along the way—also becomes a summer hotbed of nightlife. Frequent trains take 15 minutes from Stazione Principe or Brignole (buy a ticket for Genova–Nervi), or Buses 15 or 17 will take you from Brignole or Piazza de Ferrari to Nervi. Alternatively, a taxi from town center will run about 25,000 lire/€12.90 one-way. From the Nervi train station, walk east along the seaside promenade to reach beach stations, a cliff-hanging restaurant, and the 2,000 varieties of roses in the **Parco Villa Grimaldi,** all the while enjoying one of the most breathtaking views on the Riviera.

DINING AND LODGING

$$ ✕ **Marinella.** This restaurant is perched on seaside shoals a few minutes outside Genoa. Competing for attention are an impressive wrought-iron chandelier and great sea views from windows and terrace. (There's an inexpensive hotel annex, too.) Try the *zuppa di pesce* (fish soup); main dishes change according to the day's catch. Reservations are a good idea. ⊠ *Passeggiata Anita Garibaldi 18/r,* ☏ *010/3728343. MC, V. Closed Mon. and 1st 2 wks in Nov.*

$$$–$$$$ 🏨 **Romantik Hotel Villa Pagoda.** This small, top-quality hotel in sea-★ side Nervi is a majestic choice that offers the best of both worlds— luxurious peace and quiet with the city's attractions just 15 minutes away. Housed in a gated 19th-century merchant's mansion modeled after a Chinese pagoda, the hotel comes with a private park, private access to Nervi's famed cliff-top sea walk, and magnificent sea views. Request a tower room. ⊠ *Via Capolungo 15, 16167,* ☏ *010/323200,* FAX *010/321218,* WEB *www.bcedit.it/villapagoda.htm. 14 rooms, 4 suites. Restaurant, piano bar, in-room safes, minibars, meeting room, parking. AE, DC, MC, V.*

NIGHTLIFE AND THE ARTS

An **International Ballet Festival** is held every July in the Villa Gropallo park, drawing performers and audiences from all over the world. Contact the Genoa APT office (☏ 010/2462633) for ticket and schedule information.

RIVIERA DI PONENTE

The Riviera di Ponente (Riviera of the Setting Sun) stretches from Genoa to Ventimiglia on the French border. For the most part it is an unbroken chain of popular beach resorts sheltered from the north by the Ligurian and Maritime Alps, mountain walls that guarantee mild winters and a long growing season—resulting in its other nickname, the Riviera dei Fiori (Riviera of Flowers). Actually, the name is more evocative than the sight of once-verdant hillsides now swathed in plastic to form massive greenhouses. Many towns on the western Riviera have suffered from an epidemic of overdevelopment, but most have preserved their historic cores, usually their most interesting features. In major resorts, large new marinas cater to the pleasure-craft crowd. The Riviera di Ponente has both sandy and pebbly beaches with some quiet bays. Varazze, with a wide, sandy beach and many tall palm trees, is perhaps the last pleasant beach resort on the Riviera di Ponente to resist the encroachment of greater Genoa's industrial influence and the unwelcome effects of the tourist boom.

Pegli

34 *13 km (8 mi) west of Genoa.*

Once a popular summer home for many patrician Genovese families, Pegli has museums, parks, and some regal old villas with well-tended gardens. This residential suburb manages to maintain its dignity despite industrial development and the proximity of airport and port facilities. Two lovely villas make it worth an excursion. Pegli can be reached conveniently by commuter train from Stazione Porta Principe in Genoa.

Villa Doria, near the Pegli train station, has a large park. The villa itself, built in the 16th century by the Doria family, has been converted into a **naval museum.** ⊠ *Piazza Bonavino 7,* ☎ *010/6969885.* 🎫 *Villa 6,000 lire/€3.10, park free.* ☉ *Villa Tues.–Thurs. 9–1, Fri.–Sat. 9–7, 1st and 3rd Sun. of month 9–1; park daily 10–noon and 2–6.*

Villa Durazzo Pallavicini is set in 19th-century gardens with temples and artificial lakes. The villa has an **archaeological museum.** ⊠ *Via Pallavicini 11,* ☎ *010/6982776,* 🌐 *www.doit.it/pallavicini.* 🎫 *Villa 7,000 lire/€3.60, villa plus museum 10,000 lire/€5.15.* ☉ *Apr.–Sept., daily 9–7; Oct.–Mar., daily 9–5. Guided tours Apr.–Sept., at 11 (by reservation), 3, and 5; Oct.–Mar., at 11 (by reservation) and 3.*

Varazze

35 *23 km (14 mi) southwest of Pegli, 35 km (22 mi) west of Genoa.*

Varazze, known for its fine sandy beach, is a good place to stop for some sea and sun. The town, nicknamed the "city of the woman," also has well-preserved ancient ramparts, with a 10th-century church facade built into one of the rampart walls.

Albisola Marina

36 *11 km (7 mi) southwest of Varazze, 43 km (26 mi) west of Genoa.*

Albisola Marina has preserved its centuries-old tradition of ceramic making. Numerous shops here sell these distinctive wares, and even a whole sidewalk, **Lungomare degli Artisti,** has been transformed by the colorful ceramic works of well-known artists. It runs along the beachfront. The 18th-century **Villa Faraggiana** has interesting antique ceramics and exhibits on the history of the craft. ⊠ *Near the parish church on Via dell'Oratorio,* ☎ *019/480622.* 🎫 *Free.* ☉ *Apr.–Sept., Wed.–Mon. 3–7.*

Shopping
Ceramiche San Giorgio (⊠ Corso Matteotti 5, ☎ 019/482747) has been producing ceramics since the 17th century and is known for both clas-

sic and modern designs. **Mazzotti** (✉ Corso Matteotti 25, ☎ 019/481626) has an exclusive selection and a small in-house museum. In Albisola Superiore, **Ernan** (✉ Corso Mazzini 77, ☎ 019/489916) features the classic blue-and-white Old Savona patterns typical of the 18th century.

Savona

㊲ *4½ km (3 mi) southwest of Albisola Marina, 46 km (29 mi) southwest of Genoa.*

Savona is the fifth-largest seaport in Italy and handles vast oil and coal cargoes, as well as car and truck ferries. Much of the town is modern and not very interesting, although a small, austere older quarter near the harbor contains some fine homes of the town's merchant class. The large **Palazzo della Rovere** (✉ Via Pia) was designed for Pope Julius II by the Florentine Giuliano da Sangallo in 1495. Other medieval monuments include the 14th-century **Palazzo degli Anziani** and three 12th-century towers. Every other year (including in 2002) on Good Friday, antique wooden carvings depicting the Passion of Christ are carried in procession.

Shopping

Watch for shops selling crystallized fruit, a local specialty. In Millesimo, a town 4 km (2½ mi) west and 36 km (18 mi) inland from Savona, little rum chocolates known as *millesimi* are produced. Look for bargains, too, in wrought-iron work, relief work on copper plate, and pieces in local sandstone.

Finale Ligure

㊳ *24 km (15 mi) southwest of Savona, 72 km (44 mi) southwest of Genoa.*

Palms, sand strips, *gelaterie* (gelato shops), and good rock-climbing terrain make Finale Ligure a good break from gaudiness and pastel villages. Finale Ligure is made up of three villages: Finalborgo, Finalmarina, and Finalpia. The latter two have fine sandy beaches and modern resort amenities. The most attractive village is **Finalborgo,** a hauntingly preserved medieval settlement, planned to a rigid blueprint, with 15th-century walls. The village is crowned by the impressive ruins of the huge **Castel Gavone.** The Baroque church of **San Biagio** houses many works of art. The 14th- to 15th-century Dominican convent of **Santa Caterina** can be visited to enjoy the shade of the courtyard or to see the museum of paleontology and natural history, which houses prehistoric remains found in the area. ✉ *Museo Civico,* ☎ *019/690020.* 💰 *5,000 lire/€2.60.* ☉ *July–Oct., Tues.–Sat. 9–noon and 3–6, Sun. 9–noon; Nov.–June, Tues.–Sat. 9–noon and 2:30–4:30, Sun. 9–noon.*

The countryside around Finale Ligure is pierced by deep, narrow valleys and caves; the limestone outcroppings provide the warm pinkish stone found in many buildings in Genoa. Here lurk rare reptiles and exotic flora.

Dining

$$$–$$$$ ✕ **Ai Torchi.** You could easily become a homemade pesto snob at this restaurant in the center of Finalborgo. High prices are justified by excellent, inventive seafood and meat dishes. The restaurant is set in a restored 5th-century olive-oil refinery. ✉ *Via dell'Annunziata 12,* ☎ *019/690531. AE, DC, MC, V. Closed Tues. in Sept.–July, and Jan. 7–Feb. 10.*

OFF THE
BEATEN PATH

NOLI – Just 9 km (5½ mi) northeast of Finale Ligure, picturesque ruins of a castle loom benevolently over the tiny medieval gem of Noli. It is hard to imagine this charming village was—like Genoa, Venice, Pisa, and Amalfi—a prosperous maritime republic in the Middle Ages. If you don't have a car, get a bus for Noli at Spotorno, where local trains stop.

Albenga

39 *20 km (12 mi) southwest of Finale Ligure, 90 km (55 mi) southwest of Genoa.*

Albenga has a medieval core, with narrow streets laid out by the ancient Romans. A network of alleys is punctuated by centuries-old towers surrounding the 18th-century Romanesque **cathedral,** with a late-14th-century campanile and **baptistery** dating back to the 5th century AD.

OFF THE
BEATEN PATH

BARDINETO – For a look at some of the Riviera's mountain scenery, make an excursion by car to this attractive village in the middle of an area rich in mushrooms, chestnuts, and raspberries, as well as local cheese. A ruined castle stands high above the village. From Borghetto Santo Spirito (between Albenga and Finale Ligure), drive inland 25 km (15 mi).

Lodging

$$$$ 🏨 **La Meridiana.** An oasis of Italian hospitality and refinement lies 8 km (5 mi) off the Albenga exit of the A10. The handsome farmhouse compound is spread on a bucolic garden. The interiors are those of a comfortably luxe home, with tasteful, bright prints and colors; fresh flowers; and a mix of traditional and period-style furniture in the common and guest rooms. Il Rosmarino restaurant serves fine wine and seafood dishes. Nearby are the Golf Club Garlenda, a tennis club, and a country club for horseback riding. ✉ *Via ai Castelli, Garlenda 17033,* ☎ *0182/580271,* 🖷 *0182/580150. 16 rooms, 15 suites. Restaurant, pool. AE, DC, MC, V. Closed Nov.–Mar.*

Cervo

40 *23 km (14 mi) southwest of Albenga, 106 km (65 mi) southwest of Genoa.*

Cervo is the quintessential sleepy Ligurian coastal village, nicely polished for the tourists who come to explore its narrow byways and street staircases. It is a remarkably well preserved medieval town, crowned with a big Baroque church.

Nightlife and the Arts

In July and August the square in front of the church is the setting for **chamber music** concerts.

Imperia

41 *12 km (7 mi) west of Cervo, 116 km (71 mi) southwest of Genoa.*

Imperia actually consists of two towns: **Porto Maurizio,** a medieval town built on a promontory, and **Oneglia,** now an industrial center for oil refining and pharmaceuticals. Obviously, Oneglia can be skipped entirely. Porto Maurizio has a virtually intact medieval center, the Parasio quarter, an intricate spiral of narrow streets and stone portals, and some imposing 17th- and 18th-century palaces.

OFF THE
BEATEN PATH

MUSEO DELL'OLIVO – Imperia is king when it comes to olive oil, and the story of the olive—its cultivation and pressing into oil—is the theme of this small museum set up by the Fratelli Carli olive-oil company. Displays of the history of the olive tree, farm implements, types of presses, and utensils demonstrate how olive oil has been made in many countries throughout history. ☒ *Via Garessio 11,* ☎ *0183/720000,* WEB *www.museodellolivo.com.* ☞ *Free.* ⊙ *Wed.–Mon. 9–noon and 3–6:30.*

Dining

$–$$ × **Candidollo.** This charming, reasonably priced restaurant is worth a
  ★   detour to the village of Diano Borello, on the valley road a mile or so
         north of Diano Marina, 6 km (4 mi) east of Imperia. In his rustic coun-
         try inn, with checkered tablecloths and worn terra-cotta floors, host
         Bruno Ardissone depends upon locally grown ingredients and sea-
         sonal traditional recipes. The menu usually includes *coniglio al timo*
         (rabbit with thyme and other herbs) and *lumache all'agliata* (grilled
         snails in piquant sauce). Reservations are recommended. ☒ *Corso
         Europa 23, Diano Borello,* ☎ *0183/43025. No credit cards. Closed
         Tues. and Nov.–Mar. No lunch Mon.*

Taggia

42   *20 km (12 mi) west of Imperia, 135 km (84 mi) southwest of Genoa.*

The town of Taggia has a medieval core and one of the most imposing medieval stone bridges in the area. The church of **San Domenico,**
on a rise south of Taggia, was part of a monastery founded in the 15th
century and was a beacon of faith and learning in western Liguria for
300 years. An antiques market is held here on the fourth weekend of
the month.

San Remo

★ 43   *10 km (6 mi) west of Taggia, 146 km (90 mi) southwest of Genoa.*

The self-styled capital of the Riviera di Ponente is San Remo, also the
area's largest resort, lined with polished world-class hotels, exotic gardens, and seaside promenades. Renowned for its royal visitors, famous
casino, and romantic setting, San Remo still maintains some of the glamour of its heyday from the late 19th century to World War II. San Remo's
waterside palm fronds conceal a sizable historic center that, unlike in
other Ponente towns, is lively even in the off-season. Restaurants,
wine bars, and boutiques are second in Liguria only to Genoa's, and
San Remo's cafés bustle with afternoon activity. Consult www.apt.riv-
ieradeifiori.it and www.sanremonet.com for up-to-date information on
events in town.

The onion-domed Russian Orthodox church of **San Basilio** stands at
one end of the Corso dell'Imperatrice and, like this imposing seafront
promenade, is a legacy of Russian empress Maria Alexandrovna, wife
of Czar Alexander II, who built a summer house in here. San Remo is
famous for the **Mercato dei Fiori,** Italy's most important wholesale flower
market, held in a market hall between Piazza Colombo and Corso
Garibaldi and open to dealers only. More than 20,000 tons of carna-
tions, roses, mimosa flowers, and innumerable other cut flowers are
dispatched from here each year.

In the old part of San Remo, **La Pigna** ("pinecone"), explore the warren of alleyways that climbs upward to Piazza Castello, with a splendid view of the town. The newer parts of San Remo suffer from the

same epidemic of overbuilding that changed so many towns on the western Riviera for the worse. And as the center of northern Italy's flower-growing industry, the resort is surrounded by hills where once-verdant terraces are now blanketed with plastic to form immense greenhouses.

The Art Nouveau **San Remo Casino** is reminiscent of the turn of the 20th century, with a restaurant, a nightclub, and a theater that hosts concerts and the annual San Remo Music Festival. ⊠ *Corso Inglese, San Remo,* ☎ *0184/5951.* ☒ *Slot machines free, tables 15,000 lire/€7.75 weekends.* ☉ *Daily 2:30 PM–3 AM.*

OFF THE BEATEN PATH

BUSSANA VECCHIA – About 8 km (5 mi) east of San Remo, in the hills where flowers are cultivated for export, is Bussana Vecchia, a self-consciously picturesque ghost town largely destroyed by an earthquake in 1877. The inhabitants packed up and left en masse after the quake, and for almost a century the houses, church, and crumbling bell tower were empty shells, overgrown by weeds and wildflowers. Since the 1960s, an artist's colony has evolved among the ruins. Painters, sculptors, artisans, and bric-a-brac dealers have restored dwellings for themselves and sell their wares to visitors.

Dining and Lodging

$ ★ ✕ **Nuovo Piccolo Mondo.** This small, central trattoria has plenty of charm and a homey atmosphere, found in such details as the old wooden chairs dating from the 1920s, when the place opened. Family-run, it has a faithful clientele, so get there early to grab a table and order Ligurian specialties such as *sciancui* (a diamond-shape pasta with a mixture of beans, tomatoes, zucchini, and pesto) and *polpo e patate* (stewed octopus with potatoes). ⊠ *Via Piave 7,* ☎ *0184/509012. No credit cards. Closed Sun.–Mon. and July.*

$$$$ 🏨 **Royal.** It would take a dedicated hedonist to determine whether this deluxe hotel or the Splendido in Portofino is the most luxurious in Liguria. One major difference is the location: only a few paces from the casino and the train station, the Royal is definitely part of San Remo, unlike the Splendido, which is set above Portofino. Rooms here have a mixture of modern equipment and antique furnishings. The heated seawater swimming pool, open April–September, is dug into a subtropical garden. On the terrace, candlelight dining and music get under way each night under the stars in season. Keep your eyes open for spectacular off-season discounts. ⊠ *Corso Imperatrice 80, 18038,* ☎ *0184/5391,* FAX *0184/661445,* WEB *www.royalhotelsanremo.com. 121 rooms, 17 suites. Restaurant, bar, saltwater pool, miniature golf, tennis court, playground. AE, DC, MC, V. Closed Oct. 8–Dec. 20.*

$$–$$$ 🏨 **Paradiso.** This small central hotel is adjacent to a lush public park near the Royal. A quiet, palm-fringed garden gives it an air of seclusion, a plus in this sometimes hectic city. Rooms are modern and bright, and many have a little terrace. The hotel restaurant has a good fixed-price menu. ⊠ *Via Roccasterone 12, 18038,* ☎ *0184/571211,* FAX *0184/578176,* WEB *www.paradisohotel.it. 41 rooms. Restaurant, bar. AE, DC, MC, V.*

Bordighera

44 *12 km (7 mi) west of San Remo, 155 km (96 mi) southwest of Genoa.*

Bordighera, on a large, lush promontory, wears its genteel past as a famous winter resort with unstudied ease. A large English colony, attracted by the mild climate, settled here in the second half of the 19th century and is still very much in evidence today. In fin-de-siècle Bordighera, you'll regularly find people taking afternoon tea in the cafés.

This garden spot was the first town in Europe to grow date palms, and its citizens still have the exclusive right to provide the Vatican with palm fronds for Easter celebrations. Walk along the **Lungomare Argentina,** a magnificent seafront promenade, 1½ km (1 mi) long, beginning at the western end of the town, for a good view westward to the French Côte d'Azur. Thanks partly to its year-round English residents, Bordighera does not close down entirely in the off-season like some Riviera resorts but rather serves as a quiet winter haven for elderly people. With plenty of fine hotels and restaurants, Bordighera makes a good base for beachgoing and excursions and is quieter and less commercial than San Remo.

Dining and Lodging

$$–$$$ ✕ **La Reserve Restaurant.** This traditional, informal trattoria, part of the Hotel Parigi a bit out of town toward San Remo, has access to the beach and excellent views of the sea from the dining room. There are even changing rooms for anyone who wants a post-lunch dip. Concentrate on the seafood here: specialties are seafood ravioli *al finocchio selvatico* (with wild fennel) and assorted grilled fish. Reservations are recommended. ⊠ *Via Arziglia 20,* ☎ *0184/261322. AE, DC, MC, V. Closed Mon. in Sept.–June, and Nov.–Easter. No dinner Sun.*

$$–$$$ ✕ **Le Chaudron.** The charming rustic interior, with ancient Roman arches, has the look of restaurants across the French border in Provence. Ligurian specialties are featured on the predominantly seafood menu of this centrally located restaurant: try the cheese pansoti con salsa di noci and *branzino* (sea bass) with artichokes or mushrooms. A café annex serves a daily lunch special. ⊠ *Piazza Bengasi 2,* ☎ *0184/263592. Reservations essential. DC, MC, V. Closed Mon., 1st 2 wks in Feb., and 1st 2 wks in July.*

$$ ✕ **Piemontese.** Only a block from the seaside and five minutes from the train station, this simple restaurant melds Ligurian cooking and seafood with the cuisine of the neighboring Piedmont region, including *risotto al Barolo* (rice cooked with Barolo wine, sausage, and porcini mushrooms) and the winter specialty, *bagna cauda* (raw vegetables with a garlic and oil sauce). ⊠ *Via Roseto 8, off Via Vittorio Veneto,* ☎ *0184/261651. AE, MC, V. Closed Tues., sometimes mid-June–mid-July, and Nov. No dinner Mon.*

$$$$ ☷ **Grand Hotel del Mare.** Atop a steep hill rising from the beach, this tasteful hotel lives up to its name, with impeccable service and facilities. The large rooms have panoramic views of the coastline; ask for one facing the water. One floor is filled with antiques. ⊠ *Via Portico della Punta 34, 18012,* ☎ *0184/262201,* ℻ *0184/262394,* WEB *www.grandhoteldelmare.it. 74 rooms, 26 suites. Restaurant, piano bar, saltwater pool, hair salon, sauna, spa, mineral bath, tennis court, gym, beach. AE, DC, MC, V. Closed mid-Oct.–Dec. 22.*

$$$ ☷ **Grand Hotel Capo Ampelio.** This converted villa overlooks the town and the coastline. Traditional architectural details in the reception rooms and staircases are paired with convenient modern features in the rooms, all with balconies. The hotel is somewhat outside the town center, so the rooms are quiet. ⊠ *Via Virgilio 5, 18012,* ☎ *0184/264333,* ℻ *0184/264244. 104 rooms. Restaurant, bar, pool, massage, gym, recreation room. DC, MC, V. Closed Nov.–Dec. 22.*

Ventimiglia

㊺ *5 km (3 mi) west of Bordighera, 159 km (98 mi) southwest of Genoa.*

From its past life as a pre-Roman settlement known as Albintimilium, Ventimiglia possesses some important archaeological remains, including a 2nd-century AD amphitheater. A vital trade center for hundreds of years, it declined in prestige as Genoa grew and is now little more than a frontier town that lives on tourism and the cultivation of flowers. Ventimiglia is divided in two by the Roia River. The **Città Vecchia** is a well-preserved medieval Old City on the western bank. The 11th-century **Duomo** (Cathedral) has a Gothic portal dating from 1222. Walking up Via del Capo, you'll reach the **ancient walls,** which offer fine views of the coast. On Friday the large flower market, open to the trade only, is chaotic with bargain hunters from France, creating traffic gridlock; it's best to avoid Ventimiglia on that day.

OFF THE
BEATEN PATH
DOLCEACQUA – From Ventimiglia, a provincial road swings up the Nervi River valley to this lovely sounding medieval town (its name translates as Sweetwater) with its ruined castle. Liguria's best-known red wine is the local Rossese di Dolceacqua. Beyond is **Pigna,** another medieval village built in concentric circles on a hilltop.

Lodging

$$$
★
🏨 **La Riserva.** Just 5 km (3 mi) west of Ventimiglia, but more than 1,100 ft above sea level, is the village of Castel d'Appio, where you'll find this innlike establishment. The staff is very helpful, providing, for example, regular lifts into town for those without cars. In addition to its excellent restaurant, La Riserva offers numerous activities and a lovely terrace for drinks, sunbathing, or candlelight dinners. Full-board rates are a good deal. ⊠ *Via Peidago 79, Castel d'Appio, 18039,* ☎ *0184/ 229533,* FAX *0184/229712,* WEB *www.lariserva.it. 21 rooms. Restaurant, bar, pool. AE, DC, MC, V. Closed Jan. 6–Mar. and Oct.–Dec. 20. FAP.*

Giardini Botanici Hanbury

★ ㊻ *6 km (4 mi) west of Ventimiglia, 165 km (102 mi) southwest of Genoa.*

Mortola Inferiore, only 2 km (1 mi) from the French border, is the site of the world-famous Giardino Hanbury (Hanbury Garden), one of the largest botanical gardens in Italy. Planned and planted in 1867 by a wealthy English merchant, Sir Thomas Hanbury, and his botanist brother Daniel, the terraced gardens contain species from five continents, including many palms and succulents (plants of the cactus group). There are panoramic views of the sea from the gardens, which descend down to the beach. ⊠ *Giardino Hanbury, Cap Mortola, Loc. Mortola, Ventimiglia,* ☎ *0184/229507.* 🎟 *8,500 lire/€4.40.* ⊙ *Apr.–mid-June, Thurs.–Tues. 10–5; mid-June–Sept., daily 9–6; Oct.–Mar., Thurs.–Tues. 10–4. Ticket office closes 1 hr before garden.*

OFF THE
BEATEN PATH
BALZI ROSSI – At the French border, 7 km (4½ mi) from Ventimiglia and 2 km (1 mi) from the Giardino Hanbury, are the Balzi Rossi (Red Rocks), caves carved in the sheer rock in which prehistoric humans left traces of their lives and magic rites. You can visit the caves and a small museum displaying some of the objects found there. ⊠ *Via Balzi Rosso 9,* ☎ *0184/38113.* 🎟 *4,000 lire/€2.05.* ⊙ *Tues.–Sun. 9–7.*

ITALIAN RIVIERA A TO Z

To research prices, get advice from other travelers, and book travel arrangements, visit www.fodors.com.

AIR TRAVEL
CARRIERS
There is daily service between Genoa and Zurich (on Crossair), London (on British Airways), Paris (on Air France), Munich (on Air Dolomiti) and Milan and Rome (on Alitalia).

➤ AIRLINES AND CONTACTS: **Air Dolomiti** (☎ 800/013366). **Air France** (☎ 848/884466 Mon.–Fri.; 848/882255 Sat.). **Alitalia** (☎ 147/865641). **British Airways** (☎ 1478/12266). **Crossair** (☎ 848/849570).

AIRPORTS
Aeroporto Internazionale Cristoforo Colombo is only 6 km (4 mi) from the center of Genoa. The nearest airports for direct U.S. flights are Nice, in France, about 2½ hours west of Genoa (and an easy bus connection from Genoa), and Milan's Linate and Malpensa, about 2 hours northeast.

➤ AIRPORT INFORMATION: **Aeroporto Internazionale Cristoforo Colombo** (✉ Sestri Ponente, ☎ 010/6015410).

TRANSFERS

Volabus services from Cristoforo Colombo connect with Genoa's Stazione Brignole, stopping also at Piazza Acquaverde (Stazione Principe).

➤ TAXIS AND SHUTTLES: **Volabus** (☎ 010/5997414).

BOAT AND FERRY TRAVEL
Genoa is Italy's largest port and can be reached from the United States as well as other parts of Liguria and Italy (Sardinia, La Spezia, and Savona). Ships berth in the heart of Genoa, including cruise ships of the Genoa-based Costa Cruise Line. Ferries to various ports around the Mediterranean are operated by Tirrenia Navigazione, whose most popular destination is Sardinia (a 13-hour trip), and Grimaldi Lines, which sends cruise ship–like overnight ferries to Barcelona (an 18-hour trip) and Palermo, Sicily (a 20-hour trip). Popular with Genoese escapists, Corsica Ferries runs car ferries from Savona to Bastia and Ile-Rousse in Corsica.

Boat or ferry travel is the most pleasant—and, in some cases, the only—way to get from place to place within Liguria. A busy network of local services connects many of the resorts. For general information about availability of services in Liguria, contact Servizio Marittimo del Tigullio. Another source is Alimar, or contact Golfo Paradiso, which runs between Camogli, San Fruttuoso (on the Portofino promontory), and Recco. In summer there is also daily service from the port of Genoa and Nervi to Portofino, Cinque Terre, and Portovenere, stopping in Recco and Camogli. Navigazione Golfo dei Poeti runs frequent ferry-shuttle services between Portofino, Portovenere, and Cinque Terre. Cooperativa Battellieri del Porto di Genova runs a tour-boat service in Genoa's old port.

➤ BOAT AND FERRY INFORMATION: **Alimar** (✉ Calata Zingari, Genoa, ☎ 010/256775). **Cooperativa Battellieri del Porto di Genova** (☎ 0185/265712). **Corsica Ferries** (☎ 019/215511, WEB www.corsicaferries.com). **Costa Cruise Line** (✉ Via Gabriele D'Annunzio 2, ☎ 010/54831). **Golfo Paradiso** (✉ Via Scalo 3, Camogli, ☎ 0185/772091, WEB www.golfoparadiso.it). **Grimaldi Lines** (✉ Stazione Marittima, ☎ 010/589331). **Navigazione Golfo dei Poeti** (✉ Viale Mazzini 21, La Spezia, ☎ 0187/967676 or 0336/258037). **Servizio Marittimo del Tigullio** (✉ Via Palestro 8/1b, Santa Margherita Ligure, ☎ 0185/284670 or 0336/253336). **Tirrenia Navigazione** (✉ Stazione Marittima, ☎ 010/2758041).

BUS TRAVEL
The main bus station in Genoa is at Piazza Principe. Several bus lines provide connections along the Ligurian coast and link Genoa with other parts of Italy, the French Riviera, and other cities in Europe. PESCI provides reliable bus service to the Nice airport. PESCI buses run the

length of the Ligurian Coast in both directions. Local buses serve the steep valleys that run to some of the towns along the western coast. Tickets may be bought at local bus stations, or at newsstands for local buses. Buy your ticket before you board the bus.

➤ Bus Information: **Geotravels** (✉ Piazza della Vittoria 302/r, Genoa, ☎ 010/587181). **Guimar Tours** (✉ Via Balbi 192, Genoa, ☎ 010/256337). **PESCI** (✉ Piazza della Vittoria 94/r, Genoa, ☎ 010/564936).

CAR RENTAL

➤ Local Agencies: **Avis** (✉ Via delle Casaccie 3, Piazza Acquaverde, Genoa, ☎ 010/564412; 06/41999 national number; ✉ Via Fratelli Rosselli 74/76, La Spezia, ☎ 0187/770270; 06/41999 national number; ✉ Corso Imperatrice 96, San Remo, ☎ 0184/532462; 06/41999 national number). **Budget** (✉ Aeroporto Internazionale Cristoforo Colombo, Genoa, ☎ 010/6503822). **Hertz** (✉ Via delle Casaccie 3, Genoa, ☎ 010/564412; ✉ Via Casaregis 76/r, La Spezia, ☎ 010/592101; ✉ Via XX Settembre 17, San Remo, ☎ 0184/500470).

CAR TRAVEL

Autostrada A12 southeast from Genoa links up with the autostrada and superstrada network for all northern and southern destinations; Rome is a six-hour drive from Genoa. The 150-km (93-mi) trip north to Milan on A7 takes two hours. Nice is 2½ hours of tunnels west on A10.

Two good roads run parallel to each other along the coast of Liguria. Closer to shore and passing through all the towns and villages is the Via Aurelia, S1, which has excellent views at almost every turn but gets crowded in July and August. More direct and higher up than S1 is the autostrada, A10 west of Genoa and A12 to the east. This route saves a lot of time on weekends, in summer, and on days when festivals slow traffic in some resorts to a standstill. Any time of year, do your best to avoid driving in the center of Genoa.

EMERGENCY SERVICES

If you break down on the highway, walk along the side of the road until you come to a green emergency telephone. The emergency highway road service will come to your rescue and tow you to the nearest service station—for a hefty fee. On a smaller road, unless you have a cell phone, you'd be better off walking to the nearest town or gas station (not usually too far) and calling ACI Emergency Service (a free call) from any pay phone. In order to describe where you are, be prepared to seek out the help of locals. (*Dove siamo?*—Where are we?)

➤ Contacts: **ACI** (☎ 116).

EMBASSIES AND CONSULATES

➤ United Kingdom: **British Consulate** (✉ Piazza della Vittoria 15/16, 16121 Genoa, ☎ 010/564833; emergency mobile number 0337/305775, FAX 010/5531516).

EMERGENCIES

Europa and Ghersi are two late-night pharmacies in Genoa.

➤ Contacts: **Ambulance** (☎ 118). **Europa** (✉ Corso Europa 676, Genoa, ☎ 010/380239). **Genoa municipal police** (☎ 112). **Ghersi** (✉ Corte Lambruschini, Tower A, Genoa, ☎ 010/541661). **Ospedale Generale Regionale San Martino** (✉ Viale Benedetto XV, Genoa, ☎ 010/5551). **Police, doctor** (☎ 113).

MAIL AND SHIPPING

➤ Post Offices: **Genoa** (✉ Via Dante 4A/B, 16121, ☎ 010/5705913). **La Spezia** (✉ Piazza Verdi, 19121). **San Remo** (✉ Via Roma 156, 18038).

TOURS
BOAT TOURS
Informal harbor cruises or excursion cruises between coastal towns are scheduled and operated by the main ferry lines, but you can have as much fun—if not more—negotiating a price with a boat owner at one of the smaller ports. You're likely to get a boat operator with a rudimentary command of English at best. You can also take a boat tour of Genoa harbor. The tour costs 10,000 lire/€5.15, lasts about an hour, and includes a visit to the breakwater outside the harbor, the Bacino delle Grazie, and the Molo Vecchio (Old Port). For information, contact the Cooperativa Battellieri.

➤ FEES AND SCHEDULES: **Cooperativa Battellieri** (✉ Stazione Marittima, Ponte dei Mille, Genoa, ☎ 010/265712).

BUS TOURS
A bus tour of Genoa with an English-speaking guide is the good way to see the city and its panoramic upper reaches. A coach with a multilingual guide aboard leaves every day at 3 from Piazza Caricamento, by the port, and does the "Giro Giro Tour," a 1¾-hour narrated loop of the city, operated by Between Sea and Sky Tours, for 25,000 lire/€12.90. Call first to check times.

➤ FEES AND SCHEDULES: **Between Sea and Sky Tours** (☎ 010/2543431).

TRAIN TRAVEL
Frequent and fast train service connects Liguria with the rest of Italy. Genoa is 1½ hours from Milan and 5½–6 hours from Rome (4½ with the Eurostar). Many services from France (in particular, the French Riviera) pass along the Ligurian Coast on the way to all parts of Italy. Regular service, connecting all parts of Liguria, operates from Genoa's two stations, Stazione Principe and Stazione Brignole. All the coastal resorts are on this line, and many international trains stop along the coast west of Genoa on their way from Paris to Milan or Rome.

➤ TRAIN INFORMATION: **Stazione Brignole** (points east, ✉ Piazza Giuseppe Verdi, ☎ 147/888088 toll-free). **Stazione Principe** (points west, ✉ Piazza Principe, ☎ 147/888088 toll-free).

VISITOR INFORMATION
In summer, and sometimes in Easter, a provisional office is set up at the Terminale Crociere in Genoa, for the arrival of major ferries.

➤ TOURIST INFORMATION: **Genoa** (✉ Palazzina Santa Maria, Old Port, ☎ 010/248711; ✉ Stazione Principe, ☎ 010/2462633; ✉ Aeroporto Internazionale Cristoforo Colombo, ☎ 010/6015247; ✉ Via Roma 11, ☎ 010/576791). **Terminale Crociere** (☎ 010/6015247 or 010/2463686). **Alassio** (✉ Palazzo Hanbury, Via Gibb 26, 17021, ☎ 0182/647027). **Albenga** (✉ Via B. Ricci, corner of Piazza San Michele, 17031, ☎ 0182/559058). **Bordighera** (✉ Via Roberto 1, 18012, ☎ 0184/262322). **Camogli** (✉ Via XX Settembre 33, 16032, ☎ 0185/771066). **Imperia** (✉ Via Matteotti 54/a, 18100, ☎ 0183/294947). **La Spezia** (✉ Via Mazzini 47, 19100, ☎ 0187/770900). **Lerici** (✉ Via Biaggini 3, 19032, ☎ 0187/967346). **Levanto** (✉ Piazza Cavour 12, 19015, ☎ 0187/808125). **Monterosso** (✉ Via Fegina 38, 19016, ☎ 0187/817506). **Portofino** (✉ Via Roma 35, 16034, ☎ 0185/269024). **Rapallo** (✉ Lungomare V. Veneto 7, 16035, ☎ 0185/230346). **San Remo** (✉ Palazzo Riviera, Largo Nuvoloni 1, 18038, ☎ 0184/571571). **Santa Margherita Ligure** (✉ Via XXV Aprile 28, 16038, ☎ 0185/2929). **Varazze** (✉ Viale Nazioni Unite, 17019, ☎ 019/934609). **Ventimiglia** (✉ Via Cavour 61, 18039, ☎ 0184/351183).

7 FLORENCE

Florence, city of the lily, gave birth to the
Renaissance and changed the way we see
the world. For centuries its wondrous art has
captured the imagination of travelers, who
walk in the footsteps of native sons Dante,
Donatello, Botticelli, and Michelangelo;
a keystone of the Grand Tour in the 18th
century, it continues to exert the same
fascination today.

Updated by
Patricia Rucidlo

YOU CANNOT IMAGINE ANY SITUATION more agreeable than Florence," wrote the peripatetic Mary Wortley Montagu in 1740. This agreeable situation called Florence has captured the hearts and minds of just about every visitor who has ever made his or her way here. Florence (Firenze in Italian) casts a spell in the way that few cities can—perhaps because of its sublime art; perhaps because of the views at sunset over the Arno; perhaps because of the way Florentine food and wine delight the palate. Maybe it's because the city has not changed all that much since the 16th century. Though Florence was briefly the capital of a newly united Italy (1865–71), its place in the sun rests squarely on its illustrious, more distant past.

Though Florence can lay claim to a modest antique importance, it did not fully emerge into its own until the 11th century. In the early 1200s, Florence, like most of the rest of Italy, was rent by civic unrest. Two factions, the Guelphs and the Ghibellines, competed for power. The Guelphs supported the papacy, and the Ghibellines supported the Holy Roman Empire. Bloody battles—most notably the famous one at Montaperti in 1260—tore Florence and other Italian cities apart. Sometimes the Guelphs were in power and exiled the Ghibellines; at other times, the reverse was true. By the end of the 13th century the Guelphs ruled securely and Ghibellinism had been vanquished. This didn't end civic strife, however: the Guelphs split into the Whites and the Blacks for reasons still debated by historians. Dante, author of the *Divine Comedy,* was banished from Florence in 1301 because he was a White.

Local merchants had organized themselves into guilds by 1250, and in that year proclaimed themselves the *"primo popolo."* It was the first attempt at democratic, republican rule. Though the episode lasted only 10 years, it constituted a breakthrough in Western history. Such a daring stance by the merchant class can be attributed to its newfound power, as Florence was emerging as one of the economic powerhouses in 13th-century Europe. Florentines were papal bankers; they instituted the system of international letters of credit; and the gold florin became the international standard of currency. With this economic strength came a building boom. Public and private palaces, churches, and basilicas were built, enlarged, or restructured. Sculptors such as Donatello and Ghiberti were commissioned to decorate them; painters such as Giotto and Botticelli were commissioned to fresco their walls.

Though ostensibly a republic, Florence was blessed (or cursed, depending on point of view) with one very powerful family, the Medici, who came into power in the 1430s and became the de facto rulers of Florence for several hundred years. The Medici originally came from north of Florence, and it was not until the time of Cosimo Il Vecchio (1389–1464) that the family's foothold in Florence was securely established. Florence's golden age fell in the reign of his grandson Lorenzo de' Medici (1449–92). Lorenzo was not only an astute politician, he was also a highly educated man and a great patron of the arts. Called "Il Magnifico" (the Magnificent), he gathered around him poets, artists, philosophers, architects, and musicians and organized all manner of cultural events, festivals, and tournaments.

Lorenzo's son, Piero (1471–1503), proved inept at handling the city's affairs. He was run out of town in 1494, and Florence briefly enjoyed its status as a republic while dominated by the demagogic Dominican friar Girolamo Savonarola (1452–98). Savonarola preached against perceived pagan abuses and convinced his followers to destroy their books, art, women's wigs, and jewelry in public "bonfires of the vanities." Eventually, he so annoyed the pope that he was declared a heretic and hanged.

After a decade of internal unrest, the republic fell and the Medici were recalled to power. But even with the return of the Medici, Florence never regained its former prestige. By the 1530s all the major artistic talent had left the city—Michelangelo, for one, had settled in Rome. The now ineffectual Medici, eventually attaining the title of grand dukes, remained nominally in power until the line died out in 1737, after which time Florence passed from the Austrians to the French and back again until the unification of Italy (1865–70), when it briefly became the capital under King Vittorio Emanuele II (1820–78).

Florence was "discovered" in the 18th century by upper-class northerners making the grand tour. It became a mecca for travelers, particularly the Romantics, who were inspired by the elegance of its palazzi and its artistic wealth. Today, millions of modern visitors follow in their footsteps. As the sun sets over the Arno and, as Mark Twain described it, "overwhelms Florence with tides of color that make all the sharp lines dim and faint and turn the solid city to a city of dreams," it's hard not to fall under the city's magic spell.

Pleasures and Pastimes

Dining
Florentines are justifiably proud of their robust food. You can sample such specialties as creamy *fegatini* (a chicken-liver spread), and *ribollita* (minestrone thickened with bread and beans and swirled with extra-virgin olive oil) in bustling, convivial *trattorie,* where you share long wooden tables set with paper place mats. Like the Florentines, take a break at an *enoteca* (wineshop and/or wine bar) during the day and discover some little-known but excellent Chiantis and Super Tuscans.

For general information and price categories, *see* Dining *in* Smart Travel Tips.

Lodging
No stranger to visitors, Florence is equipped with hotels for all budgets, and they are found throughout the city; for instance, you can find both budget and luxury hotels in the *centro storico* (historic center) and along the Arno. Whether you are in a five-star hotel or a more modest establishment, you may have one of the greatest pleasures of all: a room with a view. Florence has so many famous landmarks that it's not hard to find lodgings with a panoramic vista. And the equivalent of the genteel pensioni of yesteryear still exist, though they are now officially classified as hotels. Usually small and intimate, they often have a quaint appeal that fortunately does not preclude modern plumbing.

For general information and price categories, *see* Lodging *in* Smart Travel Tips.

Shopping
Since the days of the medieval guilds, Florence has been synonymous with fine craftsmanship and good business. Such time-honored Florentine specialties as antiques (and reproductions), bookbinding, jewelry, lace, leather goods, silk, and straw attest to this. Lovely paper products are made here and sold all over town. The leather produced here is of especially good quality. Another medieval feature is the distinct feel of the different shopping areas, a throwback to the days when each district supplied a different product. During the Renaissance, the Oltrarno was the neighborhood where the artisans lived, and if you wander around there now you will notice that little has changed: there are still gold-

smiths, leather workers, and furniture restorers, among others, plying their trade.

EXPLORING FLORENCE

Sightseeing in Florence is space-intensive. It's likely that everything you want to see is concentrated in the relatively small historic center of the city. But there is so much packed into the area that you may find yourself slogging from one mind-boggling sight to another and feeling overwhelmed. If you are not an inveterate museum enthusiast, take it easy. Don't try to absorb every painting or fresco that comes into view. There is second-rate art even in the Galleria degli Uffizi and the Palazzo Pitti (*especially* the Pitti), so find some favorites and enjoy them at your leisure. A special museum ticket valid for three days on the Michelangelo trail includes the Galleria dell'Accademia, Cappelle Medicee, and the Museo del Bargello; it costs 25,000 lire/€12.90.

Walking through the streets and alleyways in Florence is a discovery in itself, but to save time and energy (especially after a few days in the city), make use of the efficient bus system. Buses also provide the least-fatiguing way to reach Piazzale Michelangelo, San Miniato, and the Forte di Belvedere. It is easy to make excursions to, say, Fiesole or the Medici villas by city bus. Most churches are usually open from 8 or 9 until noon or 12:30 and from 3 or 4 until about 6. The Duomo, luckily, has continuous hours.

In between your blitzes into the Renaissance and beyond, stop to breathe in the city, the marvelous synergy between history and modern Florentine life. Firenze is a living, bustling metropolis that has managed to preserve its predominantly medieval street plan and mostly Renaissance infrastructure while successfully adapting to the insistent demands of 21st-century life. During the 12th and 13th centuries, Florence, like most other Italian towns, was a forest of towers—more than 200 of them, if the smaller three- and four-story towers are included. Today only a handful survive, but if you look closely you'll find them as you explore the *centro storico* (historic center).

Numbers in the text correspond to numbers in the margin and on the Florence map.

Great Itineraries

You can see most of Florence's outstanding sights in three days. Plan your day around the opening hours of museums and churches; to gain an edge on the tour groups in high season, go very early in the morning or around closing time. If you can, allow a day to explore each neighborhood.

IF YOU HAVE 3 DAYS

Spend day one exploring Florence's centro storico, which will give you an eyeful of such masterpieces as Ghiberti's renowned bronze doors at the Battistero, Giotto's Campanile, Brunelleschi's cupola majestically poised atop the Duomo, and Botticelli's mystical *Primavera* and *Birth of Venus* at the Galleria degli Uffizi. On day two, wander north of the Duomo and take in the superb treasury of works ranging from Michelangelo's *David* at the Galleria dell'Accademia to the lavish frescoes at the Cappella dei Magi and the Museo di San Marco (don't miss San Lorenzo, Michelangelo's Biblioteca Medicea Laurenziana, and the Cappelle Medicee). On this afternoon (or on the afternoon of day three) head southeast to Santa Croce or west to Santa Maria Novella. On the third day, cross the Ponte Vecchio to the Arno's southern bank and explore the Oltrarno, being sure not to miss the Brunelleschi-designed church of Santo Spirito, Masaccio's frescoes in the church of Santa Maria del Carmine, and the colorful and lively local atmosphere.

Break down the tours in the above itinerary into shorter ones, adding a few sights such as Piazzale Michelangelo, halfway up a hill on the Arno's southern bank, and San Miniato—both with expansive views of the city that are yours to savor. Climb Giotto's Campanile (bell tower), which rewards you with sweeping views of the city and hills beyond. If you're feeling even more adventurous, climb the narrow, twisting stairs to the top of the Duomo. Take Bus 7 from the station or Piazza del Duomo to enchanting Fiesole. Spend more time in the Galleria degli Uffizi and Bargello or at one of the smaller museums such as the Museo dell'Opificio delle Pietre Dure, around the corner from the Galleria dell'Accademia. The little-visited but nevertheless wonderful Museo di Storia della Scienza is worth a trip, as is the Museo di Santa Maria Novella.

Add an all-day excursion south to the Tuscan city of Siena or a couple of half-day trips to the Medici villas around Florence. Visit more of Florence's interesting smaller churches; there's a dazzling fresco by Perguino at Santa Maria Maddalena dei Pazzi and a brilliant Pontormo in the Oltrarno's Santa Felicita. On the trail of additional and lesser-known artistic gems, check out Andrea del Castagno's fresco of the *Last Supper* in the former refectory at Sant'Apollonia, northwest of the Museo di San Marco. It's worth the trip to see Andrea del Sarto's stunning grisaille frescoes in the Chiostro dello Scalzo, just north of the Museo di San Marco. The church of Santo Spirito, west of Piazza Pitti, is a fine example of 15th-century architectural rationalism.

Centro Storico: From the Duomo to the Ponte Vecchio

Florence's centro storico, stretching from the Piazza del Duomo south to the Arno, is just possibly one of the most beautiful spots in the world. Indeed, this relatively small area is home to some very powerful artistic treasures. This smorgasbord of churches, medieval towers, Renaissance palaces, and world-class museums and galleries is not only testimony to the artistic and architectural genius of the past millennium but also a shrine to some of the most outstanding aesthetic achievements of Western history.

A Good Walk

Start at the **Duomo** ① and **Battistero** ②, climbing the **Campanile** ③ if you wish, and then visit the **Museo dell'Opera del Duomo** ④, behind the Duomo. You can go directly south from the Duomo to the Piazza della Signoria by way of Via dei Calzaiuoli. From here you can take a quick detour west on Via degli Speziali to **Piazza della Repubblica** ⑤ and take Via Orsanmichele to **Orsanmichele** ⑥ or instead go directly south from the Museo dell'Opera del Duomo along Via del Proconsolo to the **Bargello** ⑦, opposite the ancient **Badia Fiorentina** ⑧, restructured in 1285. Head west on Via della Condotta to Via Calzaiuoli, then south to discover the oddly shaped **Piazza della Signoria** ⑨, with its Loggia dei Lanzi and **Palazzo Vecchio** ⑩. The **Galleria degli Uffizi** ⑪, perhaps Italy's most important art gallery, is at the south side of the piazza. Exit from the piazza's southwest corner along Via Vaccereccia. To the left, at the corner of Via Por Santa Maria, lined with stores, is the **Mercato Nuovo** ⑫. Follow Via Por Santa Maria to the river; walk east along the north side of the Arno to Piazza dei Giudici to see the **Museo di Storia della Scienza** ⑬. Backtrack west along the Arno to the **Ponte Vecchio** ⑭.

274

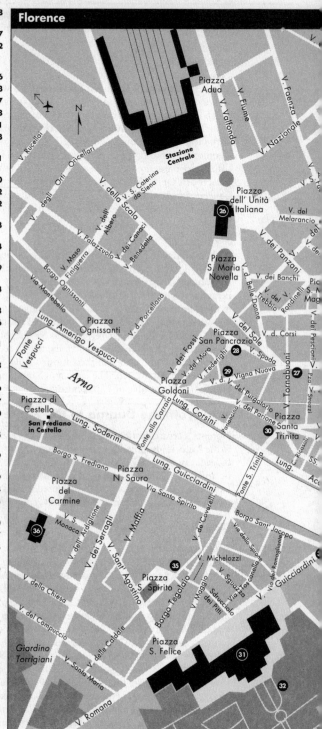

Florence

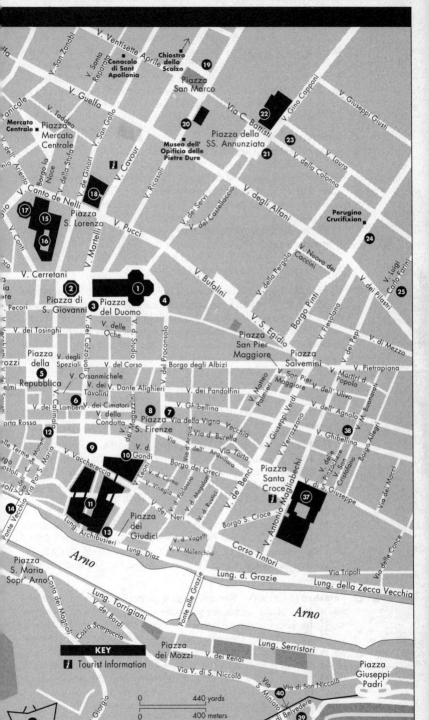

V. Zanobi

V. Ventisette Aprile

V. Santa
Reparata

**Cenacolo
di Sant
Apollonia**

**Chiostro
dello
Scalzo**

⑲

V. San Gallo

Piazza
San Marco

V. C. Battisti

V. Gino Capponi

V. Giuseppi Giusti

Via C. Battisti

㉒

㉓

V. Guelfa

V. Toddeo

**Mercato
Centrale**

Piazza
Mercato
Centrale

⑳

Museo dell'
Opificio delle
Pietre Dure

Piazza della
SS. Annunziata

㉑

V. della Colonna

V. Laura

Borgo la
Noce

V. della Stufa

V. de Ginori

V. Cavour

V. R.Ricasoli

V. dei Servi

V. degli Alfani

V. Canto de Nelli

⑰

⑮

⑱

Piazza
S. Lorenzo

V. Martelli

V. Pucci

V. dei Castellaccio

**Perugino
Crucifixion**

V. Nuova dei

㉔

⑯

V. Conti

V. Bufalini

V. Cerretani

②

①

④

Pecori

Piazza di
S. Giovanni

③

Piazza
del Duomo

V. dei Calzaiouli

V. d. Studio

V. delle
Oche

V. del Proconsolo

Piazza
San Pier
Maggiore

V. S. Egidio

Borgo Pinti

V. Fiesolana

V. della Pergola Caccini

V. Luigi
Carlo Farini

㉕

V. dei Pilastri

V. dei Tosinghi

Piazza
della
Repubblica

⑤

V. degli
Speziali

V. Orsanmichele

V. del Corso

Borgo degli Albizi

V. dei Pandolfini

Piazza
Salvemini

V. San Pier
Maggiore

V. Matteo
Palmieri

V. dell' Ulivo

V. dei Pepi

V. di Mezzo

V. Pietrapiana

V. Martiri d.
Popolo

V. dei Calimala

V. dei Lamberti

V. dei Cimatori

V. Tavolini

V. dei Dante Alighieri

V. della
Condotta

⑥

V. Ghibellina

Via della Vigna Vecchia

⑧

⑦

Piazza
S. Firenze

V. Giuseppi Verdi

V. dell' Agnolo

V. M. Buonarroti

V. Ghibellina

㊳

orta Rossa

⑫

V. Vacchereccia

⑨

V. d.
Gondi

⑩

V. Leoni

V. d'Acqua

V. d.
dell' Anguillara

Via Torta

V. d. Burella

V. Verrazzano

V. Pinzochere

V. dalle

V. Sdr

Piazza
Santa
Croce

㊲

V. di S. Giuseppe

Cristofano Borgo Allegri

Via dei Macci

⑭

Ponte Vecchio

⑪

⑬

Lung. Archibusieri

Piazza
dei
Giudici

V. d. Corno

V. Vinegia

V. d. Magliabecchi

V. de' Benci

Corso S. Croce

V. Antonio Magliabechi

V. d. Neri

V. d. Rustici

V. d. Vagelli

V. V. Malenchini

Corso Tintori

Via delle Conce

Arno

Lung. Diaz

Lung. d. Grazie

Via Tripoli

Lung. della Zecca Vecchia

Piazza
S. Maria
Sopr' Arno

Costa dei Magnoli

Lung. Torrigiani

V. dei Bardi

Costa Scarpuccia

Ponte alle Grazie

Arno

Lung. Serristori

Piazza
dei Mozzi

V. dei Renai

Piazza
Giuseppi
Padri

KEY

ℹ Tourist Information

S. Giorgio

Via V. di S. Niccolò

Via
S. Minio

Via di San Niccolò

⓪40

0   440 yards

0   400 meters

㉝

V. di Belvedere

㊴

Though much of the Florence's centro storico is closed to traffic, you still must dodge mopeds, cyclists, and masses of fellow tourists as you walk the narrow streets, especially in the area bounded by the Duomo, Piazza Signoria, Galleria degli Uffizi, and Ponte Vecchio. It takes about 40 minutes to walk the route, with 45 minutes to 1 hour each for the Museo dell'Opera del Duomo and the Palazzo della Signoria; 1 to 1½ hours for the Bargello; and a minimum of 2 hours for the Uffizi (reserve tickets in advance to avoid long lines).

Sights to See

❽ Badia Fiorentina. This ancient church was rebuilt in 1285; its graceful bell tower, best seen from the interior courtyard, is beautiful for its unusual construction—a hexagonal tower built on a quadrangular base. The interior of the church proper was halfheartedly remodeled in the Baroque style during the 17th century; its best-known work of art is the delicate *Vision of St. Bernard* by Filippino Lippi (1448/57–1504), on the left as you enter. The painting—one of Lippi's finest—is in superb condition; take a look at the Virgin Mary's hands, perhaps the most beautifully rendered in the city. ⊠ *Via Dante Alighieri 4,* ☎ *055/283451.* ▣ *Free.* ⊙ *Mon. 3–6.*

★ ❼ Bargello. During the Renaissance, this building served as the headquarters for the *podestà,* or chief magistrate. It was also used as a prison, and the exterior served as a "most wanted" billboard: effigies of notorious criminals and Medici enemies were painted on its walls. Today, it houses the **Museo Nazionale,** home to what is probably the finest collection of Renaissance sculpture in Italy. The concentration of masterworks by Michelangelo (1475–1564), Donatello (circa 1386–1466), and Benvenuto Cellini (1500–71) is remarkable, though they're distributed among an eclectic array of arms, ceramics, and enamels. For Renaissance art lovers, the Bargello is to sculpture what the Uffizi is to painting.

In 1401 Filippo Brunelleschi (1377–1446) and Lorenzo Ghiberti (circa 1378–1455) vied for the most prestigious commission of the day: the decoration of the north doors of the baptistery in Piazza del Duomo. For the competition, each designed a bronze bas-relief panel depicting the Sacrifice of Isaac; both panels are displayed, together, in the room devoted to the sculpture of Donatello on the upper floor. The judges chose Ghiberti for the commission; you can decide for yourself whether they were right. ⊠ *Via del Proconsolo 4,* ☎ *055/2388606,* 🕸 *www. arca.net/db/musei/bargello.htm.* ▣ *8,000 lire/€4.10.* ⊙ *Daily 8:30–1:50. Closed 2nd and 4th Mon. of month and 1st, 3rd, and 5th Sun. of month.*

★ ❷ Battistero (Baptistery). The octagonal Baptistery is one of the supreme monuments of the Italian Romanesque and one of Florence's oldest structures. Local legend has it that it was once a Roman temple of Mars; modern excavations, however, suggest that its foundations date from the 4th to 5th and the 8th to 9th centuries AD, well after the collapse of the Roman Empire. The round-arched Romanesque decoration on the exterior probably dates from the 11th century. The interior dome mosaics from the beginning of the 14th century are justly famous, but—glitteringly beautiful as they are—they could never outshine the building's most renowned feature: its bronze Renaissance doors decorated with panels crafted by Lorenzo Ghiberti. The doors—or at least copies of them—on which Ghiberti spent most of his adult life (1403–52) are on the north and east sides of the baptistery, and the Gothic panels on the south door were designed by Andrea Pisano (active circa 1290–1348) in 1330. The original Ghiberti doors were removed to protect them from the effects of pollution and acid rain and have been beautifully restored; some of the panels are now on display in the Museo dell'Opera del Duomo.

Ghiberti's north doors depict scenes from the *Life of Christ*; his later east doors (dating from 1425–52), facing the Duomo facade, render scenes from the Old Testament. They merit close examination, for they are very different in style and illustrate the artistic changes that marked the beginning of the Renaissance. Look at the far right panel of the middle row on the earlier (1403–24) north doors (*Jesus Calming the Waters*). Ghiberti here captured the chaos of a storm at sea with great skill and economy, but the artistic conventions he used are basically pre-Renaissance: Jesus is the most important figure, so he is the largest; the disciples are next in size, being next in importance; the ship on which they founder looks like a mere toy.

The exquisitely rendered panels on the east doors are larger, more expansive, more sweeping—and more convincing. Look at the middle panel on the left-hand door. It tells the story of *Jacob and Esau,* and the various episodes of the story—the selling of the birthright, Isaac ordering Esau to go hunting, the blessing of Jacob, and so forth—have been merged into a single beautifully realized street scene. Ghiberti's use of perspective suggests depth: the background architecture looks far more credible than on the north door panels, the figures in the foreground are grouped realistically, and the naturalism and grace of the poses (look at Esau's left leg and the dog next to him) have nothing to do with the sacred message being conveyed. Although the religious content remains, the figures and their place in the natural world are given new prominence and are portrayed with a realism not seen in art since the fall of the Roman Empire, more than a thousand years before.

As a footnote to Ghiberti's panels, one small detail of the east doors is worth a special look. Just to the lower left of the Jacob and Esau panel, Ghiberti placed a tiny self-portrait bust. From either side, the portrait is extremely appealing—Ghiberti looks like everyone's favorite uncle—but the bust is carefully placed so that there is a single spot from which you can make direct eye contact with the tiny head. When that contact is made, the impression of intelligent life—of *modern* intelligent life—is astonishing. It is no wonder that these doors received one of the most famous compliments in the history of art from an artist known to be notoriously stingy with praise: Michelangelo himself declared them so beautiful that they could serve as the Gates of Paradise. ✉ *Piazza del Duomo,* ☎ *055/2302885,* WEB *www.operaduomo.firenze.it.* ⊠ *5,000 lire/€2.60.* ⊘ *Mon.–Sat. 12:30–6:30, Sun. 8:30–1:30.*

❸ Campanile. The Gothic bell tower designed by Giotto (1266–1337) is a soaring structure of multicolored marble originally decorated with reliefs that are now in the Museo dell'Opera del Duomo. A climb of 414 steps rewards you with a close-up of Brunelleschi's cupola on the Duomo next door and a sweeping view of the city. ✉ *Piazza del Duomo,* ☎ *055/2302885,* WEB *www.operaduomo.firenze.it.* ⊠ *10,000 lire/€5.15.* ⊘ *Apr.–Oct., daily 9–7:30; Nov.–Mar., daily 9–6:50.*

★ ❶ Duomo (Cattedrale di Santa Maria del Fiore). In 1296 Arnolfo di Cambio (circa 1245–1302) was commissioned to build "the loftiest, most sumptuous edifice human invention could devise" in the Romanesque style on the site of the old church of Santa Reparata. The immense Duomo was not completed until 1436, the year when it was consecrated. The imposing facade dates only from the 19th century; it was added in the neo-Gothic style to complement Giotto's genuine Gothic 14th-century campanile. The real glory of the Duomo, however, is Filippo Brunelleschi's dome, presiding over the cathedral with a dignity and grace that few domes to this day can match.

Brunelleschi's **cupola** was an ingenious engineering feat. The space to be enclosed by the dome was so large and so high above the ground that traditional methods of dome construction—wooden centering and scaffolding—were of no use whatever. So Brunelleschi developed entirely new building methods, which he implemented with equipment of his own design (including a novel scaffolding method). Beginning work in 1420, he built not one dome but two, one inside the other, and connected them with common ribbing that stretched across the intervening empty space, thereby considerably lessening the crushing weight of the structure. He also employed a new method of bricklaying, based on an ancient Roman herringbone pattern, interlocking each new course of bricks with the course below in a way that made the growing structure self-supporting. The result was one of the great engineering breakthroughs of all time: most of Europe's later domes, including St. Peter's in Rome, were built employing Brunelleschi's methods, and today the Duomo has come to symbolize Florence in the same way that the Eiffel Tower symbolizes Paris. The Florentines are justly proud, and to this day the Florentine phrase for "homesick" is *nostalgia del cupolone* (homesick for the dome).

The interior is a fine example of Florentine Gothic. Much of the cathedral's best-known art has been moved to the nearby Museo dell'Opera del Duomo. Notable among the works that remain, however, are two towering equestrian frescoes honoring famous soldiers: *Niccolò da Tolentino,* painted in 1456 by Andrea del Castagno (circa 1419–57), and *Sir John Hawkwood,* painted 20 years earlier by Paolo Uccello (1397–1475); both are on the left-hand wall of the nave. Restorers worked from 1983 to 1995 to repair the structure of Brunelleschi's dome and clean the vast and crowded fresco of the *Last Judgment,* painted by Vasari and Zuccaro, on its interior. Originally Brunelleschi wanted mosaics to cover the interior of the great ribbed cupola, but by the time the Florentines got around to commissioning the decoration, 150 years later, tastes had changed. Too bad: it's a fairly dreadful *Last Judgment* and hardly worth the effort of craning your neck to see it.

You can explore the upper and lower reaches of the cathedral. The remains of a Roman wall and an 11th-century cemetery have been excavated beneath the nave; the stairway down is near the first pier on the right. The climb to the top of the dome (463 steps) is not for the faint of heart, but the view is superb. ⊠ *Piazza del Duomo,* ☎ *055/ 2302885,* WEB *www.operaduomo.firenze.it.* 🔛 *Excavation 5,000 lire/€2.60, Duomo 10,000 lire/€5.15.* ◷ *Mon.–Sat. 10–5 (1st Sat. of month 10–3:30), Sun. 1:30–5. Crypt Mon.–Sat. 10–5, Duomo Mon.– Sat. 8:30–6:20 (1st Sat. of month 8:30–3:20).*

★ ⓫ **Galleria degli Uffizi.** The venerable Uffizi Gallery occupies the top floor of the U-shape **Palazzo degli Uffizi** (Uffizi Palace) fronting on the Arno, designed by Giorgio Vasari (1511–74) in 1560 to hold the *uffizi* (administrative offices) of the Medici grand duke Cosimo I (1519–74). Later, the Medici installed their art collections here, creating what was Europe's first modern museum, open to the public (at first only by request, of course) since 1591. If you're a hard-core museum aficionado, you might want to pick up a complete guide to the collections, sold in bookshops and on newsstands.

Among the collection's highlights are Paolo Uccello's *Battle of San Romano,* its brutal chaos of lances one of the finest visual metaphors for warfare ever captured in paint; the *Madonna and Child with Two An-*

gels, by Fra Filippo Lippi (1406–69), in which the impudent eye contact established by the angel would have been unthinkable prior to the Renaissance; the *Birth of Venus* and *Primavera* by Sandro Botticelli (1445–1510), the goddess of the former seeming to float on air and the fairy-tale charm of the latter exhibiting the painter's idiosyncratic genius at its zenith; the portraits of the Renaissance duke Federico da Montefeltro and his wife Battista Sforza by Piero della Francesca (circa 1420–92); the *Madonna of the Goldfinch,* by Raphael (1483–1520), which though darkened by time captures an aching tenderness between mother and child; Michelangelo's *Doni Tondo* (the only panel painting that can be securely attributed to him); a *Self-Portrait as an Old Man* by Rembrandt (1606–69); the *Venus of Urbino* by Titian (circa 1485–1576); and the splendid *Bacchus* by Caravaggio (circa 1571/72–1610). In the the last two works, both very great paintings, the approaches to myth and sexuality are diametrically opposed, to put it mildly. If panic sets in at the prospect of absorbing all this art at one go, bear in mind that in the summer the Uffizi is open late, except on Sunday, and isn't usually crowded in the late afternoon. The coffee bar inside has a terrace with a fine close-up view of Palazzo Vecchio. Advance tickets can be purchased from Consorzio ITA. ✉ *Piazzale degli Uffizi 6,* ☎ *055/23885. Advance tickets:* ✉ *Consorzio ITA, Piazza Pitti 1, 50121,* ☎ *055/294883,* WEB *www.uffizi.firenze.it.* 🎫 *15,000 lire/€7.75 (3,000 lire/€1.55 reservation fee).* ⊙ *Apr.–Oct., Tues.–Sat. 8:30 AM–10 PM, Sun. 8:30–6; Nov.–Mar., Tues.–Sat. 8:30–6:50, Sun. 8:30–7.*

⑫ **Mercato Nuovo** (New Market). This open-air loggia was new in 1551. Beyond its slew of souvenir stands, its main attraction is a copy of Pietro Tacca's bronze *Porcellino* (Little Pig) fountain on the south side, dating from around 1612 and copied from an earlier Roman work now in the Uffizi. The Porcellino is Florence's equivalent of the Trevi Fountain: put a coin in his mouth, and if it lands properly, it means that one day you'll return to Florence. ✉ *Corner of Via Por Santa Maria and Via Porta Rossa.* ⊙ *Market Tues.–Sat. 8–7, Mon. 1–7.*

★ ④ **Museo dell'Opera del Duomo** (Cathedral Museum). Ghiberti's original Baptistery door panels and the *cantorie* (choir loft) reliefs by Donatello and Luca della Robbia (1400–82) keep company with Donatello's *Mary Magdalen* and Michelangelo's *Pietà* (not to be confused with his more famous *Pietà* in St. Peter's in Rome). Renaissance sculpture is in part defined by its revolutionary realism, but in its palpable suffering, Donatello's *Magdalen* goes beyond realism. Michelangelo's heartwrenching *Pietà* was unfinished at his death; the female figure supporting the body of Christ on the left was added by one Tiberio Calcagni (1532–65), and never has the difference between competence and genius been manifested so clearly. ✉ *Piazza del Duomo 9,* ☎ *055/2302885,* WEB *www.operaduomo.firenze.it.* 🎫 *10,000 lire/€5.15.* ⊙ *Mon.–Sat. 9:30–6:30, Sun. 8–2.*

⑬ **Museo di Storia della Scienza** (Museum of the History of Science). Though it tends to be obscured by the glamour of the neighboring Uffizi, this science museum has much to recommend it: Galileo's own instruments, a collection of antique armillary spheres, some of them real works of art, and a host of other reminders that the Renaissance made not only artistic but also scientific history. ✉ *Piazza dei Giudici 1,* ☎ *055/2398876 museum; 055/293493 planetarium,* WEB *www.imss.fi.it.* 🎫 *12,000 lire/€6.20.* ⊙ *Oct.–May, Mon. and Wed.–Sat. 9:30–5, Tues. 9:30–1, 2nd Sun. of the month 10–1; June–Sept., Mon. and Wed.–Fri. 9:30–5, Tues. and Sat. 9:30–1.*

⑥ **Orsanmichele.** This multipurpose structure began as an 8th-century oratory and then in 1290 was turned into an open-air loggia for selling grain. Destroyed by fire in 1304, it was rebuilt as a loggia-market. Between 1367 and 1380 the arcades were closed and two stories added above; finally, at century's end it was turned into a church. Inside is a beautifully detailed 14th-century Gothic tabernacle by Andrea Orcagna (1308–68). The exterior niches contain sculptures dating from the early 1400s to the early 1600s by Donatello and Verrocchio (1435–88), among others, that were paid for by the guilds. Though it is a copy, Verrocchio's *Doubting Thomas* (circa 1470) is particularly deserving of attention. Here you see Christ, like the building's other figures, entirely framed within the niche, and St. Thomas standing on its bottom ledge, with his right foot outside the niche frame. This one detail, the positioning of a single foot, brings the whole composition to life. Most of the sculptures have since been replaced by copies; however, it's possible to see most of them at the Museo di Orsanmichele contained within. ⊠ *Via dei Calzaiuoli; museum entrance at via Arte della Lana,* ☎ *055/ 284944.* ☉ *Daily 9–noon and 4–6; guided visits weekdays at 9, 10, and 11. Closed 1st and last Mon. of month.*

❿ **Palazzo Vecchio** (Old Palace). Florence's forbidding, fortresslike city hall was begun in 1299, presumably designed by Arnolfo di Cambio, and its massive bulk and towering campanile dominate the Piazza della Signoria. It was built as a meeting place for the heads of the seven major guilds that governed the city at the time; over the centuries it has served lesser purposes, but today it is once again City Hall. The interior courtyard is a good deal less severe, having been remodeled by Michelozzo (1396–1472) in 1453; the copy of Verrocchio's bronze *puttino* (little child), topping the central fountain, softens the space.

The main attraction is on the second floor: two adjoining rooms that supply one of the most startling contrasts in Florence. The first is the vast **Sala dei Cinquecento** (Room of the Five Hundred), named for the 500-member Great Council, the people's assembly established by Savonarola, that met here. The Sala was decorated by Giorgio Vasari, around 1563–65, with huge—almost grotesquely huge—frescoes celebrating Florentine history; depictions of battles with nearby cities predominate. Continuing the martial theme, the Sala also contains Michelangelo's *Victory* group, intended for the never-completed tomb of Pope Julius II (1443–1513), plus other sculptures of decidedly lesser quality.

The second room is the little **Studiolo,** to the right of the Sala's entrance. The study of Cosimo I's son, the melancholy Francesco I (1541–87), it was designed by Vasari and decorated by Vasari and Bronzino (1503–72). It is intimate, civilized, and filled with complex allegorical art. It makes the vainglorious proclamations next door ring more than a little hollow. ⊠ *Piazza della Signoria,* ☎ *055/2768465.* ✑ *15,000 lire/€7.75.* ☉ *Mon.–Wed. and Fri.–Sat. 9–7, Thurs. and Sun. 9–2.*

❺ **Piazza della Repubblica.** This square marks the site of the ancient forum that was the core of the original Roman settlement. The street plan in the area around the piazza still reflects the carefully plotted grid of the Roman military encampment. The Mercato Vecchio (Old Market), located here since the Middle Ages, was demolished and the current piazza was constructed between 1885 and 1895 as a neoclassical showpiece. The piazza is lined with outdoor cafés affording an excellent opportunity for people-watching.

★ ❾ **Piazza della Signoria.** This is by far the most striking square in Florence. It was here, in 1497, that the famous "bonfire of the vanities" took place, when the fanatical friar Savonarola induced his followers to hurl their worldly goods into the flames; it was also here, a year later, that he was hanged as a heretic and, ironically, burned. A bronze plaque in the pavement marks the exact spot of his execution.

The statues in the square and in the 14th-century **Loggia dei Lanzi** on the south side vary in quality. Cellini's famous bronze *Perseus* has recently returned after a painstaking restoration. Other works in the loggia include *The Rape of the Sabine* and *Hercules and the Centaur,* both late 16th-century works by Giambologna (1529–1608), and, in the back, a row of sober matrons that date from Roman times.

In the square, the Neptune Fountain, dating from between 1550 and 1575, takes something of a booby prize. It was created by Bartolomeo Ammannati, who considered it a failure himself. The Florentines call it *Il Biancone,* which may be translated as "the big white man" or "the big white lump." Giambologna's equestrian statue, to the left of the fountain, pays tribute to Grand Duke Cosimo I. Occupying the steps of the Palazzo Vecchio are a copy of Donatello's proud heraldic lion of Florence, known as the *Marzocco* (the original is now in the Bargello); a copy of Donatello's *Judith and Holofernes* (the original is inside the Palazzo Vecchio); a copy of Michelangelo's *David* (the original is now in the Galleria dell'Accademia); and Baccio Bandinelli's *Hercules* (1534).

★ ⑭ **Ponte Vecchio** (Old Bridge). This charmingly simple bridge is to Florence what the Tower Bridge is to London. It was built in 1345 to replace an earlier bridge that was swept away by flood, and its shops housed first butchers, then grocers, blacksmiths, and other merchants. But in 1593 the Medici grand duke Ferdinand I (1549–1609), whose private corridor linking the Medici palace (Palazzo Pitti) with the Medici offices (the Uffizi) crossed the bridge atop the shops, decided that all this plebeian commerce under his feet was unseemly. So he threw out all the butchers and blacksmiths and installed 41 goldsmiths and eight jewelers. The bridge has been devoted solely to these two trades ever since.

Take a moment to study the **Ponte Santa Trinita,** the next bridge downriver. It was designed by Bartolomeo Ammannati in 1567 (possibly from sketches by Michelangelo), blown up by the retreating Germans during World War II, and painstakingly reconstructed after the war. The view is beautiful from this bridge, which might explain why so many young lovers seem to hang out here.

Michelangelo Country: From San Lorenzo to the Accademia

Sculptor, painter, architect, and, yes, even poet, native son Michelangelo was a consummate genius. Some of his finest work remains in his hometown. The Biblioteca Medicea Laurenziana is perhaps his most fanciful work of architecture. The key to understanding Michelangelo's genius is in the magnificent Cappelle Medicee, where his sculptural and architectural prowess can be clearly seen. Planned frescoes were never completed, unfortunately, for they would have shown in one space the artistic triple threat that he certainly was. The towering and beautiful *David,* his most famous work, resides in the Galleria dell'Accademia.

A Good Walk

Start at the church of **San Lorenzo** ⑮, visiting the **Biblioteca Medicea Laurenziana** ⑯ and its famous anteroom before circling the church to the northwest and making your way through the San Lorenzo outdoor market on Via del Canto de' Nelli to the entrance of the **Cappelle Medicee** ⑰. Retrace your steps through the market and take Via dei Gori east to Via Cavour and the **Palazzo Medici-Riccardi** ⑱, once the home of Florence's most important family throughout the Renaissance. Follow Via Cavour two blocks north to Piazza San Marco and the church of the same name, attached to which is the **Museo di San Marco** ⑲, which houses marvelous works by the pious and exceptionally talented painter-friar Fra Angelico. If you have time, go northwest from Piazza San Marco to see Castagno's *Last Supper* at Sant'Apollonia and then north to the Chiostro dello Scalzo. From Piazza San Marco, walk a half block south down Via Ricasoli to the **Galleria dell'Accademia** ⑳. Return to the east side of Piazza San Marco and take Via Cesare Battisti east into Piazza della Santissima Annunziata, one of Florence's prettiest squares, site of the **Ospedale degli Innocenti** ㉑ and, at the north end of the square, the church of **Santissima Annunziata** ㉒. One block southeast of the entrance to Santissima Annunziata, through the arch and on the left side of Via della Colonna, is the **Museo Archeologico** ㉓. Continue down Via della Colonna to **Santa Maria Maddalena dei Pazzi** ㉔, harboring a superb fresco by Perugino. Return to Via della Colonna and continue heading southeast; take a right on Via Luigi Carlo Farini, where you'll find the **Sinagoga** ㉕ and its Museo Ebraico. If it's lunchtime, consider ending your tour with a Mediterranean-kosher meal at Ruth's.

TIMING

The walk alone takes about one hour, plus 45 minutes for the Cappelle Medicee, 20 minutes for the Palazzo Medici-Riccardi, 40 minutes for the Museo di San Marco, 30 minutes for the Galleria dell'Accademia (*David*), and 40 minutes for the Museo Archeologico. Note that the Museo di San Marco closes at 1:50 on weekdays. After visiting San Lorenzo, resist the temptation to explore the market that surrounds the church before going to the Palazzo Medici-Riccardi; you can always come back later, when the churches and museums have closed; the market is open until 7 PM.

Sights to See

⑯ **Biblioteca Medicea Laurenziana** (Laurentian Library). Michelangelo the architect was every bit as original as Michelangelo the sculptor. Unlike Brunelleschi (the architect of San Lorenzo), however, he was not obsessed with proportion and perfect geometry. He was interested in experimentation and invention and in expressing a personal vision at times highly idiosyncratic.

It was never more idiosyncratic than in the Laurentian Library, begun in 1524 and finished in 1568, and its famous **vestibolo** (anteroom). This strangely shaped anteroom has had scholars scratching their heads for centuries. In a space more than two stories high, why did Michelangelo limit his use of columns and pilasters to the upper two-thirds of the wall? Why didn't he rest them on strong pedestals instead of on huge, decorative curlicue scrolls, which rob them of all visual support? Why did he recess them into the wall, which makes them look weaker still? The architectural elements here do not stand firm and strong and tall, as inside the church next door; instead, they seem to be pressed into the wall as if into putty, giving the room a soft, rubbery look that is one of the strangest effects ever achieved by classical architecture. It is almost as if Michelangelo purposely set out to defy his predecessors, intentionally flouting the conventions of the High Renaissance in order to see what kind of bizarre, mannered effect might result. His innovations were tremendously influential and produced a period of architectural experimentation, known as Mannerism, that eventually evolved into the Baroque. As his contemporary Giorgio Vasari put it, "Artisans have been infinitely and perpetually indebted to him because he broke the bonds and chains of a way of working that had become habitual by common usage."

Nobody has ever complained about the anteroom's staircase (best viewed head-on), which emerges from the library with the visual force of an unstoppable lava flow. In its highly sculptural conception and execution, it is quite simply one of the most original and fluid staircases in the world. ⊠ *Piazza San Lorenzo 9, entrance to the left of San Lorenzo,* ☎ *055/213440.* ▨ *Free.* ⊙ *Mon.–Sat. 9–1.*

★ ⑰ **Cappelle Medicee** (Medici Chapels). This magnificent complex includes the **Cappella dei Principi,** the Medici chapel and mausoleum that was begun in 1605 and kept marble workers busy for several hundred years, and the **Sagrestia Nuova** (New Sacristy), designed by Michelangelo and so called to distinguish it from Brunelleschi's Sagrestia Vecchia (Old Sacristy).

Michelangelo received the commission for the New Sacristy in 1520 from Cardinal Giulio de' Medici (1478–1534), who later became Pope Clement VII and who wanted a new burial chapel for his father, Giuliano (1478–1534), his uncle Lorenzo the Magnificent, and two recently deceased cousins. The result was a tour de force of architecture and sculpture. Architecturally, Michelangelo was as original and inventive here as ever, but it is, quite properly, the powerful sculptural compositions of the side-wall tombs that dominate the room. The scheme is allegorical: on the wall tomb to the right are figures representing Day and Night, and on the wall tomb to the left are figures representing Dawn and Dusk; above them are idealized sculptures of the two men, usually interpreted to represent the active life and the contemplative life. But the allegorical meanings are secondary; what is most important is the intense presence of the sculptural figures, the force with which they hit the viewer. Michelangelo's contemporaries were so awed by this force (in his sculpture here and elsewhere) that they invented an entirely new word to describe the phenomenon: *terribilità* (dreadfulness). To this day it is used only when describing his work, and it is in evidence here at the peak of its power. During his stormy relations with the Medici, Michelangelo once hid out in a tiny subterranean room that is accessed from the left of the altar. Ever the artist, he drew some charcoal sketches on the wall. If you want to see them, tell the ticket vendor and pay 1,000 lire/€0.50 extra; the room is open by guided visit only. ⊠ *Piazza di Madonna degli Aldobrandini,* ☎ *055/294883 reservations.* ▨ *11,000 lire/€5.70.* ⊙ *Daily 8:15–5. Closed 1st, 3rd, and 5th Mon. and 2nd and 4th Sun. of month.*

★ ⑳ **Galleria dell'Accademia** (Accademia Gallery). The collection of Florentine paintings, dating from the 13th to the 18th century, is largely unremarkable, but the sculptures by Michelangelo are worth the price of admission. The unfinished *Slaves,* fighting their way out of their marble prisons, were meant for the tomb of Michelangelo's overly demanding patron Pope Julius II (1443–1513). But the focal point is the original *David,* moved here from Piazza della Signoria in 1873. The *David* was commissioned in 1501 by the Opera del Duomo (Cathedral Works Committee), which gave the 26-year-old sculptor a leftover block of marble that had been ruined by another artist. Michelangelo's success with the block was so dramatic that the city showered him with honors, and the Opera del Duomo voted to build him a house and a studio in which to live and work.

Today *David* is beset not by Goliath but by tourists, and seeing the statue at all—much less really studying it—can be a trial. After a 1991 attack upon it by a hammer-wielding artist who, luckily, inflicted only a few minor nicks on the toes, the sculpture has been surrounded by a Plexiglas barrier. The statue is not quite what it seems. It is so poised and graceful and alert—so miraculously alive—that it is often considered the definitive embodiment of the ideals of the High Renaissance in sculpture. But its true place in the history of art is a bit more complicated.

As Michelangelo well knew, the Renaissance painting and sculpture that preceded his work were deeply concerned with ideal form. Perfection of proportion was the ever-sought Holy Grail; during the Renaissance, ideal proportion was equated with ideal beauty, and ideal beauty was equated with spiritual perfection. But *David,* despite its supremely calm and dignified pose, departs from these ideals. Michelangelo did not give the statue perfect proportions. The head is slightly too large for the body, the arms are too large for the torso, and the hands are dramatically large for the arms. The work was originally commissioned to adorn the facade of the Duomo and was intended to be seen from a distance and on high. Michelangelo knew exactly what he was doing, calculating that the perspective of the viewer would be such that, in order for the statue to appear proportioned, the upper body, head, and arms would have to be bigger as they are farther away from the viewer's line of vision. But he also did it to express and embody, as powerfully as possible in a single figure, an entire biblical story. David's hands *are* big, but so was Goliath, and these are the hands that slew him. ✉ *Via Ricasoli 60,* ☎ *055/294883 reservations; 055/2388609 gallery.* 🎫 *15,000 lire/€7.75.* ⊗ *Apr.–Oct., Tues.–Sat. 8:30–10, Sun. 8:30–6; Nov.–Mar., Tues.–Sat. 8:30–6:50, Sun. 8:30–8.*

OFF THE
BEATEN PATH

MUSEO DELL'OPIFICIO DELLE PIETRE DURE – This fascinating small museum is attached to an Opificio, or workshop, established by Ferdinand I in 1588 to train craftsmen in the art of working with precious and semi-precious stones and marble. It is internationally renowned as a center for the restoration of mosaics and inlays in semiprecious stones. Informative exhibits include some magnificent antique examples of this highly specialized craft. ✉ *Via degli Alfani 78,* ☎ *055/289414.* 🎫 *4,000 lire/€2.10.* ⊗ *Mon. and Wed.–Sat. 8:15–2, Tues. 8:15–7, 2nd Sun. of month 8:15–2.*

㉓   Museo Archeologico (Archaeological Museum). Of the Etruscan, Egyptian, and Greco-Roman antiquities here, the Etruscan collection is particularly notable—one of the largest in Italy. The famous bronze *Chimera* was discovered (without the tail, a reconstruction) in the 16th century. ✉ *Via della Colonna 38,* ☎ *055/23575.* 🎫 *8,000 lire/€4.10.* ⊗ *Mon. 2–7, Tues. and Thurs. 8:30–7, Wed. and Fri.–Sun. 8:30–2.*

⑲   Museo di San Marco. A former Dominican convent adjacent to the church of San Marco now houses this museum, which contains many stunning works by Fra Angelico (circa 1400–55), the Dominican friar famous for his piety as well as for his painting. When the friars' cells were restructured between 1439 and 1444, he decorated many of them with frescoes meant to spur religious contemplation. His paintings are simple and direct and furnish a compelling contrast to those in the Palazzo Medici-Riccardi chapel. While Gozzoli's frescoes celebrate the splendors of the Medici, Fra Angelico's exalt the simple beauties of monastic life and quiet reflection. Fra Angelico's works are everywhere, from the friars' cells to the superb panel paintings on view in the museum. Don't miss the famous *Annunciation* on the upper floor and the works in the gallery just off the cloister as you enter. Here you can see his beautiful *Last Judgment;* as usual, the tortures of the damned are far more inventive and interesting than the pleasures of the redeemed. ✉ *Piazza San Marco 1,* ☎ *055/2388608.* 🎫 *12,000 lire/€6.15.* ⊗ *Weekdays 8:30–1:50, Sat. 8:30–6:30, Sun. 8:30–7. Closed 1st, 3rd, and 5th Sun. and 2nd, and 4th Mon. of month.*

OFF THE
BEATEN PATH

CENACOLO DI SANT'APOLLONIA – The frescoes of the refectory of a former Benedictine nunnery were painted in sinewy style by Andrea del
Castagno, a follower of Masaccio (1401–28). The *Last Supper* is a
powerful version of this typical refectory theme. From the entrance, walk
around the corner to Via San Gallo 25 and take a peek at the lovely
15th-century cloister that belonged to the same monastery but is now part
of the University of Florence. ⊠ *Via XXVII Aprile 1,* ☎ *055/2388607.*
⊙ *Daily 8:30–1:50. Closed 1st, 3rd, and 5th Sun. and 2nd and 4th
Mon. of month.*

CHIOSTRO DELLO SCALZO – Often overlooked, this small, peaceful 16th-
century cloister was frescoed in grisaille by Andrea del Sarto (1486–
1530), with scenes from the life of St. John the Baptist, Florence's patron
saint. ⊠ *Via Cavour 69,* ☎ *055/2388604.* ⊙ *Mon., Thurs., and Sat.
8:30–2.*

㉑ **Ospedale degli Innocenti.** Built by Brunelleschi in 1419 to serve as a
foundling hospital, this takes the historical prize as the very first Renaissance building. Brunelleschi designed its portico with his usual rigor,
building it out of the two shapes he considered mathematically (and
therefore philosophically and aesthetically) perfect: the square and the
circle. Below the level of the arches, the portico encloses a row of perfect cubes; above the level of the arches, the portico encloses a row of
intersecting hemispheres. The whole geometric scheme is articulated
with Corinthian columns, capitals, and arches borrowed directly from
antiquity. At the time he designed the portico, Brunelleschi was also
designing the interior of San Lorenzo, using the same basic ideas. But
since the portico was finished before San Lorenzo, the Ospedale degli
Innocenti can claim the honor of ushering in Renaissance architecture.
The 10 ceramic medallions depicting swaddled infants that decorate
the portico are by Andrea della Robbia (1435–1525/28), done in about
1487. Contained within is a small museum devoted to lesser-known
Renaissance works. ⊠ *Piazza di Santissima Annunziata 1.* 🎫 *5,000
lire/€2.60.* ⊙ *Thurs.–Tues. 8:30–2.*

★ ⑱ **Palazzo Medici-Riccardi.** The main attraction of this palace, begun in
1444 by Michelozzo for Cosimo de' Medici, is the interior chapel, the
so-called **Cappella dei Magi** on the upper floor. Painted on its walls is
Benozzo Gozzoli's famous *Procession of the Magi,* finished in 1460, which
celebrates both the birth of Christ and the greatness of the Medici family. Like his contemporary Ghirlandaio, Gozzoli was not a revolutionary painter and is today considered less interesting than other 15th-century
stars such as Masaccio, Botticelli, and Leonardo. Gozzoli's gift, however, was for entrancing the eye, not challenging the mind, and on those
terms his success here is beyond question. The paintings are full of activity yet somehow frozen in time in a way that fails utterly as realism
but succeeds triumphantly when the demand for realism is set aside.
Entering the chapel is like walking into the middle of a magnificently
illustrated children's storybook, and this beauty makes it one of the most
unpretentiously enjoyable rooms in the entire city. ⊠ *Via Cavour 1,* ☎
055/2760340. 🎫 *8,000 lire/€4.10.* ⊙ *Thurs.–Tues. 9–7.*

⑮ **San Lorenzo.** The facade of this church was never finished. Filippo
Brunelleschi designed the interior of San Lorenzo, like that of Santo
Spirito on the other side of the Arno, in the early 15th century. The
two interiors are similar in design and effect and proclaim with ringing clarity the beginning of the Renaissance in architecture. San Lorenzo
possesses one feature that Santo Spirito lacks, however, which considerably heightens the dramatic effect: the grid of dark, inlaid marble lines on the floor. The grid makes the rigorous geometry of the interior

immediately visible and offers an illuminating lesson on the laws of perspective. If you stand in the middle of the nave at the church entrance, on the line that stretches to the high altar, every element in the church—the grid, the nave columns, the side aisles, the coffered nave ceiling—seems to march inexorably toward a hypothetical vanishing point beyond the high altar, exactly as in a single-point-perspective painting. Brunelleschi's **Sagrestia Vecchia** (Old Sacristy) has stucco decorations by Donatello; it's at the end of the left transept. ✉ *Piazza San Lorenzo,* ☎ *055/216634.* ⊙ *Church Mon.–Sat. 7–noon and 3:30–5:30, Sun. 3:30–5. Old Sacristy Feb.–Nov., Mon.–Sat. 8–noon and 3:30–5:30, Sun. 3:30–5:30.*

OFF THE
BEATEN PATH
     MERCATO CENTRALE – In this huge, two-story market hall, food is everywhere, some of it remarkably exotic. The ground floor contains meat and cheese stalls, as well as some very good bars offering nice panini (sandwiches), and the second floor is teeming with vegetable stands. If you're looking for an exotic ingredient in Florence, this is most likely where you'll find it. ✉ *Piazza del Mercato Centrale.* ⊙ *Daily 7–2.*

② **Santa Maria Maddalena dei Pazzi.** One of Florence's hidden treasures, Perugino's cool and composed *Crucifixion* is in the chapter house of the monastery below this church. Here we see the Virgin Mary and St. John the Evangelist with Mary Magdalen and Sts. Benedict and Bernard of Clairvaux posed against a simple but haunting landscape. The figure of Christ crucified occupies the center of this brilliantly hued fresco. Perugino's colors radiate—note the juxtaposition of the yellow-green cuff against the orange tones of the Magdalen's robe. ✉ *Borgo Pinti 58,* ☎ *055/2478420.* 🎫 *Donation requested.* ⊙ *Daily 9–noon.*

② **Santissima Annunziata.** Dating from the mid-13th century, this church was restructured in 1447 by Michelozzo, who gave it an uncommon (and lovely) entrance cloister with lovely frescoes by Andrea del Sarto (1486–1350), Pontormo (1494–1557), and Rosso Fiorentino (1494–1540). The interior is an extreme rarity for Florence: a sumptuous example of the Baroque. But it is not really a fair example, since it is merely 17th-century Baroque decoration applied willy-nilly to an earlier structure—exactly the sort of violent remodeling exercise that has given the Baroque a bad name. The **Cappella dell'Annunziata,** immediately inside the entrance to the left, illustrates the point. The lower half, with its stately Corinthian columns and carved frieze bearing the Medici arms, was commissioned by Piero de' Medici in 1447; the upper half, with its erupting curves and impish sculpted cherubs, was added 200 years later. Each is effective in its own way, but together they serve only to prove that dignity is rarely comfortable wearing a party hat. ✉ *Piazza di Santissima Annunziata,* ☎ *055/2398034.* ⊙ *Daily 7–12:30 and 4–6:30.*

② **Sinagoga.** Jews were well settled in Florence by 1396, when the first money-lending operations became officially sanctioned. Medici patronage helped Jewish banking houses to flourish, but by 1570 Jews were required to live within the large "ghetto," near today's Piazza della Repubblica, by decree of Pope Pius V (1504–72). Construction of the modern Moorish-style Synagogue, set in its lovely garden, began in 1874 as a bequest of David Levi, who wished to endow a synagogue "worthy of the city." Falcini, Michele, and Treves designed the building on a domed Greek cross plan with galleries in the transept and a roofline bearing three distinctive copper cupolas visible from all over Florence. The exterior features alternating bands of tan travertine and pink granite, reflecting an Islamic style repeated in Giovanni Panti's ornate interior. Of particular interest are the cast-iron gates by Pasquale Franci, the eternal light by Francesco Morini, and the Murano glass mosaics by Giacomo dal Medico. The gilded doors of the Moorish ark, which fronts the pulpit and is flanked by extravagant candelabra, are decorated with symbols of the ancient Temple of Jerusalem and bear bayonet marks from vandals. The synagogue was used as a garage by the Nazis, who failed to inflict much damage in spite of an attempt to blow up the place with dynamite. Only the columns on the left side were destroyed, and, even then the Women's Balcony above did not collapse. Note the Star of David in black and yellow marble inlaid in the floor. The original capitals can be seen in the garden.

Some of the oldest and most beautiful Jewish ritual artifacts in all of Europe are displayed in the small **Museo Ebraico** upstairs, accessible by stairs or elevator in the main entrance. Exhibits document the Florentine Jewish community and the building of the synagogue. The donated objects all belonged to local families and date from as early as the late 16th century. Take special note of the exquisite needlework and silver items. A small but well-stocked gift shop is downstairs. Adjacent to the synagogue is **Ruth's** (⊠ Via Farini 2/a, ☎ 055/2480888), the only kosher-vegetarian restaurant in Tuscany. Closed for Friday dinner and Saturday lunch, it features inexpensive vegetarian and Mediterranean dishes and a large selection of kosher wines. *Synagogue and museum:* ⊠ *Via Farini 4,* ☎ *055/2346654.* 🖼 *6,000 lire/€3.10.* ⊙ *Apr.–Oct., Sun.–Thurs. 10–1 and 2–5, Fri. 10–1; Nov.–Mar., Sun.–Thurs. 10–1 and 3–5, Fri. 10–1.*

Santa Maria Novella to the Arno

Piazza Santa Maria Novella is near the train station, and like similar areas in most other European cities, it is pervaded by a certain squalor, especially at night. Nevertheless, the streets in and around the piazza are an architectural treasure trove, lined with some of Florence's most tasteful palazzi.

A Good Walk

Start in the Piazza Santa Maria Novella, its north side dominated by the church of **Santa Maria Novella** ㉖; then take Via delle Belle Donne, which leads from the east side of the piazza to a minuscule square, at the center of which stands a curious shrine known as the Croce al Trebbio. Take Via del Trebbio east and turn right onto Via Tornabuoni, Florence's finest shopping street. At the intersection of Via Tornabuoni and Via Strozzi is the overwhelming **Palazzo Strozzi** ㉗. If you want a dose of contemporary art, head straight down Via della Spada to the **Museo Marino Marini** ㉘. One block west from Via Tornabuoni and Palazzo Strozzi, down Via della Vigna Nuova, is Leon Battista Alberti's ground-breaking **Palazzo Rucellai** ㉙. Follow the narrow street opposite the palazzo (Via del Purgatorio) east almost to its end; then zigzag right and left, turning east on Via Parione to reach Piazza di Santa Trinita, where, in the middle, stands the Colonna della Giustizia, which Pope Pius IV (1499–1565) gave to Cosimo I in 1560. Halfway down the block to the south (toward the Arno) is the church of **Santa Trinita** ㉚, home to Ghirlandaio's glowing frescoes. Then go east on Borgo Santi Apostoli, a typical medieval street flanked by tower houses, and take a right on Via Por Santa Maria to get to the Ponte Vecchio. Alternatively, walk from Piazza Santa Trinita to Ponte Santa Trinita, which leads into the Oltrarno neighborhood.

TIMING

The walk takes about 30 minutes, plus 30 minutes for Santa Maria Novella and 15 minutes for Santa Trinita. A visit to the Museo di Santa Maria Novella and the cloister takes about 30 minutes.

Sights to See

Croce al Trebbio. This little granite column near Piazza Santa Maria Novella was erected in 1338 by Dominican friars (there is a Dominican church close to Santa Maria Novella) to commemorate a famous local victory: it was here in 1244 that they defeated their avowed enemies, the Patarene heretics, in a bloody street brawl. ⊠ *Via del Trebbio.*

㉘ Museo Marino Marini. Marini's life dates (1901–80) are not a misprint. One of Marini's major works, a 21-ft-tall bronze horse and rider, dominates the space of the main gallery dedicated to the painter. The museum itself is an eruption of contemporary space in a deconsecrated 9th-century church, designed with a series of open stairways, walkways, and balconies that allow you to peer at Marini's work from all angles. In addition to his Etruscanesque sculpture, the museum houses Marini's paintings, drawings, and engravings. ⊠ *Piazza San Pancrazio,* ☎ *055/219432.* 🎫 *8,000 lire/€4.10.* ⊘ *Oct.–May, Mon. and Wed.–Sat. 10–5, Sun. 10–1; June–Sept., Mon. and Wed.–Sat. 10–5, Thurs. 10–11:30, Sun. 10–1.*

㉙ Palazzo Rucellai. Architect Leon Battista Alberti (1404–72) designed perhaps the very first private residence inspired by antique models—which goes a step further than the Palazzo Strozzi. A comparison between the two is illuminating. Evident on the facade of the Palazzo Rucellai, dating between 1455 and 1470, is the ordered arrangement of windows and rusticated stonework seen on the Palazzo Strozzi, but Alberti's facade is far less forbidding. Alberti devoted a far larger proportion of his wall space to windows, which lighten the facade's appearance, and filled in the remainder with rigorously ordered classical elements borrowed from antiquity. The end result, though still severe, is less fortresslike, and Alberti strove for this effect purposely (he is on record as stating that only tyrants need fortresses). Ironically, the Palazzo Rucellai was built some 30 years *before* the Palazzo Strozzi. Alberti's civilizing ideas here, it turned out, had little influence on the Florentine palazzi that followed. To Renaissance Florentines, power—in architecture, as in life—was just as impressive as beauty. ⊠ *Via della Vigna Nuova.*

㉗ Palazzo Strozzi. This is the most imposing palazzo on Via Tornabuoni. Based on a model by Giuliano da Sangallo (circa 1445–1535) dating from around 1489 and executed between 1489 and 1504 under Il Cronaca (1457–1508) and Benedetto da Maiaino (1442–97), it was inspired by Michelozzo's earlier Palazzo Medici-Riccardi. The palazzo's exterior is simple and severe; it is not the use of classical detail but the regularity of its features, the stately march of its windows, that marks it as a product of the late-15th-century Renaissance. The interior courtyard, entered from the rear of the palazzo, is another matter altogether. It is here that the classical vocabulary—columns, capitals, pilasters, arches, and cornices—is given uninhibited and powerful expression. ⊠ *Via Tornabuoni.*

㉖ Santa Maria Novella. The facade of this church looks distinctly clumsy by later Renaissance standards, and with good reason: it is an architectural hybrid. The lower half of the facade was completed mostly in the 14th century; its pointed-arch niches and decorative marble patterns reflect the Gothic style of the day. About a hundred years later (around 1456), architect Leon Battista Alberti was called in to complete the job. The marble decoration of his upper story clearly defers to the already existing work below, but the architectural features he added evince an entirely different style. The central doorway, the four ground-floor half-columns with Corinthian capitals, the triangular pediment atop the second story, the inscribed frieze immediately below the pediment—these are classical features borrowed from antiquity, and they reflect the new Renaissance era in architecture, born some 35 years earlier at Florence's Ospedale degli Innocenti. Alberti's most important addition, however, the S-curve scrolls that surmount the decorative circles on either side of the upper story, had no precedent whatever in antiquity. The problem was to soften the abrupt transition between wide ground floor and narrow upper story. Alberti's solution turned out to be definitive. Once you start to look for them, you will find scrolls such as these (or sculptural variations of them) on churches all over Italy, and every one of them derives from Alberti's example here.

The architecture of the interior is, like the Duomo, a dignified but somber example of Florentine Gothic. Exploration is essential, however, because the church's store of art treasures is remarkable. Highlights include the 14th-century stained-glass rose window depicting the *Coronation of the Virgin* (above the central entrance); the Cappella Filippo Strozzi (to the right of the altar), containing late 15th-century frescoes and stained glass by Filippino Lippi; the *cappella maggiore* (the area around the high altar), displaying frescoes by Domenico Ghirlandaio (1449–94); and the Cappella Gondi (to the left of the altar), containing Filippo Brunelleschi's famous wood crucifix, carved around 1410 and said to have so stunned the great Donatello when he first saw it that he dropped a basket of eggs.

Of special interest, for its great historical importance and beauty, is Masaccio's *Trinity,* on the left-hand wall, almost halfway down the nave. Painted around 1426–27 (at the same time he was working on his frescoes in Santa Maria del Carmine), it unequivocally announced the arrival of the Renaissance. The realism of the figure of Christ was revolutionary in itself, but what was probably even more startling to contemporary Florentines was the barrel vault in the background. The mathematical rules for employing perspective in painting had just been discovered (probably by Brunelleschi), and this was one of the first works of art to employ them with utterly convincing success. ✉ *Piazza Santa Maria Novella,* ☎ *055/210113.* ▨ *5,000 lire/€2.60.* ☉ *Mon.–Sat. 7–12 and 3:30–5:30, Sun. 3:30–5:30*

In the cloisters of the **Museo di Santa Maria Novella,** to the left of Santa Maria Novella, is a faded fresco cycle by Paolo Uccello depicting tales from Genesis, with a dramatic vision of the Deluge. Earlier and better-preserved frescoes painted between 1348 and 1355 by Andrea da Firenze are in the chapter house, or the Cappellone degli Spagnoli (Spanish Chapel), off the cloister. ✉ *Piazza Santa Maria Novella 19,* ☎ *055/ 282187.* ▨ *5,000 lire/€2.60.* ☉ *Wed.–Mon. 9–2.*

③⓪ Santa Trinita. Started in the 11th century by Vallambrosian monks and originally Romanesque in style, this church underwent a Gothic remodeling during the 14th century. (Remains of the Romanesque construction are visible on the interior front wall.) Its major work is the cycle of frescoes and the altarpiece in the Cappella Sassetti, the second to the high altar's right, painted by Domenico Ghirlandaio from around 1480 to 1485. Ghirlandaio was a wildly popular but conservative painter for his day, and generally his paintings show little interest in the laws of perspective that other Florentine painters had been experimenting with for more than 50 years. But his work here possesses such graceful decorative appeal it hardly seems to matter. The wall frescoes illustrate the life of St. Francis, and the altarpiece, the *Adoration of the Shepherds,* veritably glows. ✉ *Piazza Santa Trinita,* ☎ *055/216912.* ☉ *Daily 7–noon and 4–7.*

In the center of Piazza Santa Trinita is a column from Rome's Terme di Caracalla, given to the Medici Grand Duke Cosimo I by Pope Pius IV in 1560. The column was raised here by Cosimo in 1565, to mark the spot where he heard the news that the Marciani had defeated the Sienese in the 1554 battle of Marciano near Prato; the victory made his power in Florence all but absolute. The column is called, with typical Medici self-assurance, the **Colonna della Giustizia,** the Column of Justice.

The Oltrarno: Palazzo Pitti, Giardini Boboli, Santo Spirito

A walk through the Oltrarno takes in two very different aspects of Florence: the splendor of the Medici, manifest in the riches of the mammoth Palazzo Pitti and the gracious Giardini Boboli; and the charm of the Oltrarno, literally "the other side of the Arno," a slightly gentrified but still fiercely proud working-class neighborhood with artisans' and antiques shops.

A Good Walk

If you start from Santa Trinita, cross the Arno over Ponte Santa Trinita and continue south down Via Maggio until you reach the crossroads of Sdrucciolo dei Pitti (on the left) and the short Via Michelozzi (on the right). Turn left onto the Sdrucciolo dei Pitti. **Palazzo Pitti** ㉛, Florence's largest palace, lies before you as you emerge onto Piazza Pitti. Behind the palace are the **Giardini Boboli** ㉜. Find time to walk through the splendidly landscaped gardens. If you have the energy, walk up the hill to the nearby **Forte di Belvedere** ㉝, which commands a wonderful view and sometimes has art exhibits. If you want to take a Mannerist detour to see the Pontormo *Deposition* at **Santa Felicita** ㉞, head northeast from Palazzo Pitti on Via Guicciardini back toward the Ponte Vecchio. Return to Via Maggio off Piazza Pitti, and then take Via Michelozzi west to Piazza Santo Spirito, dominated at its north end by the unassuming facade of the church of **Santo Spirito** ㉟. Take Via Sant'Agostino, diagonally across the square from the church entrance, and follow it west to Via dei Serragli. Cross and follow Via Santa Monaca west through the heart of the Oltrarno to Piazza del Carmine and the church of **Santa Maria del Carmine** ㊱, where the famous fresco cycle by Masaccio, Masolino, and Filippino Lippi fills the Cappella Brancacci. Go to the far end of Piazza del Carmine and turn right onto Borgo San Frediano; then follow Via di Santo Spirito and Borgo Sant'Jacopo east to reach the Ponte Vecchio.

TIMING

The walk alone takes about 45 minutes; allow one hour to visit the Galleria Palatina in Palazzo Pitti and more if you visit the other galleries. Spend at least 30 minutes to an hour savoring the graceful elegance of the Giardini Boboli. When you reach the crossroads of the Sdrucciolo dei Pitti and Via Michelozzi, you have a choice. If it's around noon, you may want to postpone the first stop temporarily to see the churches of Santo Spirito, Santa Felicita, and Santa Maria del Carmine before they close for the afternoon. Otherwise, proceed to Palazzo Pitti. The churches can be visited in 15 minutes each.

Sights to See

㉝ **Forte di Belvedere.** This impressive structure was built in 1590 to help defend the city against siege. But time has brought about a transformation, and what was once a first-rate fortification is now a first-rate exhibition venue. Farther up the hill is Piazzale Michelangelo, but, as the natives know, the best views of Florence are right here. To the north, all the city's monuments are spread out in a breathtaking panorama. To the south, the nearby hills furnish a complementary rural view, in its way equally memorable. The fortress, occasionally a setting for art exhibitions, is adjacent to the top of the Giardini Boboli. ⊠ *Porta San Giorgio.* 🖼 *Varies with exhibit.*

㉜ Giardini Boboli (Boboli Gardens). The main entrance to these landscaped gardens is from the courtyard of Palazzo Pitti. The gardens began to take shape in 1549, when the Pitti family sold the palazzo to Eleanora of Toledo, wife of the Medici grand duke Cosimo I. The initial landscaping plans were laid out by Niccolò Tribolo (1500–50). After his death work was continued by Vasari, Ammannati, Giambologna, Bernardo Buontalenti (circa 1536–1608), Giulio (1571–1635), and Alfonso Parigi (1606–56), among others, which produced the most spectacular backyard in Florence. The Italian gift for landscaping—less formal than the French but still full of sweeping drama—is displayed here at its best. A copy of the famous *Morgante,* Cosimo I's favorite dwarf astride a particularly unhappy tortoise, is near the exit. Sculpted by Valerio Cioli (circa 1529–99), the work shows a perfectly executed potbelly. ⊠ *Enter through Palazzo Pitti,* ☎ *055/2651816,* 🖼 *4,000 lire/€2.05.* ☉ *Apr.–Oct., daily 8:15–5:30; Nov.–Mar., daily 8:15–4:30. Closed 1st and last Mon. of month.*

㉛ Palazzo Pitti. This enormous palace is one of Florence's largest—if not one of its best—architectural set pieces. The original palazzo, built for the Pitti family around 1460, comprised only the main entrance and the three windows on either side. In 1549 the property was sold to the Medici, and Bartolomeo Ammannati was called in to make substantial additions. Although he apparently operated on the principle that more is better, he succeeded only in producing proof that more is just that, more.

Today it houses several museums: The **Museo degli Argenti** (🖼 4,000 lire/€2.05; ☉ Mon.–Sun. 8:30–1:50, closed 2nd and 4th Sun. and 1st, 3rd, and 5th Mon. of month) displays a vast collection of Medici household treasures. The **Galleria del Costume** (🖼 8,000 lire/€4.10; ☉ Mon.–Sun., 8:30–1:50, closed 2nd and 4th Sun. and 1st, 3rd, and 5th Mon. of month) is a showcase of the fashions of the past 300 years. The **Galleria d'Arte Moderna** (🖼 8,000 lire/€4.10; ☉ Mon.–Sun. 8:30–1:50, closed 2nd and 4th Sun. and 1st, 3rd, and 5th Mon. of month) holds a collection of 19th- and 20th-century paintings, mostly Tuscan. And, most famous of all, the **Galleria Palatina** (🖼 12,000 lire/€6.15; ☉ Nov.–Mar., Tues.–Sat. 8:30–6:50, Sun. 8:30–8; Apr.–Oct., Tues.–Sat. 8:30–10, Sun. 8:30–7), contains a broad collection of paintings from the 15th to 17th century. The rooms of the Galleria Palatina remain much as the Medici left them. Their floor-to-ceiling paintings are considered by some to be Italy's most egregious exercise in conspicuous consumption, aesthetic overkill, and trumpery. Still, the collection possesses high points, including a number of portraits by Titian and an unparalleled collection of paintings by Raphael, notably the double portraits of Angelo Doni and his wife, the sullen Maddalena Strozzi. The price of admission also allows you to explore the former **Appartamenti Reali** containing furnishings from a remodeling done in the 19th century. ⊠ *Piazza Pitti,* ☎ *055/210323.*

㉞ Santa Felicita. This late Baroque church (its facade was remodeled 1736–39) contains the Mannerist Jacopo Pontormo's (1494–1557) tour de force, the *Deposition,* the centerpiece of the Cappella Capponi (executed 1525–28), regarded as a masterpiece of 16th-century Florentine art. The remote figures, which transcend the realm of Renaissance classical form, are portrayed in an array of tangled shapes and intense pastel colors (well preserved because of the low lights in the church), in a space and depth that defy reality. Note, too, the exquisitely frescoed *Annunciation,* also by Pontormo, at a right angle to the *Deposition.*

The granite column in the piazza was erected in 1381 and marks a Christian cemetery. ✉ *Piazza Santa Felicita, Via Guicciardini.* ⊙ *Mon.–Sat. 9–noon and 3–6, Sun. 10–11 and noon–1.*

㊱ **Santa Maria del Carmine.** The Cappella Brancacci, at the end of the right transept of this church, houses a masterpiece of Renaissance painting: a fresco cycle that changed the course of Western art forever. Fire almost destroyed the church in the 18th century; miraculously, the Brancacci Chapel survived almost intact. The cycle is the work of three artists: Masaccio and Masolino (1383–circa 1440/47), who began it around 1424, and Filippino Lippi, who finished it some 50 years later, after a long interruption during which the sponsoring Brancacci family was exiled. It was Masaccio's work that opened a new frontier for painting; tragically, he did not live to experience the revolution his innovations caused, as he died in 1428 at the age of 27.

Masaccio collaborated with Masolino on several of the paintings, but by himself he painted the *Tribute Money* on the upper-left wall; *St. Peter Baptizing* on the upper altar wall; the *Distribution of Goods* on the lower altar wall; and, most famous, the *Expulsion of Adam and Eve* on the chapel's upper-left entrance pier. If you look closely at the latter painting and compare it with some of the chapel's other works, you will see a pronounced difference. The figures of Adam and Eve possess a startling presence primarily due to the dramatic way in which their bodies seem to reflect light. Masaccio here shaded his figures consistently, so as to suggest emphatically a single, strong source of light within the world of the painting but outside its frame. In so doing, he succeeded in imitating with paint the real-world effect of light on mass, and he thereby imparted to his figures a sculptural reality unprecedented in his day.

These matters have to do with technique, but with the *Expulsion of Adam and Eve* his skill went beyond mere technical innovation, and if you look hard at the faces of Adam and Eve, you see more than just finely modeled figures. You see terrible shame and suffering depicted with a humanity rarely achieved in art. ✉ *Piazza del Carmine,* ☎ *055/2382195.* 🎫 *6,000 lire/€3.10.* ⊙ *Mon. and Wed.–Sat. 10–5, Sun. 1–5.*

㉟ **Santo Spirito.** The plain, unfinished facade gives nothing away, but the interior, although it appears chilly (cold, even) compared with later churches, is one of the most important examples of Renaissance architecture in Italy. The interior is one of a pair designed in Florence by Filippo Brunelleschi in the early 15th century (the other is San Lorenzo). It was here that Brunelleschi supplied definitive solutions to the two main problems of interior Renaissance church design: how to build a cross-shaped interior using architectural elements borrowed from antiquity and how to reflect in that interior the order and regularity that Renaissance scientists (among them Brunelleschi himself) were at the time discovering in the natural world around them.

Brunelleschi's solution to the first problem was brilliantly simple: turn a Greek temple inside out. To see this clearly, look at one of the stately arch-topped arcades that separate the side aisles from the central nave. Whereas ancient Greek temples were walled buildings surrounded by classical colonnades, Brunelleschi's churches were classical arcades surrounded by walled buildings. This brilliant architectural idea overthrew the previous era's religious taboo against pagan architecture once and for all, triumphantly reclaiming that architecture for Christian use.

Brunelleschi's solution to the second problem—making the entire interior orderly and regular—was mathematically precise: he designed the ground plan of the church so that all its parts were proportionally related. The transepts and nave have exactly the same width; the side aisles are precisely half as wide as the nave; the little chapels off the side aisles are exactly half as deep as the side aisles; the chancel and transepts are exactly one-eighth the depth of the nave; and so on, with dizzying exactitude. For Brunelleschi, such a design technique would have been far more than a convenience; it would have been a matter of passionate conviction. Like most theoreticians of his day, he believed that mathematical regularity and aesthetic beauty were flip sides of the same coin, that one was not possible without the other. In the refectory of **Santo Spirito** (✉ Piazza Santo Spirito 29, ☎ 055/287043), adjacent to the church, you can see Andrea Orcagna's fresco of the *Crucifixion.* Admission is 4,000 lire/€2,05; it's open Tuesday–Sunday 10–2. *Church:* ✉ *Piazza Santo Spirito,* ☎ *055/210030.* ☉ *Thurs.–Tues. 9–noon and 4–6, Wed. 9–noon.*

From Santa Croce to San Miniato al Monte

The Santa Croce quarter, on the southeast fringe of the historic center, was built up in the Middle Ages just outside the second set of city walls. The centerpiece of the neighborhood was the basilica of Santa Croce, which could hold great numbers of worshipers and accommodate the overflow in the vast piazza, which also served as a fairground and playing field for traditional, no-holds-barred soccer games. A center of leather working since the Middle Ages, the neighborhood is still packed with leather craftsmen and leather shops.

A Good Walk

Begin your walk at the church of **Santa Croce** ㊲; from here you can take a quick jaunt up Via delle Pinzochere to **Casa Buonarroti** ㊳ to see works by Michelangelo. Return to Santa Croce, and at the southwest end of the piazza go south on Via de'Benci and cross the Arno over Ponte alle Grazie. Turn left onto Lungarno Serristori and continue to Piazza Giuseppe Poggi; a series of ramps and stairs climbs to **Piazzale Michelangelo** ㊴, where the city lies before you in all its glory. From Piazzale Michelangelo, climb the stairs behind La Loggia restaurant to the church of San Salvatore al Monte, and go south on the lane leading to the stairs that climb to **San Miniato al Monte** ㊵, cutting through the fortifications hurriedly built by Michelangelo in 1529 when Florence was threatened by troops of the Holy Roman Emperor Charles V (1500–58). You can avoid the long walk by taking Bus 12 or 13 at the west end of Ponte alle Grazie and getting off at Piazzale Michelangelo or at the stop after for San Miniato al Monte; you still have to climb the monumental stairs to San Miniato, but then the return trip will be downhill. You can take the bus from Piazzale Michelangelo back to the center of town.

TIMING

The walk alone takes about 1½ hours one way, plus 30 minutes in Santa Croce, 30 minutes in the Museo di Santa Croce, and 30 minutes in San Miniato. Depending on the amount of time you have, you can limit your sightseeing to Santa Croce and Casa Buonarroti or continue on to Piazzale Michelangelo. The walk to Piazzale Michelangelo is a long uphill hike, with the prospect of another climb to San Miniato from there. If you decide to take a bus, remember to buy your ticket before you board. Finally, since you go to Piazzale Michelangelo for the view, skip it if it's a hazy day.

Sights to See

㊳ **Casa Buonarroti.** If you are really enjoying walking in the footsteps of the great genius, you may want to complete the picture by visiting the

Buonarroti family home, even though Michelangelo never actually lived in the house. It was given to his nephew and it was the nephew's son, also called Michelangelo, who turned it into a gallery dedicated to his great-uncle. The artist's descendents filled it with art treasures, some by Michelangelo himself—a marble bas-relief, the *Madonna of the Steps,* carved when Michelangelo was just a teenager, and his wooden model for the facade of San Lorenzo—and some by other artists that pay homage to him. ✉ *Via Ghibellina 70,* ☎ *055/241752.* ✉ *12,000 lire/€6.15.* ☺ *Wed.–Mon. 9:30–1:30.*

㊱ Piazzale Michelangelo. From this lookout, you have a marvelous view of Florence and the hills around it, rivaling the vista from the Forte di Belvedere. It has a copy of Michelangelo's *David* and outdoor cafés packed with tourists during the day and with Florentines in the evening. In May, the **Giardino dell'Iris** (Iris Garden) off the piazza is abloom with more than 2,500 varieties of the flower. The **Giardino delle Rose** (Rose Garden) on the terraces below the piazza is also in full bloom in May and June.

㊵ San Miniato al Monte. This church, like the Baptistery, is a fine example of Romanesque architecture and one of the oldest churches in Florence, dating from the 11th century. The lively green-and-white marble facade has a 12th-century mosaic topped by a gilt bronze eagle, emblem of San Miniato's sponsors, the Calimala (cloth merchants' guild). Inside are a 13th-century inlaid marble floor and apse mosaic. Artist Spinello Aretino (1350–1410) covered the walls of the **Sagrestia** with frescoes on the life of St. Benedict. The adjacent **Cappella del Cardinale del Portogallo** is one of the richest Renaissance works in Florence. Built to hold the tomb of a Portuguese cardinal, Prince James of Lusitania, who died young in Florence in 1459, it has a glorious ceiling by Luca della Robbia, a sculptured tomb by Antonio Rossellino (1427–79), and inlaid pavement in multicolor marble. ✉ *Viale Galileo Galilei, Piazzale Michelangelo,* ☎ *055/2342731.* ☺ *Mon.–Sat. 8–12:30 and 2–6, Sun. 8–6.*

★ **㊲ Santa Croce.** Like the Duomo, this church is Gothic, but, also like the Duomo, its facade dates from the 19th century. The interior is most famous for its art and its tombs. As a burial place, the church is a Florentine pantheon, probably containing more skeletons of Renaissance celebrities than any other church in Italy. Among others, the tomb of Michelangelo is immediately to the right as you enter; he is said to have chosen this spot so that the first thing he would see on Judgment Day, when the graves of the dead fly open, would be Brunelleschi's dome through Santa Croce's open doors. The tomb of Galileo Galilei (1564–1642), who produced evidence that the earth is not the center of the universe, and who was not granted a Christian burial until 100 years after his death because of it, is on the left wall, opposite Michelangelo's. The tomb of Niccolò Machiavelli (1469–1527), the Renaissance political theoretician whose brutally pragmatic philosophy so influenced the Medici, is halfway down the nave on the right. The grave of Lorenzo Ghiberti, creator of the Baptistery doors, is halfway down the nave on the left. Composer Gioacchino Rossini (1792–1868) is entombed at the end of the nave on the right. The monument to Dante Alighieri (1265–1321), the greatest Italian poet, is a memorial rather than a tomb (he is actually buried in Ravenna); it is on the right wall near the tomb of Michelangelo.

The collection of art within the church complex is by far the most important of any church in Florence. Historically, the most significant works are probably the Giotto frescoes in the two adjacent chapels immediately to the right of the high altar. They illustrate scenes from the lives of St. John the Evangelist and St. John the Baptist (in the right-hand chapel) and scenes from the life of St. Francis (in the left-hand chapel). Time has not been kind to them; over the centuries, wall tombs were introduced into the middle of them, whitewash and plaster covered them, and in the 19th century they were subjected to a clumsy restoration. But the reality that Giotto introduced into painting can still be seen. He did not paint beautifully stylized religious icons, as the Byzantine style that preceded him prescribed; he instead painted drama—St. Francis surrounded by grieving friars at the very moment of his death. This was a radical shift in emphasis, and it changed the course of art. Before him, the role of painting was to symbolize the attributes of God; after him, it was to imitate life. The style of his work is indeed primitive, compared with later painting, but in the proto-Renaissance of the early 14th century it caused a sensation that was not equaled for another 100 years. He was, for his time, the equal of both Masaccio and Michelangelo.

Among the church's other highlights are Donatello's *Annunciation,* one of the tenderest and most eloquent expressions of surprise ever sculpted (on the right wall two-thirds of the way down the nave); 14th-century frescoes by Taddeo Gaddi (circa 1300–66) illustrating scenes from the life of the Virgin Mary, clearly showing the influence of Giotto (in the chapel at the end of the right transept); and Donatello's *Crucifix,* criticized by Brunelleschi for making Christ look like a peasant (in the chapel at the end of the left transept). Outside the church proper, in the **Museo dell'Opera di Santa Croce** off the cloister, is the 13th-century *Triumphal Cross* by Cimabue (circa 1240–1302), badly damaged by the flood of 1966. A model of architectural geometry, the **Cappella Pazzi,** at the end of the cloister, is the work of Brunelleschi. ⊠ *Piazza Santa Croce 16,* ☎ *055/244619.* ☒ *8,000 lire/€4.10.* ☉ *Church Mar.–Oct., Mon.–Sat. 9:30–5:30, Sun. 3–5:30; Nov.–Feb., Mon.–Sat. 9:30–12:15 and 3–5:30, Sun. 3–5:30. Cloister and museum Mar.–Oct., Thurs.–Tues. 10–7; Nov.–Feb., Thurs.–Tues. 10–6.*

DINING

A typical Tuscan repast starts with an antipasto of *crostini* (grilled bread spread with various savory toppings) or cured meats such as prosciutto *crudo* (cured ham thinly sliced) and *finocchiona* (salami seasoned with fennel). *Primi piatti* (first courses) can consist of local versions of pasta dishes available throughout Italy. Peculiar to Florence, however, are the vegetable-and-bread soups such as *pappa al pomodoro* (bread and tomato soup), ribollita, and, in the summer, a salad called *panzanella* (tomatoes, onions, vinegar, oil, basil, and bread). Before they are eaten, these are often christened with *un "C" d'olio,* a generous C-shape drizzle of the sumptuous local olive oil.

Unparalleled among the *secondi piatti* (main courses) is *bistecca alla fiorentina*—a thick slab of local Chianina beef, grilled over charcoal; seasoned with olive oil, salt, and pepper; and served rare. *Trippa alla fiorentina* (tripe stewed with tomato sauce) and *arista* (roast loin of pork seasoned with rosemary) are also regional specialties, as are many other roasted meats that go especially well with Chianti. A *secondo* is usually served with a *contorno* (side dish) of white beans, sautéed greens, or artichokes in season, all of which can be drizzled with more of that fruity olive oil. Dining hours are earlier here than in Rome, starting at 1 for the midday meal and at 8 for dinner. Many of Florence's restaurants are small, so reservations are a must.

296

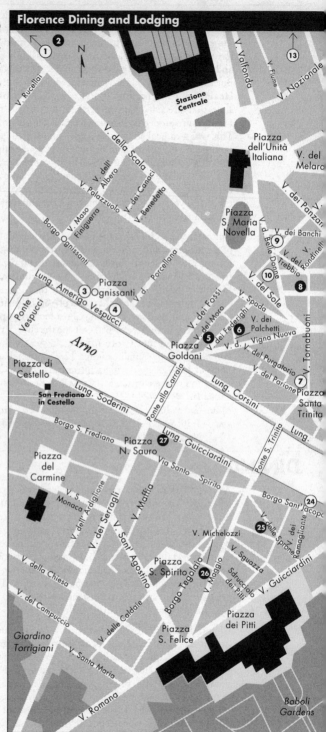

Florence Dining and Lodging

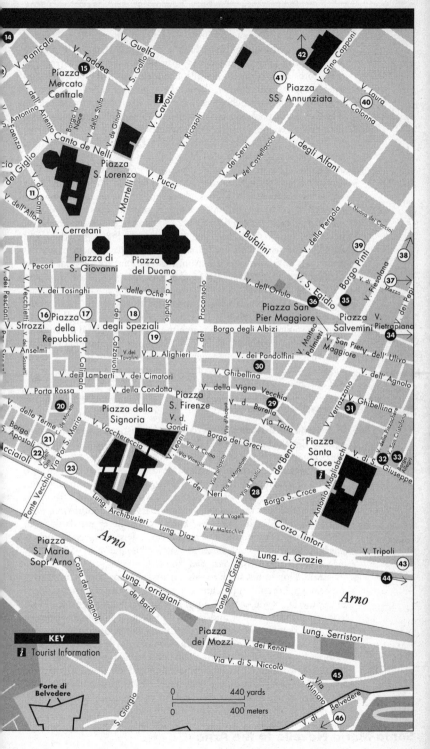

Centro Storico

$$–$$$ ✕ **Osteria n. 1.** The name "Osteria" is the only pretentious aspect of this romantic restaurant nestled in the ground floor of an old palazzo in the historic center. The place is suffused with a rosy glow from the tablecloths and cream-color walls, lined with painted landscapes and the occasional coat of arms. The food is expertly handled—try, for example, the delicate artichoke ravioli with olive oil and Parmesan or the *crespelle,* a little package of pasta stuffed with zucchini puree and topped with a subtle walnut sauce, before moving on to any of the grilled meats. ⊠ *Via del Moro 18-20/r,* ☎ *055/284897. AE, DC, MC, V. Closed Sun. and 20 days in Aug. No lunch Mon.*

$$ ✕ **Il Latini.** This may be the noisiest, most crowded trattoria in Florence. It's also a fun place to go precisely because it is so lively. Four big rooms are lined with bottles of wine and prints, and somehow they manage to feel cozy—perhaps because there are always a lot of happy Florentines tucking into their *salsicce e fagioli* (sausage and beans) or, in season, *agnello fritto* (fried lamb). Portions are big—you'll think you won't be able to eat it all, but you will. This place packs them in, tourists and locals alike, with good reason. Reservations are advised. ⊠ *Via dei Palchetti 6/r,* ☎ *055/210916. AE, DC, MC, V. Closed Mon. and 15 days at Christmas.*

$ ✕ **Pasquini.** Pasquini is a small, one-room trattoria in the heart of the centro storico. You might get the feeling you're in someone's Tuscan farmhouse kitchen—you can watch the chef cook behind garlands of garlic and hot peppers while you wait for a bowl of ribollita or a plate of carpaccio. Giacinto, manager-waiter extraordinaire, can, if in the mood, provide you with lots of laughs in between mouthfuls. ⊠ *Via Val di Lamone, 2/r,* ☎ *055/218995. AE, DC, MC, V.*

San Lorenzo and Beyond

$$$ ✕ **Taverna del Bronzino.** Want to have a sophisticated meal in a 16th-century Renaissance artist's studio? There's nothing outstanding about the decor in the former studio of Santi di Tito, a student of Bronzino's, save for its simple formality, with white tablecloths and place settings. Lots of classic, superb Tuscan food, however, graces the artful menu, and the presentation is often dramatic. A wine list of solid, affordable choices rounds out the menu. For starters try the prosciutto *e tomino alla griglia* (with broiled cheese)—ham and cheese never tasted this good. The service is outstanding. Reservations are advised, especially for eating at the wine cellar's only table. ⊠ *Via delle Ruote 27/r,* ☎ *055/495220. AE, DC, MC, V. Closed Sun. and Aug.*

$ ✕ **Mario.** Florentines flock to this narrow, unfussy, family-run trattoria near San Lorenzo at lunchtime to feast on Tuscan favorites savored at a scattering of simple tables under a wooden ceiling dating from 1536. A distinct cafeteria feel and genuine Florentine hospitality prevail: you'll be seated wherever there's room, which often means with strangers. Yes, there's a bit of extra oil in most dishes, which imparts calories as well as taste, but aren't you on vacation in Italy? Worth the splurge is *riso al ragù* (rice with ground beef and tomatoes). Come early to avoid a wait. It's open for lunch only. ⊠ *Via Rosina 2/r, corner of Piazza del Mercato Centrale,* ☎ *055/218550. Reservations not accepted. No credit cards. Closed Sun. and Aug. No dinner.*

Santa Maria Novella to the Arno

$$$ ✕ **Cantinetta Antinori.** After a rough morning of shopping on Via Tornabuoni, stop for lunch in this 15th-century palazzo in the company of Florentine ladies (and men) who lunch and come to see and be seen. The panache of the food matches its clientele, but be prepared to pay dearly for such treats as *tramezzino con pane di campagna al tartufo* (country pâté with truffles served on bread) or the *insalata di gamberoni e gamberetti con carciofi freschi* (crayfish and prawn salad with shaved raw artichokes). ✉ *Piazza Antinori 3,* ☎ *055/292234. AE, DC, MC, V. Closed weekends and Aug.*

$$–$$$ ✕ **Zibibbo.** Benedetta Vitali, chef and creative muse for many years at Florence's famed Cibrèo, has opened a restaurant of her very own. It's a welcome addition to the sometimes claustrophobic Florentine dining scene—particularly since you have to drive a few minutes out of town to get here. Off a quiet piazza, it has an unassuming facade that leads into two intimate rooms with rustic, maroon-painted wood floors and a sloped ceiling. Ms. Vitali's *tagliatelle al sugo d'anatra* (wide pasta ribbons with duck sauce) is aromatic and flavorful, and her *crocchette di fave con salsa di yogurt* (fava bean croquettes with a lively yogurt sauce) are innovative and tasty. The staff is as welcoming as the chef-owner. This place is worth the cab fare from Florence city center. ✉ *Via di Terzollina 3/r,* ☎ *055/433383. AE, DC, MC, V. Closed Mon.*

$$ ✕ **Le Fonticine.** This restaurant is a welcome oasis in a neighborhood
★ near the train station not noted for its fine dining options. Here you dine very well, since the place combines the best of two Italian cuisines: owner Silvano Bruci is from Tuscany and his wife, Gianna, is from Emilia-Romagna. Start with the mixed-vegetable antipasto plate or the delicate fried cauliflower balls before moving on to the osso buco *alla fiorentina* (in a hearty tomato sauce). The interior of the restaurant, filled with the Brucis' painting collection, provides a cheery space for the satisfying food. ✉ *Via Nazionale 79/r,* ☎ *055/282106. AE, DC, MC, V. Closed Sun. and Mon. and July 25–Aug. 25.*

The Oltrarno and Santo Spirito

$$$ ✕ **Beccofino.** Written on the menu is "*esercizi di cucina italiana*" (Ital-
★ ian cooking exercises), which is a disarmingly modest way to alert the diner that something wonderfully different is going on here. The interior has a pale-wood serpentine bar separating the ocher-walled wine bar from the green-walled restaurant. Chef Francesco Berardinelli has paid some dues in the United States, and it shows in the inventiveness of his food (such as his pairing of scallops with bitter greens), which ends up tasting wholly and wonderfully Italian. The wine bar offers a shorter and less expensive menu; in the summer, you can enjoy this food on an outdoor terrace facing the Arno. ✉ *Piazza degli Scarlatti 1/r (Lungarno Guicciardini),* ☎ *055/290076. Reservations essential. AE, DC, MC, V. Closed Mon.*

$$ ✕ **Quattro Leone.** The eclectic staff at this trattoria nestled in a small piazza is an appropriate match for the eclectic menu. In winter, you can sample the wares in one of two rooms with high ceilings, and in the summer you can sit outside and admire the scenery. Traditional Tuscan favorites, such as *taglierini con porcini* (long, thin, flat pasta with porcini), are offered, but so, too, are less typical things like the earthy cabbage salad with avocado, pine nuts, and drops of *olio di tartufo* (truffle oil). Reservations are a good idea. ✉ *Piazza della Passera, Via dei Vellutini 1/r,* ☎ *055/218562. AE, DC, MC, V.*

$ ✕ **La Casalinga.** *Casalinga* means "housewife," and this place has all the charm of a 1950s kitchen with Tuscan comfort food to match. Interior decor has largely gone by the wayside—there's nothing beyond mediocre paintings cluttering the semi-paneled walls. Tables are set close together and the place is usually jammed, with good reason. The menu is large, long, and as Tuscan as you can get; portions are plentiful; service is prompt and friendly. If you eat ribollita anywhere in Florence, eat it here—the setting couldn't be more authentic. ⊠ *Via Michelozzi 9/r,* ☎ *055/218624. AE, DC, MC, V. Closed Sun., 1 wk at Christmas, and 3 wks in Aug. No lunch in July.*

$ ✗ **Osteria Antica Mescita San Niccolò.** This bustling osteria is next to the church of San Niccolò, and if you sit in the lower part of the restaurant you will find yourself in what was once a chapel dating from the 11th century. Such subtle but dramatic background plays off nicely with the food, which is simple Tuscan style at its very best. The *pollo con limone* is tasty little pieces of chicken in a fragrant lemon-scented broth. In the winter, try the *spezzatino di cinghiale con aromi* (wild boar stew with herbs). Reservations are advised. ⊠ *Via San Niccolò, 60/r,* ☎ *055/2342836. No credit cards. Closed Sun.*

Santa Croce

$$$$ ✗ **Cibrèo.** The food at this upscale Florentine trattoria is fantastic,
★   from the first bite of seamless, creamy crostini *di fegatini* (with savory Tuscan chicken-liver spread) to the last bite of one of the meltingly good desserts. If you thought you'd never try tripe—let alone like it—this is the place to lay any doubts to rest: the *trippa in insalata* (cold tripe salad) with parsley and garlic is an epiphany. So is just about everything else on the menu. It's wise to construe owner Fabio Picchi's unsolicited advice to diners on the A to Zs of Italian eating as a manifestation of his enthusiasm about his food—which is warranted, as he serves some of the best, most creative food in town. ⊠ *Via A. del Verrocchio 8/r,* ☎ *055/2341100. Reservations essential. AE, DC, MC, V. Closed Sun. and Mon., July 25–Sept. 5, and Dec. 31–Jan. 7.*

$$$$ ✗ **Enoteca Pinchiorri.** A sumptuous Renaissance palace with high, frescoed ceilings and bouquets in silver vases provides the setting for this restaurant, one of the most expensive in Italy. Some consider it one of the best, and others consider it an expensive, non-Italian rip-off. Prices are high and portions are small; the vast holdings of the wine cellar, as well as stellar service, dull the pain, however, when the bill is presented. A variety of fish, game, and meat dishes are always on the menu, along with pasta combinations like the *ignudi*—ricotta and cheese dumplings with a lobster and coxcomb fricassee. ⊠ *Via Ghibellina 87,* ☎ *055/242777. Reservations essential. AE, MC, V. Closed Sun., Aug., and 10 days at Christmas. No lunch Mon. or Wed.*

$$$ ✗ **Alle Murate.** This sophisticated restaurant features creative versions of classic Tuscan dishes—such as *zuppa di ceci e merluzzo* (pureed chickpeas with hints of cod). The main dining room has a rich, uncluttered look, with warm wood floors and paneling and soft lights. In a smaller adjacent room called the *vineria,* you get the same splendid service and substantially reduced prices. Be warned that there's no middle ground with the wine list—only a smattering of inexpensive offerings before it soars to exalted heights. ⊠ *Via Ghibellina 52/r,* ☎ *055/240618. AE, DC, MC, V. Closed Mon. No lunch.*

$$$ ✗ **Caffè Concerto.** You might feel like you're in California on the Arno while dining at this sleek, airy restaurant a short ride from the city center. Owner-chef Gabriele Tarchiani has spent some time in the United States, which shows in the plants that fill the interior as well as the creative touches on the menu that changes monthly. It's a rare thing and a blessing in Florence to find such imagination in the *composta di cozze cavolo cinese e carciofi,* a mound of artichokes and Chinese cabbage garnished with mussels. Dessert is also enigmatic—try the sesame-seed concoction with rum-soaked dates and papaya sorbet. This is the place where Florentines come to celebrate special occasions—no wonder, as the food is delicious. ⊠ *Lungarno Colombo 7,* ☎ *055/677377. Reservations essential. AE, DC, MC, V. Closed Sun.*

$$–$$$ ✕ **La Giostra.** The clubby La Giostra, which means "carousel" in Ital-
★ ian, is owned and run by Prince Dimitri Kunz d'Asburgo Lorena, and
his way with mushrooms is as remarkable as his charm. The unusually good pastas may require explanation from Dimitri or Soldano, the
prince's twin sons. In perfect English they'll describe a favorite dish,
carbonara di tartufo, a decadently rich spaghetti with eggs and white
truffles. Try the *spianata* (slices of thinly shaved beef baked quickly
and served with fresh rosemary and sage). Leave room for dessert: this
might be the only show in town with a sublime tiramisu and a wonderfully gooey Sacher torte. ⊠ *Borgo Pinti 12/r,* ☎ *055/241341. AE,
DC, MC, V.*

$$ ✕ **Cantina Barbagianni** "Diverso dal solito" (different from the usual)
is the leitmotif here, and this attitude is reflected in the funky decor
(lots of strategically placed drapery) and in two of its subterranean rooms
adorned with avante-garde paintings. Cristina, the proprietor, pre-
sides over her guests with great ease. The menu, which changes regu-
larly, strays far from the typical Tuscan path. *L'anatra con mirtillo* (duck
with blueberries) is a rare thing in these parts, and the chef is to be
commended for his inventiveness. The *insalata del Torchio* is composed
of slivers of hearts of palm, arugula, and toasted walnuts; the *risotto
al carciofi con scamorza* (artichoke risotto with smoked cheese) is
heavenly. And so are the desserts. ⊠ *Via Sant'Egidio 13,* ☎ *055/248
0508. AE, MC, DC, V. Closed Sun.*

$$ ✕ **Cantinetta Francescani.** This unassuming trattoria with its plain
wooden tables and nondescript walls turns out some terrific twists on
Tuscan favorites. Chef Katrin Rosenthal has clearly learned her way
around a Tuscan kitchen and breathes new life into what are often tired
standards. Her *peposo,* chunks of beef simmered in a tomato sauce with
lots of black pepper, has bite and zest. The wine list is big and affordable, the staff friendly and attentive. Reservations are advised. ⊠ *Largo
Bargellini 16,* ☎ *055/241 605,* 𝖥𝖠𝖷 *055/234 7220. MC, V. Closed Tues.*

$$ ✕ **Osteria de'Benci.** Just a few minutes from Santa Croce, this charm-
★ ing osteria serves some of the most eclectic food in Florence at remarkably
low prices. Try the spicy spaghetti *dell'ubriacone* (drunkard's spaghetti),
an amazing pasta cooked in red wine that's unlike any plate of spaghetti
you've ever had. The grilled meats are justifiably famous; the *carbon-
ata* is a succulent piece of grilled beef served rare. When it's warm, you
can dine outside with a view of the 13th-century tower belonging to
the prestigious Alberti family. The English-speaking staff shouldn't scare
you off: Florentines *do* eat here. ⊠ *Via de'Benci 11/13/r,* ☎ *055/
2344923. AE, DC, MC, V. Closed Sun.*

$$ ✕ **Pallottino.** With its tiled floor, photograph-filled walls, and wooden
tables, Pallottino is the quintessential Tuscan trattoria, with hearty, heart-
warming classics like pappa al pomodoro and *peposa alla toscana* (a
beef stew laced with black pepper). Its lunch special could be, at
10,000 lire/€5.15 for primo and secondo, the best bargain in town.
⊠ *Via Isola delle Stinche 1/r,* ☎ *055/289573. AE, DC, MC, V. Closed
Mon. and 2–3 wks in Aug.*

$–$$ ✕ **Baldovino.** This lively, brightly colored spot down the street from
the church of Santa Croce is the brainchild of David and Catherine
Gardner, expat Scots. From its humble beginnings as a pizzeria, it has
evolved into something more. Happily, pizza is still on the menu, but
now it shares billing with sophisticated primi and secondi. The menu
changes monthly and offers such treats as *filetto di manzo alla Bernaise*
(filet mignon with a light béarnaise sauce). They also serve various pasta
dishes and grilled meat until the wee hours. Save room for dessert; they're
all winners. ⊠ *Via San Giuseppe 22/r,* ☎ *055/241773. AE, DC, MC,
V. Closed Mon. and 2 wks in Aug.*

Pizzerias

Pizzas in Florence can't begin to compete with their counterparts in Rome or Naples, but a good approximation may be had at **Il Pizziauolo** (⊠ Via dei Macci 113/r, ☎ 055/241171). In the Oltrarno, try **Borgo Antico** (⊠ Piazza S. Spirito 6/r, ☎ 055/210437), which serves up pizza and other trattoria fare. **Osteria del Caffè Italiano** (⊠ Isola delle Stinche 11-13/r, ☎ 055/289368) has opened a tiny, three-tabled pizzeria next door to its more formal restaurant; it defiantly serves only three types of pizza—margherita, marinara, and napoletana, all native to Naples.

Enoteche

Wine bars are popping up all over Florence, and most of them offer light fare as well as lengthy wine lists—perfect places for lunch or dinner. **Enoteca Baldovino** (⊠ Via San Giuseppe 18/r, ☎ 055/2347220), closed Monday, is a cozy little place with candlelit tiled tables just down the street from Santa Croce; try the *piatti misti* (mixed plate of various specials of the day) while sipping a glass of wine. It's hard to believe that **Coquinarius** (⊠ Via delle Oche 15/r, ☎ 055/2302153) is as close to the Duomo as it is; the place is serene and sophisticated and is a great place to rest one's soul. It's closed Sunday. **Le Volpi e l'Uva** (⊠ Piazza de' Rossi 1, ☎ 055/2398132), just off Piazza Santa Trinita, is an oenophile's dream: the waiters pour significant wines by the glass and serve equally impressive cheeses and little sandwiches to accompany them. It's closed Sunday.

Caffè

Caffè in Italy serve not only coffee concoctions and pastries but also sweets, drinks, and *panini,* and some offer hot pasta and lunch dishes. They are usually open from early in the morning to late and are closed all day Sunday. All bars in Italy ought to be like **Caffetteria Piansa** (⊠ Borgo Pinti 18/r, ☎ 055/2342362), great for breakfast, lunch, and drinks at night. **Gilli** (⊠ Piazza della Repubblica 39/r, ☎ 055/213896), closed Tuesday, has been a café, with all the amenities, since 1733. Try any of the chocolates—but avoid ordering anything from the menu. **Giacosa** (⊠ Via Tornabuoni 83/r, ☎ 055/2396226), in the heart of Florence's ritzy shopping district, serves fancy sandwiches and sweets. The Negroni (a bombshell of a drink: gin, Campari, and sweet vermouth) was supposedly invented here before WWII. **Procacci** (⊠ Via Tornabuoni 64/r, ☎ 055/211656) has been a classy Florentine institution since 1885; try one of the panini tartufati and swish it down with a glass of Prosecco. It's closed Sunday and Monday.

Gelaterie and Pasticcerie

Though the *pasticceria* (bakery) **Dolci e Dolcezze** (⊠ Piazza C. Beccaria 8/r, ☎ 055/2345458) is somewhat off the beaten path, if you walk down colorful Borgo La Croce, you'll be rewarded with the prettiest and tastiest cakes, sweets, and tarts in town. It's closed Monday. **Gran Caffè** (⊠ Piazza San Marco 11/r, ☎ 055/215833) is down the street from the Accademia, so it's a perfect stop for a marvelous panino or sweet while raving about the majesty of Michelangelo's *David*. Most people seem to think **Vivoli** (⊠ Via Isola delle Stinche 7, ☎ 055/292334) is the best gelateria in town. What with its *cioccolata con caffè* (chocolate ice cream heavily dosed with espresso), they're probably right.

Salumerie

Salumerie are gourmet food shops strong on fine fresh ingredients such as meats and cheeses; they're are great for picking up a picnic lunch or assembling dinner. If you find yourself in the Oltrarno and hungry for lunch or a snack, drop into **Azzarri Delicatesse** (⌧ Borgo S. Jacopo, 27/b–27/c, ☏ 055/2381714). You can get sandwiches made or get the fixings to go. Its list of cheeses, some of which come from France, is impressive. It's closed Sunday morning and Monday. Looking for some cheddar cheese to pile in your panino? **Pegna** (⌧ Via dello Studio 27, ☏ 055/282701), closed Saturday afternoon and Sunday, has been selling both Italian and non-Italian food since 1860. **Perini** (⌧ Mercato Centrale, enter at Via dell'Aretino, near San Lorenzo, ☏ 055/2398306), closed Sunday, sells everything from prosciutto and mixed meats to sauces for pasta and a wide assortment of antipasti. It's probably the most seductive little food shop in Florence—be prepared to drop some money.

LODGING

Florence's importance not only as a tourist city but as a convention center and the site of the Pitti fashion collections throughout the year has guaranteed a variety of accommodations, many in former villas and palazzi. However, these very factors mean that, except during the winter, reservations are a must. If you do find yourself in Florence with no reservations, go to the **Consorzio ITA** office (⌧ Stazione Centrale, ☏ 167/866022). You must go there in person to make a booking.

Centro Storico

$$$$ 🏨 **Brunelleschi.** Architects united a Byzantine tower, a medieval church, and a later building into a stunning structure in the very heart of the centro storico when creating this unique hotel. There's even a museum displaying the ancient Roman foundations and pottery shards found during restoration. Medieval stone walls and brick arches contrast pleasantly with the plush, contemporary decor. The comfortable, soundproof bedrooms are done in coordinated patterns and soft colors; the ample bathrooms feature beige travertine marble. Some complain, however, that the service isn't what it used to be. ⌧ *Piazza Sant'Elisabetta 3/r (off Via dei Calzaiuoli), 50122,* ☏ *055/27370,* ⑆ *055/219653,* 🌐 *www.hotelbrunelleschi.it. 96 rooms, 7 junior suites. Restaurant, bar, meeting room, parking (fee). AE, DC, MC, V.*

$$$$ 🏨 **Hotel Savoy.** From the outside, it looks very much like the turn-of-the-19th-century building that is is. Inside, sleek minimalism prevails at this up-to-the-minute hotel located in the heart of the centro storico. Sitting rooms have a funky edge with their cream-color walls dotted with contemporary prints and photographs. Rooms are decorated in muted colors, with streamlined furniture and soaring ceilings; many have views of the Duomo's cupola or the Piazza della Repubblica. The deep marble tubs might be reason enough to stay here—but you'll also appreciate the efficient and courteous staff. ⌧ *Piazza della Repubblica 7, 50123,* ☏ *055/27351,* ⑆ *055/2735888,* 🌐 *www.rfhotels.com/italy/florence/savoy/hotels_savoy.html. 98 rooms, 9 suites. Restaurant, bar, meeting rooms, parking (fee). AE, DC, MC, V.*

$$$ 🏨 **Hermitage.** This place is centrally located and, given the price, a
★ great bargain. All rooms are decorated differently with lively wallpaper; some have views of Palazzo Vecchio and others of the Arno. The rooftop terrace, where you can have breakfast or an aperitivi, is decked with flowers. The lobby feels like a friend's living room— its warm yellow walls are welcoming. Double glazing and air-conditioning help keep street noise at bay. (The hotel has an elevator at the top of a short flight of stairs from the street.) ⌧ *Vicolo Marzio*

1 (Piazza del Pesce, Ponte Vecchio), 50122, ☎ 055/287216, FAX 055/212208, WEB www.hermitagehotel.com. 27 rooms, 1 suite. Breakfast room, parking (fee). MC, V.

$$ 🏨 **Alessandra.** The location, a block from the Ponte Vecchio, and the clean, ample rooms make this a good choice. The building, known as the Palazzo Roselli del Turco, was designed in 1507 by Baccio d'Agnolo, a student of Michelangelo's. Though little remains of the original design save for the high wood ceilings, there's still an aura of grandeur. The English-speaking staff is friendly and helpful. ⊠ *Borgo Santi Apostoli 17, 50123,* ☎ *055/283438,* FAX *055/210619,* WEB *www.hotelalessandra.com. 25 rooms, 16 with bath. Parking (fee). AE, MC, V. Closed Dec. 10–26.*

$$ 🏨 **Pendini.** The atmosphere of an old-fashioned Florentine pensione is intact at this find in the absolute center of Florence. Public rooms are pleasant, complete with a portrait of Signora Pendini, who founded the hotel in 1879, and early 19th-century antiques or reproductions throughout. Most bedrooms have brass or walnut beds, pretty floral wallpaper, and pastel carpeting; baths are modern. Many rooms can accommodate extra beds. Rates are low for the category, and off-season rates are a real bargain. ⊠ *Via Strozzi 2, 50123,* ☎ *055/211170,* FAX *055/281807,* WEB *www.florenceitaly.net/hotel.html. 42 rooms. Breakfast room, parking (fee). AE, DC, MC, V.*

$$ 🏨 **Torre Guelfa.** Enter this hidden hotel through an immense wooden door on a narrow street, and continue through an iron gate and up a few steps to where an elevator will take you to the third floor. A few more steps will take you into the 13th-century Florentine *torre* (tower) itself. Each guest room is different, some with canopied beds, some with balconies. The Torre Guelfa once protected the fabulously wealthy Acciaiuoli family. Now it's one of the best-located small hotels in Florence, where you can have breakfast or sunset drinks on a rooftop that offers unmatched Florentine panoramas. ⊠ *Borgo Santi Apostoli 8, 50123,* ☎ *055/2396338,* FAX *055/2398577. 15 rooms, 1 suite. Bar, breakfast room, parking (fee). AE, MC, V.*

$ 🏨 **Albergo Firenze.** A block from the Duomo, this hotel is in one of the oldest piazzas in Florence. Though the reception area and hallways have all the charm of a college dormitory, the similarity ends upon entering the spotlessly clean rooms. For location and price, the place is a steal. ⊠ *Piazza Donati 4, 50122,* ☎ *055/214203,* FAX *055/212370. 61 rooms. Breakfast room, parking (fee). No credit cards.*

San Lorenzo and Beyond

$$$ 🏨 **Porta Faenza.** The 12th-century medieval well discovered during renovations has now become a focal point in the lobby. Two small pensiones were combined and a ground floor added to create this hotel, which offers good value in spacious rooms decorated in Florentine style. The friendly Italian-Canadian owners extend lots of little touches and services, including nonsmoking rooms, a cheery breakfast room, baby-sitting services, and e-mail access. ⊠ *Via Faenza 77, 50123,* ☎ *055/284119,* FAX *055/210101,* WEB *www.hotelportafaenza.it. 25 rooms. Breakfast room, baby-sitting, parking (fee). AE, DC, MC, V.*

$$ 🏨 **Bellettini.** You're in good hands here at this small, family-run hotel
★ on three floors (the top floor has two nice rooms with a view). Sisters Marcia and Gina Naldini, along with their husbands, run the place and provide a relaxed atmosphere. Attractive public rooms have a smattering of antiques. An ample buffet breakfast, including tasty homemade cakes, and air-conditioning are included in the low room rate. The good-size rooms have Venetian or Tuscan provincial decor; bathrooms are bright and modern. ⊠ *Via dei Conti 7, 50123,* ☎ *055/213561,*

FAX *055/283551,* WEB *www.firenze.net/hotelbellettini. 28 rooms. Bar, parking (fee). AE, DC, MC, V.*

Near Piazza San Marco and Beyond

$$$ 🏨 **Loggiato dei Serviti.** This hotel was not designed by Brunelleschi, Florence's architectural genius, but it might as well have been. A mirror image of the architect's famous Ospedale degli Innocenti across the way, the Loggiato is tucked away on one of the city's loveliest squares. Occupying a 16th-century former monastery, the building was originally a refuge for traveling priests. Vaulted ceilings, tasteful furnishings (some antique), canopy beds, and rich fabrics make this a find if you want to get the feel of Florence in an attractively spare Renaissance building while enjoying modern creature comforts. ✉ *Piazza Santissima Annunziata 3, 50122,* ☎ *055/289592,* FAX *055/289595. 29 rooms. Bar, breakfast room, parking (fee). AE, DC, MC, V.*

$$ 🏨 **Morandi alla Crocetta.** Near Piazza Santissima Annunziata, this is a
★ charming and distinguished residence in which guests are made to feel like privileged friends of the family. It is close to the sights but very quiet, in a former convent, and is furnished comfortably in the classic style of a gracious Florentine home. The Morandi is not only an exceptional hotel but also a good value. It's very small, so try to book well in advance. Breakfast is not included in the room rate. ✉ *Via Laura 50, 50121,* ☎ *055/2344747,* FAX *055/2480954,* WEB *www.hotelmorandi.it. 10 rooms. Breakfast room, minibars, parking (fee). AE, DC, MC, V.*

Santa Maria Novella to the Arno

$$$$ 🏨 **Excelsior.** Florentine hotels do not get much more exquisite or expensive
★ than this, which explains why world leaders stay here when they are in Florence. Though they are decorated in Empire style, the rooms still feel up-to-date. High ceilings, dramatic views overlooking the Arno, patterned rugs, tasteful prints—all these provide the rooms with a sense of extravagant well-being. ✉ *Piazza Ognissanti 3, 50123,* ☎ *055/264201,* FAX *055/ 210278,* WEB *www.luxurycollection.com/excelsiorflorence. 168 rooms. Restaurant, breakfast room, minibars, no-smoking rooms, baby-sitting, dry cleaning, laundry service, concierge, business services, meeting rooms, parking (fee). AE, DC, MC, V.*

$$$$ 🏨 **Grand.** Across the piazza from the Excelsior, this Florentine classic provides all the luxurious amenities of its slightly larger sister. Rooms are decorated in either Renaissance or Empire style; the former have deep, richly hued damask brocades and canopy beds, and the latter a lovely profusion of crisp prints and patterned fabric offsetting white walls. The overall effect is sumptuous, as is the view either of the Arno or overlooking a small rectangular courtyard lined with potted orange trees. Avoid the piano bar—it's high-price karaoke. ✉ *Piazza Ognissanti 1, 50123,* ☎ *055/288781,* FAX *055/217400,* WEB *www.luxurycollection. com/grandflorence. 107 rooms. Restaurant, breakfast room, piano bar, minibars, no-smoking rooms, baby-sitting, dry cleaning, laundry service, concierge, business services, meeting rooms, parking (fee). AE, DC, MC, V.*

$$$ 🏨 **Beacci Tornabuoni.** This is perhaps *the* classic Florentine pensione.
★ Set in a 14th-century palazzo, it has old-fashioned style and just enough modern comfort to keep you happy. The agreeable sitting room has a large fireplace, the terrace offers a tremendous view of some major Florentine monuments, and the wallpapered rooms are inviting. On Monday, Wednesday, and Friday nights nights a week, the dining room opens for guests and others, serving Tuscan specialties. ✉ *Via Tornabuoni 3, 50123,* ☎ *055/212645,* FAX *055/283594,* WEB *www.BThotel.it. 28 rooms. Restaurant, bar, parking (fee). AE, DC, MC, V. CP, MAP.*

$$ 🏨 **Le Vigne.** This small hotel on one of Florence's most beautiful and central squares has the warm atmosphere of a private home. The spacious, air-conditioned rooms are furnished in 19th-century Florentine style. The caring management and reasonable rates (at the low end of this category) make this a special place. ⊠ *Piazza Santa Maria Novella 24, 50123,* ☏ *055/294449,* FAX *055/2302263. 25 rooms. AE, DC, MC, V.*

$$ 🏨 **Villa Azalee.** Five minutes on foot from the train station and within spitting distance of the Fortezza da Basso (site of the Pitti fashion shows), this 19th-century villa deftly recalls its previous incarnation as a private residence. Furniture has casually quilted, floral-print slipcovers, and the floors are scattered with flowered throw rugs. Many of the rooms have views of the hotel's garden, and some have private terraces. ⊠ *Viale Fratelli Rosselli 44, 50018,* ☏ *055/214242,* FAX *055/ 268264,* WEB *www.villa-azalee.it. 25 rooms. Breakfast room, parking (fee). AE, DC, MC, V.*

$ 🏨 **Nuova Italia.** Near the train station and within walking distance of the sights, this hotel is run by a genial English-speaking family. It has a homey atmosphere; rooms are clean and simply furnished and have air-conditioning and triple-glazed windows to ensure restful nights. Some rooms can accommodate extra beds. Low bargain rates include breakfast. ⊠ *Via Faenza 26, 50123,* ☏ *055/268430,* FAX *055/210941. 20 rooms. Parking (fee). AE, MC, V.*

$ 🏨 **Pensione Ferretti.** Minutes away from the exquisite Renaissance Piazza Santa Maria Novella, this family-run pensione offers views onto a tiny piazza containing the Croce al Trebbio, as well as quick and easy access to the historic center. English-speaking owner Luciano Michel and his South African–born wife, Sue, do just about anything to make you feel at home (including offering 24-hour free Internet access). Though it's housed in a 16th-century palazzo, accommodations are simple and no-frills: it's a fantastic place for the budget-conscious traveler. ⊠ *Via delle Belle Donne 17, 50123,* ☏ *055/2381328,* FAX *055/ 219288. 16 rooms, 6 with bath. Breakfast room, parking (fee). AE, DC, MC, V.*

The Oltrarno

$$$$ 🏨 **Grand Hotel Villa Cora.** Built near the Boboli Gardens in 1750, the Villa Cora retains the opulence of the 18th and 19th centuries. The decor of its remarkable public and private rooms runs the gamut from neoclassical to rococo and even Moorish and reflects the splendor of such former guests as the empress Eugénie, wife of Napoléon III, and Madame von Meck, Tchaikovsky's mysterious benefactress. ⊠ *Viale Machiavelli 18, 50125,* ☏ *055/2298451,* FAX *055/229086,* WEB *www.villacora.com. 48 rooms. Restaurant, breakfast room, pool, solarium, meeting rooms, parking (fee). AE, DC, MC, V.*

$$$$ 🏨 **Lungarno.** The location couldn't be better—directly across the river from the Palazzo Vecchio and the Duomo. Rooms and suites have private terraces that jut out right over the Arno. Four suites in a 13th-century tower preserve atmospheric details like exposed stone walls and old archways and look out onto a little square with another medieval tower covered in jasmine. The very chic decor approximates a breezily elegant home, with lots of crisp white fabrics with blue trim. A wall of windows and a sea of white couches makes the lobby bar one of the nicest places in the city to stop for a drink. ⊠ *Borgo San Jacopo 14, 50125,* ☏ *055/27261,* FAX *055/268437,* WEB *www.lungarnohotels.com. 60 rooms, 11 suites. Restaurant, bar, parking (fee). AE, DC, MC, V.*

Santa Croce

$$$$ ⊡ **Hotel Regency.** The noise and crowds of Florence seem far from this
       stylish hotel in a residential district near the Sinagoga, though you're
       not more than 10 minutes from the Accademia and Michelangelo's
       David. Across the street is Piazza d'Azeglio, a small public park that
       somehow has a 19th-century Middle European feel. The public rooms,
       with their plush red carpeting and dark wood paneling, are typical of
       the taste and sophistication found here. Rooms dressed in richly col-
       ored fabrics and antique-style furniture remain faithful to the hotel's
       19th-century origins as a private mansion. Within the hotel is an
       equally sophisticated restaurant open to both guests and outsiders. ⊠
       Piazza d'Azeglio 3, 50121, ☎ *055/245247,* FAX *055/2346735,* WEB
       *www.regency-hotel.com. 34 rooms. Restaurant, parking (fee). AE,
       DC, MC, V.*

$$$$ ⊡ **J&J.** Away from the crowds, on a quiet street within walking dis-
       tance of the sights, this unusual hotel is a converted 16th-century
       monastery. Its large, suitelike rooms are ideal for honeymooners, fam-
       ilies, and small groups of friends. Some rooms are on two levels, and
       all are imaginatively arranged around a central courtyard and deco-
       rated with flair. The smaller rooms are more intimate, some opening
       onto a little shared courtyard. The gracious owners chat with guests
       in the light and airy lounge; breakfast is served in a glassed-in Renaissance
       loggia or in the central courtyard. ⊠ *Via di Mezzo 20, 50121,* ☎ *055/
       2345005,* FAX *055/240282,* WEB *www.jandjhotel.com. 20 rooms. Bar,
       breakfast room, parking (fee). AE, DC, MC, V.*

$$$$ ⊡ **Monna Lisa.** Housed in a 15th-century palazzo, with parts of the build-
  ★   ing dating from the 13th century, this hotel retains some of its original
       wood coffered ceilings from the 1500s, as well as its original marble stair-
       case. Though the rooms are on the small side, they are tastefully deco-
       rated, each with different floral wallpaper. The public rooms retain a
       19th-century aura, and the intimate bar, with its red velveteen wallpa-
       per, is the perfect place to unwind at the end of the day. ⊠ *Borgo Pinti
       27, 50121,* ☎ *055/2479751,* FAX *055/2479755,* WEB *www.monnalisa.it.
       30 rooms. Bar, parking (fee). AE, DC, MC, V.*

$$ ⊡ **Ritz.** Set in a row of buildings on the Arno, this old hotel has been
       given new energy by young owners who have worked to give it a com-
       fortable family feeling. They've decorated to make clients feel as if they
       are guests in a very pretty 19th-century Florentine home with 20th-
       century amenities. Almost all the rooms have dramatic views of the
       river or the domed, red-roofed Florentine "skyline." ⊠ *Lungarno
       Zecca Vecchia 24, 50122,* ☎ *055/2340650,* FAX *055/240863. 30 rooms.
       Bar, breakfast room, parking (fee). AE, DC, MC, V.*

NIGHTLIFE AND THE ARTS

The Arts

Festival

On June 24, Florence grinds to a halt in order to celebrate the **Festa
di San Giovanni** (Feast of St. John the Baptist) in honor of its patron
saint. Many shops and bars close, and at night a fireworks display along
the Arno attracts thousands.

Film

You can find movie listings in *La Nazione,* the daily Florentine news-
paper. Note that most American films are dubbed into Italian rather
than subtitled. English-language films are shown at the **Cinema Astro**
(⊠ Piazza San Simone near Santa Croce). Two showings of second-
and third-run English-language films are offered Tuesday through Sun-

day evenings; the cinema usually is closed for most of August. The **Odeon** (⊠ Piazza Strozzi, ☎ 055/214068) shows first-run English-language films on Monday and Tuesday at its magnificent Art Deco theater. The **Goldoni** (⊠ Via Serragli, ☎ 055/222437) screens English-language films on Wednesday. On Thursday, first-run English-language films are shown at the **Fulgor** (⊠ Via Maso Finiguerra, ☎ 055/238 1881). The **Festival del Popolo,** held in the middle of November, celebrates both feature films and documentaries and is held in the Fortezza da Basso.

Music

The **Maggio Musicale Fiorentina,** a series of internationally acclaimed concerts and recitals, is held in the Teatro Comunale (⊠ Corso Italia 16, ☎ 055/211158) from late April through June. From November to May is the concert season of the **Orchestra della Toscana** (⊠ Via Ghibellina 99, ☎ 055/210804). **Amici della Musica** organizes concerts at the Teatro della Pergola (box office: ⊠ Via Alamanni 39, ☎ 055/2479651).

Opera

Operas are performed in the **Teatro Comunale** (⊠ Corso Italia 16, ☎ 055/211158) from September through December.

Nightlife

Florentines are rather proud of their nightlife options. Most bars now have some sort of happy hour, which usually lasts for many hours often offering snacks. Discos typically don't open until very late in the evening and don't get crowded until 1 or 2 in the morning. Though the cover charges might be steep, it's fairly easy to find free passes around town.

Bars

For the swank experience, lubricated with trademark bellinis and the best martinis in town, head to **Harry's Bar** (⊠ Lungarno Vespucci 22/r, ☎ 055/2396700). **Rex** (⊠ Via Fiesolana 23–25/r, Santa Croce, ☎ 055/2480331) has a trendy atmosphere and an arty clientele. From June to September, **Via di Fuga** (⊠ Via Ghibellina, ☎ no phone) is one of the coolest spots to be; once the courtyard of Le Murate, a former Renaissance convent and 19th-century prison, it hosts big bands, performance art, movies, and more. **Zoe** (⊠ Via dei Renai 13/r, ☎ 055/243111) calls itself a "caffetteria" and, while coffee may indeed be served, twentysomething Florentines flock here for the fine (and expensive) cocktails. Here's people-watching at its very best; do it while listening to the latest CDs imported from England. **Capocaccia** (⊠ Lungarno Corsini 12-14/r, ☎ 055/210751) serves lunch, dinner, and brunch. Bloody Marys are killers here, and it's the place to be at cocktail time. **Sant'-Ambrogio Caffè** (⊠ Piazza Sant'Ambrogio 7–8/r, ☎ 055/241035) has outdoor summer seating with a view of an 11th-century church (Sant'-Ambrogio) directly across the street.

The oh-so-cool—bordering on pretentious—vibe at **La Dolce Vita** (⊠ Piazza del Carmine 6/r, ☎ 055/284595) attracts Florentines and the occasional visiting American movie star. **Danny Rock** (⊠ Via Pandolfini 13/r, ☎ 055/2340307) bills itself as a "pub-restaurant"—you can enjoy its divine cheeseburger (or have a plate of pasta) while watching Bugs Bunny cartoons on a big screen. **Il Caffe** (⊠ Piazza Pitti 9, ☎ 055/2396241) offers terrific cocktails, light lunches, and a view of Palazzo Pitti.

Nightclubs

Most clubs are closed either Sunday or Monday. **Yab** (⊠ Via Sassetti 5/r, ☎ 055/215160) is one of the largest clubs, with a young clientele. **Space Electronic** (⊠ Via Palazzuolo 37, ☎ 055/293082) has two floors, with karaoke upstairs and an enormous disco downstairs. It's full of Italian military types prowling for young foreign women. Live music, a well-stocked bar, and a cavernous underground space make for a rollicking good evening at **Loonees** (⊠ Via Porta Rossa 15, ☎ 055/212249).

Meccanò (⊠ Viale degli Olmi 1, in Le Cascine park, ☎ 055/331371) is a multimedia experience in a high-tech disco with a late-night restaurant. Young, up-to-the-minute Florentines drink and dance 'til the wee hours at **Maramao** (⊠ Via dei Macci 79/r, ☎ 055/244341). This local favorite opens at 11 and doesn't really get going until around 2. **Maracaná** (⊠ Via Faenza, 4, ☎ 055/210298) serves as a restaurant and pizzeria featuring Brazilian specialties; at 11 PM it transforms itself into a cabaret floor show and then into a disco until 4 AM. Remember to book a table if you want to eat. If you had a transvestite grandmother, her home would look like **Montecarla** (⊠ Via de' Bardi 2, ☎ 055/2340259). It's two floors crowded with people sipping cocktails, lots of exotic flowers, leopard-print chairs and chintz, and red walls and floors. **Mood** (⊠ Via Corso Tintori) has captured the fancy of young Florentines, who flock here in droves. **BeBop** (⊠ Via dei Servi 76/r) has loud, live music and Beatles nights. Those craving a night out with less raucous live music might want to check out **Jazz Club** (⊠ Via Nuova de' Caccini 3, corner of Borgo Pinti, ☎ 055/2479700). It's situated, appropriately enough, in a smoky basement. When just about everything else has closed, go where the bartenders go when they get off work, **Loch Ness** (⊠ Via de' Benci 19/r). It's the place to have that one last nightcap, which you can do until 5 AM.

OUTDOOR ACTIVITIES AND SPORTS

Participant Sports

Biking

Bikes are a great way to tour the centro storico, as the town center offers no hills. Patience, however, must be maintained while dodging hordes of tourists and those pesky *motorini* (mopeds). The Cascine, a former Medici hunting ground turned into a large public park with paved pathways and lots of trees, admits no cars. The historic center can be circumnavigated via bike paths lining the Viali, a road that runs along the center's circumference. **Florence by Bike** (⊠ Via San Zanobi 120-122/r, ☎ 055/488992) has designed some guided city rides that work quite well. They leave several times a day for one- to three-hour tours of major monuments or for tours with specific themes such as Renaissance Florence or 13th-century Florence. **I Bike Italy** (⊠ Borgo degli Albizi 11, ☎ ₣Ậ₭ 055/2342371) offers one-day tours around Fiesole and Chianti, as well as a two-day tour around Siena. The **International Kitchen** (⊠ 1209 N. Astor 11-N, Chicago, IL 60610, ☎ 800/945–8606) can arrange biking as well as walking tours of Florence and Tuscany that involve cooking and eating as well; tours should be arranged in advance through the U.S. office.

Golf

Circolo Golf dell'Ugolino (⊠ Via Chiantigiana 3, Grassina, ☎ 055/2301009) is a short (10-km [6-mi]) distance from Florence. If you're a member of any other golf club in the world, you will be welcome here. The 18-hole course is set amid the Chianti hills, teeming with cypresses and pines and natural lakes. Local wildlife—pheasants, wild hares, geese, and squirrels—have been known to make their way onto the greens. Par is 72, and the handicap standard scratch score 71. On site is a restaurant open for lunch and dinner, and a bar is open all day. There's also tennis and a swimming pool.

Tenuta di Castelfalfi (⌧ Tenuta di Castelfalfi, Montaione, ☎ 0571/698093) is fairly far out of Florence (about 50 km [31 mi]). The course, however, is open to the public; guests who stay at the **Hotel Medici Tornaquinci Golf and Country Club** (⌧ Tenuta Castelfalfi, Montaione, ☎ 0571/698093) attached to the course get a 30% discount. The course is set in rolling hills southwest of Florence; the par is 73, and the handicap standard scratch score is 71. Though there's no clubhouse, a small bar on the premises offers cold drinks and panini.

Health Clubs
Palestra Ricciardi (⌧ Borgo Pinti 75, ☎ 055/2478444 or 055/2478462), daily 20,000 lire/€10.40 or weekly 50,000 lire/€25.75, has continuous stretching, aerobics, step aerobics, and bodybuilding classes daily; it also has free weights, stationary bikes, treadmills, and rowing machines. **Centro Sportivo Fiorentino Indoor Club** (⌧ Via del Caboto 32, Via Bardazzi 15, ☎ 055/430275), daily 30,000 lire/€15.45, has all the usual gym amenities plus two pools. The only drawback is that it's far from the center.

Running
Don't even think of running on the narrow city streets, where tour buses and triple-parked Alfa Romeos leave precious little space for pedestrians. Instead, head for **Le Cascine,** the park along the Arno at the western end of the city. You can run to Le Cascine along the Lungarno (stay on the sidewalk), or take Bus 17 from the Duomo. A cinder track lies on the hillside just below **Piazzale Michelangelo,** across the Arno from the city center. The locker rooms are reserved for members, so come ready to run. A scenic, but not serene, run can be had along the Lungarno, those streets that frame both sides of the Arno.

Swimming
Piscina Bellarriva (⌧ Lungarno Aldo Moro, ☎ 055/677521) has a 50-m pool and is open daily.

Tennis
Circolo Tennis alle Cascine (⌧ Viale del Visarno 1, ☎ 055/332651) has been in existence since 1898 and is probably the most highfalutin tennis venue in town; however, the drawback is that you have to be staying at certain hotels (the Grand or the Excelsior among them), or have a member bring you in. There is also a bar and restaurant for unwinding after the match. At **Tennis Club Rifredi** (⌧ Via Facibeni 12, ☎ 055/432552) four courts are available, with lighting for nighttime play. Changing rooms are provided, and there's a bar. Membership is not a prerequisite to playing; this club's only inconvenience is that it's not in the center of town.

Spectator Sport

Soccer
Italians are passionate about *calcio* (soccer), and the Florentines are no exception; indeed, *tifosi* (fans) of the Fiorentina team are fervent supporters. The team plays its home games at the **Stadio Comunale** (Municipal Stadium, ⌧ top of Viale Manfredo Fanti, northeast of the center) in Campo di Marte. Tickets for all games except those against their biggest rivals—Juventus of Turin and A. C. Milan—are difficult but not impossible to come by. Try the ticket booth Chiosco degli Sportivi (⌧ Via Anselmi, southwest side of Piazza della Repubblica, ☎ 055/292363). Games are usually played on Sunday afternoon, from about late August to May. A medieval version of the game, **Calcio Storico,** is played around the Festa di San Giovanni each year by teams dressed in costumes representing the six Florence neighborhoods. Games take

place in Piazza Santa Croce, where they have allegedly been played since the middle of the 16th century.

SHOPPING

Window-shopping in Florence is like visiting an enormous contemporary art gallery, for many of today's greatest Italian artists are fashion designers, and most keep shops in Florence. Discerning shoppers may find bargains in the street markets. Shops are generally open 9–1 and 3:30–7:30 and are closed Sunday and Monday morning most of the year. Summer (June–September) hours are usually 9–1 and 4–8, and some shops close Saturday afternoon instead of Monday morning. When looking for addresses of shops, you will see two color-coded numbering systems on each street. The red numbers are commercial addresses and are indicated, for example, as 31/r. The blue or black numbers are residential addresses. Most shops take major credit cards and will ship purchases, but because of possible delays it's wise to take your purchases with you.

Markets

If you're looking for cheery, inexpensive trinkets to take home, you might want to stop and roam through the stalls under the loggia of the **Mercato Nuovo** (⌧ corner of Via Por Santa Maria and Via Porta Rossa). The clothing and leather-goods stalls of the **Mercato di San Lorenzo** in the streets next to the church of San Lorenzo offer bargains for shoppers on a budget. The **Mercato Centrale** (⌧ Piazza del Mercato Centrale) is a huge indoor food market that has a staggering array of things edible. You can find bargains at the **flea market** on Piazza dei Ciompi on the last Sunday of the month. An **open-air market** is held in Le Cascine park every Tuesday morning.

Shopping Districts

Florence's most fashionable shops are concentrated in the center of town. The fanciest designer shops are mainly on **Via Tornabuoni** and **Via della Vigna Nuova.** The city's largest concentration of antiques shops can be found on **Borgo Ognissanti** and the Oltrarno's **Via Maggio.** The **Ponte Vecchio** houses reputable but very expensive jewelry shops, as it has since the 16th century. The area near **Santa Croce** is the heart of the leather merchants' district.

Specialty Stores

Antiques

Galleria Luigi Bellini (⌧ Lungarno Soderini 5, ☎ 055/214031) claims to be Italy's oldest antiques dealer, which may be true, since father Mario Bellini was responsible for instituting Florence's international antiques biennial. **Giovanni Pratesi** (⌧ Via Maggio 13, ☎ 055/2396568) specializes in Italian antiques, in this case furniture, with some fine paintings, sculpture, and decorative objects turning up from time to time. Vying with Luigi Bellini as one of Florence's oldest antiques dealers, **Guido Bartolozzi** (⌧ Via Maggio 18/r, ☎ 055/215602) sells predominately period Florentine pieces. At **Paolo Paoletti** (⌧ Via Maggio 30/r, ☎ 055/214728) look for Florentine antiques with an emphasis on Medici-era objects from the 15th and 16th centuries.

Books and Paper

Pineider (⌧ Piazza della Signoria 13/r and Via Tornabuoni 76/r, ☎ 055/284 655 and 055/211605) now has shops throughout the world, but the business began in Florence and still does all its printing here. Personalized stationery and business cards are the mainstay, but the stores also sell fine leather desk accessories. **Centro Di** (⊠ Via dei Renai 20/r, ☎ 055/2342666) publishes art books and exhibition catalogs for some of the most important organizations in Europe. One of Florence's oldest paper-goods stores, **Giulio Giannini e Figlio** (⊠ Piazza Pitti 37/r, ☎ 055/212621) is *the* place to buy the marbleized stock, which comes in a variety of shapes and sizes, from flat sheets to boxes and even pencils. Long one of Florence's best art-book shops, **Libreria Salimbeni** (⊠ Via Matteo Palmieri 14–16/r, ☎ 055/2340905) has an outstanding selection. **FMR** (⊠ Via delle Belle Donne 41/r, ☎ 055/283312), the shop of the world-famous art-book editor and tastemaker Franco Maria Ricci, offers exquisite art books, handmade papers, and small works on paper. **Alberto Cozzi** (⊠ Via del Parione 35/r, ☎ 055/294968) keeps an extensive line of Florentine papers and paper products, and the artisans in the shop rebind and restore books and works on paper.

Clothing

The usual fashion suspects—Prada, Gucci, Versace, to name but a few—can all be found in Florence. The sleek, classic **Giorgio Armani** boutique (⊠ Via della Vigna Nuova 51/r, ☎ 055/219041) is a centerpiece of the dazzling high-end shops clustered in this part of town. **Emporio Armani** (⊠ Piazza Strozzi 16/r, ☎ 055/284315) offers slightly more-affordable, funky, nightclub-friendly Armani threads.

Prada (⊠ Via Tornabuoni 69/r, ☎ 055/283439), known to mix schoolmarmish sensibility with sexy cuts and funky fabrics, appeals to an exclusive clientele. Cognoscenti will drive or taxi about 45 minutes out of town to the **Prada Outlet** (⊠ Levanella Spacceo, Estrada Statale 69, Montevarchi, ☎ 055/91911). The signature **Gianni Versace** (⊠ Via Tornabuoni 13–15/r, ☎ 055/2396167) couture collection revolutionized the catwalk with rubber dresses and purple leather pants; sister Donatella continues the line of high-priced, over-the-top couture for rock stars and other celebrities. For a lighter, more affordable option, check out **Versus** (⊠ Via Vigna Nuova 36–38/r, ☎ 055/217619), the more playful Versace line created with the same sense of whimsical decadence. You can take home a custom-made suit or dress from **Giorgio Vannini** (⊠ Via Borgo Santi Apostoli 43/r, ☎ 055/293037), who has a showroom for his pret-a-porter designs. **Bernardo** (⊠ Via Porta Rossa 87/r, ☎ 055/283333) specializes in men's trousers, cashmere sweaters, and shirts with details like mother-of-pearl buttons. **Gianfranco Ferré** (⊠ Via Tosinghi 52/r, ☎ 055/292003) captures beauty and luxury in various constructions and fabrics in his couture lines; he has also created a line of sleek jeans.

The aristocratic Marchese di Barsento, **Emilio Pucci** (⊠ Via Ricasoli 36/r, ☎ 055/287622; ⊠ Via della Vigna Nuova 97–99/r, ☎ 055/294028), became an international name in the early 1960s when the stretch ski clothes he designed for himself caught on with the the dolce vita crowd—his pseudopsychedelic prints and "palazzo pajamas" became all the rage. The showroom in the family palazzo and his two boutiques (one wholesale) still sell the celebrated Pucci prints.

Embroidery and Linens

Loretta Caponi (⊠ Piazza Antinori 4/r, ☎ 055/213668) is synonymous with Florentine embroidery, and her luxury lace, linens, and lingerie have earned her worldwide renown. **Valmar** (⊠ Via Porta Rossa 53/r, ☎ 055/284493) is filled with tangled spools of cords, ribbons, and fringes, plus an array of buttons, tassels, sachets, and hand-embroidered cushions you can take home—or bring in your own fabric, choose the adornments, and you can have your cushion or table runner made.

Sant'Jacopo Show (✉ Borgo Sant'Jacopo 66/r, ☎ 055/2396912) is an offbeat shop specializing in mannequins, decorations, and shop fittings. Sumptuous silks, beaded fabrics, lace, wool, and tweeds can be purchased at **Valli** (✉ Via Strozzi 4/r, ☎ 055/282485). It carries fabrics created by Armani, Valentino, and other high-end designers.

Gifts and Housewares

The essence of a Florentine holiday is captured in the sachets of the **Officina Profumo Farmaceutica di Santa Maria Novella** (✉ Via della Scala 16/r, ☎ 055/216276), an Art Nouveau emporium of herbal cosmetics and soaps that are made following centuries-old recipes created by friars. For housewares, nothing beats **Bartolini** (✉ Via dei Servi 30/r, ☎ 055/211895) for well-designed practical items. **Sbigoli Terrecotte** (✉ Via Sant'Egidio 4/r, ☎ 055/2479713) carries traditional Tuscan terracotta and ceramic vases, pots, and cups and saucers. **Sbigoli Laboratorio** (✉ Via di Camaldoli 10/r, ☎ 055/229706) is the workshop of the mother-daughter team of Antonella Chini and Lorenza Adami, who turn out Florentine-inspired designs based on Antonella's extensive ceramics training in Faenza. What to get that gal (or guy) who has everything? Drop into the **Shabby Shop** (✉ Via del Parione 12/r, ☎ 055/294826), which specializes in antique silver—mostly English, dating from George I to George III (1698–1811)—and more recent jewelry from the 1950s. For the record: there's absolutely nothing shabby about this shop.

Jewelry

Cassetti (✉ Ponte Vecchio 54/r, ☎ 055/2396028) combines precious and semiprecious stones and metals in contemporary settings. **Gherardi** (✉ Ponte Vecchio 5/r, ☎ 055/211809), Florence's king of coral, has the city's largest selection of finely crafted pieces, as well as cultured pearls, jade, and turquoise. **Carlo Piccini** (✉ Ponte Vecchio 31/r ☎ 055/292030) has been around for several generations, selling antique jewelry as well as making pieces to order; you can also get old jewelry reset. One of Florence's oldest jewelers, **Tiffany Faraone** (✉ Via Tornabuoni 25/r, ☎ 055/215506), has supplied Italian (and other) royalty with finely crafted gems for centuries. Its selection of antique-looking classics has been updated with a choice of contemporary silver. To reach **C. O. I. Wholesale Jewelry** (✉ Via Por Santa Maria 8/r, ☎ 055/283970), you must ring the doorbell at the street and take the elevator to the second floor, where the display cases are filled with handsome handmade Florentine designs.

Gatto Bianco (✉ Borgo Santi Apostoli 12/r, ☎ 055/282989) has breathtakingly beautiful jewelry worked in semiprecious and precious stones; the feel is completely contemporary. Affordable necklaces and rings, mostly in silver, can be found at **La Gazza Ladra** (✉ Piazza Salvemini 6, ☎ 055/2466008). **Oreria** (✉ Borgo Pint, 87/a, ☎ 055/244708), run by two young women who create divine designs using silver and semiprecious stones, is the place to direct someone to buy you something significant.

Shoes and Leather Accessories

In high tourist season, status-conscious shoppers often stand in line outside **Gucci** (✉ Via Tornabuoni 73/r, ☎ 055/264011), ready to buy anything with the famous designer's initials; American Tom Ford has infused freshness into its designs, which, not surprisingly, have a decidedly American flair. Beware, however, of shop assistants with severe attitude problems. Born near Naples, the late Salvatore **Ferragamo** (✉ Via Tornabuoni 2/r, ☎ 055/292123) earned his fortune custom-making shoes for famous feet, especially Hollywood stars. The elegant store, located in a 13th-century Renaissance palazzo, displays designer clothing and accessories, but elegant footwear still underlies the Ferragamo success. **Cellerini** (✉ Via del Sole 37/r, ☎ 055/282533) is an institution in a city where it seems that just about everybody is wearing an expensive leather jacket.

For sheer creativity in both color and design, check out the shoes at **Sergio Rossi** (✉ Via Roma 15/r, ☎ 055/294873) and fantasize about having a life to go with them. Lighthearted and fun shoes for younger enthusiasts can be found at **Dominici** (✉ Via Calimala 23/r, ☎ 055/210251), which also has a lovely but limited line of clothing. **Pollini** (✉ Via Calimala 12/r, ☎ 055/214738) has beautifully crafted shoes and leather accessories for those willing to pay that little bit extra. **Romano** (✉ Via Speziali 10/r, ☎ 055/216535) has everything from the staid to the offbeat at very appealing prices. **Lily of Florence** (✉ Via Guicciardini 2/r, ☎ 055/294748) offers high-quality, classic shoe designs at reasonable prices and in American sizes.

Giotti (✉ Piazza Ognissanti 3–4/r, ☎ 055/294265) has a full line of leather goods and leather clothing. **Leather Guild** (✉ Piazza Santa Croce 20/r, ☎ 055/241932) is one of many shops that produce inexpensive, antique-looking leather goods with mass appeal, but here you can see the craftspeople at work. **Il Bisonte** (✉ Via del Parione 31/r, just off Via della Vigna Nuova, ☎ 055/215722) is known for its natural-looking leather goods, all stamped with the store's bison symbol. The ultimate fine leathers are crafted into classic shapes at **Casadei** (✉ Via Tornabuoni 33/r, ☎ 055/287240), winding up as women's shoes and bags. **Madova** (✉ Via Guicciardini 1/r, ☎ 055/2396526) has a rainbow array of high-quality leather gloves. **Furla** (✉ Via Calzaiuoli 47/r, ☎ 055/2382883) makes beautiful leather bags and wallets in up-to-the-minute designs. **Coccinelle** (✉ Via Por Santa Maria 49/r, ☎ 055/2398782) sells leather accessories in bold colors and funky designs.

SIDE TRIPS FROM FLORENCE
Fiesole and Gracious Gardens Around Florence

Fiesole

A half-day excursion to Fiesole, set in the hills 8 km (5 mi) above Florence, gives you a pleasant respite from museums and a wonderful view of the city. From here, the view of the Duomo, with Brunelleschi's powerful cupola, will give you a new appreciation for what the Renaissance accomplished. Fiesole began life as an ancient Etruscan and later Roman village that held some power until it succumbed to the barbarian invasions. Eventually it gave up its independence in exchange for Florence's protection. The medieval cathedral, ancient Roman amphitheater, and lovely old villas behind garden walls are clustered on a series of hilltops. A walk around Fiesole can take from one to two or three hours, depending on how far you stroll from the main piazza.

The trip from Florence by car or bus takes 20–30 minutes. Take Bus 7 from the Stazione Centrale di Santa Maria Novella, Piazza San Marco, or the Duomo. (You can also get on and off the bus at San Domenico.) There are several possible routes for the two-hour walk from central Florence to Fiesole. One route begins in a residential area of Florence called Salviatino (Via Barbacane, near Piazza Edison, on Bus 7 route), and after a short time it offers peeks over garden walls of beautiful villas, as well as the opportunity to look over your shoulder at the panorama of Florence nestled in the valley.

The **Duomo** reveals a stark medieval interior. In the raised presbytery, the **Cappella Salutati** was frescoed by 15th-century artist Cosimo Rosselli, but it was his contemporary sculptor Mino da Fiesole (1430–84) who put the town on the artistic map. The Madonna on the altarpiece and the tomb of Bishop Salutati are fine examples of his work. ⊠ *Piazza Mino da Fiesole,* ☎ *055/59400.* ☉ *Daily 9–12:30.*

The beautifully preserved 2,000-seat **Anfiteatro Romano** (Roman Amphitheater) nearby dates from the 1st century BC and is still used for summer concerts. To the right of the amphitheater are the remains of the **Terme Romani** (Roman Baths), where you can see the gymnasium, hot and cold baths, and rectangular chamber where the water was heated. A beautifully designed **Museo Archeologico,** an intricate series of levels connected by elevators, is built amid the ruins and contains objects dating from as early as 2000 BC. The nearby **Museo Bandini** is a small collection with a lot to offer. It is filled with the private collection of Canon Angelo Maria Bandini (1726–1803); he fancied 13th- to 15th-century Florentine paintings, terra-cotta pieces, and wood sculpture, which he later bequeathed to the Diocese of Fiesole. ⊠ *Via San Francesco 3,* ☎ *055/59477.* ✉ *10,000 lire/€5.15 (includes access to the archaeological park and the museums).* ☉ *Apr.–Sept., daily 9–7; Oct.–Mar., Wed.–Mon. 9–4:30. Closed Tues. in winter.*

Climb the hill to the church of **San Francesco** for a good view of Florence and the plain below from its terrace and benches. Halfway up the hill, you'll see sloping steps to the right; they lead to a lovely wooded **park** with trails that loop out and back to the church.

If you really want to stretch your legs, walk 4 km (2½ mi) back toward Florence center along Via Vecchia Fiesolana, a narrow lane in use since Etruscan times, to the church of **San Domenico.** Sheltered in the church is the *Madonna and Child with Saints* by Fra Angelico, who was a Dominican friar here. ⊠ *Piazza San Domenico, off Via Giuseppe Mantellini,* ☎ *055/59230.* ☉ *Daily 8–noon.*

It's only a five-minute walk northwest from the church of San Domenico to the **Badia Fiesolana,** which was the original cathedral of Fiesole. ⊠ *Via della Badia dei Roccettini,* ☎ *055/59155.* ☉ *Weekdays 9–6, weekends 9:30–12:30.*

Dining and Lodging

$$ ✕ **I' Polpa.** A short distance up the street from Fiesole's main square, this family-owned and -run restaurant offers great food and friendly service. Though it's laid out in two oddly shaped rooms, one of which has no windows, the creamy yellow walls and matching table linens impart a sunny feeling. Walls are lined with photos of famous visitors, including Luciano Pavarotti and Sting. The *carpaccio di manzo di Gorgonzola* (thinly sliced beef with a creamy Gorgonzola sauce) is a nice variation on an often trite classic. The *coniglio in porchetta* (boned rabbit, stuffed and rolled with sausage) is alone worth the trip—has rabbit ever tasted this moist? ⊠ *Piazza Mino da Fiesole 21/22,* ☎ *055/59485. AE, DC, MC, V. Closed Wed.*

$$$$ 🏨 **Villa San Michele.** The cypress-lined driveway provides an elegant preamble to this incredibly gorgeous (and expensive) hotel nestled in the hills of Fiesole. The 16th-century building was originally a Franciscan convent designed by Santi di Tito. Not a single false note is struck in the reception area (formerly the chapel), the dining rooms (a covered cloister and former refectory), or the tasteful antiques and art that decorate the rooms. The open-air loggia, where lunch and dinner are served, provides one of the most stunning views of Florence—a good thing, too, as the food is overpriced and bland. The service and the setting, however, provide a compelling distraction. ✉ *Via Doccia 4, 50014,* ☎ *055/59451,* ⟨FAX⟩ *055/598734. 41 rooms. Restaurant, piano bar, pool, gym. AE, DC, MC, V. Closed Dec.–mid-Mar. CP, MAP.*

$$ 🏨 **Villa Aurora.** On the main piazza, this attractive hotel takes advantage of its hilltop spot, with beautiful views in many of the rooms, some of which are on two levels with beamed ceilings and balconies. The building, built as a theater in 1860, was transformed into a hotel in the late 19th century. It's fit for queens, and quite a few of them—Queen Victoria and Margherita di Savoia among others—have stayed here. Rooms are sophisticated but understated, as is the hotel. ✉ *Piazza Mino da Fiesole 39, 50014,* ☎ *055/59100,* ⟨FAX⟩ *055/59587,* ⟨WEB⟩ *www.villaaurora. com. 26 rooms. Restaurant, bar, meeting room. AE, DC, MC, V.*

Nightlife and the Arts

From June through August, **Estate Fiesolana** (✉ Teatro Romano, Fiesole, ☎ 055/59611) is a festival of theater, music, dance, and film that takes place in the churches and the archaeological park of Fiesole.

Gracious Gardens Around Florence

Like any well-heeled Florentine, you, too, can get away from Florence's hustle and bustle by heading for the hills. Take a break from city sightseeing to enjoy the gardens and villas set like jewels in the hills around the city. Villa di Castello and Villa La Petraia, both just northwest of the center in Castello, can be explored in one trip. The Italian garden at Villa Gamberaia is a quick 8-km (5-mi) jaunt east of the center near Settignano. Plan for a full-day excursion, picnic lunch included, if visiting all three gardens. Spring and summer are the ideal time to visit, when flowers are in glorious bloom. For a prime taste of Medici living, venture farther afield to the family's Villa Medicea in Poggio a Caiano, just south of Prato.

Villa di Castello

A fortified residence in the Middle Ages, Villa di Castello was rebuilt by the Medici in the 15th century. The Accademia della Crusca, the 400-year-old institution that is the official arbiter of the Italian language, now occupies the palace, which is not open to the public. The gardens are the main attraction. From the villa entrance, walk uphill through the 19th-century park laid out in Romantic style, set above part of the formal garden. You'll reach the terrace, which affords a good view of the geometric layout of the Italian garden below; stairs on either side descend to the parterre.

Though the original garden design has been altered somewhat over the centuries, the allegorical theme of animals devised by Tribolo in the 1540s to the delight of the Medici is still evident. The artificial cave, Grotta degli Animali (Animal Grotto), displays an imaginative menagerie of sculpted animals by Giambologna and his assistants. An Ammannati sculpture, a figure of an old man representing *Gennaio* (January), is at the center of a pond on the terrace overlooking the Italianate garden. Two bronze sculptures by Ammannati, centerpieces of fountains studding the Italian garden, can now be seen indoors in Villa La Petraia. Allow about 45 minutes to visit the garden; you can easily visit Villa La Petraia from here, making for a four-hour trip in total.

To get to Villa di Castello by car, head northwest from Florence on Via Reginaldo Giuliani (also known as Via Sestese) to Castello, about 6 km (4 mi) northwest of the city center in the direction of Sesto Fiorentino; follow signs to Villa di Castello. Or take Bus 28 from the city center and tell the driver you want to get off at Villa di Castello; from the stop, walk north about ½ km (¼ mi) up the tree-lined allée from the main road. ✉ *Via di Castello 47, Castello,* ☎ *055/454791.* 📷 *4,000 lire/€2.05 (includes entrance to Villa La Petraia).* ☉ *Garden Nov.–Feb., daily 9–4:30, Mar.–Oct., daily 9–7. Closed 2nd and 3rd Mon. of month. Palace closed to public.*

Villa La Petraia

The splendidly planted gardens of Villa La Petraia sit high above the Arno plain with a sweeping view of Florence. The villa was built around a medieval tower and reconstructed after it was purchased by the Medici sometime after 1530. Virtually the only trace of the Medici having lived here is the 17th-century courtyard frescoes depicting glorious episodes from the clan's history. In the 1800s the villa served as a hunting lodge of King Vittorio Emanuele II (1820–78), who kept his mistress here while Florence was the temporary capital of the newly united country of Italy.

An Italian-speaking guide will take you through the 19th-century-style salons. The garden—also altered in the 1800s—and the vast park behind the palace suggest a splendid contrast between formal and natural landscapes. Allow 60 to 90 minutes to explore the park and gardens, plus 30 minutes for the guided tour of the so-called museum, the villa interior. This property is best visited after the Villa di Castello.

To reach Villa La Petraia by car, travel as though you're going to Villa di Castello, but take the right off Via Reginaldo Giuliani, following the sign for Villa La Petraia. You can walk from Villa di Castello to Villa La Petraia in about 15 minutes; turn left beyond the gate of Villa di Castello and continue straight along Via di Castello and the imposing Villa Corsini; take Via della Petraia uphill to the entrance. ✉ *Via della Petraia 40, Località Castello,* ☎ *055/451208.* 📷 *4,000 lire/€2.05 (includes entrance to Villa di Castello).* ☉ *Oct.–Mar., garden daily 9–4:30, villa tours daily at 9:15, 10, 10:45, 11:30, 12:10, 1:30, 2:20, 3, and 3:40; Apr.–May and Sept., garden daily 9–5, villa tours daily at 9:15, 10, 10:45, 11:30, 12:10, 1:30, 2:20, 3, 3:40, and 4:45; June–Aug., garden daily 9–7, villa tours daily at 9:15, 10, 10:45, 11:30, 12:10, 1:30, 2:20, 3, 3:40, 4:45, 5:35, and 6:35. Closed 2nd and 3rd Mon. of month.*

Villa Gamberaia

Villa Gamberaia, near the village of Settignano on the eastern outskirts of Florence, was the rather modest 15th-century country home of Matteo di Domenico Gamberelli, the father of noted Renaissance sculptors Bernardo, Antonio, and Matteo Rossellino. In the early 1600s the villa eventually passed into the hands of the wealthy Capponi family. They spared no expense in rebuilding it and, more importantly, creating its garden, one of the finest near Florence. Studded with statues and fountains, the garden suffered damage during World War II but has been restored according to the original 17th-century design. This excursion takes about 1½ hours, allowing 45 minutes to visit the garden.

To get here by car, head east on Via Aretina, an extension of Via Gioberti, which is picked up at Piazza Beccaria; follow the sign to the turnoff to the north to Villa Gamberaia, about 8 km (5 mi) from the center. To go by bus, take Bus 10 to Settignano. From Settignano's main Piazza Tommaseo, walk east on Via di San Romano; the second lane on the right is Via del Rossellino, which leads southeast to the entrance of Villa Gamberaia. The walk from the piazza takes about 10 minutes. ✉ *Via del Rossellino 72, near Settignano,* ☎ *055/697205.* 📷 *15,000 lire/€7.70.* ☉ *Garden Mon.–Sat. 8–6, Sun. 8–noon. Parts of villa open by appointment.*

FLORENCE A TO Z

To research prices, get advice from other travelers, and book travel arrangements, visit www.fodors.com.

AIRPORTS AND TRANSFERS

Florence's Aeroporto A. Vespucci, called Peretola, services flights from Milan and Rome, as well as Paris and Brussels. To get into the city from Peretola by car, take the autostrada A11. Pisa's Aeroporto Galileo Galilei is the closest landing point with significant international service. Driving from the airport in Pisa, take S67, a direct route to Florence. For flight information, call the Florence Air Terminal or Aeroporto Galileo Galilei.

There is local bus service from Peretola into Florence. Buy a ticket at the second-floor bar. Take Bus 62, which goes directly from the airport to the train station at Santa Maria Novella; the bus shelter is beyond the parking lot. There is no direct bus service from Pisa's airport to Florence. Buses do go to and from Pisa, but then you have to change to a slow train service.

There is no train service between downtown Florence and Peretola. A scheduled service connects the station at Pisa's Aeroporto Galileo Galilei with Florence's Stazione Centrale di Santa Maria Novella, roughly a one-hour trip. Trains start running about 7 AM from the airport, 6 AM from Florence, and continue service every hour until about 11:30 PM from the airport, 8 PM from Florence. You can check in for departing flights at the air terminal office, which is located just around the corner from train tracks 1 and 2.

➤ AIRPORT INFORMATION: **Aeroporto Galileo Galilei** (✉ 12 km [7 mi] south of Pisa and 80 km [50 mi] west of Florence, ☎ 050/500707, WEB www.pisa-airport.com). **Florence Air Terminal** (✉ Stazione Centrale di Santa Maria Novella, ☎ 055/216073). **Peretola** (✉ 10 km [6 mi] northwest of Florence, ☎ 055/373498, WEB www.safnet.it).

BIKE AND MOPED TRAVEL

Brave souls (cycling in Florence is difficult, at best) may rent bicycles at easy-to-spot locations at Fortezza da Basso, the Stazione Centrale di Santa Maria Novella, and Piazza Pitti. Otherwise try Alinari. If you want to go native and rent a noisy Vespa (Italian for "wasp") or other make of motorcycle or *motorino* (moped), you may do so at Maxirent. Massimo also rents mopeds. However unfashionable, helmets must be rented at either place. As of February 2000, helmets became mandatory, much to the chagrin of many Italians.

If you have well-exercised legs and lungs, you can also take a guided half-day bicycle tour from Florence to Fiesole with the tour group I Bike Italy.

➤ BIKE RENTALS: **Alinari** (✉ Via Guelfa 85/r, ☎ 055/280500). **I Bike Italy** (✉ Borgo degli Albizi 11, ☎ FAX 055/2342371). **Massimo** (✉ Via Cairoli 8, ☎ 055/573689). **Maxirent** (✉ Borgo Ognissanti 155/r, ☎ 055/265420).

BUS TRAVEL TO AND FROM FLORENCE

Long-distance buses offer inexpensive if somewhat claustrophobic service between Florence and other cities in Italy and Europe. One operator is SITA; you can also try Lazzi Eurolines.

➤ BUS INFORMATION: **Lazzi Eurolines** (✉ Via Mercadante 2, ☎ 055/363041, WEB www.lazzi.it). **SITA** (✉ Via Santa Caterina da Siena 17/r, ☎ 055/214721).

BUS TRAVEL WITHIN FLORENCE

Maps and timetables are available for a small fee at the ATAF (Trasporti Area Fiorentina) booth, or for free at visitor information offices. Tickets must be bought in advance at tobacco stores, newsstands, from automatic ticket machines near main stops, or at ATAF booths. The ticket must be canceled in the small validation machine immediately upon boarding. Small electric buses make the rounds of the centro storico and provide an easy alternative to footing it around town. Use the same ticket as for the regular bus.

FARES AND SCHEDULES

Two types of tickets are available, both valid for one or more rides on all lines. One costs 1,500 lire/€0.75 and is valid for one hour from the time it is first canceled; the other costs 2,500 lire/€1.30 and is valid for two hours. A multiple ticket—four tickets, each valid for 60 minutes—costs 5,800 lire/€2,60. A 24-hour tourist ticket costs 6,000 lire/€3.10. Monthly passes are also available.

➤ Bus Information: **ATAF** (⊠ next to train station; Piazza del Duomo 57/r, ☎ 800/019794 toll free).

CAR RENTAL

➤ Local Agencies: **Avis** (⊠ Via Borgo Ognissanti, 128/r, ☎ 055/2398826). **Hertz Italiana** (⊠ Via Finiguerra 33/r, ☎ 055/317543). **Maggiore-Budget Autonoleggio** (⊠ Via Termine 1, ☎ 055/311256).

CAR TRAVEL

Florence is connected to the north and south of Italy by the Autostrada del Sole (A1). It takes about 1 hour of driving on scenic roads to get to Bologna (although heavy truck traffic over the Apennines often makes for slower going), about 3 hours to Rome, and 3 to 3½ hours to Milan. The Tyrrhenian Coast is an hour west on A11. In the city, abandon all hope of using a car, since most of the downtown area is accessible only to locals with properly marked vehicles. For assistance or information, call the ACI (Automobile Club Firenze).

➤ Contacts: **ACI** (☎ 055/2486246).

EMBASSIES AND CONSULATES

➤ United Kingdom: **U.K. Consulate** (⊠ Lungarno Corsini 2, ☎ 055/284133).

➤ United States: **U.S. Consulate** (⊠ Lungarno Vespucci 38, ☎ 055/2398276).

EMERGENCIES

You can get a list of English-speaking doctors and dentists at the U.S. Consulate, or contact the Tourist Medical Service. If you need hospital treatment and an interpreter, you can call AVO, a group of volunteer interpreters; it's open Monday, Wednesday, and Friday 4–6 PM and Tuesday and Thursday 10–noon. Comunale No. 13, a local pharmacy, is open 24 hours a day, seven days a week. For a complete listing of other pharmacies that have late-night hours on a rotating basis, dial 192.

➤ Contacts: **AVO** (☎ 055/2344567). **Tourist Medical Service** (⊠ Via Lorenzo il Magnifico, 59, ☎ 055/475411).

➤ Emergency Services: **Ambulance** (☎ 118). **Emergencies** (☎ 113). **Misericordia** (Red Cross; ⊠ Piazza del Duomo 20, ☎ 055/212222). **Police** (⊠ Via Zara 2, near Piazza della Libertà, ☎ 055/49771).

➤ 24-Hour Pharmacies: **Comunale No. 13** (⊠ Stazione Centrale di Santa Maria Novella, ☎ 055/289435).

ENGLISH-LANGUAGE MEDIA
BOOKS
➤ CONTACTS: **BM Bookshop** (⊠ Borgo Ognissanti 4/r, ☎ 055/294575).
Paperback Exchange (⊠ Via Fiesolana 31/r, ☎ 055/2478154). **Seeber**
(⊠ Via Tornabuoni 70/r, ☎ 055/215697).

LODGING
VILLA RENTALS
➤ LOCAL AGENTS: **The Best in Italy** (⊠ Via Foscolo 72, 50124 Florence,
☎ 055/223064, FAX 055/2298912). **Florence and Abroad** (⊠ Via San
Zanobi 58, 50129 Florence, ☎ 055/470603). **Villas International Ltd.**
(⊠ 950 Northgate Dr., No. 206, 94903 San Rafael, ☎ 800/221–2260,
FAX 055/8244382).

MAIL AND SHIPPING
➤ POST OFFICES: **Florence** (⊠ Via Pellicceria 3, ☎ 055/211147). **Florence** (⊠ Via Pietrapiana 53/55, ☎ 055/214600).
OVERNIGHT SERVICES
➤ MAJOR SERVICES: **DHL** (⊠ Via della Cupola 234/5, ☎ 800/123800
toll-free). **Federal Express** (⊠ Via Gioberti 3, ☎ 055/8974001; 800/
123800 toll free).

SAFETY
LOCAL SCAMS
Florence is subject to the same types of petty thievery that are practiced in Italy's other large, tourist-popular cities. Pickpockets are
known to frequent crowded places, particularly buses. Purse-snatch-
ers sometimes operate on mopeds, making them quick and potentially
dangerous. Groups of gypsy children have a number of ruses to part
you from your property. While the odds are against you falling prey
to such crimes, it's always wise to keep your valuables well guarded,
to be alert to your surroundings, and to err on the side of caution if
you find yourself in suspicious circumstances.

TAXIS
Taxis usually wait at stands throughout the city (in front of the train
station and in Piazza della Repubblica, for example), or you can call
for one. The meter starts at 4,500 lire/€2.30, with a 7,000 lire/€3.60
minimum and extra charges at night, on Sunday, or for radio dispatch.
A tip of about 10% will be much appreciated.
➤ TAXI COMPANIES: **Taxis** (☎ 055/4390 or 055/4798).

TOURS
BUS TOURS
The major bus operators offer half-day itineraries, all of which use comfortable buses staffed with English-speaking guides. Morning tours begin
at 9, when buses pick visitors up at the main hotels. Stops include the
cathedral complex, the Galleria dell'Accademia, Piazzale Michelangelo,
and the Palazzo Pitti (or, on Monday, the Museo dell'Opera del Duomo).
Afternoon tours stop at the large hotels at 2 PM and take in Piazza della
Signoria, the Galleria degli Uffizi (or the Palazzo Vecchio on Monday,
when the Uffizi is closed), nearby Fiesole, and, on the return, the
church of Santa Croce. A half-day tour costs about 48,000 lire/€24.75,
including museum admissions.
➤ FEES AND SCHEDULES: **Lazzi Eurolines** (⊠ Via Mercadante 2, ☎ 055/
363041, WEB www.lazzi.it). **SITA** (⊠ Via Santa Caterina da Siena 17/
r, ☎ 055/214721).

TRAIN TRAVEL
Florence is on the principal Italian train route between most European
capitals and Rome, and within Italy it is served frequently from Milan,

Venice, and Rome by Intercity (IC) and nonstop Eurostar trains. Stazione Centrale di Santa Maria Novella is the main station and is centrally located. Be sure to avoid trains that stop only at the Campo di Marte or Rifredi stations, which are not convenient to the center.

➤ TRAIN INFORMATION: **Stazione Centrale di Santa Maria Novella** (☎ 8488/888088).

TRAVEL AGENCIES

➤ LOCAL AGENT REFERRALS: **American Express** (✉ Via Dante Alighieri 22/r, ☎ 055/50981). **CIT Italia** (✉ Piazza Stazione 51/r, ☎ 055/284145 or 055/212606). **Micos Travel Box** (✉ Via dell'Oriuolo 50–52/r, ☎ 055/2340228). **Thomas Cook** (✉ Lungarno Acciaiuoli 7/r, ☎ 055/289781).

VISITOR INFORMATION

➤ TOURIST INFORMATION: **Fiesole** (✉ Piazza Mino da Fiesole 37, 50014, ☎ 055/598720). **Florence** (Agenzia Promozione Turistica [APT]; ✉ Via Cavour 1/r, next to Palazzo Medici-Riccardi, 50100, ☎ 055/290832; ✉ Stazione Centrale di Santa Maria Novella, 50100, ☎ 055/212245; ✉ Borgo Santa Croce 29/r, ☎ 055/2340444).

8 TUSCANY

LUCCA, PISA, SIENA, CHIANTI, THE HILL TOWNS

Rolling hills, silver-green olive groves, and enchanting hill towns combine to make Tuscany one of the most beautiful places in the world. Little has changed since the Renaissance; Siena's narrow medieval streets captivate, while Chianti's narrow roads wind their way through cypress-strewn countryside. A visit here is magic and food for the soul.

USCANY, OR TOSCANA, LIES IN CENTRAL ITALY, midway down the peninsula, with miles of coastline on the Tyrrhenian Sea. Rolling hills, snowcapped mountains, and dramatic cypress trees provide breathtaking views everywhere you look. The Arno, its most famous river, stretches clear across the region from Florence before making its way to the sea just beyond Pisa. The beauty of its landscape proves a perfect foil for the abundance of superlative art and architecture found in the region. It also produces some of Italy's finest wines and olive oils. The combination of unforgettable art, sumptuous views, and eminently drinkable wines that pair beautifully with its simple food makes a trip to Tuscany something beyond special.

Updated by
Patricia Rucidlo

Tuscany was populated, at least by the 7th century BC, by the Etruscans, a mysterious lot who chose to live on hills—the better to see the approaching enemy—in such diverse places as Arezzo, Chiusi, Cortona, Fiesole, and Volterra. Some 500 years later, the Romans came, saw, and conquered; by 241 BC they had built the Aurelia, a road from Rome to Pisa that is still in use today. The crumbling of the Roman Empire and subsequent invasions by marauding Lombards, Byzantines, and Holy Roman Emperors meant centuries of turmoil. By the 12th century, the formation of city-states was occurring throughout Tuscany in part, perhaps, because it was unclear exactly who was in charge.

The two groups vying for power were the Guelphs and the Ghibellines, champions of the pope and the Holy Roman Emperor, respectively. They jostled for control of individual cities and of the region as a whole. Florence was more or less Guelph, and Siena more often than not Ghibelline. This led to bloody battles, most notably the 1260 battle of Montaperti, in which the Ghibellines roundly defeated the Guelphs.

Eventually—by the 14th century—the Guelphs became the dominant force. But this did not mean that the warring Tuscan cities settled down to a period of relative peace and tranquillity. The age in which Dante wrote his *Divine Comedy* and Giotto and Piero della Francesca created their incomparable frescoes was one of internecine strife. Florence was the power to be reckoned with; it coveted Siena, which it conquered and reconquered during the 15th and 16th centuries. Finally, in 1555, Siena fell for good, and in rapid succession Pisa, Prato, Volterra, and Arezzo succumbed as well. They were all united under Florence to form the grand duchy of Tuscany. The only city to escape Florence's dominion was Lucca, which remained fiercely independent until the arrival of Napoléon. Eventually, however, even Florence's influence waned, and the 17th and 18th centuries saw the decline of the entire region as various armies swept across it.

Some contend that the purest Italian is spoken in Tuscany. Tuscans—and Florentines, in particular—proudly claim Dante as a native son, and his *Divine Comedy* certainly did much to put the Tuscan vernacular on the map. Boccaccio followed suit with his bawdy *Decameron*, written in the 1350s. However, it was the Arezzan Petrarch (1304–74), one of the earliest of the humanists of the Italian Renaissance, whose use of the vernacular in his poetry was most widely imitated.

To many, Tuscan art is synonymous with the art of Florence, and that bias can be attributed in part to the Arezzan Giorgio Vasari (1511–74), who, in his *Lives of the Artists*, created an inescapably Florentine canon. And though Florentine art is dazzling, the rest of Tuscany should not be overlooked. Nicola Pisano (active circa 1258–78) carved a beautiful and groundbreaking pulpit in Pisa, then worked with his son Giovanni on another in Siena. Giovanni carried the tradition to

Pistoia. Ambrogio Lorenzetti (circa 1319–48) produced wonderful scenes representing *Good and Bad Government* in the Palazzo Pubblico in Siena. The frescoes of the *Legend of the True Cross* by Piero della Francesca (circa 1420–92) in Arezzo are among the 15th century's most stunning fresco cycles. Siena-born Aeneas Silvius Piccolomini (1405–64), later Pope Pius II, carried out his vision of an ideal Renaissance city in Pienza. Renaissance art was by no means exclusively Florentine.

Today many of Tuscany's cities and towns are little changed. Civic rivalries that led to bloody battles so many centuries ago have given way to soccer rivalries. Renaissance pomp lives on in the celebration of local feast days and centuries-old traditions like the Palio in Siena or the Giostra del Saraceno (Joust of the Saracen) in Arezzo. Many present-day Tuscans look as though they might have served as models for paintings produced hundreds of years ago. It often seems as though the Renaissance is within living memory.

Pleasures and Pastimes

Dining

Just as the ancient Etruscans introduced cypress trees to the Tuscan landscape, their influence on regional food—in the use of fresh herbs—still lingers after more than three millennia. Simple and earthy, Tuscan food celebrates the seasons with a host of fresh vegetable dishes, wonderful bread-based soups, and savory meats and game perfumed with sage, rosemary, and thyme. Saltless Tuscan bread is grilled and drizzled with olive oil (*crostini*), or spread with chicken liver (*crostini di fegatini*), or rubbed with garlic and topped with tomatoes (*bruschetta* or *fettunta*). For their love of beans—particularly *cannellini* (white beans) simmered in olive oil and herbs until creamy—Tuscans have been disparagingly nicknamed *mangiafagioli* (bean eaters) by Italians from other regions. Pecorino, a cheese made from sheep's milk, is particularly good in these parts—try it when it's young and in a soft, practically spreadable state, as well as when it's *stagionato*, or aged. When it's good, it's the equal of the finest Parmesan.

Grapes have been cultivated here since Etruscan times, and Chianti still dominates. The robust red wine is a staple on most tables; however, the discerning can select from a multitude of other varieties, including such reds as Brunello di Montalcino and Vino Nobile di Montepulciano and whites such as Valdinievole and Vernaccia. Super Tuscans, a fanciful name given to a group of wines by American journalists, now command attention as some of the best wines produced in Italy; they have great depth and complexity. The dessert wine *vin santo* is produced throughout the region and is often sipped with *biscotti di Prato* (twice-baked cookies), perfect for dunking. For general information and price categories, *see* Dining *in* Smart Travel Tips.

Lodging

Staying in Tuscany is not inexpensive, especially in well-visited cities such as Siena, Lucca, San Gimignano, and Arezzo. But wonderful properties abound, including medieval and Renaissance palazzi in which you'll feel more like Lorenzo de' Medici than a 21st-century visitor. To keep costs down, overnight in less-frequented towns. You might want to consider staying at an *agriturismo*, a farm that has opened its rooms or apartments to guests; choices range from rustic to stately (note that some require a minimum stay). Villa rental can also be an economical and enjoyable option for groups and families. For general information and price categories, *see* Lodging *in* Smart Travel Tips.

Exploring Tuscany

It is best to have a car when traveling in Tuscany to enjoy fully the region's riches—it's the only way to get to many small towns and vineyards. If traveling by public transportation, however, plan on going by bus rather than train. The cities west of Florence are easily reached by the A11, which heads from Florence to Lucca and then to the sea; the A1 heads south from Florence toward Arezzo. Florence and Siena are connected by a superstrada and also the panoramic S222, which threads through Chianti wine country. The hill towns north and west of Siena lie along superstradas and winding local roads—all are well marked, but you should arm yourself with a good map.

Numbers in the text correspond to numbers in the margin and on the Tuscany, Lucca, Pisa, and Siena maps.

Great Itineraries

Although Tuscany is relatively small—no important destination is more than a few hours' drive from Florence—the desire to linger is strong: can you really get enough of sitting on a *terrazza* (terrace) with a good espresso or a full-bodied Chianti and watching the evening settle over a landscape of soft-edged hills, proud medieval towns, quiet villages, and cypress-ringed villas?

It only takes a few days for the region to make an indelible mark on your memory. Seven days would allow you time to explore the main towns and meander along country roads to rustic wineries. In five days, you can see the most interesting towns, but you'll need to stick to the main sights and move briskly. If three days is the limit, you can take in all the highlights, if not the small corners.

IF YOU HAVE 3 DAYS

Florence is a practical starting point. See **Lucca** ④–⑩ and the **Leaning Tower** ⑪ in **Pisa** ⑪–⑲, and then head for ⊞ **San Gimignano** ㉒ to overnight. The next day, explore the tangle of medieval alleyways in **Siena** ㉘–㉟ for a few hours; then move on to ⊞ **Montepulciano** ㊴ for the night. The following day, detour south to the thermal waters of **Saturnia** ㊻ and stroll through the medieval town of **Pitigliano** ㊼; then go north to **Arezzo** ㊱ and head back to Florence via the A1 or, if you have time, along the twisting roads of **Chianti** ㉔–㉗ (S69 west, S408 west, S429 west, and S222 north).

IF YOU HAVE 5 DAYS

From Florence, head for industrial **Prato** ① to see its striking *centro storico*; historic **Pistoia** ②, site of bitter Guelph-Ghibelline feuding; and, if you enjoy resorts, **Montecatini Terme** ③, one of Europe's most famous spas. Stay over in ⊞ **Lucca** ④–⑩ and spend part of the next day exploring. Head for **Pisa** ⑪–⑲ to see the **Leaning Tower** ⑪; then move on to the enchanting hilltop town of **San Miniato** ⑳ and either ⊞ **Volterra** ㉑ or ⊞ **San Gimignano** ㉒, the archetypal Tuscan town and a good place to spend your second night. On the third day, either while away the morning driving through ⊞ **Chianti** ㉔–㉗ (where you will inevitably want to settle in for a night) or head directly to ⊞ **Siena** ㉘–㉟, perhaps Italy's loveliest medieval city. From Siena see the **Abbazia di Monte Oliveto Maggiore** ㊳, **Montalcino** ㊶, the **Abbazia di Sant'Antimo** ㊷, and then ⊞ **Montepulciano** ㊴, where staying in an agriturismo outside the town is a charming option. On the morning of your fifth day drive to **Saturnia** ㊻ and enjoy a hot thermal bath before moving on to ⊞ **Pitigliano** ㊼ to wander its quaint streets. Then head to **Pienza** ㊵, designed for Pope Pius II as the perfect Renaissance town. Move on to handsome and increasingly popular ⊞ **Cortona** ㊲, where you can see the lovely Fra Angelico in the Museo Diocesano; in ⊞

Tuscany

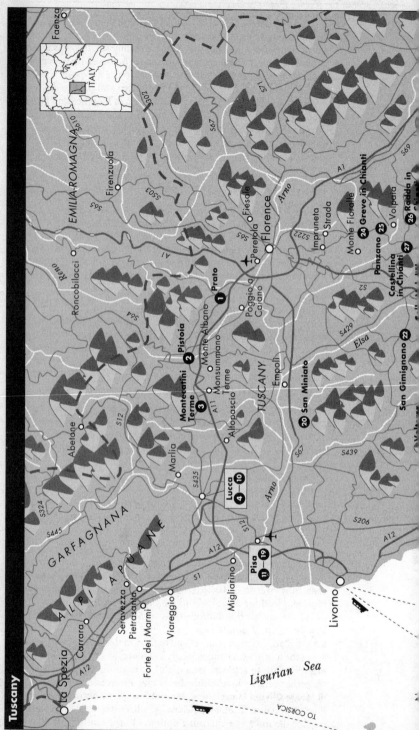

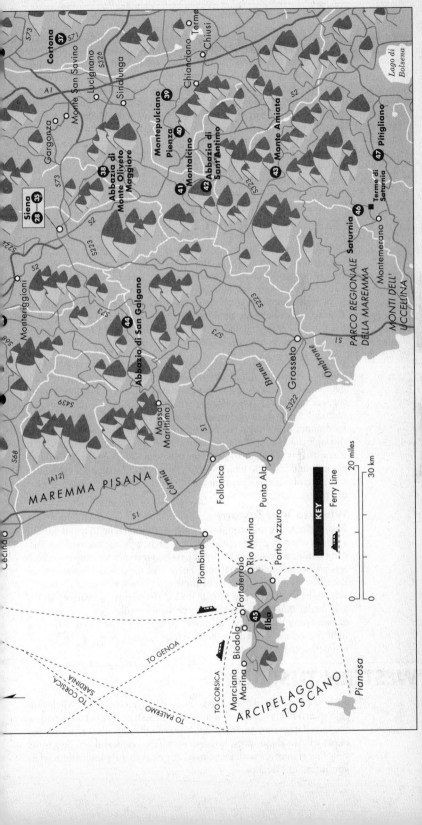

Arezzo ㊱ stop at the church of San Francesco to look at Piero della Francesca's glorious frescoed scenes of the *Legend of the True Cross*.

IF YOU HAVE 7 DAYS

As you approach **Prato** ①, you'll have time to visit the modern collection at the Centro per l'Arte Contemporanea L. Pecci. If you opt to see the resort town of **Montecatini Terme** ③, take a soak in one of the local *terme* (spas) or ride the funicular up to older Montecatini Alto. Extend your ⊞ **Pisa** ⑪–⑲ exploration beyond the Piazza del Duomo to include the Renaissance trio in **Piazza dei Cavalieri** ⑰, and then stay the night. From Pisa, you have a choice for your next day and overnight: explore timeless ⊞ **San Miniato** ⑳, ⊞ **Volterra** ㉑, and/or ⊞ **San Gimignano** ㉒, or head east to wine country. Take the S67 east toward Florence, and before entering the city turn south to pick up the meandering S222, the Strada Chiantigiana that runs through the heart of ⊞ **Chianti** ㉔–㉗ by way of **Panzano** ㉕, stopping to enjoy some of the local wine at one of the many *enoteche* (wine bars) on the main piazza. Carry on to **Castellina in Chianti** ㉗ and stay the night, perhaps in ⊞ **Radda in Chianti** ㉖. The next two days and nights, vineyard-hop in Chianti or settle into a ⊞ **Siena** ㉘–㉟ hotel, taking a day to see the city. Be sure to visit Monteriggioni, a hilltop hamlet between Siena and Colle Val d'Elsa encircled by formidable 13th-century walls. En route to Florence, stop and stroll the streets of charming **Colle Val d'Elsa** ㉓. Don't forget about the possibility of visiting the Tuscan archipelago the last two nights, including rugged ⊞ **Elba** ㊺ and Montecristo, accessible from Livorno or Piombino (by boat), and Pisa (by air).

If you're not sea bound, from Siena head south to discover **Montepulciano** ㊴, **Pienza** ㊵, and ⊞ **Montalcino** ㊶ for a night. For a moving sight, detour to the **Abbazia di San Galgano** ㊹. East of Siena and well worth the side trip and last overnight are ⊞ **Cortona** ㊲ and ⊞ **Arezzo** ㊱, the main hill towns of the province of Arezzo. For a taste of a more rugged landscape, don't take the autostrada back to Florence but detour through the Casentino, a mountainous region blanketed with a vast forest that is a far cry from the pastoral images associated with Tuscany. You'll take the winding S70, called the Consuma, a splendidly scenic road with hairpin turns and blind corners that challenge even the best drivers.

When to Tour Tuscany

In summer, try to arrive in towns early in the morning to avoid crowds and the often oppressive heat. Rising early will not be hard, as Tuscany is not about late nights; most bars and restaurants close their shutters well before midnight. If you plan to visit the frescoes in the Palazzo Pubblico in Siena at midday, be prepared to wait in line and, once inside, to be shuffled along by iron-willed attendants eager to see you in and out as quickly as possible. If you want to photograph the towers of San Gimignano from a distance, do it in early morning, when the light is good and lines of neon-color tour buses snaking up the hill will not ruin a perfect picture.

WESTERN TUSCANY

Set in the shadows of the rugged coastal Alpi Apuane, where Michelangelo quarried his marble, this area isn't as lush as southern Tuscany—the hills flatten out, and there are hints of industry. It's well worth the effort to visit these spots, however—there's wonderful art, and some very fine restaurants can be enjoyed at prices slightly lower than what you'll find in Florence.

Prato

❶ *17 km (11 mi) northwest of Florence, 60 km (37 mi) east of Lucca.*

The wool industry in this city, one of the world's largest manufacturers of cloth, was known throughout Europe as early as the 13th century. It was further stimulated in the 14th century by a local cloth merchant, Francesco di Marco Datini, who built his business, according to one of his ledgers, "in the name of God and of profit."

Prato's **Centro per l'Arte Contemporanea L. Pecci** (L. Pecci Center of Contemporary Art) has acquired a burgeoning collection of works by Italian and other artists. ⊠ *Viale della Repubblica 277,* ☎ *0574/5317,* WEB *www.comune.prato.it/pecci.* ⊡ *12,000 lire/€6.20.* ☉ *Mon. and Wed.–Sun. 10–6:15.*

Prato's Romanesque **Duomo** is famous for its **Pergamo del Sacro Cingolo** (Chapel of the Holy Girdle), to the left of the entrance, which enshrines the girdle of the Virgin Mary. It is said that the Virgin presented it to the apostle Thomas in a miraculous appearance after her Assumption. The Duomo also contains 15th-century frescoes by Prato's most famous son, Fra Filippo Lippi (1406–69), who executed scenes from the life of St. Stephen on the left wall and scenes from the life of John the Baptist on the right in the **Cappella Maggiore** (Main Chapel). ⊠ *Piazza del Duomo,* ☎ *0574/26234.* ☉ *May–Oct., daily 7–12:30 and 4–7:30; Nov.–Apr., daily 7–12:30 and 3:30–7.*

Sculptures by Donatello (circa 1386–1466) that originally adorned the Duomo's exterior pulpit are now on display in the **Museo dell'Opera del Duomo.** ⊠ *Piazza del Duomo 49,* ☎ *0574/29339.* ⊡ *10,000 lire/€5.15 (includes Museo di Pittura Murale).* ☉ *Mon. and Wed.–Sat. 9:30–12:30 and 3–6:30, Sun. 9:30–12:30.*

Installed in the **Museo di Pittura Murale** (Museum of Mural Painting) is a collection of paintings by Fra Filippo Lippi and other works from the 13th–15th centuries in a special exhibit called Treasures of the City, on view through 2002. The permanent collection contains frescoes removed from sites in Prato and environs. ⊠ *Piazza San Domenico,* ☎ *0574/440501.* ⊡ *10,000 lire/€5.15 (includes Museo dell'Opera del Duomo).* ☉ *Mon. and Wed.–Sat. 10–6, Sun. 10–1.*

The church of **Santa Maria delle Carceri** was built by Giuliano Sangallo in the 1490s and is a landmark of Renaissance architecture. ⊠ *Piazza Santa Maria delle Carceri, off Via Cairoli and southeast of the cathedral,* ☎ *0574/27933.* ☉ *Daily 7–noon and 4–7.*

Though in ruins, the formidable **Castello** (Castle) built for Frederick II Hohenstaufen, adjacent to Santa Maria delle Carceri, is an impressive sight, the only castle of its type outside southern Italy. ⊠ *Piazza Santa Maria delle Carceri,* ☎ *0574/38207.* ☉ *Nov.–Feb., Mon. and Wed.–Fri. 10–4, weekends 10–5; Mar.–Oct. Wed.–Mon. 10–7.*

OFF THE BEATEN PATH
POGGIO A CAIANO – For a look at gracious country living Renaissance style, detour south of Prato to the Villa Medicea in Poggio a Caiano. Lorenzo "il Magnifico" (1449–92) commissioned Giuliano da Sangallo (circa 1445–1516) to redo the villa, which was lavished with frescoes by important Renaissance painters such as Andrea del Sarto (1486–1530) and Pontormo (1494–1557). You can take a walk around the austerely ornamented grounds while waiting for entry. ⊠ *Poggio a Caiano, 7 km (4½ mi) south of Prato, follow signs,* ☎ *055/877012.* ⊡ *4,000 lire/€2.05.* ☉ *Apr.–May and Sept.–Oct, daily 9–5:30; June–Aug., Mon.–Sat. 9–6:30; Mar., daily 9–4:30; Nov.–Feb.,*

Mon.–Sat. 9–3:30. Guided visits only, hourly on the ½ hr (9:30–1 hr before closing). Closed 2nd and 3rd Mon. of month.

Dining

$$$ ✕ **Da Delfina.** Veer off the autostrada to this haven of Tuscan cook-
★ ing nestled amid vineyards and olive trees past Poggio a Caiano in Ar-
timino. Delfina began cooking for hungry hunters, and now she has
four comfortably rustic dining rooms in a farmhouse where you can
enjoy dishes centered on pure ingredients, seasonal vegetables, and sa-
vory meats accented with herbs. The *secondi* (second courses) such as
coniglio con olive e pignoli (rabbit sautéed with olives and pine nuts)
are a real treat. ⊠ *Via della Chiesa 1, Artimino,* ☎ *055/8718074. Reser-
vations essential. No credit cards. Closed Mon. and 1 wk in Jan. No
dinner Sun.*

$$$ ✕ **Osvaldo Baroncelli.** Polished wooden floors, subtly striped chairs, and
★ pale sponged walls bespeak the seriousness of the restaurant, which has
been in the Baroncelli family for 50-some years. In that time they've perfected their menu. You'll be tempted to eat all of the perfectly fried olives
that arrive warm, but save room for what's to come. Try the *insalata
tiepida di gamberi, calamaretti, e carciofi* (warm salad with shrimp,
squid, and artichokes) or the colorful flan *di zucca gialla e ricotta* (with
yellow squash and ricotta) in a light fish sauce. The pastas are house-
made—the *tortelli di fagiano in salsa di scalogno con pancetta* (pheas-
ant-stuffed tortelli with a shallot-infused bacon sauce) is wonderful.
Reservations are advised. ⊠ *Via Fra Bartolomeo 13,* ☎ *0574/23810.
AE, MC, DC, V. Closed Sun. and 3 wks in Aug. No lunch Sat.*

$$$ ✕ **Piraña.** Oddly named for the carnivorous fish swimming in an
aquarium with a full view of the diners, this sophisticated restaurant,
decorated in shades of blue with steely accents, is a local favorite. Seafood
is the specialty and may take the form of ravioli *di branzino in crema
di scampi* (stuffed with sea bass with a creamy shrimp sauce) and
rombo al forno (baked turbot). It's a bit out of the way for sightseers
but handy if you have a car, as it's near the Prato Est autostrada exit.
⊠ *Via G. Valentini 110,* ☎ *0574/25746. AE, DC, MC, V. Closed Sun.
and Aug. No lunch Sat.*

$$ ✕ **Baghino.** In the heart of the historic center, Baghino serves typical
Tuscan fare along with such atypical dishes as spaghetti *all'amatriciana*
(with bacon in a spicy tomato sauce) and penne *con vongole e curry*
(with clams and curry). You can dine on the lovely outdoor terrace in
summer. ⊠ *Via dell'Accademia 9,* ☎ *0574/27920, AE, DC, MC, V.
No dinner Sun., no lunch Mon.*

Shopping

Prato's biscotti (literally "twice cooked") have an extra-dense texture,
lending themselves to submersion in your caffè or vin santo. The best
in town are at **Antonio Mattei** (⊠ Via Ricasoli 20/22, ☎ 0574/25756).

The centuries-old tradition of selling fine textiles crafted into fine
clothing continues in Prato. **Ottomila** (⊠ Via Friuli-Venezia Giulia 20,
Località Macrolotto, ☎ 0574/620632) is worth a visit to check out
its lovely wholesale knitwear. **Enrico Pecci di A. Pecci & C.** (⊠ Via di
Pantano 16/e, ☎ 0574/89890) sells fabric by the meter.

Pistoia

② *18 km (11 mi) northwest of Prato, 36 km (22 mi) northwest of Florence.*

Pistoia can claim a Roman past, as well as a bloody history during the
Middle Ages when the town was rent by civil strife. Its historic center
is a jewel and little visited, which makes coming here worth the effort.

The **Cattedrale di San Zeno** in the main piazza houses the *Dossale di San Jacopo,* a magnificent silver altar. The two half-figures on the left were executed by Filippo Brunelleschi (1377–1446). ⊠ *Piazza del Duomo,* ☎ *0573/25095.* 🎟 *Illumination of altarpiece 3,000 lire/€1.55.* ☉ *Church daily 8:30–12:30 and 3:30–7; altar Mon.–Sat. 10–noon and 4–5:45, Sun. 11:20–noon and 4–5:30.*

The **Palazzo del Comune,** begun around 1295, houses the **Museo Civico,** with works by local artists from the 14th to 20th century. ⊠ *Museo Civico, Piazza del Duomo 1,* ☎ *0573/371296.* 🎟 *6,000 lire/€3.10, free Sat. 3–7.* ☉ *Tues.–Sat. 10–7, Sun. 9–12:30.*

Founded in the 13th century, the **Spedale del Ceppo** (literally, Hospital of the Tree Stump) has a glorious early 16th-century exterior terracotta frieze begun by Giovanni della Robbia (1469–1529) and completed by the workshop of Santi and Benedetto Buglioni in 1526–28. ⊠ *Piazza Ospedale, a short way down Via Pacini from Piazza del Duomo.*

An architectural gem in green-and-white marble, the medieval church of **San Giovanni Fuorcivitas** contains a *Visitation* by Luca della Robbia (1400–82), a painting attributed to Taddeo Gaddi, and a holy-water font that may have been executed by Fra Guglielmo around 1270. ⊠ *Via Cavour,* ☎ *0573/24784.* ☉ *Daily 8–noon and 5–6:30.*

Though it's not as grand as the silver altar in Pistoia's cathedral, many consider the town's greatest art treasure to be Giovanni Pisano's powerfully sculpted pulpit, executed between 1298 and 1301 in the church of **Sant'Andrea.** ⊠ *Via Sant'Andrea,* ☎ *0573/21912.* ☉ *Nov.–Mar., daily 8–12:30 and 3:30–5; Apr.–Oct., daily 8–12:30 and 3:30–7.*

☧ The **Giardino Zoologico,** a small zoo especially laid out to accommodate the wiles of both animals and children, is a 20-minute drive out of town. Take Bus 29 from the train station. ⊠ *Via Pieve a Celle 160/a,* ☎ *0573/911219.* 🎟 *14,000 lire/€7.20.* ☉ *Apr.–Sept., daily 9–7; Oct.–Mar., daily 9:30–5.*

Dining

$$ ✕ **Corradossi.** This lovely pan-Italian restaurant, a short walk from Piazza del Duomo, makes for an excellent place to break for lunch or dinner. The food is simply prepared, the service quick and attentive, and the prices are more than reasonable. Start with the *trofie e gamberi* (corkscrew-shape pasta with shrimp and sliced baby zucchini), and then follow with the *frittura di mare* (fried fish and shellfish). ⊠ *Via Frosini 112,* ☎ *0573/25683. AE, DC, MC, V. Closed Sun.*

$$ ✕ **S. Jacopo.** This charming restaurant, minutes away from the Piazza
★ del Duomo, has white walls, tiled floors, and a gracious host in Bruno Lottini, a native Pistoian fluent in English. Tasteful prints and photographs on the walls play nicely off the rustic blue linens that dress the tables. The menu has mostly regional favorites, such as the *maccheroni S. Jacopo,* wide ribbons of house-made pasta with a duck *ragù* (sauce), but the chef can turn out perfectly grilled squid as well. Save room for dessert, especially the apple strudel. ⊠ *Via Crispi 15,* ☎ *0573/27786. AE, DC, MC, V. Closed Mon. No lunch Tues.*

$ ✕ **La BotteGaia.** This tiny, popular wine bar with eight tables is located just off Piazza del Duomo. The vaulted room is narrow, with exposed brick and stone walls; jazz plays softly in the background. On offer is typical wine-bar fare: plates of *salami e formaggi* (cured hams and cheeses), assorted *carpacci* (thinly sliced cured meats or fish served over various shredded greens), and a surprisingly sophisticated list of daily specials that can include *insalatina con foie gras condita con vinaigrette* (foie gras with dressed greens). The wine list is formidable and particularly strong on Tuscany. At press time, a similarly small sister location was scheduled to open just down the street offering outdoor seating with a view of the splendid Piazza del Duomo. ⊠ *Via del Lastrone 4,* ☎ *0573/365602. Reservations essential. AE, DC, MC, V. Closed Mon. and 15 days in Aug. No lunch Sun.*

Montecatini Terme

❸ *16 km (10 mi) west of Pistoia, 49 km (30 mi) west of Florence.*

Immortalized in Fellini's 8½, Montecatini Terme is home to Italy's premier thermal baths, known for their curative powers and, at least once upon a time, for their great popularity among the wealthy. The mineral springs flow from five sources and are used to treat liver and skin disorders. Those "taking the cure" report each morning to one of the town's *stabilimenti termali* (thermal establishments; ⊠ Via Verdi 41, ☎ 0572/778509 information) to drink their prescribed cupful of water, whose curative effects became known in the 1800s. The town's wealth of Art Nouveau buildings went up during its heyday at the beginning of the 20th century. Like most other well-heeled resort towns, Montecatini attracts the leisured traveler; aside from taking the waters and people-watching in Piazza del Popolo, there's not a whole lot to do here. Of Montecatini Terme's Art Nouveau structures, the most attractive is the **Terme Tettuccio** (⊠ Viale Verdi 41, ☎ 0572/778501), a neoclassical edifice with colonnades. Here Montecatini's healthful tonic spouts from fountains set up on marble counters, the walls are decorated with bucolic scenes on painted ceramic tiles, and in the morning an orchestra plays under a frescoed dome.

The older town of **Montecatini Alto** sits atop a hill above Montecatini and is reached by a funicular from Viale Diaz. A medieval square is lined with restaurants and bars, the air is crisp, and the views of the Nievole, the valley below, are gorgeous.

LUCCA

In this picturesque fortress town, Caesar, Pompey, and Crassus agreed to rule Rome as a triumvirate in 56 BC; it was later the first town in Tuscany to accept Christianity. Lucca still has a mind of its own, and when most of Tuscany was voting communist as a matter of course, its citizens rarely followed suit. Within the city's 16th- to 17th-century ramparts, the famous composer Giacomo Puccini (1858–1924) was born. He is celebrated, along with his peers, during the summer Opera Theater of Lucca Festival.

Exploring Lucca

The historic center of Lucca is walled, and traffic is restricted—even motorbikes. Walking is therefore the best, most enjoyable way to get around. You can rent bicycles, and as the center is quite flat, getting around town on a bike is easy without the threat of traffic.

A Good Walk

Start at the **Museo Nazionale di Palazzo Mansi** ④ on Via Galli Tassi, just within the walls. Walk down Via del Toro to Piazza del Palazzo Dipinto, and follow Via di Poggio to Casa dei Puccini. Take a quick trip through the composer's house, and exit by returning to Via Poggio, which runs directly into **San Michele in Foro** ⑤. From Piazza San Michele, walk around to the back of the church and follow Via Beccheria south through Piazza Napoleone. Make a left through the smaller Piazza San Giovanni, which leads directly to the **Duomo** ⑥. Check out the charming facade before going into the church and looking at

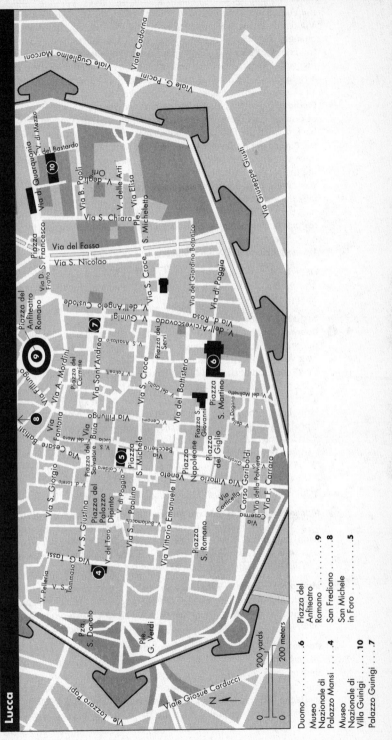

Lucca

Duomo **6**

Museo Nazionale di Palazzo Mansi **4**

Museo Nazionale di Villa Guinigi **10**

Palazzo Guinigi **7**

Piazza del Anfiteatro Romano **9**

San Frediano **8**

San Michele in Foro **5**

0 200 yards

0 200 meters

the Volto Santo crucifix and the tomb of Ilaria del Carretto. Walk down
Via dell'Arcivescovado, which is behind the Duomo; the street name
changes to Via Guinigi just after crossing Via Santa Croce. Climb the
tower of the **Palazzo Guinigi** ⑦ and admire the view. Make a right heading out of Palazzo Guinigi and proceed down via Sant'Andrea; make
a right onto via Fillungo. At Via Fontana, take a left and follow it to
Via Cesare Battisti. Make a right and head toward the church of **San
Frediano** ⑧, with its incredibly mummified Santa Zita, the patron saint
of domestic workers. From the church, walk along Via San Frediano
back toward the Fillungo; make a right and then a left, and head into
the **Piazza del Anfiteatro Romano** ⑨, where the Roman amphitheater
once stood. Relax and have an aperitivo at one of the many cafés lining the piazza. Exit the piazza through the doorway to the left where
you entered. Veer toward the right following the curve of the buildings. Make a quick left onto Via del Portico and bear right. You will
pass the church and piazza of San Pietro Somaldi on your left; just after
the piazza make a left onto Via della Fratta. Continue straight; just after
passing the church of San Francesco, you will find yourself at the
Museo Nazionale di Villa Guinigi ⑩.

TIMING

The walk will take about three hours; add a half hour for lingering in
each of the museums.

Sights to See

★ ⑥ **Duomo.** The round-arched facade of the cathedral is an example of the
rigorously ordered Pisan Romanesque style, in this case happily enlivened
by a varied collection of small carved columns. Take a closer look at
the decoration of the facade and of the portico below, which make for
one of the most entertaining church exteriors in Tuscany. The Gothic
interior contains a moving wood crucifix (called the *Volto Santo*, or
Holy Face) brought here, as legend has it, in the 8th century (though
it probably dates from between the 11th and early 13th centuries). The
marble tomb of Ilaria del Carretto (1408) is the masterpiece of the Sienese
sculptor Jacopo della Quercia (1371/74–1438). ⊠ *Piazza del Duomo,*
☏ *0583/490530.* ▭ *3,000 lire/€1.55.* ☉ *Duomo weekdays 7–6; Sat.
9:30–6:45; Sun. 9–9:50, 11:30–11:50, and 1–5. Tomb weekdays 9:30–
5:15; Sat. 9:30–6:45; Sun. 9–9:50, 11:30–11:50, and 1–5.*

④ **Museo Nazionale di Palazzo Mansi.** Highlights are the lovely *Portrait
of a Youth* by Pontormo and portraits of the Medici painted by
Bronzino (1503–72) and others. ⊠ *Palazzo Mansi, Via Galli Tassi 43,
near the west walls of the old city,* ☏ *0583/55570.* ▭ *8,000 lire/€4.10.*
☉ *Tues.–Sat. 8:30–7:30, Sun. 8:30–1:30.*

⑩ **Museo Nazionale di Villa Guinigi.** On the eastern end of the historic
center, the museum houses an extensive collection of local Romanesque
and Renaissance art. ⊠ *Villa Guinigi, Via della Quarquonia,* ☏ *0583/
496033.* ▭ *8,000 lire/€4.10.* ☉ *Tues.–Sat. 9–7, Sun. 9–2.*

⑦ **Palazzo Guinigi.** The tower of the medieval palace contains one of the
city's most curious sights: six ilex trees have established themselves at
the top, and their roots have grown into the room below. From the
tower there is a magnificent view of the city and the surrounding countryside. ⊠ *Palazzo Guinigi, Via Sant'Andrea 42,* ☏ *0583/491245.* ▭
5,000 lire/€2.60. ☉ *Nov.–Feb., daily 10–4:30; Mar.–Sept., daily 9–7:30;
Oct., daily 10–6.*

⑨ **Piazza del Anfiteatro Romano.** This is where the Roman amphitheater
once stood; the medieval buildings built over the amphitheater retain
its original oval shape and brick arches. ⊠ *Off Via Fillungo.*

8 **San Frediano.** The church contains works by Jacopo della Quercia and, bizarrely, the lace-clad mummy of the patron saint of domestic servants, St. Zita. ⊠ *Piazza San Frediano.* ☉ *Mon.–Sat. 8:30–noon and 3–5, Sun. 10:30–5.*

5 **San Michele in Foro.** This church, slightly west of the centro storico, has a facade even more fanciful than the Duomo's. Check out the superb panel painting of Sts. Girolamo, Sebastian, Rocco, and Helen in the right transept by Filippino Lippi (1457/58–1504). ⊠ *Piazza San Michele.* ☉ *Daily 7:40–noon and 3–6.*

OFF THE
BEATEN PATH

FORTE DEI MARMI – Tuscany's most exclusive summer beach resort is a favorite of moneyed Tuscans and Milanese, whose villas are neatly laid out in a vast pine woods. In summer, a beachcomber's bonanza takes place on Wednesday morning, when everything from faux designer sunglasses to plastic sandals and terry-cloth towels goes on sale. It's 35 km (22 mi) northwest of Lucca and 65 km (40 mi) northwest of Florence— also near the marble-producing towns of Carrara (where Michelangelo quarried his stone), Seravezza, and Pietrasanta.

VILLA REALE – Eight kilometers (5 miles) north of Lucca in Marlia, this villa was once the home of Napoléon's sister, Princess Elisa. Restored by the Counts Pecci-Blunt, the estate is celebrated for its spectacular gardens, originally laid out in the 16th century and redone in the middle of the 17th century. Gardening buffs adore the legendary *teatro di verdura*, a theater carved out of hedges and topiaries; concerts are occasionally held here. One of Tuscany's most popular summer events, the Festival di Marlia, is held in Marlia in July and August; contact the Lucca tourist office (⊠ *Piazzale Verdi,* ☎ *0583/419689*) for details. ⊠ *Villa Reale,* ☎ *0583/30108.* ☐ *10,000 lire/€5.15.* ☉ *Mar.–Nov., guided visits Tues.–Sun. at 10, 11, noon, 3, 4, and 5; Dec. 6–Feb., open by appointment only.*

Dining and Lodging

$$–$$$ ✕ **La Mora.** Detour to this former stagecoach station, now a gracious,
★ rustic country inn 9 km (5½ mi) outside Lucca, for local specialties— from *minestra di farro* (soup made with emmer, a wheat that resembles barley) with beans to homemade *tacconi* (a thin, short, wide pasta) with rabbit sauce to lamb raised in the nearby Garfagnana hills. You might be tempted by the varied crostini and delicious desserts. ⊠ *Via Sesto di Ponte a Moriano 1748,* ☎ *0583/406402. AE, DC, MC, V. Closed Wed. and 3 wks in Jan.*

$$ ✕ **Bucadisanantonio.** This restaurant has been around since 1782,
★ and it's easy to see why. The white-walled interior hung with copper pots, expertly prepared food, and an able staff make dining here a real treat. The menu offers something for everyone—from the simple but blissful *tortelli lucchesi al sugo* (meat-stuffed pasta with a tomato and meat sauce) to such daring dishes as roast *capretto* (kid) with herbs. ⊠ *Via della Cervia 3,* ☎ *0583/55881. AE, DC, MC, V. Closed Mon., 2 wks in Jan., and 2 wks in July. No dinner Sun.*

$$ ✕ **Il Giglio.** Just off Piazza Napoleone, this restaurant has quiet, late-19th-century charm and classic cuisine. It's a place for all seasons, with a big fireplace and an outdoor terrace in summer. Among the local specialties are *farro garfagnino* (a thick soup made with grain and beans) and *coniglio con olive* (rabbit stew with olives). ⊠ *Piazza del Giglio 2,* ☎ *0583/494058. AE, DC, MC, V. Closed Wed. and 15 days in Aug. No dinner Tues.*

$ ✕ **Da Giulio in Pelleria.** If Lucchesi businesspeople had a lunchtime cafeteria, it would be here. This loud, atmosphere-free cavernous trattoria serves tasty, traditional Tuscan favorites, as well as such Lucchesi specialties as *farinata* (vegetable soup thickened to stewlike consistency by the generous addition of cornmeal) to hordes of visitors and locals alike. Don't be at all surprised to see the affable waitstaff expertly balancing in one hand five plates brimming with food. ⊠ *Via delle Conce 45,* ☎ *0583/555948. AE, DC, MC, V. Closed Mon. and 1st, 2nd, and 4th Sun. of month.*

$ ✕ **Osteria del Neni.** Tucked away on a side street just a block from San Michele, this delightful little place offers up tasty treats in a cozy atmosphere, with paper place mats, wooden tables, and walls sponged in two different hues of warm orange. All the pasta is made in house, and if you're lucky enough to find ravioli *spinaci e anatra in salsa di noci* (stuffed with duck and spinach, with a creamy but light walnut sauce), by all means order it. The menu changes regularly; in the summer, this splendid food can be enjoyed alfresco. ⊠ *Via Pescheria 3,* ☎ *0583/492681. Reservations essential. MC, V. Closed Mon.*

$$$$ ✕ 🏨 **Locanda l'Elisa.** A refined, intimate private-home atmosphere characterizes this handsome neoclassic villa hotel set in a lush garden just outside the city. Most rooms are suites, featuring fresh flowers, antiques, and fine fabrics, and service is enhanced by a caring staff. The innovative restaurant, located in the Victorian conservatory, offers sophisticated twists on Tuscan favorites using such local ingredients as farro (emmer) and chestnuts. ⊠ *Via Nuova per Pisa 1951, 55050,* ☎ *0583/379737,* FAX *0583/379019,* WEB *www.lunet.it/aziende/locandaelisa. 2 rooms, 8 suites. Restaurant, pool. AE, DC, MC, V. Closed Jan. 7–Feb. 7.*

$$$$ 🏨 **Hotel Ilaria.** The former stables of the Villa Botini have been transformed into this modern hotel just within the historic center. Rooms are done in warm wood veneer, and the second-floor terrace overlooking the villa makes a comfortable place to relax. Free bikes are a great bonus. ⊠ *Via del Fosso, 26, 55100,* ☎ *0583/469200,* FAX *0583/991961,* WEB *www.onenet.it/lu/ilaria. 30 rooms. Breakfast room, conference room, bicycles, free parking. AE, DC, MC, V.*

$$$$ 🏨 **Palazzo Alexander.** Lucca has long been in need of a boutique hotel in the *centro storico* and now has it in this small but elegantly appointed place tucked into a quiet side street just a stone's throw from San Michele in Foro. The building, dating from the 12th century, has been restructured to create the ease common to Lucchesi nobility: timbered ceilings, warm yellow walls, and brocaded chairs adorn the public rooms, and the motif is carried into the rooms, all of which have high ceilings and that same glorious damask feel. Top-floor suites offer sweeping views of the town. ⊠ *Via S. Giustina 48, 55100,* ☎ *0583/583571,* FAX *0583/583610,* WEB *www.palazzo-alexander.it. 9 rooms, 3 suites. Breakfast room, wine bar (guests only), bicycles, parking (fee). AE, DC, MC, V.*

$$ 🏨 **La Luna.** On a quiet, airy courtyard close to historic Piazza del Mercato, this family-run hotel occupies two renovated wings of an old building. The bathrooms are modern, but some of the rooms still have the atmosphere of Old Lucca. A parking lot is a bonus. ⊠ *Corte Compagni 12, corner of Via Fillungo, 55100,* ☎ *0583/493634,* FAX *0583/490021. 30 rooms. Parking (fee). AE, DC, MC, V. Closed Jan. 7–31.*

$$ 🏨 **Piccolo Hotel Puccini.** Steps away from the busy square and church of San Michele, this little hotel is quiet, calm, and handsomely decorated. It also offers parking (which must be reserved in advance) at a reasonable fee, a great advantage. ⊠ *Via di Poggio 9, 55100,* ☎ *0583/55421,* FAX *0583/53487,* WEB *www.hotelpuccini.com. 14 rooms. Parking (fee). AE, DC, MC, V.*

Nightlife and the Arts

The **Estate Musicale Lucchese,** one of many Tuscan music festivals, runs throughout the summer in Lucca. Contact the Lucca tourist office (✉ Piazzale Verdi, ☎ 0583/419689) for details. The **Opera Theater of Lucca Festival,** sponsored by the Opera Theater of Lucca and the school of music of the University of Cincinnati, runs from mid-June to mid-July; performances are staged in open-air venues. Call the Lucca tourist office for information.

Outdoor Activities and Sports

One of the best ways to get around this lovely medieval town is on a bike. You can rent one at **Barbetti Cicli** (✉ Via Anfiteatro 23, ☎ 0583/954444). Bikes can be found at **Poli Antonio Biciclette** (✉ Piazza Santa Maria 42, ☎ 0583/493787). The centro storico is flat and easily navigated because automobile traffic is severely limited. A splendid bike ride may be had by circling the entire historic center along the top of the bastions—affording something of a bird's-eye view.

Shopping

Lucca's justly famed olive oil, available throughout the city, is exported around the world. Look for those made by Fattoria di Fubbiano and Fattoria Fabbri—-two of the best. A particularly delicious version of buccellato, a sweet, anise-flavored bread with raisins that is a specialty of Lucca, is baked at **Pasticceria Taddeucci** (✉ Piazza San Michele 34, ☎ 0583/494933). Chocoholics can get their fix at **Caniparoli** (✉ Via S. Paolino 96, ☎ 0583/53456); so serious are they about their sweets that they do not make them from June through August because of the heat. On the second Sunday of the month, there's a **flea market** in Piazza San Martino. Fashion bargain hunters should know that **Benetton** (✉ Via Fillungo 179, ☎ 0583/469608) has opened a factory outlet selling knitwear and other items at rock-bottom prices.

PISA

Pisa may have been inhabited as early as the Bronze Age. It was certainly populated by the Etruscans and, in turn, became part of the Roman Empire. In the early Middle Ages it flourished as an economic powerhouse—along with Amalfi, Genoa, and Venice, it was one of the maritime republics. The city's economic and political power ebbed in the early 15th century as it fell under the domination of Florence, though it enjoyed a brief resurgence under Cosimo I in the mid-16th century. Pisa endured heavy Allied bombing—miraculously, the Duomo and Leaning Tower were spared along with some other grand Romanesque structures. If you get beyond the kitschy atmosphere around the Leaning Tower, Pisa has much to offer. Its treasures are more subtle than Florence's, to which it is inevitably compared; the city's cathedral-baptistery-campanile complex on Piazza del Duomo is among the most dramatic in Italy.

Exploring Pisa

Pisa, like many other Italian cities, is best seen on foot, and most of what you'll want to see is within walking distance. The views along the Arno are particularly grand and shouldn't be missed—there's a feeling of spaciousness that doesn't exist along the Arno in Florence. There are several options for combination tickets to sights on the Piazza del Duomo; consider all your options when you begin your visit. (The combination tickets are sold at the sights themselves.)

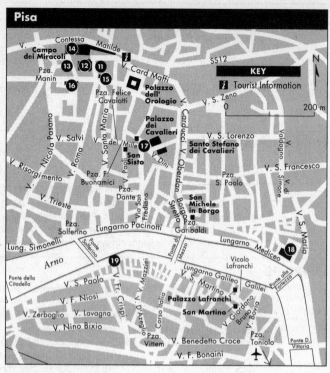

A Good Walk

Start in the Campo dei Miracoli, exploring the piazza complex containing the **Leaning Tower** ⑪, **Duomo** ⑫, **Battistero** ⑬, **Camposanto** ⑭, **Museo dell'Opera del Duomo** ⑮, and **Museo delle Sinopie** ⑯. After a coffee or gelato, walk down Via Santa Maria—the Campanile will be behind you. At Piazza Felice Cavallotti, go left onto Via dei Mille. Continue straight on Via dei Mille to **Piazza dei Cavalieri** ⑰, a study in Renaissance symmetry. Go straight through the piazza to Via Dini, and make a right onto Borgo Stretto, a major thoroughfare lined with cafés. On the left, before the river, is the church of San Michele in Borgo. With its ornate 14th-century Pisan Romanesque facade and columns, it's vaguely reminiscent of a wedding cake. Walk up to Piazza Garibaldi and turn left along the Lungarno Mediceo. Practically at the Ponte alla Fortezza, on the left, is the **Museo Nazionale di San Matteo** ⑱. After browsing in the museum, make a left and make your way to the Ponte della Fortezza. Cross the Arno, and proceed along the Lungarno, passing the Ponte di Mezzo. Just before Ponte Solferino is a Gothic jewel box of a church, **Santa Maria della Spina** ⑲.

TIMING

The walk takes a little more than an hour and a half without stops—but there's lots to see along the way; stops could take a few hours, depending upon how long you stay in the Museo Nazionale di San Matteo.

Sights to See

⑬ **Battistero.** The lovely Gothic Baptistery, which stands across from the Duomo's facade, is best known for the pulpit carved by Nicola Pisano in 1260. Ask one of the ticket takers if he'll sing for you inside the baptistery. The acoustics are remarkable; a tip of 5,000 lire/€2.60 is appropriate. ⌂ *Piazza del Duomo,* ☎ *050/561820,* WEB *www.duomo.pisa.it.* ⌨ *9,000 lire/€4.65.* ☉ *June 22–Sept. 21, daily 8–7:40; Mar. 22–June 21 and Sept. 22–Dec. 21, daily 9–5:40; Dec. 22–Mar. 21, daily 9–4:40.*

❹ **Camposanto.** According to legend, the cemetery, a walled structure on the western side of the Campo dei Miracoli, is filled with earth from the Holy Land brought back by returning Crusaders. Contained within are numerous frescoes, notably the *Drunkenness of Noah* by Renaissance artist Benozzo Gozzoli and the disturbing *Triumph of Death* (14th century), whose authorship is disputed but whose subject matter shows what was on people's minds in a century that saw the ravages of the Black Death. ⊠ *Camposanto,* ☎ *050/561 820,* WEB *www.duomo.pisa.it.* ⌷ *9,000 lire/€4.65.* ☉ *June 22–Sept. 21, daily 8–7:40; Mar. 22–June 21 and Sept. 22–Dec. 21, daily 9–5:40, Dec. 22–Mar. 21, daily 9–4:40.*

❷ **Duomo.** Pisa's cathedral was the first building to use the horizontal marble stripe motif (borrowed from Moorish architecture in the 11th century) common with Tuscan cathedrals. It is famous for the Romanesque panels depicting the life of Christ on the transept door facing the tower and for its beautifully carved 14th-century pulpit by Giovanni Pisano. ⊠ *Piazza del Duomo,* ☎ *050/561 820,* WEB *www.duomo.pisa.it.* ⌷ *3,000 lire/€1.55, free Oct.–Mar.* ☉ *June 22–Sept. 21, daily 8–7:40; Mar. 22–June 21 and Sept. 22–Dec. 21, daily 9–5:40; Dec. 22–Mar. 21, daily 9–4:40.*

❶ **Leaning Tower.** The Leaning Tower (Torre Pendente) provided the final grace note for the complex comprising the Duomo, Baptistery, and the Camposanto. Construction started in 1174, and the lopsided settling evident by the time work began on the third story. The tower's architects attempted to compensate by making the remaining floors slightly taller on the leaning side, but the extra weight only made the problem worse. The settling has continued, and a few years ago it accelerated to a point that led many to fear it would simply topple over, despite all efforts to prop the structure up. Now it has been firmly anchored to the earth. In early 2000, the final step of restoring the tower to its original tilt of 300 years ago was executed, and it appears to have been successful. This last phase involved removing some 100 tons of earth from beneath the foundation; it's hoped that the tower will lean 20 centimeters less. If all goes well, you will be able to climb it, once again, by the end of 2001. Legend holds that Galileo conducted an experiment on the nature of gravity by dropping metal balls from the top of the 187-ft-high tower; historians say this legend has no basis in fact (which is not quite to say that it is false). ⊠ *Campo dei Miracoli,* ☎ *050/560547,* WEB *torre.duomo.pisa.it.* ⌷ *25,000 lire/€12.90.*

❻ **Museo delle Sinopie.** The well-arranged museum on the south side of the Piazza del Duomo holds the *sinopie,* or preparatory drawings, for the Camposanto frescoes. Unless you're fascinated by the process of creating frescoes, you could easily give this place a miss. ⊠ *Piazza del Duomo,* ☎ *050/560547,* WEB *www.duomo.pisa.it.* ⌷ *9,000 lire/€4.65.* ☉ *June 22–Sept. 21, daily 8–7:40; Mar. 22–June 21 and Sept. 22–Dec. 21, daily 9–5:40; Dec. 22–Mar. 21, daily 9–4:40.*

❺ **Museo dell'Opera del Duomo.** At the southeast corner of the sprawling Campo dei Miracoli, the museum holds a wealth of medieval sculptures and the ancient Roman sarcophagi that inspired the figures of Nicola Pisano (circa 1220–84). ⊠ *Via Arcivescovado,* ☎ *050/ 560547,* WEB *www.duomo.pisa.it.* ⌷ *9,000 lire/€4.65.* ☉ *June 22–Sept. 21, daily 8–7:40; Mar. 22–June 21 and Sept. 22–Dec. 21, daily 9–5:40; Dec. 22–Mar. 21, daily 9–4:40.*

❽ **Museo Nazionale di San Matteo.** On the north bank of the Arno, this museum contains some beautiful early Renaissance sculpture, and a stunning reliquary by Donatello (1386?–1466). ⊠ *Lungarno Mediceo,* ☎ *050/541865.* ⌷ *8,000 lire/€4.10.* ☉ *Tues.–Sat. 9–7, Sun. 9–2.*

⓱ Piazza dei Cavalieri. The piazza, which holds the Renaissance **Palazzo dei Cavalieri, Palazzo dell'Orologio,** and **Santo Stefano dei Cavalieri,** was laid out by Giorgio Vasari in about 1560. The square was the seat of the Ordine dei Cavalieri di San Stefano (Order of the Knights of St. Stephen), a military and religious brotherhood pledged to defend the coast from possible invasion by the Turks. Also in this square is the prestigious **Scuola Normale Superiore,** founded by Napoléon in 1810 on the French model. Here graduate students pursue doctorates in literature, philosophy, mathematics, and science. In front of the school is an oversize statue of Ferdinando de' Medici dating from 1596.

⓳ Santa Maria della Spina. Originally an oratory dating from the 13th century, this gem of a church was restructured between 1323 and 1360. It's tiny and delicate and is a fine example of Tuscan Gothic. ⊠ *Lungarno Gambacorti,* ☎ *050/560464.* ☉ *Hrs vary; call in advance.*

Dining and Lodging

\$\$ ✕ Beny. Apricot walls dotted with etchings of Pisa provide a warm atmosphere in this small, single-room restaurant specializing in fish. Flavorful, fresh dishes such as the *sformato di verdura* (a flan with Jerusalem artichokes) embellished with sweet *gamberoni* (a member of the shrimp family) dot the menu. The ravioli *ripieno di polpa di pesce a pan grattato con salsa di seppie e pomodoro* (fish-stuffed ravioli with tomato and octopus sauce) is a delight. ⊠ *Piazza Gambacorti 22,* ☎ *050/25067. AE, DC, MC, V. Closed Sun., 2 wks in Aug., and 1 wk in Jan. No lunch Sat.*

\$\$ ✕ La Mescita. This cheerful trattoria has high, vaulted brick ceilings and stencilled walls lined with colorful contemporary prints. What better place to eat some of the tasty and inventive food on offer: the *tagliolini con salsiccia e porri sopra salsa di cabernet sauvignon* (house-made thin noodles with sausage and leeks in a cabernet sauvignon sauce) is extraordinary. ⊠ *Via Cavalca 2,* ☎ *050/544294. No credit cards. Closed Mon. and last 3 wks in Aug.*

\$\$ ✕ Osteria dei Cavalieri. This charming white-walled *osteria* a few
★ steps from Piazza dei Cavalieri is reason enough to come to Pisa. The chef does it all—serves up grilled fish dishes, pleases vegetarians, and prepares *tagliata* (thin slivers of rare beef) for meat lovers. There are three set menus, from the sea, garden, and earth, or you can order à la carte—which can be agonizing, because everything sounds so good. And it is. Finish your meal with a lemon sorbet bathed in Prosecco (dry sparkling wine), and walk away feeling you've eaten like a king at plebeian prices. ⊠ *Via San Frediano 16,* ☎ *050/580858. AE, DC, MC, V. Closed Sun. and July 25–Aug. 25. No lunch Sat.*

\$\$ ☷ Fattoria di Migliarino. Martino Salviati and his wife Giovanna have turned their working *fattoria,* or farm (soy, corn, and sugar beets), 15 minutes northwest of Pisa into a working inn. It now offers seven charming, spacious apartments (accommodating from two to eight people) with rustic decor, each complete with kitchen and many with fireplaces. The pool is framed by fields, and the only sound you're likely to hear is the clucking of the hens they keep for eggs. The surrounding woods can be explored on horseback or with a mountain bike. During high season, there is a one-week minimum stay. Migliarino is convenient to Lucca, and sandy beaches are a five-minute drive away. ⊠ *Viale dei Pini 289, 56010 Migliarino,* ☎ *050/803046,* ℻ *050/803170. 7 apartments. Kitchenettes, pool. MC, V.*

\$\$ ☷ Hotel Verdi. Just down the street from Teatro Verdi, this small hotel often provides lodging for actors and musicians drawn by the quiet location, clean and simple rooms with high ceilings, and an intimate feel. The small bar is well stocked, and the lounge area is a pleasant place to while away the time. ✉ *Piazza Repubblica 5/6, 56100,* ☎ *050/ 598947,* FAX *050/598944. 32 rooms. Bar, free parking. AE, MC, V. Closed 2 wks in Aug.*

$$ 🏨 **Royal Victoria.** In a pleasant palazzo facing the Arno, a 10-minute walk from the Campo dei Miracoli, this hotel has been in the same family since 1837, and such continuity probably explains why Charles Dickens and Charles Lindberg, among others, have enjoyed staying here. It's comfortably furnished, with antiques and reproductions in the lobby and in some rooms, whose style ranges from the 1800s, complete with frescoes, to the 1920s. ✉ *Lungarno Pacinotti 12, 56126,* ☎ *050/940111,* FAX *050/940180,* WEB *www.royalvictoria.it. 48 rooms, 40 with bath. Parking (fee). AE, DC, MC, V.*

Nightlife and the Arts

The **Luminaria** feast day on June 16 honors San Ranieri, the patron saint of the city. Palaces along the Arno are lit with white lights, and there's plenty of fireworks; this is the city at its best.

HILL TOWNS WEST OF SIENA

Submit to the draw of the enchanting fortified cities, many dating to the Etruscan period, crowning the hills west of Siena. San Gimignano, known as the "medieval Manhattan" because of the sprouting towers built by rival families, is perhaps the most heavily visited; but visitors are old hat to this Roman outpost, and with its tilted cobbled streets and stout medieval buildings, the days of the Guelph-Ghibelline conflicts can seem palpable. Rising from a series of bleak gullied hills and valleys, Volterra has always been popular for its minerals and stones, particularly alabaster, which was used by the Etruscans for many implements, some now displayed in the exceptional and unwieldly Museo Etrusco Guarnacci. Blissfully off the tour-bus circuit, San Miniato is a peaceful hill town with a pleasant local museum and a convent that boards guests.

San Miniato

★ ⑳ *42 km (26 mi) southeast of Pisa, 43 km (27 mi) southwest of Florence.*

Dating from Etruscan and Roman times, San Miniato was so named when the Lombards erected a church here in the 8th century and consecrated it to the saint. The Holy Roman Empire had very strong ties to San Miniato. Today the pristine, tiny hill town's narrow, cobbled streets are lined with austere facades dating from the 13th to 17th century. Its artistic treasures are on a par with some of the similar-size towns in the area, but the real reason for a trip is simply that the place is so pretty. St. Francis founded the 1211 **Convento e Chiesa di San Francesco** (Convent and Church of St. Francis), containing two cloisters and an ornate wooden choir. For a dose of monastic living, you can stay overnight. ✉ *Piazza San Francesco,* ☎ *0571/43051.* ⊙ *Daily 9–noon and 3–7 (or ring bell).*

Although the **Museo Diocesano** is small, the modest collection displays a number of subtle and pleasant works of art. Note the rather odd Fra Filippo Lippi *Crucifixion, Il Redentore* by Verrocchio (1435–88), and the small but sublime *Education of the Virgin,* by Tiepolo (1696– 1770). ✉ *Piazza del Castello,* ☎ *0571/40633.* 💶 *2,000 lire/€1.00.* ⊙ *Tues.–Sun. 10–1 and 3–6.*

Lodging

$ 🏨 **Convento San Francesco.** For a complete change of pace, you can stay in this 13th-century monastery in the company of five Franciscan friars. Rooms are simple, bordering on spartan, but clean and quiet. You are given keys, so you're not expected back by any certain time. You can partake in some spiritual activities or skip them altogether. All rooms have baths, and there are five rooms that groups can rent. It's a 10-minute walk from the town center. ✉ *Piazza San Francesco, 56020,* ☎ *0571/43051,* ℻ *0571/43398. 30 rooms. No credit cards.*

Volterra

㉑ *50 km (31 mi) west of Siena, 27 km (17 mi) southwest of San Gimignano.*

Unlike other Tuscan hill towns that rise above sprawling vineyards and rolling fields of green, Volterra—recorded by D. H. Lawrence in his *Etruscan Places* as standing "somber and chilly alone on her rock"— is surrounded by desolate terrain marred with industry and mining equipment. The fortress, walls, and gates still stand mightily over Le Balze, a stunning series of gullied hills and valleys to the west that were formed by irregular erosion. The town has long been known for its alabaster, which has been mined since Etruscan times; today the Volterrans use it to make ornaments and souvenirs sold all over town. A 12,000-lire/€6.20 combined ticket allows entry to the Museo Etrusco Guarnacci, the Pinacoteca e Museo Civico, and the Museo di Arte Sacra.

Volterra is home to some of Italy's best small museums. The extraordinarily large and unique collection of the **Museo Etrusco Guarnacci** is an enigma in a region from which many of the Etruscan artifacts have landed in state museums and at the Vatican. If only a careful curator had thought to cull the best of the 700 funerary urns rather than to display every last one of them. ✉ *Via Don Minzoni 15,* ☎ *0588/86347.* 🎟 *Combined ticket 12,000 lire/€6.20.* ☉ *Mar. 16–Nov. 1, daily 9–7; Nov. 2–Mar. 15, daily 9–2.*

The **Pinacoteca e Museo Civico** houses a highly acclaimed collection of religious art, including a *Madonna and Child with Saints* by Luca Signorelli (1445/50–1523) and a *Deposition* by Rosso Fiorentino (1494–1541), that is reason enough to visit Volterra. ✉ *Via dei Sarti 1,* ☎ *0588/87580,* WEB *www.comune.volterra.pi.it/museiit/pinac.html.* 🎟 *Combined ticket 12,000 lire/€6.20.* ☉ *Mar. 16–Nov. 1, daily 9–7; Nov. 2–Mar. 15, daily 9–2.*

The impressive facade of the medieval **Palazzo dei Priori** is adorned with Florentine coats of arms, medallions, and a large five-sided tower. Although you can go in, what's really of interest is the outside. ✉ *Piazza dei Priori,* ☎ *0588/86050.* 🎟 *Free weekdays, 2,000 lire/€1.05 weekends.* ☉ *Mon.–Fri. 9–1, Sat.–Sun. 9:30–3:30.*

Next to the altar in the town's unfinished **Duomo** is a magnificent 13th-century carved wood *Deposition*. Note the fresco by Benozzo Gozzoli (1420–97) in the Cappella della Addolorata. Along the left wall of the nave you can see the arrival of the magi. ✉ *Piazza San Giovanni,* ☎ *0588/86192.* ☉ *Daily 7–7.*

Original works from the Duomo and adjacent Baptistery are in the **Museo Diocesano di Arte Sacra.** ✉ *Via Roma 1,* ☎ *0588/86290.* 🎟 *Combined ticket 12,000 lire/€6.20.* ☉ *June 22–Sept. 21, Tues.–Sun. 9–1 and 3–6; Sept. 22–June 21, Tues.–Sun. 9–1.*

Among Volterra's best-preserved ancient remains is the Etruscan **Porta all'Arco,** an arch dating from the 4th century BC now incorporated into the city walls. The ruins of the 1st-century BC **Teatro Romano,** one of the best-preserved Roman theaters in Italy, are worth a visit. Adjacent to the theater are the remains of the **Roman Terme** (baths). The theater complex is just outside the walls past Porta Fiorentina. ✉ *Viale*

Francesco Ferrucci. ☉ *Mar.–Oct., daily 11–4; Nov.–Feb., weekends 11–4. Closed when it rains.*

Dining and Lodging

$$ ✕ **Il Sacco Fiorentino.** The understated tone of this small, two-room restaurant gives nothing away. Its white walls, tiled floors, and pink tablecloths are unremarkable; it doesn't matter, however, once the food starts arriving. The *antipasti del Sacco Fiorentino* is a medley of sautéed chicken liver, porcini, and polenta drizzled with balsamic vinegar. It just gets better: the *tagliatelle del Sacco Fiorentino* is a riot of curried spaghetti with chicken and roasted red peppers. ⊠ *Piazza XX Settembre 18,* ☎ *0588/88537. AE, DC, MC, V. Closed Wed.*

$ 🏨 **San Lino.** This hotel, once a convent, has wood beams and terra-cotta floors and offers modern-day comforts. It's within the town walls and a 10-minute walk from the main piazza. The restaurant, open only for guests and groups of 20 or more, serves regional specialties, including *zuppa alla volteranna,* a very thick vegetable soup. ⊠ *Via San Lino 26, 56048,* ☎ *0588/85250,* 𝙵𝙰𝚇 *0588/80620. 43 rooms. Restaurant, pool, parking (fee). AE, DC, MC, V. Closed Nov.*

Shopping

A number of shops in Volterra sell boxes, jewelry, and other objects made of alabaster. The **Cooperativa Artieri Alabastro** (⊠ Piazza dei Priori 5, ☎ 0588/87590) has two large showrooms in a medieval building with an array of alabaster pieces. In what was once a medieval monastery, the **Galleria Agostiniane** (⊠ Piazza XX Settembre 3, ☎ 0588/86868) crafts alabaster objects of all kinds. You can see a free video on how the mineral is quarried and carved. At the **Rossi** (⊠ Via Lungo le Mura del Mandorlo 7, ☎ 0588/86133) you can actually see the craftsmen at work; there are objects for all tastes and budgets.

San Gimignano

★ ㉒ *27 km (17 mi) east of Volterra, 57 km (35 mi) southwest of Florence.*

When you're high on a hill surrounded by centuries-old towers silhouetted against the blue sky, it's difficult not to fall under the medieval spell of San Gimignano. Its high walls and narrow streets are typical of Tuscan hill towns, but it is the surviving medieval "skyscrapers" that set the town apart from its neighbors and create its uniquely photogenic silhouette. Today 15 towers remain, but at the height of the Guelph-Ghibelline conflict there was a forest of more than 70, and it was possible to cross the town by rooftop rather than road. The towers were built partly to defend the town—they provided a safe refuge and were useful for pouring boiling oil on attacking enemies—and partly to bolster the egos of their owners, who competed with deadly seriousness to build the highest tower in town. When the Black Death devastated the population in 1348, power and independence faded fast and civic autonomy was ultimately surrendered to Florence.

Today San Gimignano isn't much more than a gentrified walled city, amply prepared for its booming tourist trade but still very much worth exploring. Despite the remarkable profusion of chintzy souvenir shops lining its main drag, there's some serious Renaissance art to be seen here and an equally important local wine (Vernaccia) to be savored. Escape at midday to the uninhabited areas outside the city walls for a hike and a picnic, and return to explore the town in the afternoon and evening, when things quiet down and the long shadows cast by the imposing towers take on fascinating shapes. You can buy two types of combination tickets for the sights; one costs 20,000 lire/€10.30 and covers just about everything, while the other costs 15,000 lire/€7.75 and is slightly more limited.

The town's most important medieval buildings are clustered around the central **Piazza del Duomo.** The imposing **Torre Grossa** is the biggest tower in town, with views that are well worth the climb. ⊠ *Piazza del Duomo 1,* ☎ *0577/940008.* 🎫 *Torre 8,000 lire/€4.10.* ☉ *Mar.–Oct., Sat.–Thurs. 9:30–7:20; Nov.–Feb., Sat.–Thurs. 10–5:30.*

The **Palazzo del Popolo** houses the **Museo Civico,** featuring Taddeo di Bartolo's celebratory scenes from the life of San Gimignano. The town's namesake was a bishop of Modena who achieved sainthood by driving hordes of barbarians out of the city in the 10th century. Dante visited San Gimignano as an ambassador from Florence for only a single day in 1300, but it was long enough to get a room named after him, which now holds a *Maestà* by 14th-century artist Lippo Memmi. A small room contains frescoes by Memmo di Filippuccio (active 1288–1324) depicting a young couple's courtship, shared bath, and wedding. The highly charged eroticism of the frescoes may be explained, in part, by the fact that they were in what were probably the private rooms of the commune's chief magistrate. ⊠ *Piazza del Duomo,* ☎ *0577/940008.* 🎫 *Museo Civico 7,000 lire/€3.60.* ☉ *Mar.–Oct., daily 9:30–7:0; Nov.–Feb., Tues.–Sun. 10–5:30.*

The Romanesque **Collegiata** is a treasure trove of frescoes, including Bartolo di Fredi's cycle of scenes from the Old Testament on the left nave wall dating from 1367. Taddeo di Bartolo's otherworldly *Last Judgment,* on the arch just inside the facade, depicts distorted and suffering nudes—avant-garde stuff for the 1390s. The New Testament scenes on the right wall, which may have been executed by Barna da Siena in the 1330s, suggest a more reserved, balanced Renaissance manner. The **Cappella di Santa Fina** contains glorious frescoes, recently restored, on the story of this local saint by Domenico Ghirlandaio (1449–94). ⊠ *Piazza del Duomo,* ☎ *0577/940316.* 🎫 *6,000 lire/€3.10.* ☉ *Apr.–Oct., weekdays 9:30–7:30, Sat. 9:30–5, Sun. 1–5; Nov.–Jan. 20, Mon.–Sat. 9:30–5, Sun. 1–5.. Closed Jan. 21–Feb. 28*

The **Museo di Criminologia Medievale** (Museum of Medieval Criminology) displays cutting-edge medieval torture technology, along with operating instructions and a clear description of the intended effect. Though some scholars dispute the historical accuracy of many of the instruments displayed, the final, very contemporary object—an electric chair imported from the United States—does give pause. ⊠ *Via del Castello 1-3,* ☎ *0577/942243.* 🎫 *15,000 lire/€7.70.* ☉ *Mar.–July 18 and mid-Sept.–Oct., daily 10–8; July 19–mid-Sept., daily 9–noon; Nov.–Feb., daily 10–6.*

Before leaving San Gimignano, be sure to see its most revered work of art, at the northern end of town, in the church of **Sant'Agostino:** Benozzo Gozzoli's utterly stunning 15th-century fresco cycle depicting scenes from the life of St. Augustine. ⊠ *Piazza Sant'Agostino,* ☎ *0577/907012.* ☉ *Nov.–Mar., daily 7–noon and 3–6; Apr.–Oct., daily 7–noon and 3–6.*

Dining and Lodging

$$ ✕ **La Mangiatoia.** Gaily colored gingham tablecloths provide an interesting juxtaposition with rib-vaulted ceilings dating from the 13th century in this cozy spot. The lighthearted feminine touch might be explained by chef Susi Cuomo, who has been presiding over her kitchen for more than 20 years. The menu is seasonal—in the autumn, don't miss her *filetto d'anatra con tartufo* (truffled duck breast), and in the summer enjoy lighter fare on the intimate, flower-bedecked, walled terrace in the back. ⊠ *Via Mainardi 5, off Via San Matteo,* ☎ *0577/941528. MC, V. Closed Tues., 3 wks in Nov., and 1 wk in Jan.*

$$ ✕ **Osteria delle Catene.** You don't come here for the ambience, because there isn't any: it's a narrow, white-walled room; accents of color are provided by the yellow tablecloths. You come here for the food: the *nana col cavolo nero* (duck with black cabbage) is a blessedly unctuous combination. Service is prompt and courteous. ⊠ *Via Mainardi 18,* ☎ FAX *0577/941966. AE, DC, MC, V. Closed Wed., Dec. 10–27, and Jan. 8–Feb. 8.*

$$$$ ✕▥ **Palazzo Mannaioni.** A 16th-century villa has been converted into a lovely, up-to-the-minute accommodation set in a small village just 10 km (6 mi) northwest of San Gimignano. Rooms are spacious, with high ceilings; the villa has a pool, an American-style bar, and a 19th-century-style atrium. The hotel's restaurant is housed in the room where olive oil was once made; the dining room's high, ribbed-vault ceilings are a perfect setting for the food, which, though often typically Tuscan, achieves heights of sophistication rarely seen in such dishes. ⊠ *Via Marconi 2, Montaione, 50050,* ☎ *0571/698300,* FAX *0571/698299. 24 rooms, 5 suites. Restaurant, bar, pool, tennis court, meeting room. AE, DC, MC, V. Closed mid.-Jan.–mid.-Feb.*

$$ ✕▥ **Bel Soggiorno.** One entire wall of this spacious restaurant is made of glass, and beyond it is a sweeping view of rolling hills. With its wooden tables and chairs, it's a simple and rustic interior. The food, however, is not: the *timballo di riso basmati con asparagi e zafferano su crema fredda di pomodorini* (a timbal of asparagus and saffron in a cherry tomato sauce) is a real treat. The restaurant, and the hotel attached to it, has been in the same family for more than 100 years. Rooms, like the restaurant, are simple and airy. If you're looking for a place right within the walls of town, look no further. ⊠ *Via San Giovanni 91, 53037,* ☎ *0577/940375,* FAX *0577/955041,* WEB *www.pescille.it. 17 rooms, 4 suites. AE, DC, MC, V. Closed Wed. and Jan. 6–Feb.*

$$$ ▥ **Pescille.** This rambling farmhouse 4 km (2½ mi) outside San Gimignano has been converted into a handsome hotel, in which restrained contemporary and country classic motifs blend well. From this charming spot, you get a splendid view of San Gimignano and her towers. ⊠ *Località Pescille, Strada Castel San Gimignano, 53037,* ☎ *0577/940186,* FAX *0577/943165,* WEB *www.pescille.it. 38 rooms, 12 suites. Pool, tennis court, gym, solarium. AE, DC, MC, V. Closed Nov.–Mar.*

Colle Val d'Elsa

㉓ *50 km (31 mi) south of Florence, 24 km (15 mi) northwest of Siena.*

On the road from Florence to Siena, Colle Val d'Elsa rises dramatically along a winding road. Its narrow streets strongly evoke the Middle Ages; they are lined with palazzi dating from the 15th to 16th century. For Renaissance art enthusiasts, it's perhaps best known as the birthplace of Arnolfo di Cambio (circa 1245–1310), architect of Florence's Duomo. Once a formidable producer of wool, the town now produces glass and crystal that can be found in local shops. Colle has two distinct parts: the relatively modern and less interesting Colle Bassa and the older Colle Alta.

The **Museo Archeologico** has an interesting collection of Etruscan artifacts, including some fascinating vases and funerary objects. ⊠ *Piazza del Duomo 42,* ☎ *0577/922954.* ☜ *3,000 lire/€1.55.* ☉ *Oct.–Apr., Tues.–Fri. 3:30–5:30, weekends 10–noon and 3:30–6:30; May–Sept., Tues.–Fri. 10–noon and 5–7, weekends 10–noon and 4–7.*

The Palazzo dei Priori houses the **Museo Civico d'Arte Sacra.** There's local art, including some 13th-century gems, and more recent work from the 18th and 19th centuries. ⊠ *Via del Castello 31,* ☎ *0577/923888.*

🕮 *5,000 lire/€2.60.* ☉ *Apr.–Oct., Tues.–Sun. 10–noon and 4–7; Nov.–Mar., weekends 10–noon and 3:30–6:30.*

Lodging

$$$$ 🏨 **La Suvera.** This luxurious estate in the lovely valley of the River Elsa,
★   28 km (17 mi) west of Siena and 56 km (33 mi) south of Florence, was
once owned by Pope Julius II. The papal villa and adjacent building
accommodate guests in magnificently furnished rooms and suites appointed with antiques and modern comforts. La Suvera's first-rate facilities, including drawing rooms, a library, an Italian garden, a park,
and the Oliviera restaurant (serving estate wines), make it hard for guests
to tear themselves away. ⊠ *Pievescola (Casola d'Elsa), off S541,
53030,* ☎ *0577/960300,* FAX *0577/960220,* WEB *www.lasuvera.it. 17
rooms, 18 suites. Restaurant, bar, pool, tennis court, library, meeting
room. AE, DC, MC, V. Closed Nov.–Easter.*

CHIANTI

Directly south of Florence is the Chianti district, one of Italy's most
famous wine-producing areas; its hill towns, olive groves, and vineyards are quintessential Tuscany. Many British and northern Europeans
have relocated here, drawn by the unhurried life, balmy climate, and
picturesque villages; there are so many Britons, in fact, that the area
has been nicknamed Chiantishire. Still, it remains strongly Tuscan in
character, and you'll be drawn to the views framing vine-quilted rolling
hills and elegantly elongated cypress trees.

The sinuous S222, known as the Strada Chiantigiana, runs from Florence through the heart of Chianti. Its most scenic section connects Strada
in Chianti, 16 km (10 mi) south of Florence, and Greve in Chianti, whose
triangular central piazza is surrounded by restaurants and vintners offering *degustazioni* (wine tastings), 11 km (7 mi) farther south.

Greve in Chianti

㉔ *27 km (17 mi) south of Florence, 40 km (25 mi) north of Siena.*

If there is a capital of Chianti, it is Greve, a friendly market town with
no shortage of cafés, enoteche, and crafts shops lining its main piazza.
The sloping, asymmetrical **Piazza Matteotti** is attractively arcaded and
has a statue of Giovanni da Verrazano (circa 1480–1528), the explorer
who discovered New York harbor, in the center. At the small end of the
piazza is the **Chiesa di Santa Croce,** with works from the school of Fra
Angelico (circa 1400–55). ⊠ *Piazza Matteotti.* ☉ *Daily 9–1 and 3–7.*

OFF THE   **MONTEFIORALLE** – Just 2 km (1 mi) west of Greve, in the tiny hilltop ham-
BEATEN PATH let of Montefioralle, you'll find the ancestral home of Amerigo Vespucci
(1454–1512), the navigator and mapmaker who named America and
whose niece Simonetta may have been the model for Venus in Sandro
Botticelli's (1445–1510) *Primavera.* Chianti's annual mid-September
wine festival, **Rassegna del Chianti Classico,** takes place here.

Lodging

$$$–$$$$ 🏨 **Villa Vignamaggio.** This historic estate has guest rooms and apart-
ments in a villa, as well as two small houses and a cottage on the grounds.
The villa, surrounded by manicured classical Italian gardens, dates from
the 14th century but was restored in the 16th. It's reputedly the birth-
place of Monna Lisa, the woman later made famous by Leonardo da
Vinci, and was the setting for Kenneth Branagh's film *Much Ado
About Nothing.* ⊠ *Via Petriolo 5, Greve in Chianti, 50022,* ☎ *055/
854661,* FAX *055/8544468,* WEB *www.vignamaggio.com. 2 rooms, 2*

suites, 15 apartments, 1 cottage. 2 pools, tennis court. AE, DC, MC, V. Closed Dec. 23–Jan. 6

$$ 🏰 **Castello Vicchiomaggio.** This castle, now a prestigious wine estate with a tasting facility you can visit, dates from 956 and was rebuilt during the Renaissance. Throughout the nine apartments and two farmhouses is wonderful heavy wooden furniture, in keeping with the estate's history. The restaurant serves homemade pastas and specialties such as *stracotto*, beef cooked in the farm's own prize-winning Chianti Classico. ✉ *Via Vicchiomaggio 4, 50022*, ☎ *055/854079*, 📠 *055/853911*, WEB *www.vicchiomaggio.it. 8 apartments, 2 farmhouses. Restaurant, pool, breakfast room. MC, V.*

Panzano

㉕ *7 km (4½ mi) south of Greve, 40 km (25 mi) south of Florence.*

With its magnificent views, Panzano is one of the prettiest stops in Chianti. The town centerpiece is the church of **Santa Maria Assunta,** where you can see an *Annunciation* attributed to Michele di Ridolfo del Ghirlandaio (1503–77). ✉ *Panzano Alto.* ⊘ *Daily 7–noon and 4–6.*

Ancient even by Chianti standards, the hilltop church of **San Leolino** probably dates from the 10th century, but it was completely rebuilt in the Romanesque style sometime in the 13th century. The 3-km (2-mi) trip south of Panzano is well worth it for the church's exterior simplicity and 14th-century cloister. The 16th-century terra-cotta tabernacles are attributed to Giovanni della Robbia, and there's also a remarkable triptych attributed to the Master of Panzano that was executed sometime in the mid-14th century. Check with the tourist office in Greve (✉ Viale Giovanni da Verrazano 33, ☎ 055/8546287) for open days and hours. ✉ *Località San Leolino,* ☎ *no phone.* 🎟 *Free.*

Dining and Lodging

$$$ ✕ **Oltre il Giardino.** An ancient stone house has been converted into a tasteful dining area with a large terrace and spectacular views of the valley. Try to book a table in time to watch the sunset. The menu captures a little more fantasy than typical Tuscan cuisine. Try the *tagliatelle all'anatra* (a flat noodle tossed with a savory duck sauce) or the *peposo* (a beef stew laced with black pepper). On the weekends, reservations are a must. ✉ *Piazza G. Bucciarelli 42,* ☎ *055/852828. AE, DC, MC, V. Closed Mon.*

$$$$ 🏰 **Villa La Barone.** This 16th-century villa was once the family residence
★ of the Viviani della Robbia. It feels very much as if you are staying in someone's private palace; you almost expect to find a member of the family strolling through the rooms. The public rooms have an intimate feel; the honor bar allows you either to enjoy an aperitivo in the tiled barroom or to take it out to the terrace and admire the view. And there are views here in abundance, from the beautiful pool to the rose garden to the back of the villa with its neatly trimmed hedges. Guest rooms have tile floors, white walls, and timbered ceilings. The meal plan is requisite for a stay here, and the restaurant is open to guests only. The food, hearty Tuscan at its best, is served in a converted stable with yellow tablecloths and red chairs. The wine list is comprehensive and well priced. ✉ *Pieve di Panzano 50020,* ☎ *055/852621,* 📠 *055/852277. 30 rooms. Restaurant, pool, tennis court. AE, MC, V. Closed Nov.–Easter. MAP.*

Radda in Chianti

㉖ *33 km (20 mi) south of Greve, 52 km (32 mi) south of Florence.*

Radda in Chianti sits on a hill that separates Val di Pesa from Val d'Arbia. It's one of many tiny Chianti villages that invite you to stroll through its steep streets and follow the signs that point you toward the *camminamento*, a covered medieval road that circles part of the city inside the walls. In Piazza Ferrucci, you'll find the **Palazzo del Podestà**, or Palazzo Comunale, the city hall that has served the people of Radda for more than four centuries. It has 51 coats of arms embedded in its facade. ⊠ *Piazza Ferrucci*.

OFF THE
BEATEN PATH

VOLPAIA – Perched atop a hill 10 km (6 mi) north of Radda is this fairy-tale hamlet, a military outpost from the 10th to 16th century and once a shelter for religious pilgrims. Every July, for the Festa di San Lorenzo, people come to Volpaia to watch for falling stars and a traditional fireworks display put on by the family that owns the adjacent wine estate and agritourist lodging, **Castello di Volpaia** (⊠ Piazza della Cisterna 1, 53017, ☎ 0577/738066).

Dining and Lodging

$$ ✕ **Il Poggio.** The spaghetti *alla Giannetto* (with bits of bacon, tomatoes, and a dash of red pepper) is a lively and piquant dish that makes the trip here well worthwhile. So, too, do the marvelous side dishes such as the broccoli *al saltati* (with extra-virgin olive oil) and the crostini di fegatini, which is served hot at the table thanks to tiny warming candles. Such fine touches are only enhanced by the three cozy rooms with their timbered ceilings. When it's warm, enjoy the fine fare on an outdoor terrace bursting with flowers. ⊠ *Località Poggio S. Polo, 53010 Lecchi, Gaiole in Chianti*, ☎ *0577/746135. AE, DC, MC, V. Closed Mon.*

$$$–$$$$ 🏠 **Relais Fattoria Vignale.** This unadorned farmhouse with an annex across the street is English-country-house comfortable on the inside—with terra-cotta floors, sitting rooms, and nice stone- and woodwork. White rooms with exposed brick and wood beams contain simple wooden bed frames and furniture, lovely rugs and prints, modern white-tile bathrooms. The grounds, lined with vineyards and plum and olive trees, are equally inviting, with various lawns, terraces, and a pool. The cavernous and rustic Ristorante Vignale serves excellent wines and various cold and warm Tuscan plates; it's perfect for a sampling of savory meats, pâtés, and cheeses. ⊠ *Via Pianigiani 9, Radda in Chianti, 53017,* ☎ *0577/738300,* 🆃🅰🆇 *0577/738592,* 🆆🅴🅱 *www.vignale.it. 34 rooms. Restaurant, bar, breakfast room, pool, library. AE, DC, MC, V. Closed Dec. 8–26 and Jan. 7–Mar.*

$$–$$$$ 🏠 **Vescine.** A former Etruscan settlement has been transformed into
★   this secluded complex of low-slung medieval stone buildings, connected by cobbled paths and punctuated by cypress trees. Unfussy white rooms have terra-cotta tile floors, attractive woodwork, and comfortable furnishings typical of Tuscany. ⊠ *Radda in Chianti, 53017,* ☎ *0577/741144,* 🆃🅰🆇 *0577/740263. 20 rooms, 5 suites. Breakfast room, pool, tennis court, library. AE, MC, V. Closed Nov.–Mar. (except over Christmas).*

Castellina in Chianti

㉗   *14 km (8 mi) west of Radda, 21 km (13 mi) north of Siena.*

Castellina in Chianti, or simply Castellina, is on a ridge above the Val di Pesa, Val d'Arbia, and Val d'Elsa, and the panorama is bucolic no matter which direction you look. The strong 15th-century medieval walls and fortified town gate give a hint of the history of this village, which was an outpost during the continuing wars between Florence and Siena.

Lodging

$$$ 🏠 **Collelungo.** One of the loveliest agriturismi in the area, Collelungo consists of a series of abandoned farmhouses that have been carefully

remodeled by Briton Tony Rocca and his Italian wife, Mira. Set amid a notable vineyard (it produces its own internationally recognized Chianti Classico), the apartments—all with cooking facilities and dining areas—have exposed stone walls and that typical Tuscan tile floor. Though there's no restaurant, if you order your panino the night before, an employee will deliver it the following morning. The *salone* (lounge), which possibly dates to the 14th century, has a satellite-dish TV; adjacent to it is an honor bar. In high season, a weeklong stay is required. ⊠ *Podere Collungo 53011*, ☎ FAX *0577/740489*, WEB *www.collelungo.it. 12 apartments. Bar, pool, laundry (fee). AE, DC, MC, V. Closed Nov.–Mar. EP.

$$$ ⊡ **Hotel Belvedere di San Leonino.** There are wonderful gardens for strolling around this restored country complex, which dates from the 14th century. The guest rooms are in two houses that look out upon vineyards to the north and Siena to the south. Homey rooms have antique furniture and exposed beams. There is a restaurant, open to guests only, with a fixed menu. In the summer you can eat dinner in the garden by the pool. ⊠ *Località San Leonino, 53011*, ☎ *0577/740887*, FAX *0577/740924. 28 rooms. Restaurant, pool. Closed mid-Nov.–mid Mar. AE, MC, V.*

$$ ⊡ **Palazzo Squarcialupi.** This refurbished 15th-century palace on the
★ main street in town offers a pleasant and restful place to stay. Rooms have high ceilings, white walls, and tile floors; bathrooms are tiled in local stone. Many of the rooms have a view of the valley below. Common areas are elegant but comfortable, and the breakfast buffet is ample. The multilingual manager, Augusto, is a font of information—an added benefit when booking a room here. Though there is no restaurant, the hotel is happy to arrange for a light lunch during the warmer months. ⊠ *Via Ferruccio 26, 53011*, ☎ *0577/741186*, FAX *0577/740386*, WEB *www.italyexpo.com/squarcialupi. 9 rooms, 8 suites. Bar. AE, DC, MC, V. Closed Nov.–Mar.*

SIENA

Italy's most enchanting medieval city, Siena is the one city you should visit in Tuscany if you visit no other. Florence's great historical rival was in all likelihood founded by the Etruscans. During the late Middle Ages, it was both wealthy and powerful, for it saw the birth of the world's oldest bank, the Monte dei Paschi, still very much in business. It was bitterly envied by Florence, which in 1254 sent forces that besieged the city for more than a year, reducing its population by half and laying waste to the countryside. The city was finally absorbed by the grand duchy of Tuscany, ruled by Florence, in 1559.

Sienese identity is still defined by its 17 medieval *contrade* (neighborhoods), each with its own church, museum, and symbol. Look for streetlights painted in the contrada's colors, plaques displaying its symbol, and statues embodying the spirit of the neighborhood. The various contrade uphold ancestral rivalries during the centuries-old Palio, a twice-yearly horse race (held in July and August) around the main square; civic pride rests on the outcome.

Exploring Siena

Practically unchanged since medieval times, Siena stretches over the slopes of three steep hills, but you will find the most interesting sights in a fairly compact area. Be sure to leave some time to wander off the main streets. Most sights are concentrated in the pedestrian-only centro storico, so you will end up walking up and down a lot of steep streets. If you only have one day in Siena, see the Piazza del Campo, the Duomo and its Museo dell'Opera Metropolitana, and the Palazzo

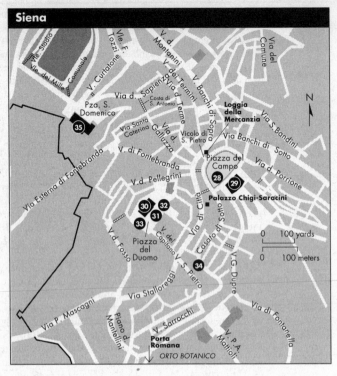

Pubblico. If you are seeing more sights, it will probably be worthwhile to buy a cumulative ticket (valid for three days, 9,500 lire/€4.90), good for entrance to the Duomo's Biblioteca Piccolomini, Battistero, and the Museo dell'Opera Metropolitana. If you have the opportunity to overnight here, by all means do so: the city is filled with day-trippers and tour buses, and in the late afternoon and evening it empties out. Siena's medieval charm and narrow streets are thrown into high relief, and Piazza il Campo positively glows.

From Florence, there are two basic routes to Siena. The speedy modern S2 is good if you're making a day trip from Florence, as it's a four-lane divided highway; for a jaunt through Chianti, take the narrower and more meandering S222, known as the Strada Chiantigiana. It's a gorgeous ride on only two lanes—patience is a necessity.

A Good Walk

Begin at the **Piazza del Campo** ㉘, one of Italy's finest squares, and visit the **Palazzo Pubblico** ㉙ and its adjacent tower, the Torre del Mangia, which you can climb. Cross the piazza and exit on the stairs to the left to Via di Città, one of Siena's main shopping streets. Up on the left is the enchanting Palazzo Chigi-Saracini, where concerts are often held. Step in to admire the especially well preserved courtyard and cistern. Continue up the hill and take the second right, Via del Capitano, which leads to Piazza del Duomo. The **Duomo** ㉚ is a must-see, along with its **Battistero** ㉛ (around the other side of the Duomo) and **Museo dell'Opera Metropolitana** ㉜. Opposite the front of the Duomo is the **Spedale Santa Maria della Scala** ㉝. Chief among Siena's other gems is the **Pinacoteca Nazionale** ㉞, several blocks straight back down Via del Capitano (which becomes Via San Pietro). The church of **San Domenico** ㉟ lies in the other direction; you could take Via della Galluzza to Via della Sapienza.

TIMING

This walk should last a full day, taken at a leisurely pace and allowing some time to relax in the Piazza del Campo. Allow two days to really explore Siena. The *passeggiata* (evening stroll) along the main shopping streets should not be missed. Keep in mind that most shops are closed on Sunday and museums have variable hours.

Sights to See

③① **Battistero.** The Duomo's 14th-century Gothic Baptistery was built to prop up one side of the Duomo. There are frescoes throughout, but the highlight is a large bronze 15th-century baptismal font designed by Jacopo della Quercia and adorned with bas-reliefs by various artists, including two by Renaissance masters: the *Baptism of Christ* by Lorenzo Ghiberti (1378–1455) and the *Feast of Herod* by Donatello. ⊠ *Piazza San Giovanni,* WEB *www.operaduomo.it.* 🔛 *3,000 lire/€1.55, combined ticket 9,500 lire/€4.90.* ⊙ *Mid-Mar.–Sept., daily 9–7:30; Oct., daily 9–6; Nov.–mid-Mar., daily 10–1 and 2:30–5.*

NEED A BREAK?	Not far from the Duomo and the Pinacoteca, Siena's **Orto Botanico** (Botanical Gardens; ⊠ Via Pier Andrea Mattioli 4, ☎ 0577/232874) is a great place to relax and enjoy views of the countryside below. It's open weekdays 8–5:30 and Saturday 8–noon.

③⓪ **Duomo.** Several blocks west of Piazza del Campo, Siena's Duomo is beyond question one of the finest Gothic cathedrals in Italy. The facade, with its multicolor marbles and painted decoration, is typical of the Italian approach to Gothic architecture, lighter and much less austere than the French. The cathedral as it now stands was completed in the 14th century, but at the time the Sienese had even bigger plans. They had decided to enlarge the building by using the existing church as a transept for a new church, with a new nave running toward the southeast. But in 1348 the Black Death decimated Siena's population, the city fell into decline, funds dried up, and the plans were never carried out. The beginnings of the new nave can be seen from the steps outside the Duomo's right transept.

The Duomo's interior, with its coffered and gilded dome, is striking. It is most famous for its unique and magnificent inlaid marble floors, which took almost 200 years to complete (beginning around 1370); more than 40 artists contributed to the work, made up of 56 separate compositions depicting biblical scenes, allegories, religious symbols, and civic emblems. They are covered for most of the year for conservation purposes but are unveiled every September for the entire month. The Duomo's pulpit, also much appreciated, was carved by Nicola Pisano between 1266 and 1268; the life of Christ is depicted on the rostrum frieze. In the **Biblioteca Piccolomini,** a room painted by Pinturicchio (circa 1454–1513) between 1502 and 1509, frescoes depict scenes from the life of native son Aeneas Sylvius Piccolomini (1405–64), who became Pope Pius II in 1458. They are in excellent condition and reveal a freshness rarely seen in Renaissance frescoes. ⊠ *Piazza del Duomo,* ☎ *0577/283048,* WEB *www.operaduomo.it.* 🔛 *Biblioteca Piccolomini 2,000 lire/€1.05, combined ticket 9,500/€4.90 lire.* ⊙ *Duomo Nov.–mid-Mar., daily 7:30–1 and 2:30–5; mid-Mar.–Oct., daily 9–7:30. Biblioteca Piccolomini Nov.–mid-Mar., daily 10–1 and 2:30–5; mid-Mar.–Oct., daily 9–7:30.*

③② **Museo dell'Opera Metropolitana.** Built into part of the unfinished new cathedral's nave, the museum contains a small collection of Sienese art and the cathedral treasury. Its masterpiece is unquestionably the *Maestà* by Duccio (circa 1255–1318), painted around 1310 and magnificently displayed in a room devoted entirely to the artist's work. There is a splendid view from the tower inside the museum. ⌧ *Piazza del Duomo, next to the Duomo,* ☎ *0577/283048,* WEB *www.operaduomo.it.* ⌧ *6,000 lire/€3.10, combined ticket 9,500 lire/€4.90.* ⊘ *Nov.–mid-Mar., daily 9–1:30; mid-Mar.–Sept., daily 9–7:30; Oct., daily 9–6.*

㉙ Palazzo Pubblico. The focal point of the Piazza del Campo, the Gothic Palazzo Pubblico has served as Siena's town hall since the 1300s. It now also contains the **Museo Civico,** its walls covered with early Renaissance frescoes. The nine governors of Siena once met in the Sala della Pace, famous for Ambrogio Lorenzetti's frescoes called *Allegories of Good and Bad Government,* painted in the late 1330s to demonstrate the dangers of tyranny. The good government side depicts a utopia, showing first the virtuous ruling council surrounded by angels and then scenes of a perfectly running city and countryside. Conversely, the bad government fresco tells a tale straight out of Dante. The evil ruler and his advisors have horns and fondle strange animals, while the town scene depicts the seven mortal sins in action. Interestingly, the bad government fresco is severely damaged, and the good government fresco is in terrific condition. The original bas-reliefs of the Jacopo della Quercia fountain, moved to protect them from the elements, are also on display. The **Torre del Mangia,** the palazzo's famous bell tower, is named after one of its first bell ringers, Giovanni di Duccio (called Mangiaguadagni, or earnings eater). The climb up to the top is long and steep, but the view makes it worth every step. ⌧ *Piazza del Campo 1,* ☎ *0577/292226.* ⌧ *Torre di Mangia 10,000 lire/€5.15, Museo Civico 12,000 lire/€6.20.* ⊘ *Torre di Mangia Nov.–Mar. 15, daily 10–4; Mar. 16–June and Sept.–Oct., daily 10–7; July–Aug., daily 10–11 PM. Museo Civico Mar. 16–June, daily 10–6:30, July–Aug., daily 10–11 PM, Sept.–Oct., daily 10–7, Nov.–Mar. 15, daily 10–4.*

㉘ Piazza del Campo. Known simply as Il Campo (The Field), this fan-shape piazza is one of the finest in Italy. Constructed toward the end of the 12th century on a market area unclaimed by any contrada, it's still the heart of town. The bricks of the Campo are patterned in nine different sections—representing each member of the medieval Government of Nine. At the top of the Campo is a copy of the **Fonte Gaia,** decorated in the early 15th century by Siena's greatest sculptor, Jacopo della Quercia, with 13 sculpted reliefs of biblical events and virtues. Those lining the rectangular fountain are 19th-century copies; the originals are in the Museo Civico. On Palio days (July 2 and August 16), Il Campo and all its surrounding buildings are packed with cheering, frenzied locals and tourists craning their necks to take it all in.

㉞ Pinacoteca Nazionale. The national picture gallery contains an excellent collection of Sienese art, including works by native sons Ambrogio Lorenzetti (documented 1319–48), Duccio (circa 1255–1318/19), and Domenico Beccafumi (1486–1551). ⌧ *Via San Pietro 29,* ☎ *0577/ 281161.* ⌧ *8,000 lire/€4.10.* ⊘ *Mon. 8:30–1:30, Tues.–Sat. 8:30–1:30 and 2:30–7, Sun. 8–1 and 2–8.*

㉟ San Domenico. In the church of San Domenico is the **Cappella di Santa Caterina,** with frescoes by Sodoma portraying scenes from the life of St. Catherine. Catherine was a much-respected diplomat, noted for ending the Great Schism by convincing the pope to return to Rome from Avignon. The saint's preserved head and finger are on display in a chapel within. ⌧ *Costa di Sant'Antonio,* ☎ *0577/280330.* ⊘ *Nov.–mid-Mar., daily 9–1 and 3–6; mid-Mar.–Oct., daily 7–1 and 2:30–6:30.*

㉝ Spedale di Santa Maria della Scala. A former hospital, built beginning in the late 9th century, is now an exhibition space hosting contempo-

rary art shows. ⊠ *Piazza del Duomo, opposite the front of the Duomo,*
☎ *0577/224811.* 🎫 *8,000 lire/€4.15.* ☉ *Nov.–Mar., daily 10:30–4:30;
Apr.–Oct., daily 10:30–6.*

Dining and Lodging

$$$$ ✕ **Antica Trattoria Botteganova.** Just outside the city walls, along the
★ road that leads north to Chianti, the Botteganova is arguably the best
restaurant in Siena. Contemporary Italian food is rarely this successful; chef Michele Sonentino's cooking is all about clean flavors, balanced combinations, and inviting presentation. The interior, with high
vaulting, is relaxed yet classy, and the service is first rate. There is a
small room for nonsmokers. ⊠ *Strada per Montevarchi SS408, 2 km
(1 mi) north of Siena,* ☎ *0577/284230. AE, DC, MC, V. Closed Mon.*

$$$ ✕ **Le Logge.** Near Piazza del Campo, this classic Sienese trattoria has
★ rustic dining rooms on two levels and tables outdoors from June to
October. Tuscan dishes are the draw, such as *malfatti all'osteria* (ri-
cotta and spinach dumplings in a cream sauce) and *anatra al finocchio*
(roast duck with fennel). Reservations are advised. ⊠ *Via del Porrione
33,* ☎ *0577/48013. AE, DC, MC, V. Closed Sun. and 2 wks in Nov.*

$$ ✕ **Osteria Castelvecchio.** Set in a stall in the oldest part of town, this
little restaurant with high ribbed vaults mixes past and present on its
menu, which changes daily. You're likely to find such Sienese standards
as spaghetti *saporiti con gli aromi* (with tomatoes and herbs) as well
as offbeat selections such as *sformatino del pastore con soia e cardi al
vino* (a ricotta and greens concoction with cardoons and tofu). Owners Mauro Lombardini and Simone Romi are committed to *piatti di
verdura* (vegetarian dishes), and they've got a great wine list. ⊠ *Via
Castelvecchio 65,* ☎ *0577/49586. AE, DC, MC, V. Closed Tues.*

$ ✕ **Enoteca Italiana.** Not far from the church of San Domenico, this fan-
tastically stocked wine cellar is in the bastions of the Medici fortress.
Here you can taste wines from all over Italy and have a light snack,
too. It's open until the wee hours (1 AM). On Friday evenings during
the winter, there's also a piano bar. ⊠ *Fortezza Medicea, Viale Mac-
cari,* ☎ *0577/288497. AE, DC, MC, V. Closed Sun.*

$ ✕ **Enoteca I Terzi.** Near the Campo and the main shopping streets, this
★ wine bar, on the ground floor of a 12th-century tower, is hard to beat
for a good glass of wine from a lengthy and well-thought-out list. Owner
Michele Incarnato offers not only a *degustazione* (tasting) menu, where
he pairs wines with dishes, but also daily pasta dishes such as a sumptuous lasagna with smoked provolone. ⊠ *Via dei Termini 7,* ☎ *0577/
44329. AE, DC, MC, V. Closed Sun.*

$$$$ 🏨 **Certosa di Maggiano.** A former 14th-century monastery converted
★ into an exquisite country hotel, this haven of gracious living is a little
more than about 1½ km (1 mi) from the center of Siena, near the Porta
Romana gate. The atmosphere is that of an exclusive retreat in which
a select number of guests enjoy the style and comfort of an aristocratic
villa. Guest rooms blend taste and comfort, with classic prints and bold
colors such as a happy daffodil yellow. Common rooms are luxurious,
with fine woods, leather, and traditional prints. In warm weather,
breakfast is served on the patio next to the garden aburst with roses,
zinnias, and other blessed friends. Half-board at 150,000 lire/€77 per
person is required in high season (and is reflected in the price category
here). ⊠ *Via Certosa 82 (take the Siena Sud exit off superstrada), 53100,*
☎ *0577/288180,* 📠 *0577/288189,* 🌐 *www.certosadimaggiano.it. 6
rooms, 11 suites. Restaurant, pool, tennis court, helipad. AE, MC, V.*

$$$$ 🏨 **Palazzo Ravizza.** There might not be a more romantic and pretty
★ place in the center of Siena than this quietly charming pensione just
outside Porta San Marco and a short 10-minute walk to the Duomo.

Rooms have high ceilings, antique furniture, big windows, and bathrooms decorated with hand-painted tiles. The attached restaurant offers up tasty Tuscan classics, which can be eaten outdoors when it's warm. Half-board is mandatory during the high season. The cost is at the low end of this price category. ⊠ *Pian dei Mantellini, 34, 53100,* ☎ *0577/280462,* FAX *0577/221597,* WEB *www.palazzoravizza.it. 30 rooms, 4 suites. Restaurant. AE, DC, MC, V.*

$$$$ 🏨 **Park.** Set among olive groves and gardens on a hillside just outside the city walls, this handsome hotel offers solid comfort and spacious double rooms with views of the grounds, which include a six-hole golf course. Public rooms in the historic medieval villa have an easy elegance and patrician antique charm. Comfortable guest rooms have bold dark fabrics, mirrors, and modern appointments. The Olivo restaurant serves regional cuisine. ⊠ *Via Marciano 18, 53100,* ☎ *0577/44803,* FAX *0577/49020,* WEB *www.parkhotelsiena.it. 69 rooms. Restaurant, bar, pool, 6-hole golf course, tennis court. AE, DC, MC, V.*

$$$ 🏨 **Duomo.** Occupying the top floor of a 300-year-old building near Piazza del Campo, this quiet hotel is furnished in a neat contemporary style, with traces of the past showing in the artfully exposed brickwork in the breakfast room. Many bedrooms have views of the city's towers and the hilly countryside. Two rooms have balconies, and there's a rooftop terrace, often with blooming flowers, that offers a splendid view. Free parking is available a short distance from the hotel. ⊠ *Via Stalloreggi 38, 53100,* ☎ *0577/289088,* FAX *0577/43043,* WEB *www.hotelduomo.it. 23 rooms. Breakfast room, free parking. AE, DC, MC, V.*

$$ 🏨 **Antica Torre.** A restored 16th-century tower within the town walls in the southeast corner of Siena, Antica Torre is a 10-minute walk from Piazza del Campo. It is the work of a cordial couple who have created the atmosphere of a private home, with only eight simply but tastefully furnished guest rooms. The old stone staircase, wooden beams, and original brick vaults here and there are reminders of the building's great age. ⊠ *Via Fieravecchia 7, 53100,* ☎ FAX *0577/222255. 8 rooms. AE, DC, MC, V.*

$$ 🏨 **Chiusarelli.** In a well-kept neoclassical villa, built in the early 1900s complete with caryatids, this hotel has functional rooms that are airy and reasonably quiet. A handy location—near the long-distance bus terminal and a parking area and only a 10-minute walk from the main sights—is the big plus here. The small garden invites reading; the restaurant caters to tour groups. ⊠ *Viale Curtatone 15, 53100,* ☎ *0577/ 280562,* FAX *0577/271177. 49 rooms. Restaurant. AE, MC, V.*

$ 🏨 **Hotel Alma Domus.** If you're after a contemplative, utilitarian convent experience, this might be the place. Run by seven Dominican nuns, it's located just around the corner from San Domenico. Rooms are spartan and very clean. Many have a view of the Duomo, which might make the 11:30 PM curfew livable. ⊠ *Via Camporegio 37, 53100,* ☎ *0577/ 44177,* FAX *0577/47601. 31 rooms. No credit cards.*

Nightlife and the Arts

Music

In last week of July, Siena hosts the **Settimane Musicali Senesi,** a series of concerts held in churches and courtyards with performances of local and other music. Contact Accademia Musicale Chigiana (⊠ via di Città 89, ☎ 0577/46152) for information.

Outdoor Activities and Sports

Siena's **Palio** horse race takes place every year on July 2 and August 16, but its spirit lives all year long. Three laps around a makeshift track in Piazza del Campo earn participants of the Palio the respect or scorn of the other 16 contrade. The event is so important to the Sienese that bribery, brutality, and kidnaping of the jockeys are commonplace—sabotaging a horse's reins is the only thing that remains taboo. A horse doesn't even need its rider to be considered a valid winner. Festivities kick off three days prior to the main event, with trial races, banquets lining the streets, and late-night celebrations. As the Palio approaches, residents don scarves with their contrada's colors and march through city streets in medieval costumes. Tickets are usually sold out months in advance; call the tourist office (⊠ Piazza del Campo 56, ☎ 0577/280551) for information. It's possible you might luck out and get an unclaimed seat or two; if not, the center of the piazza is free to all on a first-come, first-served basis, until just moments before the start.

Shopping

Siena is known for a variety of cakes and cookies, their recipes of medieval origin—*cavallucci* (sweet spice biscuits), *panforte* (Christmas fruitcake with honey, hazelnuts, almonds, and spices), and *ricciarelli* (almond-paste cookies). The best place in town to find Sienese baked goods, as well as to grab a cappuccino, is **Nannini** (⊠ Banchi di Sopra 24, ☎ 0577/41591).

Siena has excellent gourmet food and wine shops selling local products. For the finest pecorinos, try **La Antica Fattoria** (⊠ Via di Città 51, ☎ 0577/4225). **La Bottega dei Sapori Antichi** (⊠ Via delle Terme 41, ☎ 0577/285501) is a good option for local specialties. Italy's only state-sponsored enoteca, **Enoteca Italiana** (⊠ Fortezza Medicea, ☎ 0577/288497) sells wines from all over Italy. **Enoteca I Terzi** (⊠ Via dei Termini 7, ☎ 0577/44329) has a comprehensive selection of wines.

Antiche Dimore (⊠ Via di Città 115, ☎ 0577/45337) has embroidered linens and other housewares. If you've always wanted a 14th- or 15th-century Sienese painting to hang on your wall but bemoaned the high cost of an original, you can purchase superb copies by Chiara Perinetti Casoni at **Bottega dell'Arte** (⊠ Via Stalloreggi 47, ☎ 0577/40755). Her work in tempera and gold leaf on panel is of the highest quality— you might even be able to pass it off as the real thing.

AREZZO AND CORTONA

The lovely hill towns of Arezzo and Cortona carry on age-old local traditions—in June and September, for example, Arezzo's beautiful Romanesque and Gothic churches are enlivened by the Giostra del Saracino, a costumed medieval joust. Arezzo has been home to important artists, since ancient times, when Etruscan potters produced their fiery-red vessels. Fine examples of the work of Luca Signorelli are preserved in Cortona, his hometown.

Arezzo

③⑥ *81 km (50 mi) southeast of Florence, 74 km (46 mi) northwest of Perugia.*

Sleepy Arezzo was the birthplace of the poet Petrarch and the Renaissance artist and art historian Giorgio Vasari. Guido d'Arezzo, the inventor of musical notation, was also born here. Today Arezzo is best known for the magnificent frescoes by Piero della Francesca (1420–92) in the

★ church of **San Francesco.** Painted between 1452 and 1466, they depict scenes from the *Legend of the True Cross* on three walls of the *cappella maggiore,* or altar choir. What Sir Kenneth Clark called "the most perfect morning light in all Renaissance painting" may be seen in the lowest section of the right wall, where the troops of the emperor Maxentius flee before the sign of the cross. Unveiled in 2000 after a lengthy and painstaking 15-year restoration, they may now be seen in all their glory. ⊠ *Piazza San Francesco,* ☎ *0575/900404,* WEB *www.pierodellafrancesca.it.* ☜ *10,000 lire/€5.15.* ⊙ *Nov.–Mar., weekdays 9–5:30, Sat. 9–5, Sun. 1–5. Apr.–Oct., weekdays 9–7, Sat. 9–6:15, Sun. 1–6:15. Admission limited to 25 people at a time every ½ hr. Reservations required.*

With its irregular shape and sloping brick pavement, framed by buildings dating from assorted centuries, Arezzo's **Piazza Grande** is reminiscent of Siena's Piazza del Campo. Though not so grand, it is lively enough during the outdoor antiques fair held the first Sunday of every month. The **Giostra del Saracino** (Joust of the Saracen), featuring medieval costumes and competition, is held there in the middle of June and on the first Sunday of September.

The curving, tiered apse on Piazza Grande belongs to **Santa Maria della Pieve,** one of Tuscany's finest Romanesque churches, built in the 12th century. Note the 16th-century episcopal throne by Vasari to the left of the altar. ⊠ *Corso Italia,* ☎ *0575/377678.* ⊙ *Daily 8–1 and 3–6:30.*

Arezzo's medieval **Duomo** (at the top of the hill) contains a fresco of a tender *Magdalen* by Piero della Francesca; look for it next to the large marble tomb near the organ. ⊠ *Piazza del Duomo 1,* ☎ *0575/23991.* ⊙ *Daily 7–12:30 and 3–6:30.*

The church of **San Domenico,** just inside the walls, houses a 13th-century crucifix by Cimabue (circa 1240–1302). ⊠ *Piazza Fossombroni, Piazza San Domenico,* ☎ *0575/22906.* ⊙ *Daily 7–1 and 3:30–6.*

The **Casa di Giorgio Vasari** (Giorgio Vasari House) was designed and decorated by the region's leading art historian and architect around 1540 as his private home. ⊠ *Via XX Settembre 55,* ☎ *0575/409040.* ☜ *Free.* ⊙ *Mon. and Wed.–Sat. 9–7, Sun. 9–1.*

The **Museo Archeologico,** on the south side of Arezzo in the **Convento di San Bernardo,** exhibits an impressive collection of Etruscan bronzes. ⊠ *Via Margaritone 10,* ☎ *0575/20882.* ☜ *8,000 lire/€4.15.* ⊙ *Daily 8:30–7.*

Dining and Lodging

$$ ✕ **Buca di San Francesco.** A frescoed cellar restaurant in a historic building next to the church of San Francesco, this *buca* (literally "hole," figuratively "cellar") has a medieval atmosphere and serves straightforward local specialties, including *ribollita* (minestrone thickened with beans and bread). Meat eaters will find the lean Chianina beef and the *saporita di Bonconte* (a selection of several meats) succulent treats. ⊠ *Via San Francesco 1,* ☎ FAX *0575/23271. AE, DC, MC, V. Closed Tues. and 2 wks in July. No dinner Mon.*

$$ ✕ **Tastevin.** Here you'll find creative cooking that respects tradition— try risotto *alla Tastevin* (with a creamy truffle sauce) or one of the seafood dishes. Two of the dining rooms are furnished in a warm Tuscan provincial style, one in more sophisticated bistro style. At the small bar the talented owner plays and sings Sinatra and show tunes. ⊠ *Via dei Cenci 9, close to San Francesco and the central Piazza Guido Monaco,* ☎ *0575/28304. AE, DC, MC, V. Closed Sun. (except 1st Sun. of month) and 1 wk in Aug.*

$$ ⊞ **Castello di Gargonza.** Enchantment reigns at this tiny 13th-century hamlet in the countryside near Monte San Savino, part of the fiefdom of the aristocratic Florentine Guicciardini restored by the modern Count Roberto Guicciardini as a way to rescue a dying village. A cas-

tle, church, and cobbled streets set the stage. Rooms can be had for a minimum of three nights. Cottages and apartments are for rent by the week; they have one to six rooms each, sleep two to seven people, and have as many as four baths. La Torre restaurant (closed Tuesday) serves local fare. ✉ *Monte San Savino, 52048,* ☎ *0575/847021,* FAX *0575/847054,* WEB *www.gargonza.it. 7 rooms, 25 apartments. Restaurant, pool. AE, DC, MC, V. Closed 3 wks in Jan. and 3 wks in Nov.*

$$ ⊓ **Continental.** Centrally located near the train station and within walking distance of all major sights, the Continental has been a reliable and convenient place to stay since it opened in the 1950s. Bright white furnishings with yellow accents can be found throughout; gleaming bathrooms complete with hair dryers, air-conditioning in most rooms, and a pleasant roof garden are welcome pluses. Breakfast is extra. ✉ *Piazza Guido Monaco 7, 52100,* ☎ *0575/20251,* FAX *0575/350485. 73 rooms. Meeting rooms, parking (fee). AE, DC, MC, V.*

Shopping

FLEA MARKET

On the first Sunday of each month, a colorful flea market with antiques and other, less-precious objects for sale takes place in the **Piazza Grande.**

GOLD

Gold production here is on an industrial scale. **Uno-A-Erre** is the largest of several factories. Big-time baubles can be purchased in the town center. For gold jewelry set with precious or semiprecious stones, try **Il Diamante** (✉ Via Guido Monaco 69). **Borghini** (✉ Corso Italia 126) has an impressive collection of fine jewelry. **Prosperi** (✉ Corso Italia 76) works wonders in gold, silver, and platinum jewelry. Exquisite ornaments may be found at **Aurea Monilia** (✉ Piazza San Francesco 15).

KNITWEAR

A cottage knitwear industry is burgeoning in Arezzo. For sweaters, try **Maglierie Mely's** (✉ Via Romana 190). **Marika** (✉ Corso Italia 108, ☎ 0575/21000) sells beautiful household lines, as well as lace.

Cortona

🟤 *29 km (18 mi) south of Arezzo, 117 km (73 mi) southeast of Florence.*

Magnificently situated, with olive trees and vineyards creeping up to its walls, pretty Cortona commands sweeping views over Lake Trasimeno and the plain of the Valdichiana. Its two galleries and churches are rarely visited; its delightful medieval streets are a pleasure to wander for their own sake.

Cortona may be one of Italy's oldest towns—"Mother of Troy and Grandmother of Rome" is how it's popularly known. Tradition claims that it was founded by Dardanus, also the founder of Troy (and after whom the Dardanelles are named). He was fighting a local tribe, so the story goes, when he lost his helmet (*corythos* in Greek) on Cortona's hill. In time a town grew up that took its name (Corito) from the missing headgear. By the 4th century BC the Etruscans had built the first set of town walls, whose cyclopean traces can still be seen in the 3-km (2-mi) sweep of the present fortifications. As a member of the Etruscans' 12-city Dodecapolis, it became one of the federation's leading northern cities. An important consular road, the Via Cassia, which passed the foot of its hill, assured the town's importance under the Romans. Its fortunes waned in the Middle Ages, however, as the plain below reverted to marsh. After holding out against neighbors like Perugia, Arezzo, and Siena, the *comune* was captured by King Ladislas of Naples in 1409 and sold to the Florentines two years later.

The heart of Cortona is formed by **Piazza della Repubblica** and the adjacent **Piazza Signorelli.** Wander into the courtyard of the picturesque 13th-century **Palazzo Pretorio,** and if you want to see a representative collection of Etruscan bronzes, climb its centuries-old stone staircase to the Museo dell'Accademia Etrusca (Gallery of Etruscan Art). ⊠ *Piazza Signorelli 9,* ☎ *0575/630415.* 🖾 *Museo 8,000 lire/€4.15.* ⊙ *Oct.–Mar., Tues.–Sun. 10–5; Apr.–Sept., Tues.–Sun. 10–7.*

The **Museo Diocesano** (Diocesan Museum) houses an impressive number of large and splendid paintings by native son Luca Signorelli, as well as a beautiful *Annunciation* by Fra Angelico, a delightful surprise in this small, eclectic town. ⊠ *Piazza del Duomo 1,* ☎ *0575/62830.* 🖾 *8,000 lire/€4.15.* ⊙ *Nov.–Mar., Tues.–Sun. 10–1 and 3–5; Apr.–Sept., Tues.–Sun. 9:30–1 and 3:30–7.*

Dining and Lodging

\$\$ ✕ **Osteria del Teatro.** Just up the street from Teatro Signorelli, this small osteria is lined with photographs from theatrical productions spanning several decades. The food is deliciously simple—try the *filetto in crema di tartufo* (beef in a creamy tartufo sauce); service is warm and friendly. ⊠ *Via Maffei, 5,* ☎ *0575/630556. AE, DC, MC, V. Closed Wed. and 2 wks in Nov.*

\$\$\$\$ ✕🖾 **Il Falconiere.** This might be as close as you can come to dying and
   ★ going to heaven in Italy. Run by the young husband-wife team of Riccardo and Silvia Baracchi, the hotel, just minutes outside Cortona, consists of rooms in an 18th-century villa and suites in the *chiesetta* (little church) once belonging to an obscure 19th-century Italian poet and hunter. Rooms are spacious, and many have sweeping views of the plain below. The restaurant's marvelous, inventive menu is complemented by the wine list, the product of Silvia's extensive sommelier training. Massive rosemary bushes decorate the place. ⊠ *Località San Martino 370, 52044,* ☎ *0575/612679,* 🅵🅰🆇 *0575/612927,* 🆆🅴🅱 *www.ilfalconiere. com. 10 rooms, 2 suites. Restaurant, bar, minibars, 2 pools. AE, DC, MC, V.*

SOUTHERN TUSCANY

Along the roads leading south from Siena, soft green olive groves give way to a blanket of oak, dark-green cypress forests, and reddish-brown earth. Towns are the size of the roads—small—and as old as the hills. The scruffy mountain landscapes of Monte Amiata make up some of the wildest parts of Tuscany, and once you're across the mountains the landscape is still full of cliffs, like the one Pitigliano perches on. Southern Tuscany offers good wine (try Brunello di Montalcino or the exceptional Morellino di Scansano for a true treat), thermal baths at Saturnia, Etruscan ruins, and the strands and fishing villages of Elba.

Abbazia di Monte Oliveto Maggiore

㊳ *37 km (23 mi) southeast of Siena, 104 km (65 mi) south of Florence.*

This Benedictine abbey, Tuscany's most visited, is an oasis of olive and cypress trees amid the harsh landscape of a zone known as the Crete, where erosion has sculpted the hills starkly, laying open gashes of barren rock in lush farmland. Secluded amid thick woodlands in the deep-cut hills south of Siena, it is accessible by car but not easily by bus.

Olivetans, or "White Benedictines," founded the abbey in 1313; this breakaway group sought to return to the simple ideals of the early Benedictine order. The monastery's mellow brick buildings, set in one of Tuscany's most striking landscapes, protect a treasure or two. Only the **main** cloister and portions of the **park** are open to the public. The wooden choir in the church, with its intarsia designs, is an understated work of art that dates from 1503 to 1505. In the main cloister, frescoes by Luca Signorelli and Sodoma depict scenes from the life of St. Benedict with earthy realism, a quality that came naturally to Sodoma, described by Vasari as "a merry and licentious man of scant chastity." ⊠ *S451 south of Asciano*, ☎ *0577/707611.* ◷ *Daily 9:15–noon and 3:15–5:45.*

Dining

$–$$ ✕ **La Torre.** This pleasant restaurant and café in the massive tower at the abbey's entrance provides simple Tuscan fare served in a cozy dining room in winter or on an attractive terrace when it's warm. The *pici ai funghi* (thick, short spaghetti with mushroom sauce) or *zuppa di funghi* (mushroom soup) will warm your soul if you visit in the winter, and any of the grilled meats are a good bet at any time of year. There's also a remarkably good wine list. ⊠ *Abbazia di Monte Oliveto Maggiore*, ☎ *0577/707022. AE, DC, MC, V. Closed Tues.*

Montepulciano

③⑨ *13 km (8 mi) west of the A1, 119 km (74 mi) south of Florence.*

Perched high on a hilltop, Montepulciano is made up of a pyramid of redbrick buildings set within a circle of cypress trees. At an altitude of almost 2,000 ft, it is cool in summer and chilled in winter by biting winds that sweep its spiraling streets. The town has an unusually harmonious look, the result of the work of three architects, Sangallo Il Vecchio (1455–1534), Giacomo da Vignola (1507–73), and Michelozzo (1396–1472), who endowed it with palaces and churches in an attempt to impose Renaissance architectural ideals on an ancient Tuscan hill town. The pièce de résistance is the beautiful **Piazza Grande.** On the hillside below the town walls is the church of **San Biagio,** designed by Sangallo, a paragon of Renaissance architectural perfection considered to be his masterpiece. ⊠ *Via di San Biagio*, ☎ *0578/7577761.* ◷ *Daily 9–12:30 and 3:30–7:30.*

Dining and Lodging

$$$ ✕ **La Grotta.** Just across the street from the Tempio di San Biagio, this restaurant has an innocuous entrance that might lead you to pass right by. Don't. The food here is fantastic, from the house-made pastas to the sweets. The *tagliolini con carciofi e rigatino* (thin noodles with artichokes and bacon) is heavenly, as is the *tagliatelle di grano saraceno con asparagi e zucchine* (flat noodles with asparagus and zucchini). Follow with *filetto di maiale in salsa di pecorino e tartufo* (pork loin in a truffled pecorino sauce) and wash it down with the local wine, which just happens to be one of Italy's finest—Vino Nobile di Montepulciano. All this can be enjoyed in one of several large rooms with pink table linens and high vaulted ceilings. Service is impeccable. ⊠ *Località San Biagio*, ☎ *0578/757479. AE, MC, V. Closed Wed.*

$$$$ ✕🏠 **Locanda dell'Amorosa.** This "inn" occupies the 14th-century stone-and-brick hamlet of Amorosa, in the hills crowning the Valdichiana, just south of Sinalunga. The stunning setting is matched by the gorgeous, perfectly restored buildings. A lane lined with cypress trees brings you to the gateway of Amorosa, which still has its tiny little church and a group of farmers' houses for the staff. The bedrooms are handsomely decorated with antiques, and the bathrooms are large. The restaurant, housed in the old stables, serves both traditional and contemporary dishes (stick to the former). ⊠ *Località Amorosa, Sinalunga, 10 km (6 mi) from the Valdichiana exit off A1, 53048*, ☎ *0577/679497,* FAX *0577/632001,* WEB *www.amorosa.it. 9 rooms, 8 suites, 1 apartment. Restaurant, wine bar. AE, DC, MC, V.*

$$ 🏨 **Il Marzocco.** A 16th-century building within the town walls, this hotel feels like the 19th century, complete with old-fashioned parlors and a billiard room. Furnished in heavy late-19th-century style or in spindly white wood, many bedrooms have large terraces overlooking the countryside and are big enough to accommodate extra beds. ✉ *Piazza Savonarola 18, 53045,* ☎ *0578/757262,* ℻ *0578/757530. 16 rooms, 15 with bath. Restaurant. AE, DC, MC, V. Closed Jan. 20–Feb. 10.*

$$ 🏨 **La Bandita.** This attractive old farmhouse possesses great charm, with terra-cotta floors throughout, lace curtains and antiques in the bedrooms, and a fireplace and 19th-century Tuscan provincial furniture in a large, brick-vaulted living room. Some rooms can accommodate an extra bed. A garden and meals are available to guests. The restaurant is closed Tuesday. ✉ *Via Bandita 72, Bettolle, 53040, 1 km (½ mi) from Valdichiana exit off A1 autostrada,* ☎ *0577/624649,* ℻ *0577/624649,* 🖳 *www.locandalabandita.it. 9 rooms. Restaurant. AE, DC, MC, V.*

Nightlife and the Arts

The **Cantiere Internazionale d'Arte,** held in July and August, is a festival of figurative art, music, and theater, ending with a major theatrical production in Piazza Grande. Contact the Montepulciano tourist office (✉ Corso Rosellino 59, ☎ 0578/749071) for information.

Pienza

40 *120 km (75 mi) south of Florence.*

Pienza owes its urban design to Pope Pius II, who had grand plans to transform his home village of Corsignano—the town's former name—into a model Renaissance town. The man entrusted with the transformation was Bernardo Rossellino (1409–64), a protégé of the great Renaissance architectural theorist Leon Battista Alberti (1404–74). His mandate was to create a cathedral, a papal palace, and a town hall (plus miscellaneous other buildings) that adhered to the humanist pope's principles. The result was a project that expressed Renaissance ideals of art, architecture, and civilized good living in a single scheme: it stands as a sensational example of the architectural canons that Alberti formulated in the early Renaissance and that were utilized by later architects, including Michelangelo (1475–1564), in designing many of Italy's finest buildings and piazzas. Today the cool nobility of Pienza's center seems almost surreal in this otherwise unpretentious village, known locally for its *pecorino* (sheep's-milk cheese). Though it can be found elsewhere in Italy, here it is a superior gastronomic experience.

The **Palazzo Piccolomini,** the seat of Pius II's papal court, was designed by Rossellino in 1459, using Florence's Palazzo Rucellai by Alberti as a model. You can visit the papal apartments, including a beautiful library, the **Sala delle Armi,** with an impressive weapons collection, and the music room, with its extravagant wooden ceiling. ✉ *Piazza Pio II,* ☎ *0578/748503.* 🎟 *Guided tours 6,000 lire/€3.10.* ☉ *Sept.–Nov. 14, Tues.–Sun. 10–12:30 and 3–5; Dec. 2–Feb. 14, Tues.–Sun. 10–12:30 and 3–5, Mar. 8–June, Tues.–Sun. 10–12:30 and 3–5; July–Aug., Tues.–Sun. 10–12:30 and 4–7.*

The interior of the **Duomo** is simple but richly decorated with Sienese paintings. The facade is divided into three parts, with Renaissance arches under the pope's coat of arms encircled by a wreath of fruit. ✉ *Piazza Pio II.* ☉ *Daily 9–1 and 2–7.*

Dining

$ ✕ **La Chiocciola.** This no-frills trattoria a few minutes' walk from the historic center offers typical Pienza fare, including homemade local pici (thick, short spaghetti) with hare or wild boar sauce. Their take on *formaggio in forno* (baked cheese) with assorted accompaniments such as fresh porcini mushrooms is reason enough to come here. ⊠ *Via dell'Acero 2, ☎ 0578/748063. MC, V. Closed Wed. and 10 days in Feb.*

Montalcino

④ *24 km (15 mi) west of Pienza, 41 km (25 mi) south of Siena.*

Another medieval hill town with a special claim to fame, Montalcino is home to Brunello di Montalcino, one of Italy's most esteemed red wines. You can sample it in wine cellars in town or visit a nearby winery for a free guided tour and tasting; you must call ahead for reservations. One such winery is Fattoria dei Barbi e del Casato (⊠ Località Podernuovi, ☎ 0577/841200). The 14th-century Sienese **La Fortezza** has an enoteca for tasting wines. ☎ *0577/849211. ☞ 4,000 lire/€2.05. ☉ Nov.–Mar., Tues.–Sun. 9–6; Apr.–Oct., daily 9–8.*

Dining and Lodging

$$$$ ✕ **Poggio Antico.** One of Italy's renowned chefs, Roberto Minnetti, abandoned his highly successful restaurant in Rome and moved to the country just outside Montalcino. Now he and his wife, Patrizia, serve Tuscan cuisine masterfully interpreted by Roberto in a relaxed but regal dining room with arches and beamed ceilings. The seasonal menu offers *pappardelle al ragù di agnello* (flat, wide noodles in a lamb sauce) or venison in a sweet-and-sour sauce. ⊠ *Località I Poggi, 4 km (2½ mi) outside Montalcino on road to Grosseto, ☎ 0577/849200. MC, V. Closed Mon. and 20 days in Jan. No dinner Sun.*

$$
★ ✕🏠 **Fattoria dei Barbi e del Casato.** The rustic taverna of this family-owned wine estate, which produces excellent Brunello as well as its younger cousin, Rosso di Montalcino, is set among vineyards and mellow brick buildings and features a beamed ceiling, huge stone fireplace, and arched windows. The estate farm produces many of the ingredients used in such traditional specialties as *stracotto nel brunello* (braised beef cooked with beans in Brunello wine) and *ravioli ricotta e spinaci con ragù di burro e salvia* (large ravioli filled with ricotta, in butter and fresh sage). There are also six comfortable, traditionally furnished agritourist apartments next to the cantina—where you can take a tour and buy the fattoria's different labels (call ahead; there's a one-week minimum stay required). Reservations for a meal or a stay are essential. ⊠ *Località Podernuovi, 53024, ☎ 0577/841200 taverna; 0577/841111 fattoria, ℻ 0577/841112. 6 apartments. AE, DC, MC, V (no credit cards for agriturismo). Taverna closed Wed. and Jan. No dinner Tues. in Nov.–Mar.*

$$ 🏠 **La Crociona.** A quiet and serene family-owned farm, La Crociona is in the middle of a small vineyard with glorious views and all the comforts of home, including antique iron beds and 17th-century wardrobes in the rooms. There's a big terrace and you are invited to hang out around the pool and use the family barbecue as well as to sample the owner's own wine supply. ⊠ *Località La Croce, Montalcino, 53024, ☎ ℻ 0577/848007, ™ www.lacrociona.com. 6 apartments. Pool, mountain bikes. AE, DC, MC, V.*

Abbazia di Sant'Antimo

㊷ *10 km (6 mi) south of Montalcino, 51 km (32 mi) south of Siena.*

It's well worth your while to visit this abbey, a 12th-century Romanesque gem of pale stone set in the silvery green of an olive grove. The exterior and interior sculpture is outstanding, particularly the nave capitals, a combination of French, Lombard, and even Spanish influences. According to legend, the **sacristy** (rarely open) forms part of the primitive Carolingian church (founded in AD 781), its entrance flanked by 9th-century pilasters. The small **vaulted crypt** dates from the same period. An unusual element is the ambulatory, whose three radiating chapels (rare in Italian churches) were probably copied from the French model. Throughout the day, the monks fill this magnificent space with Gregorian chant. ⊠ *Castelnuovo dell'Abate,* ☎ *0577/835659.* ☉ *Daily 10–12:30 and 3–6:30.*

Monte Amiata

㊸ *86 km (52 mi) southeast of Siena, 156 km (94 mi) southeast of Florence.*

At 5,702 ft high, the dormant volcano Monte Amiata is one of Tuscany's few ski resorts, but it's no match for the Alps or the Dolomites. Its main attraction is a wide-open view of Tuscany. From here you can meander along panoramic mountaintop roads in your car and visit Castel del Piano, Arcidosso, Santa Flora, and Piancastagnaio, towns dating from the Middle Ages.

Abbazia di San Galgano

㊹ *33 km (20 mi) southwest of Siena, 70 km (43 mi) northwest of Montalcino.*

This Gothic cathedral missing its roof is a hauntingly beautiful sight. The church was built in the late 12th century by Cistercian monks, who designed it after churches built by their order in France. But starting in the 15th century it fell into ruin, declining gradually over centuries. Grass has grown through the floor, and the roof and windows are gone. What's left of its facade and walls makes a grandiose and desolate picture. Behind it, a short climb up a hill brings you to the charming little **Chiesa di San Galgano,** with frescoes by 14th-century painter Ambrogio Lorenzetti (documented 1319–48), and a sword in stone. Legend has it that Galgano, a medieval warrior, had an epiphany on this spot and gave up fighting. He thrust his sword into stone, where it remains to this day.

Elba

㊺ *Portoferraio: 1 hr by ferry from Piombino.*

The largest island in the Tuscan archipelago, ringed with pristine beaches and pocked with rugged vegetation, Elba is an hour by ferry or a half hour by Hovercraft from Piombino, or a short hop by air from Pisa. Its main port is Portoferraio, fortified in the 16th century by the Medici grand duke Cosimo I. Be sure to sample the local wines, including Moscato and Aleatico.

Lively **Portoferraio** is the best base for exploring the island. Good beaches can be found at Biodola, Procchio, and Marina di Campo. From Elba, private visits can be arranged to the other islands in the archipelago, including **Montecristo,** which inspired Alexandre Dumas's *The Count of Monte Cristo* and is now a wildlife refuge.

Victor Hugo spent his boyhood here, and Napoléon was here during his famous exile in 1814–15, which resulted in the building of the **Palazzina Napoleonica dei Mulini.** More interesting is the **Villa San Martino,** a couple of miles outside town, whose grandiose neoclassical facade was built by the emperor's nephew. *Palazzina:* ⊠ *Piazzale Napoleone 1, Portoferraio,* ☎ *0565/915846. Villa:* ⊠ *Località San Martino,* ☎

0565/914688. ⊠ *8,000 lire/€4.10 for both if visited on same day.* ☉ *Apr.–Sept., Wed.–Mon. 9–7:30, Sun. 9–1.*

The **Museo Archeologico** reconstructs the island's ancient history through a display of Etruscan and Roman artifacts recovered from shipwrecks. ⊠ *Calata Buccari, Portoferraio,* ☎ *0565/937370.* ⊠ *4,000 lire/€2.05.* ☉ *Easter–June and Sept., Fri.–Wed. 9:30–12:30 and 3–6; July–Aug., Fri.–Wed. 9:30–12:30 and 6–midnight; Nov.–Easter, Fri.–Wed. 3–6.*

Dining and Lodging

$$$ ✕ **La Canocchia.** This is in the center of Rio Marina on the eastern shore of Elba, across from a public garden. Specialties include fish-stuffed ravioli with a red shellfish sauce and *tagliolini* (thin spaghetti) with shrimp. Reservations are essential in summer. ⊠ *Via Palestro 3, Rio Marina,* ☎ *0565/962432. MC, V. Closed Mon. and Nov.–mid Feb.*

$$$ ✕ **Trattoria da Lido.** In the historic center of Portoferraio, at the beginning of the road heading up to the old Medici walls, this restaurant serves specialties such as *gnocchetti di pesce* (bite-size potato and fish dumplings) with a white cream sauce and *pesce all'elbana,* fresh whitefish baked with vegetables and potatoes. Reservations are encouraged. ⊠ *Salita del Falcone 2, Portoferraio,* ☎ *0565/914650. AE, DC, MC, V. Closed Dec. 20–Feb. 20.*

$$$$ 🏨 **Hermitage.** This hotel on the most exclusive bay on Elba, 8 km (5 ★ mi) from Portoferraio, is heavenly. It is composed of a central building with rooms and several little cottages, each with six to eight rooms and its own separate entrance. You have private access to a white sandy beach, where you'll find the hotel's own bar and restaurant. During the high season, half-board is mandatory. ⊠ *Biodola, 57037,* ☎ *0565/ 936911,* FAX *0565/969984,* WEB *www.elba4star.it. 110 rooms. 2 restaurants, 3 bars, 3 pools, 6-hole golf course, 9 tennis courts, soccer, volleyball, meeting room. AE, DC, MC, V. Closed Nov.–Apr.*

Saturnia

  ㊻ *47 km (30 mi) south of Monte Amiata, 129 km (77 mi) south of Siena.*

Etruscan and pre-Etruscan tombs cut into the local rock can be seen in this town, a lively center in pre-Etruscan times. Today it is known for its hot sulphur **thermal baths.** There is a modern spa with a luxury hotel attached to it called **Terme di Saturnia,** or you can bathe for free at the tiered natural pools of Cascate del Gorello next to the road to Montemerano.

Dining and Lodging

$$$ ✕ **Da Caino.** This excellent restaurant in the nearby town of Montemerano (on the road to Scansano) is at the high end of its price category. Specialties include tomatoes and peppers on crisp phyllo dough, lasagna with pumpkin, and such hearty dishes as *cinghiale lardolato con olive* (wild boar larded with olives). ⊠ *Via della Chiesa 4, Montemerano, 7 km (4½ mi) south of Saturnia,* ☎ *0564/602817. Reservations essential. AE, DC, MC, V. Closed Wed. No dinner Thurs.*

$$$ ✕ **I Due Cippi–Da Michele.** Owner Michele Aniello has a terrific restau-★ rant with a lengthy and creative menu; emphasis is placed on Maremman cuisine—which features game dishes such as wild boar and duck—though there are other treats as well; try the *tortelli di castagne al seme di finocchio* (chestnut-stuffed tortelli with butter sauce and fennel seeds). In good weather you can enjoy your meal on a terrace overlooking the town's main square. ⊠ *Piazza Veneto 26/a,* ☎ *0564/ 601074. Reservations essential. AE, DC, MC, V. Closed Tues. in Oct.–June; Dec. 20–26; and Jan. 10–25.*

$$$$ ⊞ **Terme di Saturnia.** Cure takers looking for a most refined approach
★ can don their bathrobes here, at the region's premier resort. The hotel,
an elegant stone building, wraps around three tufa-rock pools built over
the hot springs' source. Every imaginable type of health and beauty
treatment is available, supplemented by decidedly unspalike meals in
the restaurant. Half-board prices are a good deal. ⊠ *Saturnia, 58050,*
☎ *0564/601061,* FAX *0564/601266,* WEB *www.termedisaturnia.it. 80
rooms, 10 suites. Restaurant, bar, piano bar, in-room safes, in-room
VCRs, minibars, 4 pools, hair salon, sauna, spa, steam room, driving
range, 2 lit tennis courts, health club, shop, helipad. AE, DC, MC, V.*

$$–$$$ ⊞ **Villa Acquaviva.** This elegant villa painted antique rose is at the end
of a long tree-lined driveway, perched on top of a hill off the main road
1 km (½ mi) from Montemerano. It has lovely views and quintessential Tuscan charm. Tastefully decorated rooms are in both the main
villa and in a guest house. The farm that fans out around it produces
both wine and olive oil. ⊠ *Strada Scansanese, Montemerano, 58050,*
☎ *0564/602890,* FAX *0564/602895,* WEB *www.laltramaremma.it/
acquaviva. 24 rooms, 2 suites. Restaurant (guests only), breakfast
room, pool, free parking. AE, DC, MC, V.*

$$ ⊞ **Villa Garden.** This small, intimate hotel located a few minutes from
the center of town is a perfect place to stay if you want to take the wa-
ters. Each room is named after a flower, and the theme is continued
with floral-print bedspreads and drapes. The buffet breakfast is good
and filling, the staff courteous and efficient. ⊠ *Via Sterpeti 56, 58014,*
☎ *0564/601182,* FAX *0564/601207,* WEB *www.laltramaremma.it/villa gar-
den. 9 rooms. Breakfast room, free parking. AE, DC, MC, V. CP.*

Pitigliano

➍➐ *33 km (21 mi) east of Saturnia, 147 km (92 mi) southeast of Siena.*

From a distance, the medieval stone houses of Pitigliano look as if they
melt into the cliffs of soft tufa rock they are set on. Etruscan tombs,
which locals use to store wine, are connected by a network of caves
and tunnels. In 1293, the Orsini family moved its base from Sovana
to the more easily defended Pitigliano. They built up the town's de-
fenses and fortified their home, Palazzo Orsini. Later, in the early
1500s, Antonio da Sangallo the Younger added more to the town's
fortresslike aspect, building bastions and towers throughout the town
and adding the aqueduct as well.

Savory local specialties include the famous Pitigliano white wine, olive
oil, cured meats, and cheeses; local restaurants serve up good food at
modest prices. Note the 16th-century **aqueduct** below the fortress. Wan-
der down the narrow streets of the old **Jewish Ghetto.** Though Jews
had settled in Pitigliano as early as the 15th century, they arrived in
much greater numbers after a 1569 papal bull of Pope Pius V evicted
the Jews from Rome.

The 18th-century Baroque **Duomo** has a single nave with chapels and
various paintings on the sides. There are two altarpieces by local artist
Francesco Zuccarelli (1702–88). ⊠ *Piazza San Gregorio,* ☎ *0564/
616090.* ☾ *Daily 9–7.*

The **Palazzo Orsini Museo** features paintings by Zuccarelli, as well as
a *Madonna* by Jacopo della Quercia, a 14th-century crucifix, and
other works of interest. ⊠ *Piazza della Fortezza,* ☎ *0564/616074.* 🖻
5,000 lire/€2.60. ☾ *Jan.–Mar., daily 10–1 and 3–5; Apr.–May, daily
10–1 and 3–6; June–Dec., daily 10–1 and 3–7.*

TUSCANY A TO Z

To research prices, get advice from other travelers, and book travel arrangements, visit www.fodors.com.

AIRPORTS

The largest airports in the region are Pisa's Aeroporto Galileo Galilei and Florence's Aeroporto A. Vespucci, called Peretola, which connects to Brussels and Paris.

➤ AIRPORT INFORMATION: **Aeroporto Galileo Galilei** (☎ 050/500707, WEB www.pisa-aeroport.com). **Peretola** (✉ 10 km [6 mi] northwest of Florence, ☎ 055/373498, WEB www.safnet.it).

BIKE TRAVEL

I Bike Italy offers one-day tours of the Florence countryside. Also check out Florence by Bike, which offers several different routes in and around the city.

➤ BIKE RENTALS: **Florence by Bike** (✉ via San Zonbi 120-122/r, ☎ 055/488992). **I Bike Italy** (✉ Borgo degli Albizi 11, ☎ FAX 055/2342371).

BOAT AND FERRY TRAVEL

Boat services link the islands of Tuscany's archipelago with the mainland; passenger and car ferries leave from Piombino and Livorno for Elba.

FARES AND SCHEDULES
➤ BOAT AND FERRY INFORMATION: **Moby Lines** (✉ Piazzale Premuda, Piombino, 57037, ☎ 0565/221212; ✉ Via Ninci 1, Portoferraio, 57100, ☎ 0565/918101). **Toremar** (✉ Piazzale Premuda 13/14, Piombino, 57025, ☎ 0565/31100; ✉ Porto Mediceo, Livorno, 57123, ☎ 0586/224624; ✉ Piazzale A. Candi, Porto Santo Stefano, 58019, ☎ 0564/818803; WEB www.toremar.it).

BUS TRAVEL

Tuscany is crisscrossed by bus lines that connect the smaller towns and cities on the autostrade and superhighways. Buses can be a good mode of transport for touring, though getting information and making arrangements, particularly for a non-Italian speaker, can be a test of patience. To see the hill towns around Siena, such as San Gimignano, you can take a Siena-to-Arezzo Tra-In or Lazzi bus; at either Siena or Arezzo you can connect with the main train line. From Chiusi, on the main train line, you can take a La Ferroviaria bus to Montepulciano. From Colle Val d'Elsa you can catch a CPT bus to get to Volterra.

➤ BUS INFORMATION: **CPT** (Compagnia Pisana Transporti, ✉ Piazzale Ginori Conti 2-3, Volterra, ☎ FAX 0588/86186). **La Ferroviaria** (✉ Via Guido Monaco 37, Arezzo, ☎ 0575/39881, FAX 0575/28414). **Lazzi Eurolines** (✉ Via Mercante 2, Florence, ☎ 055/363041, WEB www.lazzi.it). **Tra-In** (✉ Statale 73, Levante 23, Due Ponti, Siena, ☎ 0577/204111).

CAR RENTAL

Hertz and Avis are the tried and true options. It is usually less expensive to arrange for car rental from the United States; explore options before traveling.

➤ LOCAL AGENCIES: **Avis** (✉ Piazza della Repubblica 1/a, Arezzo, ☎ 0575/354232; ✉ Viale Luporini 1411/a, Lucca, ☎ 0583/513614; ✉ Via Simone Martini 36, Siena, ☎ 0577/270305). **Hertz** (✉ Aeroporto Galileo Galilei, Pisa, ☎ 050/49187; ✉ Via Valentini 60, Prato, ☎ 0574/611287; ✉ Viale Sardegna 37, Siena, ☎ 0577/45085).

CAR TRAVEL

The best way to see Tuscany is by car, making it possible to explore the tiny towns and country restaurants that are so much a part of the region's charm. Drivers should be prepared to navigate through bewildering suburban sprawls around Tuscan cities; to reach the historic sections where most of the sights are, look for the CENTRO STORICO signs. In many small towns you must park outside the walls.

The Autostrada del Sole (A1) connects Florence with Bologna, 105 km (65 mi) north, and Rome, 277 km (172 mi) south, passing by Arezzo and Chiusi (where you turn off for Montepulciano). The A11 leads west from Florence and meets the coastal A12 between Viareggio and Livorno. A toll-free superstrada links Florence with Siena. For Chianti wine-country scenery, take the S222 south of Florence through the undulating hills between Strada in Chianti and Greve in Chianti.

EMERGENCY SERVICES

If you have a breakdown on the autostrada, or any toll road, you will find along the side of the road yellow "SOS" boxes placed every couple of kilometers or so. You push a button on the box, a green light pops on, and help is sent—you don't actually talk to a person. If you are on other roads, call ACI, the Italian Auto Club.

➤ CONTACTS: **ACI** (☎ 116).

EMERGENCIES

Pharmacies stay open at off hours on a rotating basis. To find out who's open, check the schedule in found in all pharmacy windows.

➤ CONTACTS: **Ambulance, medical emergency** (☎ 118). **Police, fire** (☎ 113).

MAIL AND SHIPPING

➤ POST OFFICES: **Lucca** (✉ Via Vallisneri 2, ☎ 0583/43351). **Pisa** (✉ Piazza Vittoria Emanuele, ☎ 050/43352). **Siena** (✉ Via Petrilli Savina or Via Rispini 3, ☎ 0577/50286).

OUTDOORS AND SPORTS

GOLF

Casentino Golf Club, long favored by Florentines and other ardent golfophiles, is a gorgeous 9-hole golf course set in the midst of Piero della Francesca country near Arezzo. Also on hand is a restaurant, offering the perfect spot for the "19th (or in this case 10th) hole." Though it's closed on Tuesday most of the year, in July and August it's open every day from 8 AM until sundown.

➤ CONTACTS: **Casentino Golf Club** (✉ Via Fronzola 6, Poppi, 52014, 0575/529810; 0575/5202112 restaurant, FAX 0575/520167).

HORSEBACK RIDING

Rifugio Prategiano is a hotel that offers horseback riding daily. Also try Le Cannelle, a seasonal outfit operating from Easter to September 30.

➤ CONTACTS: **Le Cannelle** (✉ Parco Naturale della Maremma, Talamone, Grosseto, ☎ 0564/887020). **Rifugio Prategiano** (✉ Montieri, Grosseto, ☎ 0566/997703), closed January 10–February 10.

HOT-AIR BALLOONING

Eyre & Humbert will arrange for a 1½-hour balloon ride over Florence. Flights depart from the Arno and sail over the rolling hills of Fiesole and Settignano. The location of touchdown depends upon local weather conditions; two cars follow the balloon and are ready for prompt pickup as well as a *brindisi*—toast upon the flight's completion. Special arrangements can be made to take a trip into the Chianti countryside. It has two balloons, each of which can hold up to four people; it's possible to arrange to have both balloons go up at the same time.

➤ CONTACTS: **Eyre & Humbert** (✉ Corso Italia 5/r, Florence, ☎ 055/ 2382251, ☎ 055/2382254).

TOURS

From Florence, American Express operates one-day excursions to Siena and San Gimignano and can arrange for cars, drivers, and guides for special-interest tours in Tuscany.
➤ FEES AND SCHEDULES: **American Express** (✉ Via Dante Alighieri 22/ r, ☎ 055/50981).

BOAT TOURS

Charters in Tuscany are available through the Centro Nautico Italiano. Depart from either Marca Marciona in Elba or Talamone (on the mainland, south of Follonica) for journeys through the Tuscan archipelago, including the islands of Giglio, Capraia, Gorgona, Pianosa, Montecristo, and Giannutri. You can either skipper your own vessel or hire a crew; fleets can accommodate as few as two people or as many as 12. Exploring the Ligurian coast, or Corsica or Sardinia, is also a possibility.
➤ FEES AND SCHEDULES: **Centro Nautico Italiano** (✉ Piazza della Signoria 31/r, Florence, ☎ 055/287419).

BUS TOURS

Bus tours can be arranged through any travel agency. Micro Travel Box, for instance, will tailor bus itineraries to suit your tastes and budget.
➤ FEES AND SCHEDULES: **Micro Travel Box** (✉ Via dell'Oriuolo 50-52/ r, Florence, ☎ 055/2340228).

WALKING TOURS

A terrific way to get a feel for Tuscany is by walking it. Several companies offer guided tours that cater to anyone from the novice hiker to the expert. Country Walkers offers weeklong (and longer) walking tours throughout Tuscany during the spring and fall. Italian Connection, Walking & Culinary Tours offers walking and culinary itineraries through Tuscan hill towns at various times between April and November.
➤ FEES AND SCHEDULES: **Country Walkers** (✉ Box 180, Waterbury, VT, 05676, ☎ 888/742–0770 or 802/244–5661). **Italian Connection, Walking & Culinary Tours** (✉ 11825-11B Ave., Edmonton, Alberta, Canada, ☎ 800/462–7911).

TRAIN TRAVEL

The coastal line from Rome to Genoa passes through Pisa and all the beach resorts. The main line from Rome to Bologna passes through Arezzo, Florence, and Prato. Call 8848/888088 for toll-free information. Italy's main rail line, which runs from Milan to Calabria, links Florence and Arezzo in Tuscany and runs past Chiusi and Cortona on its way south. Another main line connects Florence with Pisa. There's also regular, nearly hourly service from Florence to Lucca via Prato, Pistoia, and Montecatini. Call FSI, the Italian State Railway, toll-free for information.
➤ TRAIN INFORMATION: **FS** ☎ 8848/888088.

TRAVEL AGENCIES

➤ LOCAL AGENT REFERRALS: **American Express** (✉ Via Dante Alighieri 22, Florence, ☎ 055/50981). **CIT Italia** (✉ Piazza Stazione 51/r, Florence, ☎ 055/284145). **Micos Travel Box** (✉ Via dell'Oriuolo 50/52/r, Florence, ☎ 055/2340228).

VISITOR INFORMATION

➤ AGROTOURIST INFORMATION: **Terranostra** (✉ Via dei Magazzini 2, Florence, 50122, ☎ 055/280539). **Turismo Verde** (✉ Via Verdi 5, Florence, ☎ 055/2344925).

➤ TOURIST INFORMATION: **Arezzo** (✉ Piazza della Repubblica 22, ☎ 0575/377678, WEB www.turismo.tosana.it). **Colle Val d'Elsa** (✉ Via F. Campana 43, ☎ 0577/922791). **Cortona** (✉ Via Nazionale 42, ☎ 0575/630352, WEB www.cortonaweb.com). **Greve in Chianti** (✉ Viale Giovanni da Verrazzano 33, ☎ 055/8546287). **Lucca** (✉ Piazzale Verdi, ☎ 0583/419689, WEB www.lucca.turismo.toscana.it). **Montalcino** (✉ Costa del Municipio 8, ☎ 0577/442944, WEB www.montalcino.it). **Montecatini Terme** (✉ Viale Verdi 6, ☎ 0572/772244, WEB www.montecatini.it). **Montepulciano** (✉ Corso Rosellino 59, ☎ 0578/757341). **Pienza** (✉ Palazzo Pubblico, Piazza Pio II, ☎ 0578/749071). **Pisa** (✉ Via Cammao 2, ☎ 050/560464). **Pistoia** (✉ Palazzo dei Vescovi, Via Roma 1, ☎ 0573/21622, WEB www.comune.pistoia.it). **Portoferraio** (✉ Calata Italia 26, ☎ 0565/914671, WEB www.aptelba.it)). **Prato** (✉ Piazza delle Carceri 15, ☎ 0574/24112, WEB www.prato.turismo.toscana.it). **Radda in Chianti** (✉ Piazza Ferrucci 1, ☎ 0577/738494, open Mar.–Oct. only). **San Gimignano** (✉ Piazza del Duomo 1, ☎ 0577/940008, WEB www.sangimignano.com). **San Miniato** (✉ Piazza del Popolo 3, ☎ 0571/42745, WEB www.comune.san-miniato.pi.it). **Siena** (✉ Piazza del Campo 56, ☎ 0577/280551). **Volterra** (✉ Piazza dei Priori 19, ☎ 0588/87257 or 0588/86099, WEB www.comune.volterra.pi.it).

9 EMILIA-ROMAGNA

PARMA, BOLOGNA, RIMINI, RAVENNA, FERRARA

Gourmets the world over claim that Emilia-Romagna's greatest contribution to humankind has been gastronomic. Birthplace of fettuccine, tortellini, lasagna, prosciutto, and Parmesan cheese, the region is home to a bevy of great restaurants. But there are also many cultural riches in the flat, fertile Po Plain and its surroundings: Parma's Correggio paintings, Verdi's villa at Sant'Agata, the medieval splendor of Bologna's palazzi and Ferrara's castle, and the Byzantine beauty of mosaic-rich Ravenna—glittering as brightly today as it did 1,500 years ago.

Updated by
Robin S.
Goldstein

EMILIA-ROMAGNA OWES ITS BEGINNINGS to a road. In 187 BC the Romans laid out the Via Aemelia, a long highway running straight northwest from the Adriatic port of Rimini to the central garrison town of Piacenza, and it was along this central spine that the primary towns of the region developed. The old Roman road (SS9) is still called Via Emilia today, and the autostrada (A1 and A14) runs parallel to it.

Despite the unifying factor of the Via Emilia, the region has had a fragmented history. Its eastern portion, roughly the area from Faenza to the coast, known as Romagna, has looked first to the east and then to Rome for art, political power, and, some say, national character. The western portion, Emilia, from Bologna to Piacenza, had a more northern, rather dour sense of self-government and dissent. Italians say that in Romagna a stranger will be offered a glass of wine; in Emilia, a glass of water—if anything at all.

The principal city of the region is Bologna, a cultural and culinary capital less trodden but just as exciting for the visitor as Italy's more famous tourist destinations. It was founded by the Etruscans but eventually came under the influence of the Roman Empire. The Romans established a garrison there, renaming the old Etruscan settlement Bononia, the Bologna of today. It was after the fall of Rome that the region began its fragmentation. Romagna, centered in Ravenna, was ruled from Constantinople. Ravenna eventually became capital of the empire in the West in the 5th century, passing to papal rule in the 8th century. Even today, however, the city is still filled with reminders of two centuries of Byzantine rule.

The other cities of the region, from the Middle Ages on, became the fiefs of important noble families—the Este in Ferrara and Modena, the Pallavicini in Piacenza, the Bentivoglio in Bologna, and the Malatesta in Rimini. Today all these cities bear the marks of their noble patrons. When in the 16th century the papacy managed to exert its power over the entire region, some of these cities were divided among the families of the reigning popes—hence the stamp of the Farnese family on Parma, Piacenza, and Ferrara.

In the 19th century, the region was one of the first to join the fight for a unified Italy, pledging itself to the king of Italy and the forces of Garibaldi in the 1840s. Loyalty to the crown did not last long, however. The Italian socialist movement was born in the region, and throughout Italy, Bologna and Emilia-Romagna have been known for rebellion and dissent. Benito Mussolini was born here, although in keeping with the political atmosphere of his home state he was a firebrand socialist during the early part of his career. Despite being the birthplace of Il Duce, Emilia-Romagna did not take to fascism: it was in this region that the antifascist resistance was born, and during World War II the region suffered terribly at the hands of the Fascists and the Nazis.

Despite a long history of bloodletting, turmoil, and rebellion, the arts—both decorative and culinary—have always flourished in Emilia-Romagna. The great families financed painters, sculptors, and writers (Dante found a haven in Ravenna after being expelled from his native Florence). In modern times, Emilia-Romagna has given to the arts such famous sons as painter Giorgio Morandi, writer Giorgio Bassani (author of *The Garden of the Finzi-Continis*), filmmakers Michelangelo Antonioni and Federico Fellini, and tenor Luciano Pavarotti.

Nowadays, the sprawling plants of the industrial food giants of Italy, such as Barilla, Parmalat, and Fini, stand side by side with the fading villas and deteriorating farmhouses that have long punctuated the flat, fertile land of the Po Plain. Each fall, the region's trademark low-lying fog rolls in off of the Adriatic and hangs over those Romagnan flatlands for the winter, coloring cities and countryside alike with a spooky, gray glow. As Antonioni once mused: "On the plain in late September, evening comes quickly. The day ends when headlights are turned on unexpectedly. The sunset is not soft, it is mysterious. It is so hard to see what is before my eyes." Bologna is acknowledged as the leading city of Italian cuisine, and the rest of the region follows—eating is a seminal part of any Emilia-Romagnan experience. The area's history is replete with culinary legends, such as how the original tortellino was modeled on the shape of Venus's navel and the original *tagliolini* (long, thin egg pasta) was served at the wedding banquet of Annibale Bentivoglio and Lucrezia d'Este; Bologna's centuries-old nickname "the Fat" is anything but pejorative. It's impossible to eat badly here, and everything is worth trying. Parma's famed prosciutto and Parmigiano Reggiano cheese; Modena's *zampone* (pig's feet stuffed with minced meat) and sweet, jet-black balsamic vinegar; and Bologna's fettuccine, *mortadella* (smoked sausage), and *ragù* (meat sauce) are all served throughout the region, along with *tortelli alla zucca* (dumpling- or ravioli-shape pasta stuffed with squash), fresh fruits and vegetables, ancient Roman *piadina* (chewy, flat griddle bread), and a number of fine, robust wines.

Pleasures and Pastimes

Dining

Emilia-Romagna's reputation as Italy's gourmet region is well deserved, and maintaining that reputation spurs the region's chefs onto even greater heights of gastronomic achievement. For you, this means an obligation to eat lots and eat well: a trip through Emilia-Romagna wouldn't be complete without sampling what the region does best.

Emilia-Romagnan *cucina* is not without its drawbacks, however. For example, meals are not light—in Emilia-Romagna, eating light means leaving half of your tortellini *con noci e panna* (with walnuts and cream) on your plate. Ravioli stuffed with spinach and ricotta cheese, tortelli and *cappellacci* (triangular pasta dumplings) stuffed with squash, and tortellini stuffed with minced pork and beef all have in common one key word—and you'll inevitably be stuffed, too.

This is not to say that the uninitiated should be wary of the culinary delights of Bologna the Fat and its sister cities. The specialties are nothing new in name, they're just better here, where they were born: Parma's crumbly Parmigiano Reggiano cheese and world-famous Parma ham (look for prosciutto di Parma, especially the most prized version, *culatello*); Bologna's pasta (especially tagliatelle) *al ragù*, a heavenly, slow-cooked mix of onions, carrots, minced pork and beef, and fresh tomatoes that in no way resembles the Bolognese sauce served worldwide; likewise the rich, soft, garlicky mortadella sausage that has been reincarnated elsewhere to its detriment as "baloney." Although most local specialties are served throughout the region, traditionalists will have their zampone and *aceto balsamico* in Modena (the most prized version, the syrupy, cask-aged *aceto balsamico tradizionale*, commanding up to 150,000 lire/€77 for 100 ml), their risotto *in padella* (with fresh herbs and tomatoes) in Piacenza, their *brodetto* (tangy seafood stew) in Rimini, their *cappellacci di zucca* in Ferrara, and everything else in Bologna.

Emilia-Romagna's wines, fittingly, are meant to accompany the region's fine food rather than vie with it for attention and accolades. The best known is Lambrusco, a sparkling red produced on the Po plain that has some admirers and many detractors. It's praised for its tartness and condemned for the same quality. The region's best wines include Barbera, produced in the Colli Piacetini and Apennine foothills, and Sangiovese di Romagna, which can be very similar to Chianti, from the Romagnolan hills.

For general information and price categories, *see* Dining *in* Smart Travel Tips.

Lodging

Emilia-Romagna has a reputation for an efficiency uncommon in most of the rest of Italy. Even the smallest hotels are well run, with high standards of quality and service. Bologna is very much a businessperson's city, and most hotels there cater to the business traveler, but there are smaller, more intimate hotels as well. Either way, you can expect an experience delightfully free of the condescending attitude and manipulative pricing schemes that sometimes mar Italy's tourist meccas. The one exception to the rule is Rimini, whose business is tourism. Its numerous hotels, unlike those in the rest of Emilia-Romagna, offer tourist-oriented full-and half-board packages. They overflow during July and August but are closed for much of the off-season. For general information and price categories, *see* Lodging *in* Smart Travel Tips.

Exploring Emilia-Romagna

In Emilia-Romagna there's something for everyone: great art, fascinating history, fabulous food—even a busy beach scene at Rimini.

Numbers in the text correspond to numbers in the margin and on the Emilia-Romagna and Bologna maps.

Great Itineraries

Emilia-Romagna has a geographical logic—the Via Emilia (S9) and its parallel big brother, the Autostrada del Sole (highway A1), bisect through the Po Valley and Romagna plain, making it easy to cover the most of the major destinations in the region in order by driving straight through. Alternatively, you could base yourself in the regional capital, Bologna, and make forays from this hub. From Bologna there are three choices of itineraries: head north on A13 to Ferrara and then southeast on S16 to Ravenna, or continue east or west along the Via Emilia (S9), stopping for short visits at some of the smaller towns en route northwest to Piacenza or southeast to Rimini and the sea.

IF YOU HAVE 3 DAYS
Given three days, you should set aside two nights to see ⌖ **Bologna** ⑤–⑭ and its environs. The city itself has enough to fill much more than this, but while you are there, make a point of seeing the sights in and around Piazza Maggiore, including **Santo Stefano** ⑩, the **Basilica di San Petronio** ⑤, **Palazzo Comunale** ⑥, and the two towers nearby. On day two, take a train or drive the short distance to ⌖ **Ferrara** ⑲, a calm, unspoiled Renaissance city. Where you spend your third day will depend on your route out of Emilia-Romagna. If you are going to Milan or Turin, make a stop about 100 km (62 mi) northwest of Bologna at ⌖ **Parma** ③, where you could cover the major sights in two or three hours. If you are heading toward the Adriatic coast, misty, medieval ⌖ **Ferrara** ⑲ should be your priority stop.

IF YOU HAVE 5 DAYS
Bother with chaotic ⌖ **Rimini** ⑰ only if it's summer and you're looking for a hard-core resort and disco scene. Otherwise head straight for ⌖ **Ravenna** ⑱, being sure to see Sant'Apollinare in Classe, outside the

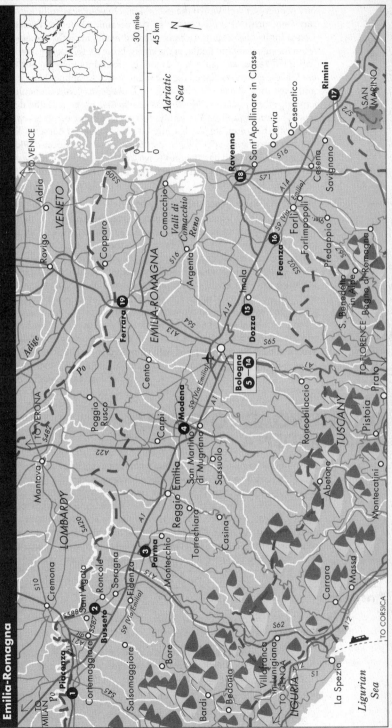

Emilia-Romagna

city proper but well worth the excursion. On your way to Bologna on day two, drop in on a factory in the ceramic center of **Faenza** ⑯, famed for its *faience* pottery. Stay two to three nights in ⊠ **Bologna** ⑤–⑭, savoring meals and taking in the sights. From there, take an overnight trip to ⊠ **Ferrara** ⑲, enjoying an amble around its turreted and towered medieval streets. Spend the last night or two sampling the fine food and wine in ⊠ **Parma** ③, stopping in ⊠ **Modena** ④, another culinary capital, along the way. Northwest of Parma, make a slight detour from the autostrada or Via Emilia to see the cluster of places associated with the composer Verdi, centered in the village of **Busseto** ②. Still heading northwest, spend your last morning or afternoon in **Piacenza** ①, an elegant and harmonious town in the typical fashion of Emilia-Romagna and a fitting exit or entrance to the region. From here, it's 66 km (41 mi) to Milan.

When to Tour Emilia-Romagna

You would never visit Emilia-Romagna for the weather. In this predominantly flat landscape, the winters are gray and cold, and summers are airless and hot, though sea breezes on the coast offer some respite. If you are here in summer, get up early and do as much as you can in the morning. Ideally, mid-afternoons in summer should be left unplanned; the hours after five are best for sightseeing and traveling. In winter, make sure you are equipped for the frequent rain and damp, penetrating cold. Dense, low-lying fog is common throughout the plains in fall and winter and can be starkly beautiful, but it can also be very hazardous on the road. No matter what the season, make sure you reserve ahead for rooms: the cities are often filled with commercial conventions and business conferences. Restaurants and hotels in Rimini are usually closed up tight during the off-season, but the rest of Emilia-Romagna offers tourists as much during the winter season as in summer.

ON THE ROAD TO PARMA AND MODENA

The Via Emilia runs through Emilia's heart in a straight shot from medieval Piacenza to thoroughly modern Modena. On the way from the past to the present you'll encounter many of Italy's cultural riches—from the culinary and artistic treasures of Parma to the birthplace and home of Giuseppe Verdi. It may be tempting to imitate Modena's Ferraris and zoom over the short (113-km [70-mi]) stretch of highway spanning the region, but if you take time to detour into the countryside, with its farmhouses and 800-year-old abbeys, or stop for a taste of prosciutto di Parma, you'll be richly rewarded.

Piacenza

① *66 km (41 mi) southeast of Milan, 150 km (94 mi) northwest of Bologna.*

The city of Piacenza has always been associated with industry and commerce. Its position on the River Po has made it an important inland port since the earliest times; the Etruscans, and then the Romans, had thriving settlements on this site. As you approach the city today, you could be forgiven for thinking that it holds little of interest. Piacenza is surrounded by ugly industrial suburbs (with particularly unlovely cement factories and a power station), but forge ahead and you'll discover that they surround a delightfully preserved medieval downtown.

The heart of the city is **Piazza dei Cavalli** (Horses' Square), dominated by the massive 13th-century **Palazzo del Comune**. This severely Gothic turreted and crenellated building was the seat of town government before Piacenza fell under the iron fists of the ruling Pallavicini and Farnese families. The flamboyant **equestrian statues** from which the piazza takes its name are depictions of members of the last and greatest of the Farnese: on the right is Ranuccio Farnese (1569–1622); on the left is his father, Alessandro (1545–92). Alessandro was a beloved ruler, enlightened and fair; Ranuccio, his successor, was less successful. Both statues are the work of Francesco Mochi, a master sculptor of the Baroque period.

Attached like a sinister balcony to the bell tower of Piacenza's 12th-century **Duomo** is a *gabbia* (iron cage), where miscreants were incarcerated naked and subjected to the scorn (and missiles) of the crowd in the marketplace below. Inside the cathedral, a less-evocative but equally impressive array of medieval stonework decorates the pillars and the crypt, and there are extravagant frescoes by Il Guercino (a.k.a. Giovanni Barbieri, 1591–1666) in the dome of the cupola. The Duomo can be reached by following Via XX Settembre from Piazza dei Cavalli. ⊠ *Piazza Duomo,* ☎ *0523/335154.* ⊙ *Daily 8:30–noon and 4–7.*

The **Museo Civico** (Civic Museum), the city-owned collection of Piacenzan art and antiquities, is housed in the vast **Palazzo Farnese.** The ruling family originally commissioned a monumental palace, but construction, begun in 1558, was never completed. The highlight of this rather eclectic exhibit is the 2nd century BC Etruscan *Fegato di Piacenza,* a bronze tablet in the shape of a *fegato* (liver), with the symbols of the gods of good and ill fortune marked on it. By comparing this master "liver" with one taken from the body of a freshly slaughtered sacrifice, the priests could predict the future. On a more humane note, the collection also contains a painting by Botticelli (1445–1510), the *Madonna with St. John the Baptist,* and a series of Roman bronzes and mosaics. There is also a collection of carriages, arms and armor, and other paraphernalia owned by the Farnese, which give life to the history of that powerful family. ⊠ *Piazza Cittadella,* ☎ *0523/326981,* WEB *www.farnese.net.* ⊡ *10,000 lire/€5.15.* ⊙ *Tues. and Thurs.–Fri. 9:30–1, Wed. and weekends 9:30–1 and 3–6; guided tours by reservation Tues.–Fri. 9:30, weekends 9:30–11 and 3–4.*

Dining

$$$$ ✕ **Antica Osteria del Teatro.** Set on a lovely piazza in the center of town,
★ this restaurant is generally touted as the best in Piacenza. It's housed in a typical 15th-century building with coffered ceilings and sober furniture, and it effuses elegance, with excellent service and an impeccable wine list. Try the rich liver with chutney and figs. ⊠ *Via Verdi 16,* ☎ *0523/323777. Reservations essential. AE, DC, MC, V. Closed Sun.–Mon., Aug. 1–25, and Jan. 1–8.*

$ ✕ **Agnello.** Central (on the corner of Piazza dei Cavalli), simple, small, and cheap, with paintings hung here and there, Agnello is an excellent place to plop down for lunch. Try the tortelli *alla Piacentina* (stuffed with ricotta and spinach and bathed in butter and Parmesan) or the *coniglio alla cacciatore* (rabbit in a tomato and white-wine sauce). Reservations are a good idea. ⊠ *Via Calzolai 2,* ☎ *0523/320874. No credit cards. Closed Mon. and Aug.*

En Route If you are driving from Piacenza, take the S10 northeast for Cremona, but turn off it just a couple of miles out of Piacenza and follow the signs for S587 to the town of Cortemaggiore. From Cortemaggiore, turn right onto a smaller rural road (not numbered) and follow the signs for Busseto, some 10 km (6 mi) away.

Busseto

❷ *30 km (19 mi) southeast of Piacenza, 15 km (9 mi) south of Cremona.*

Busseto's main claim to fame is the 15th-century **Villa Pallavicino,** where master composer Giuseppe Verdi (1813–1901) worked and lived with his mistress (and later wife), Giuseppina Strepponi. The small **Verdi museum** here displays such relics as the maestro's piano, scores, composition books, and walking sticks, and other bits of memorabilia. If you plan to visit all the area's Verdi sights, invest in an 8,000-lire/€4.15 ticket valid for the Villa Pallavicino, Palazzo Orlandi, Teatro Verdi, and Verdi's birthplace (but not Villa Sant'Agata). Call the Busseto tourist office (⊠ Comune, Piazza Giuseppe Verdi 10, ☎ 0524/931732) for more information. ⊠ *Via Provesi 36,* ☎ *0524/92239,* 🎫 *4,000 lire/€2.05.* ⊙ *Apr.–Sept., Tues.–Sun. 9–noon and 3–7; Oct.–Nov., and Mar., Tues.–Sun. 9:30–12 and 2:30–5; closed Dec.–Feb.*

Palazzo Orlandi, owned for the past century by the Orlandi family, was Verdi's home for a few years beginning in 1845. Only a few of its stately rooms are open to the public; it's a good idea to call ahead to confirm that it's open. ⊠ *Via Roma 56,* ☎ *0524/92308.* 🎫 *3,000 lire/€1.55.* ⊙ *Apr.–Sept., Tues.–Sun. 9–noon and 3–7; Oct.–Nov. and Mar., Tues.–Sun. 9:30–noon and 2:30–5.*

In the center of Busseto is the lovely **Teatro Verdi,** dedicated, as one might expect, to the works of the hamlet's famous son. Once inside the well-preserved, ornate 19th-century-style theater, use your imagination to get a feel for where he worked. Call the Busseto tourist office (⊠ Comune, Piazza Giuseppe Verdi 10, ☎ 0524/931732) for the latest word on theater performances and visiting hours. ⊠ *Piazza Verdi 10.* 🎫 *5,000 lire/€2.15.* ⊙ *Mar.–Oct., Tues.–Sun. 9:30–12:30 and 3–7; Nov.–Feb., Tues.–Sun. 9:30–12:30 and 2:30–5:30.*

OFF THE
BEATEN PATH

VILLA SANT'AGATA – Four kilometers (2½ miles) north of Busseto, Villa Sant'-Agata, also known as Villa Verdi, is the grand country home Verdi built for himself in 1849, where some of his greatest works were composed. For Verdi lovers, Sant'Agata is a veritable shrine. Tours are required, and you have to reserve your place a few days in advance, either by phone or at the Web site. ⊠ *Via Verdi 22, Sant'Agata Villanova sull'Arda, 4 km (2½ mi) north of Busseto on S588 toward Cremona,* ☎ *0523/830210,* WEB *www.villaverdi.org.* 🎫 *10,000 lire/€5.15.* ⊙ *Jan.–Mar. 15, Tues.–Sun. 10–4:30; Mar. 16–Sept., Tues.–Sun. 9–11:40 and 3–6:45; Oct., Tues.–Sun. 9–11:40 and 2:30–5:45.*

RONCOLE – Giuseppe Verdi was born in a simple farmhouse on the edge of the town of Roncole, 5 km (3 mi) southeast of Busseto. Equally modest is the church in which he took some early steps in his musical career; he was the church organist here when still in his teens. ⊠ *5 km (3 mi) east of Busseto on local road to Soragna (follow signs).* 🎫 *Verdi's birthplace 3,000 lire/€1.55.* ⊙ *Apr.–Sept., daily 9:30–12:30 and 3–7; Mar., Tues.–Sun. 9:30–12:30 and 3–7; Oct.–Nov. and Feb., Sat. 2:30–5:30, Sun. 9:30–12:30 and 2:30–5:30.*

Parma

❸ *40 km (25 mi) southeast Busseto, 97 km (61 mi) northwest of Bologna.*

Dignified, delightful Parma stands on the banks of a tributary of the River Po. Much of the lively historic center has been untouched by modern times, despite heavy damage during World War II. Almost every major European power has had a hand in ruling Parma at one time or another.

The Romans founded the city—then little more than a garrison on the Via Emilia—after which a succession of feudal lords held sway. In the 16th century came the ever-avaricious Farnese family (who are still the dukes of Parma) and then, in fast succession, the Spanish, French, and Austrians (after the fall of Napoléon). The French influence is strong. The French novelist Stendhal (1783–1842) lived in the city for several years and set his classic *The Charterhouse of Parma* here.

Bursting with gustatory delights, Parma draws crowds for its sublime cured ham, prosciutto di Parma (known locally simply as prosciutto *crudo*), of which *culatello* is the finest cut; and for the delicate, pale yellow Parmigiano Reggiano cheese, the original—and best—of a class now known around the world as Parmesan. The modern city's economic prosperity is due in no small part to the Parmalat dairy empire, which also controls a world-class soccer team.

Thanks to the efforts being made by the city fathers to control traffic, strolling Parma's cobbled streets along with the teeming masses of locals is a charming experience. The draconian traffic regulations, although a boon to pedestrians, are a nightmare for motorists.

★ The **Piazza del Duomo,** site of the cathedral, the baptistery, the church of San Giovanni, and the palaces of the bishop and other notables, is the heart of the city. This square and its buildings make up one of the most harmonious, tranquil city centers in Italy. The magnificent 12th-century **Duomo** has two vigilant stone lions standing guard beside the main door. The arch of the entrance is decorated with a delicate frieze of figures representing the months of the year, a motif repeated inside the baptistery on the right-hand side of the piazza. Some of the original artwork still exists in the church, notably the simple yet evocative *Descent from the Cross,* a carving in the right transept by Benedetto Antelami (1150–1230), a sculptor and architect whose masterwork is this cathedral's Baptistery.

It is odd to turn from this austere work of the 12th century to the exuberant fresco in the dome, the *Assumption of the Virgin,* by Antonio Correggio (1494–1534). The fresco was not well received when it was unveiled in 1530. "A mess of frogs' legs," the bishop of Parma is said to have called it. In contrast to the rather dark, somber interior of the cathedral, though, the beauty and light of the painting in the dome are a welcome relief. Today Correggio is acclaimed as one of the leading masters of Mannerist painting; his many works on view in Parma are some of the city's greatest draws. ⊠ *Piazza del Duomo,* ☎ *0521/235886.* 🎫 *Free.* ☼ *Daily 9–12:30 and 3–7.*

The **Baptistery** is a solemn, simple Romanesque building on the exterior and an uplifting Gothic building within. The doors of the Baptistery are richly decorated with figures, animals, and flowers, and the interior is adorned with figures carved by Antelami showing the months and seasons. ⊠ *Piazza del Duomo,* ☎ *0521/235886.* 🎫 *5,000 lire/€2.60.* ☼ *Daily 9–12:30 and 3–7.*

Once beyond the elaborate Baroque facade of **San Giovanni Evangelista,** the Renaissance interior reveals several works by Correggio; his *St. John the Evangelist* (left transept) is considered the finest of them. Also in this church (in the second and fourth chapels on the left) are works by Girolamo Parmigianino (1503–40)—a contemporary of Correggio's and the spearhead of the astonishing Mannerist art movement. Once seen, Parmigianino's anorexic and swan-necked Madonnas are never forgotten: they pose with all the precious élan of today's high-fashion models. ⊠ *Piazzale San Giovanni,* ☎ *0521/235592.* ☼ *Daily 9–noon and 3–6.*

In the adjoining monastery to the church of San Giovanni Evangelista is the **Spezieria di San Giovanni**—once a pharmacy where Benedictine monks mixed medicines and herbals. The 16th-century decorations survive, although the potions, which people of Parma swore by, are no longer—the pharmacy stopped production in 1881. ⊠ *Borgo Pipa 1, off Piazzale San Giovanni,* ☎ *0521/233309.* ⊐ *4,000 lire/€2.05.* ☉ *Daily 8:30–2.*

Works by Parma's own Correggio and Parmigianino as well as Leonardo da Vinci (1452–1519), El Greco (1541–1614), and Bronzino (1503–72) are the highlights of the **Galleria Nazionale,** housed in the vast but rather grim-looking **Palazzo della Pilotta,** on the bank of the river. The palace was built in about 1600 and is so big that from the air it is Parma's most recognizable sight—hence the destruction it suffered from Allied bombs in 1944. Much of the building has been restored, but not all. The palazzo takes its name from the game *pilotta,* a sort of handball played within the palace precincts in the 17th century.

To enter the Galleria Nazionale, on the ground floor of the palace, you pass through the magnificent and elaborately Baroque **Teatro Farnese,** built in 1628 and based on Palladio's theater in the northern Italian town of Vicenza. Built entirely of wood, the theater was burned badly during Allied bombing but has been flawlessly restored. ⊠ *Palazzo della Pilotta, Piazza Pilotta,* ☎ *0521/233309.* ⊐ *Teatro Farnese 4,000 lire/€2.05, Teatro and Galleria Nazionale 12,000 lire/€6.20.* ☉ *Mon. 8:30–2, Tues.–Sun. 8:30–7:30.*

The **Camera di San Paolo** is the former dining room of the abbess of the Convent of St. Paul. It was extensively frescoed by Correggio, and despite the religious character of the building, the decorations aren't Christian in nature, with ravishingly beautiful (and very worldly) depictions of mythological scenes—the *Triumphs of the Goddess Diana,* the *Three Graces,* and the *Three Fates.* It is near the Palazzo della Pilotta, off Strada Garibaldi. ⊠ *Via Melloni,* ☎ *0521/233309.* ⊐ *4,000 lire/€2.05.* ☉ *Mon. 8:30–2, Tues.–Sun. 8:30–7:30.*

Near Parma's central Piazza Garibaldi is the **Chiesa di Santa Maria della Steccata,** a delightful 16th-century domed church famous for a wonderful fresco cycle by Parmigianino. The painter took so long to complete it that his patrons imprisoned him briefly for breach of contract before releasing him so he could get back to work. ⊠ *Piazza Steccata 9, off Via Dante,* ☎ *0521/234937.* ☉ *Daily 9–noon and 3–6.*

The **Teatro Regio** opera house is a local landmark, as well as the site of regular performances. Tours are given though at press time they had been suspended due to renovation. ⊠ *Via Garibaldi 16,* ☎ *0521/218685,* WEB *www.teatroregio.parma.it.* ☉ *Tues.–Fri. 10–2 and 5–7, Sat. 9:30–12:30 and 4–7.*

Dining and Lodging

$$$–$$$$ ✕ **La Greppia.** The most elegant, most talked-about restaurant in the city is also the best. The service is extremely personal and friendly, thanks to the place's tiny size. Taste innovative treats like the *anelli con cavolo nero e mostarda della Paola* (local pasta rods with black cauliflower and caramelized fruits with mustard) and the *faraona al tartufo nero di Fragno* (guinea hen with black truffle and chestnut puree). The unpretentious decor keeps all eyes on the outstanding food. ⊠ *Via Garibaldi 39,* ☎ *0521/233686. Reservations essential. AE, DC, MC, V. Closed Mon.–Tues. and mid-July–mid-Aug.*

$$$ ✕ **Parizzi.** Named not for the city but rather for its exciting young chef, Marco Parizzi, this restaurant rivals La Greppia for the title of Parma's finest. A stylish Art Nouveau interior complements antipasti such as

culatello di Zibello, the most highly touted of Parma hams; traditional Parma classics like stuffed *tortelli*; and sublime risotto di Parmigiano Reggiano with shaved white truffle (in season). ⊠ *Via Repubblica 71,* ☎ *0521/285952. Reservations essential. AE, DC, MC, V. Closed Mon.*

$$-$$$ ✕ **Croce di Malta.** The premises of this appealing old-world restaurant once housed a convent, then an inn. Traditional local fare includes delicate homemade pasta—try the tortelli with squash filling or tagliatelle in any fashion. Second courses include well-prepared, hearty versions of classic veal and cheese dishes. ⊠ *Borgo Palmia 8,* ☎ *0521/235643. Reservations essential. AE, DC, MC, V.*

$$ ✕ **Gallo d'Oro.** Warmly colored, warmly lit, bottle-clad rooms upstairs and a multilevel bodega downstairs each house dozens of tables, which are usually filled. To go along with the atmosphere, the menu features traditional Parma specialties, like an antipasto of *salumi misti* (local hams) and several varieties of tortelli. Prices are surprisingly low, especially for Parma. ⊠ *Via Borgo della Salina 3,* ☎ *0521/208846. AE, DC, MC, V. Closed Sun.*

$$ ✕ **Parma Rotta.** An old inn about 2 km (1 mi) from downtown, the
★ Parma Rotta remains an informal neighborhood trattoria serving hearty dishes like spit-roasted lamb and roast pork, topped off with a wide array of homemade desserts. ⊠ *Via Langhirano 158,* ☎ *0521/ 966738. AE, DC, MC, V. Closed Sun. in June–Sept. and Mon. in Oct.–May.*

$-$$ ✕ **Sant'Ambrogio.** This is an ideal spot for informal dining in the cen-
★ ter of town. Duck and quail are good bets, but don't overlook the *crauti spinaci* (boiled pork sausage with pickled cabbage or spinach). ⊠ *Vicolo Cinque Piaghe 1/a,* ☎ *0521/234482. AE, DC, MC, V. Closed Mon.*

$$$$ ▥ **Palace Hotel Maria Luigia.** A top-quality hotel convenient to Old Parma and the train station, the Maria Luigia has well-furnished rooms, some with painting-like vistas of Parma. It's popular with business travelers. ⊠ *Viale Mentana 140, 43100,* ☎ *0521/281032,* ℻ *0521/ 231126,* ⟦WEB⟧ *www.venere.it/parma/maria_luigia. 102 rooms, 11 suites. Restaurant, bar, minibars, meeting room. AE, DC, MC, V.*

$$$-$$$$ ▥ **Park Hotel Stendhal.** On the edge of the historic center of town, the Stendhal is well situated whether you're here on business or pleasure—and it happens to be one of Parma's finest hotels. Rooms are thickly carpeted and spacious, some with chandeliers and antique furniture. Some rooms have views of the Palazzo della Pilotta. ⊠ *Via Bodoni 3, 43100,* ☎ *0521/208057,* ℻ *0521/285655,* ⟦WEB⟧ *www.bestwestern.it/inglese/stendhal_pr. 66 rooms. Restaurant, bar, meeting room. AE, DC, MC, V.*

$$ ▥ **Hotel Torino.** A warm reception and pleasant, relaxed surroundings are the best reasons for staying in this former convent, tucked away in a quiet pedestrian zone in the heart of town. It has modern, smallish rooms with Correggio reproductions on the walls. If traveling by car, fax ahead for a detailed map with driving directions—it's difficult to find. ⊠ *Via Mazza 7, 43100,* ☎ *0521/281046,* ℻ *0521/230725. 33 rooms. Bar. AE, DC, MC, V.*

Nightlife and the Arts

⟦BARS⟧

Before dinner, locals flock to **Enoteca Antica Osteria Fontana** (⊠ Strada Farini 24/a, ☎ 0521/286037), an atmospheric wine bar that serves up several varieties of good local wine like the sparkling Lambrusco or Sangiovese di Romagna, as well as an excellent selection of bottles from all over Italy at reasonable prices. The crowd is gregarious, whether standing or sitting. Great Parma-style grilled *panini* are also served. Closing time is early (9 PM) and it's closed all day on Sunday. After dinner, **Martinica Pub** (⊠ Viale A. Fratti 16, a bit out of town, attracts lively groups of affluent twentysomethings. It's open daily 5 PM–3 AM.

OPERA AND THEATER

Parma is the region's opera center, with performances held at the **Teatro Regio** (✉ Via Garibaldi 16, ☎ 0521/218678). Opera here is taken just as seriously as in Milan, although tickets are a little easier to come by. Playwright Dario Fo, the recipient of the 1997 Nobel Prize in Literature, helped found the **Teatro Due** (✉ Viale Basetti 12, ☎ 0521/230242), where productions are a mixture of comedy and politics—your understanding will be limited without a knowledge of Italian.

Modena

❹   *56 km (35 mi) southeast of Parma, 38 km (23 mi) northwest of Bologna.*

Old Town Modena has today gained recognition as home to three very contemporary names. The high-performance cars Maserati and Ferrari come from Modena, and so does the world-famous opera star Luciano Pavarotti. But Modena's herb-infused balsamic vinegar is still perhaps its greatest achievement. The modern town that encircles the historic center is extensive, and although the old quarter is small, it is filled with narrow medieval streets and pleasant piazzas.

The 12th-century **Duomo,** also known as the Basilica Metropolitana, is one of the finest examples of Romanesque architecture in the country. The exterior is decorated with medieval sculptures depicting scenes from the life of San Geminiano, the patron saint of Modena, and fantastic beasts, as well as a realistic-looking scene of the sacking of a city by barbarian hordes, a reminder to the faithful to be ever vigilant in defense of the church. The bell tower is made of white marble and is known as **La Ghirlandina** (The Little Garland) because of its distinctive garland-shape weather vane. The somber church interior is divided by an elaborately decorated gallery carved with scenes of the Passion of Christ. The carvings took 50 years to complete and are by an anonymous Modenese master of the 12th century. The tomb of San Geminiano is in the crypt. ✉ *Piazza Grande,* ☎ *059/216078.* ⊘ *Daily 7–12:30 and 3:30–7.*

The town's principal museum is housed in the **Palazzo dei Musei,** a short walk from the Duomo. The collection was assembled in the mid-17th century by Francesco d'Este (1610–58), Duke of Modena, and the **Galleria Estense** is named in his honor. The first room displays his portrait bust, done by Bernini (1598–1680). The duke was a man of many interests, as you can see from the collection of objets d'art—ivories, coins, medals, and bronzes, as well as fine art dating from the Renaissance to the Baroque. There are works here by Correggio and masters from other parts of Italy, such as the Venetians Tintoretto (1518–94) and Veronese (1528–88), the Bolognese Guido Reni (1575–1642), and the Carracci brothers (Annibale, 1560–1609, and Agostino, 1557–1602), and the Neapolitan Salvator Rosa (1615–73).

The gallery also houses the duke's **Biblioteca Estense,** a huge collection of illuminated books, of which the best known is the beautifully illustrated 15th-century *Bible of Borso d'Este.* A map dated 1501 was one of the first in the world to show Columbus's discovery of America. Follow Via Emilia, the old Roman road that runs through the heart of the town, to Via di Sant'Agostino. ✉ *Piazza Sant'Agostino 377,* ☎ *059/200100.* ▣ *8,000 lire/€4.15.* ⊘ *Tues. and Fri.–Sat. 9–7, Wed.–Thurs. 9–2, Sun. 9–1.*

The huge Baroque **Palazzo Ducale** now houses a military academy; once the province of the dukes only, it is still off-limits, except to flocks of cadets in elaborate uniforms. Behind the academy are Modena's large **Giardini Pubblici** (Public Gardens). ✉ *Piazza degli Estensi.*

Close-Up

BALSAMIC NECTAR

BEWARE: the balsamic vinegar you've probably tried—even the pricier Aceto Balsamico di Modena sold at specialty stores and in Italy—may be good on salads, but it bears only a minor resemblance to the real thing, **Aceto Balsamico Tradizionale di Modena.** The vinegar that passes the strict governmental standards (a winelike D.O.C.—*Denominazione di Origine Controllata*—regulation) is officially a condiment rather than a vinegar, and it is made with Trebbiano grape must, which is reduced and fermented from 12 to 25 or more years in a series of specially made wooden casks. The result is an intense and syrupy concoction best enjoyed sparingly on meats, strawberries, or Parmigiano Reggiano cheese. The vinegar has such a complexity of flavor that some even drink the stuff as an after-dinner liqueur.

The **Consorzio Produttori Aceto Balsamico Tradizionale di Modena** (⊠ Corso Cavour 60, ☎ 059/236981), which can be visited, monitors the quality of the authentic balsamic vinegar, made only by a few licensed restaurants and small producers. The consortium also limits production, keeping prices sky-high (expect to pay 80,000 lire/€41–100,000 lire/€52 for a 100-ml bottle of *tradizionale,* or 150,000 lire/€77 and up for the older *tradizionale extra vecchio* variety). In the United States, though, you'll pay double those prices—if you can even find the product.

Dining and Lodging

$$$$ ✕ **Borso d'Este.** One of the city's most highly regarded restaurants—
★ particularly with the *crema* of the region's monied set—offers some delicious variations on old themes, like ravioli stuffed with game and Parmesan. The space is ultratrendy and modern, achieved despite antiques throughout. In season don't miss the *tartufo* (truffle) specialties: ricotta- and spinach-stuffed tortelloni in a truffle-mushroom sauce, and the mushroom tart laced with the perfumy tubers. ⊠ *Piazza Roma 5,* ☎ *059/214114. Reservations essential. AE, DC, MC, V. Closed Sun. and Aug. No lunch Sat.*

$$$$ ✕ **Fini.** A Modena institution, fancy, modern Fini is widely held to be the best restaurant the city has to offer. It's Pavarotti's favorite—and you could easily gain a Pavarotti-esque figure by making a habit of the excellent local wines, *gran bollito misto,* a groaning board of boiled meats in a *salsa verde* (vegetable sauce), and homemade desserts. ⊠ *Piazzeta San Francesco,* ☎ *059/223314. Reservations essential. AE, DC, MC, V. Closed Mon.–Tues., Aug., and last wk in Dec.*

$$ ✕ **Da Enzo.** This cheerful, well-patronized trattoria is in the Old Town's pedestrian zone, close by the synagogue and a few steps from Piazza Mazzini. All the classic Modenese specialties are here, including zampone and *cotechino* (animal bladders stuffed with pork). For starters, try the tortelloni *di ricotta e spinaci* (stuffed with ricotta and spinach). Reservations are essential on weekends. ⊠ *Via Coltellini 17,* ☎ *059/225177. AE, DC, MC, V. Closed Mon. and Aug. No lunch Sun.*

$$$ ☷ **Canal Grande.** Once a ducal palace, the Canal Grande offers large, airy, well-appointed rooms with minibars. A verdant garden with a fountain in back features a pretty breakfast terrace in summer. The hotel's restaurant, La Secchia Rapita (closed Wednesday and August), gets rave

reviews. ⊠ *Corso Canalgrande 6, 41100,* ☎ *059/217160,* FAX *059/ 221674,* WEB *www.canalgrandehotel.it. 75 rooms, 3 suites. Restaurant, bar, in-room safes, minibars. AE, DC, MC, V.*

$$ 🏨 **La Torre.** Not particularly exciting, La Torre is nonetheless the best hotel choice in the low end of this price category, thanks to its being in the town center just off the Via Emilia. The somewhat stuffy rooms are functional, comfortable, and well equipped. ⊠ *Via Cervetta 5, 41100,* ☎ *059/222615,* FAX *059/216316. 26 rooms. Bar. AE, DC, MC, V.*

BOLOGNA

Through its long history, first as an Etruscan city, then a Roman one, then as an independent city-state in the Middle Ages, Bologna has always been a power in the north of Italy. Over the centuries, the city has acquired a number of nicknames: Bologna the Learned, in honor of its venerable university, the oldest in the world; Bologna the Red, for its rosy rooftops and political leanings; Bologna the Turreted, recalling the forest of medieval towers that once rose from the city center (two remarkable examples still exist); and Bologna the Fat, a tribute to its preeminent position in the world of cuisine.

Today one might be tempted to dub it Bologna the Prosperous for its immaculately kept streets, trendy boutiques, and revered restaurants exuding impeccable class. Centuries of wars, sackings, rebellions, and aerial bombing that left such dramatic evidence in other cities of the region have not taken their toll on Bologna's old city center: the narrow cobblestone streets remain as they were hundreds of years ago (except cleaner), as do the ancient churches, massive palaces, medieval towers, and famous arcaded porticoes lining many of the main thoroughfares, shading the walkways to such an extent that you can stroll around town in a rainstorm for hours without feeling a drop. The noticeable absence of foreign visitors in the city, which served as one of Europe's "cultural capitals" for 2000, is one of the more bizarre anomalies in the world of Italian tourism. Bologna's vitality is entirely locally driven.

This is due in large part to its student population. The university was founded in about the year 1088 and by the 13th century already had more than 10,000 students. It was a center for the teaching of law and theology, and it was ahead of its time in that many of the professors were women. Today the university has one of the most prominent business schools in Italy and the finest faculty of medicine in the country. Guglielmo Marconi, the inventor of the wireless telegraph, first formulated his groundbreaking theories in the physics labs of the university.

Exploring Bologna

Piazza Maggiore and the adjacent Piazza del Nettuno make up the heart of the city. Arranged around these two squares are the imposing Basilica di San Petronio, the massive Palazzo Comunale, the Palazzo del Podestà, the Palazzo di Re Enzo, and the Fontana del Nettuno—one of the most visually harmonious groupings of public buildings in the entire country. From here, sights that aren't on one of the piazzas are but a short walk away, along delightful narrow cobbled streets or under the ubiquitous porticoes that double as municipal umbrellas in case of rain.

A Good Walk

Start at the southern end of sprawling Piazza Maggiore at the 14th-century **Basilica di San Petronio** ⑤, peeking into its museum to see the church's original designs, some never realized. On the west side of Piazza Maggiore is the **Palazzo Comunale** ⑥, especially great if you like the work of modern artist Giorgio Morandi. Next, it's on to the **Palazzo del Podestà** ⑦ and its Torre dell'Arengo, at the north end of Piazza Maggiore in the adjoining Piazza Nettuno, where stands the Fontana del Nettuno, a.k.a. *Il Gigante*. To the left (west) is **Palazzo Re Enzo** ⑧, with its dark medieval associations. The busy, chic Via Rizzoli runs east from Piazza Nettuno directly into the medieval section of the city to Piazza di Porta Ravegnana, where you can climb the slightly off-kilter **Torre degli Asinelli** ⑨, next to the smaller **Torre Garisenda.** From Piazza di Porta Ravegnana, you have two choices of routes if you want a shorter walk: head south and southwest to **Santo Stefano** ⑩ and **San Domenico** ⑪, or continue northeast along Via Zamboni for the last three important sights (⑫–⑭). If you want a long walk, explore all five sights. From the piazza, walk five minutes southeast down Via Santo Stefano to the remarkable church of Santo Stefano, actually several churches in one. From there, head west on Via Farini and take a left on Via Garibaldi; a few blocks down take a left to reach Piazza San Domenico and San Domenico, containing the saint's tomb and a minor work by Michelangelo. Retrace your steps back to Piazza di Porta Ravegnana, and walk northeast on Via Zamboni a few blocks to **San Giacomo Maggiore** ⑫, haunt of the Bentivoglio. Continue up Via Zamboni to Via delle Belle Arte and the **Pinacoteca Nazionale** ⑬, with works by Raphael, Giotto, Parmigianino, and Bolognese masters (if you plan on visiting, you may want to begin your day here, as the museum closes by early afternoon). Stroll north to the **Università di Bologna** ⑭ district for a *caffè* and snack.

TIMING

You'll want at least a full day to explore Bologna; it's compact and lends itself to easy exploration, but there is plenty to see. This walk, allowing a little time to explore each sight, should take at least four hours, not including the hour you should devote to the Pinacoteca Nazionale, a half hour to climb the Torre degli Asinelli, and a lunch break to sample Bologna's culinary bounty. Note that the Pinacoteca closes at 1 or 2 PM, so plan your exploration accordingly.

Sights to See

❺ **Basilica di San Petronio.** Construction on this cathedral began in the 14th century, and work was still in progress on this vast building some 300 years later. It is not finished yet, as you can see: the wings of the transept are missing and the facade is only partially decorated, lacking most of the marble face the architects had intended. The main doorway was carved by the great Sienese master of the Renaissance, Jacopo della Quercia. Above the center of the door is a Madonna and Child, flanked by Sts. Ambrose and Petronius, patrons of the city.

The interior of the basilica is huge and echoing, 432 ft long, 185 ft wide, and 144 ft high. It's striking to note that originally the Bolognans had planned an even bigger church—you can still see the columns erected to support the larger church outside the east end—but had to tone down construction when the university seat was established next door in 1561. The **Museo di San Petronio** contains models showing how the church was originally intended to look. The most important artworks in the church are in the left aisle, frescoes by Giovanni di Modena dating from the first years of the 1400s. Also in the left aisle, laid out in the pavement of the church, is a huge sundial, placed there in 1655, showing the time and date. ✉ *Piazza Maggiore,* ☎ *051/225442.* ⌖ *Free.* ☉ *Basilica Apr.–Sept., daily 7:30–1:30 and 2:30–7:30; Oct.–Mar., daily 7–1 and 2–7. Museo di San Petronio Mon. and Wed.–Sun. 10–12:30.*

Fontana del Nettuno. Sculptor Giambologna's elaborate 1566 Baroque monument to Neptune occupying Piazza Nettuno has been aptly nicknamed *Il Gigante* (The Giant). Its exuberantly sensual mermaids and

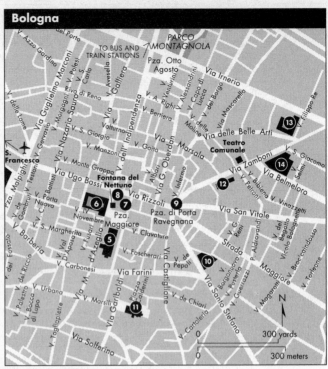

undraped God of the Sea drew fire when it was constructed, but not
enough, apparently, to dissuade the populace from using the fountain
as a public washing stall for centuries. ⊠ *Piazza Nettuno, next to the
Palazzo Re Enzo.*

⑥ Palazzo Comunale. A mélange of building styles and constant modi-
fications characterize this palace, dating from the 13th to 15th century. When Bologna was an independent city-state, this huge palace
was the seat of government, a function it still serves today. Over the
door is a statue of Bologna-born Pope Gregory XIII, most famous for
his reorganization of the calendar. ⊠ *Piazza Maggiore 6,* ☎ *051/
203111.* ☉ *Free visits of the first-floor Red Room (City Council Hall)
on advance request.*

Within the palazzo, the **Collezioni Comunali d'Arte** exhibits paintings
from the Middle Ages as well as some Renaissance works by Luca Signorelli (circa 1445–1523) and Tintoretto. On the same floor, a separate **Museo Morandi** is dedicated to the 20th-century still-life artist
Giorgio Morandi; in addition to his paintings, you'll see a re-creation
of his studio and living space. An equally good reason to come is to
get a look at the views of the piazza from the upper stories of the palace.
⊠ *Piazza Maggiore 6, west side,* ☎ *051/203629.* ☁ *8,000 lire/€4.15
each museum, 10,000 lire/€5.15 combined ticket.* ☉ *Collezioni Tues.–
Sat. 9–6:30, Sun. 10–6:30; Museo Tues.–Sun. 10–6.*

⑦ Palazzo del Podestà. This classic Renaissance palace facing the Basilica di San Petronio was erected in 1484, and attached to it is the soaring **Torre dell'Arengo.** The bells in the tower have rung since 1453
whenever the city has celebrated, mourned, or called its citizens to arms.
⊠ *Piazza Nettuno,* ☎ *051/224500.* ☉ *Visits only during exhibitions;
call for schedule.*

⑧ Palazzo Re Enzo. King Enzo of Sardinia was imprisoned in this 13th-century medieval palace for 23 years, until his death in 1272. He had waged war on Bologna and was captured after the fierce battle of Fossalta in 1249. The palace has other macabre associations: common criminals received the last rites of the church in the tiny chapel in the courtyard before being executed in Piazza Maggiore. (The courtyard is worth looking into, but there's nothing to see within the palace, which now houses government offices.) ⊠ *Piazza Re Enzo, next to the Palazzo del Podestà,* ☎ *051/224500.*

⑬ Pinacoteca Nazionale. Bologna's principal art gallery contains many works by the immortals of Italian painting, including Raphael's famous *Ecstasy of St. Cecilia.* There is also a beautiful multipanel painting by Giotto, as well as a Parmigianino *Madonna and Saints.* The centerpieces of the collection, however, are the many rooms devoted to the two most important late-16th-century Bolognese masters, Guido Reni and Annibale Carracci. Some of the most interesting works, from a historical point of view, are by Giuseppe Crespi (circa 1575–1632), a Bolognese painter who avoided grand religious or historical themes, preferring instead to paint scenes of daily life in his native city. These small canvases convey marvelously the boisterous, earthy life of Old Bologna. ⊠ *Via delle Belle Arti 56,* ☎ *051/243222.* ☞ *8,000 lire/€4.15.* ☉ *Tues.–Sat. 9–2, Sun. 9–1.*

⑪ San Domenico. The tomb of St. Dominic, who died here in 1221, is called the **Arca di San Domenico** and is found in this church in the sixth chapel on the right. Many artists participated in its decoration, notably Niccolò di Bari, who was so proud of his contribution that he changed his name to Niccolò dell'Arca to recall this famous work. The young Michelangelo carved the angel on the right. In the right transept of the church is a tablet marking the last resting place of the hapless King Enzo, the Sardinian ruler imprisoned in the Palazzo Re Enzo. In the square in front of San Domenico are two curious tombs raised above the ground on pillars, commemorating two 14th-century lawyers. ⊠ *Piazza San Domenico 13, off Via Garibaldi,* ☎ *051/6400411.* ☉ *Daily 7–1 and 2–7. Museum Tues.–Sat. 10–12:30 and 3–5, Sun. 3–5.*

⑫ San Giacomo Maggiore. Inside this church is the burial chamber of the Bentivoglio family, the city's leading family in the Middle Ages. The crypt is connected by underground passage to the Teatro Comunale across the street—a rather odd feature, until you realize that the family palazzo of the Bentivoglio used to stand on that spot. The most notable tomb is that of Antonio Bentivoglio (died 1435), carved by Jacopo della Quercia (circa 1374–1438). You can tell his profession—lecturer in law—from the group of students carved on the base. ⊠ *Piazza Rossini, off Via Zamboni,* ☎ *051/225970.* ☉ *Daily 7–noon and 3:30–6.*

★ ⑩ Santo Stefano. This splendid and unusual basilica actually contains between four and seven connected churches (authorities differ). The oldest is **Santi Vitale e Agricola,** which dates from the 8th century and contains a 14th-century nativity scene much loved by Bologna's children, who come at Christmastime to pay their respects to the baby Jesus. The church of **San Sepolcro** (12th century) contains the **Cortile di Pilato** (Courtyard of Pontius Pilate), so named for the basin in its center said to be where Pilate washed his hands after condemning Christ. Also in the building is a **museum** displaying various medieval religious works and with a shop where you can buy sundry items such as honey, shampoo, and jam made by the monks. ⊠ *Via Santo Stefano 24, Piazza Santo Stefano,* ☎ *051/223256.* ☉ *Mon.–Sat. 9–noon and 3:30–6:30, Sun. 9–12:45 and 3:30–6:30.*

⑨ Torre degli Asinelli/Torre Garisenda. The taller (320 ft) of the twin towers in the compact Piazza di Porta Ravegnana, Torre degli Asinelli leans an alarming 7½ ft off perpendicular. The Torre Garisenda (closed to visitors), now tilting 10 ft, was shortened to 165 ft for safety in the 1500s. The towers were built at the same time (1488) and are mentioned by Dante in *The Inferno*. They are two of the 60 towers that remain out of more than 200 that once presided over the city: every family of importance had a tower as a symbol of prestige and power, and as a retreat when that prestige and power were threatened. For a fine view of Bologna's rooftops, climb up the 500 steep stairs of Torre degli Asinelli. ✉ *Piazza di Porta Ravegnana.* 🎫 *Torre degli Asinelli 3,000 lire/€1.55.* ☉ *Apr.–Sept., daily 9–6; Oct.–Mar., daily 9–5.*

⑭ Università di Bologna. Take a stroll through the streets of the university district, a jumble of buildings, some dating as far back as the 15th century and most to the 17th and 18th. The neighborhood, as befits a college town, is full of bookshops, coffee bars, and cheap restaurants. None of them are particularly distinguished, but they're all characteristic of student life in the city. Try eating at the *mensa universitaria* (cafeteria) if you want to strike up a conversation with local students (most speak English). Political slogans and sentiments are scrawled on walls all around the university and tend to be ferociously leftist. The **University Museums** display scientific instruments and paleontological, botanical, and university-related artifacts. ✉ *Via Zamboni,* 🕿 *051/2049360.* 🕿 *051/2099360 museums.* 🎫 *Free.* ☉ *Weekdays; museum hrs vary.*

Dining and Lodging

$$$$ ✕ **Al Pappagallo.** Almost directly beneath Bologna's famous Asinelli
★ and Garisenda towers, the Pappagallo, facing stiff competition today, retains enough of its reputation and quality cuisine to merit at least one feast, served in a stylish, semiformal atmosphere. Try the first-course specialty, lasagna *del Pappagallo,* made with veal, sirloin of pork, and porcini mushrooms. The *filetto di tacchino al Pappagallo* (turkey stuffed with truffles, ham, and Parmesan cheese) is decadently rich. ✉ *Piazza della Mercanzia 3/c,* 🕿 *051/232807. Reservations essential. AE, DC, MC, V. Closed Sun., Dec. 25–Jan. 5, and Aug. 7–Sept. 3.*

$$$ ✕ **Rosteria Luciano.** A changing list of daily specials at this art deco–style restaurant augments what is already one of Bologna's most varied menus. Some of the best offerings are grilled lamb and beef, breast of duck, and excellent guinea fowl. Among the desserts, the *ricottina al forno* (charcoal-flavored oven-baked ricotta) is worth the splurge. ✉ *Via Nazario Sauro 19,* 🕿 *051/231249. Reservations essential. AE, DC, MC, V. Closed Wed. and Aug.*

$$–$$$ ✕ **Da Cesari.** Well-executed Bolognese classics such as tortellini *in*
★ *brodo* (in broth) and veal cutlet *Bolognese* (with ham and melted cheese) make this one of the best restaurants in Bologna in its price category. But it's the delectable appetizers—such as *coppa di testa con cipolla e aceto balsamico* (cold, sliced head meat and red onion with balsamic vinegar), white truffle with celery and shaved Parmesan, and various quiches—that make Da Cesari truly memorable. Accompany the meal with wine made by the owner's family; Cesari's Sangiovese Riserva is an excellent value, and the Liano, a Sangiovese-Cabernet blend, is world class. ✉ *Via de' Carbonesi 8,* 🕿 *051/237710. Reservations essential. AE, DC, MC, V. Closed Sun., Aug. 1–21, and Jan. 1–6.*

$$–$$$ ✕ **Rostaria Antico Brunetti.** Housed next door to a Romanesque tower and steps away from Piazza Maggiore, this wood-paneled restaurant was founded in 1873 and is known as Bologna's oldest. Specialties here range from "Mama's tortellini" to veal in a white-wine sauce, but most diners opt for the pizzas or simple pastas with seafood sauces. Dining is on two floors, but even then the restaurant fills quickly. ⊠ *Via Caduti di Cefalonia 5,* ☎ *051/234441. AE, DC, MC, V. Closed Wed. and Jan.*

$$ ✕ **Da Bertino.** Happy, gregarious diners don't seem to mind the cramped quarters in the large, bustling room here. Maybe it's because popularity hasn't spoiled this traditional neighborhood trattoria and its simple, home-style dishes. Tried-and-true highlights are the *paglia e fieno* (yellow and green pasta) with sausage and the choices on the steaming tray of bollito misto. ⊠ *Via delle Lame 55,* ☎ *051/522230. AE, DC, MC, V. Closed Sun. and Aug. No dinner Sat. in June–July, no dinner Mon.*

$$ ✕ **Da Carlo.** Dining on the medieval terrace in summer is a treat in this attractive restaurant, so be sure to reserve a table outside. The delicate game dishes, such as braised pigeon with artichokes, are favorites. ⊠ *Via Marchesana 6,* ☎ *051/233227. Reservations essential. AE, DC, MC, V. Closed Sun., Tues., Jan. 1–22, and Aug. 23–Sept. 3.*

$$ ✕ **Nuovi Notai.** If you get the timing just right, you'll hear the Angelus ring from the cathedral at this spot, just off beautiful Piazza Maggiore. The building is 14th-century, the decor 19th-century, and the food a rich, complex blend of classic regional specialties and imaginative uses of seasonal ingredients. The *tortino tiepido* (warm tartlet) of porcini mushrooms makes a good starter. ⊠ *Via de' Pignattari 1,* ☎ *051/228694. Reservations essential. AE, DC, MC, V. Closed Sun.*

$-$$ ✕ **Victoria.** It is not unusual for this unpretentious and charming
★ trattoria-pizzeria off Via dell'Indipendenza to have lines, so reserve ahead. Although locals come for the wide choice of cheap pizzas, the rest of the menu is not to be overlooked, particularly the tortellini *con noci e speck,* a ridiculously rich treatment of Bologna's classic pasta in a sauce of cream, ground walnuts, and cured ham. The back room has a lovely 17th-century painted wooden ceiling. ⊠ *Via Augusto Righi 9/ c,* ☎ *051/233548. Reservations essential. AE, DC, MC, V. Closed Thurs.*

$ ✕ **Tamburini.** This gourmet deli–cum–self-service buffet lunch spot sends the smells of all that is good about Bolognese food wafting through the room and out into the streets. Breads, numerous cheeses, *salumi* such as Parma and Bologna hams and prosciuttos, roasted peppers, inventive salads, balsamic vinegars, local olive oils, smoked salmon, and fresh pasta are among the delights. Tamburini also vacuum-packs foods for shipping or air travel. ⊠ *Via Drapperie 1,* ☎ *051/234726. AE, MC, V. Closed Sun., Tues., and Thurs. afternoons in Aug.*

$$$$ 🏨 **Grand Hotel Baglioni.** Sixteenth-century paintings and frescoes by
★ the Bolognese Carracci brothers are rarely seen outside a museum or church, but in this 15th-century palazzo they provide the stunning backdrop for the public rooms and restaurant of one of Italy's most glamorous hotels. Lady Di slept here, and you'll feel no less royal in a handsome room with antique furniture and brocaded walls. Note that although parking is available, the fee is inordinately high, at 48,000 lire/€24.80 per day. ⊠ *Via dell'Indipendenza 8, 40121,* ☎ *051/225445,* FAX *051/234840,* WEB *www.cnc.it/bologna/baglen1.htm. 140 rooms. Restaurant, bar, breakfast room, in-room safes, minibars, no-smoking room, baby-sitting, meeting room, parking (fee). AE, DC, MC, V.*

$$$–$$$$ 🏨 **Corona d'Oro 1890.** A medieval printing house in a former life, this
★ hotel has delightful, lyrical Art Nouveau decor in its public space; an atrium; and enough flowers for a wedding. Guest rooms make opulent use of original 15th- and 16th-century decorations like painted wood ceilings and Gothic-vault windows. The morning English breakfast buffet is worth getting up for. Fax ahead for driving directions. ⊠ *Via Oberdan 12, 40126,* ☎ *051/236456,* FAX *051/262679,* WEB *www.cnc. it/bologna. 35 rooms. Bar, breakfast room, in-room safes, minibars, meeting room, bicycles. AE, DC, MC, V. Closed 1st 3 wks in Aug.*

$$$–$$$$ 🏨 **Dei Commercianti.** Rooms in this hotel were designed to retain the
  ★   structural integrity of the 11th-century palace and tower the hotel oc-
           cupies and are therefore cozy and unique, with original wood beams
           built into the walls. Tower rooms and suites have balconies with mag-
           nificent views of the church; all rooms are stylishly furnished with, among
           other things, Carrara marble desks custom-built on a 15th-century de-
           sign. Fax ahead for driving directions. ⊠ *Via dei Pignattari 11, 40124,*
           ☎ *051/233052,* FAX *051/224733,* WEB *www.cnc.it/bologna. 32 rooms,*
           2 suites. Bar, breakfast room, in-room safes, minibars, bicycles. AE,
           DC, MC, V.

$$$–$$$$ 🏨 **Orologio.** Under the same management as the Corona d'Oro and
           the Dei Commercianti, the Orologio is in a quiet pedestrian zone off
           Piazza Grande and is in an ideal sightseeing location. The hotel occu-
           pies a palazzo that was originally a public building, but the interior
           achieves a contemporary effect. Top-floor rooms have good views of
           Bologna's skyline. Fax ahead for driving directions. ⊠ *Via IV Novem-*
           bre 10, 40123, ☎ *051/231253,* FAX *051/260552,* WEB *www.cnc.it/bologna.*
           29 rooms. Minibars, bicycles. AE, DC, MC, V.

$–$$ 🏨 **Accademia.** This small hotel is right in the middle of the university
           quarter, a comfortable base for exploring the area. The rooms are ad-
           equate, the staff friendly. ⊠ *Via delle Belle Arti 6, 40126,* ☎ *051/232318,*
           FAX *051/263590,* WEB *www.venere.it/bologna/accademia. 28 rooms.*
           Bar. No credit cards.

$–$$ 🏨 **San Vitale.** Modern furnishings and a garden distinguish this mod-
           est hostelry, a five-minute walk from the center of town. The service
           is courteous, and rooms are clean and bright. ⊠ *Via San Vitale 94, 40125,*
           ☎ *051/225966,* FAX *051/239396. 17 rooms. No credit cards.*

Nightlife and the Arts

The Arts

BALLET

Ballet can be found at the historic **Arena del Sole** (⊠ Via Indipendenza
44, ☎ 051/2910910).

FESTIVAL

The **Festa di San Petronio,** held each year the during the first weekend
in October, features bands, fireworks, and free *mortadella di bologna*
sandwiches in Piazza Maggiore.

MUSIC

The city hosts a wide selection of orchestral and chamber-music concerts. The 18th-century **Teatro Comunale** (⊠ Largo Respighi 1, ☎ 051/
529999) presents concerts by Italian and international orchestras
throughout the year. Check concert schedules for the **Sala Bossi** (⊠
Piazza Rossini 2, ☎ 051/233975). The **Sala Mozart** is the performance
venue for the **Accademia Filarmonica** (⊠ Via Guerazzi 13, ☎ 051/
222997), the city's principal music school.

OPERA

The acclaimed opera performances in Bologna dominate the **Teatro Co-**
munale (⊠ Largo Respighi 1, ☎ 051/529999) in the winter season.
All events sell out quickly, so be sure to reserve seats well in advance.

THEATER

The winter season at the **Europa Auditorium** (⊠ Piazza Costituzione,
☎ 051/372540) features shows from comedy to cabaret, and an occasional pop concert thrown in for good measure. A wide range of theatrical productions is staged throughout the winter at the **Teatro Duse**
(⊠ Via Cartoleria 42, ☎ 051/231836). Theater productions are staged
at the **Arena del Sole** (⊠ Via Indipendenza 44, ☎ 051/2910910).

Teatro delle Moline (✉ Via delle Moline 1, ☎ 051/235288) is just one of the many small venues where contemporary drama, dance, and comedy productions are performed. Children learning Italian may enjoy the kids' productions at the **Teatro Testoni** (✉ Via Matteotti 16, ☎ 051/377968).

Nightlife

BARS

As a university mecca, Bologna is known for its hopping nightlife. The two liveliest bars in town, frequented most often by Italian students, young adults, and the international study-abroad crowd, both have a non-Italian flavor: if you prefer an Irish pub, head for **Cluricaune** (✉ Via Zamboni 18/b, ☎ 051/263419). If your taste is for an English pub, try **Lord Lister** (✉ Via Zamboni 56).

Outdoor Activities and Sports

Swimming

The public **indoor swimming pool** (✉ Via Costa 174, ☎ 051/519107) is open June–September, Monday and Wednesday 10:30–7 and Tuesday 2–7, and October–May, weekdays noon–3, Saturday 10:30–1:30, and Sunday 9:30–12:30; admission is 9,000 lire/€4.65.

Shopping

Market

The gargantuan **City Market** (✉ Piazza VIII Agosto, off Via dell'Indipendenza north toward the train station), open daily during daylight hours, hosts vendors of every imaginable sort hawking wares of variable quality, including clothing, shoes, books, food, and every imaginable household good. Vendors also line the sidewalks of Via dell'Indipendenza on weekends.

Books

Capitalizing on the university atmosphere, **Feltrinelli** (✉ Via de' Giudei 1–2a) is the best bookstore in the region. It's open Monday–Saturday 9 AM–10 PM, Sunday 10–1:30 and 3:30–7. **Feltrinelli International** (✉ Via de' Giudei 1–2a) stocks innumerable travel guides and maps, and Italy's best selection of English and other foreign-language books. It's open Monday–Saturday 9–7:30.

Clothing

Galleria Cavour (✉ Piazza Cavour), perhaps the most upscale mall in Italy, houses many of the fashion giants, including **Gucci**, **Versace**, and the jeweler and watchmaker **Bulgari**. A host of small clothing and jewelry shops line **Via d'Azeglio** in the center of town.

Shoes

Bruno Magli (✉ Piazza della Mercanzia 1/d) showcases modern Italian fashion design at its finest. It's open Monday–Wednesday and Friday–Saturday 9–12:30 and 3:30–7:30, Thursday 3:30–7:30.

Wines

Scaramagli (✉ Strada Maggiore 31/d) offers one of the best wine selections in town—ask the owner which wines were awarded *tre bicchieri* ("three glasses" from Gambero Rosso's wine bible *Vini d'Italia*, the most prestigious award for an Italian wine). The shop is closed in the afternoon from 1 until 5, but reopens from 5 to 8 every evening except Thursday.

RIMINI, RAVENNA, AND FERRARA
Byzantine Splendors and Simple Pleasures

Heading southeast out of Bologna, Via Emilia (S9) leads to the towns of Dozza and Faenza before reaching the Adriatic coast and Rimini. From there, Ravenna and Ferrara lie to the northwest along the S16.

Dozza

⑮ *31 km (19 mi) southeast of Bologna.*

Dozza, just off the Via Emilia (S9), is a small village on a hill crowned with a splendid restored medieval castle, the **Rocca di Dozza.** Artists from all over flock to the town in September of odd years to take part in the mural competition that has left virtually every square foot of the town covered with colorful scenes executed with varying degrees of skill. **Enoteca Regionale,** housed in Dozza's castle, is the wine "library" for the region. Here you can sample the different vintages from the surrounding countryside, particularly Dozza's own Albana, a white wine that comes dry or sweet. ☎ *0542/678240 Rocca di Dozza; 0542/678089 Enoteca Regionale.* 🔳 *Rocca di Dozza 6,000 lire/€3.10.* ☉ *Apr.–Sept., Tues.–Sat. 10–noon and 3–6, Sun. 10–noon and 3–7; Oct.–Mar., Tues.–Sat. 10–noon and 2–5, Sun. 10–noon and 2–6.*

Dining

$$$$ **✕ San Domenico.** Leading food critics still count San Domenico among
★   Italy's top 10 restaurants, and so dedicated gourmands will want to make the trip to the luxe town of Imola (about 15 km [9 mi] east). Majestic decor reflects the truly royal prices you'll pay for celebrity chef Valentino Marcattilii's wondrous creations, such as homemade pâté with white truffles; hand-stuffed pasta with rabbit and eggplant in lemon-thyme sauce; and risotto with scampi, black truffle, and artichoke (not to be missed if it's available). With more than 3,000 choices, the wine list is touted as the second most extensive in Europe, after that of the Tour d'Argent in Paris. Make reservations well in advance. ✉ *Via G. Sacchi 1, Imola,* ☎ *0542/29000,* 🅵🅰🆇 *0542/39000. Reservations essential. AE, DC, MC, V. Closed Sun.–Mon. in June–July; Mon. in Sept.–May; 1st wk in Jan.; and Aug. No dinner Sun. in Sept.–May.*

Faenza

⑯ *23 km (14 mi) southeast of Dozza, 49 km (30 mi) southeast of Bologna.*

The renowned style of pottery called *faience* has been produced in Faenza, on the Via Emilia, since the 12th century. In the central **Piazza del Popolo** are dozens of shops selling the native wares. Faenza is unsurprisingly home to the **Museo delle Ceramiche** (Museum of Ceramics), one of the largest of its kind in the world, covering the potter's art in all phases of history the world over. ✉ *Viale Baccarini 19,* ☎ *0546/21240.* 🔳 *10,000 lire/€5.15.* ☉ *Apr.–Oct., Tues.–Sat. 9–7, Sun. 9:30–1; Nov.–Mar., Tues.–Fri. 9–1:30, Sat. 9–1:30 and 3–6, Sun. 9:30–1.*

OFF THE   **PREDAPPIO –** The small town of Predappio, on rural Route 9ter south of
BEATEN PATH   Forlì, is the birthplace and final resting place of Benito Mussolini, with the former dictator's crypt and a spotlighted bust on display. It is a chilling place that's become the object of pilgrimage for followers of fascism, who write repugnant political slogans in the visitors' book. ✉ *Cimitero Municipale.* ☉ *Daily 8 AM–sunset.*

SAVIGNANO – On S9 beyond Forlì, you pass through the modern towns of Forlimpopoli, Cesena, and Savignano. At this last town, there is a reminder that no matter how new the towns might look, you are still traveling in a place of great history—just outside the town is a small stream, the Rubicone. Cross it and you, too, have crossed the Rubicon, the river made famous by Julius Caesar when, in 49 BC, he defied the Senate of Rome by bringing his army across the river and plunging the country into civil war.

Dining

$$$$ ✕ **La Frasca.** This elegant countryside restaurant, by any measure one
★ of the best—and most expensive—in Romagna, and perhaps Italy, features a beautiful outdoor garden for alfresco summer dining. Chef Gianfranco Bolognesi combines fresh Adriatic seafood and local Romagnan produce in such complex and unexpected delights as *tortino di gamberi, melanzane e pomodoro* (crayfish, tomato, and eggplant pie with a ratatouille of local vegetables and delicately fried basil leaves). The wine list is, predictably, outstanding. A beautiful country drive will bring you to secluded Castrocaro Terme, 11 km (7 mi) from the town of Forlì and more or less equidistant (40 km/25 mi) from Imola and Ravenna. ⊠ *Viale Mateotti 34, Castrocaro Terme,* ☎ *0543/767471,* FAX *0543/766625. Reservations essential. AE, DC, MC, V. Closed Tues., Jan. 1–20, and Aug. 15–31.*

Rimini

🔟 *58 km (36 mi) southeast of Faenza, 121 km (76 mi) southeast of Bologna.*

Rimini is the principal summer resort on the Adriatic Coast and one of the most popular holiday destinations in Italy. Every summer, beginning in June and peaking in August, the city is flooded with vacationers, not just from Italy but from France, Austria, Germany, Scandinavia, and Great Britain as well. Be warned: the city is given over almost exclusively to tourism, with hundreds of hotels, grand and modest, and restaurants catering to virtually every national palate: you are just as likely to find a Bierkeller or an English teashop as you are an Italian restaurant. The waterfront is lined with beach clubs that rent deck chairs and umbrellas by the day, week, month, or the entire season. Hotels along the beachfront have staked out their own private turf, so the chance of swimming without having to pay for the privilege can be had only by going to one of the public beaches. Swimming on public beaches is possible, but prepare for sand that packs sunbathers in like sardines. Prepare also for murky seawater; tourists come to Rimini for the company, not an idyllic setting. In the off-season (October–March), Rimini is a ghost town. Some hotels and restaurants are open, but the majority are closed tight, hibernating until the return of the spendthrift tourists. Summers are so crowded here that it's most unwise to visit without confirmed hotel reservations.

The new town has just about swallowed the old town, but there is evidence here and there of Rimini's long and turbulent history. Rimini stands at the junction of two great Roman consular roads: the Via Emilia and the Via Flaminia. In addition, in Roman times it was an important port, making it a strategic and commercial center. From the 13th century onward, the city was controlled by the Malatesta family, an unpredictable group capable of grand gestures and savage deeds. The famous lovers immortalized in Dante's *Inferno*, Paolo and Francesca, were Malatestas. Paolo was the brother of Gianciotto Malatesta (died 1304); Francesca Polenta (died 1283 or 1284) was Gianciotto's wife. Gianciotto murdered them both for having betrayed him. Sigismondo Malatesta (1417–68), lord of the city in the middle of the 15th century, was considered a learned man of great wit and culture. He also

banished his first wife, strangled his second, and poisoned his third. He lived with his beautiful mistress, Isotta, until her death. He was so grief-stricken that he raised a magnificent monument in her honor, the
★ **Tempio Malatestiano,** the principal sight in the town.

Despite the irregular—from the church's point of view—nature of Sigismondo's relationship with Isotta, Sigismondo's memorial to his great love is today Rimini's cathedral. The building was in fact originally a Franciscan church before Sigismondo made it into a monument to his beloved. The Renaissance facade by Leon Battista Alberti (1404–72) is in the shape of a Roman triumphal arch and is considered to be one of Alberti's masterpieces.

The interior is light and spacious and contains the tombs of both the lovers. The intertwined *I*, for Isotta, and *S*, for Sigismondo, are placed everywhere and look rather like dollar signs. The carvings of elephants and roses recall the coat of arms of the Malatesta family. Sigismondo's tomb, on the right of the entrance door, is some distance from Isotta's in the second chapel on the right. (Her tomb is on the left wall of the chapel; the original inscription in marble had a pagan twist and was covered with another in bronze.) To the right of the entrance, in what is now the Tempio's book and gift shop, is a wonderful but badly damaged fresco by Piero della Francesca (1420–92) showing Sigismondo paying homage to his patron saint. When the shop is closed, one of the cathedral's staff will unlock the room containing the fresco. Over the main altar of the church is a crucifix attributed to Giotto (1266–1337); the painted feet are all but worn off from years when it was hung low enough for curious visitors to touch. ⊠ *Via IV Novembre 35,* ☎ *0541/51130.* ☉ *Mon.–Sat. 9–1 and 3:30–6, Sun. 7:50–12:30 and 3:30–6.*

Rimini's oldest monument is the **Arco d'Augusto** (Arch of Augustus), now stranded in the middle of a square just inside the city ramparts. It was erected in 27 BC, making it the oldest Roman arch in existence, and it marks the intersection of the Via Emilia and the Via Flaminia. To reach the Arch of Augustus from the Tempio Malatestiano, walk up Via Quattro Novembre to Piazza Tre Martiri (where, legend says, the mule carrying St. Anthony suddenly stopped and knelt in honor of the Holy Sacrament that was being carried past at the time) and turn left onto Corso d'Augusto. ⊠ *Largo Giulio Cesare.*

Dining and Lodging

$$–$$$ ✕ **La Locanda di San Martino.** Some have been known to drive all the
★ way from the Ligurian coast just to eat at this seafood restaurant, off the road out of Rimini heading toward Bologna. The delights of the Adriatic served here justify the trip. The setting is elegant if nondescript, but an outdoor patio in the back is a bit more romantic. *Primi piatti* such as *spaghettoni ai frutti di mare* (thick spaghetti with seafood sauce) and *secondi* like *grigliata di pesce mista* (mixed seafood grill) are uniformly superb, and the mixed antipasto served with lunch is exquisite. ⊠ *Via Emilia 226,* ☎ *0541/680127. Reservations essential. AE, DC, MC, V. Closed Mon.*

$$ ✕ **Dallo Zio.** Nothing but seafood is served here, and all of it is good
★ value. Two small rooms are unpretentiously furnished, one with antiques. Recommended treats are the *brodetto dell'Adriatica* (deliciously tangy shellfish broth), tortellini *al salmone* (in a salmon sauce), and simple grilled sole. ⊠ *Vicolo Santa Chiara 16,* ☎ *0541/786160. Reservations essential. AE, DC, MC, V. Closed Mon. No lunch Tues.–Fri.*

$$ ✕ **Taverna degli Artisti.** The row of stylish glass-and-wood doors that
★ enclose this restaurant give it the air of a French bistro, but once you're inside, the atmosphere is abundantly Italian. A local clientele of resort types and expatriates chats table-to-table over such specialties as

THE COUNTRY ON A CLIFF

"**THE WORLD'S** smallest and oldest republic" (as it dubs itself) is landlocked entirely by Italy. San Marino consists of three ancient castles perched high up on cliffs of sheer rock rising implausibly out of the flatlands of Romagna, and a tangled knot of cobblestoned streets below, which are unfortunately lined with tourist boutiques, cheesy hotels and restaurants, and gun shops. The 45-minute drive from Rimini is easily justified, however, by the castle-top view of the stunning green countryside far below the tiny country. The 1,000-meter-plus precipices of sheer rock will make jaws drop and acrophobes quiver.

San Marino was founded in the 4th century AD by a stonecutter named Marino who settled with a small community of Christians, escaping persecution by pagan emperor Diocletian. Over the millennia, largely because of the logistical and strategic nightmares associated with attacking a fortified rock, San Marino was more or less left alone by Italy's various conquerors, and continues to this day to operate as a politically independent country (population 26,000) and a member of the United Nations, economically supported almost entirely by its 3-million-visitor-per-year tourist industry.

San Marino's headline attractions are its three castles, which are medieval architectural wonders and, above all, engineering curiosities. The *tre castelli* appear on every coat of arms in the city. Starting in the center of town, you can walk along a paved cliff-top ridge from the 10th-century **Castello della Guaita** (☎ 0549/991369) to the 13th-century **Castello della Cesta** (☎ 0549/991295), which contains a museum of ancient weapons, and finally to the 14th-century **Castello Montale**, the most remote castle (closed to the public). Every step of the way affords spectacular views of Romagna and the Adriatic Sea; it is said that from the castle-top perches, on a clear day, you can see across the sea to Croatia. The

walks make for a good day's exercise but are by no means arduous. The longest—and windiest—hike is the one between the second and third castle. Even if you arrive after castle visiting hours (☉ 8–8, shorter hours in winter), the ridge walk from castle to castle is supremely worthwhile.

Another must-see while in San Marino is the **Piazza della Libertà**, whose battlemented and clock-topped Palazzo Pubblico is guarded by San Marino's real-life soldiers in their green uniforms. At the **Ferrari Museum** (✉ Maranello Rosso, V. III Settembre 3; park at the border crossing, ☎ 0549/900824) you can gaze at the automotive toys of the wealthy. As you'll notice by peering into the shops along the old town's winding streets, the republic is famous for its crossbows—and more: shopping for fireworks, firearms, and other items illegal for sale elsewhere is another popular tourist activity.

Most of the actual 26,000 residents live not in the medieval town above but rather along the more modern and accessible streets below the rock. Visiting San Marino in winter—off-season—increases the appeal of the experience, as tourist establishments shut down and you more or less have the castles to yourself. In August, on the other hand, every inch of walkway on the rock is mobbed with sightseers. To get to San Marino by car, take highway SS 72 west from Rimini. From Borgo Maggiore, at the base of the rock, a harrowing but scenic cable car will whisk you up to the castles and town. Alternatively, drive all the way up the winding road; public parking is available in the town itself. Don't worry about changing money, showing passports, learning telephone codes, and the like (although the tourist office will stamp your passport for 2,000 lire/€1.05); San Marino is, for all practical purposes, Italy—except, that is, for its majestic perch, its gun laws, and its reported 99% national voter turnout rate.

crudaiola (spicy spaghetti with tomatoes, basil, tuna, olives, and anchovies) or the Chianina steaks. An enormous wood oven and marble pizza-making counter provide a centerpiece to the sunny dining room. ⊠ *Viale Vespucci 1,* ☎ *0541/28519. AE, DC, MC, V.*

$–$$ ✕ **Picnic.** Take a break from Rimini's seaside crowds in the leafy garden of this casual restaurant in the city center, near Tempio Malatestiano. The menu is varied, with choices such as *spaghetti allo scoglio* (spaghetti with mixed seafood), *scallopine al Picnic* (veal with cream and mushrooms), and even simple pizzas. ⊠ *Via Tempio Malatestiano 30,* ☎ *0541/21916. AE, DC, MC, V. Closed Mon. in Sept.–June.*

$$$$ ☷ **Club House Hotel.** The Club House is a bit of a double-edged sword: for some, the suburban-office-building architecture may be off-putting; however, thanks to the design, all rooms have balconies right on the sea. Likewise with the hotel's location: for some, right on the main commercial strip and next door to McDonald's is a good thing. The hotel's rooms and facilities invite less debate: lovely, clean, airy rooms with green-and-white-striped ticking and across-the-street private beach access will spell summer vacation to all. ⊠ *Viale Vespucci 52, 47900,* ☎ *0541/391460,* 𝔽𝔸𝕏 *0541/391442,* 𝕎𝔼𝔹 *www.clubhouse.it. 28 rooms. Restaurant, bar, minibars, pool, beach. AE, DC, MC, V.*

$$$$ ☷ **Grand Hotel.** This fin-de-siècle extravaganza, made famous by Fellini
★ in his *Amarcord,* is grander than ever. The hyperluxe atmosphere set by enormous crystal chandeliers in the lobby and inlaid wood in the rooms seems playful rather than formal; with bright pink hallways, potted trees, and a spotless adjacent beach, the Grand is a beach resort above all else. While entourages and steamer trunks will never be out of place here, neither would it be any surprise to see a greyhound loping through the restaurant on her way to the pool. ⊠ *Via Ramusio, 1, Parco Federico Fellini, 47900,* ☎ *0541/56000,* 𝔽𝔸𝕏 *0541/56866. 117 rooms, 15 suites. 2 restaurants, 2 bars, minibars, 2 pools, hair salon, massage, sauna, tennis court, health club, beach, nightclub, meeting room. AE, DC, MC, V.*

$ ☷ **Anna Rita.** Set back on a residential road leading off the main Viale Vespucci, this hotel is small but comfortable, with a loyal clientele (availability may consequently be limited). Facilities are rudimentary, rooms are basic (though all have TVs and phones), but the main benefits here are proximity to the beach promenade and friendly price. ⊠ *Viale Misurata 24, 47900,* ☎ *0541/391044. 20 rooms. Restaurant, bar. No credit cards.*

En Route   There are two routes from Rimini to Ravenna. The coast road, S16, clings to the shoreline as far as Cervia before edging inland. Although its distance, 52 km (32 mi), is not great, this scenic route is naturally slower. The coast north of Rimini is lined with dozens of small resort towns, only one having any charm, the seaport of Cesenatico; the others are mini-Riminis, and during summer the narrow road is hopelessly clogged with traffic. A faster route is to head inland on A14 and then turn off onto the inland S71, which leads directly into Ravenna; the distance is 64 km (39 mi).

Ravenna

❶⑧   *52 km (32 mi) northwest of Rimini, 76 km (47½ mi) east of Bologna.*

Ravenna is a small, quiet city of brick palaces and cobbled streets, whose magnificent monuments are the only indicators of its storied past. The high point in Ravenna's history was 1,500 long years ago, when the city became the capital of the Roman Empire. The honor was short-lived—the city was taken by the barbarian Ostrogoths in the 5th century; in the 6th century it was conquered by the Byzantines, who ruled the city from Constantinople.

Because Ravenna spent much of its history looking to the East, its greatest art treasures show much Byzantine influence: above all, Ravenna is a city of mosaics, the finest in Western art. A single 8,000-lire/€4.15 combined ticket (available at ticket offices of all included sights) will admit you to six of Ravenna's most important monuments: the Tomba di Galla Placidia, the Basilica di San Vitale, the Battistero Neoniano, and Sant'Apollinare Nuovo, as well as the church of Spirito Santo and the Museo Arcivescovile e Cappella Sant'Andrea.

★ The **Mausoleo di Galla Placidia** and the **Basilica di San Vitale** are decorated with the best-known, and most elaborate, mosaics in the city. The little tomb and the great church stand side by side, but the tomb predates the church by at least a hundred years. Galla Placidia was the sister of Rome's emperor, Honorius, the man who moved the imperial capital to Ravenna in AD 402. She is said to have been beautiful and strong-willed and to have taken an active part in the governing of the crumbling empire. One of the most active Christians of her day, she endowed churches and supported priests and their congregations throughout the realm. This tomb, constructed in the mid-5th century, is her memorial.

Outside, the tomb is a small, unassuming building of red brick, whose seeming poverty of charm only serves to enhance the richness of the interior mosaics, in deep midnight blue and glittering gold. The tiny, low central dome is decorated with symbols of Christ and the evangelists and striking gold stars. Over the door is a depiction of the Good Shepherd. Eight of the Apostles are represented in groups of two on the four inner walls of the dome; the other four appear singly on the walls of the two transepts. Notice the small doves at their feet, drinking from the water of faith. Also in the tiny transepts are some delightful pairs of deer (representing souls), drinking from the fountain of resurrection. There are three sarcophagi in the tomb, none of which are believed to contain the remains of Galla Placidia. She died in Rome in AD 450, and there is no record of her body having been transported back to the place where she wished to lie.

The octagonal church of San Vitale, next door, was built in AD 547, after the Byzantines conquered the city, and its interior style shows a strong Byzantine influence. In the area behind the altar are the most famous works in the church, accurate portraits of the emperor of the East, Justinian, attended by his court and the bishop of Ravenna, Maximian. Facing him, across the chancel, is the emperor's wife, Theodora, with her entourage, holding a chalice containing the communion wine. The elaborate headdresses and heavy cloaks of the emperor and empress convey a marvelous sense of the grandeur of the imperial court, and of the mastery of the artisans responsible for the depictions. Presiding over the royal couple from the apse is Christ the King with San Vitale (the saint for whom the church was named) and the founder of the church, Bishop Ecclesio, who holds a model of the building. Note the way the mosaics seamlessly wrap around the columns and curved arches on the upper sides of the altar area. ⊠ *Via San Vitale off Via Salara, near Piazza del Popolo,* ☎ *0544/219938.* ▨ *8,000 lire/€4.15 (combined ticket only; includes Sant'Apollinare Nuovo, Spirito Santo, Battistero Neoniano, and others).* ☉ *Apr.–June, daily 9–6; July–Aug., daily 9–7; Sept.–Mar., daily 9–4:30.*

The **Museo Nazionale** of Ravenna, next to the Church of San Vitale, contains artifacts of ancient Rome, Byzantine fabrics and carvings, and other pieces of early Christian art. The collection is housed in a former monastery but is well displayed and artfully lit. ⊠ *Via Fiandrini,* ☎ *0544/34424.* ▨ *8,000 lire/€4.15 combined ticket.* ☉ *Tues.–Sat. 8:30–6:30, Sun. 8:30–7:30. Ticket office closes ½ hr before museum.*

Next door to Ravenna's 18th-century cathedral, the **Battistero Neoni-ano** is one of the town's most important mosaic sights. In keeping with the baptismal purpose of the building, the great mosaic in the dome shows the baptism of Christ, and beneath that scene are the Apostles. The lowest band of mosaics contains Christian symbols, the Throne of God and the Cross. Note the naked figure kneeling next to Christ—he is the personification of the River Jordan. The Battistero building is said to have been a Roman bath dating to the 5th century AD. ⊠ *Via Battistero,* ☎ *0544/219938.* ⊠ *8,000 lire/€4.15 (combination ticket only; includes Sant'Apollinare Nuovo, Galla Placidia, Spirito Santo, and others).* ☉ *Apr.–Sept., daily 9:30–7; Oct.–Mar., daily 9:30–4:30.*

The **Tomba di Dante** (tomb of Dante) is in a small neoclassical build-ing next door to the large church of St. Francis. Exiled from his native Florence, the author of *The Divine Comedy* died here in 1321. The Florentines have been trying to reclaim their famous son for hundreds of years, but the Ravennans refuse to give him up, arguing that since Florence did not welcome Dante in life it does not deserve him in death. In the church courtyard next door, note the site that served as tempo-rary, less-grand quarters for the poet's distinguished bones: a plaque identifies the mound of earth under which the Franciscan brothers put Dante's remains for safekeeping from March 1944 to December 1945. The small **Museo Dantesco** is also on the site. ⊠ *Tomba Via Dante Alighieri 9, Museo Via Dante Alighieri 4,* ☎ *0544/30252.* ⊠ *Tomb free, museum 3,000 lire/€1.55 (free Sun.).* ☉ *Tomb Apr.–Sept., daily 9–7; Oct.–Mar., daily 9–noon and 2–5. Museum Apr.–Sept., Tues.–Sun. 9–noon and 3:30–6; Oct.–Mar., Tues.–Sun. 9–noon.*

The mosaics displayed in the church of **Sant'Apollinare Nuovo** date from the early 6th century, making them slightly older than the works in San Vitale. Since the left side of the church was reserved for women, it is only fitting that the mosaic decoration on that side is a scene of 22 vir-gins offering crowns to the Virgin Mary. On the right wall are 26 men carrying the crowns of martyrdom. They are approaching Christ, who is surrounded by angels. ⊠ *Via Roma, at intersection with Via Guacci-manni,* ☎ *0544/219938.* ⊠ *8,000 lire/€4.15 (combined ticket only; includes Battistero Neoniano, Spirito Santo, Galla Placidia, and others).* ☉ *Daily 9:30–4:30.*

OFF THE
BEATEN PATH

SANT'APOLLINARE IN CLASSE – This church, about 5 km (3 mi) southeast of Ravenna, is landlocked now, but when it was built it stood in the cen-ter of the busy shipping port of Classis. The arch above and the area around the high altar are rich with mosaics. Those on the arch, older than the ones behind it, are considered superior to the rest. They show Christ in judgment and the 12 lambs of Christianity leaving the cities of Jerusalem and Bethlehem. In the apse is the figure of Sant'Apollinare himself, a bishop of Ravenna, and above him is a magnificent Transfigu-ration against blazingly green grass, animals in skewed perspective, and flowers. ⊠ *Via Romea Sud, Classe,* ☎ *0544/34057.* ⊠ *4,000 lire/€2.05 or 12,000 lire/€6.20 combined ticket with the Ravenna museums and churches, free Sun.* ☉ *Mon.–Sat. 8:30–7:30, Sun. 9–1.*

Dining and Lodging

$$ ✕ **Bella Venezia.** Graceful low archways lead into this attractive restau-rant's two small dining rooms. Try the owner's special risotto *Bazzani* (with butter, Parmesan, cured ham, mushrooms, and peas) and, for the entrée, *bistecca all'ortolana* (veal in cream sauce with cured ham and zucchini). A good-value tourist menu is available. Reservations are es-sential on weekends. ⊠ *Via IV Novembre 16,* ☎ *0544/212746. AE, DC, MC, V. Closed Sun. and Dec. 24–Jan. 24.*

$–$$ ✕ **Ca' de Ven.** A vaulted wine cellar in the heart of the old city, the Ca' de Ven is great for a hearty lunch or dinner. You sit at long tables with the other diners and feast on platters of delicious cold cuts, *piadine* (griddle breads), and cold, heady white wine. The *tortelli di radicchio e pecorino* (pasta pillows with radicchio and cheese) are the best first-course bet. ✉ *Via C. Ricci 24,* ☎ *0544/30163. AE, DC, MC, V. Closed Mon., Jan. 23–Feb. 10, and 1st wk of June.*

$$–$$$ ▥ **Hotel Bisanzio.** Just steps from San Vitale and the Tomb of Galla Placidia, this Best Western hotel is the most convenient lodging for mosaic enthusiasts. Rooms are comfortable and modern, and the lobby's Florentine lamps add a touch of style. Ask for a room on the top floor and you may get a view of the basilica. ✉ *Via Salara 30, 48100,* ☎ *0544/217111,* FAX *0544/32539,* WEB *www.bisanziohotel.com. 38 rooms. 2 bars, breakfast room, in-room safes, minibars, meeting room, parking (fee). AE, DC, MC, V.*

$$ ▥ **Hotel Centrale Byron.** In the heart of Ravenna's Old Town, this is an old-fashioned, well-managed hotel, its rooms spotless if uninspiring. Because it's in a pedestrian zone, tranquillity is assured, though you will have to leave your car in one of the nearby garages. ✉ *Via IV Novembre 14, 48100,* ☎ *0544/33479,* FAX *0544/34114,* WEB *www.hotelbyron.com. 54 rooms. Bar, in-room safes, minibars. AE, DC, MC, V.*

$ ▥ **Hotel Ravenna.** A functional stopover near the train station but still only a few minutes' walk from the center of town, this modern hotel offers smallish rooms with TVs and telephones. Two rooms are equipped for people with disabilities. ✉ *Via Maroncelli 12, 48100,* ☎ *0544/ 212204,* FAX *0544/212077. 26 rooms. Bar, parking (fee). MC, V.*

Nightlife and the Arts

The **Ravenna Festival,** a musical extravaganza held every year throughout June and July, brings in orchestras from all over the world to perform in Ravenna's mosaic-clad churches and theaters. Friday evenings in July and August you can experience **Mosaics by Night**—the byzantine masterpieces are lit up. Guided tours during the nocturnal illuminations are available; consult the tourist office (☎ 0544/35404) for information.

Ferrara

⑲ *74 km (46 mi) northwest of Ravenna, 47 km (29 mi) northeast of Bologna.*

Ferrara is a prosperous, meticulously maintained city of turrets, towers, and marvelous pleasure palaces. A mighty moated castle presides over a dark knot of winding medieval streets once inhabited by the likes of Copernicus. The ghostly low-hanging fog of the Po Plain so shrouds Ferrara in fall and winter that legendary Ferrarese filmmaker Michelangelo Antonioni has described his hometown as "a city that you can see only partly, while the rest disappears to be imagined." His 1995 film *Beyond the Clouds* lovingly traverses Ferrara's misty streets and arch-covered alleys.

Although the site was settled before the time of Christ and was once ruled by Ravenna, the history of Ferrara really begins in the 13th century, with the coming of the Este family. From 1259 until 1598, the Este dukes ruled the city, and in those 3½ centuries they left their indelible mark on it.

During the Renaissance the court of the Este came into full flower. In keeping with their time, the dukes could be politically ruthless—brother killed brother, son fought father—but they were also avid scholars and enthusiastic patrons of the arts. The cultivated Duke Nicolò III (1384–1441) murdered his wife and her lover. The greatest of all the dukes, Ercole I (1433–1505), attempted to poison a nephew who challenged his power, and when that didn't work he beheaded him. Yet it is to this pitiless man that Ferrara owes its great beauty.

One of the true jewels of Emilia-Romagna, and a UNESCO world heritage site, Ferrara draws amazingly few visitors. The city's perfectly preserved medieval and Renaissance showpieces, its cobblestone old town, excellent food, and youthful atmosphere (not to mention Europe's oldest wine bar) make the city one of Emilia-Romagna's most rewarding places to visit.

★ Naturally enough, the building that was the seat of Este power dominates the town: it is the massive **Castello Estense,** perfectly preserved and placed square in the center of the city in Piazza Castello. It is a suitable symbol for the ruling family: cold and menacing on the outside, lavishly decorated within. The public rooms are grand, but deep in the bowels of the fortress are chilling dungeons where enemies of the state were held in wretched conditions—a function these quarters served as recently as 1943, when antifascist prisoners were detained there. In particular, the **Prisons of Don Giulio, Ugo, and Parisina** have some fascinating features, like 15th-century smoke graffiti protesting the imprisonment of the young lovers Ugo and Parisina, who were beheaded in 1425.

The castle was established as a fortress in 1385, but work on its luxurious ducal quarters continued into the 16th century. Representative of Este grandeur are the **Sala dei Giochi** (Game Room), extravagantly painted with pagan athletic scenes, and the **Sala dell'Aurora,** decorated to show the times of the day. From the terraces of the castle and from the hanging garden, reserved for the private use of the duchesses, are fine views of the town and the surrounding countryside. You can cross the castle's moat, traverse its drawbridge, and wander through much of its arched interior at any time, and in the still of a misty night, the experience is haunting. ⊠ *Piazza Castello,* ☎ *0532/299233.* ☞ *8,000 lire/€4.15.* ☺ *Tues.–Sun. 9:30–5, tower visits Tues.–Sun. 10–4:30.*

The magnificent Gothic **Duomo,** a few steps away from the Castello Estense, has a three-tiered facade of bony arches and beautiful carvings over the central door. It was begun in 1135 and took more than a hundred years to complete. The interior was completely remodeled in the 17th century, and very little of the original decoration remains in place, much of it residing instead in the **cathedral museum** above the church (entrance inside the church). Displayed here are some of the lifelike carvings taken from the cathedral doors, dating from the 13th century and showing the months of the year. Also in the museum are a statue of the Madonna by the Sienese master Jacopo della Quercia (1374–1438) and two masterpieces by the Ferrarese painter Cosimo Tura, an *Annunciation* and *St. George Slaying the Dragon.* ⊠ *Piazza Cattedrale,* ☎ *0532/207449.* ☞ *Free.* ☺ *Duomo Mon.–Sat. 7:30–noon and 3–6:30, Sun. 7:30–12:30 and 3:30–7:30. Museum Mon.–Sat. 10–noon and 3–5, Sun. 10–noon and 4–6.*

The oldest and most characteristic area of Ferrara is to the south of the Duomo, stretching between the Corso Giovecca and the ramparts of the city above the river. Here various members of the Este family built pleasure palaces, the most famous of which is the **Palazzo Schifanoia** (*schifanoia* means "carefree" or, literally, "fleeing boredom"). Begun in the 14th century, the palace was remodeled in 1466 and was the city's first Renaissance palazzo. The interior is lavishly decorated, particularly the **Salone dei Mesi,** with an extravagant series of frescoes showing the months of the year and their mythological attributes. The adjacent **Museo Civico Lapidario** has a collection of coins, statuary, and paintings. ✉ *Via Scandiana 23,* ☎ *0532/64178.* 💳 *8,000 lire/€4.15 for both, free 1st Mon. of month, 10,000 lire/€5.15 combined ticket with Palazzina Marfisa d'Este.* ⊙ *Daily 9–7.*

The grand but unfinished courtyard is the most interesting part of the luxurious **Palazzo di Ludovico il Moro,** a magnificent 15th-century palace built for Ludovico Sforza, husband of Beatrice d'Este. The palazzo also houses the region's **Museo Archeologico,** a repository of relics of early man, Etruscans, and Romans found in the country surrounding the city. ✉ *Via XX Settembre 124, near the Palazzo Schifanoia,* ☎ *0532/66299.* 💳 *8,000 lire/€4.15.* ⊙ *Tues.–Sun. 9–7:30.*

The courtyard of the peaceful **Palazzo del Paradiso** contains the tomb of the great writer Ariosto (1474–1533), author of the most popular work of literature of the Renaissance, the poem *Orlando Furioso.* The building now houses the city library, called the **Biblioteca Ariostea.** ✉ *Via delle Scienze 17,* ☎ *0532/206977.* 💳 *Free.* ⊙ *Weekdays 9–7, Sat. 9–1:30.*

The writer Ariosto spent much of his life in Ferrara under the patronage of the Este. **Casa di Ludovico Ariosto,** one of his homes, has been converted into an office building but is open to the public for free tours. ✉ *Via Ariosto 67,* ☎ *0532/208564.* ⊙ *Tues., Thurs.–Fri., and Sun. 9–2; Wed. and Sat. 3–6.*

One of the best-preserved of the Renaissance palaces scattered along Ferrara's old streets is the charming **Casa Romei.** Downstairs are rooms with 15th-century frescoes and several sculptures collected from destroyed churches. The house lies not far from the Palazzo del Paradiso, in the area behind Ferrara's castle. ✉ *Via Savonarola 30,* ☎ *0532/240341.* 💳 *4,000 lire/€2.05.* ⊙ *Tues.–Sun. 8:30–7:30 (schedule varies with exhibits).*

On the busy Corso Giovecca is the **Palazzina di Marfisa d'Este,** a grandiose 16th-century home that belonged to a great patron of the arts. The house has painted ceilings, fine 16th-century furniture, and a garden containing a grotto and an outdoor theater. ✉ *Corso Giovecca 170,* ☎ *0532/207450.* 💳 *4,000 lire/€2.05, free 1st Mon. of month, 10,000/€5.15 lire combined ticket with Palazzo Schifanoia and Museo Civico.* ⊙ *Daily 9:30–1 and 3–6.*

The collection of ornate religious objects in the **Museo Ebraico** (Jewish Museum) bears witness to the long history of the city's Jewish community. This history had its high points—1492, for example, when Ercole I invited Sephardic Jews exiled from Spain to come settle here—and its lows, notably 1624, when the papal government closed the **ghetto,** which was reopened only with the advent of a united Italy in 1859. The triangular warren of narrow, cobbled streets that made up the ghetto originally extended as far as Corso Giovecca (originally Corso Giudecca, or Ghetto Street); when it was enclosed, the neighborhood was restricted to the area between Via Scienze, Via Contrari, and Via di San Romano. The museum, in the center of the ghetto, is also home to Ferrara's **synagogue.** ✉ *Via Mazzini 95,* ☎ *0532/210228.* 💳 *7,000 lire/€3.60.* ⊙ *Hour-long guided tours only, Sun.–Thurs. at 10, 11, and noon.*

The **Palazzo dei Diamanti** (Palace of Diamonds) is so called for the 12,600 faceted stone blocks that famously stud the facade. The palace was built in the 15th and 16th centuries and today contains the **Pinacoteca Nazionale,** an extensive art gallery devoted primarily to the painters of Ferrara. ⊠ *Corso Ercole I d'Este 21,* ☎ *0532/205844.* ☞ *8,000 lire/€4.15.* ☉ *Tues.–Wed. and Sat. 9–2, Thurs.–Fri. 9–7, Sun. 9–1.*

Dining and Lodging

The **Prenotel** hotel reservation hot line (☎ 0532/462046), run by the city, allows you to make reservations at any of the accommodations listed below, among many others.

$$$ ✗ **La Provvidenza.** One of the best-known restaurants in Ferrara, Provvidenza is a pleasant country-style inn with a lovely garden for summertime alfresco dining. The local specialties—fish grilled over charcoal (Thursday and Friday) and bollito misto (weekends in winter)— are the best. *Salama da sugo,* Ferrara's specialty, is a salty and oily boiled sausage served over mashed potatoes. The taste is not for everyone, but La Provvidenza executes it well. ⊠ *Corso Ercole I d'Este 92,* ☎ *0532/205187. Reservations essential. AE, DC, MC, V. Closed Mon. and 10 days in mid-Aug.*

$$$ ✗ **Trattoria La Romantica.** The former stables of a 17th-century merchant's house have been transformed into this casually elegant, wel-
★ coming restaurant, which is a great favorite among well-fed locals. While the decor (warm light and wood-beam ceilings, marred by incongruous prints and a piano) seems to be in perpetual transition, the haute-rustic food is fully realized: Ferrarese specialties like *cappellacci di zucca* (squash dumplings) in a cream-tomato-walnut-Parmesan sauce are served side by side with Texan beef and French oysters. Reservations are recommended. ⊠ *Via Ripagrande 36,* ☎ *0532/765975. AE, DC, MC, V. Closed Wed., Jan. 7–17, and July 1–17.*

$$ ✗ **Grotta Azzura.** The tender bollito misto at this elegant but reasonably priced restaurant is served with an excellent array of sauces. It's a good place to try the traditional local specialties. Although a pink-themed, chandelier-and-doily interior evokes images of wedding chapels in the Great Smoky mountains, the food here is anything but honky-tonk. ⊠ *Via Vignatagliata 61,* ☎ *0532/761052. AE, MC, V. Closed Wed. and July. No dinner Sun.*

$–$$ ✗ **Guido Ristorante.** Down a cobbled street in an atmospheric part of the old Jewish ghetto, this restaurant is a leading choice among locals. The menu is made up of Ferrarese specialties, plus some inventive dishes you won't find anywhere else. To wit: gnocchi with black olives and zucchini in curry sauce. ⊠ *Via Vignatagliata 61,* ☎ *0532/761052. Reservations essential. AE, DC, MC, V. Closed Thurs. and July.*

$$$–$$$$ ☷ **Duchessa Isabella.** Live out your Marie-Antoinette fantasies, such as they are, at this converted 16th-century mansion near Piazza Ariostea. The splendid dining rooms and entryway are sumptuously decorated in authentic style; the lacy, satiny rooms, however, teeter between royal and ridiculous. Some may find the formality wearying and the tone somewhat bogus; others will find a stay here marvelous. A horse and carriage are available. ⊠ *Via Palestro 70, 44100,* ☎ *0532/202121,* ℻ *0532/202638. 22 rooms, 5 suites. Restaurant, bar, in-room safes, minibars, meeting room. AE, MC, V.*

$$$–$$$$ ☷ **Hotel Ripagrande.** The courtyards, vaulted brick lobby, and break-
★ fast room of this 15th-century noble's palazzo retain much of their lordly pre-Renaissance flavor, but rooms are decidedly more down-to-earth. Standard doubles and many enormous bi- and tri-level suites have faux-Persian rugs, tapestries, and cozy antique furniture; top-floor rooms and suites with terraces are like a Colorado ski lodge. Unlike those of many hotels, the Ripagrande's suites are a good deal. ⊠ *Via Ripagrande 21, 44100,* ☎ *0532/765250,* ℻ *0532/764377,* 🕸 *www.4net.com/business/ripa. 20 rooms, 20 suites. Restaurant, bar, breakfast room, in-room safes, minibars, meeting room. AE, DC, MC, V.*

$$ 🖭 **Locanda Borgonuovo.** This lovely B&B is set in a 17th-century monastery on a quiet but central pedestrians-only street. It books up months in advance, partly because musicians and actors from the local theater make this their home away from home. Rooms are furnished with antiques, and one has its own kitchen for longer stays. Summer breakfasts are served in the leafy courtyard. ✉ *Via Cairoli 29, 44100,* 🕾 *0532/211100,* FAX *0532/248000. 4 rooms. Breakfast room, in-room safes, minibars, library. AE, MC, V.*

$–$$ 🖭 **Hotel San Paolo.** On the edge of the Old City, San Paolo is the best inexpensive choice in town. The 10-minute walk from the heart of Ferrara's medieval quarter is pleasant in a town so amenable to strolling, and there are good restaurants in the vicinity. ✉ *Via Baluardi 9, 44100,* 🕾 *0532/762040,* FAX *0532/762040. 47 rooms. AE, DC, MC, V.*

Nightlife

BARS

★ Europe's oldest wine bar, **Osteria Al Brindisi** (✉ Via degli Adelardi 11, 🕾 0532/209142), open Tuesday–Sunday 9 AM–1 AM, first began pouring in 1435. But this place is more than just a *Guinness Book of Records* listing. It has historic wine bottles from all over the world and early 20th-century ports lining its ancient walls, romantic ambient lighting, and a memorable spread of *salumi* and local cheeses. Al Brindisi might just be the most perfect place to drink wine in Italy—Copernicus, who once lived upstairs, seemed to think so—and perhaps the most finely realized wine bar anywhere. Even the prices (starting at 5,000 lire/€2.60 for a glass of red) and music (Otis Redding and the like) are just right. **Enoteca Due Gobbi** (✉ Via degli Adelardi 7), next door to Osteria Al Brindisi, draws a big crowd of twentysomethings after hours.

Outdoor Activities and Sports

BICYCLES

If you want to get around Ferrara the way the locals do, rent a bike at **Pirana e Bagni** (✉ Piazzale Stazione 2, 🕾 0532/772190), open weekdays 5 AM–8 PM, Saturday 6 AM–6:30 PM.

EMILIA-ROMAGNA A TO Z

To research prices, get advice from other travelers, and book travel arrangements, visit www.fodors.com.

AIR TRAVEL

Bologna is an important business and convention center and is therefore well served by European airlines linking it with other Italian cities and European capitals. There are no direct flights to the United States, however.

➤ AIRLINES AND CONTACTS: **Air France** (🕾 848/884466). **Alitalia** (🕾 848/865641). **British Airways** (🕾 848/81266). **Iberia** (🕾 848/870000). **KLM** (🕾 02/218981). **Luftansa** (🕾 0516477730).

AIRPORTS

The main airport of the region, Guglielmo Marconi, is 10 km (6 mi) northwest of Bologna. Aerobus service (Bus 54, 8,000 lire/€4.15) connects Guglielmo Marconi with Bologna's central train station as well as a downtown stop. It runs every half hour from 6 AM to 11:30 PM. Parma's small airport, Aeroporto G. Verdi, has daily flights to Milan (for Alitalia connections), Rome, Bergamo, and Bucharest. Aeradria Rimini Airport, on the Adriatic edge of the region, offers one daily London–Rimini route.

➤ AIRPORT INFORMATION: **Aeradria Rimini Airport** (🕾 0541/715711). **Aeroporto G. Verdi** (🕾 0521/982626, WEB www.aeroportoparma.it).

Guglielmo Marconi (⊠ Viale dell'Aeroporto, Bologna, ☎ 051/6479615, WEB www.bologna-airport.it).

BUS TRAVEL

Thanks to the autostrada bisecting the region and Emilia-Romagnan efficiency, bus travel in the region is easy—although the train is still easier. Private bus service links all the cities of Emilia-Romagna, with Bologna being the central hub. In Bologna, ATC buses leave from the terminal in Piazza XX Settembre, to the left upon exiting the train station. In Modena, contact ATCM; in Ferrara, ACFT, near the train station; and in Rimini, TRAM, on Via Roma.

For inner-city travel in Bologna, the *autostazione* (bus terminal) is at the top of Via dell'Indipendenza. City-run bus routes connect major towns with smaller villages and hamlets in the district, but routes are roundabout, and schedules vary from place to place.

➤ BUS INFORMATION: **ACFT** (☎ 0532/599492). **ATC** (☎ 051/290290, WEB www.atc.bo.it). **ATCM** (⊠ Via Fabriani, ☎ 059/218226). **Autostazione** (⊠ in Piazza XX Settembre, ☎ 051/290290 information, WEB www.autostazione.bo.it). **TRAM** (☎ 0541/390444).

CAR RENTAL

➤ LOCAL AGENCIES: **Avis** (⊠ Via Triumvirato 84, at the airport, Bologna ☎ 051/6472032; ⊠ Via Pietrammellara 37, Bologna, ☎ 051/255024; ⊠ Via Marco Polo 91, Bologna, ☎ 051/6341632; ⊠ Via Fratti 24, Parma; ⊠ at the airport, ☎ 0521/772418; ⊠ Viale Trieste 16D, Rimini, ☎ 0541/51256). **Europcar** (⊠ Via Amendola 12/f, Bologna, ☎ 051/247101; ⊠ Hotel Baglioni, Viale Piacenza 51/c, Parma, ☎ 0521/293035; ⊠ at the airport, ☎ 0521/293035; ⊠ Via Giovanni XXIII 126, Rimini, ☎ 0541/54746; ⊠ at the airport, ☎ 051/374606). **SIXT Autonoleggio** (⊠ Viale Mazzini 4/3, Bologna, ☎ 051/255546).

CAR TRAVEL

Bologna is on the autostrada network, so driving between cities is a breeze. The Via Emilia (SS9), one of the oldest roads in the world, runs through the heart of the region. It is a straight, low-lying modern road, the length of which can be traveled in a few hours. Ferrara and Ravenna are joined to it by good modern highways. Although less scenic, the A1 ("Autostrada del Sole") and A14 highways, which run parallel to the SS9, will get you where you're going about twice as fast. Note that much of the historic center of Bologna is closed off to cars daily 7 AM–8 PM.

ROAD CONDITIONS
Beware of low-lying fog in fall and winter, especially in Romagna nearer to the Adriatic coast. On some nights the fog can render driving an impossibility.
➤ CONTACTS: **Ambulance** (☎ 113). **Police** (☎ 112).

EMERGENCIES

For first aid, ask for "Pronto Soccorso," and be prepared to give your address. Pharmacies take turns staying open late and on Sunday; for the latest information, consult the current list posted on the front door of each pharmacy or ask at the local tourist office.
➤ CONTACTS: **Carabinieri** (☎ 112). **Police, Ambulance** (☎ 113). **Doctors and dentists** (☎ 113).

MAIL AND SHIPPING

➤ POST OFFICES: **Bologna** (⊠ Piazza Minghetti 1, 40124). **Ferrara** (⊠ Viale Cavour 27, 44100). **Modena** (⊠ Via Emilia 86, 41100). **Parma** (⊠ Via Pisacane 1, 43100). **Ravenna** (⊠ Piazza Garibaldi 1, 48100). **Rimini** (⊠ Largo G. Cesare 1, 47900).

TRAIN TRAVEL

Bologna is an important rail hub for the entire northern part of Italy and has frequent, fast train service to Rome, Milan, Florence, and Venice. The railway follows the Via Emilia (SS9), and all the cities covered can be easily reached by train. Contact Ferrovie dello Stato, the national train operator, for more information.

➤ TRAIN INFORMATION: **Ferrovie dello Stato (FS)** (☎ 848/888088, WEB www.fs-on-line.com).

TRAVEL AGENCIES

➤ LOCAL AGENT REFERRALS: **Marconi Tours** (✉ Via Marconi 47, Bologna, ☎ 051/235783). **Viaggi Urbinati** (✉ Viale Vespucci 127, Rimini, ☎ 0541/391660).

VISITOR INFORMATION

➤ TOURIST INFORMATION: **Bologna** (✉ Aeroporto Guglielmo Marconi, ☎ 051/6472036; ✉ Stazione Centrale, 40121, ☎ 051/246541; ✉ Piazza Maggiore, 40124, ☎ 051/239660; WEB www.comune.bologna.it/bolognaturismo). **Busseto** (✉ Comune, Piazza Giuseppe Verdi 10, 43011, ☎ 0524/931732). **Dozza** (✉ Via XX Settembre, 40050, ☎ 0542/678052). **Faenza** (✉ Piazza del Popolo 1, 48018, ☎ 0546/691602). **Ferrara** (✉ Castello Estense, 44022, ☎ 0532/209370, WEB www.comune.fe.it/turismo). **Modena** (✉ Piazza Grande 17, 41100, ☎ 059/206660). **Parma** (✉ Via Melloni 1/b, 43100, ☎ 0521/218889, WEB turismo.comune.parma.it/turismo). **Piacenza** (✉ Palazzo Farnese, Piazza Citadella, 29100, ☎ 0523/329324). **Ravenna** (✉ Via Salara 8, 48100, ☎ 0544/35404, WEB www.ravennaservice.net). **Rimini** (✉ Via Dante 86, 47037, ☎ 0541/51331; ✉ Piazzale Fellini 3, 47037, ☎ 0541/56902). **San Marino** (✉ Contra Omagnano 20, ☎ 0549/882400).

10 UMBRIA, THE MARCHES, AND ABRUZZO

PERUGIA, ASSISI, SPOLETO, PARCO NAZIONALE D'ABRUZZO

Central Italy's quiet valleys belie the treasures hidden in its hilltop towns. Orvieto's glittering cathedral and Assisi's miraculously restored frescoes vie for top honors with Spoleto's arts festivals and intellectual Urbino's Renaissance tradition, but every corner of the region has its delights. The riches here range from the artistic and the cultural to the culinary, in this, the home of truffles, sausage, and rich, green olive oil. Nature has its place too, in the Valnerina's lakes and the wild mountaintops and towering pines of unspoiled Abruzzo.

Updated by
Valerie
Hamilton

BIRTHPLACE OF SAINTS and home to some of the country's greatest artistic treasures, the heart of Italy is waiting to be discovered. Picture-perfect hill towns, their edges laced with terraced vineyards, whisper centuries of history; the misty green valleys below echo with the footsteps of painters, pilgrims, and saints. Umbria, the Marches, and Abruzzo are the Italian countryside as you've imagined it: verdant farmland, steep hillsides topped with fairy-tale fortresses, winding country roads traveled by horses and Fiat 500s carrying crates of fresh olives. No single town here has the extravagant wealth of art and architecture of Florence, Rome, or Venice, but this works in your favor: small jewels of towns feel manageable, knowable, not overwhelming. This is not to suggest that the cultural cupboard is bare—far from it. Orvieto's cathedral and Assisi's basilica are two of the most important sights in Italy, and Perugia, Todi, Spoleto, and Urbino are rich in art and architecture. Virtually every small town in the region has a castle, church, or museum worth a visit—but without them you'd still be compelled to stop for the picturesque streets, panoramic views, and natural beauty.

The earliest inhabitants of Umbria, the Umbri, were thought by the Romans to be the most ancient inhabitants of Italy. Little is known about them, since with the coming of Etruscan culture the tribe fled into the mountains in the eastern portion of the region. The Etruscans, who founded some of the great cities of Umbria, were in turn supplanted by the Romans. Unlike Tuscany and other regions of central Italy, Umbria had few powerful medieval families to exert control over the cities in the Middle Ages—its proximity to Rome ensured that it would always be more or less under papal domination.

Located in the center of the country, Umbria has for much of its history been a battlefield where armies from north and south clashed. Hannibal destroyed a Roman army on the shores of Lake Trasimeno, and the full and bloody course of the interminable Guelph-Ghibelline conflict of the Middle Ages was played out here. Dante considered Umbria the most violent place in Italy. Trophies of war still decorate the facade of the Palazzo dei Priori in Perugia, and the little town of Gubbio continues a warlike rivalry begun in the Middle Ages—every year it challenges the Tuscan town of Sansepolcro to a crossbow tournament. Today, of course, the bowmen shoot at targets, but neither side has forgotten that 500 years ago its ancestors shot at each other. In spite of—or perhaps because of—this bloodshed, Umbria has produced more than its share of Christian saints. The most famous is St. Francis, the decidedly pacifist saint whose life shaped the Church and the history of his time. His great shrine at Assisi is visited by hundreds of thousands of pilgrims each year. St. Clare, his devoted follower, was Umbria-born, as were St. Benedict, St. Rita of Cascia, and the patron saint of lovers, St. Valentine.

East of Umbria, the Marches (Le Marche to Italians) stretch between the hills of the southern Apennines down to the Adriatic sea. It is a scenic region of mountains and valleys, with great turreted castles standing on high peaks defending passes and roads—silent testament to the region's bellicose past. The Marches have passed through numerous hands. First the Romans supplanted the native civilizations; then Charlemagne supplanted the Romans (and gave the region its name—it was divided into "marks," or provinces, under the rule of the Holy Roman Emperor); then began the seemingly never-ending struggle between popes and local lords. Despite all this martial tussling, it was in the lonely mountain town of Urbino that the Renaissance came to its fullest flower; that small town became a haven of culture and learning that rivaled the greater, richer, and more powerful city of Florence, and even Rome itself.

Still a land of shepherds and wolves, the mountainous center of Abruzzo preserves much of its local traditions and culture. Medieval L'Aquila is a pleasant, walkable town virtually undiscovered by tourists, a lovely day trip on its own—but it's only the beginning. Craggy peaks, ruined castles, and hill towns unchanged since the Middle Ages abound in Abruzzo, but the region's real treasure is its natural beauty, preserved pristinely in the Parco Nazionale d'Abruzzo. With its hiking trails and 440 square km (170 square mi) of protected woods and wildlife, it's a must-see for nature lovers. Skiing on nearby Gran Sasso makes this a four-seasons destination.

Pleasures and Pastimes

Dining

Central Italy is mountainous, and its food is hearty and straightforward, with a stick-to-the-ribs quality that sees hardworking farmers and artisans through a long day's work and helps them make the steep climb home at night. The region has made several important contributions to Italian cuisine. Particularly prized are winter's *tartufi neri* (black truffles) from the area around Spoleto and from the hills around the tiny town of Norcia. The local pasta specialty—thick, handmade *ciriole* (roughly shaped, fat spaghetti) or *stringozzi* (long, thin homemade pasta)—is even better prepared *al tartufo*, enriched with excellent local olive oil and truffles. Norcia's pork products—especially sausages, salami, and *arista* (roast loin perfumed with rosemary)—are so famous that pork butchers throughout Italy are called *norcini,* and pork butcher shops are called *norcinerie.*

The Marches' coastline yields some of Italy's best seafood, the base for many of the region's culinary specialties. One Anconan favorite is *brodetto,* a rich fish chowder made with as many as nine types of Adriatic fish. Ascoli Piceno, inland, is known for two dishes: *olive ascolane* (batter-fried olives stuffed with meat) and the rich *vincisgrassi* (lasagna slathered with sauce enriched with innards, sometimes flavored with black truffles). Ascoli Piceno is also the home of the licorice-flavored liqueur anisette.

For general information and price categories, *see* Dining *in* Smart Travel Tips A to Z.

Hiking

Magnificent scenery makes the heart of Italy excellent hiking and mountaineering country. In Umbria, the rocky area around Spoleto is particularly good, and the tourist office supplies itineraries of walks and climbs to suit all ages and levels of ability. Abruzzo is Central Italy's wilderness region, and with a bit of luck and an early start you might cross paths with the brown bear or shy chamois of the Parco Nazionale d'Abruzzo. Find out their favorite routes on the maps sold at any of the information points inside the park, or join a guided tour to try to spot the wildlife in this beautiful protected area.

Lodging

Virtually every historic town in Umbria, the Marches, and Abruzzo has some kind of hotel, no matter how small the place may be. A popular trend in Umbria, particularly around Gubbio, Orvieto, and Todi, is the conversion of old villas, farms, and monasteries into first-class hotels. These tend to be out in the countryside, but the splendor of the settings often outweighs the problem of getting into town—although you'll

TRUFFLE TROUBLE

UMBRIA IS RICH WITH TRUFFLES—more are found here than anywhere else in Italy—and those not consumed fresh are processed into pastes or flavored oils. The primary truffle areas are around the tiny town of Norcia, which holds a truffle festival every February, and near Spoleto, where you'll see signs warning against unlicensed truffle hunting posted at the base of the Ponte delle Torri. Although grown locally, the rare delicacy can cost a small fortune, up to $200 for a quarter pound—fortunately, a little goes a long way. At such a price, there is great competition among the nearly 10,000 registered truffle hunters in the province, who use specially trained dogs to sniff them out among the roots of several trees, including oak and ilex. Despite recent incidences of poisoning truffle-hunting dogs and importing inferior tubers from China, you can be reasonably assured that the truffle shaved onto your pasta has been unearthed locally. The kind of truffle you taste will depend on the season: in summer, there's the *scorzone* (rough-skinned, dark gray–brown tuber); the fall rains bring out the *bianchetto* (small-size, smoother, and dirty-white truffle variety); and the prized *tartufo nero* (black truffle) appears from December through March. Out of season, restaurants rely on truffles preserved in olive oil, vacuum-sealed, frozen, or ground into a paste.

definitely need a car. Interestingly, hotels in town tend to be simpler than their country cousins, with notable exceptions in Spoleto, Gubbio, and Perugia. Chain are few, and most hotels are small, so it's always worth your while to call ahead and absolutely necessary when traveling in high season to Assisi, Spoleto, Orvieto, or Urbino.

For general information and price categories, *see* Lodging *in* Smart Travel Tips A to Z.

Shopping
Pottery and wine are the two most celebrated Umbrian exports, and examples of both commodities are excellent and unique to the region. Torgiano, south of Perugia, is one of the best-known centers of wine making, where you can watch the process and buy the product; you can find some of the best ceramics at Gubbio, Perugia, and Orvieto, a wine-making center in its own right. Ceramics with the most flair are found in Deruta, south of Torgiano on S3bis (in this case, "bis" means alternate highway). The red glazes of Gubbio pottery have been renowned since medieval times. The secret of the original glaze died with its inventor some 500 years ago, but some contemporary potters produce a fair facsimile.

Skiing
The same rugged mountains that make for great summer hiking make for good winter skiing, and although you won't mistake Abruzzo for Chamonix, there are plenty of opportunities for a day of snowy fun.

Exploring Umbria, the Marches, and Abruzzo
The steep hills and deep valleys that make Umbria and the Marches so picturesque also make them difficult to explore. Choose driving routes

carefully to avoid tortuous mountain roads; major towns are not necessarily linked to each other by train, bus, or highway. A detailed local road map is always helpful. If you have a car, Perugia makes a convenient base for exploring the region; without a car, plan overnights in towns farther afield.

Numbers in the text correspond to numbers in the margin and on the Umbria and the Marches, Perugia, Spoleto, and Assisi maps.

Great Itineraries

The region of Umbria is particularly suited to touring in a limited time. Basing yourself in Perugia, you can see all the major sights in the regional capital in one day, then make easy excursions to the hill towns on your other days without feeling overwhelmed by constant travel. East of Perugia, the Marches invite leisurely exploring, but expect some lengthy rides in between the main points of interest. L'Aquila is easily reachable from Rome and southern Umbria and is only a couple of hours away from the wilderness of Abruzzo's national park.

IF YOU HAVE 3 DAYS

In ⊞ **Perugia** ①–④, your main stops should be the refurbished Galleria Nazionale dell'Umbria and the Collegio del Cambio, both housed in the atmospheric **Palazzo dei Priori** ②; much of the rest of your day can be spent ambling along Corso Vannucci and toiling up and down the steep lanes on either side. Devote your second day to the medieval hill town of ⊞ **Assisi** ⑤–⑧ and its magnificently restored basilica, taking time for a stroll up through the main piazza. On your third day, get an early start and head south to **Spoleto** ⑫–⑱, where narrow streets abound with evocative views and delightful surprises.

IF YOU HAVE 5 DAYS

Given five days, you will be able to spend a couple of them exploring the unspoiled neighboring region of the Marches. The area is somewhat remote, and your means of transportation will dictate what you can see. In any case, start your tour in ⊞ **Perugia** ①–④, and follow the itinerary above for your first two days. If you are traveling by public transportation, spend your third night in ⊞ **Spoleto** ⑫–⑱, where you can jump on a train bound for **Ancona** ㉓; from here you can board a bus or a train for Pésaro and ⊞ **Urbino** ㉒. This hilltop gem retains its proud, self-contained character, almost untouched by 20th-century construction. Plan for at least half a day for reaching Urbino from Spoleto, and it's not much shorter by car, crossing the Marches border from ⊞ **Gubbio** ⑪, where you might spend your last day appreciating the views, shops, and choice hotels and restaurants.

IF YOU HAVE 7 DAYS

Reserve four days for Umbria and three for the Marches or Abruzzo. With greater flexibility you can choose how many nights you want to spend in Umbria's capital, ⊞ **Perugia** ①–④, and how many in the region's smaller centers. More time in Perugia will allow you to explore the city thoroughly, including the archaeological museum, and you might take in the easy excursion to the wine village of **Torgiano** ⑩ or the ceramics town of **Deruta** ⑪. ⊞ **Spoleto** ⑫–⑱ and ⊞ **Assisi** ⑤–⑧ are essential stops farther afield; you might stay for a night in each. ⊞ **Gubbio** ⑨ is also worth an overnight. From Spoleto, you can explore the classic hill town of **Todi** ⑳, unspoiled **Narni** ㉑, and the wine mecca **Orvieto** ⑲; they can also be seen on your way to or from Rome, only about 90 minutes away. From Spoleto, drive north to the Marches region, or south to the rugged Abruzzo for your last three days. ⊞ **Urbino** ㉒ is a must-see in the Marches. Head south for the inland town of ⊞ **Ascoli Piceno** ㉕—there is little in the way of hotels, galleries, or sophisticated shops here, but it's marvelously quaint. On the way—or on the way back—drop in at the sanctuary of **Loreto** ㉔, nestled in the mountains 24 km (15 mi) south of Ancona. If you are venturing to Abruzzo instead, 🔟 **L'Aquila** ㉖ is a pleasant base for visiting the central part of the region, including the woods of the national park.

When to Tour Umbria, the Marches, and Abruzzo

The forested hills of Umbria and the Marches ensure beguiling colors in the fall and an explosion of greenery in spring. Bear in mind that winter is longer and colder here than in nearby Rome, so bring warm clothes to enjoy the outdoors from October to April. The consolation is that winter is the high season for the region's cuisine: January to April is truffle time in Norcia and Spoleto, and October to December brings a bounty of fresh local mushrooms. Book accommodations well in advance if you are planning to visit in June and July, when the Spoleto Festival dei Due Mondi and the Jazz Festival of Perugia take place. Sightseers and pilgrims throng the streets of Assisi year-round, but the religious festivals of Christmas, Easter, the feast of St. Francis (October 4), and the Calendimaggio Festival (May 1) draw even bigger crowds.

PERUGIA

Perugino (the Perugian) filled his paintings with images of his home: soft hills with a few sparse trees, wide plains dotted with lakes. Despite the development of rather undistinguished modern suburbs, this peaceful landscape still exists, and venerable Perugia's medieval hilltop city remains almost completely intact. Perugia is the best-preserved hill town of its size, and few other places in Italy better illustrate the model of the self-contained city-state that so shaped the course of Italian history.

Exploring Perugia

The best approach to the city is by train—the station is in the unlovely suburbs, but there are frequent buses running directly to Piazza d'Italia, the heart of the Old Town. If you are driving, leave your car in one of the parking lots near the station and then take the bus or the escalator, which passes through subterranean excavations of the Roman foundations of the city, from Piazza Partigiani to the Rocca Paolina.

A Good Walk

Starting in Piazza Italia, stroll down Corso Vannucci and head to the **Duomo** ① in Piazza IV Novembre. Visit the **Palazzo dei Priori** ②, being sure to explore the Galleria Nazionale dell'Umbria and the **Collegio del Cambio** ③, with its fine Perugino frescoes. A 10-minute walk south of the center along Corso Cavour leads to the **Museo Archeologico Nazionale** ④. After perusing the Etruscan relics in the museum, return to Piazza IV Novembre, breaking for lunch or an espresso at a café.

TIMING

A thorough walk through Perugia takes about an hour, and if stopping at all sights along this itinerary, you should plan on at least a half day, plus a stop for lunch.

Sights to See

★ ❸ **Collegio del Cambio** (Bankers' Guild Hall). The series of elaborate rooms housed the meeting hall and chapel of the guild of bankers and money changers. The walls were frescoed from 1496 to 1500 by the most important Perugian painter of the Renaissance, Pietro Vannucci, better known as Perugino (circa 1450–1523). The iconography prevalent in the works includes common religious themes, like the Nativity and the

410

Umbria, the Marches, and Abruzzo

Adriatic Sea

ITALY

Numana

Ancona **23**

Loreto **24**

Recanati

Macerata

Potenza

Senigallia

Marotta

Jesi

Misa

S76

THE MARCHES

Fano

Pesaro

A14

S424

Cesano

Metauro

E78

S3

Fossombrone

Pergola

Fabriano

S76

S16

S423

San Marino

Urbino **22**

S72

E78/S73bis

S3

S258

S73

UMBRIA

Gubbio **9**

S298

Città di Castello

S3bis

Umbertide

S71

Tevere

Sansepolcro

S73

S75

411

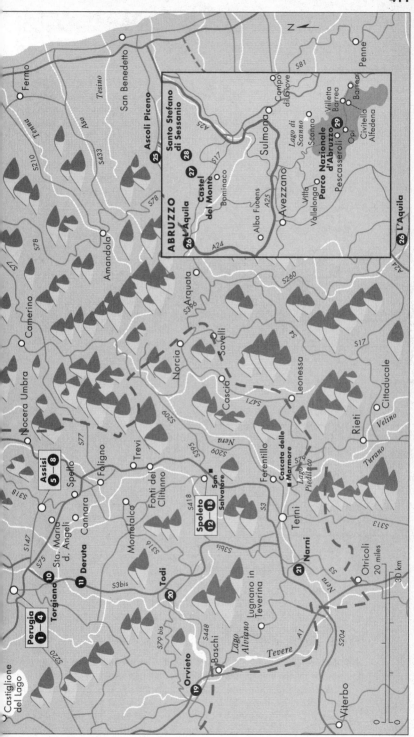

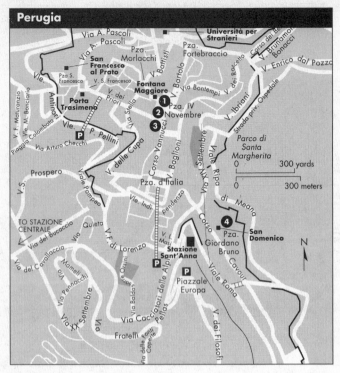

Transfiguration (on the end walls), but also figures intended to inspire
the businessmen who congregated here. On the left wall are female figures representing the Virtues, beneath them the heroes and sages of antiquity. On the right wall are the prophets and sibyls. Perugino's most
famous pupil, Raffaello Sanzio, or Raphael (1483–1520), is said to have
painted here, his hand, experts say, most apparent in the figure of For-
titude. On one of the pilasters is a remarkably honest self-portrait of
Perugino, surmounted by a Latin inscription. The Collegio is attached
to Palazzo dei Priori, but the entrance is on Corso Vannucci. ⊠ *Corso
Vannucci 25* ☎ *075/5728599,* WEB *www.comune.perugia.it.* ⧉ *5,000
lire/€2.60.* ⊙ *Mar.–Oct., Mon.–Sat. 9–12:30 and 2:30–5:30, Sun. 9–
12:30; Nov.–Feb., Tues.–Sat. 8–2, Sun. 9–12:30 (Dec. 20–Jan. 6 museum follows summer schedule).*

Corso Vannucci. The heart of the city is the broad, stately pedestrian
street that runs from Piazza d'Italia to Piazza IV Novembre. As evening
falls, Corso Vannucci is filled with Perugians out for their evening *passeggiata,* a pleasant pre-dinner stroll that may include a pause for an *aperitivo* at one of the many cafés that line the street.

❶ **Duomo.** This church's prize relic is the Virgin Mary's wedding ring,
stolen by the Perugians in 1488 from the nearby town of Chiusi. The
ring, kept in a chapel on the left aisle, is the size of a large bangle and
is kept under lock—15 locks actually—and key year-round except
July 30 and the second-to-last Sunday in January. The first date commemorates the day the ring was brought to Perugia, the second Mary's
wedding anniversary. The cathedral itself is large and rather plain, dating from the Middle Ages but with many additions from the 15th and
16th centuries. There are some elaborately carved choir stalls, executed
by Giovanni Battista Bastone in 1520. An array of precious objects associated with the cathedral is on display at the **Museo Capitolare,** in-

cluding vestments, vessels, manuscripts, and gold work. An early masterpiece by Luca Signorelli (circa 1450–1523) is the altarpiece showing the Madonna with St. John the Baptist, St. Onophrio, and St. Lawrence (1484). ⊠ *Piazza IV Novembre,* ☎ *075/5723832,* WEB *www.comune.perugia.it.* ⊙ *Mon.–Sat. 7–noon and 4–5:30.*

❹ Museo Archeologico Nazionale. This museum next to the imposing church of San Domenico contains an excellent collection of Etruscan artifacts from throughout the region. Perugia was a flourishing Etruscan site long before it fell under Roman domination in 310 BC. Other than this collection, little remains of Perugia's earliest ancestors, although the **Arco di Augusto** (Arch of Augustus), in Piazza Fortebraccio, the northern entrance to the city, is of Etruscan origin. ⊠ *Piazza G. Bruno 10,* ☎ *075/5727141,* WEB *www.archeopg.arti.beniculturali.it.* ☎ *4,000 lire/€2.05.* ⊙ *Mon.–Sat. 8:30–7:30, Sun. 9–1.*

★ **❷ Palazzo dei Priori.** The imposing palace, begun in the 13th century, has an unusual staircase that fans out into Piazza IV Novembre. The facade is decorated with symbols of Perugia's pride and past power: the griffin is the city's symbol; the lion denotes Perugia's allegiance to the medieval Guelph (or papal) cause. Both figures support the heavy chains of the gates of Siena, which fell to Perugian forces in 1358. The fourth floor of the Palazzo dei Priori contains the region's most comprehensive art gallery, the **Galleria Nazionale dell'Umbria.** Enhanced by skillfully lit displays and computers showing details of the works and background information on them, the collection includes work by native artists—most outstandingly Pinturicchio (1454–1513) and Perugino—and others of the Umbrian and Tuscan schools, including Gentile da Fabriano (1370–1427), Duccio (circa 1255–1318), Fra Angelico (1387–1455), Fiorenzo di Lorenzo (1445–1525), and Piero della Francesca (1420–92). The gallery also shows frescoes, sculptures, and some superb examples of crucifixes from the 13th and 14th centuries; other rooms are dedicated to Perugia itself, illustrating how the medieval city evolved. ⊠ *Corso Vannucci 19, Piazza IV Novembre.* ☎ *075/5741427,* WEB *www.comune.perugia.it.* ☎ *8,000 lire/€4.15.* ⊙ *Mon.–Sat. 9–7, Sun. 9–2; last admission ½ hr before closing. Closed 1st Mon. of each month.*

OFF THE
BEATEN PATH

LA CITTÀ DELLA DOMENICA – Umbria's only attraction aimed directly at the younger set is La Città della Domenica, a theme-park-style playground in the town of Montepulito, just west of Perugia on the secondary road that leads to Corciano. The 500 acres of parkland contain a variety of buildings based on familiar fairy-tale themes—Snow White's House, the Witches' Wood—as well as a reptile house, aquarium, medieval museum, exhibit of shells from all over the world, game rooms, and a choice of restaurants. ⊠ *Località Montepulito, 8 km (5 mi) west of Perugia,* ☎ *075/5054941.* ☎ *Apr.–Oct. (playground open) adults 17,000 lire/€8.80 (19,000 lire/€9.80 Sun. and holidays), children 4–10 15,000 lire/€7.75; Nov.–Mar. (playground closed) adults 6,000 lire/€3.10, children 4,000 lire/€2.05.* ⊙ *Apr.–mid-Sept., daily 10–7; mid-Sept.–Oct., weekends 10–7; Nov.–mid-Mar. (game rooms, aquarium, and reptile house only), Sat. 2–7, Sun. 10–7.*

Dining and Lodging

$$ ✗ La Rosetta. This restaurant, in the hotel of the same name, is a peaceful, elegant spot. In the winter you dine under medieval vaults; in summer, in the cool courtyard. The cuisine emphasizes regional specialties like mushrooms and truffles, simply prepared. ⊠ *Piazza Italia 19,* ☎ *075/5720841. Reservations essential. AE, DC, MC, V. Closed Mon.*

$$ ✕ **La Taverna.** Medieval steps lead to this rustic restaurant on two levels, where lots of wine bottles and artful clutter heighten the tavern atmosphere. The menu features regional specialties and better-known Italian dishes. Good choices include *chitarrini* (extra-thick spaghetti), with either *funghi* (mushrooms) or *tartufi* (truffles), and grilled meats. ⊠ *Via delle Streghe 8, next to the Teatro Pavone, off Corso Vannucci,* ☎ *075/5724128. Dinner reservations essential. AE, DC, MC, V. Closed Mon.*

$–$$ ✕ **Il Falchetto.** Here you'll find exceptional food at reasonable prices, making this Perugia's best restaurant bargain. Service is smart but relaxed in the two medieval dining rooms, with the kitchen and chef on view. The house specialty is *falchetti* (homemade gnocchi with spinach and ricotta cheese). ⊠ *Via Bartolo 20,* ☎ *075/5731775. AE, DC, MC, V. Closed Mon. and last 2 wks in Jan.*

$$$$ ▣ **Brufani Palace.** This 19th-century palazzo is an elegant lodging choice. The Brufani's public rooms and first-floor guest rooms have high ceilings and are done in the grand Belle Epoque style. Second-floor rooms are more modern, and many on both floors have a marvelous view of the Umbrian countryside or the city. ⊠ *Piazza Italia 12, 06121,* ☎ *075/5732541,* FAX *075/5720210,* WEB *www.sinahotels.com. 88 rooms. Restaurant, bar, meeting room. AE, DC, MC, V.*

$$$ ▣ **Locanda della Posta.** This luxuriously decorated small hotel in the
★ center of Perugia's historic district is a delight to behold, from its faux-marble moldings and paneled doors to the suede-upholstered elevator and fabric-covered walls. Architectural details are beautiful in the 18th-century palazzo, once Perugia's only hotel, and views of city rooftops from windows and balconies are soothing. Breakfast is included here. ⊠ *Corso Vannucci 97, 06121,* ☎ *075/5728925,* FAX *075/5732562,* WEB *www.italyhotel.com/perugia/locandadellaposta. 39 rooms, 1 suite. Breakfast room, lobby lounge. AE, DC, MC, V.*

$$ ▣ **Priori.** On an alley leading off the Corso Vannucci, this unpretentious but elegant hotel has spacious, cheerful rooms with modern furnishings. There is a partially shaded, panoramic terrace where breakfast is served in summer. If you're driving, note that for a small fee you can park in the Priori's garage. ⊠ *Via dei Priori, 06123,* ☎ *075/5723378,* FAX *075/5723213,* WEB *www.perugia.com/hotelpriori. 56 rooms, 5 suites. Bar, parking (fee). MC, V.*

$$ ▣ **Rosalba.** This is a bright and friendly choice on the fringes of Perugia's historic center. Basic rooms are scrupulously clean, and the ones at the back enjoy a view. Although somewhat out of the way, the hotel is only a matter of minutes from Corso Vannucci by virtue of the nearby escalator stop, saving a good deal of legwork. Rooms are at the low end of this price category. ⊠ *Via del Circo 7, 06121,* ☎ *075/5728285,* FAX *075/5720626. 11 rooms. Free parking. No credit cards.*

Nightlife and the Arts

The monthly *Viva Perugia* (sold at newsstands), with a section in English, is a good source of information about what's going on in town.

Music Festivals

Summer sees two international music festivals in Perugia. The **Umbria Jazz Festival** (☎ 075/5732432, FAX 075/572256, WEB www.umbria-jazz.com) is a world-famous concert series attracting jazz performers like Pat Metheny for 10 days in July. Call year-round for information about the festival or to buy tickets with a credit card as early as the end of April. The **Sagra Musicale Umbra** (☎ 075/5732800, WEB www.umbria.org/eng/eventi), which takes place over 10 days in September, celebrates traditional music of the region.

A lover of music should consider the lengthy trek to the **Festival Nazioni Musica da Camera** (Chamber Music Festival of Umbria), a two-week event held between August and September in the town of Città di Castello, about 80 km (50 mi) north of Perugia on the S3bis. For information year-round, contact the festival office (☎ 075/8521142, FAX 075/8552461).

Shopping

Chocolate
It's not hard to be tempted by Perugia's famous **Perugina chocolate,** although there's no immediate need to load yourself with presents to bring home, as the brand (a Nestlé company since the early 1990s) is easily found all over Italy. *Cioccolato al latte* (milk chocolate) and *fondente* (dark chocolate), set in tiny jewel-like boxes or in giant gift boxes the size of serving trays, are sold all over town. But the best-known chocolates made by Perugina are the round hazelnut-filled chocolate candies called Baci (literally "kisses"), which come wrapped in silver foil and, like fortune cookies, contain romantic sentiments or sayings in a variety of languages, English included. The third week in October is especially sweet, when Perugia hosts the **Eurochocolate Festival,** (WEB www.chocolate.perugia.it) and the streets are filled with stands, sculptures, and—best of all—tastings.

Shopping District
Perugia is a well-to-do town, and judging by the array of expensive shops on **Corso Vannucci,** the Perugians are not afraid to part with their lire. The main streets are lined with clothing shops selling the best-known Italian designers such as Gucci, Ferragamo, Armani, and Fendi.

ASSISI

The legacy of St. Francis, founder of the Franciscan monastic order, pervades the rosy hills of Assisi, 47 km (30 mi) north of Spoleto and 25 km (16 mi) east of Perugia. Each year, the city hosts several million pilgrims, but not even the massive flow of visitors to this town of only 3,000 residents can spoil the singular beauty of Italy's most significant religious center. The hill on which Assisi sits rises dramatically from the flat plain, and the town is dominated at the top of the mount by a medieval castle; on the lower slope of the hill is the massive Basilica di San Francesco, sitting majestically on graceful arched supports.

St. Francis was born here in 1181, the son of a well-to-do merchant. After a sinful youth, it's said, he gave up the pleasures of the flesh and adopted a life of austerity. His mystical approach to poverty, asceticism, and the beauty of man and nature struck a responsive chord in the medieval mind, and he quickly attracted a vast number of followers. Without actively seeking it (unlike many clerics of his day) he amassed great influence and political power, changing the history of the Catholic Church. He was the first saint to receive the stigmata (wounds in his hands, feet, and side corresponding to the torments of Christ on the cross). St. Francis was declared patron saint of Italy in 1939, and today the Franciscans make up the largest of the Catholic orders. And among the masses of clergy at Assisi you can identify the saint's followers by their simple, coarse brown habits girt with sashes of knotted rope.

A series of earthquakes in the fall of 1997 devastated Umbria and the Marches, rendering uninhabitable countless homes and causing the partial collapse of the ceiling of Assisi's Upper Basilica, frescoed with some of the great masterpieces of Giotto and Cimabue. It was feared that the frescoes, reduced to rubble, were beyond repair, but a massive ef-

fort by art restorers and volunteers is in the process of saving some of
them. Although the Upper Basilica has reopened, many of Assisi's medieval stone buildings are still propped up by wooden scaffolding; by
and large, however, the town has recovered.

Exploring Assisi

The train station is 4 km (2½ mi) from town, with bus service about
every half hour. The walled town is closed to outside traffic, so cars
must be left in the parking lots at Porta San Pietro, near Porta Nuova,
or beneath Piazza Matteotti. Frequent city minibuses run between the
parking lots and the center of town.

A Good Walk

Much of your visit to Assisi will likely be spent visiting churches and
walking through the quiet streets. At the top of your list should be the
Basilica di San Francesco ⑤, with its miraculously restored upstairs ceiling. Via San Francesco leads back to **Piazza del Comune** and its Pinacoteca, Museo Civico, and the **Tempio di Minerva** ⑥. From the piazza,
Via di San Rufino leads to **San Rufino** ⑦, Assisi's town cathedral. Double back to the piazza and take Corso Mazzini to **Santa Chiara** ⑧; then
continue through the Porta Nuova to the church of **San Damiano,** a
1-km (½-mi) walk a few minutes outside the walls. Also of interest outside the walls are the Eremo delle Carceri, east of the center along Via
Santuario delle Carceri, and the church of Santa Maria degli Angeli,
near the train station.

TIMING

Devote a half day or good part of the day for this walk. After seeing
the Basilica di San Francesco, you can stroll along the length of town,
stopping in at churches and shops.

Sights to See

★ ⑤ **Basilica di San Francesco.** The basilica is not one church but two, the
French Gothic upper part built on top of the Romanesque lower a scant
half-century after its completion. Work on this two-tiered monolith was
begun just a few years after the death of St. Francis. His coffin, unearthed from its secret hiding place after a 52-day search in 1818, is
on display in the crypt below the Lower Basilica. Both churches are
magnificently decorated artistic treasure houses, covered floor and
ceiling with some of Europe's finest frescoes: the Lower Basilica is dim
and full of candlelit shadows, while the Upper Basilica, restored and
reopened soon after the 1997 earthquakes, is bright and airy.

The first chapel to the left of the nave in the **Lower Basilica** was decorated by the Sienese master Simone Martini (1284–1344). Dating from
1322–26, the frescoes show the life of St. Martin—the sharing of his
cloak with the poor man, the saint's knighthood, and his death. There
is some dispute about the paintings in the third chapel on the right, which
depict the life of Mary Magdalen. Experts have argued for years as to
their authorship, with many attributing them to Giotto (1266–1337).
There is a similar dispute about the works above the high altar, depicting
the marriage of St. Francis to poverty, chastity, and obedience—some
say they are by Giotto; others claim them for an anonymous pupil. In
the right transept are frescoes by Cimabue (circa 1240–1302), including a Madonna and saints, one of them St. Francis himself. In the left
transept are some of the best-known works of the Sienese painter Pietro
Lorenzetti (circa 1280–1348). They depict the *Madonna with Sts. John
and Francis,* a *Crucifixion,* and a *Descent from the Cross.*

It's quite a contrast to climb the steps next to the altar and emerge into
the bright sunlight and airy grace of the double-arched Renaissance

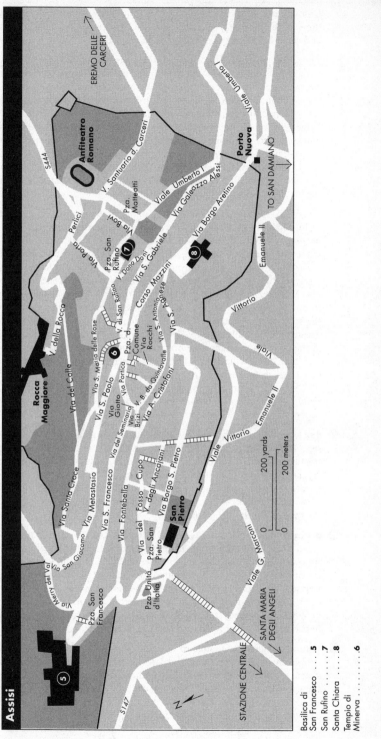

Assisi

EREMO DELLE CARCERI

Anfiteatro Romano

Porto Nuova

TO SAN DAMIANO

Viale Umberto I

V. Santuario d. Carceri

Pza. Matteotti

Via Bovi

Viale Umberto I

Via Galeazzo Alessi

Via Borgo Aretino

Pza. San Rufino

Via S. Gabriele

Corso Mazzini

V. di San Rufino V. Dono Doni

Comune

Pza. d.

Via Porta

S444

Perlici

Via della Rocca

Rocca Maggiore

V. del Colle

Via S. Maria delle Rose

Via S. Paolo

Via Giotto

Via Brizi

Via del Seminario

v. B. da Quintavalle

Via A. Cristofani

Via Rocchi

Via S. Antonio

Via S. Agnese

Vittorio

Via Santa Croce

Via San Giacomo

Via Melastasio

Via S. Francesco

Via Fontebella

Via del Fosso

Cupo

V. degli Ancajani

Via Borgo S. Pietro

Pza. San Pietro

San Pietro

Pza. Unità d'Italia

Via Merry del Val

Pza. San Francesco

S147

Viale Vittorio

Emanuele II

Emanuele II

Viale G. Marconi

SANTA MARIA DEGLI ANGELI

STAZIONE CENTRALE

200 yards

200 meters

Viale Umberto I

Chiostro dei Morti (Cloister of the Dead). A door to the right leads to the **Tesoro** (Treasury) of the church and contains relics of St. Francis and other holy objects associated with the order.

The reconstruction of the **Upper Basilica** has been hailed as proof that Italian efficiency doesn't have to be an oxymoron. Only two years after a large part of the ceiling collapsed in a series of earthquakes, reducing to rubble the Giotto and Cimabue frescoes that adorned it, the basilica reopened, little the worse for wear. Although the frescoes are still in the process of being pieced together (as the blank spaces on the vaults will attest), there is hope that even they may someday be restored. You can visit the restoration workshop behind the basilica (☎ Free, ☺ Sat. 10–5) and see how the work is going. In the meantime, there's no dearth of intact art treasures to admire, particularly Giotto's famed cycle on the life of St. Francis.

The frescoes show that Giotto, only in his twenties when he painted them, was a pivotal artist in the development of Western painting, breaking away from the stiff, unnatural styles of earlier generations and moving toward a realism and three-dimensionality that reached their peak in the Renaissance. The paintings are meant to be viewed from left to right, starting in the transept. The most beloved of the scenes is probably *St. Francis Preaching to the Birds,* a touching painting that seems to sum up the gentle spirit of the saint. It stands in marked contrast to the scene of the dream of Innocent III (circa 1160–1216). The pope dreams of a humble monk who will steady the church. Sure enough, in the panel next to the sleeping pope, you see a strong Francis supporting a church that seems to be on the verge of tumbling down—a scene that resonates with irony today. ⊠ *Piazza di San Francesco,* ☎ *075/819001.* ☺ *Lower Basilica Easter–Oct., daily 7–7; Nov.–Easter, daily 7–12:30 and 2–6. Upper Basilica (church, cloister, and treasury) Easter–Oct., daily 8:30–5:30; Nov.–Easter, daily 8:30–7.*

❼ San Rufino. St. Francis and St. Clare were among those baptized in Assisi's Duomo, the principal church in town until the 12th century. The baptismal font has since been redecorated, but it is possible to see the **crypt** of San Rufino, the martyred 3rd-century bishop who brought Christianity to Assisi. Admission to the crypt includes a look at the small **Museo Capitolare,** which features detached frescoes and artifacts. ⊠ *Piazza San Rufino.* ☺ *Daily 7–noon and 2–sunset.*

❽ Santa Chiara. This striking, red-striped 13th-century church is dedicated to St. Clare, one of the earliest and most fervent of St. Francis's followers and the founder of the Order of Poor Clares, in imitation of the Franciscans. The church contains the body of the saint, and in the **Cappella del Crocifisso** (Chapel of the Crucifix) is the crucifix that spoke to St. Francis and led him to a life of piety. A heavily veiled member of St. Clare's order is stationed before the cross in perpetual adoration of the image. ⊠ *Piazza Santa Chiara.* ☺ *Daily 7–noon and 2–sunset.*

❻ Tempio di Minerva (Temple of Minerva). Bits and pieces of a Roman temple dating from the time of Augustus (63 BC–AD 14) make up this sanctuary dedicated to the Roman goddess of wisdom. The expectations raised by the perfect classical facade are not met by the interior, subjected to a thorough Baroque assault in the 17th century, but both are worth a look. ⊠ *Piazza del Comune.* ☺ *Daily 7–noon and 2:30–sunset.*

OFF THE BEATEN PATH **CANNARA –** A pleasant excursion from Assisi leads to this tiny town 16 km (10 mi) away; a half hour's walk outside the town brings you to the fields of Pian d'Arca, the legendary site of St. Francis's sermon to the birds.

EREMO DELLE CARCERI – Just 4 km (2½ mi) east of Assisi is this monastery set in dense woodlands on the side of Monte Subasio. In the caves on the slope of the mountain, Francis and his followers established their first home, to which he returned often during his lifetime to pray and meditate. The church and monastery retain the tranquil, contemplative air St. Francis so prized. From a vantage point within the monastery, there are splendid views of the Umbrian countryside. True to their Franciscan heritage, the friars here are entirely dependent on alms from visitors. ⊠ *Via Santuario delle Carceri.* 🎟 *Donations accepted.* ⊙ *Nov.–Mar., daily 6:30–5; Apr.–Oct., daily 6:30–7.*

SANTA MARIA DEGLI ANGELI – On the outskirts of town, near the train station, this Baroque church was built over the **Porziuncola,** a little chapel restored by St. Francis. The shrine is much venerated because it was here, in the **Cappella del Transito,** then a humble cell, that St. Francis died in 1226. ⊠ *Località Santa Maria degli Angeli.* ⊙ *Daily 7 AM–sunset.*

Dining and Lodging

$$ ✕ **Buca di San Francesco.** This central restaurant is Assisi's busiest— it's no wonder, for the setting is lovely no matter what the season. In summer you dine outside in a cool green garden; in winter, under the low brick arches of the restaurant's cozy cellars. The food is first rate: try spaghetti *alla buca,* homemade pasta served with a roasted mushroom sauce. ⊠ *Via Brizi 1,* 🕾 *075/812204. AE, DC, MC, V. Closed Mon. and July.*

$$ ✕ **La Fortezza.** Parts of the walls of this modern, family-run restaurant were built by the Romans. The service is personable and the kitchen reliable. A particular standout is *anatra al finocchio selvatico* (duck cooked with wild fennel). La Fortezza also has seven simple but clean guest rooms available. ⊠ *Vicolo della Fortezza 19/b,* 🕾 *075/ 812418,* 🕸 *www.lafortezzahotel.com. Reservations essential. AE, DC, MC, V. Closed Thurs. and Feb.*

$ ✕ **La Stalla.** A kilometer or two (½–1 mile) outside the town proper, this onetime stable has been turned into a simple and rustic restaurant. In summer, enjoy a self-service lunch or dinner outside under a trellis shaded with vines and flowers. In keeping with the decor, the kitchen turns out hearty country fare. ⊠ *Via Santuario delle Carceri 8,* 🕾 *075/ 812317. No credit cards. Closed Mon. in Oct.–June.*

$$$$ 🛏 **Hotel Subasio.** Close to the Basilica di San Francesco, the Subasio, housed in a converted monastery, has counted Marlene Dietrich and Charlie Chaplin among its guests. Some of the rooms remain a little monastic, but the splendid views, comfortable old-fashioned sitting rooms, flower-decked terraces, and a lovely garden more than balance out a certain austerity in the furnishings. Ask for a room overlooking the valley. ⊠ *Via Frate Elia 2, 06081,* 🕾 *075/812206,* 🖷 *075/816691. 61 rooms. Restaurant, bar. AE, DC, MC, V.*

$$ 🛏 **Hotel Umbra.** A 16th-century town house is home to this hotel in a
★ tranquil part of the city, an area closed to traffic, near Piazza del Comune. The rooms are arranged as small apartments, each with a tiny living room and terrace. The restaurant does not serve lunch Tuesday or Wednesday. ⊠ *Via degli Archi 6, 06081,* 🕾 *075/812240,* 🖷 *075/ 813653,* 🕸 *www.caribusiness.it/carifo/az/hotelumbra. 25 rooms. Restaurant, bar. AE, DC, MC, V. Closed mid-Jan.–mid-Mar. and Dec. 1–20.*

$$$ 🛏 **San Francesco.** You can't beat the location—the roof terrace and some of the rooms look out onto the Basilica di San Francesco, which is just opposite the hotel. Rooms and facilities range from simple to homely, but you'll be reminded that looks aren't everything with nice touches like slippers, a good-night piece of chocolate, soundproofing, and that all-important rarity, air-conditioning. Fruit, homemade tarts, and fresh ricotta make for a first-rate breakfast. ⊠ *Via di San Francesco 48, 06082,* ☎ *075/812281,* FAX *075/816237,* WEB *www.krenet.it/expo/sfrancesco/home.htm. 44 rooms. Restaurant, bar, air-conditioning. AE, DC, MC, V.*

NORTHERN UMBRIA

To the north of Perugia, placid, walled Gubbio watches over green countryside, true to its nickname, "City of Silence"—except for its fast and furious festivals in May, as lively today as when they began more than 800 years ago. To the south, along the Tiber River valley, are the towns of Deruta and Torgiano, best known for their hand-painted ceramics and wine—as locals say, go to Deruta to buy a pitcher and to Torgiano to fill it.

Gubbio

9 *40 km (25 mi) northeast of Perugia, 92 km (57 mi) east of Arezzo.*

There is something otherworldly about this small jewel of a medieval town tucked away in a rugged, mountainous corner of Umbria. Even at the height of summer, the cool serenity of the City of Silence's streets remains intact. The town teeters on the slopes of Monte Ingino, and the streets are dramatically steep. Parking in the central Piazza dei Quaranta Martiri (40 Martyrs Square), named for 40 hostages murdered by the Nazis in 1944, is easy and secure, and it is wise to leave your car there and explore the narrow lanes on foot.

★ The striking Piazza Grande is dominated by the **Palazzo dei Consoli** (Palace of the Consuls), the 14th-century meeting place of Gubbio's parliament. The palace is the home of a small museum, famous chiefly for the **Tavole Eugubine** (Gubbio Tablets), seven bronze tablets written in the ancient Umbrian language, employing Etruscan and Latin characters and providing the best key to understanding this obscure tongue. Also in the museum are a captivating miscellany of coins, medieval arms, paintings, and majolica and earthenware pots, not to mention the exhilarating views over Gubbio's roofscape and beyond from the lofty loggia. For a few days at the beginning of May, the palace also displays the famous *ceri,* the ceremonial pillars that are the focus of Gubbio's annual festivities. ⊠ *Piazza Grande,* ☎ *075/9274298,* WEB *www.comune.gubbio.pg.it.* 🎫 *7,000 lire/€3.60.* ☉ *Apr.–Sept., daily 10–1 and 3–6; Oct.–Mar., daily 10–1 and 2–5.*

The **Duomo,** on a narrow street on the highest tier of the town, dates from the 12th century, with some Baroque additions—in particular, a lavishly decorated bishop's chapel. ⊠ *Via Ducale.* ☉ *Daily 8–12:45 and 3–7:30.*

The **Palazzo Ducale** (Ducal Palace) is a scaled-down copy of the Palazzo Ducale in Urbino (Gubbio was once the possession of that city's ruling family, the Montefeltro). Gubbio's palazzo contains a small **museum** and a **courtyard.** There are magnificent views from some of the public rooms. ⊠ *Via Ducale,* ☎ *075/9275872.* 🎫 *4,000 lire/€2.05.* ☉ *Tues.–Sun. 8:30–7:30.*

Just outside Gubbio's walls at the eastern end of town (follow Corso Garibaldi or Via XX Settembre to the end), a **gondola** (⊠ Via S. Girolamo, ☎ 0759/273881) provides a bracing, panoramic ride to the top of Monte Ingino. Aside from the spectacular views, Monte Ingino has the basilica of **Sant'Ubaldo,** repository of Gubbio's famous ceri, three

16-ft poles crowned with statues of Sts. Ubaldo, George, and Anthony. The pillars are transported to the Palazzo dei Consoli on the first Sunday of May to celebrate the Festival of the Ceri. ⊠ *Top of Monte Ingino.* ⊙ *Daily 9–noon and 4–7.*

Dining and Lodging

$$ ✕ **Bosone Garden.** Once the stables of the palace that now houses the Hotel Bosone, this is now a well-established Gubbio restaurant; its summer garden seats 200. Savory treats here include a two-mushroom salad with truffles, risotto *alla porcina* (with porcini mushrooms, sausage, and truffles), and leg of pork. ⊠ *Via XX Settembre 22,* ☎ *075/ 9221246. AE, DC, MC, V. Closed Wed. and 2 wks in Jan.*

$$ ✕ **Grotta dell'Angelo.** A rustic trattoria is in the lower part of the Old Town, the "Angel's Grotto" is near the main square and tourist information office. The menu features simple local specialties, including salami, stringozzi pasta, and truffled lasagna *tartufata*. A few tables welcome outdoor dining. Inexpensive guest rooms are also available. ⊠ *Via Gioia 47,* ☎ *075/9273438. Reservations essential. AE, DC, MC, V. Closed Tues. and Jan. 7–Feb. 7.*

$$ ✕ **Taverna del Lupo.** This tavern is one of the city's best, and one of the largest—it seats 150 people and can still get a bit hectic during the high season. Lasagna made in the Gubbian fashion, with ham and truffles, is an unusual indulgence. You'll also find excellent desserts and an extensive wine list. ⊠ *Via Ansidei 21,* ☎ *075/9274368. AE, DC, MC, V. Closed Mon. in Oct.–Apr.*

$$$ ▥ **Hotel Bosone Palace.** Occupying the central Palazzo Raffaelli, this old-style hotel has original frescoes in the breakfast room. The suites are particularly lavish. ⊠ *Via XX Settembre 22, 06024,* ☎ *075/ 9220688,* FAX *075/9220552. 25 rooms, 5 suites. Bar, breakfast room, minibars. AE, DC, MC, V. Closed Jan.*

$$ ▥ **Hotel Gattapone.** Right in town center is this hotel with wonderful views of the sea of rooftops. It is casual and family-run, with good-size, modern, comfortable rooms, some with well-preserved timber-raftered ceilings. ⊠ *Via Ansidei 6, 06024,* ☎ *075/9272489,* FAX *075/9272417,* WEB *www.mencarelligroup.com. 18 rooms. AE, DC, MC, V.*

Nightlife and the Arts

The silent town explodes with exuberance every May 15 during the **Corsa dei Ceri** (Race of the Poles), held every year since 1151 in honor of St. Ubaldo, Gubbio's patron saint. Three 16-ft constructions, elaborately decorated and crowned with statues of Sts. Ubaldo, George, and Anthony (representing three medieval guilds), are carried by three teams in a race up the slope of Mount Ingino. Don't place any bets, though; Ubaldo always wins.

Christmastime brings a symbol of a different kind to the slopes of Mount Ingino. Kitsch is king from December 7 to January 10, when colored lights are strung down the mountainside in a tree pattern as Gubbio stakes its claim as the home of the **world's largest Christmas tree.**

Outdoor Activities and Sports

A costumed medieval pageant with its roots in Gubbio's warring past, the **Palio della Balestra** (Crossbow Tournament) takes place on the last Sunday in May; contact the Gubbio tourist office (⊠ Piazza Oderisi 6, 06024, ☎ 075/9220693) for details.

Torgiano

⑩ *15 km (9 mi) southeast of Perugia, 18 km (11 mi) southwest of Assisi.*

Wine aficionados are certain to want to visit this home to the winery **Cantine Lungarotti,** best known for Rubesco Lungarotti, San Giorgio, and chardonnay. ⊠ *Via Mario Angeloni 12,* ☎ *075/9880348.* ☉ *Tours weekdays 8–1 and 3–6, by appointment only.*

The **Museo del Vino** (Wine Museum) has a large collection of ancient wine vessels, presses, documents, and tools that tell the story of viticulture in Umbria and beyond. The museum traces the history of wine in all its uses—for drinking at the table, as medicine, and in mythology. At the **Osteria del Museo** (☎ FAX *075/9880069*), you can taste and buy Lungarotti's award-winning wines. ⊠ *Corso Vittorio Emanuele 11,* ☎ *075/9880200.* ☞ *5,000 lire/€2.60.* ☉ *Apr.–Oct., daily 9–1 and 3–7; Nov.–Mar., daily 9–1 and 3–6.*

Deruta

🔟 *7 km (4 mi) south of Torgiano, 20 km (12 mi) southeast of Perugia.*

Deruta has been known for its ceramics since the 16th century. Notable in this medieval hill town are the 14th-century church of San Francesco and the Palazzo Comunale, but Deruta's main attraction is the magnificent ceramics collection in the **Museo Regionale della Ceramica.** ⊠ *Via Largo San Francesco,* ☎ *075/9711000.* ☞ *5,000 lire.* ☉ *Apr.–June, daily 10:30–1 and 3–6; July–Sept., daily 10–1 and 3:30–7; Oct.–Mar., Wed.–Mon. 10:30–1 and 2:30–5.*

Shopping

CERAMICS

Deruta is home to more than 70 ceramics workshops and boutiques. Start your browsing in the central Piazza dei Consoli, where you'll find a good selection at **Maioliche Cynthia** (⊠ *Via Umberto I 1,* ☎ *075/9711255*), specializing in reproductions of antique designs. **Ceramiche El Frate** (⊠ *Piazza dei Consoli 29,* ☎ *075/9711435*) sells unusual tiles and jugs. The workshop at **Fabbrica Maioliche Tradizionali** (⊠ *Via Tiberina Nord 37,* ☎ *075/9711220*) is open for visits weekdays 8:30–1 and 2:30–4:30 and also operates one of the largest shops in the area.

SPOLETO

For most of the year, Spoleto is one more in a pleasant succession of sleepy hill towns. But for three weeks every summer, it shakes off its dusty cobblestones and shifts into high gear for its turn in the spotlight: the Festival dei Due Mondi (Festival of Two Worlds), a world-class extravaganza of theater, opera, music, painting, and sculpture, where the world's top artists vie for honors and throngs of art aficionados vie for hotel rooms.

But there is good reason to visit Spoleto during the rest of the year. A solid collection of Roman and medieval attractions and superb natural surroundings make it one of Umbria's most inviting towns. From the churches set among silvery olive groves on the outskirts of town to the soaring Ponte delle Torri behind it, Spoleto offers sublime views in every direction.

Exploring Spoleto

Spoleto is small, and its noteworthy sights are clustered in the upper part of town. Like most towns made up of narrow, winding streets, Spoleto is best explored on foot. Several pedestrian walkways cut down the hill, crossing the Corso Mazzini, which turns up the hill. Parking in Spoleto is always difficult; park outside the walls in Piazza della Vittoria.

A Good Walk

Begin at Piazza del Duomo, and visit the **Duomo** ⑫, which stands against a backdrop of hill and sky with La Rocca towering overhead. Cross the

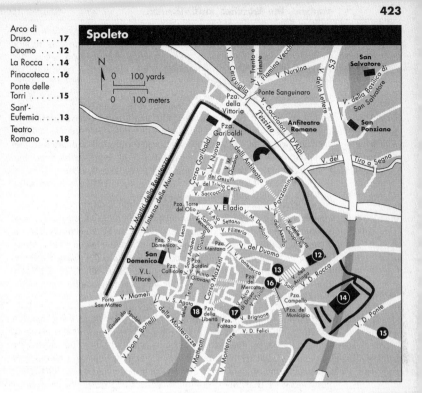

piazza and go up the stairs to Via Saffi and the church of **Sant'Eufemia** ⑬ and its museum. If you are short on time, skip Sant'Eufemia and head straight up to **La Rocca** ⑭ and **Ponte delle Torri** ⑮. Retrace your steps back to the picturesque Via Fontesecca (Sant'Eufemia), with its tempting shops selling local pottery and other handicrafts; it descends to the **Pinacoteca** ⑯ and Casa Romana. Stop in or continue on to Piazza del Mercato, built on the site of the Roman forum and home to Spoleto's open-air produce market, open Monday–Saturday 8–1:30. At the narrow end of Piazza del Mercato is the **Arco di Druso** ⑰. Turn right on Via Brignone and cross Piazza della Libertà to Via Sant'Agata, which leads to the **Teatro Romano** ⑱ and Museo Archeologico.

TIMING

Sightseeing in Spoleto is relaxed; one day will allow you to see the highlights and still have time for a leisurely lunch and a walk to the Ponte delle Torri.

Sights to See

⑰ **Arco di Druso** (Arch of Drusus). This structure was built in the 1st century AD by the Senate of Spoleto to honor the Roman general Drusus (circa 13 BC–AD 23), son of the emperor Tiberius. It once marked the entrance to the Foro Romano (Roman Forum). ⊠ *Piazza del Mercato.*

⑫ **Duomo.** The church's rather dour 12th-century Romanesque facade is lightened up by a Renaissance loggia, eight rose windows, and an early 13th-century gold mosaic of the Benedictory Christ. A stunning contrast in styles, it is one of the finest in the region. The Duomo's interior holds the most notable art in town, most notably the immaculately restored frescoes in the apse by Fra Filippo Lippi (1406–69), showing the *Annunciation,* the *Nativity,* and the *Dormition of Mary,* with a marvelous *Coronation of the Virgin* adorning the dome; be ready with a

500-lire coin to illuminate the masterpiece. The Florentine artist died shortly after completing the work, and his tomb—designed by his son, Filippino Lippi (1457–1504)—lies in the church's right transept. Another fresco cycle, including work by Pinturicchio, can be seen in the **Cappella Eroli** off the right aisle. ⊠ *Piazza Duomo,* ☎ *0743/43722.* ☉ *Mar.–Oct., daily 8–1 and 3–6:30; Nov.–Feb., daily 8–1 and 3–5:30.*

⑭ **La Rocca.** Built in 1359–63 by the Gubbio-born architect Gattapone, the fortress dominates Spoleto. Until recently it served as a high-security prison, but it now houses a small museum dedicated to medieval Spoleto. You can admire the formidable exterior from the road that circles around it. ⊠ *Take Via Saffi (off Piazza del Duomo) to Via del Ponte,* ☎ *0743/223055.* 🎫 *9,000 lire/€4.65.* ☉ *Weekdays 10–noon and 3–7, weekends 10–7; closes at sunset in winter.*

⑯ **Pinacoteca.** The town picture gallery has a small collection of works from the 12th to the 18th century. Admission to the 1st-century AD **Casa Romana,** around the corner, is included on the same ticket. *Pinacoteca:* ⊠ *Palazzo del Municipio, Via Aurelio Saffi. Casa Romana: Palazzo del Municipio, Via Visiale 9. Both:* ☎ *0743/43722.* 🎫 *5,000 lire/€2.60.* ☉ *Oct.–Apr., Tues.–Sun. 10–1 and 3–6; May–Sept., daily 10–1 and 4–7.*

★ ⑮ **Ponte delle Torri.** Standing massive and graceful through the gorge that separates Spoleto from Monteluco, this 14th-century bridge is one of Umbria's most-photographed sights, and justifiably so. The 750-ft-long bridge was built by Gattapone over the foundations of a Roman-era aqueduct and soars 262 ft above the forested gorge at its highest point—higher than the dome of St. Peter's in Rome. Postcard views over the valley and a pleasant sense of vertigo make a walk across the bridge a must, particularly on a starry night. ⊠ *Via del Ponte.*

⑬ **Sant'Eufemia.** Set in the courtyard of the archbishop's palace, this ancient, austere church dates from the 11th century. Its most interesting feature is the gallery above the nave where female worshipers were required to sit—a holdover from the Eastern Church and one of the few such galleries in this part of Italy. Enter through the Museo Diocesano, attached to the church, which contains paintings including a Madonna by Fra Filippo Lippi. ⊠ *Via Saffi, between Piazza del Duomo and Piazza del Mercato,* ☎ *0743/23101.* 🎫 *5000 lire/€2.60.* ☉ *Wed.–Mon. 10–12:30 and 3–6.*

⑱ **Teatro Romano.** The small but well-preserved Roman theater was the site of a gruesome episode in Spoleto's history. During the medieval struggle between Guelph (papal) and Ghibelline (imperial) factions for control of central and northern Italy, Spoleto took the side of the Holy Roman Emperor. And woe to those who disagreed: four hundred Guelph supporters were massacred in the theater, their bodies burned in an enormous pyre. In the end, however, the Guelphs were triumphant, and Spoleto was incorporated into the states of the Church in 1354. Through a door in the west portico, the **Museo Archeologico** displays assorted artifacts and the *Lex Spoletina* (Spoleto Law) tablets dating from 315 BC. This ancient legal document prohibited the destruction of the Bosco Sacro (Sacred Forest), just south of town on Monteluco, a pagan prayer site later frequented by St. Francis. The theater is used in summer for Spoleto's arts festival. ⊠ *Piazza della Libertà,* ☎ *0743/223277.* 🎫 *4,000 lire/€2.05.* ☉ *Mon.–Sat. 9–7, Sun. 9–1.*

OFF THE   **SAN SALVATORE** –The church and cemetery of San Salvatore seem very
BEATEN PATH much forgotten, ensconced in solitude and cypress trees on a peaceful
             hillside, with the motorway rumbling below. One of the oldest churches

in the world, it was built by eastern monks in the 4th century, largely of Roman-era materials. The highlight is the facade, with three exquisite marble doorways and windows, one of the earliest and best preserved in Umbria. It dates from a restoration in the 9th century and has hardly been touched since. ⊠ *Via della Basilica di San Salvatore, just out of town on the Via Flaminia.* ⊙ *Nov.–Feb., daily 7–5; Mar.–Apr. and Sept.–Oct., daily 7–6; May–Aug., daily 7–7.*

Dining and Lodging

$$$–$$$$ ✕ **Il Tartufo.** Spoleto's most famous restaurant has a modern dining room on the second floor and a rustic dining room downstairs—both of them incorporating ruins of a Roman villa. The traditional cooking is spiced up in summer to appeal to the cosmopolitan crowd attending (or performing in) the Festival dei Due Mondi. As its name indicates, the restaurant specializes in dishes prepared with truffles; try the risotto *al tartufo*, though there is a second menu from which you can choose items not perfumed with this expensive delicacy. ⊠ *Piazza Garibaldi 24,* ☎ *0743/40236. Reservations essential. AE, DC, MC, V. Closed Wed. and last 2 wks in July. No dinner Sun.*

$$–$$$ ✕ **Il Pentagramma.** Just off the central Piazza della Libertà, this restaurant housed in a former stable features such local dishes as fresh ravioli *alle noci* (stuffed with sage) and lamb in a truffle sauce. ⊠ *Via Martani 4,* ☎ *0743/223141. DC, MC, V. Closed Mon.*

$$ ✕ **Ristorante Panciolle.** In the heart of Spoleto's medieval quarter, this restaurant has one of the most romantic settings you could wish for. Dining outside in summer is a welcome respite, in a small piazza filled with lemon trees. Specialties include stringozzi pasta with mushroom sauce and *agnello scottadito* (grilled lamb chops). ⊠ *Vicolo degli Eroli 1,* ☎ *0743/45598. Reservations essential. AE, DC MC, V. Closed Wed. and last 2 wks in Jan.*

$$$ ✕🏨 **Hotel Dei Duchi.** This well-run hotel is a favorite among performers in the Festival dei Due Mondi. It's in town center, near the Roman theater. Some rooms have fine views of the city. A 1999 restoration focused new attention on the hotel's restaurant ($$), bringing in a new chef who turns out Umbrian treats laced with mushrooms, truffles, and even juniper berries. ⊠ *Viale G. Matteotti 4, 06049,* ☎ *0743/44541,* FAX *0743/44543,* WEB *www.hoteldeiduchi.com. 47 rooms, 2 suites. Restaurant, bar, meeting room, free parking. AE, DC, MC, V.*

$$ ✕🏨 **Hotel Clitunno.** A renovated 18th-century building houses this pleasant hotel, a five-minute walk from the town center. Bedrooms and public rooms, some with lovely timbered ceilings, evoke the atmosphere of a traditional Umbrian home (albeit one with a very good restaurant). ⊠ *Piazza Sordini 6, 06049,* ☎ *0743/223340,* FAX *0743/222663. 40 rooms. Restaurant, bar, library, meeting room. AE, DC, MC, V.*

$$$–$$$$ 🏨 **Hotel Gattapone.** The tiny hotel at the top of the Old Town, near
★ the Ponte delle Torri, has spectacular views of the bridge and the wooded slopes of Monteluco. Eclectic modern design and picture windows add character to quiet, comfortable rooms. Have breakfast overlooking the gorge on the sunny roof terrace. ⊠ *Via del Ponte 6, 06049,* ☎ *0743/ 223447,* FAX *0743/223448,* WEB *www.caribusiness.it/gattapone. 16 rooms. Bar, minibars, meeting room, free parking. AE, DC, MC, V.*

Nightlife and the Arts

The **Festival dei Due Mondi** (Festival of Two Worlds) in Spoleto, held mid-June to mid-July, features accomplished artists in all branches of the arts—particularly music, opera, and theater—and draws thousands of visitors from all over the world. Tickets for all performances should be ordered in advance from the **festival's box office** (✉ Piazza Duomo 8, ☎ 800/565600, WEB www.spoletofestival.net), which has full program information starting in February.

OFF THE
BEATEN PATH **VALNERINA –** This area southeast of Spoleto is the most beautiful of central Italy's many well-kept secrets. The twisting roads that serve the rugged landscape are poor, but a drive through the region is well worth the effort for its forgotten medieval villages and dramatic mountain scenery.

The first stop should be the **Cascata delle Marmore,** waterfalls engineered by the Romans in the 3rd century BC. You'll find them a couple of miles east of Terni, on the road to Lake Piediluco and Rieti. The waters are diverted on weekdays to provide hydroelectric power for the town of Terni, so check with the Spoleto tourist office (✉ Piazza della Libertà 7, 06049, ☎ 0743/220311) before heading here. On summer evenings, when the falls are in full spate, the cascading water is floodlit (June–August, nightly 8–10; mid-March–May and September, weekends nightly 8–9).

Close to the picturesque town of Ferentillo (northeast of Terni on S209) is the outstanding 8th-century abbey of **San Pietro in Valle,** with fine frescoes in the church nave and a peaceful cloister. One of the abbey outbuildings houses an excellent restaurant with moderate prices.

East of Spoleto in the Valnerina is **Norcia,** the birthplace of St. Benedict but better known for Umbrian pork and truffles. Norcia exports truffles to France and hosts a truffle festival, Mostra Internazionale del Tartufo Nero di Norcia, every November.

SOUTHERN UMBRIA

Orvieto, built on a tufa mount, produces one of Italy's favorite white wines and is home to one of the country's greatest cathedrals and most compelling fresco cycles. Nearby Narni and Todi are two pleasant medieval hill towns. The former stands firm over a steep gorge, its Roman pedigree evident in dark alleyways and winding streets; the latter is a fairy-tale village with incomparable Umbrian views and one of Italy's most perfect piazzas.

Orvieto

⑲ *53 km (32 mi) west of Spoleto, 86 km (53 mi) south of Perugia.*

Carved out of an enormous plateau of volcanic rock high above a green valley, Orvieto has natural defenses that made the high walls seen in many Umbrian towns unnecessary. The Etruscans were the first to take advantage of this and settled here, digging a honeycombed network of more than 1,200 wells and storage caves out of the soft stone. The Romans attacked, sacked, and destroyed the city in 283 BC; since then, it has grown up out of the rock into an enchanting maze of alleys and squares. Orvieto was solidly Guelph in the Middle Ages, and for several hundred years popes sought refuge in the city, at times needing protection from their enemies, at times from the summer heat of Rome.

When painting his frescoes inside the Duomo, Luca Signorelli asked that part of his contract be paid in Orvietan wine, and he was by no means the first or the last to appreciate the region's popular white. In past times, the caves carved underneath the town were used to ferment the Trebbiano grapes used in making Orvieto Classico; now local wine production has moved out to more traditional vineyards, but you can still while away the afternoon in tastings at any number of shops in town.

★ Orvieto's **Duomo** may be the most dazzling in all of Italy, a triumph of Romanesque-Gothic architecture. It was built to commemorate a local miracle: a priest in the nearby town of Bolsena suddenly found himself assailed by doubts about the transubstantiation—he could not bring himself to believe that the body of Christ was contained in the consecrated communion host. His doubts were put to rest, however, when a wafer he had just blessed suddenly started to drip blood onto the linen covering the altar. The pope certified the miracle and declared a new religious holiday—the Feast of Corpus Christi—and the duomo was built to celebrate the event and house the stained altar cloth.

The stunning carved-stone facade is the work of some of Italy's finest artists and took 300 years to complete. The bas-reliefs on the lower parts of the pillars by Lorenzo Maitani (circa 1275–1330), one of the original architects of the building, show well-known scenes from the Old Testament and some scary renderings of the Last Judgment and Hell, as well as a more tranquil Paradise. See how many scenes you can identify.

Inside the cathedral, a vast expanse of empty space leads to the major works, at the far end of the church in the transepts. To the left is the **Cappella del Corporale,** where the famous altar cloth is kept in a golden reliquary modeled on the cathedral, inlaid with enamel images of the miracle. The cloth is removed for public viewing on Easter and on Corpus Christi (the ninth Sunday after Easter). A trio of local artists executed frescoes depicting the miracle on the chapel walls. Signorelli's *Stories of the Antichrist,* the artistic jewel of the Duomo, deck the walls of the **Cappella Nuova** (Cappella di San Brizio), in the right transept (buy tickets in the tourist office across the square). In these delightfully gruesome works, the damned fall to hell, and lascivious demons bite off ears, step on heads, and spirit away young girls. Dante would surely have approved; in the chapel, his portrait accompanies *Scenes from Purgatorio.* Signorelli and Fra Angelico, who also worked on the chapel, witness the gory scene. ⊠ *Piazza del Duomo,* ☎ *0763/ 342477.* ☜ *Cappella Nuova 3,000 lire/€1.55.* ☉ *Nov.–Feb., daily 7:30– 12:45 and 2:30–5:15; Mar. and Oct., daily 7:30–12:45 and 2:30– 6:15; Apr.–Sept., daily 7:30–12:45 and 2:30–7:15.*

The **Museo Claudio Faina,** across the piazza from the Duomo, holds Etruscan and Roman artifacts; the museum is designed in a way that makes its Roman coins, bronze pieces, and sarcophagi particularly accessible and interesting. ⊠ *Palazzo Faina,* ☎ *0763/341511.* ☜ *8,000 lire/€4.15, 5,000 lire/€2.60 with funicular or bus ticket.* ☉ *Oct.– Mar., Tues.–Sun. 10–1 and 2:30–5; Apr.–Sept., daily 10–1 and 2–6.*

On Piazza Cahen, the **Fortezza,** built in the mid-14th century, encloses a public park with grass, benches, shade, and an incredible view. The **Pozzo di San Patrizio** (Well of St. Patrick) was commissioned by Pope Clement VII (1478–1534) in 1527 to ensure a plentiful water supply in case of siege. Descend into the well on a pair of zigzagging mule paths designed to avoid animal traffic jams. ⊠ *Viale Sangallo, off Piazza Cahen,* ☎ *0763/343768.* ☜ *6,000 lire/€3.10.* ☉ *Oct.–Mar., daily 10–5:45; Apr.–Sept., daily 9:30–6:45.*

Dining and Lodging

$$–$$$ ✕ **Le Grotte del Funaro.** This restaurant has an extraordinary location,
★ deep in a series of caves within the volcanic rock beneath Orvieto. Once you have negotiated the steep steps, typical Umbrian specialties like tagliatelle *al vino rosso* (with red wine sauce) and grilled beef with truffles await. Sample the fine Orvieto wines, either the whites or the

lesser-known reds. ⊠ *Via Ripa Serancia 41,* ☎ *0763/343276. Reservations essential. AE, DC, MC, V. Closed Mon.*

$$–$$$ ✕ **Maurizio.** In the heart of Orvieto, just opposite the cathedral, this
★ warm and welcoming restaurant gets its share of tourists as well as a local clientele. The decor is unusual, with wood sculptures by Orvieto craftsman Michelangeli. The menu offers hearty soups and homemade pastas such as *tronchetti* (a pasta roll with spinach and ricotta filling). Reservations are essential in summer. ⊠ *Via del Duomo 78,* ☎ *0763/341114. AE, MC, V. Closed Tues.*

$$$–$$$$ ⌂ **Hotel La Badia.** This is one of the best-known country hotels in Umbria. The 12th-century building, a former monastery, is set in rolling parkland that provides wonderful views of the valley and the town of Orvieto in the distance. Vaulted ceilings and exposed stone walls set a tone of rustic elegance in the rooms. ⊠ *Località La Badia, 4 km (2½ mi) south of Orvieto, 05018,* ☎ *0763/301959,* FAX *0763/305396. 26 rooms. Restaurant, bar, pool, 2 tennis courts, meeting room. AE, MC, V. Closed Feb.–Mar.*

$$ ⌂ **Grand Hotel Reale.** This hotel is in the center of Orvieto, on a square that hosts a lively market. Facing the impressive Gothic-Romanesque Palazzo del Popolo, rooms are spacious and adequately furnished, with a traditional accent. ⊠ *Piazza del Popolo 25, 05018,* ☎ *0763/341247,* FAX *0763/341247. 32 rooms. Bar. MC, V.*

$$ ⌂ **Hotel Virgilio.** The modest Virgilio is right on Piazza del Duomo, and the views of the cathedral are wonderful. The rooms are small but nicely furnished. ⊠ *Piazza del Duomo 5, 05018,* ☎ *0763/341882,* FAX *0763/343797. 13 rooms. Bar. MC, V. Closed Feb.*

$$ ⌂ **Villa Bellago.** Outside Orvieto, in a tranquil setting on a spit of land overlooking Lake Corbara, three farmhouses have been completely overhauled. The result: well-lighted and spacious guest rooms, generous facilities, and a fine restaurant (closed Tuesday) specializing in imaginatively prepared Umbrian and Tuscan dishes. Fresh fish is always on the menu. ⊠ *Outside the village of Baschi, 7½ km (4½ mi) south of Orvieto on S448, 05018,* ☎ *0744/950521,* FAX *0744/950524. 12 rooms. Restaurant, bar, pool, tennis court, gym. AE, DC, MC, V. Closed 4 wks in Jan.–Feb.*

Shopping

EMBROIDERY AND LACE

Minor arts such as embroidery and lace making flourish in Orvieto. One of the best shops for *merletto* (lace) is **Duranti** (⊠ Corso Cavour 107, ☎ no phone).

WINE

Excellent Orvieto wines are justly prized throughout Italy and the world. The whites pressed from the region's Trebbiano grapes are fruity, with a tart finish. Orvieto also produces its own version of the Tuscan dessert wine *vin santo*. It is darker than its Tuscan cousin and is aged five years before bottling. You may stop for a glass of vino at the **Wine Cellar** (⊠ Piazza del Duomo 2), where there's also a good selection of sandwiches and snacks, and vin santo is on sale.

WOODWORKING

Orvieto is a well-known center for woodworking, particularly fine inlay and veneer work. The Corso Cavour has a number of artisan shops specializing in woodwork, the best known being the **Michelangeli family studio** (⊠ Via Michelangeli 3, corner of Corso Cavour, ☎ 0763/342377), chock-full of imaginatively designed creations ranging in size from a giant *armadio* (wardrobe) to a simple wooden spoon.

Todi

⑳ *30 km (19 mi) east of Orvieto.*

As you stand on **Piazza del Popolo,** it's easy to see why Todi is often described as Umbria's prettiest hill town. The square is a model of spatial harmony with stunning views over the surrounding countryside. Todi's 12th-century Romanesque-Gothic **Duomo** is famed for its choir stalls by Antonio Bencivenni da Mercatello and his son Sebastiano, dating from 1530. Its simple square facade is echoed by the solid Palazzo dei Priori across the way. Narrow cobblestone streets go winding around the hill, every so often finishing in a tiny, quiet piazza. The Renaissance church of **Santa Maria della Consolazione,** with an elegant pale-green dome, offers a pleasant surprise on the outskirts of town.

Dining and Lodging

$$ ✕ **Ristorante Umbria.** Todi's most popular restaurant for over four decades, the Umbria is reliable for sturdy country food, plus a wonderful view from the terrace. There's always a hearty soup simmering, as well as homemade pasta with truffles, game, and the specialty of the house, *palombaccio alla ghiotta* (roasted squab). ✉ *Via San Bonaventura 13,* ☎ *075/8942737 or 075/8942390. AE, DC, MC, V. Closed Tues. and July.*

$$$ 🏠 **Tenuta di Canonica.** The affable hosts, Daniele and Maria Fano, scoured Tuscany and Umbria and returned to the first place they saw, a brick farmhouse and medieval tower with a foundation dating from the Roman period, in the Tiber Valley 5 km (3 mi) northwest of Todi. The Fanos have tastefully retained the architectural integrity of the structure: you're bound to marvel at the exposed stone walls, high beamed ceilings, brick floors, and terra-cotta tiles, all soothed by cool colors. Guest rooms are filled with family furniture and antique pieces. You can hike or ride on horseback through olive groves, orchards, and the forest on the grounds. ✉ *Località La Canonica, 75–76, follow signs to Titignano and Cordigliano, 06059,* ☎ *075/8947545,* 𝔽𝔸𝕏 *075/ 8947581,* 𝚆𝙴𝙱 *www.tenutadicanonica.com. 11 rooms, 2 apartments. Dining room, pool, library. No credit cards.*

Narni

㉑ *35 km (22 mi) south of Todi, 84 km (46 mi) southeast of Perugia.*

At the edge of a steep gorge, Narni—like so many other towns in Umbria—is a medieval city of Roman origins. Below its finely paved streets and pretty Romanesque churches, excavations offer glimpses of an intriguing past. The **Lacus,** under Piazza Garibaldi, is an ancient Roman cistern with remnants of a Roman floor that was in use until the late Middle Ages. Two cisterns and assorted Roman fragments are visible in the crypt of the 8th-century church of **Santa Maria Impensole** (✉ Via Mazzini), open daily 9:30–noon and 4:30–6:30. A macabre note is struck by the symbols and dates on the walls of the rooms under the former church of **San Domenico,** inscribed by prisoners held there during the Inquisition. The best day to visit is Sunday, when the excavated sites are open and tours are given in English. You can take a unique tour of the inside of Narni's underground **Roman aqueduct,** the only one open to the public in all of Italy, but if you have claustrophobia stay away. Contact Associazione Culturale Subterranea or call the tourist office (✉ Piazza dei Priori 3, 05035, ☎ 0744/715362) to book a visit of the excavations during the week. ✉ *Associazione Culturale Subterranea, Giardini di San Bernardo,* ☎ *0744/722292,* 𝚆𝙴𝙱 *www.narnisotterranea.it.* ☯ *Excavations Sun. 11–1 and 3–5.*

Dining

$$–$$$ ✕ **Il Cavallino.** Run by the third generation of the Bussetti family, Il Cavallino is a first-rate trattoria about 3 km (2 mi) outside Narni. There are always several pastas to choose from, but it's the meat that makes this a worthy detour. Rabbit roasted with rosemary and sage and juicy grilled T-bone steaks are house favorites. The wine list features the best of what's local. ✉ *Via Flaminia Romana 220,* ☎ *0744/761020. AE, DC, MC, V. Closed Tues., 2 wks in July, and Dec. 25–31.*

THE MARCHES
Hidden Italy

Less touristed than Tuscany or Umbria, the Marches are equally rich in diverse landscapes; as in its neighbors to the west, the region's patchwork of rolling hills is stitched with grapevines and olive trees producing delicious wine and olive oil. You're off the beaten path here, and so services tend to be less luxurious than in the regions to its west, but the advantage is that with a little luck, you'll have the place to yourself.

Travelers willing to go the extra mile will benefit from the Marches' relative remoteness, but bear in mind that traveling here is not as easy as in Umbria or Tuscany, and a car is recommended. Beyond the narrow coastal plain and away from major towns, the roads are steep and twisting. There's an efficient bus service from the coastal town of Pésaro to Urbino, the other principal tourist city of the region. Train travel in the region is slow, and stops are limited, although you can reach Ascoli Piceno by rail.

Urbino

㉒ *101 km (63 mi) northeast of Perugia, 107 km (66 mi) northeast of Arezzo.*

Majestic Urbino, atop a steep hill with a skyline of towers and domes, is something of a surprise to come upon—it's oddly remote—and it is humbling to reflect that it was once a center of learning and culture almost without rival in western Europe. The town looks much as it did in the glory days of the 15th century, a cluster of warm brick and pale stone buildings, all topped with russet-color tiled roofs. The focal point is the immense and beautiful Palazzo Ducale.

Urbino's tradition of learning continues to this day, and the city takes great pride in its intellectual and humanistic heritage. The city is home to the small but distinguished Università di Urbino—one of the oldest in the world—and during school term the streets are filled with students. It is very much a college town, with the usual array of bookshops, record stores, bars, and coffeehouses. During the summer, the Italian student population is replaced by foreigners who come to study Italian language and arts at several prestigious private fine-arts academies.

Urbino's fame rests on the reputation of three of its native sons: Duke Federico da Montefeltro (1422–82), the enlightened warrior-patron who built the Palazzo Ducale; Raffaello Sanzio (1483–1520), or Raphael, one of the most influential painters in history and an embodiment of the spirit of the Renaissance; and the architect Donato Bramante (1444–1514), who translated the philosophy of the Renaissance into buildings of grace and beauty. Unfortunately, there is little work by either Bramante or Raphael in the city, but the duke's influence can still be felt strongly, even now, some 500 years after his death.

★ The **Palazzo Ducale** holds the place of honor in the city, and in no other palace of its era are the principles of the Renaissance stated quite so clearly. If the Renaissance was, in ideal form, a celebration of the nobility of man and his works, of the light and purity of the soul, then there is no place in Italy, the birthplace of the Renaissance, where these tenets are better illustrated.

Today the palace houses the **Galleria Nazionale delle Marche** (National Museum of the Marches), with a superb collection of paintings, sculpture, and objets d'art, well arranged and properly lit. Masterworks in the collection include Paolo Uccello's *Profanation of the Host,* Titian's *Resurrection* and *Last Supper,* and Piero della Francesca's *Madonna of Senigallia.* But the gallery's highlight is Piero's enigmatic work, long known as *The Flagellation of Christ.* Much has been written about this painting, and few experts agree on its meaning. These debates notwithstanding, experts agree that the work is one of the painter's masterpieces. Piero himself thought so: it's one of the few works he signed (on the lowest step supporting the throne). ⊠ *Piazza Duca Federico,* ☎ *0722/329057,* 🕸 *www.comune.urbino.ps.it.* 🎟 *8,000 lire/€4.15.* ◷ *Tues.–Sun. 8:30–7:15 (10 PM Apr.–Oct.), Mon. 8:30–2. Ticket office closes 90 mins before Palazzo.*

The **Casa Natale di Raffaello** (Birthplace of Raphael) really is the house in which the painter was born and where he took his first steps in painting, under the direction of his artist father. There is some debate about the fresco of the Madonna here, though; some say it is by Raphael, whereas others attribute it to the father—with Raphael's mother and the young painter himself standing in as models for the Madonna and Child. ⊠ *Via Raffaello 57,* ☎ *0722/320105.* 🎟 *5,000 lire/€2.60.* ◷ *Mon.–Sat. 9–2, Sun. 10–1.*

Dining and Lodging

$$–$$$ ✕ **La Vecchia Fornarina.** The two small rooms of this trattoria, just down from Urbino's central Piazza della Repubblica, are often filled to capacity. This spot specializes in meaty country fare, such as *coniglio* (rabbit) and *vitello alle noci* (veal cooked with walnuts) or *ai porcini* (with mushrooms). There is also a good selection of pasta dishes. ⊠ *Via Mazzini 14,* ☎ *0722/320007. Reservations essential. AE, DC, MC, V.*

$ 🏨 **Hotel San Giovanni.** This hotel in the Old Town is housed in a renovated medieval building. The rooms are basic, clean, and comfortable—with a wonderful view from Rooms 24 to 30—and there is a handy restaurant-pizzeria below. ⊠ *Via Barocci 13, 61029,* ☎ *0722/2827,* 🖷 *0722/329055. 33 rooms, 17 with bath. No credit cards. Closed July and Christmas wk.*

Shopping

Historically, Urbino has been a center for the production of fine majolica ceramic designs, and you'll find pretty reproductions and new designs at shops throughout. One unique, though hard-to-carry, gift might be the Stella Ducale (Ducal Star), a complex three-dimensional decorative wooden star designed out of pyramid shapes by Renaissance mathematician Luca Pacioli.

Ancona

㉓ *87 km (54 mi) southeast of Urbino, 139 km (87 mi) northeast of Perugia.*

Set on an elbow-shape bluff (hence its name; *ankon* is Greek for "elbow") jutting out into the Adriatic, Ancona is one of Italy's most important ports. The city was the target of serious aerial bombing during World War II, and much was reduced to rubble, only to be rebuilt in a nondescript sprawl of boxy poured concrete. Just a few blocks from the main ferry terminal, however, what's left of the city's historic center remains intact, and it proves that Ancona was, and still is in parts, a lovely city. Narrow, cobbled streets wind steeply up from the waterfront, opening onto wide piazzas edged with handsome 19th-century brick-and-stucco buildings painted deep orange, pink, and ochre. The alleys leading downhill from central Piazza del Plebiscito are lined with chic shops offering everything from handmade linens to herbal cosmetics, and there are cafés and *pasticcerie* aplenty to stave off hunger before your ferry leaves. There are enough sights to fill even the longest layover, too. The 12th-century Romanesque church of **Santa Maria della Piazza** is built over a previous church of the 5th century; parts of the foundation and original hand-cut mosaic pavement are visible through handy glass cut-outs in the floor. The 2nd-century **Arco di Traiano** (Trajan's Arch) out on the point is worth a look. The **Duomo di San Ciriaco,** originally built over a Greek temple, was redesigned in the 13th century to make it more visible to ships coming in to Ancona's port. The **Loggia dei Mercanti,** dating from the 15th century, was Ancona's bazaar, home to merchants and traders dealing in all manner of goods from the Far East. The city's importance as a port means it's well served by trains, which can make it a good base for an excursion to Loreto or to Ascoli Piceno, farther south along the Adriatic coast.

Dining and Lodging

$$ ✕ **La Moretta.** This family-run trattoria is on the central Piazza del Plebiscito. In summer there is dining outside in the square, which has a fine view of the Baroque church of San Domenico. Among the specialties here are *stoccafisso all'Anconetana* (cod baked with capers, anchovies, potatoes, and tomatoes) and the famous *brodetto* fish stew. ✉ *Piazza del Plebiscito 52,* ☎ *071/202317. AE, DC, MC, V. Closed Sun. and Jan. 1–10.*

$$$ 🏨 **Grand Hotel Palace.** This old-fashioned port hotel is widely held to be the best in town. Rooms are on the small side but beautifully furnished with French beds dressed in yellow damask, and half have a view directly over the port. Extras like slippers, bath salts, and shaving kits make for a pleasant stay. Public rooms are grand and elegant, and the breakfast room is on the top floor with a panoramic view. ✉ *Lungomare Vanvitelli 24, 60100,* ☎ *071/201813,* 📠 *071/2074832,* 🌐 *www.conero.it. 39 rooms, 1 suite. Bar, breakfast room, meeting rooms, parking (fee). AE, DC, MC, V.*

Loreto

㉔ *31 km (19 mi) south of Ancona, 118 km (73 mi) southeast of Urbino.*

Thousands of pilgrims come to Loreto every year to visit one of the
★ the world's best-loved shrines, the **Santuario della Santa Casa** (House of the Virgin Mary), within the **Basilica.** According to legend, angels moved the house from Nazareth (now Loreto's sister city) to this hilltop in 1295, when Nazareth fell into the hands of Muslim invaders—not suitable landlords, the angels felt. Archaeological excavations made at the behest of the Church have since shown that the house did once stand elsewhere and was brought to the hilltop—by either crusaders or a family named Angeli—around the time the angels (*angeli*) are said to have done the job.

Easter week and the Feast of the Holy House on December 10 are marked by processions, prayers, and a deluge of pilgrims; the rest of the year, the shrine is relatively quiet. The house itself consists of three rough stone walls contained within an elaborate marble tabernacle; built around this centerpiece is the giant basilica of the Holy House, which dominates the town. The basilica was begun in Gothic style in 1468 and continued in Renaissance style through the late Renaissance with the help of some of the period's greatest architects: Bramante, Antonio da Sangallo (the Younger, 1483–1546), Giuliano da Sangallo (circa 1445–1516), and Sansovino (1467–1529). ⊠ *Piazza della Madonna,* ☎ *071/970104,* WEB *www.santuarioloreto.it.* ☉ *June–Sept., daily 6 AM–8 PM; Oct.–May, daily 6 AM–7 PM. Santuario della Santa Casa closed daily 12:30–2:30.*

Fearful flyers may take comfort from the fact that the Holy Virgin of Loreto is the patroness of air travelers. You can pick up Pope John Paul II's prayer for a safe flight in the church, where it's available in a dozen languages.

Ascoli Piceno

㉕ *105 km (65 mi) south of Ancona, 175 km (109 mi) southeast of Perugia.*

Ascoli Piceno is not a hill town; rather, it sits in a valley ringed by steep hills and cut by the fast-racing Tronto River. The town is almost unique in Italy in that it seems to have its traffic problems—in the historic center, at any rate—pretty much under control; you can drive *around* the picturesque part of the city, but driving *through* it is most difficult. This feature makes Ascoli Piceno one of the most pleasant large towns in the country for exploring on foot. True, there is traffic, but without the constant assault of jams, noise, and exhaust fumes of other Italian cities.

★ The heart of Ascoli Piceno is the majestic **Piazza del Popolo,** dominated by the Gothic church of **San Francesco** and the **Palazzo dei Capitani del Popolo,** a 13th-century town hall that contains a graceful Renaissance courtyard. The square functions as the city's living room: at dusk each evening the piazza fills with people strolling and exchanging
🖐 news and gossip. Ascoli Piceno's **Giostra della Quintana** (Joust of the Quintana) is held on the first Sunday in August. Children love this medieval-style joust and the processions of richly caparisoned horses that wind through the streets of the Old Town. Contact the Ascoli tourist office (⊠ Piazza del Popolo 1, 63100, ☎ 0736/257288) for details.

Dining and Lodging

$–$$ ✕ **Ristorante Tornasacco.** More than 60 years old, Tornasacco is one
★ of Ascoli Piceno's oldest restaurants. There's no nouvelle cuisine here: the owners pride themselves on meaty local specialties such as *olive ascolane* (olives stuffed with minced meat, breaded and deep-fried), *maccheroncini alla contadina* (homemade short pasta in a lamb, pork, and veal sauce), and *bistecca di toro* (bull steak). ⊠ *Piazza del Popolo 36,* ☎ *0736/254151. AE, DC, MC, V. Closed Fri. and July 1–15.*

$ 🏨 **Piceno.** This modest hostelry is one of the few lodgings in the historic center. It offers clean, basic amenities—no frills here. The staff is helpful and courteous, and the setting is perfect. ⊠ *Via Minucia 10, 63100,* ☎ *0736/252553. 30 rooms, 24 with bath. AE, DC, MC, V. Closed Jan.*

ABRUZZO

Central Italy isn't all tranquil rolling hills dotted with picturesque hill towns and vineyards. Just south of Umbria, the terrain of the often-overlooked Abruzzo region quickly turns more rugged and mountainous, with isolated mountain villages and some of the country's best-preserved wildlife sanctuaries. In Abruzzo, you can enjoy nature in the rough, and there's no better place than the Parco Nazionale d'Abruzzo for hiking, skiing, and horseback riding. L'Aquila, a walkable town well worth an afternoon stroll, is also a good base for exploring the central part of the region.

L'Aquila

②⑥ *58 km (36 mi) southeast of Rieti, 167 km (104 mi) southeast of Orvieto.*

Possibly the youngest regional capital in Italy, L'Aquila was founded when Emperor Frederick II (1482–1556) united the 99 surrounding kingdoms under one flag (which bore an eagle, or *l'aquila*). The town's most famous fountain, **Fontana Delle 99 Canelle,** commemorates the event with 99 spouts, and the church bells in the Duomo ring 99 times each night. A good place to begin a walk is Piazza Battaglione Alpini, which serves as a bus terminal. L'Aquila's austere **Castello** (fortress) looms above, offering sweeping vistas of the nearby Gran Sasso mountain range. Built by the Spanish rulers in the 16th century to discourage popular revolt, the Castello also served as a prison. Today it is home to the **Museo Nazionale dell'Abruzzo**, which has a good collection drawn from the region's earthquake-ravaged churches and a gallery of modern art on the top floor. The highlight of the visit is a skeleton of a million-year-old mammoth discovered nearby in 1954. ✉ *Viale delle Medaglie d'Oro,* ☎ *0862/6331.* 🎫 *8,000 lire/€4.15.* ☉ *Tues.–Sat. 9–2, Sun. 9–1 and 2–8.*

The main road from Piazza Battaglione Alpini leads to the center of town. Up on the right is the small Piazza Santa Maria Paganica; a little farther ahead is Via di San Bernardino, which climbs to the left to the Renaissance church of **San Bernardino.** It was built in honor of St. Bernardine of Siena and boasts a lovely facade featuring the classical orders of columns. The mausoleum that holds the saint's remains was built by a pupil of Donatello (circa 1386–1466), and the altarpiece is by Andrea della Robbia (1435–1525). The rest of the interior was given a Baroque makeover in the early 18th century. ✉ *Via di San Bernardino.* ☉ *Daily 8–noon and 4–6.*

A short walk from the Piazza Battaglione Alpini along Via Fontebella brings you just outside the city walls, to Santa Maria di Collemaggio, probably the most famous church in Abruzzo. It was built toward the end of the 13th century by the hermit Peter of Morrone, who was later elected Pope Celestine V, and its fame stems from Peter's. He was so attached to the church that he insisted on being crowned and buried here rather than in Rome; his remains rest in the mausoleum to the right of the altar. The church's simple Romanesque facade is strikingly laced with a geometric pattern of white and pink marble. Gothic elements include the rose windows and decorative portals. The interior is rather bare, although the floor has decorative patterns and several fine 15th-century frescoes. ✉ *Piazzale Collemaggio 1,* ☎ *0862/26744.* ☉ *Daily 9–6:30.*

Dining and Lodging

Abruzzese cooking is mountain-style—hearty, simple, local foods. You are likely to find plenty of lamb, mutton, and pork, pecorino cheese and ricotta, and wild mushrooms and lentils on restaurant menus, along with dishes spiced with saffron, which is grown near L'Aquila. The local wines tend toward the robust and the spicy; white Trebbiano and red Montepulciano d'Abruzzo are the best-known types.

$–$$ **✕ Elodia.** A local favorite for classic Abruzzese cooking, Elodia spe-
★ cializes in hard-to-find traditional dishes such as *crespelle di ricotta alla montanara* (thin ricotta pancakes), simple flavors like chickpea and chestnut soup (in winter), and foodie touches like an olive oil list and wine-tasting menus. The small dining room is no-smoking, a rarity in Italy. Delicious homemade desserts such as apple-chocolate cake and pears baked in Montepulciano d'Abruzzo wine should not be missed. After

dinner, ask for a tour of the wine cellar. ✉ *Frazione Camarda, S17bis del Gran Sasso,* ☎ *0862/606219. AE, DC, MC, V. Closed Mon. and 1st 2 wks in July. No dinner Sun.*

$ ✗ **Trattoria del Giaguaro.** In the most evocative square in town, this trattoria will welcome you with an array of homemade pasta dishes, including *maccheroni a chitarra al sugo* (macaroni with lamb sauce) and ravioli filled with first-rate fresh sheep's-milk ricotta. A selection of grilled meat or the popular osso buco *agli ortaggi* (veal shank in a tomato sauce, served with mixed vegetables) will fill you up fast, although you should try to save room for homemade crème brûlée. ✉ *Piazza Santa Maria Paganica 4,* ☎ *0862/28249. MC, V. Closed Tues., 2 wks in July–Aug., and over Christmas.*

$$ 🏨 **Duomo.** The quiet Duomo, housed in 18th-century quarters, is as central as it can be. Many rooms have a view of the lovely square below, and the decor is a nice blend of traditional touches and modern comforts: expect terra-cotta floors and wrought-iron beds matched with practical wooden furniture. Buffet breakfast includes local honey, cakes, and cookies. ✉ *Via Dragonetti 10, 67100,* ☎ *0862/410893,* FAX *0862/413058. 27 rooms. Bar. AE, MC, V.*

Shopping

There's a good **antiques market** in Piazza Santa Maria della Paganica the second weekend of each month. Piazza del Duomo is home to the town's **produce market** Monday–Saturday 8–1.

Medieval Abruzzo

The landscape surrounding L'Aquila is studded with old castles, guard towers, and tiny hamlets, some perfectly preserved and still inhabited, others in ruins, haunted by the ghosts of past battles. Castel del Monte and Santo Stefano di Sessanio are two medieval *borghi* (hamlets) east of L'Aquila on the S17bis that make a pleasant half-day excursion.

㉗ Castel del Monte is an unusual example of a *ricetto,* a type of fortified village without external walls. A single steep access road rises to the center of the town, which is crossed by narrow alleys and dark tunnels leading to the more distant houses. In case of attack, the inhabitants could barricade themselves in their houses, block the narrow streets, and pour hot oil down the main street.

㉘ Santo Stefano di Sessanio, 26 km (17 mi) east of Castel del Monte on the S17bis, was first the property of the powerful Roman Piccolomini family, then passed to the Medici. It features the most sophisticated guard tower in the area, built with rounded instead of squared sides to make an attack more difficult. Climb to the top to enjoy a panoramic view of the Campo Imperatore valley and its striking rock formations.

Skiing

The area around L'Aquila is dominated by the Apennines, central Italy's greatest mountains. The Alps they're not, but winter visitors to Abruzzo and day-trippers from Rome will find ample choice for a day's skiing at **Campo Imperatore** (☎ 0862/22146), **Campo Felice** (☎ 0862/917803), and **Ovindoli** (☎ 0863/705087), which have a total of 60 km (40 mi) of runs and 100 km (60 mi) of cross-country trails.

Parco Nazionale d'Abruzzo

★ ㉙ *Pescasseroli 109 km (68 mi) southeast of L'Aquila.*

Italy's national park system is for the most part underdeveloped, but the 440-square-km (170-square-mi) Abruzzo National Park (WEB www.pna.it) is a notable exception. Full of lakes, streams, ruined castles, wildlife, and rugged terrain crossed by hiking trails and ski runs, the park is home to Apennine wolves, Marsican brown bears, Abruzzan chamois, lynx, and more than 200 species of birds. The Carta Turistica, on sale at local tobacconists or news agents, is a comprehensive topographical map with nearly 150 trails marked and identified with symbols indicating their relative difficulty and the animals that you're most likely to meet on the way. One of the most popular short walks (2½ hours) begins near Opi (path F2) and crosses the lovely Valle Fondillo, with chamois to be spotted in the early morning (should you miss them, the Opi entrance is home to a semi-enclosed chamois preserve). For a full-day loop in the green, try path I1 to the Val di Rosa forest, and then head up to Passo Cavuto and return to town via Valle Ianna'nghera (path K6). The park is open year-round, although it is best appreciated in the off-season, as during Easter week and between July and September the crowds of visitors often scare the animals away and popular hiking routes are accessible by reservation only in an attempt to limit congestion.

Helpful information offices at the edges of the park in the towns of Pescasseroli, Civitella Alfedena, and Villetta Barrea (☞ Visitor Information *in* Umbria, the Marches, and Abruzzo A to Z, *below*) have all the information you will need for a hike through the scenery and can also arrange guided tours in English. The visitor centers, open daily 10–1 and 3–7, each themed toward a different kind of wildlife found inside the park, provide great opportunities for children to learn about animals. There's a wolf reserve and wolf museum with exhibits and films at Civitella Alfedena, and Pescasseroli has a nature reserve for injured animals and a nature museum and eco-lab with interactive displays for kids.

Dining and Lodging

$$ ✕ 🏠 **Plistia.** Pescasseroli's oldest inn has 10 rooms and a low-key, small restaurant with a mission to keep old, traditional recipes alive. Get the eight-course tasting menu for a full session on Abruzzese cuisine, or select from a list of little-known dishes like *carratelli* (pasta with wild spinach) or *cotturo* (lamb slowly simmered in a spiced broth). For dessert, the apple cake and almond tart are delightful. ✉ *Via Principe di Napoli 28, 67032 Pescasseroli,* ☎ *0863/910732,* FAX *0863/911741. 10 rooms. Restaurant. AE, DC, MC, V. Restaurant closed Mon.*

Skiing

Pescasseroli's **ski area** (☎ 0863/910461) is the best-developed in the region, with 14 downhill runs of varying difficulty and great views all around. Two cross-country trails, 10 km (6 mi) and 30 km (18 mi) long, wind through the park and afford wildlife-spotting opportunities.

UMBRIA, THE MARCHES, AND ABRUZZO A TO Z

To research prices, get advice from other travelers, and book travel arrangements, visit www.fodors.com.

AIRPORTS
Central Italy's closest major airports are in Rome, Pisa, and Florence. Perugia's tiny Aeroporto Sant'Egidio has flights to and from Milan, Rome Ciampino, and Palermo.

➤ AIRPORT INFORMATION: **Aeroporto Sant'Egidio** (☎ 075/592141, WEB www.airport.umbria.it). **Florence** (Peretola, ☎ 055/3061700). **Pisa** (Galileo Galilei, ☎ 050/500707). **Rome** (Fiumicino, ☎ 06/65953640).

BUS TRAVEL

Perugia is served by the Sulga Line, with daily departures from Rome's Stazione Tiburtina and from Piazza Adua in Florence. The central bus station in Abruzzo's L'Aquila sends hourly ARPA buses to Rome; buy tickets in the small ARPA kiosk on the piazza.

There is good local bus service between all the major and minor towns of Umbria. Some of the routes in rural areas, especially in the Marches, are designed to serve as many destinations as possible and are, therefore, quite roundabout and slow. Schedules often change, so consult with local tourist offices before setting out.

➤ BUS INFORMATION: **ARPA** (✉ P. Battaglione Alpini, ☎ 0862/412808). **Sulga Line** (☎ 075/5009641, WEB www.sulga.it).

CAR RENTAL

➤ LOCAL AGENCIES: **Avis** (✉ Sant'Egidio airport, Perugia, ☎ 075/6929796; ✉ Stazione Ferroviaria Fontivegge, Perugia, ☎ 075/5000395; ✉ Località S. Chiodo 164, Spoleto, ☎ 0743/46272; ✉ Via XX Settembre 80/d, Terni, ☎ 0744/287170). **Hertz** (✉ Via dell'Arcone 13, Orvieto, ☎ 0763/301303; ✉ Piazza Vittorio Veneto 4, Perugia, ☎ 075/5002439; ✉ Via Cerquiglia 144, Spoleto, ☎ 0743/46366).

CAR TRAVEL

On the western edge of the region is the Umbrian section of the Autostrada del Sole (A1), the principal north–south highway in Italy. It links Florence and Rome with Orvieto and passes near Todi and Terni. The S3 intersects with A1 and leads on to Assisi and Urbino. The Adriatica superhighway (A14) runs north–south along the coast, linking the Marches to Bologna and Venice. The A24 runs from Rome to L'Aquila and up to the Adriatic.

Umbria has an excellent, modern road network. Central Umbria is served by a major highway, S75bis, which passes along the shore of Lake Trasimeno and ends in Perugia. Assisi is served by the modern highway S75; S75 connects to S3 and S3bis, which cover the heart of the region. Major inland routes connect coastal A14 to large towns in the Marches, including Urbino, Jesi, Macerata, and Ascoli Piceno, but inland secondary roads in mountain areas can be tortuous and narrow.

EMERGENCY SERVICES

When you're on the road, always carry a good road map, a flashlight, and, if possible, a cellular phone so that in case of a breakdown you can call ACI for towing and repairs—ask and you will be transferred to an English-speaking operator. Be prepared to tell the operator which road you're on, the direction you're going (e.g., "*verso* [in the direction of] Perugia") and the *targa* (license plate number) of your car. The great majority of Italians carry cellular phones, so if you don't have one, flag down someone who does for help.

➤ CONTACTS: **ACI dispatchers** (☎ 116).

EMERGENCIES

Emergency numbers (listed below) are accessible from every phone, including cellular phones, all over Italy. If you have ongoing medical concerns, it's a good idea to make sure someone is on duty all night where you're staying—not a given in Umbria, less so in Le Marche and Abruzzo. As elsewhere in Italy, every pharmacy in Umbria, Le Marche, and Abruzzo bears a sign at the door listing area pharmacies open in off-hours. Perugia, Spoleto, Assisi, Gubbio, and Urbino all have at least one so-called "night" pharmacy, but out in the countryside you may need a car to get to one. Try to bring extras with you of all medications you take regularly.

➤ CONTACTS: **Emergencies** (☎ 113). **Ambulance** (☎ 118). **Carabinieri** (Military Police; ☎ 112). **Fire** (☎ 115).

MAIL AND SHIPPING

➤ POST OFFICES: **Assisi** (✉ P. del Comune 23, ☎ 075/812355). **Perugia** (✉ P. Matteotti 1, ☎ 075/5720395). **Spoleto** (✉ P. della Libertà 12, ☎ 0743/223198).

TRAIN TRAVEL

Assisi lies on the Terontola–Foligno rail line, with almost hourly connections to Perugia and direct trains to Rome and Florence several times per day. The main rail line from Rome to Ancona passes through Narni, Terni, Spoleto, and Foligno. Travel time from Rome to Spoleto is a little less than 90 minutes on intercity trains. The main Rome–Florence line stops at Orvieto. With a change of trains at the small town of Terontola, one can travel by rail from Rome or Florence to Perugia and Assisi. Trains run to L'Aquila via Sulmona, which is on the Rome–Pescara line (the bus from Rome's Stazione Tiburtina is much faster, however).

Branch lines link Ancona with the inland towns of Fabriano and Ascoli Piceno. In Umbria, a small, privately owned railway operated by Ferrovia Centrale Umbra (FCU) runs from Città di Castello in the north to Terni in the south via Perugia.

➤ TRAIN INFORMATION: **Ferrovia Centrale Umbra** (FCU; ☎ 075/5729121, WEB www.fcu.it). **Ferrovie dello Stato (State Railways)** (☎ 848/888088, WEB www.fs-on-line.com).

VISITOR INFORMATION

➤ AGROTOURIST INFORMATION: **Turismo Verde** (✉ Via Campo di Marte 14/1, 06100 Perugia, ☎ 075/5002953, FAX 075/5002956, WEB www.turismoverde.it).

➤ TOURIST INFORMATION: **Abruzzo** (WEB www.abruzzo2000.com). **Ancona** (✉ Via Thaon de Revel 4, 60100, ☎ 071/358991, WEB www.comune.ancona.it). **Ascoli Piceno** (✉ Piazza del Popolo 1, 63100, ☎ 0736/257288, www.data.it/marche/provap/ascoli/ascoli.htm, WEB www.ascolipiceno.com). **Assisi** (✉ Piazza del Comune 12, 06081, ☎ 075/812534, WEB www.comune.assisi.pg.it). **Civitella Alfedena** (✉ Via Santa Lucia, 67030, ☎ FAX 0864/890141, WEB www.pna.it). **Gubbio** (✉ Piazza Oderisi 6, 06024, ☎ 075/9220693, WEB www.comune.gubbio.pg.it). **L'Aquila** (✉ Via XX Settembre 8, 67100, ☎ 0862/22306, www.comune.laquila.it/turismo/turismo_e_cultura.htm; ✉ Centro Turistico del Gran Sasso, Corso Vittorio Emanuele 49, 67100, ☎ 0862/22146, WEB www.comune.laquila.it/turismo). **Loreto** (✉ Via Solari 3, 60025, ☎ 071/920276, WEB www.turismo.marche.it). **Narni** (✉ Piazza dei Priori 3, 05035, ☎ 0744/715362, WEB www.comune.narni.tr.it). **Orvieto** (✉ Piazza Duomo 24, 05018, ☎ 0763/341772, WEB www comune.orvieto.tr.it). **Perugia** (✉ Piazza IV Novembre, 06123, ☎ 075/5042546; ✉ Via Mazzini 21, 06100, ☎ 075/5725341, WEB www.comune.perugia.it). **Pescasseroli** (✉ Via Vico Consultore, 67032, ☎ 0863/91955, WEB www.pna.it). **Spoleto** (✉ Piazza della Libertà 7, 06049, ☎ 0743/220311, WEB www.spoleto1.com). **Todi** (✉ Piazza Umberto I 6, 06059, ☎ 075/8943395, WEB www.argoweb.it/tuderte/itinerari.uk.html). **Urbino** (✉ Via Puccinotti 35, 61029, ☎ 0722/2613, WEB www.comune.urbino.ps.it). **Villetta Barrea** (✉ Via Roma 1, 67030, ☎ 0864/89102, WEB www.pna.it).

11 ROME

In Rome, Nero fiddled, Mark Antony praised Caesar, and Charlemagne was crowned. Today, you can walk in their footsteps past the masterpieces of Michelangelo, sip your *caffè* in the shadow of Mussolini, and dodge Vespas speeding by Baroque *palazzi* and Egyptian obelisks. The ages of history live on in this, the Eternal City.

R OME'S 2,700 YEARS OF HISTORY are laid open with every step. Ancient Rome rubs shoulders with the medieval, the modern runs into the Renaissance, and the result is like nothing so much as an open-air museum, a city that glories in its glories and is a monument to itself. Senators, emperors, vandals, popes and the Borgias, Michelangelo and Bernini, Napoléon, and Mussolini all left their physical, cultural, and spiritual stamps on the city—and what stamps they are. More than Florence, more than Venice, Rome is Italy's treasure trove, packed as it is with masterpieces from more than two millennia of artistic achievement. This is where a metropolis once bustled around the carved marble monuments of the Roman Forum, where centuries later Michelangelo Buonarroti painted Christian history in the Sistine Chapel, where Gian Lorenzo Bernini's nymphs and naiads dance in their fountains, and where an empire of gold was worked into the crowns of centuries of rulers.

Updated by
Valerie
Hamilton

Today Rome's formidable legacy is upheld by its people, their history knit into the fabric of their everyday lives. Students walk dogs in the park that was once the mausoleum of the family of the emperor Augustus; Raphaelesque madonnas line up for buses on busy corners; a priest in flowing robes walks through a medieval piazza talking on a cell phone. Modern Rome has one foot in the past, one in the present— a delightful stance that allows you to have an espresso in a square designed by Bernini, then take the metro back to your hotel room in a renovated Renaissance palace. "When you first come here you assume that you must burrow about in ruins and prowl in museums to get back to the days of Numa Pompilius or Mark Antony," Maud Howe observes in her book *Roma Beata*. "It is not necessary; you only have to live, and the common happenings of daily life—yes, even the trolley car and your bicycle—carry you back in turn to the Dark Ages, to the early Christians, even to prehistoric Rome."

Pleasures and Pastimes

Il Caffè (Coffee)

The Roman day begins and ends with coffee, and more cups of coffee punctuate the time in between. To live like the Romans do, drink as they drink, standing at the counter or sitting at outdoor tables of the corner *bar.* (In Italy, the term always means coffee bar—establishments focusing on alcoholic beverages are called *pubs* or *American bars.*) A primer: *Caffè* means coffee, and Italian standard issue is what Americans call espresso—short, strong, and usually drunk very sweet. *Cappuccino* is a foamy half-and-half of espresso and steamed milk; cocoa powder (*cacao*) on top is acceptable, cinnamon not. If you're thinking of having a cappuccino for dessert, think again—Romans drink only caffè or *caffè macchiato* after lunchtime. Confused? Homesick? Order *caffè americano* for a reasonable facsimile of good old filter joe.

Dining

Rome is distinguished more by its good attitude toward eating out than by a multitude of outstanding restaurants. Don't look for star chefs here, or the latest trends—with a few notable exceptions, the city's food scene is a bit like its historical sights, well worn but still standing. But food lovers nonetheless have much to look forward to. Romans have been known since ancient times for great feasts and banquets, and though the days of the triclinium and the saturnalia are long past, dining out is still Rome's favorite pastime. Many of the city's restaurants cater to a clientele of regulars, and atmosphere and attitude are usually friendly and informal. The flip side is that in Rome, the customer is not always right—the chef and waiters are in charge, and no one will beg forgiveness if you wanted *skim* milk in that cappuccino. Be flexible, and you're sure to *mangiar bene* (eat well). Lunch is served from noon to 2:30 and dinner from 8 until 10:30 or 11, but some restaurants stay open later, especially in summer, when patrons linger at sidewalk tables to enjoy the *ponentino* (evening breeze). For general information and price categories, *see* Dining *in* Smart Travel Tips.

Lodging

Rome has the range of accommodations you would expect of any great city, from the squalid little hotels and *pensioni* (pensions) around the railway station to the grand monuments to luxury and elegance on and around Via Veneto. Appearances can be misleading here: crumbling stucco facades may promise little from the outside, but they often hide interiors of considerable elegance. For general information and price categories, *see* Lodging *in* Smart Travel Tips.

Motorbikes

Buzzing, roaring, zipping, honking, swerving, and (occasionally) crashing, *motorini* (motorbikes) are an inescapable part of Roman daily life. One look at the traffic will tell you why: with the city's narrow streets already jammed with pedestrians, buses, and triple-parked cars, motorini are the fastest and easiest way to get around town. If you want to join the fray, or just go for a spin, there are numerous places to rent a scooter and mandatory helmet, but keep in mind that Roman traffic is not for the faint of heart. And no matter what you may see others doing, remember that traffic laws apply to cars *and* motorini and that contravention may get you slapped with a stiff fine.

Opera Alfresco

Roman nightlife moves outdoors in summertime, and that goes not only for pubs and discos but for higher culture as well. Open-air opera is one venerable Italian tradition that has recently staged a comeback. Competing opera companies commandeer everything from church courtyards to the soccer stadium for performances that range from student-run mom-and-poperas to full-scale extravaganzas. The quality of performances is generally quite high, even if small productions often resort to school-play scenery and folding chairs to cut costs. Tickets run from about 25,000 lire/€12.90 to 80,000 lire/€41.30, making a night at the opera alfresco an affordable evening's entertainment. Look for old-fashioned posters, plastered all over the city, advertising classics like *Tosca* and *La Traviata,* or contact the companies directly to find out what's on.

The Passeggiata (Strolling)

A favorite pastime of Romans (and most Italians) is the *passeggiata,* literally, the promenade. In the late afternoon, especially on weekends, couples, family groups, and packs of teenagers stroll in the main streets and piazzas. It's not hard to join in—just dress up in your finest and hit the streets for a bit of aimless wandering, with a little window-shopping or a gelato stop thrown in for fun. As you amble down the narrow streets, take time to peek into courtyards and look up at open windows as dusk falls to see lights go on, illuminating carved or frescoed ceilings on upper floors.

Politics

Walking through its ancient ruins, strolling past its quiet squares, you might forget that Rome is the capital of a vibrant, noisy, and often messy modern democracy. After 57 postwar governments (and counting), however, Italians have developed a flair for protest, and you'll see it proudly paraded should you happen upon one of the innumerable political demonstrations that descend upon the city each year. Whether it's dairy farmers depositing cows at St. Peter's, teachers blocking traffic, or leftists marching on the Senate, someone seems to be complaining about something nearly every day. Demonstration locales vary, but Via Cavour, Via dei Fori Imperiali, Corso Rinascimento, and Piazza del Parlamento are popular sites, particularly on weekend mornings.

Shopping

The city's most famous shopping district is conveniently compact, fanning out at the foot of the Spanish Steps in a galaxy of boutiques offering gorgeous wares with glamorous labels. Here you can ricochet from Gucci to Prada to Valentino to Versace with less effort than it takes to pull out your platinum credit card. Even if your budget is designed for lower altitudes, you can find great clothes and accessories at prices you can afford. But buying is not necessarily the point. The greatest pleasure is in browsing, admiring window displays that are works of art, imagining you or yours in a little red dress by Valentino or a lean Armani suit.

EXPLORING ROME

Visitors to Rome often face a conundrum: the more you see of the city, the more you'll realize how little you have time to see. Take heart; Rome wasn't built in a day. The Italian author Silvio Negro said it best: "*Roma, non basta una vita*" (Rome, a lifetime is not enough). It's wise to start out knowing this and to have a focused but flexible itinerary. A ramble through a picturesque quarter of Old Rome can be just as enchanting as the quiet contemplation of a chapel or a trek through marbled miles of museum corridors.

Though spread out, Rome invites walking, and taxis are rarely far off for the weary. Plan your day taking into account the varying opening hours of the sights you plan to visit, which usually means mixing the ancient, classical, and Baroque, museums and parks, the center and the environs. Most churches are usually open from 8 or 9 until noon or 12:30 and from 3 or 4 until about 6:30 or 7.

A combination ticket for the Colosseum, Palatine, and the various branches of the Museo Nazionale Romano (including Palazzo Altemps, Terme di Diocleziano and Palazzo Massimo alle Terme), valid for five consecutive days, is available at each participant's ticket office for 30,000 lire/€15.50, making it a good deal for ancient-history buffs.

Great Itineraries

IF YOU HAVE 3 DAYS

Begin your first day at Piazza Venezia and survey Rome from atop the Campidoglio. Next, explore the Roman Forum and see the Palatine Hill and the Colosseum. In the afternoon, combine sightseeing with shopping and make your way through the neighborhood around the Spanish Steps and the Trevi Fountain. The following day, visit St. Peter's and the Vatican Museums and Sistine Chapel, breaking between the two for lunch. Take it easy on your third morning: explore a museum or sight of interest and then relax at a café and watch the passing parade. Spend your final afternoon and evening exploring the picturesque Ghetto and Trastevere neighborhoods.

IF YOU HAVE 5 DAYS

On the morning of the fourth day wander through Villa Borghese and see the Canova and Bernini sculptures in the Galleria Borghese (make reservations ahead of time). On the fifth day, make an early morning

excursion either along Via Appia Antica or to Ostia Antica, an ancient city comparable to Pompeii in atmosphere. After a sustaining lunch back in town, see some of Rome's most historic churches, with Michelangelo's *Moses* in San Pietro in Vincoli a highlight.

IF YOU HAVE 7 DAYS
Devote more time to the museums and galleries that interest you most. Explore a neighborhood you have not seen yet, or return to one you liked best, allowing plenty of time for poking into odd corners and courtyards and churches, and for café-sitting. Make a couple of excursions outside Rome, to Tivoli or perhaps to Tarquinia and Cerveteri.

Ancient Rome: Glories of the Caesars

A walk through the very core of Roman antiquity, through what was once the capital of the Western world, the Roman Forum, is an impressive introduction to the glories of the ancient city. Although the millennia have reduced this grand complex to fields of picturesque ruins, it is enough to consider that this square was the birthplace of Western civilization. Roman law and powerful armies were created here, banishing the barbarian world for a millennium. Here, all Rome shouted as one, "Caesar has been murdered," and crowded to hear Mark Antony's eulogy for the fallen leader. Legend has it that St. Paul traversed the Forum en route to his audience with Nero. Up on the Campidoglio, the harmony of Michelangelo's Renaissance piazza is appropriate testament to the seat of the ancient governments based here 2,000 years before. In the heyday of the Empire, the Forum below occasionally became an enormous banquet hall, where imperial Rome could be entertained in one place (as our times have observed thanks to such Hollywood epics as *Quo Vadis, Ben-Hur,* and *Cleopatra*). After 27 centuries of such a parade of pageantry, it is fitting that Shelley and Gibbon reflected here on the meaning of *sic transit gloria mundi* (so passes away the glory of the world).

Numbers in the text correspond to numbers in the margin and on the Rome map.

A Good Walk

Begin your walk on the **Campidoglio** ①—the site of Michelangelo's spectacular piazza and Rome's city hall, Palazzo Senatorio, which was built over the Tabularium, the ancient hall of records. Flanking the palazzo are both halves of Rome's most noteworthy museum complex, the **Musei Capitolini** ②, made up of the Museo Capitolino and the Palazzo dei Conservatori, which contain works of art gathered by Pope Sixtus IV, one of the earliest papal patrons of the arts. Off to the side of the Campidoglio, at the head of its formidable flight of steps, stands the ancient redbrick church of **Santa Maria d'Aracoeli** ③. Walk down the road to the left of Palazzo Senatorio, behind the piazza, and look out over the remains of the Roman Forum. From here, steps descend to the gloomy **Carcere Mamertino** ④, the Mamertine Prison. The road leads out past the Forum of Caesar to Via dei Fori Imperiali. Across the street are the Forum of Trajan and the **Column of Trajan** ⑤. Continue along the Via dei Fori Imperiali, passing the fora built by Augustus and Nerva, and cross back over the road to the entrance of the **Roman Forum** ⑥. At the end of the ancient Via Sacra inside the Forum is the entrance to the **Palatine Hill** ⑦, site of Rome's earliest settlement. Take the ramp that leads from the Forum–Palatine Hill area to the **Arch of Constantine** ⑧ and, beyond it, the **Colosseum** ⑨, one of antiquity's most famous monuments. Don't forget to check out the view from the park laid out over the ruins of Nero's **Domus Aurea** ⑩, his sumptuous palace, behind the Colosseum.

TIMING

It takes about 45 minutes to walk the route, plus one hour to visit the Musei Capitolini, from two to three hours to explore the Roman Forum and Palatine Hill and a half hour to see the Colosseum.

Sights to See

❽ Arch of Constantine (Arco di Costantino). This imposing arch was erected in AD 315 to celebrate the victory of the emperor Constantine (280–337) over Maxentius (died 312). The best-preserved of Rome's triumphal arches, it is also the largest (69 ft high, 85 ft wide, and 23 ft deep) and one of the last great monuments of ancient Rome.

★ **❶ Campidoglio** (Capitoline Hill). Though most of the buildings on Michelangelo's piazza date from the Renaissance, this hill was once the nerve center of the Roman Empire, the place where the city's first and holiest temples stood, including its most sacred, the Tempio di Giove (Temple of Jupiter). The city's archives were kept in the Tabularium (hall of records), the tall, gray-stone structure that forms the foundation of today's city hall, the **Palazzo Senatorio.** By the Middle Ages, Capitol Hill, as the hill was already called, had fallen into ruin. In 1537, Pope Paul III (1468–1549) decided to restore its grandeur for the triumphal entry into the city of Charles V (1500–58), the Holy Roman Emperor, and called upon Michelangelo to create the staircase ramp; the buildings and facades on three sides of Capitol Hill; the slightly convex pavement and its decoration; and the pedestal for the bronze equestrian statue of Marcus Aurelius. A work from the 2nd century AD, the statue stood here from the 16th century until 1981. The statue—the most celebrated equestrian bronze to survive from classical antiquity—was mistakenly believed to represent the Christian emperor Constantine rather than the pagan Marcus Aurelius, hence its survival through the centuries. A legend foretells that some day the statue's original gold patina will return, heralding the end of the world. To forestall destiny, the city fathers had it restored and placed in the courtyard of the Museo Capitolino, saving not only what was left of the gold but also the statue's bronze, once seriously menaced by air pollution. A copy was placed on the original pedestal in 1997. As Michelangelo's preeminent urban set piece, the piazza sums up all the majesty of High Renaissance Rome.

❹ Carcere Mamertino (Mamertine Prison). This series of gloomy, subterranean cells under a 17th-century church is where Rome's vanquished enemies were finished off. Some historians believe that St. Peter was held prisoner here, and legend has it that he miraculously brought forth a spring of water with which to baptize his jailers. ⊠ Via del Tulliano. 🖾 Donation requested. ☉ Daily 9–noon and 2:30–5.

Circus Maximus (Circo Massimo). In the giant arena laid out between Palatine and Aventine hills, more than 300,000 spectators watched chariot races while the emperor surveyed the scene from his palace on the Palatine Hill.

★ **❾ Colosseum** (Colosseo). Massive and majestic, ancient Rome's most famous monument was begun by the Flavian emperor Vespasian (AD 7–79) in AD 72 and inaugurated eight years later with a program of games and shows lasting 100 days. More than 50,000 spectators could sit within the arena's 573-yard circumference, which was faced with marble, accented with hundreds of statues, and had a velarium—an ingenious system of sail-like awnings rigged on ropes manned by imperial sailors—to protect the audience from the sun and rain. Before the imperial box, gladiators would salute the emperor and cry, "*Ave, imperator, morituri te salutant*" (Hail, emperor, men soon to die

salute thee); it is said that when one day they heard the emperor Claudius respond "Or maybe not," they were so offended that they called a strike.

Originally known as the Flavian Amphitheater, it was called the Colosseum, as reported by the Venerable Bede in 730, after a truly colossal gilt bronze statue of Nero that stood in the vicinity until the end of the 6th century. The arena later served as a quarry from which materials were filched to build Renaissance-era churches and palaces. Finally, it was declared sacred by the Vatican in memory of the many Christians believed martyred here (scholars now maintain that Christians met their death not here but rather in Rome's imperial circuses). During the 19th century, romantic poets lauded the glories of the amphitheater when viewed by moonlight. Now its arches glow at night with mellow golden spotlights—less romantic, perhaps, but still impressive. ⊠ *Piazza del Colosseo,* ☎ *06/7004261.* ✆ *10,000 lire/€5.15, 30,000 lire/€15.50 for multisight ticket.* ☉ *Daily 9–2 hrs before sunset.*

❺ Column of Trajan (Colonna di Traiano). The ashes of Trajan (AD 53–117) were buried inside the base of this column, built to commemorate the emperor and his military campaigns in Dacia (Romania). It stands in what was once the **Forum of Trajan** (Foro di Traiano), with its huge semicircular market building, adjacent to the ruins of the **Forum of Augustus** (Foro di Augusto). ⊠ *Entrance: Via dei Fori Imperiali and Via IV Novembre 6,* ☎ *06/67102802.* ✆ *3,750 lire/€1.95.* ☉ *Tues.–Sun. 9–2 hrs before sunset.*

❿ Domus Aurea. Nero's "Golden House" is a spectacular example of the excesses of Imperial Rome. After fire destroyed much of the city in AD 64, Nero took advantage of the resulting open space to construct a lavish palace so large that contemporary accounts complained, "All Rome has become a villa." In this sort of Roman White House, one wing was given over to public functions, and the other was the emperor's private residence, which included a revolving dining room. Today the palace is a wonderfully well preserved trove of ancient architecture, painting, and sculpture. The site is kept cool and damp, so you should dress accordingly. Reservations are strongly recommended. ⊠ *Via della Domus Aurea,* ☎ *06/6990110 information; 06/39967700 reservations,* 🌐 *www.archeorm.arti.beniculturali.it/sar2000/domus/Domus_aurea.htm.* ✆ *10,000 lire/€5.15, plus 2,000 lire/€1.05 reservation fee.* ☉ *Wed.–Mon. 9–7:45.*

Forum of Caesar (Foro di Cesare). Caesar built this forum, including a temple dedicated to himself and the goddess Minerva, to expand the then-crowded original Roman Forum, which had been built up over the preceding 500 years. In doing so, Caesar set a trend that several emperors followed, building what are now called the Imperial Fora.

★ ❷ Musei Capitolini (Capitoline Museums). The collections in the twin Museo Capitolino and Palazzo dei Conservatori were assembled in the 15th century by Pope Sixtus IV (1414–84), one of the earliest of the great papal art patrons. Although parts of the collection may excite only archaeologists and art historians, others contain some of the most famous pieces of classical sculpture, such as the poignant *Dying Gaul,* the regal *Capitoline Venus* (recently identified as another Mediterranean beauty, Cleopatra herself), and the delicate *Marble Faun* that inspired Nathaniel Hawthorne's novel of the same name. Remember that many of the works here and in Rome's other museums were copied from Greek originals. For hundreds of years, craftsmen of ancient Rome prospered by producing copies of Greek statues using a process called "pointing," by which exact replicas could be created to order.

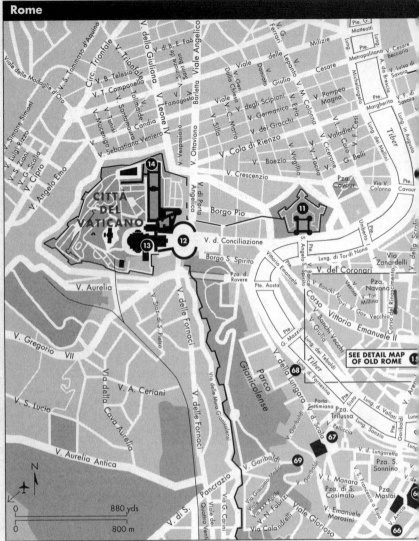

Portraiture, however, was one area in which the Romans outstripped the Greeks. The hundreds of Roman portrait busts of emperors in the Sala degli Imperatori and of philosophers in the **Museo Capitolino's** Sala dei Filosofi constitute a Who's Who of the ancient world. Within these serried ranks are 48 Roman emperors, ranging from Augustus to Theodosius (346–95). On one console, you'll see the handsomely austere Augustus, who "found Rome a city of brick and left it one of marble." On another rests Claudius "the stutterer," an indefatigable builder brought vividly to life in the novel *I, Claudius*, by Robert Graves (1895–1985). Also in this company is Nero, most notorious of the emperors—though by no means the worst—who built for himself the fabled Domus Aurea. And, of course, there are the baddies: cruel Caligula (AD 12–41) and Caracalla (AD 186–217), and the dissolute, eerily modern boy-emperor, Heliogabalus (AD 203–22).

Unlike the Greeks, whose portraits are idealized and usually beautiful, the Romans belonged to the "warts and all" school of representation. Many of the busts that have come down to us, notably that of Commodus (AD 161–92), the emperor-gladiator (found in a gallery on the upper level of the museum), are nearly savage in the relentlessness of their portrayals. As you leave the museum, be sure to stop in the courtyard. To the right is the original equestrian statue of Marcus Aurelius, restored and safely kept behind glass. At the center of the courtyard is the gigantic, reclining figure of Oceanus, found in the Roman Forum and later dubbed *Marforio*, one of Rome's famous "talking statues" to which citizens from the 1500s up to the 20th century affixed anonymous notes of political protest and satirical verses (a talking statue is still in use near Piazza Navona, at Piazza Pasquino).

The **Palazzo dei Conservatori** is a trove of ancient and Baroque treasures. Lining the courtyard are the colossal fragments of a head, leg, foot, and hand—all that remains of the famous statue of the emperor Constantine the Great, who believed that Rome's future lay with Christianity. These immense effigies were much in vogue in the later days of the Roman Empire. The resplendent Salone dei Orazie Curiazi (Salon of Horatii and Curatii) on the first floor is a ceremonial hall with a magnificent gilt ceiling, carved wooden doors, and 16th-century frescoes. At either end of the hall reign statues of the Baroque era's most charismatic popes, a marble Urban VIII (1568–1644) by Bernini (1598–1680) and a bronze likeness of Innocent X (1574–1655) by Bernini's rival Algardi (1595–1654). The renowned symbol of Rome, the *Capitoline Wolf,* a 6th-century-BC Etruscan bronze, holds a place of honor in the museum; the suckling twins were added during the Renaissance to adapt the statue to the legend of Romulus and Remus. Recently reopened after restorations, the museum's Pinacoteca, or painting gallery, holds some of Baroque painting's great masterpieces, including Caravaggio's *La Buona Ventura* (1595) and *San Giovanni Battista* (1602), Peter Paul Rubens's (1577–1640) *Romulus and Remus* (1614), and Pietro da Cortona's (1627) sumptuous portrait of Pope Urban VIII. Admission to the Pinacoteca is included in your ticket. ✉ *Piazza del Campidoglio,* ☎ *06/39967700.* 🎫 *12,000 lire/€6.20, free last Sun. of month.* ⊙ *Tues.–Fri. and Sun. 9:30–7:30, Sat. 9:30 AM–11 PM.*

❼ Palatine Hill. A lane known as the Clivus Palatinus, whose worn paving stones were once trod by emperors and their slaves, climbs from the Forum area to a site that historians identify with Rome's earliest settlement. About a century ago, illustrious archaeologist Rodolfo Lanciani excavated a site on the Palatine Hill and found evidence testifying to Romulus's historical presence, thereby contradicting early critics who deemed Romulus to a mythical figure. The story goes that the twins

Romulus and Remus were abandoned as infants but were nursed by a she-wolf on the banks of the Tiber and adopted by a shepherd. Encouraged by the gods to build a city, the twins chose a site in 735 BC, fortifying it with a wall that Lanciani identified by digging on the Palatine Hill. During the building of the city, the brothers quarreled, and in a fit of anger Romulus killed Remus.

Despite its location overlooking the Forum with its traffic, congestion, and attendant noise, the Palatine Hill was the most coveted address for ancient Rome's rich and famous. More than a few of the 12 Caesars called the Palatine Hill home—including Caligula, who met his premature end in the Cryptoporticus tunnel, which today still stands and remains unnerving. The palace of Tiberius was the first to be built here; others followed, most notably the gigantic extravaganza constructed for Emperor Domitian. Views from the ruins of the imperial palaces extend over the Circus Maximus. Today the Palatine is one of the most tranquil places in town, its Renaissance gardens a welcome respite, especially on a hot day. The Palatine Antiquarium holds relics found during excavations on the hill. ⊠ *Entrances at the Arch of Titus in the Roman Forum and Via S. Gregorio 30,* ☎ *06/39967700.* 🎫 *12,000 lire/€6.20.* 🕙 *Mon.–Sat. 9–2 hrs before sunset, Sun. 9–2.*

★ ❻ **Roman Forum** (Foro Romano). Built in what was once a marshy valley between the Capitoline and Palatine hills, the Forum was the civic heart of Republican Rome, the austere enclave that preceded the hedonistic society that grew up under the emperors in the 1st to 4th centuries AD. The area once was filled with stately and magnificent buildings—temples, palaces, shops—and crowded with people from all corners of the world. Today this series of ruins and marble fragments interspersed with crumbling columns is impressive, but it's not easy to envision the grandeur that once was. It may help to bear in mind that what you see today are the ruins not of one period but of almost 900 years, from about 500 BC to AD 400. Rome's timeless landscape is suggestive enough that you will probably be content to wander, letting your imagination dwell on Cicero (106–43 BC), Julius Caesar (100–44 BC), and Mark Antony (circa 81–30 BC), who delivered the funeral address in Caesar's honor from the rostrum just left of the **Arco di Settimio Severo** (Arch of Septimius Severus).

This arch, one of the grandest of all antiquity, was built in AD 203 to celebrate the victory of the emperor Severus (AD 146–211) over the Parthians, and was topped by a bronze equestrian statuary group with six horses. Most visitors also explore the reconstruction of the large brick senate hall, the **Curia**; the three Corinthian columns (a favorite of 19th-century poets), all that remains of the **Tempio di Vespasiano** (Temple of Vespasian); the circular **Tempio di Vesta** (Temple of Vesta), where the highly privileged vestal virgins kept the sacred flame alive; and the **Arco di Tito** (Arch of Titus), which stands in a slightly elevated position on a spur of the Palatine Hill. The view of the Colosseum from the arch is superb and reminds us that it was the Emperor Titus (AD 39–81) who helped finish the vast amphitheater begun by his father, Vespasian. Now cleaned and restored, the arch was erected in AD 81 to celebrate the sack of Jerusalem 10 years earlier, after the great Jewish revolt. A famous relief shows the captured contents of Herod's Temple—including its huge seven-branched menorah—being carried in triumph down Rome's Via Sacra. Audio guides are available at the bookshop–ticket office at the Via dei Fori Imperiali entrance. ⊠ *Entrances at Via dei Fori Imperiali and Piazza del Colosseo,* ☎ *06/69905110.* 🎫 *Free.* 🕙 *Daily 9–2 hrs before sunset.*

❸ **Santa Maria d'Aracoeli.** This stark redbrick church was one of the first Christian churches in Rome. Legend recounts that it was on this spot that the Sibyl predicted to Augustus the coming of a redeemer. The emperor responded by erecting the Ara Coeli, the Altar of Heaven. The church is best known for its seemingly endless, steep stairs climbing from Piazza Venezia and for the 15th-century frescoes by Pinturicchio (1454–1513) in the first chapel on the right. ⊠ *Piazza d'Aracoeli.* ☉ *Oct.–May, daily 7–noon and 4–6; June–Sept., daily 7–noon and 4–6:30.*

The Vatican: Rome of the Popes

This tiny walled city-state, capital of the Catholic world, draws millions of visitors every year to its wealth of treasures and spiritual monuments. You might go to the Vatican for its exceptional art holdings—Michelangelo's frescoes, rare archaeological marbles, or Bernini's statues—or to immerse yourself in the unique and grandiose architecture of St. Peter's square. Or you may go in pilgrimage, spiritual or otherwise, to the most overwhelming architectural achievement of the Renaissance and the seat of world Catholicism, St. Peter's Basilica. In between the sacred and the profane lie sights for every taste and inclination: magnificent rooms decorated by Raphael, sculptures like the *Apollo Belvedere* and the *Laocoön,* frescoes by Fra Angelico, paintings by Giotto and Leonardo, and the celebrated ceiling of the Sistine Chapel. The power that emerged as the Rome of the emperors declined— the Church—gave impetus to a profusion of artistic expression and shaped the destiny of the city for a thousand years. Note that there is a strict dress code for all interior Vatican sights.

A Good Walk

Start your walk at the **Castel Sant'Angelo** ⑪, the fortress that once served as the pope's refuge, and take in the stage-set beauty of the Ponte Sant'Angelo before turning right onto Via della Conciliazione (or taking the more picturesque route west along Borgo Pio) to the Vatican. Once inside **Piazza San Pietro** ⑫, rich architectural detail awaits at **St. Peter's Basilica** ⑬, the grand and magnificent seat of the Catholic Church. Below the basilica, visit the Vatican Grottoes, the last repose of many of the popes, and, if you have time, arrange a tour of the excavations below the church and the Vatican Gardens.

TIMING

Allow an hour for a visit to Castel Sant'Angelo. You'll also need an hour to see St. Peter's, plus 30 minutes for the Museo Storico, 15 minutes for the Vatican Grottoes, and an hour to climb to the top of the dome. Note that free one-hour English-language tours of the basilica are offered Monday–Saturday at 10 and 3, Sunday at 2:30 (sign up at the little desk under the portico).

Sights to See

⟲ ⑪ **Castel Sant'Angelo.** For hundreds of years, this fortress guarded the Vatican, to which it is linked by the Passetto, an arcaded passageway. According to legend, Castel Sant'Angelo got its name during the plague of 590, when Pope Gregory the Great (circa 540–604), passing by in a religious procession, had a vision of an angel sheathing its sword atop the stone ramparts. Though it may look like a stronghold, Castel Sant'Angelo was in fact built as a tomb for the emperor Hadrian (76–138) in AD 135. By the 6th century, it had been transformed into a fortress, and it remained a refuge for the popes for almost 1,000 years. It has dungeons, battlements, cannons and cannonballs, and a collection of antique weaponry and armor.

The upper terrace, below the massive angel statue commemorating Gregory's vision, evokes memories of Tosca, Puccini's poignant heroine in the opera of the same name, who threw herself off these ramparts with the cry, "*Scarpia, avanti a Dio!*" (Scarpia, we meet before God). One of Rome's most beautiful bridges, **Ponte Sant'Angelo** spans the Tiber in front of the fortress and is studded with graceful angels designed by Bernini.

The lower levels formed the base of Hadrian's mausoleum; ancient ramps and narrow staircases climb through the castle's core to courtyards and frescoed halls and rooms holding a collection of antique arms and armor. Off the loggia is a café. ⊠ *Lungotevere Castello 50,* ☎ *06/6819111,* WEB *www.vatican.va.* 🎟 *10,000 lire/€5.15.* ☉ *Tues.–Sun. 9–8.*

Papal Audience. The pope holds audiences in a large, modern audience hall (or in St. Peter's Square in summer) on Wednesday morning at 10. You must apply for tickets in advance; there are several sources, but if you are pressed for time it may be easier to arrange for them through a travel agency. You can avoid the formalities by seeing the pope when he makes his weekly appearance at the window of the Palazzo Vaticano on Sunday at noon when he is in Rome to bless the crowd. On summer Sundays he may give the blessing at his summer residence at Castel Gandolfo. For audience tickets, apply in writing at least 10 days in advance to the **Papal Prefecture** (Prefettura della Casa Pontificia, ⊠ 00120 Vatican City, ☎ 06/69883273, FAX 06/69885863), indicating the date you prefer, the language you speak, and the hotel where you will be staying. Or go to the prefecture, through the Porta di Bronzo, the bronze door at the end of the colonnade on the right side of the piazza; the office is open Monday–Saturday 9–1, and last-minute tickets may be available. You can also arrange to pick up free tickets on Tuesday afternoon at the office of **Santa Susanna American Church** (⊠ Via XX Settembre 15, ☎ 06/42014554); call first. For a fee, travel agencies make arrangements that include transportation.

⑫ **Piazza San Pietro** (St. Peter's Square). As you enter the square you are entering Vatican territory. This square (actually an oval) is one of Bernini's most spectacular masterpieces. Completed in 1667 after 11 years' work—a relatively short time in those days, considering the vastness of the task—the square can hold 400,000 people. It is surrounded by a curving pair of quadruple colonnades, which are topped by a balustrade and statues of 140 saints. Look for the two disks set into the pavement on either side of the obelisk. If you stand on one disk, a trick of perspective makes the colonnades seem to consist of a single row of columns. Bernini had an even grander visual effect in mind when he designed the square. By opening up this immense, airy, and luminous space in a neighborhood of narrow, shadowy streets, he created a contrast that would surprise and impress anyone who emerged from the darkness into the light, in a characteristically Baroque metaphor. But in the 1930s, Mussolini ruined it all. To celebrate the "conciliation" between the Vatican and the Italian government under the Lateran Pact of 1929, he conceived of the Via della Conciliazione, the broad, rather soulless avenue that now forms the main approach to St. Peter's and gives the eye time to adjust to the enormous dimensions of the square and church, nullifying Bernini's grand Baroque effect.

★ ⑬ **St. Peter's Basilica** (Basilica di San Pietro). The physical statistics of Rome's sublime sanctuary are staggering: it covers about 18,100 square yards, extends 212 yards in length, and carries a dome that rises 435 ft and measures 138 ft across its base. Its history is equally impressive: no fewer than five of Italy's greatest artists—Donato Bramante (1444–1514), Raphael (1483–1520), Baldassare Peruzzi (1481–1536), Antonio Sangallo the Younger (1483–1546), and Michelangelo (1475–1564)—died while working on the construction of this new St. Peter's. The history of the original St. Peter's goes back to the year AD 319, when the emperor Constantine built a basilica over the site of the tomb of St. Peter (died AD 64). This early church stood for more than 1,000 years, undergoing a number of restorations, until it was on the verge of collapse. Reconstruction began in 1452 but was abandoned for lack of funds. In 1506 Pope Julius II (1443–1513) instructed the architect Bramante to raze the existing structure and build a new and greater basilica. In 1546 Pope Paul III persuaded the aging Michelangelo to take on the job of completing the building. Returning to Bramante's ground plan, Michelangelo designed the dome to cover the crossing, but his plans, too, were modified after his death. The cupola, one of the most beautiful in the world, was completed by Giacomo della Porta (circa 1537–1602) and Fontana. The new church wasn't completed and dedicated until 1626—by that time the ground plan had shifted from a Greek cross to a Latin one, creating a longer nave but obscuring the view of the dome from the piazza. Under the portico, Filarete's 15th-century bronze doors, salvaged from the old basilica, fill the central portal. Off the entry portico, Bernini's famous *Scala Regia,* the ceremonial entryway to the Vatican Palace and one of the most magnificent staircases in the world, is graced with Bernini's dramatic statue of Constantine the Great.

The cherubs over the holy-water fonts will give you an idea of just how huge St. Peter's is: the sole of the cherub's foot is as long as the distance from your fingers to your elbow. It is because the proportions of this giant building are in such perfect harmony that its vastness may escape you at first. But in its megascale—inspired by the spatial volumes of ancient Roman ruins—it reflects Roman *grandiosità* in all its majesty.

Over an altar in a side chapel near the entrance is Michelangelo's **Pietà.** Legend has it that the artist, only 22 at the time the then-unsigned work was completed, overheard passersby expressing scepticism that such a young man could have executed such a sophisticated and moving piece. Offended at the implication, he crept back that night and signed the piece—in big letters, right on Mary's sleeve, where no one could possibly miss it. His name is there today.

Four massive piers support the dome at the crossing, where the mighty Bernini **baldacchino** (canopy) rises high above the papal altar. "What the barbarians didn't do, the Barberini did," 17th-century wags quipped when Barberini Pope Urban VIII had the bronze stripped from the Pantheon's portico and melted down to make the baldacchino (using what was left over for cannonballs). The pope celebrates mass here, over the grottoes holding the tombs of many of his predecessors. Deep in the excavations under the foundations of the original basilica is what is believed to be the tomb of St. Peter. The bronze throne above the main altar in the apse, the Cathedra Petri (Chair of St. Peter), is Bernini's work (1656), and it covers a wooden and ivory chair that St. Peter himself is said to have used. However, scholars tell us that this throne probably dates only from the Middle Ages. See how the adoration of a million lips has completely worn down the bronze on the right foot of the statue of St. Peter in front of the near right pillar in the transept. Note: ushers at the entrance of St. Peter's Church and the Vatican Museums will not allow entry to persons with inappropriate clothing (no bare knees or shoulders). ☉ *Apr.–Sept., daily 7–7; Oct.–Mar., daily 7–6. Closed during ceremonies in the piazza.* WEB *www.vatican.va*

The entrance to the **Vatican Grottoes** (Grotte Vaticane), which hold the tombs of many popes, is at the crossing. The only exit from the grottoes leads outside St. Peter's, to the courtyard that holds the entrance to the roof and dome. ☉ *Apr.–Sept., daily 7–6; Oct.–Mar., daily 7–5.*

A small but rich collection of Vatican treasures is housed in the **Museo Storico** (Historical Museum) in the Sacristy, among them precious antique chalices and the massive 15th-century sculptured bronze tomb of Pope Sixtus V (1520–90) by Antonio del Pollaiuolo (1431–98). ⊠ *8,000 lire/€4.05.* ⊙ *Apr.–Sept., daily 9–6; Oct.–Mar., daily 9–5.*

The roof of the church, reached by elevator or stairs, is a landscape of domes and towers. A short interior staircase leads to the base of the dome for a dove's-eye view of the interior of St. Peter's. Then, only if you are stout of heart and sound of lung should you attempt the very taxing and claustrophobic climb up the narrow stairs—there's no turning back!—to the balcony of the lantern, where the view embraces the Vatican Gardens and all of Rome. ☎ *06/69883462,* ⊠ *Elevator 6,000 lire/€3.05, stairs 5,000 lire/€2.50.* ⊙ *Apr.–Sept., daily 7–7; Oct.–Mar., daily 7–6. Closed during ceremonies in the piazza.*

OFF THE BEATEN PATH	**VATICAN NECROPOLIS –** Visit the pre-Constantine necropolis under St. Peter's for a fascinating glimpse of the underpinnings of the great basilica, which was built over the cemetery where archaeologists believe they have found St. Peter's tomb. Apply in advance by sending a fax with the name of each visitor, language spoken, possible days for the visit, and a local phone number. Reservations will be confirmed a few days in advance. No children under 15 are admitted. Tickets are sometimes available for same-day tours; apply in person at the Ufficio Scavi (Excavations Office), on the right beyond the Arco delle Campane (Arch of the Bells) entrance to the Vatican, which is left of the basilica. Tell the Swiss Guard you want the Ufficio Scavi, and he will let you by. ☎ *06/ 69885318,* FAX *06/69885518,* WEB *www.vatican.va.* ⊠ *15,000 lire/€7.75.* ⊙ *Ufficio Scavi Mon.–Sat. 9–5.*

Vatican Gardens (Giardini Vaticani). A tour offers a two-hour jaunt through the pope's backyard, half by bus and half on foot, with a guide. Tickets are available at the **Vatican Information Office** (⊠ Piazza San Pietro, ☎ 06/69884466), open Monday–Saturday 8:30–7. Make reservations two or three days in advance. WEB *www.vatican.va* ⊠ *20,000 lire/€10.30.* ⊙ *Apr.–Oct., Mon.–Tues. and Thurs.–Sat. at 10; Nov.–Mar., Sat. at 10, weekdays by request for groups.*

Vatican Museums: Beyond the Sistine Ceiling

The Vatican Palace has been the papal residence since 1377. Actually, it represents a collection of buildings that cover more than 13 acres, containing an estimated (no one has bothered to count them) 1,400 rooms, chapels, and galleries. Other than the pope and his court, the occupants are some of art's greatest masterpieces. The main entrance to the museums, on Viale Vaticano, is a long walk from Piazza San Pietro. Some city buses stop near the museums' main entrance on Viale Vaticano: Bus 49 from Piazza Cavour stops right in front; Buses 81 and 492 and Tram 19 stop at Piazza Risorgimento, halfway between St. Peter's and the museums. The Ottaviano–S. Pietro stop on metro A also is in the vicinity.

A Good Tour

There are many sections of the **Vatican Museums** ⑭ besides the Sistine Chapel that are not to be overlooked: the Museo Egiziano; the Chiaramonti and Museo Pio Clementino, which are given over to classical sculptures (among them some of the best-known statues in the world—the *Laocoön*, the *Belvedere Torso*, and the *Apollo Belvedere*—which with their vibrant humanism had a tremendous impact on Renaissance art); and the Museo Etrusco. Finally, you should make sure to visit the Stanze di Raffaello and see Raphael's paintings in the Pinacoteca.

TIMING

Plan on about an hour if you just want to see highlights; an in-depth visit will take at least a full morning. To minimize time spent in line, it is usually a good idea to get here just before opening time.

Sights to See

★ ⑭ **Vatican Museums** (Musei Vaticani). The immense collections housed here are so rich that unless you are an art history buff, you will probably just want to skim the surface, concentrating on pieces that strike your fancy. The Sistine Chapel is a must, of course, and that's why you may have to wait in line to see it; after all, every tourist in Rome has the same idea. Pick up a leaflet at the main entrance to the museums to see the overall layout. The Sistine Chapel is at the far end of the complex, and the leaflet charts two abbreviated itineraries through other collections to reach it. You can rent a taped commentary (6,000 lire/€3.05, about 90 minutes) in English for the Sistine Chapel, the Stanze di Raffaello, and the other main attractions.

The **Stanze di Raffaello** (Raphael Rooms) are second only to the Sistine Chapel in artistic interest. In 1508, Pope Julius II employed Raphael, on the recommendation of Bramante, to decorate the rooms with biblical scenes. The result was a Renaissance tour de force. Of the four rooms, the second and third were decorated mainly by Raphael. The others were decorated by Giulio Romano (circa 1499–1546) and other assistants of Raphael; the first room is known as the Stanza dell'Incendio, with frescoes of the fire (*incendio*) in the Borgo by Romano.

The frescoed **Stanza della Segnatura** (Room of the Signature), where papal bulls were signed, is one of Raphael's finest works; indeed, they are thought by many to be some of the finest paintings in the history of Western art. This was Julius's private library, and the room's use is reflected in the frescoes' themes, philosophy, and enlightenment. A paradigm of High Renaissance painting, the works here demonstrate the revolutionary ideals of the time: naturalism (Raphael's figures lack the awkwardness of those painted only a few years earlier); humanism (the idea that man is the noblest and most admirable of God's creations); and a profound interest in the ancient world, the result of the 15th-century rediscovery of classical antiquity. Theology triumphs in the fresco known as the *Disputa,* or *Debate on the Holy Sacrament.* The *School of Athens* glorifies some of philosophy's greats, including Plato and Aristotle at the fresco's center. The pensive figure on the stairs is sometimes thought to be modeled after Michelangelo, who was painting the Sistine Ceiling at the same time Raphael was working here.

The tiny **Cappella di Nicholas V** (Chapel of Nicholas V) is aglow with frescoes by Fra Angelico (1387–1455), the Florentine monk whose sensitive paintings were guiding lights for the Renaissance. The **Appartamento Borgia** (Borgia Apartment) is worth seeing for the elaborately painted ceilings, designed and partially executed by Pinturicchio, but the rooms have been given over to the Vatican's large, but not particularly impressive, collection of modern religious art.

In 1508, while Raphael was put to work on his series of rooms, the redoubtable Pope Julius II commissioned Michelangelo to paint single-handedly the more than 10,000-square-ft ceiling of the **Sistine Chapel** (Cappella Sistina). The task cost the artist four years of mental and physical anguish. It's said that for years afterward Michelangelo couldn't read anything without holding it up over his head. The result, however, was the masterpiece that you now see, its colors cool and brilliant after restoration. Bring a pair of binoculars to get a better look at this incredible work (unfortunately, you're not allowed to lie down on the floor to study the frescoes above, the viewing position of choice in decades past; by the time you leave the chapel, your neck may feel like Michelangelo's, so you may also want to study it—to take a cue from 19th-century visitors—with the aid of a pocket mirror).

The ceiling is in essence a painted Bible: Michelangelo's subject was the story of humanity before the coming of Christ, seen through Augustinian tenets of faith popular in early 16th-century theological circles. While some of the frescoed panels are veritable stews of figures, others—especially the depiction of God's outstretched hand giving Adam the spark of life in the *Creation of Adam*—are forcefully simple, revealing how much Michelangelo brought to painting from the discipline of sculpture. In 1541, some 30 years after completing the ceiling, Michelangelo was commissioned to paint the *Last Judgment* on the chapel's altar wall. If the artist's ceiling may be taken as an expression of the optimism of the High Renaissance, the *Last Judgment*, by contrast, is a virtual guided tour through hell. This is not surprising, since in the intervening years Rome had been sacked and pillaged by the French, who had used the Sistine Chapel to stable their horses.

In only a few years, the grim Counter-Reformation began, and suddenly the nudity in Michelangelo's *Last Judgment* was so repugnant to the papal court that the artist Daniele da Volterra (1509–66)—forever after known as *il braghettone* (the breeches-maker)—was retained to paint loincloths over the offending parts. The aged and embittered Michelangelo painted his own face on the wrinkled human skin in the hand of St. Bartholomew, below and to the right of the figure of Christ, which he clearly modeled on the *Apollo Belvedere* (now on exhibit in the Vatican galleries). Like the ceiling, the *Last Judgment* has been cleaned; the restoration was unveiled in April 1994, surprising viewers with its clarity and color. Was Michelangelo truly a master of vibrant color? Or is the "new" Sistine a travesty of the artist's intentions? Opinions remain divided, but most art historians believe the restoration is true to Michelangelo's original vision.

The exhibition halls of the **Biblioteca Vaticana** (Vatican Library) are bright with frescoes and contain a sampling of the library's rich collections of precious manuscripts. Room X, the Room of the Aldobrandini Marriage, holds a beautiful Roman fresco of a nuptial rite. More classical statues are on view in the new wing. At the Quattro Cancelli, a cafeteria offers a well-earned break. The **Pinacoteca** (Picture Gallery) displays mainly religious paintings by such artists as Giotto (circa 1266–1337), Fra Angelico, and Filippo Lippi (circa 1406–69), and Raphael's exceptional *Transfiguration, Coronation,* and *Foligno Madonna.*

In the **Museo Profano** (Pagan Antiquities Museum), modern display techniques enhance another collection of Greek and Roman sculptures. The **Museo Pio Cristiano** (Christian Antiquities Museum) has early Christian and medieval art (its most famous piece is the 3rd-century-AD statue the *Good Shepherd*). The **Museo Missionario-Etnologico** (Ethnological Museum) exhibits art and artifacts from exotic places throughout the world; it's open Wednesday and Saturday only. The complete itinerary ends with the **Museo della Storia** (Historical Museum), whose collection of carriages, uniforms, and arms can be opened by a custodian on request. In all, the Vatican Museums offer a staggering foray into the realms of art and history; it's foolhardy to try to see all the collections in one day. ⊠ *Viale Vaticano,* ☎ *06/69883041,* WEB *www.vatican.va.* 🎫 *18,000 lire/€9.30, free last Sun. of month.* ☉ *Easter wk and mid-Mar.–Oct., weekdays 8:45–3:45, Sat. 8:45–12:45; Nov.–mid-Mar. (except Easter), Mon.–Sat. 8:45–12:45; last Sun. of every month*

8:45–12:45. *Note: Ushers at the entrance of St. Peter's Church and the Vatican Museums will not allow entry to persons with inappropriate clothing (no bare knees or shoulders).*

Neighborhood trattorias that are far better and far less popular with tourists than those opposite the Vatican Museums entrance include the **Hostaria Dino e Toni** (⊠ Via Leone IV 60), where you can dine on typical Roman fare at moderate, even inexpensive prices. **La Caravella** (⊠ Via degli Scipioni 32, at Via Vespasiano, off Piazza Risorgimento) serves Roman specialties, including pizza during lunch, every day but Thursday, when it's closed.

Old Rome: Gold and Grandeur

The neighborhood between the Corso and the Tiber bend is one of Rome's most beautiful districts, filled with narrow streets with curious names, airy Baroque piazzas, and picturesque courtyards. It has been an integral part of the city since ancient times, and its position between the Vatican and the Lateran palaces, both seats of papal rule, put it in the mainstream of Rome's development from the Middle Ages onward. It includes such world-famous sights as the Pantheon, but it is mainly an excursion into the 16th and 17th centuries, when Baroque art triumphed. Some of Rome's most coveted residential addresses are here.

The most important clue to the Romans is their Baroque art—not its artistic technicalities but its spirit. When you understand this, you will no longer be a stranger in Rome. Flagrantly emotional, heavily expressive, and sensuously visual, the 17th-century artistic movement known as the Baroque was born in Rome, the creation of three geniuses, the sculptor and architect Gianlorenzo Bernini and the painters Annibale Carracci (1560–1609) and Caravaggio (1573–1610). From the austere drama found in Caravaggio's paintings to the jewel-laden, gold-on-gold detail of 17th-century Roman palaces, Baroque style was intended both to shock and delight by upsetting the placid, "correct" rules of the Renaissance. By appealing to the emotions, it became a powerful weapon in the hands of the Counter-Reformation.

Numbers in the text correspond to numbers in the margin and on the Old Rome map.

A Good Walk

Start on Via del Plebiscito, near Piazza Venezia, at the huge church of **Il Gesù** ⑮, the grandmother of all Baroque churches. Walk north to Piazza della Minerva, where in the church of **Santa Maria sopra Minerva** ⑯ you will find the tomb of Fra Angelico. Turn down Via della Minerva to reach the **Pantheon** ⑰. From Piazza della Rotonda, in front of the Pantheon, take Via Giustiniani onto Via della Dogana Vecchia to the church of **San Luigi dei Francesi** ⑱, a pilgrimage spot for art lovers everywhere. Just north is the church of **Sant'Agostino** ⑲, in the piazza of the same name. Visit historic **Palazzo Altemps** ⑳, off Piazza Sant'Apollinare, before arriving at **Piazza Navona** ㉑, one of Rome's showpiece piazzas, home to Bernini's Fontana dei Quattro Fiumi and the church of Sant'Agnese in Agone, the quintessence of Baroque architecture. Take Via Tor Millina west to Via della Pace and follow it north to Piazza della Pace, where a semicircular portico stands in front of the 15th-century church **Santa Maria della Pace** ㉒. Explore the byways on the north side of Corso Vittorio Emanuele II before crossing over one of Rome's great thoroughfares and take a side street south to aristocratic Via Giulia. Continue south to the **Palazzo Falconieri** ㉓ and the

Palazzo Farnese ㉔, perhaps the most beautiful Renaissance palace in Rome. On your way back to Corso Vittorio Emanuele II along Via Farnese, go through **Campo dei Fiori** ㉕ before coming to the **Museo Baracco** ㉖. Across the way, note one of the outstanding architectural monuments of Renaissance Rome, the **Palazzo Massimo alle Colonne** ㉗, and, two blocks east along the bustling street, the huge, 17th-century church of **Sant'Andrea della Valle** ㉘. Finally, head down Corso del Rinascimento to No. 40, the church of **Sant'Ivo alla Sapienza** ㉙, with a golden lantern atop the dome in the shape of a spiral.

TIMING

Allow about three hours for this walk.

Sights to See

★ ㉕ **Campo dei Fiori.** This bustling square is home to a famed morning market, a must-see dose of local culture for any Roman holiday. Each morning, vendors fill temporary stalls with all manner of local produce, nuts, cheese, spices, flowers, and seafood; by early afternoon, it's all gone, to resurface in the city's homes and restaurants at dinnertime. If you don't want to join the fray, step back and take a break at one of the many pleasant cafés that edge the market. The view has certainly improved since the Middle Ages, when the square was the scene of public executions, including that of philosopher-monk Giordano Bruno (1548–1600). His statue still broods in the center of the square.

NEED A BREAK?

Some of Rome's best pizza comes out of the ovens of the **Antico Forno** (☎ 06/68806662) on Campo dei Fiori. Choose between pizza *bianca* (topped with olive oil) or *rossa* (with tomato sauce), or any of a half dozen baked goodies on hand. The benches at the foot of Palazzo Farnese in the adjacent piazza make a good place to enjoy your snack.

⑮ **Il Gesù.** Grandmother of all Baroque churches, this huge structure was designed by Giacomo da Vignola (1507–73) to be the tangible symbol of Jesuits, a major force in the Counter-Reformation in Europe. It remained unadorned for about 100 years, but when it finally was decorated, no expense was spared. Its interior drips with gold and lapis lazuli, gold and precious marbles, gold and more gold—all covered by a fantastically painted ceiling by Baciccia (1639–1709) that seems to swirl down to merge with the painted stucco figures at its base. ⊠ *Piazza del Gesù,* ☎ 06/697001. ⊘ *Daily 7–noon and 4–7.*

㉖ **Museo Baracco.** Located in a Renaissance town house around the corner from Campo dei Fiori, the collection here is meant to trace the development of sculpture throughout the ancient Mediterranean. There's the usual complement of Roman and Etruscan works, contrasted with ancient Egyptian, Sumerian, Assyrian, Cypriot, and Greek pieces dating back to the 5th century BC. ⊠ *Corso Vittorio Emanuele II 166,* ☎ *06/68806848.* ▨ *5,000 lire/€2.60.* ⊘ *Tues.–Sat. 9–7, Sun. 9–1.*

⑳ **Palazzo Altemps.** If you're interested in ancient sculpture, you should not miss one of Rome's greatest collections of classical antiquities, housed in this 16th-century building. Opened in 1997, it displays the collections of ancient Roman and Egyptian sculpture of the **Museo Nazionale Romano.** Look for two works in the famed Ludovisi collection: the large, intricately sculptured *Ludovisi Sarcophagus,* and *Galata,* a poignant work portraying a barbarian warrior who chooses death for himself and his wife rather than humiliation by the enemy. The palace's stunning courtyard and gorgeously frescoed ceilings and loggia make an impressive setting for the sculptures. ⊠ *Piazza Sant'Apollinare 46,* ☎ *06/6833566.* ▨ *10,000 lire/€5.15.* ⊘ *Tues.–Sun. 9–7:45.*

National
Museo
Romano

Parked
Car

PIAZZA DI
S. APOLLINARE

Old Rome

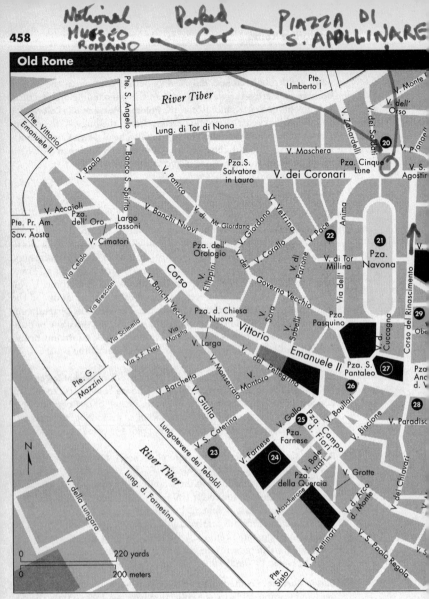

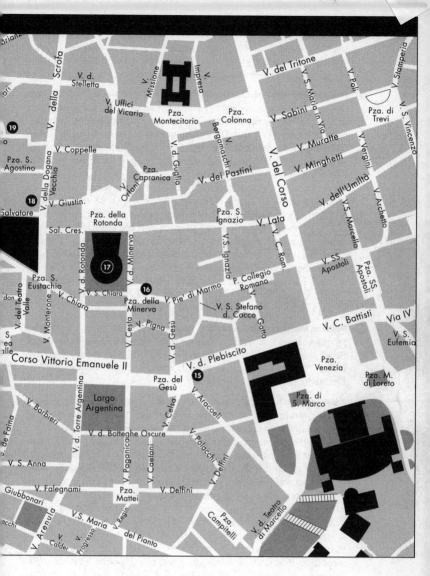

㉓ Palazzo Falconieri. Francesco Borromini's (1599–1667) masterful work of architecture houses nothing of interest to the visitor, but the building itself is one of Rome's most elegant attractions. In order to get a good look at this gracefully imposing building, go around the block and view the palace from along the Tiber embankment. ⊠ *Via Giulia 1.*

㉔ Palazzo Farnese. Michelangelo had a hand in building what is now the French Embassy and perhaps the most beautiful Renaissance palace in Rome. Within is the **Galleria Carracci** vault painted by Annibale Carracci between 1597 and 1604—the second-greatest ceiling in Rome. It depicts the loves of the gods, a supremely pagan theme that the artist painted in a swirling style that announced the birth of Baroque. It's said that Carracci was so dismayed at the miserly fee he received—the Farnese family was extravagantly rich even by the standards of 15th- and 16th-century Rome's extravagantly rich—that he took to drink and died shortly thereafter. Those who sympathize with the poor man's plight will be further dismayed to learn that the French government pays 1 lira every 99 years as rent for its sumptuous embassy. For special permission to view it, write in advance to the embassy, specifying the number in your party, when you wish to visit, and a local phone number, for confirmation a few days before the visit. ⊠ *Servizio Culturale, French Embassy, Piazza Farnese 67, 00186 Rome,* ☎ *06/686011.* ▭ *Free.* ◷ *By appointment only.*

㉗ Palazzo Massimo alle Colonne. A graceful columned portico marks this inconspicuous but seminal architectural monument of Renaissance Rome, built by Baldassare Peruzzi in 1527. Via del Paradiso, across Corso Vittorio Emanuele II, affords a better view. ⊠ *Corso Vittorio Emanuele II 141.*

★ **⑰ Pantheon.** Paradoxically, one of Rome's most perfect and best-preserved ancient monuments is perhaps its least appreciated. The emperor Hadrian designed the Pantheon himself in around AD 120 and had it built on the site of an earlier temple that had been destroyed by fire. The most striking thing about the Pantheon is not its size, immense though it is (until 1960 the dome was the largest ever built); rather, it is the remarkable harmony of the building. Notice that the height of the dome is equal to the diameter of the circular interior. The oculus, or opening in the ceiling, is meant to symbolize the all-seeing eye of heaven; in practice, it illuminates the building and lightens the heavy stone ceiling. Note the original bronze doors, which have survived more than 1,800 years, centuries more than the interior's rich gold ornamentation, long since plundered by popes and emperors. ⊠ *Piazza della Rotonda,* ☎ *06/68300230.* ◷ *Mon.–Sat. 9–6:30, Sun. 9–1.*

★ ◷ **㉑ Piazza Navona.** This famed 17th-century piazza, built over the site and following the form of the 1st-century Stadium of Domitian, is one of Rome's showpiece attractions. It still has the carefree air of the days when it was the scene of Roman circus games, medieval jousts, and 17th-century carnivals. Today, this renowned spot often attracts fashion photographers and Romans out for their evening *passeggiata* (promenade). The Christmas fair held in the piazza from early December through January 6 is lively and fun for children, with games and nativity scenes, and the Befana—the ugly but good witch who brings candy and toys to Italian children on the Epiphany. (Her name is a corruption of the Italian word *Epifania*.) Bernini's splashing **Fontana dei Quattro Fiumi** (Fountain of the Four Rivers), with an enormous rock squared off by statues representing the four corners of the world, makes a fitting centerpiece. Behind the fountain is the church of **Sant'Agnese in Agone,** an outstanding example of Baroque architecture built by the Pamphili Pope Innocent X and still owned by his descendants, the Doria Pamphili. The facade—a wonderfully rich mélange of bell towers, concave spaces, and dovetailed stone and marble—is by Carlo Rainaldi (1611–91) and Francesco Borromini (1599–1667), a contemporary and sometime rival of Bernini. One story has it that the Bernini statue nearest the church, which represents the River Plate, has its hand up before his eye because it can't bear the sight of the Borromini facade. Though often repeated, the story is a fiction: the facade wasn't built until after the fountain was installed.

NEED A
BREAK? **Tre Scalini** café (⊠ Piazza Navona 30), closed Wednesday, is the birth-place of the *tartufo*, a luscious chocolate-covered ice cream treat named after the truffles, or *tartufi*, it resembles.

🔞 **San Luigi dei Francesi.** The clergy of San Luigi considered Caravaggio's roistering and unruly lifestyle scandalous enough, but his realistic treatment of sacred subjects—seen in three paintings in the last chapel—was too much for them. They rejected outright his first version of the altarpiece, and they weren't especially happy with the other two works. Thanks to the intercession of Caravaggio's patron, the influential Cardinal Francesco del Monte, they were persuaded to keep them—a lucky thing, since they are now thought to be among the artist's finest paintings. Have a few 500-lire coins handy for the light machine. ⊠ *Piazza San Luigi dei Francesi,* ☎ 06/688271. ☾ *Fri.–Wed. 7:30–12:30 and 3:30–7, Thurs. 7:30–12:30.*

🔞 **Sant'Agostino.** Caravaggio's celebrated *Madonna of the Pilgrims*—which scandalized all Rome because it pictured pilgrims with dirt on the soles of their feet—can be found in this small church, over the first altar on the left. ⊠ *Piazza di Sant'Agostino,* ☎ 06/68801962. ☾ *Mon.–Sat. 7:45–noon and 4–7:30, Sun. 4–6.*

🔞 **Sant'Andrea della Valle.** This huge 17th-century church looms mightily over a busy intersection. Aficionados of Puccini, who set the first act of his opera *Tosca* here, have been known to hire a horse-drawn carriage at night for an evocative journey that traces the course of the opera (from Sant'Andrea up Via Giulia to Palazzo Farnese—Scarpia's headquarters—to the locale of the opera's climax, Castel Sant'Angelo). ⊠ *Corso Vittorio Emanuele II,* ☎ 06/6861339. ☾ *Daily 7–noon and 4–7:30.*

🔞 **Sant'Ivo alla Sapienza.** Borromini's eccentric church has what must surely be Rome's most unusual dome—topped by a golden spiral said to have been inspired by a bee's stinger. ⊠ *Corso Rinascimento 40.* ☾ *Sun. 10–noon.*

🔞 **Santa Maria della Pace.** Hidden away in a corner of Old Rome, gracing Piazza Santa Maria della Pace, are a semicircular portico and 15th-century church. In 1656, Pietro da Cortona (1596–1669) was commissioned by Pope Alexander VII (1599–1667) to enlarge its tiny piazza to accommodate the carriages of the church's wealthy parishioners. The result was one of Rome's most delightful little architectural stage sets, complete with bijou-size palaces. Within the church are two Renaissance treasures: Raphael's frescoes of the Sibyls (above the first altar on the right near the front door) and the cloister designed by Bramante, the very first expression of High Renaissance style in Rome. It's rarely open except for guided visits (call to make arrangements), but the cloister is used in the summer for concerts. ⊠ *Piazza Santa Maria della Pace,* ☎ 06/6861156.

🔞 **Santa Maria sopra Minerva.** In practically the only Gothic-style church in Rome, the attractions are Michelangelo's *Risen Christ* and the tomb of the gentle 15th-century artist Fra Angelico. Have some coins handy to light up the **Carafa Chapel** in the right transept, where exquisite 15th-century frescoes by Filippino Lippi (circa 1457–1504) are well worth the small investment. (Lippi's most famous student was Botticelli.) In front of the church, Bernini's charming elephant bearing an Egyptian obelisk has an inscription on the base stating something to the effect that it takes a strong mind to sustain solid wisdom. ⊠ *Piazza della Minerva,* ☎ *06/6793926.*

Via Giulia. Named after Pope Julius II and having functioned for more than four centuries as the "salon of Rome," this street is still the address of choice for Roman aristocrats. It is lined with elegant palaces, including the Palazzo Falconieri, and old churches (one, San Eligio, reputedly designed by Raphael himself). The area around Via Giulia is a wonderful place to wander in to get the feeling of daily life as carried on in a centuries-old setting—an experience enhanced by the dozens of antiques shops in the neighborhood.

Vistas and Views: From the Spanish Steps to the Trevi Fountain

Though it has a bustling commercial air, this part of the city also holds great visual allure, from the gaudy marble confection that is the monument to Vittorio Emanuele II to the theatrical Piazza di Sant'Ignazio. Among the things to look for are stately palaces, Baroque ballrooms, and the greatest example of portraiture in Rome, Velázquez's incomparable *Innocent X* at the Galleria Doria Pamphili. Those with a taste for the sumptuous theatricality of Roman ecclesiastical architecture—heroic illusionistic ceiling painting in particular—will find this a rewarding stop. The highlights are the Trevi Fountain and the Spanish Steps, 18th-century Rome's most famous example of city planning.

Numbers in the text correspond to numbers in the margin and on the Rome map.

A Good Walk

Start at the flamboyant **Monument to Vittorio Emanuele II** ㉚ in Piazza Venezia, a mass of marble studded with statuary that has the city's best view from its top. As you look up Via del Corso, to your left is **Palazzo Venezia** ㉛, an art-filled Renaissance palace from whose balcony Mussolini once addressed the crowds. On Saturday, you can visit the picture gallery, known as the Galleria Colonna, in the **Palazzo Colonna** ㉜, east of Piazza Venezia. From Piazza Venezia head north on Via del Corso, one of the city's busiest shopping streets, to the **Palazzo Doria Pamphili** ㉝, home to an important painting gallery. A quick detour west will bring you to the sumptuous 17th-century church of **Sant'Ignazio** ㉞. If you continue north on Via del Corso you will reach Piazza Colonna and the ancient **Column of Marcus Aurelius** ㉟. Continue north on Via del Corso and take a right onto chic Via Condotti, which gives you a head-on view of the **Spanish Steps** ㊱ and Piazza di Spagna; to the right of the steps, at No. 26, is the **Keats-Shelley Memorial House** ㊲, where the English Romantic poet Keats died. A great view across Rome's skyline awaits at the top of the Spanish Steps. From the narrow (southern) end of Piazza di Spagna, take Via Propaganda to Sant'Andrea delle Fratte, take a left onto Via del Nazareno, and then cross busy Via del Tritone to Via della Stamperia. This street leads to the **Trevi Fountain** ㊳, one of Rome's most famous landmarks.

TIMING

The walk takes approximately three hours.

Sights to See

③⑤ Column of Marcus Aurelius. This ancient column—like the one Trajan erected—is an extraordinary stone history book. Its detailed reliefs spiraling up to the top illustrate the victorious campaigns of emperor Marcus Aurelius (AD 121–80) against the barbarians. ⊠ *Piazza Colonna.*

③⑦ Keats-Shelley Memorial House. English Romantic poet John Keats (1795–1821) lived in what is now a museum dedicated to him and his great contemporary and friend Percy Bysshe Shelley (1792–1822). You can visit his tiny rooms, preserved as they were when he died here in 1821. ⊠ *Piazza di Spagna 26, next to the Spanish Steps,* ☏ *06/ 6784235,* WEB *www.Keats-Shelley-House.org.* 🎫 *5,000 lire/€2.52.* ☽ *Weekdays 9–1 and 3–6, Sat. 11–2 and 3–6.*

OFF THE
BEATEN PATH

CIMITERO PROTESTANTO – Behind the Piramide, a stone pyramid built in 12 BC at the order of the Roman *praetor* (senior magistrate) who was buried here, is a cemetery reminiscent of a country churchyard that was for non-Catholics. You'll find Keats's tomb and the place where Shelley's heart was buried. It's about a 20-minute walk south from the Arch of Constantine along Via San Gregorio and Viale Aventino. ⊠ *Via Caio Cestio 6,* ☏ *06/5741141 (ring bell for custodian).* 🎫 *Donation of 500–1,000 lire/€0.25–50.* ☽ *Tues.–Sun. 9–4.*

③⓪ Monument to Vittorio Emanuele II. The huge bronze sculpture group atop this vast marble monument is visible from many parts of the city, making this modern Rome's most flamboyant landmark. It was erected in the late 19th century to honor Italy's first king, Vittorio Emanuele II (1820–78), and the unification of Italy. Sometimes said to resemble a wedding cake or a typewriter in the Victorian style, it also houses the **Tomb of the Unknown Soldier** with its eternal flame. The "Vittoriano" reopened to the public in 2000 after 30 years; the views from the top are unforgettable. Opposite the monument, note the enclosed wooden veranda fronting the palace on the corner of Via del Plebiscito and Via Corso. For the many years that she lived in Rome, Napoléon's mother had a fine view from here of the local goings-on. ⊠ *Entrance at Piazza Ara Coeli, next to Piazza Venezia,* ☏ *06/6781848,* WEB *www.ambienterm.arti.beniculturali.it/vittoriano/index.html.* ☽ *Tues.– Sun. 10:30–1 hr before sunset.*

③② Palazzo Colonna. This fabulous private palace is opened to the public once a week. The entrance to the picture gallery, the **Galleria Colonna**, is a secondary one, behind a plain, obscure-seeming door. The old masters are lackluster, but the gallery should be on your must-see list because the **Sala Grande** is truly the grandest 17th-century room in Rome. More than 300 ft long, with bedazzling chandeliers, colored marble, and enormous paintings, it is best known today as the site where Audrey Hepburn met the press in *Roman Holiday.* ⊠ *Via della Pilotta 17,* ☏ *06/6794362,* WEB *web.tin.it/galleriacolonna.* 🎫 *10,000 lire/€5.15.* ☽ *Sept.–July, Sat. 9–1.*

③③ Palazzo Doria Pamphili. The 18th-century facade of this palazzo on Via del Corso is only a small part of a bona fide patrician palace, still the residence of a princely family that rents out many of the palazzo's 1,000 rooms. A few of those rooms are remarkably well preserved as the **Galleria Doria Pamphili**, a picture gallery that gives you a sense of the sumptuous surroundings of a Roman noble family and how art was once put on display: numbered paintings (the museum catalog, available from the book shop, comes in handy) are packed onto every available wall space. Pride of place is given to the famous (and pitiless) portrait of the 17th-century Pamphili pope Innocent X by Diego

Velázquez (1599–1660), but don't overlook Caravaggio's poignant *Rest on the Flight into Egypt*—and, time permitting, catch the guided tour of the state apartments, which gives a discreet glimpse of an aristocratic lifestyle. Pundits say most Roman palazzi consist of one bathroom, two bedrooms, and 40 ballrooms, and after this tour, you can understand why. ⊠ *Piazza del Collegio Romano 2,* ☎ *06/6797323,* WEB *www.doriapamphilj.it.* 🖼 *Galleria Doria Pamphili 13,000 lire/€6.70 (includes audio guide), private-apartments tours 6,000 lire/€3.05.* ☉ *Fri.–Wed. 10–5; private-apartments tours at 10:30, 11, 11:30, noon.*

③① **Palazzo Venezia.** A blend of medieval solidity and genuine Renaissance grace, this building houses a good collection of mostly early Renaissance paintings, sculptures, and objets d'art in its grand salons, some of which Mussolini (1883–1945) used as his offices. Notice the balcony over the main portal, from which Il Duce addressed huge crowds in **Piazza Venezia** below. ⊠ *Piazza San Marco 49,* ☎ *06/69994319.* 🖼 *8,000 lire/€4.15.* ☉ *Tues.–Sat. 9–2.*

③④ **Sant'Ignazio.** The false interior dome in this sumptuous 17th-century church is a trompe-l'oeil oddity among the lavishly frescoed domes of the Eternal City. To get the full effect of the illusionistic ceiling painted by Andrea del Pozzo (1642–1709), stand on the small disk set into the floor of the nave to view his *Glory of St. Ignatius Loyola.* The church contains some of Rome's most splendorous, jewel-encrusted altars. If you're lucky, you might be able to catch an evening concert performed here. The church is the focus of Filippo Raguzzini's 18th-century rococo piazza, where the buildings are arranged almost as in a stage set, reminding us that theatricality was a key element of almost all the best Baroque and rococo art. ⊠ *Piazza Sant'Ignazio,* ☎ *06/6794406.* ☉ *Daily 7:30–12:30 and 4–7:30.*

NEED A BREAK?
     The **Antico Caffè Greco** (⊠ Via Condotti 86, ☎ 06/6791700), a 200-year-old institution, ever a haunt of artists and literati, has tiny, marble-top tables and velour settees. Goethe, Byron, and Liszt were habitués; Buffalo Bill stopped in when his Wild West road show hit Rome. It's closed Sunday.

★ **③⑥** **Spanish Steps** (Scalinata di Trinità dei Monti). Both the steps and **Piazza di Spagna** get their names from the Spanish Embassy to the Vatican on the piazza, opposite the American Express office, though the staircase was built with French funds in 1723. In an allusion to the church of Trinità dei Monti at the top of the hill, the staircase is divided by three landings (beautifully banked with blooming azaleas from mid-April to mid-May). This area has always welcomed tourists: 18th-century dukes and duchesses on their Grand Tour, 19th-century artists and writers in search of inspiration—among them, Stendhal, Balzac, Thackeray, and Byron—and today's enthusiastic hordes. The **Fontana della Barcaccia** (Fountain of the Old Boat) at the base of the steps is by Pietro Bernini, father of the famous Gian Lorenzo. ⊠ *Piazza di Spagna.*

★ **③⑧** **Trevi Fountain** (Fontana di Trevi). Tucked away on a small piazza off Via del Tritone, this huge fountain, designed by Nicola Salvi (1697–1751), is a spectacular fantasy of mythical sea creatures amidst cascades of splashing water. It was featured in the 1954 film *Three Coins in the Fountain* and, of course, was the scene of Anita Ekberg's aquatic frolic in Fellini's *La Dolce Vita.* The fountain is the world's most spectacular wishing well: legend has it that you can ensure your return to Rome by tossing a coin into the fountain. At night, the spotlit piazza takes on the festive air of a crowded outdoor party. ⊠ *Piazza Fontana di Trevi.*

MUSEO NAZIONALE DELLE PASTE ALIMENTARI – For a food-history inter-
lude, try the National Museum of Pasta, a showcase of Italy's most famous culinary contribution. Small galleries named the Wheat Room and
the Ligurian Room unfold the compelling saga of pasta and its present-
day production. ✉ *Piazza Scanderbeg 117,* ☎ *06/6991120.* ✉
12,000 lire/€6.20. ☉ *Daily 9:30–5:30.*

Historic Churches: Heavenly Monuments of Faith

Rome's history can be told through its churches. In both their historical import and artistic mastery, the ubiquitous and unique buildings bear
witness to the centuries they have withstood, and far from being only
religious monuments, they have something for every visitor. The churches
that highlight this walk date to the early centuries of Christianity.

A Good Walk

Not far from the Colosseum and the Roman Forum is the church of
San Pietro in Vincoli ㊟, up a steep hill off Via Cavour. Look for Via
San Francesco di Paola, a street staircase that leads off of Via Cavour
on the right as you go uphill, passes under the old Borgia palace, and
leads to the church. Return to Via Cavour, which veers northeast to
Santa Maria Maggiore ㊵, and from here go south on Via Merulana,
which leads straight to **San Giovanni in Laterano** ㊶. The adjoining
Palazzo Laterano houses the Museo Storico Vaticano; across the street,
a small building houses the **Scala Santa** ㊷, or Sacred Stairs, supposedly from Pilate's Jerusalem palace. Circle Palazzo Laterano to see the
4th-century octagonal Battistero di San Giovanni, forerunner of many
such buildings throughout Italy. Follow Via San Giovanni in Laterano
to San Clemente, and explore the ancient church buried underground.

TIMING

The walk alone takes approximately 90 minutes, plus 15–20 minutes
in each of the churches. Allow at least an hour to explore San Clemente.
A visit to the Museo Storico Vaticano will take you about 30 minutes.

Sights to See

㊶ **San Giovanni in Laterano.** Many are surprised when they discover that
the cathedral of Rome is not St. Peter's but this church. (St. Peter's is
in Vatican City, technically not a part of Rome.) Dominating the piazza whose name it shares, this immense building is where the present
pope officiates in his capacity as bishop of Rome. The towering facade
and Borromini's cool Baroque interior emphasize the majesty of its proportions. The **cloister** is one of the city's finest, with beautifully carved
columns surrounding a peaceful garden.

The adjoining **Palazzo Laterano** (Lateran Palace) was the official papal
residence until the 13th century and is still technically part of the Vatican. It houses the offices of the Rome Diocese and the rather bland **Museo
Storico Vaticano** (Vatican Historical Museum). Behind the palace is the
4th-century octagonal **Battistero di San Giovanni** (St. John's Baptistery),
forerunner of many similar buildings throughout Italy, and Rome's
oldest and tallest obelisk, brought from Thebes and dating from the 15th
century BC. ✉ *Piazza San Giovanni in Laterano,* ☎ *06/69886433.* ✉
Cloister 4,000 lire/€2.05, museum 6,000 lire/€3.05. ☉ *Church Apr.–
Sept., daily 7–7; Oct.–Mar., daily 7–6. Cloister 9–½ hr before church
closing. Museum Sat. guided tours at 9:15, 10:30, and noon. 1st Sun.
of each month 8:45–1. Baptistery daily 9–1 and 5–1 hr before sunset.*

SAN CLEMENTE – The remains of ancient Roman dwellings and a 4th-
century church below the upper church of San Clemente are among
Rome's most intriguing subterranean sights. ✉ *Via San Giovanni in Lat-*

erano 108, ☎ *06/70451018.* 🖬 *3,000 lire/€1.55.* ⊙ *Mon.–Sat. 9–noon and 3:30–6, Sun. 10–12:30 and 3–6.*

SANTI QUATTRO CORONATI – The 12th-century Four Crowned Saints church, part of a fortified abbey that provided refuge to early popes and emperors, is in an unusual corner of Rome, a quiet island that has resisted the tide of time and traffic flowing beneath its ramparts. Few places in Rome are so reminiscent of the Middle Ages. Don't miss the cloister with its well-tended gardens and 12th-century fountain. The entrance is the door in the left nave; ring if it's not open. You can also ring at the adjacent convent for the key to the Oratorio di San Silvestro (Oratory of St. Sylvester), with 13th-century frescoes. ✉ *Largo Santi Quattro Coronati,* ☎ *06/70475427.* ⊙ *Easter–Christmas, daily 9:30–12:30 and 3:30–6; Christmas–Easter, daily 9:30–12:30.*

㊴ San Pietro in Vincoli. The church takes its name from the *vincoli* (chains) that once held St. Peter (in the case under the altar), but the throngs of tourists come to see Michelangelo's *Moses,* a powerful statue almost as famed as his frescoes in the Sistine Chapel. The *Moses* was destined for the tomb of Julius II, designed to be the largest in St. Peter's Basilica. But Julius's successors had Michelangelo work on other projects, and the tomb was never finished. ✉ *Piazza San Pietro in Vincoli,* ☎ *06/4882865.* ⊙ *Daily 7–12:30 and 3:30–6:30.*

㊵ Santa Maria Maggiore One of Rome's four great pilgrimage churches was built on the spot where a 3rd-century pope witnessed a miraculous midsummer snowfall. The gleaming mosaics on the arch in front of the main altar date from the 5th century. The apse mosaic dates from the 13th century, and the opulently carved wood ceiling is believed to have been gilded with the first gold brought from the New World. ✉ *Piazza Santa Maria Maggiore, off Via Cavour,* ☎ *06/4881094.* ⊙ *Daily 7–1 hr before sunset.*

㊷ Scala Santa (Sacred Stairs). A small building opposite the Lateran Palace houses what is claimed to be the staircase from Pilate's palace in Jerusalem. The faithful climb the staircase on their knees. ✉ *Piazza San Giovanni in Laterano.* ⊙ *Daily 6:15–noon and 3:30–6:30.*

From the Quirinal Hill to Piazza della Repubblica: Princely Palaces and Romantic Fountains

You'll see ancient Roman sculptures and early Christian churches, but concentrate on the 16th and 17th centuries, when Rome was conquered by the Baroque—and by Bernini.

A Good Walk

Begin on **Quirinal Hill** ㊸, the highest of Rome's seven hills. Here you'll find the Palazzo Quirinale, official residence of the president of Italy. Along Via del Quirinale (which becomes Via XX Settembre) is the church of **Sant'Andrea** ㊹, considered by many to be Bernini's finest work, and, at the Quattro Fontane (Four Fountains) crossroads, the church of **San Carlino alle Quattro Fontane** ㊺, designed by Bernini's rival Borromini. Take a left on Via delle Quattro Fontane to reach the imposing **Palazzo Barberini** ㊻, where the Galleria Nazionale d'Arte Antica houses splendid masterpieces by Raphael and Caravaggio. Down the hill is Piazza Barberini and the **Fontana del Tritone** ㊼, another Bernini design. Cross the piazza and begin your gradual climb up Via Vittorio Veneto, which bends past **Santa Maria della Concezione** ㊽ and the U.S. Embassy, and turn off onto Via Bissolati. On the corner of Piazza San Bernardo is the church of **Santa Maria della Vittoria** ㊾, known for Bernini's Baroque decoration. It's not far down Via Orlando to **Piazza della Repub-**

blica ⑤⓪. On one side of the square is an ancient Roman brick facade that marks the church of Santa Maria degli Angeli. Beyond, on the near corner of Piazza del Cinquecento, the vast square in front of Stazione Termini, is the last stop. **Palazzo Massimo alle Terme** ⑤① houses part of the Museo Nazionale Romano's collections, highlighting examples of the fine mosaics and masterful paintings that decorated ancient Rome's villas and palaces.

<u>TIMING</u>

The walk takes approximately 90 minutes, plus 10 to 15 minutes for each church visited, and 1½ hours each for visits to the Galleria Nazionale in Palazzo Barberini and Palazzo Massimo alle Terme.

Sights to See

㊼ Fontana del Tritone (Triton Fountain). The centerpiece of Piazza Barberini is Bernini's graceful fountain, designed in 1637 for the sculptor's patron, Pope Urban VIII, whose Barberini coat of arms, featuring bees, is at the base of the large shell. ⊠ *Piazza Barberini.*

㊻ Palazzo Barberini. Along with architect Carlo Maderno (1556–1629), Borromini helped make the splendid 17th-century Palazzo Barberini a residence worthy of Rome's leading art patron, Pope Urban VIII, who began this palazzo for his family in 1625. Inside, the **Galleria Nazionale d'Arte Antica** offers some fine works by Raphael (the *Fornarina*) and Caravaggio. Rome's biggest ballroom is here; its ceiling, painted by Pietro da Cortona (1596–1669), depicts Immortality bestowing a crown upon Divine Providence escorted by a "bomber squadron"—to quote Sir Michael Levey—of mutant bees (bees featured prominently in the heraldic device of the Barberini). ⊠ *Via Barberini 18,* ☎ *06/4824184,* WEB *www.galleriaborghese.it.* ⊡ *12,000 lire/€6.19.* ☉ *Tues.–Sat. 9–7:30, Sun. 9–1.*

㊶ Palazzo Massimo alle Terme. This 19th-century palace in early Baroque style holds part of the collections of antiquities belonging to the Museo Nazionale Romano (also exhibited in the Palazzo Altemps). Here you can see extraordinary examples of the fine mosaics and masterful paintings that decorated ancient Rome's palaces and villas. Don't miss the fresco—depicting a lush garden in bloom—that came from the villa that Livia, wife of Emperor Augustus, owned outside Rome. ⊠ *Largo Villa Peretti 2,* ☎ *06/48903501.* ⊡ *12,000 lire/€6.20 (includes Museo delle Terme di Diocleziano).* ☉ *Tues.–Sun. 9–7:45.*

㊿ Piazza della Repubblica. This piazza has a typical 19th-century layout, but the curving porticoes echo the immense **Terme di Diocleziano** (Baths of Diocletian), which once stood here. Built in the 4th century AD, they were the largest and most impressive of the baths of ancient Rome, and their vast halls, pools, and gardens could accommodate 3,000 people at a time. Also part of the great baths was an **Aula Ottagonale** (Octagonal Hall), which now holds a sampling of ancient sculptures found there, including two beautiful bronzes. ⊠ *Via Romita 8,* ☎ *06/4870690.* ⊡ *Free.* ☉ *Tues.–Sat. 9–2, Sun. 9–1.*

The racy **Fontana delle Naiadi** (Fountain of the Naiads), an 1870 addition to the piazza, depicts voluptuous bronze ladies wrestling happily with marine monsters. The curving ancient Roman brick facade on one side of the piazza marks the church of **Santa Maria degli Angeli,** adapted by Michelangelo from the vast central chamber of the colossal baths. The scale of the church's interior gives you an idea of the grandeur of the ancient structure.

㊸ Quirinal Hill. The highest of ancient Rome's seven hills, this is where ancient Romans, and later popes, built their residences in order to escape the deadly miasmas and the malaria of the low-lying area around the Forum. The fountain in the square has ancient statues of Castor and Pollux reining in their unruly steeds and a basin salvaged from the Roman Forum. **Palazzo del Quirinale** passed from the popes to Italy's kings in the 19th century; it's now the official residence of the nation's president. Every day at 4 PM, the ceremony of the changing of the guard at the portal includes a miniparade, complete with band.

⑤ San Carlino alle Quattro Fontane. Borromini's church at the Four Fountains crossroads is an architectural gem. In a space no larger than the base of one of the piers of St. Peter's, Borromini attained geometric perfection. Characteristically, he chose a subdued white stucco for the interior decoration, so as not to distract from the form. The exterior of the church is Borromini at his bizarre best, all curves and rippling movement. Outside, four charming fountains frame views in four directions. ⊠ *Via del Quirinale 23,* ☎ *06/4883261.* ☉ *Daily 9–noon and 3–7.*

⑱ Santa Maria della Concezione. In the crypt under the main Capuchin church, the bones of some 4,000 dead Capuchin monks are arranged in odd decorative designs around the shriveled and decayed skeletons of their kinsmen, a macabre reminder of the impermanence of earthly life. Signs declare, "WHAT YOU ARE, WE ONCE WERE. WHAT WE ARE, YOU SOMEDAY WILL BE." Although not for the easily spooked, the crypt is touching and oddly beautiful. ⊠ *Via Veneto 27,* ☎ *06/4871185.* ☞ *Donation requested.* ☉ *Fri.–Wed. 9–noon and 3–6.*

⑲ Santa Maria della Vittoria. This church is known for Bernini's Baroque decoration of the **Cappella Cornaro,** an exceptional fusion of architecture, painting, and sculpture, in which the *Ecstasy of St. Teresa* is the focal point. Bernini's audacious conceit was to model the chapel as a theater: members of the Cornaro family—sculpted in white marble—watch from theater boxes as, center stage, St. Teresa, in the throes of mystical rapture, is pierced by a gilded arrow held by an angel. To quote one 18th-century observer, President de Brosses: "If this is divine love, I know it well." ⊠ *Via XX Settembre 17,* ☎ *06/4826190.* ☉ *Daily 7–noon and 4–7:30.*

⑭ Sant'Andrea. This small but imposing Baroque church was designed and decorated by Bernini, who considered it one of his finest works. ⊠ *Via del Quirinale,* ☎ *06/48903187.* ☉ *Mon. and Wed.–Sat. 8–noon and 4–6, Sun. 4–6.*

Amid Sylvan Glades: From the Villa Borghese to the Ara Pacis

Touring Rome's artistic masterpieces while staying clear of its hustle and bustle can be, quite literally, a walk in the park. Some of the city's finest sights are tucked away in or next to green lawns and pedestrian piazzas, offering a breath of fresh air for weary sightseers. **Villa Borghese,** one of Rome's largest parks, can alleviate gallery gout by offering an oasis in which to cool off under the ilex trees. Just be sure to pick up your picnic in advance, whether ready-to-go from the snack bars or do-it-yourself from *alimentari* (food shops), as you'll find only fast-food carts within the park itself.

A Good Walk

Start at **Porta Pinciana** ㊾, one of the entrances to Villa Borghese. Follow Viale del Museo Borghese to the **Museo e Galleria Borghese** ㊿ and its fabulous art collection in an extraordinary setting (make sure to reserve a ticket for your visit in advance). Head to the southwest corner of the park to enjoy the view of Rome from the **Pincio** ㊼ belvedere before descending the ramps to all-pedestrian **Piazza del Popolo** ㊺. At the north end of the piazza, next to the 400-year-old city gate, the Porta del Popolo, is the church of **Santa Maria del Popolo** ㊻, with one of the richest art collections of any church in the city. Stroll south along Via di Ripetta to the **Augusteum,** built by Caesar Augustus; next to it is the **Ara Pacis Augustae** ㊼, built in 13 BC.

TIMING

The walk takes approximately two hours; allow an additional 1½ hours for the Galleria Borghese and another 45 minutes for the stroll past the Augusteum and then the Ara Pacis.

Sights to See

㊼ Ara Pacis Augustae (Altar of Augustan Peace). This altar, sheltered in a modern glass edifice on the northwest corner of Piazza Augusto Imperatore, was erected in 13 BC to celebrate the era of peace ushered in by Augustus's military victories. The reliefs showing the procession of the Roman imperial family are magnificent and moving. Notice the poignant presence of several forlorn children; historians now believe they attest to the ambition of Augustus's wife, Empress Livia, who succeeded in having her son Tiberius ascend to the throne by dispatching his family rivals with poison. Next to it is the imposing bulk of the marble-clad **Mausoleo di Augusto** (Mausoleum of Augustus) built by the emperor for himself and his family. The Ara Pacis is closed for restoration, but you may be able to take a look through the glass enclosure. ✉ *Ara Pacis: Via Ripetta,* ☎ *06/68806848.* 🎟 *3,750 lire/€1.95.* ☉ *Closed for restoration. Mausoleum:* ✉ *P. Augusto Imperatore,* ☎ *06/ 67103819.* 🎟 *3,750 lire/€1.95.* ☉ *Weekends 10–1.*

★ ㊾ Museo e Galleria Borghese (Borghese Museum and Gallery). The 1613 palace of Cardinal Scipione Borghese (1576–1633)—a place to flaunt his fabulous antiquities collection and hold elegant fêtes—is today a monument to 18th-century Roman interior decoration at its most luxurious, dripping with porphyry and alabaster. Throughout the grand salons are ancient Roman mosaic pavements and statues of various deities, including one officially known as *Venus Vincitrix.* There has never been any doubt, however, as to the statue's real subject: Pauline Bonaparte, Napoléon's sister, who married Prince Camillo Borghese in one of the storied matches of the 19th century. Sculpted by Canova (1757–1822), the princess reclines on a chaise longue, bare-bosomed, her hips swathed in classical drapery, the very model of haughty detachment and sly come-hither. Pauline is known to have been shocked that her husband took pleasure in showing off the work to his guests. This coyness seems all the more curious given the reply she is supposed to have made to a lady who asked her how she could have posed for the work: "Oh, but the studio was heated." But then it was exactly the combination of aristocratic disdain and naïveté that is said to have made her irresistible in the first place. Other rooms hold important sculptures by Bernini, including *David* and *Apollo and Daphne.* The renowned picture collection has splendid works by Titian, Caravaggio, and Raphael, among others. ✉ *Piazza Scipione Borghese 5, off Via Pinciana,* ☎ *06/8548577 information; 06/328102 reservations (press 2 for English),* 🌐 *www.galleriaborghese.it information, www.beniculturali.it ticketing.* 🎟 *12,000 lire/€6.20, plus 2,000 lire/€1.05 reservation fee.* ☉ *Winter Tues.–Sun. 9–7, summer Tues.– Fri. 9–9, Sat. 9 AM–midnight, Sun. 9–8; reservations required.*

㊺ Piazza del Popolo. Designed by neoclassical architect Giuseppe Valadier (1762–1839) in the early 1800s, this square is one of the largest in Rome, and it has a 3,000-year-old obelisk in the middle. Always a favorite spot for café-sitting and people-watching, the square is closed to automotive traffic, creating a pedestrian oasis. The bookend Baroque churches **Santa Maria dei Miracoli** and **Santa Maria in Montesanto** at the southern end of the piazza are not, first appearances to the contrary, twins. On the plaza's eastern side, stairs lead uphill to the Pincio. To the north, at the end of the square is the 400-year-old **Porta del Popolo,** Rome's northern city gate.

NEED A
BREAK?   **Rosati** (✉ Piazza del Popolo 5, ☎ 06/3225859) café, with a tearoom and upstairs dining room, has never gone out of style, forever a rendezvous of literati, artists, and actors.

☺ ㊿ **Pincio.** At the southwestern corner of Villa Borghese, the Pincio belvedere and gardens were laid out by Valadier as part of his overall plan for Piazza del Popolo. Back then, counts and countesses liked to take their evening passeggiata here in the hope of meeting Pius IX (1792–1878), the last pope to go about Rome on foot. Nowadays you're more likely to see runners and in-line skaters, as well as throngs of Romans out for a stroll.

㊾ **Porta Pinciana** (Pincian Gate). One of the historic city gates in the Aurelian Walls surrounding Rome, it was built in the 6th century AD, about three centuries after the walls were built to keep out the barbarians. These days it is one of the entrances to Villa Borghese.

㊽ **Santa Maria del Popolo.** This church next to the Porta del Popolo goes almost unnoticed, but it has one of the richest art collections of any church in Rome. Here you'll find Raphael's High Renaissance masterpiece the **Chigi Chapel,** as well as two stunning Caravaggios in the **Cerasi Chapel.** ✉ *Piazza del Popolo,* ☎ *06/3610836.* ☉ *Mon.–Sat. 7–7, Sun. 8–2 and 4:30–7:30.*

Across the Tiber: The Ghetto, Tiberina Island, and Trastevere

This walk takes you through separate communities, each staunchly resisting the tides of change, including the old Jewish Ghetto. In picturesque Trastevere you will find a resident colony of foreigners coexisting with "the Romans of Rome." Despite rampant gentrification, Trastevere remains about the most tightly knit community in the city, its natives proudly proclaiming their descent from the ancient Romans.

A Good Walk

Begin at Largo Argentina and take Via Paganica to Piazza Mattei, where one of Rome's loveliest fountains, the 16th-century **Fontana delle Tartarughe** ㊾, is tucked away. Take Via della Reginella into Via Portico d'Ottavia, heart of the Jewish Ghetto. On the Tiber is the **Sinagoga** ㊾. The **Teatro di Marcello** ㊿, behind the Portico d'Ottavia, was originally a theater designed to hold 20,000 people. Follow Via di Teatro di Marcello south, passing the ruins of two small temples: the **Tempio della Fortuna Virilis** ㊽ and the circular **Tempio di Vesta** ㊾. Across **Piazza Bocca della Verità** ㊿ is the 12th-century church of Santa Maria in Cosmedin, with the marble Bocca della Verità. Retracing your steps, walk upstream along the Tiber, cross Ponte Fabricio over **Isola Tiberina** ㊾, and then head into Trastevere.

Begin your exploration of Trastevere at Piazza in Piscinula (you will need a good street map to make your way around this intricate maze of winding side streets), take Via dell'Arco dei Tolomei, cross Via dei Salumi, and turn left onto Via dei Genovesi and then right to the piazza in front of **Santa Cecilia in Trastevere** ㊿. Baroque enthusiasts will want to walk several blocks southwest down Via Anicia to **San Francesco**

a Ripa ⑥⑥ to see a famous Bernini sculpture. Follow Via San Francesco a Ripa to the very heart of Trastevere, to **Piazza di Santa Maria in Trastevere** ⑥⑦, site of the lovely 12th-century church of the same name. With a detailed map, find your way through the narrow byways to Piazza Sant'Egidio and Via della Scala, continuing on to Via della Lungara and **Villa Farnesina** ⑥⑧, where you can see frescoes by Raphael. From Trastevere, climb Via Garibaldi to the Janiculum Hill, which offers views spanning the whole city, and where you'll find the church of **San Pietro in Montorio** ⑥⑨, built in 1481.

TIMING

The walk takes approximately three hours, plus 10 to 15 minutes for each church visited, and about 30 minutes for a visit to Villa Farnesina.

Sights to See

⑤⑧ **Fontana delle Tartarughe.** The 16th-century Fountain of the Turtles in Piazza Mattei is one of Rome's loveliest. Designed by Giacomo della Porta (1539–1602) in 1581 and sculpted by Taddeo Landini (1550–96), the piece revolves around four bronze boys, each clutching a dolphin that jets water into marble shells. Several bronze tortoises, thought to have been added by Bernini, are held in each of the boys' hands and drink from the fountain's upper basin. The piazza is named for the Mattei family, which built **Palazzo Mattei** on Via Caetani, worth a peek for its sculpture-rich courtyard and staircase. ⊠ *Piazza Mattei, Ghetto.*

⑥④ **Isola Tiberina** (Tiber Island). Ancient Ponte Fabricio and Ponte Cestio link the old Jewish Ghetto and the neighborhood of Trastevere to this island, where a city hospital stands on a site that has been dedicated to healing ever since a temple to Aesculapius was erected here in 291 BC. If you have time, and if the river's not too high, walk down the stairs for a different perspective on the island and the Tiber.

Jewish Ghetto. Rome has had a Jewish community since the 1st century BC, and from that time until the present its living conditions have varied widely according to its relations with the city's rulers. In 1555, Pope Paul II established Rome's Jewish "ghetto" in the neighborhood marked off by the Portico d'Ottavia, the Tiber, and Via Arenula. The area quickly became Rome's most squalid and densely populated. At one point, Jews—formerly farmers of the fertile land across the Tiber—were limited to the sale of used clothing as a trade. The Ghetto laws were rescinded around the time of the Risorgimento in the 1870s, and not much remains of it as it was, but some of Rome's 15,000 Jews still live in the area, and a few families still run clothing shops on the Via di Portico d'Ottavia. German troops occupied Rome during World War II, and on October 16, 1943, many of Rome's Jews were rounded up and deported to Nazi concentration camps. In 1982, the synagogue here was bombed by anti-Semitic Romans, and in 1986, as a gesture of reconciliation, Pope John Paul II paid a visit to Rabbi Elio Toaff, becoming the first pope ever to pray in a Jewish synagogue. Today, the ghetto is home to Rome's few judaica shops and kosher groceries, bakeries, and restaurants, as well as linen and shoe stores and the trendy cafés and bars that have moved in with gentrification. Quiet, winding alleys are a shady respite from the center's hustle and are well worth a half hour's stroll.

Palazzo Corsini. This elegant palace holds the 16th- and 17th-century painting collection of the **Galleria Nazionale d'Arte Antica**; even if you're not interested in the paintings, stop in to climb the extraordinary 17th-century stone staircase, itself a drama of architectural shadows and sculptural voids. ⊠ *Via della Lungara 10, Trastevere,* ☎ *06/68802323,* WEB *www.galleriaborghese.it.* 🎫 *8,000 lire/€4.15.* ☉ *Tues.–Sun. 8:30–7:30.*

63 **Piazza Bocca della Verità.** On the site of the Forum Boarium, ancient Rome's cattle market, this square was later used for public executions. Its name is derived from the marble **Bocca della Verità** (Mouth of Truth) set into the entry portico of the 12th-century church of **Santa Maria in Cosmedin.** In the Middle Ages, legend had it that any person who told a lie with his hand in the mouth of the ancient drain hole cover would have it chomped off; today tour groups line up to give this ancient lie detector a try.

OFF THE
BEATEN PATH

AVENTINE HILL – One of the seven hills of ancient Rome, the Aventine is now a quiet residential neighborhood that most tourists don't see. It's home to some of the city's oldest and least-visited churches and some unusual views: peek through the keyhole in the gate to the garden of the **Knights of Malta** (⊠ Piazza Cavalieri di Malta) for a surprise view of the dome of St. Peter's. The city panorama from the walled park next to the church of Santa Sabina, off Via Santa Sabina, is wider, if more conventional.

TERME DI CARACALLA – The scale of the towering ruins of ancient Rome's most beautiful and luxurious public baths, the Baths of Caracalla, hints at their past splendor. Inaugurated by Caracalla in 217, the baths were used until the 6th century. An ancient version of a swank athletic club, the baths were open to all, though men and women used them separately; citizens could bathe, socialize, and exercise in huge pools and richly decorated halls. ⊠ *Via delle Terme di Caracalla.* 🕾 *8,000 lire/€4.15.* ⊙ *Apr.–Sept., Tues.–Sat. 9–6, Sun. and Mon. 9–1; Oct.–Mar., Tues.–Sat. 9–3, Sun. and Mon. 9–1.*

★ **67** **Piazza di Santa Maria in Trastevere.** This piazza is a popular spot for afternoon coffees and evening cocktails at its outdoor cafés, but the showpiece of the square is the 12th-century church of **Santa Maria in Trastevere.** The 13th-century mosaics on the church's facade—which add light and color to the piazza, especially at night when they are spotlit—are believed to represent the Wise and Foolish Virgins. Inside, the enormous golden mosaic in the apse is the city's finest, a shining burst of Byzantine color and light set off by a processional of giant columns. There are larger naves in Rome, but none quite so majestic. 🕾 *06/5814802.* ⊙ *Daily 9–noon and 4–9.*

66 **San Francesco a Ripa.** This church in Piazza San Francesco d'Assisi is a must for fans of the Baroque. It holds one of Bernini's most dramatic sculptures, a statue of the Blessed Ludovica Albertoni, ecstatic at the prospect of entering heaven as she expires on her deathbed. ⊠ *Piazza San Francesco d'Assisi,* 🕾 *06/5819020.* ⊙ *Mon.–Sat. 8–noon and 4–6, Sun. 4–6.*

69 **San Pietro in Montorio.** One of Rome's key Renaissance buildings stands in the cloister of this church, built by order of Ferdinand and Isabella of Spain in 1481 over the spot where St. Peter was thought to have been crucified. Bramante's **Tempietto** is an architectural gem and was one of his earliest and most successful attempts to design a building in an entirely classical style. ⊠ *Via Garibaldi, Gianicolo,* 🕾 *06/5813940.* ⊙ *Daily 9–noon and 4–6.*

65 **Santa Cecilia in Trastevere.** Mothers and children love to dally in the delightful little garden in front of this church in Piazza Santa Cecilia. Duck inside for a look at the very grand 18th-century interior and the languid statue of St. Cecilia under the altar. Fragments of a *Last Judgment* fresco cycle by Cavallini, dating from the late 13th century, remain one of his most important works. Though the Byzantine-influenced fragments are obscured by the structure, what's left reveals a rich luminosity in the seated apostles' drapery and a remarkable depth in their expressions. ✉ *Piazza Santa Cecilia,* ☎ *06/5899289.* 🎫 *Frescoes 3,000 lire/€1.55.* ⏲ *Daily 8–12:30 and 2:30–7; frescoes Tues. and Thurs. 10–11:30, Sun. 11:30–noon.*

(59) **Sinagoga** (Synagogue). The large, bronze-roofed synagogue on the Tiber is a Roman landmark. The **Museo Ebraico** (Museum of the Jewish Community) documents the history of the Jewish community in Rome. Most of the decorative crowns, prayer books, holy chairs, and tapestries, dating from the 17th century, were donated by prominent Jewish families whose ancestors once lived in the Ghetto. The collection offers a refreshing change from the predominantly Christian art found elsewhere in Rome. ✉ *Lungotevere Cenci 15,* ☎ *06/68400661.* 🎫 *10,000 lire/€5.15.* ⏲ *Mon.–Thurs. 9–6, Fri. 9–2, Sun. 9–12:30.*

(60) **Teatro di Marcello.** The Teatro, hardly recognizable as a theater today, was originally designed to hold 20,000 spectators. It was begun by Julius Caesar; today, the medieval apartments that sprout out of its remains have become one of Rome's most prestigious residential addresses. The theater makes a grand stage for chamber music concerts in the summer. ✉ *Via del Teatro di Marcello,* ☎ *06/67103819.* ⏲ *Open during concerts only.*

(61) **Tempio della Fortuna Virilis** (Temple of Manly Fortune). This rectangular temple dates from the 2nd century BC and is built in the Greek style, as was the norm in the early years of Rome. For its age, it is remarkably well preserved, in part due to its subsequent consecration as a Christian church. ✉ *Piazza Bocca della Verità.*

(62) **Tempio di Vesta.** All but one of the 20 original Corinthian columns in Rome's most evocative small ruin remain intact. Like the Temple of Manly Fortune, it was built in the 2nd century BC, long before the ruins in the Roman Forum. ✉ *Piazza Bocca dell Verità.*

Trastevere. This area consists of a maze of narrow streets that is still, despite evident gentrification, one of the city's most authentically Roman neighborhoods. Literally translated, its name means "across the Tiber," and indeed Trastevere and the Trasteverini—the neighborhood's natives—are a breed apart. The area is hardly undiscovered, but among its self-consciously picturesque trattorias and trendy tearooms you'll also find old shops and dusty artisans' workshops in alleys festooned with laundry hung out to dry. One of the least affected parts of Trastevere centers on **Piazza in Piscinula,** where the tiny **San Benedetto,** the smallest medieval church in the city, is opposite the restored medieval Casa dei Mattei. Take a stroll along Via dell'Arco dei Tolomei and Via dei Salumi, shadowy streets showing the patina of the ages.

Via del Portico d'Ottavia. Along this street in the heart of the Jewish Ghetto are buildings where medieval inscriptions, ancient friezes, and half-buried classical monuments attest to the venerable history of the neighborhood. The old **Chiesa di Sant'Angelo in Pescheria** was built right into the ruins of the Portico d'Ottavia, which was a monumental area enclosing a temple, library, and other buildings within colonnaded porticoes.

(68) **Villa Farnesina.** Money was no object to extravagant host Agostino Chigi, a Sienese banker who financed many a papal project. His munificence is evident in his elegant villa, built about 1511. When Raphael could steal some precious time from his work on the Vatican Stanze and from his wooing of the Fornarina, he executed some of the frescoes, notably a luminous *Galatea.* Chigi delighted in impressing guests

by having his servants clear the table by casting precious dinnerware into the Tiber. Naturally, the guests did not know of the nets he had stretched under the waterline to catch everything. ⊠ *Via della Lungara 230,* ☎ *06/68801767,* WEB *www.lincei.it/english.version/farnesina.html.* 🎫 *8,000 lire/€4.15.* ☉ *Mon.–Sat. 9–1.*

Quo Vadis? The Catacombs and the Via Appia Antica

The Early Christian sites on the ancient Appian Way are some of the religion's oldest. Catacombs, where early Christians (whose religion prohibited cremation) buried their dead and gathered to worship in secret, lie below the very road where tradition says Christ appeared to St. Peter. The Via Appia Antica, built 400 years before, offers a quiet, green place to walk and ponder the ancient world. The Rome APT office offers an informative free pamphlet for this itinerary.

A Good Tour
Resist any temptation to undertake the 1½-km (1-mi) walk between Porta San Sebastiano and the catacombs; it is a dull and tiring hike on a heavily trafficked cobblestone road, with stone walls the only scenery. Instead, hop on Bus 660 from the Colli Albani metro stop on Line A to the **Via Appia Antica** ⑦⓪. (Bus 218 from San Giovanni in Laterano also passes near the catacombs, but you have to walk about ½ km [¼ mi] east from Via Ardeatina to Via Appia Antica.)

TIMING
Allow one hour for this tour, plus one hour for the catacombs.

Sights to See
★ ⑦⓪ **Via Appia Antica.** his Queen of Roads, "Regina Viarium," was the most important of the extensive network of roads that traversed the Roman Empire, a masterful feat of engineering that made possible Roman control of a vast area, by allowing efficient transport of armies and commercial goods. Completed in 312 BC by Appius Claudius, the road was ancient Europe's first highway, connecting Rome with Brindisi, 584 km (365 mi) away on the Adriatic coast. Today, part of the route still exists (as Via Appia, SS7), but most of it is a paved, modern highway. The stretch indicated here is the opposite: closed to traffic, the ancient roadway passes through grassy fields and shady groves, and is still paved with the ancient *basoli* (basalt stones) over which the Romans drove their carriages. Taverns, houses, temples, and tombs flanked the ancient road, and the occasional lone statue, crumbling wall, or column is still visible, draped in ivy or alone in a patch of wildflowers. Pick a sunny day for your visit, wear comfortable shoes, and bring plenty of water. **San Callisto** is one of the best-preserved of the underground catacombs. A friar will guide you through its crypts and galleries. ⊠ *Via Appia Antica 110,* ☎ *06/51301580.* 🎫 *8,000 lire/€4.15.* ☉ *Feb.–Dec., Mon.–Sat. 8:30–noon and 2:30–5:30.*

The 4th-century **San Sebastiano** (St. Sebastian) catacomb, named for the saint who was buried here, burrows underground on four levels. The only one of the catacombs to remain accessible during the Middle Ages, it is the origin of the term "catacomb," for it was in a spot where the road dips into a hollow, a place the Romans called *catacumbas* ("near the hollow"). Eventually, the Christian cemetery that had existed here since the 2nd century came to be known by the same name, which was applied to all underground cemeteries discovered in Rome in later centuries. ⊠ *Via Appia Antica 136,* ☎ *06/7850350.* 🎫 *8,000 lire/€4.15.* ☉ *Mar.–Jan., Mon.–Sat. 8:30–noon and 2:30–5:30.*

On the east side of Via Appia Antica are the ruins of the **Circo di Massenzio** (Circus of Maxentius), where the obelisk now in Piazza Navona once stood. ⊠ *Via Appia Antica 153,* ☎ *06/7801324.* ☉ *Oct.–Mar., Tues.–Sun. 9–5; Apr.–Sept., Tues.–Sun. 9–7.*

The circular **Tomba di Cecilia Metella** (Tomb of Cecilia Metella), the mausoleum of a Roman noblewoman who lived at the time of Julius Caesar, was transformed into a fortress in the 14th century. It marks the beginning of the most evocative stretch of Via Appia Antica, lined with tombs and fragments of statuary. Cypresses and umbrella pines stand guard over the ruined sepulchers, and the occasional tracts of ancient paving stones are the same ones trod by triumphant Roman legions. ⊠ *Via Appia Antica 161,* ☎ *06/7802465.* ☞ *Free.* ☉ *Weekdays 9–1 hr before sunset, weekends 9–1.*

DINING

Roman cooking is simple. Dishes rarely have more than a few ingredients. Meat and fish are most often roasted, baked, or grilled. Although many traditional recipes are based on innards, you won't find much of that on the menu in restaurants in the city center, with the exception of *trippa alla romana* (tripe stewed in tomatoes with wild mint).

The typical Roman fresh pasta is fettuccine, golden egg noodles that are at their classic best when laced with *ragù*, a thick, rich tomato and meat sauce. Spaghetti *alla carbonara* is spaghetti tossed with a sauce of egg yolk, chunks of rendered *guanciale* (cured pork cheek) or *pancetta* (salt-cured bacon), pecorino Romano cheese, and lots of freshly ground black pepper. *Pasta all'amatriciana* has a sauce of tomato, guanciale, and onion. Potato gnocchi, served with a tomato sauce and a dusting of Parmesan or pecorino, are a Roman favorite for Thursday dinner. The best meat on the menu is often *abbacchio*, milk-fed lamb. Legs of lamb are usually roasted with rosemary and potatoes, and the chops are grilled *alla scottadito* (literally "burn your finger," for small chops eaten with your fingers hot off the grill). Most Mediterranean fish are light yet flavorful, among them *spigola* (sea bass), *orata* (bream), and *rombo* (turbot or flounder).

Local cheeses are made from sheep's milk; the best-known is the aged, sharp pecorino Romano. Fresh ricotta is a treat all on its own, and finds its way into a number of dishes and desserts. Many restaurants make a specialty of the *fritto misto* (literally "mixed fried") with whatever vegetables are in season. Rome is famous for *carciofi* (artichokes)— the season runs from November to April—traditionally prepared *alla romana* (stuffed with garlic and mint and braised in oil), or *alla giudia* (fried whole, making each petal crisp). A special springtime treat is *vignarola*, a mixture of tender peas, fava beans, and artichokes, cooked with bits of guanciale.

Typical wines of Rome are those of the Castelli Romani, the towns in the hills to the southeast: Frascati, Colli Albani, Marino, and Velletri. Though the water in Rome is good to drink, restaurants will usually have you choose between bottled waters, either *gassata* (sparkling) or *liscia* (not).

Old Rome

\$\$\$\$
★ ✕ **El Toulà.** Rome's prestigious El Toulà has the warm, welcoming comforts of a 19th-century country house, with white walls, antique furniture in dark wood, heavy silver serving dishes, and spectacular fruit and flower arrangements. There's a cozy bar off the entrance, where you can sip a Prosecco, the Venetian sparkling wine best paired with the chef's Venetian specialties that are always on offer, along with con-

476

Rome Dining

Viale delle Belle Arti
Botanical Gardens
V. Pietro Raimondi
V. dell'Uccelliera
Viale P. Canonica
Viale dell'Uccelliera
V. Salaria
Vle. G. Washington
Villa Borghese
Viale d. Museo Borghese
V. di Villa Albani
Viale Regina Margherita
V. Po
Vle. G. Annunzio
V. d. Magnolie
Galoppatoio
V. Pinciana
Vicolo d'Emilia
Via Savoia
Via Nizza
V. Alessandro
Nomentana
Pincio
Porta Pinciana
Corso d'Italia
Pza. Fiume
Pza. Alessandria
34
Villa Medici
Viale del Muro Torto
Viale Trinità d'Monti
V. Campania
Ple. di Porta Pia
V. del Babuino
V. di Pta. Pinciana
32
33
V. Piemonte
V. Romagna
V. Piave
Del Corso
V. Vittoria
6
Pza. di Spagna
7
V. Ludovisi
V. Boncompagni
V. della Croce
V. delle Carozze
V. Condotti
V. Borgognona
V. Frattina
V. F. Crispi
V. Sistina
Vitt. Veneto
V. L. Bissolati
V. Sallustiana
V. Quintino Sella
V. XX Settembre
V. Castelfidardo
V. Goito
35
V. Polestro
V. Gaeta
V. S. Martino
V. Cernaia
V. Volturno
V. Vicenza
V. Marghera
36
Campo Marzio
V. Gambero
V. del Tritone
Pza. Barberini
V. Barberini
Nicolò da Tolentino
Vicolo d. Bottino
V. d. Quattro Fontane
V. Milazzo
QUIRINAL HILL
31
V. d. Scuderie
Giardini del Quirinale
Pza. d. Repubblica
V. Torino
Stazione Termini
V. Marsala
Pza. Colonna
V. della Murate
V. dell'Umiltà
Pza. di Trevi
Pza. del Quirinale
Via Nazionale
Via Viminale
Via d'Azeglio
14
Pastini
V. del seminario
a. della tonda
Collegio Romano
V. d. Plebiscito
V. C. Battisti
Pza. Venezia
Novembre
V. IV
V. d. Serpenti
V. Panisperna
V. Napoli
V. A. Depretis
V. di S. Maria Maggiore
Pza. S. Maria Maggiore
V. Cavour
V. G. Amendola
V. D. Morin
V. G. Giolitti
V. F. Turati
Vega Oscure
V. Celsa
V. d. Gesù
Via
VIMINAL HILL
V. Milano
V. Cavour
Quattro Cantoni
V. Carlo Alberto
V. Napoleone III
30
V. del Pianto
V. dei Fori Imperiali
V. Cavour
V. Giovanni Lanza
ESQUILINE HILL
V. d. Statuto
Pza. Vittorio Emanuele II
Fabricio
Lung. d. Pierleoni
Pza. d. Campidoglio
CAPITOLINE HILL
Foro Romano
Pza. del Colosseo
Viale del Monte Oppio
V. Mecenate
Merulana
V. Emanuele Filiberto
3
Pte. Palatino
V. S. Teodoro
V. d. Domus Aurea
V. Rugg. Bonghi
V. Manzoni
Tiber
PALATINE HILL
V. Labicana
V. S. Giovanni in Laterano
V. di S. Gregorio
V. dei Cerchi
V. Claudia
Pza. S. Giovanni in Laterano
AVENTINE HILL
V. del Circo Massimo
Ple. Remolo e Remo
Circo Massimo
CELIAN HILL
V. di S. Stefano Rotondo
V. dell'Amba Aradam
V. di S. Sabina
V. A. Magno
V. S. Prisca
V. di S. Erasmo
V. d. Navicella
AVENTINE HILL
Viale Aventino
V. delle Terme Caracalla
Pza. di Porta Metronia
V. Pannonia
Parco di Porta Capena
28
29
V. Gallia

temporary interpretations of Italian classics. Jacket and tie are required in winter months. ⊠ *Via della Lupa 29/b,* ☎ *06/6873750. Reservations essential. AE, DC, MC, V. Closed Sun. and Aug. No lunch Mon. or Sat.*

$$$$ ✕ **La Rosetta.** The city's most elegant (and priciest) seafood restaurant, La Rosetta is still the place to go in Rome for artful presentations of first-rate fish. The space is refined in its simplicity, with warm woods, fresh flowers, and a stunning display of fish at the entrance. Particularly good are the *vongole veraci* (sautéed clams), *tonnarelli ai frutti di mare* (poached fish on artichokes or potatoes), and sea bass with black truffles. Homemade desserts are worth saving room for. ⊠ *Via della Rosetta 9,* ☎ *06/6861002. Dinner reservations essential. AE, DC, MC, V.* ☉ *Closed Sun. and 2–3 wks in Aug. No lunch Thurs. or Fri.*

$$$ ✕ **Sangallo.** Small and intimate, this is an old-fashioned restaurant where
★ the owner buys the fish himself and where dinner is meant to last all night. The traditional menu leans heavily toward the gourmet, with dishes like oysters tartare, snapper with foie gras, Texas steaks, and a fixed-price menu based on truffles. There are few tables in the tiny dining room, so make sure to book ahead. ⊠ *Vicolo della Vaccarella 11/a,* ☎ *06/6865549. AE, DC, MC, V. Closed Sun., 1 wk in Jan., and 2 wks in Aug. No lunch Mon.*

$$ ✕ **Dal Bolognese.** Long a haunt of the art crowd, this classic restau-
★ rant on Piazza del Popolo is a trendy choice for a leisurely lunch between sightseeing and shopping. An array of contemporary paintings decorates the dining room, but the real attraction is the lovely pedestrian piazza—prime people-watching real estate. As the name promises, the cooking here adheres to the hearty tradition of Bologna, with delicious homemade tortellini *in brodo* (in broth), fresh pastas in creamy sauces, and steaming trays of boiled meats. Among the desserts, try the *dolce della mamma* (a concoction of gelato, zabaglione, and chocolate sauce) and the fruit-shape gelato. ⊠ *Piazza del Popolo 1,* ☎ *06/ 3611426. AE, DC, MC, V. Closed Mon. and Aug.*

$$ ✕ **L'Eau Vive.** This restaurant with classic French food and unusual tropical specialties is run by a society of French missionary nuns, who serve up one of Rome's more unusual dining experiences. Sisters in their habits wait on tables to the tune of hymnal music; the eclectic menu spans from hamburgers to lobster thermidor. Some nights the sisters put on a sort of devotional dinner theater, and they take a pause before dessert to sing "Ave Maria"—you are welcome to join in. The upstairs rooms, reserved for nonsmokers, have beautiful frescoes. ⊠ *Via Monterone 85,* ☎ *06/68801095. AE, DC, MC, V. Closed Sun. and Aug.*

$$ ✕ **Myosotis.** The menu here rides a delicate line between tradition and
★ innovation, focusing more on the freshness and quality of the ingredients than on elaborate presentation. Fresh pasta gets special attention: it's rolled out by hand to order for the *stracci alla delizia di mare* (pasta with seafood). There's a wide choice of fish, meat, and seasonal vegetables to choose from. The wine list is ample, and the prices are honest. ⊠ *Vicolo della Vaccarella 3/5,* ☎ *06/6865554. AE, DC, MC, V. Closed Sun. and 2 wks in Aug.*

$$ ✕ **Otello alla Concordia.** The clientele in this popular spot off a shopping street near Piazza di Spagna is about evenly divided between tourists and businesspeople. The former like to sit outdoors in the courtyard in any weather; the latter have their regular tables in one of the inside dining rooms. The menu offers classic Roman and Italian dishes, and service is friendly and efficient. Since the regulars won't relinquish their niches, you may have to wait for a table; go early. Reservations are not accepted after 8:30. ⊠ *Via della Croce 81,* ☎ *06/6791178. AE, DC, MC, V. Closed Sun.*

$$ ✕ **Sora Lella.** What was once a simple trattoria ensconced on the Tiberina Island (great view from the bathroom) is now a monument to the late founder herself, a beloved example of true Roman warmth and personality. Inside, two small dining rooms are lined with wood paneling and bottles of wine. Although prices are much higher than when Sora Lella presided over the cash desk, the cooking is still 100% Roman. Daily specials as well as menu standards are written on the chalkboard, but you'll usually find rigatoni all'amatriciana and *maialino all'antica roma* (suckling pig with prunes and baby onions). Leave room for the quintessential Roman ricotta cake. ⊠ *Via Ponte Quattro Capi 16,* ☏ *06/6861601. AE, DC, MC, V. Closed Sun. and Aug.*

$$ ✕ **Vecchia Roma.** Consistent food, sure-handed service, and a romantic atmosphere make this restaurant still worthy of attention, even if it's a bit pricey. With tables outside on a quiet, narrow square close to Capitol Hill, Vecchia Roma is one of the best places in town to eat alfresco. The tasteful interior proceeds through several small rooms, some with floral frescoes, others with stucco panel reliefs. Unlike those of a great many "old Roman restaurants," its menu covers the classics without being stale. ⊠ *Piazza Campitelli 18,* ☏ *06/6864604. Reservations essential. AE, DC. Closed Wed. and mid-Aug.*

$ ✕ **Ditirambo.** Don't let the country-kitchen ambience fool you; this lit-
★ tle spot off Campo dei Fiori is anything but traditional. A constantly changing selection of offbeat takes on Italian classics is a step beyond ordinary Roman fare. Try a sweet fettuccine *di castagne con funghi porcini* (chestnut-flour fettuccine with porcini mushrooms) or mousse *di stoccafisso su crostoni di polenta* (codfish mousse on polenta toast). A whole page of the menu is set aside for vegetarians, with treats like *sformato di zucca* (pumpkin flan) high on the list. Reservations are a good idea. ⊠ *Piazza della Cancelleria 74,* ☏ *06/6871626. AE, MC, V. Closed Aug. No lunch Mon.*

$ ✕ **Orso 80.** The good kind of tourist restaurant, this bright and bustling trattoria near Piazza Navona is well known for its wide assortment of fresh seafood and fabulous antipasto table. Also worth trying are the homemade egg pasta or the *bucatini* (thick, hollow spaghetti) all'amatriciana. For dessert, the *torta di ricotta* (sheep's-milk cheesecake), a genuine Roman specialty, is always good. ⊠ *Via dell'Orso 33,* ☏ *06/6864904. AE, DC, MC, V. Closed Mon. and Aug.*

Veneto

$$$$ ✕ **La Terrazza dell'Eden.** The Hotel Eden's La Terrazza restaurant has
★ an unparalleled view of Rome's seven hills, but don't let that distract you from some of the best food in the city. A sort of Italian nouvelle cuisine—high on flavor and herbs and low on butter and cream—is the vision of chef Enrico Derflingher. Always on the prowl for superior fresh ingredients, he has taken the search to a new level: how many other restaurants have their own fishing boat, which reserves the best of the day's catch for the chef? The luxuriously spacious interior is a welcome change from Rome's often-cramped quarters. ⊠ *Hotel Eden, Via Ludovisi 49,* ☏ *06/47812752. Dinner reservations essential. Jacket and tie. AE, DC, MC, V.*

$$$$ ✕ **Le Sans Souci.** All the glitz and glamour of the 1950s dolce vita days lives on in this overdecorated but superb subterranean sanctuary of French and Italian gourmet delights. Impeccably dressed waiters slide over the carpeted floor with unparalleled grace, their gait reminiscent of Swiss walking lessons. An elaborate coffered ceiling, mirrors, and painted ceramics from Perugia decorate the main room. Carved wooden busts of Roman emperors gaze over tables, set in the French fashion, where couples share a couch rather than sit opposite one another (so much easier to see the show). Among the delectable dishes are truffled terrine of foie gras and various sweet and savory soufflés. ✉ *Via Sicilia 20,* ☎ *06/42014510. Reservations essential. Jacket and tie. AE, DC, MC, V. Closed Aug. 10–20. No lunch.*

$$$ ✕ **Papá Baccus.** Italo Cipriani takes his meat as seriously as any Tuscan. He uses real Chianina beef, the prized breed traditionally used for the *bistecca alla fiorentina,* a thick, bone-in steak, grilled but rare in the middle, a house specialty. In this, Rome's best Tuscan restaurant, you can depend on the genuineness of the rest of the dishes, too. Cipriani brings many ingredients from his hometown in northern Tuscany. Try the sweet and delicate prosciutto from Pratomagno. The welcome is warm, the service excellent. ✉ *Via Toscana 36,* ☎ *06/42742808. AE, DC, MC, V. Closed Sun., 2 wks in Aug., and at Christmas. No lunch Sat.*

$$ ✕ **Colline Emiliane.** Expect a reliable neighborhood trattoria, not far from Piazza Barberini. Behind an opaque glass facade are a couple of plain dining rooms, where you are served light homemade pastas, *tortelli di zucca* (squash-filled ravioli), and meats from *bollito misto* (boiled beef) to *cotoletta alla Bolognese* (fried veal cutlet with cheese and prosciutto). Family run, it's quiet and soothing—a good place to rest after a sightseeing stint. Service is cordial and discreet. ✉ *Via degli Avignonesi 22,* ☎ *06/4817538. Reservations essential. MC, V. Closed Fri. and Aug.*

Near Termini

$ ✕ **Pommidoro.** Mamma's in the kitchen and the rest of the family greets, serves, and keeps you happy and well fed at this popular trattoria near Rome's main university, a short cab ride east of Stazione Termini. The menu—not so well translated—offers especially good grilled meats and game birds as well as classic home-style *cucina* (cooking). You can dine outside in warm weather. ✉ *Piazza dei Sanniti 44,* ☎ *06/4452692. AE, DC, MC, V. Closed Sun.*

Vatican

$$$$ ✕ **La Pergola.** High atop Monte Mario, the Cavalieri Hilton's rooftop La Pergola restaurant offers a commanding view onto the city below. The dining room is warmly elegant with trompe-l'oeil ceilings, handsome wood paneling, and large windows. Amply spaced tables and low lighting create an intimate atmosphere not matched by other restaurants in town. Celebrated Wunder-chef Heinz Beck is a skilled technician and brings Rome its finest example of Mediterranean *alta cucina* (haute cuisine); dishes are balanced and light, and presentation is striking. The wine list and the cheese cart offer ample and interesting choices from Italy and France. ✉ *Cavalieri Hilton, Via Cadlolo 101,* ☎ *06/3509221. Reservations essential. Jacket and tie. AE, DC, MC, V. Closed Sun. and Mon. No lunch.*

$$ ✕ **Dal Toscano.** An open wood-fired grill and classic dishes like *ribollita* (a thick bread and vegetable soup) and *pici* (fresh thick pasta, served with a wild hare sauce) are the draw at this great family-run Tuscan trattoria near the Vatican. The cuts of beef visible in the refrigerator opposite the entrance tell you right away that the house special is the prized bistecca alla fiorentina. Wash it all down with a strong Chianti or ½ liter of the Tuscan house wine. Desserts such as pastry-cream tarts, apple strudel, and *castagnaccio* (a tasty chestnut and pine-nut treat) in wintertime are all homemade. Service is friendly and speedy. ✉ *Via Germanico 58,* ☎ *06/39725717. DC, MC, V. Closed Mon., Aug., and 2 wks in Dec.*

$$ \times$$ **Mare e Vino.** In this small, serene restaurant, fanciful, lightened-up versions of traditional Roman fare are beautifully presented on king-size plates. The menu—a selection of composed salads, vegetable soups, and pastas—always has a few suggestions from the chef. Try the *vermicelli cacio e pepe* (pasta with pecorino cheese and black pepper) or ravioli *di borragine* (filled with borage leaves), and various vegetable *sformati* (flans). ⊠ *Via dei Sediari 2,* ☎ *06/6869336. AE, DC, MC, V. Closed Sun.*

$ $$ \times$$ **Alfredo e Ada.** There's no place like home, and you'll feel like you're back there from the moment you squeeze into a table at this hole in the wall just across the river from Castel Sant'Angelo. There's no menu, just plate after plate of whatever Ada thinks you should try, from hearty, classic pastas to *involtini di vitello* (savory veal rolls with tomato) and home-made sausage. Sit back, relax, and enjoy—it's all good. By the time you leave, you may have made some new friends, too. ⊠ *Via dei Banchi Nuovi 14,* ☎ *06/6878842. No credit cards. Closed weekends.*

$ $$ \times$$ **Tre Pupazzi.** The "three puppets," after which the trattoria is named, are the worn stone figures on a fragment of an ancient sarcophagus that embellishes a building on this byway near the Vatican. Little has changed here since the place was built in 1625, and the restaurant upholds a tradition of good food, courteous service, and reasonable prices. The menu offers classic Roman and Abruzzese trattoria fare, including fettuccine and abbacchio, plus pizzas at lunchtime, a rarity in Rome. The restaurant opens early, at noon for lunch and 7 for dinner. ⊠ *Via dei Tre Pupazzi at Borgo Pio,* ☎ *06/6868371. AE, DC, MC, V. Closed Sun.*

Trastevere/Testaccio

$$–$$$ $$ \times$$ **Paris.** On a small square just off Piazza Santa Maria in Trastevere, Paris (named for a former owner) has a reassuring, understated ambience, without the hokey flamboyance of so many other eateries in this neighborhood. The menu features the best of classic Roman cuisine: homemade fettuccine, delicate fritto misto, and, of course, baccalà. You can also choose from a good wine list. In fair weather opt for tables on the piazza. ⊠ *Piazza San Calisto 7/a,* ☎ *06/5815378. AE, DC, MC, V. Closed Mon. and 3 wks in Aug. No dinner Sun.*

$$ $$ \times$$ **Checchino dal 1887.** Carved out of a hillside made of potsherds from Roman times, Checchino turns out the most traditional Roman cuisine served without fanfare in a clean, austere space. Though the slaughterhouses of Rome's Testaccio quarter—a short cab ride from the city center—are long gone, daring diners can still try the variety meats that make up the soul of Roman cooking: *trippa* (tripe), *testina* (head), *pajata* (intestine), *zampa* (trotter), and *coratella* (sweetbreads). There's also plenty to choose from if you're uninterested in innards: house specialties include *coda alla vaccinara* (stewed oxtail), a popular Roman dish the owners claim was invented here, and abbacchio *alla cacciatora* (braised in tomato sauce). Desserts are very good. ⊠ *Via di Monte Testaccio 30,* ☎ *06/5746318. AE, DC, MC, V. Closed Sun. and Mon., Aug., and at Christmas.*

$–$$ $$ \times$$ **Antico Arco.** Run by three friends with a passion for wine and fine
★ food, the Antico Arco, at the top of the Janiculum Hill, has won the hearts of Roman foodies with innovative dishes and moderate prices. There are always 30 wines to choose from by the glass, plus an excellent list of Italian and French labels. Particularly good are starters like soufflé *di parmigiano e cipolle verdi* (with and green onion) and second courses like *petto d'anatra con salsa di lamponi* (duck breast with raspberry sauce). Don't miss dessert. ⊠ *Piazzale Aurelio 7,* ☎ *06/ 5815274. AE, DC, MC, V. Closed Sun. No lunch.*

$ ✕ Perilli. A bastion of authentic Roman cooking since 1911 (the decor has changed very little), this trattoria is the place to go to try rigatoni *con pajata* (with calves' intestines)—if you're into this sort of thing. Otherwise pasta all'amatriciana and carbonara are classics. The house wine is a golden nectar from the Castelli Romani. ⊠ *Via Marmorata 39,* ☎ *06/5742415. AE, DC, MC, V. Closed Wed.*

Along Via Appia Antica

$$ ✕ Cecilia Metella. From the entrance on Via Appia Antica, practically opposite the catacombs, you walk uphill to a low-lying but sprawling construction designed for wedding feasts and banquets. There's a large terrace shaded by vines for outdoor dining. Although obviously geared to larger groups, Cecilia Metella also gives couples and small groups full attention, good service, and traditional Roman cuisine. The specialties are the searing-hot *crespelle* (crepes), served in individual casseroles, and *pollo al Nerone* (chicken à la Nero—flambéed, of course). ⊠ *Via Appia Antica 125,* ☎ *06/5136743. AE, DC, MC, V. Closed Mon. and last 2 wks in Aug.*

$$ ✕ L'Archeologia. In this farmhouse just beyond the catacombs, you dine indoors beside the fireplace in cool weather or in the garden under age-old vines in the summer. The atmosphere is friendly and intimate. Specialties include homemade pastas, abbacchio alla scottadito, and fresh seafood. ⊠ *Via Appia Antica 139,* ☎ *06/7880494. AE, MC, V. Closed Thurs.*

Pizzerias

It may have been invented somewhere else, but in Rome it's hard to walk a block without passing pizza in one form or another. Pizza from a bakery is usually made without cheese—pizza *bianca* (with olive oil and salt) or pizza *rossa* (with tomato sauce). Many small shops specialize in pizza *al taglio* (by the cut), priced by the *etto* (100 grams, about a ¼ pound), according to the kind of topping. Both of these make a great snack any time of day. Some good places to find the real thing on the go: **Il Forno di Campo dei Fiori** (⊠ Campo dei Fiori), closed Sunday, makes hot pizza bianca and rossa all day. **Antico Forno Roscioli** (⊠ Via dei Chiavari 34) is a truly excellent kosher bakery and pizzeria, closed weekends. **Zi Fenizia** (⊠ Via Santa Maria del Pianto 64) makes kosher pizza in the old Jewish Ghetto; it closes Friday at sundown, Saturday, and Jewish holidays.

But don't leave Rome without sitting down to a classic, wafer-thin, crispy Roman pizza in a lively, no-frills pizzeria. Most are open only for dinner, usually from 8 PM to midnight. Look for a place with a *forno a legna* (wood-burning oven), a must for a good thin crust on your plate-size Roman pizza. Standard models are the *margherita* (tomato, mozzarella, and basil) and the *capricciosa* (a little bit of everything, depending upon the "caprices" of the pizza chef: tomato, mozzarella, sausage, olives, artichoke hearts, prosciutto, even egg), but most pizzerias have a long list of additional options, including tasty mozzarella *di bufala* (buffalo-milk cheese).

$ ✕ Baffetto. Down a cobblestone street not far from Piazza Navona, this is Rome's best-known pizzeria and a summer favorite for streetside dining. The plain interior is mostly given over to the ovens, but there's another room with more paper-covered tables. Turnover is fast; this is not the place to linger. ⊠ *Via del Governo Vecchio 114, Old Rome,* ☎ *06/6861617. Reservations not accepted. No credit cards. Closed Sun. and Aug. No lunch.*

$ ✕ **Da Gino.** Trastevere's most elegant pizzeria serves all the classics, but with a style that sets it apart from its more rough-and-tumble neighbors. Delectably thin wood-oven pizza shares menu space with treats like *fritto di moscardini* (fried baby octopus). The wine list shows a sommelier's touch. Outdoor tables on a bustling pedestrian street are refreshing in summer. ✉ *Via della Lungaretta 85, Trastevere,* ☎ *06/5803403. AE, MC, V. Closed Wed. No lunch Mon.–Sat.*

$ ✕ **Dar Poeta.** Romans drive across town for great pizza, a bit cheaper than average, from this neighborhood joint on a small street in Trastevere. Maybe it's the dough—made from a secret blend of flours reputed to be easier to digest than that of the competition. For dessert, an unusual calzone is baked with Nutella (a chocolate and hazelnut spread) and ricotta. ✉ *Vicolo del Bologna 45, Trastevere,* ☎ *06/5880516. Reservations not accepted. AE, MC, V. Closed Mon. No lunch.*

$ ✕ **Il Leoncino.** Lines out the door on weekends attest to the popularity of this fluorescent-lit pizzeria in the otherwise big-ticket neighborhood around Piazza di Spagna. This is one of the few pizzerias open for lunch as well as dinner. ✉ *Via del Leoncino 28, near the Corso, Old Rome,* ☎ *06/6876306. Reservations not accepted. No credit cards. Closed Sun. and Aug.*

$ ✕ **La Soffitta.** You pay more, but hey, it's imported. This is Rome's hottest spot for classic Neapolitan pizza (thick, though crunchy on the bottom, rather than paper thin and crispy like the Roman kind) and one of the few *pizzerie* in town certified by the True Neapolitan Pizza Association. Desserts are brought in daily from Naples. ✉ *Via dei Villini 1/e, near Termini,* ☎ *06/4404642. Reservations not accepted. No credit cards. Closed Sun. and Aug. No lunch.*

Enoteche

It was not so long ago that wine in Rome (and other towns) was strictly local; you didn't have to walk far to find an *osteria,* a tavern-like establishment where you could buy wine straight from the barrel or sit down to drink and nibble a bit, chat, or play cards. The tradition continues today, as many Roman wineshops are also open as *enoteche* (wine bars). They've done away with the folding chairs and rickety tables—now it's designer interiors and chic ambience. Shelves are lined with hundreds of bottles from all over the country, representing the best in Italian wine making, many available by the glass. Behind the bar you'll find a serious wine enthusiast, maybe even a sommelier. There's usually a selection of carefully selected cheeses and cured meats and sometimes a short menu of simple dishes and desserts.

$$$ ✕ **Il Simposio di Costantini.** At the classiest wine bar in town, done out in wrought-iron vines, wood paneling, and velvet, you can choose from about 30 wines. Food is appropriately fancy: marinated and smoked fish, composed salads, top-quality salami and cured meats (classical and wild), terrines and pâtés, and several gussied-up hot vegetable and meat dishes. It has 80 assorted cheeses, grouped according to origin or type (French, Italian, goat, hard, herb crusted). ✉ *Piazza Cavour 16, Vatican,* ☎ *06/3211502. AE, DC, MC, V. Closed Thurs.*

$ ✕ **Enoteca degli Spiriti.** This tiny wine bar behind the Pantheon has been winning fans with a daily menu of homemade treats, served inside at small wooden tables or outside under umbrellas. Get cozy in winter with *polenta ai funghi porcini* (polenta with porcini mushrooms) and a glass of Brunello, or cool off in summer with *involtini di mozzarella di bufala* (buffalo-milk mozzarella rolls) and a crisp chardonnay. Service is friendly, and the price is right. ✉ *Via S. Eustachio 5,* ☎ *no phone. No credit cards. Closed Sun. No lunch Sat.*

$ ✕ **L'Osteria dell'Ingegno.** This trendy spot with a casual ambience is great for a glass of wine or a light meal in the center. The menu is eclectic, with simple but innovative dishes that change weekly. The walls are hung with colorful paintings by local artists, and service is friendly. ⊠ *Piazza di Pietra 45, Old Rome,* ☎ *06/6780662. Reservations essential. AE, DC, MC, V. Closed Sun.*

$ ✕ **Trimani Il Winebar.** This is a handy address for diners in a town where most restaurants don't unlock the door before 8 PM. Trimani opens up at 6 PM for snacks and cold plates, at 7:30 for hot food, and stays open until 11:30. The feeling is modern and casually reserved. There's always a choice of a soup and a few pasta plates, as well as second courses and *torte salate* (savory tarts). Around the corner is a wineshop, one of the oldest in Rome, of the same name. Call about wine tastings and short courses (in Italian). ⊠ *Via Cernaia 37/b, near Termini,* ☎ *06/ 4469630. AE, DC, MC, V. Closed Sun. and 2 wks in Aug.*

Cafés

As elsewhere in Italy, there is a *bar* (café-bar) on nearly every corner in Rome where you can get coffee drinks, fruit juices, pastries, sandwiches, liquor, and beer. Locals usually stop in for a quickie at the counter—prices are two to three times higher when sitting at a table. Pricey **Antico Caffè Greco** (⊠ Via Condotti 86, ☎ 06/6791700) is a national landmark; its red-velvet chairs and marble tables have hosted the likes of Byron, Shelley, Keats, Goethe, and Casanova. **Caffè Sant'Eustachio** (⊠ Piazza Sant'Eustachio 82, ☎ 06/6861309) claims its blend makes Rome's best coffee and points to the thick umber foam on top to prove it. **Tazza d'Oro** (⊠ Via degli Orfani 84, near the Pantheon, ☎ 06/6789792) contends that its coffee is the best in the city—but why not see for yourself? If you want your *caffè* (espresso) without sugar at either Tazza d'Oro or Sant'Eustachio, ask for it *amaro.* You can sit back and watch the world go by at **Rosati** (⊠ Piazza del Popolo 5, ☎ 06/3225859). **Antico Caffè della Pace** (⊠ Via della Pace 3, ☎ 06/ 6861216), near Piazza Navona, has an ornate, old-fashioned atmosphere. **Caffè Teichner** (⊠ Piazza Santa Maria in Lucina 17, ☎ 06/6871449), just off the Corso, is a good spot to take a break from shopping.

Gelaterie and Pasticcerie

Gelato is more a snack for Italians than a serious dessert. **Il Gelato di San Crispino** (⊠ Via della Panetteria 42, near the Trevi Fountain, ☎ 06/6793924), closed Tuesday, is perhaps the most celebrated gelato in all of Italy, made without artificial colors or flavors. It's worth crossing town for. **Fiocco di Neve** (⊠ Via del Pantheon 51, ☎ 06/6786025) is convenient to the Pantheon. **Fonte della Salute** (⊠ Via Cardinal Marmagi 2, ☎ 06/5897471), literally, "fountain of health," serves frozen yogurt as well as traditional gelato. It's closed Tuesday in winter. The historic **San Filippo** (⊠ Via di Villa S. Filippo 8, ☎ 06/8079314), closed Monday, is renowned for flavors like chestnut and clementine in winter, watermelon and peach in summer. **Giolitti** (⊠ Via Uffici del Vicario 40, ☎ 06/6991243), just off of Via Campo Marzio, has an old-fashioned tearoom and traditional atmosphere.

Romans are not known for their sweet tooths, and there are few *pasticcerie* (pastry shops) in town that distinguish themselves with particularly good examples of the few regional desserts. One exception is the **Forno del Ghetto** (⊠ Via del Portico d'Ottavia 1, ☎ 06/6878637), closed Friday at sundown, Saturday, and Jewish holidays. This hole in the wall—no sign, no tables, just a take-away counter—is an institution, preserving a tradition of Italian-Jewish sweets that cannot be found anywhere else. The ricotta cake (with sour cherry jam or chocolate) is unforgettable. For a change of pace, try the Austrian cakes and American pies at **Dolceroma** (⊠ Via del Portico d'Ottavia 20/b, ☎ 06/6892196); the apple strudel and Sacher torte may not be Italian, but Romans flock here in droves just the same. It's closed Sunday afternoon and Monday and four weeks July–August.

Salumerie

There are several hundred *salumerie* (gourmet food shops) in town, but a few stand out for a particularly ample selection and items of rare, superior quality. Foodies should head straight for **Franchi** (⊠ Via Cola di Rienzo 200, ☎ 06/6864576), closed Sunday, with the city's best takeout, gourmet treats like salmon mousse, roast beef and vegetable fritters, and an endless selection of sliced meats and cheeses that you can have vacuum-packed for safe transport home. **Castroni** (⊠ Via Cola di Rienzo 196, ☎ 06/6864383), closed Sunday, is a fine general food shop with lots of imported items. It's right next door to Franchi. **Volpetti** (⊠ Via Marmorata 47, ☎ 06/5742352), closed Thursday afternoon and Sunday, has the highest-quality meats and specializes in aged cheeses from small producers.

LODGING

Updated by
Jude Barrand

Palatial surroundings, luxurious comfort, and high standards of service can be found at the city's pricier establishments, but standards vary considerably; quality and good value should not be taken for granted in any category. Note that the star rating system used by all Italian hotels is based on facilities and services offered but is no indication of the quality of those facilities and services. Generally, rooms tend to be small by U.S. standards. Many of the lower-priced hotels are actually old-fashioned *pensioni* set on one or several floors of a large building. One disadvantage of staying in central hotels in lower categories is noise; ask for an inside room if you are a light sleeper, but don't be disappointed if it faces a dark courtyard.

Because Rome's religious importance makes it a year-round tourist destination, there is never a period when hotels are predictably empty, so you should always try to make reservations, even if only a few days in advance, by phone or fax. Always inquire about special low rates, often available in both winter and summer if occupancy is low. If you do arrive without reservations, try **Hotel Reservation Service** (☎ 06/6991000), with an English-speaking operator available daily 7 AM–10 PM, and with desks at Aeroporto Fiumicino and Stazione Termini. A list of all the hotels in Rome, with prices and facilities, is available from the main **EPT** information office (⊠ Via Parigi 5, ☎ 06/48899255).

Old Rome

$$$$ 🏢 **Dei Borgognoni.** This quietly chic hotel is on a byway in the heart of the smart shopping district near Piazza San Silvestro. The centuries-old building has been remodeled to provide spacious lounges, a glassed-in garden, and stylishly furnished rooms that are cleverly arranged to create an illusion of space, though they are actually compact. Some rooms have balconies or terraces on an interior court. The hotel has a garage, a rarity in such a central location. ⊠ *Via del Bufalo 126, 00187,* ☎ *06/69941505,* FAX *06/69941501,* WEB *www.borgognoni.it. 51 rooms. Parking (fee). AE, DC, MC, V. EP.*

$$$$ 🏢 **Holiday Inn Crowne Plaza Minerva.** This hotel is the very stylish reincarnation of the hostelry that occupied this 17th-century palazzo

486

Rome Lodging

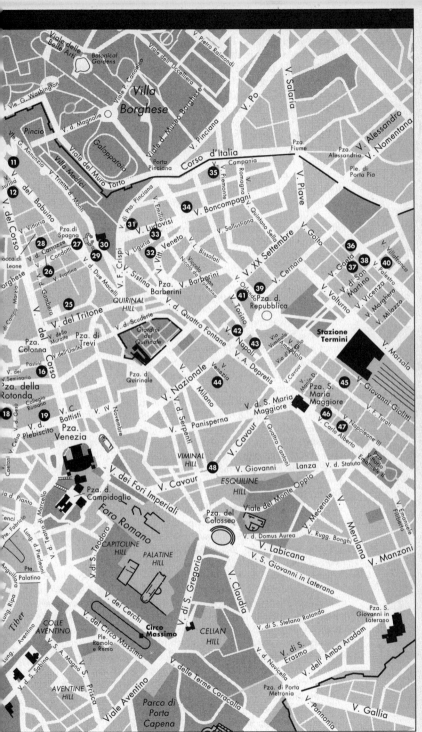

for centuries, hosting literati from Stendhal to Sartre and de Beauvoir. Entirely redone, with a stunning stained-glass lobby ceiling designed by renowned architect Paolo Portoghesi, the Minerva has everything a guest could want in the way of comfort, all in an absolutely central location. And from the roof terrace, open for summer dining in fair weather, you can almost touch the immense, flattened dome of Hadrian's Pantheon. ✉ *Piazza della Minerva 69, 00186,* ☎ *06/695201,* ℻ *06/6794165,* WEB *www.crowneplaza.com. 118 rooms, 17 suites. Restaurant, bar. AE, DC, MC, V. EP.*

$$$$ **Raphaël.** This may be Rome's most fascinating hotel. The location
★ is perfect—tucked away behind Piazza Navona—and the vine-covered facade creates a feeling of cozy mystery. The extensive lobby features an array of sculpture, genuine antiques, and a collection of original Picasso ceramics. Each room is uniquely designed and decorated with its own treasures, and bathrooms are finished with travertine marble or hand-painted tiles. The bi-level Bramante Terrace, where guests can arrange to have meals, offers great city views. The Raphaël Restaurant is memorable, serving French and Mediterranean cuisine on Picasso-inspired dinnerware. Some suites have private terraces. ✉ *Largo Febo 2, 00186,* ☎ *06/682–831,* ℻ *06/687–8993,* WEB *www.raphaelhotel.com. 51 rooms, 7 suites, 10 apartments. Restaurant, bar, sauna, gym, parking (fee). AE, DC, MC, V. EP.*

$$$ **Cardinal.** Staying at this hotel is like stepping inside a Renaissance painting—it was built by Bramante and is set on magnificent Via Giulia, whose immutable vistas have scarcely changed since the 15th century. Cardinals would feel right at home: the lobby is a riot of red, while the rooms upstairs are almost ascetic. Serene, severe, and subdued, many of them feature antique engravings and Olympian-high ceilings. Of course, the interiors don't matter so much when Via Giulia—lined with beautiful palazzi and opulent antiques stores—is right outside your doorstep. ✉ *Via Giulia 62, 00186,* ☎ *06/68802719,* ℻ *06/6786376. 71 rooms. Bar. AE, DC, MC, V. EP.*

$$$ **Cesàri.** From the traffic-free street in front of this intimate and
★ quiet hotel in the center of Rome you can see the columns of an ancient temple that were incorporated into the side of the stock exchange. The hotel's exterior is as it was when Stendhal stayed here in the 1800s, but the interior has been thoroughly renovated and redecorated, with cream-color walls embellished with old prints of Rome and soft-green drapes and bedspreads. A few rooms are furnished with antiques; all have smart two-tone blue-marble bathrooms. ✉ *Via di Pietra 89a, 00186,* ☎ *06/6792386,* ℻ *06/6790882. 47 rooms. Parking (fee). AE, DC, MC, V.*

$$$ **Santa Chiara.** Three historic buildings form this gracious hotel be-
★ hind the Pantheon. It has been in the same family for 200 years, and its personal attention shows in meticulously decorated and maintained lounges and rooms. Though not all the rooms are spacious, all have character and are quiet and well organized. Each has built-in oak headboards, a marble-top desk, and an elegant travertine bath. Double-glazed front windows overlook Piazza della Minerva. The excellent location and low rates in this category give it a good quality-for-price ratio. The hotel also has three apartments, for two to five people, with full kitchens. The topmost has beamed ceilings, a fireplace, and a huge terrace with a view of the Pantheon's dome. ✉ *Via Santa Chiara 21, 00186,* ☎ *06/6872979,* ℻ *06/6873144,* WEB *www.albergosantachiara.com. 100 rooms, 4 suites, 3 apartments. Bar, kitchenettes (some), parking. AE, DC, MC, V. CP.*

$$ **Arenula.** This hotel—with a luminous and cheerful all-white interior—is one of Rome's best values. Rooms have pale-wood furnishings and gleaming bathrooms, as well as double-glazed windows

and air-conditioning (summer only; no help on warm spring or fall days). Two rooms accommodate four beds. The catch at the four-story Arenula is that the graceful oval staircase of white marble and wrought iron is the only way up—there is no elevator. The hotel is on an age-worn byway off central Via Arenula, on the edge of the Ghetto. ⊠ *Via Santa Maria dei Calderari 47 (at Via Arenula), 00186,* ☎ *06/6879454,* FAX *06/6896188,* WEB *www.hotelarenula.com. 50 rooms. DC, MC, V.*

$$ ☷ **Campo dei Fiori.** Frescoes, exposed brickwork, and picturesque effects throughout this little hotel in Old Rome could well be the work of a set designer. There's an aura of fantasy and romanticism in the decoration, with the layout cleverly designed to make the most of limited space. A few rooms are so compact they're almost claustrophobic; other rooms are larger, and all have an unusual decorative feature of some kind to remind you that you are in the heart of Rome. The hotel has no elevator, but the climb to the roof terrace rewards you with a marvelous view. Rates for the best rooms exceed parameters in this price category. ⊠ *Via del Biscione 6, 00186,* ☎ *06/68806865,* FAX *06/6876003. 27 rooms, 14 with bath. MC, V. EP.*

$$ ☷ **Cronet.** You, too, can be a guest in the vast Palazzo Doria Pamphili off Piazza Venezia. This small hotel occupies part of a floor in one wing of the palace; seven interior rooms overlook the aristocratic family's lovely private garden court. Antique-style stuccoes and moldings in the carpeted halls and beamed ceilings in several rooms are in keeping with the historic surroundings. The good-size rooms have oldish baths, some very small; several rooms can accommodate three or four beds. ⊠ *Piazza Grazioli 5, 00186,* ☎ *06/6792341,* FAX *06/69922705. 13 rooms, 10 with bath. AE, DC, MC, V. CP.*

$$ ☷ **Portoghesi.** In the heart of Old Rome, the Portoghesi is a small hotel
★ with big atmosphere. From a tiny lobby, an equally tiny elevator takes you to the quiet bedrooms. It has a charming roof garden with a view of the city's domes and rooftops. ⊠ *Via dei Portoghesi 1, 00186,* ☎ *06/6864231,* FAX *06/6876976,* WEB *www.hotelportoghesiroma.com. 22 rooms, 6 suites. MC, V.*

$$ ☷ **Teatro di Pompeo.** Where else can you breakfast under the ancient
★ stone vaults of Pompey's Theater, historic site of Julius Caesar's assassination? At this intimate and refined little hotel in the heart of Old Rome you are part of that history; at night, you sleep under restored beamed ceilings that date from the days of Michelangelo. The tastefully furnished rooms offer comfort as well as charm. Book well in advance. ⊠ *Largo del Pallaro 8, 00186,* ☎ *06/68300170,* FAX *06/ 68805531. 12 rooms. AE, DC, MC, V.*

Spanish Steps

$$$$ ☷ **Hassler.** Positioned at the top of the Spanish Steps, the Hassler has
★ sweeping views of Rome from its front rooms and rooftop restaurant; other rooms overlook the Villa Medici gardens. The hotel is run by the distinguished Wirth family of hoteliers, which assures a cordial atmosphere and imperial service from the well-trained staff. The public rooms have an extravagant 1950s elegance—especially the glass-roofed lounge. There is a clubby winter bar as well as a pretty summer garden bar. The comfortable guest rooms, some with frescoed walls, have been undergoing a decorating renovation that was close to complete at press time. (Ask for a renovated room.) The penthouse suite is resplendent with antiques and has a huge terrace. ⊠ *Piazza Trinità dei Monti 6, 00187,* ☎ *06/699340,* FAX *06/6789991,* WEB *www.hotelhasslerroma.com. 85 rooms, 15 suites. Restaurant, 2 bars, lobby lounge, hair salon. AE, DC, MC, V. EP.*

$$$$ ⊞ **Hotel de Russie.** In the 19th century, this historic hostelry counted Russian princes among its guests. Later Picasso and Cocteau leaned out the windows to pick oranges from the trees in the stunning, terraced garden, a lush oasis just a few steps from Piazza del Popolo. Now Sir Rocco Forte of the hotel dynasty has restored the de Russie to a superlative standard of accommodations and service, introducing today's comforts (including faxes and voice messaging) into rooms decorated in chic Italian contemporary style, with Roman mosaic motifs in bathrooms. Many rooms have garden views, and several suites have panoramic terraces. In fair weather you can dine in the splendid garden setting. Even the spa–fitness center is luxurious. ⊠ *Via del Babuino 9, 00187,* ☎ *06/328881,* FAX *06/32888888,* WEB *www.rfhotels.com. 130 rooms, 27 suites. Restaurant, bar, hair salon, spa, health club. AE, DC, MC, V.*

$$$$ ⊞ **The Inn at the Spanish Steps.** The name of this small, exclusive hotel, which opened in 2000, tells it all. Staying here is like having your own little place on fabled Via Condotti, the elegant shopping street crowned by the Spanish Steps. The hotel shares a centuries-old palazzo with historic Caffè Greco and is arranged on the upper floors. Rooms, all junior suites, are handsomely decorated with damask fabrics and antiques. ⊠ *Via Condotti 85, 00187,* ☎ *06/69925657,* FAX *06/6786470,* WEB *www.atspanishsteps.com. 22 rooms. Airport shuttle. AE, DC, MC, V.*

$$$–$$$$ ⊞ **D'Inghilterra.** Legendary names like Liszt, Mendelssohn, Hans
★   Christian Andersen, Mark Twain, and Hemingway litter the guest book here. With a residential feel and a staff that is as warm as the surroundings are velvety, this hotel near the Spanish Steps has nearly everything. Even a pedigree: before 1845, it had been the guest house of the fabulously rich Prince Torlonia. The outside still looks suitably vintage, and inside there's 19th-century elegance. Just beyond the tiny lobby is the Lounge, a favored luncheon spot whose decor of framed prints and Biedermeier-style furniture is a connoisseur's joy. Upstairs, guest rooms are so full of stylishly arranged carpets, gilt-framed mirrors, and cozy bergères you'll hardly notice the snug dimensions. ⊠ *Via Bocca di Leone 14, 00187,* ☎ *06/699811,* FAX *06/6798601,* WEB *www.charminghotels.it/inghilterra. 90 rooms, 12 suites. 2 restaurants, bar. AE, DC, MC, V.*

$$$ ⊞ **Carriage.** The Carriage's location is what makes it special: it's just two blocks from the Spanish Steps, in the heart of Rome. The stylish decor uses subdued Baroque accents and antique reproductions to give the hotel a touch of elegance. Though some of the rooms are pint-size, and a couple open onto an air shaft, several have little terraces; a roof garden adds to the appeal. ⊠ *Via delle Carrozze 36, 00187,* ☎ *06/6990124,* FAX *06/6788279,* WEB *www.hotelcarriage.net. 24 rooms, 2 suites. AE, DC, MC, V.*

$$–$$$ ⊞ **Locarno.** Art aficionados have long appreciated this hotel's fin-de-siècle charm, intimate feel, and central location off Piazza del Popolo. Rooms have coordinated wallpaper and fabric prints, lacquered wrought-iron beds, and some antiques juxtaposed with modern features (electronic safes and air-conditioning). Amenities include an ample buffet breakfast, bar service on the panoramic roof garden, and complimentary bicycles. ⊠ *Via della Penna 22, 00186,* ☎ *06/3610841,* FAX *06/3215249,* WEB *www.hotellocarno.com. 46 rooms, 2 suites. Bar, breakfast room, lobby lounge, bicycles. AE, DC, MC, V.*

$$–$$$ ⊞ **Scalinata di Spagna.** An old-fashioned pensione loved by generations of romantics, this tiny hotel is booked solid for months—even years—ahead. Its location at the top of the Spanish Steps, inconspicuous little entrance, and view from the terrace where you breakfast make it seem like your own special, exclusive inn. And that's why rates for some rooms are at the top of this category. ⊠ *Piazza Trinità dei Monti*

17, 00187, ☎ *06/6793006,* FAX *06/69940598,* WEB *www.hotelscali-nata.com. 15 rooms. Parking (fee). MC, V.*

$ ☆ **Margutta.** The lobby and halls in this small hotel are unassuming,
★ but rooms are a pleasant surprise, with a clean and airy look, attractive wrought-iron bedsteads, and modern baths. Though it's in an old building, there is an elevator. It's centrally located, on a quiet side street between the Spanish Steps and Piazza del Popolo. ⊠ *Via Laurina 34, 00187,* ☎ *06/3223674,* FAX *06/3200395. 24 rooms. AE, DC, MC, V.*

Veneto

$$$$ ☆ **Eden.** A superlative hotel that combines dashing elegance and stun-
★ ning vistas of Rome with the warmth of Italian hospitality, the Eden was once the preferred haunt of Hemingway, Ingrid Bergman, and Fellini and of many other celebrities before them. Precious antiques, sumptuous Italian fabrics, linen sheets, and marble baths have an understated elegance. The views from the rooftop bar and terrace will take your breath away, and the hotel's top-floor restaurant, La Terrazza dell'Eden, merits raves, too. ⊠ *Via Ludovisi 49, 00187,* ☎ *06/478121,* FAX *06/4821584,* WEB *www.hotel-eden.it. 101 rooms, 12 suites. Restaurant, bar, gym, free parking. AE, DC, MC, V. EP.*

$$$$ ☆ **Excelsior.** To Romans and many others, the white Victorian cupola of the Excelsior is a symbol of Rome at its most cosmopolitan. The hotel's porte cochere has long sheltered Europe's aristocrats and Hollywood's royalty as they alighted from their Rollses and Ferraris. They entered the polished doors that still open onto a world of luxury lavished with mirrors, carved moldings, Oriental rugs, crystal chandeliers, and huge, baroque floral arrangements. The theme of gracious living prevails throughout the hotel in splendidly appointed rooms and marble baths. ⊠ *Via Veneto 125, 00187,* ☎ *06/47081,* FAX *06/4826205,* WEB *www.westin.com. 286 rooms, 35 suites. Restaurant, bar, barbershop, hair salon, free parking. AE, DC, MC, V. EP.*

$$$$ ☆ **Majestic.** In the 19th-century tradition of grand hotels, this establishment on Via Veneto offers sumptuous furnishings and spacious rooms, with up-to-date accessories such as CNN, minibars, strongboxes, and white marble bathrooms. There are authentic antiques in the public rooms, and the excellent restaurant looks like a Victorian conservatory. The Ninfa grill-café on street level is an intimate spot for light meals and drinks. Many suites have whirlpool baths. ⊠ *Via Veneto 50, 00187,* ☎ *06/421441,* FAX *06/4880984,* WEB *www.hotelmajestic.com. 100 rooms, 18 suites. 2 restaurants, bar, café, in-room safes, minibars, parking (fee). AE, DC, MC, V.*

$$$ ☆ **La Residenza.** Mainly Americans frequent this hotel in a converted
★ town house near Via Veneto, with first-class comfort and a great atmosphere. The canopied entrance, spacious and well-furnished lounges, and the bar and terrace are of the type you would expect to find in a deluxe lodging. Rooms have bentwood armchairs, large closets, color TVs, refrigerator-bars, air-conditioning, and heated towel racks. Rates include a generous American-style buffet breakfast and an in-house movie every night. ⊠ *Via Emilia 22, 00187,* ☎ *06/4880789,* FAX *06/485721. 21 rooms, 6 suites. Bar. V.*

$$$ ☆ **Victoria.** A 1950s luxury in the public rooms, solid comfort throughout at reasonable rates, and impeccable management are the main features of this hotel near Via Veneto. Oriental rugs, oil paintings, and fresh flowers add charm to the public spaces, and the rooms are well furnished with armchairs and other amenities ignored by many modern decorators. American businesspeople, who prize the hotel's personalized service and restful atmosphere, are frequent guests. Some upper rooms and the roof terrace overlook the majestic pines of the Villa Borgh-

ese. ✉ *Via Campania 41, 00187,* ☎ *06/473931,* FAX *06/4871890. 110 rooms. Restaurant, bar. AE, DC, MC, V. FAP, MAP.*

Near Termini

$$$$ 🏨 **Mascagni.** Outside is one of Rome's busiest, most central streets, but not a sound filters into the interior of this elegant establishment. It has a cheerful staff and the particular charm of the small hotel. Decorated in early 1920s style, it has handsome mahogany furnishings and coordinated fabrics. The intimate lounges and pleasant bar mirror the same decorating scheme, as does the breakfast room, where a lavish buffet is laid in the morning. ✉ *Via Vittorio Emanuele Orlando 90, 00185,* ☎ *06/48904040,* FAX *06/4817637,* WEB *www.hotelmascagni.com. 40 rooms. Bar, breakfast room, business services. AE, DC, MC, V.*

$$$$ 🏨 **St. Regis Grand.** A 100-year-old establishment of class and style, this hotel caters to an elite international clientele. Recently totally renovated as part of the Sheraton group, it reopened in 2000 but preserves the grand manner that has always distinguished its posh salons and rooms, all sumptuously decorated in Empire and Regency style. Over each bed is a large original fresco of a Roman scene. Murano glass chandeliers, a 24-hour butler-service floor of suites, and Bulgari bathroom amenities are just some of the features of this deluxe establishment. Le Grand Bar is a popular rendezvous; afternoon tea and Sunday brunch are served in the Grand Hall Café. ✉ *Via Vittorio Emanuele Orlando 3, 00185,* ☎ *06/47091,* FAX *06/4747307,* WEB *www.stregis.com. 130 rooms, 31 suites. Restaurant, bar, café, gym, parking (fee). AE, DC, MC, V. EP.*

$$$–$$$$ 🏨 **Art Deco.** This hotel's name tells all about its glamorous decor, attuned to the elegance of the 1920s, with whimsical accents in Deco paintings and antiques. Underlying the style is reassuring technology: a fail-safe electrical system, air-conditioning, and whirlpool baths. The hotel is in a residential neighborhood 10 minutes from Stazione Termini and handy to public transport. Book through Best Western or directly for the best rates. ✉ *Via Palestro 19, 00185,* ☎ *06/4457588,* FAX *06/4441483. 49 rooms. Restaurant, bar, hot tub. AE, DC, MC, V. EP.*

$$$ 🏨 **Britannia.** This fine small hotel, with frescoed halls and breakfast
★   room, is a very special place, offering superior quality at moderate rates. Its quiet but central location is one attraction; a caring management is another. You are coddled with such service as English-language dailies and local weather reports delivered to your room each morning, with sybaritic marble bathrooms (some with whirlpool baths) and compact rooms furnished with luxury fabrics and original art. The fine rooftop suite has an ample terrace. ✉ *Via Napoli 64, 00184,* ☎ *06/4883153,* FAX *06/4882343. 32 rooms, 1 suite. Breakfast room, free parking. AE, DC, MC, V.*

$$$ 🏨 **D'Este.** The fresh-looking decor in this distinguished 19th-century hotel evokes solid comfort, with brass bedsteads and lamps and rustic darkwood furniture. Rooms are quiet, light, and spacious; many can accommodate family groups. The attentive owner-manager likes to have fresh flowers in the halls and sees that everything works. He encourages inquiries about special rates, particularly during the slack summer months. It's within hailing distance of Santa Maria Maggiore and close to Stazione Termini (you can arrange to be picked up there by the hotel car). Under the same management is the newer, more intimate Hotel Giubileo ($$), across the street. ✉ *Via Carlo Alberto 4/b, 00185,* ☎ *06/4465607,* FAX *06/4465601. 37 rooms. Bar. AE, DC, MC, V.*

$$$ 🏨 **Duca d'Alba.** This elegant hotel has made a stylish contribution to the ongoing gentrification of the Suburra neighborhood, near the Colosseum and the Roman Forum. The tasteful neoclassical decor is in character with ancient Roman motifs. with custom-designed fur-

nishings and marble bathrooms. All rooms are entirely soundproofed; a few have tiny terraces. The four-bed suite with kitchenette is a bargain for a family or a group of friends. This well-run establishment offers exceptionally good value: rates are at the lowest rung in the category. The attentive staff is another plus. ⊠ *Via Leonina 14, 00184,* ☎ *06/484471,* FAX *06/4884840,* WEB *www.hotelducadalba.com. 27 rooms, 1 suite. Kitchenettes (some). AE, DC, MC, V.*

$$$ ⊞ **Morgana.** After enjoying the richly marbled lobby, comfortable
★ lounges, antique accents in fully carpeted halls, and soundproofed rooms decorated with fine fabrics, you'll agree this is an elegantly conceived hotel. The Morgana offers excellent value and shows the management's attention to comfort and detail. The atmosphere is cordial and the rates are low in this category. It's also convenient to Stazione Termini. ⊠ *Via Filippo Turati 33, 00185,* ☎ *06/4467230,* FAX *06/ 4469142,* WEB *www.hotelmorgana.com. 100 rooms, 2 suites. Bar, airport shuttle, parking (fee). AE, DC, MC, V.*

$$ ⊞ **Des Artistes.** This no-smoking hotel run by the three personable young
★ Riccioni brothers offers probably the best quality–price ratio in the Termini Station neighborhood. Together with soundproofing, air-conditioning, minibars, and safety features, rooms have attractive fabrics and furnishings, copies of master paintings, and marble baths. On one floor, 13 equally well furnished rooms share baths in a three-to-one ratio and have ceiling fans and even lower rates. And there are a few dorm rooms at rock-bottom prices. The roof terrace is fitted out for fair-weather relaxing, and the little lounge has computer facilities for guests. ⊠ *Via Villafranca 20, 00185,* ☎ *06/4454365,* FAX *06/ 4462368,* WEB *www.hoteldesartistes.com. 40 rooms, 27 with bath. Bar, in-room data ports, minibars. AE, DC, MC, V. CP.*

$$ ⊞ **Miami.** Its location in a dignified 19th-century building on Rome's important Via Nazionale puts this hotel in a strategic spot for sightseeing, shopping, and getting around in general; it is on main bus lines and near Stazione Termini and the metro. The marble floors, chrome trim, and dark colors are brightened by the friendly family-style management. Rooms on the courtyard are quieter. ⊠ *Via Nazionale 230, 00184,* ☎ *06/4817180,* FAX *06/484562,* WEB *www.hotelmiami.com. 48 rooms, 2 suites. AE, DC, MC, V.*

$$ ⊞ **Montreal.** This is a compact hotel on a central avenue across the square from Santa Maria Maggiore, only three blocks from Stazione Termini, with bus and subway lines close by. On three floors of an older building, it has been totally renovated and offers fresh-looking rooms. The owner-managers are pleasant and helpful, and the neighborhood has plenty of reasonably priced restaurants. ⊠ *Via Carlo Alberto 4, 00185,* ☎ *06/4457797,* FAX *06/4465522,* WEB *www.hotelmontreal-roma.com. 27 rooms. Parking (fee). AE, DC, MC, V.*

$$ ⊞ **Siviglia.** You are transported back to a more opulent era in this 19th-century mansion in the quieter residential fringe of the Stazione Termini area. Like the several embassies in the neighborhood, it, too, has bright flags flying at the entrance. Inside, Venetian glass chandeliers and antique reproduction furniture give the lounges considerable character; rooms are simpler, with a light, airy touch. ⊠ *Via Gaeta 12, 00185,* ☎ *06/4441197,* FAX *06/4441195. 42 rooms. Bar. AE, MC, V.*

$ ⊞ **Italia.** Off Via Nazionale, this family-run hotel offers freshly painted, luminous rooms with big windows, desks, parquet floors, new baths with faux-marble tiles, and attractive art on the walls, along with a generous buffet breakfast. Three rooms are triples. An eight-room annex across the street has high ceilings, double-glazed windows, and a slightly more upscale look. Ask for low August and winter rates. ⊠ *Via Venezia 18, 00184,* ☎ *06/4828355,* FAX *06/4745550,* WEB *www.hotelitaliaroma.com. 31 rooms. AE, DC, MC, V.*

$ 🏨 **Romae.** In the better part of the Stazione Termini neighborhood, the Romae has the advantages of a strategic location, a very friendly and helpful management, and good-size rooms. The color scheme is Roman pink, with fragments of faux antiquities throughout. Amenities such as satellite TV, safes, and hair dryers in every room, and free Internet access, make this hotel a very good value. Families benefit from special rates and services. ⊠ *Via Palestro 49, 00185,* ☎ *06/4463554,* FAX *06/4463914,* WEB *www.hotelromae.com. 38 rooms. Breakfast room, in-room safes. AE, MC, V.*

Vatican

$$$$ 🏨 **Cavalieri Hilton.** Though the Cavalieri is outside the imaginary confines of the city's center, distance has its advantages, one of them being the magnificent view from the hotel's hilltop position (ask for a room facing the city). This hotel is a stylish oasis of quiet and comfort, with good taste and a distinctive Italian flair. If you can tear yourself away from your balcony, the terraces, gardens, and swimming pools, you will find a courtesy shuttle bus leaving for downtown Rome every hour. Don't miss the deservedly acclaimed rooftop restaurant, La Pergola. ⊠ *Via Cadlolo 101, 00136,* ☎ *06/35091,* FAX *06/35092241,* WEB *www.cavalieri-hilton.com. 357 rooms, 17 suites. 3 restaurants, bar, indoor pool, hair salon, spa, tennis court, health club. AE, DC, MC, V.*

$$$$ 🏨 **Giulio Cesare.** An aristocratic town house with a garden in the residential but central Prati district, the Giulio Cesare is a 10-minute walk across the Tiber from Piazza del Popolo. It's beautifully run, with a friendly staff and a quietly luxurious air. The rooms are elegantly furnished, with chandeliers, thick rugs, floor-length drapes, and rich damasks in soft colors. Public rooms have Oriental carpets, old prints and paintings, marble fireplaces, and a grand piano. The buffet breakfast is a veritable banquet. ⊠ *Via degli Scipioni 287, 00192,* ☎ *06/3210751,* FAX *06/3211736. 90 rooms. Bar. AE, DC, MC, V.*

$$$-$$$$ 🏨 **Atlante Star.** The lush rooftop-terrace garden café and the restaurant of this comfortable hotel near St. Peter's have a knockout view of the basilica and the rest of Rome. In a distinguished 19th-century building, the rooms are attractively decorated with striped silks and prints for an old-world atmosphere; many bathrooms have hot tubs. The friendly family management is attentive to guests' needs and takes pride in offering extra-virgin olive oil from its own trees in the country. A sister hotel, the **Atlante Garden** ($$–$$$), just around the corner, has larger rooms and the same prerogatives at slightly lower rates. ⊠ *Via Vitelleschi 34, 00193,* ☎ *06/6873233,* FAX *06/6872300,* WEB *www.atlantehotels.com. 60 rooms, 10 suites. Restaurant, café, airport shuttle. AE, MC, V.*

$$$ 🏨 **Farnese.** A late-19th-century mansion, the Farnese is near the metro
★   and within walking distance of St. Peter's. Furnished with great attention to detail in art deco style, it has an intimate atmosphere, dazzling modern baths, charming fresco decorations, and a roof garden. ⊠ *Via Alessandro Farnese 30, 00193,* ☎ *06/3212553,* FAX *06/3215129. 24 rooms. Bar, free parking. AE, DC, MC, V. EP.*

$$$ 🏨 **Sant'Anna.** An example of the gentrification of the picturesque old Borgo neighborhood in the shadow of St. Peter's, this fashionable small hotel has ample, air-conditioned bedrooms in art deco style. The frescoes in the breakfast room and fountain in the courtyard are typical Roman touches. The spacious attic rooms have tiny terraces. ⊠ *Borgo Pio 134, 00193,* ☎ *06/68801602,* FAX *06/68308717,* WEB *www.hotelsantanna.com. 20 rooms. Breakfast room, parking (fee). AE, DC, MC, V.*

$$ 🏨 **Alimandi.** On a side street a block from the Vatican Museums, this
★   family-operated hotel offers excellent value in a neighborhood with moderately priced shops and restaurants. A spiffy lobby and ample lounges,

Close-Up

CONVENTS AND CURFEWS

ROME HAS AT LEAST 150 convents and religious institutes that offer accommodations, usually quite plain but clean and inexpensive. Beds are usually singles. Generally, unmarried couples are not accepted. Most institutes have a strict curfew, usually about 10 or 10:30 PM. To book by phone, you may need to speak Italian, or have someone standing by who does. A list is available from the Vatican Information Office. Rates range from 60,000 to 100,000 lire/€31–52 for a single, from 85,000 to 120,000 lire/€44–62 for a double. Meals are usually available for a modest extra charge.

Casa di Santa Brigida. Book well in advance, for this is one of the best and best-known of the convents that take paying guests. It has an enviable location off Piazza Farnese in the heart of Old Rome. The address is that of the church of Santa Brigida, but the guest-house entrance is around the corner at Via Monserrato 54. There are comfortable lounges and a roof terrace. Rooms have small private baths. The Brigidine sisters are known for their gentle manner; they wear a distinctive habit and veil with a caplike headband. ⊠ *Piazza Farnese 96, 00186,* ☎ *06/68892497. 24 rooms with bath. AE, DC, MC, V.*

Fraterna Domus. Located on a byway near Piazza Navona, this guest house is run by nuns who do not wear religious habits. Rooms are spartan but have the essentials, including small private bathrooms. Meals are hearty and inexpensive, and the curfew is 11 PM. ⊠ *Vicolo del Leonetto 16, 00186.* ☎ *06/68802727. 20 rooms with bath.*

San Giuseppe della Montagna. This convent is just outside the Vatican walls, near the entrance to the Vatican Museums. Some of the guest rooms have three beds and all have private bathrooms. Here there is no curfew; guests are given keys. ⊠ *Viale Vaticano 87, 00165,* ☎ *06/39723807. 15 rooms with bath.*

—Barbara Walsh Angelillo

a tavern, terraces, and roof gardens are some of the perks. Rooms are spacious, airy, and well furnished; many can accommodate extra beds. Handy public transportation gets you downtown in 10 minutes or so. ⊠ *Via Tunisi 8, 00192,* ☎ *06/39723948,* FAX *06/39723943,* WEB *www.alimandi.org. 35 rooms. Bar, parking (fee). AE, DC, MC, V. EP.*

$$ 🏨 **Amalia.** Handy to St. Peter's, the Vatican, and the Cola di Rienzo shopping district, this small hotel is owned and operated by the Consoli family—Amalia and her brothers. On several floors of a 19th-century building, it has large rooms with functional furnishings, TV sets, minibars, pictures of angels on the walls, and gleaming marble bathrooms (hair dryers included). The Ottaviano stop of Metro A is a block away. ⊠ *Via Germanico 66, 00192,* ☎ *06/39723356,* FAX *06/39723365,* WEB *www.hotelamalia.com. 30 rooms, 23 with bath. Minibars, parking (fee). AE, MC, V.*

Fiumicino

$$$$ 🏨 **Hilton Rome Airport.** Rome finally has a hotel within the precincts of Leonardo da Vinci Airport at Fiumicino. The Hilton's premier-standard comforts and style are only two minutes away from the passenger terminals by courtesy bus, and there's an elevated walkway connection with the terminals, too. Fast airport train connections with downtown Rome make it easy to visit the city, and as soon as you see the lobby's stylish vaulted Roman arches and gleaming travertine marble, you know you're in the Eternal City. The Executive Floor features private concierge, check-in, and club-room facilities. ⊠ *Via Arturo Ferrarin 2, Fiumicino, 00050,* ☎ *06/65258,* FAX *06/65256525,* WEB *www.hilton.com/hotels/ROMAPTW. 509 rooms, 8 suites. 3 restaurants, bar, no-smoking floor, indoor-outdoor pool, hair salon, tennis court, health club, airport shuttle, free parking.*

NIGHTLIFE AND THE ARTS

The Arts

Rome has a varied and vibrant cultural life, with music, dance, theater, film, and socializing opportunities for every taste. Trends and offerings change constantly, so the best way to take stock of the leisure activities at hand is to avail yourself of one of the many local publications devoted entirely to free time. You'll find listings in English in the back of the weekly *Roma c'è* booklet, along with handy bus and metro information. A new issue is on sale at newsstands every Thursday. The weekly *Time Out Roma* gives comprehensive event schedules as well as editors' picks; listings are in Italian but easy to decipher. Schedules of events are also published in daily newspapers; pick up *Trovaroma,* the weekly entertainment guide published in Italian every Thursday as a supplement to the daily newspaper *La Repubblica.* The *Guest in Rome* booklet is distributed free at hotels. Brochures are available at APT and city tourist-information offices. An English-language biweekly, *Wanted in Rome,* is sold at central newsstands and has good listings of events.

Dance

The **Rome Opera Ballet** performs regularly at the Teatro dell'Opera (⊠ Via Firenze 72, ☎ 06/48160255 or 06/481601), often with leading international guest stars. Rome is regularly visited by classical and modern ballet companies from Russia, the United States, and Europe; performances are at the Teatro dell'Opera, **Teatro Olimpico** (⊠ Piazza Gentile da Fabriano 17, ☎ 06/326–5991), or at one of the open-air venues in summer. Small dance companies from Italy and abroad perform in various places; check concert listings for details.

Film

Rome has dozens of movie houses, but the only one that shows exclusively English-language films, in English, is the **Pasquino** (⊠ Piazza Sant'Egidio 10, near Piazza Santa Maria in Trastevere, ☎ 06/5803622). The **Quirinetta** (⊠ Via M. Minghetti 4, off Via del Corso, ☎ 06/6790012) shows films in their original language, usually English but occasionally Spanish, French, or other. A few other theaters in the center reserve one night a week for original-language movies: check listings in *Roma c'è.* Tickets are usually 8,000 lire/€4.15 for matinees and all day Wednesday, 12,000 lire/€6.20 the rest of the week.

Music

CLASSICAL

Despite the long-standing criticism that Rome doesn't have a central concert hall, a wide variety of classical music concerts are held at numerous small venues throughout the city. This can result in memorable performances in smaller halls and churches whose ambience makes up for the less grand spaces, particularly at Christmastime, an especially busy concert season in Rome. Of the larger companies, one principal concert series is organized year-round by the **Accademia di Santa Ce-**

cilia (concert hall and box office: ✉ Via della Conciliazione 4, ☎ 06/68801044 or 06/3611064). The **Accademia Filarmonica Romana** (✉ Via Flaminia 118, ☎ 06/3201752) concerts are performed at the Teatro Olimpico. **Istituzione Universitaria dei Concerti** (✉ Aula Magna, Piazzale Aldo Moro 5, ☎ 06/4990175) is a solid company. The internationally respected **Oratorio del Gonfalone** (✉ Via del Gonfalone 32, ☎ 06/687–5952) series focuses on Baroque music. **Il Tempietto** (✉ Area Archaeolica del Palatino, Cortile di San Teodoro, Via di San Teodoro 7, ☎ 06/87131590) organizes music festivals and concerts throughout the year. Depending on the venue, tickets run from about 15,000 lire/€7.75 to 50,000 lire/€25.82.

In addition to the formal concert companies, many small concert groups perform in cultural centers and churches. Many concerts are free, including all those performed in Catholic churches, where a special ruling permits only concerts of religious music. Look for posters outside churches announcing free concerts, particularly at the church of **Sant'Ignazio** (✉ Piazza Sant'Ignazio, near the Pantheon, ☎ 06/679–4560), which often hosts concerts in a spectacularly frescoed setting.

ROCK, POP, AND JAZZ

Pop, jazz, and world music concerts are frequent, especially in summer, although even performances by big-name stars may not be well advertised. Most of the bigger-name acts perform outside the center, so it's worth asking about transportation *before* you buy your tickets. Tickets for for major events are usually handled by **Orbis** (✉ Piazza Esquilino 37, ☎ 06/4744776). **Ricordi** music stores (✉ Via del Corso 506, ☎ 06/3612331; ✉ Viale Giulio Cesare 88, ☎ 06/3720216) usually sell tickets.

Opera

Rome's opera season runs from November or December to May, and performances are staged in the **Teatro dell'Opera** (✉ Via Firenze 72, ☎ 06/48160255 or 06/481601). Prices range from about 30,000 lire/€15.50 to 220,000 lire/€113.50 for regular performances; they can go much higher for an opening night or an appearance by an internationally acclaimed guest singer. Standards may not always measure up to those set by Milan's fabled La Scala, but, despite strikes and shortages of funds, most performances are respectable. The summer opera season was evicted from the ruins of the ancient **Terme di Caracalla,** and temporary venues have been created in **Villa Borghese** and most recently at one end of the **Stadio Olimpico**, Rome's soccer stadium. Small, private companies hold sporadic performances of the classics in venues ranging from school auditoriums to church courtyards. **Mendelflor Musica** (☎ 06/21707618) usually has something in production; call for program information.

Nightlife

La Dolce Vita notwithstanding, Rome's nightlife is not the world's most exciting, but discos, live-music spots, and quiet late-night bars have proliferated in recent years. In keeping with the changing times, the "flavor of the month" factor works here, too, and many places fade into oblivion after their five minutes of fame. The best source for an up-to-date list of late-night spots is the "Night Scene" section of *Roma c'è,* but if you'd prefer to see where the night takes you, head to Trastevere or the area around Piazza Navona, both filled with bars, restaurants, and people after dark. In summer, all discos and many bars and music clubs close to beat the heat (although some simply relocate to the beach, where many Romans spend their summer nights). The city-sponsored Roma Estate (Rome Summer) festival takes over, lighting up hot city nights with concerts, bars, and discos, all in the open air. Pick up the Roma Estate event guide at newsstands.

Bars

The last few years have brought an inexplicable inundation of English- and Irish-style pubs to Rome, and judging from their popularity among young Italians and foreigners, it looks like Guinness is here to stay. One of the first of the Irish invasion, **Flann O'Brien** (⊠ Via Napoli 29, ☎ 06/4480418) has the look and atmosphere of a good Irish pub but also serves decent cappuccino. **Trinity College** (⊠ Via del Collegio Romano 6, near Piazza Venezia, ☎ 06/6786472) has two floors of university-style pub trappings (and Italian snacks all day), with an old-school look and convivial music and drinks until 2 AM. The granddaddy of Rome's authentic Hibernian-style pubs, **Fiddler's Elbow** (⊠ Via dell'Olmata 43, ☎ 06/4872110) encourages singing and good *craic* (lively chat). **Four Green Fields** (⊠ Via Costantino Morin 42, off Via della Giuliana, ☎ 06/3595091) features live music and is open until 2 AM.

So where do you go for a cocktail? **Bar della Pace** (⊠ Piazza della Pace, ☎ 06/6861216) is still the people-watching cocktail bar of choice, near stylish Piazza Navona. **Bar del Fico** (⊠ Piazza del Fico 26, ☎ 06/6865205) is a down-to-earth, authentically Roman alternative to Bar della Pace around the corner, but expect huge crowds on weekend and summer nights. **Taverna del Campo** (⊠ Piazza Campo dei Fiori 16, ☎ 06/6874402), at Campo dei Fiori, is the spot of the moment for wine and elegant hors d'oeuvres.

Music Clubs

Jazz, folk, pop, and Latin music clubs are flourishing in Rome, particularly in Trastevere and Testaccio. Jazz clubs are especially popular, and talented local groups may be joined by visiting musicians from other countries. As admission, many clubs require that you buy a membership card for 10,000 lire/€5.15 to 20,000 lire/€10.30. For popular shows or weekend nights, it's a good idea to reserve a table in advance no matter where you're going.

In the Trionfale district near the Vatican, **Alexanderplatz** (⊠ Via Ostia 9, ☎ 06/39742171), Rome's most famous jazz club, has a bar and a restaurant and features live jazz and blues played nightly by both local and internationally known musicians; it's closed Sunday. **Big Mama** (⊠ Vicolo San Francesco a Ripa 18, Trastevere, ☎ 06/5812551) offers live blues, R&B, African, jazz, and rock. Latin rhythms are the specialty at **Berimbau** (⊠ Via dei Fienaroli 30/b, Trastevere, ☎ 06/5813249), closed Monday and Tuesday, a live-music club with a Brazilian accent and disco dancing after the show.

In trendy Testaccio, **Four XXXX Pub** (⊠ Via Galvani 29, ☎ 06/5757296) is a combination restaurant–beer hall–jazz club, with live jazz groups and no-smoking sections downstairs. **Il Locale** (⊠ Vicolo del Fico 3, near Piazza Navona, ☎ 06/6879075), closed Monday, pulls in a lively crowd for new rock sounds from both sides of the Atlantic. The **Jazz Club** (⊠ Via Zanardelli 12, ☎ 06/6861990), near Piazza Navona, is a classic watering hole with seating at the bar or in leather-upholstered booths. Light meals are available, and there's live music a few nights a week. Live performances of jazz, soul, funk, and dance music get people moving at **Jam Session** (formerly St. Louis Music City, ⊠ Via del Cardello 13/a, ☎ 06/4745076), closed Monday and Tuesday. There is also a restaurant.

Nightclubs

Most clubs open about 10:30 PM and charge an entrance fee of around 30,000 lire/€15.50 to 35,000 lire/€18.05, which may include the first drink; subsequent drinks cost about 10,000 lire/€5.16 to 15,000 lire/€7.75. Most clubs are closed Monday, and all those listed here close during the summer months, some opening instead at the beaches of Ostia or Fregene. **Jackie O'** (⊠ Via Boncompagni 11, ☎ 06/42885457) is an upscale favorite with the rich and famous for dinner and disco dancing. At **Gilda** (⊠ Via Mario de' Fiori 97, near Piazza di Spagna, ☎ 06/6797396), you may spot Italian actors and politicians and American celebrities. This sophisticated nightspot has a piano bar, as well as a restaurant, dance floors, and live music. Jackets are required. **Bella Blu** (⊠ Via Luciani 21, ☎ 06/3230490) is an exclusive Parioli club that caters to Rome's thirtysomething elite.

One of Rome's first discos, **Piper** (⊠ Via Tagliamento 9, ☎ 06/8555398), is still hot and a magnet for young movers and shakers. It has disco music, live bands, and pop videos as well as Latin nights once a week. Occasionally, there's ballroom dancing for an older crowd, and Sunday afternoons it's open for teenagers. Testaccio's the **Saint** (⊠ Via Galvani 46, ☎ 06/5747945) is a three-level complex with two discos that play everything from house to new age music; it also has rooms designated Paradiso and Inferno (Heaven and Hell). The under-25 crowd lets loose to indie rock and weekend live shows at postindustrial **Black Out** (⊠ Via Saturnia 18, ☎ 06/70496791). **Follia** (⊠ Via Ovidio 17, ☎ 06/68805682), a favorite for film parties, lures celebrities and a tony young crowd with disco music and a piano bar.

Dancing starts late in Rome; most discos don't rev up until at least midnight and keep thumping until dawn and beyond. A young and alternative crowd frequents the row of discos on Via di Monte Testaccio; in addition to the usual loud techno-music spots there are a few standouts: **Caruso** (⊠ Via di Monte Testaccio 36, ☎ 06/5745019) is a club that has proven its staying power; it's a Latin alternative to the many rock clubs that line this strip. **Alibi 2000** (⊠ Via di Monte Testaccio 39, 06/5743448) is a multilevel complex that caters to a mixed gay and straight crowd. The **Open Gate** (⊠ Via San Nicola da Tolentino 4, ☎ 06/42000848), open every night, is near Via Veneto and swings to a Latin beat, with disco and live music in a splashy tropical setting complemented by Cuban, Brazilian, and Mexican food.

OUTDOOR ACTIVITIES AND SPORTS

Participant Sports

Biking
You can rent a bike at **Collalti** (⊠ Via del Pellegrino 82, ☎ 06/68801084), closed Monday, which is also a reliable bike repair shop. **St. Peter's Motor Rent** (⊠ Via di Porta Castello 43, ☎ 06/6875714) is a good place to rent scooters as well as bikes.

Golf
Nonmembers are welcome in these clubs, all with 18 holes, but must show the membership cards of their home golf or country clubs. The oldest and most prestigious golf club here is the **Circolo del Golf Roma** (⊠ Via Appia Nuova 716/a, ☎ 06/7803407), closed Saturday–Monday. Among the newest clubs is **Golf Club Parco de' Medici** (⊠ Viale Parco de' Medici 165, ☎ 06/6553477), closed Tuesday. You can get into the swing at **Country Club Castel Gandolfo** (⊠ Via Santo Spirito 13, Castel Gandolfo, ☎ 06/9312301). The **Golf Club Fioranello** (⊠ Via della Falcognana 61, ☎ 06/7138080), closed Wednesday, is at Santa Maria delle Mole, off Via Appia Antica. Also try **Olgiata Golf Club** (⊠ Largo Olgiata 15, Via Cassia, ☎ 06/30889141), closed Monday.

Health Clubs

The **Cavalieri Hilton** (✉ Via Cadlolo 101, ☎ 06/35091) has a running path on its grounds as well as outdoor and indoor pools, two clay tennis courts, and a luxurious spa, fitness center, and hair salon, all open to nonguests. The **Sheraton Roma** (✉ Viale del Pattinaggio 100, ☎ 06/5453) has a heated outdoor pool, a tennis court, two squash courts, and a sauna, but no gym. The **Sheraton Golf** (✉ Viale Parco de' Medici 22, ☎ 06/658588) has a fitness center and 18-hole golf course. Two tennis courts and a 25-m pool are at the **St. Peter's Holiday Inn** (✉ Via Aurelia Antica 415, ☎ 06/6642). The **Roman Sport Center** (✉ Via del Galoppatoio 33, ☎ 06/3201667) is a vast, full-fledged health club next to the underground parking lot in Villa Borghese; it has two swimming pools, a gym, aerobic workout areas, squash courts, and saunas. It is affiliated with the **American Health Club** (✉ Largo Somalia 60, ☎ 06/86212411). Day passes at all of the above cost between 40,000 lire/€20.65 and 60,000 lire/€32.00.

Horseback Riding

There are numerous riding clubs in Rome. The most central is the **Centro Ippico Villa Borghese** (✉ Via del Galoppatoio 18, ☎ 06/3200487). Also try the **Società Ippica Romana** (✉ Via Monti della Farnesina 18, ☎ 06/3240591). The **Circolo Ippico Olgiata** (✉ Largo Olgiata 15, ☎ 06/30888792) is outside the city on residential Via Cassia.

Running

The best bet for running in central Rome is the **Villa Borghese,** with an approximately ⅔-km (½-mi) circuit of the Pincio, among the marble statuary. A longer run in the park itself might include a loop around **Piazza di Siena,** a grass riding arena. Although most traffic is barred from Villa Borghese, government and police cars sometimes speed through. Be careful to stick to the sides of the roads. For a long run away from all traffic, try **Villa Ada** and **Villa Doria Pamphili** on the Janiculum. History-loving runners should do as the chariot horses did and run at the old **Circus Maximus,** or along **Via delle Terme di Caracalla,** flanked by a park.

Swimming

The outdoor pool of the **Cavalieri Hilton** (✉ Via Cadlolo 101, ☎ 06/35091) is a summertime oasis open to nonguests for a fee. The **Hotel Aldovrandi** (✉ Via Ulisse Aldovrandi 15, ☎ 06/3223993) charges slightly less for a dip. The **Roman Sport Center** (✉ Via del Galoppatoio 33, ☎ 06/3201667) has two swimming pools. Expect to pay from 50,000 lire/€25.80 to 70,000 lire/€36.15 for a day pass.

Spectator Sports

Basketball

Games are played, usually on Sunday, at the **Palazzo dello Sport** in the EUR district (✉ Piazzale dello Sport, ☎ 06/5925107).

Horseback Riding

The **International Riding Show,** held in May, draws a stylish crowd to the amphitheater of Piazza di Siena in Villa Borghese. The competition is stiff, and the program features a cavalry charge staged by the dashing mounted corps of the *carabinieri* (military police). Check with the tourist office (✉ Via Parigi 5, ☎ 06/48899255) for details.

Soccer

Italy's favorite spectator sport stirs passionate enthusiasm among partisans. Games are usually held on weekend afternoons throughout the fall-to-spring season. Two teams—Roma and Lazio—play their home games in the Olympic Stadium at the extensive **Foro Italico** sports complex (✉ Via dei Gladiatori, ☎ 06/3336316), built by Mussolini on the banks of the Tiber. There is a chance of tickets being on sale at the box office before the games, but it's a better idea to buy them in advance from **Lazio Point** (✉ Via Farini 34, ☎ 06/4826688) to see the Lazio team play. Go to **Orbis** (✉ Piazza Esquilino 37, ☎ 06/4744776) for tickets to see the Roma team.

SHOPPING

When in Rome, do as the Romans do—and the Romans love to shop. Shops are open from 9 or 9:30 to 1 and from 3:30 or 4 to 7 or 7:30. There's a tendency in Rome for shops in central districts to stay open all day, and hours are generally becoming more flexible throughout the city. Remember that many stores are closed Sunday, though this is changing, too. Generally, with the exception of food and technical-supply stores, most stores also close on Monday morning from September to mid-June and Saturday afternoon from mid-June through August. You can save some money taking advantage of the Tax-Free for Tourists VAT tax refunds, available at most large stores for purchases over 300,000 lire/€155. Or hit Rome at the end of January and beginning of February, when stores clean house with the justly famous annual sales.

Bargains

You can often find good buys in knitwear and silk scarves at stands on the fringes of outdoor food markets. Bargaining is still an art at the **Porta Portese** flea market and is routine when purchasing anything from a street vendor. On **Via Cola di Rienzo** there are stands selling everything from CDs to handicrafts. The market at **Via Sannio** (San Giovanni in Laterano) features job lots of designer shoes and ranks of stalls selling new and used clothing at bargain prices; it's a great place to hunt for used leather jackets. Hours are weekdays 10–1, Saturday 10–6. The morning market in **Piazza Testaccio,** in the heart of the neighborhood of the same name, is known for stands selling designer shoes. Bargain hunters will also love **Vesti a Stock** (✉ Via Germanico 170), a mini-outlet for designer casual wear, coats, shoes, and accessories.

Department Stores and Malls

Italian department stores have virtually nothing in common with their American and English cousins; they're comparatively small and old-fashioned. Still, they're worth a stop if you're looking for something in a hurry, as their selection still seems to be broader than at traditional boutiques. **Rinascente** (✉ Near Piazza Colonna, ☎ 06/6797691) sells clothing and accessories only. Another Rinascente (✉ Piazza Fiume, ☎ 06/8841231) has the same stock, plus furniture and housewares. Both stores are open daily 9–9. **Coin** (✉ Piazzale Appio, near San Giovanni in Laterano, ☎ 06/7080020; ✉ Cinecittà Due, ☎ 06/7220931) carries housewares, as well as fashions for men and women. The **UPIM** and **Oviesse** chains offer low-end to moderately priced goods ranging from bathing suits to first-aid supplies and have while-you-wait shoe-repair service. **Cinecittà Due** (✉ Piazza di Cinecittà, at Viale Palmiro Togliatti, ☎ 06/7220902) was the first of several megamalls, with 100 stores; take Metro A to the Subaugusta stop.

Markets

All outdoor food markets are open Monday–Saturday from early morning to about 1 PM (a bit later on Saturday), but get there in the

Rome Shopping

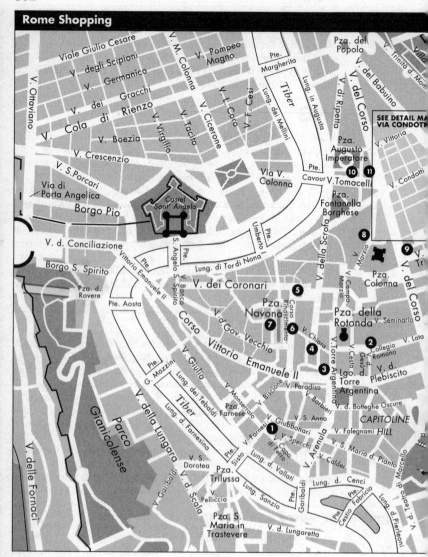

Viale Giulio Cesare
V. M. Colonna
V. Pompeo Magno
V. degli Scipioni
V. Germanico
V. dei Gracchi
V. Cola di Rienzo
V. Tacito
V. L. Coro
V.- F. Cesi
Lung. dei Mellini
Tiber
Lung. in Augusta
Pte. Margherita
Pza. del Popolo
V. di Trinità d'. Mon
Villa
V. del Babuino
V. del Corso
V. di Ripetta
V. Ciceroni
V. Ottaviano
V. Boezia
V. Virgilio
V. Crescenzio
Via di Porta Angelica
Borgo Pio
V. S. Porcari
V. d. Conciliazione
Borgo S. Spirito
Pza. d. Rovere
Pte. Aosta
Castel Sant'Angelo
Vittorio Emanuele II
S. Angelo S. Spirito
V. Banco S. Spirito
Pte.
Pte. Umberto
Lung. di Tor di Nona
V. dei Coronari
Via V. Colonna
Pte. Cavour
V. Tomacelli
Pza. Augusto Imperatore
SEE DETAIL MA VIA CONDOTT
V. Vittoria
V. Condotti
Pza. Fontanella Borghese
Pza. Navona
Corso Rinascimento
V. d. Gov. Vecchio
Corso Vittorio Emanuele II
V. Chiara
V. della Scrofa
V. Campo Marzio
Marzio
Pza. Colonna
V. Tr
V. del Corso
Pza. della Rotonda
V. Seminario
Collegio Romano
V. Lata
Lgo. d. Torre Argentina
V. d. Plebiscito
V. Torre Argentina
V. Cesio
V. d. Gesù
V. Paradiso
V. Barbieri
V. d. Bottegghe Oscure
CAPITOLINE HILL
V. S. Anna
V. Monserrato
V. Giulia
V. G. Mozzini
Lung. dei Tebaldi
Lung. d. Farnesina
Pza. Farnese
Tiber
Parco Gianicolense
V. della Lungara
V. S. Dorotea
Pza. Trilussa
V. d. Scala
V. Garibaldi
V. Pelliccia
Pza. S. Maria in Trastevere
V. delle Fornaci
V. Giubbonari
V. Farnesi
V. Biscione
V. Specchi
V. Capo di Ferro
Pte. Sisto
Lung. d. Vallati
Lung. Sanzio
V. Arenula
V. Calder
V. S. Maria d. Pianto
V. Falegnami
Lung. d. Cenci
Pte. Garibaldi
Pte. Cestio
Pte. Fabricio
Lung. d. Pierleoni
V. d. Lungaretta
CAPITOLINE HILL
V. Teatro di p. n.

Ai Monasteri 5	Nardecchia 7	
Aston 14	Officina Farmaceutica di Santa Maria Novella 6	
Bruno Magli 13		
Cinecittà Due 16		
Coin 17	Rinascente 9	
Fratelli Bassetti ...3	Sac Joli 10	
Furla 11	Tanca 4	
Lavori Artigianali Femminili 12	Volterra 15	
Le Tartarughe 2	Wazoo 1	
Myricae 8		

Pza.
Fiume

0   440 yards

0   400 meters

N

Cafoppatora

Viale del Muro Torto

Medici

Porta
Pinciana

Corso d'Italia

V. Campania

Ple. di
Porta Pia

Viale Castro Pretorio

V. di Pta. Pinciana

V. Lazio

V. Piemonte

V. Romagna

V. Piave

14

V. Boncompagni

V. Quintino Sella

V. Goito

V. Ludovisi

13

V. Liguria

Vitt. Veneto

V. Sallustiana

V. Lucullo

V. Carducci

V. XX Settembre

V. Cernaia

V. Gaeta

V. Palestro

V. F. Crispi

V. S. Basilio

V. S. Nicola
da Tolen.

Bissolati

V. Volturno

V. Vicenza

V. Sistina

V. S. Nicolo

V. Barberini

15

V. Castro Pretorio

12

Pza.
Barberini

V. Marsala

QUIRINAL
HILL

V. d. Quattro Fontane

V. Torino

Pza. d.
Repubblica

V. d. Scuderie

Giardini
del
Quirinale

V. Quirinale

Stazione
Termini

Pza. di
Trevi

V. Piacenza

dell'Umiltà

Pza. d.
Quirinale

V. Nazionale

Milano

V. A. Depretis

Napoli

V. G. Amendola

V. Giovanni Giolitti

C.
attisti

V. IV
Novembre

V. d. Serpenti

Panisperna

V. d. S. Maria
Maggiore

Pza. S.
Maria
Maggiore

V. F. Turati

za.
Venezia

V. dei Fori Imperiali

VIMINAL
HILL

V. Cavour

V. Giovanni

Quattro Cantoni

V. Napoleone III

V. Carlo Alberto

16

Pza. d.
Campidoglio

V. Cavour

ESQUILINE
HILL

Lanza

V. d. Statuto

Pza
Vittorio
Emanuele II

V. Emanuele Filiberto

Foro Romano

Pza. del
Colosseo

Viale del Monte Oppio

V. Mecenate

V.

Merulana

PALATINE
HILL

V. d. Domus Aurea

V. Rugg. Bonghi

V. Labicana

V. Manzoni

V. S. G. in Laterano

17

early part of the day for the best selection. Beware of pickpockets and don't go if you can't stand crowds. Downtown Rome's most colorful outdoor food market is at **Campo dei Fiori** (⊠ south of Piazza Navona), at Piazza della Cancelleria. The so-called **Trionfale market** (⊠ Via Andrea Doria), officially called the Mercato di Via Andrea Doria, is big and bustling; it's located about a five-minute walk north of the entrance to the Vatican Museums. Smaller markets can be found throughout the city. There's room for bargaining at the Sunday-morning flea market at **Porta Portese** (⊠ Via Ippolito Nievo, off Viale Trastevere); it offers seemingly endless rows of dealers in new and secondhand clothing, bootleg CDs, old furniture, car stereos of suspicious origin, and all manner of old junk. Keep an eye on your wallet—the crowds and money changing hands draw some of Rome's most skillful pickpockets.

Shopping Districts

If your shopping list starts with Gucci, Prada, Fendi, and the other big names, start your shopping day at **Piazza di Spagna,** in the vicinity of which are most of fashion's top shops. **Via Condotti** is the neighborhood's central axis, but you'll find elegant designer clothing and accessories on every block of this area, bordered by Piazza di Spagna on the east, Via del Corso on the west, from Piazza San Silvestro to Via della Croce.

There are so many hole-in-the-wall boutiques selling top-quality merchandise in Rome's center that even just wandering, you're sure to find something that catches your eye. Shops along **Via Campo Marzio** and adjoining **Piazza San Lorenzo in Lucina** stock eclectic and high-quality clothes and accessories, although without the big names and at slightly lower prices. Running from Piazza Venezia to Piazza del Popolo lies **Via del Corso,** the center's main shopping avenue, more than a mile of clothing, shoes, leather goods, and home furnishings from classic to cutting-edge. **Via Cola di Rienzo,** across the Tiber from Piazza del Popolo, has block after block of boutiques and department stores, as well as street stalls and gourmet food shops. For top-quality antiques, look in shops along **Via del Babuino,** near Piazza di Spagna. **Via Coronari,** across the Tiber from Castel Sant'Angelo, has quirkier antiques and home boutiques. Nearby **Via Giulia** and surrounding streets are also good bets for decorative arts. Should your gift list include religious souvenirs, you'll find everything from rosaries to Vatican golf balls at the shops between Piazza San Pietro and **Borgo Pio.** Liturgical vestments and statues of saints made for good window-shopping on **Via dei Cestari** near the Pantheon.

Specialty Stores

Antiques and Prints

For old prints and antiques, **Tanca** (⊠ Salita dei Crescenzi 12, near the Pantheon, ☎ 06/6875272) is a good hunting ground. Early photographs of Rome and views of Italy from the archives at **Alinari** (⊠ Via Alibert 16/a, ☎ 06/6792923) make memorable souvenirs. **Nardecchia** (⊠ Piazza Navona 25, ☎ 06/6869318) is reliable for prints. Stands in **Piazza della Fontanella Borghese** sell prints and old books.

Crafts and Gifts

For fine pottery, handwoven textiles, and other handicrafts, **Myricae** (⊠ Piazza del Parlamento 38, ☎ 06/6873643) has a good selection. A bottle of liqueur, jar of marmalade, or bar of chocolate handmade by Cistercian monks in several monasteries in Italy makes an unusual, tasty gift to take home; pick from among these and other goodies at **Ai Monasteri** (⊠ Piazza Cinque Lune 66, ☎ 06/68802783). Herbal and

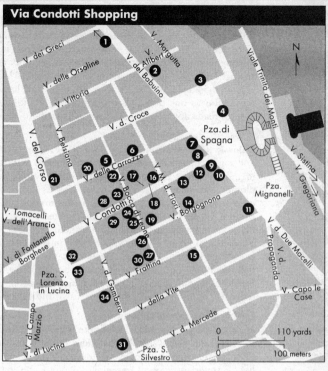

Via Condotti Shopping

floral soaps, lotions, perfumes, and potpourri are easily carried gifts for yourself or a friend and can be found near Piazza Navona in the Rome branch of Florence's historic apothecary, the **Officina Farmaceutica di Santa Maria Novella** (⊠ Corso Rinascimento 47, ☎ 06/6872446). Pricey **C.u.c.i.n.a.** (⊠ Via del Babuino 118/a, ☎ 06/6791275) is one of the better kitchen-supply stores in town, great for those handsome Italian designs.

Designer Clothing

All of Italy's top fashion houses and many international designers have stores near Piazza di Spagna. **Dolce & Gabbana** (⊠ Piazza di Spagna 82, ☎ 06/6792294), a spin-off of the top-of-the-line D&G store on Via Borgognona, shows the trendiest designer fashions in casual wear and accessories for men and women. **Fendi** (⊠ Via Borgognona 40, ☎ 06/696661) has several stores in Rome; all stock a wide assortment of the Fendi sisters' signature furs and print fashions. Magnificent silk scarves and sexy shoes are on offer at **Ferragamo** (⊠ Via Condotti 74, ☎ 06/6791565). Sleek, vaguely futuristic **Prada** (⊠ Via Condotti 92, ☎ 06/6790897) is divided into two entrances, the men's boutique to the left of the women's. The shop is as understated and elegant as the designs at **Giorgio Armani** (⊠ Via Condotti 77, ☎ 06/6991460). **Gucci** (⊠ Via Condotti 8, ☎ 06/6789340) often has lines out the door of its two-story shop, testament to the continuing popularity of its rich leathers, hot designs, and edgy clothing fashions.

The trio of Gianni Versace stores, **Versace Uomo** (⊠ Via Borgognona 24, ☎ 06/6795037), **Versace Donna** (⊠ Via Bocca di Leone 26, ☎ 06/6780521), and **Versus** (⊠ Via Borgognona 33, ☎ 06/6783977), offers the rock-star styles that made the house's name. Don't miss **La Perla** (⊠ Via Condotti 79, ☎ 06/69941933) for luscious lingerie.

Ermenegildo Zegna (⊠ Via Borgognona 7/e, ☎ 06/6789143) has the finest in elegant men's styles and accessories. **Il Portone** (⊠ Via delle Carrozze 71, ☎ 06/6793355) embodies a tradition in custom shirt-making. For decades a man was a fashion flop without Portone's classic cuts and signature stripes in his closet. **Brioni** (⊠ Via Condotti 21, ☎ 06/6783428; ⊠ Via Barberini 79, ☎ 06/484517) has a well-deserved reputation as one of Italy's top tailors. In addition to impeccable custom-made apparel, you can suit up in ready-to-wear garments.

Galassia (⊠ Via Frattina 21, ☎ 06/6791351) has expensive, extreme, and extravagant women's styles by Gaultier, Westwood, and Ya-mamoto—this is the place for feather boas and hats with ostrich plumes. **Mariselaine** (⊠ Via Condotti 70, ☎ 06/6795817) is a top-quality women's fashion boutique. **Le Tartarughe** (⊠ Via del Piè di Marmo 17, ☎ 06/6792240) has understated and versatile garments for women, including packable knits and jerseys. **Mariella Burani** (⊠ Via Bocca di Leone 28, ☎ 06/6790630) mixes classy chic with judicious high-fashion overtones. **Wazoo** (⊠ Via dei Giubbonari 28, ☎ 06/6869362) is one of Rome's trendiest boutiques for designer pieces, funky shoes, and special dresses. **Marisa Padovan** (⊠ Via delle Carrozze 81, ☎ 06/6793946) shows exclusive and expensive lingerie.

Embroidery and Linens
Frette (⊠ Piazza di Spagna 11, ☎ 06/6790673) is a Roman institution for luxurious linens. **Venier Colombo** (⊠ Via Frattina 79, ☎ 06/6787705) has a selection of exquisite lace goods, including lingerie and linens. **Lavori Artigianali Femminili** (⊠ Via Capo le Case 6, ☎ 06/6781100) offers delicately embroidered household linens, infants' and children's clothing, and blouses.

Jewelry and Silver Objects
What Cartier is to Paris, **Bulgari** (⊠ Via Condotti 10, ☎ 06/6793876) is to Rome; the shop's elegant display windows hint at what's beyond the guard at the door. **Buccellati** (⊠ Via Condotti 31, ☎ 06/6790329) is a tradition-rich Florentine jewelry house renowned for its silver work; it ranks with Bulgari for quality and reliability. You'll find a tempting selection of small silver objects at **Fornari** (⊠ Via Frattina 133, ☎ 06/6780105). **Bozart** (⊠ Via Bocca di Leone 4, ☎ 06/6781026) features dazzling costume jewelry in keeping with the latest fashions.

Shoes and Leather Accessories
Roland's (⊠ Piazza di Spagna 74, ☎ 06/6790391) has an extensive stock of good-quality leather fashions and accessories, as well as stylish casual wear in wool and silk. For the latest styles in handbags and a selection of scarves and costume jewelry at reasonable prices, go to **Furla** (⊠ Piazza di Spagna 22, ☎ 06/6878230), which has several stores in downtown Rome. **Sac Joli** (⊠ Via Tomacelli 154, ☎ 06/6878431), despite its French name, displays a large collection of fine Italian-made handbags in up-to-the-minute styles. Offbeat and trendy, one-of-a-kind handbags in leather and/or fabrics are made and sold by **Amadei** (⊠ Via delle Carrozze 20, ☎ 06/67833452). **Volterra** (⊠ Via Barberini 102, ☎ 06/4819315) is well stocked and offers a wide selection of handbags at moderate prices. For gloves as pretty as Holly Golightly's, head to **Sermoneta** (⊠ Piazza di Spagna 61, ☎ 06/6791960). **Di Cori** (⊠ Piazza di Spagna 53, ☎ 06/6784439) has a spectrum of gloves in every color imaginable. **Merola** (⊠ Via del Corso 143, ☎ 06/6791961) carries a line of expensive top-quality gloves and scarves. **Charles** (⊠ Via del Corso 109, ☎ 06/6792345) has a broad range of shoes, handbags, leather clothing and accessories, and a bilingual sales staff. **Bruno Magli** (⊠ Via del

Gambero 1, ☎ 06/6793802; ✉ Via Veneto 70, ☎ 06/4884355) is known for well-made shoes and matching handbags at moderate to high prices. **Campanile** (✉ Via Condotti 58, ☎ 06/6790731) has four floors of shoes in the latest—as well as classic—styles and other leather goods. **Tod's** (✉ Via Borgognona 45, ☎ 06/6786828) might sound British, but the signature button-soled moccasins are strictly Italian made. This exclusive Tod's carries every model and style as well as its line of hand-made bags spotted on the arms of celebrities.

Silks and Fabrics

Fratelli Bassetti (✉ Corso Vittorio Emanuele II 73, ☎ 06/6892326) has a vast selection of world-famous Italian silks and fashion fabrics in a rambling palazzo. **Aston** (✉ Via Boncompagni 27, ☎ 06/42871227) stocks couture-level fabrics for men and women. You can find some real bargains when *scampoli* (remnants) are on sale.

SIDE TRIPS FROM ROME

Ostia Antica: A Prettier Pompeii

One of the easiest excursions from the capital takes you west to the sea, where tall pines stand among the well-preserved ruins of Ostia Antica, the main port of ancient Rome.

Founded around the 4th century BC, Ostia served as Rome's port city for several centuries until the Tiber changed course, leaving the town high and dry. What has been excavated here is a remarkably intact Roman town in a pretty, parklike setting. Fair weather and good walking shoes are essential. On hot days, be here when the gates open or go late in the afternoon. A visit to the excavations takes two to three hours, including 20 minutes for the museum.

Numbers in the margin correspond to numbers on the Side Trips from Rome map.

❶ **Ostia Antica** was inhabited by a cosmopolitan mix of rich businessmen, wily merchants, sailors, and slaves. The great *horrea* (warehouses) were built in the 2nd century AD to handle huge shipments of grain from Africa; the *insulae* (forerunners of the modern apartment building) provided housing for the growing population. Under the combined assaults of the barbarians and the *anopheles* mosquito, and after the Tiber changed course, the port was eventually abandoned. Tidal mud and windblown sand covered the city, which lay buried until the beginning of this century. Now it has been extensively excavated and is well maintained. **Porta Romana,** one of the city's three gates, opens onto the **Decumanus Maximus,** the main thoroughfare crossing the city from end to end. Black-and-white mosaic pavements representing Neptune and Amphitrite decorate the **Terme di Nettuno** (Baths of Neptune). Directly behind the baths is the barracks of the fire department, which played an important role in a town with warehouses full of valuable goods and foodstuffs.

On one side of the Decumanus Maximus is the beautiful **theater,** built by Agrippa and completely restored by Septimius Severus in the 2nd century AD. In the vast Piazzale delle Corporazioni, where trade organizations similar to guilds had their offices (notice the floor mosaics, which correspond to the various trades), is the **Tempio di Cerere** (Temple of Ceres): this is appropriate for a town dealing in grain imports, since Ceres, who gave her name to cereal, was the goddess of agriculture. You can visit the **Casa di Apuleio** (House of Apuleius), built in Pompeiian style, built lower to the ground and with fewer windows than was characteristic of Ostia. Next to it is the **Mithraeum,** with balconies and a hall dec-

Side Trips from Rome

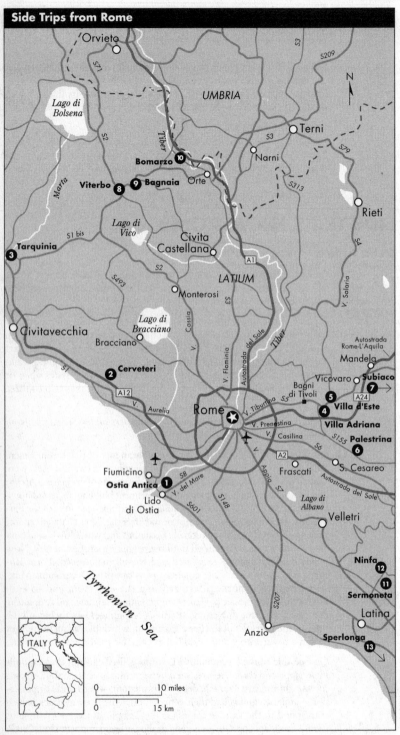

Orvieto

Lago di Bolsena

UMBRIA

S71

S2

Tiber

Bomarzo 10

Orte

Terni

S3

S209

Narni

S79

S313

Viterbo 8 9 **Bagnaia**

Lago di Vico

Marta

S1 bis

Tarquinia 3

S493

S2

Civita Castellana

A1

LATIUM

S3

Rieti

V. Salaria

V. Solaria

Monterosi

Cassia

Lago di Bracciano

Civitavecchia

Bracciano

V.

Aurelia

A12

Cerveteri 2

S1

V. Flaminia

Autostrada del Sole

Tiber

Autostrada Rome–L'Aquila

Mandela

Vicovaro

Subiaco 7

Bagni di Tivoli

S5

5 A24

4 **Villa d'Este**

Villa Adriana

Rome ★

V. Tiburtina

V. Prenestina

V. Casilina

S155

Palestrina 6

S6

Fiumicino

Ostia Antica 1

S8

V. del Mare

Lido di Ostia

S601

A2

Appia S7

Frascati

S. Cesareo

Autostrada del Sole

Lago di Albano

Velletri

Ninfa 12

11

Sermoneta

Latina

S148

Tyrrhenian Sea

S207

Anzio

Sperlonga 13

ITALY

0 ___ 10 miles

0 ___ 15 km

N

orated with symbols of the cult of Mithras. This men-only religion, imported from Persia, was especially popular with legionnaires.

On Via dei Molini you can see a **mill,** where grain for the warehouses next door was ground with the stones that are still there. Along Via di Diana you come upon a *thermopolium* (bar) with a marble counter and a fresco depicting the fruit and food that were sold here. At the end of Via dei Dipinti is the **Museo Ostiense,** which displays some of the ancient sculptures and mosaics found among the ruins. The **Forum** holds the monumental remains of the city's most important temple, dedicated to Jupiter, Juno, and Minerva; other ruins of baths; a basilica (which in Roman times served as a secular hall of justice); and smaller temples. **Via Epagathiana** leads toward the Tiber, where there are large warehouses erected in the 2nd century AD to deal with the enormous amounts of grain imported into Rome during the height of the Empire.

The **Casa di Cupido e Psiche** (House of Cupid and Psyche), a residential house, was named for a statue found there (now on display in the museum); you can see what remains of a large pool in an enclosed garden decorated with marble and mosaic motifs. Even in ancient times a premium was placed on water views: the house faces the shore, which would have been only about ⅓ km (¼ mi) away. On Via della Foce are the **Casa del Serapide** (House of Serapis), a 2nd-century multilevel dwelling, and the **Terme dei Sette Sapienti** (Baths of the Seven Wise Men), named for a fresco found here. There is another apartment building on Cardo degli Aurighi.

The **Porta Marina** leads to what used to be the seashore. In the vicinity are the ruins of the **Jewish Synagogue,** one of the oldest in the Western world. On Via Semita dei Cippi you can see the **Casa di Fortuna Annonaria,** the richly decorated house of a wealthy Ostian. This is another place to marvel at the skill of the mosaic artists and, at the same time, to realize that this really was someone's home. One of the rooms opens onto a secluded garden. The **Museo Ostiense** is also on the grounds. ⊠ *Via dei Romagnoli 717,* ☎ *06/58358099,* WEB *www.itnw.roma.it/ostia/scavi.* ⌫ *8,000 lire/€4.15 includes excavations and museum.* ☉ *Excavations Tues.–Sun. 9 AM–1 hr before sunset, museum Tues.–Sun. 9–1:30.*

Ostia Antica A to Z

CAR TRAVEL

From Porta San Paolo, next to the Piramide in the southern part of Rome's center, Via Ostiense leads southwest and becomes Via del Mare, which leads directly to Ostia (a 30- to 40-minute trip). Signs indicate the turnoff for Ostia Antica, which comes before the modern town of Ostia.

TRAIN TRAVEL

There is regular train service to the Ostia Antica station from Rome's Ostiense train station, near Porta San Paolo; the ride takes about 30 minutes. Contact Ferrovie dello Stato (FS) for information. Another way to go is to take Metro Line B to the Magliana station and switch to the Ostia line (trains every half hour).

➤ TRAIN INFORMATION: **Ferrovie dello Stato** (☎ 848/888088, WEB www.fs-on-line.com).

Cerveteri and Tarquinia: Etruscan Landscapes

The rolling landscape along the coast northwest of Rome was once Etruscan territory, and at Cerveteri and Tarquinia it holds some intriguing reminders of a people who taught the ancient Romans a thing or two about religion, art, and a pleasurable way of life.

The Etruscans were an apparently peaceable and pleasure-loving people who held sway over what is now central and southern Tuscany and northern Lazio before the rise of the Roman Republic. They loved life and they were sure that they would enjoy the afterlife, too. The Etruscan necropolis, or "city of the dead," was a cemetery faithfully reproducing the homes and lifestyles of the living. Both of the sites you visit are necropolises.

Beyond Rome's city limits, the countryside is green with pastures and endless fields of artichokes, a premium crop in these parts. You catch glimpses of the sea to the west, where the coast is dotted with suburban developments. Because the beaches in this area are popular with Romans, highways and public transportation can be uncomfortably crowded on weekends from spring to fall. Exploring the Etruscan sites requires some agility in climbing up and down uneven stairs, and you need shoes suitable for walking on rough dirt paths.

Cerveteri is the principal Etruscan site closest to Rome and features the Necropoli della Banditaccia, a sylvan setting among mossy stones and variously shaped monuments that are memorials to revered ancestors. Tarquinia is farther north but has even better tombs, as well as an excellent museum full of objects recovered from tombs throughout the region. On the way, you'll pass Civitavecchia, Rome's principal port. From the highway or train you can see the port installations, which include a fort designed by Michelangelo. The low mountains to the east are the Tolfa range, where the Etruscans mined metals for export to ancient Mediterranean markets.

❷ Cerveteri

The nucleus of the town, in the shadow of a medieval castle, stands on a spur of tufa rock that was the site of the Etruscan city of Caere, a thriving commercial center in the 6th century BC. The necropolis is about 2 km (1 mi) from Cerveteri's main piazza, a trip you can make on foot or by taxi.

In the **Necropoli della Banditaccia** (Banditaccia Necropolis), the Etruscan residents of Caere left a heritage of great historical significance. In this monumental complex of tombs set in parklike grounds, they laid their relatives to rest, some in simple graves, others in burial chambers that are replicas of Etruscan dwellings. In the round tumulus tombs you can recognize the prototypes of Rome's tombs of Augustus and Hadrian (in the Mausoleo di Augusto and Castel Sant'Angelo) and the Tomb of Cecilia Metella on the Via Appia. Look for the **Tomba dei Capitelli,** with carved capitals; the **Tomba dei Rilievi,** its walls carved with reliefs of household objects; and the similar **Tombe degli Scudi e delle Sedie.** The **Tomba Moretti** has a little vestibule with columns. Some tombs have several chambers. ⊠ *Necropoli della Banditaccia.* ☎ *8,000 lire/€4.15.* ☉ *May–Sept., Tues.–Sun. 9–7; Oct.–Apr., Tues.–Sun. 9–4.*

In Cerveteri's medieval castle, the **Museo Nazionale Cerite** is a small archaeological museum with some of the finds, mostly pottery, from the various Etruscan cemeteries that have been located in the area. ⊠ *Piazza della Necropoli,* ☎ *06/9940001,* WEB *www.etruschi.it/cittadine/cerveter.html.* ☎ *Free.* ☉ *Tues.–Sun. 9–7.*

❸ Tarquinia

Tarquinia sprawls on a hill overlooking the sea. Once a powerful Etruscan city, it was a major center in the Middle Ages, too. Though it lacks the harmony of better-preserved medieval towns, Tarquinia offers unexpected pleasures, among them views of narrow medieval streets opening onto quaint squares dominated by palaces and churches, and the sight of the majestic, solitary church of Santa Maria di Castello encircled by medieval walls and towers. To focus on Tarquinia's Etruscan heritage, visit the museum in Palazzo Vitelleschi, and then see the frescoed underground tombs in the fields east of the city. You can walk to the necropolis from town. From Piazza Matteotti, the town's main square, take Via Porta Tarquinia south past the church of San Francesco; go through the Porta Tarquinia, also known as Porta Clementina, and continue south on Via Ripagrotta. At the intersection with Via delle Croci, head east on the main road to reach the necropolis. There is infrequent bus service from Piazza Cavour to the necropolis, with only a couple of morning and afternoon departures.

The **Museo Nazionale Tarquiniense** (National Museum of Tarquinia) is housed in the Palazzo Vitelleschi, a splendid 15th-century building that contains a wealth of Etruscan treasures. Even if pottery vases and endless ranks of stone sarcophagi leave you cold, what makes a visit here memorable are the horses. A pair of marvelous golden terra-cotta winged horses gleam warmly against the gray stone wall on which they have been mounted in the main hall. They are from a frieze that once decorated an Etruscan temple, and they are strikingly vibrant proof of the degree of artistry attained by the Etruscans in the 4th century BC. The museum and its stately courtyard are crammed with sarcophagi from the underground tombs found under the meadows surrounding the town. The figures of the deceased recline casually on their stone couches, mouths curved in enigmatic smiles. Upstairs are vases and other Etruscan artifacts, together with some of the more precious frescoes from the tombs. The frescoes were removed to keep them from deteriorating. ⊠ *Piazza Cavour,* ☎ *0766/856036.* ⌑ *8,000 lire/€4.15, 12,000 lire/€6.20 including necropolis.* ⊘ *Tues.–Sun. 8:30–7:30.*

The entrance to the **Necropoli** (Necropolis), the Etruscan city of the dead, is about 1 km (½ mi) outside the town walls. Frequent, regularly scheduled guided tours—not mandatory—leave from the ticket office, visiting about 10 of the 100 most interesting tombs on a rotating basis. The tombs date from the 7th to the 2nd century BC, and they were painted with lively scenes of Etruscan life. The colors are amazingly fresh in some tombs, and the scenes show the vitality and highly civilized lifestyle of this ancient people. Of the thousands of tombs that exist throughout the territory of Etruria (there are 40,000 in the vicinity of Tarquinia alone), only a small percentage have been excavated scientifically. Many more have been found and plundered by "experts" called *tombaroli,* who dig illegally, usually at night. The tombs in the Tarquinia necropolis are bare; the only evidence of their original function is the stone platforms on which the sarcophagi rested. But the wall paintings are intriguing and in many cases quite beautiful. The visit takes about 90 minutes, and good explanations in English are posted outside each tomb. ⊠ *Monterozzi, on the Strada Provinciale 1/b (Tarquinia–Viterbo),* ☎ *0766/856308; 06/9941098 for English-language tours.* ⌑ *8,000 lire/€4.15, 12,000 lire/€6.20 including museum.* ⊘ *Tues.–Sun. 9 AM–1 hr before sunset.*

Cerveteri and Tarquinia A to Z

BUS TRAVEL

COTRAL buses leave every 30 minutes from the Lepanto stop of Metro A for Cerveteri (about 80 minutes) and for Tarquinia (about two hours, sometimes with a bus change in Civitavecchia).

CAR TRAVEL

For Cerveteri, take either the A12 Rome–Civitavecchia toll highway to the Cerveteri-Ladispoli exit, or take the Via Aurelia. The trip is about 40 minutes. To get to Tarquinia, take the A12 Rome–Civitavecchia highway all the way to the end, where you continue on the Via Aurelia to Tarquinia. The trip is about 60 minutes.

TRAIN TRAVEL

Hourly trains from Termini, Ostiense, and Trastevere stations take you to the Cerveteri-Ladispoli station (50 minutes) and Tarquinia (70 minutes). Both stations are a short bus ride out of their respective towns.

VISITOR INFORMATION

➤ TOURIST INFORMATION: **Cerveteri** (✉ Piazza Risorgimento 19, ☎ 06/99551971). **Tarquinia** (✉ Piazza Cavour 1, ☎ 0766/856384), open Monday–Saturday 8–2.

Tivoli, Palestrina, and Subiaco: Fountains, Villas, and Hermitages

East of Rome are two of Lazio's star attractions—the Villa Adriana and the Villa d'Este in Tivoli—and, in the mountains beyond them, the lesser-known and wonderfully peaceful Palestrina and Subiaco. The road from Rome to Tivoli passes through some uninspiring industrial areas and burgeoning suburbs that used to be lush countryside. You'll know you're close to Tivoli when you see vast quarries of travertine marble and smell the sulfurous vapors of the little spa, Bagni di Tivoli. Both sites in Tivoli are outdoors and entail walking.

With a car, you can continue your loop through the mountains east of Rome, taking in two very different sights that are both focused on religion. The ancient pagan sanctuary at Palestrina is set on the slopes of Mt. Ginestro, from which it commands a sweeping view of the green plain and distant mountains. Subiaco, the cradle of Western monasticism, is tucked away in the mountains above Tivoli and Palestrina. Unless you start out very early and have lots of energy, plan an overnight stop along the way if you want to take in all three.

Tivoli

❹ **Villa Adriana** (Hadrian's Villa), 3 km (2 mi) south of Tivoli, should be visited early, especially in summer, to take advantage of cool mornings. Hadrian's Villa was an emperor's theme park, a retreat where the marvels of the classical world were reproduced for a ruler's pleasure. Hadrian, who succeeded Trajan as emperor in AD 117, was a man of genius and intellectual curiosity. Fascinated by the accomplishments of the Hellenistic world, he decided to re-create it for his own enjoyment by building this villa over a vast tract of land below the ancient settlement of Tibur. From AD 118 to 130, architects, laborers, and artists worked on the villa, periodically spurred on by the emperor himself as he returned from another voyage full of ideas for even more daring constructions. After his death in AD 138, the fortunes of his villa declined. It was sacked by barbarians and Romans alike; many of his statues and decorations ended up in the Vatican Museums, but the expansive ruins are nonetheless compelling. A visit here can take anywhere from two hours to all day, depending on how much time you want to leave just to wander the site, a delightful activity all its own. ✉ *Via di Villa Adriana 1,* ☎ *0774/530203.* ✆ *8,000 lire/€4.15.* ☉ *Daily 9 AM–90 mins before sunset.*

❺ **Villa d'Este,** a late-Renaissance estate, is a playground of artistic whimsy, manifested in the 80-some fountains of all shapes and sizes that tumble down the vast, steep hillside garden. Cardinal Ippolito d'Este (1509–72), an active figure in the political intrigues of mid-16th-century Italy, set about proving his dominance over man and nature by commissioning this monument to architectural excess. His builders tore down part of a Franciscan monastery to clear the site, then diverted the Aniene River to water the garden and feed the fountains. History shows it was worth the effort—the Villa d'Este is still considered one of Italy's most beautiful spots. Tiny drinking fountains, massive reflecting pools, a fountain that once played music through organ pipes, and one that's a scale model of the great monuments of Rome show their years but are still a sight to see, and the green of the gardens is a pleasant break in summer. Allow an hour for this visit, and bear in mind that you'll be climbing a lot of stairs. ⊠ *Piazza Trento 1,* ☎ *0774/312070.* ⊠ *8,000 lire/€4.15.* ☉ *Tues.– Sun. 9 AM–90 mins before sunset.*

➏ Palestrina

Giovanni Pierluigi da Palestrina, born in Palestrina in 1525, was the renowned composer of 105 masses, as well as madrigals, magnificats, and motets. But the town was celebrated long before the composer's lifetime. Ancient Praeneste, modern Palestrina, was founded much earlier than Rome. It was the site of the Temple of Fortuna Primigenia, which dates from the beginning of the 2nd century BC. This was one of the biggest, richest, and most-frequented temple complexes in all antiquity. People came from far and wide to consult its famous oracle, yet in modern times no one had any idea of the extent of the complex until World War II bombings exposed ancient foundations that stretched into the plain below the town. It has since become clear that the temple area was larger than the town of Palestrina is today. Now you can make out the four superimposed terraces that formed the main part of the temple; they were built up on great arches and were linked by broad flights of stairs. The whole town sits on top of what was once the main part of the temple.

Large arches and terraces scale the hillside up to the **Palazzo Barberini,** built in the 17th century along the semicircular lines of the original temple. It's now a museum containing material found on the site, some dating back to the 4th century BC. The collection of splendid engraved bronze urns, plundered by thieves in 1991 and later recovered, takes second place to the chief attraction, a 1st-century BC mosaic representing the Nile in flood. This delightful work—a large-scale composition in which form, color, and innumerable details captivate the eye—is alone worth the trip to Palestrina. But there's more: a model of the temple as it was in ancient times helps you appreciate the immensity of the original construction. ⊠ *Museo Nazionale Archeologico, Palazzo Barberini,* ☎ *06/9538100.* ⊠ *4,000 lire/€2.05.* ☉ *Mid-Sept.–mid-Nov. and mid-Mar.–May, daily 9–6; June–mid-Sept., daily 9–7:30; mid-Nov.–mid-Mar., daily 9–4.*

➐ Subiaco

Between the town and St. Benedict's hermitage on the mountainside is the **Convento di Santa Scolastica,** the only one of the hermitages founded by St. Benedict to have survived the Lombard invasion of Italy in the 9th century. It has three cloisters; the oldest dates from the 13th century. The library was the site of the first print shop in Italy, set up in 1474. ⊠ *Subiaco,* ☎ *0774/85525.* ☉ *Daily 9–12:30 and 4–7 (6:30 in winter).*

The 6th-century **Monastero di San Benedetto** (Monastery of St. Benedict), a landmark of Western monasticism, was built over the grotto where the saint lived and meditated. Clinging to the cliff on nine great arches, it has resisted destruction for almost 800 years. Over the little wooden veranda at the entrance, a Latin inscription augurs PEACE TO THOSE WHO ENTER. Every inch of the upper church is covered with frescoes by Umbrian and Sienese artists of the 14th century. In front of the main altar, a stairway leads down to the lower church, carved out of the rock, with yet another stairway down to the grotto where Benedict lived as a hermit for three years. The frescoes here are even earlier than those above; look for the portrait of St. Francis of Assisi, painted from life in 1210, in the Cappella di San Gregorio, and for the oldest fresco in the monastery, in the Shepherd's Grotto. ⊠ *Subiaco,* ☎ *0774/85039.* ⊙ *Daily 9–12:30 and 3–6.*

Tivoli, Palestrina, and Subiaco A to Z

BUS TRAVEL

COTRAL buses leave for Tivoli every 15 minutes from the terminal at the Rebbibia stop on Metro B, but not all take the route that passes near Hadrian's Villa. Ask which bus passes closest to Villa Adriana and tell the driver to let you off there. The ride takes about an hour. From Rome to Palestrina, take the COTRAL bus from the Anagnina stop on Metro A. From Rome to Subiaco, take the COTRAL bus from the Rebbibia stop on Metro B; buses leave every 40 minutes; the circuitous trip takes one hour and 45 minutes. There is local bus service between Tivoli and Palestrina, but check with COTRAL before you go.
➤ Bus Information: **COTRAL** (☎ 800/431784 toll free).

CAR TRAVEL

For Tivoli, take Via Tiburtina or the Rome–L'Aquila autostrada (A24). To get to Palestrina directly from Rome, take either Via Prenestina or Via Casilina, or take the Autostrada del Sole (A2) to the San Cesareo exit and follow signs for Palestrina; this trip takes about one hour. (The autostrada is longer but can be quicker at nonpeak hours.) It's best to drive from Rome to Subiaco. Take S155 east for about 40 km (25 mi) before turning left onto S411 for the remaining 25 km (15 mi) to Subiaco; the trip takes about 70 minutes.

From Tivoli to Palestrina, follow signs for Via Prenestina and Palestrina. To get to Subiaco from either Tivoli or Palestrina, take the autostrada for L'Aquila (A24) to the Vicovaro–Mandela exit, and then follow the local road to Subiaco.

TOURS

CIT (Compagnia Italiana Tourismo) has half-day excursions to Villa d'Este in Tivoli. American Express, Appian Line, and Carrani Tours have tours that include Hadrian's Villa.
➤ Fees and Schedules: **American Express** (☎ 06/67641). **Appian Line** (☎ 06/487861). **Carrani Tours** (☎ 06/4880510). **CIT** (☎ 06/4620311, WEB www.citonline.it).

TRAIN TRAVEL

FS trains connect Rome's Termini and Tiburtina stations with Tivoli in about 30 minutes; Villa d'Este is about a 20-minute walk from the station in Tivoli. The FS train from Stazione Termini to Palestrina takes about 40 minutes; you can then board a bus from the train station to the center of town.

VISITOR INFORMATION

➤ Tourist Information: **Palestrina** (⊠ Piazza Santa Maria degli Angeli, ☎ 06/9573176). **Tivoli** (⊠ Largo Garibaldi, ☎ 0774/334522). **Subiaco** (⊠ Via Cadorna 59, ☎ 0774/822013).

Viterbo, Bagnaia, and Bomarzo: Where Popes and Prelates Took Their Ease

The Viterbo region, 104 km (64 mi) north of Rome, is rich in history embodied in cameo scenes of dark medieval stone, dappled light on wooded paths, a prelate's palace worthy of Rome itself, and another prelate's pleasure garden, where splashing fountains were aquatic jokes played on unsuspecting guests. The city of Viterbo, which overshadowed Rome as a center of papal power for a time during the Middle Ages, lies in the heart of Tuscia, the modern name for the Etruscan domain of Etruria, a landscape of dramatic beauty punctuated by thickly forested hills and deep, rocky gorges. Lake Bolsena is an extinct volcano, and the sulfur springs still bubbling up in Viterbo's spas were used by the ancient Romans. Bagnaia is the site of Villa Lante, where there are Italian gardens and a vast park.

The ideal way to explore this region is by car, making Bomarzo your first stop. By train, you can start at Viterbo and get to Bagnaia by local bus. If you're driving between Rome and Florence, an overnight in Viterbo is a good way to break up the trip and makes it easier to see all the attractions.

★ ➑ **Viterbo**

Viterbo's moment of glory was in the 13th century, when it became the seat of the papal court. The medieval core of the city still nestles within 12th-century walls. You can get the feel of the Middle Ages in the **San Pellegrino** district, where daily life is carried on in a quaint, peaceful setting that has remained practically unchanged over the centuries. The Palazzo Papale and the cathedral enhance the effect. Since medieval times, the city has remained a renowned spa center, for its natural **hot springs** just outside of town.

The Gothic **Palazzo Papale** (Papal Palace) was built in the 13th century as a residence for the popes who chose to sojourn here. At that time Rome was a notoriously unhealthy place, ridden with malaria and plague and rampaging factions of rival barons. In 1271 the palace was the scene of a novel type of rebellion. A conclave held here to elect a new pope had dragged on for months, apparently making no progress. The people of Viterbo were exasperated by the delay, especially as custom decreed that they had to provide for the cardinals' board and lodging for the duration of the conclave. So they tore the roof off the great hall where the cardinals were meeting and put them on bread and water. A new pope—Gregory X—was elected in short order. ⊠ *Piazza San Lorenzo.*

The facade and interior of the cathedral, **Chiesa di San Lorenzo** (Church of St. Lawrence) date from the Middle Ages. On the ancient columns inside the church you can see the chips that an exploding bomb took out of the stone during World War II. ⊠ *Piazza San Lorenzo.*

The medieval district of **San Pellegrino** is one of the best-preserved in Italy. It has charming vistas of arches, vaults, towers, exterior staircases, worn wooden doors on great iron hinges, and tiny hanging gardens. You pass many an antiques shop as you explore the little squares and byways. The **Fontana Grande** in the piazza of the same name is the largest and most extravagant of Viterbo's authentic Gothic fountains. ⊠ *Via San Pellegrino.*

Viterbo has been a spa town for centuries, and the **Terme dei Papi** continues the tradition. This excellent spa offers the usual rundown of health and beauty treatments with an Etruscan twist: try a facial with local volcanic mud, or a steam bath in an ancient cave, where scalding hot mineral water direct from the Bullicam spring splashes down a waterfall to a pool under your feet. The Terme dei Papi's main draw, however, is the *terme* (baths) themselves: a 100,000 square-ft **outdoor limestone pool** of Viterbo's famous hot water, which pours in at 59°C (138°F). Floats and deck chairs are for rent, but bring your own bathrobe or towel. ⊠ *Strada Bagni 12, Viterbo,* ☎ *0761/3501,* WEB *www.termedeipapi.it.* 🎟 *Mon.–Fri. 20,000 lire/€10.30, Sat.–Sun. 25,000 lire/€12.90.* ☾ *Pool daily 9–4:30; spa daily 9–5:30.*

$$ ✕ **Enoteca La Torre.** Foodie paradise is found here, in a simple but el-
★ egant temple to good eating that's a real surprise so far off the beaten
path. In addition to an ever-changing menu and a wine list cross-
referenced with ratings from Italian wine guides, there are lists for cheeses,
mineral waters, oils, and vinegars, the latter two from a stock kept in
an old wooden chest in the front of the dining room. Chestnut fritters
and rabbit stew are unusual delicacies, but rest assured that whatever
you choose, it will be local, traditional, and of the highest quality. Next
door you can sample a reduced version of the restaurant menu at the
casual La Cantina wine bar ($) or stop in for a wine-and-olive-oil tast-
ing before dinner. ✉ *Via della Torre 5,* ☎ *0761/226467. AE, DC, MC,
V. Closed Sun.*

$$$ 🏨 **Hotel Niccolò V.** This peaceful, airy hotel attached to the spa at Terme
★ dei Papi would be a delight even without its views over the massive
thermal pool that is its raison d'être. Marble baths and wooden floors
give the quiet rooms an air of country-house elegance. Breakfast, a sumptuous buffet, is taken in an unusual wood-beamed gallery overlooking a small garden in back. Hotel guests are allowed free use of the
pool and get a 15% discount on spa treatments. ✉ *Strada Bagni 12,
01100,* ☎ *0761/3501,* FAX *0761/352451,* WEB *www.terme.it 20 rooms,
3 suites. Restaurant, bar, breakfast room, in-room safes, minibars, pool,
meeting rooms. AE, DC, MC, V.*

❾ **Bagnaia**

The village of Bagnaia, 5 km (3 mi) east of Viterbo, is the site of 16th-
century cardinal Alessandro Montalto's summer retreat. Small twin residences are but an excuse for the hillside garden and park that surround
them, designed by Vignola for a member of the papal court.

Villa Lante is a terraced extravaganza. On the lowest level, a delightful Italian garden has a centerpiece fountain fed by water channeled
down the hillside. On another, higher terrace a stream of water runs
through a groove carved in a long stone table where the cardinal entertained his friends alfresco, chilling wine in the running water. And
that is only one of the most evident and innocent of the whimsical water
games that were devised for the cardinal. The symmetry of the formal
gardens contrasts with the wild, untamed park adjacent to it, reflecting the paradoxes of nature and artifice that are the theme of this pleasure garden. ✉ *Via J. Barozzi 71,* ☎ *0761/288008.* 🎫 *4,000 lire/€2.05.*
🕐 *Open Tues.–Sun. 9 AM–1 hr before sunset.*

👆 ❿ **Bomarzo**

The eerie 16th-century **Parco dei Mostri** (Monster Park), 15 km (9 mi)
east of Viterbo, is populated by weird and fantastic sculptures of mythical creatures and eccentric architecture. It was created by Prince Vi-
cino Orsini for his wife, Giulia Farnese, who is said to have taken one
look at the park and died of heart failure. No one really knows why
the prince had the sculptures carved in outcroppings of stone in a dusky
wood on his estate, but it probably has something to do with the ar-
tifices that were an artistic conceit of his time. Children love it, and
there are photo ops galore. ✉ *1½ km (1 mi) west of town.* 🎫 *15,000
lire/€7.75.* 🕐 *Daily 8:30 AM–1 hr before sunset.*

Viterbo, Bagnaia, Bomarzo A to Z

COTRAL buses for Viterbo depart from the Saxa Rubra stop of the
Ferrovie COTRAL train. The *diretta* (direct) bus takes about 75 minutes. Other buses are slower. Bagnaia can be reached from Viterbo by
local city bus.

➤ BUS INFORMATION: **COTRAL** (☎ 800/431784 toll free).

Head out of Rome on the A1 autostrada, exiting at Attigliano. Bomarzo is only 3 km (2 mi) from the autostrada. The trip takes one hour. It takes about 20 minutes to get to Viterbo from Bomarzo. Bagnaia, just east of Viterbo, can be visited before entering Viterbo.

For Viterbo, authorized guides are available through the APT office.

For schedules and information, contact Ferrovie COTRAL.
➤ TRAIN INFORMATION: **Ferrovie COTRAL** (✉ Piazzale Flaminio, ☎ 1674/31784).

➤ TOURIST INFORMATION: **APT Viterbo** (✉ Piazza San Carluccio, ☎ 0761/220957).

Sermoneta, Ninfa, and Sperlonga: Picturesque Towns and Romantic Ruins

A trio of romantic places south of Rome, set in a landscape defined by low mountains and a broad coastal plain, lure you into a past that seems centuries away from the city's bustle. Sermoneta is a castle town. Ninfa, nearby, is a noble family's fairy-tale garden that is open to the public only at certain times. Sperlonga is a hilltop village overlooking the sea and site of one of emperor Tiberius's most fabulous villas. You need a car to see them all in a day or so, and to get to Ninfa. But Sermoneta and Sperlonga are accessible by public transportation.

⑪ **Sermoneta**

In Sermoneta, 80 km (50 mi) southeast of Rome, the town and castle are one. Within concentric rings of walls, in medieval times, townspeople lived and farmers came to take shelter from marauders. The lords—in this case the Caetani family—held a last line of defense in the tall tower, where if necessary they could cut themselves off by pulling up the drawbridge.

The **Castello Caetani** (Caetani Castle) dates from the 1200s. In the 15th century, having won it by ruse from the Caetani, the Borgia pope Alexander VI transformed it into a formidable fortress and handed it over to his son Cesare. The chiaroscuro of dark and light stone, the quiet of the narrow streets, and the bastions that hint at siege and battle take you back in time. ✉ *Via della Fortezza.* ☎ *5,000 lire/€2.60. Guided tours only.* ⊙ *Apr.–Sept., Fri.–Wed. 10–11, 3–4, and 5–6; Nov.–Mar., Fri.–Wed. 10–11:30, 2–3, and 4–5.*

⑫ **Ninfa**

In the Middle Ages Ninfa was a thriving village, part of the Caetani family's vast land holdings around Sermoneta. It was abandoned when malaria-carrying mosquitoes infested the plain, and it fell into ruin. Now it is a place of rare beauty, a dream garden of romantic ruins and rushing waters, of exotic species and fragrant blooms. Ninfa is part of a World Wildlife Fund Oasis, managed in collaboration with the Caetani heirs. Earlier generations of the Caetani family, including English and American spouses and gardening buffs, created the garden over the course of the 20th century. ✉ *Via Ninfina, Doganella di Ninfa,* ☎ *0773/695407 (APT Latina-Provincial Tourist Office).* ☎ *12,000 lire/€6.20. Guided tours only.* ⊙ *Apr.–June, call for designated days; July–Sept., 1st weekend of month 9–noon and 2:30–6.*

⑬ Sperlonga

Sperlonga, 127 km (79 mi) southeast of Rome, is a labyrinth of white-washed alleys, arches, and little houses, like a casbah wrapped around a hilltop overlooking the sea, with broad, sandy beaches on either side. Long a favorite haunt of artists and artisans in flight from Rome's quick pace, the town has ancient origins. The medieval town gates, twisting alleys, and watchtower were vital to its defense when pirate ships came into sight. Now they simply make this former fishing town even more picturesque.

Under a cliff on the shore only 1 km (½ mi) south of Sperlonga are the ruins of **Grotta di Tiberio** (Grotto of Tiberius). The villa incorporated several natural grottoes, in one of which Tiberius dined with guests on an artificial island. The various courses were served on little boats that floated across the shallow seawater pool to the emperor's table. Showpieces of the villa were the colossal sculpture groups embellishing the grotto. The **Museo Nazionale** (National Museum) was built on the site especially to hold the fragments of these sculptures, discovered by chance by an amateur archaeologist. The huge statues had been smashed to pieces centuries earlier by Byzantine monks unsympathetic to pagan images. For decades, the subject and appearance of the originals remained a mystery, and the museum was a work in progress as scholars there tried to put together the 7,000 pieces of this giant puzzle. Their achievement, the immense Scylla group, largest of the sculptures, is on view here. ⊠ *Via Flacca,* ☎ *0771/54028.* ☎ *4,000 lire/€2.05.* ☉ *Daily 9 AM–1 hr before sunset.*

DINING

$$–$$$ ✕ **Gli Archi.** Tucked into a landing of Old Sperlonga's myriad stairways, this attractive restaurant has brick-arch interiors and a courtyard for fair-weather dining. A touch of refinement puts it a cut above the establishments closer to the beach, and its owners take pride in serving high-quality ingredients with culinary simplicity. Seafood, including pasta with seafood sauces, predominates on the menu, but there are a few meat courses, too. ⊠ *Via Ottaviano 17,* ☎ *0771/54300. AE, DC, MC, V. Closed Wed. and Jan.*

$–$$ ✕ **La Bisaccia.** A favorite with locals, La Bisaccia is popular with seasonal residents, too. It's near the beach in the newer part of town, and you can walk to it in 10–15 minutes from the center of Old Sperlonga. Book a table for lunch on weekends and in summer. Seafood comes just about any way you want it, from pasta with scampi to fried, baked, or grilled fish. And if you don't want fish, the menu has some basic meat dishes and a local specialty, tangy buffalo-milk mozzarella. ⊠ *Via Romita 19,* ☎ *0771/584576. AE, DC, MC, V. Closed Tues. in Oct.–mid-June, and Nov.*

Sermoneta, Ninfa, and Sperlonga A to Z

BUS TRAVEL
COTRAL buses for Sermoneta leave Rome from the EUR Fermi stop of Metro B. The ride takes about one hour. For Sperlonga, COTRAL buses leave from the same stop. The trip takes about 1½ hours.
➤ BUS INFORMATION: **COTRAL** (☎ 800/431784, toll free).

CAR TRAVEL
The fastest route south is the Via Pontina, an expressway. An alternative is the Via Appia. For Sermoneta, turn east at Latina. The trip takes about 50 minutes. For out-of-the-way Ninfa, proceed as for Sermoneta, but before getting there follow the signs for Doganella/Ninfa. An alternative is to follow the Via Appia to Cisterna and then look for signs for Doganella/Ninfa. The trip takes about one hour. For Sperlonga, take the Via Pontina to Latina, then the Via Appia to Terracina and Sperlonga. The trip takes about 1½ hours.

FS trains on the Rome–Formia–Naples line stop at Latina Scalo, where you can get a local bus to Sermoneta, though service is sketchy. Traveling time is about one hour. For Sperlonga, on the same line, get off at the Itri station, from which buses leave for Sperlonga. The trip takes about 1½ hours.

VISITOR INFORMATION

➤ TOURIST INFORMATION: **APT Latina** (✉ Via Duca del Mare 19, Latina, ☎ 0773/695–407).

ROME A TO Z

To research prices, get advice from other travelers, and book travel arrangements, visit www.fodors.com.

AIRPORTS AND TRANSFERS

Most international flights and all domestic flights arrive at Aeroporto Leonardo da Vinci, also known as Fiumicino, 30 km (19 mi) southwest of Rome. Some international and charter flights land at Ciampino, a civil and military airport 15 km (9 mi) southeast of Rome. To get to the city from Fiumicino by car, follow the signs for Rome on the expressway from the airport, which links with the GRA, the beltway around Rome. The direction you take on the GRA depends on where your hotel is, so get directions from the car-rental people at the airport. A taxi from Fiumicino to the center of town costs 70,000 lire/€36.15–80,000 lire/€41.25, including *supplementi* (extra charges) for airport service and luggage, and the ride takes 30–40 minutes, depending on traffic. Private limousines can be hired at booths in the arrivals hall; they charge a little more than taxis but can take more passengers. Ignore gypsy drivers who approach you inside the terminal; stick to the licensed cabs, yellow or white, that wait by the curb. A booth inside the arrivals hall provides taxi information.

You have a choice of two trains to get to downtown Rome from Fiumicino Airport. Ask at the airport (at APT or train information counters) which takes you closer to your hotel. The nonstop Airport-Termini express (marked FS and run by the state railway) takes you directly to Track 22 at Stazione Termini, Rome's main train station, which is well served by taxis and is the hub of metro and bus lines. The ride to Termini takes 30 minutes; departures are hourly, beginning at 7:50 AM from the airport, with a final departure at 10:05 PM. Tickets cost 15,000 lire/€7.75. FM1, the other airport train, runs from the airport to Rome and beyond, with its terminal in Monterotondo, a suburban town to the east. The main stops in Rome are at Trastevere, Ostiense, and Tiburtina stations; at each you can find taxis and bus and/or metro connections to other parts of Rome. This train runs from Fiumicino from 6:35 AM to 12:15 AM, with departures every 20 minutes, a little less frequently in off-hours. The ride to Tiburtina takes 40 minutes. Tickets cost 8,000 lire/€4.15. For either train buy your ticket at automatic vending machines (you need Italian currency). There are ticket counters at some stations (at Termini/Track 22, Trastevere, Tiburtina). Date-stamp the ticket at the gate before you board.

➤ AIRPORT INFORMATION: **Aeroporto Leonardo da Vinci** (☎ 06/65953640). **Ciampino** (✉ Via Appia Nuova, ☎ 06/794941, WEB www.adr.it).

BIKE AND MOPED TRAVEL

Pedaling through Villa Borghese, along the Tiber, and through the center of the city when traffic is light is a pleasant way to see the sights, but remember: Rome is hilly. Enjoy Rome organizes all-day bike tours of Rome for small groups covering major sights and some hidden ones. The same tours are available by moped. You can rent a moped or scooter and mandatory helmet at Scoot-a-Long. Also try St. Peter's Motor Rent and Happy Rent.

➤ BIKE RENTALS: **Enjoy Rome** (✉ Via Varese 39, 00185 Rome, ☎ 06/4451843, WEB www.enjoyrome.com). **Happy Rent** (✉ Piazza Esquilino 8/h, ☎ 06/4818185, WEB www.happyrent.it). **Scoot-a-Long** (✉ Via Cavour 302, ☎ 06/6780206). **St. Peter's Motor Rent** (✉ Via di Porta Castello 43, ☎ 06/6875714).

BUS TRAVEL TO AND FROM ROME

There is no central bus terminal in Rome. COTRAL is the suburban bus company that connects Rome with outlying areas and other cities in the Lazio region. Long-distance and suburban buses terminate either near Tiburtina Station or near outlying metro stops such as Rebbibia and Anagnina. For COTRAL bus information, call weekdays 8 AM–8 PM.

FARES AND SCHEDULES
➤ BUS INFORMATION: **COTRAL** (☎ 800/431784, toll free).

BUS TRAVEL WITHIN ROME

ATAC city buses and tram lines run from about 6 AM to midnight, with night buses (indicated N) on some lines. A 75-minute ticket costs 1,500 lire/€0.75. The compact electric buses of Lines 117 and 119 take handy routes through the center of Rome that can save lots of walking. Orange-and-blue J-Line buses are a handy alternative way to get across town; route information and tickets are available at newsstands and tobacconists. The J-Line buses, which are not part of the ATAC system, are a big help to visitors; from 7 to 11, you can ride directly from San Giovanni in Laterano to the Vatican and back, stopping off at the Colosseum and the Circus Maximus. Tickets cost 1,900 lire/€1.00 at newsstands and tobacconists; ATAC tickets are not valid.

FARES AND SCHEDULES
➤ BUS INFORMATION: **ATAC** (☎ 800/431784 toll free). **J-Line** (☎ 800/076287).

CAR RENTAL

➤ LOCAL AGENCIES: **Avis** (☎ 06/42824728). **Eurodollar** (☎ 167/018668). **Hertz** (☎ 199/112211). **Maggiore** (☎ 147/867067). **Thrifty** (☎ 06/4820966).

CAR TRAVEL

The main access routes from the north are A1 (Autostrada del Sole) from Milan and Florence and the A12/E80 highway from Genoa. The principal route to or from points south, including Naples, is the A2. All highways connect with the Grande Raccordo Anulare (GRA), which channels traffic into the center. Markings on the GRA are confusing: take time to study the route you need.

EMBASSIES AND CONSULATES

➤ AUSTRALIA: **Australian Consulate** (✉ Via Alessandria 215, ☎ 06/852721).
➤ CANADA: **Canadian Consulate** (✉ Via Zara 30, ☎ 06/445981).
➤ NEW ZEALAND: **New Zealand Consulate** (✉ Via Zara 28, ☎ 06/4417171).
➤ UNITED KINGDOM: **U.K. Consulate** (✉ Via Venti Settembre 80/a, ☎ 06/4825441).
➤ UNITED STATES: **U.S. Consulate** (✉ Via Veneto 121, ☎ 06/46741).

EMERGENCIES

Farmacia Internazionale Capranica, Farmacia Internazionale Barberini, and Farmacia Cola di Rienzo are pharmacies that have some English-speaking staff. Most pharmacies are open 8:30–1 and 4–8; some are open all night. A schedule posted outside each pharmacy indicates the nearest pharmacy open during off-hours (afternoons, through the night, and Sunday). Dial ☎ 1100 for an automated list of three open pharmacies closest to the telephone from which you call. The hospitals listed below have English-speaking doctors. Rome American Hospital is about 30 minutes by cab from the center of town.

➤ EMERGENCY SERVICES: **Ambulance** (☎ 118). **Police** (☎ 113). **Red Cross** (☎ 06/5510).

➤ HOSPITALS: **Rome American Hospital** (✉ Via Emilio Longoni 69, ☎ 06/22551, WEB www.rah.it). **Salvator Mundi International Hospital** (✉ Viale delle Mura Gianicolensi 66, ☎ 06/588961, WEB www.smih.pcn.net).

➤ PHARMACIES: **Farmacia Cola di Rienzo** (✉ Via Cola di Rienzo 213, ☎ 06/3243130). **Farmacia Internazionale Barberini** (✉ Piazza Barberini 49, ☎ 06/4825456). **Farmacia Internazionale Capranica** (✉ Piazza Capranica 96, ☎ 06/6794680).

ENGLISH-LANGUAGE MEDIA

BOOKS

English-language books in Rome are expensive; most are imported from England, so prices in Rome reflect the strong pound and shipping costs. The Anglo-American Bookstore and the Economy Book and Video Center have the widest selection of genres. Trastevere's Corner Bookstore carries lots of offbeat new fiction and has a vast history section. For used books at lower prices, try the Open Door.

➤ CONTACTS: **Anglo-American Bookstore** (✉ Via della Vite 102, ☎ 06/6795222, WEB www.aab.it). **Corner Bookstore** (✉ Via del Moro 48, Trastevere, ☎ 06/5836942). **Economy Book and Video Center** (✉ Via Torino 136, ☎ 06/4746877, WEB www.booksitaly.com). **Lion Bookshop** (✉ Via dei Greci 33/36, ☎ 06/32654007). **Open Door** (✉ Via della Lungaretta 25, Trastevere, ☎ 06/5896478).

NEWSPAPERS AND MAGAZINES

The ubiquitous *International Herald Tribune* is published in Italy with the four-page *Italy Daily* insert, an English-language summary of main Italian news stories and local cultural events. Major English and American newsmagazines and a few daily papers are available at some newsstands, including those on Via Veneto, Via del Corso (at Via del Tritone), and Campo dei Fiori.

LODGING

APARTMENT AND VILLA RENTALS

For stays of a week or more, especially for families or groups of friends, an apartment or villa rental may be more convenient than a hotel. Always insist on photos, a map with indication of location, and a detailed description of the property. Homes International offers short- and long-term accommodations in Rome. Property International handles monthly and weekly rentals in Rome and Tuscany. The English-language biweekly *Wanted in Rome* lists rentals available privately.

➤ LOCAL AGENTS: **Homes International** (✉ Via Bissolati 20, 00187, ☎ 06/4881800, FAX 06/4881808). **Property International** (✉ Viale Aventino 79, 00153, ☎ 06/5743170, FAX 06/5743182).

➤ RENTAL LISTINGS: **Wanted in Rome** (WEB www.wantedinrome.it).

MAIL AND SHIPPING
➤ Post Offices: **Main post office** (✉ Piazza San Silvestro 19, ☎ 06/6798495).

OVERNIGHT SERVICES
While DHL and UPS offices are far out of the city center, FedEx has walk-in service on Via Barberini; all three companies will pick up packages from anywhere in Rome.
➤ Major Services: **DHL** (800/345345). **Federal Express** (✉ Via Barberini 115, ☎ 800/123800). **UPS** (☎ 800/877877

SAFETY
LOCAL SCAMS
A word of caution: "gypsy" children, who hang around sights popular with tourists throughout Europe, are rife in Rome and are adept pickpockets. One modus operandi is to approach a tourist and proffer a piece of cardboard with writing on it. While the unsuspecting victim attempts to read the message *on* it, the children's hands are busy *under* it, trying to make off with purses or valuables. If you see such a group (recognizable by their unkempt appearance), do not even allow them near you—they are quick and know more tricks than you do. Also be aware of persons, usually young men, who ride by on motorbikes, grab the shoulder strap of your bag or camera, and step on the gas. Wear or carry your bag on the side away from the street edge of the sidewalk, or, best of all, wear a concealed money belt. Don't carry more money than you need, and don't carry your passport unless you need it to exchange money. A useful expression to ward off pesky panhandlers or vendors is "*Vai via!*" (Go away!).

WOMEN IN ROME
Foreign women can expect to attract extra attention from Italian men, but this is usually harmless flirtation, and rarely will become a safety issue. Use common sense.

SUBWAY TRAVEL
The metro (subway) is the easiest and fastest way to get around and there are stops near most of the main tourist attractions. Service begins at 5:30 AM, and the last trains leave the most distant station at 11:30 PM (on Saturday night, trains run until 12:30 AM). There are two lines—A and B—which intersect at Stazione Termini. The fare is 1,500 lire/€0.75.

TAXIS
Taxis in Rome do not cruise, but if empty (look for an illuminated TAXI sign on the roof) they will stop if you flag them down. Taxis wait at stands and can also be called by phone, in which case you're charged a bit more. The meter starts at 4,500 lire/€2.65; there are extra charges for night service (5,000 lire/€2.50 extra from 10 PM to 7 AM) and on Sunday and holidays, as well as for each piece of baggage. Use only licensed, metered yellow or white cabs, identified by a numbered shield on the side, an illuminated taxi sign on the roof, and a plaque next to the license plate reading SERVIZIO PUBBLICO. Avoid unmarked, unauthorized, unmetered gypsy cabs (numerous at airports and train stations), whose renegade drivers actively solicit your trade and may demand astronomical fares. Some taxis accept some credit cards, but you must specify when calling that you will pay that way.
➤ Taxi Companies: **Taxi** (☎ 06/5551, 06/3570, 06/4994, or 06/88177).

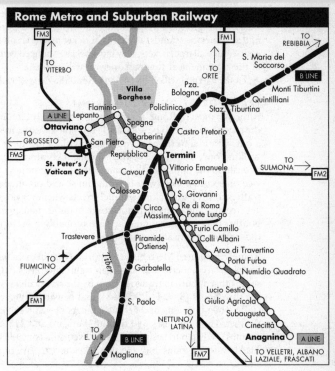

Rome Metro and Suburban Railway

TOURS

BUS TOURS

American Express and CIT offer general orientation tours of the city, as well as specialized tours of particular areas such as the Vatican or Ancient Rome.

➤ FEES AND SCHEDULES: **American Express** (☎ 06/67641). **Appian Line** (☎ 06/4884151). **ATAC** (☎ 800/431784). **CIT** (✉ Piazza della Repubblica 64, ☎ 06/4620311, WEB www.citonline.it).

WALKING TOURS

American Express, Enjoy Rome, and Scala Reale offer walking tours of Rome.

➤ FEES AND SCHEDULES: **American Express** (☎ 06/67641). **Enjoy Rome** (✉ Via Varese 39, 00185, ☎ 06/4451843, WEB www.enjoyrome.com). **Scala Reale** (✉ Via dell'Olmata 30, 00184, ☎ 06/4745673 or 800/732–2863 ext. 4052, WEB www.scalareale.org).

TRAIN TRAVEL

Stazione Termini is Rome's main train terminal; the Tiburtina and Ostiense stations serve some long-distance trains, many commuter trains, and the FM1 line to Fiumicino Airport. Some trains for Pisa and Genoa leave Rome from, or pass through, the Trastevere Station. You can find English-speaking staff at the information office at Stazione Termini, or ask for information at travel agencies. You can purchase tickets up to two months in advance either at the main stations or at travel agencies bearing the FS (Ferrovie dello Stato) emblem. Lines at station ticket windows may be very long, and electronic ticket machines are complex, though they have instructions in English; you can save time by buying your ticket at a travel agency. Remember that you can reserve a seat up to one day in advance at a travel agency or up to three hours in advance at a train station. Tickets for train rides within a radius of 100 km (62 mi) of Rome can be purchased at tobacco shops and at some newsstands, as well as at ticket machines on the main concourse. Like all train tickets, they must be date-stamped before you board, at the machine near the track, or you will be fined.

➤ TRAIN INFORMATION: FS (☎ 848/888088, 7 AM–9 PM).

TRANSPORTATION AROUND ROME

Although most of Rome's sights are in a relatively circumscribed area, the city is too large to be seen solely on foot. Take the metro (subway), a bus, or a taxi to the area you plan to visit, and expect to do a lot of walking once you're there. Wear a pair of comfortable, sturdy shoes to cushion the impact of the *sampietrini* (cobblestones). Heed our advice on security. Get away from the noise and polluted air of heavily trafficked streets by taking parallel streets whenever possible. You can get free city and transportation-route maps at municipal information booths; the transportation maps are probably more up-to-date than those you can buy at newsstands.

Rome's integrated Metrebus transportation system includes buses and trams (ATAC), metro and suburban trains and buses (COTRAL), and some other suburban trains (FS) run by the state railways. Try to avoid the rush hours (8–9, 1–2:30, 7–8), and beware of pickpockets, especially when boarding and getting off cars or vehicles, particularly on the metro and on Buses 64 (Termini–Vatican) and 218 and 660 (Catacombs). When purchasing tickets for excursions outside Rome on CO-TRAL buses or trains, buy a return ticket, too, to save time at the other end.

FARES AND SCHEDULES

A ticket valid for 75 minutes on any combination of buses and trams and one entrance to the metro costs 1,500 lire/€0.80. You are supposed to date-stamp your ticket when you board the first vehicle, stamping it again when boarding for the last time within 75 minutes (the important thing is to stamp it the first time). Tickets for the metrebus system are sold at tobacconists, newsstands, some coffee bars, automatic ticket machines positioned in metro stations and some bus stops, and at ATAC and COTRAL ticket booths (in some metro stations, on the lower concourse at Stazione Termini, and at a few main bus terminals). A BIG tourist ticket, valid for one day on all public transport, costs 6,000 lire/€3.05. A weekly ticket (Settimanale, also known as CIS) costs 24,000 lire/€12.40 and can be purchased only at ATAC booths.

TRAVEL AGENCIES

➤ LOCAL AGENT REFERRALS: **American Express** (☎ 06/67641). **Appian Line** ((☎ 06/4884151). **Carrani Tours** (✉ Via Vittorio Emanuele Orlando 95, ☎ 06/4880510). **CIT** (✉ Piazza della Repubblica 64, ☎ 06/4620311, WEB www.citonline.it).

VISITOR INFORMATION

➤ TOURIST INFORMATION: **Tourist office** (Azienda Provinciale di Turismo/APT; ✉ Via Parigi 5, ☎ 06/48899255, open weekdays 8:15–7:15 and Sat. 8:15–1:30; ✉ Stazione Termini, near Track 4, ☎ 06/4871270, open daily 8:15–7:15; ✉ Aeroporto Leonardo da Vinci, ☎ 06/65956074, open daily 8:15–7); general English-language information (☎ 06/36004399).

12 CAMPANIA

NAPLES, POMPEII, CAPRI, THE AMALFI COAST

Emperors, kings, and artists have all made Campania's sea-wreathed resorts and starlit isles their abodes for more than 2,000 years. And well they might, for this region is a compact realm of undiluted beauty. Naples—the most operatic of cities—rules over its breathtaking bay. Nearby, ancient Romans once led carefree lives at Pompeii just as today's travelers now soak up the 24-karat sun in Capri, Positano, and Ravello.

Updated by
Robert
Andrews

CAMPANIA IS A REGION OF NAMES—Capri, Sorrento, Pompeii, Paestum—that evoke visions of cliff-shaded coves, sun-dappled waters, and mighty ruins. And Naples, a tumultuous, animated city, the very heart of Campania, stands guard over these treasures. Campania stretches south in flat coastal plains and low mountains from Baia Domizia, Capua, and Caserta to Naples and Pompeii on the magnificent bay; past the isles of Capri and Ischia; along the rocky coast to Sorrento, Amalfi, and Salerno; and farther still past the Cilento promontory to Sapri and the Calabria border. Inland lie the bleak fringes of the Apennines and the rolling countryside around Benevento.

On each side of Naples the earth fumes and grumbles, reminding us that all this beauty was born of cataclysm. Toward Sorrento, Vesuvius smolders sleepily over the ruins of Herculaneum and Pompeii, while west of Naples, beyond Posillipo, the craters of the Solfatara spew steaming gases. And nearby are the dark, deep waters of Lago d'Averno, legendary entrance to Hades. With these reminiscences of death and destruction so close at hand, it's no wonder that the southerner in general, and the Neapolitan in particular, takes no chances, plunging enthusiastically into the task of living each moment to its fullest.

Campania was probably settled by the ancient Phoenicians, Cretans, and Greeks. Traces of their presence here date from approximately 1000 BC, some 250 years before the legendary founding of Rome. Herculaneum is said to have been established by Hercules himself, and as excavation of this once-great city—Greek and later Roman—progresses, further light will be thrown on the history of the whole Campania region. The origin of Naples, once called Partenope and later Neapolis, presumably can be traced to what are now the ruins of Cumae nearby, which legend tells us was already in existence in 800 BC. Here, in a dark vaulted chamber, the Cumaean Sibyl pronounced her oracles. Greek civilization flourished for hundreds of years all along this coastline, but there was nothing in the way of centralized government until centuries later, when the Roman Empire, uniting all Italy for the first time, surged southward and absorbed the Greek colonies with little opposition. The Romans were quick to appreciate the sybaritic possibilities of such a lovely land, and it was in this region that the wealthy of the empire built their palatial country residences. Generally, the peace of Campania was undisturbed during these centuries of Roman rule.

Naples and Campania, with the rest of Italy, decayed with the Roman Empire and collapsed into the abyss of the Middle Ages. Naples itself regained some importance under the rule of the Angevins in the latter part of the 13th century and continued its progress in the 1440s under Aragonese rule. The nobles who served under the Spanish viceroys in the 16th and 17th centuries, when their harsh rule made all Italy quail, enjoyed their pleasures, and taverns and gaming houses thrived, even as Spain milked the area with its taxes. After a short-lived Austrian occupation, Naples—Napoli in Italian—became the capital of the Kingdom of the Two Sicilies, which the Bourbon kings established in 1738. Their rule was generally benevolent, as far as Campania was concerned, and their support of papal authority in Rome was an important factor in the development of the rest of Italy. Their rule was important artistically, too, for not only did it contribute greatly to the architectural beauty of the region, but it attracted great musicians, artists, and writers only too willing to enjoy the easy life at court in such magnificent natural surroundings. Finally, Giuseppe Garibaldi launched his famous expedition, and in 1860 Naples was united with the rest of Italy.

Times were relatively tranquil through the years that followed—with visitors of one nation or another thronging to Capri, to Sorrento, to Amalfi, and, of course, to Naples—until World War II. Allied bombings did considerable damage in Naples and the bay area. At the fall of the fascist government, the sorely tried Neapolitans rose up against Nazi occupation troops and in four days of street fighting drove them out of the city. A monument was raised to the *scugnizzo* (the typical Neapolitan street urchin), celebrating the youngsters who participated in the battle. The war ended. Artists, tourists, writers, and other lovers of beauty began to flow again into the Campania region that one ancient writer called "most blest by the Gods, most beloved by man." As the years have gone by, some parts gained increased attention from knowing visitors, while others lost the cachet they once had. The balance is maintained, with a steady trend toward more and more tourist development.

Pleasures and Pastimes

Dining

Campania's simple cuisine relies heavily on the bounty of the region's fertile farmland. Locally grown tomatoes are exported all over the world, but to try them here is a new experience. Even during the winter you can find tomato sauce made with small sun-dried tomatoes plucked from bright red strands that you can see hanging outdoors on kitchen balconies. Pasta is a staple here, and spaghetti *al pomodoro* (with tomato sauce) and spaghetti *alle vongole* (with clam sauce, either white or red, depending on the cook's whim) appear on most menus.

Naples is the homeland of pizza, and you'll encounter it here in two classic forms: *alla margherita* (with tomato, mozzarella, and basil) and marinara (with tomato, garlic, and oregano). Locally produced mozzarella is used in many dishes; one of the most gratifying on a hot day is *insalata caprese* (salad with mozzarella, tomatoes, and basil). *Melanzane* (eggplant) and even zucchini are served *parmigiana* (fried and layered with tomato sauce and mozzarella). Meat may be served *alla pizzaiola* (cooked in a tomato-and-garlic sauce). Fish and seafood in general can be expensive, though fried calamari and *totani* (cuttlefish) are usually reasonably priced. Lemons, grown locally, are widely used in cooking and for the sweet and heady liqueur *limoncello,* especially popular around Sorrento and on the Amalfi Coast. Among the region's wines, Gragnano, Falerno, Lacrima, Cristi, and Greco di Tufo are fine whites. Ischia and Ravello also produce good white wine. Campania's best-known reds are Aglianico, Taurasi, and the red version of Falerno. For general information and price categories, *see* Dining *in* Smart Travel Tips.

Lodging

All areas have fine accommodations in all categories, but they get very busy (especially the small establishments), so reserve well in advance. High-season rates apply at all coastal resorts from April or May through September, and Christmas and Easter also draw crowds and command top rates. Whereas coastal resorts elsewhere close up tight from fall to spring, some hotels and restaurants are open in Sorrento and on the Amalfi Coast year-round (many lodgings reopen just for the Christmas and New Year period). It's always a good idea to book far in advance, and it's imperative in high season (July to September). During the summer, hotels on the coast that serve meals almost always require that you take half-board. For general information and price categories, *see* Lodging *in* Smart Travel Tips.

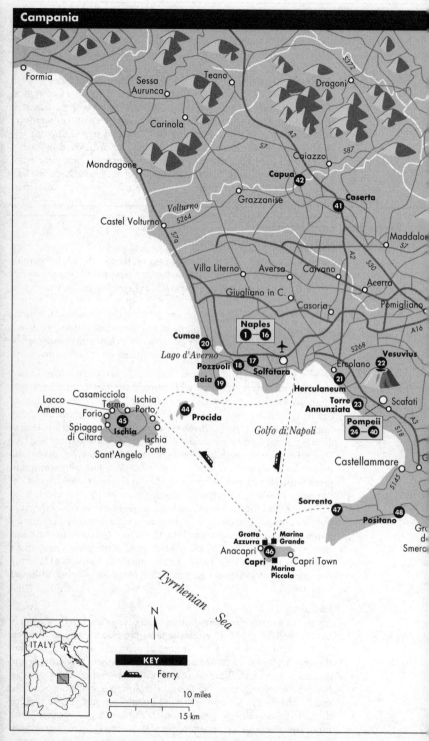

Campania

Formia

Sessa Aurunca

Teano

Dragoni

Carinola

S372

Mondragone

S7

A2

Caiazzo

S87

Capua 42

41 **Caserta**

Grazzanise

Castel Volturno

Volturno

S264

S7a

Maddaloni

S7

Villa Literno

Aversa

Caivano

Giugliano in C.

Casoria

Acerra

Pomigliano

Cumae 20

Lago d'Averno

Naples
1 — 16

A16

Pozzuoli 18 17 **Solfatara**

Baia 19

S268

Vesuvius 22

Ercolano

21

Herculaneum

Torre Annunziata 23 Scafati

Casamicciola

Lacco Ameno

Terme

Forio

Ischia Porto

44 **Procida**

Golfo di Napoli

Pompeii
24 — 40

A3

Spiagga di Citara

45 **Ischia**

Ischia Ponte

S18

Sant'Angelo

Castellammare

S145

Sorrento 47

48 **Positano**

Grotta Azzurra

Marina Grande

Gr
d
Smera

Anacapri

46

Capri

Capri Town

Marina Piccola

Tyrrhenian Sea

N

ITALY

KEY

🚢 Ferry

0 ——— 10 miles

0 ——— 15 km

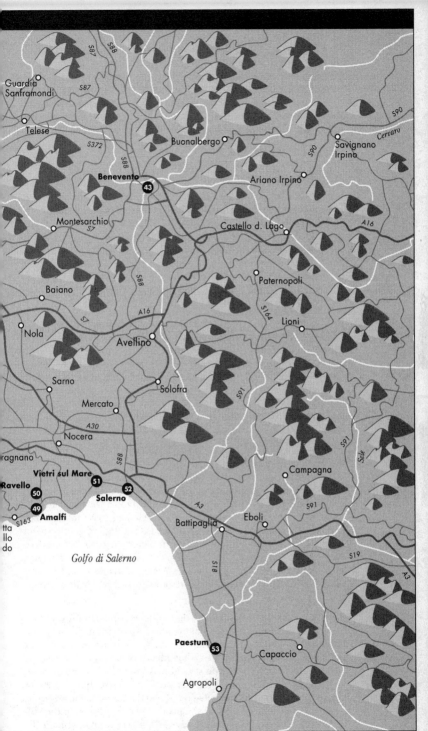

Guardia
Sanframondi

Telese

S87

S88

S87

S372

Buonalbergo

S90

Savignano
Irpino

Cervaro

Benevento

43

Ariano Irpino

S88

S90

Montesarchio

S7

Castello d. Lago

A16

Baiano

S88

Paternopoli

A16

S164

Lioni

Nola

S7

Avellino

Sarno

Solofra

S91

Mercato

A30

Nocera

S91

Sele

ragnano

S88

Campagna

Vietri sul Mare

51

Ravello

50

52

Salerno

A3

49

Amalfi

S163

Battaglia

Eboli

S91

tta
llo
do

Golfo di Salerno

S18

S19

A3

Paestum

53

Capaccio

Agropoli

Exploring Campania

Many of Campania's attractions are on the Golfo di Napoli (Bay of Naples)—including the city itself and its satellite islands, Capri and Ischia, and the archaeological sites of Pompeii, Herculaneum, and the Campi Flegrei (Phlegrean Fields) at the northern end of the bay. At the southern end, Sorrento also lies in this charmed circle, within easy distance of Positano, Amalfi, and the pleasures of the Amalfi Coast. Farther afield, Paestum offers more classical sights, and inland, Caserta and Benevento have a Bourbon palace and more majestic Roman remains.

Numbers in the text correspond to numbers in the margin and on the Campania, Naples, and Pompeii maps.

Great Itineraries

If art and antiquities are high on your list, consider spending a few days in Naples before retreating to the beauty of Capri, Ischia, or the Amalfi Coast. Few fall in love with Naples at first sight, and many complain about its obvious flaws: urban decay and delinquency. But practically everyone who takes the time and trouble to discover its artistic riches and appreciate its vivacious nature considers it worth the effort. Naples is close to Italy's most fabled classical ruins, and you should dedicate at least a morning or afternoon to Pompeii or Herculaneum.

IF YOU HAVE 3 DAYS

In ⊞ **Naples** ①–⑯, a visit to the **Museo Archeologico Nazionale** ⑮ is an essential preparation (or follow-up) for an expedition to **Herculaneum** ㉑ and **Pompeii** ㉔–㊵, indispensable sights for anyone visiting Campania. The islands of ⊞ **Ischia** ㊺ and ⊞ **Capri** ㊻ can also be reached from Naples and make an ideal antidote to the city's noise. It is worth spending at least one night out of Naples, and a good alternative to the islands would be ⊞ **Sorrento** ㊼, an easy hydrofoil ride away and a good base from which to tour the nearby Amalfi Coast, where you could visit small towns—⊞ **Positano** ㊽, ⊞ **Amalfi** ㊾, ⊞ **Ravello** ㊿, and/or **Vietri sul Mare** ⑤, for instance—on a third day's excursion.

IF YOU HAVE 5 DAYS

In ⊞ **Naples** ①–⑯, more time will enable you to take in one of the region's greatest palace-museums, the **Museo di Capodimonte** ⑯, housed in one of the Bourbon royal palaces. Outside of town you could also see more than just one of the classical sights, including a visit to the Greek temples of **Paestum** ㉝, highly recommended for a glimpse at some of Magna Graecia's most stunning relics. You might also venture north to **Caserta** ㊶ to wander around the royal palace. Back in the Bay of Naples, spend your fourth and fifth days exploring ⊞ **Ischia** ㊺ and ⊞ **Sorrento** ㊼, both undemanding holiday resorts with plenty of natural beauty.

IF YOU HAVE 7 DAYS

A week in Campania will allow you to discover some of the more esoteric pleasures that Naples has to offer. Apart from the sheer vibrancy of its shopping streets and alleys, and the glorious views over the waterfront, ⊞ **Naples** ①–⑯ has plenty of diversions within its tight mesh of streets, and you should make time for visiting some of its many famous churches—the **Duomo** ⑬, of course, but also **Santa Chiara** ⑩, **Santa Maria Donna Regina** ⑭, and the **Cappella Sansevero** ⑪, with its 18th-century sculptures. Outside town, head west to the volcanic region of the **Phlegrean Fields** ⑰–⑳, where Roman remains lie within a smoking, smoldering area rich with classical history. Spend three nights on the Amalfi Coast, making sure to visit inland ⊞ **Ravello** ㊿ and pass some time in pretty ⊞ **Positano** ㊽, which requires at least a day and a half. ⊞ **Capri** ㊻, too, deserves a couple of nights to appreciate fully its beauty—of secluded coves and beaches, not to mention the famous Blue Grotto—easily eclipsing the island's more lurid tourist trappings. You might pass a last day, perhaps en route out of Campania, in **Benevento** ㊸, which holds a well-preserved Roman theater and the renowned Arco di Traiano.

When to Tour Campania

Campania is not at its best in high summer: Naples is a sweltering inferno, the archaeological sites are swarmed, and the islands and Amalfi Coast resorts are similarly overrun with tour buses and bad tempers. Any other time of year would be preferable, including even winter, when the temperature rarely falls below the comfort threshold and rain is relatively rare. Swimming is possible year-round, though you will only see the hardiest bathers out between October and May.

Summer is also the worst time for ascents to Vesuvius; the best visibility occurs around spring and fall. Watch the clock, however, as the days get shorter; excursions to Vesuvius, Pompeii, Herculaneum, and the islands all require some traveling, and it's easy to get caught with little daylight left. At most archaeological sites you are rounded up two hours before sunset, so the earlier you arrive the better. Remember, too, that the majority of hotels, restaurants, and other tourist facilities in Sorrento, the Amalfi Coast, and the islands close down from November until around Easter.

NAPLES

"Built like a great amphitheater around her beautiful bay, Naples is an eternally unfolding play acted by a million of the best actors in the world," Herbert Kubly observes in his *American in Italy.* "The comedy is broad, the tragedy violent. The curtain never rings down." Is it a sense of doom, living in the shadow of Vesuvius, that makes many Neapolitans so volatile, so seemingly blind to everything but the pain or pleasure of the moment? Poverty and overcrowding are the more likely causes, but whatever the reason, Naples is a difficult place for the casual tourist to take a quick liking to. Much restoration is being done, particularly in the *centro storico* (historical center), under the auspices of UNESCO and the EU. If you have the time and if you're willing to work at it, you'll come to love Naples as a mother loves her reprobate son; but if you're only passing through and hoping to enjoy a hassle-free vacation, spend as little time here as you can. Why visit Naples at all? First, Naples is the most sensible base—particularly if you're traveling by public transportation—from which to explore Pompeii, Herculaneum, Vesuvius, and the Phlegrean Fields. Second, it's the home of the Museo Archeologico Nazionale. The most important finds from Pompeii and Herculaneum are on display here—everything from sculpture to carbonized fruit—and seeing them will add to the pleasure of your trip to Pompeii and Herculaneum. Third, there are many fascinating buildings—once you look behind the grimy facades.

Exploring Naples

In Naples you need a good sense of humor and a firm grip on your pocketbook and camera. Better still, leave all your valuables, including your passport, in the hotel safe. You'll probably be doing a lot of walking (take care crossing the chaotic streets), for buses are crowded and taxis get stalled in traffic. If you come to Naples by car, park it in a garage, agree on the cost in advance, and then keep it there for the duration of your stay. (If you park it on the street, smashed windows and theft are constant risks.) Use the funiculars to get up and down the hills, and take the quick Metropolitana (the city's subway system)

Naples

TO ORTO BOTANICO

Corso Giuseppi

Via S. Antonio Abate

Via S. benedetta

Via Cesare Rosaoli

Via Foria

Via Carbonara

Pza. E. De Nicola

Principe Umberto

Stazione Centrale

Via Poerio

Pza. P.S. Mancini

Pza. Garibaldi

Garibaldi

Via Nolana

Beato Cesare Carmigiano

V. Giacomo Savarese

V.S. Giovanni a Mare

Pza. del Mercato

Pza. Masanieollo

MUSEO NAZIONAL FERROVIARIA

Bacino del Piåer

Corso Umberto I

Via P. Colletta

Via Miracoli

Via Cristallini

Via

Via della Sanita

S. Margherita

Via Antonio Villari

Via a Fonseca

Via Stella

Via Matteo

Fontanelle

TO CATACOMBE DI SAN GENNARO

DI MOD

Corso Amedeo di Savoia

Via S. Teresa degli Scalzi

Via Materdei

Via S. Giuseppi dei Nudi

Salita S. Raffaele

Via Salvator Rosa

Via E.S. Carrera Cavoney

Santa Ponteciovo

Salita Trisia

Via Materdei

Via Matteo Renato Imbriani

Vico Nocelle

Via S. Mandato

Via Salvator Rosa

V. Battista lo Caracciolo

Via Salvator Rosa

Piazza Leonardo

Via Grachio

Via G. Cosi

Via. U. Nutta

Piazza Med D'oro

Via. M. Fiore

Viale Michelangelo

Viale Raffaello

Via Tito Angelini

FUNICOLARE DI MONTESANITO

Via Tito Angelini

Morghen

R.

Via A. Scalatli

Via G.L. Bernini

VOMERO

Via tino di Camalino

Via Giolto

Via S. Gennaro al Vomero

Via Luca Giordano

Via Solimente

Via F. Cilea

Via Cimarosa

Via Luigia

Flaridiana

Villa Floridiana

santelia

Foria

Via S. Apostili

Via S. Agostili

Via Anticaglia

Via Duomo

Via S. Maria Antica

Via Vicaria Vecchia

Museo Filangieri

Grand Archivio

Via Lucano

Via S. Paola

Via Armani

Via Pisanelli

Via Atri

Via L. de Crecchio

Via S. Maria di Constantinopoli

Piazza Bellini

Piazza Dante

SPACCANAPOLI

Via de Sanctis

Via Nilo

Via Tribunali

San Domenico Maggiore

Croce di Lucca

Via S. Geronimo

Via S. Chiara

Via Giovanni Paladino

Via Mezzocanone

SANTA CHIARA

Via S. Sebastiano

Via Danangelo

Via G. Sanfelice

Via B. Croce

Via Benedetto Croce

Via del Gesù

Via Toledo

Via Capitelli

Via Montealiveto

Via Monteoliveto

Piazza del Gesù

Piazza Carità

Piazza Matteotti

Via A. Diaz

Via G. Oberdan

Via R. Bracco

Via Medina

Via W.

Via R. Bracco

Toledo

Pza. N. Amore

V.L. Bianchini

V. A. Troya

Corso Umberto I

V. Marotta

Via Nuova Marina

Via A. Depretis

Via V. A. di Costanzo

Via G. Sanfelice

Via di Vria

V. A. De Gaspari

Stazione Cumana

Piazza Montesanto

Via Pasquale Scura

Via F. Girardi

QUARTIERI SPAGNOLI

Via E. De Dio

Via Ventaglieri

Corso Vitt. Emanuele

Piazza

Via

Scaccioro

Via

V. Scalato

Via Gramo

Via Sponecorvo

Via Pessina

Via E.

① ⑦

⑧

⑨

⑩

⑪

⑫

⑬

⑭

⑮

⑯

TO ORTO BOTANICO

Pza. Cavour

M

M

M

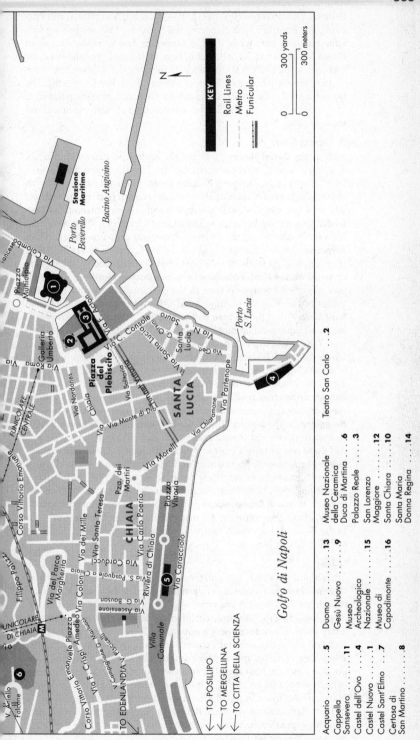

Golfo di Napoli

Acquario	5	
Cappella Sansevero	11	
Castel dell'Ovo	4	
Castel Nuovo	1	
Castel Sant'Elmo	7	
Certosa di San Martino	8	
Duomo	13	
Gesù Nuovo	9	
Museo Archeologico Nazionale	15	
Museo di Capodimonte	16	
Museo Nazionale della Ceramica Duca di Martina	6	
Palazzo Reale	3	
San Lorenzo Maggiore	12	
Santa Chiara	10	
Santa Maria Donna Regina	14	
Teatro San Carlo	2	

TO POSILLIPO
TO MERGELLINA
TO CITTÀ DELLA SCIENZA

KEY
— Rail Lines
--- Metro
▬ Funicular

0   300 yards
0   300 meters

to distant destinations (Piazza Garibaldi, Chiaia, Mergellina, and Pozzuoli. For Pompeii, Herculaneum, and Sorrento, take the private Circumvesuviana line, while the Circumflegrea and Cumana lines from Piazza Montesanto take in Pozzuoli, Baia, and Cumae. Bus and funicular fares are 1,500 lire/€0.80, valid for 90 minutes; 4,500 lire/€2.30 buys a ticket for the whole day. Subway tickets cost 1,500 lire/€0.80. The tourist information office at Piazza del Gesù can provide pamphlets with itineraries tracing the city's development in ancient, medieval, and modern times.

A Good Tour

Start at the **Castel Nuovo** ①, facing the harbor on Piazza Municipio, housing a museum of mainly religious art. Pass the **Teatro San Carlo** ② on your way to the imposing **Palazzo Reale** ③, a royal palace rich with the indulgences of Naples's past rulers. Next, turn back to the seafront where, a few minutes' walk south, is another royal fortress, the **Castel dell'Ovo** ④, overlooking the Santa Lucia waterfront. Walking or taking a bus farther along the seafront, you might drop into the extensive **Acquario** ⑤ before turning inland. Take Via Carducci to Via dei Mille, turn left, and go to the funicular stop at Piazza Amedeo; take a ride up to the **Museo Nazionale della Ceramica Duca di Martina** ⑥—though you might be content to take in the extraordinary views from the slopes of the Vomero neighborhood. Also on Vomero are the **Castel Sant'Elmo** ⑦ and the **Certosa di San Martino** ⑧, set in the same parkland and commanding magnificent vistas over city and sea to Vesuvius. Take a funicular ride down—this time to Piazza Montesanto—from which you are well placed to stroll northeast along Spaccanapoli, a group of streets cutting a straight line through the heart of Old Naples, taking in the churches of **Gesù Nuovo** ⑨ and **Santa Chiara** ⑩ en route. Farther up Spaccanapoli, you need only detour a few steps to see some other art-rich religious monuments: **Cappella Sansevero** ⑪, **San Lorenzo Maggiore** ⑫, the **Duomo** ⑬, and **Santa Maria Donna Regina** ⑭. Continuing north on Via Duomo, take a left onto Via Foria, and you will end up at one of Italy's most important museums, the **Museo Archeologico Nazionale** ⑮, packed with archaeological relics of the classical era and a must before venturing out of town to see Pompeii and Herculaneum. From here, footsore and weary, you deserve a taxi or bus to reach **Museo di Capodimonte** ⑯, the greatest of the Bourbon palaces, where, after ogling at the artistic masterpieces on display, you can siesta in the Bosco di Capodimonte (park) and admire the wonderful views over the Bay of Naples.

TIMING

You should start early to fit all these sights into just one day. The best option would be to split it between two days, ending one at the Certosa di San Martino (seeing sights ①–⑧), then tackling the rest on the other, including the Museo Archeologico Nazionale, which merits half a day itself. Make sure you do not end up at the archaeological museum on a Tuesday, when it's closed, or at any churches at lunchtime, when they close for two or three hours. The views over the bay are good at any time but especially at sunset. Another, very appealing approach would be to spend a morning at the Museo Archeologico Nazionale followed by an afternoon visiting either the Phlegrean Fields or Herculaneum and Vesuvius. Return to Naples for the evening, perhaps best spent at the world-famous Teatro San Carlo; the following morning, set out for Pompeii.

Sights to See

⑤ **Acquario** (Aquarium). Children and art-exhausted adults adore the aquarium in the public gardens on Via Caracciolo. Founded by a German naturalist in the late 19th century, it's the oldest in Europe. About 200 species of fish and marine plants thrive in large tanks, undoubtedly better off here than in the highly polluted Bay of Naples, their natural habitat. If you have time you may want to wander in the gardens of the Villa Comunale—where there are a bandstand and play areas for children. On the third and fourth weekends of the month, antiques markets are held here. ⊠ *Stazione Zoologica, Viale A. Dohrn,* ☎ *081/5833111.* ⊡ *3,000 lire/€1.55.* ☉ *May–Sept., Tues.–Sat. 9–6, Sun. 10–6; Oct.–Apr., Tues.–Sat. 9–5, Sun. 9–2.*

OFF THE
BEATEN PATH

EDENLANDIA – This is the largest amusement park in Campania. It's in the Mostra d'Oltremare area of Naples, near the Stadio San Paolo, southwest of the center. ⊠ *Viale Kennedy,* ☎ *081/2391182.* ⊡ *4,000 lire/€2.05 admission, 16,000 lire/€8.25 all rides.* ☉ *Oct.–Mar., weekends 10:30 AM–midnight; Apr.–Sept., weekdays 1–8 or 9, weekends 10:30 AM–midnight.*

MUSEO NAZIONALE FERROVIARIO – Children love to see the old-fashioned engines, cars, and railroad equipment on display in the restored railway works, east of the center, founded by the Bourbon rulers of Naples in the last century. ⊠ *Corso San Giovanni a Teduccio,* ☎ *081/472003.* ⊡ *Free.* ☉ *Mon.–Sat. 9–2.*

⓫ Cappella Sansevero. Off Spaccanapoli, the Cappella di Santa Maria della Pietà dei Sangro, better known as the Cappella Sansevero, holds the tombs of the noble Sangro di San Severo family. Much of it was designed in the 18th century by Giuseppe Sammartino, including the centerpiece, a striking *Dead Christ,* carved from a single block of alabaster. If you can stomach it, take a peek in the crypt, where some of the anatomical experiments conducted by Prince Raimondo, a scion of the family and noted 18th-century alchemist, are gruesomely displayed. ⊠ *Via de Sanctis 19,* ☎ *081/5518470.* ⊡ *8,000 lire/€4.15.* ☉ *Mon. and Wed.–Sat. 10–8, Sun. 10–1:30.*

❹ Castel dell'Ovo. Dangling over the Porto Santa Lucia on a thin promontory, this 12th-century fortress built over the ruins of an ancient Roman villa commands a view of the whole harbor—proof, if you need it, that the Romans knew a premium location when they saw one. For the same reason, some of the city's top hotels share the site. It's a peaceful spot for strolling and enjoying the views. ⊠ *Santa Lucia waterfront, Via Caracciolo,* ☎ *081/7640590.* ⊡ *Free.* ☉ *Mon.–Sat. 9–6, Sun. 9–1:30.*

❶ Castel Nuovo. Also known as the Maschio Angioino, this massive fortress was built by the Angevins (related to the French monarchy) in the 13th century and completely rebuilt by the Aragonese rulers (descendants of an illegitimate branch of Spain's ruling line) who succeeded them. The decorative marble triumphal arch that forms the entrance was erected during the Renaissance in honor of King Alfonso V of Aragón (1396–1458), and its rich bas-reliefs are credited to Francesco Laurana (circa 1430–1502). Set incongruously into the castle's heavy stone walls, the arch is one of the finest works of its kind. Within the castle, you can see sculptures and frescoes from the 14th and 15th centuries, as well as the city's **Museo Civico,** comprising mainly local artwork from the 15th to 19th century. It's hard to avoid the impression that these last were rejects from the much finer collection at the Museo di Capodimonte, though there are also regular exhibitions worth visiting, and the windows offer views over the piazza and the port below. You can also visit the Palatine Chapel and the octagonal **Sala dei Baroni,** where Ferrante I disposed of a group of rebellious barons in 1485 by inviting them to a mock wedding party and then pouring boiling oil on their heads from the ceiling. The room is still occasionally used for city council meetings. There are also some Greco-Roman remains, recently discovered underneath the castle during restoration work and opened to the public in 2000. ⊠ *Castel Nuovo, Piazza Municipio,* ☎ *081/7952003.* ☒ *10,000 lire/€5.15, free Sun.* ⊙ *Whole building Mon.–Sat. 9–7, courtyard only Sun. 9–1.*

❼ Castel Sant'Elmo. Perched on Vomero, the castle was built by the Angevins in the 14th century to dominate the port and the Old City and remodeled by the Spanish in 1537. The stout fortifications are still in use today by the military, and are the occasional setting for performances, exhibitions, and fairs. ⊠ *Largo San Martino,* ☎ *081/5784020.* ☒ *2,500 lire/€1.30.* ⊙ *Tues.–Sun. 9–7.*

❽ Certosa di San Martino. A Carthusian monastery restored in the 17th century in exuberant Neapolitan Baroque style, this structure now houses the **Museo Nazionale di San Martino,** an eclectic collection of ships' models, antique *presepi* (Christmas crèches), and Neapolitan landscape paintings. The main reason to come, however, is to see the splendidly decorated church and annexes, the pretty garden, and the view from the balcony off Room 25. There's another fine view from the square in front of the Certosa. Take the funicular from Piazza Montesanto to Vomero. ⊠ *Museo Nazionale di San Martino,* ☎ *081/5781769.* ☒ *11,000 lire/€5.70.* ⊙ *Tues.–Fri. 8:30–7:30, weekends 9–7:30.*

⑬ Duomo. Though the Duomo was established in the 1200s, the building you see was erected a century later and has since undergone radical changes, especially during the Baroque age. Inside the cathedral, 110 ancient columns salvaged from pagan buildings are set into the piers that support the 350-year-old wooden ceiling. Off the left aisle, you step down into the 4th-century church of **Santa Restituta,** which was incorporated into the cathedral; though Santa Restituta was redecorated in the late 1600s in the prevalent Baroque style, a few very old mosaics remain in the **Battistero** (Baptistery). The chapel also gives access to an archaeological zone, a series of paleochristian rooms dating from the Roman era.

On the right aisle of the cathedral, in the **Cappella di San Gennaro,** are multicolor marbles and frescoes honoring St. Januarius, miracle-working patron saint of Naples, whose altar and relics are encased in silver. Three times a year—on September 19 (his feast day); on the Saturday preceding the first Sunday in May, which commemorates the transference of his relics to Naples; and on December 16—his dried blood, contained in two sealed vials, is believed to liquefy during rites in his honor. On these days large numbers of devout Neapolitans offer up prayers in his memory. ⊠ *Via del Duomo,* ☎ *081/449097.* ☒ *Duomo and Cappella di San Gennaro free, Battistero 2,000 lire/€1.05, Battistero and archaeological zone 5,000 lire/€2.60.* ⊙ *Duomo and Cappella di San Gennaro daily 8–12:30 and 4:30–7; Battistero and archaeological zone Mon.–Sat. 9–noon and 4:30–7, Sun. 9–noon.*

OFF THE
BEATEN PATH

MUSEO FILANGIERI – This Neapolitan museum contains Prince Gaetano Filangieri's private collection of arms, armor, furniture, paintings, and fascinating other memorabilia. It's housed in the Florentine-style Renaissance Palazzo Cuomo. ⊠ *Palazzo Cuomo, Via Duomo 288,* ☎ *081/203175.* ☒ *5,000 lire/€2.60.* ⊙ *Tues.–Sat. 9:30–2 and 3:30–7, Sun. 9:30–1:30.*

❾ Gesù Nuovo. The oddly faceted stone facade of the church was designed as part of a palace dating from between 1584 and 1601, but plans were changed as construction progressed, and it became the front of an elaborately decorated Baroque church. ⊠ *Piazza Gesù Nuovo,* ☎ *081/5518613.* ☉ *Mon.–Sat. 6:30–12:45 and 4:15–7:30, Sun. 6:30–1:30.*

OFF THE
BEATEN PATH

SEAFRONT TOURS – Summer evening boat tours take in the waterfront of Naples, from the port at Mergellina to Cape Posillipo, with a view of Castel dell'Ovo on the way back. Ask for information at the port or in the tourist office (⊠ Piazza del Gesù, ☎ 081/5523328).

★ ⓯ **Museo Archeologico Nazionale** (National Archaeological Museum). The huge red building, a cavalry barracks in the 16th century, is dusty and unkempt, but it holds one of the world's great collections of Greek and Roman antiquities, including such extraordinary sculptures as the *Hercules Farnese,* an exquisite Aphrodite attributed to the 4th-century BC Greek sculptor Praxiteles, and an equestrian statue of Roman emperor Nerva. Vividly colored mosaics and countless artistic and household objects from Pompeii and Herculaneum provide insight into the life and art of ancient Rome. The most recent addition to the treasures on permanent display is an entire fresco sequence—more than 300 ft wide—discovered in 1765 in perfect condition at the Temple of Isis in Pompeii. Invest in an up-to-date printed museum guide, because exhibits are poorly labeled. ⊠ *Piazza Museo,* ☎ *081/440166.* 🖃 *12,000 lire/€6.20.* ☉ *Wed.–Mon. 9–7.*

NEED A
BREAK?

Rescigno (⊠ Via Foria 40, ☎ 081/2110810) is a family bakery that has been in business for more than 200 years. It includes a shop and café, a great place to sample the many different breads and cakes and tasty local snacks.

OFF THE
BEATEN PATH

ORTO BOTANICO – A short walk from the Museo Archeologico Nazionale, these botanical gardens, founded in 1807, belong to the Science Faculty of the University of Naples and contain numerous rare plants, trees, and shrubs. You can also visit the library, seed museum, and laboratory. ⊠ Via Foria 223, ☎ 081/449759. 🖃 Free. ☉ By appointment.

★ ⓰ **Museo di Capodimonte.** The grandiose 18th-century neoclassical Bourbon royal palace, in the vast Bosco di Capodimonte (Capodimonte Park), which served as the royal hunting preserve and later as the site of the Capodimonte porcelain works, houses an impressive collection of fine and decorative art. Capodimonte's greatest treasure is the excellent collection of paintings well displayed in the **Galleria Nazionale,** on the palace's first and second floors. Before you arrive at the collection, a magnificent staircase leads to the **royal apartments,** where you'll find beautiful antique furniture, most of it on the splashy scale so dear to the Bourbons, and a staggering collection of porcelain and majolica from the various royal residences. The walls of the apartments are hung with numerous portraits, providing a close-up of the unmistakable Bourbon features, a challenge to any court painter. The main galleries on the first floor are devoted to work from the 13th to 18th century, including many familiar masterpieces by Dutch and Spanish masters, as well as by the great Italians. Look out for some stunning paintings by Caravaggio (1573–1610), originally found in the city's churches. The second floor features mainly Neapolitan works of the 19th century, including plenty of dramatic renditions of Vesuvius in all its raging glory. When you've had your fill of these, take time to admire the genuine article from the shady parkland outside, which affords a sweeping view of the bay. ⊠ *Parco di Capodimonte,* ☎ *081/7499111.* 🖃 *14,000 lire/€7.25, 12,000 lire/€6.20 after 2 PM.* ☉ *Tues.–Sun. 8:30–7:30.*

CATACOMBE DI SAN GENNARO – Many of the catacombs in Naples pre-
date the Christian era by two centuries. These are found behind an
18th-century church built over 5th-century foundations and inspired by
the design of St. Peter's in Rome. The niches and corridors of the catacombs are hung with early Christian paintings. ⊠ *Via Capodimonte,
next to Madre di Buon Consiglio church on Via Capodimonte,* ☎ *081/
7411071.* ≞ *5,000 lire/€2.60.* ◷ *Guided tour (required) daily every
45 mins 9:30–11:45* AM.

❻ Museo Nazionale della Ceramica Duca di Martina. The lushly shaded
park and the view over Naples are two reasons to venture up the Chiaia funicular from Via del Parco Margherita. Set on the slopes of the
Vomero hill in a park known as Villa Floridiana, it houses thousands
of ceramic pieces, including local majolica, a fine collection of European and Asian porcelain, and other objets d'art in a neoclassical residence built in the early 19th century by King Ferdinand I for his wife,
Lucia Migliaccio. Their portraits greet you as you enter. Enjoy the view
from the terrace behind the museum. ⊠ *Via Cimarosa 77,* ☎ *081/
5788418.* ≞ *5,000 lire/€2.60.* ◷ *Tues.–Sun. 9–2; visits only at 9:30,
11, and 12:30.*.

❸ Palazzo Reale (Royal Palace). Dominating Piazza del Plebiscito, the huge
palace—best described as overblown imperial—dates from the early
1600s. It was renovated and redecorated by successive rulers, including Napoléon's sister Caroline and her ill-fated husband, Joachim
Murat (1767–1815), who reigned briefly in Naples after the French
emperor had sent the Bourbons packing and before they returned to
reclaim their kingdom. Don't miss seeing the **royal apartments,** sumptuously furnished and full of precious paintings, tapestries, porcelains,
and other objets d'art. The monumental marble staircase gives you an
idea of the scale on which Neapolitan rulers lived. ⊠ *Piazza del Plebiscito,* ☎ *081/7944021.* ≞ *8,000 lire/€4.15.* ◷ *Thurs.–Tues. 9–8.*

Besieged by the traffic swirling around the Teatro San Carlo and
Palazzo Reale, the **Caffè Gambrinus** (⊠ Piazza Trieste e Trento, ☎
081/417582) is a haven of old-style Naples and the onetime haunt of
artists and intellectuals of every persuasion. Gilded and mirrored, this
gran caffè continues to serve top-quality pastries and gelato alongside
savories and the never-ending cappuccinos.

Piazza Dante. Students from the nearby music conservatory like to hang
out in this semicircular hub, though presently fenced off for long-term
work on the subway system. The area is filled with inexpensive trattorias and pizzerias.

Piazza del Plebiscito. The vast square next to the Palazzo Reale was
laid out by order of Murat, whose architect was clearly inspired by
the colonnades of St. Peter's in Rome. The large church of **San Francesco
di Paola** in the middle of the colonnades was added as an offering of
thanks for the Bourbon restoration by Ferdinand I, whose titles reflect
the somewhat garbled history of the Kingdom of the Two Sicilies,
made up of Naples (which included most of the southern Italian mainland) and Sicily. They were united in the Middle Ages, then separated,
then unofficially reunited under Spanish domination during the 16th
and 17th centuries. In 1816, with Napoléon out of the way on St. He-
lena, Ferdinand IV (1751–1825) of Naples, who also happened to be
Ferdinand III of Sicily, officially merged the two kingdoms, proclaiming himself Ferdinand I of the Kingdom of Two Sicilies. His reac-
tionary and repressive rule earned him a few more colorful titles among
his rebellious subjects.

Quartieri Spagnoli (Spanish Quarter). The Spanish garrison was quartered in the now-decaying tenements aligned in a tight-knit grid along incredibly narrow alleys in this neighborhood roughly between Via Toledo (downhill border) and Via Pasquale Scura (western leg of Spaccanapoli). It's a hectic, impoverished (sometimes dangerous) area—chock-full of local color—brooding in the shadow of Vomero, but it's showing signs of improvement. This area is a five-minute walk west of Piazza Municipio, accessible from Via Toledo.

⓬ San Lorenzo Maggiore. It is unusual to find French Gothic style in Naples, but it has survived to great effect in this church. Built in the Middle Ages and decorated with 14th-century frescoes, it is supposed to be where the poet Boccaccio (1313–75) first saw the model for his *Fiammetta*. Outside the 17th-century cloister is the entrance to **excavations** revealing what was once part of the Roman forum, and before that the Greek agora. You can walk among the streets, shops, and workshops of the ancient city and see a model of how the Greek *Neapolis* might have looked. ⊠ *Via Tribunali,* ☎ *081/290580.* ⊡ *Excavations 5,000 lire/€2.60.* ☉ *Daily 9–1 and 3–5:30; excavations weekdays 9–1 and 3–5:30 (4–6:30 in summer), Sat. 9–5:30, Sun. 10–1:30.*

⓾ Santa Chiara. The monastery church is a Neapolitan landmark and the subject of a famous old song. It was built in the 1300s in Provençal Gothic style, and it's best known for the quiet charm of its cloister garden, with columns and benches sheathed in 18th-century ceramic tiles painted with delicate floral motifs and vivid landscapes. An adjoining museum traces the history of the convent; the entrance is off the courtyard at the left of the church. ⊠ *Piazza Gesù Nuovo,* ☎ *081/5526209.* ⊡ *Museum and cloister 6,000 lire/€3.10.* ☉ *Church Apr.–Sept., daily 8:30–noon and 4–7; Oct.–Mar., daily 8:30–noon and 4–6. Museum and cloister Mon.–Sat. 9:30–1 and 3:30–5:30, Sun. 9:30–1.*

NEED A
BREAK?

Walking up Via Santa Maria di Costantinopoli, which is lined with antiques shops, you'll come upon Piazza Bellini, a leafy square that holds **Intra Moenia** (☎ 081/290720), a bookstore café open every day from 10 AM to 3 AM, serving snacks, salads, and drinks—and selling books, prints, and postcards of Naples. It also stages art exhibitions and has one Internet terminal.

⓮ Santa Maria Donna Regina. The towering Gothic funeral monument to Mary of Hungary, wife of Charles II of Anjou (circa 1254–1309), who is said to have commissioned the frescoes in the church at a cost of 33 ounces of gold, is contained within this church. Don't confuse this church with another of the same name nearby in the piazza, but Baroque. ⊠ *Vico Donnaregina.* ☉ *Daily 8–noon.*

Spaccanapoli. Nowhere embodies the spirit of backstreet Naples better than the arrow-straight street divided into tracts bearing several names. It runs through the heart of the old city (*spacca* means "cut through") from west to east, retracing one of the main arteries of the Greek, and later Roman, settlement. **Via Benedetto Croce** was named in honor of the illustrious philosopher born here in 1866, in the building at No. 12. You'll walk past peeling palaces, dark workshops where artisans ply their trades, and many churches and street shrines. Where the street changes to **Via San Biagio dei Librai** and **Via San Gregorio Armeno** the shops stage special exhibitions of nativity scenes (*presepi*) in the weeks before Christmas. The figures may be carved of wood or made of terra-cotta. ⊠ *Beginning with Via Pasquale Scura, just west of Via Toledo, and ending with Via Vicaria Vecchia just east of Via del Duomo.*

NEED A
BREAK?

While you're exploring the old part of town, take a break at what the Neapolitans call "the best pastry shop in Italy"—**Scarturchio** (⊠ Piazza S. Domenico Maggiore 19, ☎ 081/5516944), closed Tuesday. The café was founded in 1918 by two brothers, one of whom, Francesco, invented the cakes called *ministeriali* to attract Anna Fouché, a famous actress of the time. You can still buy these cakes today, along with other Neapolitan specialties such as *baba*, *rafiol*, and *pastiera*, which you can either eat there with a coffee or have specially gift-wrapped in the room at the back.

❷ **Teatro San Carlo.** This large theater was built in 1737, 40 years earlier than Milan's La Scala—though it was destroyed by fire and had to be rebuilt in 1816. You can visit the impressive interior, decorated in the white-and-gilt stucco of the neoclassical era, as part of a guided group, and visitors are sometimes allowed in during morning rehearsals. ⊠ *Via San Carlo, between Piazza Municipio and Piazza Plebiscito,* ☎ *081/ 7972331 or 081/7972412,* WEB *www.teatrosancarlo.it.* ⊠ *5,000 lire/€2.60.* ◷ *Tours weekends 2–3:30.*

NEED A
BREAK?

Across from the Teatro San Carlo towers the imposing entrance to the glass-roofed neoclassical **Galleria Umberto** (⊠ Via San Carlo), a shopping arcade where you can sit at one of several cafés and watch the vivacious Neapolitans as they go about their business.

Via Toledo. Sooner or later you'll wind up at one of the busiest commercial arteries, also known as Via Roma, in this perennially congested city. However, don't avoid dipping into this parade of shops and coffee bars where plump pastries are temptingly arranged.

Vomero. Heart-stopping views of the Bay of Naples are framed by this gentrified neighborhood on a hill served by the Montesanto, Centrale, and Chiaia funiculars. Stops for all three are an easy walk from Piazza Vanvitelli, a good starting point for exploring this thriving district with no shortage of smart bars and trattorias to pause in.

OFF THE
BEATEN PATH

CITTA DELLA SCIENZA – Though open since 1998, Italy's first science museum is now finally fully operational, on the outskirts of town in a former industrial area by the sea. Child-friendly, it features exhibitions on astronomy, robotics, and the environment, among others. The best way to get here is by taxi. ⊠ *Via Coroglio 104,* ☎ *081/7352260,* WEB *www. cittadellascienza.it.* ⊠ *8,000 lire/€4.15.* ◷ *Tues.–Sun. 9–7.*

NAPLES UNDERGROUND – Take a revelatory trip exploring the foundations of the city, some of which date back as much as 4,000 years. Forty meters underground, informed guides will show you ancient aqueducts built by the Greeks and Romans, which later served as a bomb shelter during World War II. The commentary is normally in Italian, though with advance notice an interpreter can be hired. ⊠ *Vico S. Anna di Palazzo 52,* ☎ *081/400256.* ⊠ *10,000 lire/€5.15.* ◷ *Tours Sat. at 10, noon, and 6; Sun. at 10, 11, noon, and 6; Thurs. at 9 PM; or call to arrange at other times. Meet at Piazza Trieste e Trento (by Bar Gambrinus).*

Dining and Lodging

$$$ ✕ **La Bersagliera.** You'll inevitably be drawn to eating at the Santa Lucia waterfront, in the shadow of the looming medieval Castel dell'Ovo. This spot is big and touristy but fun, with an irresistible combination of spaghetti and mandolins. The menu suggests uncomplicated, time-worn classics, such as spaghetti *alla pescatora* (with seafood sauce) and

DISCIPLINED PIZZAS

THERE'S NO PIZZA like real Neapolitan pizza. If you don't believe it, try one at **Ciro a Santa Brigida** (⊠ Via Santa Brigida 71, ☎ 081/5524072). This restaurant is a little more upscale than a typical Neapolitan pizzeria, but its pizza is the real thing, and it's proper to eat it with your napkin stuffed into your shirt to avoid tomato stains. The restaurant's owner, Antonio Pace, president of the True Neapolitan Pizza Association, is behind an unusual initiative to upgrade the quality of pizza worldwide. Mr. Pace and Professor Carlo Mangoni di Santo Stefano, a nutritionist at the University of Naples, have written what they call a Pizza Discipline, a treatise that discusses everything from the history of pizza to the perfect ingredients for the perfect Neapolitan pie. Based on the Pizza Discipline, the city of Naples recently registered a logo that pizzerias can hang in their window if, and only if, they serve true Neapolitan pizza. That means using sinfully luscious buffalo-milk mozzarella made in certain areas near Naples, kneading the dough for exactly 30 minutes, and letting it rise for four hours. (The "discipline" includes photos of dough taken through a microscope before and after it has risen.)

It may take awhile before pizzerias around the globe actually hang the logo in their windows. But the city of Naples wants it eventually to be a sign of quality as distinctive as the DOC (Denominazione di Origine Controllata, or denomination of controlled origin) on wine labels. The logo will be blue, with Mt. Vesuvius in the background, a red pizza with mozzarella in the center, and PIZZA NAPOLETANA written across the foreground. Make sure you're the first to spot it!

Some pizza history, as recounted by Professor Mangoni (who scoffs at claims that pizza was invented in the United States): Pizza marinara, which doesn't have mozzarella at all but is simply a pie with tomatoes, garlic, oregano, and olive oil, first appeared in Naples around 1760. King Ferdinand of Naples liked the pizza, but his wife, a Habsburg princess, wouldn't allow pizza in the palace. The king would often sneak out to some of the world's first pizzerias, making the places famous. Even earlier, there's a mention of plates of flour with other food on top in Homer's *Iliad*, but Professor Mangoni says this was just a precursor to pizza, not the real thing. Tomato sauce, says Mangoni, dates back to 1733.

Mozzarella came later. The pizza margherita was invented in 1889, when Naples chef Raffaele Esposito was called on to prepare a meal for the Italian queen Margherita. He made a pizza with tomato sauce and mozzarella, and his wife had the idea of adding basil to honor Italy's red, white, and green flag.

According to the Pizza Discipline, the only true pizzas are marinara and margherita. Anchovies, pepperoni, and so on are heresy. (It should be noted that some Neapolitan pizzerias of very respectable heritage don't take such a puritanical approach when it comes to ingredients.)

In Antonio Pace's family, pizza goes back a long way. He claims his grandfather's grandfather made pizza in 1856. Pizza fact or fiction aside, at Ciro a Santa Brigida everything is delicious. Ask for a taste of plain buffalo mozzarella and just savor it in your mouth. If you have a lactose intolerance, there's still hope—Professor Mangoni and his team of scientists are developing lactose-free mozzarella. If they manage to match the taste of real mozzarella, he says, pizzerias will be allowed to use it and still display the Pizza Napoletana logo. Go figure.

melanzane alla parmigiana. ⊠ *Borgo Marinaro 10,* ☎ *081/7646016. AE, DC, MC, V. Closed Tues. and 2 wks in late Jan.*

$$$ ✕ **La Sacrestia.** Neapolitans flock to this upscale patrician villa for the
★ restaurant's location—on the slopes of the Posillipo hill—and high culinary standards. The seafood and meat specialties range from tasty antipasti to linguine in *salsa di scorfano* (scorpion-fish sauce). ⊠ *Via Orazio 116,* ☎ *081/7611051. AE, DC, MC, V. Closed Sun. in July–Aug. and 2 wks in mid-Aug. No lunch Mon., no dinner Sun.*

$$–$$$ ✕ **Mimì alla Ferrovia.** Near the central station, this bustling fish restaurant has scooped plenty of plaudits in recent years. The service is polite without being obsequious, the atmosphere relaxed, sometimes noisy. Try the *céfalo* (mullet) when it's in season, or the lobster. Other sure bets are *peperoni ripieni* (stuffed peppers) and grilled mushrooms. ⊠ *Via Alfonso D'Aragona 21,* ☎ *081/5538525. AE, DC, MC, V. Closed Sun. and 10 days in mid-Aug.*

$$ ✕ **Antonio e Antonio.** This relatively new ristorante-pizzeria (opened in 1999) attracts crowds of Neapolitans for its huge range of pizzas and typical dishes such as spaghetti *alle vongole* (with clams) and *orecchiette con broccoletti* (little-eared pasta with broccoli). On the site of a former nightclub right on the Santa Lucia waterfront, it has a modern blue and yellow decor that is easy on the eye. There's another branch at Via Francesco Crispi 89. ⊠ *Via Partenope 24/27,* ☎ *081/2451987. AE, DC, MC, V. Closed Mon.*

$$ ✕ **Ciro a Santa Brigida.** Off Via Toledo near the Castel Nuovo, Ciro is a straightforward restaurant popular with business travelers, artists, and journalists who prefer food over frills. In dining rooms on two levels, customers dine on classic Neapolitan cuisine. The *polpette alla Ciro* (meatballs) are wonderful. ⊠ *Via Santa Brigida 71,* ☎ *081/5524072. AE, DC, MC, V. Closed Sun. and 2 wks in Aug.*

$ ✕ **Cibo.** Young, noisy, and hip, this restaurant-bar is a friendly mixing spot at night and a great place for a take-out pizza or sandwich at lunch while you're discovering Spaccanapoli. There is a wide and innovative selection of pizzas and a stimulating selection of sandwiches for vegetarians who are tired of tomato and mozzarella. ⊠ *Piazza del Gesù Nuovo 26,* ☎ *081/5518427. No credit cards.*

$ ✕ **Da Michele.** One of Naples's original pizzerias, with chunky marble-topped tables, this old haunt has preserved the tradition of serving only two kinds of pizza, *margherita* (with tomatoes, mozzarella and Parmesan cheese) and *marinara* (sailor-style, with garlic, tomatoes, anchovies, and olive oil). ⊠ *Via Sersale 1,* ☎ *081/5539204. No credit cards. Closed Sun.*

$ ✕ **Di Matteo.** Right in the old part of Naples, this pizzeria was founded in 1936 and has been the location for many movies. Jack Lemmon and Marcello Mastroianni ate here when filming *Maccheroni,* and when President Clinton came to the conference of the G7 in 1994, this was the pizzeria he chose. ⊠ *Via Tribunali 94,* ☎ *081/455262. No credit cards. Closed Sun.*

$$$$ 🏠 **Excelsior.** The lobby and lounges of this Starwood Luxury Collection hotel in Santa Lucia are lavishly furnished with Oriental carpets and gilt or glass chandeliers. Rooms are either in the Empire style, with neoclassical furniture and brocades, or of a Neapolitan floral-print persuasion. Off the large, semicircular lounge is a chic little bar. There is also a rooftop restaurant, La Terrazza, situated at the angle of the bay, with views over to both Castel Nuovo and Vesuvius and to Castel dell'Ovo and Posillipo. In Liberty style, it is tranquil, elegant, and discreet. Guests also have access to an off-site health club with excellent amenities including spa treatments and exercise machines. ⊠ *Via Partenope 48, 80121,* ☎ *081/7640111,* FAX *081/7649743,* WEB *www.excelsior.it. 136 rooms. Restaurant, bar, parking (fee). AE, DC, MC, V.*

$$$$ ⊞ **Grand Hotel Vesuvio.** One of the top Naples hotels, this place on the Santa Lucia waterfront has attracted artists, royalty, and dignitaries—including the Clintons—to relax in its luxury. Many are lured by its superb facilities, chief among which are its Caruso rooftop restaurant and its extremely comprehensive health club, offering exercise facilities as well as sauna, massage therapies, and beauty treatments. It also has a dedicated children's room with mobiles, a rocking horse, and baby-sitting services. ⊠ *Via Partenope 45, 80121,* ☎ *081/7640044,* FAX *081/7644483,* WEB *www.vesuvio.it. 171 rooms, 16 suites. Restaurant, bar, health club, baby-sitting, meeting room, parking (fee). AE, DC, MC, V.*

$$$$ ⊞ **Paradiso.** You can take a taxi or funicular from downtown to the ★ modern, air-conditioned building perched on a hill above the port of Mergellina. Huge window walls in the lobby and front rooms provide gorgeous views. The decor, in tones of blue and beige, is restful and attractive. Smallish rooms are smart, with built-in furnishings of rosy wood with marble surfaces. A roof terrace invites sitting, dining, and contemplating the entire bay and Vesuvius. ⊠ *Via Catullo 11, 80122,* ☎ *081/7614161,* FAX *081/7613449. 74 rooms. Restaurant, bar, minibars, parking (fee). AE, DC, MC, V.*

$$$$ ⊞ **Parker's.** Gracefully old-fashioned, this is a sumptuous home away from home, tucked halfway between the Spanish Quarter and Vomero. Its hillside location affords wonderful views, which can be appreciated from the rooftop restaurant. The lobby and guest rooms reflect the general finery, and you can indulge bookish pursuits in the library filled with rare editions. ⊠ *Corso Vittorio Emanuele 135, 80121,* ☎ *081/ 7612474,* FAX *081/663527. 80 rooms. Restaurant, bar, library. AE, DC, MC, V.*

$$$ ⊞ **Parteno.** This B&B on the waterfront is in a beautifully restored 18th-century building. The style owes much to the design skills of local sculptor and architect Luigi Mazzella; his presence is felt in the beautiful brass ceiling and door panels and various sculptured lamps, mirrors, and beds, creating an elegant, peaceful atmosphere in the style of patrician houses. From the breakfast room there are views to the sea, and all rooms have balconies. ⊠ *Lungomare Partenope 1, 80121,* ☎ FAX *081/2452095. 6 rooms. Breakfast room, room service. AE, DC, MC, V.*

$$$ ⊞ **Splendid.** The light, airy, modern accommodations here are an excellent value. Located in the Posillipo district, this hotel has inspiring views over the Phlegrean Fields and across to Ischia and Capri. ⊠ *Via Manzoni 96, 80123,* ☎ *081/645462,* FAX *081/7146431. 45 rooms. Restaurant, bar, dance club, meeting room, free parking. AE, DC, MC, V.*

$$ ⊞ **Belvedere.** In the center of the airy Vomero district, opposite the Carthusian monastery of San Martino, the Belvedere makes the most of its position high above the Spanish Quarter. Each of the spacious, comfortable rooms—half with balconies—comes equipped with a minibar. ⊠ *Via Tito Angelini 51, 80129,* ☎ *081/5788169,* FAX *081/ 5785417. 27 rooms. Restaurant, bar. AE, DC, MC, V.*

$$ ⊞ **Donna Regina.** This bed-and-breakfast is in part of the 14th-century monastery of Donna Regina and has been lovingly restored by a family of Neapolitan artists. In the old part of town, it has views of the cloisters and the two churches of Santa Maria Donna Regina. Inside it's filled with antique Neapolitan furniture and family works of art. Donna Gabriella will cook delightful traditional evening meals on request. With only four rooms, it requires that you book well in advance throughout the year. ⊠ *Via Settembrini 80, 80139,* ☎ FAX *081/ 446799. 4 rooms. Breakfast room, lounge. No credit cards.*

$$ ⊞ **Le Fontane al Mare.** Come here for semi-luxurious accommodations at a relatively low price. Most of the elegant rooms have balconies overlooking the sea (although only seven rooms have private bath), and you're a short walk from the Villa Comunale, the pleasant park on the bay. ⊠ *Via Niccolò Tommaseo 14, 80121,* ☎ *081/7643811,* FAX *081/ 7643470. 20 rooms, 7 with bath. AE, DC, MC, V.*

$ 🖪 **Pensione Mancini.** Situated at the heart of the action just off the Piazza Mancini market on the west side of Piazza Garibaldi, this modest, family-run pensione is a safe outpost in the daily carnival of Neapolitan life. Rooms are very plain but clean, some with a balcony, and there are also dormitories. ⊠ *Via Mancini 33, 80120,* ☎ *081/5536731,* FAX *081/ 5546675. 6 rooms, 3 with bath. Bar. No credit cards.*

Nightlife and the Arts

The Arts

MUSIC

A classical music festival known as **International Music Weeks** takes place throughout May in Naples. Concerts are held at the Teatro San Carlo, the Teatro Mercadante, and in the neoclassical Villa Pignatelli. For information, contact the Teatro San Carlo box office (☎ 081/ 7972331 or 081/7972412).

OPERA

Naples has a full opera season from fall through spring. The **Teatro San Carlo** (⊠ Via San Carlo, ☎ 081/7972331 or 081/7972412, WEB www.teatrosancarlo.it), where the season runs throughout the year apart from July and August, is one of Italy's top opera houses.

Nightlife

TRADITIONAL NEAPOLITAN DANCE

There are several restaurants where you can eat and then enjoy traditional Neapolitan entertainment—singing and dancing in folk costumes. In all cases it is best to reserve first and confirm what is on offer, as it varies from night to night. Three places worth trying are **Rosolino** (⊠ Lungomare Santa Lucia, ☎ 081/7649873), **'A Canzuncella** (⊠ Piazza Santa Maria Nova 18, ☎ 081/5519018), and **Girulà** (⊠ Via Vetriera 7, ☎ 081/425511).

NIGHTCLUBS

Nightclubs and bars are found in many areas around Naples. The sophisticated crowd heads toward the areas of Posillipo, the Vomero, or along the seafront (Via Partenope), and behind the Villa Comunale (Riviera di Chiaia). A more bohemian and literary crowd makes for the *centro storico* and the area around Piazza Bellini. Bear in mind that clubs, and their clientele, may change rapidly, so do some investigating before you hit the town. Following are specific venues to check out:

Tongue (⊠ Via Manzoni 207, ☎ 081/7690800) appeals especially to gays and techno-heads. The sophisticated **Chez Moi** (⊠ Via del Parco Margherita 13, ☎ 081/407526) has a dress code—casual is okay, as long as it's style-conscious—and is popular with the fashion jet set. **La Mela** (⊠ Via dei Mille 40, ☎ 081/413881) is for the more aristocratic set. **Accademia** (⊠ Via Porta Posillipo 43, ☎ 081/7692500) is a fashionable venue in the Posillipo district.

Outdoor Activities and Sports

Beaches

If you want a beach near Naples, many private lidos provide chairs, cabins, and bar service from May to October, charging a small fee for the use of their services for the day. The best ones include **Elena** (⊠ Via Posillipo 14, ☎ 081/5755058), **Le Rocce Verdi** (⊠ Via Posillipo 68, ☎ 081/5756716), and **Marechiaro** (⊠ Discesa Marechiaro, ☎ 081/ 7691215).

Sailing
Club Nautico (✉ Borgo Marinari, ☎ 081/7645829) offers courses for sailors or would-be sailors all year round. **Canottieri Savoia** (✉ Borgo Marinari, ☎ 081/7646162) offers courses from October through June.

Swimming Pool
If you prefer a pool to the beach, you'll find a good-size outdoor one in Fuorigrotta, **Piscina Scandone** (✉ Via Giochi del Mediterraneo, ☎ 081/5702636).

Thermal Baths
With all the volcanic activity in the area, sulfur baths have been enjoyed here for centuries. There are two ancient Roman-period structures (*sudatoria*) that offer spa facilities, ideal both in summer and winter. **Stuffe di Neroni** (✉ Via Stuffe di Neroni 37, 80074 Bacoli, ☎ 081/8688006) has two pools, one outside where you can sit and sunbathe, another inside with a sauna and various thermal treatments. **Stuffe di San Germano** (✉ Via Agnano Astroni 24, ☎ 081/5702122) has thermally heated spring pools and natural steam caves, as well as mud baths and massages with eucalyptus leaves.

Waterskiing and Scuba Diving
Sci Nautico Partenopeo (✉ Lago d'Averno, Pozzuoli, ☎ 081/8662214) offers waterskiing at Lago d'Averno, once believed the mouth of hell, west of Naples. **Subacquei Napoletani** (✉ Via Caracciolo 2, ☎ 081/7611985) arranges scuba diving.

Shopping

Leather goods, jewelry, and cameos are some of the best items to buy in Campania. In Naples, where many of the top leather and fashion houses have their factories, you'll find good buys in handbags, shoes, and clothing. If you want the real thing, make your purchases in shops, but if you don't mind imitation goods, rummage around at the various street-vendor *bancherelle* (stalls). Most boutiques and department stores are closed until about 4:30 on Monday (hours are roughly Monday 4:30–8, Tuesday–Saturday 9:15–1 and 4:30–8), though food shops are open Monday morning, too.

Shopping Districts
The immediate area around **Piazza dei Martiri** has the densest concentration of luxury shopping, with perfume shops, fashion outlets, and antiques on display. Browse **Via Chiaia, Via dei Mille,** and **Via Filangieri.** The most expensive street is the small, pedestrian-only **Via Calabritto,** where you'll find Prada, Gucci, Versace, Vuitton, Cacharel, Damiani, and Cartier. The **Vomero** district also yields more luxury shops—especially in the **Galleria Scarlatti,** on Via Scarlatti, and the **Galleria Vanvitelli,** in Piazza Vanvitelli. If you're looking for cheaper stores, try **Via Toledo** for the department store La Rinascente and other smaller fashion shops. The *centro storico* area, running down from the Museo Nazionale and Via Duomo, is packed with street markets and also has a fair choice of arts and crafts stores. **Via Santa Maria di Costantinopoli** is the street for antiques shops, and you'll find an antiques market on the third weekend of each month in the gardens of Villa Comunale and a flower market every day in the Castel Nuovo moat.

Shopping Mall
The **Galleria Umberto** (✉ Via Roma at Via S. Carlo) is a good introduction to shopping in Naples; a wide variety of retail outlets is found in the four glass-roofed arcades.

Specialty Stores

Arte Antica (⊠ Via Domenico Morelli 6, ☎ 081/7643704) is famous for Italian antiques, especially flamboyant, richly decorated porcelain. **Eddy Monetti** sells a range of elegantly tailored togs for men (⊠ Via Scarlatti 171, ☎ 081/5780009) and women (⊠ Via Merliani 34, ☎ 081/5788463). **Gay Odin** (⊠ Via Toledo 291, ☎ 081/421867; ⊠ Via Toledo 427, ☎ 081/5513491) produces handmade chocolates that you can only find in its Naples shops. Buy a delicious chocolate Mount Vesuvius, or try the famous *foresta* (flaked chocolate). You can also visit the **Gay Odin factory** (⊠ Via Vetriera 12, ☎ 081/417843). **Mario Raffone** (⊠ Via Santa Maria di Costantinopoli 102, ☎ FAX 081/459667) is a family printing business where they still use old presses. They sell prints of nativity figures and Vesuvius and have a catalogue of old prints from the 20th century. **Keramos** (⊠ Via Porta Posillipo 40/b, ☎ 081/7692950), a local artists' studio, is worth visiting if you're interested in modern ceramic work. **Marinella** (⊠ Via Riviera di Chiaia 287/a, ☎ 081/2451182) sells made-to-measure ties, supposedly the best in the world.

THE PHLEGREAN FIELDS

The name Campi Flegrei—the fields of fire—was once given to the entire region west of Naples, including the island of Ischia. The whole area floats freely on a mass of molten lava very close to the surface. The fires are still smoldering. Greek and Roman notions of the Underworld were not the blind imaginings of a primitive people; they were the creations of poets and writers who stood on this very ground and wrote down what they saw. Today, it should take about a half of a day to assess it yourself.

Solfatara

17 *8 km (5 mi) west of Naples.*

Here at the sunken volcanic crater Solfatara you can experience firsthand the volcanic nature of this otherworldly terrain. In fact, the only eruption of this semiextinct volcano was in 1198, though according to one legend, every crater in the Phlegrean Fields is one of the mouths of a hundred-headed dragon named Typhon that Zeus hurled down the crater of Epomeo on the island of Ischia. According to another, the sulfurous springs of the Solfatara are poisonous discharges from the wounds the Titans received in their war with Zeus. The stark, scorched area, slightly marred by the modern apartment blocks peering over the rim, exerts a strange fascination. The area is safe for walking if you stick to the path. ☎ 081/5262341. ◪ 8,000 lire/€4.15. ⊙ Daily 8:30–1 hr before sunset.

Pozzuoli

18 *2 km (1 mi) west of Solfatara, 8 km (5 mi) west of Naples.*

The **Anfiteatro Flavio** (Flavian Amphitheater) here is the third-largest arena in Italy, after the Colosseum and Santa Maria Capua Vetere, and once held 40,000 spectators, who were sometimes treated to mock naval battles when the arena was filled with water. The well-preserved underground passages and chambers are fascinating and give a good sense of how wild animals were hoisted up into the arena. ☎ 081/5266007. ◪ 4,000 lire/€2.05. ⊙ Daily 9–1 hr before sunset.

You may want to make a short side trip to the town's harbor and imagine St. Paul landing here en route to Rome in AD 61, only 18 years before the eruption of Vesuvius. His own ship had been wrecked off Malta, and he was brought here on the *Castor and Pollux*, a grain ship from Alexandria.

Baia

⑲ *7 km (4½ mi) south of Pozzuoli, 12 km (7 mi) west of Naples.*

Now largely under the sea, this was once the most opulent and fashionable resort area of the Roman Empire, a place where Sulla, Pompey, Julius Caesar, Tiberius, Nero, and Cicero all built holiday villas. Petronius's *Satyricon* is a satire on the corruption and intrigue, the wonderful licentiousness of Roman life at Baia. (Petronius was hired to arrange parties and entertainments for Nero, so he was in a position to know.) It was here at Baia that Emperor Claudius built a great villa for his wife Messalina (who spent her nights indulging herself at public brothels); here that Agrippina poisoned her husband and was, in turn, murdered by her son Nero; and here that Cleopatra was staying when Julius Caesar was murdered on the Ides of March in 44 BC. You can visit the excavations of the famous *terme* (baths). ✉ *Via Fusaro 35,* ☎ *081/8687592.* ⊠ *4,000 lire/€2.07.* ☉ *Tues.–Sun. 9–2 hr before sunset.*

En Route Follow the southern loop around Lago Miseno (a volcanic crater believed by the ancients to be the Styx, across which Charon ferried the souls of the dead) and Lago del Fusaro. You'll take in some fine views of the Golfo di Pozzuoli (Bay of Pozzuoli).

Cumae

⑳ *5 km (3 mi) north of Pozzuoli, 16 km (10 mi) west of Naples.*

Perhaps the oldest Greek colony in Italy, Cumae overshadowed the Phlegrean Fields, including Naples, in the 7th and 6th centuries BC. The **Antro della Sibilla** (Sibyl's Cave) is here—one of the most venerated sites in antiquity. In the 6th or 5th century BC, the Greeks hollowed the cave from the rock beneath the present ruins of Cumae's acropolis. You walk through a dark, massive stone tunnel that opens into a vaulted chamber where the Sibyl uttered her oracles. Standing here, the sense of mystery, of communication with the invisible, is overwhelming. "This is the most romantic classical site in Italy," wrote the English travel writer H. V. Morton (1892–1979). "I would rather come here than to Pompeii."

Virgil (70–19 BC) wrote his epic *Aeneid*, the story of the Trojan prince Aeneas's wanderings, in part to give Rome the historical legitimacy that Homer had given the Greeks. On his journey, Aeneas had to descend to the Underworld to speak to his father, and to find his way in, he needed the guidance of the Cumaean Sibyl. Virgil did not dream up the Sibyl's cave or the entrance to Hades—he must have stood both in her chamber and along the rim of Lago d'Averno, as you yourself will stand. When he wrote *"Facilis descensus Averno"*—"The way to hell is easy"—it was because he knew the way. In Book VI of the *Aeneid*, Virgil described how Aeneas, arriving at Cumae, sought Apollo's throne (remains of the **Tempio di Apollo** can still be seen) and "the deep hidden abode of the dread Sibyl / An enormous cave . . ."

The Sibyl was not necessarily a charlatan; she was a medium, a prophetess, an old woman whom the ancients believed could communicate with the Other World. The three most famous Sibyls were at Erythrae, Delphi, and Cumae. Foreign governments consulted the Sibyls before mounting campaigns. Wealthy aristocrats came to consult with their dead relatives. Businessmen came to get their dreams interpreted or to seek favorable omens before entering into financial agreements or setting off on journeys. Farmers came to remove curses on their cows. Love potions were a profitable source of revenue. Women from Baia lined up for potions to slip into the wine of handsome charioteers who drove up and down the street in their gold-plated four-horsepower chariots.

With the coming of the Olympian gods, the earlier gods of the soil were discredited or given new roles and names. Ancient rites, such as those surrounding the Cumaean Sibyl, were now carried out in secret and known as the Mysteries. The Romans—like the later Soviets—tried in vain to replace these Mysteries by deifying the state in the person of its rulers. Yet even the Caesars appealed to forces of the Other World. And until the 4th century AD the Sibyl was even consulted by the Christian bishop of Rome. ⊠ *Via Acropoli,* ☎ *081/8543060.* 🎫 *4,000 lire/€2.05.* ☉ *Daily 9–2 hrs before sunset.*

Lago d'Averno

4 km (2½ mi) south of Cumae, 11 km (7 mi) west of Naples.

The best time to visit the fabled Lago d'Averno (Lake Avernus) is at sunset or when the moon is rising. There's a restaurant on the west side, where you can dine on the terrace. Forested hills rise on three sides; the menacing cone of Monte Nuovo rises on the fourth. The smell of sulfur hangs over this sad, lonely landscape seemingly at the very gates of hell. No place evokes Homer, Virgil, and the cult of the Other World better than this silent, mysterious setting. ⊠ *Drive west from Pozzuoli on S7 toward Cumae and then turn left (south) on the road to Baia. About 1 km (½ mi) along, turn right and follow signs to Lake Avernus.*

HERCULANEUM, VESUVIUS, POMPEII

Ancient Inspirations

Volcanic ash and mud preserved the Roman towns of Herculaneum and Pompeii almost exactly as they were on the day Mt. Vesuvius erupted in AD 79, leaving them not just archaeological ruins but museums of daily life in the ancient world. The two buried cities and the volcano responsible can be visited from either Naples or Sorrento, thanks to the Circumvesuviana, the suburban railway that provides fast, frequent, and economical service.

Herculaneum

★ ㉑ *10 km (6 mi) south of Naples.*

Lying more than 60 ft below the town of Ercolano, the ruins of Herculaneum are set among the acres of greenhouses that make this area one of Europe's principal flower-growing centers. Hercules himself is said to have founded the town, which became a famous weekend retreat for the Roman elite. It had about 5,000 inhabitants when it was destroyed; many of them were fishermen, craftsmen, and artists. A lucky few patricians owned villas overlooking the sea. Herculaneum was damaged by an earthquake in AD 63, and repairs were still being made 16 years later when the gigantic eruption of Vesuvius (which also destroyed Pompeii) sent a fiery cloud of gas and pumice hurtling onto the town, which was completely buried under a tide of volcanic mud. This semiliquid mass seeped into the crevices and niches of every building, covering household objects and enveloping textiles and wood—sealing all in a compact, airtight tomb.

Casual excavation—and haphazard looting—began in the 18th century, but systematic digs were not initiated until the 1920s. Today less than half of Herculaneum has been excavated; with present-day Ercolano and the unlovely Resina Quarter (famous among bargain hunters as the area's largest secondhand-clothing market) sitting on top of the site, progress is limited. From the ramp leading down to Herculaneum's neatly laid out streets and well-preserved edifices, you get a good overall view of the site, as well as an idea of the amount of rock that had to be removed to bring it to light.

If you feel closer to the past at Herculaneum than at Pompeii, it's in part because there are fewer hawkers here. Also, though Herculaneum had only one-fourth the population of Pompeii and has only been partially excavated, what has been found is generally better preserved. In some cases, you can even see the original wooden beams, staircases, and furniture. Much excitement is presently focused on one excavation in a corner of the site, the Villa dei Papiri, built by Julius Caesar's father-in-law. The building is named for the 1,800 carbonized papyrus scrolls dug up here in the 18th century, leading scholars to believe that this may have been a study center or library. Now Italian geologists and archaeologists have uncovered part of the villa itself and hope to unearth more of the library—given the right funds and political support. Little of the site can be seen aboveground, though visitors to the Getty Villa (formerly the J. Paul Getty Museum) in Malibu, California, can see a modern version, built following drawings made by the Swiss archaeologist Carl Weber in the 18th century.

At the entrance to the archaeological park you should pick up a map showing the gridlike layout of the dig. Decorations are especially delicate in the **Casa del Atrio Mosaico** (House of the Mosaic Atrium), with a pavement in a black-and-white checkerboard pattern, and in the **Casa del Nettuno ed Anfitrite** (House of Neptune and Amphitrite), named for the subjects of a still-bright mosaic on the wall of the nymphaeum (a recessed grotto with a fountain). Annexed to the latter house is a remarkably preserved wineshop, where amphorae still rest on carbonized wooden shelves. And in the **Casa del Tramezzo di Legno** (House of the Wooden Partition), one of the best-preserved of all, there is a carbonized wooden partition with three doors. In the **terme,** where there were separate sections for men and women, you can see benches, basins, and the hot, warm, and cold rooms, embellished with mosaics. The **Casa del Bicentenario** (House of the Bicentenary) was a patrician residence with smaller rooms on the upper floor, which may have been rented out to artisan-tenants who were probably Christians, as they left an emblem of the cross embedded in the wall. The palaestra and 2,500-seat theater, the sumptuously decorated suburban baths, and the **Casa dei Cervi** (House of the Stags), with an elegant garden open to the sea breezes, are all evocative relics of a lively and luxurious way of life.

Until a few years ago it was believed that most of Herculaneum's inhabitants had managed to escape by sea, since few skeletons were found in the city. Excavations at Porta Marina, the gate in the sea wall leading to the beach, have revealed instead that many perished there, a few steps from the only escape route open to them. Most important buildings can be seen in about two hours. The site entrance is a short walk south from the Circumvesuviana station. ⊠ *Corso Ercolano,* ☎ *081/ 8575347,* WEB *www.pompeiisites.org.* ✉ *16,000 lire/€8.30, including Oplontis; 26,000 lire/€13.50 including Oplontis, Pompeii, and 2 other sites over 3 days.* ☉ *Apr.–Oct., daily 8:30–7:30 (ticket office closes at 6); Nov.–Mar., daily 8:30–5 (ticket office closes at 3:30).*

Vesuvius

㉒   *8 km (5 mi) northeast of Herculaneum, 16 km (10 mi) east of Naples.*

The profile of Vesuvius is so inseparable from the Bay of Naples area, and the ferocious power it can unleash so vivid as you tour the sights of the cities that it destroyed, you may be overwhelmed by the urge to explore the crater itself. In summer especially, the prospect of rising above the sticky heat of the city and sights below is a heady one. The view when clear is magnificent, with the curve of the coast and the tiny white houses among the orange and lemon blossoms. If the summit is lost in mist, you'll be lucky to see your hand in front of your face. When you see the summit clearing—it tends to be clearer in the afternoon—head for it. If possible, see Vesuvius after you've toured the ruins of buried Herculaneum to appreciate the magnitude of the volcano's power.

Reaching the crater takes some effort. From the Ercolano stop of the Circumvesuviana, take scheduled buses (trip takes one hour; departures currently four or five times a day—check locally for the latest times) or your own car to the Seggovia station, the lower terminal of the defunct chairlift. (Though there's talk of putting it back in working order, no one is optimistic about the possibility.) From here you must climb the soft, slippery cinder track on foot, a 30-minute ascent, and you must pay about 12,000 lire/€6.20 for compulsory guide service, though the guides don't do much more than tell you to stay away from the edge of the crater. If you're not in shape, you'll probably find the climb tiring. Wear nonskid shoes (not sandals). ☎ *081/7775720.* ✆ *Guide service 12,000 lire/€6.24.*

You can visit **Osservatorio Vesuviano** (the old observatory)—2,000 ft up—and view instruments used to study the volcano, some dating back to the mid-19th century. ☎ *081/7390644.* ☉ *By appointment only.*

Torre Anunziata (Oplontis)

★ **㉓**   *20 km (12 mi) southeast of Naples, 5 km (3 mi) west of Pompeii.*

Surrounded by the fairly drab urban landscape of Torre Annunziata, thrown up in the 1960s, Oplontis justifies its reputation as one of the most spectacular archaeological sites to be unearthed in the 20th century. The villa complex has been imaginatively ascribed—from a mere inscription on an amphora—to Nero's second wife, Poppaea Sabina, whose family was well known among the landed gentry of neighboring Pompeii. As Roman villas go, Poppaea's Villa, or Villa A, as it is called more prosaically by archaeologists, is truly exceptional. Excavation so far has uncovered an area of more than 325 ft by 225 ft, and because the site is bound by a road to the west and a canal to the south, we are unlikely ever to gauge its full extent. What's been found includes porticoes, a large peristyle, a *piscina* (pool), baths, and extensive gardens, as well as the standard atria, triclinia, and a warren of cubicula. The villa is thought by some to have been a training school for young philosophers and orators. Certainly, for those overwhelmed by the throngs at Pompeii, a modern-day visit to the site of Oplontis offers a chance for contemplation and intellectual refreshment.

Access is easiest from the Circumvesuviana station of Torre Annunziata (about 200 yards away). Outside the station turn left and then right downhill, and the site is just after the crossroads down on the left. If coming by car, take the Torre Annunziata turnoff from the Naples–Salerno autostrada, turn right, and then look for signs on the left for Oplontis at the first major crossroads. The main entrance to the site is from the north—you basically go into the villa through the gardens, with the atrium on the southern side lying under about 16 ft of pumice and pyroclastic material from Vesuvius. This is a good time to have a close look at the stratigraphy of the volcanic deposits: note the thin layers of the lighter surge-flow deposit near the base of the profile. Pumice fallout presented few problems for local inhabitants during the eruption, but the surge cloud proved lethal, leading rapidly to asphyxiation.

Oplontis offers the full gamut of Roman wall paintings, with its occupants showing a particular penchant for the illusionist motifs of the so-called Second Pompeian Style. There are some good examples in the west wing of the villa, especially in the triclinium (Room 14—look for the room numbers above the doors) giving onto the small portico (Room 13), which abuts the west end of the site and the road above. Although the stucco work in the thermae, or baths, is less impressive than in Pompeii and Herculaneum, the calidarium (Room 8) has a delightful miniature landscape scene surmounted by a peacock in a niche at its eastern end. Nearby, in the tepidarium (Room 8), there is an interesting glimpse into the structural design of Roman baths; here the floor is raised by *suspensurae*, small brick supporting pilasters, enabling warm air to pass beneath.

Such opulence is found throughout the site, although there are exceptions to the rule—for example, the relatively small *cubicula*, or bedrooms, are conspicuous by their simplicity. In the eastern wing, a warren of rooms gives way to much larger spaces, featuring long corridors, peristyles fit for large gaggles of stoics, and a large piscina, with its complement of porticoes and terraces, at the eastern end. ⊠ *Via Sepolcri 1, Torre Annunziata,* ☎ *081/8575347,* WEB *www.pompeiisites.org.* 🎟 *10,000 lire/€5.15; 16,000 lire/€8.30 including Herculaneum or Pompeii; 26,000 lire/€13.50 including Herculaneum, Pompeii, and 2 other sites over 3 days.* ☉ *Apr.–Oct., daily 8:30–7:30 (ticket office closes at 6); Nov.–Mar., daily 8:30–5 (ticket office closes at 3:30).*

Pompeii

★ *11 km (7 mi) northeast of Herculaneum, 24 km (15 mi) southeast of Naples.*

Ancient Pompeii was much larger than Herculaneum; a busy commercial center with a population of 10,000–20,000, it covered about 160 acres on the seaward end of the fertile Sarno Plain. In 80 BC the Roman general Sulla turned Pompeii into a Roman colony, where wealthy patricians came to escape the turmoil of city life. The town was laid out in a grid pattern, with two main intersecting streets. The wealthiest took a whole block for themselves; those less fortunate built a house and rented out the front rooms, facing the street, as shops. The facades of these houses were relatively plain and seldom hinted at the care and attention lavished on the private rooms within. When visitors arrived, they passed the shops and entered an open atrium. In the back was a receiving room. Behind was another open area, called the peristyle, with rows of columns and perhaps a garden with a fountain. Only good friends ever saw this private part of the house, which was surrounded by bedrooms and the dining area.

Pompeiian houses were designed around an inner garden, so that families could turn their backs on the world outside. Today we install picture windows that break down visual barriers between ourselves and our neighbors; the people in these Roman towns had few windows, preferring to get their light from the central courtyard—the light within. How pleasant it must have been to come home from the forum or the baths to one's own secluded kingdom, with no visual reminders

Pompeii

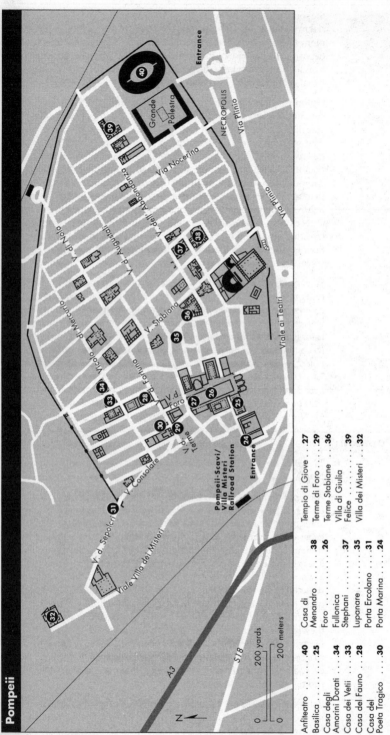

of a life outside one's own. Not that public life was so intolerable. There were wineshops on almost every corner, and frequent shows at the amphitheater. The public fountains and toilets were fed by huge cisterns connected by lead pipes beneath the sidewalks. Since garbage and rainwater collected in the streets of Pompeii, the sidewalks were raised, and huge stepping stones were placed at crossings so pedestrians could keep their feet dry. Herculaneum had better drainage, with an underground sewer that led to the sea.

The ratio of freemen to slaves was about three to two. A small, prosperous family had two or three slaves. Since all manual labor was considered degrading, the slaves did all housework and cooking, including the cutting of meat, which the family ate with spoons or with their hands. Everyone loved grapes, and figs were popular, too. Venison, chicken, and pork were the main dishes. People ate quinces (a good source of vitamin C) to guard against scurvy. Bread was made from wheat and barley (rye and oats were unknown) and washed down with wine made of grapes grown on the slopes of Vesuvius.

The town was considered a democracy, but women, children, gladiators, and Jews couldn't vote. They did, however, express their opinions on election day, as you'll see in campaign graffiti left on public walls. Some 15,000 graffiti have been found in Pompeii and Herculaneum. Many were political announcements—one person recommending another for office, for example, and spelling out his qualifications. Some were announcements of upcoming events—a play at the theater, a gladiatorial show at the amphitheater. Others were public notices— that wine was on sale, that an apartment would be vacant on the Ides of March. A good many were personal and lend a human dimension to the disaster that not even the sights can equal. Here are a few:

At the baths: "What is the use of having a Venus if she's made of marble?"

At a hotel: "I've wet my bed. My sin I bare. But why? you ask. No pot was anywhere."

At the entrance to the front lavatory at a private house: "May I always and everywhere be as potent with women as I was here."

(24) Enter through **Porta Marina,** so called because it faces the sea. It is near the Pompeii–Villa Misteri Circumvesuviana station. Past the Temple **(25)** of Venus is the **Basilica,** the law court and the economic center of the city. These oblong buildings ending in a semicircular projection (apse) were the model for early Christian churches, which had a nave (central aisle) and two side aisles separated by rows of columns. Standing in the Basilica, you can recognize the continuity between Roman and Christian architecture.

(26) The Basilica opens onto the **Foro** (Forum), the public meeting place, surrounded by temples and public buildings. It was here that elections were held and speeches and official announcements made. At the far **(27)** (northern) end of the forum is the **Tempio di Giove** (Temple of Jupiter). **(28)** The renowned **Casa del Fauno** (House of the Faun) displays wonderful mosaics, though the originals are in the Museo Archeologico Nazionale in Naples.

(29) The **Terme di Foro** (Forum Baths) on Via delle Terme is smaller than the Terme Stabiane, but with more delicate decoration. The **Casa del** **(30)** **Poeta Tragico** (House of the Tragic Poet) is a typical middle-class house from the last days of Pompeii. On the floor is a mosaic of a chained dog and the inscription CAVE CANEM ("Beware of the dog").

㉛ The beautiful **Porta Ercolano** (Gate of Herculaneum) was a main gate
㉜ that led to Herculaneum and Naples. The **Villa dei Misteri** (Villa of the
Mysteries), outside Pompeii's walls, contains what some consider the greatest surviving group of paintings from the ancient world, telling the story
of a young bride (Ariadne) being initiated into the mysteries of the cult
of Dionysus. Bacchus (Dionysus), the god of wine, was popular in a town
so devoted to the pleasures of the flesh. But he also represented the triumph of the irrational—of all those mysterious forces that no official
state religion could fully suppress. The cult of Dionysus, like the cult of
the Cumaean Sibyl, gave people a sense of control over fate and, in its
focus on the Other World, helped pave the way for Christianity.

㉝ The **Casa dei Vetii** (House of the Vetii) is the best example of a rich mer-
㉞ chant's house, faithfully restored with vivid murals. The **Casa degli Amor-
ini Dorati** (House of the Gilded Cupids) is an elegant, well-preserved
home with original marble decorations in the garden. On the walls of
㉟ **Lupanare** (brothel) are scenes of erotic games in which clients could en-
㊱ gage. The **Terme Stabiane** (Stabian Baths) had underground furnaces,
the heat from which circulated beneath the floor, rose through flues in
the walls, and escaped through chimneys. The water temperature could
be set for cold, lukewarm, or hot. Bathers took a lukewarm bath to prepare themselves for the hot room. A tepid bath came next, and then a
plunge into cold water to tone up the skin. A vigorous massage with
oil was followed by rest, reading, horseplay, and conversation.

㊲ Togas were washed at **Fullonica Stephani**. The cloth was dunked in a
tub full of water and chalk and stomped on like so many grapes. Once
clean, the material was stretched across a wicker cage and exposed to
sulfur fumes. The fuller (cleaner) carded it with a long brush, then placed
it under a press. The harder the pressing, the whiter and brighter it be-
㊳ came. Many paintings and mosaics were executed at **Casa di Menan-
㊴ dro**, a patrician's villa. The **Villa di Giulia Felice** (House of Julia Felix)
has a large garden with a lovely portico. The wealthy woman living here
ran a public bathhouse annex and rented out ground-floor rooms as shops.

㊵ The **Anfiteatro** was the stage for chariot races and games between animals and gladiators. When an important person such as the emperor was
in attendance, exotic animals—lions and tigers, panthers, elephants,
and rhinos—were released. Teams of gladiators worked for impresar-
ios, who hired them out to wealthy citizens, many of whom were running for office and hoping that the gory entertainment would buy them
some votes. Most gladiators were slaves or prisoners, but a few were Germans or Syrians who enjoyed fighting. When a gladiator found himself
at another's mercy, he extended a pleading hand to the president of the
games. If the president turned his thumb up, the gladiator lived; if he
turned his thumb down, the gladiator's throat was cut. The arena got
pretty bloody after a night's entertainment and was sprinkled with red
powder to camouflage the carnage. The victorious gladiator got money
or a ribbon exempting him from further fights. If he was a slave, he was
often set free. Pompeii had a gladiatorial school (Caserma dei Gladiatori), which you can visit on your way back to Porta Marina.

To get the most out of Pompeii, buy a detailed printed guide and map
and allow plenty of time—at least three or four hours. You should have
a pocketful of small change for tipping the guards who are on duty at
the most important villas. They will unlock the gates for you, insist on
explaining the attractions, show you some soft Pompeiian pornogra-
phy if you ask for it, and expect a tip for their services. Make sure the
guide is registered and standing inside the gate; agree beforehand on
the length of the tour and the price. Pompeii has its own stop (Pompeii–Villa dei Misteri) on the Circumvesuviana, close to the main en-

trance at the Porta Marina (there are other entrances to the excavations at the far end of the site, near the amphitheater). ✉ *Pompeii Scavi,* ☎ *081/8575347,* WEB *www.pompeiisites.org.* 🎫 *16,000 lire/€8.30, including Oplontis; 26,000 lire/€13.50 including Oplontis, Herculaneum, and 2 other sites over 3 days.* ○ *Apr.–Oct., daily 8:30–7:30 (ticket office closes at 6); Nov.–Mar., daily 8:30–5 (ticket office closes at 3:30).*

Many visitors to Pompeii are unaware of the modern pilgrimage that many Italians make to visit the **Sanctuario,** consecrated in 1891, which dominates the central square in modern Pompeii. Its main altar contains a painting, *The Virgin of the Rosary with Child,* that has been worshiped all over the world since it was claimed to have healing powers in 1876. The bell tower stands more than 250 ft high and has great views over the Lattari Mountains, Mount Vesuvius, the Sorrento coast, the ruins of Pompeii, and modern Pompeii. ✉ *Piazza Bartolo Longo,* ☎ *081/8577111.* 🎫 *Bell tower elevator 1,000 lire/€0.50.* ○ *Church daily 6:30–2 and 3–7:30; bell tower May–Sept., Sat.–Thurs. 9–1 and 3–6, Oct.–Apr. 9–1 and 3–5.*

Anyone interested in Vesuvius will find the **Museo Vesuviano** in modern Pompeii well worth a visit. It was originally set up as a research center, and today this small museum houses a collection of 200 rocks as well as old drawings, prints, and photographs, chronicling eruptions from 79 BC to the last one in 1944. ✉ *Via Colle San Bartolomeo 10,* ☎ *081/8507255.* 🎫 *Free.* ○ *Mon.–Sat. 9–1.*

Dining and Lodging

$$$ ✕ **President.** A classic restaurant in the heart of Pompeii, President is run by a father and son who have drawn on traditional recipes to create modern dishes made from local produce. Fish is a specialty—try *cicinielli alla brace in foglia di limone* (small fish served in lemon leaves). There is also a good selection of local wines. ✉ *Piazza Schettini 12, 80045,* ☎ *081/8507245. AE, DC, MC, V. Closed Mon. and mid-Aug.*

$$–$$$ 🏨 **Amleto.** This elegant hotel, restored by the current owner in 1997, offers excellent accommodation near the archaeological site (there aren't many hotels in the area). The hotel's pillars, mosaics, and murals evoke ancient Pompeii, and bedrooms are in either Venetian or Neapolitan style. From the roof garden you can enjoy views over ancient and modern Pompeii. There is no restaurant, but a generous buffet breakfast is served in the mornings. ✉ *Via Bartolo Longo 10, 80045,* ☎ *081/8631004,* FAX *081/8635585,* WEB *www.hotelamleto.it. 24 rooms, 2 junior suites. Bar, breakfast room, solarium, meeting room, free parking. AE, DC, MC, V.*

CASERTA AND BENEVENTO

From Caserta, the Italian answer to Versailles, if you proceed to Benevento you'll view an almost perfectly preserved Roman arch. Benevento was badly damaged by World War II bombings, but among the modern structures there are some medieval and even older relics still standing in the Old Town. If you go by car, make a brief detour to the medieval hamlet of Caserta Vecchia on the hillside, where there are one or two good restaurants and a very old cathedral.

Caserta

★ ④ *11 km (7 mi) northeast of Herculaneum, 25 km (16 mi) northeast of Naples.*

The palace known as the **Reggia** shows how Bourbon royals lived in the mid-18th century. Architect Luigi Vanvitelli devoted 20 years to its construction under Bourbon ruler Charles II, whose son, Charles III (1716–88), moved in when it was completed in 1774. Both king and architect were inspired by Versailles, and the rectangular palace was conceived on a massive scale, with four interconnecting courtyards, 1,200 rooms, and a vast park. Though the palace is not as well maintained as its French counterpart, the main staircase puts the one at Versailles to shame, and the **royal apartments** are sumptuous. It was here, in what Eisenhower called "a castle near Naples," that the Allied High Command had its headquarters in World War II, and here German forces in Italy surrendered in April 1945. There is also a museum showing items relating to the palace and the Caserta area. Most enjoyable are the gardens and parks, particularly the Cascades, adorned by the classical goddess Diana and her maidens. ⊠ *Piazza Carlo III,* ☎ *0823/ 321400.* ⊠ *Royal apartments 8,000 lire/€4.15; museum 4,000 lire/€2.05; park 4,000 lire/€2.05; minibus 1,500 lire/€0.80.* ⊙ *Royal apartments Tues.–Sun. 8:30–7:30. Park Mar., Tues.–Sun. 8:30–5; Apr., Tues.–Sun. 8:30–6; May and Aug., Tues.–Sun. 8:30–6:30; June and July, Tues.–Sun. 8:30–7; Sept. and Oct., Tues.–Sun. 8:30–5:30; Nov.–Feb., Tues.–Sun. 8:30–3:30; ticket office closes 1 hr before closing.*

Capua

42   *11 km (7 mi) northwest of Caserta, 33 km (20 mi) north of Naples.*

The nondescript town of Capua is home to the **Museo Campano,** a provincial museum collection that includes *Le Madri (The Mothers),* 200 eerily impressive stone votive statues representing highly stylized mother figures. They were found on the site of a sanctuary devoted to Matuta, the ancient goddess of childbirth, and date from the 7th to 1st century BC. ⊠ *Via Roma,* ☎ *0823/961402.* ⊠ *8,000 lire/€4.15.* ⊙ *Tues.–Sat. 9–1:30, Sun. 9–1, other times by appointment.*

Benevento

43   *35 km (22 mi) east of Caserta, 60 km (37 mi) northeast of Naples.*

Benevento owes its importance to its establishment as the capital of the Lombards, a northern tribe that invaded and settled what is now Lombardy when they were forced to move south by Charlemagne's conquests in the 8th century. Tough and resourceful, the Lombards moved south and set up a new duchy in Benevento, later moving its seat south to Salerno, where they saw the potential of the natural harbor. Under papal rule in the 13th century, Benevento built a fine cathedral and outfitted it with bronze doors that were a pinnacle of Romanesque art. The cathedral, doors, and a large part of the town were blasted by World War II bombs. The **Duomo** has been rebuilt, with the remaining panels of the original bronze doors in the chapter library. Fortunately, the majestic 2nd-century AD **Arco di Traiano** survived 20th-century bombs unscathed. Roman emperor Trajan, who sorted out Rome's finances, brought parts of the Middle East into the empire, and extended the Appian Way through Benevento to the Adriatic. The ruins of the **Teatro Romano,** which had a seating capacity of 20,000, is still in good enough shape to host a summer opera and theater season. ⊠ *Take Via Carlo from the Duomo.* ⊠ *4,000 lire/€2.05.* ⊙ *Daily 9–1 hr before sunset.*

PROCIDA, ISCHIA, AND CAPRI
Swept Away

History's hedonists have long luxuriated on Campania's famous islands. The Roman emperor Tiberius built a dozen villas on Capri in which to indulge his sexual whims. Later residents have included dancer Rudolf Nureyev and droves of artists and writers. These days, day-trippers make up the majority of visitors, diminishing the islands' social cachet. Ischia, less pretty and less chic than Capri, is still a popular destination on account of its spas, beaches, and hot springs. Procida, for long the poor relation of the three, and the closest to Naples, is starting to capitalize on its chief natural asset, the unspoiled isle of Vivara. The pastel colors of Procida's main harbor may be familiar to anyone who has seen the widely acclaimed film *Il Postino*, scenes of which were shot here.

Procida

44 *35 mins by hydrofoil, 1 hr by car ferry from Naples.*

Lying barely 3 km (2 mi) from the mainland and 10 km (6 mi) from the nearest port of Pozzuoli, Procida is an island of enormous contrasts. It is the most densely populated island in Europe—almost 11,000 people crammed into less than 3½ square km (2 square mi)—and yet there are oases like Marina Corricella and Vivara, which seem to have been bypassed by modern civilization. It's no surprise that picturesque Procida has strong artistic traditions and is widely considered the painters' island par excellence.

Corricella

Singled out for the waterfront scenes in *Il Postino*—the 1995 Oscar winner for Best Foreign Film—Corricella has been relatively immune to life in the limelight, and apart from the opening of an extra restaurant and bar, there have been few changes in this sleepy fishermen's village. This is the type of place where even those with failing grades in art class feel like reaching for a paintbrush to record the delicate pinks and yellows of the waterfront buildings.

Dining and Lodging

$$–$$$ ✕ **La Gorgonia.** This atmospheric restaurant sits right on the waterfront down at Corricella. The specialty here is a combination of seafood and locally grown vegetables, such as pasta *con fagioli e cozze* (with beans and mussels). ⊠ *Marina Corricella 50,* ☎ *081/8101060. AE, DC, MC, V. Closed Mon. and Nov.–Jan.*

$$ 🏨 **Casa Gentile.** This very quiet hotel, with spacious rooms overlooking Corricella, is designed to blend in tastefully with the local Mediterranean architecture. If interested in fishing, ask the owner, Vincenzo, if you can join him on his nighttime travels around the Bay of Naples. The hotel offers a water-taxi service to and from port. ⊠ *Marina Corricella 88, Procida 80079,* ☎ *081/8967799,* FAX *081/ 8969011. 10 rooms. MC, V. Closed Nov.–mid-Mar.*

Ischia

45 *45 mins by hydrofoil, 90 mins by car ferry from Naples; 60 mins by ferry from Pozzuoli.*

While Capri wows you with its charm and beauty, Ischia takes its time in casting its spell. In fact, an overnight stay is probably not long enough for the island to get into your blood. It does have its share of wine-growing villages beneath the lush volcanic slopes of Monte Epomeo, and unlike Capri, it enjoys a life of its own that survives when the tourists head home. But there are few signs of antiquity here, the architecture is unremarkable, the beaches are small and pebbly, there's little shopping beyond gift shops, and most visitors are either German (off-season) or Italian (in-season). On the other hand, some will delight in finding an island not yet discovered by tourists. Ischia also has some lovely hotel-resorts high in the mountains, offering therapeutic programs and rooms with breathtaking views. Should you want to plunk down in the sun for a few days and tune out the world, this is an ideal place to go; just don't expect Ischia to be an unspoiled, undiscovered Capri. When Augustus gave the Neapolitans Ischia for Capri, he knew what he was doing.

Ischia is volcanic in origin. From its hidden reservoir of seething molten matter come the thermal springs said to cure whatever ails you. As early as 1580, a doctor named Lasolino published a book about the mineral wells at Ischia. "If your eyebrows fall off," he wrote, "go and try the baths at Piaggia Romano. Are you unhappy about your complexion? You will find the cure in the waters of Santa Maria del Popolo. Are you deaf? Then go to Bagno d'Ulmitello. If you know anyone who is getting bald, anyone who suffers from elephantiasis, or another whose wife yearns for a child, take the three of them immediately to the Bagno di Vitara; they will bless you." Today the island is covered with thermal baths surrounded by tropical gardens.

Ischia Porto is the largest town on the island and the usual point of debarkation. It's no workaday port, however, but a pretty resort with plenty of hotels and low, flat-roofed houses on terraced hillsides above the water. Its narrow streets often become flights of steps that scale the hill, and its villas and gardens are framed by pines.

Most of the hotels are along the beach in the part of town called **Ischia Ponte,** which gets its name from the *ponte* (bridge) built by Alfonso of Aragón in 1438 to link the picturesque castle on a small islet offshore with the town and port. For a while, the castle was the home of Vittoria Colonna, poetess, platonic soul mate of Michelangelo, with whom she carried on a lengthy correspondence, and granddaughter of Renaissance Duke Federico da Montefeltro (1422–82). You'll find a typical resort atmosphere: countless cafés, shops, and restaurants, and a 1-km (½-mi) stretch of fine-sand beach. **Casamicciola,** a popular beach resort, is just 5 km (3 mi) west of Ischia Porto. Chic and upscale **Lacco Ameno,** next to Casamicciola, is distinguished by a mushroom-shape rock offshore and some of the island's best hotels. Here, too, you can enjoy the benefits of Ischia's therapeutic waters.

The far western and southern coasts of the island are more rugged and attractive. **Forio,** at the extreme west, is an ideal stop for lunch or dinner. Try **La Tinaia** (✉ Via M. Verde 39, ☎ 081/998448) for simple trattoria fare. The sybaritic hot pools of the **Giardini Poseidon Terme** (Poseidon Gardens) spa establishment are on the Citara beach, south of Forio. You can sit like a Roman senator on a stone chair recessed in the rock and let the hot water cascade over you—all very campy, and fun. **Sant'Angelo,** on the southern coast, is a charming village; the road doesn't reach all the way into town, so it's free of traffic, and it's a five-minute boat ride from the beach of Maronti, at the foot of cliffs. The inland towns of **Serrara, Fontana,** and **Barano** are all high above the sea. Fontana is the base for excursions to the top of **Monte Epomeo,** the long-dormant volcano that dominates the island landscape. You can reach its 2,585-ft peak in less than 1½ hours of relatively easy walking.

A good 35-km (22-mi) road makes a circuit of the island; the ride takes most of a day at a leisurely pace, if you're stopping along the way to enjoy the views and perhaps have lunch. You can book a **boat tour** around the island at the booths in various ports along the coast; there's a one-hour stop at Sant'Angelo. The information office is at the harbor. You may drive on Ischia year-round. There's also fairly good bus service, and you'll find plenty of taxis.

Dining and Lodging

$$ ✕ **Bar-Ristorante Bagno Teresa.** This is an unpretentious restaurant on Citara Beach (no dress code) that offers a range of fresh seafood at reasonable prices served with lively local wine. It's the place to come if you want to eat lightly before the afternoon swim—there's no need to order a full Mediterranean splurge. ⊠ *Baia di Citara,* ☎ *081/907647. No credit cards. Closed Nov.–Mar.*

$$ ✕ **Gennaro.** This small family restaurant on the seafront in Ischia Porto serves excellent fish in a convivial atmosphere. Specialties include spaghetti alle vongole and linguine *all'aragosta* (with lobster). ⊠ *Via Porto 66, Ischia Porto,* ☎ *081/992917. AE, DC, MC, V. Closed Nov.–mid-Mar.*

$$$$ 🏨 **Hotel San Montano.** Modern San Montano, replete with nautical motifs and ceramic-tile floors, overlooks the sea in a quiet spot. The rooms have color TVs and minibars, and there are resort facilities and spa treatments available. Note that half-board is required in high season. ⊠ *Via Montevico 20, 80076, Lacco Ameno,* ☎ *081/994033,* FAX *081/980242,* WEB *www.ischiagrandialberghi.it. 67 rooms. Restaurant, minibars, 2 pools, spa, tennis court. AE, DC, MC, V. Closed Nov.– Mar. MAP.*

$$$$ 🏨 **Regina Isabella.** Tucked away in an exclusive corner of the beach
★ in Lacco Ameno, Ischia's top luxury hotel has full resort facilities and pampers you with spa treatments as well. The rooms are ample and decorated in warm Mediterranean colors, and most have terraces or balconies. Don't miss the fun of socializing with chic vacationers in the elegant bar or restaurant or at poolside. Half-board or full board is required. ⊠ *Lacco Ameno, 80076,* ☎ *081/994322,* FAX *081/900190,* WEB *www.reginaisabella.it. 134 rooms. 2 restaurants, 2 bars, 3 pools, spa, 2 tennis courts, beach. AE, DC, MC, V. Closed Oct.–Mar.*

$$$ 🏨 **Villarosa.** A highlight at this gracious family-run hotel—a villa with
★ bright and airy rooms—is the thermally heated pool in the villa garden. In high season, half-board is required, and you must reserve well in advance. It's in the heart of Ischia Porto and only a short walk from the beach. ⊠ *Via Giacinto Gigante 5, 80077 Ischia Porto,* ☎ *081/ 991316,* FAX *081/992425,* WEB *www.lavillarosa.it. 37 rooms. Restaurant, pool. AE, DC, MC, V. Closed Nov.–Mar.*

$$ 🏨 **Del Postiglione.** This attractive, pink, Mediterranean-style edifice, a couple of minutes from the seafront, is smaller than it appears, with only 15 guest rooms. Its aura of understated luxury is created with tropical plants outside, marble floors, and generous balconies overlooking one of Ischia Porto's quiet backstreets. ⊠ *Via Giacinto Gigante 19, 80077 Ischia Porto,* ☎ *081/991579,* FAX *081/985956. 15 rooms. Restaurant, bar. MC, V. MAP.*

Capri

⑯ *74 mins by boat, 40 mins by hydrofoil from Naples.*

Erstwhile pleasure dome to Roman emperors, and now Italy's most glamorous seaside getaway, Capri (pronounced with an accent on the first syllable) is a craggy island at the southern approach to the Bay of Naples. The summer scene on Capri calls to mind the stampeding of bulls through the narrow streets of Pamplona: if you can visit in the spring or fall, do so. Yet even the crowds are not enough to destroy Capri's very special charm. The town is a Moorish opera set of shiny white houses, tiny squares, and narrow medieval alleyways hung with flowers. You can take a bus or the funicular to reach the town, which rests on top of rugged limestone cliffs, hundreds of feet above the sea, and on which huge herds of *capre* (goats) once used to roam (giving the name to the island). Unlike the other islands in the Bay of Naples, Capri is not of volcanic origin but is an integral part of the limestone chain of the Apennines, left above water when some subterranean cataclysm sank its connecting link with the mainland.

The Phoenicians were the earliest settlers of Capri. The Greeks arrived in the 4th century BC and were followed by the Romans, who made it their playground. Emperor Augustus vacationed here; Tiberius built 12 villas scattered over the island, and here he spent the later years of his life, refusing to return to Rome even when he was near death. Capri was one of the strongholds of the 16th-century pirate Barbarossa, who first sacked it and then made a fortress of it. Moors and Greeks had previously established their citadels on its heights, and pirates from all corners of the world periodically raided it. In 1806 the British wanted to turn it into another Gibraltar and were beginning to build fortifications when the French took it away from them in 1808. But the Roman influence has remained the strongest, reflecting a sybaritic way of life inherited from the Greek colonists on the mainland.

Thousands of legends concerning the lives and loves of mythological creatures, Roman emperors, Saracen invaders, and modern eccentrics combine to give Capri a voluptuous allure—sensuous and intoxicating—like the island's rare and delicious white wine. (Most of the wine passed off as "local" on Capri comes from the much more extensive vineyards of Ischia.)

You may have to wait in line for the cog railway (3,600 lire/€1.85 round-trip) to **Capri Town** from the harbor. If it's not operating, there's bus and taxi service. From the upper station, walk out into Piazza Umberto I, much better known as the Piazzetta, the island's social hub. You can window-shop in expensive boutiques and browse in souvenir shops along Via Vittorio Emanuele, which leads south toward the many-domed **Certosa di San Giacomo.** The church and cloister of this much-restored monastery can be visited, and you should also pause long enough to enjoy the breathtaking view of Punta Tragara and the Faraglioni, three towering shoals, from the viewpoint at the edge of the cliff. ⊠ *Via Certosa,* ☎ *081/8376218.* ☉ *Tues.–Sun. 9–2.*

★ Only when the spectacular **Grotta Azzurra** was "discovered" in 1826 by the Polish poet August Kopisch and his Swiss friend, the artist Ernest Fries—it had long been known to the island residents—did Capri become a tourist heaven. The watery cave's breathlessly blue beauty quickly became a symbol of the era of Romanticism—a monument in man's return to nature and revolt from reason. The pair's discovery triggered widespread interest and began the flow of Grand Tour visitors to the island. In fact, however, the grotto had been an island landmark since time immemorial. In the Roman era, as testified by the extensive remains primarily below sea level together with several large statues, now at the Certosa di San Giacomo, it had been the elegant, mosaic-decorated nymphaeum of the adjoining roman villa of Gradola. Historians can't quite agree if it was simply a lovely little pavilion where rich patricians would cool themselves for midday picnics or if it was truly a religious site where sacred mysteries were practiced. The extraordinary sapphire color makes the Mediterranean itself look gray and is caused by a hidden opening beneath the surface of the walls that refracts light through the blue water from the outside. At highest illumination, the very air inside looks tinted blue.

The Grotta Azzurra can be reached from Marina Grande or from the small embarkation point below Anacapri on the northwest side of the island, reached by bus from Anacapri. If you're pressed for time, however, skip this sometimes frustrating and disappointing excursion. You board one boat to get to the grotto, then have to transfer to another smaller boat to take you inside the grotto. If there's a backup of boats waiting to get in, you'll be given precious little time to enjoy the gorgeous color of the water and its silvery reflections. Adventurists can hike to the grotto area from Anacapri. ⊠ *Marina Grande.* 🚢 *About 23,000 lire/€11.95, including 8,000 lire/€4.15 admission to grotto.* ⊙ *Apr.–Sept., daily 9:30–2 hrs before sunset; Oct.–Mar., daily 10–noon.*

OFF THE
BEATEN PATH

BELVEDERE AND ARCO NATURALE – A short walk along Via Tragara leads to a belvedere overlooking the Faraglioni; another takes you out of town on Via Matermania to the so-called Natural Arch, an unusual rock formation near a natural grotto that the Romans transformed into a shrine. The 20-minute walk from the Piazzetta along picturesque Via Madre Serafina and Via Castello to the belvedere at Punta Cannone gives you a panoramic view of the island.

From the terraces of **Giardini di Augusto** (Gardens of Augustus), a beautifully planted public garden with excellent views, you can see the village of Marina Piccola below—restaurants, cabanas, and swimming platforms huddle among the shoals. This is the best place on the island for swimming; you can reach it by taking a bus or by following the steep and winding Via Krupp, actually a staircase cut into the rock, all the way down. (Friedrich Krupp, the German arms manufacturer, loved Capri and became one of the island's most generous benefactors.) ⊠ *Via Matteotti, beyond the monastery of San Giacomo.* ⊙ *Daily dawn–dusk.*

OFF THE
BEATEN PATH

VILLA JOVIS – From Capri Town, the 45-minute hike east to Villa Jovis, the grandest of those built by Tiberius, is strenuous but rewarding. Follow the signs for Villa Jovis, taking Via Le Botteghe from the Piazzetta, then continuing along Via Croce and Via Tiberio. At the end of a lane that climbs the steep hill, with pretty views all the way, you come to the precipice over which the emperor reputedly disposed of the victims of his perverse attentions. From a natural terrace above, near a chapel, are spectacular views of the entire Bay of Naples and (on clear days) part of the Gulf of Salerno. Below are the ruins of Tiberius's palace. Allow 45 minutes each way for the walk alone. ⊠ *Via Tiberio,* ☎ *081/8370381.* 🚢 *4,000 lire/€2.05.* ⊙ *Daily 9–1 hr before sunset.*

A tortuous road leads up to **Anacapri,** the island's second town, about 3 km (2 mi) from Capri Town. To get there, you can take a bus from Marina Grande (1,800 lire/€0.95) or a taxi (about 20,000 lire/€10.35 one-way; agree on the fare before starting out). Crowds are thick around the square that's the starting point of the chairlift to the top of Monte Solaro. Elsewhere, Anacapri is quietly appealing. It's a good starting point for walks, such as the 80-minute round-trip journey to the **Migliara Belvedere,** on the island's southern coast.

An impressive limestone formation and the highest point on Capri (1,932 ft), **Monte Solaro** affords gasp-inducing views toward both bays of Naples and Salerno. A 12-minute chairlift ride will take you right to the top (refreshments available at bar), which is a starting point for a number of scenic trails on the western side of the island. Picnickers should note that even in the summer it can get windy at this height, and there are few trees to provide shade or refuge. ⊠ *Piazza Vittoria, Anacapri,* ☎ *081/8371428.* 🚢 *5,9,500 lire/€4.95 round-trip.* ⊙ *Daily 9–5:30.*

In the heart of Anacapri, the octagonal Baroque church of **San Michele,** finished in 1719, is best known for its exquisite majolica pavement, designed by Solimena and executed by the *mastro-riggiolaro* (master tiler) Chiaiese from Abruzzo. A walkway skirts the rich ceramic carpet depicting Adam and a duly contrite Eve being expelled from the Garden of Eden, but you can get a breathtaking overview from the organ loft, reached by a winding staircase near the ticket booth (a privileged perch you have to pay for). Outside the church is the Via Finestrale, which leads to Anacapri's noted **Le Boffe quarter.** This section of town, slightly lower on the hillside, is centered on the Piazza Ficacciate and the Church of Santa Sophia and owes its name to the distinctive domestic architecture prevalent here, which uses vaults and sculpted groins instead of cross beams. The word *boffe*, as it turns out, comes from the Neapolitan dialect for "swollen." ✉ *Piazza Nicola, Anacapri,* ☎ *081/8372396.* 🎫 *2,000 lire/€1.05.* 🕐 *Nov.–Mar. daily 9:30–5; Apr.–Oct., daily 9–7.*

One of the best excursions from Anacapri is to the ruins of the Roman **Villa di Damecuta.** Sited strategically on a ridge with views sweeping across the Bay of Naples toward Procida and Ischia, the villa would have had its main access point at the landing stage right by the Blue Grotto at Gradola. This was probably one of the villas mentioned by Tacitus in his *Annals* as having been built by Tiberius: "Here on Capreae, in twelve spacious, separately named villas, Tiberius settled." Like Villa Jovis to the east, Villa di Damecuta was extensively plundered over the centuries prior to its proper excavation in 1937. Below the medieval tower (Torre Damecuta) there are two rooms (*domus* and *cubiculum*) that are thought to have been Tiberius's secret summer refuge. Affinities with Villa Jovis may be seen in the *ambulatio* (walkway) complete with seats and a stunning backdrop. To reach Villa Damecuta, get the bus from Anacapri to Grotto Azzurra and ask the driver to let you off at the proper stop. Alternatively, you can walk from the center of Anacapri down the bus route (about 30 minutes, but no sidewalks) or try your luck in the network of virtually traffic-free little alleyways running parallel to the main road. ✉ *Via A. Maiuri.* 🎫 *Free.* 🕐 *Daily 9–1 hr before sunset.*

From Anacapri's Piazza della Vittoria, picturesque Via Capodimonte leads to **Villa San Michele,** the charming former home of Swedish scientist Axel Munthe (1857–1949). Henry James called this villa and garden "the most fantastic beauty, poetry, and inutility that one had ever seen clustered together," and this encomium can't be topped. At the ancient entranceway to Anacapri just at the top of the Scala Fenicia and occupying the site of an ancient Roman villa, Villa San Michele was built (beginning in 1896) in accordance with Muthe's instructions. Physician to the Swedish royal family, Munthe practiced both in Paris and in Rome, thereby building up a substantial fortune, much of which he plowed into real estate in Anacapri. He was also a philanthropist with a lifelong dedication to the sick and destitute. Munthe's *The Story of San Michele* is an evocative—if not entirely reliable—autobiography.

Those 19th-century artists Alma-Tadema and Lord Leighton—specialists in painting scenes *all'antica*—would have set up their easels in a minute at the villa, since it is set around Roman-style courtyards, marble walkways, and atriums. Rooms display the doctor's varied collections, which range from bric-a-brac to antiquities (once thought so important J. Pierpont Morgan arrived to spend millions on them, but the good doctor knew that most were fakes so refused all offers). Medieval choir stalls, Renaissance lecterns, and gilded statutes of saints compose the aesthetic setting, with some rooms preserving the doctor's personal memorabilia, enabling the visiting public to find out more about this enigmatic patron of the arts and humanist. The villa is connected by a spectacular pergola path overlooking the entire Bay of Naples. This leads to the famous Sphinx Parapet, where an ancient Egyptian sphinx sits and looks out over to Sorrento (you cannot see its face— on purpose). It is said that if you touch the sphinx's hindquarters with your left hand while making a wish, it will come true. The parapet is connected to the little Chapel of San Michele, which once stood on the grounds of one of Tiberius's villas.

Besides hosting summer concerts, the Axel Munthe Foundation has an ecomuseum that fittingly reflects Munthe's fondness for animals, where you can learn about various bird species—accompanied by their songs— found on Capri. Not only did Munthe aid people, he bought up the hillside as a sanctuary for birds, which prevented the Caprese from capturing the resident quail. Today, thanks to the good Dr. Munthe, this little realm is still an Eden. ⊠ *Via Axel Munthe,* ☎ *081/837401.* 🖃 *8,000 lire/€4.15.* ⊙ *May–Sept., daily 9–6; Mar., daily 9:30–4:30; Apr. and Oct., daily 9:30–5; Nov.–Feb., daily 10:30–3:30.*

Dining and Lodging

$$$–$$$$ ✕ **La Capannina.** One of Capri's finest restaurants, La Capannina is
★ only a few steps from the busy social hub of the Piazzetta. It has a vine-draped veranda for dining outdoors by candlelight in a garden setting. The specialties, aside from an authentic Capri wine with the house label, are homemade ravioli alla caprese and regional dishes, especially fish. ⊠ *Via Le Botteghe 12 bis and 14, Capri Town,* ☎ *081/8370732. Reservations essential. AE, DC, MC, V. Closed mid-Nov.–mid-Mar. (except a week at New Year), and Wed. in Mar. and Oct.–mid-Nov.*

$$$ ✕ **I Faraglioni.** With natural shade provided by a 100-year-old wisteria plant, this is a popular, fairly stylish restaurant that is both centrally located and yet immersed in Mediterranean greenery. Meals here usually kick off with *uovo alla Monachina,* an egg-shape dish stuffed with mystery ingredients. For first course, try the *straccetti con gamberi e pomodorini* (fresh green pasta with shrimp and small tomatoes). ⊠ *Via Camerelle 75, Capri Town,* ☎ *081/8370320. Reservations essential. AE, DC, MC, V. Closed Nov.–Mar.*

$$$ ✕ **La Canzone del Mare.** This is the legendary bathing lido of the Marina Piccola, erstwhile haunt of Grace Fields, Emilio Pucci, Noël Coward, and any number of 1950s and '60s glitterati. The VIPs may have departed for the Bagni di Tiberio beach, but the setting is as magical as ever: Enjoy luncheon (no dinner served) in the thatched-roof pavilion looking out over the sea and I Faraglioni in the distance—this is Capri as picture-perfect as it comes. You need to pay a fee to use this bathing *stabilimenti,* but why not make a day of it—after all, the menu comes with a beach mattress. ⊠ *Via Marina Piccola 93, Capri Town,* ☎ *081/8370104. AE, DC, MC, V. Closed Nov.–Mar. No dinner.*

$$–$$$ ✕ **Al Grottino.** This small and friendly family-run restaurant, near the Piazzetta, has arched ceilings and lots of atmosphere; autographed photos of celebrity customers cover the walls. House specialties are gnocchi with tomato sauce and mozzarella, and linguine *agli scampi.* ⊠ *Via Longano 27, Capri Town,* ☎ *081/8370584. Reservations essential. AE, DC, MC, V. Closed Tues. and Nov. 3–Mar. 20.*

$$–$$$ ✕ **La Pigna.** Ensconced in a glassed-in veranda and offering outdoor dining in a garden shaded by lemon trees, La Pigna is one of Capri's most popular restaurants. The specialties are a house-produced wine, *farfalle impazzite* (bow-tie pasta with seafood and tomato), and aragosta *alla luna caprese* (with mozzarella, tomato, and basil). The cordial host organizes party evenings with feasts of seasonal specialties and seafood. ⊠ *Via Lo Palazzo 30, Capri Town,* ☎ *081/8370280. Reservations essential. AE, DC, MC, V.*

$$ ✕ **Da Tonino.** It is well worth making the short detour off the beaten track to the Arco Naturale to be pampered by creative chef Tonino. With the emphasis more on land-based dishes, try the *testina di coniglio* (rabbit terrine) or ask for the pigeon dish with pesto, rosemary, and pine nuts, accompanied by wine from a well-stocked cellar. ⊠ *Via Dentecala 34, Capri Town,* ☎ *081/8376718. AE, DC, MC, V. Closed Jan. 10–Mar. 15.*

$$ ✕ **La Giara.** Only about two minutes' walk from the bustling Piazza Vittoria in Anacapri, this pizzeria-ristorante has a wide range of palatable piatti served briskly and courteously. For a change from seafood, try the *pennette aum aum,* pasta pleasingly garnished with eggplant, mozzarella, cherry tomatoes, and basil. ⊠ *Via Orlandi 67, Anacapri,* ☎ *081/8373860. AE, DC, MC, V. Closed Dec.–Jan. and Wed.*

$$ ✕ **Mamma Giovanna.** This ristorante-pizzeria sits just below Piazza Diaz in the heart of the old town of Anacapri, facing the 16th-century church of Santa Sofia. The no-frills ambience belies the quality of the cucina: besides *pizze* (served midday and evenings), Mamma Giovanna specializes in *primi piatti,* such as *maccheroncelle al cartoccio* (pasta cooked in the oven with seafood). Reservations are essential for dinner. ⊠ *Via Boffe 3/5, Anacapri,* ☎ *081/8372057. No credit cards. Closed Dec.–Jan.*

$$$$ ✕🏠 **Villa Brunella.** This opulent, family-run gem is nestled in a garden setting just below the lane leading to the Faraglioni. Comfortable and tastefully furnished, the hotel has spectacular views and a swimming pool overlooking the sea. The terrace restaurant ($$$) also benefits from the superb panorama and is renowned for its seafood and other local dishes. ⊠ *Via Tragara 24, 80073 Capri Town,* ☎ *081/ 8370122,* FAX *081/8370430,* WEB *www.caprionline.com/villabrunella. 20 rooms. Restaurant, bar, pool. AE, DC, MC, V. Closed Nov.–Mar.*

$$$$ 🏠 **Capri Palace.** A modern resort atmosphere pervades this large Mediterranean-style hotel set in lovely gardens. Each of four junior suites has a private swimming pool and terrace. The bedrooms are tastefully decorated in bright contemporary style, with white predominating, and have marble bathrooms. The location in Anacapri offers relative seclusion from the summer crowds. ⊠ *Via Capodimonte 2 bis, 80071 Anacapri,* ☎ *081/8373800,* FAX *081/8373191,* WEB *www.capri-palace. com. 83 rooms. Restaurant, bar, pool, spa. AE, DC, MC, V. Closed mid-Nov.–Mar.*

$$$$ 🏠 **Quisisana.** Catering largely to Americans, this is the most luxurious and traditional hotel in the center of Capri Town. Spacious rooms have some antique accents. Many have arcaded balconies with views of the sea or the charming enclosed garden, surrounding a swimming pool. ⊠ *Via Camerelle 2, 80073 Capri Town,* ☎ *081/8370788,* FAX *081/ 8376080,* WEB *www.quisi.com. 149 rooms. Restaurant, bar, pool, sauna, tennis court. AE, DC, MC, V. Closed Nov.–mid-Mar.*

$$$$ 🏠 **Scalinatella.** The name means "little stairway," and that's how this
★ charming but modern small hotel is built, on terraces following the slope of the hill, overlooking the gardens, pool, and sea. The bedrooms are intimate, with alcoves and fresh, bright colors; the bathrooms feature whirlpool baths. ⊠ *Via Tragara 8, 80073 Capri Town,* ☎ *081/8370633,* FAX *081/8378291. 30 rooms. Bar, pool, tennis court. AE, DC, MC, V. Closed Nov.–mid-Mar.*

$$$ 🏠 **San Michele.** You'll find this large white villa-hotel next to Axel Munthe's home. Surrounded by luxuriant gardens, the San Michele offers solid comfort and good value to go with spectacular views. It's modern, with some Neapolitan antiques adding atmosphere. Most rooms have a terrace or balcony overlooking either the sea or island landscapes. ⊠ *Via G. Orlandi 5, 80071 Anacapri,* ☎ *081/8371427,* FAX *081/8371420,* WEB *www.sanmichele-capri.com. 59 rooms. Restaurant, pool. AE, DC, MC, V. Closed Nov.–Mar.*

$$-$$$ ⌧ **Villa Krupp.** Occupying a quiet location overlooking the Gardens of Augustus, this historic hostelry was the onetime home of Maxim Gorky, whose guests included Lenin. Rooms are plain but spacious. ⊠ *Viale Matteotti 12, 80073 Capri Town,* ☎ *081/8370362,* FAX *081/8376489. 12 rooms. MC, V. Closed Nov.–Feb.*

$$-$$$ ⌧ **Villa Sarah.** This whitewashed Mediterranean building has a homey look and bright, simply furnished rooms. It's close enough to the Piazzetta (a 10-minute walk) to give easy access to the goings-on there, yet far enough away to ensure restful nights. There is a garden and a small bar. ⊠ *Via Tiberio 3/a, 80073 Capri Town,* ☎ *081/8377817,* FAX *081/8377215,* WEB *www.villasarah.it. 20 rooms. Bar. AE, DC, MC, V. Closed Nov.–Mar.*

$$ ⌧ **Aida.** A 10-minute walk from the town center, on a tiny lane that borders the Gardens of Augustus, the Aida offers a tranquil haven from Capri's bustle and hard sell. The staff is sociable, and the rooms, which look onto a small garden, are spacious, comfortably furnished, and immaculately clean. The beach at Marina Piccola is only 20 minutes away. ⊠ *Via Birago, 80073 Capri Town,* ☎ *081/8370366. 10 rooms. No credit cards. Closed Oct.–Mar.*

$$ ⌧ **Villa Eva.** Named after its dynamic owner-manager, this is a popular international stopover for young *Wandervögel* (travelers) who have a more laid-back approach to traveling. Accommodation is in small, low-impact villas set in luxuriant gardens. When not tending the grounds, Vincenzo, Eva's husband, will take you down to the nearby Blue Grotto for a late-afternoon swimming expedition. ⊠ *Via La Fabbrica 8, 80071 Anacapri,* ☎ *081/8371549,* FAX *081/8372040,* WEB *www.villaeva.com. 24 rooms. Bar, pool. AE, DC, MC, V. Closed mid-Nov.–mid-Feb.*

Nightlife and the Arts

Capri's New Year's Eve celebrations last all night, with dancing and music in the Piazzetta and magnificent fireworks from the numerous private parties illuminating the night sky. On New Year's Day there are marching bands, pageants, and all the revelry you would expect on this exuberant island.

THE AMALFI COAST

Sorrento to Salerno

As travelers journey down the fabled Amalfi Coast, their route takes them past rocky cliffs plunging into the sea and small boats lying in sandy coves like brightly colored fish. Erosion has contorted the rocks into shapes like figures from mythology and hollowed out fairy grottoes where the air is turquoise and the water an icy blue. In winter, nativity scenes of moss and stone are created in the rocks. White villages dripping with flowers nestle in coves or climb like vines up the steep, terraced hills. Lemon trees abound, loaded with blossom or fruit—and in winter they are covered by netting to protect the fruit. The inhabitants jest that they look after their lemons better than their children. The road must have a thousand turns, each with a different view, on its dizzying 69-km (43-mi) journey from Sorrento to Salerno.

Sorrento

④ *50 km (31 mi) south of Naples, 50 km (31 mi) west of Salerno.*

Sorrento is across the Bay of Naples from Naples itself, on autostrada A3 and S145. The Circumvesuviana railway, which stops at Herculaneum and Pompeii, provides another connection. The coast between Naples and Castellammare, where road and railway turn off onto the Sorrento peninsula, seems at times depressingly overbuilt and industrialized. Yet Vesuvius looms to the left, you can make out the 3,000-ft-high mass of Monte Faito ahead, and on a clear day you can see Capri off the tip of the peninsula. The scenery improves considerably as you near Sorrento, where the coastal plain is carved into russet cliffs rising perpendicularly from the sea. This is the Sorrento (north) side of the peninsula; on the other side is the Amalfi Coast, more dramatically scenic. But Sorrento has at least two advantages over Amalfi: the Circumvesuviana railway terminal and a fairly flat terrain. A stroll around town is a pleasure—you'll encounter narrow alleyways and interesting churches, and the views of the Bay of Naples from the Villa Comunale and the Museo Correale are priceless.

Until the mid-20th century, Sorrento was a small, genteel resort favored by central European princes, English aristocrats, and American literati. During World War I, American soldiers came to recuperate at the Hotel Vittoria. Now the town has grown and spread out along the crest of its famous cliffs, and apartments stand where citrus groves once bloomed. Like most resorts, Sorrento is best off-season, either in spring and early autumn or in winter, when Campania's mild climate can make a stay pleasant anywhere along the coast.

A highlight of Sorrento is **Museo Correale di Terranova,** an 18th-century villa with a lovely garden on land given to the patrician Correale family by Queen Joan of Aragón in 1428. It has an excellent private collection amassed by the count of Terranova and his brother. The building itself is fairly charmless, with few period rooms, but the garden offers an allée of palm trees, citrus groves, floral nurseries, and an esplanade with a panoramic view of the Sorrento coast. The collection itself is one of the finest devoted to Neapolitan paintings, decorative arts, and porcelains, so for connoisseurs of the Seicento (Italian 17th century), this museum is a must. Magnificent 18th-century inlaid tables by Giuseppe Gargiulo, Capodimonte porcelains, and rococo portrait miniatures remind us of the age when pleasure and delight were all. Also on view are regional Greek and Roman archaeological finds, medieval marble work, glasswork, old master paintings, 17th-century majolicas—even Tasso's death mask. ⊠ *Via Correale,* ☏ *081/8781846.* 🎫 *Museum and gardens 10,000 lire/€5.15.* ⊙ *Wed.–Mon. 9–2.*

Worth checking out is the **Museo Bottega della Tarsialignea,** set up by local craftspeople to ensure the continuity of the intarsia (wood inlay) tradition. It houses historical collections as well as exhibitions of modern work. There's a shop if you fancy taking home an unusual souvenir. ⊠ *Via San Nicola 28,* ☏ *081/8771942.* 🎫 *15,000 lire/€7.80.* ⊙ *Museum guided visits (required) every ½ hr Apr.–Oct., Tues.–Sun. 9:30–noon and 5–7; Nov.–Mar., Tues.–Sun. 9:30–noon and 3–5. Shop Tues.–Sun. 9:30–1 and 5–8, or 3–6 in winter.*

Via Marina Grande turns into a pedestrian lane, then a stairway leading to Sorrento's only real beach at **Marina Grande,** where fishermen pull up their boats and there are some good seafood restaurants. A frequent bus also plies this route, if you don't fancy the legwork (tickets are bought at the *tabacchi*).

....

OFF THE
BEATEN PATH   **CAPO DI SORRENTO AND THE BAGNO DELLA REGINA GIOVANNA** – Just 2 km (1 mi) west of Sorrento, turn right off Statale 145 toward the sea, and then park and walk a few minutes through citrus and olive groves to get to Capo di Sorrento, the craggy tip of the cape, with the most interesting ancient ruins in the area. They were identified by the Latin poet Publio Pa-

pinio Stazio as the ancient Roman villa of historian Pollio Felice, patron
of the great authors Virgil and Horace. Next to the ruins is Bagno della
Regina Giovanna (Queen Joan's Bath). A cleft in the rocks allows the sea
to channel through an archway into a clear, natural pool, with the water
turning iridescent blue, green, and violet as the sunlight changes angles.
The easiest way to see all this is to rent a boat at Sorrento, and later you
can go on to the fishermen's haven of Marina di Puolo by sailing westward for lunch at a modest restaurant with fresh catch.

Dining and Lodging

$$$-$$$$ ✗ **Antica Trattoria.** An old-world dining room inside and garden tables
in fair weather make this a pleasant place to enjoy the local cooking.
The atmosphere is homey and hospitable. The menu is voluminous and
your choice will be difficult, but the specialties include spaghetti alle von-
gole and *gamberetti all'Antica Trattoria* (shrimp in tomato sauce). You
can also opt for one of the four prix-fixe menus. ⊠ *Via Giuliani 33,* ☎
081/8071082. AE, DC, MC, V. Closed Mon. and 4 wks in Jan.–Feb.

$$$ ✗ **Zi 'ntonio.** The sixth generation of Uncle Tony's family now runs
this rustic restaurant, serving huge portions of sensational food. Choose
antipasti from a spread of more than 25 dishes, and then try specialties including St. Peter's fish with artichokes; lobster and lemon risotto;
and savory Parma ham served with mozzarella (*delizioso!*—from the
same distributor since the 1950s). Local wines are well priced. Up a
chestnut-wood staircase, it's fun to eat aloft in the balcony, but any of
the three floors and several rooms is evocative, filled with tiles, flags,
murals, plates, and hearty diners. ⊠ *Via Luigi de Maio 11,* ☎ *081/
8781623. AE, DC, MC, V. Closed Tues.*

$$ ✗ **Parrucchiano.** Central and popular, this is one of Sorrento's oldest
and best restaurants. You walk up a few steps to glassed-in veranda
dining rooms filled, like greenhouses, with vines and plants. The menu
offers classic local specialties, among them *panzerotti* (pastry shells filled
with tomato and mozzarella) and *scaloppe alla sorrentina* (scallops with
tomato and mozzarella). ⊠ *Corso Italia 71,* ☎ *081/8781321. MC, V.
Closed Wed. in Nov.–Mar.*

$$ ✗ **Trattoria da Emilia.** You can sit outside here, right on the Marina
Grande, and watch the life of the port go by. This simple, rustic restau-
rant with wooden tables has been run by Donna Emilia and her off-
spring since 1947 and provides typical Sorrento home cooking and a
family atmosphere. Fried seafood is the specialty. Sofia Loren came to
eat here while filming *Pane, amore, ...* ⊠ *Via Marina Grande 62,*
☎ *081/8072720. No credit cards. Closed Tues. in Oct.–Mar. No dinner Oct.–Mar.*

$$$$ ☷ **Bellevue Syrene.** This exclusive hotel is set in a cliff-top garden close
to the center of Sorrento. It retains its solid, old-fashioned comforts
and sumptuous charm, with Victorian nooks and alcoves, antique
paintings, and exuberant frescoes. You can find interior-facing rooms
at lower prices, if you are willing to forgo the splendid views over the
sea. ⊠ *Piazza della Vittoria 5, 80067,* ☎ *081/8781024,* FAX *081/
8783963,* WEB *www.sorrentopalace.it. 73 rooms. Restaurant, bar, beach.
AE, DC, MC, V.*

$$$$ ☷ **Cocumella.** A grand hotel in every sense, the Cocumella seems lit-
★   tle changed since the days when Goethe and Napoléon's enemy, the
Duke of Wellington, stayed here. Set in the blissfully tranquil hamlet
of Sant'Agnello, in a cliff-top garden overlooking the Bay of Naples,
this extraordinary hotel occupies a historic 17th-century monastery complete with frescoed ceilings, antique reliquaries, and a marble cloister.
The Del Papa family has seen fit to gild this lily with the last word in
luxuries: a spectacular pool area, a workout room, a summer season
of concerts held in the hotel's Baroque church, and palatial suites that

offer fireplaces and Empire-style ambience. For around 200,000 lire/€104 per person, guests can spend a day on the hotel's 90-ft-long 19th-century yacht. ⊠ *Via Cocumella 7, 80065 Sant'Agnello (Sorrento),* ☎ *081/8782933,* FAX *081/8783712. 45 rooms, 15 suites. Restaurant, bar, spa, gym, pool. AE, DC, MC, V. Closed Nov.–Mar.*

$$$$ 🏠 **Excelsior Vittoria.** Magnificently set overlooking the Bay of Naples,
★ this is a Belle Epoque dream come true. Gilded salons, stunning gardens, and an impossibly romantic terrace where orchestras lull you twice a week with Neapolitan and modern music: in all, it's a truly intoxicating experience. Caruso stayed here and, more recently, Pavarotti and Princess Margaret. Save your pennies, splurge—but come! There's a 15% discount from November to February and a 10% discount in March. ⊠ *Piazza Tasso 34, 80067,* ☎ *081/8071044,* FAX *081/8771206,* WEB *www.exvitt.it. 109 rooms, 14 suites. Restaurant, bar, pool, meeting room. AE, DC, MC, V.*

$$$$ 🏠 **Imperial Hotel Tramontano.** The birthplace of the poet Torquato Tasso (the first of an impressive list of literary credentials), this palatial villa lies within a semitropical garden in the center of Sorrento. The sumptuous furnishings and Belle Epoque tone are set off by the spectacular views out to sea. ⊠ *Via Veneto 1, 80067,* ☎ *081/8782588,* FAX *081/8072344,* WEB *www.tramontano.com. 120 rooms. Restaurant, bar, pool, beach, meeting room. AE, MC, V. Closed Jan. and Feb.*

$$ 🏠 **Mignon Meublé.** This centrally located hotel is an especially good find for the price category, so it's advisable to book well in advance. You'll find spacious and simple yet stylish accommodations in a friendly atmosphere. Breakfast is served in your room, but there's a small sitting area where you can also relax. ⊠ *Via Sersale 9, 80067,* ☎ *081/8073824,* FAX *081/5329001. 23 rooms. Air-conditioning. AE, DC, MC, V.*

$$ 🏠 **Nice.** This modest pensione is comfortable and close to the bus and train stations. The rooms are somewhat dull but airy, with marble floors. The friendly management will provide a wealth of information about the area. ⊠ *Corso Italia 257, 80067,* ☎ *081/8781650,* FAX *081/8783086. 12 rooms. AE, DC, MC, V. Closed Dec.–Feb.*

$$ 🏠 **Settimo Cielo.** This hotel, with a swimming pool and gardens, is an excellent choice (and great value) if you want to stay on the water but your budget doesn't extend to one of the luxury hotels. The beach is just a few steps away. The rooms, which all face the sea, are simple and modern. ⊠ *Via Capo 27, 80060,* ☎ *081/8781012,* FAX *081/8073290. 20 rooms. Restaurant, bar, pool, parking. AE, DC, MC, V. Closed Nov.–mid-Mar.*

Nightlife and the Arts

BAR

At **Circolo dei Forestieri** (⊠ Via de Maio 35, ☎ 081/8773263), you'll get a memorable view of the Bay of Naples from the terrace. Drinks are moderately priced, and there is live music nightly in summer and every weekend the rest of the year. It's closed January and February.

DISCOS

For the younger set, or the young at heart, there are a couple of discos worth visiting: the **Club** (⊠ Piazza Tasso, ☎ 081/8773236) and **Il Mito** (⊠ Via Fuori Mura 47, ☎ 081/8782506).

FILM

Every October, the **International Cinema Convention** in Sorrento draws an elite collection of producers, directors, and stars in a less frantic atmosphere than what's found at Cannes. While much of the activity revolves around deal making, a number of previews are screened. For details, contact the Sorrento tourist office (⊠ Via de Maio 35, ☎ 081/80740330).

MUSIC

MUSIC

July and August welcome the **Summer Music Festival,** held in the 12th-century cloister of St. Francis. There's a wide choice of music to enjoy, from classical and Baroque to jazz and folk. Contact the tourist office (⊠ Via de Maio 35, ☎ 081/8074033) for information.

SHOWS

The following clubs put on **Tarantella Shows,** which consist of traditional Neapolitan songs and dances performed in typical 19th-century costumes of Sorrento. Shows usually run from 9 PM until about 11 PM and are followed by disco dancing. Admission prices (around 35,000 lire/€18.20) include one drink. **Fauno Notte Club** (⊠ Piazza Tasso 13/a, ☎ 081/8781021). **La Mela Due** (⊠ Corso Italia 263, ☎ 081/8781917).

Shopping

LOCAL CRAFTS

Around **Piazza Tasso** are a number of shops selling embroidered goods and *intarsia* (wood inlay) work, a centuries-old tradition here. Along narrow **Via San Cesareo,** where the air is pungent with the perfumes of fruit and vegetable stands, there are shops selling local and Italian crafts—everything from jewelry boxes to trays and coffee tables with intarsia decoration. **Ferdinando Corcione,** in his shop on Via San Francesco, gives demonstrations of intarsia work, producing decorative plaques with classic or contemporary motifs. You may want to stop in one of the many shops selling the famous lemon liqueur *limoncello*; highly recommended brands include **Piemme** and **Villa Massa,** the latter of which is exported to the United States.

Positano

★ ④ *14 km (9 mi) east of Sorrento, 57 km (34 mi) south of Naples.*

When John Steinbeck lived here in 1953, he wrote that it was difficult to consider tourism an industry because "there are not enough *tourists.*" Alas, Positano, a village of white Moorish-style houses clinging dramatically to slopes around a small sheltered bay, has since been discovered. The artists came first, and, as happens wherever artists go, the wealthy followed and the artists fled. Another Steinbeck observation still applies, however: "Positano bites deep. It is a dream place that isn't quite real when you are there and becomes beckoningly real after you have gone. Its houses climb a hill so steep it would be a cliff except that stairs are cut in it. I believe that whereas most house foundations are vertical, in Positano they are horizontal. The small curving bay of unbelievably blue and green water laps gently on a beach of small pebbles. There is only one narrow street and it does not come down to the water. Everything else is stairs, some of them as steep as ladders. You do not walk to visit a friend, you either climb or slide."

In the 10th century, Positano was part of Amalfi's Maritime Republic, which rivaled Venice as an important mercantile power. Its heyday was in the 16th and 17th centuries, when its ships traded in the Near and Middle East, carrying spices, silks, and precious woods. The coming of the steamship in the mid-19th century led to the town's decline; some three-fourths of its 8,000 citizens emigrated to America, most to New York. One of the major tasks of Positano's mayor has been finding space in the overcrowded cemetery for New York Positanesi who want to spend eternity here.

What had been reduced to a forgotten fishing village is now the number one attraction on the coast, with hotels for every budget, charming restaurants, and dozens of boutiques. From here you can take hydrofoils to Capri during the summer, escorted bus rides to Ravello, and tours of the Grotta dello Smeraldo. If you're staying in Positano, check whether your hotel has a parking area. If not, you will have to pay for space in a parking lot, which is almost impossible to find during the high season, from Easter to September. The best bet for day-trippers is to arrive by bus—there is a good, regular service—or else get to Positano early enough so that space is still available.

No matter how much time you spend in Positano, make sure you have some comfortable walking shoes (no heels) and that your back and legs are strong enough to negotiate those daunting *scalinatelli* (little stair-ways). If not, ride the municipal bus, which frequently plies along the one-and-only-one-way Via Pasitea, hairpinning from Positano's central Piazza dei Mulini to the mountains and back, making a loop through the town every half hour. Heading down from the Sponda bus stop toward the beach, you pass Le Sirenuse, the hotel where John Steinbeck stayed in 1953. Its stepped terraces offer vistas over the town, so you might splurge on lunch or a drink here on the pool terrace, a favorite gathering place for Modigliani-sleek jet-setters. Continue to Piazza dei Mulini, and make a left turn onto Via dei Mulini. If you want to catch your breath after a bus ride to Positano, take a quick time-out for an espresso, a slice of Positanese (a chocolate cake as delectable as its namesake), or a fresh-fruit iced "granite" in the lemon-tree garden at **Bar-Pasticceria La Zagara** (✉ Via Mulini 8, ☎ 089/875964). Past a bevy of resort boutiques, head to Via dei Mulini 23 to view the prettiest garden in Positano—the 18th-century courtyard of the **Palazzo Murat,** originally built by Prince Joachim Murat, whom Napoléon designated as King of Naples in 1808. Murat wanted to forget the demands of power and escaped to Positano to lead the simple life. Since Murat was one of Europe's leading style setters, it couldn't be *too* simple, and he wound up building a grand abode (now a hotel) just steps from the main beach.

Just beyond the Palazzo Murat is the Chiesa Madre, or parish church of **Santa Maria Assunta,** its green and yellow majolica dome, topped by a perky cupola, visible from just about anywhere in town. Built on the site of the former Benedictine abbey of St. Vito, the 13th-century Romanesque structure was almost completely rebuilt in 1700. The last piece of the ancient mosaic floor can be seen under glass near the apse. Note the carved wooden Christ, a masterpiece of devotional religious art, with its bathetic face and bloodied knees, on view before the altar. At the altar is a Byzantine 13th-century painting on wood of Madonna with Child, known as the Black Virgin, carried to the main beach every August 15 to celebrate the Feast of the Assumption. Legend claims that the painting was once stolen by Saracen pirates, who, fleeing in a raging storm, heard from a voice on high, *"Posa, posa"*—"Put it down, put it down." When they placed the statue on the beach near the church, the storm calmed, as did the Saracens. Positano was saved, and the town's name was established (yet again). Embedded over the doorway of the church's bell tower, set across the tiny piazza, is a medieval bas-relief of fishes, a fox, and a Pistrice, the mythical half-dragon, half-dog sea monster. This is one of the sole relics of the medieval abbey of St. Vito. ✉ *Piazza Flavio Gioia, just above the main beach.*

The walkway from the Piazza Flavio Gioia leads down to the **Spaggia Grande,** or main beach, bordered by an esplanade and some of Positano's best restaurants. Head over to the stone pier to the far right of the beach as you face the water. A staircase leads to the **Via Positanesi d'America,** a lovely seaside walkway. Halfway up the path you'll find the Torre Trasìta, the most distinctive of Positano's three coastline defense towers, which define the edges of Positano in various states of repair. The Trasìta—now a residence occasionally available for summer rental—was one of the defense towers used to warn of pirate raids. Just beyond the tower is O'Guaraccino, an arbor-covered restaurant. Continuing along the Via Positanesi d'America, you pass tiny inlets and emerald coves until the large Spaggia di Fornillo beach comes into view.

Dining and Lodging

$$$ ✕ **Buca di Bacco.** After an aperitif at the town's most famous and fashionable café downstairs, you dine on a veranda overlooking the beach. The specialties include spaghetti alle vongole and *grigliata mista* (mixed grilled seafood). ⊠ *Via Rampa Teglia 8,* ☎ *089/875699. AE, DC, MC, V. Closed Nov.–Mar.*

$$$ ✕ **'O Capurale.** Among the popular restaurants on the beach promenade, this one just around the corner has the best food and lowest prices. Tables are set under vines on a breezy sidewalk in the summer, indoors and upstairs in winter. Spaghetti *con melanzane* (with eggplant) and crepes *al formaggio* (with cheese) are among the specialties. ⊠ *Via Regina Giovanna 12,* ☎ *089/875374. AE, DC, MC, V. Closed Nov.–mid-Feb.*

$$–$$$ ✕ **Donna Rosa.** This minimalist little hideaway in one-street Montepertuso, the hamlet high over Positano, is truly original. Everybody gets into the act: Mamma does the creative cooking, to order; Pappa "makes noise"; and the daughters rule out front—Rosa is the namesake nonna. Homemade pasta is the house specialty—it may have arugula *in* it, mixed with clams, mussels, porcini mushrooms, and artichokes—along with the delectable desserts, which may include walnut or strawberry mousse and *crostata all'arancio* (orange tart). A wide selection of fine wines is on hand, live music can be anything from jazz to Australian gospel (with a daughter singing sweetly), and free car service is provided. There is a terrace, but the better view is from the kitchen. A reservation is essential for dinner. ⊠ *Via Montepertuso,* ☎ *089/811806. AE, DC, MC, V. Closed Mon.*

$$$$ ⌂ **Casa Albertina.** Clinging to the cliff, this little house is well loved for its Italianate charm, its homey restaurant, and its owners, the Cinque family. Rooms have high ceilings, bright fabrics, tile flooring, and sunny terraces or balconies overlooking the sea and coastline. Car or motorboat excursions to surrounding towns and attractions can be arranged. Cars can't drive to the doorway, but porters will ferry your luggage. Note: it's 300 steps down to the main beach. Half- or full board is required in summer (and is reflected in the price category here). ⊠ *Via Tavolozza 4, 84017,* ☎ *089/875143,* FAX *089/811540,* WEB *www. casalbertina.it. 21 rooms. Restaurant, air-conditioning, parking (fee). AE, DC, MC, V.*

$$$$ ⌂ **Le Sirenuse.** A handsome 18th-century palazzo in the center of
★ town is the setting for this luxury hotel, in which bright tiled floors, precious antiques, and tasteful furnishings are featured in ample and luminous salons. The bedrooms have the same sense of spaciousness and comfort; most have splendid views from balconies and terraces. The top-floor suites have huge bathrooms and whirlpool baths. One side of a large terrace has an inviting swimming pool; on the other is an excellent restaurant. ⊠ *Via Cristoforo Colombo 30, 84017,* ☎ *089/ 875066,* FAX *089/811798,* WEB *www.sirenuse.it. 60 rooms. Restaurant, bar, pool, sauna, gym. AE, DC, MC, V.*

$$$$ ⌂ **Palazzo Murat.** The location is perfect—in the heart of town, near the beachside promenade, but set in a quiet, walled garden. The old wing is a historic palazzo with tall windows and wrought-iron balconies; the new wing is a whitewashed Mediterranean building with arches and terraces. You can relax in antiques-accented lounges or in the charming vine-draped patio, and enjoy gorgeous views from the comfortable bedrooms. ⊠ *Via dei Mulini 23, 84017,* ☎ *089/875177,* FAX *089/*

811419, WEB *www.starnet.it/murat. 31 rooms. Restaurant, bar. AE, DC, MC, V. Closed Jan.–mid-Mar.*

$$$$ 🏨 **San Pietro.** Extraordinary is the word for this luxurious oasis for
★   the affluent international set. Outside the town and set high above the
       sea with garden terraces, the San Pietro has sumptuous Neapolitan
       Baroque decor and masses of flowers in the lounges, elegantly under-
       stated rooms (most with terraces), and marvelous views. There's a pool
       on an upper level, and an elevator whisks you down to the private beach
       and beach bar. The proprietors organize boating excursions and par-
       ties and provide car and minibus service into town. ⊠ *Via Laurito 2,
       84017,* ☎ *089/875455,* FAX *089/811449,* WEB *www.ilsanpietro.it. 60
       rooms. Restaurant, 2 bars, pool, tennis court, beach, dock. AE, DC,
       MC, V. Closed Nov.–Mar.*

$$–$$$ 🏨 **La Fenice.** This tiny, friendly, unpretentious hotel on the peaceful
★   outskirts of town beckons with bougainvillea-laden vistas, castaway
        cottages, and a turquoise pool (available only in summer), all perched
        over a private beach. Guest rooms—accented with coved ceilings,
        whitewashed walls, and native folk art—are simple havens of tranquillity
        (book the best, those closest to the sea, only if you can handle *very*
        steep walkways). ⊠ *Via G. Marconi 4, 84017,* ☎ *089/875513,* FAX *089/
        811309. 15 rooms. Pool. No credit cards.*

Nightlife

L'Africana (⊠ Vettica Maggiore, Praiano, 10 km [6 mi] east of Positano on the coast road, ☎ 089/874042) is the premier nightclub on
the Amalfi Coast, built into a fantastic grotto above the sea.

Grotta dello Smeraldo

13 km (8 mi) east of Positano, 27 km (17 mi) east of Sorrento.

A peculiar green light that casts an eerie emerald glow over impressive
formations of stalagmites and stalactites, many of them underwater,
inspired the name of the Grotta dello Smeraldo (Emerald Grotto).
You can park at the signposts for the grotta along the coast road and
take an elevator down, or you can drive on to Amalfi and return to
the grotto by the more romantic route—via boat. Boat tours leave from
the Amalfi seafront regularly, according to demand; the charge is
10,000 lire/€5.15 per person. Call ahead, as hours are subject to
change. 🎫 *Grotto 10,000 lire/€5.15.* 🕐 *Apr.–Sept., daily 9–5; Oct.–
Mar., daily 10–4.*

Amalfi

④⑨ *4 km (2½ mi) east of Grotta dello Smeraldo, 35 km (22 mi) east of
Sorrento.*

"The sun—the moon—the stars and—Amalfi," Amalfitans used to say.
During the Middle Ages, Amalfi was an independent maritime state—
a little Republic of Venice—with a population of 50,000. The ship com-
pass, trivia fans will be interested to know, was invented here in 1302.
The Republic also brought the art of papermaking to Europe from Ara-
bia. Before World War II there were 13 mills making paper by hand
in the Valle Molini, but now only two small ones remain. The town is
romantically situated at the mouth of a deep gorge and has some
good-quality hotels and restaurants. It's also a convenient base for excursions to Capri and the Emerald Grotto. The parking problem here
is as bad as that in Positano. The small lot in the center of town fills
quickly; if you can afford the steep prices, make a luncheon reservation at one of the hotel restaurants and have your car parked for you.

Amalfi's main historical sight is its **Duomo** (Cathedral of St. Andrew), which shows an interesting mix of Moorish and early-Gothic influences. The interior is a 10th-century Romanesque skeleton in 18th-century Baroque dress. The transept and the choir date from the 13th century. The handsome 12th-century campanile has identical Gothic domes at each corner. Don't miss the beautiful late-13th-century Moorish **cloister**, with its slender double columns. At least one critic has called the cathedral's facade the ugliest piece of serious architecture in Italy—decide for yourself. The same critic snickers at the tourists who fail to note the cathedral's greatest treasure, the 11th-century bronze doors from Constantinople. Turn right out of the doors for the cloister, with whitewashed arches and palms, and a small **museum** in the adjoining crypt. ⊠ *Piazza del Duomo,* ☎ *089/871059.* 🎫 *Cloister and museum 3,000 lire/€1.55.* ☉ *Apr.–June and Oct., daily 9–7; July–Sept., daily 9–9; Nov.–Mar., daily 10–12:30 and 2:30–5:30.*

Valle dei Mulini (Valley of the Mills), uphill from town, was for centuries Amalfi's center for papermaking, an ancient trade learned from the Arabs (who learned it from the Chinese). Beginning in the 12th century, former macaroni mills in the town were converted to produce paper made from cotton and linen, being among the first in Europe to do so. In 1211 Frederick II of Sicily prohibited this lighter, more readable paper for use in the preparation of official documents, favoring traditional sheepskin parchment, but by 1811 more than a dozen mills here, with more along the coast, were humming. Natural waterpower ensured that the handmade paper was cost-effective, but catastrophic flooding in 1954 closed most of the mills for good, and many of them have now been converted into private housing. The **Museo della Carta** (Museum of Paper) opened in 1971 in a 15th-century mill; paper samples, tools of the trade, old machinery, and the audiovisual presentation are all enlightening. A 20-minute stroll from the Piazza Duomo will take you to the valley via the main thoroughfare of Via Genoa, turning onto Via Capuano at the edge of town. ⊠ *Valle dei Mulini.* 🎫 *3,000 lire/€1.55.* ☉ *Tues.–Thurs., weekends 9–1.*

Dining and Lodging

$$$–$$$$ ✕ **Da Gemma.** Amalfi's oldest restaurant, in a side street opposite the Duomo, was established in 1872 by the great-grandmother of the current owner. Here you can dine on traditional Campanian dishes surrounded by photos of Old Amalfi on the walls. Recommended choices include *zuppa di pesce* (fish soup) and the traditional Amalfi dessert, *melanzane al cioccolato* (eggplant in chocolate). ⊠ *Via Fratello Gerardo Sasso 9,* ☎ *089/871345. AE, DC, MC, V. Closed Wed. and mid-Jan.–mid-Feb.*

$$$–$$$$ ✕ **Eolo.** Built into the rocks, this restaurant, with a delightful terrace for alfresco dining, has panoramic views over Amalfi. A tank of live fish greets you at the entrance, while ceramic fish and stars from Vietri dance on the walls. Fish is of course the main feature here, complemented by the freshest local produce and homemade bread and pasta. ⊠ *Via P. Comite 3,* ☎ *089/871241. AE, DC, MC, V. Closed Tues. in Sept.–July, and Nov.–Mar.*

$$$–$$$$ ✕ **La Caravella.** You'll find this welcoming establishment tucked under arches lining the coast road, next to the medieval Arsenal, where Amalfi's mighty fleet was once provisioned. La Caravella has a nondescript entrance but a pleasant interior decorated with paintings of Old Amalfi. It's small and intimate; specialties include linguine *alla colatura di alici* (with anchovies, based on a medieval recipe) and *calamari ripieni* (stuffed squid). ⊠ *Via M. Camera 12,* ☎ *089/871029. AE, MC, V. Closed Tues. and Nov.*

$$$ ✕ **Trattoria di Maria.** This is a popular local haunt, and Enzo (son of Maria), a convivial host, creates a friendly and inviting atmosphere. Sample the delicious pizza cooked in a wood oven or enjoy local fish dishes and lemon profiteroles. Ask for a glass of the limoncello or one of the other homemade liqueurs made from bay leaves, fennel, or bilberries (similar to blueberries). ⊠ *Piazza ad Amalfi,* ☎ *089/871880. AE, DC, MC, V. Closed Mon. and Nov.*

$$$$ 🏨 **Santa Caterina.** A large mansion perched above a terraced and flow-
★ ered hillside on the coast road just outside Amalfi proper, the Santa Caterina is one of the best hotels on the entire coast, attracting the likes of Claudia Schiffer, Karl Lagerfeld, and Hillary Clinton to name only a few. The rooms are tastefully decorated; most have small terraces or balconies with great views. There are lovely lounges, gardens, and terraces for relaxing, and an elevator delivers you to the seaside saltwater pool, bar, and swimming area. On grounds lush with lemon and orange groves, there are two romantic villa annexes. ⊠ *Strada Amalfitana 9, 84011,* ☎ *089/871012,* FAX *089/871351,* WEB *www.hotelsantacaterina.it. 66 rooms. 2 restaurants, 2 bars, saltwater pool, gym, beach, meeting room, free parking. AE, DC, MC, V.*

$$$ 🏨 **La Bussola.** This capacious hotel right in the center of Amalfi is built in an old pasta factory. The rooms, most of which overlook the sea, are simply furnished, but nearly all have balconies. The lounge, bar, and restaurant areas downstairs are elegant and roomy, and the staff is extremely helpful. If you don't fancy sunbathing on the roof terrace, there's access to a private platform that serves in lieu of a beach here. ⊠ *Lungomare dei Cavalieri 16, 84011,* ☎ *089/871533,* FAX *089/871369,* WEB *www.amalficoast.it/hotel/labussola. 62 rooms. Restaurant (closed Nov.), bar, beach, meeting rooms, free parking. AE, DC, MC, V.*

$$$ 🏨 **Piccolo Paradiso.** A location in the Amalfi harbor area just across from the Arsenale already makes this upscale B&B a special choice. A small elevator deposits you in the cozy house, sunny yellow with green shutters, with a casually furnished sea-air and sun-bright terrace. The atmosphere is more pleasing and elegant than that of a typical pensione. A common area has tile flooring, and rooms are smallish but comfortable, with wicker seating and wrought-iron headboards, even some private terraces. ⊠ *Via M. Camera 5, 84011,* ☎ *089/873001. 5 rooms. No credit cards.*

$$–$$$ 🏨 **Hotel dei Cavalieri.** This terraced white Mediterranean-style hotel on the main road outside Amalfi has three villa annexes on grounds just across the road that extend all the way to a beach below. Bright rooms are functionally furnished, with splashy majolica tile floors. An ample buffet breakfast is served. ⊠ *Via M. Comite 32, 84011,* ☎ *089/ 831333,* FAX *089/831354,* WEB *www.hoteldeicavalieri.it. 54 rooms. Restaurant (May–Oct.), bar, air-conditioning. AE, DC, MC, V.*

Shopping

Drop in on **Antonio Cavaliere** (⊠ Via Fiume, ☎ 089/871954), an elderly resident still making paper by hand, with products for sale. You'll find paper creations, maps, and other souvenirs near the Duomo at **Amalfi nelle Stampe Antiche** (⊠ Piazza Duomo 10, ☎ 089/872368).

Ravello

★ 🔟 *5 km (3 mi) northeast of Amalfi, 40 km (25 mi) east of Sorrento.*

Perched on a ridge high above Amalfi and the neighboring town of Atrani, the enchanting village of Ravello has stupendous views, quiet lanes, two important Romanesque churches, and several irresistibly romantic gardens. Set "closer to the sky than the sea," according to André Gide, the town has been the ultimate aerie ever since it was founded as a smart suburb for the richest families of Amalfi's 12th-century maritime republic. Rediscovered by English aristocrats a century ago, the town now hosts one of Italy's most famous music festivals.

Here, pride of place is taken by the **Duomo,** or town cathedral, dedicated to patron saint Pantaleone and founded in 1086 by Orso Papiro, the first bishop of Ravello. Rebuilt in the 12th and 17th centuries, it retains traces of medieval frescoes in the transept, an original mullioned window, a marble portal, and a three-story 13th-century bell tower playfully interwoven with mullioned windows and arches. The 12th-century bronze door (1179) features 54 embossed panels depicting Christ's life, and saints, prophets, plants, and animals, all narrating biblical lore. It was crafted by Barisano da Trani, who also fashioned the doors of the cathedrals of Train and Monreale. The nave's three aisles are divided by ancient columns, and treasures include sarcophagi from Roman times and paintings by southern Renaissance artist Andrea da Salerno. Most impressive are the two 12th-century *ambos,* or pulpits: The earliest one, used for reading the Epistles, is inset with a mosaic scene of Jonah and the whale, symbolizing death and redemption. The more famous one, used for reading the Gospels, was commissioned by Nicolo Rufolo in 1272 and created by Niccolo di Bartolomeo da Foggia. An eagle grandly tops the colonnette fronting the inlaid marble lectern. Here in 1149, Adrian IV, the English pope, crowned William the Bad, king of Sicily.

A chapel is dedicated to the left of the apse to St. Pantaleone, a physician, who was beheaded in the 3rd century in Nicomedia. Every July 27 devout believers gather in hope of witnessing a miracle (similar to that of St. Gennaro in Naples), in which the saint's blood, collected in a vial and set out on an inlaid marble altar, appears to liquefy and come to a boil (it hasn't happened in recent years). In the crypt is the **Museo del Duomo,** which displays treasures from around the 13th century, during the reign of Frederick II of Sicily, in an elegant setting. ⊠ *Museo del Duomo, Piazza del Duomo.* 🖃 *2000 lire/€1.05.* ☉ *Summer, daily 9–1 and 3–7.*

★ Directly off the main piazza is the **Villa Rufolo,** built in the 13th century by Landolfo Rufolo, whose immense fortune stemmed from trade with Moors and Saracens. Within is a scene from the earliest days of the Crusades. Norman and Arab architecture mingle in profusion in a welter of color-filled gardens so lush that composer Richard Wagner used them as his inspiration for the home of the Flower Maidens in his opera *Parsifal.* Beyond the Arab-Sicilian cloister and the Norman tower are two flower-bedded terraces that offer a splendid vista of the Bay of
★ Salerno; the lower "Wagner Terrace" is the site for the year-long **Festival Musicale di Ravello** (for information, contact the Ravello Concert Society, ☎ 089/858149 or 081/857657, FAX 089/858249). ⊠ *Piazza Vescovado, 84010.* 🖃 *6,000 lire/€3.10.* ☉ *Daily 9–sunset.*

From Ravello's main piazza, head west along Via San Francesco and
★ Via Santa Chiara to the **Villa Cimbrone,** a medieval-style fantasy that sits 1,500 ft above the sea. Created in 1905 by England's Lord Grimthorpe and made world-famous when Greta Garbo stayed here in 1937, the Gothic *castello-palazzo* is set in fragrant rose gardens that lead to the **Belvedere of Infinity,** a grand stone parapet that overlooks the impossibly blue Gulf of Salerno and frames a panorama that noted writer and Ravello resident Gore Vidal has called "the most beautiful in the world." The villa itself is now a hotel. ⊠ *Via Santa Chiara 26,* ☎ *089/857459.* 🖃 *8,000 lire/€4.15.* ☉ *Daily 9–sunset.*

Dining and Lodging

$$ **✕ Cumpà Cosimo.** This family-run restaurant a few steps from the cathe-
★ dral square offers a cordial welcome in two simple but attractive din-
ing rooms. There's no view, but the food is excellent, most of it coming
from owner Donna Netta's garden or her butcher shop next door. Among
the specialties are cheese crepes, roast lamb, and a dish including seven
types of homemade pasta. ⊠ *Via Roma 44,* ☎ *089/857156. AE, DC,
MC, V. Closed Mon. in Jan.–Mar.*

$$ **✕ Vittoria.** Between the Duomo and the gardens of the Villa Rufulo,
this is a good place for a return to reality and an informal bite. Vitto-
ria's thin-crust pizza with loads of fresh toppings is the star attraction,
and locals praise it *molto.* But also try the pasta, maybe fusilli with
tomatoes, zucchini, and mozzarella. Decor is extremely simple, with
white walls and a few etchings of Ravello. ⊠ *Via dei Rufulo 3,* ☎ *089/
857947. AE, DC, MC, V. Closed Tues.*

$$$$ **🏨 Hotel Palumbo.** Occupying a 12th-century patrician palace furnished with antiques and outfitted with modern comforts, this hotel
has an elegant, warm atmosphere that gives you the feeling of being a
guest in a lovely private home, under the personal care of courtly host
Signor Vuilleumier. With beautiful garden terraces, breathtaking views,
and a sumptuous upstairs dining room, the hotel is a memorable one.
Guest rooms in the modern annex are considerably cheaper. Note that
half-board is compulsory, except in winter, when the restaurant is
closed. ⊠ *Palazzo Confalone, Via San Giovanni del Toro 16, 84010,*
☎ *089/857244,* 𝔽𝔸𝕏 *089/858133,* 𝕎𝔼𝔹 *www.hotel-palumbo.it. 20 rooms.
Restaurant (closed Nov.–Easter), bar. AE, DC, MC, V. MAP.*

$$$$ **🏨 Palazzo Sasso.** In this 12th-century palace, inhabited in the 18th
century by the aristocratic Sasso family, Wagner penned part of his opera
Parsifal in the 1880s, and in the 1950s the Sasso family hosted Ingrid
Bergman and Roberto Rossellini. On reopening in July 1997, after a
20-year hiatus, the hotel is still luring the glitterati—its first guests were
Placido Domingo and his entourage. Ordinary mortals, too, can come
for a peek at the marble atrium and lofty coastal views. All of the individually designed guest rooms are immaculately furnished, with the
latest computer-operated lighting systems, but extra-special rooms include 201, for its wide terrace, and 213, for its architectural detail. The
rooftop terrace has two hot tubs. The Rossellini restaurant is also nothing
to sneeze at; it is open to nonresidents. ⊠ *Via San Giovanni del Toro
28, 84010,* ☎ *089/818181,* 𝔽𝔸𝕏 *089/858900,* 𝕎𝔼𝔹 *www.palazzosasso.com.
38 rooms, 5 suites. Restaurant, bar, pool, outdoor hot tub, library. AE,
DC, MC, V. Closed Nov.–Feb.*

$$$$ **🏨 Villa Cimbrone.** This magical place will take your breath away: sus-
★ pended over the azure sea and set amid rose-laden gardens, it was once
the home of Lord Grimthorpe and the holiday hideaway of Greta
Garbo. Now exquisitely transformed into a hotel, the Gothic-style *castello*
has guest rooms ranging from palatial to cozy (opt for the Peony
Room, which has its own terrace). The villa is a strenuous hike from
the town center. ⊠ *Via Santa Chiara 26, 84010,* ☎ *089/857459,* 𝔽𝔸𝕏
089/857777, 𝕎𝔼𝔹 *www.villacimbrone.it. 13 rooms. Breakfast room, minibars, library. AE, DC, MC, V. Closed Nov.–Easter.*

$$$–$$$$ **🏨 Caruso Belvedere.** Charmingly old-fashioned, spacious, and com-
★ fortable, this rambling villa hotel has plenty of character and a full share
of Ravello's spectacular views from its terraces and balconied rooms.
Relax in the garden belvedere with its memorable vistas. The restau-
rant is known for fine food and locally made house wine. It's hoped
that a major refurbishment will have been completed by the end of 2001.
⊠ *Via Toro 52, 84010,* ☎ *089/857111,* 𝔽𝔸𝕏 *089/857372. 24 rooms.
Restaurant, room service, baby-sitting, laundry service, free parking.
AE, DC, MC, V.*

$$ 🏨 **Villa Amore.** A 10-minute walk from the Piazza Duomo, this hotel is family run, with a garden and an exhilarating view of the sea from most of its bedrooms. If you're looking for tranquillity, you've found it, especially at dusk, when the valley is tinged with a glorious purple light. Rooms are small, with modest if modern furnishings, and one of the treats at breakfast is delicious homemade jam. Full board is available here, and at least half-board is required in the summer. Reserve ahead, and specify time of arrival if you need help with luggage from the parking lot or bus stop (you pay 7,000/€3.60 lire per bag). ✉ *Via Santa Chiara, 84010,* ☎ 🆁🆇 *089/857135. 12 rooms. Restaurant, bar. DC, MC, V. FAP.*

Vietri sul Mare

51 *20 km (12 mi) east of Amalfi, 60 km (37 mi) east of Sorrento.*

This Amalfi Coast town is a major ceramics center, and its distinctive pottery, with sunny motifs and bright colors, is sold in towns along the coast. The shops and factories are concentrated in the lively Old Town, surrounding a majolica-domed church, but the seafront below is dull.

Shopping

CERAMICS

Many small shops in Vietri sul Mare offer goods from local pottery workshops. You can pick over all kinds of wares at the **Solimene works** (✉ Vietri sul Mare).

Salerno

52 *6 km (4 mi) east of Vietri sul Mare, 56 km (35 mi) southeast of Naples.*

Spread out along its bay, Salerno was long a sad testimony to years of neglect and overdevelopment, but the antique port is now reevaluating its artistic heritage. It makes an ideal base for exploring the Cilento area to the south, which boasts such lovely sea resorts as Castellabate and Palinuro, and inland some fine mountain walks and spectacular gorges and caves, such as Castelcivita and Pertosa.

Salerno itself has an imposing **Romanesque cathedral,** built in 1085 and remodeled in the 18th century with Byzantine doors (1099) from Constantinople and an outstanding 12th-century pulpit. ✉ *Via Duomo* ☎ *089/231387.* ☉ *Daily 8–noon and 4–7.*

In the **Museo Diocesano,** behind the cathedral, is a collection of medieval carved tablets. ✉ *Piazza Plebiscito,* ☎ *089/239126.* 🆁 *Free.* ☉ *Daily 9–6:30.*

Occupying two floors of the **Abbazia di San Benedetto** (San Benedetto Monastery), the **Museo Provinciale** houses a handsome bronze head of Apollo fished out of the bay in the 1930s. ✉ *Via San Benedetto,* ☎ *089/231135.* 🆁 *Free.* ☉ *Mon.–Sat. 9–1 and 4:30–7:30, Sun. 9–1.*

Lodging

$$ 🏨 **Plaza.** This central hotel, in a quiet residential area convenient to the train station, is modern and uncluttered. The interior is decorated in warm, mellow tones throughout, and guest rooms are spacious, some with air-conditioning and all with TVs. Breakfast costs an additional 10,000 lire/€5.15 extra. ✉ *Piazza Vittorio Veneto 42, 84123,* ☎ 🆁🆇 *089/224477. 42 rooms. Breakfast room, lobby lounge, air-conditioning. AE, DC, MC, V.*

$ 🖵 **Santa Rosa.** This small, family-run pensione-style hotel near the train station offers simple and friendly accommodation on a second floor. Note that breakfast is not provided, and there are no TVs in the rooms. ⊠ *Corso Vittorio Emanuele 14, 84123,* ☏ ⅭAX *089/225346. 12 rooms, 6 with bath.*

Paestum

★ ⑤ *42 km (26 mi) southeast of Salerno, 99 km (62 mi) southeast of Naples.*

One of Italy's most majestic sights lies on the edge of a flat coastal plain: the remarkably well preserved **Greek temples** of Paestum. S18 from the north passes the train station (Stazione di Paestum), which is about 800 yards from the ruins, through the perfectly preserved archway **Porta Sirena.** The ruins stand on the site of the ancient city of Poseidonia, founded by Greek colonists in the 7th century BC. When the Romans took over the colony in 273 BC and called it Paestum, they enlarged the settlement, adding an amphitheater and a forum. Much of the archaeological material found on the site is displayed in the **Museo Nazionale,** and several rooms are devoted to the unique tomb paintings discovered in the area, rare examples of Greek and pre-Roman pictorial art. About 200 yards from the museum (in front of the main entrance), framed by banks of roses and oleanders, is the **Tempio di Poseidone** (Temple of Poseidon), a magnificent Doric edifice, with 36 fluted columns and an extraordinarily well preserved entablature. Greece itself does not have such a fine monument of Hellenic architecture. To the left of the temple is the so-called **Basilica,** the earliest of Paestum's standing edifices; it dates from very early in the 6th century BC. The name is an 18th-century misnomer, for the structure was in fact a temple sacred to Hera, the wife of Zeus. Behind it, an ancient road leads to the **Foro Romano** (Roman forum) and the single column of the **Tempio della Pace** (Temple of Peace). Beyond is the **Tempio di Cerere** (Temple of Ceres). Try to see the temples in the late afternoon, when the light enhances the deep gold of the stone and the air is pierced with the cries of the crows that nest high on the temples. ☏ *0828/811023.* 🖾 *Excavations 8,000 lire/€4.15, museum 8,000 lire/€4.15.* ☉ *Excavations July–Sept., daily 9 AM–10 PM; Oct.–June, daily 9–1 hr before sunset. Museum July–Sept., daily 9 AM–10 PM; Oct.– June, daily 9–6:30; closed 1st and 3rd Mon. of each month.*

Dining and Lodging

$$ ✕🖵 **Helios.** Directly across the road from the Porta della Giustizia and only a few steps from the temples, the Helios has cottage-type rooms in a garden setting. Seven rooms have whirlpool baths. A pleasant restaurant serves local specialties and seafood. The home-produced ricotta and mozzarella are especially recommended. ⊠ *Via Principe di Piemonte 1, Zona Archeologica, 84063,* ☏ *0828/811451,* ⅭAX *0828/811600. 27 rooms. Restaurant, pool. AE, DC, MC, V.*

CAMPANIA A TO Z

To research prices, get advice from other travelers, and book travel arrangements, visit www.fodors.com.

AIRPORTS

Aeroporto Capodichino, 8 km (5 mi) north of Naples, serves the Campania region. It handles domestic and international flights, including several daily between Naples and Rome (flight time 45 minutes). From May to September there is direct helicopter service with Cab Air between Aeroporto Capodichino and Capri or Ischia. The cost is about 1,760,000 lire/€915, with larger copters running 2,530,000/€1,315.

Taxis are available at the airport for the ride downtown (about 30,000 lire/€15.60), or else there is a private bus service, CLP, leaving roughly every hour with stops at Piazza Garibaldi and Piazza Muncipio (3,000 lire/€1.55). The more frequent but slightly slower buses 14 and 15 also ply the route to Piazza Garibaldi (tickets from the newsagent inside the airport run 1,500 lire/€0.78).

➤ AIRPORT INFORMATION: **Aeroporto Capodichino** (☎ 081/7896259). **Cab Air** (☎ 081/5844355 or 081/2587110). **CLP (Consorzio Linee Provinciali)** (☎ 081/5311646).

BOAT AND FERRY TRAVEL

Hydrofoils and passenger and car ferries connect the islands of Capri and Ischia with Naples and Pozzuoli year-round. In summer, Capri and Ischia are serviced by boats from the Amalfi Coast. Boats and hydrofoils for these islands and for Sorrento leave from Naples's Molo Beverello. They also leave from Mergellina.

Information on departures is available at the tourist office or at the port, or contact the companies—Caremar, Navigazione Libera del Golfo, SNAV, and Alilauro—directly. Always double-check schedules in stormy weather. The Coop Sant'Andrea, a boat company based in Amalfi, organizes trips to many places along the coast, as well as special disco and fireworks cruises.

FARES AND SCHEDULES

➤ BOAT AND FERRY INFORMATION: **Alilauro** (☎ 081/5522838). **Caremar** (☎ 081/5513882). **Coop Sant'Andrea** (☎ 089/873190). **Mergellina** (✉ about 1½ km [1 mi] to the west of Piazza Municipio). **Molo Beverello** (✉ southeast of Piazza Municipio). **Navigazione Libera del Golfo** (NLG; ☎ 081/5527209). **SNAV** (☎ 081/7612348).

BUS TRAVEL

Marozzi, a Rome-based line, runs direct, air-conditioned buses from Rome to Pompeii, Salerno, Sorrento, and Amalfi. Buses leave Rome's Stazione Tiburtina weekdays at 3 PM, weekends at 7 AM.

There is an extensive network of local buses in Naples and throughout Campania. ACTP buses connect Naples with Caserta in one hour, leaving every 20 minutes from Piazza Garibaldi in Naples (every 40 minutes on Sunday). There are six buses a day Monday to Saturday from Piazza Garibaldi to Benevento. The trip takes 90 minutes. SITA buses for Salerno leave every 30 minutes Monday to Saturday and every two hours on Sunday from the SITA terminal on Via Pisanelli. SITA buses also serve the Amalfi Coast, connecting Sorrento with Salerno. Curreri operates a service between Sorrento and Aeroporto Capodichino.

➤ BUS INFORMATION: **ACTP** (☎ 081/7001111). **Curreri** (☎ 081/8015420). **Marozzi** (☎ 06/4076140). **SITA** (✉ Via Pisanelli, near Piazza Municipio, ☎ 081/5522176).

CAR RENTAL

➤ LOCAL AGENCIES: **Avis** (✉ Stazione FS, Caserta, ☎ 0823/443756; ✉ Stazione Centrale, Naples, ☎ 081/5537171; ✉ Via Piedigrotta 44, Naples, ☎ 081/7611365; ✉ Viale Nizza 53, Sorrento, ☎ 081/8782459). **Hertz** (✉ Via G. Bosco, Caserta, ☎ 0823/356383; ✉ Aeroporto Capodichino, Naples, ☎ 081/7802971; ✉ Piazza Garibaldi 91/b, Naples, ☎ 081/206228; ✉ Garage Di Leva, Via degli Aranci 9, Sorrento, ☎ 081/8071646).

CAR TRAVEL

Italy's main north–south route, the A2 (also known as the Autostrada del Sole), connects Rome with Naples and Campania. In good traffic the drive to Naples takes less than three hours. Autostrada A3, a southern continuation of the A2 from Rome, runs through Campania and into Calabria. It also connects with the autostrada A16 to Bari, which passes Avellino and is linked with Benevento by expressway. Take S18 south from Naples for Herculaneum, Pompeii, and the Sorrento peninsula; for the Sorrento peninsula and the Amalfi Coast, exit at Castellammare di Stabia. To get to Paestum, take A3 to the Battipaglia exit and take the road to Capaccio Scalo–Paestum.

GARAGES
In Naples, Garage dei Fiori is near Villa Pignatelli, Grilli is near Stazione Centrale, and Turistico is near the port.
➤ CONTACTS: **Garage dei Fiori** (⊠ Via Colonna 21, ☎ 081/414190). **Grilli** (⊠ Via Ferraris 40, ☎ 081/264344). **Turistico** (⊠ Via de Gasperi 14, ☎ 081/5525442).

ROAD CONDITIONS
All roads on the Sorrento peninsula and Amalfi Coast are narrow, serpentine, and tortuous, but they have outstanding views. In high season, from about April through October, only residents' cars are allowed on Ischia and Capri.

EMBASSIES AND CONSULATES
➤ UNITED KINGDOM: **U.K. Consulate** (⊠ Via Crispi 122, Naples, ☎ 081/663511).
➤ UNITED STATES: **U.S. Consulate** (⊠ Piazza della Repubblica 2, Naples, ☎ 081/5838111).

EMERGENCIES
➤ CONTACTS: **Police** (☎ 112). **Ambulance** (in Naples, ☎ 081/7520696, 081/7528282, or 081/7520850).
➤ PHARMACIES: **Farmacia Helvethia** (⊠ Piazza Garibaldi 11, opposite Stazione Centrale, ☎ 081/5548894).

ENGLISH-LANGUAGE MEDIA
The monthly *Qui Napoli,* free from tourist offices, has useful information on museums, exhibitions, and transportation.

MAIL AND SHIPPING
➤ POST OFFICES: **Naples Main Post Office** (⊠ Piazza Matteotti, off Via Toledo, ☎ 081/5511456).

OVERNIGHT SERVICES
UPS has a location in Casoria, near Naples, but shipping services should be arranged using the toll-free number. Federal Express doesn't have a Naples office but works in conjunction with the service SDA. The main Naples post office is open Monday–Saturday 9 to 7.
➤ MAJOR SERVICES: **Federal Express** (☎ 02/25088001; 800/123800 toll free). **SDA** (⊠ Via Botteghelle di Portici 203/a, Naples, ☎ 081/2583411). **UPS** (⊠ Via Pascoli 8, Casoria, ☎ 02/25088001; 800/877877 toll free).

SAFETY
LOCAL SCAMS
The main risks in Naples are purse-snatching and car break-ins.

SUBWAY TRAVEL
Naples's rather old Metropolitana (subway system) provides frequent service and can be the fastest way to get across the traffic-clogged city. Tickets cost 1,500 lire/€0.80, and trains run from 5 AM until midnight.
➤ SUBWAY INFORMATION: **FS** (☎ 147/888088).

TOURS

The Associazione di Donnaregina, run by two Neapolitan artists, organizes small group tours (six to eight people) of Naples and surroundings, offering insights into the culture, traditions, and lesser-known places of the region. Other operators include Carrani Tours, Milleviaggi, Tourcar, and STS.

➤ CONTACTS: **Associazione di Donnaregina** (✉ Via Luigi Settembrini 80, Naples, ☎ 081/446799 or 0338/6401301). **Carrani Tours** (✉ Via Vittorio Emanuele Orlando 95, Rome, ☎ 06/4880510 or 06/4742501). **Milleviaggi** (✉ Riviera di Chiaia 252, Naples, ☎ 081/7642064). **Tourcar** (✉ Piazza Matteotti 1, Naples, ☎ 081/5520429). **STS** (✉ Piazza Medaglie d'Oro 41, Naples, ☎ 081/5789292).

TRAIN TRAVEL

There are trains every hour between Rome and Naples. Intercity trains make the trip in less than two hours. Trains take either the inland route (through Cassino) or go along the coast (via Formia). Intercity and express trains to Naples stop at Stazione Centrale.

A network of suburban trains connects Naples with several points of interest. The line used most by visitors is the Circumvesuviana, which runs from Corso Garibaldi Station and stops at Stazione Centrale before continuing to Ercolano (Herculaneum), Pompeii, and Sorrento. Frequent local trains connect Naples with Caserta and Salerno. Travel time between Naples and Sorrento on the Circumvesuviana line is one hour. Benevento is on the main line between Naples and Foggia. The Circumflegrea runs from Piazza Montesanto Station in Naples to the archaeological zone of Cumae, with three departures in the morning. The Ferrovia Cumana runs from Piazza Montesanto Station to Pozzuoli and Baia.

➤ TRAIN INFORMATION: **Circumflegrea** (☎ 081/5513328). **Circumvesuviana** (☎ 081/7722444). **Ferrovia Cumana** (☎ 081/5513328). **Stazione Centrale** (✉ Piazza Garibaldi, ☎ 147/888088).

VISITOR INFORMATION

The EPT (Ente Provinciale per il Turismo) handles information for the province—which in this case could be the province of Naples or that of Salerno—while information offices run by the local tourist organizations are more ubiquitous, though they cover much the same ground.

➤ TOURIST INFORMATION: **EPT** (✉ Piazza dei Martiri 58, 80121 Naples, ☎ 081/405311; ✉ Stazione Centrale, 80142 Naples, ☎ 081/268779; ✉ Stazione Mergellina, 80122 Naples, ☎ 081/7612102; ✉ Aeroporto Capodichino, 80133 Naples, ☎ 081/7805761, WEB www.ept.napoli.it). **Amalfi** (✉ Corso delle Repubbliche 27, 84011, ☎ 089/871107). **Benevento** (✉ Piazza Roma, 82100, ☎ 0824/319938). **Capri** (✉ Marina Grande pier, 80073, ☎ 081/8370634; ✉ Capri Town, Piazza Umberto I, 80073, ☎ 081/8370686, WEB www.capritourism.com). **Caserta** (✉ Piazza Dante, 81100, ☎ 0823/321137). **Ercolano** (✉ Via 4 Novembre 82, 80056, ☎ 081/7881243). **Naples** (✉ Piazza del Gesù, 80135, ☎ 081/5523328). **Pompeii** (✉ Via Sacra 1, 80045, ☎ 081/8507255). **Porto d'Ischia** (✉ Via Iasolino, Porto Salvo, 80077, ☎ 081/5074231). **Ravello** (✉ Piazza Duomo, 84010, ☎ 089/857096). **Salerno** (✉ Piazza Vittorio Veneto, 84100, ☎ 800/213289 toll free in Italy, 089/231432; WEB www.crmpa.it/ept). **Sorrento** (✉ Via de Maio 35, 80067, ☎ 081/8074033, WEB www.sorrentotourism.com).

13 APULIA AND MOLISE

BARI, GARGANO PROMONTORY,
TRULLI DISTRICT, LECCE, ISERNIA

Steeped in relics from millennia of history,
Apulia invites intrepid exploration of its
whitewashed ports, imposing castles, and
trulli, strange beehive-shape dwellings. The
cities of Brindisi and Bari have fascinating
medieval centers, although the real cultural
gem is the Baroque city of Lecce. To the west,
the region of Molise has long lived in the
shadow of its more glamorous neighbor. This
has thankfully spared the region many of the
ravages of late-20th-century development,
preserving the area's natural attractions and
archaeological sites.

Updated by
Mark Walters

ONCE MERELY ASSOCIATED WITH TRAIN OR CAR JOURNEYS for Greece-bound travelers, Apulia (called Puglia by the Italians—English speakers are really using the Latin term) has now gained credentials as a destination in its own right.

This ancient land, the heel and spur of Italy's boot, has some of the country's most unspoiled scenery, most fascinating artistic and historical sites, and finest beaches. What's more, beyond the increasingly popular seaside resorts and the few major sights lies sunbaked countryside where expanses of silvery olive trees and giant prickly-pear cacti fight their way through the rocky soil, as if in defiance of the relentless summer heat. Local buildings, too, do their best to dispel the effects of the sun: whitewashed ports stand coolly over the turquoise Mediterranean; the landscape is studded with the odd stone *trulli,* curious limestone structures dating from the Middle Ages.

Apulia had long before then been inhabited, conquered, and visited. On sea voyages to their colonies and trading posts in the west, the ancient Greeks invariably headed for Apulia first—it was the shortest crossing—before filtering southward into Sicily and westward to the Tyrrhenian coast. In turn, the Romans—often bound in the opposite direction—were quick to recognize the importance of this strategic peninsula. Later centuries were to see a procession of other nations raiding or colonizing Apulia: Byzantines, Saracens, Normans, Swabians, Turks, and Spaniards all swept through at some stage, each group leaving its mark. Romanesque churches and the powerful castles built by 13th-century Holy Roman Emperor Frederick II of Swabia (part of present-day Bavaria), king of Sicily and Jerusalem, are among the most impressive of the buildings in the region. Frederick II, dubbed *Stupor mundi* (Wonder of the World) for his wide-ranging interests in literature, science, mathematics, and nature, was an outstanding personality in the Middle Ages.

The last 50 years have seen a huge economic revival after the centuries of neglect that followed Apulia's golden age under the Normans and Swabians. Having benefited from EU and state incentive programs and subsidies for irrigation, Apulia is now Italy's biggest producer of wine, with most of the rest of the land devoted to olives, citrus fruits, and vegetables. The main ports of Bari, Brindisi, and Taranto are lively and economically thriving centers, though there remain serious problems of unemployment and poverty. However, the much publicized arrival of thousands of asylum seekers from Eastern Europe and beyond has not significantly destabilized these cities, as had been feared, and the economic and political refugees have been dispersed throughout Italy. Compared with neighboring Albania a mere 70 km (44 mi) away across the Straits of Otranto, Apulia oozes with prosperity: it is blessed with plenty of high-quality restaurants and shops, though don't always expect to find an abundance of lodging facilities outside the business circuit.

Though bypassed by the Appian Way under the Roman Empire and with the main towns of Isernia and Campobasso still relatively isolated from Italy's north–south network of *autostrade,* the region of Molise is no backwater. This was homeland to the Samnites, who, according to the Romans at least, were warlike and ungovernable. Fortunately the Samnites have bequeathed some wondrous archaeological sites in breathtaking settings, while the benign influence of subsequent millennia have ensured that you'll enjoy the region's good cultural pedigree in a fairly unspoiled environment.

Pleasures and Pastimes

Beaches

Italians and foreign visitors alike return summer after summer to Apulia, drawn by the sea. Though no longer "undiscovered," the shores of the Gargano Promontory offer safe swimming and sandy beaches. The whole coastline between Bari and Brindisi is well served with beach facilities. In even the smallest villages you'll find beaches with changing rooms and—essential in the blazing Apulian sun—beach umbrellas. If you don't mind venturing farther afield, Gallipoli, on the south coast of the heel, has exceptional strands.

Dining

Anyone who likes to eat will find pleasure in Apulia, where the cuisine has evolved from more than 2,000 years of foreign influences. Southern cuisine is hearty and healthy, based around homemade pastas and cheeses, fresh vegetables, seafood, and local olive oil. Open-air markets and delicatessens overflow with local fruits, vegetables, pastries, sausages, smoked meats, and cheeses. Here you will find dishes unavailable elsewhere in Italy, such as *'ncapriata,* also called *favi e fogghi* (a first-course fava-bean puree with bitter chicory or other cooked vegetables). Focaccia *barese* (stuffed with fried onions, black olives, anchovies, and ricotta) makes a great snack or lunch.

Apulia's pasta specialties include *orecchiette* (ear-shape pasta), *troccoli* (homemade noodles cut with a special ridged rolling pin), and *strascenate* (rectangles of pasta with one rough side and one smooth side). Among the many typical sauces is *salsa alla Sangiovanniello* (sauce of olive oil, capers, anchovies, parsley, and hot peppers) from Brindisi. Don't miss the dairy products, such as ricotta and buttery *burrata* cheese. And be sure to sample Apulia's wealth of excellent local wines, ranging from the strong white wine of Martina Franca to the sweet white Moscato di Trani, from the rich dry red Castel del Monte to the sweet red Aleatico di Puglia.

In smaller, family-run restaurants and *trattorie,* don't expect to find menus. You are likely to get a verbal list of exotic-sounding dishes; ordering is largely an act of faith in the chef's bravura.

For general information and price categories, *see* Dining *in* Smart Travel Tips A to Z.

Festivals

In keeping with the provincial nature of Apulia, the arts take on a folk flavor, with processions on religious occasions more prevalent than performing arts in theaters or opera houses. Still, there are some good festivals and pageants to help broaden your experience of life in Italy's deep south. The best newspaper for listings is the daily *Gazzetta del Mezzogiorno* (www.gdmland.it), which covers the entire region. Local crafts range from lace, wood carvings, and baskets to ceramic pots and painted clay whistles.

Lodging

Outside the larger cities, hotel accommodations are limited and modest—both in amenities and price—though this may be more than compensated for by friendly service. Along the miles of sandy beaches on the Gargano spur and elsewhere on the coast, big, white, Mediterranean-style beach hotels have sprung up in profusion. Most are similar in design, price, and quality. In summer, many cater only to guests paying full board (lodging plus three meals per day) or half board (lodging plus breakfast and one other meal) for longer stays. If you are traveling to the Gargano Promontory in summer, you should reserve through a travel agent to avoid complications with limited lodging and public transportation. During Easter, rooms in the Alberobello area may be at a premium.

In some cases, such as when visiting Bari during the annual Trade Fair in September, you must make reservations. Throughout the region, hotels are often booked up with commercial travelers, so reserve well in advance. Many establishments, particularly the beach resorts, close during the winter months. And remember that in a region like this—blazing hot in summer and bitter cold in winter—air-conditioning and central heating are important.

Agriturismo in Apulia is an increasingly popular lodging—and dining—option. Most farms offering accommodation are listed at local tourist information offices, and they vary widely in cost, facilities, and English-language competence. But this may be the closest you get to experiencing the trademark Apulian rural lifestyle.

For general information and price categories, *see* Lodging *in* Smart Travel Tips A to Z.

Shopping

Apulia is rich in folk art, reflecting the influences of the many nations that have passed through the region or ruled it. Don't expect boutiques; instead, look for handmade goods, such as pottery with traditional designs, baskets, textiles, and carved-wood figures, at modest shops and open-air markets, where some bargaining can enter into the purchase.

Exploring Apulia

Driving is the best way to get around the region. The autostrada and superstrada networks connect the hubs of Bari and Brindisi and the smaller towns. If you are mainly interested in spending time at the beach, the Gargano Promontory is lined with some of Apulia's best coastline, although there are pleasant beach resorts within easy reach of most of the region's attractions. Convenient travel bases include Alberobello and Martina Franca in the trulli country; Lecce and Otranto near the tip of the heel; and the small coastal towns of Trani and Polignano, within easy reach of Bari.

Bari and Brindisi are notorious for purse-snatchings, car thefts, and break-ins. If you are driving in these cities, do not leave valuables in the car or trunk, and find a guarded parking space if possible.

Numbers in the text correspond to numbers in the margin and on the Apulia and Bari maps.

Great Itineraries

Apulia's attractions are so varied and scattered that you may want to take a full week or more to explore it at a leisurely pace, selecting two or three bases in different parts of the region and taking day trips to nearby sights.

IF YOU HAVE 3 DAYS
With three days in Apulia, you should make the southeastern part of the region your priority. If your first landfall in Apulia is ⊞ **Bari** ①–③, leave on the Brindisi road and head into the trulli district toward ⊞ **Martina Franca** ㉒ or ⊞ **Alberobello** ⑱, good bases for the first night. Then make for your second base, ⊞ **Lecce** ㉕, spending the day in this glorious Baroque town. On the morning of the third day, explore the Salentine peninsula, visiting the well-preserved historic towns of ⊞ **Gallipoli** ㉗ and ⊞ **Otranto** ㉖.

Apulia

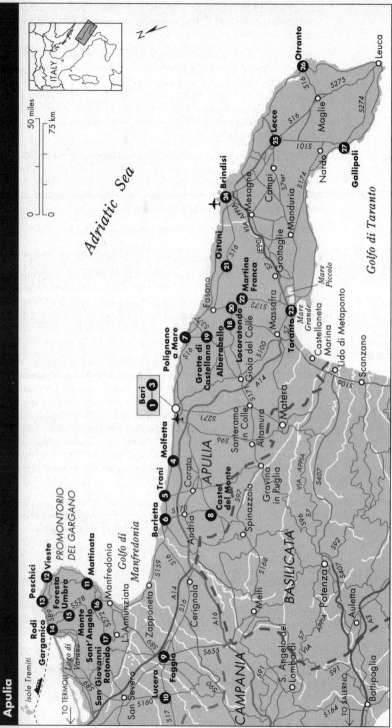

IF YOU HAVE 5 DAYS

Spend a couple of days exploring the forested **Gargano Promontory** ⑨–
⑰ and the coastline northwest of **Bari** ①–③ along the Adriatic. Take the
coast road (S16) from Bari toward **Trani** ⑤, a historic port with a famed
waterside cathedral. After **Barletta** ⑥, the coast road (S159) heads northwest through abandoned salt pans and marshes, now nature preserves
of international importance. The seaside fishing villages–cum–resorts of
the Gargano Promontory— 🏨 **Vieste** ⑫, 🏨 **Peschici** ⑬, and 🏨 **Rodi Garganico** ⑭—offer the best choice of accommodations, although 🏨 **Foggia** ⑨ and nearby 🏨 **Lucera** ⑩ make good bases, too. Aim to spend your
fourth night in 🏨 **Alberobello** ⑱, the capital of trulli country—touristy,
but engaging—or in whitewashed **Ostuni** ㉑. From Alberobello, it's a short
run to **Taranto** ㉓ for a look around the archaeological museum. Break
your journey for an hour or two in **Brindisi** ㉔, stopping at the famous
column marking the end of the Via Appia, but save your last night for
the Salentine peninsula and 🏨 **Lecce** ㉕, a treat that will provide some
of your most abiding memories of Apulia.

IF YOU HAVE 7 DAYS

For a more in-depth visit to Apulia, choose 🏨 **Polignano a Mare** ⑦ as
your base, an atmospheric seaside town with good road and rail links
with the regional capital. Having devoted about a half day to **Bari** ①–
③, venture up to the Gargano Promontory. A car is indispensable since
transport connections are tortuous and slow, but be prepared to abandon it for a half-day ramble through the **Foresta Umbra** ⑮ and **Monte
Sant'Angelo** ⑯, dominated by a large Norman castle that was once host
to crusaders setting off for the East, and **San Giovanni Rotondo** ⑰. Proceed down the Adriatic Coast back toward Bari, with a stopover in
Trani ⑤, perhaps taking in the fine cathedrals of **Barletta** ⑥ and **Molfetta** ④, and making an inland detour to view the fascinatingly geometri-
cal **Castel del Monte** ⑧. Head southeast toward trulli country, spending
a night in 🏨 **Alberobello** ⑱ or 🏨 **Martina Franca** ㉒. At some point take
a trip underground at the **Grotte di Castellana** ⑲, a soothing respite from
the summer heat. The bustling cities of **Taranto** ㉓ and **Brindisi** ㉔ are
worth a stop for their archaeological relics. Spend your last two nights
in the heel of Italy, dividing your time between the Baroque pleasures
of 🏨 **Lecce** ㉕ (your best lodging option from October through March)
and the seaside town of 🏨 **Otranto** ㉖ or 🏨 **Gallipoli** ㉗ (both of which
are good for overnights in late spring and summer).

When to Tour Apulia

Summers are torrid this far south, and even the otherwise perfect villages of the interior are too dazzlingly white for easy comfort from July
to early September. So unless you are planning to be thoroughly idle—
always an alluring prospect in Apulia—avoid the hot season. Of course,
if you're on the Gargano Promontory, which has Apulia's only significant elevation, you'll be able to appreciate the forested interior during these months. And the Gargano and Bari-to-Brindisi coastal regions
are strictly summer-holiday zones.

Wintertime in Apulia can see heavy bursts of rain, often lasting several days at a time. However, the temperatures rarely fall to freezing.
In spring, days are usually warm and the light crystal clear; you can
generally find water warm enough for comfortable bathing into October. Note that lodging availability can be limited off-season.

BARI AND THE ADRIATIC COAST

The coast has a strong flavor of the Norman presence in the south,
embodied in the distinctive Apulian-Romanesque churches, the most

atmospheric being in Trani. The busy, commercial port of Bari offers architectural nuggets in its compact, labyrinthine Old Quarter abutting the sea, while Polignano a Mare combines accessibility to the major centers with the charm of a medieval town. For a unique excursion, drive inland to the imposing Castel del Monte, an enigmatic 13th-century octagonal fortification.

Bari

260 km (162 mi) southeast of Naples, 450 km (281 mi) southeast of Rome.

Bari is a big, hectic, rough-and-tumble port and a transit point for travelers catching ferries across the Adriatic to Greece. Most of the city is set out in a logical 19th-century grid pattern, following the designs of Joachim Murat (1767–1815), Napoléon's brother-in-law and King of the Two Sicilies. The heart of the modern town is Piazza della Libertà, but just beyond it, across Corso Vittorio Emanuele, is the *città vecchia* (Old Town), a maze of narrow, crooked streets on the promontory that juts out between Bari's old and new ports. In the *città vecchia*, over-

❶ looking the sea and just off Via Venezia, is the **Basilica di San Nicola,** built in the 11th century to house the bones of St. Nicholas, better known to us as St. Nick, or Santa Claus. His remains, buried in the crypt, are said to have been stolen by Bari sailors from Myra, in what is now Turkey. The basilica, of solid and powerful construction, was the only building to survive the otherwise wholesale destruction of Bari by the Normans in 1152. ✉ *Piazza San Nicola.* ☉ *Daily 7–noon and 4–6:30.*

❷ The 12th-century **Cattedrale** is the seat of the local bishop and was the scene of many significant political marriages between important families in the Middle Ages. The cathedral's solid architecture reflects the Romanesque style favored by the Normans of that period. ✉ *Piazza dell'Odegitria.* ☉ *Daily 7–1:30 and 4–7.*

❸ Looming over Bari's cathedral is the huge **Castello.** The current building dates from the time of Holy Roman Emperor Frederick II (1194–1250), who rebuilt an existing Norman-Byzantine castle to his own exacting specifications. Designed more for power than beauty, it looks out beyond the cathedral to the small Porto Vecchio (Old Port). Inside is a collection of medieval Apulian art. ✉ *Piazza Federico II di Svevia.* 🎫 *4,000 lire/€2.05.* ☉ *Tues.–Sun. 8:30–7:30.*

Dining and Lodging

$$–$$$ ✕ **Ristorante al Pescatore.** This is one of Bari's best fish restaurants, in the Old Town opposite the castle and just around the corner from the cathedral. Summer cooking is done outside, where you can sit amid a cheerful clamor of quaffing and dining. Try the *céfalo* (mullet) if it is available, accompanied by crisp salad and a carafe of invigorating local wine. ✉ *Piazza Federico II di Svevia,* ☎ *080/5237039. Reservations essential in high season. AE, DC, MC, V. Closed Mon.*

$$$$ 🏨 **Sheraton Nicolaus.** This large, modern hotel on the edge of the city is easily reached by car from Highway S16, which skirts the congested town center. It caters mainly to businesspeople and is well equipped for meetings, conferences, and banquets. Rooms are spacious and comfortable, with the usual amenities of an international chain hotel. ✉ *Via Agostino Ciasca 9, 70124,* ☎ *080/5042626,* 🖷 *080/5042058,* 🌐 *www.sheraton.com. 175 rooms. Restaurant, bar, indoor pool, sauna, convention center, meeting room. AE, DC, MC, V.*

$$ 🏨 **Adria.** This lodging's virtues are its convenience to the train station and relative low cost in a city sadly short on inexpensive lodgings. Fa-

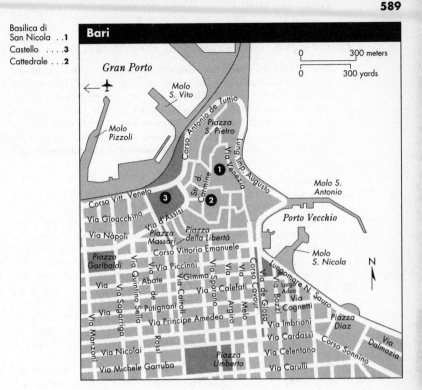

Bari

Gran Porto

Molo S. Vito

Molo Pizzoli

Corso Antonio de Tuttio

Piazza S. Pietro

Via Venezia

Lung. Imp. Augusto

Str. d. Carmine

Corso Vitt. Veneto

Via Gioacchino

Via d'Assisi

Via Napoli

Piazza Massari

Piazza della Libertà

Corso Vittorio Emanuele

Piazza Garibaldi

Via Quintino Sella

Via Piccinni

Via Gimma

Abate

Via Carioli

de Putignani

Via Sparano

Via Sagarriga

Via Manzoni

Via Principe Amedeo

Rossi

Via Nicolai

Via Michele Garruba

Calefati

Argiro

Melo

Corso Cavour

Via de Giosa

Via Bozzi

Lungomare N. Sauro

Largo Adua

Via Cognetti

Via Imbriani

Via Cardassi

Via Celentano

Corso Sonnino

Via Carulli

Piazza Umberto

Molo S. Antonio

Porto Vecchio

Molo S. Nicola

Piazza Diaz

Via Dalmazia

N

0   300 meters
0   300 yards

cilities are adequate if undistinguished, but this is primarily a one-night stopover. Guest rooms are basic but fine. Turn right out of the station to find it. ⊠ *Via L. Zuppetta 10, 70121,* ☎ *080/5246699,* ℻ *080/5213207. 35 rooms. Restaurant, bar. AE, DC, MC, V.*

Nightlife and the Arts

While Bari's famous Teatro Petruzzelli awaits restoration after a devastating fire in 1991, most top-notch drama and ballet has been diverted to the **Teatro Piccinni** (⊠ Corso Vittorio Emanuele 84, ☎ 080/5210878).

Outdoor Activities and Sports

BIKING

G. S. De Benedictis (⊠ Via Nitti 23, ☎ 080/5744345) rents bikes, which are a great way to explore the flat roads winding through the trulli region.

FISHING

For information on approved spots and license applications, contact **Federazione Italiana Pesca Sportiva** (⊠ Molo Pizzoli, Bari, ☎ 080/5210685).

Molfetta

❹ *25 km (16 mi) northwest of Bari, 108 km (67 mi) east of Foggia.*

The unusual 12th-century **Duomo Vecchio** of Molfetta reveals distinct Byzantine features, such as the pyramid-shape covers of the three main domes. If you are in the area around Easter, don't miss Molfetta's colorful Holy Week processions, a surefire hit for young and old alike. ⊠ *Banchina Seminario.* ☉ *Daily 7–noon and 4–7.*

Trani

⑤ *18 km (11 mi) northwest of Molfetta, 43 km (27 mi) northwest of Bari.*

Smaller than the other ports along this coast, Trani has a quaint Old
Town with polished stone streets and buildings, medieval churches, and
a harbor filled with fishing boats. The 11th-century **Duomo,** considered one of the finest in Apulia, is built on a spit of land jutting into
the sea. The Jewish community flourished here in medieval times, and
on Via Sinagoga (Synagogue Street) two of the four synagogues still
exist: the 13th-century **Santa Maria Scolanova** and **Santa Anna,** which
still bears a Hebrew inscription.

Dining and Lodging

$$ ✕ **La Regia.** Just in front of the cathedral, on a swath of land jutting
★   out into the sea, La Regia has an antique feel, with stonework, vaulted
ceilings, and terra-cotta tile floors. Regional specialties are presented
imaginatively: try the baked crepes (similar to cannelloni); risotto
made with salmon, crab, and cream; lobster; or grilled fish. Reserva-
tions are essential for Sunday lunch and dinner on summer weekends.
⊠ *Piazza Duomo 2,* ☎ *0883/584444. AE, DC, MC, V. Closed Mon.*

$$$ 🏠 **La Regia.** This small hotel occupies a 17th-century palazzo; it's
above the restaurant of the same name and under the same ownership.
Don't expect grand or spacious rooms, though they are perfectly adequate; the best take full advantage of the hotel's superb setting opposite Trani's cathedral. ⊠ *Piazza Duomo 2, 70059,* ☎ *0883/584444,*
FAX *0883/506595. 10 rooms. Restaurant, bar. AE, DC, MC, V.*

$$$ 🏠 **Royal.** This is an unpretentious and modern hotel near the train sta-
tion. Furnishings are trim and tidy, suited to brief stopovers rather than
extended stays. ⊠ *Via De Robertis 29, 70059,* ☎ *0883/588777,* FAX
0883/582224. 40 rooms. Restaurant, meeting room. AE, DC, MC, V.

Barletta

⑥ *13 km (8 mi) northwest of Trani, 56 km (35 mi) northwest of Bari.*

The **Colossus,** a bronze statue more than 15 ft tall, is thought to be of
the Byzantine emperor Valentinian and to date from the 5th century
AD. Part of Venice's booty after the sack of Byzantium's capital, Con-
stantinople, in the 1200s, the Colossus was abandoned on the beach
near Barletta when the ship carrying it to Venice foundered in a storm.
⊠ *Next to the church of San Sepolcro, Corso Vittorio Emanuele.*

Dining

$$ ✕ **La Casaccia.** Near a picturesque castle, this restaurant prides itself
on its *zuppa di pesce* (fish soup), made fresh every day, as well as de
rigueur local dishes like orecchiette. There's nothing fancy here: the
tone is calm and down-home, most tables occupied by discriminating
regulars who appreciate the good Apulian cooking and the moderate
prices. ⊠ *Corso Cavour 40,* ☎ *0883/334065. No credit cards.*

Nightlife and the Arts

The **Disfida a Barletta,** held on the last Sunday in August, is a reen-
actment of an event that took place in 1503. Every Italian child is taught
in school that the *disfida* (challenge) of a duel was issued by 13 Italian officers to 13 French officers, after one of the French insulted the
Italians by stating that Italy would always be under foreign domination. The Italians taught the Frenchman and his compatriots a lesson.

Polignano a Mare

❼ *40 km (24 mi) southeast of Bari, 14 km (9 mi) north of Castellana.*

With a well-preserved Old Town perched on impressive limestone cliffs overlooking the Adriatic, Polignano a Mare makes an atmospheric base for exploring the surrounding area and Bari, only a half hour's train ride up the coast.

Dining and Lodging

$$ ✕ **Le Antiche Mura.** Built into the 16th-century walls of the Old Town, this recently established family-run restaurant is popular with locals and visitors alike. Specialties here are mainly—but not exclusively— seafood platters like *cozze a gratin* (mussels filled with bread crumbs) and *seppie al forno* (baked cuttlefish). ⊠ *Via Roma 11,* ☎ *080/ 4242476. Reservations essential weekends. AE, DC, MC, V.*

$$$ ⌂ **Grotta Palazzese.** Toward the lower end of the price category and willing to offer off-peak discounts, this hotel makes the most of its sea- cliff location in the Old Town, with a summer restaurant in the large grotto beneath the hotel. Ask for one of the stylishly refurbished apart- ments across the road rather than the more boxlike rooms in the main 1960s block. ⊠ *Via Narciso 59, 70059,* ☎ *080/4240677,* FAX *080/ 4240767,* WEB *www.grottapalazzese.it. 14 rooms, 14 small apartments. 2 restaurants, bar, air-conditioning, meeting room, parking (fee). AE, DC, MC, V.*

Castel del Monte

★ **❽** *30 km (19 mi) south of Barletta, 56 km (35 mi) southwest of Bari.*

Built by Frederick II in the first half of the 13th century on an isolated hill, Castel del Monte is a huge, bare, octagonal castle with eight tow- ers. Very little is known about the structure, since virtually no records exist. It has none of the usual defense features associated with medieval castles, so it probably had little military significance. Some theories sug- gest it might have been built as a hunting lodge or may have served as an astronomical observatory or a stop for pilgrims on their quest for the Holy Grail. ⊠ *On signposted minor road 18 km (11 mi) south of Andria.* ☎ *6,000 lire/€3.10.* ☉ *Mar.–Sept., 10–1:30 and 2:30–7; Oct.– Feb., 9–1:30 and 2:30–6.* WEB *www.castelli-puglia.org/it/monte.html.*

Shopping

In Andria, between Castel del Monte and Barletta, **copper** objects and containers are made and sold by local craftsmen.

GARGANO PROMONTORY

Forming the spur of Italy's boot, the Gargano Promontory (Promon- torio del Gargano) provides a striking contrast to the Adriatic's gen- erally flat, unenthralling coastline. This is the land of whitewashed coastal towns, wide sandy beaches interspersed with secluded coves, and craggy limestone cliffs topped by deep-green pine and lush Mediter- ranean *maquis*. Not surprisingly it pulls in the crowds in the high sea- son. For the kids, the beaches and forests of the newly created Gargano National Park are great places for letting off steam, and many towns stage puppet shows in their public gardens.

Foggia

❾ *95 km (60 mi) west of Bari.*

Foggia, the chief city in Apulia's northernmost province, is not the most inspiring destination, though it makes a useful overnight stop for visitors to the Gargano. On the main line from Rome and Naples, and easily accessible from the autostrada, Foggia has all the amenities one might expect from a major commercial center hosting numerous fairs and conventions throughout the year. This means that, although it enjoys a decent selection of lodgings and restaurants, you'll need to reserve to make sure of accommodations. This is the place to get or exchange cash or rent a car for excursions to the Gargano.

Dining and Lodging

$$ ✕ **Mangiatoia.** In an old farmhouse, this rustic restaurant has lovely
★   arches, white walls, and wood-beamed ceilings. You can dine outdoors in a large garden, where tables made from wagon wheels surround an old well. Seafood is the specialty; fish and shellfish are displayed live in tanks. The chef will supply recipes for dishes, such as spaghetti *ai datteri di mare al cartoccio* (with razor clams) and fettuccine in a creamy scampi sauce. It's on the main road to Bari, near the Foggia Agricultural Fairgrounds. ⊠ *Via Virgilio 2,* ☎ *0881/634457. Reservations essential on weekends. AE, DC, MC, V. Closed Mon.*

$$$ 🏨 **Cicolella.** This 1920s hotel near the station has tasteful rooms with floor-length curtains, regal wallpaper, and restful, discreet lighting. Some have balconies. The suites, which fall into the $$$$ category, are particularly recommended. The restaurant (closed weekends) specializes in international cuisine as well as well-prepared local dishes. ⊠ *Viale Ventiquattro Maggio 60, 71100,* ☎ *0881/688890,* 🆕 *0881/778984. 106 rooms. Restaurant, meeting room. AE, DC, MC, V.*

Lucera

🔟 *18 km (12 mi) northwest of Foggia.*

Occupying a commanding position over the Tavoliere, Apulia's flat coastal plains, Lucera flourished during the Roman era, long before Frederick II—in what was considered an enlightened gesture for the 13th century—relocated over 10,000 Sicilian Arabs here in 1224. Though subsequent decades of religious intolerance removed the Arab mosques, Lucera has retained an impressive complement of historical sites and an attentively preserved Old Town.

After you've explored Lucera's cobblestone streets and narrow corridors, head for the 14th-century **Cattedrale** a curious blend of Romanesque and Gothic architecture, commissioned by Charles II of Anjou to replace an earlier mosque. ⊠ *Piazza Duomo,* ☎ *0881/ 520880.* ⊙ *Daily 9–12:30 and 4:30–7.*

The small **Museo Civico G. Fiorelli,** housed in a fine 17th-century palazzo east of Lucera's cathedral, has a representative selection of Roman inscriptions, sculpture, and mosaics, as well as several finds from the Saracen period. ⊠ *Via De Nicastri 36,* ☎ *0881/547041.* 🖅 *1,500 lire/€0.75.* ⊙ *Tues.–Fri. 9–1 and 4–7, weekends 9–1.*

Lying rather incongruously beyond one of the poorer parts of the modern town is Lucera's partially reconstructed **Anfiteatro Romano,** built at the end of the 1st century BC. Although much of the superstructure has been lost, the grandiose entrance gates have been rebuilt, complete with dedication inscriptions. ⊠ *Viale Augusteo,* ☎ *0881/548626.* ⊙ *Oct.–Apr., Tues.–Sun. 8:30–2:30; May–Sept., Tues.–Sun. 8:30–7.*

The so-called **Castello Svevo-angioino,** a 10-minute walk northwest of the Old Town, is an impressive sight. It was plundered for building material up to relatively modern times, and little but the base remains of Frederick's *palatium,* a palace built in 1233. The castle owes its present form to the Angevins, who transformed it over the next century into a military stronghold, complete with drawbridge, moat, 24 towers, and a wall more than 1 km (½ mi) long. ⊠ *Via Castello,* ☎ *0881/548626.* ⊙ *Tues.–Sun. 8–2:30 and 4:30–8.*

In the spirit of cultural enlightenment that pervades Lucera, **guided tours** (in Italian and occasionally English; ☎ 0881/548626 for bookings) are available free of charge, subject to availability, at the museum, amphitheater, and castle.

Lodging

$$ 🏨 **La Balconata 2.** This family-run hotel occupies part of a modern condominium and is strategically located two minutes' walk from the south gate of Porta Troia leading to the Old Town. When booking, ask for the quieter rooms away from the main road. The restaurant's regional cuisine is also well worth a try, but you'll need to be immune to cigarette smoke. ⊠ *Viale Ferrovia 15, 71036,* ☎ FAX *0881/520998,* ☎ *0881/546725,* WEB *www.labalconata.it. 49 rooms. Restaurant, bar, air-conditioning. AE, DC, MC, V.*

Mattinata

⓫ *53 km (32 mi) northeast of Foggia, 138 km (86 mi) northwest of Bari.*

Just inland from a fine sandy beach, where you'll find most of the campsites and hotels, this is a generally quiet village that comes into its own in the summer season.

Lodging

$$–$$$ 🏨 **Baia delle Zagare.** On the shore road around the Gargano Promontory, north of Mattinata, Baia delle Zagare is a secluded, modern group of cottages overlooking an inlet. An elevator takes you down to a private beach, and the hotel restaurant is good enough to warrant staying on the premises all day. (You're expected to take full board in August.) ⊠ *Località Valle dei Mergoli, 17 km (10 mi) northeast of Mattinata, 71030,* ☎ *0884/550155,* FAX *0884/550884. 144 rooms. Restaurant, pool, tennis court, beach. MC, V. Closed Oct.–May. FAP.*

$–$$ 🏨 **Alba del Gargano.** Although it's in the town center, the modern Alba provides a restful atmosphere. Large balconies overlook a quiet courtyard garden, and a frequent (and free) bus service connects with a private beach, where you can use the hotel's beach chairs and umbrellas. Rooms are comfortably furnished, and there is a good restaurant. ⊠ *Corso Matino 102, 71030,* ☎ *0884/550771,* FAX *0884/550772,* WEB *www.albadelgargano.it. 40 rooms, 3 suites. Restaurant, bar, beach. MC, V.*

Vieste

⓬ *93 km (58 mi) northeast of Foggia, 179 km (111 mi) northwest of Bari.*

This large town on the tip of the spur is the Gargano's main commercial center and an attractive place to wander around. Though slightly less accessible from the autostrada and main-line rail stations than Peschici and Mattinata, the range of accommodations (including camping) makes it a useful base for exploring Gargano. Make for the **castle,** not open to the public but offering good views from its high position overlooking the beaches and town. The resort attracts legions of tourists in summer, some bound for the **Isole Tremiti,** a tiny archipelago connected to Vieste by regular ferries.

Lodging

$$$$ 🏨 **Pizzomunno.** Probably the most luxurious resort on the Gargano, ★ Pizzomunno is right on the beach and is surrounded by an extensive park. It is large, white, modern, air-conditioned, and well equipped.

The rooms are ample and plush, all with terraces. Here you can unwind, or try your hand at tennis or archery. ✉ *Lungomare di Pizzomunno, 71019,* ☎ *0884/708741,* FAX *0884/707325,* WEB *www.pizzomunno.it. 190 rooms. 3 restaurants, air-conditioning, 2 pools, sauna, 3 tennis courts, archery, health club, cinema, dance club, children's programs. AE, DC, MC, V. Closed Nov.–Mar..*

$–$$ 🏨 **Punta San Francesco.** After starting its life as an olive-oil factory, this hotel was tastefully refurbished in the mid-1990s. Thanks to its location near the waterfront in the heart of old Vieste, it is both quiet and strategically close to the action. ✉ *Via San Francesco 2, 71019,* ☎ *0884/701422,* FAX *0884/701424. 14 rooms. Air-conditioning. MC, V.*

Peschici

⑬   *22 km (14 mi) northwest of Vieste, 199 km (124 mi) northwest of Bari.*

Though it has no outstanding historical monuments, Peschici is a pleasant resort on Gargano's north shore, with some surrounding areas particularly popular with campers from northern Europe. Development has not wreaked too much havoc on this whitewashed town, and the mazelike center retains its characteristic low houses topped with little domes.

Rodi Garganico

⑭   *20 km (12 mi) west of Peschici, 40 km (25 mi) west of Vieste.*

This fishing village squeezed between the hills and the sea takes its name from the island of Rhodes, recalling its former Greek population. Ringed by pine woods and citrus groves, Rodi is linked by hydrofoils with the Isole Tremiti, and things can get hectic in high summer.

OFF THE BEATEN PATH   **ISOLE TREMITI –** A ferry service from Termoli, west of the Gargano (1 hr, 40 mins), and hydrofoil service from Vieste, Peschici, Rodi Garganico, and Manfredonia (40 mins to 1 hr) connect the mainland with these three small islands north of the Gargano. Although somewhat crowded with Italian tourists in summer, they are famed for their sea caves, pine forests, and craggy limestone formations. Interesting medieval churches and fortifications dot the islands.

Dining

$$ ✕ **Gabbiano.** Admire the view facing the sea in Rodi Garganico at this cheerful restaurant while savoring freshly caught seafood. ✉ *Via Trieste 16,* ☎ *0884/965283. AE, V. Closed Thurs. in Nov.–Mar.*

Foresta Umbra

★ **⑮**   *25 km (16 mi) south of Rodi Garganico, 30 km (19 mi) southwest of Vieste.*

In the middle of the Gargano Promontory is the majestic Foresta Umbra (Shady Forest), a dense growth of beech, maple, sycamore, and oak generally found in more northerly climates, thriving here because of the altitude, 3,200 ft above sea level. Between the trees in this newly created national park are occasional dramatic vistas opening out over the Golfo di Manfredonia. From the north coast, take S528 (midway between Peschici and Rodi Garganico) south to head through the interior of the Gargano, or try the gentler ascent from Vieste on S89.

Monte Sant'Angelo

★ ⑯ *16 km (10 mi) north of Manfredonia, 60 km (19 mi) southwest of Vieste.*

Perched amid olive groves on the rugged white limestone cliffs overlooking the gulf is the town of Monte Sant'Angelo. Pilgrims have flocked here for nearly 1,500 years—among them, St. Francis of Assisi and the crusaders setting off for the Holy Land from the then-flourishing port of Manfredonia. Monte Sant'Angelo is centered on the **Santuario di San Michele** (Sanctuary of San Michele), built over the grotto where the archangel Michael is believed to have appeared before shepherds in the year 490. Walk down a long series of steps to get to the grotto itself—on the walls you can see the hand tracings left by pilgrims as votive symbols.

The **Tomba di Rotari** (Tomb of Rotari), believed to have been a medieval baptistery, has some remarkable 12th-century reliefs. It's reached by steps down and to the left from the Santuario di San Michele. Steep steps lead up to the large, ruined **Castello Normano** (Norman Castle) that dominates the town, with a view of the intricate pattern of the streets and steps winding their way up the side of the valley. Monte Sant'Angelo's medieval quarter, the **Rione Junno,** is a maze of little white houses squeezed into a corner of the narrow valley.

Lodging

$$ 🏨 **Hotel Rotary.** This simple but welcoming modern hotel is set amid olive and almond groves just outside town. Most rooms have basic decor and terraces with a good view of the Golfo di Manfredonia. ⊠ *Via Pulsano, km 1, 71037,* ☎ *0884/562147* FAX *0884/562146. 24 rooms. Restaurant. AE, MC, V.*

Shopping

Most food shops in the Junno sell a local specialty called *ostia piena* (filled host), a pastry made with candied almonds and wafers of a type similar to communion hosts. The best place to get them—and munch on them—is at the southern end of the Junno, by the Villa Comunale.

Shoemaker **Domenico Palena** displays his unique leather sculptures at his tiny shop in the Junno quarter. Local craftsmen make and sell wooden utensils, wooden furniture, and wrought-iron work.

San Giovanni Rotondo

⑰ *25 km (16 mi) west of Monte Sant'Angelo, 85 km (52 mi) southwest of Vieste.*

The ancient village of San Giovanni Rotondo, on the winding S272, is a relatively recent center of religious pilgrimage. Devotees have flocked here to pay their respects to the shrine and **Tomba di Padre Pio** (1887–1968; ⊠ Chiesa Santa Maria delle Grazie, Piazzale Santa Maria delle Grazie), a monk revered for his pious life, his miraculous intercessions, and his having received the stigmata, the signs of Christ's wounds. The **Casa Sollievo della Sofferenza** (Foundation for the Mitigation of Suffering, ⊠ Piazzale Santa Maria delle Grazie), supported through contributions from around the world, is a testament to the enduring appeal of this holy man.

En Route A short ride south on S273, and then east (left) at L'Annunziata, will take you back to Manfredonia, where you can link up with the coastal road to return to Bari.

TRULLI DISTRICT

Alberobello, Locorotondo, Ostuni, and Martina Franca

The inland area to the southeast of Bari is one of Italy's oddest enclaves, a flat land given over to olive cultivation and interspersed with the idiosyncratic habitations that have lent their name to the district. The origins of the beehive-shape trulli go back to the 13th century and maybe further. The trulli are built of local limestone, without mortar, and with a hole in the top for escaping smoke. Some are painted with mystical or religious symbols; some are isolated, and others are joined together with roofs on various levels. The center of trulli country is Alberobello, with the greatest concentration of the buildings, though you will spot scores of them all over this region, some in states of disrepair but always adding a quirky charm to the landscape.

Alberobello

⑱ *59 km (37 mi) southeast of Bari, 45 km (28 mi) north of Taranto.*

The trulli zone of Alberobello, where more than 1,000 trulli huddle together along steep, narrow streets, is a national monument. It is also one of the most popular tourist destinations.

Dining and Lodging

$$–$$$ ✕ **Il Poeta Contadino.** Proprietor Marco Leonardo serves "creative regional cooking" in this rustic-style restaurant. In the heart of the attractive trulli zone, it features candlelit tables and a refined, understated ambience. Specialties to look for are fish platters and antipasti, accompanied by an extensive range of fine wines. ⊠ *Via Indipendenza 21,* ☎ *080/4321917. Reservations essential. AE, DC, MC, V. Closed Mon. in Oct.–June, Jan. 7–22, and 10 days at end of June.*

$$ ✕ **Trullo d'Oro.** This welcoming, rustic restaurant set in five trulli
★ houses has dark-wood beams, whitewashed walls, and an open hearth. Local country cooking includes dishes using lamb and veal, vegetable and cheese antipasti, pasta dishes with crisp raw vegetables on the side, and almond pastries. Among the specialties are roast lamb with *lampasciuni* (a type of wild onion) and spaghetti *al trullo,* made with tomatoes, *rughetta* (arugula), and four cheeses. ⊠ *Via F. Cavallotti 27,* ☎ *080/4321820. Reservations essential. AE, DC, MC, V. Closed Mon. and Jan. 8–Feb. 3.*

$$$ ▥ **Dei Trulli.** Trulli-style cottages in a pine wood near the trulli zone make this a pleasant hotel. It is decorated with rustic furnishings and folk-art rugs. The modestly priced restaurant serves local specialties. You're expected to take half or full board in high season. ⊠ *Via Cadore 28-32, 70011,* ☎ *080/4323555,* ℻ *080/4323560,* 🕸 *www.inmedia.it/ hoteldeitrulli. 33 rooms. Restaurant, pool. AE, MC, V. FAP, MAP.*

Shopping

In the trulli zone, you'll find small shops selling hand-painted clay figurines. Rugs and fabrics are good bets here, but there is also a good deal of shoddy merchandise.

Grotte di Castellana

⑲ *20 km (12 mi) northwest of Alberobello, 63 km (52 mi) southeast of Bari.*

The Grotte di Castellana is a huge network of caves discovered in 1938. You can take one of the hourly guided tours through the grottoes, filled with fantastically shaped stalagmites and stalactites, forming part of the largest network of caves on the Italian mainland. On site are a speleological museum and an astronomical observatory. ☎ 080/4998211, WEB *www.grottedicastellana.it.* 🖼 *15,000 lire/€7.75 (1-hr tour), 25,000 lire/€12.90 (2-hr tour).* ☉ *Apr.–Oct., daily 8:30–1 and 2:30–7; Nov.–Mar., daily 8:30–1 and 2:30–6.*

Dining

$$ ✕ **Al Parco Chiancafredda.** The refined ambience and cuisine of this restaurant, set apart from the tourist haunts, make it pricier than its neighbors. But the food and service are worth it: try such regional dishes as *sformato di verdura* (vegetable stew) and *agnello alla castellanese* (local lamb). ✉ *Via Chiancafredda 12,* ☎ *080/4968710. Reservations essential. AE, MC, V. Closed Tues. and Nov.*

$ ✕ **Taverna degli Artisti.** Near the caves, this rustic tavern-style restaurant with a big garden specializes in local home cooking, such as roast lamb, homemade orecchiette, and dishes with ominous names like *timballo fine del mondo* (end-of-the-world timbale) and *involtini al purgatorio* (purgatory roulades). ✉ *Via Vito Matarrese 27,* ☎ *080/4968234. AE, DC, MC, V. Closed Thurs. in Oct.–June, and mid-Dec.–mid-Jan.*

Locorotondo

⓴ *9 km (5½ mi) southeast of Alberobello, 40 km (25 mi) north of Taranto.*

Locorotondo is an attractive hillside town within the trulli district in the Itria Valley (take S172 from Alberobello). The *rotondo* in the town's name refers to the circular pattern of the houses, apparent from any vantage point at the top of the town.

Ostuni

㉑ *50 km (30 mi) west of Brindisi, 40 km (25 mi) northeast of Locorotondo.*

This sun-bleached, picturesque medieval town lies on three hills a short distance from the coast. The **Old Town,** on the highest of the hills, has steep cobbled lanes and stupendous views out over the coast and the surrounding plain.

Dining and Lodging

$$ ✕ **Vecchia Ostuni.** In the heart of the Old Town, enjoy regional specialties from this well-established trattoria, whose grills and seafood dishes are renowned among locals. Let yourself go on the antipasti table before settling down with a *sarago alla brace* (char-grilled bream) or *lombate e salsicce alla brace* (loin and sausages char-grilled). The homemade desserts are also worth some attention, and there is a good selection of local wines. Reservations are recommended weekends. ✉ *Largo Lanza 9,* ☎ *0831/303308. AE, DC, MC, V. Closed Tues. and Jan.*

$$–$$$ 🏨 **Incanto.** At this modest hotel outside the Old Town, you can admire the countryside and the sea in the distance from many of its rooms. It makes a basic but adequate overnight base for seeing the area. ✉ *Via dei Colli, 72017,* ☎ *0831/301781,* FAX *0831/338302. 65 rooms. 2 restaurants, 2 bars. AE, DC, MC, V.*

Martina Franca

㉒ *6 km (4 mi) south of Locorotondo, 36 km (22 mi) north of Taranto.*

Martina Franca is an appealing town with a dazzling mixture of medieval and Baroque architecture in the light-color local stone. Ornate balconies hang above the twisting, narrow streets, with little alleys leading off into the surrounding hills. Martina Franca was developed as a military stronghold in the 14th century, when a surrounding wall with 24 towers was built, but now all that remains are the four gates that had been the only entrances to the town. Each July and August Martina Franca holds a music festival.

Dining and Lodging

$–$$ ✕ **La Tavernetta.** This small restaurant with a vaulted ceiling in the Old Town center serves large portions of good home cooking, starting with a pottery bowl full of local olives and excellent house wine. Specialties include favi e fogghi and, in summer, orecchiette with *cocomero* (a vegetable that looks like a miniature watermelon and tastes like a cross between cucumber and honeydew melon). Main courses include a mixed grill of lamb, liver, and spicy local sausage. ⊠ *Corso Vittorio Emanuele 30,* ☎ *080/4306323. MC, V. Closed Mon.*

$$–$$$ 🏨 **Park Hotel San Michele.** This garden hotel makes a pleasant base in the warm months, thanks to its pool. The two categories of rooms have a small price difference; opt for the higher-priced ones. All are spacious, some embellished with handsome furniture and including complimentary bowls of fruit. ⊠ *Viale Carella 9, 74015,* ☎ *080/4807053,* 🖷 *080/4808895,* 🌐 *www.parkhotelsm.it. 86 rooms. Restaurant, bar, pool. AE, DC, MC, V.*

Nightlife and the Arts

Martina Franca concentrates on music in its annual **Festa della Valle Itria** (Festival of the Itria Valley) each July and August.

ACROSS THE HEEL AND SOUTH TO LECCE

Taranto, Brindisi, Lecce, Otranto, and Gallipoli

This far south, the mountains run out of steam and the land is uniformly flat, although agriculturally quite important. The monotonous landscape, however, is redeemed by some of the region's best sandy coastline and a handful of alluring small towns. Taranto and Brindisi don't quite fit this description: both are big ports where historical importance is obscured by unsightly heavy industry. Nonetheless, Taranto has its special attractions, not the least of them its archaeological museum; Brindisi marks the end of the Via Appia. Farther south, in Il Salento (the Salentine Peninsula), Lecce is an unexpected oasis of grace and sophistication, and its swirling architecture will melt even the most uncompromising critic of the Baroque.

Taranto

❷❸   *100 km (62 mi) southeast of Bari, 40 km (25 mi) south of Martina Franca.*

Taranto—the stress is on the first syllable—was an important port even in Roman times. It lies toward the back of the instep of the boot on the broad Mare Grande bay, which is connected to a small internal Mare Piccolo basin by two narrow channels, one artificial and one natural. The Old Town is on an island between the larger and smaller bodies of water; the modern city stretches inward along the mainland. Little remains of Taranto's past except the 14th-century church of **San Domenico** (⊠ Via Duomo 33) at one end of the island, and its famous naval academy.

★ A compendium on the millennia of local history, the **Museo Nazionale** has a large collection of prehistoric, Greek, and Roman artifacts, discovered mainly in the immediate vicinity. The museum is just over the bridge from the Old Town on the promontory. Some of the prehistoric items from Apulian tombs date from before 1000 BC, but more plentiful are the examples of intricately crafted Greek jewelry from around 500 BC. The museum is a testament to the importance of this ancient port, which has always taken full advantage of its unique trading position at the end of the Italian peninsula. If you are making a special journey to see the museum, telephone beforehand to avoid disappointment—the building is currently undergoing major renovation and some displays may not be on view. ⊠ *Corso Umberto 41,* ☎ *099/ 4532112.* ⌑ *4,000 lire/€2.05.* ⊙ *Daily 8:30–7:30.*

Dining and Lodging

$ ✕ **Da Basile.** Here's an ideal spot, just a couple of blocks from the museum, for a quick lunch or a good, straightforward (and cheap!) evening meal. You'll be sharing the four small rooms with families, crowds of youths, solitary businessmen, and groups of women, and you may have to wait for a table. Pizzas with fresh vegetables, no-frills pasta dishes, fish and meat, and delicious homemade gelato round out the menu. Service is fast and attentive. ⊠ *Via Pitagora 76,* ☎ *099/ 4526240. V. Closed Sat.*

$$$$ ⊞ **Golf Hotel.** Less than an hour's drive along the coast from Taranto, this hotel, as its name implies, caters to golf enthusiasts, with apartments in a modern, well-equipped annex overlooking the links. Guests are entitled to a 20% reduction on fees for the 18-hole course, and a shuttle bus plies between hotel, golf course, and beaches. Guests are required to take half or full board in high season, with minimum stays of a week. ⊠ *Località Riva dei Tessali, 74011 Castellaneta Marina,* ☎ *099/8439251,* FAX *099/8439255,* WEB *www.rivadeitessali.it. 70 rooms, 20 apartments. Dining room, bar, pool, golf privileges, tennis court. AE, DC, MC, V. FAP, MAP.*

$$$ ⊞ **Grand Hotel Delfino.** This big, well-equipped hotel downtown caters to business clients. Airy rooms have balconies. The restaurant features regional seafood. ⊠ *Viale Virgilio 66, 74100,* ☎ *099/7323232,* FAX *099/ 7304654,* WEB *www.grandhoteldelfino.it. 198 rooms. Restaurant, minibars, pool, meeting room. AE, DC, MC, V.*

The Arts

Taranto has Easter processions on Holy Thursday and Good Friday, the Processione dei Misteri (Procession of the Mysteries) and the Processione dell'Addolorata (Procession of Our Lady of Sorrows).

Outdoor Activities and Sports

GOLF

Apulia's only 18-hole golf course is the **Riva dei Tessali** (⊠ Marina di Castellaneta, 40 km [25 mi] west of Taranto along the coast road, ☎ 099/8431844), where even experienced golfers may find it challenging to negotiate their way through the groves of Aleppo pines.

SAILING

Sailors should contact the **Lega Navale** (⊠ Lungomare Vittorio Emanuele II, ☎ 099/4593801), the focal point for sailing and canoeing courses.

Brindisi

24 *114 km (71 mi) southeast of Bari, 72 km (45 mi) east of Taranto.*

Occupying the head of a deep inlet on the eastern Adriatic coast, Brindisi (stress placed on first syllable) has long been one of Italy's most important ports, and today most people think of the town only as a terminus for the ferry crossing that links Italy with Greece. Although this impression fails to give credit to the broader importance of the city (it has a population of nearly 100,000), it is a present-day reminder of the role Brindisi has always played as gateway to the eastern Mediterranean and beyond. Brindisi has seen a constant flow of naval and mercantile traffic over the centuries, and in the Middle Ages it was an important departure point for several crusades to the Holy Land.

The core of Brindisi is at the head of a deep channel, which branches into two harbors with the city between them. Look for the steeple of the cathedral to get your bearings, but go beyond it and down the steps to the water's edge. Just to the left is a tall **Roman column** and the base of another one next to it. These were built in the 2nd century AD and marked the end of the **Via Appia** (Appian Way), the Imperial Roman road that led from the capital to this important southeastern seaport. ⊠ *Viale Regina Margherita.*

The **Duomo,** a short walk from the Roman column, has a mosaic floor in its apse that is worth the stop; the floor dates from the 12th century, although much of the rest of the cathedral was rebuilt in the 18th. ⊠ *Piazza Duomo.* ☉ *Daily 7–noon and 4–8.*

The **Castello Svevo,** one of the defense fortifications built by the illustrious Frederick II in the 13th century, guards the larger of Brindisi's two inner harbors. It isn't accessible to the public. ⊠ *Piazza Castello.*

Lodging

$$ ☷ **Mediterraneo.** Comfort and a convenient central location are the advantages of this modern hotel. Rooms have double-glazed windows and most have balconies, though for the best views it's worth heading up to the restaurant on the seventh floor. ⊠ *Viale Aldo Moro 70, 72100,* ☎ *0831/582811,* 𝖥𝖠𝖷 *0831/587858,* 𝖶𝖤𝖡 *www.hotelmediterraneo.it. 65 rooms. Restaurant, air-conditioning. AE, DC, MC, V.*

Nightlife and the Arts

The **Festa della Città di Brindisi** (City of Brindisi Festival), July–September, is a citywide display of art and folklore; contact the **tourist office** (⊠ Piazza Dionisi, ☎ 0831/523072).

Outdoor Activities and Sports

SAILING

Contact Brindisi's **Lega Navale** (⊠ Via Vespucci, ☎ 0831/418824), which offers canoe and sailing courses.

Lecce

㉕ *40 km (25 mi) southeast of Brindisi, 87 km (54 mi) east of Taranto.*

Although Lecce, the crown jewel on the tour of Apulia, was founded before the time of the ancient Greeks, it is almost always associated with the term Lecce Baroque. This is because of a citywide impulse in the 17th century to redo the town in the Baroque fashion. But this was Baroque with a difference. Although Baroque architecture is often heavy and monumental, here it took on a lighter, more fanciful air. Just

★ look at the **Basilica di Santa Croce,** with the **Palazzo della Prefettura** abutting it. Although every column, window, pediment, and balcony is given a curling Baroque touch—and then an extra one for good measure—the overall effect is lighthearted. The buildings' scale is unintimidating and the local stone is a glowing honey color: it couldn't look menacing if it tried. ⊠ *Via Umberto I.* ☉ *Daily 7:30–noon and 5–7:30.*

In the middle of **Piazza Sant'Oronzo** is a **Roman column** of the same era and style as the one in Brindisi, but imaginatively surmounted by an 18th-century statue of the city's patron saint, Orontius. Next to the column, the shallow rows of seats in the **Anfiteatro Romano** suggest a small-scale Roman Colosseum or Verona's arena.

Dining and Lodging

$–$$ ✕ **Plaza.** Tucked away behind Lecce's castle, this high-quality restaurant has been keeping the city's gourmets happy for 30 years. Regional dishes are given a personal touch. Try the *tubettini alle cozze* (pasta with clams) and the antipasti, worth dipping into. ⊠ *Via 140 Fanteria 10,* ☎ *0832/305093. AE, DC, MC, V. Closed Sun. and Aug.*

$$ 🏨 **Risorgimento.** An old-fashioned Liberty-style hotel in a converted palace in the heart of the Baroque old town, the Risorgimento combines historic charm with modern comfort. For undisturbed sleep and summer-time siestas during longer stays, ask for rooms overlooking the backstreets or the courtyard. The roof garden has great town views. ⊠ *Via Augusto Imperatore 19, 73100,* ☎ *0832/242125,* 🖷 *0832/ 245571. 57 rooms. Restaurant, lounge, meeting room, air-conditioning. AE, DC, MC, V.*

$ 🏨 **Cappello.** This popular hotel is close to the train station but outside the old city walls, about a 10-minute walk from the town center. Space is confined in the upstairs guest rooms, but they are perfectly fine for a short stay and fully equipped with TV, telephone, and air-conditioning. Those at the back can get noise from the nearby railroad. Reservations are advised. ⊠ *Via Montegrappa 4, 73100,* ☎ *0832/308881,* 🖷 *0832/ 301535. 32 rooms. Bar, air-conditioning. AE, DC, MC, V.*

Nightlife and the Arts

In July, the public gardens are the setting for productions of drama and, sometimes, opera. A **Baroque music festival** is held in churches throughout the city in September. For details on forthcoming events call the Tourist Information Office (☎ 0832/248092).

Otranto

㉖ *36 km (22 mi) southeast of Lecce, 188 km (117 mi) southeast of Bari.*

As the easternmost point in Italy—and therefore closest to the Balkan peninsula—Otranto has often borne the brunt of foreign invasions during its checkered history. A flourishing port from ancient Greek times, Otranto (the Roman *Hydruntum*) has a history like that of most of southern Italy: after the fall of the western Roman Empire, centuries of Byzantine rule interspersed with Saracen incursions, followed by the arrival of the Normans and other dynasties from northern Europe. The town was sacked by Turkish forces in 1480, occupied for a year, and never recovered its former glory. The *centro storico* (Old Town) nestles within impressive city walls and bastions, dominated by the **Castello,** most of which are attributed to engineers working under the Spanish viceroys in the 16th century. The real jewel in Otranto is the **Cattedrale,** originally begun by the Normans and conserving an extraordinary 12th-century mosaic pavement in the nave and aisles. ⊠ *Piazza Basilica,* ☎ *0836/802720.* ⏰ *Daily 8:30–noon and 5–7:30.*

Lodging

$ 🏨 **La Fattoria.** This working farm (dairy cows and olives) lies in open country 3 km (2 mi) southwest of Otranto, just off the road to Uggiano. It makes an excellent base for visiting Lecce, Gallipoli, and other sights in the Salentine Peninsula. The restaurant specializes in organic food but operates only weekends (and evenings in summer), which means you have to fend for yourself the rest of the time. Bring bath towels

and soap! ⊠ *SS Otranto–Uggiano Bivio Casamassetta, 73028,* ☎
0836/804651, FAX *0836/804651. 5 self-catering mini-apartments, 5
bungalows. Restaurant, playground. AE, DC, MC, V.*

Shopping

Otranto's Old Town has been tastefully gentrified in recent years and
has an array of shops displaying local products. **Texum** (⊠ Corso
Garibaldi 43) specializes in objets d'art sculpted from *pietra leccese,*
the soft local limestone used for much of the Baroque architecture in
the Salentine Peninsula. If you need to stock up on fine wines and olive
oil, stop off at **Il Giardino del Re** (⊠ Corso Garibaldi 64), where wine-
tasting sessions are frequently arranged.

Gallipoli

㉗ *37 km (23 mi) south of Lecce, 190 km (118 mi) southeast of Bari.*

The modern section of the town of Gallipoli, on the Golfo di Taranto,
lies on the mainland; turn right on the main street at the end of the central square and cross a 17th-century bridge to the Old Town, crowded
onto its own small island in the gulf. The Greeks called it Kallipolis, the
Romans Anxa. Like the famous Turkish town of the same name on the
Dardanelles, the Italian Gallipoli occupies a strategic location and thus
was repeatedly attacked through the centuries—by the Normans in
1071, the Venetians in 1484, the British in 1809. The historic quarter,
a mesh of narrow alleys and squares, is guarded by a formidable **Castello
Aragonese,** a massive fortification that grew out of an earlier Byzantine
fortress that you can still see at the southeast corner. After being an op-
erative base for the busy *Guardia di Finanza* (revenue police), it is now
being renovated and adapted for future use as a public monument. Gallipoli's **Duomo** (⊠ Via Antonietta De Pace, ☎ 0833/261987) open daily
9–noon and 5–8, is a notable Baroque church. The church of **La Puris-
sima** (⊠ Riviera Nazario Sauro, ☎ 0833/261699) has a stuccoed interior as elaborate as a wedding cake, with an especially noteworthy tiled
floor. You can visit daily 9–noon and 5–7:30.

Dining and Lodging

\$\$ ★ ✕ **Marechiaro.** You have to cross a little bridge to reach this simple
port-side restaurant, actually not far from the town's historic center.
It's built out onto the sea, replete with wood paneling, flowers, and
terraces with panoramic coastal views. Try the renowned *zuppa di pesce
alla gallipolina* (fish stew), succulent shellfish, and linguine with
seafood. ⊠ *Lungomare Marconi,* ☎ *0833/266143. AE, DC, MC, V.
Closed Tues. in Oct.–May.*

\$\$\$ ★ 🏨 **Costa Brada.** The rooms all have terraces with sea views at this
modern white beach hotel of classic Mediterranean design. The interiors are uncluttered and tasteful; rooms 110–114 are particularly
spacious and overlook the beach. The hotel accepts only half-board
or full-board guests in high season. ⊠ *Baia Verde, Litoranea Santa
Maria di Leuca, 73014,* ☎ *0833/202551,* FAX *0833/202555,* WEB *www.
grandhotelcostabrada.it. 89 rooms. 2 restaurants, snack bar, indoor and
outdoor pools, sauna, gym, shop. AE, DC, MC, V. FAP, MAP.*

\$\$–\$\$\$ 🏨 **Le Sirenuse.** A private beach and a pine forest distinguish this gleam-
ing white Mediterranean-style hotel complex. The pleasant rooms
have terraces. Half or full board is required in high season. ⊠ *Riserva
Naturalistica Torre del Pizzo, Litorana Santa Maria di Leuca, 73014,*
☎ *0833/202536,* FAX *0833/202539,* WEB *www.caroli.net. 120 rooms.
Restaurant, air-conditioning, pool, tennis court, beach. AE, DC, MC,
V. FAP, MAP.*

Outdoor Activities and Sports

Ample swimming, water sports, and clean, fine sand make Gallipoli a good choice for families. The 5-km- (3-mi-) long expanse of sand sweeping south from town has both public and private beaches, the latter equipped with changing rooms, sun beds, and umbrellas. Water sports equipment can be bought or hired at the waterfront shops in town.

MOLISE

Established in 1965 after splitting from Abruzzo to the north, the region of Molise has long lived in the shadow of its more glamorous neighboring regions like Campania and Apulia. This has spared it many of the ravages of late-20th-century development: its mountains have a good endowment of their original woodland and grassland, the hill villages are generally well preserved, the archaeological sites are delightfully undervisited, and the *cucina* has retained its distinct *molisano* flavor with the best of local ingredients. With the exception of Valle d'Aosta, Molise is Italy's smallest region and lends itself to a few days' exploration from a single base. Of the two provincial centers, Isernia has a greater historical pedigree and far more character than its rather brash counterpart to the east, Campobasso.

Isernia

111 km (70 mi) north of Naples, 176 km (110 mi) southeast of Rome.

Isernia perches at just under 1,500 ft above sea level on what in the distant past must have been an easily defensible ridge, overlooking river valleys and busy viaducts. The town suffered severe collateral damage during Allied bombing raids in World War II—they were aiming for the bridge down in the valley. The northern part of the town is laid out in the standard grid pattern of Italian postwar development. Previous damage had been wrought by an earthquake in 1837, a notable victim being the **Cattedrale,** rebuilt in rather incongruous neoclassical style shortly afterward. Beneath the campanile to the east of the cathedral are four marble statues (in desperate need of restoration) from the Roman era positioned at the corners of the gateway.

In the heart of the Old Town is the **Museo Nazionale,** which houses finds from Roman necropolises outside ancient Aesernia. You can view an impressive array of funerary sculptures and the remarkably preserved remains of local fauna (including elephant and rhino species) hunted by *Homo aeserniensis* on a grassy river plain more than 700,000 years ago. Ask to see the helpful video (in good English) contextualizing the finds. ✉ *Ex-convento Santa Maria delle Monache, Corso Marcelli 48,* ☎ *0865/415179.* ☞ *4,000 lire/€2.05.* ♁ *Daily 9–1 and 3–7.*

....

OFF THE
BEATEN PATH
PESCHE – Travel 4 km (2 mi) northeast of Isernia to Pesche, a village clinging both to its past and the steep limestone slope beneath it. From here, two paths head up and around the Riserva Naturale di Pesche above the village, mainly through holm-oak and deciduous oak forests. In springtime look for orchids among the bare limestone rocks, and enjoy the woodland concert of blackcaps and finches.

....

Dining and Lodging

$$ ✕ **Taverna Maresca.** Don't be misled by the rustic, unassuming air of this family restaurant in the heart of Isernia's Old Town. This is an excellent place for sampling local *cucina*. Warming dishes in winter include the northern-sounding polenta *al sugo* (with meat sauce), and

involtini di melanzane (eggplant rolls stuffed with meat and cheese) are thankfully served throughout the year. ✉ *Via Marcelli 186,* ☎ *0865/3976. Reservations essential Sat. dinner. AE, DC, MC, V. Closed Sun., Dec. 24–Jan. 2, and Aug. 8–24.*

$–$$ 🏨 **Hotel S. Maria del Bagno.** Though not the last word in traditional *molisano* decor, this quiet, well-run hotel lies just outside the picturesque medieval hill village of Pesche and makes a perfect base for local country walks exploring nearby Isernia (3 km [2 mi]) and excursions into the rest of Molise. ✉ *Viale S. Maria del Bagno 1, 86090 Pesche,* ☎ *0865/460136,* 𝔽𝔸𝕏 *0865/460129. 45 rooms. Restaurant, bar, meeting room, playground, parking. AE, DC, MC, V.*

Outdoor Activities and Sports

SKIING
Monte Capraro (✉ Capracotta, ☎ 0865/949043, WEB www.capracotta. com) runs ski lifts up to 5,000 ft and will also rent out equipment. It's best to phone beforehand and check on snow depth before you make the journey up here (one hour's drive north of Isernia).

Pietrabbondante

26 km (17 mi) northeast of Isernia, 25 km (16 mi) south of Agnone.

Identified by some scholars as Bovianum Vetus, the capital of Samnium in antiquity, the site of Pietrabbondante consists of a theater and temple complex built between the 4th and 1st centuries BC, 3,000 ft up in the wilds of Molise. Though recent attempts to restore two of the monuments are in questionable taste, seeing a **Hellenistic theater** this high up verges on a numinous experience. ✉ *Via Macere,* ☎ *0865/76129.* 🎟 *4,000 lire/€2.05.* ⊘ *May–Sept., daily 9–7; Oct.–Apr., daily 9–1:15.*

Agnone

43 km (27 mi) north of Isernia.

Known since medieval times for its thriving production of bells, Agnone has a rambling Old Town that invites exploration. Make a stop at the **Museo Storico della Campana,** which chronicles the history of campanology in the area. ✉ *C/o Fonderia Marinelli, Via F. D'Onofrio 14,* ☎ *0865/78235.* 🎟 *8,000 lire/€4.15.* ⊘ *Guided tours daily at noon and 4 (currently Italian only).*

Lodging

$$ 🏨 **Albergo Sammartino.** Strategically located just at the entrance to the Old Town and with views from most rooms sweeping over the Verrino valley, this hotel has been run by the Sammartino family for almost 90 years. It is usually quiet, except for Sunday mornings, when church bells start up their concerto around dawn. ✉ *Via Pietro Micca 44, 86081,* ☎ *0865/77577,* 𝔽𝔸𝕏 *0865/78239. 22 rooms. Restaurant, bar, meeting room. AE, DC, MC, V.*

Sepino

41 km (26 mi) southeast of Isernia, 25 km (16 mi) south of Campobasso.

The hill town of Sepino takes its name from the ancient Roman town of **Saepinum,** situated just off the main S17 near the village of Altìlia. The site, whose monuments were mainly laid out in the Augustan age (27 BC–AD 14), is like a miniature Pompeii, but refreshingly without the hordes of visitors. Saepinum is best tackled by entering through the Porta Tammaro 300 ft from the main road and working your way round counterclockwise via the theater, the baths (note the original stucco on the walls), the *decumanus* (main street) to the basilica (identified by its peristyle of columns), and then out onto the forum, with its standard complement of civic buildings. Southwest of the forum, just off the *cardo* (main cross street) leading to the southwestern gate of Porta Terravecchia are the administrative offices and visitor center, where site maps and descriptions (in Italian) can be obtained. ✉ *Contrada Altilia, Sepino,* ☎ *0874/790207.* 🎟 *Free.* ☼ *Daily 8–8.*

Termoli

69 km (43 mi) northeast of Campobasso, 105 km (66 mi) northeast of Isernia, 110 km (69 mi) southeast of Pescara.

Built on a promontory overlooking the Adriatic, Termoli is the only port along the region's 32-km (20-mi) coastline. The entrance to the Old Town is dominated by the 13th-century **Castello** built in the reign of Frederick II, now a military meteorological station and sadly—like so many other vantage points on the sensitive Adriatic coast—closed to the public. Except when overwhelmed by large numbers of sun seekers frequenting its lidos in the height of summer, Termoli makes a good base for day trips to the unspoiled Tremiti islands situated 42 km (26 mi) offshore.

Dining and Lodging

$$ ✕ **Zio Gianni.** Attractive vaulted spaces in Termoli's Old Town house this small restaurant specializing in freshly caught Adriatic seafood. Try the sublime *orecchiette allo scoglio* (fish soup served with pasta), which the locals wash down with a fruity red wine, Montepulciano del Molise. ✉ *Via Duomo 30,* ☎ *0875/704593. Reservations essential weekends. AE, DC, MC, V. Closed Mon. and 2 wks in Jan.–Feb.*

$$–$$$ 🏨 **Grand Hotel Sømerist.** Enjoying a rather bizarre seafront location below a 1970s condominium, this small but well-appointed hotel is both close to the port and the railway station yet in a very quiet area of town. ✉ *Via V. Cuoco 14, 86039,* ☎ *0875/706760,* 📠 *0875/706760,* WEB *www.somerist.it. 20 rooms. Restaurant, air-conditioning, meeting room. AE, DC, MC, V.*

APULIA AND MOLISE A TO Z

To research prices, get advice from other travelers, and book travel arrangements, visit www.fodors.com.

AIR TRAVEL

CARRIERS
Several airlines serve the cities of Bari and Brindisi: Alitalia flies regularly from Rome and Milan; Air Europe connects Milan and Bari; Airone serves both Bari and Brindisi, with flights from Turin, Milan, and Rome; and Airdolomiti flies between Verona and Bari.
➤ AIRLINES AND CONTACTS: **Airdolomiti** (☎ 800/013366). **Air Europe** (☎ 848/848130). **Airone** (☎ 848/848130). **Alitalia** (☎ 848/865641).

AIRPORTS

A regular bus service connects the two airports, Bari-Palese (about 10 km [7 mi] northwest of the city center) and Brindisi-Papola (8 km [5 mi] to the north), with their respective cities. Bari-Palese lies. Brindisi-Papola is 8 km (5 mi) to the north. Alitalia buses provide service from the cities to arrivals and departures at both airports.
➤ AIRPORT INFORMATION: **Bari-Palese** (☎ 080/583–5204). **Brindisi-Papola** (☎ 0831/411–7208).

BOAT AND FERRY TRAVEL

Ferries ply the waters from Bari and Brindisi to Greece (Corfu, Igou-
menitsa, Patras, and Kephalonia), Turkey, Albania, and even Egypt and
Croatia.

➤ BOAT AND FERRY INFORMATION: **Adriatica di Navigazione** (agents at
A. Galli e Figlio, ✉ Corso Manfredi 4, 71043 Manfredonia, ☎ 0884/
582520; Gargano Viaggi, ✉ Piazza Roma 7, 71019 Vieste, ☎ 0884/
708501). **Blue Star Ferries** (agents at Il Globo, ✉ Corso Garibaldi 65,
72100 Brindisi, ☎ 0831/527684).

BUS TRAVEL

Compared to rail, travel times by bus into Apulia from Naples on the
far side of the Apennines are substantially shorter. From Rome, contact Autolinee Marozzi, at their Rome office or in Bari. If traveling between Naples and Foggia, contact CLP; Miccolis runs a daily Naples-Lecce
service which takes five hours, about half as long as by train.

Direct, if not always frequent, connections operate between most destinations in Apulia. SITA is the main bus company operating in the region. In many cases the bus service is actually the backup to the train
service.

➤ BUS INFORMATION: **Autolinee Marozzi** (☎ 06/4424–9519 in Rome,
☎ 080/556–2446 in Bari). **CLP** (☎ 081/5311706). **Miccolis** (☎ 081/
200380). **SITA** (✉ Piazza Aldo Moro 15/a, ☎ 080/5213714).

CAR RENTAL

➤ LOCAL AGENCIES: **Avis** (✉ Via Zuppetta 5/a, Bari, ☎ 080/5247154;
✉ Aeroporto Palese, Bari, ☎ 080/5316168; ✉ Piazza Cairoli 25,
Brindisi, ☎ 0831/526407; ✉ train station, Foggia, ☎ 0881/778912;
✉ Viale Grassi 158, Lecce, ☎ 0832/228585; ✉ Corso Umberto 61,
Taranto, ☎ 099/4532278; WEB www.avisautonoleggio.italia.it). **Hertz**
(✉ Aeroporto Palese, Bari, ☎ 080/5316171; ✉ Aeroporto Papola, Brin-
disi, ☎ 0831/413060; ✉ Viale Virgilio 51, Taranto, ☎ 099/7362290;
WEB www.hertz.com). **Maggiore-Budget** (✉ Viale Ventiquattro Mag-
gio 76, Foggia, ☎ 0881/773173).

CAR TRAVEL

Driving is the best way to get around Apulia and Molise and the only
way to see remote sights. Apulia is linked with the Italian autostrada
system, making it just a four- or five-hour drive from Rome to the
Gargano Promontory or Bari. Roads are good, and major cities are linked
by fast autostrade. Secondary roads connect the whole region; more
direct—but sometimes less scenic—routes provide a convenient link between Bari, Brindisi, and Lecce. Don't plan on any night driving in the
countryside, because the roads can become confusing without the aid
of landmarks or large towns.

EMERGENCY SERVICES

ACI Emergency Service offers 24-hour roadside assistance.

➤ CONTACTS: **ACI dispatchers** (☎ 116).

EMERGENCIES

Pharmacies take turns staying open late and on Sunday. A list of hours
is posted on each *farmacia* (pharmacy).

➤ CONTACTS: **General Emergencies** (☎ 113).

MAIL AND SHIPPING

➤ POST OFFICES: **Bari** (✉ Via Amendola 116, ☎ 080/550–7236). **Brindisi** (✉ Piazza Vittoria 8, ☎ 0831/525058).

SAFETY

WOMEN IN APULIA AND MOLISE

The usual precautions apply here as throughout the south of Italy. Curb-crawlers still abound—local women just ignore them and continue on their way—and evening outings are best done in groups.

TOURS

The Azienda di Promozione Turistica in Bari is the best connection for guided tours in Apulia, otherwise poorly served by tour operators. The office can put you in touch with one of a number of local operators that offer everything from chauffeur-driven cars to a quick regional primer as part of a longer excursion.

➤ FEES AND SCHEDULES: **Azienda di Promozione Turistica della Provincia di Bari** (⊠ Piazza Moro 32/a, 70122, ☎ 080/5242244, WEB www.pugliaturismo.it).

TRAIN TRAVEL

Bari is a transit hub for train connections with northern Italy. Good train service, operated by FS (Italian State Railways), links Bari to Brindisi, Lecce, and Taranto, but smaller destinations can often be reached only by completing the trip on a connecting bus operated by the railroad. The private Ferrovie Sud-Est (FSE) line connects the trulli area and Martina Franca with Bari and Taranto, and the fishing port of Gallipoli with Lecce.

➤ TRAIN INFORMATION: **Italian State Railways** (☎ 848/888088). **Ferrovie Sud-Est** (FSE; (080/5462111)).

TRAVEL AGENCIES

➤ LOCAL AGENT REFERRALS: **Carlson Wagonlit Travel** (⊠ Via Cardassi 56, Bari, ☎ 080/5540588, WEB www.ewt.it). **Crusi Viaggi e Turismo** (⊠ Piazza S. Oronzo 21, Lecce 73100, ☎ 0832/305522, FAX 0832/306208). **Sestante** (⊠ Via Abate Gimma 150, Bari, ☎ 080/5213552). **Silver Viaggi** (⊠ Corso Garibaldi 95, 72100, Brindisi, ☎ 0831/528333). **Utac Viaggi** (⊠ Via Santa Lucia 11, Brindisi 72100, ☎ 0831/560780, FAX 0831/529040 WEB www.utacviaggi.it).

VISITOR INFORMATION

➤ TOURIST INFORMATION: **Bari** (⊠ Piazza Moro 32/a, 70122, ☎ 080/5242244, WEB www.pugliaturismo.it). **Brindisi** (⊠ Piazza Dionisi, 72100, ☎ 0831/523072). **Campobasso** (⊠ Piazza della Vittoria 14, 86100, ☎ 0874/95662). **Foggia** (⊠ Via Perrone 17, 71100, ☎ 0881/723650). **Isernia** (⊠ Via Farinacci 11, 86170, ☎ 0865/3992). **Lecce** (⊠ Via Vittorio Emanuele 24, 73100, ☎ 0832/248092). **Ostuni** (⊠ Corso Mazzini 6, 72017, ☎ 0831/301268). **San Giovanni Rotondo** (⊠ Piazza Europa 104, 71013, ☎ 0882/456240). **Taranto** (⊠ Corso Umberto I 113, 74100, ☎ 099/4532392). **Trani** (⊠ Via Cavour 140, 70059, ☎ 0883/588830). **Vieste** (⊠ Piazza Kennedy, 71019, ☎ 0884/708806; ⊠ kiosk in Piazza della Repubblica, summer only, ☎ 0883/43295).

14 BASILICATA AND CALABRIA

MATERA, COSENZA, THE TYRRHENIAN COAST

The lure of Italy's deep south, a magical combination of mountain and sea, has eluded visitors so far. It's their loss, for here sprawls untrammeled scenery that's hardly been altered since the city-states of Magna Graecia ruled the coasts. Their vestiges are here, as are the bizarre cave dwellings of Matera, a shining example of Byzantine church-building at Stilo, and the tranquil, sun-drenched beaches of Tropea and Scilla.

T HE *MEZZOGIORNO,* the informal name for Italy's south, reaches
its full apotheosis in the regions of Basilicata and Calabria, often
referred to as the instep and toe of Italy's boot. Here, in an area
of Italy off most tourist itineraries, the southern sun burns on a sparsely
populated landscape where government neglect and archaic social patterns have prevented the kind of industrialization and rush to moder-
nity experienced in other parts of the country. Despite the undeveloped
state of large tracts of these two regions, however, Basilicata and Calabria have become increasingly popular among Italians, and a good
infrastructure of hotels and leisure facilities won't make your stay in
any sense deprived. On the contrary, the combination of superlative
beaches, spectacular mountain ranges, and the ubiquitous relics of Magna
Graecia (Greek colonies) and the Norman and Spanish occupations,
makes a visit here a worthwhile component to any trip to Italy.

By Robert
Andrews

Pleasures and Pastimes

Beaches

The lack of industry in Basilicata and Calabria has one positive result
for beach fans—acres of sand and a largely unpolluted sea running almost continuously down both coasts of the peninsula. This is not the
place for you if you like your beaches impeccably tended but crowded
with regimented lines of sunbathers and ranks of uniform beach umbrellas. Here you can pick and choose strands at whim and spread out.
What's more, there is a pronounced difference between the two coasts:
the more developed Tyrrhenian littoral, on the western side, has more
villages and facilities and is more scenic, with the mountains a constant backdrop; the eastern Ionian shore, on the other hand, is flatter
and wilder, has fewer towns and villages, and holds less visual interest. The best Tyrrhenian spots are around Maratea, Praia a Mare, Amantea, Tropea, and Scilla. On the Ionian, head for Lido di Metaponto,
Sibari, Capo Rizzuto, and Soverato. Remember that if you don't have
your own beach umbrella, the summer sun can be oppressive and even
dangerous: borrow or buy one if you can, and arm yourself with plenty
of sunscreen. Alternatively, stick to your hotel beach or seek out those
few spots where there are lidos and amenities to rent, such as at
Metaponto, Soverato, and around Tropea.

Dining

Basilicata and Calabria are renowned for both their seafood—calamari,
bream, sea bass, and swordfish to name a few—and their produce. Look
for various types of *funghi* (mushrooms), particularly in the fall, and
pork in its many forms. Food production has not reached the industrial level of Italy's north, and consequently you will find much greater
variety in the methods of preparing and even naming the dishes, leaving much scope for adventurous eating and the discovery of new tastes.
One taste experience you will find universally available, however, is
that of *peperoncini* (small dried hot chile peppers), whose sweat-in-
ducing seeds are often added to pasta dishes. For general information
and price categories, *see* Dining *in* Smart Travel Tips.

Hiking and Skiing

Most vacationers in Basilicata and Calabria think of only swimming
and sunbathing as the main pastimes, unaware of the hiking and skiing that can be done in the forested or craggily bare peaks and valleys
of the predominantly mountainous landscape. Three zones have been
made into nature reserves, with facilities set up to cater to outdoors enthusiasts. All three areas see plenty of cross-country and downhill skiing; the best slopes are at Camigliatello and Gambarie, where you can

rent equipment. Farthest north, the Parco Nazionale del Monte Pollino, riddled with lush canyons and marked paths, straddles the boundary between Basilicata and Calabria and is a good place to spot eagles and even wild boars. The villages of Morano Calabro, off the A3 autostrada to the south, and San Severino Lucano, off S653 to the north, are good starting points for these mountains, which reach up to 7,500 ft. Occupying the widest part of the Calabrian peninsula, the Sila Massif (which rises to 6,300 ft) attracts most visitors, though the thick pine, beech, and chestnut forests are vast enough for you to find your own space. The Sila Grande, accessible from Lorica or Camigliatello, offers the most rewarding exploring within this extensive range. Farthest south, the Aspromonte Massif, soaring above Reggio di Calabria, is a welcome retreat from summer temperatures, also with peaks as high as 6,500 ft; access is easiest from the S183 between Melito di Porto Salvo and Gambarie. For further information, including walking and hiking itineraries and the state of the slopes, contact local tourist offices.

Lodging

Hotels are generously distributed throughout this region. They range from high-class, professionally run complexes with pools, tennis courts, and copious grounds to family-run places where the famous southern hospitality compensates for a lack of amenities. Note that many hotels close during the winter months, especially those by the sea, and that hotels in skiing areas will be open in summer and winter but are closed for the rest of the year. Children are welcomed everywhere and are usually a prominent presence in the region's hotels. Many families vacation in the numerous campsites along both coasts, most fully equipped and often with bungalows or apartments for rent by the week or less; these can get congested in August. Most campsites are closed in the winter months. For general information and price categories, *see* Lodging *in* Smart Travel Tips.

Exploring Basilicata and Calabria

The regions of Basilicata and Calabria can be toured as either brief side trips from Campania, Apulia, or Sicily or as a series of select stops en route to these other regions. The best and fastest way to explore these regions is to stick to the coasts, making inland jaunts from there. West of Taranto, follow the Ionian coast for the classical remains at Metaponto, Locri, and other Greek sights strung along the S106, making brief detours to visit such curiosities as the troglodyte city of Matera and the Norman stronghold of Gerace. South of Salerno, the route along the Tyrrhenian coast takes in a brief stretch of Basilicata— among whose cliffs nestles the smart resort of Maratea—before swooping down into Calabria, where you can divide your time between first-class beaches on the Tropea promontory, or at Scilla, and the high inland ranges of Sila and Aspromonte.

Basilicata and Calabria are well served by transport connections, and drivers and bus and train passengers alike will find no difficulty circulating within these regions. The toll-free A3 autostrada gives a clear run from Salerno all the way down to Reggio di Calabria; the S106 traces the Ionian coast from Taranto to Reggio and is often empty of traffic. Trains also follow these coastal routes, with frequent connections on the Naples–Villa San Giovanni line and fewer trains on the Ionian side. Things get much busier, of course, in midsummer, when beaches and resorts burst into activity and hotel rooms can be hard to find.

Numbers in the text correspond to numbers in the margin and on the Basilicata and Calabria map.

Basilicata and Calabria

Adriatic Sea

Andria · Bari
A14 · Monópoli
A16 · S96 · S16
Spinazzola · Fasano
Melfi · Gravina in Puglia · Altamura · Ostuni
APULIA · Gioia del Colle
Matera ② · Massafra · Francavilla
Potenza · Grassano · Via Appia · Taranto
Bradano · S407
Auletta · Ferrandina · **Metaponto** ①
BASILICATA · Pisticci · Lido di Metaponto
Sala Consilina · Viggiano · **Aliano** ③
CAMPANIA · Colobraro · Gulf of Taranto
Francaville in Sinni · Parco Nazionale del Pollino · Amendolara
Lagonegro · San Severino Lucano
Marina di Camerota · Acquafredda · Rotonda · S106
Maratea ④ · Sibari
Marina di Maratea · Morano Calabro · Castrovillari
Praia a Mare · Rossano
Scalea
Cirella · CALABRIA
Diamante ⑤ · Parco Nazionale della Calabria
Cetraro · **Camigliatello** ⑦ · San Giovanni in Flore
Paola · **Cosenza** ⑥ · SILA GRANDE · Crotone
Lorica
Amantea · SILA MASSIF
Falerna · Catanzaro
S280 · Capo Rizzuto
Lamezia Terme
Pizzo ⑧ · Soverato
Tropea ⑨ · **Stilo** ⑰
Nicotera · A3 · Marina di Monasterace
Rosarno · S106
Bagnara Calabra ⑩ **Palmi** · **Gerace**
Villa **Scilla** ⑪ · S112 · **Locri** ⑮ · ⑯
San Giovanni · ⑫ · ⑭ **Aspromonte**
Milazzo · Messina · **Reggio di Calabria** ⑬ · Gambarie · Parco Nazionale della Calabria
Barcellona · Gallico · Ionian Sea
SICILY · A18 · Melito di Porto Salvo
Stromboli · Panarea · Salina · Lipari · Vulcano
Tyrrhenian Sea

N

KEY
----- Ferry Lines

0 — 30 miles
0 — 50 km

Great Itineraries

Your itinerary while exploring Basilicata and Calabria will depend on the direction you're traveling. An ideal route is to come from the north either along the Tyrrhenian coast—from Campania on the S18 or the faster A3 highway—or from Apulia on the S106. If you're traveling in Basilicata, you can cross over to the Tyrrhenian coast without any difficulty on the panoramic S653, passing through the Pollino range and enabling you to make a stop at Maratea. Farther south, you can change coasts at Sibari, Catanzaro, Stilo, and Locri. From the Tyrrhenian coast, head inland at Paola to go through the Sila range to Crotone on the Ionian Sea.

IF YOU HAVE 2 OR 3 DAYS

If heading south from Campania, you should consider a night in the beautifully sited resort of ⊡ **Maratea** ④, a perfect marriage of cliffs and beaches. On your second day, stop for lunch at **Diamante** ⑤, and then move on to your next hotel stop at ⊡ **Tropea** ⑨, close to some of Calabria's best beaches. From here, it's a short run down to the Sicily ferries at Villa San Giovanni.

Alternatively, coming from Apulia, make a stop at the archaeological site at **Metaponto** ① before crossing over to Basilicata's west coast for an overnight at Maratea; then continue south as above. With an extra day at your disposal, you might return to the Ionian coast to see the lovely Byzantine La Cattólica church at ⊡ **Stilo** ⑰. Spend the night here, and then drive the brief distance down the coast to see the classical ruins of **Locri** ⑮ before heading west to the archaeological museum at ⊡ **Reggio di Calabria** ⑬.

IF YOU HAVE 4 OR 5 DAYS

A greater amount of time will allow you to form a closer acquaintance with Basilicata and Calabria. From Apulia, allow two or three hours to explore the classical remains at **Metaponto** ① before heading inland on the fast S407 to ⊡ **Matera** ②, a must for its fascinating *sassi,* prehistoric rock dwellings, and an ideal first overnight stop. The next day, cross over to the Tyrrhenian side, making a brief diversion in deepest Basilicata to see **Aliano** ③, the minuscule village made famous by Carlo Levi. Spend your second night at ⊡ **Maratea** ④, and then head south via **Diamante** ⑤. At Paola, veer east across the coastal chain to get a taste of inland Calabria, spending your third night in either ⊡ **Camigliatello** ⑦ or ⊡ **Cosenza** ⑥. Explore Cosenza's old town, or take some time to hike or ski in the area. The next day, make your way south to the attractive seaside town of ⊡ **Pizzo** ⑧, and later head to beautiful ⊡ **Tropea** ⑨, either of which makes a good fourth-night stop. If you can pull yourself away, continue down the coast the following day; you might stop at the eclectic museum at **Palmi** ⑩, lunch by the harbor at **Bagnara Calabra** ⑪, siesta on the beach at **Scilla** ⑫, and check in for the night at ⊡ **Reggio di Calabria** ⑬, where the archaeological museum is one of southern Italy's best. If you have time left over, either make an excursion on to the brooding massif of **Aspromonte** ⑭ or skirt south around this range to the Greek site at **Locri** ⑮ and the nearby Norman town of **Gerace** ⑯. Otherwise, it's just a short hop over the Straits to Messina and Sicily.

When to Tour Basilicata and Calabria

The regions of Basilicata and Calabria suffer from intense heat in summer and, away from the coasts, bitter winter cold. If you don't mind sacrificing the Ferragosto (Festival of the Assumption) celebrations in the middle of the month, avoid August, since accommodations can be limited and facilities generally strained; any time on either side, though, would be ideal for touring these regions. Beaches are comparatively empty and the water temperature is comfortable in June, July, and September. Avoid the coastal resorts in winter if you want to find hotels open and anything more than a lonely dog on the streets. The months of January and February see snow inland, which is great if you want to ski but can make for dangerous driving conditions. Spring and fall see the forests of Basilicata and Calabria at their best.

BASILICATA

Occupying the instep of Italy's boot, Basilicata has long been one of Italy's poorest regions, memorably described by Carlo Levi in his *Christ Stopped at Eboli*, a book that brought home to the majority of the Italians the depths of deprivation to which this forgotten region was subject. (The tale of Levi's internment was poignantly filmed by Francesco Rosi in 1981.) Basilicata was not always so desolate, however. For the ancient Greeks, the area formed part of Magna Graecia, the loose collection of colonies founded along the coasts of southern Italy whose wealth and military prowess rivaled those of the city-states of Greece itself. Metaponto (formerly Metapontion or Metapontum) was one of the most important of these colonies; its remains easily reached along the coastal S106. You could visit the sights and museum en route to Matera, inland from here. This town is built on the side of an impressive ravine that is honeycombed with prehistoric dwellings (*sassi*), some of them still occupied, forming a separate enclave that contrasts vividly with the attractive Baroque town above.

Metaponto

❶ *48 km (30 mi) southwest of Taranto, 114 mi south of Bari.*

Greek Metapontion was founded around 700 BC by an Achaean colony from the city-states of Sybaris and Kroton (farther down the coast, in what is now Calabria). The great mathematician and philosopher Pythagoras, banished from Kroton, established a school here in about 510 BC and eventually died in the city. Punished for its support of the Carthaginian general Hannibal (247–183 BC) after his victory over Rome at Cannae (216 BC), Metapontum, as it was known by the Romans, endured long years of decline—sacked by the slave-rebel Spartacus (died 71 BC) and subsequently ravaged both by malaria and Saracen raids. Most of what remained was used for building elsewhere in the region, but the *zona archeologica* (archaeological zone), which covers a vast area, retains enough interest to merit a visit. You'll need a car: allow about an hour for the museum, which is best seen before the sight, to view the plans and maps and put it all into context, and then an hour or two for the excavations. When you've finished here, you might take a dip at Lido di Metaponto, where there are sandy, well-equipped beaches.

The modern **Museo Archeologico Nazionale** displays 4th- and 5th-century statuary, ceramics, jewelry, and coins on a rotating basis—sadly, representing only a tiny fraction of the total number of finds until work on a new wing is completed. Perhaps most interesting are examples of coins stamped with images of grain, symbolizing the cereal production to which Metapontion owed its prosperity. Also noteworthy is the section showing how the study of fingerprints on shards found in the artisans' quarter has revealed new information on the social makeup of the ancient city. Maps and aerial photographs of the site with accounts of the excavations are useful for your visit. The museum lies about 2 km (1 mi) outside Lido di Metaponto (look out for the scanty signs). ⊠ *Metaponto Borgo,* ☎ *0835/745327.* ▨ *5,000 lire/€2.60.* ⊘ *Mon. 2–8, Tues.–Sun. 9–8.*

Highlights of the sprawling **zona archeologica,** accessible to the east of the Museo Archeologico Nazionale, include the **Santuario di Apollo Licio** (Sanctuary of Apollo Lykaios), a 6th-century BC Doric temple which, archaeologists have deduced, once boasted 32 columns. Only the foundations and a few capitals and shafts are to be seen today. Nearby, encircled by an expanse of grass, lie the remains of a 4th-century BC **Teatro,** much restored. More compelling is the better-preserved Tempio di Hera (Temple of Hera), commonly known as **Tavole Palatine,** found 2–3 km (1–2 mi) north, where the main S106 crosses the Bradano River. With 15 of its fluted Doric columns surviving, it is the most evocative remnant of this once mighty state. ⊠ *Metaponto Borgo,* ☎ *0835/ 745327.* ⌕ *Free.* ☉ *Daily 9–1 hr before sunset.*

Matera

❷ *45 km (28 mi) north of Metaponto, 62 km (39 mi) south of Bari.*

Matera is one of southern Italy's most unusual towns. On their own, the elegant Baroque churches, palazzi, and broad piazzas—filled to bursting during the evening *passeggiata,* when the locals turn out to stroll the streets—would make Matera stand out in Basilicata's impoverished landscape. But what really sets this town apart is its *sassi,* rock-hewn dwellings piled chaotically atop one other and straggling along the sides of a steep ravine. Until relatively recently, these troglodytic abodes presented a Dante-esque vision of squalor and poverty, graphically described in Carlo Levi's *Christ Stopped at Eboli,* but in the 1960s most of them were emptied of their inhabitants, who were largely consigned to the ugly blocks you saw on your way into town. Today, however, having been designated a World Heritage Site in 1993, the area has been cleaned up and is gradually being populated once again. A Strada Panoramica highway leads you safely through this desolate region, which still retains its eerie atmosphere and panoramic views. To get the most out of the whole area, pick up an *itinerario turistico* (tourist itinerary) from the tourist office. For a commentary and access to parts of the sassi you might otherwise miss, you can join a guided tour or hire a guide.

There are two areas of sassi, the **Sasso Caveoso** and the **Sasso Barisano,** and both can be viewed from vantage points in the upper town. Follow the Strada Panoramica down and feel free to ramble among the strange structures, which, in the words of H. V. Morton in his *A Traveller in Southern Italy,* "resemble the work of termites rather than of man." Among them, you will find several *chiese rupestri,* or rock-hewn churches, some of which have medieval frescoes, notably **Santa Maria de Idris,** right on the edge of the Sasso Caveoso, near the ravine. A few minutes east of Santa Maria, in the so-called Albanian quarter (settled by refugees in the 15th century), the 10th-century **Santa Lucia alle Malve** has Byzantine-style frescoes dating from 1250. Hours for both churches may vary, as you have to get the custodian to open them up. ⊠ *Sasso Caveoso.* ⌕ *Gratuity expected.* ☉ *Daily 9–1 and 3:30–dusk.*

When you've had your fill of the sassi, take a leisurely stroll around the upper town. The **Duomo,** which occupies a prominent position between the two areas of sassi, was built in the late 13th century. It has a pungent Apulian-Romanesque flavor; inside, some of the columns came from Metaponto, and there is a recently recovered fresco, probably painted in the 14th century, showing scenes from the *Last Judgment.* On the Duomo's facade, the figures of Sts. Peter and Paul stand on either side of a sculpture of Matera's patron, Madonna della Bruna. Her feast day, the Sagra di Santa Bruna, is celebrated on July 2, when her statue is carried in procession three times around the piazza before being stormed by the onlookers, who are allowed to break up the float and carry off bits as mementos. ⊠ *Via Duomo.* ⊙ *Daily 8–noon and 4–7.*

In town you'll find the 17th-century church of **San Francesco d'Assisi,** which contains eight panels of a polyptych by Bartolomeo Vivarini (circa 1432–99), set above the altar. The church's ornate Baroque style was superimposed on two older churches that can be visited through a passage in the third chapel on the left; inside are traces of some 11th-century frescoes. ⊠ *Piazza San Francesco.* ⊙ *Daily 8–noon and 4–7.*

The graceful **conservatory,** behind the church of San Francesco, is dedicated to the 18th-century composer Egidio Duni (1708–75), a native of Matera who settled in Paris, where he helped to popularize Neapolitan comic opera during the ancien régime. The building was formerly a convent, then the town hall, before assuming its present role. ⊠ *Piazza Sedile.*

Allow time to view Matera's excellent **Museo Ridola,** housed in the ex-monastery of Santa Chiara. Illustrating the human and geological history of the area, the museum includes an extensive selection of prehistoric and classical finds, notably an array of Bronze Age weaponry and beautifully decorated Greek plates and amphoras. ⊠ *Via Ridola 24,* ☎ *0835/310058.* ▦ *5,000 lire/€2.60.* ⊙ *Mon. 2–8, Tues.–Sun. 9–8, longer hrs in summer.*

The **Palazzo Lanfranchi,** at the end of Via Ridola, holds a **Pinacoteca** with an assortment of 17th- and 18th-century paintings. The real draw here is the **Centro Carlo Levi,** containing a good cross section of Levi's vivid canvases, as well as the long mural *Lucania 1961.* The palace's open hours may be restricted while it undergoes restoration work (which is supposed to be completed by the end of 2002). ⊠ *Piazzetta Pascoli,* ☎ *0835/310468.* ▦ *Free.* ⊙ *Tues.–Sat. 9–1, Sun. 9–noon.*

Dining and Lodging

$$ ✕ **Il Terrazzino.** This is a wonderfully atmospheric spot, its "little terrace" well positioned for dining alfresco with unrivaled views over the sassi. The ambience is equally appealing inside, a cavernous space with niches and a cheerful buzz of tourists and locals. The food isn't bad either—specialties include *minestra di grano e ceci* (grain and chickpea soup) and homemade spumoni ice cream. A very reasonable tourist menu is offered. Book ahead to get one of the best tables. ⊠ *Vico San Giuseppe 7,* ☎ *0835/332503. AE, DC, MC, V. No dinner Tues. Closed 1 wk in June.*

$$ ✕ **Trattoria Lucana.** This trattoria is a simple family-run place in the center of town, where you can enjoy local recipes in a friendly, rustic environment—try out the *agnello allo spiedo* (lamb on the spit) or *bocconcini di vitello* (veal). ⊠ *Via Lucana 48,* ☎ *0835/336117. Reservations essential. AE, DC, MC, V. Closed Sun. and 2 wks in Sept.*

$$ ▦ **Albergo Italia.** Central and stylish, the Italia is a reliably comfortable accommodation choice, housed in a well-preserved old building just steps away from the sassi and Museo Ridola. The best rooms are ornate but unfussy, with pastel color-coordinated curtains and comforters, and some have balconies. There's a small, elegant restaurant and a modern bar. ⊠ *Via Ridola 5, 75100,* ☎ *0835/333561,* FAX *0835/330087. 46 rooms. Restaurant (closed 2 wks in Aug.). AE, DC, MC, V.*

$$ ▦ **Sassi Hotel.** For the full sassi experience, this place can't be beat—it's right in the heart of the Sasso Barisano, directly across to the Duomo. The whole place has a raw, cavelike design, with rough-hewn walls and stairs (and so not advised for anyone with mobility difficulties). Facilities are minimal (there's no restaurant) and the few guest rooms—on different levels and served by separate steps—are small and plain

but clean, comfortable, and air-conditioned. The hotel's position at the bottom of the valley means that it's not always quiet, but the views are supreme. One room is set aside for hostel-type bunk accommodation at budget rates. ⊠ *Via San Giovanni Vecchio 89, 75100,* ☎ *0835/ 331009,* 𝔽𝔸𝕏 *0835/333733. 10 rooms. Bar. AE, DC, MC, V.*

Outdoor Activities and Sports

WALKING TOUR

The agency **Nuovi Amici dei Sassi** (⊠ Piazza Sedile 20, 75100, ☎ 0835/ 331011) arranges up to four tours of the sassi area a day, charging around 15,000 lire/€7.80 per person for a group of four or more. There are also independent guides who offer their services on the spot, asking from 15,000 lire/€7.80 to 30,000 lire/€15.60, according to length of tour and the number in your party.

Aliano

❸ *127 km (79 mi) southwest of Matera, 102 km (63 mi) southeast of Potenza.*

This remote village off S598 in the center of Basilicata's empty interior was the site of Carlo Levi's internment during 1936 and 1937. After the war, Levi (1902–75) published his account of that time in his classic *Christ Stopped at Eboli*, later filmed by Francesco Rosi. Not significantly different from any of the countless villages scattered over the featureless clay gullies and outcrops stretching out on all sides, Aliano (called Gagliano by Levi) has not altered much, and readers can identify the church, the piazza where the Fascist mayor addressed the impassive peasants, and the timeless views. The house where Levi stayed has been preserved as the **Museo Storico Carlo Levi,** displaying some personal items of Levi's as well as other articles of local interest. It's best to phone first or stop in the Bar Centrale in the center of the village for the custodian. ⊠ *Palazzo Caporale,* ☎ *0835/568074 or 0360/ 506548.* 🖼 *Free.* ☺ *By appointment.*

Maratea

❹ *103 km (64 mi) southwest of Aliano, 217 km (135 mi) south of Naples.*

When encountering Maratea for the first time, you can be forgiven for thinking they've somehow arrived at the French Riviera. The high, twisty road resembles nothing so much as a corniche, complete with glimpses of a turquoise sea below. Divided by the craggy rocks into various separate localities—Maratea, Maratea Porto, Maratea Marina—the sequence ends above the main inland village (*paese*) where the ruins of a much older settlement can be seen (Maratea Antica). At the summit of the hill a dramatic, gigantic Christ stands, reminiscent of the one in Rio de Janeiro. Most of the area's hotels and restaurants lie in the Fiumicello–Santa Venere neighborhood, a short walk from an enticing beach. But there's no shortage of secluded sandy strips in between the rocky headlands, which can get crowded in August. A summer minibus service connects all of the various points once or twice an hour.

Dining and Lodging

$$ ✕ **Taverna Rovita.** Housed in a former convent with exposed beams, this restaurant in the heart of the old town offers a menu based on traditional recipes, but the food here is in a different league from that of Maratea's other eateries. The *antipasti,* for a start, are various and abundant, and the homemade pasta comes with a selection of rich sauces that changes according to the season. Choose a locally caught fish or a grand and meaty mixed grill for the main course, and then succumb to a decadent dessert.

Reservations are advised. ⊠ *Via Rovita 13, Maratea,* ☎ *0973/876588. AE, DC, MC, V. Closed Tues. and Nov.–Feb.*

$$$$ 🏨 **Santavenere.** This deluxe hotel is worth fasting for, if only for the opulent architectural style of the public rooms. The guest rooms are disappointingly ordinary, but most enjoy an incredible panorama of rock and sea. A tennis court, private beach, and round pool complete the picture. The high tab is reduced by up to 50% outside the summer months. ⊠ *Località Fiumicello di Maratea, 85040,* ☎ *0973/876910,* FAX *0973/877654,* WEB *www.santaverenehotel.com. 40 rooms. 2 restaurants, bar, pool, tennis court, beach. AE, DC, MC, V. Closed Nov.–Mar.*

CALABRIA

Italy's southernmost mainland region has seen more than its fair share of oppression, poverty, and natural disaster, but the region of Magna Graecia, mountains, and *mare* (sea) also has more than its share of fantastic scenery and great beaches. The accent here is on the landscape, the sea, and the constantly changing dialogue they create together. Don't expect much in the way of high culture in this most neglected of regions, but be open to the simple pleasures to be found—the food, the friendliness, the disarming hospitality of the people. This little-traveled region also boasts some sights worth going out of your way for, from the vividly colored murals of Diamante to the ruins of Magna Graecia at Locri. The drive on the southbound autostrada alone is a breathtaking experience, the more so as you approach Sicily, whose image is glimpsed tantalizingly as the road dips in and out of long tunnels through the mountain. This is the road you should take for the big picture—but don't forget to stop awhile to get a closer view of this fascinating land.

Diamante

❺ *51 km (32 mi) south of Maratea, 225 km (140 mi) south of Naples.*

One of the most fashionable of the string of small resorts lining Calabria's north Tyrrhenian coast, Diamante makes a good stop for its whitewashed maze of narrow alleys, brightly adorned with a startling variety of large-scale murals. The work of various local artists, the murals depict a range of subjects and give a sense of wandering through a huge open-air art gallery. Flanking the broad seaside promenade are sparkling beaches to the north and south.

Dining and Lodging

$$ ✕ **Taverna del Pescatore.** One of a pair of good, moderately priced fish restaurants down by the seafront at Diamante's Spiaggia Piccola (the other is Lo Scoglio), this is the less formal of the two, and the more welcoming, with spartan but bright decor. Naturally, fish predominates— whatever's hauled in is cooked in a variety of ways. Phone first to secure a table outside. ⊠ *Via Calvario,* ☎ *0985/81482. MC, V. Closed Tues. in Oct.–May.*

$$$$ 🏨 **Grand Hotel San Michele.** A survivor from a vanishing age of hotels, the San Michele occupies a Belle Epoque–style, cliff-top ex-hunting lodge near the village of Cetraro, 20 km (12 mi) south of Diamante on SS18. Mingling Mediterranean charm with old-style elegance, the hotel is set within extensive grounds that include semitropical gardens and a small golf course, and an elevator takes you down to the private beach at the base of the cliff. The only downside is its isolation—you need a car to do anything, if you can ever be lured away from this palatial retreat. ⊠ *Località Bosco, 87022 Cetraro,* ☎ *0982/91012,* FAX *0982/91430,* WEB *www.sanmichele.it. 73 rooms. Restaurant, bar, tennis court, 9-hole golf course, beach. AE, DC, MC, V. Closed Nov.*

Cosenza

❻ *75 km (48 mi) south of Diamante, 185 km (115 mi) north of Reggio di Calabria.*

If you're traveling from the north, Cosenza is the first sizable town you'll encounter in Calabria. It's worth a stop to explore the *centro storico*. The town also provides the best gateway for the mountains of the Sila, whose steep walls rear up to the town's eastern side. Though much modern, often ugly, building has sprouted in recent years, investment has not been spared in renovating the old part of town, where you can easily spend half a day wandering around.

Crowning the Pancrazio hill above the Old City, with views across to the Sila mountains, **Castello Svevo** is largely in ruins, having suffered successive earthquakes and a lightning strike that ignited gunpowder stored within. The castle takes its name from the great Swabian emperor Frederick II (1194–1250), who added two octagonal towers, though it dates back originally to the Normans, who fortified the hill against their Saracen foes. Occasional exhibitions and concerts are staged here in summer. ⌂ *Porta Piana.* ☒ *Free.* ☉ *Apr.–Sept., weekdays 9–12:30 and 4–6.*

Cosenza's noblest square, **Piazza XV Marzo** (commonly known as Piazza della Prefettura), houses government buildings as well as the elegant **Teatro Rendano.** From the square, the **Villa Comunale** (public gardens) provides plenty of shady benches for a rest.

NEED A BREAK? In the heart of the *centro storico*, the charming and historic **Gran Caffè Renzelli** (⌂ Corso Telesio 46, ☎ 0984/412538) makes a fine spot for a pause in your perambulations. At tables inside or out (there is a no-smoking room as well as an outside terrace), you can enjoy *varciglia* (a dry almond cake) along with your *gran caffè* (large black coffee with cream floating on the top, served in a tall glass). Join in the *chiacchiere al caffè* (talks over coffee), echoing the discussions of the literary salon that once met here.

Cosenza's original **Duomo** was probably built in the middle of the 11th century but was destroyed by the earthquake of 1184. A new cathedral was consecrated in the presence of Emperor Frederick II in 1222. After many Baroque additions, later alterations have restored some of the Provençal Gothic style. Inside, look for the lovely tomb of Isabella of Aragon, who died after falling from her horse en route to France in 1271. ⌂ *Piazza del Duomo,* ☎ *0984/77864.* ☉ *Daily 7:30–noon and 3:30–7.*

Dining and Lodging

$-$$ ✕ **Calabria Bella.** On two floors of an 18th-century building to the left of the Duomo, this restaurant and pizzeria offers typical Calabrian cuisine. Pasta is homemade—try the fusilli *al ferretto con salsiccia, funghi e porcini* (with sausage, mushrooms, and pork)—and pizzas (evenings only) are cooked over a wood fire. Tables spill out onto the piazza in summer. ⌂ *Piazza Duomo 20,* ☎ *0984/793531. AE, DC, MC, V.*

$-$$ ✕ **Da Giocondo.** In the new part of town, but near the *centro storico*, you can sample simple homemade dishes in a modern yet homey atmosphere. Go for the local freshly picked mushrooms from the Sila as an antipasto, followed by *polpettine* (meatballs), washed down with local Cirò wine. ⌂ *Via Piave 53,* ☎ *0984/29810. AE, MC, V. Closed Sun. and 2–3 wks in Aug.*

$$ **Excelsior.** Used for years as an army barracks, this 1900 Liberty-style building was restored in 1999 to its former grandeur. The public areas are imposing, retaining their original style, while the spacious guest rooms have a modern feel. It's close to the shops of Cosenza's main drag, Corso Mazzini, and an easy walk across the Busento river from the *centro storico.* ⊠ *Piazza Matteotti 14, 87100,* ☎ FAX *0984/74383. 44 rooms. Restaurant, bar, meeting room. AE, DC, MC, V.*

$$ **Royal.** Though lacking much character, this modern hotel in the new part of town is handy for buses departing for the Sila. The public spaces have a classical style with columns and Persian carpets on the marble floor. The restaurant specializes in local Calabrian dishes. ⊠ *Via Molinella 24/E, 87100,* ☎ *0984/412165,* FAX *0984/412461. 50 rooms. Restaurant, bar, meeting room. AE, DC, MC, V.*

Camigliatello

❼ *36 km (22 mi) east of Cosenza.*

Lined with chalets, Camigliatello, between Crotone and Cosenza, is one of the Sila Massif's major resort towns. Most of the Sila is not mountainous at all; it is, rather, an extensive, sparsely populated plateau with areas of thick forest. Unfortunately, the region has been exploited by construction and fuel industries, resulting in considerable deforestation. However, since 1968, when the area was designated a national park (Parco Nazionale delle Calabria), strict rules have limited the felling of timber, and forests are now regenerating. There are well-marked trails through pine and beech woods, and ample opportunities for horseback riding. Fall and winter see droves of locals hunting mushrooms and gathering chestnuts, while ski slopes near Camigliatello also draw crowds. A couple of miles east of town, **Lago Cecita** makes a good starting point for exploring **La Fossiata,** a lovely wooded conservation area within the park.

Lodging

$$ **Tasso.** On the edge of Camigliatello, less than 1 km (½ mi) from the ski slopes, this hotel is in a peaceful, picturesque location. It's modern and well equipped, with plenty of space for evening entertainment, including live music, and relaxation after a day of hiking or skiing. The restaurant has a terrace shaded by a walnut tree, and all rooms have balconies. ⊠ *Via degli Impianti Sportivi, 87058,* ☎ FAX *0984/578113. 85 rooms. Restaurant, bar, lounge, nightclub, recreation room, meeting room, free parking. AE, DC, MC, V. Closed Mar.–May and Nov.*

Outdoor Activities and Sports

HIKING AND WALKING

One of the best hikes around Camigliatello is the **Strada delle Vette** (Peaks Road), a 13-km (8-mi) route that links the Sila's highest mountains. For maps and itineraries, contact the Camigliatello tourist office (⊠ Via Roma 5, ☎ 0984/578243).

HORSEBACK RIDING

With plenty of trails winding through woods and around lakes, horseback riding is one of Sila's year-round attractions. Contact **Maneggio Sila** (⊠ Via Molarotta, 3 km [2 mi] outside Camigliatello, ☎ 0360/283252).

SKIING

The slopes in the area are small and get quite crowded. The best place to rent equipment is at the **ski lift.** Call for rental information and slope conditions (☎ 0984/578037).

Pizzo

❽ *148 km (92 mi) south of Diamante, 107 km (66 mi) north of Reggio di Calabria.*

Overlooking the coast and a fishing port, Pizzo has a good selection of seafood restaurants and a small cliff-top Aragonese castle near the center of town. Here the French general Joachim Murat (1767–1815) was imprisoned, tried, and shot in October 1815, after a bungled attempt to rouse the people against the Bourbons and reclaim the throne of Naples given him by his brother-in-law Napoléon.

The **Chiesetta di Piedigrotta,** a little over a mile north of Pizzo's castle, at the bottom of a flight of steps leading down to the beach, is a 17th-century church hewn out of rock by shipwrecked Neapolitan sailors in thanks for their rescue. They filled it with statues of biblical figures; the collection was added to by a local father-and-son team at the beginning of this century, and in 1969 another scion of the family contributed some of his own, including a bizarre ensemble showing Fidel Castro kneeling before Pope John XXIII (1881–1963) and President Kennedy (1917–63). ✉ *Via Nazionale.* ⏱ *Daily 9–1 and 3–7:30.*

Before you leave Pizzo, make sure you sample the renowned gelato *di Pizzo,* a rich, creamy delight available in many flavors at any of the outdoor bars in the central Piazza della Repubblica.

Lodging

$$ 🏨 **Hotel Murat.** Here's a good, central choice for accommodation should you decide to overnight in Pizzo. Right in the town's main square, a stone's throw from the castle, the Murat has comfortable rooms, of which the ones on the sides are biggest and have the best views (ask for No. 207). ✉ *Piazza della Repubblica 41, 89812,* ☎ *0963/534201,* 📠 *0963/534469. 12 rooms. Restaurant, bar. AE, DC, MC, V.*

Tropea

❾ *28 km (17 mi) southwest of Pizzo, 107 km (66 mi) north of Reggio di Calabria.*

Ringed by cliffs and wonderful sandy beaches, the Tropea promontory is still undiscovered by the big tour operators. The main town, Tropea, easily wins the contest for prettiest town on Calabria's Tyrrhenian coast, its old palazzi built in simple golden stone on an elevation above the sea. On a clear day, the seaward views extend to embrace Stromboli's cone and perhaps some of the other Aeolians, too—the islands can be visited by motorboats that depart daily from Tropea in summer. Beach addicts will not be disappointed by the choice of magnificent sandy bays within easy reach of here—some of the best are south at Capo Vaticano and north at Briatico—and there are numerous hotels and restaurants in town to satisfy every taste.

In Tropea's harmonious warren of lanes, seek out the old Norman **Cattedrale,** whose interior displays a couple of unexploded U.S. bombs from World War II, with a grateful prayer to the Madonna attached to each. ✉ *Piazza Sedile.* ⏱ *Daily 7–noon and 4–6.*

From the belvedere at the bottom of the main square, Piazza Ercole, the church and Benedictine monastery of **Santa Maria della Isola** glistens on a rocky promontory above an aquamarine sea. Stroll out to visit the church on a path lined with fishermen's caves. Of Basilian origin, the church was remodeled in the Gothic style, then given another face-lift after an earthquake in 1905. The interior has an 18th-century nativity and some fragments of medieval tombs. ✉ *Santa Maria della Isola.* ⏱ *Daily 7–noon and 4–7.*

Dining and Lodging

$$$ ✕ **Pimm's.** Centrally located in Tropea's historic center, this restaurant offers the town's top dining experience. Seafood is the best choice, with such specialties as pasta with sea urchins, smoked swordfish, and stuffed squid. The splendid sea views are an extra enticement. ⊠ *Corse Vittorio Emanuele 2,* ☎ *0963/666105. AE, DC, MC, V. Closed Mon. in Oct.–May, and Jan.*

$$ 🏨 **Torre Ruffa.** Near the beach 6 km (4 mi) south of Tropea, this whitewashed hotel has everything you need for a quiet sojourn away from the madding crowd. Cane furniture, banana trees, and bright wisteria help to create a luxurious enclave. It also makes a great center for sports enthusiasts, offering weekly packages that include sailing, windsurfing, tennis, aerobics, and diving, with the opportunity to gain PADI certification. Round out the day with an evening cabaret show. ⊠ *Località Torre Ruffa 1, 88036 Ricadi,* ☎ *0963/663006,* 🄵🄰🄷 *0963/ 663942,* 🅆🄴🄱 *www.torreruffa.com. 42 rooms. Restaurant, bar, tennis court, beach. AE, DC, MC, V. Closed Oct.–May.*

Palmi

⑩ *60 km (37 mi) south of Tropea, 47 km (29 mi) north of Reggio di Calabria.*

The small town of Palmi is worth a stop for its excellent **Casa della Cultura Leonida Repaci** museum complex. Named after a local writer and artist, the wide-ranging collection includes an archaeological section, displaying pottery and other items dredged up from the sea bed; paintings by old masters, including Tintoretto (circa 1518–94) and Il Guercino (1591–1666); a gallery of modern art, mainly by southern Italian artists such as Renato Guttuso but also by Modigliani (1884–1920), Giorgio de Chirico (1888–1978), and Carlo Levi; a section devoted to local composer Francesco Cilea (1866–1950); and Calabria's best collection of folklore items. The museum is a little above the town, close to the S18. ⊠ *Via San Giorgio, Palmi,* ☎ *0966/262250.* 🎟 *3,000 lire/€1.55.* ☉ *Tues., Wed., and Fri. 8–2, Mon. and Thurs. 8–2 and 3–6.*

Bagnara Calabra

⑪ *11 km (7 mi) south of Palmi, 36 km (22 mi) north of Reggio di Calabria.*

Fishing is in the blood of the local villagers in Bagnara Calabra, particularly when in pursuit of swordfish, for which the town has long enjoyed widespread fame. Casual trattorias make this a great lunch stop.

Dining

$$ ✕ **Taverna Kerkira.** Centrally located on Bagnara's main street, this restaurant owes its name to the mother of the chef, who hails from Corfu. Accordingly, you'll see such Greek dishes as moussaka slipped in among the local choices on the menu. In season (April–September) you can be sure to find *pescespada* (swordfish) prepared in a variety of ways. ⊠ *Corso Vittorio Emanuele 217,* ☎ *0966/372260. AE, DC, MC, V. Closed Mon.–Tues., Aug. or Sept., and Dec. 20–Jan. 12.*

Scilla

⑫ *10 km (6 mi) south of Bagnara Calabra, 26 km (16 mi) north of Reggio di Calabria.*

According to Homer's *Odyssey,* ancient Scylla was where one of two monsters resided, dreaded by passing sailors. The other was Charybdis, modern-day Cariddi, on the Messina side of the Straits. Today, nothing in Scilla looks remotely threatening, especially in summer, when the broad, sandy beach is the focus for sunning and swimming by day, and carousing by night. At the northern end of the bay, a castle rises loftily on a rocky spur—a grand vantage point for watching the tall-masted *felucche* swordfish boats patrolling the Straits. Most of these are based in Bagnara Calabra, to the north.

Reggio di Calabria

⑬ *26 km (16 mi) south of Scilla, 499 km (311 mi) south of Naples.*

Reggio di Calabria, the city on Italy's toe tip, was laid low by the same catastrophic earthquake that struck Messina in 1908. The city has a run-down, nondescript appearance, though it does possess one of southern Italy's most important archaeological museums, the **Museo Nazionale della Magna Grecia.** Prize exhibits here are two statues, known as the **Bronzi di Riace,** found by accident by an amateur deep-sea diver off Calabria's Ionian coast in 1972. Black in color and flaunting physiques that gym enthusiasts would die for, the pair are thought to date from the 5th century BC and have been attributed to both Phidias and Polyclites. It is possible that they were destined for the temple at Delphi when the vessel that carried them was shipwrecked. Coins and votive tablets are among the numerous other treasures from Magna Graecia contained in the museum, and there are also prehistoric remnants, Byzantine items, and some fine medieval artwork. ⊠ *Piazza de Nava, Corso Garibaldi,* ☎ *0965/812255.* ⌑ *8,000 lire/€4.15.* ☉ *Daily 9–7. Closed 1st and 3rd Mon. of month.*

Lodging

$$$ 🏨 **Miramare.** On the seafront midway between the port and the station, Miramare has one of the best locations in Reggio. It has been restored to evoke the charm of the early 20th century yet has all modern facilities. ⊠ *Via Fata Morgana 1, 89127,* ☎ *0965/812444,* FAX *0965/ 812450,* WEB *www.reggiocalabriahotels.it. 96 rooms. Restaurant, bar, parking (fee). AE, DC, MC, V.*

$$ 🏨 **Palace Masoanri's.** Right behind the Museo Nazionale, this modern hotel sits on a quiet side street with seaward views. Rooms are uninspiring though adequate for a night or two, and many have views over the Straits. There's no restaurant, but you can eat at the Excelsior across the street— which is under the same management—or choose one of many other nearby restaurants. ⊠ *Via Vittorio Veneto 95, 89121,* ☎ *0965/26433,* FAX *0965/26436,* WEB *www.reggiocalabriahotels.it. 65 rooms. Bar, breakfast room, meeting room, parking (fee). AE, DC, MC, V.*

Aspromonte

⑭ *Gambarie: 42 km (26 mi) northeast of Reggio di Calabria.*

Rising to the east of Reggio di Calabria, Aspromonte is the name of the sprawling massif that dominates mainland Italy's southern tip. Long the haunt of brigands and still the refuge of modern-day kidnapers— for whom industrialists, not tourists, are the usual targets—this thickly forested range reaches nearly 6,560 ft and is popular with skiers in winter. In summer, it makes a cool respite from the heat of the coast, offering endless opportunities for hiking and shady picnicking. On a clear day, you can see right across to Mt. Etna, 60 km (36 mi) south. Ask at Reggio's tourist office (⊠ Corso Garibaldi 329, ☎ 0965/892012) for walking itineraries. To get here going north from Reggio, turn inland off the autostrada or coast road at Gallico, 12 km (7 mi) north of town; driving east from Reggio on S184, turn left onto the S183 at Melito di Porto Salvo.

En Route The fast S106 hugs Calabria's Ionian coast, leading south out of Reggio di Calabria and curving around Aspromonte to your left. Having rounded Capo Spartivento, the road proceeds north. If you don't want to continue farther northward, turn left onto the S112dir, shortly before Bovalino and 14 km (9 mi) before reaching Locri. This winding mountain road takes you round the rugged northern slopes of Aspromonte, a highly scenic route but not recommended for anyone who suffers from car sickness.

Locri

⑮ *100 km (62 mi) east of Reggio di Calabria.*

Just south of the seaside town of Locri, visit the excavations of **Locri Epizefiri,** where one of the most important of Magna Graecia's city-states stood. Founded around the 7th century BC, Locris became a regional power when—apparently assisted by Castor and Pollux—10,000 Locrians defeated an army of 130,000 from Kroton on the banks of the Sagra River, 25 km (16 mi) north. Founding colonies and gathering fame in the spheres of horse-breeding and music, Locris was responsible for the first written code of law in the Hellenic world. The walls of the city, parts of which are still visible, measured some 8 km (5 mi) in circumference, and the archaeological site within is spread over a wide area among farms and orchards. The best-preserved remains are a 5th-century BC Ionic temple, a Roman necropolis, and a Graeco-Roman theater. There's also an on-site museum, though some of the best finds are now at Reggio's Museo Nazionale. ☎ 0964/390023. ✉ *Site free, museum 4,000 lire/€2.05.* ⊙ *Site daily 9–1 hr before sunset; museum daily 9–8; museum and archaeological zone closed 1st and 3rd Mon. of month.*

Gerace

⑯ *10 km (6 mi) west of Locri, 110 km (68 mi) east of Reggio di Calabria.*

When the Saracens plundered Locri in the 7th century AD, the survivors fled inland to found Gerace, on an impregnable site that was later occupied and strengthened by the Normans. It's worth the short detour to visit this redoubt, its ruined castle tottering precariously on a jagged outcrop. Gerace's **Duomo** was founded in 1045 by Robert Guiscard (circa 1015–85), enlarged by Frederick II two centuries later, and today is still the biggest church in Calabria. Its simple, well-preserved interior has 20 columns of granite and marble, each different, and the 10th on the right, in verd antique (a green marble), changes tone according to the weather. ✉ *Piazza Vittorio Emanuele.* ⊙ *Apr.–July, daily 9:30–1 and 3–8; Aug., daily 9:30–1 and 3–9; Sept.–Oct., daily 9:30–1 and 3–7; Nov.–Mar., daily 9:30–1 and 3–6.*

Stilo

⑰ *50 km (31 mi) north of Locri, 138 km (86 mi) northeast of Reggio di Calabria.*

Grandly positioned on the side of the rugged Monte Consolino, the village of Stilo is famous on two accounts. First, it was the birthplace and home of the philosopher Tommaso Campanella (1568–1639), whose magnum opus was the socialistic *La Città del Sole* (*The City of the Sun*, 1602)—for which he spent 26 years as prisoner of the Spanish Inquisition. A tangible reason to visit the village is the tiny 10th-century Byzantine temple **La Cattólica.** Standing on a ledge above the town, this tiled and turreted building is believed to be the best-preserved monument of its kind. ⊠ *Via Cattólica.* 🎫 *Free (donation).* ☉ *Easter–Sept., daily 8–8; Oct.–Easter, daily 7–7.*

Lodging

$ 🏨 **San Giorgio.** Tucked away off Stilo's main Via Campanella, this hotel is housed in a 17th-century cardinal's palace and decked out in the style of that period, with elegantly furnished guest rooms. There are exhilarating views seaward from the garden. Half or full board is required—the food is acceptable, and there's nowhere else in town to eat anyway. ⊠ *Via Citarelli 8, 89049,* 🕾 FAX *0964/775047. 10 rooms. Restaurant, bar, pool. Closed Oct.–May. FAP, MAP.*

En Route From Stilo you can take the S110 inland—a long, twisty road that takes you through the high Serra region, covered with a thick mantle of chestnut forest. There are terrific views to be enjoyed over the Ionian coast, and you can continue across the peninsula to Calabria's Tyrrhenian littoral, emerging at Pizzo. The total road distance between Stilo and Pizzo is around 80 km (50 mi).

BASILICATA AND CALABRIA A TO Z

To research prices, get advice from other travelers, and book travel arrangements, visit www.fodors.com.

AIRPORTS

Twenty-seven kilometers (17 miles) north of Pizzo, Aeroporto di Lamezia caters to international charters and domestic flights, with connections to Milan, Bologna, and Rome; airlines servicing the airport are Alitalia and Airone. Reggio di Calabria's Aeroporto dello Stretto handles Alitalia domestic flights only, with five departures daily to Rome, two to Milan.

➤ AIRPORT INFORMATION: **Aeroporto di Lamezia** (🕾 0968/51766 or 0968/51205). **Aeroporto dello Stretto** (call Alitalia, 🕾 8488/65641). **Airone** (🕾 1478/48880). **Alitalia** (🕾 8488/65641).

BOAT AND FERRY TRAVEL

Hydrofoils, ferries, and fast ferries ply the Straits of Messina once or twice hourly from Reggio di Calabria and from Villa San Giovanni, day and night (reduced service in winter). Crossings take about 20 minutes from Reggio, about 40 minutes from Villa. In Reggio contact SNAV, FS, and Meridiano Ferries; in Villa, FS and Caronte.

➤ BOAT AND FERRY INFORMATION: **Caronte** (🕾 0965/793111 or 🕾 0965/756725). **FS** (🕾 0965/863545). **Meridiano Ferries** (🕾 0965/712208). **SNAV** (🕾 0965/29568).

BUS TRAVEL

Matera is linked with Bari and Metaponto by frequent buses operated by Ferrovie Appulo-Lucane, and with Taranto by SITA buses. In Calabria, various bus companies make the north–south run with stops along both coasts; Ferrovie della Calabria operates many of the local services. In Reggio di Calabria, contact Lirosi for buses to Rome, leaving three times daily. From Reggio di Calabria, Salzone runs to Scilla, and Federico to Locri and Stilo.

➤ BUS INFORMATION: **Federico** (🕾 0965/590212). **Ferrovie Appulo-Lucane** (🕾 0835/332861). **Ferrovie della Calabria** (🕾 0984/36851). **Lirosi** (🕾 0966/575552). **Salzone** (🕾 0965/751586). **SITA** (🕾 0835/835007).

CAR RENTAL

Cars can be rented at airports and at downtown locations in Matera and Reggio di Calabria and also from Cosenza train station and Lamezia airport.

➤ LOCAL AGENCIES: **Avis** (✉ Vico XX Settembre 8, Matera, ☎ 0835/336632; ✉ Aeroporto dello Stretto, Reggio di Calabria, ☎ 0965/643023; WEB www.avisworld.com). **Damasco** (✉ Vico XX Settembre 12, Matera, ☎ 0835/334605). **Hertz** (✉ Aeroporto dello Stretto, Reggio di Calabria, ☎ 0965/643093; ✉ Via Florio 17, Reggio di Calabria, ☎ 0965/332222, WEB www.hertz.it). **Maggiore-National** (✉ Aeroporto dello Stretto, Reggio di Calabria, ☎ 0965/643148, WEB www.maggiore.it).

CAR TRAVEL

Metaponto is a major road and rail junction for routes along the coast and inland. To get to Metaponto by car from Apulia's Taranto, take the S106 southwest for 45 km (28 mi). From Apulia's Bari, take the S96 south for 44 km (28 mi) to Altamura, then the S99 south 19 km (12 mi) to Matera. The A3 Autostrada del Sole runs between Salerno and Reggio di Calabria, with exits for Pizzo, Rosarno (for Tropea), Palmi, and Scilla; it takes an inland route as far as Falerna, then tracks the Tyrrhenian coast south (except for the bulge of the Tropea promontory). Take the S18 for coastal destinations on the Tyrrhenian side, S106 (which is uncongested and fast) for the Ionian. To drive from Basilicata's Metaponto to Matera, take the S175 northwest for 45 km (28 mi). You can cross the Straits of Messina from Villa San Giovanni or Reggio.

EMERGENCY SERVICES

When you're on the road, always carry a good road map, a flashlight, and, if possible, a cellular phone so that in case of a breakdown you can call ACI for towing and repairs—ask and you will be transferred to an English-speaking operator. Be prepared to tell the operator which road you're on, the direction you're going (e.g., *verso* (in the direction of) Pizzo") and the *targa* (license plate number) of your car.

➤ CONTACTS: **ACI dispatchers** (☎ 116).

EMERGENCIES

In Reggio di Calabria, the pharmacies Curia and Caridi are open at night. Elsewhere, late-night pharmacies are open on a rotating basis; information on current schedules is posted on any pharmacy door.

➤ CONTACTS: **Police, Ambulance, Fire** (☎ 113). **Hospital** (☎ 0965/8501 in Reggio di Calabria, ☎ 0835/2431 in Matera). **Curia** (✉ Corso Garibaldi 455, ☎ 0965/332332). **Caridi** (✉ Corso Garibaldi 327, ☎ 0965/24013).

LANGUAGE

The dialects of Basilicata and Calabria, which vary from village to village, are impenetrable to anyone with a knowledge only of textbook Italian. Most locals can also communicate in the standard language, however, and you'll find a considerable number of older people, returned emigres from the U.S. or Canada, who are happy to show off their rusty English.

MAIL AND SHIPPING

➤ POST OFFICES: **Cosenza** (✉ Via Vittorio Veneto). **Matera** (✉ Via Vittorio Veneto). **Reggio** (✉ Via Miraglia).

SAFETY

LOCAL SCAMS

The area is not noticeably more crime-ridden than any other Italian region, as far as foreign visitors are concerned. Car crime is probably the biggest threat: don't leave anything visible in the car overnight, and never leave it unlocked.

WOMEN IN BASILICATA AND CALABRIA

The south is more old-fashioned about independent women than other parts of Italy, though things have improved dramatically in recent years, and women can expect nothing more menacing than stares from men.

TOURS

Foderaro organizes bus tours of Reggio di Calabria, Scilla, Pizzo, Locri, and Gerace and boat tours to the Aeolian Islands. The tourist office recommends touring Matera with an official guide agency, preferably the English-language Itinera, which always has access to sights.
➤ FEES AND SCHEDULES: **Foderaro** (✉ Corso Mazzini 185, Catanzaro 88100, ☎ 0961/726006). **Itinera** (✉ Via La Martella 43, Matera, ☎ 0835/334761).

TRAIN TRAVEL

The main north–south FS line has hourly services from Reggio north to Palmi, Pizzo, Diamante, and Maratea, continuing on as far as Salerno, Naples, and Rome. There are nine daily Intercity or Eurocity trains linking Reggio di Calabria with Naples (4–5 hours) and Rome (6–7 hours). All trains, which are run by FS, also stop at Villa San Giovanni (for connections to Sicily), a 20-minute ride from Reggio. Two fast FS trains run daily between Metaponto and Naples (about 4 hours) and Rome (5½–6 hours), and three others connect Metaponto and Salerno (about 3½ hours), from which there are frequent connections to Naples and Rome. Two trains daily go as far as Milan, fastest time 13¼ hrs.

With the region, the main FS (Italian State Railways) line from Taranto stops in Metaponto, from which there are regular departures to Matera on Ferrovie Appulo-Lucane (FAL) trains. The FAL rail line links Matera to Altamura in Apulia (for connections to Bari) and to Ferrandina (for connections to Metaponto or Potenza). South of Metaponto, FS trains run into Calabria, either following the Ionian coast as far as Reggio di Calabria or swerving inland to Cosenza and the Tyrrhenian coast at Paola. Main FS services run along both coasts but can be crowded along the Tyrrhenian. Call for information on times and frequencies.
➤ TRAIN INFORMATION: **Ferrovie Appulo-Lucane** (☎ 0835/332861). **FS** (Italian State Railways; ☎ 147/888088).

TRAVEL AGENCIES

➤ LOCAL AGENT REFERRALS: **Simonetta** (✉ Corso Garibaldi 521, Reggio di Calabria, ☎ 0965/331444).

VISITOR INFORMATION

➤ TOURIST INFORMATION: **Camigliatello** (✉ Via Roma 5, 87052, ☎ 0984/578243). **Cosenza** (✉ Corso Mazzini 92, 87100, ☎ 0984/27485). **Maratea** (✉ Piazza del Gesù, 85046, ☎ 0973/876908). **Matera** (✉ Via de Viti de Marco 9, off Via Roma, 75100, ☎ 0835/331983). **Pizzo** (✉ Piazza della Repubblica, 88026, ☎ 0963/531310). **Reggio di Calabria** (✉ Corso Garibaldi 329, 89100, ☎ 0965/892012). **Tropea** (✉ Piazza Ercole, 88038, ☎ 0963/61475).

15 SICILY

PALERMO, AGRIGENTO, SIRACUSA,
THE AEOLIAN ISLANDS

On this fabled island you can ski down a snow-muffled volcano, wander through palm and orange groves, and swim within sight of majestic ruins. It has a stubborn personality: cynical yet passionate, languorous yet industrious. But the ethereal subtleties of this seemingly far-off kingdom reveal themselves in panoramic Taormina, the Valley of the Temples, and the unforgettable rose-tinted moon rising over Mount Etna.

Updated by
Robert
Andrews

ARRIVING IN SICILY for the first time, you may be surprised to see so many people with blond hair and blue eyes, and to learn that two of the most popular boys' names are Ruggero (Roger) and Guglielmo (William), but these sorts of surprises are what Sicily is all about. For 2,000 years it has been an island where unexpected contrasts somehow come together peacefully. Lying in a strategic position between Europe and Africa, Sicily at one time hosted two of the most advanced and enlightened capitals of Europe—a Greek one in Siracusa and an Arab-Norman one in Palermo. (The Normans are responsible for the blond-haired Rogers and blue-eyed Williams.) Sicily was one of the great melting pots of the ancient world and home to every great civilization that existed in the Mediterranean: Greek and Roman; then Arab and Norman; and, finally, French, Spanish, and Italian. Something of all of these peoples was absorbed into the island's artistic heritage, a rich tapestry of art and architecture that includes massive Romanesque cathedrals, two of the best-preserved Greek temples in the world, Roman amphitheaters, and delightful Baroque palaces and churches.

Modern Sicily is still a land of surprising contrasts. The traditional graciousness and nobility of the Sicilian people exist side by side with the atrocities and destructive influences of the Mafia, although recent events suggest that the Mafia's grip on the island is slowly being loosened. Alongside some of the most exquisite architecture in the world are the shabby products of some of the worst speculation imaginable. In recent years, Sicily, like much of the Mediterranean coast, has experienced a boom in tourism and a surge in condominium development that has only now begun to be checked. The chic boutiques purveying lace and linen in jet-set resort towns like Taormina give no clue to the poverty in which their wares are produced.

In Homer's *Odyssey,* Sicily represented the unknown end of the world, yet the region eventually became the center of the world under the Normans, who recognized a paradise in its deep blue skies and temperate climate, its lush vegetation and rich marine life. Much of this paradise does still exist today. Add to it Sicily's unique cuisine—another harmony of elements, mingling Arab and Greek spices with Spanish and French influences, and using some of the world's tastiest seafood—and you can understand why those who arrived here were often reluctant to leave.

You do not have to be paranoid about safety in Sicily, but you do have to be careful: do not flaunt jewelry, and keep your handbag securely strapped across your chest. Leaving valuables visible in your car while you go sightseeing is inviting trouble. Be careful; then enjoy the company of the Sicilians. You will find them to be friendly and often willing to go out of their way to help you. It is not uncommon in small towns for visitors to receive invitations to a local's house for dinner. It doesn't matter if you don't speak Italian or speak only a little: they usually aren't offended if your pronunciation isn't perfect. One of the reasons for this, no doubt, is the fact that many Sicilians or their close relatives have themselves been strangers in foreign lands, and empathy goes a long way.

Pleasures and Pastimes

Beaches
There is a surfeit of beaches in Sicily, but many of them are too rocky, too crowded, or too dirty to be enjoyed for long. Among the exceptions are Mondello, near Palermo, a popular sandy beach on a tiny

peninsula jutting out into the Mediterranean; Sant'Alessio and Santa Teresa, north of Taormina (the beaches just below Taormina itself are disappointing); and Capo San Vito, on the northern coast, near Erice, a sandy beach on a promontory overlooking a bay in the Gulf of Castellammare.

Camping

Sicily has excellent camping facilities on both the main island and its satellite islands. The two best are El Bahira, in San Vito Lo Capo, and Bazia, in Furnari Marina, west of Milazzo. Both have restaurants and showers, as well as swimming pools, tennis courts, and discos.

Dining

Sicilian cooking reflects the various Mediterranean influences that have left their mark on the island. Fish, vegetables, and grains are used in imaginative combinations, sometimes served with Italian pastas or Arab or North African ingredients such as couscous. Sweet and sour tastes are deftly mingled, and cooks have distinctive touches, so that *caponata* (an antipasto of eggplant, capers, olives, and, in eastern Sicily, peppers) is different at every restaurant.

Sicily has always been one of Italy's poorest areas, so meat is not the centerpiece on menus. It is usually prepared *alla brace* (skewered) or in *falso magro* (a thin slice of meat rolled around sausage, onion, bacon, bits of egg, and cheese). In Sicily, naturally, you'll enjoy the freshest seafood in all of Italy, and you'll also find the most variety. *Tonno* (tuna) is a staple in many coastal areas, and *pesce spada* (swordfish) is equally common, if more expensive. Try *ricci* (sea urchins), a specialty of Mondello, near Palermo. Fish sauces are often tossed on pasta: pasta *con le sarde* is made with fresh sardines, olive oil, anchovies, raisins, and pine nuts and has the distinctive flavor of wild fennel. In Catania, spaghetti *alla Norma,* named for the heroine in the opera by local composer Vincenzo Bellini, is prepared with a sauce of tomato and fried eggplant.

Desserts from Sicily are famous. The traditional Easter cake is the *cassata siciliana,* a rich sponge cake with candied fruit, marzipan, and icing. From behind bakery windows and glass cases beam tiny marzipan sweets, fashioned into brightly colored apples, cherries, corncobs, hamburgers, and more. Local gelato is excellent and is usually homemade, as are brilliant *granite* (granitas) in flavors such as lemon. Gooey cakes and very sweet desserts such as chestnut ice cream covered with hot zabaglione provide a sugar fix. The sweet dessert wine Marsala is Sicily's most famous, but there is a range of other local wines, from the dark red Faro to the sparkling dry Regaleali, excellent with fish.

For general information and price categories, *see* Dining *in* Smart Travel Tips A to Z.

Kids' Stuff

Almost every major city in Sicily has a theater giving performances of the world-famous Sicilian *pupi* (marionettes), and it is worth going to at least one show during your trip. Adults as well as children will enjoy the colorful shows, the most popular of which are in Palermo, Acireale, and Taormina. Stories center on heroes from the Norman fables, distressed damsels, and Saracen invaders. Even if you can't understand Italian, the action is fast and furious, so it's easy to figure out what's going on. Palermo has an international museum dedicated to these and other types of marionettes. If you are in Sicily at Carnival time (the week before Ash Wednesday, about 45 days before Easter), Acireale has one of Italy's best celebrations, when dozens of colorful torch-lit floats, with papier-mâché characters aboard, are pulled through the streets by costumed revelers.

Lodging

Sicily is Italy's largest region, with some of the most remote countryside. The good-quality hotels tend to be limited to the major cities and resorts of Palermo, Taormina, Siracusa, and Agrigento. There are, of course, some superb establishments, such as converted villas with sea views and well-equipped modern hotels, but it is best not to expect to come across some enchanting oasis in the middle of nowhere. If you want to get away from the major centers, make reservations well in advance.

Hotels in the $$$$ category provide comfort and services to match those in other Italian regions; they are usually the older, more established hotels. In the $$–$$$ range, you'll find newer hotels built to cater to the increased tourist trade of the past 20 years. In recent years, some of these newer hotels have shown style and character rather than the bland modernity of chains, such as the Jolly, which have seen better days. Inexpensive establishments are usually family-run, but even these offer private baths and often TVs and air-conditioning. Recently there has been an explosion in the development of *agriturismo* lodgings (rural B&Bs), many of them quite basic, though others providing the same facilities found in hotels.

For general information and price categories, *see* Lodging *in* Smart Travel Tips A to Z.

Scuba Diving

Scuba diving and other water sports have become popular on the Sicilian coast, but the most important center is on the island of Ustica, north of Palermo. Its rugged coast is dotted with grottoes that are washed by crystal-clear waters and filled with an incredible variety of interesting marine life. In July, Ustica hosts the International Meeting of Marine Fishing, which attracts sportsmen as well as marine biologists from all over the world.

Shopping

Sicily is one of the leaders in the Italian ceramics industry, with important factories at Caltagirone, in the interior, and Santo Stefano di Camastra, along the northern coast between Messina and Cefalù. Colorful Sicilian folk pottery can still be bought at bargain prices. Place mats, tablecloths, napkins, and clothing decorated with fine petit point are good buys in Cefalù, Taormina, and Erice, but they are not cheap. Make sure that any linen you buy is produced in Sicily and not on another continent. Collectors have been combing Sicily for years for pieces of the colorful *carretti siciliani* (Sicilian carts). Before the automobile, these were the major form of transportation in Sicily, and they were decorated in bright primary colors and in primitive styles, with scenes from the Norman troubadour tales. The axles of these carts were ornamented with open filigree work, which was also brightly painted.

Exploring Sicily

Sicily is about 180 km (112 mi) north to south and 270 km (168 mi) across. The island is so dense with places of interest that not even a week is sufficient to explore it in depth, though with a car at your disposal you will be able to cover all the most important sights. The best way to visit it is to travel counterclockwise along the coast by car, bus, or train, making occasional detours inland. You needn't visit all of the Isole Eolie individually. In summer, hydrofoils and ferries connect all seven, so one or two of them can be admired from the sea. Lipari is the most equipped of the islands for tourism, though all of the islands except Stromboli offer some kind of accommodation, from small, family-run guest houses to beds in private homes.

Numbers in the text correspond to numbers in the margin and on the Sicily, Palermo, Agrigento, and Siracusa maps.

Great Itineraries

In nine days, you can do a thorough loop around the island, which starts in Palermo, moves west and south to the stunning Greek cities of Selinunte and Agrigento, then dips inland and continues southeast to Siracusa, and finally heads north to Acireale and the picturesque Taormina and the Isole Eolie. Explorations concentrated around Palermo and environs can be done in three or five days.

IF YOU HAVE 3 DAYS

A three-day sojourn on the island should not necessitate renting a car if you base yourself in Sicily's capital, ☷ **Palermo** ①–⑪. In this hub of Norman Sicily, the highlights include the **Palazzo dei Normanni** ① and the **Museo Archeologico Regionale** ⑩, as well as a handful of churches. Head out to **Monreale** ⑫ to admire the splendid cathedral, and compare it with the slightly earlier mosaic-laden monument at ☷ **Cefalù** ⑮. Spend your last day exploring this seaside resort.

IF YOU HAVE 5 DAYS

A longer time on the island will allow you to add choice excursions to the three-day itinerary, but you'd still be wise not to be over-ambitious, confining your tour to western Sicily. Spend your first two nights in ☷ **Palermo** ①–⑪; then head west, dropping in on the imposing half-finished temple of **Segesta** ⑰, a short detour from the autostrada, and making panoramic ☷ **Erice** ⑱ your next overnight stop. From Erice, you can take a quick glance at the port city of **Trapani** ⑲, just down the road, and the old Phoenician town of **Marsala** ㉑, before swinging eastward to the ruins of **Selinunte** ㉒, whose remarkable metopes you will have seen in Palermo's archaeological museum. Following the coast down, aim for the Greek temple site at ☷ **Agrigento** ㉓–㉙, for which you should allow a full day. Next, strike north on the S640 to meet the A19 autostrada near Caltanisetta, which will bring you back up to the Tyrrhenian coast. There you can spend your last night at ☷ **Cefalù** ⑮ before turning westward back to Palermo.

IF YOU HAVE 9 DAYS

Begin by following the five-day itinerary above, but at Agrigento make for inland **Enna** ㊻, worth a quick whirl around; then spend the afternoon viewing the exuberant mosaics of the Roman villa at **Casale** ㊼. If you have time, stop off to see the Museo della Ceramica at **Caltagirone** ㊽ before continuing on the S124 to ☷ **Siracusa** ㉚–㊺ for a full day's exploring. From here, head north up the coast—a visit to **Catania** ㊿ may be more hassle than it's worth if time is short—and continue on to the Baroque town of **Acireale** ㊾, perhaps stopping for a fish lunch before landing for two nights at ☷ **Taormina** ㊾. From here, it's a brief drive or walk up to the village of **Castelmola** ㊾, with its memorable views over Taormina and **Mt. Etna** ㊾, whose silhouette will have accompanied you on your progress through eastern Sicily. You'll be hard put to resist an excursion onto the volcano (most cloud-free in the morning), either a drive round its lower slopes or an expedition to the top—either way, it'll take you the better part of a day. From Taormina, drive up the coast to **Messina** ㊾, where the Museo Regionale will give you a last blast of Sicilian art before crossing—either from Messina or Milazzo, on the north coast—to the Aeolian archipelago, where ☷ **Lipari** ㊾ has the biggest selection of accommodations and boasts a superb Museo Archeologico. From here, you can

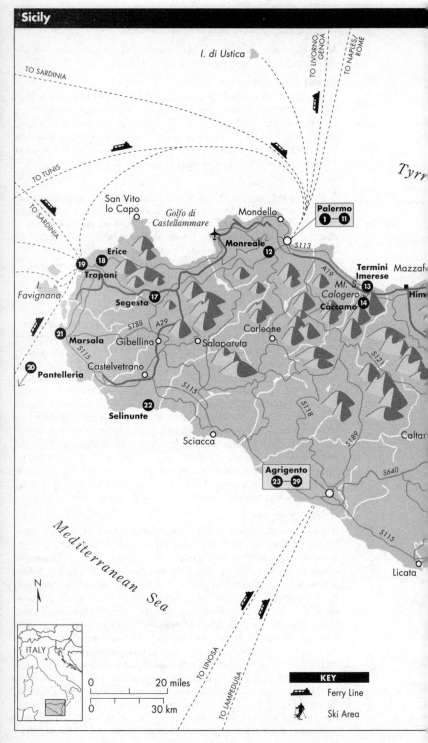

TO LIVORNO, GENOA

TO NAPLES/ ROME

I. di Ustica

TO SARDINIA

Tyrr

TO TUNIS

TO SARDINIA

San Vito lo Capo

Golfo di Castellammare

Mondello

Palermo
① — ⑪

I. Favignana

Erice

⑲ ⑱

Trapani

Monreale

⑫

S113

A19

Termini Imerese

⑬

Mazzafo

Mt. S. Calogero

Segesta

⑰

Cáccamo

⑭

Him

S188

A29

Corleone

⑳

⑳

Marsala

Gibellina

Salaparuta

S115

S121

Castelvetrano

S118

S189

Pantelleria

Selinunte

⑳

Sciacca

Caltar

S640

Agrigento
㉓ — ㉙

Licata

S115

Mediterranean Sea

N

ITALY

0   20 miles

0   30 km

TO LINOSA

TO LAMPEDUSA

KEY

Ferry Line

Ski Area

TO NAPLES

Stromboli 61

Panarea 60

Alicudi 62 **Filicudi** 63

Salina 59

TO NAPLES

ISOLE EOLIE

57 **Lipari**

58

Golfo di Gióia

Vulcano

nian Sea

Milazzo

Mortelle

Capo d'Orlando

S113

Patti

A20

Messina 56

Reggio
di Calabria

Cefalù Caldura

15

S113

**Santo Stefano
di Camastra**

16

S117

Castelmola

55

54

Bronte

Mt. Etna 52

Taormina

Riposto

Adrano

Giarre

Biancavilla

Acireale

46

Enna

S192

Paterno

53

A19

Catania 51

S288

*Golfo di
Catania*

ta

47

Casale

Ionian Sea

48

Caltagirone

S124

S114

Gela

**Palazzolo
Acreide**

Euryalus

49

Golfo di Gela

Comiso

S124

Siracusa

Ragusa

30 45

Noto

50

Avola

Modica

S115

*Golfo
di Noto*

*Capo
Passero*

TO MALTA

opt to explore the remaining six Aeolian islands of **Vulcano** ⑱, **Salina** ⑲, **Panarea** ⑳, **Stromboli** ㉑, **Alicudi** ㉒, and **Filicudi** ㉓, or else return to reality and the Sicilian mainland for your last night at ⌧ **Cefalù** ⑮.

When to Tour Sicily

Sicily comes into its own in the spring, but you're not alone in knowing this. Taormina and Erice attract a flood of visitors around Easter, and any visit scheduled for this time should be backed up by solid advance bookings. Many sights, such as inland Segesta, are at their best in the clear spring light and are far enough off the beaten track to ensure a fairly hassle-free time. August, on the other hand, is hellish wherever you choose to roam—not just for the presence of fellow travelers but for the extreme, uncomfortably hot temperatures. Cities should be avoided. Beaches don't necessarily offer refuge from the sizzling heat; they can get pretty clogged with Italian and foreign vacationers. Come in September or October, and you'll find acres of beach space. Cefalù, like Taormina, sees year-round tourism, though some of the luxury hotels close down for the winter. As with Easter, Christmas and New Year's draw visitors to the island, and reservations should always be made as early as possible. Other festivals, such as Agrigento's almond festival in February and the *Carnevale* in Acireale, can also mean a dearth of vacancies.

PALERMO

Palermo's heritage encompasses all of Sicily's varied ages, but its distinctive aspect is its Arab-Norman identity, an improbable marriage that, mixed in with Byzantine and Jewish elements, created some resplendent works of art. These are most notable in the churches, from small jewels such as San Giovanni degli Eremiti to larger-scale works such as the cathedral.

Once the intellectual capital of southern Europe, Palermo has always been at the crossroads of civilization. Favorably situated on a crescent-shape bay at the foot of Monte Pellegrino, it has attracted almost every people and culture touching the Mediterranean world. To Palermo's credit, it has absorbed these diverse cultures into a unique personality that is at once Arab and Christian, Byzantine and Roman, Norman and Italian. Palermo was first colonized by Phoenician traders in the 6th century BC, but it was their descendants, the Carthaginians, who built the important fortress here that caught the covetous eye of the Romans. After the First Punic War, the Romans took control of the city in the 3rd century BC. Following several invasions by the Vandals, Sicily was settled by Arabs, who made the country an emirate and established Palermo as a showpiece capital that rivaled both Cordoba and Cairo in the splendor of its architecture. Nestled in the fertile Conca d'Oro (Golden Conch) plain, full of orange, lemon, and carob groves and enclosed by limestone hills, Palermo became a magical world of palaces and mosques, minarets and palm trees.

It was so attractive and sophisticated a city that the Norman ruler Roger de Hauteville (1031–1101) decided to conquer it and make it his capital (1072). The Norman occupation of Sicily resulted in the Golden Age of Palermo (1072–1194), a remarkable period of enlightenment and learning in which the arts flourished. The city of Palermo, which in the 11th century counted more than 300,000 inhabitants, became the center of the Norman court in all Europe and one of the most important ports of trade between East and West. Eventually the Normans were replaced by the Swabian ruler Frederick II (1194–1250), the Holy Roman Emperor, and incorporated into the Kingdom of the Two Sicilies. You will also see plenty of evidence in Palermo of the Baroque art and architecture of the long Spanish rule, which followed the bloody Sicilian Vespers uprising of 1282, in which the French Angevin dynasty was overthrown. The Aragonese viceroys also brought the Spanish Inquisition to Palermo, which some historians believe helped foster the protective secret societies that eventually evolved into today's Mafia.

Exploring Palermo

The Sicilian capital is a multilayered, vigorous metropolis, packed with interest. Approach the city with an open mind, and you'll find it an enriching and enjoyable place to explore, with a strong historical profile. Be aware that you're likely to encounter some frustrating instances of inefficiency and, depending on the season, stifling heat. Regulate your pace, don't attempt to see too much too quickly, and keep your head. If you have a car, park it in a garage as soon as you can, and don't take it out until you are ready to depart.

Palermo is easily explored on foot, though you may choose to spend a morning taking a city bus tour to help you get oriented. The Quattro Canti, or Four Corners, is the hub that separates the four sections of the old city: La Kalsa to the southeast, Albergheria to the southwest, Capo to the northwest, and Vucciria to the northeast. Each of these is a tumult of activity during the day, though at night the narrow alleys empty out and are best avoided altogether in favor of the more animated avenues of the new city, north of Piazza Castelnuovo. Sights you will want to see by day are scattered along three major streets: Corso Vittorio Emanuele, Via Maqueda, and Via Roma. The tourist information office in Piazza Castelnuovo will give you a map and a valuable handout that lists opening and closing times, which sometimes change with the seasons.

A Good Tour

Start at the **Palazzo dei Normanni** ①, at the far west end of Corso Vittorio Emanuele, to see the mosaics in the Cappella Palatina and the royal apartments. Walk down Via dei Benedettini, following the five pink domes of **San Giovanni degli Eremiti** ②. Back east on the Corso stands Palermo's **Cattedrale** ③, a cacophony of Arab, Norman, and Gothic influences. Farther east is Piazza Vigliena, better known as **Quattro Canti** ④, the intersection of Via Maqueda and Corso Vittorio Emanuele. Just east off Quattro Canti is Piazza Pretoria, adjacent to which Piazza Bellini holds a trio of eminent churches: the Baroque **Santa Caterina** ⑤ and, up the stairs, **San Cataldo** ⑥ and **La Martorana** ⑦, which form a delightful Norman complex. Walk northeast along Via Alloro to **Palazzo Abatellis** ⑧ and its Galleria Regionale, holding a fine collection of medieval and Renaissance art. If you like puppets, take Via Alloro east and go northwest (left) on Via Butera to the **Museo delle Marionette** ⑨. Then, either take Bus 104 or 105 back along Corso Vittorio Emanuele to transfer to 101 heading north along Via Roma, or take a 40-minute walk: cross Corso Vittorio Emanuele to reach Via Cala, follow this busy road around the old port (it will become Via Barilai), and turn left at Piazza XIII Vittime onto Via Cavour. Follow this as far as Via Roma, where you turn left, walking south 165 ft to the **Museo Archeologico Regionale** ⑩. (If you're more adventurous and want a shortcut, you can turn left off the noisy Via Cala, though you need a good sense of direction to negotiate the labyrinth of the Vucciria.) Cut through Via Bara all'Olivella to Piazza Verdi and the **Teatro Massimo** ⑪.

636

Palermo

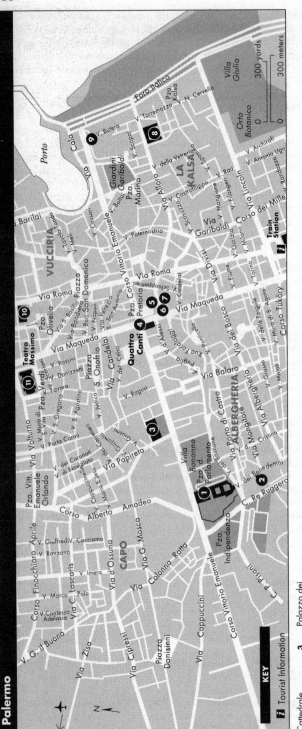

KEY

i Tourist Information

Catedrale **3**
La Martorana **7**
Museo
Archeologico
Regionale **10**
Museo delle
Marionette **9**
Palazzo Abatellis . . **8**

Palazzo dei
Normanni **1**
Quattro Canti **4**
San Cataldo **6**
San Giovanni degli
Eremiti **2**
Santa Caterina **5**
Teatro Massimo . . . **11**

TIMING

Allow the better part of a day for this tour, with lunch around the Quattro Canti. Check first with the tourist office to see if all the sights on your itinerary are open, as they tend to close on short notice and on national holidays, or for renovations or staff shortages.

Sights to See

❸ Cattedrale. This church is a lesson in Palermitan eclecticism—originally Norman (1182), then Catalan Gothic (14th–15th century), then fitted out with a Baroque and neoclassical interior (18th century). Its turrets, towers, dome, and arches come together in the kind of meeting of diverse elements that King Roger II (1095–1154), whose tomb is inside along with that of Frederick II, fostered during his reign. Be sure to walk outside and look at the back of the apse, which is gracefully decorated with interlacing Arab arches, inlaid with limestone and black volcanic tufa. ⊠ *Corso Vittorio Emanuele,* ☎ *091/334376.* ⊠ *Crypt 1,000 lire/€0.50.* ☉ *Church Mon.–Sat. 7–7, Sun. 8–1:30 and 4–7; crypt Mon.–Sat. 9:30–5:30.*

❼ La Martorana. Distinguished by an elegant campanile, this church was erected in 1143 but had its interior altered considerably during the Baroque period. High along the western wall, however, is some of the oldest mosaic artwork of the Norman period. Near the entrance is an interesting mosaic of Roger being crowned by Christ. In it, Roger is dressed in a bejeweled Byzantine stole, reflecting the Norman court's penchant for all things Byzantine. Archangels along the ceiling wear the same stole, wrapped around their shoulders and arms. Like the archangels, the Norman monarchs preferred to think of themselves as emissaries from heaven, engaged in defending Christianity by ridding the island of infidel invaders. ⊠ *Piazza Bellini 3,* ☎ *091/6161692.* ☉ *Apr.–Sept., Mon.–Sat. 9:30–1 and 3:30–7, Sun. 9–1; Oct.–Mar., Mon.–Sat. 9:30–1 and 3:30–5:30, Sun. 9–1.*

❿ Museo Archeologico Regionale. Especially interesting pieces in this small but excellent collection are the examples of prehistoric cave drawings and a marvelously reconstructed Doric frieze from the Greek Temple at Selinunte that gives you a good idea of the high level of artistic culture attained by the Greek colonists in Sicily some 2,500 years ago. ⊠ *Piazza Olivella 24, Via Roma,* ☎ *091/6116805.* ⊠ *8,000 lire/€4.15.* ☉ *Sun., Mon., Thurs., and Sat. 9–1:15; Tues., Wed., and Fri. 9–1:15 and 3–6:15.*

 ❾ Museo delle Marionette (Museum of Marionettes). The traditional Sicilian *pupi,* with their glittering armor and fierce expressions, have become a symbol of Norman Sicily. Plots center on the chivalric legends of the troubadours, who, before the puppet theater, kept alive tales of Norman heroes in Sicily, such as Orlando Furioso and William the Bad (1120–66). Along with the displays there are weekly performances; the day and time of performance varies. ⊠ *Via Butera 1,* ☎ *091/328060.* ⊠ *5,000 lire/€2.60.* ☉ *Weekdays 9–1 and 4–7, Sat. 9–1.*

NEED A BREAK?

If you're a lover of Sicilian pastries, then don't miss **Pasticceria Alba.** You'll find all your favorites, like the famous *cassata siciliana* (ice cream with sponge cake, candied fruit, and marzipan), *cannoli,* and *frutta di Martorana* (fruits and other shapes made out of almond paste), as well as original creations. It's at the top of Via della Libertà, several miles north of Teatro Massimo, near the entrance to La Favorita Park. ⊠ *Piazza Don Bosco 7/c,* ☎ *091/309016.*

❽ Palazzo Abatellis. Housed in this late-15th-century Catalan Gothic palace with Renaissance elements is the **Galleria Regionale.** Among its treasures are an *Annunciation* (1474) by Sicily's prominent Renaissance master Antonello da Messina (1430–79) and an arresting fresco by an unknown painter, titled *The Triumph of Death*, a macabre depiction of the plague years. ✉ *Via Alloro 4,* ☎ *091/6230000.* 🎫 *8,000 lire/€4.15.* ⊙ *Mon., Wed., Fri., and Sat. 9–1:30; Tues. and Thurs. 9–1:30 and 3–7:30; Sun. 9–12:30.*

★ **❶** **Palazzo dei Normanni** (Norman Palace). This historic palace, for centuries the seat of Sicily's rulers, currently houses the Sicilian Parliament, so that little, unfortunately, is viewable by the public. However, the **Cappella Palatina** (Palatine Chapel) remains open, built by Roger II in 1132 and a dazzling example of the unique harmony of artistic elements produced under the Normans. In it, the skill of French and Sicilian masons was brought to bear on the decorative purity of Arab ornamentation and the splendor of Greek Byzantine mosaics. The interior is covered with glittering mosaics and capped by a splendid Arab honeycomb stalactite wooden ceiling. Biblical stories blend happily with scenes of Arab life—look for one showing a picnic in a harem—and Norman court pageantry. Stylized Moorish palm branches run along the walls below the mosaics and recall the battlements on Norman castles—each one a different mosaic composition.

Upstairs are the royal apartments, including the **Sala di Ruggero** (King Roger's Hall), decorated with medieval murals of hunting scenes. Tour guides escort you around these halls, which once hosted one of the most splendid courts in Europe. French, Latin, and Arabic were spoken here, and Arab astronomers and poets exchanged ideas with Latin and Greek scholars in what must have been one of the most interesting marriages of culture in the Western world. ✉ *Piazza Indipendenza,* ☎ *091/7054317.* 🎫 *Free.* ⊙ *Chapel weekdays 9–noon and 3–5, Sat. 9–noon, Sun. 9–10 and noon–1. Apartments Mon., Fri., and Sat. 9–noon. Tours must be arranged in advance. Closed during religious services and for weddings.*

Piazza Pretoria. The square's centerpiece, a lavishly decorated fountain originally intended for a Florentine villa, underwent extensive restoration in 1999 and 2000. Its abundance of nude figures so shocked some Palermitans when it was unveiled in 1575 that it got the nickname "Fountain of Shame." It is even more of a sight when illuminated at night.

❹ **Quattro Canti.** The Four Corners is the intersection of Corso Vittorio Emanuele and Via Maqueda. Four rather traffic-blackened Baroque palaces from the Spanish rule meet at concave corners, each with its own fountain and representations of a Spanish ruler, patron saint, and one of the four seasons.

❻ **San Cataldo.** Orange-red domes mark this church, built in 1160. Its spare but intense interior, punctuated by antique Greek columns, retains much of its original medieval simplicity. If the church is closed, the custodian at La Martorana will let you in during public hours. ✉ *Piazza Bellini.* ⊙ *Weekdays 9–3:30, Sat. 9–12:30, Sun. 9–1.*

❷ **San Giovanni degli Eremiti.** Distinguished by its five pink domes, this 12th-century church was built by the Normans on the site of an earlier mosque—one of 200 that once stood in Palermo. The emirs ruled Palermo for almost two centuries and brought to it their passion for lush gardens and fountains. One is reminded of this while sitting in San Giovanni's delightful cloister of twin half-columns, surrounded by palm trees, jasmine, oleander, and citrus trees. ✉ *Via dei Benedettini,* ☎ *091/6515019.* 🎫 *8,000 lire/€4.15.* ⊙ *Mon.–Sat. 9–7, Sun. 9–1.*

⑤ **Santa Caterina.** The walls of this splendid Baroque church (1596) in Piazza Bellini are covered with decorative 17th-century inlays of precious marble. ⊠ *Piazza Bellini,* ☎ *091/6162488.* ☼ *Open by appointment for groups only.*

⑪ **Teatro Massimo.** Construction of this formidable neoclassic theater was started in 1875 by Giovanni Battista Basile and completed by his son, Ernesto, in 1897. Claimed to be Italy's largest, the theater was featured in scenes in *The Godfather Part III.* ⊠ *Piazza Verdi, at the top of Via Maqueda,* ☎ *091/6053515,* ᵂᴱᴮ *www.teatromassimo.it.* ☎ *5,000 lire/€2.60.* ☼ *Tues.–Sat. 10–3:30, except during rehearsals.*

★ **Vucciria outdoor market.** "Vucciria," in dialect, means "voices" or "hubbub," and it's easy to see why. In the maze of side streets around Piazza San Domenico, hawkers everywhere deliver their unceasing chants from behind stands brimming with mounds of olives, blood oranges, wild fennel, and long-stemmed artichokes. One of them goes at the trunk of a swordfish with a cleaver, while across the way another holds up a giant squid or dangles an octopus. It may be Palermo, but this is really the Casbah. Morning is the best time to see the market in full swing. ⊠ *Around Piazza San Domenico.* ☼ *Daily dawn–dusk.*

NEED A BREAK?	If you're a street-food fanatic, **Vucciria** is your Eden. Stalls around the neighborhood sell everything from *calzoni* (deep-fried meat- or cheese-filled pockets of dough) to *panelle* (chickpea-flour fritters). If you're feeling adventurous for something typically Palermitan, look for a stall with a big cast-iron pot selling *guasteddi* (fresh buns filled with thin strips of calf's spleen, ricotta cheese, and a delicious hot sauce).

Dining and Lodging

$$$ ✕ **Charleston.** You'll feel pampered by the discreet service and elegant surroundings in this famous Palermo restaurant, located in a pavilion on the sea 8 km (5 mi) north at Mondello. Impeccably outfitted waiters coast effortlessly through the high-ceiling rooms, producing a range of Sicilian and international dishes with an emphasis on seafood. Try the delicious spaghetti *all'aragosta* (with lobster sauce) or the pesce spada *arrosto* (roasted), but leave room for the house dessert, *semifreddo alle mandorle* (a soft ice cream made with almonds). ⊠ *Viale Regina Elena, Mondello,* ☎ *091/450171. Reservations essential. AE, DC, MC, V. Closed Sun. in Oct.–Easter.*

$$–$$$ ✕ **Strascinu.** The specialty in this informal and busy restaurant is pasta *con le sarde* (with sardines), the region's ubiquitous Arab-Sicilian dish. Amphoras, Sicilian ceramics, and even a miniature, electrically operated puppet theater enliven the rustic decor, and there's a large garden with gazebos. ⊠ *Viale Regione Siciliana 2286,* ☎ *091/401292. AE, DC, MC, V. Closed 2 wks in mid-Aug.*

$$ ✕ **Capricci di Sicilia.** It's said that this spot, in the heart of Palermo next to the Teatro Politeama, is the best place in town for cassata siciliana. You'll find only typical Sicilian specialties here, such as pasta with sardines or with a ragù of sausage and fresh ricotta. ⊠ *Piazza Luigi Sturzo,* ☎ *091/327777. AE, DC, MC, V.*

$$ ✕ **Santandrea.** A chic clientele frequents this trattoria, where home
★ cooking is the rule and most ingredients come from the Vucciria market just around the corner. There is no written menu, as the dishes available depend on what is in season, but if lucky you'll find the delectable *tagliatelli con triglie, zucchini, e mandorle* (pasta with red mullet, zucchini, and almonds). You can always count on a good choice of fresh fish for a main course and some delicious homemade desserts, such as black chocolate mousse. It's a few steps down from Piazza San

Domenico. ⊠ *Piazza Sant'Andrea 4,* ☎ *091/334999. AE, DC, MC, V. Closed Tues. and Jan.*

$–$$ ✕ **Stella.** Though located in Kalsa, a run-down and occasionally spooky area of town, Stella is a real find (leave your valuables at the hotel). With a large leafy courtyard and a choice of well-prepared dishes (mainly seafood) on the menu, it has an enthusiastic following among locals, so reservations are advised in summer. ⊠ *Via Alloro 104,* ☎ *091/6161136. AE, DC, MC, V. Closed Sun. in summer, Mon. in winter.*

$–$$ ✕ **Trattoria ai Normanni.** This is a good spot for lunch after visiting the Palazzo dei Normanni, just off Piazza Indipendenza. In the tall-ceilinged interior with internal balcony the ambience is casual and the service polite. Try the house specialty, spaghetti *ai Normanni* (with fresh tomatoes, shrimp, eggplant, and grated peanuts, smothered with fennel). Other choices include *zuppa di cozze* (mussel soup), and there are pizzas in the evening. Sit inside or out—but arrive early or reserve if you want an outdoor table. ⊠ *Piazza della Vittoria 25,* ☎ *091/ 6516011. AE, DC, MC, V. Closed Mon. in winter.*

$ ✕ **Antica Focacceria San Francesco.** This place in Palermo's heart is an institution, as you can see from the turn-of-the-20th-century wooden cabinets and fixtures of what is still a neighborhood bakery. It serves the snacks that locals love—and from which you can make an inexpensive meal. The big pan on the counter holds the regional specialty guasteddi, but for the squeamish, try the *panelle* (potato croquette) instead. You can sit at marble-topped tables or take food out. The good gelateria in the piazza is under the same management. ⊠ *Via Paternostro 58,* ☎ *091/320264. Reservations not accepted. No credit cards.*

$ ✕ **Bellini.** The pizzas are good, the pastas are better, but the best reason to eat in this former theater is the location, overlooking the churches of San Cataldo and La Martorana in the heart of old Palermo. Get a seat next to the window—or better still, in summer, eat alfresco. Trade is brisk, and so is the service, which can be offhand. ⊠ *Piazza Bellini 6,* ☎ *091/6165691. MC, V. Closed Tues.*

$ ✕ **Casa del Brodo.** On the edge of the Vucciria and dating back to 1890, this restaurant—its two small rooms usually crowded with a mix of tourists and locals—is one of Palermo's oldest. Typical Sicilian dishes are on offer; try the *carni bollite* (boiled meats). The risotto with mushrooms or asparagus is also a standout. ⊠ *Corso Vittorio Emanuele 175,* ☎ *091/321655. AE, DC, MC, V. Closed Tues. in Oct.–Easter.*

$$$$ ⊞ **Grand Hotel et des Palmes.** This grande dame hotel had an extensive face-lift in 2000, and its fabled (but recently faded) charm glows once more. The public rooms suggest the elegant life of Palermo society before World War I, when they were alive with tea dances and balls. Guest rooms are filled with antiques and heavy fabrics. There's an American-style cocktail bar and a couple of banquet halls. Wagner finished writing the opera *Parsifal* during a stay here. ⊠ *Via Roma 398, 90139,* ☎ *091/583933,* FAX *091/331545,* WEB *www.thi.it/despalmes.htm. 183 rooms, 4 suites. Restaurant, bar, parking (fee). AE, DC, MC, V.*

$$$$ ⊞ **Hotel Principe di Villafranca.** Not far from Palermo's glitzy shopping district, this hotel has put a great deal of thought into creating the feel of a private home—and with fine Sicilian antiques, imperial striped silks, creamy marble floors, and vaulted ceilings, a museum-quality home indeed. But you will feel comfortable in the understated surroundings: relax in the library with an aperitif or savor an authentic meal in the rustic adjoining Ristorante dei Vecchi Monsù. Rooms are elegant, with fine linens, wardrobes painted by local artists, lovely handmade porcelain pieces (which you can order for your own casa), and more antiques. ⊠ *Via G. Turrisi Colonna 4, 90140,* ☎ *091/6118523,* FAX *091/588705,* WEB *www.principedivillafranca.it. 34 rooms. Restaurant, breakfast room, café, gym, library, meeting room, free parking. AE, DC, MC, V.*

$$$$ ⊞ **Mondello Palace.** This is the leading hotel at the Mondello resort,
★ making the best use of its location near the beach. The private beach
has cabins and changing rooms for the use of Mondello Palace guests.
The rooms are large, with luxury baths, and most have balconies. In
summer you can choose between the hotel's own restaurant or the beachside venue of Palermo's excellent Charleston—just across the road. ⊠
Viale Principe di Scalea, 90139 Mondello Lido, just north of Palermo,
☎ *091/450001,* FAX *091/450657. 84 rooms, 9 suites. Restaurant, bar,
pool, gym, beach, windsurfing, boating. AE, DC, MC, V.*

$$$$ ⊞ **Villa Igiea.** A short taxi ride through some rough-looking districts
★ of Palermo takes you to this oasis of luxury and comfort in its own
tropical garden at the edge of the bay. A meander through the grounds
reveals such relics as an ancient Greek temple at the water's edge. Large
rooms are furnished individually, the nicest with an Italian Art Nouveau flavor. Spacious lobbies and public rooms unfold onto a terrace
and restaurant. Sports facilities help make this elegant villa a self-contained enclave in frenetic Palermo. ⊠ *Salita Belmonte 43, Acquasanta,
3 km (2 mi) north of Palermo, 90142,* ☎ *091/543744,* FAX *091/547654,*
WEB *www.thi.it/igea.htm. 110 rooms, 6 suites. Restaurant, bar, pool,
gym, tennis court. AE, DC, MC, V.*

$$$ ⊞ **Massimo Plaza Hotel.** This hotel boasts one of Palermo's best lo-
cations—right opposite the renovated Teatro Massimo. It is small and
select, its few rooms spacious, comfortably furnished, and—most im-
portant—well insulated from the noise on Via Maqueda. Service is per-
sonal and polite. ⊠ *Via Maqueda 437, 90133,* ☎ *091/325657,* FAX *091/
325711. 15 rooms. Bar, parking (fee). AE, DC, MC, V.*

$$ ⊞ **Posta.** A night here may bring you face to face with one of the famous Italian singers or actors who frequent this hotel, as the numer-
ous photographs in the foyer testify. Centrally located off Via Roma,
yet undisturbed by the racket of traffic along that main road, this is
an unpretentious place, its guest rooms simply furnished but well
equipped. Friendly service and a soothing atmosphere set the tone
here. There is no restaurant, but breakfast is available in the bar. ⊠
Via Antonio Gagini 77, 90133, ☎ *091/587338,* FAX *091/587347. 26
rooms. Bar. AE, DC, MC, V.*

$$ ⊞ **Principe di Belmonte.** This is a tasteful choice among Palermo's cheaper
hotels (it's at the low end of this price category). It's family-run,
friendly, and central—a convenient walk both from the port and Pi-
azza Castelnuovo—but is on a relatively quiet street. Rooms are small-
ish. Advance reservations are advised. ⊠ *Via Principe di Belmonte 25,
90139,* ☎ *091/331065,* FAX *091/6113424. 17 rooms, 14 with bath. Bar.
AE, DC, MC, V.*

Nightlife and the Arts

The Arts

CONCERTS AND OPERA

Teatro Massimo (⊠ Piazza Verdi, at the top of Via Maqueda, ☎ 091/
6053515, WEB www.teatromassimo.it) reopened in summer 1997 after
23 years of restoration. A program of concerts and operas is presented
throughout the year. The grandiose **Politeama Garibaldi** (⊠ Piazza Rug-
gero Settimo, ☎ 091/6053315) stages a winter season of opera and
orchestral works. Choral and chamber recitals are performed at the
Teatro Golden (⊠ Via Terrasanta 60, ☎ 091/305217).

FESTIVALS

Palermo stages the **Festa di Santa Rosalia**, a street fair held July 11–
15 in honor of the city's patron saint. There are fireworks displays in
the evenings. **Epiphany** (January 6) is celebrated with Byzantine rites

and a procession of townspeople in local costume through the streets of Piana degli Albanesi, 24 km (15 mi) south of Palermo. The village is named for the Albanian immigrants who first settled there, bringing with them the Byzantine Catholic rites.

PUPPET SHOWS

Children and adults alike will enjoy Palermo's tradition of puppet theater. Often you see street artists performing outside the **Teatro Massimo** in summer. Contact the **Opera dei Pupi, Cuticchio Mimmo** (⊠ Via Bara all'Olivella 52, ☎ 091/323400), or **Teatro Ippogrifo** (⊠ Vicolo Ragusi 4, ☎ 091/329194) to see what's playing. Check with the tourist office for details.

THEATER

Palermo's **Teatro Biondo** (⊠ Via Roma, ☎ 091/582364) is Sicily's foremost theater. Its season of plays lasts from November to May.

Nightlife

NIGHTCLUBS

Apart from some trendy bars lining Via Principe del Belmonte, intersecting with Via Roma and Via Ruggero Settimo (a northern extension of Via Maqueda), nightlife is concentrated in the nightclubs and discotheques scattered around the northern, newer end of town, a taxi ride away. Check out **Il Cerchio** (⊠ Viale Strasburgo 312, ☎ 091/6885421), **Paramatta** (⊠ Viale Lazio 51, ☎ 091/513621), and **Kandisky** (⊠ Discesa Tonnara 4, ☎ 091/6375611). In summer, the scene shifts to Mondello, Palermo's seaside satellite on the other side of Monte Pellegrino.

Outdoor Activities and Sports

Bowling

Bowling enthusiasts should seek out **Bowling and Games** (⊠ Via L. di Scalea 781, ☎ 091/6716078) or **Bowling la Favorita** (⊠ Viale del Fante 1, ☎ 091/6375056) at the Favorita sport center.

Sailing and Windsurfing

Sailing and windsurfing facilities and instruction are available in Mondello at **Albaria** (⊠ Viale Regina Elena 89/a, ☎ 091/453595) and **Euro-Yachting Sports** (⊠ Presso L'Antico Stabilimento Balneare, Viale Regina Elena, ☎ 091/455851).

Swimming

Palermo has two public outdoor swimming pools: the **Piscina Comunale** (⊠ Viale del Fante, ☎ 091/6703558) at the sport center at Parco Favorita and the **Piscina Polisportiva** (⊠ Via Belgio 2, ☎ 091/6703078).

Tennis

The best of Palermo's tennis clubs are the **Country Club** (⊠ Viale Olimpo 12, ☎ 091/454886), **Circolo del Tennis TC1** (⊠ Via del Fante 3, ☎ 091/544517), and **Circolo del Tennis TC2** (⊠ Via San Lorenzo, ☎ 091/6885360). Call first to confirm court availability.

Shopping

Most shops in Palermo are open 9–1 and 4–8 but close Sunday; in addition, most food shops close Wednesday afternoons, while other shops normally close Monday mornings. The main shopping area is around Piazza Castelnuovo, especially on the two parallel streets connecting the square with the train station, **Via Roma** and **Via Maqueda,** where there is a good range of boutiques and shoe shops that becomes increasingly upmarket as you move on to **Via Ruggero Settimo.** North of Piazza Castelnuovo, **Via della Libertà** and the streets around it represent the luxury end of the scale, with some of Palermo's best-known stores.

Markets

Looking to pick up antique marionettes of the Norman cavaliers or brilliantly colored pieces from the carretti siciliani? Head to the **flea market,** held daily behind Palermo's Cattedrale, on Via Papireto. Don't miss the raucous outdoor market around Vucciria's **Piazza San Domenico,** every day but Sunday.

Nearby, between Via Roma and Via Maqueda, **Via Bandiera** is a riot of *bancherelle*—market stalls selling everything from clothes to imitation designer handbags.

Specialty Stores

ANTIQUES

The area behind the Cattedrale, in the midst of the flea market on Via Papireto and spreading to the next street, Corso Amedeo, is the antiques-store neighborhood.

CERAMICS

De Simone has a wide selection of ceramics decorated in a modern style reminiscent of Picasso. You can browse through the workshop (⊠ Via Lanza di Scalea 698) or see what's on offer at a more central retail outlet (⊠ Via Daita 13/b, near Piazza Ruggero Settimo).

MONREALE AND THE TYRRHENIAN COAST

Sicily's northern shore, the Tyrrhenian coast, is almost entirely dedicated to vacationing. Mostly a succession of small holiday towns interspersed with stretches of sand, it's often hard to find a calm spot among the thousands of other tourists and locals in high summer, though the scene quiets down considerably after August. The biggest attraction is the old town of Cefalù, with one of Sicily's most remarkable medieval cathedrals, encrusted with mosaics. The coast on either side is dotted with ancient archaeological remains and Arab-Norman buildings. You need only venture a couple of miles south of Cefalù to explore the Monti Madonie national park, which contains the highest peak in Sicily after Mount Etna—Pizzo Carbonara at 6,500 ft. For skiers, Piano della Battaglia offers a fully equipped ski resort with lifts. The area has a very un-Sicilian aspect with Swiss-type chalets and even alpine churches. In spring and summer, there are many good paths for hiking.

From Palermo, it's an easy drive or bus ride to the high fastness of Monreale, whose cathedral provides an instructive comparison to the one at Cefalù, built at around the same time. The glittering mosaics here are among the finest in the whole Mediterranean. Fans of military architecture and great views should make the short drive inland to the castle of Cáccamo, site of a formidable Norman castle midway between Palermo and Cefalù.

Monreale

⑫ *10 km (6 mi) southwest of Palermo.*

★ Don't miss Monreale's splendid **Duomo,** lavishly executed with mosaics depicting events from the Old and New Testaments. After the Norman conquest of Sicily, the new princes showcased their ambitions through monumental building projects. William II (1154–89) built the church complex with a cloister and palace between 1174 and

1185, employing Byzantine craftsmen. The result was a glorious fusion of Eastern and Western stylistic influences, widely regarded as the finest example of Norman architecture in Sicily.

The major attraction is the 68,220 square ft of glittering gold mosaics decorating the cathedral interior. The commanding image of Christ Pantocrator overlooks the apse area, which also contains mosaics of the Virgin and Child, the archangels, prophets, and saints. The nave contains two narrative bands, starting adjacent to the central apse, illustrating the book of Genesis from the Creation of Heaven and Earth and continuing through Jacob Wrestling with the Angel. Scenes from the life of Christ adorn the walls of the aisles and the transept. The painted wooden ceiling, a reconstruction of the original following a fire in 1811, dates from 1816 to 1837. Bring 500-lire coins to illuminate the mosaics. (How the lighting will be handled with the transfer to the euro was an unresolved issue at press time.) A small pair of binoculars will make it easier to read the Latin inscriptions. The roof commands a great view if you are up to climbing the 172 stairs.

Bonnano Pisano's **bronze doors**, completed in 1186, depict 42 biblical scenes and are considered among the most important of medieval artifacts. Note the Norman heraldic symbols of lions and griffins on the bottom of the doors. Barisano da Trani's 42 panels on the north door, dating from 1179, present saints and evangelists. ⊠ *Piazza del Duomo,* ☎ *091/6404413.* ⊘ *Daily 8–6.*

Don't miss the lovely **cloister** of the abbey adjacent to the Duomo. It was built at the same time as the church but enlarged in the 14th century. The beautiful square enclosure is surrounded by 216 double columns, every other one decorated in a unique glass mosaic pattern. Note the intricate carvings on the bases and the capitals of the columns. In one of the corners, by the stylized palm-tree fountain, look for a capital showing William II offering the cathedral to the Virgin Mary. ⊠ *Piazza del Duomo,* ☎ *091/6404403.* ▣ *8,000 lire/€4.15.* ⊘ *Mon.– Sat. 9–7, Sun. 9–1.*

Afterward, don't forget to walk behind the cloisters to the **belvedere,** with stunning panoramic views over the Conca d'Oro (Golden Conch) valley toward Palermo.

You'll find a variety of water-based amusements at **Acqua Park** (⊠ Via Pezzingoli 172, ☎ 091/6460246), daily from June through September.

Dining

$$ ✕ **La Botte.** It's worth the short drive or inexpensive taxi fare from Monreale to reach this restaurant, a good value for well-prepared local specialties. Dine alfresco on daily specials such as *pennette agli odori* (little penne with tomato, garlic, parsley, basil, mint, and oregano) or regular favorites, such as *involtini* (meat or fish roulades). Local wines are a good bet. ⊠ *Contrada Lenzitti 20, S186,* ☎ *091/414051. AE, DC, MC, V. Closed Mon. and Aug. No dinner Sun., no lunch Tues.–Fri.*

Termini Imerese

⑬ *40 km (25 mi) east of Palermo.*

This port town takes its name from the Greeks who founded it (refugees from nearby Himera), and the natural spa baths, or *terme,* that helped to make it an important Roman city. Termini's upper town, occupying a high promontory above the port, holds the few survivals from the town's classical period—the ruins of an amphitheater and the foundations of a public building, enveloped among the trees of the public gardens. More compelling are the outstanding vistas to be enjoyed from the belvedere, the extensive views along the coast only partly marred by the industry surrounding the port below.

Sit down and have a gelato before wandering around Termini's elegant Baroque churches, making a stop at the **Museo Civico,** housed in a 14th-century palazzo that incorporates a self-contained chapel. There is some impressive religious art to be seen here, including sculpture by 15th-century artist Antonello Gagini and a triptych, *Madonna with Child and Saints,* attributed to Gaspare da Pésaro (active 1413–60). Other rooms in this well-displayed collection hold prehistoric and archaeological material, including finds from Himera. ⊠ *Via Civico,* ☎ *091/ 8128279.* 🎟 *Free.* ⊙ *Apr.–mid-Oct., Tues.–Sat. 9–1:30 and 4–7, Sun. 9–1:30; mid-Oct.–Mar., Tues.–Sat. 9–1:30 and 3–6, Sun. 9–1:30.*

OFF THE
BEATEN PATH
HIMERA – From Termini Imerese, drive or take a taxi to the site of ancient Himera, 15 km (8 mi) east along the coast, site of the original 7th-century BC Chalcidinian (Greek) settlement. All that's left of the city that once stood here is the massive **Tempio della Vittoria** erected to commemorate the Greek victory over a huge Carthaginian army in 480 BC and built by the Carthaginian prisoners themselves. The Carthaginian leader Hamilcar had intended to take Himera and probably the rest of Sicily, too, but his defeat by the combined armies of Akragas (Agrigento), Gela, and Syracuse led him to throw himself onto the pyre. The victory marked the beginning of Greek ascendancy in Sicily, though for Himera the celebrations were short lived: Hamilcar's nephew, Hannibal, wreaked his revenge in 409 BC by razing the city to the ground, forcing the surviving citizens west to what is now Termini Imerese. Little remains above knee-level of the original Doric monument, but it's a poignant sight, redolent of ancient glory. Above the temple on the site of Himera's acropolis, a modern **antiquarium** shows diagrams of the temple as it once appeared, together with some remnants of the Greek city; the rest is in the museums at Termini and Palermo. ⊠ *Buonfornello,* ☎ *091/8140128.* 🎟 *4,000 lire/€2.05.* ⊙ *Apr.–Sept., daily 9–6; Oct.–Mar., daily 9–5.*

Lodging

$$$ 🏨 **Grand Hotel delle Terme.** Dominating Termini's lower town, this hotel was built at the end of the 19th century right over the spring from which Termini's famous spa waters—praised by Plutarch, among others—gush forth. You can take full advantage of the curative waters in the classically styled thermal complex in the basement, where treatments include massage and mud therapy. Aboveground, public rooms are sumptuously furnished, with a grand staircase and a wealth of paintings and potted plants scattered around, but guest rooms tend to be on the small side. A rooftop pool provides a pleasant lounging area even if you aren't tempted to take a dip. ⊠ *Piazza delle Terme, 90018,* ☎ *091/8113557,* 🆋 *091/8113107. 69 rooms, 11 suites. Restaurant, bar, pool, hair salon, massage, spa, health club. AE, DC, MC, V.*

Cáccamo

⓮ *12 km (8 mi) south of Termini Imerese, 52 km (32 mi) southeast of Palermo.*

The quiet village of Cáccamo rises on an inland spur that the Normans could not resist fortifying, and the mighty **Castello** that they raised here in the 12th century still stands, superbly restored, its sheer white walls a landmark from miles around. It's one of Sicily's largest and most impressive bastions, bristling with turrets and crenellations, and among its 130 rooms is the **Sala della Congiura,** where a baron's plot against William I was hatched in 1160. If the castle's entrance gate isn't open, ring at Corso Umberto 6 (the door nearest the war memorial opposite the main entrance). ⊠ *Corso Umberto,* ☎ *091/810–3248.* 🎫 *Free (gratuity requested).* ⊙ *Daily 9:30–12:30 and 3:30–7.*

Dining

$ ✕ **A Castellana.** For a meal by the castle, this medieval-looking pizzeria-restaurant is ideal. Have a simple pizza or pasta con le sarde. ⊠ *Piazza Monumento 4,* ☎ *091/8148667. AE, DC, MC, V. Closed Mon.*

Cefalù

★ ⓯   *38 km (24 mi) northeast of Termini Imerese, 70 km (42 mi) east of Palermo.*

Cefalù is a charming town built on a spur jutting out into the sea and dominated by a massive 12th-century Romanesque **Duomo,** one of the finest Norman cathedrals in Italy. (Note that visitors are expected to wear proper attire—don't come in shorts or beachwear.) King Roger began it in 1131 as an offering of thanks for having been saved here from a shipwreck. Its mosaics rival those of Monreale. Like the one in Monreale, this cathedral is dominated by a colossal mosaic figure of the Byzantine Pantocratic Christ, high in the bowl of the apse. While the Monreale figure is an austere and powerful image, emphasizing Christ's divinity, the Cefalù Christ is softer, more compassionate, and more human. The traffic going in and out of Cefalù town can be heavy in summer; you may want to take the 50-minute train ride or 40-minute bus ride from Palermo instead of driving. ⊠ *Piazza Duomo,* ☎ *0921/ 421293.* ⊙ *Daily 8–noon and 3:30–5 (3:30–9 in summer). No shorts or beachwear.*

OFF THE   **REGIONAL PARK OF THE MADONIE –** This park is a great place to ski or
BEATEN PATH hike; **Piano Battaglia** provides the best base. For maps and more information contact the **Club Alpino Italiano Rifugio Marini** (☎ 0921/ 649994) or the office of the **Parco Regionale** (⊠ Corso Pietro Agliata 16, Petralia Sottana, ☎ 0921/684011).

Dining and Lodging

$$$ ✕ **Gabbiano.** "Seagull" is an appropriate name for a beach-side seafood restaurant with a nautical theme. House specialties are *involtini di pesce spada* (swordfish roulades) and spaghetti marinara. ⊠ *Via Lungomare Giardina 17,* ☎ *0921/421495. AE, DC, MC, V. Closed Wed. in mid-Sept.–June, and mid-Dec.–Jan.*

$$ ✕ **La Brace.** This bistro-style restaurant near the cathedral has been serving upscale dishes in a lively atmosphere since 1977. Graceful ceiling vaults and rustic walls give it an informal air. Dutch proprietor Dietmar Beckers and his team pride themselves on creatively reworking local ingredients. Savor the excellent grills, and save room for the *parfait di vaniglia* (vanilla parfait). There's an extensive wine list. ⊠ *Via Venticinque Novembre 10,* ☎ *0921/423570. AE, DC, MC, V. Closed Mon. and mid-Dec.–mid-Jan.*

$$$ 🏨 **Kalura.** Caldura, 3 km (2 mi) east along the coast, is the setting for
★   this modern hotel on a small promontory that's hard to reach without a car; it's only a few minutes by taxi from Cefalù, though. Sports facilities keep you from getting too sedentary, and the private beach is ideal for swimming. Rooms are bright and cheerful. Rates are low in this price category. ⊠ *Via V. Cavallaro 13, 90015 Contrada Caldura,* ☎ *0921/421354,* 📠 *0921/423122,* 🌐 *www.kalura.it. 65 rooms. Restaurant, bar, pool, tennis court, beach. AE, DC, MC, V.*

$$–$$$ 🏨 **Baia del Capitano.** The peaceful district of Mazzaforno, about 5 km
★   (3 mi) outside town, sets the stage for this handsome hotel with great

amenities. The ranch-style building is less than 30 years old, but it blends in with the rural surroundings. The colorful gardens, extending to the surrounding olive groves, are ideal for quiet reading or an afternoon siesta in the shade. A good sandy beach is an easy walk away. The rooms are large and quiet. You must pay half board in high season. ⊠ *Contrada Mazzaforno, 90015 Mazzaforno,* ☎ *0921/420005,* FAX *0921/420163. 39 rooms. Restaurant, bar, pool, tennis court, Ping-Pong, playground. AE, DC, MC, V. MAP.*

Santo Stefano di Camastra

16   *33 km (20 mi) east of Cefalù, 152 km (95 mi) west of Messina.*

When the original village of Santo Stefano di Camastra was destroyed in a landslide in 1682, the local duke, Giuseppe Lanza, rebuilt it on the coast according to strict military principles—a geometric street-grid, and artery roads connecting the center with the periphery. His innovations led directly to the duke's being entrusted with the rebuilding of Catania and Noto following the destruction of those cities by a catastrophic earthquake 10 years later. Today, Santo Stefano looks like any of the other resorts along the coast but for the abundance of ceramics shops lining every street, filled with the vividly colored pottery for which the town has an international reputation. Quality, of course, is variable, and you will need a discriminating eye to pick out the best items. And then, haggle like mad. If you want an overview of some of the possibilities of pottery, the range of uses to which it can be put and the heights of mastery in the genre, drop in on the **Museo della Ceramica,** housed in the 18th-century Palazzo Trabia in the center of town. Plates, figurines, extravagant sculptures, and diverse exhibitions are arranged in a well-lit environment, along with explanations of the processes and techniques involved. ⊠ *Via Palazzo,* ☎ *0921/331110.* ⌨ *Free.* ☽ *May–Sept., weekdays 9–1 and 4–8; Oct.–Apr., weekdays 9–1 and 3:30–7:30.*

Shopping
CERAMICS

The Franco family has a long tradition of creating ceramic *objets* by borrowing styles from past eras. Thus, Renaissance Madonnas rub shoulders with florid Baroque vases, all richly colored and skillfully finished. View them at the two outlets of **Ceramiche Franco** (⊠ Via Nazionale 8, ☎ 0921/337222; ⊠ Via Nazionale 40, ☎ 0921/339925) on Santo Stefano's main street.

WESTERN COAST TO AGRIGENTO
Land of Temples

Western Sicily has a remote air, less developed than the eastern coast, and bearing traces of the North African culture that for centuries exerted a strong influence on this end of the island. Influences are most tangible in the coastal towns of Trapani and Marsala, and the outlying island of Pantelleria, nearer to the Tunisian coast than the Sicilian. In contrast, the cobbled streets of the hilltop town of Erice, outside Trapani, retain a strong medieval complexion, giving the town the air of a last outpost gazing out over the Mediterranean. The Greek presence is still strong, however, in the splendidly isolated site of Segesta, and the cluster of ruined temples at Selinunte. The crowning glory of this tour is the concentration of Greek temples at Agrigento, occupying a fabulous position on a height between the modern city and the sea.

Segesta

⑰ *30 km (19 mi) east of Trapani, 85 km (53 mi) southwest of Palermo.*

Segesta is the site of one of the most impressive of Sicily's **Greek temples,** constructed on the side of a windswept barren hill overlooking a valley of wild fennel. Virtually intact today, the temple is considered by some to be finer, in its proportions and setting, than any other Doric temple left standing. The Greeks started the temple in the 5th century BC but never finished it. The walls and roof never materialized, and the columns were never fluted. Just over 1 km (½ mi) away, near the top of the hill, are the remains of a fine **Greek theater,** with impressive views, especially at sunset, of nearby Monte Erice and the sea. ☎ 0924/46277. ☞ *8,000 lire/€4.15.* ☉ *Daily 9–2 hrs before sunset.*

OFF THE
BEATEN PATH

GIBELLINA AND SALAPARUTA – On the night of January 14, 1968, a fierce earthquake devastated the wine-producing district of the Valle del Belice, causing 400 deaths and displacing more than 50,000 mostly poor inhabitants of the area. Two of the towns most affected were Gibellina and Salaparuta, and while most other damaged centers were (eventually) rebuilt, these were left as a memorial to the catastrophe. It's a disturbing, rather grim, though deeply peaceful landscape to visit today, a tangle of destruction in which broken walls protrude from mountains of rubble. In Gibellina, part of one hillside has been covered with a mantle of white concrete in which the lanes of the old town have been symbolically cut through, which you can wander among. Elsewhere, an amphitheater of scaffolding has been improvised where dramatic performances are enacted each summer, mainly of classical plays and concerts. Contact the **Fondazione Orestiadi** (✉ Baglio di Stefano, 91024 Gibellina Nuova, ☎ 0924/67844, FAX 0924/67855) for details. Gibellina Nuova itself, a new town built to accommodate the former residents 18 km (12 mi) to the west, is also worthy of a passing visit to see the collection of huge and diverse modern sculptures displayed here—a giant star built over the main S188, white spheres, a plough, a snail, and much more.

Erice

⑱ *35 km (22 mi) west of Segesta, 112 km (70 mi) west of Palermo.*

Erice is perched 2,450 ft above sea level, an enchanting medieval mountaintop aerie of castles and palaces, fountains, and cobblestone streets. Erice was the ancient Eryx and was dedicated to the fertility goddess whom the Phoenicians called Astarte, the Greeks Aphrodite, and the Romans Venus. According to Virgil, Aeneas built a temple to the goddess here, but it was destroyed when the Arabs took over and renamed the place Mohammed's Mountain. When the Normans arrived, they built a castle where today you'll find a public park with benches and belvederes, from which there are striking views of Trapani, the Egadi Islands, and, on a *very* clear day, Cape Bon and the Tunisian coast.

NEED A
BREAK?

Fans of Sicilian sweets will make a beeline for **Pasticceria Grammatico** (✉ Via Vittorio Emanuele 14, ☎ 0923/869390), run by Maria Grammatico, a former nun who gained international fame with *Bitter Almonds,* her life story co-written with Mary Taylor Simeti. She learned how to make her sweet confections in the convent where she was brought up. Molded into a variety of shapes, including dolls and animals, her almond-paste creations are works of art. The balcony from the tearoom upstairs has wonderful views. At **Pasticceria del Convento** (✉ Via Guarnotte 1), Maria

Grammatico's sister sells the same delectable treats that are found at Pasticceria Grammatico.

Dining and Lodging

$$ ✕ **Monte San Giuliano.** Buried within the labyrinth of lanes that makes up Erice, this restaurant has a satisfying traditional feel. Sit out on the stone patio and sample such house specialties as the spicy Arab-influenced seafood couscous or the risotto with *rucola* (arugula) and swordfish. Wash it all down with a bottle of Donnafugata, a good white from the Rallo vineyards at Marsala. ✉ *Vicolo San Rocco 7,* ☎ *0923/869595. AE, DC, MC, V. Closed Mon., 2 wks in Jan., and 2 wks in Nov.*

$$$ ✕🏨 **Moderno.** Local crafts and some antiques decorate the gracious
★ rooms of this intimate, well-run hotel on the cobblestone streets of the medieval town. Some rooms are in the modern annex. Open to guests and nonguests alike, the renowned restaurant ($$) serves seafood pasta and homemade desserts. In winter, a fire is always blazing. ✉ *Via Vittorio Emanuele 67, 91016,* ☎ *0923/869300,* 🖷 *0923/869139,* 🌐 *www.pippocatalano.it. 40 rooms. Restaurant, bar. AE, DC, MC, V.*

$$ 🏨 **Ermione.** Spectacular views and cool breezes are the rewards of a visit to Erice, and this 1960s hotel overlooking the Tyrrhenian Sea is in a position to offer both. Nearly every room has a good view, although some would say that the terrace bar has the most panoramic vista. The hotel restaurant is popular locally, with fish couscous a standout. ✉ *Via Pineta Comunale 43, 91016,* ☎ *0923/869138,* 🖷 *0923/869587. 46 rooms. Restaurant, bar, pool. AE, DC, MC, V.*

Trapani

⓳ *30 km (18 mi) west of Segesta, 107 km (67 mi) west of Palermo.*

The modern town of Trapani, below Erice, is the departure point for ferries to the Egadi Islands and the island of Pantelleria, near the African coast. The lanes near Corso Italia hold a handful of churches worth wandering into. **Santa Maria di Gesù,** on Via San Pietro, has Gothic and Renaissance doors and a Madonna by Andrea della Robbia (1435–1525). **Sant'Agostino,** on Piazzetta Saturno, behind the town hall, has a 14th-century rose window. This rugged western end of Sicily is reminiscent of the terrain in American Westerns—as well it should be, for many "spaghetti Westerns" were filmed here. If you fancy North African couscous, Trapani is the place to try the Sicilian version, made with fish instead of meat. The result is a kind of fish stew with semolina, laced with cinnamon, saffron, and black pepper.

Dining

$$–$$$ ✕ **P&G.** Opposite the Villa Margherita public gardens near the train
★ station, this small restaurant has a quiet, dignified air and attentive service. The local pasta, *busiate,* is cooked with swordfish and eggplant, while the couscous features fish in summer (Friday only) and meat in winter. A mixed grill of meats in a zesty orange sauce will revive any appetite suffering from fish fatigue. Reservations on a good idea on weekends. ✉ *Via Spalti 1,* ☎ *0923/547701. MC, V. Closed Sun. and mid-Aug.–mid-Sept.*

Pantelleria

⓴ *100 km (62 mi) southwest of Sicily, 6 hrs by ferry from Trapani.*

Pantelleria, near the Tunisian coast, is one of Sicily's most evocative islands, although some find its starkness unappealing. If you're travel-weary and need a place to hole up for a few days in blissfully calm surroundings, however, this makes an ideal spot, its few hotels and restaurants catering to your basic needs. Many opt to rent accommodations in the traditional dammuso houses, with stout walls and domes for maximum coolness in the fierce summer heat. There are no beaches, but the hilly terrain offers plenty to explore, either on foot or astride a rented moped. Its volcanic formations, scant patches of forest, prehistoric tombs, and dramatic seascapes constitute an otherworldly landscape. From its grapes—the *zibibbo*—the locals make an amber-color dessert wine and a strong, sweet wine called Tanit. Daily ferries and, in summer, hydrofoils connect the island with Trapani.

Marsala

㉑ *30 km (18 mi) south of Trapani, 140 km (87 mi) southwest of Palermo.*

The quiet seaside town of Marsala was once the main Carthaginian base in Sicily, from which Carthage fought for supremacy of the island against Greece and Rome. Some of the flavor of those times is recaptured by the well-preserved Punic warship displayed in the town's **Museo Archeologico Baglio Anselmi,** along with some of the amphoras and other artifacts recovered from the wreck. The vessel, which was probably sunk during the great sea battle that ended the First Punic War in 241 BC, was dredged up from the mud near the Egadi Islands in the 1970s and is now installed under a climate-controlled plastic tent. ⊠ *Via Boeo 30,* ☎ *0923/952535.* 🎫 *4,000 lire/€2.05.* ☉ *Mon., Tues., and Thurs. 9–1:30; Wed, Fri., and weekends 9–1:30 and 4–7 (6:30 in winter).*

Nowadays, Marsala is more readily associated with the world-famous, rich-color, sweet-tasting wine named after the town. In 1773 a British merchant named John Woodhouse happened upon Marsala and discovered that the wine here was as good as the port the British had long imported from Portugal. Two other wine merchants, Whitaker and Ingram, rushed in, and by 1800 Marsala was exporting its wine all over the British Empire.

Selinunte

㉒ *88 km (55 mi) southeast of Marsala, 114 km (71 mi) south of Palermo.*

Near the town of Castelvetrano, an overwhelming array of ruined **Greek temples** is perched on a plateau overlooking the Mediterranean at Selinunte. The city was one of the most superb colonies of ancient Greece. The original complex held seven temples scattered over two sites separated by a harbor. Of the seven, only one—reconstructed in 1958—stands. Founded in the 7th century BC, Selinunte became the rich and prosperous rival of Segesta, which in 409 BC turned to the Carthaginians for help. The Carthaginians sent an army commanded by Hannibal to destroy the city. The temples were demolished, the city was razed, and 16,000 of Selinunte's inhabitants were slaughtered. The beautiful metopes preserved in Palermo's Museo Archeologico Regionale come from the frieze of Temple E here. A small **museum** on the site contains other excavated pieces. Selinunte is named after a local variety of wild celery that in spring still grows in profusion among the ruined columns and overturned capitals. ☎ *0924/46251.* 🎫 *8,000 lire/€4.15.* ☉ *Daily 9–1 hr before sunset.*

Agrigento

100 km (60 mi) southeast of Selinunte, 126 km (79 mi) south of Palermo.

The natural defenses of Akragas, the Greek city today called Agrigento, depended on its secure, and quite lovely, position between two rivers on a flood plain a short distance from the sea. Akragas was settled by

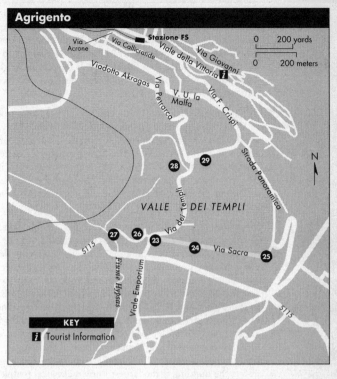

Agrigento

the Greeks in 582 BC and grew wealthy through trade with Carthage, just across the Mediterranean. Despite attacks from the Carthaginians at the end of the 5th century BC, the city survived through the Roman era, the Middle Ages (when it came under Arab and Norman rule), and into the modern age. Famous sons include the ancient Greek philosopher Empedocles (circa 490–430 BC) and the Italian playwright Luigi Pirandello (1867–1936).

★ In Agrigento you will be treated to what is considered by many experts the best-preserved collection of buildings from classical Greece in existence today. Whether you first come upon the **Valle di Templi** (Valley of the Temples) in the early morning light, bathed by golden floodlights at night, or at very their best in February, when the valley is awash in the fragrant blossoms of thousands of almond trees during the Festa delle Mandorle, it is easy to see why Agrigento was celebrated by Pindar as "the most beautiful city built by mortal men." Exit from the highway, walk down from the parking lot on Via dei Templi, and turn left. The ridge holding the temples of Hercules, Concord, and Juno is in front of you.

23 The eight pillars of the **Tempio di Ercole** (Temple of Hercules) make up Agrigento's oldest temple complex, dating from the 6th century BC. Partially reconstructed in 1922, it reveals the remains of a large Doric temple that originally had 38 columns. Like all the area temples, it faces east. The Museo Archeologico Nazionale contains some of the marble warrior figures that once decorated its pediment.

24 The beautiful **Tempio di Concordia** (Concord), up the hill from the Temple of Hercules, owes its exceptional state of preservation to the fact that it was converted into a Christian church in the 6th century and was extensively restored in the 18th. The structure dates from about 430 BC, and, like most of the temples here, was constructed of the local soft oolitic limestone that was originally coated in white stucco and brightly painted. The name of the temple, based on a Latin inscription found nearby, is in fact an error. It is now accepted that the inscription bears no relation to the building. To this day, however, it remains a well-established tradition in Agrigento for couples to visit the temple on their wedding day. On the left of the temple is a Paleochristian **necropolis.** Early Christian tombs were both cut into the rock and dug into underground catacombs.

㉕ The **Tempio di Giunone** (Juno), east on the Via Sacra from the Temple of Concord, commands an exquisite view of the valley, especially at sunset. It is similar to but smaller than the Concordia and dates from about 450 BC. Traces of a fire that probably occurred during the Carthaginian attack in 406 BC, which destroyed the ancient town, can be seen on the walls of the cellar. Thirty of the original 34 columns still stand, of which 16 still retain their capitals. ⊠ *Zona Archeologica,* ☎ *0922/497221.* ☜ *4,000 lire/€2.05.* ⊙ *Daily 8:30 AM–9 PM.*

From the parking lot in the Piazzale dei Templi, where a bar sells drinks and ice cream, cross to the opposite side of the road to enter ㉖ the western archaeological zone. Though never completed, the **Tempio di Giove** (Jupiter) was considered the eighth wonder of the world. The temple was probably built in gratitude for victory over Carthage and was constructed by prisoners captured in that war. Basically Doric in style, it did not have the usual colonnade of freestanding columns but rather a series of half-columns attached to a solid wall. Inside the excavation you can see one of the 38 colossal figures, or telamones, of Atlas that supported the massive roof of the temple. This design is unique among known Doric temples, and with a length of more than 330 ft the building is the largest known classical temple. Note that it usually closes at 5.

㉗ The four columns supporting part of an entablature of the **Tempio di Castore e Polluce** (Castor and Pollux) have become emblematic of Agrigento, but, in fact, the reconstruction of 1836 haphazardly put together elements from diverse buildings. The **Santuario delle Divinita Ctonie** (Sanctuary of the Cthonic Divinities) has cultic altars and eight small temples dedicated to Demeter, Persephone, and other Underworld deities have been found. It's located to the north of the Temple of Castor and Pallux; in the vicinity are two columns of a temple dedicated to Hephaestus (Vulcan). ⊠ *Zona Archeologica,* ☎ *0922/497221.* ☜ *Free.* ⊙ *Daily 8:30–7 in summer, 8:30–5:30 in winter.*

At the end of Via dei Templi, where it turns left and becomes Via Petrarca, stands the **Museo Archeologico Nazionale.** An impressive col-㉘ lection of antiquities includes vases, votives, everyday objects, weapons, statues, and models of the temples as they once stood. ⊠ *Contrada San Nicola,* ☎ *0922/401565.* ☜ *8,000 lire/€4.15.* ⊙ *Daily 9–1 and 3:30–5:30.*

㉙ The **Hellenistic and Roman Quarter,** across the road from the archaeological museum, consists of four parallel streets, running north and south, that have been uncovered, along with the foundations of some houses from the Roman settlement (2nd century BC). Some of these streets still have their original mosaic pavements.

There is little reason to go up the hill to the rather dreary modern city of Agrigento, where industrial speculation threatens to encroach upon the Valley of the Temples below—except to ring the doorbell at the **Convento di Santo Spirito** on the Salita di Santo Spirito off Via Porcello and try the almond cakes and the *kus-kus* (sweet cake), made of pistachio nuts and chocolate, that the nuns there prepare.

OFF THE
BEATEN PATH

CASA PIRANDELLO – One of Agrigento's native sons was the distinguished dramatist Luigi Pirandello (1867–1936), whose plays, such as *Six Characters in Search of an Author,* express the fundamental ambiguity of life. Pirandello's ashes lie under a pine tree behind the house where he was born, in Piazzale Caos, a couple of miles west of town. His house has been made into a museum of Pirandello memorabilia. Every year, a festival of Pirandello's plays is held in Agrigento from late July to early August. ☎ 0922/511102. ☞ 5,000 lire/€2.60. ☉ Mon.–Sat. 8:30–1 and 4–7.

Dining and Lodging

$$$ ✕ **Trattoria dei Templi.** Located near the archaeological area, this simple restaurant can get very busy in the early evening, when it becomes too dark for temple exploring. The menu has all the classic Sicilian dishes, with plenty of grilled fish on offer, and there's an exceptional array of antipasti. ⊠ *Via Panoramica dei Templi 15,* ☎ *0922/403110. AE, DC, MC, V. Closed Thurs. in Sept.–June and 2 wks between Nov. and Jan.*

$$ ✕ **Ambasciata di Sicilia.** This tiny restaurant in the heart of Old Agrigento gets busy, so be sure to book a table in advance. It specializes in typical local dishes and serves a good *antipasto rustico.* On a hot day, choose a table on the outside terrace—perfect for cool summer meals. ⊠ *Via Gianbertoni 2, off Via Atenea,* ☎ *0922/20526. AE, DC, MC, V. Closed Mon. and Nov.*

$$ ✕ **Kokalos.** Eight kilometers (5 miles) southeast of town in the Villagio Mosè, this restaurant in an old village house has serenely beautiful views over the temples. As well as serving local specialties in the restaurant, Kokalos includes a pizzeria and *enoteca* (wine shop). ⊠ *Via Cavaleri Magazzeni 3, Villagio Mosè,* ☎ *0922/606427. AE, MC, V.*

$$ ✕ **Le Caprice.** The high points of this popular restaurant in the temple area are the overflowing trays of antipasti and abundant plates of seafood, including pesce spada. The waiters—when they are not rushed—are proud to explain some of the less-familiar entries on the wine list, which is relatively extensive. ⊠ *Via Panoramica dei Templi 51,* ☎ *0922/26469. AE, DC, MC, V. Closed Fri. and 1st 2 wks in July.*

$$$$ ▥ **Foresteria Baglio della Luna.** Fiery sunsets and moonlight cast a glow over this hotel in the valley below the temples, a couple of miles from town and easily accessible by taxi. A tower dating from the 8th century is central to the stone farmhouse complex, set around a peaceful geranium- and ivy-filled courtyard and a garden beyond. Standard rooms are cozy but nothing fancy, with mellow walls, bright flowered prints, and wooden furniture. The intimate, rustic restaurant serves Sicilian and Italian specialties, including superb pasta dishes. ⊠ *Contrada Maddalusa, Valle dei Templi, 92100,* ☎ *0922/511061,* ℻ *0922/598802. 22 rooms, 3 suites. Restaurant, bar, air-conditioning, minibars. AE, DC, MC, V.*

$$$$ ▥ **Villa Athena.** There is much demand for this former villa, the only hotel right in the midst of the archaeological zone, so make reservations as early as possible. The price reflects its privileged position, as the hotel itself, although pleasant, is not outstanding. Many rooms have terraces overlooking the large gardens and the swimming pool. The temples are an easy walk away, and there is a convivial atmosphere in the bar, where a multinational crowd swaps stories. ⊠ *Via dei Templi 33, 92100,* ☎ *0922/596288,* ℻ *0922/402180. 40 rooms. Restaurant, bar, pool. AE, DC, MC, V.*

$$ ▥ **Tre Torri.** This is the place to stay if you are sports minded and bent on exploring the countryside around Agrigento. The owner, a keen cyclist, provides special weekly half-board packages for bikers, hikers, and equestrians. A boat can also be booked for fishing trips, and water sports can be arranged. Public areas are spacious, and the modern rooms

simply furnished. The hotel's location, Villagio Mosè (8 km [5 mi] south-east of town), is on a regular bus route. ⊠ *Villagio Mosè, 92100,* ☎ *0922/606733,* ℻ *0922/607839,* Ⅶℰℬ *www.mediatel.it/public/tre-torri. 118 rooms. Restaurant, bar, pool, sauna, gym, bicycles, nightclub, meeting room. AE, DC, MC, V.*

Nightlife and the Arts

On the first weekend in February, Agrigento hosts a **Festa delle Mandorle,** or Almond Blossom Festival, with international folk dances, a costumed parade, and the sale of marzipan and other sweets made from almonds.

SIRACUSA

Greek Sicily began along the Ionian coast, and some of the finest examples of Baroque art and architecture were also created here, particularly in Siracusa. The city was founded in 734 BC by Greek colonists from Corinth and soon grew to rival, and even surpass, Athens in splendor and power. Siracusa became the largest, wealthiest city-state in Magna Graecia and a bulwark of Greek civilization. Although it suffered from tyrannical rule, kings such as Dionysius filled their courts in the 5th century BC with Greeks of the highest artistic stature—among them, Pindar, Aeschylus, and Archimedes. The Athenians did not welcome the rise of Siracusa and sent a fleet to destroy the rival city, but the natives outsmarted them in what was one of the greatest naval battles of ancient history (413 BC). Siracusa continued to prosper until it was conquered two centuries later by the Romans.

There are essentially two areas to explore in Siracusa: the Parco Archeologico, on the mainland; and the island of Ortygia, the ancient city first inhabited by the Greeks, which juts out into the Ionian sea and is connected to the mainland by two small bridges.

Exploring Siracusa

Siracusa's old nucleus of Ortygia is a compact area, a pleasure to amble around without getting unduly tired. In contrast, mainland Siracusa is predominantly a grid of right-angled streets through which the main roads Corso Gelone and Viale Cadorna channel most of the traffic. At the northern end of Corso Gelone, above Viale Paolo Orsi, the orderly grid gives way to the ancient quarter of Neapolis, where the sprawling Parco Archeologico is accessible from Viale Teracati (an extension of Corso Gelone). East of Viale Teracati, about a 10-minute walk from the Parco Archeologico, the district of Tyche holds the archaeological museum and the church and catacombs of San Giovanni, both off Viale Teocrito. You *could* walk to these far-flung sites from Ortygia, but it's not an inspiring hike, and you'd do better to take either a taxi or a city bus. Coming from the train station, it's a 15-minute trudge to Ortygia along Via Francesco Crispi and Corso Umberto.

Note that you can purchase combined tickets at a discount for three of Siracusa's major sights: a ticket for Parco Archeologico and Museo Archeologico is 12,000 lire/€6.25; for Parco Archeologico, Museo Archeologico, and Museo Regionale, 15,000 lire/€7.80. Tickets are valid for two days.

A Good Walk: Parco Archeologico and Museo Archeologico

Start your tour of mainland Siracusa at the Parco Archeologico (entrance from Largo Anfiteatro). Before reaching the ticket booth, pause briefly at the meager remains of the **Ara di Ierone** ㉚. Beyond the ticket

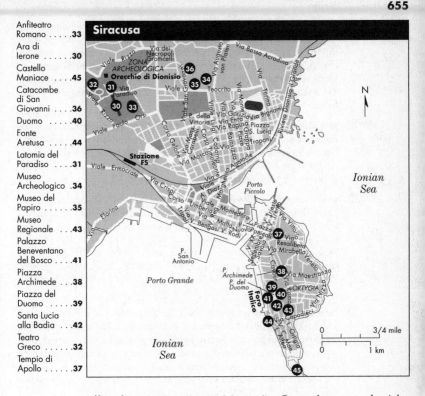

Siracusa

office, the extensive **Latomia del Paradiso** ㉛ stretches out on the right, while the archaeological park's pièce de résistance lies to the left: the awesome expanse of the **Teatro Greco** ㉜. Leave by the same way you entered, making a diversion before the park's exit (you'll need to show your entry ticket) to view the elliptical **Anfiteatro Romano** ㉝. From Largo Anfiteatro, head east along the busy Viale Teocrito, where, after a few minutes, you'll pass the **Museo Archeologico** ㉞. A few steps beyond is the much smaller but still intriguing **Museo del Papiro** ㉟. From here, retrace your steps along Viale Teocrito before turning right up Via San Giovanni to visit the church of San Giovanni and the **Catacombe di San Giovanni** ㊱ beneath. From here, drive or take one of the frequent city buses down Corso Gelone and Corso Umberto for the old city.

TIMING

Allow at least a full day for this tour, which can be quite taxing. In view of the fact that the Parco Archeologico has little or no shade, early morning or late afternoon would be the best times to visit on a hot day. You'll probably want to spend three or four hours here, with perhaps an hour afterward to recuperate over lunch or a *birra* (beer). The archaeological museum might easily take another two or three hours, though the tour of the refreshingly cool catacombs lasts less than half an hour, and you will probably spend a similar amount of time in the Museo del Papiro.

Sights to See

㉝ **Anfiteatro Romano** (Roman Amphitheater). A comparison of this and the Teatro Greco reveals much about the differences between the Greek and Roman personalities. In the Roman amphitheater, the emphasis was on the spectacle of combative sports and the circus. The arena is one of the largest of its kind and was built around the 2nd century AD. The corridor where gladiators and beasts entered the ring is still intact, and the seats, some of which still bear the occupants' names, were hauled in and constructed on the site from huge slabs of limestone. A crowd-pleasing show, and not the elevation of men's minds, was the intention here. If the Parco Archeologico (Archaeological Park) is closed, go up Viale G. Rizzo from Viale Teracati, to the belvedere overlooking the ruins, which are floodlit at night. ⊠ *Parco Archeologico: Viale Augusto,* ☎ *0931/66206.* ☒ *8,000 lire/€4.15.* ⊘ *Daily 9–1 hr before sunset (last tickets sold 2 hrs before sunset).*

㉚ Ara di Ierone (Altar of Hieron). Near the entrance to the Archaeological Park is the gigantic Altar of Hieron, which was once used by the Greeks for spectacular sacrifices involving hundreds of animals. ⊠ *Parco Archeologico: Viale Augusto,* ☎ *0931/66206.* ☒ *8,000 lire/€4.15.* ⊘ *Daily 9–1 hr before sunset (last tickets sold 2 hrs before sunset).*

㊱ Catacombe di San Giovanni. Not far from the Archaeological Park, off Viale Teocrito, the catacombs below the church of San Giovanni are one of the earliest-known Christian sites in the city. Inside the crypt of San Marciano is an altar where St. Paul preached on his way through Sicily to Rome. The frescoes in this small chapel are still bright and fresh, though some dating from the 4th century AD show their age. ⊠ *Piazza San Giovanni.* ☎ *0931/66571.* ☒ *6,000 lire/€3.10.* ⊘ *Tues.– Sun. 9–12:30 and 2:30–5:30 (hrs subject to change).*

㉛ Latomia del Paradiso. Just beyond the ticket office of the Archaeological Park you will come upon a lush tropical garden full of palm and citrus trees. This series of quarries served as prisons for the defeated Athenians, who were enslaved; the quarries once rang with the sound of their chisels and hammers. At one end is the Orecchio di Dionisio, with an ear-shape entrance and unusual acoustics inside, as you'll discover if you clap your hands. The legend is that Dionysius used to listen in at the top of the quarry to hear what the slaves were plotting below. ⊠ *Parco Archeologico: Viale Augusto,* ☎ *0931/66206.* ☒ *8,000 lire/€4.15.* ⊘ *Daily 9–1 hr before sunset (last tickets sold 2 hrs before sunset).*

㉞ Museo Archeologico. The impressive collection of Siracusa's splendid archaeological museum is organized by region around a central atrium and ranges from neolithic pottery to fine Greek statues and vases. You will want to compare the *Landolina Venus*—a headless, stout goddess of love who rises out of the sea in measured modesty (she is a 1st century AD Roman copy of the Greek original)—with the much earlier (300 BC), elegant Greek statue of Hercules in Section C. Of a completely different style is a marvelous fanged Gorgon, its tongue sticking out, that once adorned the cornice of the temple of Athena to ward off evildoers. One exhibit depicts the Temple of Apollo, the oldest Doric temple in Sicily, on the island of Ortygia. ⊠ *Viale Teocrito,* ☎ *0931/464022.* ☒ *8,000 lire/€4.15.* ⊘ *Mon. 3:30–7:30 (6:30 in winter); Tues., Thurs., Fri., and weekends 9–1; Wed. 9–1 and 3:30–7:30 (6:30 in winter).*

㉟ Museo del Papiro. Close to Siracusa's Museo Archeologico, the Papyrus Museum demonstrates how papyruses are prepared from reeds and then painted—an ancient tradition in the city. Siracusa, it seems, has the only climate outside the Nile Valley in which the papyrus plant—from which we get our word "paper"—thrives. ⊠ *Viale Teocrito 66,* ☎ *0931/ 61616.* ☒ *Free.* ⊘ *Tues.–Sun. 9–1.*

㉜ Teatro Greco (Greek Theater). The chief monument in the Archaeological Park—and indeed one of Sicily's greatest classical sites—is this most complete Greek theater surviving from antiquity. Climb to the top of the seating area for a fine view: all the seats converge upon a single point—the stage—which has the natural scenery and the sky as its background. Hewn out of the hillside rock in the 5th century BC, the theater, which could accommodate 15,000, saw the premieres of the plays of Aeschylus, and in May and June of even-numbered years Greek tragedies are still performed here. Drama as a kind of religious ritual was the intention when the theater was built. ✉ *Parco Archeologico: Viale Augusto,* ☎ *0931/66206.* 🎫 *8,000 lire/€4.15.* ⏲ *Daily 9–1 hr before sunset (last tickets sold 2 hrs before sunset).*

NEED A BREAK? For some great Sicilian cakes and ice cream on your way to the archaeological park, visit the bar-cum-*pasticceria* **Leonardi** (✉ Viale Teocrito 123, ☎ 0931/61411). It's popular with the locals, so you may have to queue for your cakes in holiday times. It's closed Wednesday.

A Good Walk: Ortygia Island

The central part of Siracusa is a modern city, with Corso Gelone its main shopping street. At its southern end, Corso Umberto leads to the Ortygia Island bridge, which crosses a harbor lined with fish restaurants. Begin at Piazza Pancali, the square where you arrive after crossing the bridge. Behind the piazza stand the scanty remains of the **Tempio di Apollo** ㊲. Proceed from here to **Piazza Archimede** ㊳, from which it's a brief walk to **Piazza del Duomo** ㊴, the main square of the old town and site of Siracusa's ancient and splendid **Duomo** ㊵. Other impressive buildings to see in the piazza include the **Palazzo Beneventano del Bosco** ㊶ and the church of **Santa Lucia alla Badia** ㊷; the Palazzo Bellomo, housing the **Museo Regionale** ㊸, is just around the corner. After you've had your fill of this, stroll onto the waterfront where several bars cluster around the lovely **Fonte Aretusa** ㊹, a perfect spot for a break. Walking along the seafront promenade to the southern tip of Ortygia will bring you to the **Castello Maniace** ㊺. Ortygia's backstreets are largely composed of elegant Baroque palazzi whose uniformity is the result of the major reconstruction that took place following an earthquake in 1693, at a time when this style of Baroque was de rigueur. Be sure to wander along Via della Maestranza, the main lateral street of the island, or Via Veneto, on the eastern side, where you'll notice the bulbous wrought-iron balconies, said to have been fashioned to accommodate ladies' billowing skirts, and facades embellished with mermaids and gargoyles—and don't miss the stucco decoration on Palazzo Lantieri, on Via Roma (off Piazza Archimede).

TIMING

You'll need the better part of a day to do justice to Ortygia. Obviously, the more detours you make—and there are distractions aplenty here—the longer you'll spend. The Duomo alone can take an hour or so to see properly, while you could easily spend two more hours in the Museo Regionale. Fortunately, there is no lack of inviting bars and restaurants to break up your tour.

Sights to See

㊺ **Castello Maniace.** The southern tip of Ortygia island is occupied by a castle built by Frederick II (1194–1250), now an army barracks, from which there are fine views of the sea.

★ ㊵ **Duomo.** Siracusa's Duomo is an archive of island history, beginning with the bottommost excavations that have unearthed remnants of Sicily's distant past, when the Siculi inhabitants worshiped their deities here. During the 5th century BC, the Greeks built a temple to Athena over it, and in the 7th century, Siracusa's first Christian cathedral was built on top of the Greek structure. The massive columns of the original temple were incorporated into the present structure and are clearly visible, embedded in the exterior wall along Via Minerva. The Greek columns were also used to dramatic advantage inside, where on one side they form chapels connected by elegant wrought-iron gates. The

Baroque facade, added in 1700, displays a harmonious rhythm of concaves and convexes. In front, the piazza is encircled by pink and white oleanders and elegant buildings ornamented with filigree grillwork. ⊠ *Piazza del Duomo.* ☎ *0931/65328.* ⊙ *Daily 8–noon and 4–7:30.*

44 **Fonte Aretusa.** Just off the promenade along the harbor you'll find the Fountain of Arethusa, a freshwater spring next to the sea. This anomaly is explained by a Greek legend that tells how the nymph Arethusa was changed into a fountain by the goddess Artemis (Diana) when she tried to escape the advances of the river god Alpheus. She fled from Greece, into the sea, with Alpheus in close pursuit, and emerged in Sicily at this spring. Supposedly even today, if you throw a cup into the Alpheus River in Greece, it will emerge here at this fountain, which is home to a few tired ducks and some dull-colored carp—but no cups. If you want to stand right by the fountain, you need to gain admission through the aquarium; otherwise look down on it from Largo Aretusa.

43 **Museo Regionale.** Siracusa's principal museum of art is housed inside Palazzo Bellomo, a lovely Catalan-Gothic building with mullioned windows and an elegant exterior staircase. Among the select group of paintings and sculptures inside is a *Santa Lucia* by Caravaggio (1573–1610) and a damaged but still brilliant *Annunciation* by Antonello da Messina. There are also exhibitions of Sicilian nativity figures, silver, furniture, ceramics, and religious vestments. ⊠ *Via Capodieci 14,* ☎ *0931/69511.* 🖃 *5,000 lire/€2.60.* ⊙ *Tues., Thurs., Fri., and weekends 9–1:30; Wed. 9–1:30 and 3–6. Sometimes open later in summer.*

41 **Palazzo Beneventano del Bosco.** On a corner of the Piazza del Duomo, this elegant palazzo, a private residence, has an impressive interior courtyard ending in a grand winding staircase. ⊠ *Piazza del Duomo.*

38 **Piazza Archimede.** One of Ortygia's two main piazzas has at its center a Baroque fountain, the *Fontana di Diana,* festooned with fainting sea nymphs and dancing jets of water.

39 **Piazza del Duomo.** In the heart of Ortygia, this ranks as one of Italy's most beautiful piazzas, its elongated space lined with Sicilian Baroque gems.

NEED A BREAK? | When you're in need of refreshment, the elegant **Antico Caffè Minerva** (⊠ Via Minerva 15, ☎ 0931/22606), around the corner from the Duomo, will satisfy your cravings. It's closed on Wednesday.

42 **Santa Lucia alla Badia.** This Baroque church stands at one end of Piazza del Duomo, featuring an engaging wrought-iron balcony and pleasant facade. ⊠ *Piazza del Duomo. Closed for restoration.*

37 **Tempio di Apollo.** In the piazza just across the bridge to Ortygia you'll find the ruins of a temple dedicated to Apollo, a model of which is in the Museo Archeologico. In fact, little of this noble Doric temple still remains today, except for some crumbled walls and shattered columns; the window in the south wall belongs to a Norman church that was built much later on the same spot. ⊠ *Piazza Pancali.*

OFF THE BEATEN PATH | **CASTELLO EURIALO –** West of the city, on the highlands that overlook the sea, the Euryalus Castle was created by Dionysius, with the help of Archimedes, for protection against the Carthaginians. This astonishing boat-shape structure once covered 135,000 square ft. The intricate maze of tunnels is fascinating, and the view from the heights is superb. ⊠ Belvedere, 8 km (5 mi) northwest of Siracusa. 🖃 Free. ⊙ Daily 9–1 hr before sunset.

Dining and Lodging

$$–$$$ ✕ Ionico. Enjoy seaside dining in the coastal Santa Lucia district. The
★ Ionico boasts a terrace and veranda for alfresco meals, and the interior is plastered with diverse historical relics and has a cheerful open
hearth for the winter. Chef-proprietor Roberto Giudice cooks meals
to order or will suggest a specialty from a selection of market-fresh ingredients. Try the pasta *con acciughe e il pan grattato* (in an anchovy
sauce). ⊠ *Riviera Dionisio il Grande 194,* ☎ 0931/65540. AE, DC,
MC, V. Closed Tues.

$$ ✕ Archimede. The *antipasto misto* (mixed antipasto) should whet
your appetite for the predominantly seafood menu of this small es-
tablishment in the *città vecchia* (Old Town), Ortygia. Risotto di mare
and pesce spada are specialties. Sample the *involtini all'Archimede*
(roulades stuffed with fish and bread crumbs) or the *tagliatelli al-
l'Archimede* (a fish and pasta dish). ⊠ *Via Gemmellaro 8,* ☎ 0931/
69701. AE, DC, MC, V. No dinner Sun. in Oct.–Easter.

$$ ✕ Minosse. You'll find this small, old-fashioned restaurant in the heart
of Siracusa's Old Town. Fish is the specialty, and it comes broiled, baked,
stuffed, and skewered. For an introduction to the local seafood, try the
antipasto misto di frutti di mare. Ask for the daily special as your main
course, or try the pesce spada alla brace. The *zuppa di pesce* (fish soup)
is a local favorite. ⊠ *Via Mirabella 6,* ☎ 0931/66366. AE, MC, V. Closed
Mon. Oct.–Mar., and 2 wks in July.

$ ✕ La Siciliana. This is an ideal spot in Ortygia for an inexpensive
pizza and a cool beer or white wine. There are more than 50 varieties
of pizza to choose from, from the most exotic to the local fried variety, *Siciliana,* crusty and flavorful, stuffed with *tuma* (fresh, unsalted
cheese), anchovies, and black pepper (evenings only). There are also
nonpizza choices on the menu including pasta and fish. ⊠ *Via Savoia
17,* ☎ 0931/68944. No credit cards.

$$$$ 🏨 Grand Hotel. An elegant, fantasy-inspired design that would feel at
home in Gotham prevails at this venerable institution, which has enjoyed
a prime position overlooking the Porto Grande since 1898. A modern
seascape sets a dreamy tone in the lobby, which is decked out in peri-
winkle leather club chairs, antiques, gilt mirrors, and marble inlay floors
lined with lights. Beyond the leather doors, rooms display fine wood floors,
modern fixtures, and stained-glass windows. The Piccolo Museo (Little
Museum) downstairs displays columns from the original structure. The
roof-garden restaurant has superb views over the Grand Harbor and
seafront of Ortygia as well as excellent food. A shuttle service is provided to the hotel's nearby private beach. ⊠ *Viale Mazzini 12, 96100,*
☎ 0931/464600, FAX 0931/464611. 39 rooms, 19 suites. Restaurant, bar,
beach, meeting room, free parking. AE, DC, MC, V.

$$$$ 🏨 Grand Hotel Villa Politi. This grand 18th-century villa was frequented
by European royalty and various VIPs, including Winston Churchill. Lovingly restored in 1998, and now equipped with modern luxuries, it still
retains its charm and elegance. The hotel is centrally located near the archaeological zone but set back from the road in the ancient extensive
gardens of the Latomie dei Cappuccini, overlooking a small archaeological
site. High-quality service and all the trimmings are guaranteed. ⊠ *Via
M. Politi Laudien 2, 96100,* ☎ 0931/412121, FAX 0931/36061, WEB
www.grandhotelvillapoliti.it. 100 rooms. 2 restaurants, bar, in-room
safes, pool, library, free parking. AE, DC, MC, V.

$$$ 🏨 Domus Mariae. You can see the sea at the end of the corridor as
you enter this hotel on Ortygia's eastern shore. In an unusual twist, it
is run by nuns of the Ursuline order, who help to create a placid and
peaceful ambience. Don't expect monastic conditions, however: rugs
and refined decor distinguish the public rooms, and guest rooms—four

with sea views—are bright, modern, and comfortable. ✉ *Via Vittorio Veneto 76, 96100,* ☎ *0931/24854,* 𝖥𝖠𝖷 *0931/24858,* 𝖶𝖤𝖡 *www.sistemia. it/domusmariae. 16 rooms. Restaurant, bar, reading room, chapel. AE, DC, MC, V.*

$$ 🏨 **Il Limoneto.** Awash with orchards and citrus groves, this *agriturismo*
★   9 km (5 mi) from Syracuse on SP14 Mare-Monti offers a haven of peace after the rigors of sightseeing in the city. Expect splendid home cooking; the renowned Adele will let you watch her make pasta and even induct you into the secrets of Mama's recipes. In the evenings, guests are encouraged to gather and may be regaled with Sicilian poetry. Guest rooms are furnished in a rustic style, and some have mezzanine floors (perfect for children). With only eight rooms available, be sure to book far in advance; if there are no beds, you can always come just for a meal. ✉ *Via del Platano 3, 96100,* ☎ 𝖥𝖠𝖷 *0931/717352. 8 rooms. Restaurant, bowling, bicycles, playground. DC, MC, V. Closed Nov.*

$$ 🏨 **Park Hotel Helios.** This unpretentious hotel is in a quiet part of town north of the archaeological zone. Rooms are spacious and warmly lit, the foyer bedecked with potted palms and Persian rugs. Outside are a barbecue and a play area for children. ✉ *Via Filisto 80, 96100,* ☎ *0931/ 412233,* 𝖥𝖠𝖷 *0931/38096. 143 rooms. Restaurant, pool, meeting room, free parking. AE, DC, MC, V.*

Nightlife and the Arts

The feast of the city's patroness, St. Lucy, is held on December 13 at **Santa Lucia alla Badia** (✉ Piazza del Duomo). A splendid silver statue of the saint is carried from the cathedral to the church on the site of her martyrdom, near the Catacombs of San Giovanni. A torchlight procession and band music accompany the bearers. In May and June of even-numbered years only, Siracusa's impressive **Teatro Greco** (✉ Parco Archeologico, ☎ 0931/67710) is the setting for performances of classical drama and comedy.

Shopping

The specialty of Siracusa is papyrus paper. But beware—most of what you buy is commercially produced, hard, and of inferior quality to the handmade paper, which feels like fabric. One of the best, and few, places to buy the genuine article is **Galleria Bellomo** (✉ Via Capodieci 15, ☎ 0931/61340), opposite the Museo Regionale on Ortygia. It is run by an artist who sells cards and paintings and will also give a demonstration of how to make the paper.

EASTERN SICILY

On the Road to Taormina

Sicily's interior is for the most part underpopulated and untrammeled, though the Imperial Roman Villa at Casale, outside Piazza Armerina, gives precious evidence from an epoch gone by. Don't miss Caltagirone, a ceramics center of renown. Halfway up the eastern coast, Catania packs the vivacity of Palermo, if not the artistic wealth; the city makes a good base for exploring lofty Mt. Etna, as does Taormina. Messina's scant attractions include its unparalleled position opposite the mountains of Calabria and one of the island's best museum collections.

Enna

🏵 *105 km (63 mi) northeast of Agrigento, 136 km (85 mi) southeast of Palermo.*

Deep in Sicily's interior, the fortress city of Enna commands exceptional views of the surrounding rolling plains, and, in the distance, Mt. Etna. The narrow, winding streets are dominated at one end by an impressive castle built by Frederick II, easily visible as you approach town.

Lodging

$$ ⊞ **Grande Albergo Sicilia.** Sicily's interior has a dearth of decent accommodations, so it's a relief to find Enna's only hotel a reliable and comfortable choice—it was restored and modernized in 2000. Centrally located, the Sicilia has bright, clean rooms, some with excellent views. ⊠ *Piazza Napoleone Colaianni 7, 94100,* ☎ *0935/500850,* FAX *0935/ 500488. 76 rooms. Bar, parking (fee). AE, DC, MC, V.*

Casale

❹❼ *6 km (4 mi) southwest of Piazza Armerina, 120 km (75 mi) west of Catania.*

The exceptionally well preserved **Imperial Roman Villa** here is thought to have been a hunting lodge of the emperor Maximianus Heraclius (4th century AD). The excavations were not begun until 1950, and the wall decorations and vaulting have been lost. However, some of the best mosaics of the Roman world cover more than 12,000 square ft under a shelter that hints at the layout of the original buildings. The mosaics were probably made by Carthaginian artisans, because they are similar to those in the Tunis Bardo Museum. The entrance was through a triumphal arch that led into an atrium surrounded by a portico of columns. Through this the *thermae,* or bathhouse, is reached. It's colorfully decorated with mosaic nymphs, a Neptune, and slaves massaging bathers. The peristyle leads to the main villa, where in the Salone del Circo you look down on mosaics illustrating Roman circus sports. Another apartment shows hunting scenes of tigers, elephants, and ostriches; the gym shows girls exercising; the private apartments are covered with scenes from Greek and Roman mythology; and Room 38 even reveals a touch of eroticism. ⊠ *Imperial Roman Villa,* ☎ *0935/ 680036.* 🎟 *8,000 lire/€4.15.* ☉ *Daily 9–6:30.*

Caltagirone

❹❽ *30 km (18 mi) southeast of Piazza Armerina, 60 km (37 mi) southwest of Catania.*

Built over three hills, this charming Baroque town of Caltagirone is a leader in the Sicilian ceramics industry. Here you will find majolica balustrades, tile-decorated windowsills, and a monumental tile staircase of 142 steps—each decorated with a different pattern—leading up to the neglected **Santa Maria del Monte.** On the feast of San Giacomo (July 24), the staircase is illuminated with candles that form a tapestry design over the steps. It is the result of months of work preparing the 4,000 *coppi,* or cylinders of colored paper that hold oil lamps. At 9:30 PM on July 24, a squad of hundreds of boys springs into action to light the lamps, so that the staircase flares up all at once. ☉ *Daily 7–noon and 4–7.*

There is an interesting **Museo della Ceramica** (Ceramics Museum) in Caltagirone's public gardens, which were designed by Ernesto Basile (1857–1932), the master of Sicilian Art Nouveau. The exhibits in the museum trace the history of the craft from specimens excavated from the earliest settlements through the influential Arab period to the present. ⊠ *Giardino Pubblico,* ☎ *0933/21680.* 🎟 *5,000 lire/€2.60.* ☉ *Daily 9–6:30.*

Shopping

CERAMICS

Of the numerous ceramic shops and workshops in Caltagirone's old center, **Branciforti** (✉ Scala Santa Maria del Monte 3, ☎ 0933/24427), right on Caltagirone's fabled ceramic steps, is one of the best, selling eye-catching work with deep shades of blue and swirling arabesques. **Laureanti** (✉ Via Duomo 6, ☎ 0933/53931), opposite the Duomo on the main square, uses rich yellows and oranges for its ceramics done predominantly following 18th-century patterns.

Palazzolo Acreide

49 *60 km (40 mi) southeast of Caltagirone, 40 km (25 mi) west of Siracusa.*

This small inland town is best known for its archaeological zone, the old Greek *Akrai,* containing the foundations of a temple dedicated to Aphrodite, and a well-preserved theater.

Dining

$ ✕ **Da Alfredo.** This one-man show (Alfredo is the owner-chef) is on one of the most attractive streets of this Baroque town between Caltagirone and Siracusa. Specialties depend on the season and Alfredo's whims. Homemade pastas, such as penne and cheese-filled ravioli, are specialties, and the sauces are hearty and spicy. ✉ *Via Duca d'Aosta 27,* ☎ *0931/883266. No credit cards. Closed Wed.*

Noto

50 *34 km (21 mi) southeast of Palazzolo Acreide, 32 km (19 mi) southwest of Siracusa.*

Modeled on a hierarchical plan following the destruction of the ancient town during the great earthquake of 1693, Noto presents a pleasing ensemble of honey-color Baroque architecture, strikingly uniform in style but never dull. Disaster struck again in March 1996, when the dome of the majestic cathedral, Noto's centerpiece (completed in 1776), collapsed during a thunderstorm, probably due to a previous botched restoration. Repairs are currently under way, but it may take several years to complete the work, adding to the rebuilding that has consistently blighted this otherwise delightful town center.

Dining

$$ ✕ **Trattoria del Carmine.** Simple but ever reliable local dishes are the staples at this affable eatery in the center of town. If you're not tempted by the fish of the day, you can choose between the various land-based dishes on offer, such as ravioli with a pork sauce, *salsiccia al finocchietto* (sausage cooked with fennel), and *coniglio* (rabbit). ✉ *Via Ducezio 1/a,* ☎ *0931/838705. AE, MC, V. Closed Mon.*

Catania

51 *60 km (37 mi) north of Siracusa, 94 km (59 mi) south of Messina.*

The chief wonder of Catania, Sicily's second city, is that it is there at all. Its successive populations were deported by one Greek tyrant, sold into slavery by another, and driven out by the Carthaginians. Every time the city got back on its feet, it was struck by a new calamity: plague decimated the population in the Middle Ages, a mile-wide stream of lava from Mt. Etna swallowed most of the city in 1669, and 25 years later a disastrous earthquake forced the Catanese to begin again. Today the city needs considerable renovation. Traffic flows in ever-increasing volume and adds to the smog from the industrial zone between Catania and Siracusa, but the views of Mt. Etna from Catania are superb. To Mt. Etna, Catania also owes a fertile surrounding plain and its site on nine successive layers of lava. Many of Catania's buildings are constructed from solidified lava, and the black lava stone has given the city a singular appearance. As a result, Catania is known as the city of lava and oranges. Catania's greatest native son was the composer Vincenzo Bellini (1801–35), whose operas have thrilled audiences since their premieres in the first half of the 19th century. His home, now the **Museo Belliniano,** in Piazza San Francesco, preserves memorabilia of the man and his work. ⊠ *Piazza San Francesco 3,* ☎ *095/7150535.* 🎟 *Free.* ⊗ *Wed. and Fri.–Mon., 9–1, Tues. and Thurs. 9–1 and 3–6.*

The **Villa Bellini** (⊠ To the north, just off Via Etnea), Catania's public gardens, has lovely views of snowcapped Mt. Etna on clear days. The **Duomo** is a fine work by Vaccarini (1736), as is the obelisk-balancing elephant carved out of lava stone in the piazza before it. Bellini is buried inside the cathedral. Also inside is the sumptuous Cappella di Sant'Agata, honoring Catania's patron saint, who is credited with having held off, more than once, the fiery flows of lava that threatened the city. During her feast (February 3–5), 16-ft-tall, highly ornate carved wooden *cannelore* (large bundles of candles) are paraded through the streets at night. ⊠ *Bottom end of Via Etnea,* ☎ *095/320044.* ⊗ *Daily 8–noon and 4–7.*

Dining and Lodging

If you haven't had cannoli in Sicily yet, the pastry shops along Via Etnea are good places to try one of these wafer tubes filled with silky-smooth ricotta cheese. If you're in need of something more substantial, duck into one of the trattorias along this street and order a dish of pasta *alla Norma.* It's named after one of Bellini's most famous operas and consists of short pasta with a rich eggplant-and-tomato sauce, garnished with basil leaves, and ricotta cheese—a quintessential Sicilian pasta dish.

$$–$$$ ✕ **Costa Azzurra.** At this seafood restaurant in the Ognina district, re-
★ serve a table on the veranda by the edge of the sea with good views of the harbor. The fritto misto can be ordered as an antipasto or a main course, and the pesce spada steak is a simple classic, served grilled with a large slice of lemon. ⊠ *Via De Cristofaro 4, Ognina, just north of the center, on the way to the Taormina road,* ☎ *095/494920. AE, DC, MC, V. Closed Mon. and 2 wks in Aug.*

$$ ✕ **Da Rinaldo.** A popular restaurant with the locals, Da Rinaldo has a welcoming and rustic atmosphere created by wooden tables and local art on the walls. You can't go wrong with the local specialties such as grilled fish and meat. ⊠ *Via G. Simili 59,* ☎ *095/532312. AE, MC, V. Closed Aug.*

$$ ✕ **Pagano.** This restaurant behind the Hotel Excelsior has been around since the 1950s and remains a favorite with locals for genuine Catanese cooking. Seafood is the specialty, but it's the unpretentious kind that won't send the check orbiting into the stratosphere. Try *insalata di polipo* (octopus salad) as a starter and then sarde or *acciughe* (anchovies) in a variety of sauces. Like the sober, rather dated decor, the service is formal. ⊠ *Via De Roberto 37,* ☎ *095/537045. AE, MC, V. Closed 1 wk in mid-Aug. No lunch Sat., no dinner Sun.*

$$$$ 🏨 **Excelsior.** Ask for a room facing Piazza Verga, a neat tree-lined square in this quiet but central district of Catania. The Excelsior, which completed an extensive renovation in 2001, has air-conditioning and sound-insulated windows in all rooms. The American Bar should provide solace to anyone waxing nostalgic for a Manhattan. ⊠ *Piazza Verga 39, 95129,* ☎ *095/7476111,* FAX *095/537015,* WEB *www.thi.it/exe-catania.htm. 176 rooms, 13 suites. Restaurant, bar, gym, parking (fee). AE, DC, MC, V.*

$$ ⌶ **Savona.** Refurbished in 2001, this is a conveniently located hotel a stone's throw from Piazza del Duomo. The rooms are spacious and comfortable, solidly furnished, and well equipped. Reception can help with parking suggestions. ⊠ *Via Vittorio Emanuele 210, 95124,* ☎ *095/326982,* FAX *095/7158169. 30 rooms. Bar. MC, V.*

Nightlife and the Arts

The opera season at the **Teatro Bellini** (⊠ Piazza Bellini, Catania, ☎ 095/7306111), October to mid-June, attracts top singers and productions to the birthplace of the great composer.

PUBS

There are many pubs and piano bars around the Teatro Massimo; try **Ixtlan** (⊠ Via Teatro Massimo 33, ☎ no phone), where you can drink and listen to piano music late into the night.

Mt. Etna

★ ❺❷ *30 km (19 mi) north of Catania, 60 km (37 mi) south of Messina.*

Mt. Etna is one of the world's major active volcanoes and is the largest and highest in Europe—the cone of the crater rising to 10,958 ft above sea level. It has erupted 10 times in the past 30 or so years, most spectacularly in 1971 and 1983, when rivers of molten lava destroyed the two highest stations of the cable car that rises from the town of Sapienza. Travel in the proximity of the crater depends on Mt. Etna's temperament, but you can walk up and down the enormous lava dunes and wander over its moonlike surface of dead craters. The rings of vegetation change markedly as you rise, with vineyards and pine trees gradually giving way to growths of broom and lichen. Catania is the departure point for excursions around—but not always to the top of—Mt. Etna. Buses leave from Catania's train station in the early morning. There's **gondola service** (⊠ Piazza Vittorio Emanuele 45, ☎ 095/911158 or 095/914209) from the town of Nicolosi, which can take you to an altitude of 8,200 ft; the cost is approximately 72,000 lire/€37 for the two- to three-hour round-trip, including cable car, jeep and, guide. For personalized guided tours, contact Nicolosi's **information office** (⊠ Via Garibaldi 63, ☎ 095/911505) or call the **Gruppo Guide Alpine Etna** (☎ 095/7914755). Closer to the ground, an alternative view of the volcano can be had from the **Circumetnea railroad** (⊠ Via Caronda 352, Catania, ☎ 095/541243), which runs near the volcano's base. The private railway runs 114 km (71 mi) between Giarre-Riposto and Catania—30 km (19 mi) apart on the coast—almost circling Mt. Etna. The line is small, slow, and only single track but offers some dramatic vistas of the volcano and goes through lava fields. The round-trip takes about five hours, there are about 10 departures a day, and tickets cost 10,000 lire/€5.15 one-way.

For a bird's-eye view of Mt. Etna, you may be tempted to try paragliding or hang-gliding; contact **No Limits Etna Center** (⊠ Via Milano 6/a, Catania, ☎ 095/7213682, FAX 095/7212447, WEB www.etnacenter.net). For nonpilots, there are tandem flights and microlight trips, as well as courses of varying lengths. The company also organizes free climbing, caving, and diving expeditions.

OFF THE
BEATEN PATH   **BRONTE –** On the slopes of Mt. Etna, Bronte was where Admiral Nelson was given a duchy by the grateful Bourbon monarchy, but it's better known as Italy's center for pistachio cultivation. The pistachio was introduced to Sicily with the Roman and Arab conquests. The bars here offer various pistachio delicacies such as nougat, *colomba, panettone* (both cakes), and ice cream.

Acireale

🟢 *16 km (10 mi) north of Catania.*

Acireale sits amid a clutter of rocky pinnacles and lush lemon groves. The craggy coast is known as the Riviera dei Ciclopi, after the legend narrated in the *Odyssey,* in which the blinded cyclops Polyphemus hurled boulders at the retreating Ulysses, thus creating spires of rock, or *faraglioni.* Tourism has not yet taken off here, so it's a good destination if you feel the need to put some distance between yourself and the busloads of tourists in Taormina. And though the beaches are rocky, there is good swimming here, too.

Begin your visit with a stroll down to the public gardens, **Villa Belvedere,** at the end of the main Corso Umberto, for superb coastal views. There's also a good vista from **Belvedere di Santa Caterina,** near the Terme, visited by Lord Byron (1788–1824) during his Italian wanderings.

Almost totally destroyed by the earthquake that ravaged so much of eastern Sicily in 1693, the town was rebuilt in Sicilian Baroque style and contains a cluster of fine buildings, most of them on or around Piazza Duomo.

With its cupola and twin turrets, Acireale's **Duomo** is an extravagant Baroque construction dating back to the 17th century. In the chapel to the right of altar, look for the 17th-century silver statue of Santa Venera, patron saint of Acireale, made by Mario D'Angelo, and the early 18th-century frescoes by Antonio Filocamo. ⊠ *Piazza Duomo,* ☎ *095/601797.* ⊘ *Daily 8–noon and 4–7.*

Inside the **Basilica dei Santi Pietro e Paolo,** with its ornate facade, there are paintings and frescoes by the eminent local painter Pietro Paolo Vasta (1697–1760). ⊠ *Piazza Duomo,* ☎ *095/601834.* ⊘ *Daily 8–noon and 4–7.*

The **Palazzo Comunale,** near Piazza Duomo, is famous for its wrought-iron balconies supported by stone creatures. In Piazza Vigo, the **Basilica di San Sebastiano,** is regarded as one of the most beautiful Baroque churches in Sicily. Its facade is richly adorned with statues from the Old Testament, sculpted by Giovan Battista Marini. ⊠ *Piazza Vigo,* ☎ *095/601313.* ⊘ *Daily 8–noon and 4–7.*

NEED A BREAK?

Acireale is renowned in Sicily for its marzipan, made into fruit shapes and delicious biscuits. You'll find the tasty treat in pasticcerias such as **El Dorado** (⊠ Corso Umberto 5, ☎ 095/601464) and **Castorina** (⊠ Piazza del Duomo 25, ☎ 095/601546). Both also serve delicious ice creams, and the *granita di mandorle* (almond granita) invites a first-hand acquaintance.

The town comes into its own during Carnival celebrations, considered the best in Sicily. Streets are jammed with thousands of fancy-dressed revelers and floats dripping with flowers and gaudy papier-mâché models.

Acireale is also known for its puppet theater, a Sicilian tradition that has all but died out in other parts. See shows at **Coop E. Magri** (⊠ Corso Umberto 11, ☎ 095/606272). The **Teatro dell'Opera dei Pupi** (⊠ Via Nazionale 95, Turi Grasso, ☎ 095/7648035) has puppet shows and also an exhibition of puppets.

The small but entertaining collection at the **Museo della Civiltà Contadina** shows local life as it was once lived. Though poorly labeled, there's a variety of tools, presses, and household implements. ⊠ *Via Vittorio Emanuele III 124,* ☎ *095/801433.* ☑ *Free.* ☉ *Visits by appointment.*

The sulphur-rich volcanic waters from Mount Etna found at **Terme di Acireale** were first used by the Greeks. In the 2nd century AD, Acireale's patron saint, Venera, was martyred, after which the waters were accorded miraculous powers. After 1873, when the Santa Venera bathing establishment was created with its park, the baths attracted a stream of celebrated visitors including Wagner. Present-day patrons can book in advance to use the baths and have mud treatments and massages (multiday treatment packages are available). Nonpatrons can wander the gardens for free (open 9–8). The complex was sold to private ownership in 1999 and some of the facilities are due to be modernized. ⊠ *Via delle Terme 47,* ☎ *095/601508,* FAX *095/606468.* ☑ *Free.* ☉ *Daily 7–1 and 2–8.*

OFF THE
BEATEN PATH

SANTA MARIA DELLA SCALA – A half hour's walk from Acireale's center, the picturesque harbor of Santa Maria is the place to watch fishermen unloading their brightly colored boats and to enjoy a fine and inexpensive lunch in one of the many restaurants along the harbor. Remember that the price of your fresh fish dish depends upon its weight.

Dining and Lodging

$$ ✗ **All'Antica Osteria.** This restaurant-pizzeria specializes in grilled food. Other local delicacies include risotto *alla zarina* (with salmon, cream, and pistachio) and *saraceni con ragù di pesce* (buckwheat with fish sauce). ⊠ *Via Carpinati 34,* ☎ *095/7634135. AE, DC, MC, V. Closed Mon.*

$$ ✗ **Al Molino.** Right next to the old water mill on the *lungomare,* this stylish local haunt is devoted to fish, from the antipasto and pasta to the main course. Follow local tradition and finish the meal with a lemon sorbet. ⊠ *Via Molino 106,* ☎ *095/7648116. AE, MC, V. Closed Wed.*

$$ ✗ **La Grotta di Carmelo.** It's only when you enter this conventional-looking trattoria that you realize you'll be dining in a cave with an actual rock-face wall. Try the *insalata di mare* (a selection of delicately steamed fish served with lemon and olive oil) or fish grilled over charcoal. The menu is small but immaculate; you will need to book in advance. ⊠ *Via Scala Grande 56,* ☎ *095/7648153. Reservations essential. AE, MC, V. Closed Tues. and mid-Oct.–early Nov.*

$$ ✗ **L'Oste Scuro.** Near the Basilica di San Sebastiano, this is a good place for the local *antipasto di frutti di mare* (shellfish antipasto) and fresh fish including *spigola* (sea bass) with the sauce of the day. Leave some room for the delectable *fichi d'India* (prickly pears). ⊠ *Piazza L. Vigo 5–7,* ☎ *095/7634001. AE, DC, MC, V. Closed Wed.*

$$$ 🛏 **Aloha D'Oro.** Unusual for a modern hotel, this place uses local building methods and materials, incorporating traditional wooden windows, wrought-iron work, rustic tiles, arches, and towers. Try to secure a room at the back, which overlooks a nature reserve and has views to the sea. The Aloha D'Oro is a stone's throw from the beach and is conveniently located near the town center and the thermal baths. ⊠ *Via dei Gasperi 10, 95024,* ☎ *095/604344,* FAX *095/606984,* WEB *www.hotel-aloha.com. 119 rooms. Restaurant, bar, pizzeria, 2 pools, beach, dance club, free parking. AE, DC, MC, V.*

Shopping

At **Bottega d'Arte** (⊠ Via Vittorio Emanuele 86, ☎ 095/606805), you can see a local artist at work, carving wood statues and traditional carts, as his father and grandfather did before him. He also makes brass and wooden puppets.

Taormina

★ ㊿ *43 km (27 mi) southwest of Messina, 50 km (31 mi) north of Catania.*

The natural beauty of the medieval mountaintop town of Taormina is so great that even the considerable overdevelopment that it has suffered in the past 50 years has not spoiled its grandeur. The view of the sea and Mt. Etna from its jagged cactus-covered cliffs is as close to perfection as a panorama can get, especially on clear days when the snow-capped volcano's white puffs of smoke are etched against the blue sky. Writers have extolled Taormina's beauty almost since its founding in the 6th century BC by Greeks from Naples. Goethe and D. H. Lawrence were among its enthusiasts. The Greeks put a premium on finding impressive locations to stage their dramas, and Taormina's **Teatro Greco** occupies one of the finest of theater sites. It was built during the 3rd century BC and rebuilt by the Romans during the 2nd century AD. Its acoustics are exceptional: even today a stage whisper can be heard in the last rows. In summer, Taormina hosts an arts festival of music, film, and dance events, many of which are held in the Teatro Greco. ⊠ *Via Teatro Greco,* ☎ *0942/232220.* ⊡ *8,000 lire/€4.15.* ☉ *Daily 9–1 hr before sunset.*

Taormina's many 14th- and 15th-century palaces have been carefully preserved. Especially beautiful is the **Palazzo Corvaja** (⊠ Largo Santa Caterina, ☎ 0942/23243), with characteristic black-lava and white-limestone inlays. Today it houses the tourist office and the **Museo di Arte e Storia Popolare,** which has a collection of cribs, carts, puppets, and folklore. ⊠ *Palazzo Corvaja.* ⊡ *5,000 lire/€2.60.* ☉ *Tues.–Sun. 9–1 and 4–8.*

The medieval **Castello Saraceno** (⊠ Monte Tauro), enticingly perched on an adjoining cliff above town, can be reached by footpath or car.

From the main Corso Umberto, stroll down Via Bagnoli Croce to the **Parco Duca di Cesarò,** the public gardens designed by Florence Trevelyan Cacciola, a Scottish lady "invited" to leave England following a romantic liaison with the future Edward VII (1841–1910). Arriving in Taormina in 1889, she married a local professor and devoted herself to the gardens, filling them with Mediterranean plants, ornamental pavilions (known as the Beehives), and fountains. Stop by the panoramic bar, which has stunning views.

NEED A BREAK? A marzipan devotee should not leave Taormina without trying one of the gooey sweets—maybe in the guise of the ubiquitous *fico d'India* (prickly pear)—at **Bar Mocambo** (⊠ Piazza 9 Aprile, ☎ 0942/23350).

Dining and Lodging

$$$–$$$$ ✕ **La Giara.** Although opened in 1953, this is one of Taormina's oldest restaurants, elegant and classical in style, and enhanced by columns of Syracuse stone sculpted by local master stonecutters. It has been frequented by the rich and famous including Peter O'Toole, Alain Delon, and Ava Gardner. Known throughout southern Italy for its fine cuisine, the kitchen here blends upscale dishes with the simple flavors of local specialties from the past. Try the *involtini di cernia al finocchietto selvatico* (stuffed grouper with wild fennel). You can extend your evening by taking an after-dinner drink at the piano bar. ⊠ *Vico La Floresta 1,* ☎ *0942/23360. AE, DC, MC, V. No lunch. Closed Mon. in Sept.–July, 2 wks in Nov., and Sun.–Thurs. in Feb.–Mar.*

$$-$$$ ✕ **Luraleo.** You can dine indoors by candlelight or, in summer, in the vine-covered garden. It's touristy, but the food is of a high standard, with the accent on fish—delight in the unusual risotto with salmon and pistachios, a house specialty, or choose a live lobster. There is a rich selection of antipasti. Service can be slow. ⊠ *Via Bagnoli Croce 27,* ☎ *0942/24279. AE, DC, MC, V. Closed Wed. in Oct.–June and 3 wks in Feb.–Mar.*

$$ ✕ **Granduca.** There's an antiques shop in the entrance of this tastefully decorated restaurant, where cane chairs and luxurious plants jostle for space among the objets d'art, carrying the antiques theme throughout. Your attention, however, will be principally occupied by the riveting views from the terrace. In summer, you can eat outside in the floral gardens. Try such well-executed dishes as *fettuccine al Granduca* (wide-ribbon pasta with a creamy vegetable sauce) or *involtini alla Siciliana* (grilled meat rolls). There's also a wood-fired oven for pizzas. ⊠ *Corso Umberto 172,* ☎ *0942/24983. AE, DC, MC, V. Closed Tues. in Dec.–Easter., Nov., and 3 wks in Feb.–Mar.*

$$ ✕ **La Dracena.** Just behind the castle, this place takes its name from the dragon tree in the garden and is ideal for an alfresco meal. The *mezze lune* (half-open ravioli) and dishes with zucchini are very good. ⊠ *Via Michele Amari,* ☎ *0942/23491. AE, DC, MC, V. Closed Mon. and mid-Jan.–mid-Mar.*

$$$$ ⊡ **Grand Hotel Timeo.** Even though it reopened in 1998 after a 14-year hiatus, the deluxe Timeo wears a handsome confidence and graceful patina that suggests it's been here—in a princely perch overlooking the town and just below the Teatro Greco—untouched since the dolce vita days. A splash of Baroque mixes with an old-world Mediterranean flavor in the lobby, with wooden floors, tile- and brickwork, and vaulting. Wrought iron and wicker chairs surround marble tables in the bar and on the adjoining palatial patio. The rooms are luxuriously decorated with fine earth-tone linens and drapes, Oriental rugs, gilt-framed prints, and exquisite moldings on butter-color walls. ⊠ *Via Teatro Greco 59, 98039,* ☎ *0942/23801,* FAX *0942/628501,* WEB *www.framon-hotels.com. 34 rooms, 22 suites. Restaurant, bar, air-conditioning, in-room safes, minibars, room service, convention center. AE, DC, MC, V. FAP, MAP.*

$$$$ ⊡ **Romantik Villa Ducale.** Formerly the summer residence of a local aristocrat, this stupendously sited villa 10 km (6 mi) outside Taormina has been converted into a comfortable hotel by his great-grandson. Individually styled rooms furnished with antiques and an intimate wood-paneled library create an atmosphere at once homelike and palatial, while the vast roof terrace takes full advantage of the wide panorama embracing Etna and the bay below. There is no restaurant, but snacks are always available, and breakfast is on the terrace. In summer months, a free shuttle bus connects the hotel with the area's best beaches. ⊠ *Via Leonardo da Vinci 60, 98039,* ☎ *0942/28153,* FAX *0942/28710. 15 rooms, 1 suite. Bar. AE, DC, MC, V. Closed Dec.–Feb.*

$$$$ ⊡ **San Domenico Palace.** Sweeping views from this converted 15th-
  ★ century convent will linger in your mind long after you're gone. And the gardens—full of red trumpet flowers, bougainvillea, and lemons—are heaven, with a dramatic vista of the castle, the sea, and Mt. Etna. Luxury and comfort are bywords in this deluxe hotel, which has managed to sneak in a number of unobtrusive 20th-century comforts (such as wheelchair access and climate control). The essential Renaissance flavor is preserved, however, with the cloisters and the chapel, now a bar. Rooms are brimming with antiques and fresh flowers. ⊠ *Piazza San Domenico 5, 98039,* ☎ *0942/23701,* FAX *0942/625506, www.hotelvilladucale.it,* WEB *www.thi.it/domenico.htm. 111 rooms. 2 restaurants, bar, pool, gym. AE, DC, MC, V.*

$$$$ ⊞ **Villa Diodoro.** High on a cliff near the Greek amphitheater, this hotel commands superlative views. One of its most attractive features is the relaxing, sprightly garden, where you can have a drink and watch the play of light over the sea. A regular hotel bus service runs to the beach (5,000 lire/€2.60). ⊠ *Via Bagnoli Croce 75, 98039,* ☎ *0942/23312,* FAX *0942/23391,* WEB *www.gaishotels.com. 99 rooms. Restaurant, bar, pool. AE, DC, MC, V.*

$$$ ⊞ **Aratena Rocks Hotel.** Here's a good choice if you want to stay near the sea, escaping the worst of Taormina's scrum. In fact, Giardini-Naxos—the resort at the foot of Taormina—makes a great base, in summer just as lively as Taormina, and the broad, sandy beach is a bonus. The hotel stands at one end of the bay, right on the cape where Greek settlers first landed in Sicily. If you don't fancy swimming off the rocks here, there's a splendid pool, around which Sicilian singers and musicians entertain you every other night in summer. A twice-daily free bus service links the hotel to Taormina. Half-board is mandatory. ⊠ *Via Calcide Eubea 55, 98035 Giardini-Naxos,* ☎ *0942/51348,* FAX *0942/51690. 49 rooms. Restaurant, bar, pool, free parking. AE, DC, MC, V. Closed Nov.–Easter.*

$$ ⊞ **Villa Fiorita.** This converted private home near the Greek amphitheater has excellent northerly coastal views from nearly every room. Rooms vary in size and furnishings, but most are bright, breezy, and colorful, with large windows and balconies (do ask). Prices are reasonable considering the compact swimming pool and garden. The elevator is at the top of 65 steps. ⊠ *Via Pirandello 39, 98039,* ☎ *0942/24122,* FAX *0942/625967. 25 rooms. Pool, parking (fee). AE, MC, V.*

Nightlife and the Arts

FESTIVALS

The Greek Theater and the Palazzo dei Congressi, near the entrance to the theater, are the main venues for the summer festival dubbed **Taormina Arte** (☎ 0942/21142, WEB www.taormina-arte.com) held each year from May to September and encompassing classical music, ballet, theater, and also the famous **film festival** in June and July.

MUSIC

Free classical music concerts take place in the Duomo and some of Taormina's other churches during December and January, as part of **Natale a Taormina** (Christmas in Taormina), an initiative sponsored by the tourist office (⊠ Palazzo Corvaja, Largo Santa Caterina, ☎ 0942/23243). Performances usually start at around 7 PM and last about an hour.

Outdoor Activities and Sports

BICYCLING

If you feel like braving the ups and downs of Taormina and its surroundings by bike, you can have one delivered by **Rent a Bike** (⊠ Via Naxos 39–41, ☎ 0942/56090; 0942/23193 Nov.–Easter).

GOLF

Twenty-five kilometers (15 miles) west of Taormina, on the slopes of Mt. Etna, is the 18-hole **Picciolo Golf Club** (⊠ Via Picciolo 1, 95012 Castiglione di Sicilia, ☎ 0942/986252). It's both scenic and cool. The clubhouse has a restaurant and some guest rooms.

HEALTH CLUB

As well as providing conventional medical treatments, the **Taormina Health Center** (⊠ Corso Umberto 119, ☎ 0942/23904) is a place to unwind; it offers various forms of massage, holistic medicine, thermal baths, and beauty treatments.

TENNIS

Right in the heart of Taormina, next to the public gardens, you can play tennis on clay courts at **Taormina Sporting Club** (⊠ Via Bagnoli Croce 71, ☎ 0942/23282). You'll need to book in advance.

WATER SPORTS

At the **Naxos Diving Centre** (⊠ Baia Mazzarò, ☎ 0942/24464) you can take introductory dives and courses, as well as rent boats.

Shopping

Ceramics shops abound, but **G. di Blasi** (⊠ 103 Corso Umberto, ☎ 0942/24671) is a standout in both quantity and quality. A small stock of the rustic white country pottery in traditional shapes from Caltagirone is very special. Via Teatro Greco, which winds up to the ancient amphitheater, is lined with tiny shops and stalls selling the ubiquitous cameos, glass beads, lava items, and coral necklaces. You can bargain. You can find more unusual gift shops at Via Teatro Greco 39. Check out the **Macchia L'Artigiana** (⊠ Via Teatro Greco 39, ☎ 0942/625110), where traditional designs are given a new twist. The **linen shops** here have nice cotton damask napkins bordered in grosgrain and pastel jacquard linen tablecloths that are worth investigating.

Castelmola

55　*5 km (3 mi) west of Taormina, 65 km (40 mi) south of Messina.*

If your passion for heights hasn't been quelled, visit Castelmola, the tiny town above Taormina, where local bars make their own refreshing almond wine—the perfect complement to the spectacular 360-degree panorama.

En Route　The 50-km (30-mi) stretch of road between Taormina and Messina is flanked by lush vegetation and seascapes. Inlets punctuated by gigantic, oddly shaped rocks distract from the road. It was along this coast, legend says, that the giant one-eyed Cyclops hurled his boulders down on Ulysses and his terrified men as they fled to the sea in Homer's *Odyssey.*

Messina

56　*43 km (27 mi) northeast of Taormina, 94 km (59 mi) northeast of Catania.*

Messina's ancient history lists a series of disasters, but the city nevertheless managed to develop a fine university and a thriving cultural environment. But at 5 o'clock in the morning on December 28, 1908, Messina changed from a flourishing metropolis of 120,000 to a heap of rubble, shaken to pieces by an earthquake that turned into a tidal wave and left 80,000 dead and the city almost completely leveled. As you approach the sickle-shape bay, through which ferries connect Sicily to the mainland, you won't notice any outward indication of the disaster, except for the modern countenance of a 3,000-year-old city. The somewhat flat look is a precaution of seismic planning: tall buildings are not permitted.

The reconstruction of Messina's Norman and Romanesque **Duomo,** originally built by the Norman king Roger II in 1197, has retained much of the original plan, including a handsome crown of Norman battlements, an enormous apse, and a splendid wood-beam ceiling. The adjoining **bell tower**—of a much later date—is one of the city's principal attractions. It contains one of the largest and most complex mechanical clocks in the world, constructed in 1933 with a host of gilded automatons—a roaring lion, a crowing rooster, and numerous biblical figures—that spring into action every day at the stroke of noon. ✉ *Piazza del Duomo*, ☎ *090/675175.* ✆ *Daily 8–12:30 and 4–7.*

NEED A
BREAK? **Billé** (✉ corner of Piazza Cairoli and Via Cannizzaro) proffers good lunchtime snacks, if you don't mind standing up. You can sample (or take away) such typical Sicilian items as *arancini* (deep-fried, breaded rice balls stuffed with cheese or meat sauce), *mozzarella in carrozza* (deep-fried bread pockets), and *piddoni* (savory parcels of mozzarella or vegetables).

Messina is the birthplace of the great Renaissance painter Antonello da Messina, whose *Polyptych of the Rosary* (1473) can be viewed along with two large Caravaggios in the **Museo Regionale,** along the sea in the northern outskirts of the city. ✉ *Viale della Libertà,* ☎ *090/ 361292.* ✆ *8,000 lire/€4.15.* ✆ *Mon., Wed., and Fri. 9–1:30; Tues., Thurs., and Sat. 9–1:30 and 4–6:30 (Oct.–May, 3–5:30); Sun. 9–12:30.*

Dining and Lodging

$$$ ✕ **Da Piero.** An institution in Messina for decades, this centrally located restaurant (four blocks up from Piazza Cairoli) trades on its well-deserved reputation for classic Sicilian dishes, particularly seafood. In season, try the *involtini di pesce spada* (stuffed swordfish), while the exquisite *calamari* are good at any time. Marsala sipped with one of the rich homemade desserts makes for a grand finale. ✉ *Via Ghibellina 119,* ☎ *090/718365. AE, DC, MC, V. Closed Sun. and Aug.*

$$$$ 🏨 **Grand Hotel Liberty.** A complete renovation has raised this hotel to the top rank of Messina's lodgings. Conveniently located across the piazza from the train station, it offers a cool haven from the bustle of the surrounding streets. The entrance and public rooms are sumptuously fitted out in a white marbled neoclassical style with a meticulous attention to detail, while bedrooms are plainer but comfortably equipped. ✉ *Via I Settembre 15, 98122,* ☎ *090/6409436,* FAX *090/ 6409340,* WEB *www.framon-hotels.com. 51 rooms. Restaurant, bar, meeting rooms. AE, DC, MC, V.*

Nightlife and the Arts

Messina stages a folklore parade of huge traditional effigies, called **Giganti,** each year on August 13 and 14.

THE AEOLIAN ISLANDS

Just off Sicily's northeast coast lies an archipelago of seven spectacular islands of volcanic origin. The Isole Eolie (Aeolian Islands), also known as the Isole Lipari (Lipari Islands), were named after Aeolus, the Greek god of the winds, who is said to keep all the earth's winds stuffed in a bag in his cave here. The Aeolians are a fascinating world of grottoes and clear-water caves carved by waves through the centuries. Superb snorkeling and scuba-diving opportunities abound in the clearest and cleanest of Italy's waters. Of course, the beautiful people of high society discovered the archipelago years ago—since Roberto Rossellini courted his star Ingrid Bergman, prior to marrying her, in 1950—and you should not expect complete isolation, at least on the main islands. August, in particular, can get unpleasantly overcrowded, and lodging and travel should always be booked as early as possible.

Lipari provides the best range of accommodations and is a good jumping-off point for day trips to the other islands. Most exclusive are Vulcano and Panarea, the former noted for its black sands and stupendous sunsets (and prices), as well as the acrid smell of its sulphur emissions, while the latter is, according to some, the prettiest. Most spectacular is Stromboli (pronounced with the accent on the first syllable) with its constant eruptions, and remotest are Filicudi and Alicudi, where electricity has only recently been introduced. Access to the islands is via ferry and hydrofoil from Sicily or Naples. The bars in the Aeolian Islands, and especially those on Lipari, are known for their granite of fresh strawberries, melon, peaches, and other fruits. Many Sicilians, especially Aeolians and in Messina, Taormina, and Catania, begin the hot summer days with a *granita di caffe* (a coffee ice topped with whipped cream), into which they dunk their breakfast rolls. You can get one any time of day.

Lipari

⑤⑦ *37 km (23 mi) north of Milazzo (2 hrs 10 mins by ferry, 1 hr by hydrofoil); Milazzo: 41 km (25 mi) west of Messina.*

The largest and most developed of the Aeolians, Lipari welcomes you with distinctive pastel-color houses. Fields of spiky agaves dot the northernmost tip of the island, **Acquacalda,** indented with pumice and obsidian quarries. In the west is **San Calogero,** where you can explore hot springs and mud baths. From the red lava base of the island rises a plateau crowned with a 16th-century castle and a 17th-century **cathedral.** The **Museo Eoliano** is one of the best archaeological museums in Europe, with an intelligently arranged collection of prehistoric finds—some dating as far back as 4000 BC—from various sites in the archipelago. ⊠ *Via Castello,* ☎ *090/9880174.* 🎫 *8,000 lire/€4.15.* ☉ *Daily 9–1:30 and 3–7.*

Dining and Lodging

$$$ ✕🏨 **Il Filippino.** The views from the flower-strewn outdoor terrace of this restaurant in the upper town are a fitting complement to the superb fare on offer. Founded in 1910, the restaurant is rated one of the archipelago's best and on the whole lives up to expectations. Top choice is seafood, especially the zuppa di pesce, and the smoked pesce spada is a must in season. Just leave some room for the local version of cassata, accompanied by sweet Malvasia wine from Salina. The restaurant has recently opened comfortable B&B ($–$$) facilities 300 yards away. ⊠ *Piazza Municipio,* ☎ *090/9811002. 22 rooms. AE, DC, MC, V. Closed Mon. in Oct.–Mar., and Nov. 10–Dec. 20.*

$$–$$$$ 🏨 **Gattopardo Park Hotel.** Bright bougainvillea and fiery hibiscus set
★ the tone in this grand villa, whose restaurant enjoys sweeping views out to sea. Guest quarters are in the 19th-century main building or in whitewashed bungalows in the surrounding tranquil parkland. Public rooms have wood-beamed ceilings and rustic-style furnishings. A minibus shuttles between the hotel and Spiagge Bianche. There are also trips round the island, boat excursions, and folklore evenings. Half-board is required in summer. ⊠ *Via Diana, 98055,* ☎ *090/9811035,* 🅵🅰🆇 *090/9880207. 53 rooms. Restaurant, bar. MC, V. Closed Nov.–Mar. MAP.*

$$$ 🏨 **Villa Augustus.** Tucked away off a side street in the center of Lipari's old town, this is a peaceful enclave, where a simple homey spirit prevails, with friendly service and a discreet attention to detail. In addition to a palm-shaded garden, there is a roof-garden offering good views. The rooms are bright and spacious and fully equipped. ⊠ *Vico Ausonia 16, 98055,* ☎ *090/9811232,* 🅵🅰🆇 *090/9812233. 34 rooms. Piano bar, free parking. AE, DC, MC, V. Closed Nov.–Feb.*

Vulcano

⑤⑧ *18 km (11 mi) northwest of Lipari (25 mins by ferry, 10 mins by hydrofoil), 55 km (34 mi) northwest of Milazzo.*

True to its name, Vulcano has a profusion of fumaroles sending up jets of hot vapor, but the volcano here has long been dormant. Many come to soak in the strong-smelling sulfur baths, whose odors will greet you, when the wind is in the right direction, long before you disembark. The island has some of the archipelago's best beaches, though the volcanic black sand can be off-putting at first. You can ascend to the crater (1,266 ft above sea level) on muleback for a wonderful view or take boat rides into the grottoes around the base. From Capo Grillo there is a view of all the Aeolians.

Lodging

$$$$ ⊡ **Les Sables Noires.** Named for the black sands of the beach in front,
★ this luxury hotel is superbly sited on the beautiful Porto di Ponente. The cool modern decor, wicker furniture, and inviting pool (for those unwilling to lounge on the private beach) induce a sybaritic mood, while the white-walled guest rooms are also tasteful and spacious. The restaurant, naturally, looks out over the bay: sunsets, framed by the towering faraglioni (pillars of rock rising dramatically out of the sea), are sublime. ⊠ *Porto di Ponente, 98050,* ☎ *090/9850,* FAX *090/9852454,* WEB *www.framon-hotels.com. 48 rooms. Restaurant, bar, pool, beach. AE, DC, MC, V. Closed mid-Oct.–mid-Apr.*

Salina

⑤⑨ *15 km (9 mi) north of Lipari (50 mins by ferry, 20 mins by hydrofoil), 52 km (38 mi) northwest of Milazzo.*

The second largest of the Aeolian Islands, Salina is also the most fertile—which accounts for its good wine, the golden Malvasia. Excursions go up Mt. Fossa delle Felci, which rises to more than 3,000 ft. It is also the highest of the islands, and the vineyards and fishing villages along its slopes add to its allure. Malvasia wine here is locally produced, unlike that found on other islands. Salina has a good range of reasonably priced accommodations and restaurants—and fewer crowds than Lipari.

Lodging

$$–$$$ ⊡ **Bellavista.** This is a quiet hotel in a quiet location, even though it's right next to the port. Rooms are simply furnished and cheerfully decorated with bright materials and ceramic tiles. Almost all have sea views, which can be enjoyed from the balconies. The management provides you with a list of things to do while on Salina and can organize boat excursions and transport around the island, though you may well opt for the *dolce far niente* (idle life). ⊠ *Via Risorgimento, Santa Marina Salina, 98050,* ☎ FAX *090/9843009. 13 rooms. No credit cards. Closed Nov.–Mar.*

Panarea

⑥⓪ *18 km (11 mi) north of Lipari (2 hrs by ferry, 25–50 mins by hydrofoil), 55 km (33 mi) north of Milazzo.*

Panarea has some of the most dramatic scenery of the islands: wild caves carved out of the rock and dazzling flora. The exceptionally clear water and the richness of life on the sea floor make Panarea especially suitable for underwater exploration, though there is little in the way of beaches. The outlying rocks and islets make a gorgeous sight, and you can enjoy the panorama on an easy excursion to the small Bronze Age village at Capo Milazzese.

Lodging

$$$$ ⊡ **La Raya.** This discreetly expensive hotel is perfectly in keeping with the elite style of Panarea, most exclusive of the Aeolian islands. Public

rooms, including bars, a broad terrace, and an open-air restaurant, are right on the port; the residential area is a 10-minute walk inland, though the rooms still enjoy the serene prospect of the sea and Stromboli from their balconies. The decor is elegant and understated, with Moorish-type hangings and low divans helping to create a tone of serene luxury. Families with young children are asked to book elsewhere. ⊠ *San Pietro, 98050,* ☎ *090/983013,* ⅎⅩ *090/983103,* ⷔⷕ *www.hotelraya.it. 29 rooms. Restaurant, bar, nightclub. AE, DC, MC, V. Closed mid-Oct.–mid-Apr.*

Stromboli

⓫ *40 km (25 mi) north of Lipari (3 hrs 45 mins by ferry, 65–90 mins by hydrofoil), 63 km (40 mi) north of Milazzo.*

This northernmost of the Aeolians (also accessible from Naples) consists entirely of the cone of an active volcano. The view from the sea—especially at night, as an endless stream of glowing red-hot lava flows into the water—is unforgettable. Stromboli is in a constant state of mild dissatisfaction, and every now and then its anger flares up, so authorities insist that you climb to the top (about 3,031 ft above sea level) only with a guide. The round-trip—climb, pause, and descent—usually starting at around 6 PM, takes about four hours. You will find a small selection of reasonably priced hotels and restaurants in the main town, and a choice of lively clubs and cafés for the younger set. In addition to the round-island tour, excursions include boat trips around the naturally battlemented isle of Strombolicchio. Numerous tour operators are available for Stromboli, among them Società Navigazione Pippo (☎ 090/986135 or 0338/985–7883). Rates are around 25,000 lire/€13 per person for three hours.

Alicudi

⓬ *65 km (40 mi) west of Lipari (3 hrs 25 mins–3 hrs 50 mins by ferry, 60–95 mins by hydrofoil), 102 km (68 mi) northwest of Milazzo.*

The farthest outpost of the Aeolians remains sparsely inhabited, wild, and at peace. Here and on Filicudi there is a tiny selection of accommodations, but you can rent rooms cheaply. Only the coming and going of hydrofoils disturbs the rhythm of life here, and the only noise is the occasional braying of donkeys.

Filicudi

⓭ *30 km (16 mi) west of Salina (3 hrs 25 mins–3 hrs 50 mins by ferry, 90 mins–2 hrs by hydrofoil), 82 km (54 mi) northwest of Milazzo.*

Just a dot in the sea, Filicudi is famous for its unusual volcanic rock formations and the enchanting **Grotta del Bue Marino** (Grotto of the Sea Ox). At Capo Graziano is a prehistoric village. The island has a handful of hotels and pensions, and some local families put up guests.

Lodging

$$ ⌂ **La Canna.** Set on a height above the tiny port, this *pensione* commands fabulous views of sky and sea from its flower-filled terrace. It's a wonderful prospect to wake up to and a fit setting for the utter tranquillity that characterizes any sojourn on this island. Rooms are small but adequate, kept clean and tidy by the friendly staff, and the cooking is exquisite (half- or full board required in peak season—and recommended at any time). Arrange to be collected at the port. ⊠ *Via Rosa 43, 98050,* ☎ *090/9889956,* ⅎⅩ *090/9889966. 10 rooms. Restaurant. MC, V. FAP, MAP.*

SICILY A TO Z

To research prices, get advice from other travelers, and book travel arrangements, visit www.fodors.com.

AIRPORTS

Sicily can be reached from all major cities via Rome, Milan, or Naples. Planes land at Aeroporto Falcone-Borsellino, 32 km (19 mi) west of Palermo at Punta Raisi. Catania's Aeroporto Fontanarossa, 5 km (3 mi) south of city center, is the main airport on Sicily's eastern side. In high season there are also direct charter flights to Sicily from New York, London, and Paris.

➤ AIRPORT INFORMATION: **Aeroporto Falcone-Borsellino** (☎ 091/ 591698). **Aeroporto Fontanarossa** (☎ 095/7306266).

TRANSFERS

Hourly Prestia & Comandè buses ply between Palermo's Falcone-Borsellino airport and the city center (Piazza Castelnuovo and the central station); tickets cost 7,500 lire/€3.90. Taxis charge around 65,000 lire/€33.80 for the same 45-minute trip. Catania's Fontanarossa airport is served by Alibus, which leaves about every half hour from the airport and the central train station, with a stop at Piazza Stesicoro, on Via Etnea. The journey takes around 25 minutes; tickets cost 1,300 lire/€0.70. Taxis cost around 40,000 lire/€20.65.

➤ TAXIS AND SHUTTLES: **Alibus** (☎ 095/7360450). **Prestia & Comandè** (☎ 091/580457).

BOAT AND FERRY TRAVEL

Frequent car ferries cross the strait between Villa San Giovanni in Calabria and Messina on the island. The crossing usually takes about half an hour, but during the summer months there can be considerable delays. Overnight car ferries operated by Tirrenia run daily all year between Naples and Palermo. In the summer (April–October), SNAV has a daytime service by faster catamarans, which also carry vehicles. Passenger-only *aliscafi* (hydrofoils) also cross the strait from Reggio di Calabria to Messina in about 15 minutes. The Aeolian Islands are reachable by hydrofoil from Naples, Messina, Palermo, and Milazzo. From Messina you can get ferry service to the islands. Call Siremar and SNAV.

FARES AND SCHEDULES

➤ BOAT AND FERRY INFORMATION: **Siremar** (☎ 081/5800340). **SNAV** (☎ 091/6118525 Palermo; 081/7612348 Naples). **Tirrenia** (☎ 081/ 7201111 Naples; 091/6021111 Palermo).

BUS TRAVEL

Air-conditioned coaches connect major and minor cities and are often faster and more convenient than local trains but slightly more expensive. Various companies serve the different routes. SAIS plies frequently between Palermo and Catania, Messina, and Siracusa, in each case arriving at and departing from near the train stations. Cuffaro runs between Palermo and Agrigento. On the south and east coasts and in the interior, SAIS connects the main centers, including Catania, Agrigento, Enna, Taormina, and Siracusa. Etna Trasporti operates between Catania, Caltagirone, Piazza Armerina, and Taormina. Interbus serves the routes between Messina, Taormina, Catania, and Siracusa.

➤ BUS INFORMATION: **Cuffaro** (☎ 091/6161510). **Etna Trasporti** (☎ 095/530396). **Interbus** (☎ 095/532716). **SAIS** (☎ 091/6166028 Palermo; 095/536168 or 095/536201 Catania).

CAR RENTAL

Renting a car is definitely the best way to get around Sicily. Trains are unreliable and slow, and buses, though faster and air-conditioned in summer, can be subject to delays and strikes. Cars can be rented at airports and downtown locations in every major city.

➤ LOCAL AGENCIES: **Avis** (✉ Aeroporto Fontanarossa, Catania, ☎ 095/340500; ✉ Via V. Giuffrida 19/21, Catania, ☎ 095/445536; ✉ Aeroporto Falcone-Borsellino, Palermo, ☎ 091/591684; ✉ Via E. Amari 91, Palermo, ☎ 091/586940). **Hertz** (✉ Aeroporto Fontanarossa, Catania, ☎ 095/341595; ✉ Via Toselli 16/c, Catania, ☎ 095/322560; ✉ Aeroporto Falcone-Borsellino, Palermo, ☎ 091/213112; ✉ Via Messina 7/e, Palermo, ☎ 091/331668). **Maggiore** (✉ Aeroporto Fontanarossa, Catania, ☎ 095/340594; ✉ Piazza Verga 48, Catania, ☎ 095/536927; ✉ Aeroporto Falcone-Borsellino, Palermo, ☎ 091/591681; ✉ Stazione Marittima, Palermo ☎ 091/6810801).

CAR TRAVEL

This is the ideal way to explore Sicily. Modern highways circle and bisect the island, making all main cities easily reachable. A20 (supplemented by S113 at points) connects Messina and Palermo; Messina and Catania are linked by A18; running through the interior, from Catania to west of Cefalù, is A19; threading west from Palermo, A29 runs to Trapani and the airport, with a leg stretching down to Mazara del Vallo. The superstrada S115 runs along the southern coast, and connecting superstrade lace the island. Cars can be rented at airports and downtown locations in every major city.

EMERGENCY SERVICES

If you have trouble on the road, contact the Polizia Stadale (Road Police) by phone. (A cell phone is invaluable in such situations.)
➤ CONTACTS: **Polizia Stadale** (☎ 116).

RULES OF THE ROAD

The basic rules of the road are the no different here than elsewhere in Italy, but be aware that Sicilians are the country's most aggressive drivers.

EMBASSIES AND CONSULATES

➤ UNITED KINGDOM: **U.K. Consulate** (✉ Via Cavour 117, Palermo, ☎ 091/326412).
➤ UNITED STATES: **U.S. Consulate** (✉ Via Vaccarini 1, Palermo, ☎ 091/305857).

EMERGENCIES

➤ CONTACTS: **Ambulance, Police, Fire** (☎ 113). **Hospital** (☎ 091/288141 Palermo; 095/7591111 Catania).

LANGUAGE

The Sicilian language (considered by some an Italian dialect) is still strong on the island and varies enormously from town to town and from village to village. To hear it, it's nothing like standard Italian; however, most Sicilians will speak to strangers in standard Italian.

MAIL AND SHIPPING

OVERNIGHT SERVICES

In Palermo, the local courier used by UPS is Randazzo. The local FEDEX courier in Palermo is SDA. To call for pickups or information from either Federal Express or UPS, use their national service numbers.
➤ MAJOR SERVICES: **Federal Express** (☎ 800/123800). **Randazzo** (✉ Via Sturzo 260, Zona Industriale, Carini, ☎ 091/868–0200). **SDA** (✉ Via Pablo Picasso, Palermo). **UPS** (☎ 02/25088001).

➤ POST OFFICES: **Palermo** (✉ Via Roma 322, ☎ 091/7531111). **Siracusa** (✉ Piazza delle Poste, Ortygia, ☎ 0931/489111).

OUTDOORS AND SPORTS

Tours are organized in the Sicilian national parks by Biosport. Walking expeditions by the day or week, as well as canoeing and biking in the Etna, Nebrodi, Madonie, and Peloritani parks, can all be arranged. ➤ HIKING AND WALKING: **Biosport** (✉ Via Garibaldi 110, 98100 Messina, ☎ 090/6409800 or 091/545623, FAX 090/6409497).

SAFETY

Although you are unlikely to be a victim of any of Sicily's fabled Mafia clans, there are some elementary rules which travelers to Sicily should follow to ensure a hassle-free holiday. In the cities, it is not recommended to wander around those parts of Palermo and Catania where there are not plenty of other people about, particularly at night, and you should never flaunt expensive watches, jewelry, and the like. Women traveling alone should keep out of deserted areas at all times. Watch your bags constantly, especially at airports.

TOURS

Tours of Palermo and Monreale are provided by the Italian tour operator CST on Friday afternoon and Saturday morning, with pickups from your hotel or a central location such as outside the Politeama theater. Contact the agency to confirm details. CST also arranges tours of Taormina and Etna, bookable from their office in Taormina, as well as to Piazza Armerina, Agrigento, and western Sicily, or you can join a seven-day tour of all Sicily's major sights in a comfortable air-conditioned coach with an English-speaking guide, with weekly departures from either Palermo or Catania; the cost includes all meals and accommodations in luxury hotels. ➤ FEES AND SCHEDULES: **CST** (✉ Via E. Amari 124, Palermo, ☎ 091/7439611; ✉ Corso Umberto 101, Taormina, ☎ 0942/23301).

TRAIN TRAVEL

There are direct express trains from Milan and Rome to Palermo, Catania, and Siracusa. The Rome–Palermo and Rome–Siracusa trips take at least 11 hours. After Naples, the run is mostly along the coast, so try to book a window seat on the right if you're not on an overnight train. At Villa San Giovanni, in Calabria, the train is separated and loaded onto a ferryboat to cross the strait to Messina.

Main lines connect Messina, Taormina, Siracusa, and Palermo. Secondary lines are generally very slow and unreliable. The Messina–Palermo run, along the northern coast, is especially scenic. Call FS for information. ➤ TRAIN INFORMATION: **FS** (Italian State Railways; ☎ 147/888088).

VISITOR INFORMATION

➤ TOURIST INFORMATION: **Acireale** (✉ Corso Umberto 177, 95024, ☎ 095/892129). **Agrigento** (✉ Viale della Vittoria 255, 92100, ☎ 0922/401352; ✉ Via Cesare Battisti 15, 92100, ☎ 0922/20454). **Caltagirone** (✉ Via V. Libertini 3, 95041, ☎ 0933/53809). **Caltanisetta** (✉ Corso Vittorio Emanuele 109, 93100, ☎ 0934/530411). **Catania** (✉ Via Cimarosa 10, 95124, ☎ 095/7306233, WEB www.apt.catania.it; ✉ Stazione Centrale, 95129, ☎ 095/7306255; ✉ Aeroporto Fontanarossa, 95121, ☎ 095/7306266). **Cefalù** (✉ Corso Ruggero 77, 90015, ☎ 0921/21050 or 0921/21458). **Enna** (✉ Via Roma 413, 94100, ☎ 0935/528228; ✉ Piazza Napoleone Colaianni 6, 94100, ☎ 0935/500875). **Erice** (✉ Via Conte Pepoli 11, 91016, ☎ 0923/869388).

Lipari (⊠ Corso Vittorio Emanuele 202, 98055, ☎ 090/9880095, WEB www.tau.it/aapitme/isole.html). **Marsala** (⊠ Via XI Maggio 100, 91025, ☎ 0923/714097). **Messina** (⊠ Piazza della Repubblica, 98122, ☎ 090/672944; ⊠ Via Calabria 301/b, 98123, ☎ 090/674236; ⊠ Piazza Cairoli 45, 98123, ☎ 090/2936294). **Monreale** (⊠ Piazza Duomo, 90046, ☎ 091/6564570). **Palermo** (⊠ Piazza Castelnuovo 35, 90141, ☎ 091/583847, WEB www.aapit.pa.it; ⊠ Aeroporto Falcone-Borsellino, 90045, ☎ 091/591698). **Piazza Armerina** (⊠ Via Cavour 1, 94015, ☎ 0935/680201). **Siracusa** (⊠ Via San Sebastiano 43, 96100, ☎ 0931/67710; ⊠ Via Maestranza 33, 96100, ☎ 0931/464255). **Taormina** (⊠ Palazzo Corvaja, Largo Santa Caterina, 98039, ☎ 0942/23243, WEB www.taormina-ol.it). **Trapani** (⊠ Piazza Saturno, 91100, ☎ 0923/29000; ⊠ Via Francesco d'Assisi 27, 91100, ☎ 0923/545511).

16 SARDINIA

CAGLIARI, SU NURAXI, PORTO CERVO

An uncut jewel of an island, Sardinia remains unique and enigmatic. Too distant from Rome to be influenced by the character of the mainland, this island is as fascinating as its prehistoric stone structures, the *nuraghi*. Modern luxury can also be found here: just follow the jet-setters who sail their yachts to the Costa Smeralda. Beautiful in its severity, Sardinia is a prime destination if you're seeking a getaway.

T HE SECOND-LARGEST ISLAND in the Mediterranean—just smaller than Sicily—Sardinia is about 180 km (112 mi) from mainland Italy and very much off the beaten track. A Phoenician stronghold in ancient times and later a Spanish dominion, Sardinia doesn't seem typically "Italian" in its color and flavor. It lies just a bit too far from the mainland—from imperial and papal Rome and from the palaces of the Savoy dynasty—to have been transformed by the events that forged a national character. Yet Giuseppe Garibaldi, the charismatic national hero who led his troops in fervid campaigns to unify Italy in the mid-19th century, chose to spend his last years in relative isolation on the small island of Caprera, just off the coast of Sardinia.

Updated by
Robert
Andrews

Although Sardinia (Sardegna in Italian) is less than an hour by air and only several hours by boat from mainland Italy, it is removed from the mainstream of tourism except for July and August, when Italians take its beautiful coasts and clean waters by storm. The interior is *never* crowded; Italian tourists in Sardinia come for the sea, less for the rugged and deserted mountain scenery.

Sardinia closely resembles Corsica, the French island across the 16-km-wide (10-mi-wide) windswept Strait of Bonifacio to the north. A dense bush, or *macchia*, barely penetrable in some districts, covers large areas. The terrain is rough, like the short, sturdy shepherds you see in the highlands—impassive figures engaged in one of the few gainful oc-cupations the stony land allows. Shaggy flocks of sheep and goats are familiar features in the Sardinian landscape, just as their meat and cheese are staples of the island's cuisine. The main highway linking Cagliari with Sassari was begun in 1820 by the Savoy ruler Carlo Felice; des-ignated S131, but still referred to as the Strada Carlo Felice by the is-landers, it runs through the fertile Campidano Plain for 216 km (134 mi) between the two cities.

Aside from the chic opulence of the Costa Smeralda, there's little so-phistication in Sardinia, but the cost of living on the island is typically higher than on the mainland. The sprawling cities of Cagliari and Sas-sari have a distinctly provincial air. Newer hotels may seem a little old-fashioned, and hotels of any vintage are hard to find inland. There's little traffic on the roads, and trains, buses, and people in general move at a gentle pace. In hamlets, women swathed in black shawls and long, full skirts look with suspicion upon strangers passing through. Sardinians are courteous but remote, perhaps because of their innate dignity.

Like mainland Italians, the Sardinians are of varied origin. On the northwest coast, fine traceries of ironwork around a balcony underscore the Spanish influence. In the northeast, the inhabitants boast Genoese or Pisan ancestry, and the headlands display the ruined fortresses of the ancient Pisan duchy of Malaspina on the Italian mainland. As you ex-plore the southern coast, you'll come upon the physiognomies, customs, dialects, place names, and holy buildings of the Turks, Moors, Phoeni-cians, Austrians, and mainland Italians. If there are any pure Sardini-ans—or Sards—left, perhaps they can be found in the south-central mountains, south of Nuoro, under the 6,000-ft crests of the Gennar-gentu Massif, in the rugged country still ironically called Barbagia, "Land of Strangers."

Pleasures and Pastimes

Beaches

For their fine sand and lack of crowds, Sardinia's beaches are among the best in the Mediterranean; its waters are among the cleanest, with the exception of those in the immediate vicinity of Cagliari, Arbatax, and Porto Torres. The beach resorts of the Costa Smeralda, on the northeastern tip of the island, are exclusive and expensive, but elsewhere on the island you can find beach areas with a wide range of prices.

Many agree that the most beautiful beaches on the island are those of Cala di Luna and Cala Sisine, hidden among the rocky cliffs between Baunei and Dorgali, on the eastern coast; these remote strands can be reached only by boat from Cala Gonone or Arbatax. For more accessible beaches with more amenities, go to Santa Margherita di Pula, near Cagliari, where you'll find several hotels; to Villasimius and the Costa Rei, on the southeastern coast; or to the sandy coves sheltered by wind-carved granite boulders on the northern coast in the Gallura district and the archipelago of La Maddalena. There are also beaches around Olbia and Alghero, and on the Costa Paradiso, near Castelsardo.

Dining
In the island's restaurants you'll find that Sardinian regional cuisine is basically Italian, with interesting local variations. Meat dishes are usually veal, lamb, or *porcheddu* (roast suckling pig). On the coast, seafood is king and is served in great variety. Langouste or *aragosta* (lobster) is a specialty of the northern coast and can get pricey. Foreign conquerors left legacies of bouillabaisse (known here as *zimino*), couscous, and paella, but there are also native pastas: *malloreddus* (small shells of bran pasta sometimes flavored with saffron) and *culurgiones* (the Sardinian version of ravioli). Sharp pecorino cheese made from sheep's milk and thin, crispy bread called *carta di musica* are typical island fare. Try the *sebadas* (fried cheese-filled ravioli doused with honey) for dessert. The local red wines are sturdy and strong, while the whites tend toward the light and delicate. Amber-color Vernaccia is dry and heady. For general information and price categories, *see* Dining *in* Smart Travel Tips A to Z.

Festivals
As one of Italy's most—perhaps *the* most—remote regions, Sardinia is not really a prime spot for sophisticated visual or performing arts. This same remoteness, however, can prove fruitful for sampling some of the culture here, sometimes natively inspired, sometimes drawing on the influences of the traders and invaders who have left their mark on the island over the millennia. Sardinia's own brand of Catholicism—occasionally bordering on the grotesque—can be witnessed in the local *feste*, or festivals. Ostensibly, the festivals celebrate a saintly or religious occasion, but often they are imbued with an almost pagan feeling.

The main festivals are at Cagliari (Festa di Sant'Efisio, May 1), Sassari (Ascension Day, the 40th day after Easter; La Cavalcata, penultimate Sunday of May, and I Candelieri, August 14), and Nuoro (penultimate Sunday in August). Some of the best are the smaller festivals in the scattered mountain villages of the interior; in Fonni, in the heart of the Barbagio, locals celebrate the Festa di San Giovanni, held June 24, in traditional costume. These festivities are not just expressions of religious devotion but also an explicit statement of community identity.

Fishing
Check locally for regulations on deep-sea fishing. Underwater fishing is restricted to the daylight hours, and no more than 5 kilos (11 pounds) of fish and shellfish may be taken. No oxygen tanks or nets may be used for underwater fishing. Freshwater fishing is good along the Flumendosa, Tirso, Rio Mannu, and other rivers rising in the mountainous interior and in the artificial basins of Flumendosa and Omodeo.

Golf

Sardinia has two world-class golf courses, the Pevero Golf Club on the Costa Smeralda, which was designed by Robert Trent Jones, and the Is Molas 18-hole course at Santa Margherita di Pula.

Horseback Riding

Spaghetti Westerns were once filmed in Sardinia, and it's easy to imagine why: the rugged, mountainous terrain of the inland is the perfect frontier setting for an adventure on horseback. On the barren hilltops of the Barbagio you may even catch a glimpse of the wild dwarf horse that is native to these parts, though numbers have dwindled over the years. If you prefer a more sedate way of seeing the island on horseback, you can stick to the coast, where the riding is easier but the scenery is still magnificent. Group itineraries and horse rentals can be arranged.

Kids' Stuff

Sardinia is a vast playground where children can explore and swim in season. There's nothing like a long hike along deserted beaches or through herb-perfumed hills to send them to bed early. Let them clamber over the nuraghi and poke into the countless *domus de janas* (witches' houses) and *tombe di giganti* (giants' tombs), fancifully named grottoes hewn in the rock by the island's prehistoric inhabitants. Near Alghero, at Anghelu Ruiu, and near the Costa Smeralda, at Arzachena, they served as burial places, but with a little imagination you can make up some fanciful fairy tales.

Lodging

The island's most luxurious hotels are on the Costa Smeralda. They have magnificent facilities but close from fall to spring; many are too out of the way to be good touring bases. Other, equally attractive coastal areas have seen a spate of resort hotels and villa colonies sprouting up; they, too, close from October through April, which narrows the choice of hotels considerably during the other months. In the cities suggested as touring bases, you can expect to find standards of comfort slightly below those on the mainland. The best accommodations may be available at commercial hotels, which can mean little atmosphere. In smaller towns throughout the island, you'll find modest hotels offering basic accommodations, restrained but genuine hospitality, and low rates. For general information and price categories, *see* Lodging *in* Smart Travel Tips A to Z.

Sailing

Sailing enthusiasts tack for Sardinia in droves for of its craggy coast full of wildly beautiful inlets only accessible by sea. You can watch the very rich engage in one of their favorite sports—yachting—at the posh resorts of Costa Smeralda each August, when a number of regattas are held.

Berthing and provisions facilities are available on all coasts, though concentrated in the area around the Costa Smeralda and La Maddalena areas in the northeast. Altogether, there are 15 nautical schools, nearly half of these in the northeast. The harbor master, or *capitano di porto,* can issue permits for anchorage. The **Lega Navale Italiana** at Marina Piccola in Cagliari (☎ 070/303794) has information on the island's facilities.

Shopping

Sardinia is crafts heaven. Locally produced goods include bright woolen shawls and rugs, hand-carved wooden objects, gold filigree jewelry in traditional designs, coral jewelry, and, above all, handwoven baskets in all shapes and sizes. The best places to go for crafts are the various government-sponsored ISOLA centers in Cagliari, Sassari, Castelsardo, and Nuoro.

Exploring Sardinia

The island is about 260 km (162 mi) from north to south and takes three to four hours to drive; it's roughly 120 km (75 mi) across. Driving is the best way to see the island's most interesting sights, though Sardinia's mountainous terrain can make driving rigorous and slow. Local transportation is not geared to the needs of visitors, so you can cover more ground in less time if you have a car. If you don't have a car, establish yourself in one of the larger towns and make excursions to as many attractions as time and schedules allow. There are bus and train connections to most places, except some areas of the Costa Smeralda and Su Nuraxi nuraghe.

Numbers in the text correspond to numbers in the margin and on the Sardinia and Cagliari maps.

Great Itineraries

Three days in Sardinia will give you only enough time to see one corner of the island. In five days, you will be able to venture out to some of the attractions in the north of the island. A fairly comprehensive tour taking in the coastline and interior can be accomplished in seven days.

IF YOU HAVE 3 DAYS

You would do well to confine your visit to ☷ **Cagliari** ①–⑥ and its environs. In Sardinia's capital you'll find Italianate architecture, churches of all styles, and the **Museo Archeologico** ①, with the island's best antiquities collection. If you do not have your own transport, you can use taxis or buses to make easy day trips from Cagliari. Your priority should be **Su Nuraxi** ⑪, the island's most imposing nuraghic monument. On your second or third day, head out to the small coastal village of ☷ **Pula** ⑧; great beaches rim the coast, and just outside is Nora, a Carthaginian and Roman archaeological site.

IF YOU HAVE 5 DAYS

Stay in ☷ **Cagliari** ①–⑥ two days, still leaving enough time for a visit to **Pula** ⑧. Spend your third night in ☷ **Alghero** ⑰, an appealing walled town about three hours from Cagliari on the northwest coast with a distinctly Spanish flavor, perhaps stopping for lunch en route at ⊠ **Oristano** ⑬. For your last two nights you have a choice. You could spend them in the lap of luxury in one of the hotels in or outside ☷ **Porto Cervo** ㉒, which is about three hours from Alghero, or, if you are on a limited budget and/or prefer adventure, make ☷ **Nuoro** ⑮ your base from which to explore the rugged interior of the island. Spend as little time as possible exploring the provincial capital before veering south into the mountainous Barbagia region, the island's most primitive district.

IF YOU HAVE 7 DAYS

Spend your first two days exploring ☷ **Cagliari** ①–⑥ and the beaches at **Villasimius** ⑦, on the southeastern tip of the island. On your third day, go southwest from Cagliari, taking in the ancient remains outside **Pula** ⑧, and follow along the western coast on the Strada Carlo Felice as far as the sleepy village of **Sant'Antioco** ⑨. Here you can take a 20-minute ferry ride over to the small island of ☷ **San Pietro** ⑩ for the night, a favorite weekend retreat of wealthy Cagliarans, with delightful picnic and swimming spots. Continue up toward Oristano, making an inland detour to the fascinating nuraghe of **Su Nuraxi** ⑪, off the main road outside the quiet town of Barumini. Wildlife enthusiasts may want to take another jaunt north of Barumini to the **Giara di Gesturi** ⑫, a basalt plateau with the island's more exotic wildlife. On your fourth night, stay in ☷ **Oristano** ⑬, which saw its heyday in the Middle Ages but now merits a cursory walk through town and a

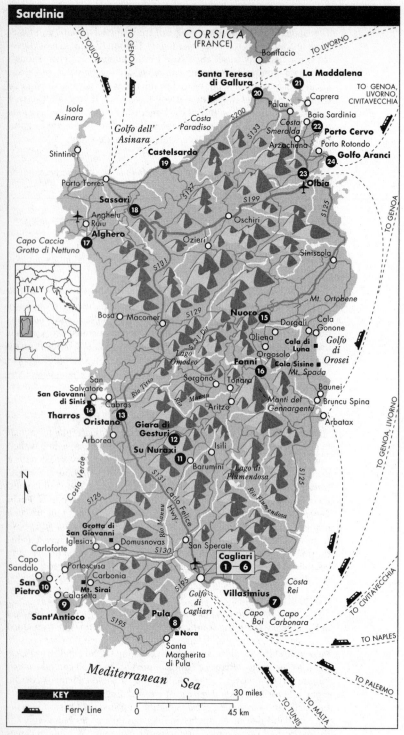

CORSICA
(FRANCE)

Bonifacio

Santa Teresa di Gallura
La Maddalena
20
21
Caprera
Palau
TO LIVORNO
TO GENOA, LIVORNO, CIVITAVECCHIA
Costa Paradiso
Baia Sardinia
Costa Smeralda
22
Porto Cervo
Arzachena
Porto Rotondo
Golfo Aranci
Castelsardo
19
24
23 ✈ **Olbia**
Isola Asinara
Golfo dell' Asinara
Stintino
S200
S133
S127
S199
TO TOULON
TO GENOA
Sassari
18
Anghelu Ruiu
Porto Torres
Oschiri
S125
TO GENOA
Ozieri
Capo Caccia
Grotto di Nettuno
17 ✈
Alghero
Siniscola
S131
Mt. Ortobene
Bosa
Macomer
S129
Nuoro
15
Dorgali
Cala Gonone
Golfo di Orosei
S127 Dir
Oliena
Cala di Luna ■
Lago Omodeo
Orgosolo
Fonni
16
Cala Sisine ■
Mt. Spada
San Salvatore
Sorgono
Tonara
Baunei
San Giovanni di Sinis
Rio Tirso
Bruncu Spina
14
Cabras
13
Aritzo
Monti del Gennargentu
Arbatax
Tharros
Oristano
Rio Mannu
Isili
Giara di Gesturi
12
Arborea
Su Nuraxi
11
Barumini
Lago di Flumendosa
S131
S125
Costa Verde
Carlo Felice Hwy.
Rio Flumendosa
S126
Rio Mannu
Grotta di San Giovanni
Iglesias ■
Domusnovas
San Sperate
S130
Carloforte
Capo Sandalo
Portoscusa
Carbonia
S195
Cagliari
1 6 ✈
San Pietro
10
■ **Mt. Sirai**
Calasetta
9
Villasimius
7
Costa Rei
Sant'Antioco
Golfo di Cagliari
Capo Boi
Capo Carbonara
Pula
8
S195
■ **Nora**
Santa Margherita di Pula
TO CIVITAVECCHIA
TO NAPLES
TO PALERMO

N

Mediterranean Sea

TO MALTA
TO TUNIS

KEY
🚢 Ferry Line

0 — 30 miles
0 — 45 km

ITALY

glimpse of the Carthaginian ruins at **Tharros** ⑭, just outside the city. Head northeast for **Nuoro** ⑮ and its fascinating museum of folk culture before striking south into the Barbagia region. Torturous roads wind their way over a wild and primitive terrain that seems impervious to the 20th century, let alone the 21st. If you prefer coastal attractions to the inland ones, spend no more than half a day exploring the region; then head west from Nuoro on road 129 to Bosa, where you turn right into hilly and arid scrub country that eventually brings you to ⊞ **Alghero** ⑰, on the northwest coast. Consider spending your fifth night here. While heading northeast across an area fringed with low cliffs, inlets, and small bays, don't be distracted by **Sassari** ⑱, but stop to appreciate the exquisite seaside resorts, including **Castelsardo** ⑲, a walled citadel that is a delight for basket lovers. Conitue along to the relaxed fishing village of ⊞ **Santa Teresa di Gallura** ⑳, surrounded fine beaches and well-equipped hotels. Spend your last day pampering yourself on the sun-kissed beaches of one of Europe's premier summer holiday meccas, the Costa Smeralda, its most exclusive address being ⊞ **Porto Cervo** ㉒, a great place for a final splurge in Sardinia before taking the ferry back to the mainland from Olbia.

When to Tour Sardinia

If you can help it, avoid Sardinia in steamy August, when the island is swamped not only with tourists from the mainland but the Sards, too, taking their annual break. A combination of unbearable heat, crowded beaches, accommodation shortages, and shuttered shops and offices can make for a less-than-idyllic vacation. May and September are much quieter and still temperate. Sudden storms can be a hazard, but these quickly blow over. The sea remains warm enough for swimming well into October. The mountainous interior is probably at its best in the spring, when the woods and valleys are alive with color and burgeoning growth. For the gradations of color, the fall is also a good time. In winter, rain and clouds are common over high ground—and most of Sardinia is mountainous—and it snows most years in the Barbagia region. In the south, the weather rarely turns cold, but winter is not beach weather. (Additionally, many resorts are closed from October to April, limiting lodging possibilities.) Try to schedule your visit to Sardinia to coincide with one of the famous annual festivals. They are mega-affairs, with accommodation and restaurant space at a premium, so plan well ahead.

CAGLIARI AND THE SOUTHERN COAST

Sardinia's southern coast is a stunning succession of wild rocky inlets and pristine beaches. Though blissfully uncommercialized for the most part, there are pockets of development that have sprouted as tourism has found a niche. However, you'll find hotels artfully concealed behind thick swathes of eucalyptus and lush pine groves at Santa Margherita di Pula, one of Sardinia's most luxurious holiday enclaves. The main center in these parts is Pula, an inland town within easy reach of both good beaches and what is Sardinia's most important archaeological site, the Carthaginian and Roman city of Nora. South and west of Santa Margherita, the protected coast has few beaches but no lack of jaw-dropping vistas, unspoiled by any construction.

North and east of Pula is Sardinia's largest city, Cagliari (the stress is on the first syllable). The island's capital is characterized by its busy commercial center and waterfront with broad avenues, as well as by the typically narrow streets of the old hilltop citadel. This is where you'll find Sardinia's principal art and archaeology museums, as well as its old cathedral and the medieval towers, which have lofty views of the surrounding sea, lagoons, and mountains.

East of Cagliari, the coast is no less scenic, though more built up, especially around the resort of Villasimius, also within a short distance of some first-class sandy beaches.

Cagliari

268 km (166 mi) south of Olbia.

The island's capital has impressive Italianate architecture and churches in a variety of styles. Medieval Spanish conquerors from Aragon as well as Pisans and Piemontese all left their marks.

❶ Begin your visit at the **Museo Archeologico,** within the walls of the castle that the Pisans erected in the early 1300s to ward off attacks by the Aragonese and Catalans, from what is now Spain. Among the intriguing artifacts from Nuraghic, Carthaginian, and Roman times are bronze statuettes from the tombs and dwellings of Sardinia's earliest inhabitants, who remain a prehistoric enigma. These aboriginal people left scant clues to their origins. Ancient writers called them the Nuraghic people, from the name of their stone dwellings, the nuraghi. The structures are unique to Sardinia, just as the Aztec pyramids are to Mexico. Archaeologists date the nuraghi from about 1300–1200 BC, a time when the ancient Israelites were establishing themselves in Canaan; when the Greeks were besieging Troy; when the Minoan civilization collapsed in Crete; when the Ramses pharaohs reigned in Egypt; and when many migrations were taking place along the shores and water routes of the Mediterranean. During the next 1,000 years, the Nuraghic people gradually withdrew to the island's highland fastnesses to avoid more disciplined and better-armed invaders. (Their only weapons, say the chroniclers, were stones and boulders they hurled down from the hilltops.) They eventually succumbed when the Romans, following on the heels of Carthaginian invaders, conquered the island in the 3rd century BC. ✉ *Cittadella dei Musei, Piazza Arsenale,* ☎ *070/ 655911.* 💶 *5,000 lire/€2.60.* 🕐 *Tues.–Sun. 9–7.*

❷ The medieval **Torre di San Pancrazio** (Tower of St. Pancras), part of the imposing Pisan defenses, is just outside Cagliari's archaeological museum. You can climb up the tower for a fabulous panorama of the city and its surrounds. ✉ *Piazza Indipendenza,* ☎ *070/655911.* 💶 *Free.* 🕐 *Apr.–Sept., Tues.–Sun. 9–1 and 3–7; Oct.–Mar., Tues.–Sun. 9–4:30.*

❸ The **Torre dell'Elefante** (Tower of the Elephant), twin to the tower of San Pancrazio, is at the seaward end of Cagliari's bastions. ✉ *Via Università,* ☎ *070/659674.* 💶 *Free.* 🕐 *Apr.–Sept., Tues.–Sun. 9–1 and 3–7; Oct.–Mar., Tues.–Sun. 9–4:30.*

❹ **Piazza Palazzo,** at the top of Via Martini, is where you'll find the **Duomo,** which has been extensively rebuilt and restored. The tiers of columns on the facade echo those of medieval Romanesque Pisan churches, but only the central portal is an authentic relic of that era. ✉ *Piazza Palazzo,* ☎ *070/663837.* 🕐 *Daily 8–12:30 and 4–8.*

On the narrow streets of the **Castello quarter,** below the Duomo, humble dwellings still open directly onto the sidewalk and the wash is hung out to dry on elaborate wrought-iron balconies.

❺ The Bastion of St. Remy, better known as the **Terrazza Umberto I,** is a monumental neoclassical staircase and arcade. It was added in the 19th century to the bastion built by the Spaniards 400 years earlier. ✉ *Piazza Costituzione.*

❻ Below the Museo Archeologico are the **Anfiteatro Romano,** some very old churches, and a few good restaurants near the waterfront. The am-

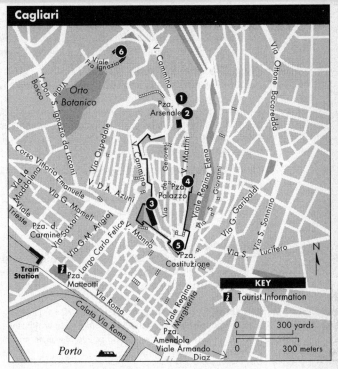

phitheater, which dates from the 2nd century AD, is a well-preserved arena complete with underground passages and a beasts' pit, evidence of the importance of this Roman outpost. ⊠ *Viale Fra Ignazio,* ☎ *070/ 652130.* 🖾 *Free.* ☉ *Apr.–Sept., Mon.–Sat. 9–1 and 4–8, Sun. 9–1 and 2:30–5; Oct.–Mar., daily 9–5.*

Dining and Lodging

$$$ ✕ **Dal Corsaro.** This formal restaurant near the port is one of the island's most commended eating places, so make reservations. The decor is refined, the welcome cordial. The menu features seafood and meat specialties, such as seafood antipasto and porcheddu. ⊠ *Viale Regina Margherita 28,* ☎ *070/664318. Reservations essential. AE, DC, MC, V. Closed Sun., 2 wks in Aug., and 1 wk at Christmas.*

$$ ✕ **Il Gatto.** "The Cat," near the train station and the central Piazza del Carmine, is popular with locals; make sure you have reservations, because the place can fill up quickly. It serves some of the best Sardinian seafood, such as risotto with shellfish, but for a change of pace try the zesty *insalata di funghi, rucola, e grana padano* (salad of mushrooms, arugula, and a young Parmesan cheese). ⊠ *Viale Trieste 15,* ☎ *070/ 663596. AE, DC, MC, V. No lunch weekends.*

$$$ 🏨 **Panorama.** With its unprepossessing exterior, this hotel in downtown Cagliari is geared toward the business class. Rooms are functional, spacious, and comfortable. Try to reserve one on the higher of the nine floors and enjoy the view over the harbor and bay. ⊠ *Viale Armando Diaz 231, 09100,* ☎ *070/307691,* 𝔽𝔸𝕏 *070/305413. 90 rooms. Restaurant, bar, pool, meeting room, parking (fee). AE, DC, MC, V.*

$$ 🏨 **AeR Bundes Jack.** Despite the unprepossessing entrance under the arcades of Via Roma, this central third-floor pensione (there's an elevator) is impeccably clean and guarantees simply furnished rooms, sheltered from the hubbub of traffic. The port is directly opposite (though rooms are all inward-facing), the bus and train stations steps away, and

Via Roma itself presents an entertaining parade of shops and sit-down bars. You can also expect polite service and reams of information from the kind family that runs it. Rates are low in the category. ⊠ *Via Roma 75, 09100,* ☎ ℻ *070/657970. 14 rooms. No credit cards.*

Nightlife and the Arts

Sardinia's greatest annual festival, the **Festa di Sant'Efisio**, May 1–4, involves thousands of costumed villagers, many of them on horseback, parading through town, and a four-day procession between Cagliari and Pula. It's a good chance to take part in the centuries-old folklore. Cagliari's **university** (⊠ Via Università) holds concerts throughout the academic year; contact the tourist office for information.

Outdoor Activities and Sports

FISHING

For information on obtaining a fishing license, contact the **Assessorato Regionale alla Difesa dell'Ambiente** (⊠ Via Biasi 7/9, Cagliari, 09100, ☎ 070/6066620).

Shopping

The best place for crafts is **ISOLA** (⊠ Via Bacaredda 176, ☎ 070/492756; ⊠ Via Santa Croce 34, ☎ 070/651488), a government-sponsored exhibition of artisanal crafts where most of the work is for sale.

OFF THE BEATEN PATH

SAN SPERATE – Walls throughout this town 20 km (12 mi) north of Cagliari have been brightened with *murales* (mural paintings) by local artists and some well-known Italian painters, transforming the entire town into an open-air art gallery.

Villasimius

❼ *50 km (31 mi) east of Cagliari, 296 km (184 mi) south of Olbia.*

The eastern route takes you through some dismal industrial suburbs on the road that leads to the scenic coast and beaches of Capo Boi and Capo Carbonara. Villasimius ranks as the chief resort here, but the beautiful beaches lie a couple of miles north of town, on the golden sands of the Costa Rei.

Pula

❽ *29 km (18 mi) southwest of Cagliari, 314 km (195 mi) southwest of Olbia.*

Resort villages sprawl along the coast southwest of the capital, which has its share of fine scenery and good beaches. On the marshy shoreline between Cagliari's Aeroporto di Elmas and Pula, huge flocks of flamingos are a common sight.

The **Is Molas** championship golf course near Pula has won tributes from Tom Watson, Jack Nicklaus, and other professionals of the sport.

The small **Museo Archeologico Comunale** (archaeological museum) has finds from the Nora site, including amphoras, anchors, and inscribed stones, mostly dredged up from the sea. ⊠ *Corso Vittorio Emanuele 67,* ☎ *070/9209610.* 🎫 *5,000 lire/€2.60, 8,000 lire/€4.15 including Nora.* ☉ *Apr.–Oct., daily 9–8; Nov.–Mar., daily 9–7.*

The narrow promontory called ★**Nora,** less than 3 km (2 mi) outside the town of Pula, was the site of a Phoenician, then Carthaginian, and later a Roman settlement. Extensive excavations have shed light on life in this ancient city from the 8th century BC onward. Many of the exhibits in Cagliari's archaeological museum were found here. An old

Roman road passes the moss-covered ruins of temples, an amphitheater, and a small Roman theater. You can make out the channels through which hot air rose to warm the Roman baths; watch for the difference between the simple mosaic pavements laid by the Carthaginians and the more elaborate designs of the Romans. Taking in the views from Nora, you can see why the Phoenicians chose the site for settlement. They always scouted for locations with good harbors, cliffs to shelter their craft from the wind, and an elevation such as a promontory, from which they could defend themselves against attack. If the sea is calm, look under the clear waters along the shore for more **ruins** of the ancient city, submerged by earthquakes, rough seas, and erosion. ☏ *070/9209138.* ⊠ *5,000 lire/€2.60, 8,000/€4.15 including Museo Archeologico Comunale.* ☉ *Excavations Apr.–Sept., daily 9–8; Oct.–Mar., daily 9–6. Guided tours hourly.*

Sant'Efisio, the little Romanesque church at the base of the Nora promontory, plays a part in one of the island's most colorful annual events. Efisio, the patron saint of Sardinia, was a 3rd-century Roman soldier who converted to Christianity. A procession in early May accompanies a statue of the saint all the way from Cagliari and back again. The processional round-trip takes four days, with festive stops along the way, and culminates in a huge parade down Cagliari's main avenue. If you're in Sardinia from May 1 to May 4, don't miss it. ⊠ *Nora,* ☏ *070/9208473.* ☉ *Apr.–Sept., Sat. 3–6, Sun. 9:30–1 and 3–7:30; Oct.–Mar., Sun. 9:30–noon and 3–5; other times by appointment.*

Lodging

The lodgings and beaches that cater to the summer crowds visiting Pula and Nora are concentrated a little over a mile south, in a conglomeration of hotels that makes up the town of Santa Margherita di Pula.

$$$$ 🏨 **Is Morus Relais.** A luxurious enclave, the Is Morus is on a sandy
★ cove and offers all the amenities of a fine beach resort, with low, attractive buildings shaded by pinewoods, plus the option (for guests taking half- or full board) of golfing at the fine Is Molas course, about 11 km (7 mi) away. ⊠ *Santa Margherita di Pula, 09010,* ☏ *070/921171,* FAX *070/921596. 85 rooms. Restaurant, bar, pool, golf privileges, miniature golf, tennis court, beach. AE, DC, MC, V. Closed mid-Oct.–mid-Apr. FAP, MAP.*

$$$ 🏨 **Flamingo.** Directly on the beach and in a shady setting, this resort hotel features a main building and several two-story cottages nestled among eucalyptus trees. Balconied rooms are light and airy, overlooking park or sea, and full sports facilities are offered, including diving and windsurf. ⊠ *Santa Margherita di Pula, 09010,* ☏ *070/9208361,* FAX *070/9208359. 134 rooms. Restaurant, piano bar, pool, miniature golf, tennis court, dance club. AE, DC, MC, V. Closed Nov.–Apr.*

Outdoor Activities and Sports

GOLF

Guests at any of the hotels in Santa Margherita di Pula can avail themselves of the international-standard 18-hole **Is Molas** course (☏ 070/9241014). The **Is Molas Golf Hotel** (⊠ Località Is Molas, Santa Margherita di Pula, ☏ 070/9241006) lies adjacent to the Is Molas golf course and includes the greens fee if you book half-board.

Sant'Antioco

❾ *75 km (47 mi) west of Pula, 100 km (62 mi) west of Cagliari.*

Off the southwest coast is Sant'Antioco, a popular holiday spot with good beaches. You drive over a causeway to get on the island, where the most hectic activity seems to be the silent repairing of nets by local fishermen who have already pulled in their daily catch. Before leaving the main town, also called Sant'Antioco, take time to visit the **zona archeologica** at the top of the old section, affording terrific views over to the Sardinian mainland. Here you can see a Punic necropolis, and a tophet, or burial site, dedicated to the Carthaginian goddess Tanit, scattered with urns that contained the cremated remains of stillborn children. ▨ *8,000 lire/€4.15, including guided tour of site, and ethnographic and archaeological museums.* ☉ *Apr.–Sept., daily 9–1 and 3:30–7; Oct.–Mar., daily 9–1 and 3:30–6.*

OFF THE BEATEN PATH **CARBONIA AND IGLESIAS –** If your curiosity prods you to explore more esoteric places, you could go just inland from Sant'Antioco to explore the rugged, once-booming mining country around Carbonia (14 km [9 mi] northeast of Sant'Antioco), a town built by Mussolini in 1938 to serve as an administrative center for the coal miners and their families. With its time-frozen fascist architecture—ordered rows of houses around a core of monumental public buildings on the broad main piazza—it has been called an urban UFO set down in the Sardinian landscape. **Monte Sirai,** near Carbonia and open daily 9–1 hour before sunset, holds the remains of Sardinia's most important Carthaginian military stronghold, impregnably sited atop a hill that dominates the outlook inland and far out to sea; admission is 5,000 lire/€2.60. **Iglesias,** 20 km (12 mi) north of Carbonia, is an authentic Sardinian town, with a medieval cathedral; traveling east past Domusnovas on the Cagliari–Iglesias highway, you can detour and drive right through an immense cave, the Grotta di San Giovanni.

San Pietro

🔟 *5 km (3 mi) northwest of Sant'Antioco.*

A ferry at the small northern port of Calasetta connects Sant'Antioco with the smaller island of San Pietro at the main town of Carloforte. This is a favorite of wealthy Cagliarians, many of whom have built weekend cottages here. The best views are from Capo Sandalo, on San Pietro's rugged western coast, but head to the island's southern tip for the beaches. The ferry departs every 20 minutes in summer and every 30 in winter—the trip takes 20 minutes.

Lodging

$$ 🏨 **Hieracon.** This ornate, Art Nouveau lodging sits on the harbor in Carloforte. Rooms are modern, with whitewashed walls, TVs, telephones, and air-conditioning. A small internal garden is home to a few palms. Try to get a front-facing room, though there may be some traffic noise; the ones at the top have low ceilings and no view. The central location means that you're a short walk from some good restaurants if you don't want to eat in. ✉ *Corso Cavour 68, 09014,* ☎ *0781/854028,* ℻ *0781/854893. 17 rooms. Restaurant, bar, air-conditioning, minibars. AE, MC, V.*

BARUMINI TO THE COSTA SMERALDA
The Barren and the Beautiful

A more traditional—and wild—Sardinia awaits the traveler who ventures into the mountainous inland of the island. The Italian film directors the Taviani brothers made the hinterland of the Barbagia region, where traditional Sardinian customs are maintained in remote hilltop villages, the subject of the extraordinary film *Padre Padrone* (1977). Inland Sardinians are hardy souls, used to living in a climate that is as unforgiving in winter as it is intolerable in summer. Old traditions, including the vendetta, are firmly rooted in the social fabric of this mountainous land, which is both barren and beautiful. Here, rare species of wildlife share the rocky uplands with sturdy medieval churches and mysterious nuraghi, ancient stone citadels left by prehistoric people. You may want to make your base Oristano, on the west coast and the medieval center of Sardinian nationalism.

As you move northward the timeless beauty of the landscape begins to show greater signs of 20th-century development. The sunny resort of Alghero, the Spanish-influenced port on the west coast, is one of the island's premier holiday spots. In the 1960s and '70s, the Costa Smeralda, the luxury resort complex developed by the Aga Khan on the northeast corner of Sardinia, was *the* place to summer, along with the Côte d'Azur.

Su Nuraxi

★ ⓫ *60 km (37 mi) north of Cagliari.*

It is worth making a detour to the fascinating **nuraghe** of Su Nuraxi, off the main road outside the quiet little town of Barumini. You could spend hours clambering over this extraordinary structure of concentric rings of stone walls, chambers, passages, wells, and a beehive tower. The main nuraghe is probably about half its original height, and some of the smaller towers around it have been reduced by pillaging and erosion to mere circles of stones on the ground.

The nuraghi vary from single defensive towers to multitowered complexes sheltering whole communities, prehistoric versions of medieval walled towns and the forts of the American West. Though this particular type of construction is unique to Sardinia, similar buildings dating from the same era are found in other parts of the Mediterranean, such as Cyprus and the Balearic islands off Spain. Of the 7,000 nuraghi on Sardinia, Su Nuraxi is the most impressive, with those of Sant'Antine and Losa, both near Macomer, close runners-up. It's a good idea to take a flashlight along. *1 km (½ mi) west of Barumini.* ☎ *0337/813087.* 🎟 *8,000 lire/€4.15.* ☉ *Apr.–Sept., daily 9–7:30; Oct.–Mar., daily 9–5.*

Giara di Gesturi

⓬ *8 km (5 mi) north of Barumini, 68 km (42 mi) north of Cagliari.*

On the basalt plateau of Giara di Gesturi roam some of the island's more exotic wildlife, including a species of wild dwarf horse. Another rare species in the Giara is the mouflon, a wild sheep distinguishable from its domesticated counterpart by its long, curving horns and skittishness. Long hunted for their horns, the mouflon are now an endangered species, with only a few surviving on Sardinia and Corsica.

Costa Verde

80 km (50 mi) northwest of Cagliari, 40 km (25 mi) south of Oristano.

If you've come to Sardinia in search of untrammeled wilderness and sweeping sands as far as the eye can see, this deserted coast is the place to find them. Hidden away in the forgotten northwest corner of Cagliari province, the Costa Verde is accessible only by a bumpy, unpaved track. The effort is worth it. The dune-backed sands shelter a range of rare grasses and bird life, as well as providing magnificent swimming.

You can approach the coast either from the town of Guspini, on the straggling S126, or from a turnoff a couple of miles farther south, which will lead you through the abandoned mining town of **Ingurtosu.** It's a strange, ghostly cluster of chimneys and workers' dwellings, forlorn amid the encroaching scrubland. Drive down the dirt track another 10 km (6 mi) or so, through woods of lentisk and juniper, to reach the sea.

Lodging

$$–$$$ ⛤ **Hotel Le Dune.** A remote oasis on the beach, this hotel was formerly
★   a deposit for the minerals dug out from the surrounding hills, and you can still see the remains of wagons, rails, and other mining bric-a-brac scattered about, which only add to the desolate allure of the place. The simple, TV-less guest rooms have a light, spacious feel from the bamboo furnishings; 11 of the rooms have their own sitting rooms. Though facilities are minimal, they include a good cocktail bar where you can contemplate the limitless sands stretching out on either side. Both the bar and the restaurant—which serves up Sardinian specialties as well as the regular Italian menu—are open to all. Itineraries and guides for exploring the area are available on request. ⊠ *Piscinas di Ingurtosu, 09030,* ☎ *070/977130,* ℻ *070/977230. 26 rooms. Restaurant, bar, air-conditioning, free parking. AE, DC, MC, V.*

Oristano

⑬   *25 km (16 mi) north of Giara di Gesturi, 93 km (58 mi) northwest of Cagliari.*

Oristano, on the west coast, shone in the Middle Ages when it was capital of the Giudicato of Arborea, an independent duchy led by Sardinia's own Joan of Arc–type heroine, Eleanora di Arborea (circa 1340–1402). In the 14th century, Eleanora inherited the difficult task of defending the duchy's freedom, constantly undermined by the superior military might of Spanish troops from Aragon. Although the duchy eventually reverted to Aragonese rule, Eleanora made a lasting contribution to Sardinia by implementing a code of law that was adopted throughout the island and remained in effect until Sardinia's unification with Italy in 1847. Now an important but slow-paced agricultural center, Oristano is the scene of livestock fairs and a rousing series of horse races, called Sa Sartiglia, marking the end of February's Carnival.

OFF THE   **CABRAS –** Ten kilometers (6 miles) northwest of Oristano you can see
BEATEN PATH extensive marshlands where fishermen pole round-bottomed rush boats through shallow ponds teeming with eels and crayfish.

Dining and Lodging

$$$ ✕ **Il Faro.** Locals and visiting foodies consider this elegant seafood restau-
★   rant to be one of the best in the area, as it offers authentic and well-prepared seasonal dishes. The service is impeccable, the decor simple. There's *capretto allo spiedo* (spit-roasted goat) around Easter, *porchetto* (roast suckling pig, also known as porcheddu) in the fall, *agnello* (lamb) in winter, and an aromatic *zuppa di fave* (fava-bean soup) with bacon and fennel in the spring. ⊠ *Via Bellini 25,* ☎ *0783/70002. AE, DC, MC, V. Closed 2 wks in Jan., and July. No lunch Sun. in Oct.–Mar.*

$$ ✕ **Da Gino.** Extremely central (off Piazza Roma), this simple trattoria has authentic local dishes including seafood. Try the delicious spaghetti *alla bottarga* (with smoked fish roe). The service is friendly and attentive, making this a popular spot for locals and an ideal lunch stop. ⊠ *Via Tirso 13,* ☎ *0783/71428. MC, V. Closed Sun., 1 wk in Jan., and 3 wks in Aug.*

$$ ✕ **Salvatore.** This seafood restaurant near the church of Sacra Cuore isn't full of surprises—it's predictable, but the food is cooked to perfection. Seafood from the lagoons of Cabras and Santa Giusta is im-

peccably fresh. Specialties include grilled *anguillara* (eel). ✉ *Via Carbonia 1,* ☎ *0783/357134. No credit cards. No dinner Sun.*

$$–$$$ 🏨 **Ala Birdi.** Buried within a thick belt of pinewoods fringing the Golfo di Oristano—4 km (2½ mi) outside Arborea and 15 km (9 mi) south of Oristano—this family hotel doubles as the island's premier center for horseback riding. In addition to the stables, a cornucopia of other sports facilities make this spot ideal for family stays. Although the guest rooms and the food from the three restaurants tend to be blandly institutional, the nearby sandy beach, not to mention the excursions by day and nightly entertainment, ensure a good time. ✉ *Strada a Mare 24, Arborea 09092,* ☎ *0783/80500,* FAX *0783/801086,* WEB *www.alabirdi-arborea.it. 385 rooms. 3 restaurants, 2 bars, 3 pools, tennis court, horseback riding, gym, recreation room. AE, DC, MC, V.*

$$ 🏨 **Mistral 2.** Oristano's most comfortable hotel is primarily oriented toward business travelers, with first-class facilities. A modern, seven-story block, well maintained and efficiently run, it is located on the western outskirts of town (well signposted) on its own grounds, and convenient for drivers. If you wish to stay closer to the center, opt instead for the original **Mistral** (✉ Via Mártiri di Belfiore, ☎ 0783/212505), with older facilities but lower rates. ✉ *Via XX Settembre, 09170,* ☎ *0783/210389,* FAX *0783/211000. 132 rooms. Restaurant, bar, pool, meeting rooms, free parking. AE, DC, MC, V.*

Nightlife and the Arts

The **Sartiglia** festival, on the last Sunday of Carnival season, includes rich costumes and a ritual joust. Each summer, the town holds an **arts-and-crafts exhibition,** with local foods and wines given prominence. Contact the **tourist office** (✉ Via Cagliari 278, ☎ 0783/74191) for information.

Tharros

⑭ *20 km (12 mi) west of Oristano, 113 km (70 mi) northwest of Cagliari.*

The **ruins** of the Carthaginian and Roman city of Tharros are along the road marked San Giovanni di Sinis; its position afforded it a strategic view over scenic Sinis peninsula. Like Nora to the south, the site was chosen because it commanded the best views of the harbor and could provide an easy escape route if inland tribes threatened. Four Corinthian columns still stand, and there are baths and fragments of mosaics from the Roman city. As at Nora, there is much more submerged under water. ✉ *20 km (12 mi) west of Oristano.* 💰 *8,000 lire/€4.15.* ⊙ *Daily 9–1 hr before sunset.*

On your way to Tharros, you'll pass the ghost town of **San Salvatore,** revived briefly in the 1960s as a locale for spaghetti Westerns and since abandoned. The saloon of the movie set still stands. Among the dunes farther along past San Salvatore are large **rush huts** formerly used by fishermen and now much in demand as back-to-nature vacation homes. The 5th-century church of **San Giovanni di Sinis,** on the Sinis peninsula, is the oldest Christian church in Sardinia.

Nuoro

⑮ *89 km (56 mi) northeast of Oristano, 181 km (113 mi) north of Cagliari.*

The somewhat shabby provincial capital of Nuoro is on the edge of a gorge in the harsh mountainous area that culminates in **Gennargentu,** the island's highest massif (6,000 ft). The only things likely to interest you are the views from the park on Sant'Onofrio hill and the exhibits in the **Museo della Vita e delle Tradizioni Popolari Sarde** (Museum of

Sardinian Life and Folklore), where you can see a fabulous array of local costumes, domestic and agricultural implements, and traditional jewelry. ⊠ *Via Mereu 56,* ☎ *0784/31426.* 🖾 *5,000 lire/€2.60.* ⊙ *Mid-June–Sept., daily 9–8; Oct.–mid-June, daily 9–1 and 3–7.*

Make an excursion about 3 km (2 mi) east of Nuoro to **Monte Ortobene** (2,900 ft) for some lofty views over the gulch below. Here you can also see up close the imposing statue of Christ the Redeemer overlooking the city. Picnic tables make this a handy spot for an alfresco lunch stop.

OFF THE
BEATEN PATH

ORGOSOLO – This old center of banditry halfway between Nuoro and Fonni is still a poor and undeveloped village, but the houses have been daubed with *murales* (mural paintings) vividly depicting political and cultural issues. The effect is startling and lively. The forest and grassy plane above the village make fine walking country.

Dining and Lodging

$$–$$$ ✕🏨 **Su Gologone.** Despite attracting tourists in droves, this bustling
★   country inn (20 km [12 mi] southeast of Nuoro) still manages a friendly atmosphere. The restaurant ($$$) alone is worth a detour for an authentic Sardinian meal. Island specialties include *maccarones de busa* (thick homemade pasta), culurgiones, porcheddu, and sebadas. Wash it all down with the local Vernaccia. The hotel organizes jeep and hiking expeditions and has bikes for guests' use. ⊠ *Località Su Gologone, 08025,* ☎ *0784/287512,* 📠 *0784/287668,* 🌐 *www.sugologone.it. 68 rooms, 8 junior suites. Restaurant, bar, pool, miniature golf, 2 tennis courts, gym, bicycles. AE, DC, MC, V. Closed Nov.–Mar.*

Nightlife and the Arts

Nuoro's **Festa del Redentore** (Feast of the Redeemer) is held on the next-to-last Sunday in August. It's the best time to view the various traditional costumes of Sardinia's interior all in one place.

Shopping

Crafted for local festivals, wooden masks are available at local shops and make unusual and festive souvenirs. The local **ISOLA** shop (⊠ Via Monsignor Bua 10, ☎ 0784/31507) is in the heart of the Old Town.

Fonni

🔟 *30 km (19 mi) south of Nuoro, 137 km (85 mi) south of Olbia.*

In the heart of the Barbagia region, Fonni is the highest town on the island and a good base for excursions by car to all sights of interest, including Monte Spada and the Bruncu Spina refuge on the Gennargentu Massif, in this mountainous district that is Sardinia's most primitive. Life in some villages seems not to have changed much since the Middle Ages. Here a rigidly patriarchal society perpetuates the unrelenting practice of vendetta, and strangers are advised to mind their own business. High mountain roads wind and loop their way through the landscape; towns are small and undistinguished, their social fabric seemingly untouched by the 21st, or 20th, century. On feast days elaborate regional costumes are taken out of mothballs and worn as an explicit statement of community identity.

OFF THE
BEATEN PATH

ARBATAX – If you have the stamina, take the rickety old train on a leg of the journey that runs on a single-gauge track between Cagliari and Arbatax, midway up the east coast (involving a change at Mandas). If all goes well, it takes about seven hours to cover the approximately 250 km (155 mi) of track, guaranteeing you a look at a Sardinia few tourists ever see. With daily, early-morning departures, the train rattles up into the Barbagia district through some breathtaking mountain scenery, then eases down into the desert landscape inland from Arbatax, where the trip ends on the dock next to the fishing boats. The train is run by the **Ferrovie Complementari** (☎ 070/491304), and the ticket costs around 30,000 lire/€15.60. In Tortoli, just outside Arbatax, **Dolce Casa** (✉ Via Sarcidano 3, ☎ 0782/624235, ℻ 0782/623484) is a modest, one-star hotel, scrupulously clean, run by an English-speaking couple. It's open June–September only.

Nightlife and the Arts
You can see one of the most characteristic of the Barbagia's celebrations in local costume in Fonni during the **Festa di San Giovanni,** held June 24.

Shopping
Special candies are made from honey and nougat and sold in hilltop Tonara, southwest of Fonni. In the mountain village of Aritzo, about 45 km (28 mi) south of Fonni, high up in the Barbagia, you'll find hand-crafted wooden utensils and furniture.

En Route From Nuoro, take S129 west about 65 km (40 mi) to coastal Bosa, where you turn right into hilly and arid scrub country, with its abundance of cactus and juniper. Pines and olive trees shelter low buildings from the steady winds that make these parts ideal for sailing. About the only cash crop here is cork from the cork trees dotting the landscape. Yet in the low valleys and along the riverbeds, masses of oleanders bloom in the summer, creating avenues of color.

Alghero

⑰ *40 km (25 mi) north of Bosa, 137 km (85 mi) southwest of Olbia.*

Among the larger centers on the northwest coast is Alghero, an appealing walled resort town with a distinctly Spanish flavor. It was built and inhabited in the 14th century by the Aragonese and Catalans, who constructed seaside ramparts and sturdy towers encompassing an inviting nucleus of narrow, winding streets. Rich wrought-iron scrollwork decorates balconies and screened windows; Spanish motifs appear in stone portals and in bell towers. The dialect spoken here is a version of Catalan, not Italian: attend one of the masses conducted in Algherese to hear it.

Near Alghero are broad sandy beaches and the spectacular heights of **Capo Caccia,** an imposing limestone headland to the west. At the base of the sheer cliff, the pounding sea has carved an entrance to the vast **Grotta di Nettuno,** a fantastic cavern that you must visit with a guide. By land, you reach the entrance at the base of the cliff by descending the more than 600 steps of the aptly named *escala del cabirol* (mountain goat's stairway), a dizzying enterprise—and the ascent is just as daunting. The excursion by sea is much less fatiguing but is not possible in winter or when seas are rough. Boats leave the port of Alghero four times daily, or every hour or so in peak season, and the trip takes 2½ hours. *Boat tour:* ✉ *Navisarda,* ☎ *079/950603.* 🎫 *Grotto 15,000 lire/€7.80 (includes mandatory tour), boat tour 17,000 lire/€8.85 (excluding ticket for grotto).* ☉ *Grotto Apr.–Sept., daily 9–7; Oct., daily 10–5; Nov.–Mar., daily 9–2; tours on the hr. Boat tours Apr., May, and Oct., daily at 9, 10, 3, and 4; June–Sept., daily 9–5 on the hr.*

Dining and Lodging
$$–$$$ ✕ **Al Tuguri.** The name is dialect for "old abandoned house," though in fact the building has been sensitively renovated, retaining a rustic

but smart ambience. Space is limited to one small upstairs room, and an even smaller attic, but this only enhances the feeling of friendly intimacy, fostered by the charming host, Benito Carbonella. He will explain the finer points of Catalan cookery, whose traditional recipes he has adapted, or "revisited." Ask for the sampling menu to see what he means. Seafood is the main ingredient, artfully prepared and presented in a variety of ways, for example mousse *de ricci* (with sea urchins). The desserts, too, are exceptional. ⊠ *Via Maiorca 113,* ☎ *079/976772. No credit cards. Closed Sun. and 4 wks in Dec.–Jan.*

$$ ✕ **Da Pietro.** On a narrow street in the picturesque old town near Largo San Francesco, this seafood restaurant has vaulted ceilings and a bustling atmosphere. The menu features *bucatini all'algherese* (pasta with a sauce of clams, capers, tomatoes, and olives) and baked fish with a white-wine sauce. ⊠ *Via Ambrogio Machin 18,* ☎ *079/979645. AE, DC, MC, V. Closed Wed. and 1 wk at Christmas.*

$$ ✕ **La Lepanto.** A covered veranda by the seafront marks out Alghero's top seafood restaurant, usually thronged with locals. The specialty is aragosta cooked in a variety of ways, including *alla catalana* (with tomato and onions). For starters, try risotto *nero di seppia* (with cuttlefish ink). ⊠ *Via Carlo Alberto 125,* ☎ *079/979116. AE, DC, MC, V. Closed Mon. in Oct.–May.*

$$$$ ⊞ **Villa Las Tronas.** The villa is a former royal mansion on a rocky bluff
★   above the sea but still near the center of town. The gardens sheltering the hotel from the road impart a regal sense of seclusion, and there are great views across the water to the Old Town. Inside, the Belle Epoque atmosphere is complemented by modern comforts and good en-suite facilities. The restaurant is open in summer only. ⊠ *Lungomare Valencia 1, 07041,* ☎ *079/981818,* ℻ *079/981044. 28 rooms, 1 suite. Restaurant, pool, gym, beach. AE, DC, MC, V.*

$$–$$$ ⊞ **Carlos V.** Right opposite the Villa Las Tronas on the shore boulevard, about 1 km (½ mi) from the center of town, this modern hotel (pronounced Carlos Quinto) has gardens, porticoes, and terraces, one of which has a good-size swimming pool. All rooms—airy and modern but lacking in character—have a balcony, but don't settle for the slightly cheaper ones facing the back; the pleasure here is all in the magnificent sea view. Low-season rates are a bargain, and there are discounts for longer stays. Note that both pool and restaurant are closed in winter. ⊠ *Lungomare Valencia 24, 07041,* ☎ *079/979501,* ℻ *079/975886,* ⟨WEB⟩ *www.hotelcarlosv.it. 110 rooms. Restaurant, pool, 2 tennis courts, miniature golf, meeting rooms. AE, DC, MC, V.*

$$ ⊞ **San Francesco.** Centrally located in Alghero's Spanish quarter, this hotel occupies the convent that was once attached to the church of San Francesco. The rooms are grouped around the 14th-century cloister and, though somewhat cramped, are modern and quiet. ⊠ *Via Machin 2, 07041,* ☎ ℻ *079/980330. 21 rooms. Bar, meeting room, parking (fee). DC, MC, V. Closed Nov.*

Shopping

Coral, still harvested in the bay, and gold jewelry are displayed in many specialty shops as well as more touristy outlets throughout Alghero's old quarter.

Sassari

❶⑧   *34 km (21 mi) northeast of Alghero, 212 km (132 mi) north of Cagliari.*

Inland Sassari is an important university town and administrative center, notable for its historic, ornate cathedral and a good archaeological museum. Sassari is the hub of several highways and secondary roads leading to various coastal resorts, among them Stintino and Castelsardo.

Shopping

Sassari has Sardinia's main **ISOLA** outlet (⊠ Giardini Pubblici, ☎ 079/230101), an exhibition center in the public gardens next to Viale Mancini built specifically as a showcase for gifts and souvenirs.

Castelsardo

⑲ *32 km (20 mi) northeast of Sassari, 100 km (62 mi) west of Olbia.*

The walled seaside citadel of Castelsardo is a delight for basket lovers. Roadside stands and shops in the old town sell tons of island crafts: rugs, wrought iron, and baskets—in myriad shapes and colors. Take the children to see the **Elephant Rock** on the road into Castelsardo; hollowed out by primitive man to become a *domus de janas* (literally, "fairy house," in fact a neolithic burial chamber), it resembles an elephant, trunk and all.

Shopping

There is an **ISOLA** workshop (⊠ Via Roma 104, ☎ 079/471413), where local handicrafts can be bought. The local specialty is a brightly colored basket made of dwarf palms.

Santa Teresa di Gallura

⑳ *68 km (42 mi) northeast of Castelsardo, 65 km (41 mi) northwest of Olbia.*

At the northern tip of Sardinia, Santa Teresa di Gallura retains the relaxed, carefree air of an authentic fishing village turned resort.

Dining and Lodging

$–$$ ✕⌂ **Canne al Vento.** This cheerful, family-run hotel and restaurant on the main road into town is a quiet, tasteful haven. The restaurant specializes in authentic island cuisine, for example *zuppa cuata* (bread, cheese, and tomato soup), porcheddu, or seafood. The hotel has a defiantly rustic feel, despite the bland, modern exterior, with a bamboo-roofed restaurant and the odd ornamental wagon wheel. Rooms are sparsely furnished but cool and comfortable. Ask for one of the quieter ones at the back. ⊠ *Via Nazionale 23, 07028,* ☎ *0789/754219,* FAX *0789/754948. 22 rooms. Restaurant. MC, V. Closed Mon. and Oct.–Easter.*

$$–$$$ ⌂ **Grand Hotel Corallaro.** This hotel offers luxury accommodations in a panoramic spot right by the beach, a brief walk from the town center. Rooms are functional and some have balconies. Public rooms are much grander, furnished with wicker chairs, and there are terraces and lawns where you can sip preprandial drinks. Half- or full board is required in peak season. ⊠ *Località Rena Bianca, 07028,* ☎ *0789/755475,* FAX *0789/755431,* WEB *www.hotelcorallaro.it. 82 rooms. Restaurant, indoor pool, Turkish baths, gym. MC, V. Closed mid-Oct.–Easter. FAP, MAP.*

La Maddalena

㉑ *30 km (19 mi) east of Santa Teresa di Gallura, 45 km (20 mi) northwest of Olbia.*

From the port of Palau you can visit the archipelago of La Maddalena, seven granite islands embellished with lush green scrub and wind-bent pines. Pilgrims pay homage to **Garibaldi's tomb** (1807–82) on the grounds of his hideaway on Isola Caprera, the island to the east of Isola Maddalena. ☎ *0789/727162.* ⊡ *4,000 lire/€2.10.* ☉ *Apr.–Sept., daily 9–5:30; Oct.–Mar., daily 9–1:30.*

Porto Cervo

★ ㉒ *30 km (19 mi) north of Olbia.*

Sardinia's northeastern coast is fringed with low cliffs, inlets, and small bays. This has become an upscale vacationland, with glossy resorts such as Baia Sardinia and Porto Rotondo, just outside the confines of the famed Costa Smeralda, developed by the Aga Khan (born 1936), who accidentally discovered its charms—and potential—in 1965, when his yacht took shelter here from a storm. The Costa Smeralda is still dominated by his personality; its attractions remain geared to those who can measure themselves by the yardstick of his fabled riches. Sardinia's most expensive hotels are here, and the world's most magnificent yachts anchor in the waters of Porto Cervo. The trend has been to keep this enclave of the really rich an exclusive haven by encouraging more multimillionaires to build discreetly luxurious villas and planning four more golf courses for their leisure.

All along the coast, carefully tended lush vegetation surrounds vacation villages and elaborate villa colonies that have sprung up over the past decade in a range of spurious architectural styles best described as bogus Mediterranean. Outside the peak season, however, the majesty of the natural surroundings shines through, justifying all the hype and giving grounds for the Emerald Coast's fame as one of the truly romantic corners of the Mediterranean.

Lodging

$$$$ 🏨 **Cala di Volpe.** Long a magnet for the beautiful people, this luxury establishment, now part of ITT Sheraton, was built to resemble an ancient Sardinian village. The hotel's decor is rustic-elegant, with beamed ceilings, Sardinian arts and crafts, and porticoes overlooking the sea. The presidential suite in the highest tower has a private pool. ⊠ *Cala di Volpe, 07020,* ☎ *0789/976111,* 🅵🅰🆇 *0789/976617. 123 rooms. Restaurant, bar, air-conditioning, pool, 3 tennis courts, gym, beach. AE, DC, MC, V. Closed mid-Oct.–Mar.*

$$$$ 🏨 **Cervo.** Low Mediterranean buildings surround a large pool and garden in the heart of the Costa Smeralda's Porto Cervo. This complex is next to the marina and *piazzetta* (small piazza), a popular spot to see and be seen. The rooms are large and most have a terrace. Guests have access to five good tennis courts in summer. ⊠ *Porto Cervo, 07020,* ☎ *0789/931111,* 🅵🅰🆇 *0789/931613. 111 rooms. 5 restaurants, piano bar, 3 pools, 5 tennis courts, gym, squash, beach. AE, DC, MC, V.*

$$$–$$$$ 🏨 **Nibaru.** Pinkish-red brick buildings with tiled roofs stand in a secluded inlet set in lush gardens—not bad for a hotel that enjoys all the best features of the Costa Smeralda at comparatively low rates. Guest rooms are just a few yards from the sea and some superb swimming spots and also within easy access of the Pevero Golf Club and the tennis courts of Porto Cervo. ⊠ *Località Cala di Volpe, 07020,* ☎ *0789/ 96038,* 🅵🅰🆇 *0789/96474. 45 rooms. Restaurant, bar, pool. AE, DC, MC, V. Closed mid-Oct.–mid-Apr.*

Outdoor Activities and Sports

GOLF

An 18-hole, world-class **Pevero Golf Course** (☎ 0789/958020), designed by Robert Trent Jones, is on the Bay of Pevero, near Porto Cervo.

SAILING

The **Yacht Club Costa Smeralda** (☎ 0789/902200) at Porto Cervo offers use of its pool, restaurant, bar, and guest rooms to those with memberships at other yacht clubs.

Shopping

Contemporary pottery displaying traditional motifs is a hot item, snatched up at whim along the Costa Smeralda. Porto Cervo's Sottopiazza has some big-name boutiques, and there's an **ISOLA** (⊠ Villaggio Sottopiazza, ☎ 0789/94428) outlet here, too.

Olbia

㉓ *30 km (19 mi) south of Porto Cervo, 106 km (66 mi) north of Nuoro.*

Set amid the resorts of Sardinia's northeastern coast, Olbia is a lively little seaport, not heavily industrialized, at the head of a long, wide bay. The little basilica of **San Simplicio,** a short walk behind the main Corso Umberto, is worth searching out if you have any spare time in Olbia. The simple granite structure dates from the 11th century, part of the great Pisan church-building program, using pillars and columns recycled from Roman buildings. ⊠ *Via San Simplicio.* ☯ *Daily 6:30– 12:30 and 4–7.*

Lodging

$$–$$$ 🏨 **Martini.** Olbia's newest hotel, opened in 1997, is an eye-catching site on the shore of a lagoon north of town. It's convenient to the port and center, though still a taxi ride away (it's about a 20-minute walk). Plush, modern, and businesslike, the hotel has lounge chairs on the roof with views of the port but is thankfully detached from the early morning and late-night comings and goings of ferries embarking. Most bedrooms benefit from the excellent vista. There is no restaurant, but just next door there's the elegant Delle Rose ($$$, ☎ 0789/24545), serving classic Italian fare. ⊠ *Via G. D'Annunzio, 07026,* ☎ *0789/26066,* ☏ *0789/26418. 66 rooms. Bar, air-conditioning, meeting room. AE, DC, MC, V.*

Golfo Aranci

㉔ *19 km (12 mi) northeast of Olbia.*

At the mouth of the Gulf of Olbia, Golfo Aranci is a small-scale resort and major debarkation point for ferries from the mainland. The craggy headland west of town has been left undeveloped as a nature reserve, and there are some inviting beaches within an easy drive.

SARDINIA A TO Z

To research prices, get advice from other travelers, and book travel arrangements, visit www.fodors.com.

AIR TRAVEL

Alitalia and Meridiana connect Rome, Milan, Pisa and other cities on the mainland and in southern Europe with Sardinia. Flying is by far the fastest and easiest way to get to the island. The Rome–Cagliari flight takes about an hour. Sardinia's major airports are at Cagliari and Alghero, with another, smaller one, at Olbia, providing access to the Costa Smeralda.

➤ AIRLINES AND CONTACTS: **Alitalia** (☎ 800/223–5730 in U.S.; 020/ 7602–7111 or 0990/448–259 in U.K.; 06/65641 in Rome; 848/865641 elsewhere in Italy, ☒ www.alitalia.it).

AIRPORTS

Cagliari's Aeroporto di Elmas is about 6 km (4 mi) west of town center, and there is regular bus service from the airport to Piazza Matteotti, in front of the train station. Alghero's Aeroporto Fertilia is 13 km (8 mi) from the city. A bus links the airport with the main bus station in the center of town. Aeroporto Costa Smeralda is 4 km (2½ mi) southeast of Olbia, linked by local bus to Olbia.

➤ AIRPORT INFORMATION: **Aeroporto Costa Smeralda** (☎ 0789/52634). **Aeroporto di Elmas** (☎ 070/240119). **Aeroporto Fertilia** (☎ 079/935282 or 079/935033).

BOAT AND FERRY TRAVEL

Large modern ferries run by Tirrenia Lines, Moby Lines, and the FS (Italian State Railways) connect Sardinia (ports at Porto Torres, Olbia, Arbatax, and Cagliari) with the mainland. These ferries are a popular mode of transport. Tirrenia sails to several ports in Sardinia from Genoa, La Spezia, Civitavecchia, Fiumicino, Naples, Palermo, and Trapani. Moby Lines transports passengers and cars between Livorno and Olbia and between Civitavecchia and Olbia. FS ferries carry trains as well as passengers and cars; they sail from Civitavecchia to Golfo Aranci, near Olbia.

FARES AND SCHEDULES

The ferry ride on Tirrenia from Naples takes about 17 hours and costs approximately 100,000 lire/€52 for second-class passage in mid- or high season, with a berth. The Civitavecchia–Olbia/Golfo Aranci run takes about eight hours and there are overnight sailings, or take a more expensive high-speed ferry (summer only), which takes just four to six hours but costs more and gets booked up weeks ahead during the peak of the season in mid-August. According to the time of year, the normal ferry service is scheduled two or three times a week, while high-speed ferries depart one to four times daily in season; reservations are essential in the summer.

➤ BOAT AND FERRY INFORMATION: **FS** (☎ 1478/88088). **Moby Lines** (☎ 06/4201 1455 or 0586/826824, WEB www.mobylines.it). **Tirrenia** (☎ 800/824079 toll free in Italy; 1478/99000 or 081/3172999 from cellular phones or from abroad, WEB www.tirrenia.it).

BUS TRAVEL

Cagliari is linked with the other towns of Sardinia by a network of buses. Local destinations are served by ARST. Major cities, excluding Olbia, are served by PANI. The heart of the Sardinian bus system is the Stazione Autolinee, across the square from the main tourist office in Cagliari. City buses in Cagliari and Sassari operate on the same system as those on the mainland: buy your ticket first, at a tobacco shop or machine, and cancel it by punching it in the machine on the bus. Fares are 1,300 lire/€0.65 per ride.

➤ BUS INFORMATION: **ARST** (☎ 070/4098324 or 1678/65042). **PANI** (☎ 070/652326). **Stazione Autolinee** (✉ Piazza Matteotti).

CAR RENTAL

➤ LOCAL AGENCIES: **Avis** (✉ Via Sonnino 87, Cagliari, ☎ 070/668128; ✉ Aeroporto di Elmas, Cagliari, ☎ 070/240081; ✉ Via Genova 67, Olbia, ☎ 0789/22420; ✉ Aeroporto Costa Smeralda, Olbia, ☎ 0789/69540; ✉ Via Mazzini 2, Sassari, ☎ 079/235547, WEB www.avis.com). **Hertz** (✉ Aeroporto di Fertilia, Alghero, ☎ 079/935054; ✉ Piazza Matteotti 8, Cagliari, ☎ 070/651078; ✉ Aeroporto di Elmas, Cagliari, ☎ 070/240037; ✉ Aeroporto Costa Smeralda, Olbia, ☎ 0789/66024, WEB www.hertz.com). **Maggiore** (✉ Via Sassari 87, Alghero, ☎ 079/979375; ✉ Aeroporto di Fertilia, Alghero, ☎ 079/935045; ✉ Viale Monastir 116, Cagliari, ☎ 070/273692; ✉ Aeroporto di Elmas, Cagliari, ☎ 070/240069; ✉ Via D'Annunzio, Olbia, ☎ 0789/22131; ✉ Aeroporto Costa Smeralda, Olbia, ☎ 0789/69457; ✉ Piazza Santa Maria 6, Sassari, ☎ 079/235507, WEB www.maggiore.it).

CAR TRAVEL

The best way to get around Sardinia is to drive. Cars may be taken on board most of the ferry lines connecting Sardinia with the mainland. The north–south S131 (Strada Carlo Felice) connects Cagliari, Oristano, Sassari, and Porto Torres. The S131 Dir and S129 connect the Carlo Felice Highway with Nuoro and the Barbagia. The S597 connects Sassari and Olbia.

EMERGENCY SERVICES

If you have trouble on the road, contact the Polizia Stadale (Road Police) by phone. (A cell phone is invaluable in such situations.)
➤ CONTACTS: **Polizia Stadale** (☎ 116).

ROAD CONDITIONS

The roads are generally in good condition, but bear in mind that such roadside conveniences as gas stations and refreshment stands are infrequent on some routes, especially in the east. Try to avoid driving at night, when mountain roads are particularly hazardous and slow.

RULES OF THE ROAD

In general, Sardinia is a much calmer place to negotiate than elsewhere in southern Italy, whether you're driving or trying to cross the road. Cagliari and Sassari can get busy, but elsewhere there's normally less traffic and people are more patient.

EMERGENCIES

Late-night pharmacies are open on a rotating basis; information on current schedules is pinned up on any pharmacy door or can be obtained by calling 192.
➤ CONTACTS: **Ambulance** (✉ Cagliari, ☎ 070/4092901). **Hospital** (Ospedale Civile San Michele, ✉ Via Peretti, Cagliari, ☎ 070/543266). **Police** (☎ 112 or 113).

LANGUAGE

Although the Sard dialect is incomprehensible to mainland Italians, let alone to foreigners, most locals can switch from dialect to perfect standard Italian with ease. In Alghero, the Catalan dialect is practically extinct nowadays, though the tourist office can tell you where you can attend Catalan-language church services if you're interested. In the main tourist areas, most people you deal with will have a smattering of English.

MAIL AND SHIPPING

OVERNIGHT SERVICES

The local courier used by Federal Express is SDA, inFangario, near Cagliari. The local courier used by UPS is La Freccia, in Cagliari. To call for pickups or information from either Federal Express or UPS, use their national service numbers.
➤ MAJOR SERVICES: **Federal Express** (☎ 800/123800). **La Freccia** (✉ Viale Monastir, Kilometro 7,382, Cagliari, ☎ 070/23622310). **SDA** (✉ Viale Elmas, Kilometro 1.5, Fangario). **UPS** (☎ 02/25088001).
➤ POST OFFICES: **Cagliari** (✉ Piazza del Carmine, ☎ 070/663356). **Sassari** (✉ Via Brigata Sassari, ☎ 079/231609).

TOURS

Guided tours are a good introduction to Sardinia. Travel from the Italian mainland is included, as are travel and accommodations on Sardinia. They must be booked through a travel agent, such as Viaggi Orru. Appian Line has a fly-drive package on the Costa Smeralda; transportation is by air, the rental car is picked up at the airport at Olbia.

Accommodations are in good but not outlandishly expensive hotels on this famous coastline for the rich.

➤ FEES AND SCHEDULES: **Viaggi Orru** (✉ Via Roma 95, ☎ 070/659858).

BUS TOURS

Chiariva offers two group tours of Sardinia by bus with guide. A nine-day tour leaves from Genoa; an eight-day tour departs from Rome. Both operate April–September. Aviatour has a similar eight-day tour leaving from either Milan or Rome. The tour also runs from April to September only. All bus tours must be booked through a travel agent.

HORSEBACK RIDING TOURS

The Associazione Nazionale di Turismo Equestre can provide information on renting mounts and joining riding parties with itineraries along the coast or into the heart of the island. The Centro Vacanze Ala Birdi organizes riding vacations.

➤ FEES AND SCHEDULES: **Associazione Nazionale di Turismo Equestre** (✉ Via Carso 35/a, Sassari, ☎ 079/299889). **Centro Vacanze Ala Birdi** (✉ Arborea, near Oristano, ☎ 0783/801083, WEB www.alabirdi-arborea.it).

TRAIN TRAVEL

The Stazione Centrale in Cagliari is next to the bus station on Piazza Matteotti. There are fairly good connections between Olbia, Cagliari, Sassari, and Oristano. You can reach Nuoro via Macomer; Alghero is reached via Sassari. Service on the few other local lines is infrequent and slow. The fastest train between Olbia and Cagliari takes more than four hours. Local trains connect Golfo Aranci, the Ferrovie dello Stato (FS) port for the train ferry, with Olbia (20 minutes) and Sassari with Alghero (35 minutes).

➤ TRAIN INFORMATION: **FS** (☎ 8848/888088, WEB www.fs-on-line.com).

TRAVEL AGENCIES

➤ LOCAL AGENT REFERRALS: **Cagliari** (Viaggi Orru, ✉ Via Roma 95, ☎ 070/659858).

VISITOR INFORMATION

➤ TOURIST INFORMATION: **Alghero** (✉ Piazza Porta Terra 9, 07041, ☎ 079/979054). **Cagliari EPT, regional information** (✉ Piazza Deffenu 9, 09100, ☎ 070/654811; 800/013153 toll free; ✉ Aeroporto di Elmas, ☎ 070/240200). **Cagliari ESIT, Sardinia-wide information** (✉ Via Mameli 97, 09124, ☎ 070/60231, WEB www.esit.it). **Golfo Aranci** (✉ City Hall, 07026, ☎ 0789/21672 June–Aug. only). **Nuoro** (✉ Piazza Italia 19, 08100, ☎ 0784/30083). **Olbia** (✉ Via Catello Piro, 07026, ☎ 0789/21453; ✉ Aeroporto Costa Smeralda, ☎ 0789/21453). **Oristano** (✉ Via Cagliari 278, 09170, ☎ 0783/74191). **Sassari** (✉ Viale Umberto 72, 07100, ☎ 079/231331; ✉ Viale Caprera 36, 07100, ☎ 079/299544).

17 BACKGROUND AND ESSENTIALS

Portraits of Italy

Books and Videos

Chronology

Map of Italy

Smart Travel Tips A to Z

Italian Vocabulary

THE PALMS OF SICILY

Excerpted from Bella Tuscany: The Sweet Life in Italy (1999), *by Frances Mayes*

I'm not off the plane in Palermo five minutes before I have an arancino in my hand, ready to taste the signature dish of Sicily. Ed has gone to find the rental car office and I head to the bar right in the center of the airport. There they are, a line of the deep-fried risotto balls formed into the size and shape of oranges. "What's inside?" I ask.

A man with those amazing black, Sicilian deep-as-wells eyes points to the round ones. "Ragà, signora. And the oval ones—besciamella e prosciutto." His eyes fascinate me as much as the arancini. All through the airport I've seen the same Byzantine, hidden, historical eyes. At the bar, savoring the crisp creamy texture of the rice, I'm watching a parade of these intensely Italian-looking Italians. Women with gobs of dark curls cascading and flowing, slender men who seem to glide instead of walk. Tiny girls with miniature gobs of the same dark curls, and old men formed by stoop labor, carrying their hats in their hands. Crowds surge to meet planes coming in from Rome, which is only an hour away. They're all waving and shouting greetings to deplaning Sicilians who probably have been gone a few days, judging from their carry-on bags. Ed comes back, bearing keys. He, too, polishes off an arancino and orders an espresso. He looks startled when he sees how small it is, barely a spoonful, with rich crema. One taste and he's transported.

The waiter sees his surprise. He's about 5'3". He looks up at Ed, almost a foot taller. "The farther south you go, signore, the smaller and the stronger."

Ed laughs, "È fantastico." He wheels our bag out to the green Fiat and zooms out of the garage.

Along the coastal road to Palermo, we glimpse the sea and cubical north African-style houses in a rocky landscape. The instant we enter Palermo, we're in wild traffic, careening traffic, traffic moving too fast for us to locate where we are going. Lanes disappear, avenue names keep changing, we turn and turn in mazes of one-way streets. "That barista should have said 'smaller, stronger, and faster,'" Ed shouts. At a light, he rolls down the window and calls desperately to a man revving his motorcycle in anticipation of the green, "Per favore, which way to Hotel Villa Igiea?"

"Follow me," he shouts back and he's off, spiraling among cars and glancing back now and then to see if we're behind him. Somehow we are. Ed seems to be in his wake, just going. At highway speeds on city streets, cars are neck-and-neck. On all four sides, we are two inches from other bite-sized cars. If someone braked, we'd be in a hundred-car pile-up. But no one brakes. At an intersection, the motorcyclist points to the left then waves. He swerves right so hard his ear almost touches the ground. We're tossed into a roundabout, spun, and emptied suddenly onto a quiet street. And there's the hotel. We creep into the parking lot and stop.

"Let's don't get in this car again until we leave. That was absolutely the worst."

"Suits me," Ed agrees. He's still gripping the wheel. "Let's take taxis. Everywhere. This is more like the running of the bulls than driving." We grab our bag, lock the Fiat, and don't look at the car again until we check out.

The taxi arrives quickly and we launch into the bumper-car traffic. Yes, it's always like this, the driver tells us. No, there aren't many accidents. Why?

He shrugs, everybody is used to it. We sit back, and he's right, we begin to feel the double-time rhythm of driving here. Drivers look alert, as though engaging in a contact sport. He drops us in the center near an esplanade closed to traffic. Out of the street's chaos, we're greeted by the scent of flowers. Vendors are selling freesias in all the Easter colors, purple, yellow, and white. Instead of the puny bouquets I buy at home, these are sold in armfuls, wrapped in a ruff of brazen pink foil and trailing ribbons.

Not wanting to take time for lunch, we sample sfincione, pizza with big bread crumbs on top, then keep going—palms, outdoor tables filled with people, small shops of luxurious bags and shoes, waiters with trays aloft carrying pastries and espresso.

Pastries! Every pasticceria displays an astonishing variety. We're used to drier Tuscan pastries; these are mounded with cream. A woman arranges her shop window with realistic marzipan pineapples, bananas, prickly pears, lemons, cherries, and, for the Easter season, lambs complete with curls. Inside, her cases display almond cakes, wild strawberry tarts, biscotti, and, of course, cannoli, but in all sizes, from thumb-sized to a giant as large as a leg of lamb. Two bakers pause in the kitchen doorway and all the customers step back as they gingerly balance and step. They bring out a three-foot tree made from small cannoli, a stiff pyramid like a French croquembouche at Christmas. Sfince, rice fritters filled with ricotta, cinnamon, candied oranges or strawberries, honor San Giuseppe, whose onomastico, name day, is March 19, when Italians also celebrate Father's Day.

The freezers glow with sorbetti—pistachio, lemon, watermelon, cinnamon, jasmine, almond, as well as the usual fruits. Most children seem to prefer gelato, not in a cup or cone, but stuffed inside a brioche. Just looking at the almond cake is almost enough satisfaction, but we instead split one of the crisp cannoli lined with chocolate and heavenly, creamy ricotta. No harm done; we're planning to walk for the rest of the afternoon.

On the first day in a new place, it's good to wander, absorb colors, textures, and scents, see who lives here, and find the rhythm of the day. We'll crank into tourist mode later, making sure we don't miss the great sights. Dazed by actually coming to Palermo, by the flight, the espresso, and the day, we just take the appealing street, turning back if it begins to look dicey. Palms are everywhere. I wish I could take one back to Bramasole to replace the one December's freeze probably killed. Not only do I love palms because they mean tropical air, I love the image Wallace Stevens made: "the palm at the end of the mind." To imagine the end of the mind and to see not a blank wall or a roadblock or an abyss but a tall swaying palm seems felicitous to me.

We come upon a botanical park, dusty and empty except for cacti, carob, mulberry, agave, and shrubs with primitive, broad leaves. The palm looks native but was brought by Arabs in the ninth century, along with their fountains, spices, arabesques, ice cream, mosaics, and domes. Palms and domes—gold, pomegranate, aqua, verdigris—characterize Palermo. How bold to color the five domes of San Giovanni degli Eremiti a burnt red. Inside, aromatic citrus blossoms and jasmine suffuse a cloister garden, a secretive respite from the tortured road outside.

On the map, we see that the Palazzo dei Normanni is nearby and decide to go in the famous Cappella Palatina today. The subjects of the mosaics, the guidebook says, seem to have been chosen with reference to the Holy Spirit and the theology of light. I'm intrigued, since these two concepts seem identical in my mind.

Originally built by those busy Arabs in the ninth century, the palace was expanded by the Normans in the twelfth century and established as the residence for their kings. Later residents and royalty left their bits and pieces, and today the styles have so long overlapped that the architecture simply looks like itself. Byzantine Greeks began the mosaic decoration in the twelfth century. Tessera by tessera, it must have taken them forever; every Bible story I ever heard glitters around this room. The floors, too, are mosaic or inlaid marble in designs like Oriental rugs.

The Holy Spirit and theology of light are only a layer. A lot is going on. It's like Palermo—each square inch occupied with life. I love the word "tesserae." It seems to shower silver and gold on its own. There's the whole Adam and Eve saga, the flood, there's Jacob wrestling with the angel, and in the dome and apse, Christ. In the dome he's surrounded by foreshortened angels, each in intricate clothes. Christ offers a blessing in the apse. In both mosaics, he has long, long fingers. Looking through my opera glasses, I focus for a long time on his right hand, just this one small moment in the entire chapel—the hand held up, the thumb holding down the next-to-last finger, the other three straight, all formed with delicacy and subtle coloration. Late afternoon sun has a weak hold on the walls but still the gold around him sings with burnished amber light.

The rest of the Palazzo is closed. Walking back toward the center of Palermo, we pass rubble-filled lots still unrestored since World War II bombings. We look in open storefronts where hideous junk is sold and step off crowded sidewalks with frystations selling chickpea fritters. People are out gathering last minute food for dinner. About their business, the people look contained, silent, often weary. When they meet an acquaintance their faces break into vibrant expression. In the taxi back to the hotel, we hardly notice the near-death encounters.

The first two restaurants Ed selects for dinner are nixed by the hotel desk clerk. Dangerous areas, he tells us, making the motion of someone slicing a throat. He takes a ballpoint and scribbles out whole areas of our map. "What about this one?" Ed asks, pointing in our Italian restaurant

guide to the highly regarded, unpronounceable N'grasciata. "And what does that mean?"

"In local dialect that means 'dirty' but don't be alarmed, just a way of speaking."

Speaking of what? I think. Dirty means dirty. "Your highest recommendation?"

"Sì, authentic. They have their own fishing boat. You won't see tourists there. I will call and they will expect you."

We're dropped off at a plain place which is even plainer inside. No tablecloths, a TV somewhere, no decor, no menu, harsh lighting and the buzz of bugs hitting the zapper. The waiter starts bringing out the food. I'm crazy about the panelli, chickpea fritters, and the platter of fried artichokes. Then comes pasta with pomarola, that intense, decocted tomato sauce, and baby octopus. I'm not so sure about this dish. I chew for a long time. The platter comes round again and Ed has more. We're offered another pasta, this one bucatini with sardines, currants, and fennel. The next dish is a grilled orata, which my dictionary translates as "gilthead," surrounded by fried frutta di mare—just various fish. I'm slowing down. I like a little bit of fish, not a lot. Ed loves anything that comes from the sea and is so obviously relishing the food that the waiter starts to hover, commenting on each morsel. He's pouring wine to the brim of the glass. His dolorous eyes look like Jesus' in the mosaic dome. His long fingers have tufts of black curly hair on each digit, and a matt of hair escapes the collar of his shirt. He has the long, four-inch-wide face I associate with newspaper photos of hijackers.

I revive briefly for the spicy melanzane—here's a touch of the Arabic, eggplant with cinnamon and pine nuts—but balk at the appearance of the stuffed squid (all those suction cups on the arms) and the sea bream sausage. Is he bringing us everything in the kitchen? Next comes a plate of fried potatoes. "Signora," our waiter says. "Signora." He can't believe that I have stopped eating. He pulls up a chair and sits down. "You must."

I smile and shake my head. Impossible. He rolls those dolorous eyes to heaven. "Ho paura," I'm afraid, I try to joke, pointing at the squid. He takes me literally and eats a bite himself to prove there's no cause for alarm. Still, I shake my head no. He takes my fork, gently grabs a handful of my hair and starts to feed me. I am so astonished I open my mouth and eat. I really hate the texture, like tenderized erasers.

As an afterthought, he brings out involtini, veal rolled around a layer of herbs and cheese, but even Ed has stopped by now. He's thanking the waiter. "The best fish in Palermo," he tells him.

"How do you know?" I ask him on the way out. The waiter bares his teeth in a big grin. No, he looks more like a wolf than Jesus.

"It had to be. That was a down-home place."

We're out early. In the Vucciria quarter, the market is stupendous. I've been to markets in France, Spain, Peru, San Francisco, all over Italy. This is the market. For the senses, ecstasy and assault. Because Palm Sunday is this weekend, perhaps it is more of an assault than usual. Lines of lambs, gutted and dripping, eyeballs bulging, hang by their feet. Their little hooves and tails look so sad. Their little guts look so horrifying. The rainbows of shining fish on ice, the mounds of shrimp still wiggling their antennae, painted carts of lemons, jewel-colored candied fruits, bins of olives, nuts, seeds—everything is presided over by dealers who shout, sing, cajole, joke, curse, barter, badger. They're loud and raucous. Could it be true, as I've read, that the Mafia runs the heroin trade out of here? A vendor holds out a basket of eels that look like live sterling silver. He gyrates his hips to emphasize their movement. This feels more like a carnival than the more decorous Tuscan markets we're used to. I wish for a kitchen so I could gather some of the lustrous eggplants and clumps of field greens. My stomach is growling so loud it sounds like a tiny horse neighing. Cooks here are in paradise. I'll never eat lamb again.

Ed refuses to go to the Catacombe dei Cappuccini, where 8,000 desiccated corpses are on exhibit. I have already bought a postcard of a red-haired girl under glass for decades, her delicate nostrils still stuffed with cotton, a ribbon in her hair. We have visited the same sort of place in Guanajuato, Mexico. I was fascinated; he was revolted. We decide on the Museo Archeologico, and we don't come out until it closes. I find this one of the best museums I've ever visited—so much of what interests me is gathered in this old convent. Phoenician anchors and amphoras dredged from the sea lie around the courtyard. Mysterious stelae painted with portraits were found on ancient grave sites in Marsala. Etruscan treasures, some with traces of paint, from the tombs at Chiusi, near us in Tuscany, somehow have ended up in Sicily. Here we get to see the sixth- and fifth-century BC metopes (panels of the temple frieze) removed from the Greek site at Selinunte, one of the most important Greek sites on the island. We find Demeter, the Cretan bull; Perseus, Hercules, and Athena star in various triumphs. Hera marries Zeus, and Actaeon becomes a stag. Seeing the familiar mythic players as they actually were on temples brings the legends closer to my imagination. These images come from the time when they were real to people, not just characters from the history of myth—an astounding telescoping of distance. The enormous scale, too, prepares us for the dimensions of the ruins we'll see.

We can't look at all 12,000 of the votive figures also excavated at Selinunte but we look until we can't look anymore. That only leaves rooms and rooms of Roman sculpture, Greek vases, and more and more. We meander through, stopped by painted fragments from Pompeii, a fantastic third century BC Bronze ram, and a blur of mosaic pavements. Then, out.

Onto the plain sidewalk, dazed and dazzled by what we've seen.

As the freesias begin to wilt in our room, we decide to start our tour of the island tomorrow morning. We have a glass of blood orange juice on our balcony. All we can hear is the rattle of palms below us in the breeze and the jingle of rigging on the sailboats in the bay. "Do you want to come back?" I ask.

"Yes. We haven't seen whole areas of Palermo."

"It's hard to get a sense of the place. So layered, so crude, so complex—a daunting city."

"My core impression is of a chaos everyone here has learned how to survive."

But I suddenly remember a story a woman I met in Milwaukee told me about someone she knew. "This Midwestern soldier in World War II was on a ship which was bombed by retreating Germans in the harbor of Palermo," I tell Ed. "He survived even though almost everyone else was killed. He swam to shore and was stranded here. I think the Germans were retreating by then. One night he went to the opera—he'd never been before. At the end, he was so moved by the music he started to cry. All the horrors caught up with him. He just stood there during the applause and afterwards, openly crying. The audience started to file out. A man looked at him, paused, and touched him on the head, as though he were bestowing a benediction. As all the people passed him, each one stopped and touched him on the head."

"That's one of the best things I've ever heard. So that's Palermo."

Each succeeding conqueror of Sicily—Greeks, Carthaginians, Romans, Arabs, Normans, and all the rest—must have brought pocketfuls of wildflower seeds. The countryside in primavera is solidly in flower, rivers of yellow, purple cascading around rocks, roadsides lined with tiny blue-eyed blooms, and almond orchards whose long grasses are overtaken by white daisies. We made an easy exit, considering. We were only lost half an hour. Even though Ed was intimidated by traffic in Palermo, once we were out on the open road, I noticed his new skills, learned from the back seat of the taxis. He's relaxing into the concept that lanes do not exist much; the road is an open field for getting where you're going. The white line is the center of an imaginary lane to be used as needed.

Driving along the coast and meandering inland, the Mar Tirreno seven shades of blue out one window, and rampantly flowering hills out the other, it is easy to see why all those conquering hoards wanted this island. The landscape is everywhere various or dramatic. Anytime the perfume of orange and lemon groves wafts in the window, the human body has to feel suffused with a languorous well-being.

Soon we come to the turn-off for Segesta, first of the many Greek temples we hope to see in Sicily—the number rivals Greece itself. The Doric temple rises, just off the highway, where it has loomed on the hillside since the fifth century BC, which is close to forever. Along the climbing path, we see gigantic fennel growing, ten feet, even more. I always wondered how Prometheus took fire back to the Greeks in a fennel stalk. In these you could stash quite a few coals. In the process, maybe he invented grilled fennel.

The guidebook says of Segesta: "It is peripteral and hexastyle with 36 unfluted columns (9 m high, 2 m wide at base) on a stylobate 58 m by 23 m. The high entablature and the pediments are intact. The bosses used for maneuvering the blocks of the stylobate into position remain. Refinements include the curvature of the entablature and the abaci." Well, yes, but it's beautiful.

So is the equally ancient theater a short hike away. Greece was the first country I ever wanted to see. My longing was produced by a total immersion in Lord Byron when I was a senior in high school. In college, my friend Rena and I took a course in

Greek drama. We wrote for brochures from Greek freighters and decided to drop out and see the world. We wanted to book passage on Hellenic Destiny, until our parents said absolutely not. I've never yet been to Greece. A few years ago I saw the magnificent temples at Paestum in the south of Italy and the longing was reawakened. "The mountains look on Marathon / and Marathon looks on the sea / and musing there an hour alone, / I dreamed that Greece might still be free." Something like that—it seems to scan into iambic tetrameter.

Like Paestum, Segesta is stripped down to pure silence, its skeletal purity etched against the sky. No one is here, though there were several people in the gift shop. We're alone with history and swallows swooping from their nests.

I'm glad I don't have to take a test on Agrigento. For an American used to a comparatively straightforward history, all the Italian past seems hopelessly convoluted. The saga of the Greek ruins multiplies this complexity. Agrigento, since its Greek founding in the sixth century BC has been tossed among Carthaginians, Romans, Swabians, Arabians, Bourbons and Spaniards. Subjected to a name change during Mussolini's zeal to Italianize all things, the old name Akragas became Agrigento. I've seen the same zeal on the plaque outside where John Keats lived in Rome, cut off from his love and dying from tuberculosis. He's called Giovanni Keats, which somehow makes him seem more vulnerable than ever.

Akragas/Agrigento was Luigi Pirandello's birthplace. Travelling in Sicily casts his plays and stories, with their quirky sense of reality, in quite a natural light. The coexistence of the Greek ruins, the contemporary ruins, the tentacles of the Mafia, and the mundane day-to-day would skew my sense of time and place, too. The sun, Pirandello wrote, can break stones. Even in March, we feel the driving force on our heads as we walk in the Valley of the Temples.

All over a valley of almond trees and wildflowers stand a mind-boggling array of remains from an ancient town, from temples to sewer pipes. You could stay for days and not see everything. Unlike other sites, this one is quite populated with visitors. The Temple of Concordia is the best-preserved temple we've seen. Patch up the roof and the populace could commune with Castor and Pollux, to whom it probably was dedicated.

Five days ago I knew almost nothing about these ruins. Now the ancient dust covers my feet through my sandals; I have seen the unlikely survival of these buildings through rolls and rolls of time. These temples, men selling woven palm fronds for Palm Sunday, schoolchildren hiding among the columns, awed travellers like us with dripping gelato—all under the intense Sicilian sky. I'm thrilled. Just as I think that, Ed says, "This is a thrill of a lifetime."

Meandering, we stop at a cypress-guarded cemetery near Modica. Extravagant tombs are elaborately carved miniature houses laid along miniature streets. Here's the exuberance of Modica's art of the Baroque in microcosm. Through the grates or gates, the little chapels open to linen-draped altars with framed portraits of the dead and potted plants or vases of flowers. At thresholds, a few cats sun on the warmed marble. A woman is scrubbing, as she would her own stoop. With a corner of her apron, she polishes the round photo of a World War I soldier. A young girl weeds the hump of earth over a recent grave in the plain old ground. These dead cool off slowly; someone still tends flowers on plots where the inhabitants have lain for fifty years.

Cortona's cemetery, too, reflects the town, although not as grandly. A walled city of the dead situated just below the live city, it glows at night from the votive lights on each grave. Looking down from the Piazza del Duomo, it's hard not to imagine the dead up and about, visiting each other as their relatives still do right up the hill. The dead here probably would want more elaborate theatrical entertainments.

Next on our route, Avola retains some charm. One-room-wide Baroque houses line the streets. Could we take home at least a dozen of the gorgeous children in their white smocks? On the corners men with hand-held scales scoop cockles from a mound on the sidewalk. Open trucks selling vegetables attract crowds of women with baskets. We keep turning down tiny roads to the sea. We can't find the beaches we expect—the unspoiled littoral dream of the island's limpid waters—only bleak beach towns, closed and depressing out of season.

It's only in Siracusa that I finally fall in love. In my Greek phase in college, I took Greek and Roman History, Greek and Roman Drama, Greek Etymology. At that point, my grandfather who was sending me to college, drew a line. "I am not paying for you to stick your head in the clouds. You should get a certificate for teaching so you have something to fall back on." The message being, if your husband—whom you have gone to college to acquire, and no Yankees, please—dies or runs off. Meanwhile, I was loving Aeschylus, the severe consequences of passion, pure-as-milk marble sculptures, the explorative spirit of the Greeks. Siracusa, therefore, is tremendously exciting to visit. Mighty Siracusa, ancient of ancients. Second to Athens in the classical world. We opt for a super-luxurious hotel on the connecting island of Ortigia, with a room surrounded by views of the water. We're suddenly not tired exactly, but saturated. We spend the afternoon in the huge bed, order coffee sent up, pull back the curtains and watch the fishing boats nosing—isn't that a Greek blue—into the harbor.

After siesta, we find Ortigia in high gear for Easter. Bars display chocolate eggs two feet tall, wrapped in purple cellophane and ribbons. Some are open on one side to reveal a marzipan Christ on the cross. Others have a surprise inside. I'd love to buy marzipan doves, lambs in baskets, chocolate hens. The lambs are like stuffed animals, large, decorated from nose to tail with fanciful marzipan curls. At the Antica Dolceria, they've gone into marzipan frenzy: Noah's ark complete with animals, the Greek temples, olives, pencils. Marzipan—called pasta reale—we realize is a serious folk art form. For me, three bites will suffice; maybe you have to have been born in Sicily to be able to eat more.

Ortigia is fantastic. The vague, intuitive sense of oppression I've felt in Sicily entirely lifts. Is the Mafia not in control here? People seem more lighthearted, playful, and swaggering. They look you in the eye, as people do in the rest of Italy. In the late afternoon, we walk all over the small island. It has its own Greek ruins just lying in a grassy plot at an intersection. An inscription carved into steps identifies the site as a temple to Apollo. Dense ficus trees along a walkway bordering the water are home to thousands of birds singing their evening doxology. Views across the water, Baroque iron balconies, Venetian Gothic windows, boarded up palazzi, and intricate medieval streets—layers and layers of architecture and time. Suddenly the streets intersect and widen at the Piazza del Duomo. The Baroque facade and entrance of the church in no way prepares you for the stunning surprise inside. Along one wall, the building incorporates a row of twelve majestic columns from the fifth-century BC Tempio di Atene. At evening, spikes of sunlight fall across the piazza, lighting the faces of those having an aperitivo at outdoor tables. Ordinary people, with the sun, like the sheen of gold mosaics, transforming their faces.

We're ready to put in a full day on foot. In the museum on Ortigia, Caravaggio's painting of the burial of Santa Lucia, a local martyr in 304, who cut out her own eyes when a suitor admired them, occasioned a lecture from the guard worthy of any docent. And where are we from? Ah, he has a cousin in California; we should meet him when we return. Ed loves Annunciation paintings and the peeling one by da Messina enthralls him. Small local museums are my favorite kind. They stay close to the source, usually, and deepen a tourist-level connection with a place.

We walk across the bridge and through a park then through a honeycomb of streets. The Museo Archeologico in Siracusa proper is world class. Intelligently arranged and exhibited, the art and craft of succeeding waves of life in this area are displayed. Beginning with prehistory we trace the history through one stunning room after another. Artifacts, statues, lion faces from the temple in ruins in Ortigia, Greek ex-votos, and an amazing bronze horse—oh, so much.

The amphitheater in Siracusa—what fabulous siting. The stone cup of the hill was chopped out into natural seating, a 300-degree arrangement focusing on a stage. Corridors were carved out for gladiators to enter and exit. In summer, the Greek plays are still performed here. What fun it would be to act in one. The ruins we've seen are the major ones; hundred of other temples, foundations, baths, and unknown stones cover the island. This must be the ideal time to see them because hardly anyone is around. The solitude of these places sharpens the experience of happening upon them, the sense of discovery that for me lies at the heart of travel.

Frances Mayes is also the author of the best-selling Under the Tuscan Sun: At Home in Italy (1996) *and* In Tuscany (2000), *with photographs by Bob Krist. Her books are available from Broadway Books and in audio from Bantam, Doubleday, Dell.*

THE ARTLESS ART OF ITALIAN COOKING

You are staying with friends in their villa in a windswept olive orchard above Florence. After a day in town—a morning at the Palazzo Pitti, afternoon in the Brancacci Chapel—you have returned to rest. In the garden, you find your hostess lifting heavy tomatoes into a basket, the acrid smell of their skins wafting up in the gentle September heat. You pick basil and tug figs from a tree that warms its back against the 14th-century kitchen wall. Inside, you watch while your hostess rinses the greens in the quarried stone sink. The tomatoes are still sun-warm when she scoops them, chopped, into a blender with the basil and a stream of olive oil; she pours the mixture into a faience bowl over steaming pasta. You eat at the kitchen table, pour wine from a crockery pitcher, and wipe your bowl with torn chunks of flour-flecked bread. Over the greens your hostess drizzles more olive oil and a bit of rock salt pinched from an open bowl. The figs melt in your mouth like chocolate. A scalding syrup of Arabic coffee streams from the *macchinetta,* and you're ready for a midnight survey of the olive groves.

Simple, earthy, at once wholesome and sensual, as sophisticated in its purity as the most complex cuisine, as inspired in its aesthetics as the art and architecture of its culture, Italian cooking strikes a chord that resonates today as it did in the Medici courts. Its enduring appeal can be traced to an ancient principle: respect for the essence of the thing itself—nothing more, nothing less. Like Michelangelo freeing the prisoners that dwelt within the stone—innate, organic—an Italian chef seems intuitively to seek out the crux of the thing he is about to cook and flatter it, subtly, with the purest of complements. To lay a translucent sheet of prosciutto—earthy, gamey, faintly redolent of brine—across the juicy pulchritude of a melon wedge is a stroke of insight into the nature of two ingredients as profound as the imaginings of Galileo.

Considering the pizzas, lasagnas, and red-drenched spaghetti that still pass for Italian food abroad (despite a wave of enlightenment that revived "northern" techniques in the 1980s), it's no surprise that visitors to Italy are often struck by the austerity of the true Italian dishes put before them. The pasta is only lightly accented, not drowning in an industrial ladle-full of strong, soupy sauce. And while there may have been a parade of vegetable *antipasti,* the salad itself bears no resemblance to the smorgasbord of Anglo-American salad bars—it's a simple mix of greens, a drizzle of oil, a spritz, perhaps, of red-wine vinegar. If you've just come from Germanic countries, you'll notice a lack of Maggi, the bottled brown "flavor enhancer" that singes the tongue with monosodium glutamate, on the table. If you've come from Belgium, you'll miss the sauceboat of Hollandaise. And if you've come from France, you may shrug dismissively at the isolated ingredients you're served, saying as other Frenchmen before you, "But this is not really a true *cuisine. . . .*"

Ah, but it is. Shunning the complexities of heavy French sauces and avoiding the elaborate farce, Italian cuisine—having unloaded the aspirations of *alta cucina* onto its northern neighbors when Catherine de' Medici moved (chefs and all) to Paris—stands alone, proud, purist, unaffected.

The Italians' pride comes in part from a confidence in their raw ingredients, an earthiness that informs the appreciation of every citizen-connoisseur, from the roughest peasant in workers' blue to the vintner in shoulder-tied cashmere: they are in touch with land and sea. In the country, your host can tell you the source of every ingredient on the table, from the neighbor's potted goose to the porcini gathered in the beech grove yesterday. In the city, the market replaces the country network, and aggressive shopping will trace the genealogy of every mushroom, every artichoke, every wooden scoop of olives. And in balconies overhanging the seashore, the squid floating in their rich, blue-black ink were bought from a fisherman on the beach at dawn.

The spectrum of Italian regional cooking is as broadly varied as Italy's terrain, and cuisine and countryside are intimately allied. Emerging into sunlight from the Great St. Bernard pass into the Valle d'Aosta, the Piedmont, the hills of Lombardy, you'll find wood-lined alpine trattorias offering rib-sticking gnocchi and air-dried beef, bubbling pots of *bagna cauda* (hot dipping sauce of olive oil and garlic), slabs of polenta, hearty walnut *torta* (cake). The pearl-spotted rice of Arborio, in the Po Valley, fuels an extraordinary array of risottos in Milan, where chefs shun olive oil in favor of the region's rich butter. Descend to Alba and savor the earthy perfume of truffles, the muscular Barolo wines. Cross over into Liguria and the cuisine changes as abruptly as the landscape: wild herbs, greens, and ground nuts flavor a panoply of sauces (consider the famous pesto, flavored with a "riviera" basil rarely found elsewhere), served as condiments to meat as often as over pasta. The succulent pink pork of a Parma ham, the golden butterfat in a Reggiano cheese were nurtured on the same fertile soil of Emilia-Romagna, both the culinary and agricultural heart of Italy, while the *bistecca* of Tuscany comes from Chianina beef, pampered on local prairie grass and slaughtered at a tender age. Head south for sun-plumped eggplant, and quasi-tropical artichokes—in Rome, fried in delicate batter; in Calabria, stuffed with meat and sharp Pecorino from its hillside sheep herds. The chickpeas in Sicilian dishes remind you you're nearly in North Africa. And, of course, on this slender leg of land you are never far from the sea, and the harvest of its *frutti di mare* graces nearly every region—but none more than the islands and tide-washed shores of the south.

Careening in your rental car down the western coast, clinging to the waterfront through sea-shanty villages that cantilever over the roaring surf, you feel a morning lag: your breakfast of *latte macchiato* and sugary *cornetto* has worn away. A real espresso would hit the spot; you hurtle down a web of switchbacks and pull into a seaside inn. You sip aromatic coffee and watch the waves. An hour passes in reverie—an aperitif, perhaps? Another hour over the Martini rosso, and you give in to the impulse, adjourning to the dining room. The odor of wood smoke drifts from the kitchen. A nutty risotto with a blush of tomato precedes a vast platter—austere, unembellished—of smoke-grilled fish, still sizzling, lightly brushed with oil, and glittering with rock salt. At the table beside yours, when the platter arrives, the woman rises and fillets the fish dexterously, serving her husband and sons.

There's a wholesomeness in the way Italians eat that is charming and contagious. If American foodies pick and kvetch and French gastronomes worship, Italians plunge into their meal with frank joy, earnest appreciation, and ebullient conversation. Yet they do not overindulge: portions are light, the drinking gentle, late suppers spartan with concern for digestion uppermost. It's as if the voice of Mamma still whispers moderation in their ear. They may, on the other hand, take disproportionate pleasure in watching guests eat, in surrounding them with congenial company, in pouncing on the bill. (This wholesome spirit even carries into the very bars: unlike the dark, louche atmosphere of Anglo lounges and pubs, in Italy you'll drink your *amaro* in a fluorescent-lit coffee bar without a whiff of sin in the air.)

Yet for all their straightforwardness, Italians are utterly at ease with their heritage, steeped from birth in the art and architecture that surrounds them. Without a hint of the grandiose, they'll construct a still life of figs and Bosc pears worthy of Caravaggio; a butcher will drape iridescent pheasants and quail, heads dangling, with the panache of a couturier. Consider the artless beauty of ruby-raw beef on an emerald bed of arugula, named for the preferred colors of the Venetian painter Carpaccio; pure white porcelain on damask; a mosaic of olives and pimientos in blown glass; a flash of folkloric pottery on a polished plank of oak.

In fact, it must be said: a large part of the pleasure of Italian dining is dining in Italy. We have all eaten in Italian restaurants elsewhere. The food can be superb, the ingredients authentic, the pottery and linens imported by hand. Yet who can conjure the blood-red ocher crumbling to gold on a Roman wall, the indigo and pastel hues of fishing boats rocking in a marina, the snow flurry of sugar papers on a café floor? These impart the essence that—as much as the basil on your *bruschetta*—flavors your Italian dining experience.

Inside the great walls of Lucca, you are lunching—slowly, copiously, and at length—in the shade of a vaulted portico. Strips of roasted eggplant and pepper steeped in garlic and oil; tortelloni stuffed with squab in a pool of butter and sage; roasted veal laced with green peppercorns; blackberries in thick cream. The bottle of Brunello di Montalcino, alas, is drained. It has been a perfect morning, walking the ramparts, and you have found the perfect restaurant: a Raphaelesque perspective of arcades and archways, pillars, porches, and loges spreads before you. The shadows and lines are strong in the afternoon sun; you admire from your seat in the cross breeze. It's only slowly that you realize that this Merchant/Ivory moment has a sound track, so organic to the scene you hadn't noticed—but now you feel goose bumps rising on your neck. It is Puccini: a young woman is singing, beautifully, from a groined arcade across the square, accompanied by a portable tape player.

". . . Ma quando vien lo sgelo . . . il primo sole è mio . . ."

Your coffee goes cold, untouched until the song, the moment, are over—and, in all its multifaceted magnificence, your Italian meal as well.

–Nancy Coons

THE PASSIONATE EYE: ITALIAN ART THROUGH THE AGES

Italian art flows as naturally as its wine, its sunshine, and its amore, and it has been springing from the Italian spirit for nearly as long. Perhaps nowhere else in the world has such a vital creative impulse flourished so bountifully within the noble sweep of the classical tradition. Perhaps no other country's cultural life has been so inextricably interwoven with its history.

And yet, Italy lives comfortably in the midst of all her accumulated treasures. She accepts them casually and affectionately, as she does her children and her flowers. True, some of her precious store has been gathered into world-famous museums, but Italians know best and love most intimately the art that surrounds their daily activity. They go to church among thousand-year-old mosaics, buy their groceries in a shop open since the time of Columbus, picnic on the steps of a temple that was old when Christ was born, and attend the opera in the same theaters where Rossini and Verdi saw their works premiered. Italy wears the raiment of her heritage with a light and touching grace. She must: it is the very fabric of her life. For travelers from other countries, however, Italian art remains unique, extraordinary, worthy of worship. Here we offer a short history, focusing on Italy's greatest artistic achievement, the Renaissance—often called the nursery of Western art. The discoveries of 14th- and 15th-century Italian artists making it possible to render a realistic image of a person or an object determined the course of Western art right up until the late 19th century. Following the essay is a glossary of art and architectural terms that will prove useful in understanding the artistic treasures of Italy.

Art in the Middle Ages

The eastern half of the Roman Empire, based in Constantinople (Byzantium), was powerful long after the fall of Rome in AD 476: Italy remained influenced—and at times ruled—by the Byzantines. The artistic revolution began when artists started to rebel against the Byzantine ethic, which dictated that art be exclusively Christian and that its aim be to arouse a sensation of mystical awe and reverence in the onlooker. This ethic forbade frivolous pagan portraits, bacchanalian orgy scenes, or delicate landscapes with maidens gathering flowers, as painted and sculpted by the Romans. Instead, biblical stories were depicted in richly colored mosaics—rows of figures against a gold background. (You can see some of the finest examples of this art at Ravenna, once the Western capital of the Empire, on the Adriatic coast.) Even altarpieces, painted on wood, followed the same model—stiff figures surrounded by gold, with no attempt made at an illusion of reality.

In the 13th century, the era of St. Francis and of a new humanitarian approach to Christianity, artists in Tuscany began to portray real people in real settings. Cimabue was the first to feel his way in this direction, but it was Giotto who broke decisively with the Byzantine style. Even if his sense of perspective is nowhere near correct and his figures still had typically Byzantine slanting eyes, he painted palpably solid people who, presumably, experienced real emotions.

By the end of the 14th century, the International Gothic Style (which had arrived in Italy from France) had made further progress toward realism, but more with depictions of plants, animals, and clothes than of the human figure. And, as you can see from Gentile da Fabriano's *Adoration of the Magi,* housed in the Galleria degli Uffizi in Florence, it was mainly a decorative art, still very much like a Byzantine mosaic.

Italian architecture during the Middle Ages followed a number of different trends. In the south, the solid Norman Romanesque style was dominant; towns such as Siena and Pisa in central Italy had their own Romanesque style, more graceful than its northern European counterparts. Like northern Romanesque, it was dominated by simple geometric forms, but buildings were covered with decorative toylike patterns done in multicolored marble. In northern Italy, building was in a more solemn red brick.

In Tuscany, the region around Florence, the 13th century was a time of great political and economic growth, and there was a desire to celebrate the new wealth and power in the region's buildings. This is why such civic centers as the Palazzo Vecchio in Florence are so big and fortresslike. Florence's cathedral, the Duomo, was built on a colossal scale mainly in order to outdo the Pisans and the Sienese, Florence's rivals. All these Tuscan cathedrals are in the Italian version of Gothic, a style that originated in France and found its expression there in tall, soaring, light-and-airy verticality, intended to elevate the soul. The spiritual aspect of Gothic never really caught on in Italy, where the top priority for a church (as representative of a city) was to be grander and more imposing than the neighboring cities' churches.

Art in the Renaissance

The Renaissance, or "rebirth," did not evolve simply from a set of newfound artistic skills; the movement represented a revolution in attitudes whereby each individual was thought to play a specific role in the divine scheme of things. By fulfilling this role, it was believed the individual gained a new dignity. It was no coincidence that this revolution took place in Florence, which in the 15th century was an influential, wealthy, highly evolved city-state. Artists here had the leisure, prestige, and self-confidence to develop their talent and produce works that would reflect this new dignity and strength as well as their own prowess.

The sculptor Donatello, for example, wanted to astound, rather than please, the spectator with his defiant warts-and-all likenesses and their intense, heroic gazes. In painting, Masaccio's figures have a similarly assured air.

Art had changed gears in the early Renaissance: the Classical Age was now the model for a noble, moving, and realistic art. Artists studied ancient Roman ruins for what they could learn about proportion and balance. They evolved the new science of perspective and took it to its limits with sometimes bizarre results, as in Uccello's dizzily receding *Deluge* (in Florence's church Santa Maria Novella) or his carousel-like *Battle of San Romano* (in the Uffizi in Florence). One of the most frequently used perspective techniques was that of foreshortening, or making an object seem smaller and more contracted, to create the illusion of distance. From this technique emerged the *sotto in su* effect—literally, "from below upward," meaning that the action in the picture takes place above you, with figures, buildings, and landscapes correspondingly foreshortened. It's a clever visual trick that must have delighted visitors who walked into, for example, Mantegna's Camera degli Sposi in Mantua and saw what appeared to be people curiously looking down at them through a gap in the ceiling.

The concept of the universal man was epitomized by the artist who was at home with an array of disciplines, including the science of perspective, Greek, Latin, anatomy, sculpture, poetry, architecture, philosophy—even engineering, as in the case of Leonardo da Vinci, the universal man par excellence. Not surprisingly, there was a change in attitude toward artists: whereas previously they had been considered merely anonymous workmen trained to carry out commissions, now they were seen as giant personalities, immensely skillful and with highly individual styles.

The new skills and realistic effects of Florentine painting rapidly found a sympathetic response among Venetian painters. Gentile Bellini and Antonio Carpaccio, just two of the many whose work fills the Accademia, took to covering their canvases with crowd scenes, buildings, canals, processions, dogs, ships, parrots, and chimneys. These were generally narrative paintings, telling the story of a saint's life or simply depicting everyday scenes.

It was the emphasis on color, though, that made Venetian art Venetian, and it was the 15th-century masters of color, preeminently Giovanni Bellini and Giorgione, who began to use it no longer as decoration but as a means to create a particular atmosphere. How different the effect of Giorgione's *Tempest* (in the Accademia) would be with a sunny blue sky instead of the ominous grays and dark greens that fill the background! For the first time, the atmosphere, not the figures, became the central focus of painting.

In architecture the Gothic excesses of the 13th century were toned down in the 14th, while the 15th ushered in a completely new approach. The humanist ideal was expressed through classical Roman design. In Florence, Brunelleschi used Roman columns for the basilica of San Lorenzo; Roman-style rustication (massive exterior blocks) for the Pitti Palace; and Roman round arches—as opposed to pointed Gothic ones—for his Ospedale degli Innocenti (Foundling Hospital), which is generally considered the first truly classical building of the Renaissance. Leon Battista Alberti's treatise on ideal proportion was even more influential as a manifesto of the Renaissance movement. Suddenly, architects had become erudite scholars and architecture far more earnest.

High Renaissance and Mannerism

Florence in the late 15th century and Rome in the early 16th (following its sacking in 1527) underwent a trau-matic political and religious upheaval that naturally came to be reflected in art. Classical proportion and realism no longer seemed enough. The heroic style suddenly looked hollow and outdated. Tuscan artists such as Pontormo and Rosso Fiorentino found expression for their unease in discordant colors, elongated forms, tortured looks in staring eyes. Giambologna carved his *Hercules and the Centaur* (in Florence's Museo del Bargello) at the most agonizing moment of their battle, when Hercules bends the Centaur's back to the point where it is about to snap. This is Mannerism, a style in which optimism and self-confidence are gone. What remains is a self-conscious, stylized show of virtuosity, the effect of which is neither to please (like Gothic) nor to impress (like Renaissance art) but to disquiet. Even Bronzino's portraits are cold, unsmiling, and far removed from the relaxed mood of the Renaissance portrait. By the 1530s an artistic exodus from Florence had taken place; Michelangelo had left for Rome, and Florence's golden age was over.

Venice, meanwhile, was following its own path. Titian's painting was a more virtuoso version of Bellini's and Giorgione's poetic style, but Titian later shifted the emphasis back to figures, rather than atmosphere, as the central focus of his paintings. Titian's younger contemporaries in Venice—Veronese, Tintoretto, and Bassano—wanted to make names for themselves. They started working on huge canvases—which gave them more freedom of movement—playing all sorts of visual games: juggling with viewpoints and perspective and using dazzlingly bright colors. This visual trickery suggests a natural parallel with the self-conscious artifice of Florentine painting of the same period, but the exuberance of these Venetian painters, and the increasingly emotional quality of their work, remained significantly more vital than the arid and ever more sterile works of central Italy toward the end of the 16th century.

Mannerism found a fairly precise equivalent in architecture. In Florence the rebellious younger generation (Michelangelo, Ammanati, Vasari) used the same architectural vocabulary as the Renaissance architects but distorted it deliberately and bizarrely in a way that would have made Alberti's hair stand on end. Michelangelo's staircase at the Biblioteca Laurenziana in Florence, for example, spills down like a gush of stone water, filling almost the entire floor space of the vestibule. Likewise, the inside walls are treated as if they were facades, though with columns and niches disproportionately large for the size of the room.

Andrea del Palladio, whose theories and elegant palaces were to be immensely influential on architecture elsewhere in Europe and as far north as England, was one of the greatest architects of the period.

The 17th and 18th Centuries

In the second half of the 16th century, Italy was caught up in the Counter-Reformation. This movement was a reaction against the Protestant Reformation of the Christian church that was sweeping through Europe. The Counter-Reformation enlisted art as a weapon, an instrument for the diffusion of the Catholic faith. Artists were discouraged from expressing themselves as freely as they had been before and from creating anything that was not of a religious nature. But within this religious framework they were able to evolve a style that appealed to the senses.

The Baroque—an emotional and heroic style that lasted through most of the 17th century—was propaganda art, designed to overwhelm the masses through its visual illusion, dramatic lighting, strong colors, and violent movement. There was an element of seduction in this propaganda: the repressive religiosity of the Counter-Reformation went hand in hand with a barely disguised eroticism. The best-known example of this ambiguity is Bernini's sculpture of the *Ecstasy of Santa Teresa* in Rome, in which the saint sinks back in what could be a swoon of either pain or pleasure, while a smiling angel stands over her holding an arrow. Both the painting and architecture of this period make extensive use of sensuous curves.

The cradle of the Baroque was Rome, where Pietro da Cortona and Bernini channeled their genius into spectacular theatrical frescoes, sculptures, palaces, and churches. Rome had become the artistic center of Italy. Florence was politically and artistically dead by this time, and Venice was producing only hack imitations of Titian's and Tintoretto's paintings.

In the 18th century, Venice came back into its own and Rome was practically finished as an artistic center. Venetian artists adopted the soft, overripe version of Baroque—known as rococo—that had originated in France. Free from the spiritual ideals that motivated the Baroque style, rococo celebrated sensuousness (and sensuality) for its own sake. Although Venice was nearing the last stages of its political decline, there was still immense wealth in the city, mostly in the hands of families who wished to make the world know about it—and what better way than through vast, dazzling rococo canvases, reassuringly stylized and removed from reality? The revival began with Sebastiano Ricci and was expertly elaborated on by Tiepolo. But it could never have taken place had there not been a return to the city's great artistic traditions. Late-16th-century color technique and expertise were drawn on and fused with what had been learned from the Baroque to create the breathtaking, magical, decadent world of the Venetian Rococo.

This was the final flowering of Venetian painting. The death of Francesco Guardi in 1793, compounded by the fall of the Republic of Venice in 1797, marked the effective end of the city's artistic life. Neoclassicism found no champion here, except for the sculptor Canova, who, in any case, did his finest work after he left Venice.

Today, the great tradition of Italian art is widely diffused, perhaps diluted, but it is certainly too early to write its obituary. That has been done periodically over the past 20 centuries, inevitably to the chagrin of the mistaken commentator. In the midst of the burgeoning vitality, which charms and occasionally maddens the visitor, the arts are not long to be neglected. Italians live the tradition too deeply.

—Sheila Brownlee

ARTISTICALLY SPEAKING: A GLOSSARY

The eloquence of the world's greatest masterpieces can be deafening, and Italy's treasures—their message made manifest in marble, pigment, and precious metals—instill a spirit of awe. The privilege of enjoying this bounty of the ages can be greatly deepened and enhanced by a familiarity with the language and terms of art-speak. Here is a limited glossary for the interested layman. Many of these Italian words are now part of the basic art-history vocabulary.

Acanthus: Sculptural ornamentation from antiquity; it's based on the foliage of the acanthus plant.

Apse: A semicircular terminus found behind the altar in a church.

Atrium: The courtyard in front of the entrance to an ancient Roman villa or an early church.

Badia: Abbey.

Baldacchino: A canopy—often made of stone—above a church altar, supported by columns.

Baptistery: A separate structure or area in a church where rites of baptism are held.

Baroque: A 17th-century European art movement in which dramatic, elaborate ornamentation was used to stir viewers' emotions. The most famous Italian Baroque artists were Carracci and Bernini.

Basilica: A rectangular Roman public building divided into aisles by rows of columns. Many early churches were built on the basilican plan, but the term is also applied to some churches without specific reference to architecture.

Belvedere: Usually a lookout point for vistas; the word means "beautiful view."

Campanile: A bell tower of a church.

Capital: The crowning section of a column, usually decorated with Doric, Ionic, or Corinthian ornament.

Chiaroscuro: Meaning "light/dark;" refers to the distribution of light and shade in a painting, either with a marked contrast or a muted tonal gradation.

Cinquecento: Literally, "five hundred," used in Italian to refer to the 16th century.

Contrapposto: A dramatic pose of a sculpted figure in which the upper portion of the body is placed in opposition to the lower portion.

Cortile: Courtyard.

Cupola: Dome.

Duomo: Cathedral.

Fresco: A wall-painting technique, used in Roman times and again in the early Renaissance, in which pigment was applied to wet plaster.

Gothic: Medieval architectural and ornamental style featuring pointed arches, high interior vaulting, and flying buttresses to emphasize height and, symbolically, an ascension to heaven. The term is also used to describe the painting style made famous by Giotto and Simone Martini.

Grotesques: Decorations of fanciful human and animal forms, embellished with flowers; first used in Nero's Golden House and rediscovered during the Renaissance.

Loggia: Roofed balcony or gallery.

Maestà: Majestic image of the Virgin Mary enthroned and surrounded by angels.

Mannerism: Style of the mid-16th century, in which artists—such as Bronzino and Il Rosso—sought to replace the warm, humanizing ideals of Leonardo and Raphael with super-elegant, emotionally cold forms. Portraits in the Mannerist style feature florid colors, high-fashion anatomies, and frosty demeanors.

Nave: The central aisle of a church.

Palazzo: A palace, or more generally, any large building.

Perspective: The illusion of three-dimensional space that was obtained in the early 15th century with the discovery that all parallel lines running in one direction meet at a single point on the horizon known as the vanishing point. Leonardo da Vinci later perfected aerial perspective, in which gradations of *sfumato* (haze) and color can be used to create the illusion of distance.

Piano nobile: The main floor of a palace (the first floor above ground level).

Pietà: Literally "piety"; refers to an image of the Virgin Mary holding the crucified body of Christ on her lap.

Polyptych: A painting—often an altarpiece—on multiple wooden panels that are joined.

Predella: A series of small paintings found below the main section of an altarpiece.

Putti: Cherubs, cupids, or other images of infant boys in painting.

Quattrocento: Literally "four hundred"; refers to the 15th century.

Renaissance: Major school of Italian art, literature, and philosophy (14th century–16th century) that fused innovations in realism with the rediscovery of the great heritage of classical antiquity. After Giotto introduced a new naturalism into painting in the 14th century, Florentine artists of the 1430s, such as Masaccio and Fra Filippo Lippi, paved the way for the later 15th-century realism of Botticelli and Signorelli. While reaching first flower in Florence, the movement culminated in Rome with the High Renaissance (circa 1490–1520) and the masterpieces of Leonardo, Raphael, and Michelangelo.

Rococo: Light, dainty 18th-century art and architectural style created in reaction to heavy Baroque. Tiepolo is the leading painter of the rococo style.

Romanesque: Architectural style of the 11th and 12th centuries that reworked ancient Roman forms, particularly barrel and groin vaults. Stark, severe, and magisterial, Romanesque basilicas are among Italy's most awe-inspiring churches.

Sacra conversazione: The motif of the "holy conversation," showing the Madonna and Child in the midst of and/or interacting with saints.

Tondo: Circular painting or sculpture.

Trompe l'oeil: An artistic technique employed to "fool the eye" into believing that the object or scene depicted is actually real.

Tryptych: A three-panel painting executed on wood.

Veduta: A painting of a city or landscape as viewed from afar, popular in the 18th century.

WHAT TO READ AND WATCH BEFORE YOU GO

Books

The Italians, by Luigi Barzini, is a comprehensive, lively analysis of the Italian national character, still worthy reading although published in 1964 (Atheneum). More recent musings on Italian life include *Italian Days,* by Barbara Grizzuti Harrison (Ticknor & Fields), and *That Fine Italian Hand,* by Paul Hofmann (Henry Holt), for many years *New York Times* bureau chief in Rome.

Novels and historical fiction often impart a greater sense of a place than straight history books: Irving Stone's best-selling *The Agony and the Ecstasy* (NAL) romanticizes the life of Michelangelo but paints an enduring picture of Renaissance Florence; Umberto Eco's *The Name of the Rose* (Harcourt Brace) is a gripping murder mystery that will leave you with tremendous insight into monastic life in Italy. On the lighter side, Florence is the setting for two of Magdalen Nabb's entertaining thrillers: *Death in Autumn* and *Death of a Dutchman* (HarperCollins).

Classics of the travel essay genre include James Morris's *World of Venice* (Harcourt Brace), Mary McCarthy's *Venice Observed* and *The Stones of Florence* (both Harcourt Brace also), Lawrence Durrell's *Sicilian Carousel* (out of print), Elizabeth Bowen's *A Time in Rome* (Penguin), and James Lees-Milne's *Roman Mornings* and *Venetian Mornings* (New Amsterdam). Historic musings about Italy are offered in Henry James's perceptive *Italian Hours* (offered in many editions, including *Traveling in Italy with Henry James: Essays,* William Morrow), Edith Wharton's *Italian Backgrounds* and *Italian Villas and their Gardens* (Ecco Press), and Axel Munthe's *Story of San Michele* (out of print) about his celebrated villa on Capri.

If you are looking for a general historical and art history framework, Harry Hearder's *Italy, A Short History* (Cambridge) cuts right to the chase, with 2,000 years covered in less than 300 pages, and Michael Levey's clear and concise treatment of the Renaissance (*Early Renaissance* and *High Renaissance,* Penguin) are good places to begin. A comprehensive introduction to Italian art is Frederick Hartt's *History of Italian Renaissance Art* (Abrams).

For more historical background, Edward Gibbon's *Decline and Fall of the Roman Empire* is available in three volumes (Modern Library). Consult Giorgio Vasari's *Lives of the Artists* and *The Autobiography of Benvenuto Cellini,* and Machiavelli's *The Prince* (all available in Penguin Classics) for eyewitness accounts of the 16th century. Otherwise, *The Civilization of the Renaissance in Italy,* by 19th-century Swiss historian Jacob Burckhardt (Modern Library), offers a classic foundation. Christopher Hibbert's *House of Medici* (Quill/William Morrow) details the family's rise and fall.

For aficionados of Rome's artistic treasures, Georgina Masson's *Companion Guide to Rome* (Penguin) is a must. Eloquent writing as well as important scholarship is found in the works of such celebrated art historians as Richard Krautheimer, John Pope-Hennessy, John Shearman, Irving Lavin, Charles de Tolnay, and André Chastel. *Inside Rome* (Phaidon Press) is a picture book that gives you a tantalizing peek into the sumptuous palaces, galleries, private homes, athletic clubs, and even historic coffeehouses of the eternal city. Fodor's *Holy Rome: A Millennium Guide to the Christian Sights* traces Christianity in Rome, as it can be seen today, through gorgeous photography, thematic essays, easy-to-follow itineraries, and biographical sketches. Palladio's architecture is beautifully distilled in James Ackerman's *Palladio* (Penguin). To some observers, the most beautiful book about the most beautiful city in the world is Richard de Combray's *Venice, Frail Barrier* (Doubleday).

Susan Sontag's *Volcano Lover* (Farrar Straus Giroux), set in 18th-century Naples, is about Sir William Hamilton, his wife Emma, and Lord Nelson. *The Leopard*, by Giuseppe di Lampedusa (Pantheon), is a compelling portrait of Sicily during the political upheavals of the 1860s. Historical fiction set in World War II includes *History: A Novel*, by Elsa Morante (Vintage Aventura), about the fate of inhabitants of wartime Rome, and *Bread and Wine* by Ignazio Silone (Signet Classics), about Italian peasants under the control of the Fascists. Anne Cornelison's nonfiction *Women of the Shadows* portrays the life of peasant women in early post–World War I southern Italy (Vintage). More recently, mysteries set in Italy have found great popularity, including the Urbino Macintyre series of Edward Sklepowich and the Lovejoy series of Jonathan Gash.

Many English and American expatriates have chronicled their experiences restoring a farmhouse and making sense of the local culture and color in Tuscany and Umbria. Among the better examples in this genre are Frances Mayes's *Bella Tuscany, Under the Tuscan Sun: At Home in Italy,* and *In Tuscany* (Broadway Books), Matthew Spender's *Within Tuscany: Reflections on a Time and Place* (Viking), and Lisa St. Aubin de Terán's *A Valley in Italy: The Many Seasons of a Villa in Umbria* (HarperCollins). Tim Parks's *Italian Neighbors* (Grove) gives accounts of life in rural Tuscany and Verona by British expatriates. Fodor's Escape Guides illuminate two of Italy's special regions in photos and prose: in the pages of Fodor's *Escape to Tuscany,* stay at the convent where *The English Patient* was filmed and go ballooning over Chianti's vineyards. The Amalfi Coast is captured in an impossible array of blues in *Escape to the Amalfi Coast.*

To catch glimpses of the Tuscan landscape, pick up Harold Acton's *Great Houses of Tuscany: The Tuscan Villas* (Viking) or Carey More's *Views from a Tuscan Vineyard* (Pavillion). For a recent look at Umbrian life, try Lisa St. Aubin de Terán's *A Valley in Italy: The Many Seasons of a Villa in Umbria* (HarperCollins). The glories of historic Italian gardens are caught in the ravishing photographs of three recent volumes: Judith Chatfield's *Gardens of the Italian Lakes* (Rizzoli), Ethne Clark's *Gardens of Tuscany* (Weidenfeld & Nicolson), and Nicolas Saphiena's *Gardens of Naples* (Scala Books).

Although every year there are more and more cookbooks on Tuscan food, Waverley Root's *Food of Italy* (Vintage), published in 1977, is still a handy (if not infallible) reference. Take Faith Heller Wilinger's *Eating in Italy* (Morrow) to guide you to the good food and restaurants, and Burton Anderson's *Pocket Guide to Italian Wines* (Little, Brown) to sort your way through the wine lists.

Videos

You'll recognize the idyllic scenery of central Italy in numerous English-language films, including the Academy Award–winning *The English Patient* (1996), Kenneth Branagh's *Much Ado About Nothing* (1993), Bernardo Bertolucci's *Stealing Beauty* (1996), and Merchant/Ivory's *A Room with a View* (1986). Italian filmmaking has been prolific and often excellent. The acknowledged master is Federico Fellini, creator of the classics *Nights of Cabiria, La Strada,* and *La Dolce Vita,* among many others. More recent favorites include *Cinema Paradiso* (1990), *Il Postino* (The Postman, 1995), and *La Vita è Bella* (Life Is Beautiful, 1997), Roberto Benigni's tale of the Holocaust in fascist Italy.

ITALY AT A GLANCE

ca. 1000 BC Etruscans arrive in central Italy.

ca. 800 Rise of Etruscan city-states.

753 Traditional date for the founding of Rome.

750 Greek city-states begin to colonize Sicily and southern Italy.

600 Latin language becomes dominant in Etruscan League; Rome becomes established urban center.

510 Foundation of the Roman republic; expulsion of Etruscans from Roman territory.

410 Rome adopts the 12 Tables of Law, based on Greek models.

343 Roman conquest of Greek colonies in Campania.

312 Completion of Via Appia (Appian Way) to the south of Rome; an extensive Roman road system begins to develop.

264–241 First Punic War (with Carthage): increased naval power helps Rome gain control of southern Italy and then Sicily.

218–200 Second Punic War: Hannibal's attempted conquest of Italy, using elephants, is eventually crushed.

176 Roman Forum begins to take shape as the principal civic center in Italy.

146 Third Punic War: Rome razes city of Carthage and emerges as the dominant Mediterranean force.

133 Rome rules entire Mediterranean Basin except Egypt.

49 Julius Caesar conquers Gaul.

45 Civil War leaves Julius Caesar as sole ruler; Caesar's Forum is established.

44 Julius Caesar is assassinated.

31 The Battle of Actium resolves the power struggle that continued after Caesar's death; Octavian becomes sole ruler.

27 Rome's Imperial Age begins; Octavian (now named Augustus) becomes the first emperor and is later deified. The Augustan Age is celebrated in the works of Virgil (70 BC–AD 19), Ovid (43 BC–AD 17), Livy (59 BC–AD 17), and Horace (65–8 BC).

14 AD Augustus dies.

29 Jesus is crucified in the Roman colony of Judea.

43 Rome invades Britain.

50 Rome is the largest city in the world, with a population of a million.

65 Emperor Nero begins the persecution of Christians in the empire; Saints Peter and Paul are executed.

70–80 Vespasian builds the Colosseum.

98–117 Trajan's military successes are celebrated with his Baths (98), Forum (110), and Column (113); the Roman Empire reaches its apogee.

ca. 150–200 Christianity gains a foothold within the Empire, with the theological writings of Clement, Tertullian, and Origen.

165 A smallpox epidemic ravages the Empire.

212 Roman citizenship is conferred on all nonslaves in the Empire.

238 The first wave of Germanic invasions penetrates Italy.

293 Diocletian reorganizes the Empire into West and East.

313 The Edict of Milan grants toleration of Christianity within the Empire.

330 Constantine founds a new Imperial capital (Constantinople) in the East.

410 Rome is sacked by Visigoths.

476 The last Roman Emperor, Romulus Augustus, is deposed. The Empire of Rome falls.

552 Eastern emperor Justinian (527–565) recovers control of Italy.

570 Lombards gain control of much of Italy, including Rome.

590 Papal power expands under Gregory the Great.

610 Heraldius revives the Eastern Empire, thereafter known as the Byzantine Empire.

774 Frankish ruler Charlemagne (742–814) invades Italy under papal authority and is crowned Holy Roman Emperor by Pope Leo III (800).

ca. 800–900 The breakup of Charlemagne's (Carolingian) realm leads to the rise of Italian city-states.

811 Venice is founded by mainlanders escaping Barbarian invasions.

1054 The Schism develops between Greek (Orthodox) and Latin churches.

ca. 1060 Europe's first university is founded in Bologna.

1077 Pope Gregory VII leads the Holy See into conflict with the Germanic Holy Roman Empire.

1152–90 Frederick I (Barbarossa) is crowned Holy Roman Emperor (1155); punitive expeditions by his forces (Ghibellines) are countered by the Guelphs, creators of the powerful Papal States in central Italy. Guelph–Ghibelline conflict becomes a feature of medieval life.

1204 Crusaders, led by Venetian doge Dandolo, capture Constantinople.

1257 The first of four wars is declared between Genoa and Venice; at stake is the maritime control of the eastern Mediterranean.

1262 Florentine bankers issue Europe's first bills of exchange.

1264 Charles I of Anjou invades Italy, intervening in the continuing Guelph–Ghibelline conflict.

1275 Marco Polo (1254–1324) reaches the Orient.

1290-1375 Tuscan literary giants Dante Alighieri (1265–1321), Francesco Petrarch (1304–74), and Giovanni Boccaccio (1313–75) give written imprimatur to modern Italian language.

1309 The pope moves to Avignon in France, under the protection of French kings.

1355 Venetian doge Marino Falier is executed for treason.

1376 The pope returns to Rome, but rival Avignonese popes stand in opposition, creating the Great Schism until 1417.

1380 Venice finally disposes of the Genovese threat in the Battle of Chioggia.

1402 The last German intervention into Italy is repulsed by the Lombards.

1443 Brunelleschi's (1377–1446) cupola is completed on Florence's Duomo.

1447 Nicholas V founds the Vatican Library. This begins an era of nepotistic popes who devalue the status of the papacy but greatly enrich the artistic and architectural patronage of the Holy City.

1469-92 Lorenzo "Il Magnifico" (1449–92), the Medici patron of the arts, rules in Florence.

1498 Girolamo Savonarola (1452–98), the austere Dominican friar, is executed for heresy after leading Florence into a drive for moral purification, typified by his burning of books and decorations in the "Bonfire of Vanities."

1499 Leonardo da Vinci's (1452–1519) *Last Supper* is completed in Milan.

1508 Michelangelo (1475–1564) begins work on the Cappella Sistina.

1509 Raphael (1483–1520) begins work on his *Stanze* in the Vatican.

1513 Machiavelli's (1469–1527) *The Prince* is published.

1521 The Pope excommunicates Martin Luther (1483–1546) of Germany, precipitating the Protestant Reformation.

1545-63 The Council of Trent formulates the Catholic response to the Reformation.

1546 Andrea Palladio (1508–80), architectural genius, wins his first commission in Vicenza.

1571 The combined navies of Venice, Spain, and the Papacy defeat the Turks in the Battle of Lepanto.

1626 The Basilica di San Pietro is completed in Rome.

1633 Galileo Galilei (1564–1642) faces the Inquisition.

1652 Sant'Agnese in Agone church, Borromini's (1599–1667) Baroque masterpiece, is completed in Rome.

1667 The Piazza di San Pietro, designed by Bernini (1598–1680), is completed.

ca. 1700 Opera develops as an art form in Italy.

1720–90 The Great Age of the Grand Tour: northern Europeans visit Italy and start the vogue for classical studies. Among the famous visitors are Edward Gibbon (1758), Jacques-Louis David (1775), and Johann Wolfgang von Goethe (1786).

1778 Teatro alla Scala is completed in Milan.

1796 Napoléon begins his Italian campaigns, annexing Rome and imprisoning Pope Pius VI four years later.

1815 Austria controls much of Italy after Napoléon's downfall.

1848 Revolutionary troops under Risorgimento (Unification) leaders Giuseppe Mazzini (1805–72) and Giuseppe Garibaldi (1807–82) establish a republic in Rome.

1849 French troops crush rebellion and restore Pope Pius IX.

1860 Garibaldi and his "Thousand" defeat the Bourbon rulers in Sicily and Naples.

1870 Rome is finally captured by Risorgimento troops and is declared capital of Italy by King Vittorio Emanuele II.

1900 King Umberto I is assassinated by an anarchist; he is succeeded by King Vittorio Emanuele III.

1915 Italy enters World War I on the side of the Allies.

1922 Fascist "black shirts" under Benito Mussolini (1883–1945) march on Rome; Mussolini becomes prime minister and later "Il Duce" (head of Italy).

1929 The Lateran Treaty: Mussolini recognizes Vatican City as a sovereign state, and the Church recognizes Rome as the capital of Italy.

1940–44 In World War II, Italy fights on the side of the Axis powers until its capitulation (1943), when Mussolini flees Rome. Italian partisans and Allied troops from the landings at Anzio (January 1944) win victory at Cassino (March 1944) and force the eventual withdrawal of German troops from Italy.

1957 The Treaty of Rome is signed, and Italy becomes a founding member of the European Economic Community.

1966 November flood damages many of Florence's artistic treasures.

1968–79 The growth of left-wing activities leads to the formation of the Red Brigades and provokes right-wing reactions.

Bombings and kidnapings culminate in the abduction and murder of Prime Minister Aldo Moro (1916–1978).

1980 Southern Italy is hit by a severe earthquake.

1991 Waves of refugees from neighboring Albania flood southern ports on the Adriatic. Mt. Etna erupts, spewing forth a lava stream that threatens the Sicilian town of Zafferana.

1992 The Christian Democrat Party, in power throughout the postwar period, loses its hold on a relative majority in Parliament.

1993 Italians vote for sweeping reforms after the Tangentopoli (Bribe City) scandal exposes widespread political corruption, including politicians' collusion with organized crime. A bomb outside the Galleria degli Uffizi in Florence kills five but spares the museum's most precious artwork; authorities blame the Cosa Nostra, flexing its muscles in the face of a crackdown.

1994 A center-right coalition wins in spring elections, and media magnate Silvio Berlusconi becomes premier—only to be deposed within a year. Italian politics seem to be evolving into the equivalent of a two-party system.

1995 Newly appointed Lamberto Dini takes hold of the government's rudder and, as president of the Council of Ministers, institutes major reforms and replaces old-line politicians.

1996 A league of center-left parties wins national elections and puts together a government coalition that sees the Democratic Party of the Left (PDS), the former Communist party, into power for the first time ever in Italy. Thousands of Romans gathered in Piazza del Campidoglio to bid farewell to the late beloved actor Marcello Mastroianni, revered for his portraits of the consummate Italian charmer in films such as *La Dolce Vita*, *8½*—both Federico Fellini films—and *Divorce Italian Style*.

1997 Political stability and an austerity program put Italy on track toward the European Monetary Union and adoption of the single euro currency. Though only a copy, the statue of Roman emperor Marcus Aurelius is returned to its pedestal on the Campidoglio as a symbol of Rome's historic grandeur. A series of earthquakes hit the mountainous interior of central Italy, severely damaging villages and some historic towns. In Assisi, portions of the vault of the Basilica di San Francesco crumble, destroying frescoes by Cimabue.

1998 In February a U.S. Navy jet fighter on a low-flying training mission through the Italian Alps cuts a ski gondola cable, killing 20 people. Romano Prodi's center-left government, widely praised for its economic policies and lack of scandals, is brought down by a no confidence vote in October, after the Reformed-Communist Party (PCI) withdraws its support for Prodi. The center-left regroups and forms a new government under Massimo D'Alema, leader of the former Communist Party, who in large part continues Prodi's policies. The Pope visits Cuba, and more than a million people see the Shroud of Turin, on display for a just a few months.

1999 Italy serves as a principal base for NATO air raids against Serbia. Rome continues preparations for the Giubileo (Holy Year) celebrations in 2000 with an array of public works projects. The International Olympic Committee chooses Turin to host the 2006 Winter Olympics.

2000 The Jubilee of the third milennium is proclaimed by Pope John Paul II. Millions of pilgrims flock to Rome.

2001 Media mogul Silvio Berlusconi elected prime minister.

2002 The lira is subplanted by the euro as the currency of the land.

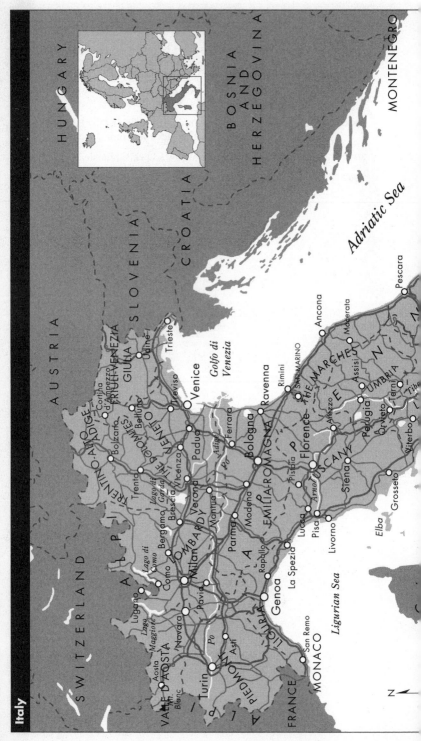

Italy

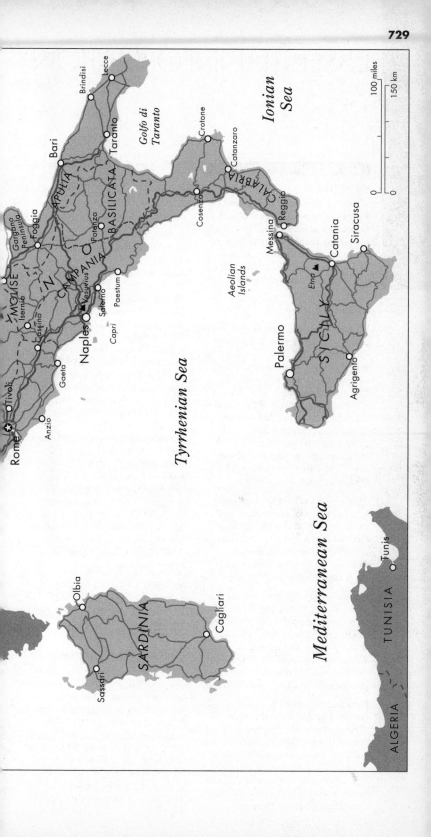

Ionian Sea

Lecce
Brindisi
Golfo di Taranto
Crotone
Bari
Taranto
Catanzaro
APULIA
BASILICATA
CALABRIA
Foggia
Gargano Peninsula
Potenza
Cosenza
Reggio
Messina
MOLISE
Isernia
CAMPANIA
Vesuvius
Paestum
Salerno
Etna
Catania
Siracusa
Cassino
Naples
Capri
SICILY
Tivoli
Gaeta
Palermo
Rome
Anzio
Agrigento

Aeolian Islands

Tyrrhenian Sea

100 miles
150 km

Olbia
SARDINIA
Cagliari
Sassari

Mediterranean Sea

Tunis
TUNISIA

ALGERIA

ESSENTIAL INFORMATION

AIR TRAVEL

BOOKING

When you book **look for nonstop flights** and **remember that "direct" flights stop at least once.** Try to avoid connecting flights, which require a change of plane. For more booking tips and to check prices and make on-line flight reservations, log on to www.fodors.com.

CARRIERS

When flying internationally, you must usually choose between a domestic carrier, the national flag carrier of the country you are visiting, and a foreign carrier from a third country. You may, for example, choose to fly Alitalia to Italy. National flag carriers have the greatest number of nonstops. Domestic carriers may have better connections to your hometown and serve a greater number of gateway cities. Third-party carriers may have a price advantage.

Alitalia—in addition to other major European airlines and smaller, privately run companies such as Meridiana and Air One—offers an extensive network of internal flights in Italy. Ask your domestic or Italian travel agent about discounts.

On international flights, Alitalia serves Rome, Milan, and Venice. The major international hubs in Italy are Milan and Rome, served by Continental Airlines, Delta Air Lines, and TWA. American Airlines, United Airlines, and Northwest Airlines fly into Milan. US Airways serves Rome.

Direct service from Heathrow is provided by Alitalia and British Airways. From Manchester, there are three direct BA flights daily to Milan, and daily flights to Rome. Privately run Meridiana has two or three direct flights between London and Olbia on Sardinia weekly in summer and three direct flights daily to Florence

throughout the year. Meridiana also connects London with Catania and Turin. Lower-priced charter flights to a range of Italian destinations are available throughout the year.

➤ MAJOR AIRLINES: **Alitalia** (☎ 800/223–5730 or 020/7602–7111; 0990/448–259 in Britain; 06/65641 in Rome; 848/865641 elsewhere in Italy, WEB www.alitalia.it). **American Airlines** (☎ 800/433–7300; 02/679141 in Milan, WEB www.aa.com). **British Airways** (☎ 0345/222–111; 06/6501–1575 in Rome; 848/812266 elsewhere in Italy, WEB www.britishairways.com). **Continental Airlines** (☎ 800/231–0856; 06/4767–5205 in Rome; 800/296–230 toll-free elsewhere in Italy, WEB www.flycontinental.com). **Delta Air Lines** (☎ 800/241–4141; 800/864–114 toll-free in Italy, WEB www.deltaairlines.com). **Northwest Airlines** (☎ 800/225–2525, WEB www.nwa.com). **TWA** (☎ 800/892–4141; 06/47241 in Rome; 800/841843 toll-free in Italy, WEB www.twa.com). **United Airlines** (☎ 800/538–2929; 02/667481 in Milan, WEB www.unitedairlines.com). **US Airways** (☎ 800/428–4322; 848/813177 in Italy, WEB www.usairways.com).

➤ SMALLER AIRLINES: **Air One** (☎ 06/488–800 in Rome; 848/848880 elsewhere in Italy, WEB www.flyairone.it). **Meridiana** (☎ 06/478–041, WEB www.meridiana.it).

CHECK-IN & BOARDING

Assuming that not everyone with a ticket will show up, airlines routinely overbook planes. When everyone does, airlines ask for volunteers to give up their seats. In return, these volunteers usually get a certificate for a free flight and are rebooked on the next flight out. If there are not enough volunteers, the airline must choose who will be denied boarding. The first to get bumped are passengers who checked in late and those flying on discounted tickets, so **get to the gate and check in as early as possible,** especially during peak periods.

Always **bring a government-issued photo ID to the airport;** even when it's not required, a passport is best.

CUTTING COSTS

The least expensive airfares to Italy must usually be purchased in advance and are nonrefundable. It's smart to **call a number of airlines, and when you are quoted a good price, book it on the spot**—the same fare may not be available the next day. Always **check different routings** and look into using different airports. Travel agents, especially low-fare specialists (☞ Discounts & Deals, *below*), are helpful.

Consolidators are another good source. They buy tickets for scheduled international flights at reduced rates from the airlines, then sell them at prices that beat the best fare available directly from the airlines, usually without restrictions. Sometimes you can even get your money back if you need to return the ticket. Carefully read the fine print detailing penalties for changes and cancellations, and **confirm your consolidator reservation with the airline.**

➤ CONSOLIDATORS: **Cheap Tickets** (☎ 800/377–1000). **Discount Airline Ticket Service** (☎ 800/576–1600). **Unitravel** (☎ 800/325–2222). **Up & Away Travel** (☎ 212/889–2345). **World Travel Network** (☎ 800/409–6753).

ENJOYING THE FLIGHT

All flights within Italy are smoke free. However, smoking is allowed on a limited number of international flights; **contact your carrier about its smoking policy.** For more legroom, **request an emergency-aisle seat.** Don't sit in the row in front of the emergency aisle or in front of a bulkhead, where seats may not recline. If you have dietary concerns, **ask for special meals when booking.** These can be vegetarian, low-cholesterol, or kosher, for example. On long flights, try to maintain a normal routine, to help fight jet lag. At night, **get some sleep.** By day, **eat light meals, drink water** (not alcohol), and **move around the cabin** to stretch your legs. For additional jet-lag tips consult *Fodor's FYI: Travel Fit & Healthy* (available at bookstores everywhere).

FLYING TIMES

Flying time is 8½ hours from New York, 10–11 hours from Chicago, 11½ hours from Dallas (via New York), 11½ hours from Los Angeles, 2 hours from London (to Milan), and 23½ hours from Sydney to Rome via Milan.

HOW TO COMPLAIN

If your baggage goes astray or your flight goes awry, complain right away. Most carriers require that you **file a claim immediately.**

➤ AIRLINE COMPLAINTS: U.S. Department of Transportation **Aviation Consumer Protection Division** (✉ C-75, Room 4107, Washington, DC 20590, ☎ 202/366–2220, WEB www.dot.gov/airconsumer). **Federal Aviation Administration Consumer Hotline** (☎ 800/322–7873).

AIRPORTS

The major gateways to Italy include Rome's **Aeroporto Leonardo da Vinci,** better known as **Fiumicino,** and Milan's **Aeroporto Malpensa 2000** (MXP). If you are going directly to Florence and landing at Rome's Fiumicino or at Milan's Malpensa, you can make connections at the airport for a flight to Florence; you can also take airport trains to Rome's Termini Station or to central Milan, where fast trains for Florence are frequent during the day. Smaller, minor gateways are served by domestic and some international flights.

➤ AIRPORT INFORMATION: **Aeroporto Leonardo da Vinci** or **Fiumicino** (✉ 35 km [20 mi] southeast of Rome, ☎ 06/6595–3640, WEB www.adr.com). **Aeroporto Malpensa 2000** (✉ 45 km [28 mi] north of Milan, ☎ 02/7485–2200, WEB www.sea-aeroportimilano.it). **Bologna: Aeroporto Guglielmo Marconi** (✉ Borgo Panigale, 7 km [4½] mi from Bologna, ☎ 051/647–9615, WEB www.bologna-airport.it). **Florence: Aeroporto A. Vespucci,** called Perétola (✉ 6 km [4 mi] northwest of Florence,

☎ 055/30615, WEB see link in www. firenze.turismo.toscana.it) and **Aero-porto Galileo Galilei** (✉ Pisa, 80 km [50 mi] west of Florence, ☎ 050/500–707, WEB www.pisa-airport.com).
Milan: Aeroporto Linate (✉ 10 km [6 mi] east of Milan, ☎ 02/7485–2200, WEB www.sea-aeroportimilano.it).
Naples: Aeroporto Capodichino (✉ 8 km [5 mi] north of Naples, ☎ 081/789–6111, WEB www.gesac.it).
Palermo: Aeroporto Punta Raisi (✉ 32 km [20 mi] west of Palermo, ☎ 091/591–698 [information about arrivals only] or 091/702–0111).
Venice: Aeroporto Marco Polo (✉ Tessera, about 10 km [6 mi] north of Venice, ☎ 041/260–9260, WEB www.veniceairport.it).

DUTY-FREE SHOPPING

Duty-free shopping in airports has been eliminated in Italy (and other EC countries); you can still make in-flight duty-free purchases, however.

BEACHES

With 7,420 km (4,610 mi) of coast-line facing three seas—the Adriatic to the Northeast, the Ionian to the Southeast, and the Tyrrhenean to the West—Italy offers every type of beach scene. Italy has several world-famous beaches, like those along the Costa Esmeralda in Sardinia and the town of Portofino in Liguria, and great stretches of deserted and untouched coastline, many found in eastern Calabria, Sardinia, and the islands around Sicily. In Emilia-Romagna, Riccione and Rimini are famous for their nightlife and seaside fitness programs ("spinning" classes to weightlifting, water gymnastics to Latin dance classes). The Tremiti Islands (off the Adriatic coast, be-tween Molise and Puglia), the Gargano Peninsula (in Puglia), Tropea (in Calabria), Taormina (in Sicily), the islands of Capri and Ischia (in the Gulf of Naples), the Amalfi Coast (in Campania), Ponza (off the coast of Lazio), and the island of Elba (off the coast of Livorno in Tuscany) bring together a natural beauty with a low-key worldliness that includes discos and stylish restaurants.

For most Italians who live along the coast, going to the beach is more a part of the regular summer routine

than a vacation: locals head to the nearest beach during the long Italian lunch break and for the evening *passeggiata*. In Italy a healthy suntan is still much sought after, although awareness of the dangers of long-term overexposure is spreading. Cremes and sunblocks are available, but read the labels carefully to make sure you are getting the protection you desire and don't underestimate the scorching power of the Italian sun. The "tan-ning season" begins in early May, when bathing suits by the major designers begin to appear in the windows of Italian shops, and beach life starts in earnest in early June, with the opening of beaches run by concessionaires.

It is essential to distinguish between the private and public beaches. The former are free and open to the pub-lic, but offer no services. Although on the most popular public beaches it's sometimes possible to buy sandwiches and soft drinks from kiosks or roam-ing vendors, as a general rule you shouldn't expect such comforts, let alone pay telephones, toilets, or show-ers. Private beaches charge admission, and range from the downright spartan (cold showers and portable toilets) to the luxurious (with gardens, stylish bars, fish restaurants, and private guest huts). Admission policies and prices vary accordingly: although most establishments offer day passes costing from 10,000 lire/€5.15 to 50,000 lire/€25.80 per person and include a chaise lounge and an um-brella, some of the most exclusive places cater only to patrons who pay by the week or month. Inquire at local tourist offices for details.

The summer season ends on Septem-ber 15. During weekends and holi-days and in August, most sea resorts and beaches tend to be very crowded, some posting no-vacancy signs by 10 AM, so an early start is essential. If in northern and central Italy sunbathing topless is common practice, in the south it could lead to undesired attention from local men. Nowhere in Italy, except in the rare nudist beach, is it common practice to walk around topless, and beach attire (bare chests and thighs) worn in town can still earn you a fine in some places.

BIKE TRAVEL

Italians are great bicycling enthusiasts, and there are satisfying bicycling itineraries throughout the country. Given the generally hilly terrain, it's essential to have a good map with elevations, distances, and the various types of roads clearly marked. An excellent map choice is the green regional series issued by the Italian Touring Club, available at major book stores. Road conditions are generally good throughout Italy, but, as you move along, it's always a good idea to ask local tourist information offices about cyclist-friendly routes. Especially in the smaller towns and villages, cyclists do not go unnoticed, and if you speak a little Italian you'll be likely to meet sympathetic native cyclists eager to give valuable tips about the region. Always park (and lock) your bike inside your hotel for the night. And a small but important matter: laundromats are rare in Italy and can be found only in the bigger cities.

The Federazione Italiana Amici della Bicicletta (FIAB) will help you plan your itinerary. The site www.cycling.it, under Itinerari Italiani, contains an interesting selection of articles (in Italian) from the publication *La Bicicletta,* with detailed descriptions of itineraries across national parks and areas of natural beauty.

➤ LOCAL RESOURCES: **FIAB** (✉ Viale Venezia 7, 30170 Mestre, Veneto, ☎ FAX 041/938092, WEB www. fiab-onlus.it).

➤ RENTALS: **Happy Rent** (✉ Via Farini 3 Rome, ☎ 06/481–8185). **I Bike Rome** (✉ underground parking lot at Villa Borghese, Via del Galoppatoio 33, Rome, ☎ 06/322–5240). **St. Peter Moto Rent** (✉ Via di Porta Castello 43, Rome, ☎ 06/687–5714 or 06/488–5485; ✉ Via Fosse di Castello 7, ☎ 06/687–4909).

➤ BIKE TOURS: **Backroads** (✉ 801 Cedar St., Berkeley, CA 94710, ☎ 510/527–1555 or 800/462–2848, FAX 510/527–1444). **Bike Riders** (✉ Box 130254, Boston, MA 02113, ☎ 617/723–2354 or 800/473–7040, FAX 617/723–2355). **Butterfield & Robinson** (✉ 70 Bond St., Suite 300, Toronto, Ontario, Canada M5B 1X3, ☎ 416/864–1354 or 800/678–1147, FAX 416/864–0541). **Ciclismo Classico** (✉ 30 Marathon St., Arlington, MA 02474, ☎ 781/646–3377 or 800/866–7314, FAX 781/641–1512). **Classic Adventures** (✉ Box 143, Hamlin, NY 14464-0143, ☎ 716/964–8488 or 800/777–8090, FAX 716/964–7297). **Euro-Bike Tours** (✉ Box 990, De Kalb, IL 60115, ☎ 800/321–6060, FAX 815/758–8851). **Europeds** (✉ 761 Lighthouse Ave., Monterey, CA 93940, ☎ 831/646–4920 or 800/321–9552, FAX 831/655–4501). **Himalayan Travel** (✉ 110 Prospect St., Stamford, CT 06901, ☎ 203/359–3711 or 800/225–2380, FAX 203/359–3669). **Naturequest** (✉ 30872 South Coast Hwy., Suite 185, Laguna Beach, CA 92651-8162, ☎ 949/499–9561 or 800/369–3033, FAX 949/499–0812). **Progressive Travels** (✉ 224 W. Galer Ave., Suite C, Seattle, WA 98119, ☎ 206/285–1987 or 800/245–2229, FAX 206/285–1988). **Uniquely Europe/Europe Express** (✉ 19805 North Creek Pkwy., Suite 100, Bothell, WA 98011, ☎ 425/487–6711 or 800/426–3615, FAX 425/487–3750 or 800/270–0509).

BIKES IN FLIGHT

Most airlines accommodate bikes as luggage, provided they are dismantled and boxed. Airlines sell bike boxes, which are often free at bike shops, for about $5 (it's at least $100 for bike bags). International travelers can sometimes substitute a bike for a piece of checked luggage at no charge; otherwise, the cost is about $100. Domestic and Canadian airlines charge $25–$50.

BOAT & FERRY TRAVEL

Ferries connect the mainland with all major islands. To many destinations there is also hydrofoil (*aliscafo*) service, which is generally twice as fast as ferries and double the price. Service is considerably more frequent during the summer months. Car ferries operate to Sicily and Sardinia and many islands, including Elba, Ponza, Capri, Ischia, the Lido near Venice, and other islands. If you are traveling in July–August, try to make reservations at least a month ahead.

Tirrenia operates ferries to Liguria, Tuscany, Naples, Sicily, Sardinia, and Tunisi. SNAV operates high-speed ferries between Naples and Palermo (only from April to early October) and hydrofoils between Naples and Capri. Lauro has hydrofoils and car ferries to Ischia from Naples, and Capri is reached by Caremar. Adriatica connects Italy with Greece. FS ferries sail from Civitavecchia to Golfo Aranci, near Olbia. Moby Lines and Toremar serve Elba from Piombino. For the Lake District contact Navigazione Laghi.

➤ BOAT & FERRY INFORMATION: **Adriatica** (✉ Via San Nicola da Tolentino 27, Rome, ☎ 06/481–8341, WEB www.adriatica.it). **Caremar** (✉ Molo Beverello, Napoli, ☎ 081/551–3882). **FS** (☎ 848/8888088). **Lauro** (✉ Molo Beverello, Napoli, ☎ 081/552–2838, WEB www.lauro.it). **Moby Lines** (✉ Viale Regina Margherita, Piombino, ☎ 0565/225–211). **Navigazione Laghi** (✉ Viale Baracca 1, Arona (Novara), ☎ 800/551–801 toll-free within Italy, WEB www.navlaghi.it). **SNAV** (✉ Via Giordano Bruno 84, Napoli, ☎ 081/761–2348, WEB www.snavali.com). **Tirrenia** (✉ Rione Sirignano 2, Napoli, ☎ 199/123199 within Italy; 081/3172999 from abroad and on cell phones, WEB www.tirrenia.it). **Toremar** (✉ Piazzale Premuda 13, Piombino, ☎ 0565/31100, WEB www.etruscan.it).

BUS TRAVEL

Italy's bus network is extensive, although buses are not as attractive an option as in other European countries, partly because of the low cost and convenience of train travel. However, in some areas buses can be faster and more direct than local trains, so it's a good idea to **compare bus and train schedules.** Bus service outside cities is organized on a regional level and often operated by private companies.

If you're traveling by bus from the United Kingdom, **bring a few French francs to spend en route.** And be sure to consider the train (☞ Train Travel, *below*), as bus fares are quite high, especially when you take the long and tiring overnight journey into account. Eurolines runs a weekly bus service to

Rome that increases to three times a week between June and September.

TICKETS & SCHEDULES

Unlike city buses, for which you must buy your ticket from a machine, newsstand, or tobacconist and stamp it after you board, private bus lines usually have a ticket office in town or allow you to pay when you board.

➤ BUS INFORMATION: **Eurolines** (✉ 52 Grosvenor Gardens, London SW1W 0AU, ☎ 020/7730–8235 or 020/7730–3499; or contact any National Express agent).

BUSINESS HOURS

BANKS & POST OFFICES

Banks are open weekdays 8:30 to 1:30 and 2:45 to 3:45. Most churches are open from early morning until noon or 12:30, when they close for three hours or more; they open again in the afternoon, closing about 7 PM or later.

Post offices are open Monday–Saturday 9–2; central and main district post offices stay open until 6:30 PM weekdays, 9–2 on Saturday. On the last day of the month all post offices close at midday.

MUSEUMS & SIGHTS

A few major churches, such as St. Peter's in Rome and San Marco in Venice, are open all day. Note that sightseeing in churches during religious rites is discouraged. Museum hours vary and often change with the seasons. Many museums are closed one day a week, often on Monday. Always check locally. Most shops are open from 9 to 1 and from 3:30 or 4 to 7:30, Monday–Saturday.

PHARMACIES

Pharmacies are generally open Monday–Friday from 8:30 until 1 and from 4 until 8, and Saturday mornings 9 until 1. Local pharmacies cover the off-hours in shifts: on the door of every pharmacy is a list of which pharmacies in the vicinity will be open on Saturday afternoon, Sunday, or 24 hours.

SHOPS

Clothing shops are generally closed on Monday mornings. Barbers and hairdressers, with some exceptions, are closed Sunday and Monday. Some bookstores and fashion and tourist-oriented shops in places such as Rome and Venice are open all day, also on Sunday, as are some department stores and supermarkets.

CAMERAS & PHOTOGRAPHY

The *Kodak Guide to Shooting Great Travel Pictures* (available at bookstores everywhere) is loaded with tips.

➤ PHOTO HELP: **Kodak Information Center** (☎ 800/242–2424). *Kodak Guide to Shooting Great Travel Pictures,* available in bookstores or from Fodor's Travel Publications (☎ 800/533–6478; $18 plus $5.50 shipping).

EQUIPMENT PRECAUTIONS

Don't pack film and equipment in checked luggage, where it is much more susceptible to damage. X-ray machines used to view checked luggage are becoming much more powerful and therefore are much more likely to ruin your film. Always **keep film and tape out of the sun.** Carry an extra supply of batteries, and **be prepared to turn on your camera or camcorder** to prove to security personnel that the device is real. Always **ask for hand inspection of film,** which becomes clouded after repeated exposure to airport X-ray machines, and **keep videotapes away from metal detectors.**

FILM & DEVELOPING

In Rome and most major cities you'll see scores of photo developing shops, many with service in one hour (or less). In smaller cities look for a shop with a Kodak sign outside its door. Although it's not expensive to develop film in Italy (around 12,000 lire/€6.20 per 36-exposure roll), film is considerably more expensive than in the United States (around 17,000 lire/€8.30 for a color 36-exposure roll), so it's a good idea to **stock on film before you leave.**

VIDEOS

While VHS videotapes and players are common, be forewarned that Italy, like other countries in Europe, uses a different video system than the one used in the United States. This means that you won't be able to play the videotapes that you bring from home on Italian equipment, and tapes purchased in Italy won't work in an American VCR.

CAR RENTAL

Renting a car in Italy is essential for exploring the countryside, but not if you plan to stick to city travel. Signage on country roads is usually pretty good, but be prepared for fast and impatient fellow drivers. Major car-rental companies have boxy Ford-type cars (such as Astras) and FIATs in various sizes that are always in good condition.

➤ MAJOR AGENCIES: **Alamo** (☎ 800/ 522–9696; 020/8759–6200 in the U.K., WEB www.alamo.com). **Avis** (☎ 800/331–1084; 800/879–2847 in Canada; 02/9353–9000 in Australia; 09/525–1982 in New Zealand; 0870/ 606–0100 in the U.K., WEB www.avis. com). **Budget** (☎ 800/527–0700; 0870/156–5656 in the U.K., WEB www.budget.com). **Dollar** (☎ 800/ 800–6000; 0124/622–0111 in the U.K., where it's affiliated with Sixt; 02/9223–1444 in Australia, WEB www.dollar.com). **Hertz** (☎ 800/654– 3001; 800/263–0600 in Canada; 020/ 8897–2072 in the U.K.; 02/9669– 2444 in Australia; 09/256–8690 in New Zealand, WEB www.hertz.com). **National Car Rental** (☎ 800/227– 7368; 020/8680–4800 in the U.K., WEB www.nationalcar.com).

CUTTING COSTS

Most major American car-rental companies have offices or affiliates in Italy, but the rates are generally better if you make a reservation from abroad rather than from within Italy. To get the best deal, **book through a travel agent who will shop around.** In Italy, you can save up to 30% by renting your car on-line pretending you are still abroad. Weekend rates with limited mileage are usually good deals. Note that in Italy car-rental companies usually make it mandatory to purchase the collision-damage waiver, regardless of what coverage may be provided by your credit card.

Do **look into wholesalers,** companies that do not own fleets but rent in bulk from those that do and often offer better rates than traditional car-rental operations. Payment must be made before you leave home.

➤ WHOLESALERS: **Auto Europe** (☎ 207/842–2000 or 800/223–5555, FAX 207/842–2222, WEB www.autoeurope.com). **Europe by Car** (☎ 212/581–3040 or 800/223–1516, FAX 212/246–1458, WEB www.europebycar.com). **DER Travel Services** (✉ 9501 W. Devon Ave., Rosemont, IL 60018, ☎ 800/782–2424, FAX 800/282–7474 information; 800/860–9944 brochures, WEB www.dertravel.com). **Kemwel Holiday Autos** (☎ 800/678–0678, FAX 914/825–3160, WEB www.kemwel.com).

INSURANCE

When driving a rented car you are generally responsible for any damage to or loss of the vehicle. Before you rent, see what coverage your personal auto-insurance policy and credit cards provide.

Before you buy collision coverage, check your existing policies—you may already be covered. However, collision policies that car-rental companies sell for European rentals usually do not include stolen-vehicle coverage. Note that in Italy, all car-rental companies make you buy theft-protection policies.

REQUIREMENTS & RESTRICTIONS

In Italy your own driver's license is acceptable. An International Driver's Permit is a good idea; it's available from the American or Canadian Automobile Association and, in the United Kingdom, from the Automobile Association or Royal Automobile Club. These international permits are universally recognized, and having one in your wallet may save you a problem with the local authorities. In Italy you must be 21 years of age to rent an economy or subcompact car, and most companies require customers under the age of 23 to pay by credit card. Upon rental, all companies require credit cards as a warranty; to rent bigger cars (2,000 cc or more), you must often show two credit cards. Call local agents for details. No restrictions apply to senior-citizen drivers.

SURCHARGES

Before you pick up a car in one city and leave it in another, **ask about drop-off charges or one-way service fees,** which can be substantial. Note, too, that some rental agencies charge extra if you return the car before the time specified in your contract. To avoid a hefty refueling fee, **fill the tank just before you turn in the car,** but be aware that gas stations near the rental outlet may overcharge.

CAR TRAVEL

There is an extensive network of *autostrade* (toll highways), complemented by equally well maintained but free *superstrade* (expressways). The ticket you are issued upon entering an autostrada must be returned when you exit and pay the toll; on some shorter autostrade, mainly connecting highways, the toll is paid upon entering. Viacard cards, on sale at many autostrada locations, make paying tolls easier and faster. A *raccordo* is a ring road surrounding a city. *Strade statali* (state highways, denoted by *S* or *SS* numbers) may be single-lane roads, as are all secondary roads; directions and turnoffs are not always clearly marked.

AUTO CLUBS

➤ IN AUSTRALIA: **Australian Automobile Association** (☎ 02/6247–7311).

➤ IN CANADA: **Canadian Automobile Association** (CAA; ☎ 613/247–0117).

➤ IN NEW ZEALAND: **New Zealand Automobile Association** (☎ 09/377–4660).

➤ IN THE U.K.: **Automobile Association** (AA; ☎ 0990/500–600). **Royal Automobile Club** (RAC; ☎ 0990/722–722 membership; 0345/121–345 insurance).

➤ IN THE U.S.: **American Automobile Association** (AAA; ☎ 800/564–6222).

➤ IN ITALY: **Automobil Club Italiano** (ACI; ☎ 06/49982389 daily 8 AM–8 PM) gives travel tips and information in English about rules of the road, road conditions, and car insurance.

EMERGENCY SERVICES

➤ CONTACTS: **ACI Emergency Service** offers 24-hour road service. Dial 116 from any phone, 24 hours a day, to reach the ACI dispatch operator. Also, your rental car company may have an emergency tow service that can be reached with a toll-free call. Check your paperwork or ask when renting.

GASOLINE

Gas stations are generally open Monday–Saturday 7–7 with a break at lunchtime. Many stations have automatic self-service pumps that only accept bills of 10,000 lire and 50,000 lire (the standard euro denominations are still being established); only a few also take also credit cards. Gas stations on autostrade are open 24 hours. Gas costs about 2,250 lire/€1.20 per liter.

PARKING

Parking space is at a premium in most towns, especially in the *centri storici* (historic centers), which are filled with narrow streets and restricted circulation zones. It is often a good idea (if not the only option) to park your car in a designated (preferably attended) lot. Parking in an area signposted ZONA DISCO (disk zone) is allowed for limited periods (from 30 minutes to two hours or more—the limit is posted); if you don't have the cardboard disk (inquire at the local tourist office) to show what time you parked, you can use a piece of paper. The *parcometro,* the Italian version of metered parking in which you put coins into a machine for a stamped ticket that you leave on the dashboard, has been introduced in some cities. It's advisable to **leave your car only in guarded parking areas.**

ROAD CONDITIONS

Autostrade are well maintained, as are most interregional highways. The condition of provincial (county) roads varies, but road maintenance at this level is generally good in Italy. Street and road signs are often challenging—a good map and patience are essential.

RULES OF THE ROAD

Driving is on the right. Regulations are largely as in Britain and the United States, except that the police have the power to levy on-the-spot fines. In most Italian towns the use of the horn is forbidden in certain, if not all, areas; a large sign, ZONA DI SILENZIO, indicates where. Speed limits are 130 kph (80 mph) on autostrade and 110 kph (70 mph) on state and provincial roads, unless otherwise marked. Fines for driving after drinking are heavy, including the suspension of license and the additional possibility of six months' imprisonment.

Italians drive fast and are impatient with those who don't. Tailgaiting is the norm here—the only way to avoid it is to get out of the way.

CHILDREN IN ITALY

Although Italians love children and are generally very tolerant and patient with them, they provide few amenities for them. Discounts do exist. Always ask about a *sconto bambino* (child's discount) before purchasing tickets. Children under a certain height ride free on municipal buses and trams. Children under 18 who are EU citizens are admitted free to state-run museums and galleries, and there are similar privileges in many municipal or private museums. If you are renting a car, don't forget to **arrange for a car seat** when you reserve.

Fodor's Around Rome with Kids (available in bookstores everywhere beginning in March 2002) can help you plan your days together.

FLYING

If your children are two or older, **ask about children's airfares.** As a general rule, infants under two not occupying a seat fly at greatly reduced fares or even for free. When booking, **confirm carry-on allowances** if you're traveling with infants. In general, for babies charged 10% of the adult fare you are allowed one carry-on bag and a collapsible stroller; if the flight is full, the stroller may have to be checked or you may be limited to less.

Experts agree that it's a good idea to use safety seats aloft for children weighing less than 40 pounds. Airlines set their own policies: U.S. carriers usually require that the child be ticketed, even if he or she is young enough to ride free, since the seats must be strapped into regular seats. Do **check your airline's policy about using safety seats during takeoff and landing.** And since safety seats are not allowed everywhere in the plane, get your seat assignments early.

When reserving, **request children's meals or a freestanding bassinet** if you need them. But note that bulkhead seats, where you must sit to use the bassinet, may lack an overhead bin or storage space on the floor.

FOOD

In restaurants and trattorias you may find a high chair or a cushion for the child to sit on, but rarely do they offer a children's menu. **Order a _mezza porzione_** (half-portion) of any dish, or **ask the waiter for a _porzione da bambino_** (child's portion).

LODGING

Most hotels in Italy allow children under a certain age to stay in their parents' room at no extra charge, but others charge for them as extra adults; be sure to **find out the cutoff age for children's discounts.** The Luxury Collection of Sheraton Hotels has more than 20 properties in Italy, all of which welcome families. Club Med has a "Mini Club" (for ages 4–9) and a "Kids Club" (for ages 10 and 11) at its ski village in Sestriere. There are also kids' programs at summer resort villages in Metaponto (Basilicata) and on the islands of Sicily and Sardinia, marketed mainly to Europeans. Some of the Valtur vacation villages also have special facilities and activities for children.

➤ BEST CHOICES: **Club Med** (✉ 40 W. 57th St., New York, NY 10019, ☎ 800/258–2633, WEB www.clubmed. com). **Sheraton Hotels** (☎ 800/ 221–2340, WEB www.sheraton.com). **Valtur** (✉ Via Milano 46, Rome 00184, ☎ 06/482–1000, FAX 06/ 474–2466, WEB www.valtur.com).

SIGHTS & ATTRACTIONS

Places that are especially appealing to children are indicated by a rubber-duckie icon (🦆) in the margin.

COMPUTERS ON THE ROAD

Getting on-line in Italian cities isn't difficult: public Internet stations and Internet cafés, some open 24 hours a day, are becoming more and more common. Prices differ from place to place, so **spend some time to find the best deal.** This isn't always readily apparent: a place might have higher rates, but because it belongs to a chain you won't be charged an initial flat fee again when you move to a different city with the same chain. Some hotels have in-room modem lines, but, as with phones, using the hotel's line is relatively expensive. Always check modem rates before plugging in. You may need an adapter for your computer for the European-style plugs. As always, if you are traveling with a laptop, carry a spare battery and an adapter. Never plug in your computer into any socket before asking about surge protection. IBM sells a pea-size modem tester that plugs into a telephone jack to check if the line is safe to use.

CONSUMER PROTECTION

Whenever shopping or buying travel services in Italy, **pay with a major credit card,** if possible, so you can cancel payment or get reimbursed if there's a problem. If you're doing business with a particular company for the first time, **contact your local Better Business Bureau and the attorney general's offices** in your state and (for U.S. businesses) the company's home state as well. Have any complaints been filed? Finally, if you're buying a package or tour, always **consider travel insurance** that includes default coverage (☞ Insurance, _below_).

➤ BBBs: **Council of Better Business Bureaus** (✉ 4200 Wilson Blvd., Suite 800, Arlington, VA 22203, ☎ 703/ 276–0100, FAX 703/525–8277, WEB www.bbb.org).

CUSTOMS & DUTIES

When shopping, **keep receipts** for all purchases. Upon reentering the country, **be ready to show customs officials what you've bought.** If you feel a duty is incorrect or object to the way your clearance was handled, note the inspector's badge number and ask to see a supervisor. If the problem isn't resolved, write to the appropriate authorities, beginning with the port director at your point of entry.

IN AUSTRALIA

Australian residents who are 18 or older may bring home $A400 worth of souvenirs and gifts (including jewelry), 250 cigarettes or 250 grams of tobacco, and 1,125 ml of alcohol (including wine, beer, and spirits). Residents under 18 may bring back $A200 worth of goods. Prohibited items include meat products. Seeds, plants, and fruits need to be declared upon arrival.

➤ INFORMATION: **Australian Customs Service** (Regional Director, ✉ Box 8, Sydney, NSW 2001, Australia, ☎ 02/9213–2000, FAX 02/9213–4000, WEB www.customs.gov.au).

IN CANADA

Canadian residents who have been out of Canada for at least seven days may bring home C$750 worth of goods duty-free. If you've been away fewer than seven days but more than 48 hours, the duty-free allowance drops to C$200; if your trip lasts 24–48 hours, the allowance is C$50. You may not pool allowances with family members. Goods claimed under the C$750 exemption may follow you by mail; those claimed under the lesser exemptions must accompany you. Alcohol and tobacco products may be included in the seven-day and 48-hour exemptions but not in the 24-hour exemption. If you meet the age requirements of the province or territory through which you reenter Canada, you may bring in, duty-free, 1.14 liters (40 imperial ounces) of wine or liquor *or* 24 12-ounce cans or bottles of beer or ale. If you are 19 or older you may bring in, duty-free, 200 cigarettes and 50 cigars. Check ahead of time with the Canada Customs Revenue Agency or the Department of Agriculture for policies regarding meat products, seeds, plants, and fruits.

You may send an unlimited number of gifts worth up to C$60 each duty-free to Canada. Label the package UNSOLICITED GIFT—VALUE UNDER $60. Alcohol and tobacco are excluded.

➤ INFORMATION: **Canada Customs Revenue Agency** (✉ 2265 St. Laurent Blvd. S, Ottawa, Ontario K1G 4K3, Canada, ☎ 204/983–3500 or 506/636–5064; 800/461–9999 in Canada, FAX 613/991–4126, WEB www.ccra-adrc.gc.ca).

IN ITALY

Of goods obtained anywhere outside the EU, the allowances are: (1) 200 cigarettes or 100 cigarillos (under 3 grams) or 50 cigars or 250 grams of tobacco; (2) 2 liters of still table wine or 1 liter of spirits over 22% volume; and (3) 50 milliliters of perfume and 250 milliliters of toilet water.

Of goods obtained (duty and tax paid) within another EU country, the allowances are: (1) 800 cigarettes or 400 cigarillos (under 3 grams) or 200 cigars or 1 kilogram of tobacco; (2) 90 liters of still table wine or 10 liters of spirits over 22% volume or 20 liters of spirits under 22% volume or 110 liters of beer.

➤ INFORMATION: **Ministero delle Finanze, Direzione Centrale dei Servizi Doganali, Divisione I** (✉ Via Carucci 71, 00143 Rome, Italy, ☎ 06/5024–2117). **Dogana Sezione Viaggiatori** (✉ Aeroporto Leonardo da Vinci, Fiumicino 00054 Rome, ☎ 06/6595–4343).

IN NEW ZEALAND

Homeward-bound residents 17 or older may bring back $700 worth of souvenirs and gifts. Your duty-free allowance also includes 4.5 liters of wine or beer; one 1,125-ml bottle of spirits; and either 200 cigarettes, 250 grams of tobacco, 50 cigars, or a combination of the three up to 250 grams. Prohibited items include meat products, seeds, plants, and fruits.

➤ INFORMATION: **New Zealand Customs** (Custom House, ✉ 50 Anzac Ave., Box 29, Auckland, New Zealand, ☎ 09/300–5399, FAX 09/359–6730), WEB www.customs.govt.nz).

IN THE U.K.

If you are a U.K. resident and your journey was wholly within the European Union (EU), you won't have to pass through customs when you return to the United Kingdom. If you plan to bring back large quantities of alcohol or tobacco, check EU limits beforehand.

➤ INFORMATION: **HM Customs and Excise** (✉ Dorset House, Stamford St., Bromley, Kent BR1 1XX, U.K., ☎ 020/7202–4227, WEB www.hmce. gov.uk).

IN THE U.S.

U.S. residents who have been out of the country for at least 48 hours (and who have not used the $400 allowance or any part of it in the past 30 days) may bring home $400 worth of foreign goods duty-free.

U.S. residents 21 and older may bring back 1 liter of alcohol duty-free. In addition, regardless of your age, you are allowed 200 cigarettes and 100 non-Cuban cigars. Antiques, which the U.S. Customs Service defines as objects more than 100 years old, enter duty-free, as do original works of art done entirely by hand, including paintings, drawings, and sculptures.

You may also mail or ship packages home duty-free: up to $200 worth of goods for personal use, with a limit of one parcel per addressee per day (except alcohol or tobacco products or perfume worth more than $5); label the package PERSONAL USE and attach a list of its contents and their retail value. Do not label the package UNSOLICITED GIFT or your duty-free exemption will drop to $100. Mailed items do not affect your duty-free allowance on your return.

➤ INFORMATION: **U.S. Customs Service** (✉ 1300 Pennsylvania Ave. NW, Washington, DC 20229, WEB www.customs.gov; inquiries ☎ 202/354–1000; complaints c/o ✉ 1300 Pennsylvania Ave. NW, Room 5.4D, Washington, DC 20229; registration of equipment c/o ✉ Office of Passenger Programs, ☎ 202/927–0530).

DINING

The restaurants we list are the cream of the crop in each price category. Properties indicated by an ✕🏠 are lodging establishments whose restaurant warrants a special trip.

CATEGORY	ROME, FLORENCE, VENICE, AND MILAN*	ELSEWHERE IN ITALY*
$$$$	over 45,000 lire/€23	over 35,000 lire/€18
$$$	35,000 lire–45,000 lire/€18–€23	25,000 lire–35,000 lire/€13–€18
$$	25,000 lire–35,000 lire/€13–€18	15,000 lire–25,000 lire/€8–€13
$	under 25,000 lire/€13	under 15,000 lire/€8

Prices are for main courses (secondi piatti).

A few pointers on Italian dining etiquette: Menus are posted outside most restaurants (in English in tourist areas); if not, you might step inside and ask to take a look at the menu, but don't ask for a table unless you intend to stay. Italians diners tend to know exactly how they like their food, so **don't be afraid to ask the waiter for what you want** (salt, extra Parmesan cheese or olive oil on the side), or to have a dish prepared without ingredients you do not care for (for example, *senz'aglio, per favore*—without garlic, please). Although mineral water makes its way to almost every table, you can always order a carafe of tap water (*acqua di rubinetto* or *acqua semplice*) instead. Italians order their food first, then wine and beverages. Children's menus are practically unheard of in Italy, but most restaurants will have no problem making simple dishes such as *pasta con olio e parmigiano* (pasta with olive oil and Parmesan), *pesce bollito* (steamed fish), *riso al burro* (boiled rice with butter), *verdura lessa* (boiled vegetables), *uova* (eggs), and so on. Wiping your bowl clean with a (small) piece of bread is considered a sign of appreciation, not bad manners. Spaghetti should be eaten with a fork only, although a little help from a spoon will not horrify the locals the way cutting spaghetti into little pieces might. When you finish eating and are ready to have your plate cleared, **rest your utensils together on your** plate at about five o'clock. Order your espresso (Italians do not drink a cappuccino after dinner) after dessert, not with it. When you are ready for the check *(il conto)*, **ask for it:** unless it's well past closing time, no waiter will put a bill on your table without you having asked first. Don't ask for a doggy bag.

MEALS & SPECIALTIES

What's the difference between a ristorante and a trattoria? Can you order food at an enoteca? Can you go to a restaurant just for a snack, or order just a salad at a pizzeria? The following definitions should help.

Not too long ago, restaurants tended to be more elegant and expensive than trattorie and osterie, which served more traditional, home-style fare in an atmosphere to match. But the distinction has blurred considerably, and an osteria in the center of town might be far fancier (and pricier) than a ristorante across the street. In all these types of places, you are generally expected to order at least a two-course meal, such as: a *primo* (first course) and a *secondo* (main course); an antipasto (starter) followed by either primo or secondo; or a secondo and a *dolce* (dessert).

In an *enoteca* (wine bar) or pizzeria, it's not inappropriate to order just one dish. An enoteca menu is often limited to a selection of cheese, cured meats, pickles, salads, and desserts, but if there is a kitchen, you'll also find vegetable soups, pasta, meat, and fish. Venetian *bacari* are something between an old-style osteria and a wine bar: here it's possible to grab a fast snack *(cicheto)* at the counter to be swallowed down with a glass of wine *(ombra),* or to sit down for a quick meal. Most pizzerie don't offer just pizza, and although the other dishes on the menu are supposed to be starters, there's no harm in skipping the pizza. The typical pizzeria fare includes *affettati misti* (selection of cured pork meats), simple salads, various kinds of bruschetta and *crostino* (similar to bruschetta, but baked) and, in Rome, *olive ascolane* (green olives with a meat stuffing, deep fried) and *filetti di baccalà* (fried cod fillet). All pizzerie have fresh fruit, ice cream, and simple desserts.

Throughout the country, the handiest and least expensive places for a quick snack between sights are probably bar, caffè, and pizza al taglio spots. Most bars have a selection of *panini* (sandwiches, often warmed up on the griddle—*piastra*) and *tramezzini* (sandwiches served on untoasted white bread triangles). In larger cities, bars also serve prepared salads, fruit salads, cold pasta dishes, and yogurt around lunchtime. Most bars offer beer and a variety of alcohol, but very few bars (except in Venice) sell wine by the glass. A caffè is like a bar but usually with more tables to sit down at. Pizza at a caffè is to be avoided— it's usually frozen and reheated in a microwave oven. If you place your order at the counter, ask if you can sit down: some places charge extra for table service, others do not. In self-service bar and caffès, it's good manners to clean up your table before you leave. Note that in some places you have to pay before you place the order and then show your *scontrino* (receipt) when you move to the counter. Pizza al taglio shops are easy. They sell pizza by weigh: just point out which kind you want and how much. Very few pizza al taglio shops have places to sit down.

MEALTIMES

Breakfast is usually served from 7 to 10:30; in the north, lunch is served from 12:30 to 2:30, dinner from 7:30 to 10, while in the center and south lunch is served from 1 to 3, dinner from 8–8:30 to 10:30–11. Enoteche and bacari are open also in the morning and late afternoon for a snack at the counter. Most pizzerie open at 8 PM and close around midnight–1 AM, or later in the summer and on weekends. Most bars and caffè are open nonstop from 7 AM until 8–9 PM; a few stay open until midnight or so.

Unless otherwise noted, the restaurants listed in this guide are open daily for lunch and dinner.

PAYING

Prices for goods and services in Italy include tax. Restaurant menu prices include service *(servizio)* unless indicated on the menu (in which case it is added on to the prices listed on the menu). It is customary to leave a small tip (a few thousand lire/a euro or two) in appreciation of good service. Tips are always given in cash. Some restaurants still charge a separate "cover" charge per person, usually listed on the menu as *"pane e coperto."* It should be a modest charge (from 2000 lire/€1.00 to 5,000 lire/€2.50 per person), except at the most expensive restaurants. Some restaurants instead charge for bread, which should be brought to you (and paid for) only if you order it. Whenever in doubt, ask about the servizio, pane, and coperto policy upon ordering to avoid unpleasant discussions about payment later. The price of fish dishes is often given by weight (before cooking), so the price you see on the menu is for 100 grams of fish, not for the whole dish. An average fish portion is about 350 grams.

RESERVATIONS & DRESS

Reservations are always a good idea in restaurants and trattorias, especially over weekends and holidays. We mention them only when they are essential or not accepted. Book as far ahead as you can, and reconfirm as soon as you arrive in town. Pizzerie and enoteche accept reservations only for large groups. We mention dress only when men are required to wear a jacket or a jacket and tie. But unless they are at a sea resort eating outdoors and perfectly tanned, Italian men never wear shorts or running shoes in a restaurant—no matter how humble—or in an enoteca. Shorts are acceptable in pizzerie and side caffè. The same "rules" apply to ladies' casual shorts, running shoes, plastic sandals, and clogs.

DISABILITIES & ACCESSIBILITY

Italy has only recently begun to provide facilities such as ramps, telephones, and rest rooms for people with disabilities; such things are still the exception, not the rule. Travelers' wheelchairs must be transported free of charge, according to Italian law, but the logistics of getting a wheelchair on and off trains and buses can make this requirement irrelevant. Seats are reserved for people with disabilities on public transportation, but few buses have lifts for wheelchairs. High, narrow steps for boarding trains create additional problems. In many monuments and museums, even in some hotels and restaurants, architectural barriers make access difficult.

Contact the nearest Italian consulate about bringing a Seeing Eye dog into Italy. This requires an import license, a current certificate detailing the dog's inoculations, and a letter from your veterinarian certifying the dog's health.

LODGING

The Italian Government Travel Office (ENIT; ☞ Visitor Information, *below*) can give you a list of hotels that provide access and addresses of Italian associations for travelers with disabilities.

RESERVATIONS

When discussing accessibility with an operator or reservations agent, **ask hard questions.** Are there any stairs, inside *or* out? Are there grab bars next to the toilet *and* in the shower/tub? How wide is the doorway to the room? To the bathroom? For the most extensive facilities meeting the latest legal specifications, **opt for newer accommodations.**

➤ COMPLAINTS: **Aviation Consumer Protection Division** (☞ Air Travel, *above*) for airline-related problems. **Civil Rights Office** (✉ U.S. Department of Transportation, Departmental Office of Civil Rights, S-30, 400 7th St. SW, Room 10215, Washington, DC 20590, ☎ 202/366–4648, FAX 202/366–9371, WEB www.dot.gov/ost/docr/index.htm) for problems with surface transportation. **Disability Rights Section** (✉ U.S. Department of Justice, Civil Rights Division, Box 66738, Washington, DC 20035-6738, ☎ 202/514–0301 or 800/514–0301; 202/514–0383 TTY; 800/514–0383 TTY, FAX 202/307–1198, WEB www.usdoj.gov/crt/ada/adahom1.htm) for general complaints.

TRAVEL AGENCIES

In the United States, the Americans with Disabilities Act requires that travel firms serve the needs of all travelers. Some agencies specialize in working with people with disabilities.

➤ TRAVELERS WITH MOBILITY PROB-LEMS: **Access Adventures** (⌧ 206 Chestnut Ridge Rd., Scottsville, NY 14624, ☎ 716/889–9096, dltravel@prodigy.net), run by a for-mer physical-rehabilitation counselor. **CareVacations** (⌧ No. 5, 5110–50 Ave., Leduc, Alberta, ☎ 780/986–6404 or 877/478–7827, FAX 780/986–8332, WEB www.carevacations.com), for group tours and cruise vacations. **Flying Wheels Travel** (⌧ 143 W. Bridge St., Box 382, Owatonna, MN 55060, ☎ 507/451–5005 or 800/535–6790, FAX 507/451–1685, WEB www.flyingwheelstravel.com).

➤ TRAVELERS WITH DEVELOPMENTAL DISABILITIES: **New Directions** (⌧ 5276 Hollister Ave., Suite 207, Santa Bar-bara, CA 93111, ☎ 805/967–2841 or 888/967–2841, FAX 805/964–7344, WEB www.newdirectionstravel.com).

DISCOUNTS & DEALS

Be a smart shopper and **compare all your options** before making decisions. A plane ticket bought with a promo-tional coupon from travel clubs, coupon books, and direct-mail offers or on the Internet may not be cheaper than the least expensive fare from a discount ticket agency. And always keep in mind that what you get is just as important as what you save.

DISCOUNT RESERVATIONS

To save money, **look into discount reservations services** with toll-free numbers, which use their buying power to get a better price on hotels, airline tickets, even car rentals. When booking a room, always **call the hotel's local toll-free number** (if one is available) rather than the central reservations number—you'll often get a better price. Always ask about special packages or corporate rates.

When shopping for the best deal on hotels and car rentals, **look for guar-anteed exchange rates,** which protect you against a falling dollar. With your rate locked in, you won't pay more, even if the price goes up in the local currency.

➤ AIRLINE TICKETS: ☎ 800/FLY–ASAP.

➤ HOTEL ROOMS: **Hotel Reservations Network** (☎ 800/964–6835, WEB www.hoteldiscount.com). **Interna-tional Marketing & Travel Concepts** (☎ 800/790–4682, WEB www.imtc-travel.com). **Players Express Vacations** (☎ 800/458–6161, WEB www.playersexpress.com). **Steigen-berger Reservation Service** (☎ 800/223–5652, WEB www.srs-worldhotels.com). **Travel Interlink** (☎ 800/888–5898, WEB www.travelinterlink.com). **Turbotrip.com** (☎ 800/473–7829, WEB www.turbotrip.com).

PACKAGE DEALS

Don't confuse packages and guided tours. When you buy a package, you travel on your own, just as though you had planned the trip yourself. Fly/drive packages, which combine airfare and car rental, are often a good deal. If you **buy a rail/drive pass,** you may save on train tickets and car rentals. All Eurail- and Europass holders get a discount on Eurostar fares through the Channel Tunnel.

ELECTRICITY

To use electric-powered equipment purchased in the United States or Canada, **bring a converter and adapter.** The electrical current in Italy is 220 volts, 50 cycles alternating current (AC); wall outlets take Conti-nental-type plugs, with two or three round prongs.

If your appliances are dual-voltage, you'll need only an adapter. Don't use 110-volt outlets marked FOR SHAVERS ONLY for high-wattage appliances such as blow-dryers. Most laptops operate equally well on 110 and 220 volts and so require only an adapter.

EMBASSIES

➤ AUSTRALIA: **Australian Consulate** (⌧ Via Borgogna 2, Milan, ☎ 02/777–041).

➤ CANADA: **Canadian Embassy** (⌧ Via G.B. de Rossi 27, Rome, ☎ 06/445–981).

➤ NEW ZEALAND: **New Zealand Embassy** (⌧ Via Zara 28, Rome, ☎ 06/441–7171).

➤ UNITED KINGDOM: **British Embassy**
(✉ Via XX Settembre 80A, Rome,
☎ 06/482–5441).

➤ UNITED STATES: **U.S. Embassy** (✉
Via Veneto 121, Rome, ☎ 06/46741).

EMERGENCIES

No matter where you are in Italy, **dial
113 for all emergencies,** or find
somebody (your concierge, a
passerby) who will call for you, as
not all 113 operators speak English;
the Italian word to use to draw people's attention in an emergency is
"Aiuto!" (Help!, pronounced "ah-
YOU-toh"). *"Pronto soccorso"*
means "first aid" and when said to an
operator will get you an *ambulanza*
(ambulance). If you just need a doctor, you should ask for *"un medico"*;
most hotels will be able to refer you
to a local doctor. Don't forget to ask
the doctor for *una ricevuta* (an invoice) to show to your insurance
company in order to get a reimburse-
ment. Other useful Italian words to
use in an emergency are: *"Al fuoco!"*
(Fire!, pronounced "ahl fuh-WOE-
co"), and *"Al ladro!"* (Follow the
thief!, pronounced "ahl LAH-droh").

Italy has a national police force
(carabinieri) as well as local police
(polizia). Both are armed and have
the power to arrest and investigate
crimes. **Always report the loss of
your passport to either the carabinieri
or the police,** as well as to your
embassy. Local traffic officers are
known as *vigili* (though their official
name is *polizia municipale*)—they are
responsible for, among other things,
giving out parking tickets and clamp-
ing cars, so before you even consider
parking the Italian way, make sure
you are at least able to spot their
white (in summer) or black uniforms
(many are women). Should you find
yourself involved in a minor car
accident in town, you should contact
the vigili. A country-wide toll-free
number is used to call the carabinieri
in case of emergency.

➤ CONTACTS: **Carabinieri** (☎ 112).

GAY & LESBIAN TRAVEL

➤ GAY- & LESBIAN-FRIENDLY TRAVEL
AGENCIES: **Different Roads Travel** (✉
8383 Wilshire Blvd., Suite 902, Bev-
erly Hills, CA 90211, ☎ 323/651–
5557 or 800/429–8747, FAX 323/651–
3678, lgernert@tzell.com). **Kennedy
Travel** (✉ 314 Jericho Turnpike,
Floral Park, NY 11001, ☎ 516/352–
4888 or 800/237–7433, FAX 516/354–
8849, WEB www.kennedytravel.com).
Now Voyager (✉ 4406 18th St., San
Francisco, CA 94114, ☎ 415/626–
1169 or 800/255–6951, FAX 415/626–
8626, WEB www.nowvoyager.com).
Skylink Travel and Tour (✉ 1006
Mendocino Ave., Santa Rosa, CA
95401, ☎ 707/546–9888 or 800/
225–5759, FAX 707/546–9891, WEB
www.skylinktravel.com), serving
lesbian travelers.

➤ LOCAL CONTACTS: **Circolo di
Cultura Omosessuale Mario Mieli**
(✉ Via Corinto 5, Rome, ☎ 06/
5960–4622). **Arci Gay** (✉ Via
Bezzecca 3, Milan, ☎ 02/5412–2225,
cig-milano@libero.it).

GUIDEBOOKS

Plan well and you won't be sorry.
Guidebooks are excellent tools—and
you can take them with you. You may
want to check out Fodor's regional
gold guides: *Fodor's Rome, Fodor's
Florence, Tuscany, and Umbria,
Fodor's Naples and the Amalfi Coast,*
and *Fodor's Venice and the Veneto.*
Or study color-photo-illustrated
guides such as *Fodor's Exploring
Italy, Exploring Rome, Exploring
Venice* and *Exploring Tuscany,* thorough on culture and history; *Escape
to the Amalfi Coast, Escape to the
Riviera,* and *Escape to Tuscany,*
highlighting unique experiences; or
pocket-size *Citypack Florence, Citypack Rome,* and *Citypack Venice,*
which include supersize city maps.
Fodor's Holy Rome, also with color
photos, explores the city's Christian
heritage. *Fodor's upCLOSE Italy* is
loaded with budget options. All are
available at on-line retailers and
bookstores everywhere.

HEALTH

The Centers for Disease Control and
Prevention (CDC) in Atlanta caution
that most of Southern Europe is in the
"intermediate" range for risk of
contacting traveler's diarrhea. Part of
this risk may be attributed to an
increased consumption of olive oil

and wine, which can have a laxative effect on stomachs used to a different diet. The CDC also advises all international travelers to swim only in chlorinated swimming pools, unless they are absolutely certain the local beaches and freshwater lakes are not contaminated.

In 2001, mad cow disease had a significant impact on Italian dining habits. Although into the summer there were not any cases of the disease in humans in Italy, and only two Italian cows were found infected, most Italians stopped eating beef altogether. News stories regularly reported that butchers were being driven out of business in the early part of the year. The beloved *bistecca alla fiorentina*, the thick T-bone steak cut from Tuscan beef, was banned by the European Union; restaurants famous for this specialty have switched to grilled pork. Other traditional dishes at least temporarily unavailable include *osso buco* (braised veal shank), oxtail, and offal specialties prepared throughout the country. *Vitello* (veal), *vitellone* (young beef), and *manzo* (beef) are considered safe to eat by both the Italian government and the European Union (these are cuts that don't come in touch with spinal marrow). Yet consumers tend to trust veal only. As a result, some restaurants are experimenting with "alternative meats" such as *struzzo* (ostrich) and *canguro* (kangaroo). *Cavallo* (horse meat, which is sweet and lean), *buffalo* (buffalo, like beef but less tender), and *coniglio* (rabbit) can be found at many butchers. The price of lamb and pork has risen 20%, while the price of fish has remained stable.

As of the summer of 2001, hoof-and-mouth disease had yet to have an impact on the Italian table.

HIKING AND WALKING

Italy has many good places to hike and an extensive network of long trails. The Sentiero Italia is a national trail running from Reggio Calabria on the toe of the Italy's boot to the central section of the Apennine mountains. There are plans to lengthen it farther north and to the western Alps, and from there to the Dolomites and Udine in the Friuli region. For detailed information on the Sentiero Italia contact the CAI (Club Alpino Italiano) headquarters or local offices. Local tourist information offices can also be helpful.

➤ HIKING ORGANIZATIONS: **CAI** (✉ via Petrella 19, 201124 Milan, ☎ 02/2057231, FAX 02/205723201).

➤ HIKING AND WALKING TOURS: **Abercrombie & Kent** (☞ Group Tours, Super-Deluxe, *above*). **Above the Clouds Trekking** (✉ Box 398, Worcester, MA 01602-0398, ☎ 508/799–4499 or 800/233–4499, FAX 508/797–4779). **Backroads** (☞ Bike Travel, *above*). **Butterfield & Robinson** (☞ Bike Travel, *above*). **Ciclismo Classico** (☞ Bike Travel, *above*). **Country Walkers** (✉ Box 180, Waterbury, VT 05676-0180, ☎ 802/244–1387 or 800/464–9255, FAX 802/244–5661). **Euro-Bike Tours** (☞ Bike Travel, *above*). **Mountain Travel-Sobek. Progressive Travels** (☞ Bike Travel, *above*). **Uniquely Europe/Europe Express** (☞ Bike Travel, *above*). **Wilderness Travel** (✉ 1102 Ninth St., Berkeley, CA 94710, ☎ 510/558–2488 or 800/368–2794, FAX 510/558–2489).

HOLIDAYS

National holidays include January 1 (New Year's Day); January 6 (Epiphany); March 31 and April 1 (Easter Sunday and Monday); April 25 (Liberation Day); May 1 (Labor Day or May Day); August 15 (Assumption of Mary, better known as Ferragosto); November 1 (All Saints' Day); December 8 (Immaculate Conception); December 25 and 26 (Christmas Day and Boxing Day).

The feast days of patron saints are observed locally. Many businesses and shops may be closed in Florence, Genoa, and Turin on June 24 (St. John the Baptist); in Rome on June 29 (Sts. Peter and Paul); in Palermo on July 15 (Santa Rosalia); in Naples on September 19 (San Gennaro); in Bologna on October 4 (San Petronio); in Trieste on November 3 (San Giusto); and in Milan on December 7 (St. Ambrose). Venice's feast of St. Mark is April 25, the same as Liberation Day, so the Madonna della

Salute on November 21 makes up for the lost holiday. (*Also see* Festivals and Seasonal Events *in* When to Go, *below*.)

INSURANCE

The most useful travel-insurance plan is a comprehensive policy that includes coverage for trip cancellation and interruption, default, trip delay, and medical expenses (with a waiver for preexisting conditions).

Without insurance you will lose all or most of your money if you cancel your trip, regardless of the reason. Default insurance covers you if your tour operator, airline, or cruise line goes out of business. Trip-delay covers expenses that arise because of bad weather or mechanical delays. Study the fine print when comparing policies.

If you're traveling internationally, a key component of travel insurance is coverage for medical bills incurred if you get sick on the road. Such expenses are not generally covered by Medicare or private policies. U.K. residents can buy a travel-insurance policy valid for most vacations taken during the year in which it's purchased (but check preexisting-condition coverage). British and Australian citizens need extra medical coverage when traveling overseas.

Always **buy travel policies directly from the insurance company**; if you buy them from a cruise line, airline, or tour operator that goes out of business you probably will not be covered for the agency or operator's default, a major risk. Before making any purchase, **review your existing health and home-owner's policies** to find what they cover away from home.

➤ TRAVEL INSURERS: In the United States: **Access America** (✉ 6600 W. Broad St., Richmond, VA 23230, ☎ 800/284–8300, FAX 804/673–1491, WEB www.etravelprotection.com), **Travel Guard International** (✉ 1145 Clark St., Stevens Point, WI 54481, ☎ 715/345–0505 or 800/826–1300, FAX 800/955–8785, WEB www.noelgroup.com).

➤ INSURANCE INFORMATION: In the United Kingdom: **Association of**

British Insurers (✉ 51–55 Gresham St., London EC2V 7HQ, U.K., ☎ 020/7600–3333, FAX 020/7696–8999, WEB www.abi.org.uk). In Canada: **RBC Travel Insurance** (✉ 6880 Financial Dr., Mississauga, Ontario L5N 7Y5, Canada, ☎ 905/791–8700; 800/668–4342 in Canada, FAX 905/816–2498, WEB www.royalbank.com). In Australia: **Insurance Council of Australia** (✉ Level 3, 56 Pitt St., Sydney NSW 2000, ☎ 02/9253–5100, FAX 02/9253–5111, WEB www.ica.com.au). In New Zealand: **Insurance Council of New Zealand** (✉ Box 474, Wellington, New Zealand, ☎ 04/472–5230, FAX 04/473–3011, WEB www.icnz.org.nz).

LANGUAGE

In the main tourist cities, language is not a big problem. Most hotels have English speakers at their reception desks, and you can always find someone who speaks at least a little English otherwise. Remember that the Italian language is pronounced exactly as it is written (many Italians try to speak English by enunciating every syllable, with disconcerting results). You may run into a language barrier in the countryside, but a phrase book and close attention to the Italians' astonishing use of pantomime and expressive gestures will go a long way. Try to **master a few phrases for daily use** and familiarize yourself with the terms you'll need for deciphering signs and museum labels.

LANGUAGES FOR TRAVELERS

A phrase book and language-tape set can help get you started. *Fodor's Italian for Travelers* (available at bookstores everywhere) is excellent.

➤ PHRASE BOOKS & LANGUAGE-TAPE SETS: *Fodor's Italian for Travelers* (☎ 800/733–3000 in the U.S.; 800/668–4247 in Canada; $7 for phrase book, $16.95 for audio set plus $5.50 for shipping).

LODGING

The lodgings we list are the cream of the crop in each price category. We always list the facilities that are available—but we don't specify whether they cost extra: when pricing accommodations, always ask what's included and what costs extra. Properties indicated by an ✕🏠 are lodging establishments whose restaurants warrant a special trip.

CATEGORY	ROME, FLORENCE, VENICE, AND MILAN*	ELSEWHERE IN ITALY*
$$$$	over 500,000 lire/€260	over 300,000 lire/€155
$$$	350,000 lire– 500,000 lire/ €180–€260	200,000 lire– 300,000 lire/ €105–€155
$$	200,000 lire– 350,000 lire/ €105–€180	100,000 lire– 200,000 lire/ €105–€50
$	under 200,000 lire/€105	under 100,000 lire/€50

Prices are for a standard double room for two including tax and service.

Assume that hotels operate on the Continental Plan (CP, with a Continental breakfast daily), unless we specify that they use the Modified American Plan (MAP, with breakfast and dinner daily), or the Full American Plan (FAP, with all meals).

APARTMENT & VILLA RENTALS

If you want a home base that's roomy enough for a family and comes with cooking facilities, **consider a furnished rental.** These can save you money, especially if you're traveling with a group. Home-exchange directories sometimes list rentals as well as exchanges.

➤ INTERNATIONAL AGENTS: **At Home Abroad** (⊠ 405 E. 56th St., Suite 6H, New York, NY 10022, ☎ 212/421–9165, FAX 212/752–1591, WEB www. athomeabroadinc.com). **Drawbridge to Europe** (⊠ 98 Granite St., Ashland, OR 97520, ☎ 541/482–7778 or 888/268–1148, FAX 541/482–7779, WEB www.drawbridgetoeurope.com). **Hideaways International** (⊠ 767 Islington St., Portsmouth, NH 03801, ☎ 603/430–4433 or 800/843–4433, FAX 603/430–4444, WEB www.hideaways.com; membership $129). **Hometours International** (⊠ Box 11503, Knoxville, TN 37939, ☎ 865/690–8484 or 800/367–4668, WEB thor.he.net/~hometour/). **Interhome** (⊠ 1990 N.E. 163rd St., Suite 110, N. Miami Beach, FL 33162, ☎ 305/940–2299 or 800/882–6864, FAX 305/

940–2911, WEB www.interhome.com). **Vacation Home Rentals Worldwide** (⊠ 235 Kensington Ave., Norwood, NJ 07648, ☎ 201/767–9393 or 800/633–3284, FAX 201/767–5510, WEB www.vhrww.com). **Villanet** (⊠ 11556 First Ave. NW, Seattle, WA 98177, ☎ 206/417–3444 or 800/964–1891, FAX 206/417–1832, WEB www. rentavilla.com). **Villas and Apartments Abroad** (⊠ 1270 Avenue of the Americas, 15th floor, New York, NY 10020, ☎ 212/897–5045 or 800/433–3020, FAX 212/897–5039, WEB www.vaanyc.com). **Villas International** (⊠ 950 Northgate Dr., Suite 206, San Rafael, CA 94903, ☎ 415/499–9490 or 800/221–2260, FAX 415/499–9491, WEB www.villasintl.com).

➤ LOCAL AGENTS: **Cuendet USA** (⊠ 165 Chestnut St., Allendale, NJ 07041, ☎ 201/327–2333; ⊠ Suzanne T. Pidduck, c/o Rentals in Italy, 1742 Calle Corva, Camarillo, CA 93010, ☎ 800/726–6702). **Eurovillas** (⊠ 3212 Jefferson St., Suite 298, Napa, CA 94558, ☎ 800/767–0275, ☎ FAX 707/648–2066). **Rentvillas.com** (⊠ 1742 Calle Corva, Camarillo, CA 93010-8428, ☎ 805/987–5278 or 800/726–6702, FAX 805/482–7976). **Vacanze in Italia** (⊠ 22 Railroad St., Great Barrington, MA 01230, ☎ 413/528–6610 or 800/533–5405).

➤ IN THE U.K.: **CV Travel** (⊠ 43 Cadogan St., London SW3 2PR, England, ☎ 020/7581–0851). **Magic of Italy** (⊠ 227 Shepherds Bush Rd., London W6 7AS, England, ☎ 020/8748–7575).

FARM HOLIDAYS & AGRITOURISM

Rural accommodations in the *agriturismo* (agritourism) category are increasingly popular with both Italians and visitors to Italy. You stay on a working farm or vineyard, often in stone farmhouses that accommodate a number of guests. Contact local APT tourist offices, or you can buy *Agriturism,* compiled by Agriturist, which includes more than 1,600 farms in Italy. Although it is available in Italian only from major bookstores, pictures and the use of international symbols describing facilities make the guide a good tool to use.

➤ AGENCIES: **Essentially Tuscany**
(⊠ 30 York St., Nantucket, MA,
☎ FAX 508/228–2514). **Italy Farm
Holidays** (⊠ 547 Martling Ave.,
Tarrytown, NY 10591, ☎ 914/631–
7880, FAX 914/631–8831).

HOME EXCHANGES

If you would like to exchange your
home for someone else's, **join a home-
exchange organization,** which will
send you its updated listings of available exchanges for a year and will
include your own listing in at least
one of them. It's up to you to make
specific arrangements.

➤ EXCHANGE CLUBS: **HomeLink
International** (⊠ Box 47747, Tampa,
FL 33647, ☎ 813/975–9825 or 800/
638–3841, FAX 813/910–8144, WEB
www.homelink.org; $98 per year).
Intervac U.S. (⊠ Box 590504,
San Francisco, CA 94159, ☎ 800/
756–4663, FAX 415/435–7440, WEB
www.intervacus.com; $93 yearly fee
includes one catalogue and on-line
access).

HOSTELS

No matter what your age, you can
**save on lodging costs by staying at
hostels.** In some 4,500 locations in
more than 70 countries around the
world, Hostelling International (HI),
the umbrella group for a number of
national youth-hostel associations,
offers single-sex, dorm-style beds and,
at many hostels, rooms for couples
and family accommodations. Membership in any HI national hostel
association, open to travelers of all
ages, allows you to stay in HI-affili-
ated hostels at member rates; one-
year membership is about $25 for
adults (C$26.75 in Canada, £9.30 in
the U.K., $30 in Australia, and $30 in
New Zealand); hostels run about
$10–$25 per night. Members have
priority if the hostel is full; they're
also eligible for discounts around the
world, even on rail and bus travel in
some countries.

➤ ORGANIZATIONS: **Australian Youth
Hostel Association** (⊠ 10 Mallett St.,
Camperdown, NSW 2050, Australia,
☎ 02/9565–1699, FAX 02/9565–1325,
WEB www.yha.com.au). **Hostelling
International—American Youth
Hostels** (⊠ 733 15th St. NW, Suite

840, Washington, DC 20005, ☎ 202/
783–6161, FAX 202/783–6171, WEB
www.hiayh.org). **Hostelling International—Canada** (⊠ 400–205 Catherine St., Ottawa, Ontario K2P 1C3,
Canada, ☎ 613/237–7884, FAX 613/
237–7868, WEB www.hostellingintl.ca).
**Youth Hostel Association of England
and Wales** (⊠ Trevelyan House, 8 St.
Stephen's Hill, St. Albans, Hertford-
shire AL1 2DY, U.K., ☎ 0870/
8708808, FAX 01727/844126, WEB
www.yha.org.uk). **Youth Hostels
Association of New Zealand** (⊠
Level 3, 193 Cashel St., Box 436,
Christchurch, New Zealand,
☎ 03/379–9970, FAX 03/365–4476,
WEB www.yha.org.nz).

HOTELS

Italian hotels are awarded stars (one
to five) based on their facilities and
services. Keep in mind, however, that
these are general indications and that
a charming three-star might make for
a better stay than a more expensive
four-star. In the major cities, room
rates are on a par with those of other
European capitals: deluxe and four-
star rates can be downright extravagant. In those categories, **ask for one
of the better rooms,** since less desir-
able rooms—and there usually are
some—don't give you what you're
paying for. Except in deluxe and some
four-star hotels, rooms may be very
small by U.S standards, and bathrooms usually have showers rather
than bathtubs. Hotels with three or
more stars always have bathrooms in
all rooms.

In all hotels there is a rate card inside
the door of your room or inside the
closet door; it tells you exactly what
you will pay for that particular room
(rates in the same hotel may vary
according to the location and type of
room). On this card, breakfast and
any other optionals must be listed
separately. Any discrepancy between
the basic room rate and that charged
on your bill is cause for complaint to
the manager and to the police.

Although, by law, breakfast is supposed to be optional, most hotels
quote room rates including breakfast.
When you book a room, specifically
**ask whether the rate includes break-
fast** (*colazione*). You are under no

obligation to take breakfast at your hotel, but in practice most hotels expect you to do so. The trick is to "offer" guests "complimentary" breakfast and have its cost built in the rate. However, it is encouraging to note that many of the hotels we recommend provide generous buffet breakfasts instead of simple, even skimpy "Continental breakfasts." Remember, if the latter is the case, you can eat for less at the nearest coffee bar.

Hotels that we list as (\$\$) and (\$) may charge extra for optional air-conditioning. In older hotels the quality of the rooms may be very uneven; if you don't like the room you're given, request another. This applies to noise, too. Front rooms may be larger or have a view, but they also may have a lot of street noise. If you're a light sleeper, **request a quiet room when making reservations.** Rooms in lodgings listed in this guide have a shower and/or bath, unless noted otherwise. Remember to **specify whether you care to have a bathtub or shower,** since not all rooms have both. It is always a good idea to have your reservation, dates, and rate confirmed by fax or e-mail.

During low season and whenever a hotel is not full, it is often possible to negotiate a discounted rate. Major cities, such as Rome and Milan, have no official off-season as far as hotel rates go, though some hotels do offer substantial discounts during the slower parts of the year and on weekends. Always **inquire about special rates.** Major cities have hotel-reservation service booths in train stations.

The Sheraton/The Luxury Collection has more than 20 Italian properties, almost all five-star deluxe. Jolly has 32 four-star hotels in Italy. Atahotels has 20 mostly four- and five-star hotels. Starhotels has 14 mainly four-star hotels. Space Hotels has 80 independently owned four- and three-star hotels. Prima Hotels has about 20 independently owned four- and five-star hotels. AGIP Motels is a chain of about 50, mostly four-star motels on main highways; the motels are commercial, functional accommodations for business travelers and

tourists needing 40 winks, but they—and the Jolly hotels—can be the best choice in many out-of-the-way places. The **Forte** group has taken over some top-of-the-line AGIP properties throughout Italy.

Best Western, an international association of independently owned hotels, has some 75 mainly three- and four-star hotels in Italy; call to request the *Europe and Middle East Atlas* that lists them. **Family Hotels,** which groups about 80 small (maximum 35 rooms) family-run, one-, two-, and three-star hotels, offers good value. A spin-off of this group, the **Sun Rays Pool,** comprises four- and five-star hotels, as well as several *agriturismi* with horseback riding.

➤ TOLL-FREE NUMBERS: **Atahotels** (✉ Via Lampedusa 11/a, 20141 Milan, ☎ 02/895261, FAX 02/89503643; E&M Associates, ☎ 212/599–8280 or 800/223–9832). **Best Western** (☎ 800/528–1234, WEB www.bestwestern.com). **Choice** (☎ 800/221–2222, WEB www.hotelchoice.com). **Clarion** (☎ 800/252–7466, WEB www.hotelchoice.com). **Comfort** (☎ 800/228–5150, WEB www.comfortinn.com). **Family Hotels** (✉ Via Faenza 77, 50100 Florence, ☎ FAX 055/2381905). **Forte** (☎ 800/225–5843, WEB www.forte-hotels.com). **Four Seasons** (☎ 800/332–3442, WEB www.fourseasons.com). **Hilton** (☎ 800/445–8667, WEB www.hilton.com). **Holiday Inn** (☎ 800/465–4329, WEB www.basshotels.com). **Jolly** (☎ 800/247–1277 in New York; 800/221–2626 elsewhere in U.S.; 800/237–0319 in Canada; 800/017–703 toll-free in Italy). **Marriott** (☎ 800/228–9290, WEB www.marriott.com). **Le Meridien** (☎ 800/543–4300, WEB www.lemeridien-hotels.com). **Quality Inn** (☎ 800/228–5151, WEB www.qualityinn.com). **Radisson** (☎ 800/333–3333, WEB www.radisson.com). **Ramada** (☎ 800/228–2828, WEB www.ramada.com). **Sheraton** (☎ 800/325–3535, WEB www.starwood.com). **Sheraton/The Luxury Collection** (☎ 800/221–2340; 800/835035 toll-free in Italy, FAX 212/421–5929). **Space Hotels** (☎ 800/813–013 toll-free in Italy). **Starhotels** (✉ Viale Belfiore 27, 50144 Firenze, ☎ 055/36921; 800/860–200 toll-free in Italy;

800/448–8355, FAX 055/36924).
Supranational (☎ 416/927–1133 or
800/843–3311). **Westin Hotels &
Resorts** (☎ 800/228–3000, WEB www.
westin.com).

MAIL & SHIPPING

The Italian mail system is notoriously
slow. Allow up to 15 days for mail
to and from the United States and
Canada, about a week to and from
the United Kingdom and within Italy.
Posta Prioritaria (for Italy only) and
Postacelere (for Italy and abroad) are
new special-delivery services from the
post office that guarantee delivery
within 24 hours in Italy and three to
five days abroad.

OVERNIGHT SERVICES

Private courier companies make
sending overnight mail internationally
from major cities in Italy fairly easy.
Most couriers have a morning dead-
line for fastest service (next day or
two-day delivery). For information
from DHL, Federal Express, or SDA
regarding rates and drop-off points, or
to schedule a pick-up, you can use the
services' national toll-free numbers

➤ MAJOR SERVICES: **DHL** (☎ 800/
345345, 24 hrs a day). **Federal Express** (☎ 800/123800, Mon.–Fri. 8–
7). **SDA** (☎ 800/016027, Mon.–Fri.
8:30–7:30, Sat. 8:30–1:30).

POSTAL RATES

Airmail letters and postcards
(lightweight stationery) to the United
States and Canada cost 1,300 lire/
€0.67 for the first 20 grams; for
heavier stationery you should go to the
post office. Always stick the blue
airmail tag on your mail, or write
"Airmail" in big, clear characters to
the side of the address. Postcards and
letters (for the first 20 grams) to the
United Kingdom, as well as to any
other EU country, including Italy, cost
800 lire/€0.41.

Posta Prioritaria (stationery and small
packages up to 2 kilograms) and the
more expensive Postacelere (up to 20
kilograms) are special delivery services from the post office that guarantee delivery within 24 hours in Italy
and three to five days abroad.
Lightweight stationery sent as Posta
Prioritaria to the United States and

Canada costs 1,500 lire/€0.77 (for
the first 20 grams, double that for
parcels up to 100 grams); to the
United Kingdom, Italy, and all other
EU countries it costs 1,200 lire/
€0.62. As regular stamps are not
valid for this service, make sure you
buy the special golden Posta Prioritaria stamps. Postacelere rates to the
United States and Canada range
between 46,000 lire/€23.76 (30,000
lire/€15.49 to the United Kingdom
and Europe) for parcels up to 500
grams (a little over a pound) and
358,000 lire/€184.90 (148,000
lire/€76.44 to the United Kingdom
and Europe) for packages weighing
20 kilos.

You can buy stamps at tobacconists
and post offices.

Informazioni Poste Italiane ☎ 160;
600 lire/€0.31 for information in
Italian about rates and local post
offices' opening hours; toll-free 800/
009–966 for information about
Postacelere, WEB www.poste.it for
information in Italian about postal
codes, rates, post offices' addresses,
and for tracing information on packages sent as Postacelere.

RECEIVING MAIL

Correspondence can be addressed to
you in care of the Italian post office.
Letters should be addressed to your
name, "c/o Ufficio Postale Centrale,"
followed by "Fermo Posta" on the
next line, and the name of the city
(preceded by its postal code) on the
next. You can **collect it at the central
post office** by showing your passport
or photo-bearing I.D. and paying a
small fee. American Express also has
a general-delivery service. There's no
charge for cardholders, holders of
American Express Traveler's checks,
or anyone who booked a vacation
with American Express.

MONEY MATTERS

As in most countries, prices vary from
region to region and are substantially
lower in the countryside than in
touristy cities. Good value for the
money can be had in the scenic
Trentino–Alto Adige region and the
Dolomites, in Umbria and the
Marches, and on the Amalfi Coast.
With a few exceptions, southern Italy,

Sicily, and Sardinia also offer good values, but hotels are not always up to par. Of Italy's major cities, Venice and Milan are the most expensive. Resorts such as the Costa Smeralda, Portofino, and Cortina d'Ampezzo cater to the rich and famous and charge top prices.

Admission to the Vatican Museums is 18,000 lire/€9.30; to the Galleria degli Uffizi, 12,000 lire/€6.20. The cheapest seat at Rome's Teatro dell'-Opera runs 32,000 lire/€16.55. A movie ticket is 13,000 lire/€6.70. Getting into a Milan nightclub will set you back about 35,000 lire/€18.00. A daily English-language newspaper is 2,500 lire/€1.30. A Rome taxi ride (1⅓ km, or 1 mi) costs 10,000 lire/€5.15. An inexpensive hotel room for two, including breakfast, in Rome is about 190,000 lire/€98; an inexpensive Rome dinner is 40,000 lire/€21, and a ½ liter carafe of house wine, 6,000 lire/€3.10. A simple pasta item runs about 13,000 lire/€6.70, a cup of coffee 1,200–1,400 lire/€0.60–0.70, and a rosticceria lunch, about 15,000 lire/€7.75. A Coca-Cola (standing) at a café is 2,500–3,500 lire/€1.30–1.80 and a pint of beer is 7,000 lire/€3.60.

Prices throughout this guide are given for adults. Substantially reduced fees are almost always available for children, students, and senior citizens. For information on taxes, *see* Taxes, *below.*

ATMS

Fairly common in Rome and in any other town as well as in airports and train stations, ATMs are the easiest way to get euros in Italy. Don't, however, count on finding ATMs in tinier towns and rural areas.

CREDIT CARDS

All over Italy, Visa and MasterCard are preferred to American Express, but in tourist areas American Express is usually accepted. While increasingly common, not all establishments and stores take credit cards, and some require a minimum expenditure. If you want to pay with a card in a small hotel, store, or restaurant, it's a good idea to make your intentions known early on.

Throughout this guide, the following abbreviations are used: **AE,** American Express; **DC,** Diners Club; **MC,** MasterCard; and **V,** Visa.

➤ REPORTING LOST CARDS: **American Express** (☎ 336/668–5110 international collect). **Diners Club** (☎ 702/797–5532 collect). **MasterCard** (☎ 800/870–866 toll-free within Italy). **Visa** (☎ 800/821–001).

CURRENCY

Up to January 1, 2002, the lira will remain the main unit of currency in Italy, but after that date, the new single European Union (EU) currency, the euro, will take over. While the lira still exists, it is found in bills of 500,000 (practically impossible to change outside of banks), 100,000, 50,000, 10,000, 5,000, 2,000, and 1,000 lire. Coins are 1000, 500, 200, 100 and 50 lire.

Lire will stay in circulation through March 2002. After January 1, 2002, participating European national currencies will no longer be listed on foreign exchange markets. Note that prices in euros correspond generally to the U.S. dollar as their exchange rates are relatively close.

Under the euro system, there are eight coins: 1 and 2 euros, plus 1, 2, 5, 10, 20, and 50 centimes, or cents, of the euro. All coins have one side that has the value of the euro on it and the other side with each country's own unique national symbol. There are seven notes: 5, 10, 20, 50, 100, 200, and 500 euros. Notes are the same for all countries.

CURRENCY EXCHANGE

For the most favorable rates, **change money through banks.** Although ATM transaction fees may be higher abroad than at home, ATM rates are excellent because they are based on wholesale rates offered only by major banks. You won't do as well at exchange booths in airports or rail and bus stations, in hotels, in restaurants, or in stores. To avoid lines at airport exchange booths, **get a bit of local currency before you leave home.**

At press time, the exchange rate was about 2,222 lire/1.15 euros to the U.S. dollar; 1,446 lire/0.75 euros to the Canadian dollar; 3,154 lire/1.63 euros to the pound sterling; 1,143 lire/0.59 euros to the Australian dollar; and 920 lire/0.47 euros to the New Zealand dollar.

➤ EXCHANGE SERVICES: **International Currency Express** (☎ 888/278–6628 for orders, WEB www.foreignmoney. com). **Thomas Cook Currency Services** (☎ 800/287–7362 for telephone orders and retail locations, WEB www. us.thomascook.com).

TRAVELER'S CHECKS

Do you need traveler's checks? It depends on where you're headed. If you're going to rural areas and small towns, go with cash; traveler's checks are best used in cities. Lost or stolen checks can usually be replaced within 24 hours. To ensure a speedy refund, buy your own traveler's checks— don't let someone else pay for them: irregularities like this can cause delays. The person who bought the checks should make the call to request a refund.

PACKING

The weather is considerably milder, in the winter at least, in Italy than in the north and central United States or Great Britain. In summer, stick with very light clothing, as things can get steamy at the height of summer; a sweater may be necessary for cool evenings, especially in the mountains and on islands even during the hot months. Sunglasses, a hat, and sunblock are essential. Brief summer afternoon thunderstorms are common in Rome and inland cities, so an umbrella will come in handy. In winter bring a medium-weight coat and a raincoat for Rome and farther south. Northern Italy calls for heavier clothes, gloves, hats, scarves, and boots. Even in Rome and other milder areas, central heating may not be up to your standards, and interiors can be cold and damp; take wools or flannel rather than sheer fabrics. Bring sturdy shoes for winter and comfortable walking shoes in any season.

Italians dress exceptionally well. They do not usually wear shorts. Men aren't required to wear ties or jackets anywhere, except in some of the grander hotel dining rooms and top-level restaurants, but are expected to look reasonably sharp—and they do. Formal wear is the exception rather than the rule at the opera nowadays, though people in expensive seats usually do get dressed up.

A certain modesty of dress (no bare shoulders or knees) is expected in churches, and strictly enforced in many, especially in Rome at St. Peter's and the Vatican Museums and at the Basilica di San Marco in Venice.

For sightseeing, **pack a pair of binoculars;** they will help you get a good look at painted ceilings and domes. If you stay in budget hotels, **take your own soap.** Many such hotels do not provide it or give guests only one tiny bar per room.

In your carry-on luggage, **pack an extra pair of eyeglasses or contact lenses** and **enough of any medication you take** to last the entire trip. You may also ask your doctor to write a spare prescription using the drug's generic name, since brand names may vary from country to country. In luggage to be checked, **never pack prescription drugs or valuables.** To avoid customs delays, carry medications in their original packaging. And don't forget to carry with you the addresses of offices that handle refunds of lost traveler's checks. Check *Fodor's How to Pack* (available in bookstores everywhere) for more tips.

CHECKING LUGGAGE

How many carry-on bags you can bring with you is up to the airline. Most allow two, but not always, so make sure that everything you carry aboard will fit under your seat or in the overhead bin, and get to the gate early. Note that if you have a seat at the back of the plane, you'll probably board first, while the overhead bins are still empty.

If you are flying internationally, note that baggage allowances may be determined not by piece but by weight—generally 88 pounds (40 kilograms) in first class, 66 pounds (30 kilograms) in business class, and 44 pounds (20 kilograms) in economy.

Airline liability for baggage is limited to $1,250 per person on flights within the United States. On international flights it amounts to $9.07 per pound or $20 per kilogram for checked baggage (roughly $640 per 70-pound bag) and $400 per passenger for unchecked baggage. You can buy additional coverage at check-in for about $10 per $1,000 of coverage, but it excludes a rather extensive list of items, shown on your airline ticket.

Before departure, **itemize your bags' contents** and their worth, and label the bags with your name, address, and phone number. (If you use your home address, cover it so potential thieves can't see it readily.) Inside each bag, **pack a copy of your itinerary.** At check-in, **make sure that each bag is correctly tagged** with the destination airport's three-letter code. If your bags arrive damaged or fail to arrive at all, file a written report with the airline before leaving the airport.

PASSPORTS & VISAS

When traveling internationally, **carry your passport** even if you don't need one (it's always the best form of ID) and **make two photocopies of the data page** (one for someone at home and another for you, carried separately from your passport). If you lose your passport, promptly call the nearest embassy or consulate and the local police.

ENTERING ITALY

➤ AUSTRALIAN CITIZENS: Citizens of Australia need only a valid passport to enter Italy for stays of up to 90 days.

➤ CANADIAN CITIZENS: Citizens of Canada need only a valid passport to enter Italy for stays of up to 90 days.

➤ NEW ZEALAND CITIZENS: Citizens of New Zealand need only a valid passport to enter Italy for stays of up to 90 days.

➤ U.K. CITIZENS: Citizens of the United Kingdom need only a valid passport to enter Italy for an unlimited stay.

➤ U.S. CITIZENS: All U.S. citizens, even infants, need only a valid passport to enter Italy for stays of up to 90 days.

PASSPORT OFFICES

The best time to apply for a passport or to renew is in fall and winter. Before any trip, check your passport's expiration date, and, if necessary, renew it as soon as possible.

➤ AUSTRALIAN CITIZENS: **Australian Passport Office** (☎ 131–232, WEB www.dfat.gov.au/passports).

➤ CANADIAN CITIZENS: **Passport Office** (☎ 819/994–3500; 800/567–6868 in Canada, WEB www.dfait-maeci.gc.ca/passport).

➤ NEW ZEALAND CITIZENS: **New Zealand Passport Office** (☎ 04/494–0700, WEB www.passports.govt.nz).

➤ U.K. CITIZENS: **London Passport Office** (☎ 0870/521–0410, WEB www.ukpa.gov.uk) for fees and documentation requirements and to request an emergency passport.

➤ U.S. CITIZENS: **National Passport Information Center** (☎ 900/225–5674; calls are 35¢ per minute for automated service, $1.05 per minute for operator service; WEB www.travel.state.gov/npicinfo.html).

REST ROOMS

Public rest rooms are rather rare in Italy; the locals seem to make do with well-timed pit stops and rely on the local bar. While private businesses can refuse to make their toilets available to the passing public, most bars will allow you to use the rest room if you ask politely. Alternatively, it is not uncommon to pay for a little something—a few cents for a mineral water or espresso—in order to get access to the facilities. Standards of cleanliness and comfort vary greatly. In cities, restaurants, hotel halls, department stores like La Rinascente and Coin, and McDonald's restaurants tend to have the cleanest rest rooms. Pubs and bars rank among the worst. In general, it is in your interest to carry tissues with you. There are bathrooms in all airports and train stations (in major train stations you'll also find well-kept pay toilets for 500–1,000 lire/€0.25–0.50) and in most museums. There are also bathrooms at highway rest stops and gas stations: a small tip to the cleaning person is always appreciated. There are no bathrooms in churches, post offices, public beaches, or subway stations. Aside from in Venice, pay toilets scattered through the city center of Italian towns are the exception, not the rule. In Venice, pay toilets are well posted and strategically located along the main drags which link Piazzale Roma and the train station with the city center; the cost is 1,000 lire/€0.50.

SAFETY

The best way to **protect yourself against purse snatchers and pick-pockets** is to wear a money belt or a pouch on a string around your neck, both concealed. If you carry a bag or camera, be absolutely sure it has straps; you should sling it across your body bandolier-style. Always be astutely aware of stealthy pickpockets, especially when in jam-packed city buses and metros, when making your way through train corridors, and in busy piazzas.

LOCAL SCAMS

A word of caution: "gypsy" children are rife in Rome, especially around the Colosseum, and are adept pickpockets. One tactic is to approach a tourist and proffer a piece of cardboard with writing on it. While you attempt to read the message *on* it, the children's hands are busy *under* it, trying to make off with purses or valuables. If you see such a group, avoid them—they are quick and know more tricks than you do.

WOMEN IN ITALY

The difficulties encountered by women traveling alone in Italy are often overstated. Younger women have to put up with much male attention, but it is rarely dangerous. Ignoring whistling and questions is the best way to get rid of unwanted attention.

SENIOR-CITIZEN TRAVEL

To qualify for age-related discounts, **mention your senior-citizen status up front** when booking hotel reservations (not when checking out) and, if you are EU citizens over 65, before buying museum tickets. When renting a car, ask about promotional car-rental discounts, which can be cheaper than senior-citizen rates.

➤ EDUCATIONAL PROGRAMS: **Elderhostel** (✉ 11 Ave. de Lafayette, Boston, MA 02111-1746, ☎ 877/426–8056, FAX 877/426–2166, WEB www.elderhostel.org). **Interhostel** (✉ University of New Hampshire, 6 Garrison Ave., Durham, NH 03824, ☎ 603/862–1147 or 800/733–9753, FAX 603/862–1113, WEB www.learn.unh.edu).

SHOPPING

The notice PREZZI FISSI (fixed prices) means just that—it's a waste of time to bargain unless you're buying a sizable quantity of goods or a particularly costly object. Always try to bargain, however, at outdoor markets (except food markets) and when buying from street vendors. For information on VAT refunds, *see* Taxes, *below.*

SMOKING

To the dismay of many clean-air-loving travelers, Italians are unrepentant smokers. Although the number of smokers is dropping slowly each year, Italians are known for disregarding the many no-smoking laws that do exist, but are seldom seriously enforced. If you ask someone to smoke elsewhere or not to smoke in no-smoking areas, don't expect them to respond or respect your request. By Italian law, restaurants and bars should be equipped with ventilation systems, but many restaurants seem not to comply adequately. Your best bet for finding as smoke-free an environment as possible is to stick to large establishments and, weather permitting, to eat outside. All FS trains have no-smoking cars: always specify when you make reservations.

STREET ADDRESSES

Addresses in Italy are fairly straightforward: the street is followed by the street number. However, you might see an address with a number plus "bis" or "A," for instance, "Via Verdi 3/bis" or "Via Mazzini 8/A." This indicates that 3/bis or 8/A are the next entrance or door down from Via Verdi 3 and Via Mazzini 8 respectively. In central Florence, addresses with a number followed by "r" (e.g., Via Santo Spirito 35/r), refer to "rosso" (red), the color of the number painted on the wall.

In rural areas, some addresses give only the route name or the distance in kilometers along a major road (e.g., Via Fabbri, km. 4.3), or sometimes only the name of the small village in which the site is located.

In Venice addresses are made up of the name of one the city's six neighborhoods and a number. The hitch is that the numbers don't go in any sequential order, so San Marco 3672 and 3673 might well be several narrow winding streets away from one another. Accordingly, when helpful the Venetian addresses in this book include the nearest campo, bridge, or calle.

STUDENTS IN ITALY

In the major art cities there are plenty of facilities in the way of information and lodging geared to students' needs. Students with I.D. cards may obtain discounts at museums, galleries, exhibitions, and entertainment venues, and on some transportation.

LOCAL RESOURCES

The Centro Turistico Studentesco is a student and youth travel agency with offices in major Italian cities. CTS helps its clients find low-cost accommodations and bargain fares for travel in Italy and elsewhere. CTS is also the Rome representative for EuroTrain International.

TRAVEL AGENCIES

To save money, **look into deals available through student-oriented travel agencies.** To qualify you'll need a student ID card. Members of international student groups are also eligible.

➤ IDs & SERVICES: **Centro Turistico Studentesco** (CTS; ✉ Corso Vittorio Emanuele II 297, Rome, 00186, ☎ 06/687–2672); **Council Travel** (CIEE; ✉ 205 E. 42nd St., 15th floor, New York, NY 10017, ☎ 212/822–2700 or 888/268–6245, FAX 212/822–2699, WEB www.councilexchanges.org) for mail orders only, in the United States; **Travel Cuts** (✉ 187 College St., Toronto, Ontario M5T 1P7, Canada, ☎ 416/979–2406 or 800/667–2887 in Canada, FAX 416/979–8167, WEB www.travelcuts.com).

TAXES

HOTEL

The service charge and the 9% IVA, or VAT tax, are included in the rate except in five-star deluxe hotels, where the IVA (12% on luxury hotels) may be a separate item added to the bill upon departure.

RESTAURANT

A service charge of approximately 15% is added to all restaurant bills; in some cases the menu may state that the service charge is already included in the menu prices.

VALUE-ADDED TAX

Value-added tax (IVA, or VAT) is 20% on clothing, wine, and luxury goods. On consumer goods, it is already included in the amount shown on the price tag, whereas on services it may not be.

To **get an IVA refund,** when you are leaving Italy take the goods and the invoice to the customs office at the airport or other point of departure and have the invoice stamped. (If you return to the United States or Canada directly from Italy, go through the procedure at Italian customs; if your return is via any of the EC countries, for instance, via France, take the Italian goods and invoice to French customs.) Under Italy's IVA-refund system, a non-EU resident is entitled to a VAT refund. Shop with your passport and ask the store for an invoice itemizing the article(s), price(s), and the amount of tax. Once back home—and within 90 days of the date of purchase—mail the stamped invoice to the store, which will send the IVA rebate to you.

Global Refund is a VAT refund service that makes getting your money back hassle-free. The service is available Europe-wide at 130,000 affiliated stores. In participating stores, **ask for the Global Refund refund form** (called a Shopping Cheque). Have it stamped like any customs form by customs officials when you leave the European Union (be ready to show customs officials what you've bought). Then take the form to one of the more than 700 Global Refund counters—conveniently located at every major airport and border crossing—and your money will be refunded on the spot in the form of cash, check, or a refund to your credit-card account (minus a small percentage for processing).

➤ VAT REFUNDS: **Global Refund** (✉ 99 Main St., Suite 307, Nyack, NY 10960, ☎ 800/566–9828, FAX 845/348–1549, WEB www. globalrefund.com).

TELEPHONES

AREA & COUNTRY CODES

The country code for Italy is 39. Here are area codes for major cities: Bologna, 051; Brindisi, 0831; Florence, 055; Genoa, 010; Milan, 02; Naples, 081; Palermo, 091; Perugia, 075; Pisa, 050; Rome, 06; Siena, 0577; Turin, 011; Venice, 041; Verona, 045. For example, a call from New York City to Rome would be dialed as 011 + 39 + 06 + phone number.

When dialing an Italian number from abroad, you no longer drop the initial 0 from the local area code. The country code is 1 for the United States and Canada, 61 for Australia, 64 for New Zealand, and 44 for the United Kingdom.

DIRECTORY & OPERATOR ASSISTANCE

For general information in English, dial 176. To place international telephone calls via operator-assisted service, dial 170 or long-distance access numbers (☞ International Calls *below*).

INTERNATIONAL CALLS

Since hotels tend to overcharge for long-distance and international calls, it is best to make such calls from public phones, using telephone cards.

You can **make collect calls from any phone by dialing 172-1011,** which will get you an English-speaking operator. Rates to the United States are lowest on Sunday around the clock and 10 PM–8 AM (Italian time) on weekdays and Saturday.

From major Italian cities, you can place a direct call to the United States by reversing the charges or using your

phone credit card number. When calling from pay telephones, insert a 200-lire coin, which will be returned upon completion of your call. You automatically reach an operator in the country of destination and thereby avoid all language difficulties.

LOCAL AND LONG-DISTANCE CALLS

For all calls within Italy—local and long distance—you must dial the regional area code (*prefisso*), which begins with a 0, as 06 for Rome, 041 for Venice. If you are calling from a public phone you must deposit a coin or use a calling card to get a dial tone.

LONG-DISTANCE SERVICES

AT&T, MCI, and Sprint access codes make calling long distance relatively convenient, but you may find the local access number blocked in many hotel rooms. First ask the hotel operator to connect you. If the hotel operator balks, ask for an international operator, or dial the international operator yourself. One way to improve your odds of getting connected to your long-distance carrier is to travel with more than one company's calling card (a hotel may block Sprint, for example, but not MCI). If all else fails, call from a pay phone.

➤ ACCESS CODES: **AT&T Direct** (☎ 172–1011). **MCI WorldPhone** (☎ 172–1022). **Sprint International Access** (☎ 172–1877).

PHONE CARDS

Prepaid *carte telefoniche* (calling cards) are prevalent throughout Italy and more convenient than coins. You buy the card (values vary—5,000 lire, 10,000 lire, and so on; euro values had not yet been determined at press time) at post offices, tobacconists, most news stalls, and bars. Tear off the corner of the card and insert it in the slot. When you dial, its value appears in the window. After you hang up, the card is returned so you can use it until its value runs out. The phone card called Time Europa (50,000 lire) is a good value, allowing you to call Europe and the United States at only 540 lire/€0.28 per minute during peak hours.

PUBLIC PHONES

Some pay phones accept only coins (50 centimes is likely to be the cost in the new currency), others only *carte telefoniche,* so be smart and always have both ready in your pockets (☞ Phone Cards, *above*).

TIME

The time difference between New York and Rome is 6 hours (so when it's 1 PM in New York is 7 PM in Rome). The time difference between London and Rome is 1 hour; between Sydney and Rome 10 hours; between Aukland and Rome 12 hours. Italy, like the rest of Europe, uses the 24-hour (or "military") clock, which mean that after 12 noon you continue counting forward: 13:00 is 1 PM, 23:30 is 11:30 PM.

TIPPING

The following guidelines apply in major cities, but Italians tip smaller amounts in smaller cities and towns. In restaurants a service charge of about 15% usually appears as a separate item on your check. Some restaurants state on the menu that cover and service charge are included. Either way, it's customary to leave an additional 5%–10% tip for the waiter, depending on the service. Tip check-room attendants 500 lire/€0.30 per person and rest-room attendants 200 lire/€0.10 (more in expensive hotels and restaurants). Tip 100 lire/€0.05 for whatever you drink standing up at a coffee bar, 500 lire/€0.25 or more for table service in cafés. At a hotel bar, tip 1,000 lire/€0.50 and up for a round or two of cocktails.

Italians rarely tip taxi drivers. Railway and airport porters charge a fixed rate per bag. Tip an additional 500 lire/€0.25 per person, and more if the porter is very helpful. Give a barber 2,000 lire/€1–3,000 lire/€1.50 and a hairdresser's assistant 3,000 lire/€1.50–8,000 lire/€4.15 for a shampoo or cut, depending on the type of establishment.

On sightseeing tours, tip guides about 2,000 lire/€1.05 per person for a half-day group tour, more if they are very good. In monasteries and other sights where admission is free, a contribution (500 lire/€0.26–1,000 lire/€0.52) is expected. Service station attendants are tipped only for special services, for example, 1,000 lire/€0.52 for checking your tires.

In hotels, give the *portiere* (concierge) about 15% of his bill for services, or 5,000 lire/€2.60–10,000 lire/5.00 if he has been generally helpful. For two people in a double room, leave the chambermaid about 1,500 lire/€0.75 per day, or about 8,000 lire/€4.15–10,000 lire/€5.15 a week, in a moderately priced hotel; tip a minimum of 1,000 lire/€0.52 for valet or room service. Double amounts in a very expensive hotel. In very expensive hotels, tip doormen 1,000 lire/€0.50 for calling a cab and 2,000 lire/€1.05 for carrying bags to the check-in desk, bellhops 3,000 lire/€1.55–5,000 lire/€2.60 for carrying your bags to the room, and 3,000 lire/€1.55–5,000 lire/€2.60 for room service.

TOURS & PACKAGES

Because everything is prearranged on a prepackaged tour or independent vacation, you'll spend less time planning—and often get it all at a good price.

BOOKING WITH AN AGENT

Travel agents are excellent resources. But it's a good idea to collect brochures from several agencies, as some agents' suggestions may be influenced by relationships with tour and package firms that reward them for volume sales. If you have a special interest, **find an agent with expertise in that area**; ASTA (☞ Travel Agencies, *below*) has a database of specialists worldwide.

Make sure your travel agent knows the accommodations and other services of the place being recommended. Ask about the hotel's location, room size, beds, and whether it has a pool, room service, or programs for children, if you care about these. Has your agent been there in person or sent others whom you can contact?

Do some homework on your own, too: local tourism boards can provide information about lesser-known and small-niche operators, some of which may sell only direct.

BUYER BEWARE

Each year consumers are stranded or lose their money when tour operators—even large ones with excellent reputations—go out of business. So **check out the operator.** Ask several travel agents about its reputation, and try to **book with a company that has a consumer-protection program.** (Look for information in the company's brochure.) In the United States, members of the National Tour Association and the United States Tour Operators Association are required to set aside funds to cover your payments and travel arrangements in the event that the company defaults. It's also a good idea to choose a company that participates in the American Society of Travel Agents' Tour Operator Program (TOP); ASTA will act as mediator in any disputes between you and your tour operator.

Remember that the more your package or tour includes the better you can predict the ultimate cost of your vacation. Make sure you know exactly what is covered, and **beware of hidden costs.** Are taxes, tips, and transfers included? Entertainment and excursions? These can add up.

➤ TOUR-OPERATOR RECOMMENDATIONS: **American Society of Travel Agents** (☞ Travel Agencies, *below*). **National Tour Association** (NTA; ✉ 546 E. Main St., Lexington, KY 40508, ☎ 859/226–4444 or 800/682–8886, WEB www.ntaonline.com). **United States Tour Operators Association** (USTOA; ✉ 342 Madison Ave., Suite 1522, New York, NY 10173, ☎ 212/599–6599 or 800/468–7862, FAX 212/599–6744, WEB www.ustoa.com).

TRAIN TRAVEL

The fastest trains on the Ferrovie dello Stato (FS), the Italian State Railways, are the Eurostar trains, operating on several main lines, including Rome–Milan via Florence and Bologna. Supplement is included in the fare; although seat reservations are mandatory only during weekends and holidays, they are always advisable. Ask for seats located away from the smoking car, as the poorly designed partitions are not smoke proof. Some Eurostar trains (the ETR 460 trains)

have little aisle and luggage space (though there is a space near the door where you can put large bags). To avoid having to squeeze through narrow aisles, board only at your car (look for the number on the reservation ticket). Car numbers are displayed on their exterior. Next-fastest trains are the Intercity (IC) trains, for which you pay a supplement and for which seat reservations may be required and are always advisable. *Interregionale* trains usually make more stops and are a little slower. *Regionale* and *locale* trains are the slowest; many serve commuters.

Note that in some Italian cities—Milan, Turin, Genoa, Naples, and Rome included—there are two or more main-line stations, although one is usually the principal terminal or through-station. Be sure of the name of the station at which your train will arrive, or from which it will depart.

There is refreshment service on all long-distance trains, with mobile carts and a cafeteria or dining car. Tap water on trains is not drinkable.

Traveling by night is inexpensive, but never leave your belongings unattended (even for a minute!) and make sure the door of your compartment is well locked. More comfortable trains run on the longer routes (Sicily–Rome, Sicily–Milan, Sicily–Venice, Rome–Turin, Lecce–Milan); ask for the good value T3, Intercity Notte, and Carrozza Comfort. The Vagone Letto Excelsior has private bathrooms, coffee machines, microwave ovens, refrigerators, and a suite with a double bed and a VCR.

➤ FROM THE U.K. : **British Rail** (☎ 020/7834–2345). **French Railways** (☎ 0891/515–477); calls charged at 49p a minute peak rate, 39p all other times.

CLASSES

All Italian trains have first and second classes. On local trains the higher first-class fare gets you little more than a clean doily on the headrest of your seat, but on long-distance trains you get wider seats and more legroom and better ventilation and lighting. At peak travel times, first-class train travel is worth the difference. Remember **always to make seat reservations in advance,** for either class.

CUTTING COSTS

To save money, **look into rail passes.** But be aware that if you don't plan to cover many miles you may come out ahead by buying individual tickets.

If Italy is your only destination in Europe, **consider purchasing an Italian Railpass (Italy Railcard),** which allows unlimited travel on the entire Italian Rail network for 8 ($299 first class, $199 second class), 15 ($373 first class, $249 second class), 21 ($433 first class, $289 second class), or 30 consecutive days ($522 first class, $348 second class). The Italy Flexi Rail Card allows a limited number of travel days within one month: for 4 days of travel ($239 first class, $159 second class); 8 days of travel ($334 first class, $223 second class); and 12 days of travel ($429 first class, $286 second class).

The Italian Kilometric Ticket (*biglietto chilometrico*) is valid for two months and can be used by as many as five people to travel a maximum of 20 journeys covering an overall distance of 3,000 km (1,800 mi). The price is 350,000 lire/€180.75 lire for first class and 214,000 lire/€110.50 for second class.

Once in Italy, **inquire about the Cartaverde (Green Card) if you're under 26** (45,000 lire/€23.25 for one year), which entitles the holder to a 30% discount on first-class travel and a 20% discount on second-class tickets. Those under 26 should also inquire about discount travel fares under the Billet International Jeune (BIJ) and Euro Domino Junior schemes. Also in Italy, you can **purchase the Carta d'Argento (Silver Card) if you're over 60** (45,000 lire/€23.25 for one year), which allows a 30% discount on first-class rail travel and a 20% discount on second-class travel. **Biglietti per mini-gruppi** entitle parties of three to five people traveling together to a 30% discount on all tickets except during Easter holidays, July–August, October 27–November 5, and December–January 14. Finally, disabled travelers in need of assistance can acquire the **Carta Blu (Dark-blue Card)**

(10,000 lire/€5.15 for five years), which entitles their companions to free tickets. For further information, check out the Ferrovie dello Stato (FS) Web site (www.fs-on-line.com).

Italy is one of 17 countries in which you can **use Eurailpasses,** which provide unlimited first-class travel in all of the participating countries. If you plan to rack up the miles, get a standard pass. Train travel is available for 15 days ($554), 21 days ($718), one month ($890), two months ($1,260), and three months ($1,558). You can also receive free or discounted fares on some ferry lines.

If your plans call for only limited train travel, **look into the Europass,** which costs less than a Eurailpass and allows train travel in France, Germany, Italy, Spain, and Switzerland within a two-month period ($348 for 5 days of travel; $368 for 6 days; $448 for 8 days; $528 for 10 days; and $728 for 15 days). Rail travel to Austria, Hungary, Portugal, Greece, and Benelux can be added for additional fees ($60 one country, $100 two countries). You can receive discounts for two or more people. Please note that these fares are subject to change in 2002.

In addition to standard Eurailpasses, **ask about special rail-pass plans.** Among these are the Eurail Youthpass (for those under age 26), Eurail Saverpass and Eurail Saver Flexipass (which give a discount for two or more people traveling together), Eurail Flexipass (which allows a certain number of travel days within a set period), and the EurailDrive Pass (which combines travel by train and rental car).

Whichever pass you choose, remember that you must **purchase your Eurailpass or Europass before you leave** for Europe. You can get further information and order tickets at the Rail Europe Web site (www.raileurope.com).

Many travelers assume that rail passes guarantee them seats on the trains they wish to ride. Not so. You need to **book seats ahead even if you are using a rail pass.** Seat reservations are required on some European trains, particularly high-speed trains, and are a good idea on trains that may be crowded—particularly in summer on popular routes. You will also need a reservation if you purchase sleeping accommodations.

➤ INFORMATION AND PASSES: **CIT Rail** (✉ 9501 W. Devon Ave., Suite 502, Rosemont, IL 60018, ☎ 800/248–7245). **DER Tours** (✉ Box 1606, Des Plaines, IL 60017, ☎ 800/782–2424, ℻ 800/282–7474). **Rail Europe** (✉ 226-230 Westchester Ave., White Plains, NY 10604, ☎ 914/682–5172 or 800/438–7245, WEB www.raileurope.com; ✉ 2087 Dundas E., Suite 105, Mississauga, Ontario L4X 1M2, ☎ 416/602–4195).

TICKETS, SCHEDULES, AND RESERVATIONS

Trains can be very crowded; it is always a good idea to make a reservation. To avoid long lines at station windows, **buy tickets and make seat reservations up to two months in advance** at travel agencies displaying the FS emblem. Tickets can be purchased at the last minute, but seat reservations can be made at agencies (or the train station) up until about three hours before the train departs from its city of origin. For trains that require a reservation (all Eurostar and some Intercity), you may be able to get a seat assignment just before boarding the train; look for the conductor on the platform.

Tickets are good for two months after the date of issue, but right before departure **they must be validated in the yellow machines located in the departure area.** Once stamped, tickets are valid for 6 hours on distances of less than 200 km (124 mi) or for 24 hours on distances of 200 km or more. If you wish to stop along the way and your final destination is more than 200 km away, you can stamp the ticket a second time before it expires so as to extend its validity to a maximum of 48 hours from the time it was first stamped. If you forget to stamp your ticket in the machine, or you didn't make it to the station in time to buy the ticket, you must actively seek out a conductor and pay a 10,000 lire/€5.15 fine. Don't wait for the conductor to find

out that you are without a valid ticket (unless the train is overcrowded and walking becomes impossible), as he might charge you a much heavier fine. You can buy train tickets for nearby destinations (within a 200-km [124-mi] range) at tobacconists and at ticket machines in stations.

➤ TRAIN INFORMATION: **Ferrovie dello Stato** (FS; ☎ 147/888–088 in Italy, WEB www.fs-on-line.com).

TRANSPORTATION
AROUND ITALY

Public transportation is the fastest way to travel between Italy's cities. It is also relatively inexpensive compared to the cost of renting a car and paying for gas and tolls. Italy's cities are served by an extensive state railway system (FS; ☞ Train Travel, *above*), with fast service on main lines (Milan–Venice–Florence–Rome–Naples) that in some cases beats plane travel in time and cost. A complete schedule of all trains in the country and fares can be bought from most newsstands for about $8, or check it on-line at www.fs-on-line.com.

Buses (☞ Bus Travel, *above*), less roomy but slightly less expensive than trains, offer more frequent service to certain smaller cities and towns that are served only by secondary train lines. Buses are also a better option in more rugged areas where train service is spotty: the Dolomites, Liguria, Tuscany, and the Amalfi Coast, for instance. Ferries and hydrofoils (☞ Boat & Ferry Travel, *above*) ply between islands; some islands, such as Capri and Ischia, have helicopter service, a more expensive alternative.

Getting around in Italy by plane (☞ Air Travel, *above*) is an expensive but viable option, and it is the fastest means of traveling long distances, as to Sicily and Sardinia. Look for special bargain rates that can defray costs. Train and bus connections between airports and city centers are usually smooth.

Italy has an intricate network of autostrade routes, good highways, and secondary roads, making renting a car (☞ Car Rental, *above*) for travel between most cities a doable but more expensive alternative to public transportation (due to high gas prices and freeway tolls). A car can be a good investment if you are interested in carefree countryside rambles, offering time to explore more remote towns. Having a car in major cities, however, often leads to parking and traffic headaches, plus additional expense in the form of garage and parking fees.

TRAVEL AGENCIES

A good travel agent puts your needs first. Look for an agency that has been in business at least five years, emphasizes customer service, and has someone on staff who specializes in your destination. In addition, **make sure the agency belongs to a professional trade organization.** The American Society of Travel Agents (ASTA), with more than 26,000 members in some 170 countries, is the largest and most influential in the field. Operating under the motto "Without a travel agent, you're on your own," it maintains and enforces a strict code of ethics and will step in to help mediate any agent-client disputes if necessary. ASTA also maintains a Web site that includes a directory of agents. (If a travel agency is also acting as your tour operator, *see* Buyer Beware *in* Tours & Packages, *above*.)

➤ LOCAL AGENT REFERRALS: **American Society of Travel Agents** (ASTA; ☎ 800/965–2782 24-hr hot line, FAX 703/739–7642, WEB www.astanet.com). **Association of British Travel Agents** (⊠ 68–71 Newman St., London W1T 3AH, U.K., ☎ 020/7637–2444, FAX 020/7637–0713, WEB www.abtanet. com). **Association of Canadian Travel Agents** (⊠ 130 Albert St., Ste. 1705, Ottawa, Ontario K1P 5G4, Canada, ☎ 613/237–3657, FAX 613/237–7502, WEB www.acta.net). **Australian Federation of Travel Agents** (⊠ Level 3, 309 Pitt St., Sydney NSW 2000, Australia, ☎ 02/9264–3299, FAX 02/9264–1085, WEB www.afta.com.au). **Travel Agents' Association of New Zealand** (⊠ Level 5, Paxus House, 79 Boulcott St., Box 1888, Wellington 10033, New Zealand, ☎ 04/499–0104, FAX 04/499–0827, WEB www.taanz.org.nz).

VISITOR INFORMATION

➤ TOURIST INFORMATION: **Italian Government Tourist Board** (ENIT; ⊠ 630 5th Ave., New York, NY 10111, ☎ 212/245–4822, FAX 212/586–9249; ⊠ 401 N. Michigan Ave., Chicago, IL 60611, ☎ 312/644–0990, FAX 312/644–3019; ⊠ 12400 Wilshire Blvd., Suite 550, Los Angeles, CA 90025, ☎ 310/820–0098, FAX 310/820–6357; ⊠ 1 Pl. Ville Marie, Suite 1914, Montréal, Québec H3B 3M9, ☎ 514/866–7667, FAX 514/392–1429; ⊠ 1 Princes St., London W1R 8AY, ☎ 020/7408–1254, FAX 020/7493–6695, WEB www.italiantourism.com).

➤ TOURIST OFFICES IN ITALY: **Florence** (⊠ Via Cavour 1/r, next to Palazzo Medici–Riccardi, 50129, ☎ 055/290–832, WEB www.firenze.turismo. toscana.it). **Milan** (⊠ Via Marconi 1, 20121, ☎ 02/7252–4301, WEB www. mimu.it, www.provincia.milano.it). **Naples** (⊠ Piazza dei Martiri 58, 80121, ☎ 081/405311, WEB www.ept. napoli.it). **Palermo** (⊠ Piazza Castelnuovo 35, 90141, ☎ 091/583–847, WEB www.aapit.pa.it). **Rome** (⊠ Via Parigi 5, 00185, ☎ 06/3600–4399, WEB www.comune.roma.it, www.in-Roma.it). **Venice** (⊠ San Marco 71/f, near the Museo Correr, 30124, ☎ 041/041/5298711, WEB www.venezia. provincia/apt.it).

➤ U.S. GOVERNMENT ADVISORIES: **U.S. Department of State** (⊠ Overseas Citizens Services Office, Room 4811 N.S., 2201 C St. NW, Washington, DC 20520, ☎ 202/647–5225 for interactive hot line, WEB travel.state. gov/travel/html); enclose a self-addressed, stamped, business-size envelope.

WEB SITES

Do check out the World Wide Web when planning your trip. You'll find everything from weather forecasts to virtual tours of famous cities. Be sure to **visit Fodors.com** (www.fodors.com), a complete travel-planning site. You can research prices and book plane tickets, hotel rooms, rental cars, vacation packages, and more. In addition, you can post your pressing questions in the Travel Talk section and, in the site's Rants & Raves section, read comments about some of the restaurants and hotels in this book—and chime in yourself. Other planning tools include a currency converter and weather reports, and there are loads of links to travel resources.

WHEN TO GO

The main tourist season runs from April to mid-October. For serious sightseers the best months are from fall to early spring. The so-called low season may be cooler and inevitably rainier, but it has its rewards: less time waiting on lines and closer-up, unhurried views of what you want to see.

Tourists crowd the major art cities at Easter, when Italians flock to resorts and to the country. From March through May, busloads of eager schoolchildren on excursions take cities of artistic and historical interest by storm.

CLIMATE

Weatherwise, the best months for sightseeing are April, May, June, September, and October—generally pleasant and not too hot. The hottest months are July and August, when

humidity can make things unpleasant. Winters are relatively mild in most places on the main tourist circuit but always include some rainy spells. In general, the northern half of the peninsula and the entire Adriatic Coast, with the exception of Apulia, are rainier than the rest of Italy.

If you can avoid it, don't travel at all in Italy in August, when much of the population is on the move, especially around Ferragosto, the August 15 national holiday, when cities such as Rome and Milan are deserted and many restaurants and shops are closed. (Of course, with residents away on vacation, this makes crowds less of a bother for tourists.) Except for a few year-round resorts, such as Taormina and some towns on the Italian Riviera, coastal resorts usually close up tight from October or November to April; they're at their best in June and September, when everything is open but uncrowded.

➤ FORECASTS: **Weather Channel Connection** (☎ 900/932–8437), 95¢ per minute from a Touch-Tone phone.

ROME

Jan.	52F	11C	May	74F	23C	Sept.	79F	26C
	40	5		56	13		62	17
Feb.	55F	13C	June	82F	28C	Oct.	71F	22C
	42	6		63	17		55	13
Mar.	59F	15C	July	87F	30C	Nov.	61F	16C
	45	7		67	20		49	10
Apr.	66F	19C	Aug.	86F	30C	Dec.	55F	13C
	50	10		67	20		44	6

FLORENCE

Jan.	48F	9C	May	73F	23C	Sept.	79F	26C
	36	2		54	12		59	15
Feb.	52F	11C	June	81F	27C	Oct.	68F	20C
	37	3		59	15		52	11
Mar.	57F	14C	July	86F	30C	Nov.	57F	14C
	41	5		64	18		45	7
Apr.	66F	19C	Aug.	86F	30C	Dec.	52F	11C
	46	8		63	17		39	10

VENICE

Jan.	42F	6C	May	70F	21C	Sept.	75F	24C
	33	1		56	13		61	16
Feb.	46F	8C	June	76F	25C	Oct.	65F	19C
	35	2		63	17		53	12
Mar.	53F	12C	July	81F	27C	Nov.	53F	12C
	41	5		66	19		44	7
Apr.	62F	17C	Aug.	80F	27C	Dec.	46F	8C
	49	10		65	19		37	3

FESTIVALS AND SEASONAL EVENTS

Italy's top seasonal events are listed below, and any one of them could provide the stuff of lasting memories. It is revealing that the Italian "festa" can be translated either as "festival" or "holiday" or "feast"—food is usually fundamental to Italian celebrations. Contact the **Italian Government Travel Office** (☞ Visitor Information, *above*) for exact dates and further information.

➤ EARLY DEC.: The **Feast of St. Ambrose** (Festa di Sant'Ambrosio) in Milan officially opens La Scala's opera season.

➤ DEC.–JUNE: The **Opera Season** is in full swing at La Scala in Milan and elsewhere, notably in Turin, Rome, Naples, Parma, Venice, and Genoa.

➤ DEC. 31: Rome stages a rousing **New Year's Eve** celebration, dubbed the Festa di San Silvestro, with fireworks in Piazza del Popolo.

➤ JAN. 5–6: Roman Catholic **Epiphany (Epifania) Celebrations** and decorations are evident throughout Italy. Notable is the Epiphany Fair at Piazza Navona in Rome.

➤ EARLY FEB.: The **Almond Blossom Festival** (Festa del Fiore di Mandorlo) in Agrigento is a week of folk music and dancing, with groups from many countries, in the Valley of the Temples.

➤ FEB. 28–MAR. 6: A big do in the 18th century, revived in the last half of the 20th century, **Carnival (Carnevale) in Venice** includes concerts, plays, masked balls, fireworks, and indoor and outdoor happenings of every sort. It is probably Italy's most famous festival, bringing in hundreds of thousands. During **Carnival in Viareggio,** masked pageants, fireworks, a flower show, and parades are among the festivities.

➤ FEB. 28–MAR. 6: The **Carnival in Ivrea,** near Turin, includes three days of folklore, costumes, parades, and cooking in the streets. The party culminates with the Battle of the Oranges, on Quinquagesima Sunday (March 4) and Shrove Monday (March 5), which features real fruit flying through the air.

➤ APR. 16–22: **Settimana Santa** (Holy Week) features parades and outdoor events at every major city and most small towns in Italy, but Rome, Naples, Assisi, and Florence have particularly notable festivities.

➤ APR. 13: In Rome, a torchlit nighttime **Good Friday Procession** (Venerdì Santo) led by the pope winds from the Colosseum past the Roman Forum and up the Palatine Hill.

➤ APR. 15: The Easter Sunday **Scoppio del Carro,** or Explosion of the Cart, in Florence, is the eruption of a cartful of fireworks in the Piazza del Duomo, set off by a mechanical dove released from the altar during High Mass. Needless to say, **Easter Mass at the Vatican** in Rome is long, intense, and packed, with many people attending in elaborate holiday costumes.

➤ LATE APR.–EARLY JULY: The **Florence May Music Festival** is the oldest and most prestigious Italian festival of the performing arts.

➤ MAY 1: The **Feast of Sant'Efisio** in Cagliari sees a procession of marchers and others in splendid Sardinian costume.

➤ MID-MAY: During the **Race of the Candles** (Corsa dei Ceri) in Gubbio, a procession to the top of Mt. Ingino features young men in local costume carrying huge wooden pillars.

➤ MAY 19–20: The **Sardinian Cavalcade** (Cavalcata Sarda) is a traditional procession of more than 3,000 people in Sardinian costume winding through Sassari.

➤ LAST SUN. IN MAY: The **Palio of the Archers** (Palio della Balestra) is a medieval crossbow contest in Gubbio, dating back to 1461.

➤ JUNE: On three consecutive days in June, usually on the third week of the month, the **Flower Festival** (Infiorata), in Genzano (Rome), is a religious procession along streets carpeted with flowers in splendid designs.

➤ LATE MAY/EARLY JUNE: The **Regatta of the Great Maritime Republics** sees keen competition among the four former maritime republics—Amalfi, Genoa, Pisa, and Venice. The 2002 event takes place in Pisa.

➤ 1ST AND 2ND SUN. IN JUNE AND JUNE 24: **Soccer Games in 16th-Century Costume**, in Florence, commemorate a match played in 1530. Festivities include fireworks displays.

➤ JUNE: The **Umbria Jazz Festival**, in Perugia (WEB www.umbriajazz.com), brings in many of the biggest names in jazz each summer.

➤ LAST SUN. IN JUNE: The **Battle of the Bridge** (Gioco del Ponte), in Pisa, is a medieval parade and contest.

➤ LATE JUNE–MID-JULY: The **Festival of Two Worlds** (Festa dei Due Mondi), in Spoleto, is perhaps Italy's most famous performing-arts festival, bringing in a worldwide audience for concerts, operas, ballets, film screenings, and crafts fairs. Plan well in advance.

➤ JUNE–EARLY AUG.: The **Summer Operetta Festival** (Festival Internazionale dell'Operetta) is held in Trieste.

➤ JULY 2 AND AUG. 16: The world-famous **Palio Horse Race**, in Siena, is a colorful bareback horse race with ancient Sienese factions showing their colors and participants competing for the *palio* (banner).

➤ EARLY JULY–LATE AUG.: The **Arena of Verona Outdoor Opera Season** heralds spectacular productions in the 22,000-seat Roman amphitheater of Verona.

➤ 3RD SAT. IN JULY: The **Feast of the Redeemer** (Festa del Redentore) is a procession of gondolas and other craft commemorating the end of the epidemic of 1575 in Venice. The fireworks over the lagoon are spectacular.

➤ LATE JULY–MID-SEPT.: The **Stresa Musical Weeks** comprise a series of concerts and recitals in Stresa.

➤ LATE AUG.–EARLY SEPT.: The **Venice Film Festival**, oldest of the international film festivals, takes place mostly on the Lido.

➤ 1ST SUN. IN SEPT.: The **Historic Regatta** (Regata Storica) includes a traditional competition between two-oar gondolas in Venice. The **Joust of the Saracen** is a tilting contest with knights in 13th-century armor in Arezzo.

➤ SEPT. 16: The **Joust of the Quintana** is a 17th-century-style joust and historical procession in Foligno.

➤ 1ST SUN. IN OCT.: Alba's **100 Towers Tournament** (Giostra delle Cento Torri) features costumes and races and is held a week before the opening of the **Truffle Fair** (Fiera del Tartufo), a food fair centered on the white truffle.

➤ OCT. 4: The **Feast of St. Francis** (Festa di San Francesco) is celebrated in Assisi, his birthplace.

WORDS AND PHRASES

English	Italian	Pronunciation
Basics		
Yes/no	Sí/No	see/no
Please	Per favore	pear fa-**vo**-ray
Yes, please	Sí grazie	see **grah**-tsee-ay
Thank you	Grazie	**grah**-tsee-ay
You're welcome	Prego	**pray**-go
Excuse me, sorry	Scusi	**skoo**-zee
Sorry!	Mi dispiace!	mee dis-spee-**ah**-chay
Good morning/ afternoon	Buon giorno	bwohn **jor**-no
Good evening	Buona sera	**bwoh**-na **say**-ra
Good bye	Arrivederci	a-ree-vah-**dare**-chee
Mr. (Sir)	Signore	see-**nyo**-ray
Mrs. (Ma'am)	Signora	see-**nyo**-ra
Miss	Signorina	see-nyo-**ree**-na
Pleased to meet you	Piacere	pee-ah-**chair**-ray
How are you?	Come sta?	**ko**-may **stah**
Very well, thanks	Bene, grazie	**ben**-ay **grah**-tsee-ay
And you?	E lei?	ay **lay**-ee
Hello (phone)	Pronto?	**proan**-to
Numbers		
one	uno	**oo**-no
two	due	**doo**-ay
three	tre	tray
four	quattro	**kwah**-tro
five	cinque	**cheen**-kway
six	sei	say
seven	sette	**set**-ay
eight	otto	**oh**-to
nine	nove	**no**-vay
ten	dieci	dee-**eh**-chee
eleven	undici	**oon**-dee-chee
twelve	dodici	**doe**-dee-chee
thirteen	tredici	**tray**-dee-chee
fourteen	quattordici	kwa-**tore**-dee-chee
fifteen	quindici	**kwin**-dee-chee
sixteen	sedici	**say**-dee-chee
seventeen	diciassette	dee-cha-**set**-ay

eighteen	diciotto	dee-**cho**-to
nineteen	diciannove	dee-cha-**no**-vay
twenty	venti	**vain**-tee
twenty-one	ventuno	vain-**too**-no
twenty-two	ventidue	vayn-tee-**doo**-ay
thirty	trenta	**train**-ta
forty	quaranta	kwa-**rahn**-ta
fifty	cinquanta	cheen-**kwahn**-ta
sixty	sessanta	seh-**sahn**-ta
seventy	settanta	seh-**tahn**-ta
eighty	ottanta	o-**tahn**-ta
ninety	novanta	no-**vahn**-ta
one hundred	cento	**chen**-to
ten thousand	diecimila	dee-eh-chee-**mee**-la
one hundred thousand	centomila	chen-to-mee-la

Useful Phrases

Do you speak English?	Parla inglese?	par-la een-glay-zay
I don't speak Italian	Non parlo italiano	non **par**-lo ee-tal-**yah**-no
I don't understand	Non capisco	non ka-**peess**-ko
Can you please repeat?	Può ripetere?	pwo ree-**pet**-ay-ray
Slowly!	Lentamente!	**len**-ta-men-tay
I don't know	Non lo so	noan lo **so**
I'm American/ British	Sono americano(a)	**so**-no a-may-ree-**kah**-no(a)
	Sono inglese	**so**-no een-**glay**-zay
What's your name?	Come si chiama?	**ko**-may see kee-**ah**-ma
My name is . . .	Mi chiamo . . .	mee kee-**ah**-mo
What time is it?	Che ore sono?	kay **o**-ray **so**-no
How?	Come?	**ko**-may
When?	Quando?	**kwan**-doe
Yesterday/today/ tomorrow	Ieri/oggi/domani	**yer**-ee/**o**-jee/ do-**mah**-nee
This morning/ afternoon	Stamattina/Oggi pomeriggio	sta-ma-**tee**-na/**o**-jee po-mer-**ee**-jo
Tonight	Stasera	sta-**ser**-a
What?	Che cosa?	kay **ko**-za
What is it?	Che cos'è?	kay ko-**zay**
Why?	Perché?	pear-**kay**
Who?	Chi?	kee
Where is . . .	Dov'è . . .	doe-**veh**
the bus stop?	la fermata dell'autobus?	la fer-**mah**-ta del ow-toe-**booss**
the train station?	la stazione?	la sta-tsee-**oh**-nay
the subway station?	la metropolitana?	la may-tro-po-lee-**tah**-na
the terminal?	il terminal?	eel ter-mee-**nahl**
the post office?	l'ufficio postale?	loo-**fee**-cho po-**stah**-lay

the bank?	la banca?	la **bahn**-ka
the . . . hotel?	l'hotel . . .?	lo-**tel**
the store?	il negozio?	ell nay-**go**-tsee-o
the cashier?	la cassa?	la **kah**-sa
the . . . museum?	il museo . . .?	eel moo-**zay**-o
the hospital?	l'ospedale?	lo-spay-**dah**-lay
the first aid station?	il pronto soccorso?	eel **pron**-to so-**kor**-so
the elevator?	l'ascensore?	la-shen-**so**-ray
a telephone?	un telefono?	oon tay-**lay**-fo-no
Where are the restrooms?	Dov'è il bagno?	do-**vay** eel **bahn**-yo
Here/there	Qui/là	kwee-la
Left/right	A sinistra/a destra	a see-**neess**-tra/ a **des**-tra
Straight ahead	Avanti dritto	a-**vahn**-tee **dree**-to
Is it near/far?	È vicino/lontano?	ay vee-**chee**-no/ lon-**tah**-no
I'd like . . .	Vorrei . . .	vo-**ray**
a room	una camera	**oo**-na **kah**-may-ra
the key	la chiave	la kee-**ah**-vay
a newspaper	un giornale	oon jor-**nah**-lay
a stamp	un francobollo	oon-frahn-ko-**bo**-lo
I'd like to buy . . .	Vorrei comprare . . .	vo-**ray** kom-**prah**-ray
a cigar	un sigaro	oon see-**gah**-ro
cigarettes	delle sigarette	day-lay see-ga-**ret**-ay
some matches	dei fiammiferi	day-ee fec-ah-**mea**-fer-ee
some soap	una saponetta	**oo**-na sa-po-**net**-a
a city plan	una pianta della città	**oo**-na **pyahn**-ta day-la chee-**tah**
a road map of . . .	una cara stradaleldi . . .	**oo**-na **cart**-a stra-**tah**-lay dee
a country map	una carta geografica	**oo**-na **cart**-a jay-o-**grah**-fee-ka
a magazine	una rivista	**oo**-na rec-**voess**-ta
envelopes	delle buste	day-lay **booss**-tay
writing paper	della carta da lettere	**day**-la **cart**-a da **let**-air-ay
a postcard	una cartolina	**oo**-na car-toe-**lee**-na
a guidebook	una guida turistica	**oo**-na **gwee**-da too-**reess**-tee-ka
How much is it?	Quanto costa?	**kwahn**-toe **coast**-a
It's expensive/ cheap	È caro/economico	ay **car**-o/ay-ko-**no**-mee-ko
A little/a lot	Poco/tanto	**po**-ko-**tahn**-to
More/less	Più/meno	pee-**oo**/**may**-no
Enough/too (much)	Abbastanza/troppo	a-bas-**tahn**-sa/**tro**-po
I am sick	Sto male	sto **mah**-lay
Please call a doctor	Chiami un dottore	kee-**ah**-mee oon doe-**toe**-ray

Help!	Aiuto!	a-**yoo**-toe
Stop!	Alt!	ahlt
Fire!	Al fuoco!	ahl **fwo**-ko
Caution/Look out!	Attenzione!	a-ten-**syon**-ay

Dining Out

A bottle of . . .	Una bottiglia di . . .	**oo**-na bo-**tee**-lee-ah dee
A cup of . . .	Una tazza di . . .	**oo**-na **tah**-tsa dee
A glass of . . .	Un bicchiere di . . .	oon bee-key-**air**-ay dee
Bill/check	Il conto	eel **cone**-toe
Bread	Il pane	eel **pah**-nay
Breakfast	La prima colazione	la **pree**-ma ko-la-**tsee**-oh-nay
Cocktail/aperitif	L'aperitivo	la-pay-ree-**tee**-vo
Dinner	La cena	la **chen**-a
Fixed-price menu	Menù a prezzo fisso	may-**noo** a **pret**-so **fee**-so
Fork	La forchetta	la for-**ket**-a
I am diabetic	Ho il diabete	o eel dee-a-**bay**-tay
I am vegetarian	Sono vegetariano/a	**so**-no vay-jay-ta-ree-**ah**-no/a
I'd like . . .	Vorrei . . .	vo-**ray**
I'd like to order	Vorrei ordinare	vo-**ay** or-dee-**nah**-ray
Is service included?	Il servizio è incluso?	eel ser-**vee**-tzee-o ay een-**kloo**-zo
It's good/bad	È buono/cattivo	ay **bwo**-no/ka-tee-vo
It's hot/cold	È caldo/freddo	ay **kahl**-doe/**fred**-o
Knife	Il coltello	eel kol-**tel**-o
Lunch	Il pranzo	eel **prahnt**-so
Menu	Il menù	eel may-**noo**
Napkin	Il tovagliolo	eel toe-va-lee-**oh**-lo
Please give me . . .	Mi dia . . .	mee **dee**-a
Salt	Il sale	eel **sah**-lay
Spoon	Il cucchiaio	eel koo-kee-**ah**-yo
Sugar	Lo zucchero	lo **tsoo**-ker-o
Waiter/Waitress	Cameriere/cameriera	ka-mare-**yer**-ay/ka-mare-**yer**-a
Wine list	La lista dei vini	la **lee**-sta **day**-ee **vee**-nee

INDEX

NOTES

FODOR'S ITALY 2002

EDITOR: Matthew Lombardi

Editorial Contributors: Robert Andrews, Barbara Walsh Angelillo, Jude Barrand, Robin S. Goldstein, Valerie Hamilton, Carla Lionello, Heather O'Brian, Caragh Matthews Rockwood, Patricia Rucidlo, Mark Walters

Editorial Production: Stacey Kulig

Maps: David Lindroth, Inc., Mapping Specialists, *cartographers*; Rebecca Baer and Bob Blake, *map editors*

Design: Fabrizio La Rocca, *creative director*; Guido Caroti, *art director*; Jolie Novak, *senior picture editor*; Melanie Marin, *photo editor*

Cover Design: Pentagram

Production/Manufacturing: Yexenia Markland

COPYRIGHT

ISBN 0–679–00865–9

ISSN 0361–977X

SPECIAL SALES

Fodor's Travel Publications are available at special discounts for bulk purchases for sales promotions or premiums. Special editions, including personalized covers, excerpts of existing guides, and corporate imprints, can be created in large quantities for special needs. For more information, contact your local bookseller or write to Special Markets, Fodor's Travel Publications, 280 Park Avenue, New York, NY 10017. Inquiries from Canada should be directed to your local Canadian bookseller or sent to Random House of Canada, Ltd., Marketing Department, 2775 Matheson Boulevard East, Mississauga, Ontario L4W 4P7. Inquiries from the United Kingdom should be sent to Fodor's Travel Publications, 20 Vauxhall Bridge Road, London SW1V 2SA, England.

PRINTED IN THE UNITED STATES OF AMERICA

10 9 8 7 6 5 4 3 2 1

IMPORTANT TIP

Although all prices, opening times, and other details are based on information supplied to us at press time, changes occur all the time in the travel world, and Fodor's cannot accept responsibility for facts that become outdated or for inadvertent errors or omissions. So **always confirm information when it matters,** especially if you're making a detour to visit a specific place.

PHOTOGRAPHY

The Image Bank: *Bullaty/Lomeo*, cover. (Umbria)

Art Resource: *Nimatallah*, 29 bottom.

G. Carfagna & Associati: *Giuseppe Carfagna*, 7A, 12B, 22B, 23A, 23B, 30C. *Marina Di Marco*, 17 bottom right.

Corbis: *Archivo Iconografico, S.A.*, 30J. *Kea Publishing Services Ltd.*, 30E.

Da Cesari, 30B.

Robert I.C. Fisher, 2 top, 4–5, 21 top left, 21C, 26A, 30A.

Hotel Accademia, 30G.

The Image Bank: *Gio Barto*, 9 center right. *Antonio Bignami*, 8B. *Bullaty/Lomeo*, 1, 6B, 6C, 7C, 13D, 14A, 15D, 15 bottom left. *Marco Cappelli*, 9C, 10A. *M.J. Cardenas*, 17A. *Kay Chernush*, 2 bottom right. *Giuliano Colliva*, 18A, 22A, 24C. *Paolo Curto*, 25 top. *Stuart Dee*, 28C. *Grant V. Faint*, 6A. *Froomer Pictures*, 25A. *David W. Hamilton*, 16A, 20B. *R. Johnson*, 10 top right, 10B, 11B, 14B. *Paul Loven*, 12A. *Mahaux Photography*, 24B. *Aris Mihich*, 14C. *Giuseppe Molteni*, 22D. *Alberto Nardi*, 25B. *Carlos Navajas*, 19D. *Marvin E. Newman*, 30I. *Photo H.B.*, 9B. *Andrea Pistolesi*, 9A, 11A, 12C, 16C, 19 bottom left, 22C, 24A, 27B. *F. Reginato*, 7B. *Antonio Rosario*, 30H. *Francesco Ruggeri*, 29D. *Stefano Scata*, 23C, 30D. *Bernard Van Berg*, 18C. *R. Vignoli*, 20A. *Hans Wolf*, 3 top left, 8A.

Italian Government Tourist Board, 2 bottom left, 2 bottom center, 3 top right, 3 bottom left, 3 bottom right, 16B, 17B, 18B.

Gualtiero Marchesi, 30F.

Andrea Pistolesi, 32.

Antonio Sferlazzo, 15 top, 19E, 28 bottom.

ABOUT OUR WRITERS

The more you know before you go, the better your trip will be. Italy's most fascinating small museum (or its chicest boutique or coziest trattoria) could be just around the corner from your hotel, but if you don't know it's there, it might as well be on the other side of the globe. That's where this book comes in. It's a great step toward making sure your next trip lives up to your expectations. As you plan, check out the Web as well. Guidebooks have been helping smart travelers find the special places for years; the Web is one more tool. Whatever reference you consult, be savvy about what you read, and always consider the source. Images and language can be massaged to make places appear better than they are. Here at Fodor's, and at our on-line arm, Fodors.com, our focus is on providing you with information that's not only useful but accurate and on target. Every day Fodor's editors put enormous effort into getting things right, beginning with the search for the right contributors—people who have objective judgment, broad travel experience, and the writing ability to put their insights into words. There's no substitute for advice from a like-minded friend who has just come back from where you're going, but our writers, having seen all corners of Italy, are the next best thing. They're the kind of people you'd poll for tips yourself if you knew them.

After six-years in Calabria, **Robert Andrews**—who covers Italy's *mezzogiorno* (south) for Fodor's—considers himself an honorary Italian. He has written guidebooks on Sicily and Sardinia and now lives in Bristol, England, where he compiles anthologies when he isn't travel writing.

British-born journalist **Jude Barrand** has crossed the globe, filing reports on developing nations for the UN and writing travel articles. She now resides in Rome, where she works for Vatican Radio when she's not out enjoying the best that the Eternal City has to offer.

Fresh pesto, fishing villages, and Sampdoria soccer lured **Robin Goldstein** from his roots in Calabria and Apulia to the Italian Riviera, where he took up residence in Genoa.

His previous travel-writing stints include Spain, Mexico, and Ecuador.

Five years ago, **Valerie Hamilton** turned in her surfboard and moved from San Francisco to Rome, where she is a journalist and TV producer. She holds a degree in art history and archaeology, but her first love is travel; she has been covering Italy for Fodor's for the past three years.

Carla Lionello grew up in Venice, where she received a degree in English literature. In 1989 she traded Piazza San Marco for the Spanish Steps and moved to Rome, where she writes for food magazines and guidebooks. Carla also teaches Italian cooking workshops to culinary-inspired visitors.

Heather O'Brian's first year in Italy was spent in Bologna, where she earned a master's degree in international relations and played on the local soccer team. She returned a few years later and is now settled in Milan, where she writes about finance, fashion, and tourism.

Patricia Rucidlo lives in Florence with her dog, Tillie, who occasionally accompanies her on the Tuscan art history and food circuit. Though she has master's degrees in Italian Renaissance history and art history, Patti's true love is Italian food (as is Tillie's), and from time to time she even works as a pastry chef.

An editor, travel writer, and naturalist, British-born **Mark Walters** first settled in Naples as a British Council lecturer in the 1980s. He completed his graduate studies in classics and now, when not hiking or playing field hockey, he leads study tours around the Mediterranean.

Don't Forget to Write

We love feedback—positive and negative—and follow up on all suggestions. So contact the Italy editor at editors@fodors.com or c/o Fodor's, 280 Park Avenue, New York, NY 10017. Have a wonderful trip!

Karen Cure
Editorial Director